International Directory of

COMPANY
HISTORIES

International Directory of

COMPANY HISTORIES

VOLUME 50

Editor

Thom Votteler

ST. JAMES PRESS®

Detroit • New York • San Diego • San Francisco • Cleveland • New Haven, Conn. • Waterville, Maine • London • Munich

International Directory of Company Histories, Volume 50

Thom Votteler, Editor

Project Editor
Miranda H. Ferrara

Editorial
Erin Bealmear, Joann Cerrito, Jim Craddock,
Stephen Cusack, Peter M. Gareffa,
Kristin Hart, Melissa Hill,
Margaret Mazurkiewicz, Carol A. Schwartz,
Christine Tomassini, Michael J. Tyrkus

Imaging and Multimedia
Randy Bassett, Dean Dauphinais, Robert
Duncan, Lezlie Light

Manufacturing
Rhonda Williams

LIBRARY OF CONGRESS CATALOG NUMBER 89-190943

ISBN: 1-55862-476-7

BRITISH LIBRARY CATALOGUING IN PUBLICATION DATA

International directory of company histories. Vol. 50
I. Thom Votteler
33.87409

Printed in the United States of America
10 9 8 7 6 5 4 3 2 1

CONTENTS _____

Company Histories

PREFACE

The St. James Press series *The International Directory of Company Histories (IDCH)* is intended for reference use by students, business people, librarians, historians, economists, investors, job candidates, and others who seek to learn more about the historical development of the world's most important companies. To date, *IDCH* has covered over 5,775 companies in 50 volumes.

Inclusion Criteria

Most companies chosen for inclusion in *IDCH* have achieved a minimum of US$25 million in annual sales and are leading influences in their industries or geographical locations. Companies may be publicly held, private, or nonprofit. State-owned companies that are important in their industries and that may operate much like public or private companies also are included. Wholly owned subsidiaries and divisions are profiled if they meet the requirements for inclusion. Entries on companies that have had major changes since they were last profiled may be selected for updating.

The *IDCH* series highlights 10% private and nonprofit companies, and features updated entries on approximately 45 companies per volume.

Entry Format

Each entry begins with the company's legal name, the address of its headquarters, its telephone, toll-free, and fax numbers, and its web site. A statement of public, private, state, or parent ownership follows. A company with a legal name in both English and the language of its headquarters country is listed by the English name, with the native-language name in parentheses.

The company's founding or earliest incorporation date, the number of employees, and the most recent available sales figures follow. Sales figures are given in local currencies with equivalents in U.S. dollars. For some private companies, sales figures are estimates and indicated by the abbreviation *est.* The entry lists the exchanges on which a company's stock is traded and its ticker symbol, as well as the company's NAIC codes.

Entries generally contain a *Company Perspectives* box which provides a short summary of the company's mission, goals, and ideals, a *Key Dates* box highlighting milestones in the company's history, lists of *Principal Subsidiaries, Principal Divisions, Principal Operating Units, Principal Competitors,* and articles for *Further Reading.*

American spelling is used throughout *IDCH*, and the word ''billion'' is used in its U.S. sense of one thousand million.

Sources

Entries have been compiled from publicly accessible sources both in print and on the Internet such as general and academic periodicals, books, annual reports, and material supplied by the companies themselves.

Cumulative Indexes

IDCH contains three indexes: the **Index to Companies**, which provides an alphabetical index to companies discussed in the text as well as to companies profiled, the **Index to Industries**, which allows researchers to locate companies by their principal industry, and the **Geographic Index**, which lists companies alphabetically by the country of their headquarters. The indexes are cumulative and specific instructions for using them are found immediately preceding each index.

Suggestions Welcome

Comments and suggestions from users of *IDCH* on any aspect of the product as well as suggestions for companies to be included or updated are cordially invited. Please write:

> The Editor
> *International Directory of Company Histories*
> St. James Press
> 27500 Drake Rd.
> Farmington Hills, Michigan 48331-3535

ABBREVIATIONS FOR FORMS OF COMPANY INCORPORATION

A.B.	Aktiebolaget (Sweden)
A.G.	Aktiengesellschaft (Germany, Switzerland)
A.S.	Aksjeselskap (Denmark, Norway)
A.S.	Atieselskab (Denmark)
A.Ş.	Anomin Şirket (Turkey)
B.V.	Besloten Vennootschap met beperkte, Aansprakelijkheid (The Netherlands)
Co.	Company (United Kingdom, United States)
Corp.	Corporation (United States)
G.I.E.	Groupement d'Intérêt Economique (France)
GmbH	Gesellschaft mit beschränkter Haftung (Germany)
H.B.	Handelsbolaget (Sweden)
Inc.	Incorporated (United States)
KGaA	Kommanditgesellschaft auf Aktien (Germany)
K.K.	Kabushiki Kaisha (Japan)
LLC	Limited Liability Company (Middle East)
Ltd.	Limited (Canada, Japan, United Kingdom, United States)
N.V.	Naamloze Vennootschap (The Netherlands)
OY	Osakeyhtiöt (Finland)
OAO	Otkrytoe Aktsionernoe Obshchestve (Russia)
OOO	Obshchestvo s Ogranichennoi Otvetstvennostiu (Russia)
PLC	Public Limited Company (United Kingdom)
PTY.	Proprietary (Australia, Hong Kong, South Africa)
S.A.	Société Anonyme (Belgium, France, Switzerland)
SpA	Società per Azioni (Italy)
ZAO	Zakrytoe Aktsionernoe Obshchestve (Russia)

ABBREVIATIONS FOR CURRENCY

$	United States dollar	KD	Kuwaiti dinar
£	United Kingdom pound	L	Italian lira
¥	Japanese yen	LuxFr	Luxembourgian franc
A$	Australian dollar	M$	Malaysian ringgit
AED	United Arab Emirates dirham	N	Nigerian naira
		Nfl	Netherlands florin
B	Thai baht	NIS	Israeli new shekel
B	Venezuelan bolivar	NKr	Norwegian krone
BFr	Belgian franc	NT$	Taiwanese dollar
C$	Canadian dollar	NZ$	New Zealand dollar
CHF	Switzerland franc	P	Philippine peso
COL	Colombian peso	PLN	Polish zloty
Cr	Brazilian cruzado	PkR	Pakistan Rupee
CZK	Czech Republic koruny	Pta	Spanish peseta
DA	Algerian dinar	R	Brazilian real
Dfl	Netherlands florin	R	South African rand
DKr	Danish krone	RMB	Chinese renminbi
DM	German mark	RO	Omani rial
E£	Egyptian pound	Rp	Indonesian rupiah
Esc	Portuguese escudo	Rs	Indian rupee
EUR	Euro dollars	Ru	Russian ruble
FFr	French franc	S$	Singapore dollar
Fmk	Finnish markka	Sch	Austrian schilling
GRD	Greek drachma	SFr	Swiss franc
HK$	Hong Kong dollar	SKr	Swedish krona
HUF	Hungarian forint	SRls	Saudi Arabian riyal
IR£	Irish pound	TD	Tunisian dinar
K	Zambian kwacha	W	Korean won

International Directory of

COMPANY HISTORIES

ABN AMRO Holding, N.V.

Gustav Mahlerlaan 10
1082 PP Amsterdam
The Netherlands
Telephone: (31) 20-628-9393
Fax: (31) 20-629-9111
Web site: http://www.abnamro.com

Public Company
Employees: 111,710
Sales: EUR 18.8 billion (US $16.8 billion) (2001)
Stock Exchanges: Amsterdam Frankfurt London
    New York Paris
Ticker Symbol: ABN (New York)
NAIC: 522110 Commercial Banking

Rooted in 19th-century Dutch East Indies trade, ABN AMRO Holding, NV has grown into a major international bank with operations in more than 60 countries. The Amsterdam-based holding company is the top banking group in the Netherlands, where it has one-quarter of its 3,400 branches. With $600 billion in total assets, it stands as the seventh largest bank in Europe, and 13th largest in the world. ABN AMRO is the biggest foreign bank in the United States where it maintains a robust Midwest presence. American subsidiaries include Michigan's largest bank, Standard Federal, and LaSalle Bank NA, a leading bank in the Chicago area. The bank also has significant operations in Brazil. ABN AMRO reorganized at the start of 2001, dividing its operating divisions into a trio of strategic business units. At the same time it sold many non-core operations around the world and withdrew from investment banking in the United States. The company has about 111,000 employees worldwide.

Holland's King Launches ABN in 1824

The 1991 marriage of the two largest banks in the Netherlands—Amsterdam-Rotterdam Bank (AMRO) and Algemene Bank Nederland (ABN)—gave rise to ABN AMRO. However, each bank arrived at the wedding as a product of previous banking mergers. ABN's original ancestor was The Netherlands Trading Society (Nederlandsche Handel-Maatschapijj), a company created in 1824 by decree of the Netherlands' King Willem I—Holland's Merchant Monarch. The King and company founders intended to revive the trading in the Dutch East Indies (Indonesia) that had flourished during the 17th and 18th centuries with the Dutch East Indies Company. The Netherlands Trading Society (NTS) managed its operations from the Dutch colony on Java, Indonesia's largest island and commercial hub. It financed the export of agricultural products which, between 1840 and 1880, brought the Dutch treasury an average of 18 million guldens a year, about one-third of the country's budget. NTS opened offices in Shanghai (1825), Singapore (1858), Hong Kong (1906), and elsewhere around Asia, and soon expanded into traditional banking operations with credits, time deposits, and security orders. In 1926, NTS founded Saudi Hollandi Bank in Jeddah to serve the Islamic pilgrims from the Dutch East Indies. For many years it operated as Saudi Arabia's central bank maintaining the gold stock of the country, and processing its first oil-related transactions.

NTS survived both World War I and worldwide depression in the 1930s. World War II, however, crippled the company. Germany occupied the Netherlands and Japan controlled Indonesia. NTS attempted to recover by focusing on expansion and opening branches throughout the Netherlands. But by the early 1960s, competition among the numerous Dutch banks had escalated and produced a period of consolidation. In 1964, NTS opted to merge with Twentsche Bank, a 100-year-old Dutch agriculture bank, and took on the new moniker—Algemene Bank Nederland (ABN). Seeking more international balance, ABN in 1967 acquired Hollandsche Bank Unie, which had a large presence in South America. In 1975, ABN bought Mees & Hope Bankiers, a Dutch bank with significant investment banking business and solid network of branches. Mees & Hope continued to do business under its own name, and later added private asset management and fiduciary services for international clients. ABN's international reach also extended to the United States. In 1972, the bank formed ABN Corporation to represent its North American subsidiaries. The bank secured a firm foothold in the Midwest in 1979 when it purchased LaSalle National Bank, the sixth largest bank in the Chicago area with 700 employees. Two years later, in a restructuring move, La-Salle Bank became part of the ABN holding company LaSalle

Company Perspectives:

The goal of ABN AMRO is to create value for its clients. The key to our relationship approach is a constant focus on the financial services needs of our chosen client segments. It is through the professionalism and motivation of our staff across the globe that we realize this value. By strict adherence to financial targets these efforts produce maximum economic value for our shareholders. The ABN AMRO Values and Business Principles provide the framework within which we carry out our operations. We operate in three principal customer segments, namely Consumer and Commercial Clients, Wholesale Clients, and Private Clients and Asset Management. The objective is to maximize the value of each of these businesses as well as the synergies between them. Excellence of service to our clients and leadership in our chosen markets are of paramount importance to our long-term success.

National Corporation. The holding company went on to acquire six other Midwest banks including Exchange Bancorporation.

AMRO Is Born in Rotterdam: 1863

AMRO, ABN's merger partner, also began by financing Dutch East Indies trade. In 1863, a group of Rotterdam businesspeople and bankers created the Rotterdamsche Bank, lending funds to Dutch companies operating in Indonesia. The bank expanded its local lending activity to other businesses in the Netherlands, then added brokerage and securities firms to the banking operations through mergers. By the early 1900s, the company had a listing on the Amsterdam Stock Exchange. Renamed the Rotterdamsche Bankvereeniging, or Robaver, the bank continued to acquire local banks and also establish overseas bank branches in the West Indies (Antilles and the Bahamas) and Russia. By the early 1920s, Robaver stood as one of the largest banks in the Netherlands, and one of the more progressive banks as well. In 1928 it opened Vrouwenbank, a bank specifically for women.

Robaver persevered through the Depression and World War II, and in 1948 became the Netherlands' largest bank in when it merged with Incasso Bank, a Dutch institution founded in 1891. The same 1960s bank consolidation movement that produced ABN also swept up Robaver and Amsterdamsche Bank, another Dutch bank founded in the previous century. In 1964, Amsterdamsche Bank and Robaver merged to become the Amsterdam-Rotterdam Bank, or AMRO.

AMRO made a foray into the U.S. market in 1968. In a joint purchase with three other European banks, it bought New York-based European American Bank and Trust Company (EAB). AMRO continued building its retail banking business during the 1970s, and in 1975 acquired Dutch investment bank Pierson, Heldring & Pierson. In the 1980s, AMRO proposed the first sizable cross-border merger in European banking when it made a bid for Belgium's largest bank, Generale de Banque. But the deal collapsed with both parties citing legal, accounting and cultural difficulties. In the aftermath, AMRO bought Frankfurter Kreditbank, a German industrial bank.

1990: ABN and AMRO Merge

In the late 1980s the Dutch government softened its merger and acquisition laws. The deregulation paved the way for its national banks to pursue global operations and to sidestep takeovers by dominant global banking players in United States, Japan, and Great Britain. As with the banking consolidation frenzy of 1964, ABN and AMRO proved prominent players.

In March 1990, ABN and AMRO—now the two largest commercial banks in the Netherlands—announced their plan to merge. Consolidation promised to strengthen their domestic dominance in the face of increased competition from NMB-Postbank and Rabobank, two other leading Dutch banks. The merger was also expected to create economies of scale in retail bank networks and technology, along with reductions in staff and overlapping businesses. But the merger was not an entirely defensive or a cost-cutting maneuver. Officials at both banks aspired to take advantage of the strong combined capital base and become a global player and bank for the world's biggest international companies. With European monetary unification on the horizon, the combined companies were especially keen on extending their reach into Europe. Although legal unification was not finalized until September 1991, the banks reached a merger agreement and incorporated in the Netherlands in the summer of 1990. The newfound bank attained instant prominence. ABN AMRO was not only the largest bank in the Netherlands, but also controlled half of the Dutch corporate banking market and two-fifths of securities trading on the Amsterdam Stock Exchange. Outside the country, it ranked as the sixth largest bank in Europe, and one of the top 20 banks in the world. It had combined assets of $233 billion, well exceeding the balance sheet of Citibank, the largest U.S. bank with assets of $214 billion.

To add to its global expansion war chest, ABN AMRO immediately raised $650 million with the sale of preferred stock. However, the new bank first moved to enlarge its markets in the United States rather than advance into Europe. Intent on creating an East Coast financial center to complement its Midwest operations, the bank bought out AMRO's European American Bank partners in July 1991. It then bolstered its stake in the Midwest the following year. ABN AMRO North America—the new holding company controlling U.S. and Canadian operations—spent $430 million to takeover Talman Home Federal Savings and Loan Association, the largest savings and loan in Illinois.

Integration of the banks proceeded smoothly during the first years following the merger as executives from the partnering banks shared top executive roles. ABN AMRO avoided massive layoffs by managing staff reduction through attrition. In 1993, it merged its two independent Dutch—AMRO-owned Pierson, Heldring & Pierson and ABN-owned Mees & Hope—into a new bank called MeesPierson. MeesPierson remained independent from ABN AMRO, until it was sold to financial conglomerate Fortis Group four years later.

1994–1999: CEO Kalff Drives Expansion

Peter Jan Kalff, the banker responsible for the success and growth of ABN's LaSalle acquisition, became the ABN AMRO chief executive in 1994. Kalff guided the bank through a strong expansion period by adding smaller lending institutions to exist-

Key Dates:

1824: Dutch King Willem I creates The Netherlands Trading Society (NTS), parent company of ABN.

1863: Rotterdamsche Bank (Robaver) is founded and lends funds to Dutch companies operating in Indonesia.

1928: The progressive Robaver opens Vrouwenbank, a bank specifically for women.

1948: Robaver merges with Incasso Bank and becomes the Netherlands' largest bank.

1964: NTS merges with 100-year-old Dutch agriculture Twentsche Bank forming Algemene Bank Nederland (ABN); and Amsterdamsche Bank and Robaver merge and form the Amsterdam-Rotterdam Bank (AMRO).

1975: ABN buys Dutch investment banking specialist Mees & Hope Bankiers; AMRO acquires Dutch investment bank Pierson, Heldring & Pierson.

1979: ABN acquires Chicago-based LaSalle Bank and gains strong foothold in the United States.

1990: ABN and AMRO, the two largest banks in the Netherlands, agree to merge and form ABN AMRO Bank.

1991: The merger of ABN and AMRO is completed, and the company acquires Talman Home Federal Savings and Loan Association, the largest savings and loan in Illinois.

1994: Peter Jan Kalff becomes chief executive.

1995: *International Financing Review* designates ABN AMRO as the 1995 Bank of the Year.

1996: ABN AMRO purchases Standard Federal Bancorporation of Michigan.

1998: ABN AMRO buys Brazil's fourth largest public bank, Banco Real.

2000: ABN AMRO buys commercial bank holding company Michigan National Corporation; and Rijkaman Groenink becomes chairman and chief executive.

2002: ABN AMRO closes its U.S. investment bank and brokerage businesses; and U.K.-based ABN AMRO Asset Management and Artemis Investment Management merge operating under the Artemis name with ABN AMRO as majority owner.

ing networks, and allowing new properties to operate with considerable autonomy. The LaSalle subsidiary continued to snap up credit, financial, savings and other banking operations during the mid-1990s, merging and remerging companies until in 2000 all operations fell under the LaSalle Bank NA. Kalff also drove the Dutch bank into investment banking and brokerage services. In 1992, ABN AMRO had acquired Hoare Govett, a U.K.-based international corporate investment bank. In 1995 it announced plans to buy the Nordic investment bank Alfred Berg from Sweden's Volvo group, and also The Chicago Corp, a New York-based securities operation.

In 1996, *International Financing Review* designated ABN AMRO as the 1995 Bank of the Year for meeting rigorous financial objectives created after the 1991 merger. Yet the year was filled with far more momentous events. In the United

States, ABN AMRO made headlines when in late 1996 it agreed to pay US$1.9 billion for Standard Federal Bancorporation of Michigan, a large, profitable mortgage lender with US$15.5 billion in assets and over 180 branches in Michigan, Ohio, and Indiana. The highest price ever paid for a savings and loan, the sale further fortified its Midwest operations and caused ABN AMRO's stock to soar to a record high of 109.7 guilders. The deal made ABN AMRO the 12th largest bank in the United States. The same year the Dutch bank strengthened its position in Central and Eastern Europe by paying $90 million for a majority interest in Magyar Hitel Bank, Hungary's fifth largest commercial bank. It then purchased Australian-based Lloyds Bank, with branches in both Australia and New Zealand, for $868 million.

Kalff also pursued out-of-favor banking markets in Latin America and Asia. In 1998, ABN AMRO bought Brazil's fourth largest public bank, Banco Real, for $2.1 billion and went on to take a controlling interest in Bandepe Bank. It established residential mortgage financing, asset management, and insurance activities in Brazil and five other Latin American and Caribbean countries. The same year it paid $183 million for a 75 percent stake in Thailand's Bank of Asia, one of the healthier financial institutions in the nation's struggling banking industry.

Yet ABN AMRO's plan to establish a borderless, Pan-European bank remained illusive. Nationalistic regulators threw up hurdles regularly. In 1998 the bank looked at creating a second European home market in France by bidding on the French government's sale of Credit Industriel & Commerical. But French authorities opted instead to sell to a national institution with a lower bid than the Dutch bank's offer. The scene was repeated later that year when ABN AMRO endeavored to take over Belgium's Generale de Banque. The Dutch bank countered the $10.7 billion offer made by the Dutch-Belgian Fortis Group, but Generale's shareholders preferred not to be bought by their Dutch rivals even for more money. Declaring ABN AMRO's $12.2 billion bid a hostile takeover, Fortis anteed up $13 billion to buy Generale. ABN AMRO finally established a small foothold in a Western European financial center in 1999, taking a 10 percent minority position in Italy's Banca di Roma. Late in the year it also purchased the Netherlands' fifth largest mortgage lender, Bouwfounds Nederlandse Gemeenten.

New Millennium Brings Profit Declines and Restructuring

ABN AMRO's goal to become a powerful, full-service European bank had failed to materialize by the end of decade, yet the bank had charted considerable success by other measures. At the end of 1999 the bank had logged ten consecutive years of profit growth, with an overall rise of 40.6 percent that year, the highest since the two Dutch banks merged. However, concerns about maintaining profit growth surfaced as ABN AMRO entered the new millennium. Midyear of 2000, it announced a restructuring plan that divided operations into three client-based strategic business units: Consumer and Commercial Clients, Wholesale (Corporate) Clients, and Private Clients and Asset Management. It also outlined a plan to cut costs by closing full-service branches and investing in electronic Internet banking. The bank planned to eliminate about 10 percent, or 2,500 jobs from its Netherlands' workforce, and close 150 of its 900 branches over the next five years.

Heading up the restructuring was new ABN AMRO chairman and chief executive Rijkaman Groenink, a management board member who replaced the retiring Kalff in May 2000. Analysts depicted Groenink as more aggressive than his predecessor, and in the fall of 2000 two significant acquisitions were underway. The bank agreed to pay $825 million for New York-based Allegheny Asset Management. The move was an effort to remedy ABN AMRO's slim asset management business and lack of European investment channels to supplement underfunded government pensions. Allegheny managed about $45 billion in assets and the acquisition increased the bank's global assets under management to $155 billion. A month later ABN AMRO struck an agreement with National Australia Bank to buy U.S. commercial bank holding company Michigan National Corporation, based in Farmington Hills, Michigan. The $2.75 billion deal was again intended to bolster the Dutch bank's already solid banking franchise in the Midwest. Michigan National Corporation had assets amounting to $11.6 billion and its primary subsidiary, Michigan National Bank had 3,600 employees and 184 branches. ABN AMRO merged the bank with its Standard Federal holding.

Groenink painted a fuller picture of the changes coming later in the year when he reported a 21 percent decline in the bank's second-quarter profit for 2001. He said that ABN AMRO would not only monitor the growth of its corporate and investment banking but also look for a merger or an alliance, with Fortis as a possible candidate. Meanwhile, the bank continued to adjust its holdings to help cut costs and improve profits. To finance the acquisition of Allegheny and Michigan National, and focus exclusively on the Midwest, ABN AMRO sold New-York based European American Bank (EAB) to Citibank for $1.6 billion. It also reached agreement with Dutch rival ING Group to purchase the North American brokerage, corporate finance, domestic equities, and futures and options businesses of subsidiary ING Barings for $275 million. Late in the year the bank began divesting global units outside its home markets and business focus. Bank operations were sold in Sri Lanka, Morocco, Panama, Argentina, Kenya, Bahrain, Malaysia, the Philippines, and elsewhere. Yet the sluggish economy and terrorist attacks on the United States in September 2001 combined to produce disappointing year-end results. Revenues for 2001 rose only 2 percent to $16.8 billion (EUR 18.8 billion) and net profits dropped 24 percent to $2.8 billion (EUR 2.4 billion) excluding the sale of European American Bank and restructuring charges.

Refocusing on Retail Banking

In 2002, the pullback in securities and investment banking business outside Europe continued. Only a year after acquiring ING Barings, ABN AMRO decided to close its U.S. equities and corporate finance operations in the United States, cutting 550 trading, research and back-office jobs. Analysts estimated these operations were losing $100 million a year, and bank officials admitted their U.S. operations were too small and weak to compete with the larger Wall Street firms. Meanwhile, bank closures in the Netherlands continued to move ahead with an announcement that it would shut down 250 more branches in the Netherlands by the year's end. The bank's assets manage-

ment business suffered a blow after two of its high-profile fund managers left to work for a rival firm, but recovered to a degree when ABN AMRO Asset Management and Artemis Investment Management, both located in the United Kingdom, agreed to merge. The enlarged business operated under the Artemis name, but ABN AMRO maintained majority ownership.

A slow economy and ambitions to compete in U.S. corporate and investment banking caused ABN AMRO to stumble in the first years of the new millennium. Analysts praised the retreat from the U.S. markets, believing the Dutch bank was better suited to building securities and corporate brokerage business in Europe and Asia. ABN AMRO executives seemed to agree that a transition back to the profitable retail and commercial banking it was most familiar with made sense in the near term.

Principal Subsidiaries

ABN AMRO Asset Management Ltd.; ABN AMRO Bank NV; ABN AMRO Bouwfonds Nederlandse Gemeenten NV (50%); ABN AMRO Lease Holding NV; ABN AMRO North America, Inc.; Banco ABN AMRO Real SA (88%); LaSalle Bank NA; LaSalle National Corporation; Standard Federal Bancorporation.

Principal Competitors

Deutsche Bank; ING; Societe Generale; Credit Suisse; HypoVereinsbank.

Further Reading

"ABN AMRO and Artemis to Merge," *Sunday Telegraph* (London), June 16, 2002, p. 9.
"ABN-AMRO Digs in to Europe," *The Banker* (London), December 1996, p. 6.
"ABN AMRO in Takeover Spree," *Euroweek* (London), April 13, 1995, p. 1.
"ABN AMRO's Profit Falls," *New York Times*, February 23, 2001, p. W1.
"ABN AMRO Targets Latin American Bank," *Mergers and Acquisitions*, September/October 1998, p. 8.
"ABN AMRO to Close 2 Units in United States," *New York Times*, March 26, 2002, p. C4.
"AMRO and ABN Head for the Altar," *Mergers & Acquisitions International*, August 1, 1990, posted August 29, 2000, http://www.lexux-nexus.com.
Bakker, Tino, "Dutch Take the Fast Track," *The Banker* (London), April 1998, pp. 35–37.
"A Bank Ahead of Its Time," *Forbes.com*, posted June 14, 1999, http://www.forbes.com.
Burgess, Kate, "ABN AMRO Loses Two Top Fund Managers to Rival," *Financial Times*, April 3, 2002, p. 25.
Cowell, Alan, "ABN AMRO Shifts Focus Back to Traditional Banking," *New York Times*, August. 17, 2001, p. W1.
——, "Bank Expects Income to Fall," *New York Times*, October 24, 2001, p. W1.
Currie, Antony, "Enter Fortis—The Fourth Force," *Euromoney* (London), November 1996, pp. 65–68.
"Everyone Gunning for ABN-AMRO," *Euromoney* (London), October 1993, p. 64.
"Fortis Victorious in the Battle for Generale Bank," *The Banker* (London), July 1998, p. 7.

Gearing, Julian, ''Meet My Protection: Bank of Asia Finds a Heavy-weight Partner,'' *Asiaweek.com*, accessed June 24, 2002, http://www.asiaweek.com.

Hakim, Danny, ''Europeans Buy 2 U.S. Money Managers,'' *New York Times*, October 19, 2000, p. C19.

Hansell, Saul, ''Dutch Bank in $1.9 Billion Deal for S&L,'' *New York Times*, November 23, 1996, p. 31.

''History,'' *ABN AMRO*, accessed June 24, 2002, http://www.abnamro.com.

''History,'' *MeesPierson*, accessed June 24, 2002, http://www.meespierson.com.

Hoare, Michael, ''Analysts Call for More Cuts at ABN,'' *eFinancial News*, posted April 2, 2002, http://www.efinancialnews.com.

Hobson, Dominic, ''Dutch Treat,'' *Asset International Online*, posted March 1992, http://www.assetpub.com.

Hungry Dutch Bankers, *United States Banker*, April 1993, p. 31.

''Interview: Jan Kalff, Chairman, ABN AMRO,'' *Euromoney* (London), September 1995, p. 64.

Kantrow, Yvette, ''ABN AMRO/Chicago Corp. Will Expand 'Significantly' in N.Y.,'' *The Investment Dealers' Digest*, October 2, 1995, p. 8.

Kapner, Suzanne, ''Dutch Bank Says Profit Is Down 12%,'' *New York Times*, May 10, 2001 p. W1.

Kerr, Ian, ''ABN AMRO Should Be Cautious in the U.S.,'' *eFinancial News*, posted April 15, 2002, http://www.efinancialnews.com.

Marshall, Jeffrey, ''A Dutch Treat in America,'' *U.S. Banker,* April 1997, pp. 32–42.

Merrell, Caroline, ''ABN to Shut 250 Branches as Profits Take a 42% Fall,'' *The Times* (London), April 30, 2002, p. 25.

''New Chief at ABN AMRO,'' *New York Times*, November 13, 1999, p. 2.

Pechter, Kerry, ''Enjoying Dutch Treats,'' *International Business*, July 1993, p. 25.

Pohl, M., and S. Freitag, S., eds., ''ABN AMRO Bank,'' *Handbook on the History of European Banks,* 1994, pp. 749–760.

Saigol, Lina, and Mary Chung, ''Closure of U.S. Units Meets with Relief,'' *Financial Times*, March 26, 2002, p. 30.

Serenvi, Peter, ''Uphill Struggle to Make Profits,'' *Euromoney* (London), May 2000, p. 18.

Sorkin, Andrew Ross, ''ABN AMRO Set to Trim 10% of Work Force,'' *New York Times*, January 19, 2000, p. C4.

Van de Krol, Ronald, ''Move Signals Bank's Expansionist Mood,'' *Financial Times* (London), July 17, 1991, p. 28.

——, ''The Netherlands: Merger Pace Accelerates,'' *Financial Times* (London), September 4, 1991, p. 31.

Van de Krol, Ronald, and George Graham, ''ABN AMRO Buys Complete Control of U.S. Bank,'' *Financial Times* (London), July 3, 1991, p. 24.

''World Banking: The New Landscape,'' *Euromoney* (London), December 1992, p. 58.

—Douglas Cooley

AEGON N.V.

Mariahoeveplein 50
2501 TV The Hague
The Netherlands
Telephone: (31) 70-344-3210
Fax: (31) 70-344-8445
Web site: http://www.aegon.com

Public Company
Incorporated: 1983
Employees: 24,109
Sales: EUR 31.895 billion (2001)
Stock Exchanges: Amsterdam Euronext Frankfurt
    London New York Tokyo Zurich
Ticker Symbol: AGN (Euronext), AEG (NYSE)
NAIC: 524114 Direct Health and Medical Insurance
    Carriers; 524128 Other Direct Insurance (except Life,
    Health, and Medical) Carriers; 524126 Direct Property
    and Casualty Insurance Carriers; 524210 Insurance
    Agencies and Brokerages

AEGON N.V., one of the world's ten largest listed life insurance groups, is a prime example of the move toward larger units in the insurance industry. The company's formation is due to the merger in the late 1960s of two insurance firms, AGO and Ennia. The history of these firms is the story of combining smaller companies into larger and more competitive organizations— AGO is the product of the merger of Algemeene Friesche, Groot-Noordhollandsche, and Olveh; and Ennia is the product of the merger of Eerste Nederlandsche, Nieuwe Eerste Nederlandsche, and Nillmij. AEGON's name, is made up of the initials of its major predecessors. The name reflects its roots; and its locally managed structure is designed to help the company compete successfully in a mature, internationalized market. The company operates in three major markets: the Americas, including the United States, Canada, and Mexico; The Netherlands; and the United Kingdom. AEGON is also present in a number of other countries, including Hungary, Spain, Belgium, Germany, Hong Kong, Italy, Luxembourg, the Philippines, Taiwan, and has representative offices in China and India.

AEGON's Predecessors: Dutch Insurance Through 1870

The company's earliest predecessors were burial funds such as the Broederlijke Liefdebeurs (the Fraternal Fund of Love), which was established in Haarlem in 1759. Burial funds were set up to serve a locality or industry and offered some protection from a city-provided pauper's funeral. The funds became increasingly common in the 19th century. The burial funds had a number of distinctive characteristics. Statutes limited them to operate in only one Dutch province. Low premiums that appealed to working people were collected weekly at the insured's home, and fixed premiums did not always mean a fixed-death payment. Burial funds also traditionally insured young children free.

One such fund was started when J. Oosterhoff, a civil servant and former burial-fund agent, decided to go into business for himself in 1844. He and another civil servant founded Algemeene Friesche in Friesland. After several years of growth, Oosterhoff wanted to expand nationwide. In 1860 the company passed a government examination of its actuarial practices and became a full-fledged mutual insurance company, and all the people it insured gained equal rights. Ordinary life insurance companies could become national entities and offer a broader range of insurance products, including annuities, term policies, whole life policies, endowment policies, and group life insurance. When Algemeene Friesche's organizational form changed, it continued to offer basically the same product but in a broader market.

Groot-Noordhollandsche also began as a burial fund. A local vicar in the western Netherlands established this fund in 1845, a year after Oosterhoff set up Algemeene Friesche. In 1918, Groot-Noordhollandsche also became an ordinary life insurance company.

Another burial fund that grew into a life insurance company was the Dordrecht. The Dordrecht's main competitor in the 1880s was an ordinary insurance company, so the burial fund's managers reorganized to remain competitive. In 1883 the Dordrecht became an industrial life insurer, underwriting low-cost policies aimed at working men, basically the same market it had served as a burial fund.

Key Dates:

1968: Algemeene Friesche, Groot-Noordhollandsche, and the Olveh merge to form AGO.

1969: Eerste Nederlandsche, NIEUWE Eerste Nederlandsche, and Nillmij merge to form Ennia.

1983: AEGON incorporates in The Netherlands through the merger of AGO Holding N.V. and Ennia N.V.

1985: Company is listed on the NASDAQ.

1986: Company acquires Monumental Corporation and is listed on the Tokyo Stock Exchange.

1988: AEGON USA is formed from the merger of Life Investors, Monumental Corporation, and National Old Life.

1991: Company acquires Western Reserve Life and is listed on the New York Stock Exchange.

1993: Company signs an agreement with Scottish Equitable Life Assurance Society of Edinburgh to establish a new company, Scottish Equitable PLC.

1994: Subsidiary AEGON UK signs an agreement with the Independent Insurance Group PLC enabling AEGON UK to disengage from the U.K. property and casualty market.

1997: Company acquires U.S.-based Providian Corporation for NLG 6.7 billion (US $3.5 billion).

1999: Company acquires Transamerica Corporation and the life insurance business of Guardian Royal Exchange UK.

2001: Company acquires J.C. Penney Direct Marketing Services, Inc.

Other life insurance predecessors of AEGON, however, did not come out of the burial fund tradition. Vennootschap Nederland was set up to offer a complete line of life insurance products, the first firm to be able to make that claim.

Count A. Langrand-Dumonceau established Vennootschap Nederland in 1858. Langrand-Dumonceau was a colorful European financier who had begun his career selling pencils, paper, and wallets as a youngster. As soon as possible, he left his native Belgium to join the French Foreign Legion, but his career there was short—Langrand-Dumonceau was one of the few legionnaires ever to have his legion contract annulled. Back home in Belgium, he founded a number of life insurance companies, the most important of which was the Royal Belge. In 1858 he established Vennootschap Nederland, and that same year became one of the founding directors of Der Anker in Vienna. At age 32 he headed four insurance companies and was a self-made millionaire.

Langrand-Dumonceau's companies sold a very popular tontine, a policy in which the capital of group savings was divided among the survivors after a specified period. The right to claim the surrender value of a policy or to borrow on the policy made the product attractive to small savers with few options. About 1860, however, the Belgian millionaire began to expand into mortgage banking throughout Western Europe. When an economic crisis hit in the late 1860s his empire crumbled. While his insurance companies survived because

they had been more carefully managed, they were no longer as sound as they had been before Langrand-Dumonceau's entry into banking. In 1913, Vennootschap Nederland merged with Eerste Nederlandsche, an almost unheard-of step in an industry that generated growth from within.

Another insurance firm, the Olveh, began as a self-help organization for civil servants in 1877. The Olveh was patterned after a similar Austrian union, which had been very successful in promoting the interests of its members. The group's goal was to reduce the cost of living and provide some security for members by setting up consumer cooperatives, a savings plan, and a life insurance program. In 1878 the life insurance end of the Olveh became a separate company, and in 1879 it began to offer the same coverage for members and nonmembers of its parent organization. By 1909 all ties with the original self-help organization had been cut, but it retained the association form.

Another of AEGON's predecessors was the Nillmij. The Nillmij was established in the Dutch East Indies in 1859 by C.F.W. Wiggers van Kerchem, one of the colony's foremost financiers who had set up the first general bank in the Indies. The Nillmij was successful because of its unique relationship with the colonial government. Van Kerchem used his influence to win the active support of authorities. Some premiums were collected by government tax collectors and military paymasters; the governor and commanders of the colonial army and navy recommended the Nillmij as a way for civil servants and military personnel to save outside of their pension systems. The Nillmij's monopoly continued until the 1880s. In 1883 the government stopped helping the company collect premiums, and competition from the Dordrecht, the Olveh, Eerste Nederlandsche, and others gained a foothold in the colony.

While the Nillmij's special relationship with the government initially made it successful, government regulation of the life insurance industry at home made operation more difficult for domestic companies. State regulation of life insurance dated to special decrees issued by Napoléon Bonaparte in 1809. Royal decrees of 1830 and 1833 strengthened these controls. Under them, the government controlled entry into the field and defined what constituted life insurance. In 1860 the government formulated the mortality table to be used and the interest rate to be charged. Foreign life insurance companies operating in the country were exempt from these rules, which often meant that they could charge lower rates.

Developments Through World War I

In 1880 the Dutch Supreme Court ruled that the royal decrees were not binding, and government regulation ended. Although the regulated system had been criticized, life insurers were concerned that the public would lose faith in an unregulated industry. It was not until 1922—a year after the bankruptcy of the largest Dutch life insurance company, the Algemeene Maatschappij van Levensverzekering en Lijfrente (the General Company for Life Insurance and Superannuation)—that new regulations of the industry were passed, with input from life insurance companies.

Despite the problems of life insurance regulation, Dutch life insurers generally did not offer any other type of insurance product, just as other insurers did not offer life insurance. Another of AEGON's predecessors, Eerste Nederlandsche, had pioneered nonlife coverage, specifically accident and health insurance.

Eerste Nederlandsche introduced accident insurance in The Netherlands about 1880. The company's founder brought the concept to The Netherlands after a visit to England, where he became familiar with the Railway Passengers Assurance Company. Eerste Nederlandsche filled another niche as well, offering collective accident insurance for factory and construction workers. Since health and accident insurance was still new, however, the new company's directors decided to also provide life insurance for security.

Although Eerste Nederlandsche was involved in administering payments when the Workmen's Compensation Act was passed in 1901, government social insurance was the impetus for a reorganization of the company. The accident and health department became a separate company, the Nieuwe Eerste Nederlandsche, whose shares were held by the parent firm. The company also decided to diversify at this time, becoming one of the first to offer insurance against liability and burglary. It also began to insure bicycles, and in 1911 wrote its first motor vehicle policy.

By 1913, AEGON's predecessors, Algemeene Friesche, Eerste Nederlandsche, Groot-Noordhollandsche, Olveh, and Nillmij were strong competitors in the life insurance field, while Nieuwe Eerste Nederlandsche was successfully staking out new areas of insurance. Algemeene was by far the largest Dutch insurer, the Dordrecht was second, and Eerste Nederlandsche, Nillmij, and Olveh all had places in the top ten. All of these companies except the Dordrecht were primarily domestic firms. The Dordrecht had successfully established a presence in Hungary, Italy, and northern France. Other companies' attempts to sell insurance abroad, especially Vennootschap Nederland's efforts in Prussia and New York, were not as successful.

During World War I, Dordrecht's foreign interests meant that it was more seriously hurt than companies with primarily domestic operations. Even in neutral Holland, war led to interruptions in premium collection and mobilization of part of the staff.

The postwar years meant growth for the larger insurance companies. An increased emphasis on security and sharing risks increased profits for these companies. Acquisitions became a more acceptable way to put profits to work. Algemeene Friesche and Groot-Noordhollandsche especially grew through acquisitions between the wars, and Eerste Nederlandsche took over the Dordrecht in 1919. When Algemeene Maatschappij van Levensverzekering en Lijfrente failed in 1921, Algemeene Friesche took over its Dutch business, and the Nillmij acquired its business in the East Indies.

World War II and Recovery: The Mergers Continue Through 1980

Expansion and profitability came to an abrupt end with the Depression and then World War II. The German Army occupied The Netherlands on May 10, 1940. Communications abroad were cut off, as eventually were communications within the country as well. Nearly all men were sent to work in Ger-

many or went underground to avoid being transported to work camps. Potential customers concentrated on survival in a time of chronic food shortages. Eerste Nederlandsche's headquarters was among the many buildings destroyed when Germans bombed The Hague in March 1945.

The German occupying force also required that Jewish employees be dismissed and that all Jewish insurance policies be surrendered. While the insurance board unofficially asked for inconspicuous noncooperation and the Dutch government in exile declared the measures null and void, companies did not always avoid compliance. The war reached the Dutch East Indies in 1942, with even more devastating results. The European population there was interned, and the companies that operated there simply vanished.

Postwar rebuilding offered new opportunities for insurance companies to test their flexibility. Premium income expanded rapidly between 1945 and 1950, by approximately 13 percent overall. Increases in group insurance and insurance-based pension plans contributed to this growth. Government involvement in social programs increased in the aftermath of World War II, and the impact was mixed. The state's social security program, enacted in 1957, promoted financial planning with social insurance as one basis and supplementary private insurance as another. Compulsory car insurance offered new opportunities in 1961. The Disability Law of 1967, however, ended group disability insurance, a concept the Nieuwe Eerste Nederlandsche had pioneered.

In this new environment, the division between general and life insurance became less pronounced. Large life insurance companies such as Algemeene Friesche and Groot-Noordhollandsche gained experience in general insurance by acquiring smaller firms. Insurance companies also began to diversify into noninsurance areas, especially mortgage banking.

The insurance companies that operated in the Dutch East Indies, however, faced more difficult postwar problems. Operations had to be rebuilt from scratch. Currency restrictions and inflation drastically cut profits. Finally, the colony became independent in 1949 and the Indonesian government in 1957 nationalized Dutch concerns. The Nillmij, which had originated in the Dutch East Indies, had to change dramatically to continue to operate. Its subsidiary in The Netherlands was made the parent company, and the assets of the former parent in Indonesia were nationalized.

The movement toward combining companies accelerated during the 1960s. Postwar emphasis on European cooperation culminated in the establishment of the European Economic Community in 1957. The movement toward a single European market gave larger companies a competitive edge. Inflation and rising operation costs—especially the cost of computerizing operations—also made bigger companies more profitable.

Mergers in the United States, Great Britain, and Canada were followed in 1963 by the merger of the largest and second-largest Dutch insurance companies: The Netherlands Insurance Company and the Nationale Levensverzekering-Bank. Algemeene Friesche, Groot-Noordhollandsche, and the Olveh merged in 1968 to form AGO; and Eerste Nederlandsche, Nieuwe Eerste Nederlandsche, and Nillmij merged in 1969 to form Ennia.

Both mergers involved major organizational changes, but the AGO merger proved especially difficult because the firms involved had different structures. Algemeene Friesche and the Olveh were mutuals, while Groot-Noordhallandsche had retained *vereniging*, or association, structure. In a series of steps, the new company became a holding company with subsidiaries concentrating on different aspects of the insurance market. AGO Life Insurance Company and AGO General Insurance Company operated as limited companies, while AGO Holding Company retained the *vereniging* structure and was not owned by shareholders.

The mergers were completed as the Dutch insurance market was contracting. Pension-linked insurance business dropped, and the collapse of the housing market undermined mortgage operations. High interest rates also had an adverse impact. In this domestic climate, worldwide insurance expansion was attractive. Attempts to establish foreign branches or subsidiaries during the 1950s and 1960s had not been successful. Europe and the United States, the largest single insurance market in the world, offered potential for expansion as domestic opportunities diminished.

In 1979, AGO acquired a majority interest in Life Investors in Cedar Rapids, Iowa. Ennia began its foreign acquisitions in earnest when it established operations in Spain in 1980. In 1981, Ennia purchased National Old Line Insurance Company of Little Rock, Arkansas. In 1982, the year before AEGON was formed, 50 percent of AGO's life insurance income came form foreign sources, as did 46 percent of its general insurance income. For Ennia, 55 percent of general insurance premiums were foreign, although its foreign life insurance business remained small.

AEGON's Continued Success after the 1980s

The mergers that formed AGO and Ennia had made both companies more effective competitors at home and abroad. By 1983, however, the companies were exploring other opportunities to remain competitive. And with European integration looming in 1992, competitive advantage was becoming increasingly important. Soon, their attentions turned to each other, and for the same reasons that these two companies sprung from previous mergers—cost reduction, the economies of combining technology infrastructure, a better basis for foreign expansion—AGO and Ennia merged to form AEGON in November 1983, becoming the second largest Dutch insurance firm behind Nationale-Nederlanden.

The new company continued to pursue a strategy of expansion at home and abroad. In 1986 AEGON purchased the troubled Friesch-Groningsche Hypotheek-bank and improved earnings there by the end of the decade. That same year it increased its presence in Spain, buying Union Levantina de Seguros. AEGON's chairman, J.F.M. Peters, said Spain's entry into the European common market and the country's economic development made it an attractive market. Citing opportunities for growth in the United States, Peters announced the purchase of Monumental Corporation of Baltimore, Maryland, the same year. In 1985, the company was first listed on the NASDAQ.

By the end of the 1980s, management reorganization and cost controls had led to rising profits. European deregulation with its increasing competition had some short-term impact on profits. AEGON adopted a policy of selective expansion in profitable markets and cost-reduction measures assisted the company to meet those challenges, while continuing to merge and consolidate smaller companies.

In 1988, AEGON introduced AEGON Aandelenfonds N.V., an open-end investment fund on the Amsterdam Stock Exchange, and a year later the company merged three subsidiaries—Life Investors, Monumental Corporation, and National Old Line—to form the holding company AEGON USA. In 1990, AEGON acquired J.P. Morgan Nederland, but with this acquisition, the company also sold some of its less profitable interests, such as LeaseAmerica and Gebam B.V. Later that year, AEGON reduced its ownership interest in the AEGON Aandelenfonds N.V.

In the United Kingdom, AEGON announced a cooperation agreement with the Scottish Equitable Life Assurance Society of Edinburgh, and established a new company, the Scottish Equitable PLC, in 1993. Through Scottish Equitable that same year, AEGON started a strategic alliance with ONVZ and established Scottish Equitable International in Luxembourg.

In 1994 one of the company's subsidiaries, AEGON UK, signed an agreement with the Independent Insurance Group PLC, another U.K. based company, in which Independent acquired assets from AEGON UK and was able to offer renewals on general insurance policies previously underwritten by AEGON UK. This agreement was not a sale of AEGON UK, but a controlled disengagement by AEGON from the UK property and casualty market.

Acquisitions continued, as the company moved toward the millennium. In 1997, AEGON purchased the Dutch funeral insurance company Levob Uitvaartverzekering N.V., a nod to their burial fund origins. Later that June, they made a large stateside acquisition: the insurance operations of Providian Corporation, a transaction valued at the time at NLG 6.7 billion (US $3.5 billion). The 1999 acquisitions of Transamerica and the Guardian Royal Exchange UK life insurance businesses, as well as the 2001 acquisition of the assets of J.C. Penney Direct Marketing Services, Inc, helped drive increases in premium income and other revenues in the Americas and the United Kingdom.

The strategies appeared successful. In 1999, AEGON announced that since it was formed in 1983, the company has consistently reported profit growth. Their compound annual growth in net earnings over their first ten years amounted to 17 percent, and 22 percent over the most recent five years.

Principal Operating Units

AEGON America; AEGON Nederland; AEGON UK; AEGON Taiwan.

Principal Subsidiaries

AEGON Bank N.V.; AEGON UK PLC; AEGON Union Aseguradora S.A. de Seguros y Reaseguros; AEGON USA,

Inc.; Afore Banamex AEGON S.A. (48%); AMVEST Vastgoed B.V.; AXENT/AEGON Leven N.V.; AXENT/AEGON Schade N.V.; Bankers United Life Assurance Company; Commonwealth General Corporation; First AUSA Life Insurance Company; Guardian Assurance PLC; Life Investors Insurance Company of America; Monumental Life Insurance Company; Nederlandse Verzekeringsgroep Leven N.V.; Nederlandse Verzekeringsgroep Schade N.V.; Peoples Benefit Life Insurance Company; PFL Life Insurance Company; Scottish Equitable International Holding PLC; Spaarbeleg Kas N.V.; Transamerica Corporation; USA Life Insurance Company, Inc.; Van Nierop Assuradeuren N.V.

Further Reading

"AEGON Agrees to Sell Container-Transport Unit," *New York Times,* July 25, 2000 p. C4(N).

"AEGON Buys Transamerica," *European Report,* March 3, 1999, p. 1.

"AEGON Launches 20-Year Insurance Product," *BusinessWorld,* October 12, 1998; p. 1.

"Aegon Sells Its Stakes in Two Mexican Firms to Citigroup," *Wall Street Journal,* Jan 21, 2002, p. C13.

Barney, Lee, "Impact of Aegon's Deal Remains to Be Seen," *Mutual Fund Market News,* March 1, 1999.

"Best Is Saved until Last as Aegon Serves Up Dutch Treat," *Euroweek,* December 15, 2000, p. 45.

Evans, Richard, "AEGON Sallies Out from Its Dykes," *Euromoney,* December 1985; pp. 157–159.

Harris, Elizabeth, "Satisfying 2 Cravings: Yield and Safety," *New York Times,* January 6, 2002, p. 3.21.

"Health Insurance Alliance with Aegon Being Studied," *Wall Street Journal,* June 22, 1990, p. A6(W).

"Icon Group International, Inc Staff, Aegon N.V.: Labor Productivity Benchmarks and International Gap Analysis," Icon Group International, Incorporated, October, 2000.

Lumenthal, Robin Goldwyn, "California Victory: Dutch Insurers to Provide List of Holocaust claims," *Barron's,* December 6, 1999, p. 16.

McGonegle, Kim, "Taking Work Off-Site—AEGON's Telecommuting Program," *Employment Relations Today,* Spring 1996, pp. 25–39.

Meakin, Thomas K., "Life & Health Stocks Lead November Rally," *National Underwriter,* December 14, 1998, pp. 29–31.

"Monumental in Aegon Deal," *New York Times,* May 28, 1986, p. N25.

Racanelli, Vito J, "European Trader: Show Us the Earnings," *Barron's,* March 18, 2002; p. MW6, 1.

Reier, Sharon, "Marathon Man," *Financial World,* September 1, 1992, p. 56.

Rescigno, Richard, "Old World, New Vitality: A Fund Chief Sees Some Bargains," *Barron's National Business and Financial Weekly,* April 27, 1992, pp. M12–17.

Reynolds, Simon, "Dutch Caution," *Reactions,* October 1993, pp. 44–47.

"Storm across America," *The Economist,* February 20, 1999.

"Teachers, Aegon to Team Up on Securitization," *Commercial Mortgage Alert,* July 23, 2001, pp. 1–3.

"Working for Security," The Hague, AEGON, 1983.

—Ginger G. Rodriguez
—update: C.J. Gussoff

Allied Waste Industries, Inc.

15880 N. Greenway-Hayden Loop, Suite 100
Scottsdale, Arizona 85260
U.S.A.
Telephone: (480) 627-2700
Toll Free: (888) 208-1000
Fax: (480) 627-2701

Public Company
Incorporated: 1987
Employees: 29,000
Sales: $5.6 billion (2001)
Stock Exchanges: New York
Ticker Symbol: AW
NAIC: 562212 Solid Waste Landfills Combined with Collection and/or Local Hauling of Non-Hazardous Waste Material

Allied Waste Industries, Inc. (AWI) is the second largest non-hazardous solid waste company in the United State (the largest company is Waste Management). AWI serves approximately 10 million customers in 39 states. The company is actually comprised of 355 collection companies (which AWI bought or merged with), 181 transfer stations, 167 landfills, and 65 recycling facilities. Allied Waste's customer base is residential, commercial, and industrial.

Allied Waste's Roots: 1987–1990

Bruce Lessey serviced garbage trucks in Houston when he decided to become part of the industry itself. He founded Allied Waste in 1987 as a public company, and began buying waste companies. In 1989 his company was in financial trouble. Roger Ramsey, a cofounder of garbage industry giant Browning-Ferris Industries, Inc. (BFI), and a partner in Houston Partners, LP, an investment company that owned part of AWI, joined Allied Waste's board of directors in August 1989. At the time, Lessey said that Ramsey brings "significant knowledge and experience to the organization." He felt confident that Ramsey would help Allied Waste become a national company.

The young company experienced difficult years during 1989 and 1990. In September 1989, Lessey was appointed vice-chairman and CFO. In its place as president AWI selected Fred Ferreira, a man who brought over 20 years of industry experience (many of them with Waste Management, the largest company in the field) to his new position. By the end of October 1989, Lessey left AWI, the company announcing only that he was returning "to the venture capital industry." Ramsey became the company's CEO in 1990.

Early Company Growth: 1990

Allied Waste started the 1990s with its acquisition of Sanco, a solid waste company that served northeast New Mexico. Fred Ferreira said of the acquisition: "Sanco exemplifies AWI's acquisition strategy; to continue with a national expansion program of acquiring profitable and well-managed waste collection and disposal companies."

In early 1990, Daniel J. Ivan joined AWI as vice-president of Market Development. Ivan came from industry leader Waste Management, where he worked with Ferreira. In October 1990, Ivan was promoted to president, in place of Ferreira who resigned "for personal reasons." At that time, AWI was poised to begin a program of mergers and acquisitions that would lead it from a small solid waste handler to a giant rivaling Waste Management, all in a relatively short period of time. Interestingly enough, the company first concentrated on markets small enough (communities of less that 50,000 people), so as not to compete with the big names, according to Ivan.

In March 1991, AWI purchased 80 percent of CRX, a solid waste company headquartered in Fremont, Nebraska. This purchase was the first step to an eventual complete acquisition of CRX by AWI. CRX owned and operated landfills, transfer stations and collection services in Nebraska and Iowa. AWI viewed CRX's assets as a base "from which to expand into surrounding market areas."

In September 1991, with markets in Iowa, Missouri, Nebraska, New Mexico, and, of course, Texas, AWI was listed on NASDAQ under the ticker symbol AWIN. The company than purchased Super Services Waste Management, Inc., headquartered in Flagstaff, Arizona. The Super Services acquisition gained Allied Waste entry into new markets in Northern Arizona, and Nevada, and expanded their operations in New Mexico. Other purchases in 1991 expanded the existing markets in the above five states.

In 1992, AWI purchased two Illinois companies that, according to Ramsey, established "a new regional base for Allied's continued growth into a national solid waste management company." While the companies, National Scavenger Service, Inc. (hauling and transfer station), and R.18 (landfill), indeed established a new regional base for the growing Allied Waste, the purchase's true significance was bringing together Thomas Van Weelden and Roger Ramsey.

Van Weelden comes from a family with deep roots in the waste industry. At one time, 25 people in his family worked in this industry. His father owned a garbage hauling company in Chicago. Van Weelden started a small company of his own in 1975, working the trucks until noon and soliciting new accounts for the rest of the day.

He built up his company and caught Ramsey's attention in the early 1990s. Van Weelden and Ramsey found they had a lot in common, and Ramsey recalled that the first time they got together, "One of us would start a sentence and the other could finish it. It was incredible." Their business sense was so compatible that they shared an office for seven years, to cut down on meetings time. It was the combination of Ramsey and Van Weelden that took AWI to its place as one of the leaders in its industry.

Thomas Van Weelden was an unusual leader. "In my family," he said in a 1997 interview with *Forbes*, "there is nothing wrong with being a garbage man." Consequently, Van Weelden required his management trainees to spend a year on the trucks. And he did not like to micromanage. In 1999 he said: "If I need a staff meeting every week to tell my guys what to do the following week, I got the wrong guys." His unorthodox methods also included taking huge risks. When AWI bought Laidlaw's North American solid waste business for a staggering $1.5 billion, the resulting debt the company carried was three times its equity.

While the garbage industry shied away from vertical integration, Ramsey and Van Weelden based their rapid growth strategy on exactly that concept. The strategy proved successful. When Van Weelden joined Allied Waste, annual revenues were $35 million. By the end of 2001, revenues reached roughly $5.6 billion.

Rapid Expansion and Growth: 1993–1996

With Van Weelden and Ramsey at the helm, the company continued to grow. Van Weelden's philosophy was to not set limits on its expansion. The company increased its landfill area by 53 percent in 1993. Also in 1993, due to intense competition from Browning-Ferris Industries, AWI moved its headquarters from Houston to Scottsdale, Arizona. New acquisitions throughout the early 1990s expanded Allied Waste's role in established markets (such as Illinois), and gained it new major markets, such as Georgia (with the acquisition of Southern States Environmental Services, Inc. and related companies), and St. Louis, Missouri (with the acquisition of Midwest Waste Inc. and related companies).

In 1996, during a time of rapid consolidation in the waste industry (the result of tightening environmental control regulations), Allied Waste announced what was, according to Roger Ramsey, "the biggest deal ever in the industry." AWI paid $1.5 billion ($1.2 billion in cash, the rest in stock and notes) for the North American solid waste unit of Laidlaw, Inc., a Toronto-based company. The acquisition was completed on December 30, 1996. Laidlaw, also a provider of school bus and ambulance services, saw its solid waste business constantly underperforming. The purchase brought AWI into 17 new markets, and made it the fourth largest trash-disposal company in the United States. AWI's annual revenues shot from $169 million to approximately $1 billion as a result of the purchase. While many analysts were alarmed by the debt Allied Waste took on (its debt-to-capital ratio rose to 82 percent as a result of the purchase), Ramsey was confident the decision was right. "We wouldn't have taken on this risk if we didn't think we could manage the debt," he said. In 1997, AWI sold the Canadian operations it bought from Laidlaw to USA Waste Services, Inc, for $518 million. Ramsey noted that in the rapidly changing garbage-disposal industry, "We've created a new force. We believe this transaction will ensure our survival."

The BFI and Rabanco Acquisitions: 1997–1998

Browning-Ferris Industries, Inc. (BFI) was at one time the second largest solid waste disposal company in the world. In addition to its formidable presence in the United States, by the mid-1990s, BFI had contracts in Asia, the Middle East, Europe, New Zealand, and Australia. The company was founded in 1966, just as regulations regarding waste disposal were changing. Unlike many family operations, BFI managed to raise capital, through shrewd financing and acquisitions, which allowed it to stay in business and prosper. But by the end of the 1980s, the company was experiencing trouble. It was facing charges of price-fixing and illegal hazardous waste handling. And while BFI seemed to have rebounded in the mid-1990s, the late 1990s found it struggling again. In 1997 it sold its properties outside the United States. Two years later, the smaller AWI came calling, with a roughly $9 billion offer, and BFI became a wholly owned subsidiary of AWI. The deal increased AWI's debt to a staggering $10.2 billion, and brought its revenues to $6.3 billion when the deal was finalized. With BFI now part of AWI, the latter jumped from the fourth largest waste disposal company in the United States to the second largest, swallowing a company that had been in business for some 30 years.

Allied Waste's acquisition of BFI came shortly after USA Waste Services purchased the formidable Waste Management, the largest waste handling company in the United States (USA Waste kept the Waste Managment name intact). At that time, the Justice Department came under fire for being too easy on USA Waste Services—to gain the buyout approval, USA Waste only had to divest assets that totaled $275 million in annual revenue. Perhaps due to that criticism, the Justice Department was tougher in its requirement when it came to AWI's purchase of BFI. In July 1999, AWI agreed to divest some 50 landfills, transfer stations, and hauling operations. These assets totaled roughly $197 million in annual revenues, a proportionally much bigger divestiture than the one required of USA Waste. In addition, AWI had to sell its interest in three American Ref-Fuel plants (American Ref-Fuel specializes in the conversion of waste to energy). As AWI always shied away from hazardous waste, BFI's medical waste unit was sold to Stericycle of Illinois, and the proceeds, some $440 million, were used to trim AWI's debt resulting from the BFI deal.

In 1998, Allied Waste expanded into the Pacific Northwest buy acquiring the Rabanco Company for $400 million. That same year, the company growth reached a point where its upper management felt it was appropriate to transfer their listing to the New York Stock Exchange. AWI started trading on NYSE on December 30, 1998.

Changing Focus: 1999 and Beyond

While BFI's purchase was a major triumph for Allied Waste, the resulting financial burden made for a difficult year in 1999. The company was unable to divest assets as quickly as it had anticipated, and as a result of the BFI transaction, its size tripled in a very short period of time. In AWI's 1999 annual report, Van Weelden said: "Going forward, it all comes down to our ability to control costs and deliver margins on a much larger asset base than before. The focus will be on operating efficiently."

AWI moved forward with trying to bring up its internalization rate—the rate of collected trash dumped in the company's own landfills. The rate had dropped substantially following the Laidlaw acquisition, to about 50 percent. At the time BFI was purchased, the rate was 57 percent. AWI targeted its internaliza-

tion rate at around 70 percent. Other plans for the company included asset swaps and acquisitions in select markets, while divesting of assets that were not fully integrated into the company's operations or vertical integration strategy. As then COO Larry Henk said: "Today, acquisitions will be the icing on the cake, rather than the cake itself." More emphasis was placed on paying down debt and increasing free cash flow.

The strategy seemed to have worked. By the third quarter of 2000, the company's internalization rate was up to 65 percent, ahead of schedule. Of course, cost-cutting measures had to include reduction in headcount, and the company cut some 2,900 jobs in 2000.

The economic recession in 2001, combined with the dramatic reduction in travel and tourism following the tragic events of September 11, 2001, affected AWI just as it was outgrowing its post-BFI-acquisition growing pains. Third quarter net income in 2001 was $.13 a share, as opposed to $.27 per share in the same quarter in 2000. Shortly after these results were announced, Larry Henk, AWI's president and COO resigned, citing personal reasons. Van Weelden became president, in addition to his roles as Chairman and CEO. Yet not all the news was bad. Despite the sagging economy and the effects of September 11, AWI generated an impressive $480 million of free cash flow and reduced its debt by $389 million that same year.

As Allied Waste entered 2002, it appeared that the second largest solid waste disposal company in the United States was working its magic again. Net income for the first quarter was $32.4 million, compared to a loss of $36 million for the same period the previous year. To accommodate its growth, the company was revamping its infrastructure, expanding from two areas, eight regions, and 46 districts to four areas, 12 regions, and 58 districts. Internalization rate increased to 67 percent by the end of 2001. Unlike BFI, which moved away from decentralized management and became stagnant, AWI stuck with its decentralized model and continued to grow. With a proven strategy, an experienced management team, and with the mad rush to consolidate finished for now, AWI seems well positioned for long-term success.

Principal Subsidiaries

Allied Waste Industries of Illinois; Allied Waste North America; Allied Waste Systems; Browning-Ferris Industries.

Principal Competitors

Republic Services; Waste Management.

Further Reading

"Allied Waste Earnings Rebound," *The Business Journal of Phoenix,* April 30, 2002, http://phoenix.bizjournals.com.

"Allied Waste Industries Announces Election of Ramsey to Board of Directors." *PR Newswire,* August 18, 1989, http://www.prnewswire.com.

"Allied Waste Industries Announces Election of President and Board of Directors," *PR Newswire,* September 27, 1989, http://www.prnewswire.com.

"Allied Waste Industries, Inc. Announces Resignation of Bruce G. Lessey," *PR Newswire*, October 27, 1989, http://www.prnewswire.com.

"Allied Waste Industries Announces the Acquisition of Sanco for Stock and Cash," *PR Newswire*, January 16, 1990, http://www.prnewswire.com.

"Allied Waste Industries Inc. Promotes Daniel J. Ivan," *PR Newswire*, October 19, 1990, http://www.prnewswire.com.

"Allied Waste Acquires Interest in CRX," *PR Newswire*, March 29, 1991, http://www.prnewswire.com.

"Allied Waste Industries Begins Trading on NASDAQ," *PR Newswire*, September 10, 1991.

"Allied Waste Enters New Markets," *PR Newswire*, December 9, 1991, http://www.prnewswire.com.

Balzer, Stephanie, "Allied Waste: Rising Stars: A Look at What's Behind the Remarkable Success of Two Arizona Companies," *The Business Journal of Phoenix*, May 14, 1999, Vol.19, Is.31, p. 1.

Barrett, William P., "Talking Trash: As a Teen, Tom Van Weelden.," *Forbes*, October 20, 1997, Vol. 160, n. 9, p. 258.

"BFI to Shed Medical Waste Assets to Stericycle in Pending Stock Swap," *Hazardous Waste News*, May 24, 1999, Vol. 21, Is. 21.

"Interview with Tyler Mathisen, Allied Waste Chairman and CEO," *CNBC Anchor: Power Lunch*, audio transcript, November 8, 2000, http://www.djinteractive.com.

Johnson, Jim, "Longtime Exec Henk Exits Allied." *Waste News*, November 12, 2001, Vol. 7, Is. 14, p. 3.

Lowry, Tom, "Talking Trash Turns to Some Serious Cash," *USA Today*, September 19, 1996, p. O3B.

—Adi R. Ferrara

American Cast Iron Pipe Company

1501 31st Avenue North
Birmingham, Alabama 35207
U.S.A.
Telephone: (205) 325-7701
Fax: (205) 325-1942
Web site: http://www.acipco.com

Private Company
Incorporated: 1905
Employees: 2,300 (2001)
Sales: $600 million (2000)
NAIC: 331511 Iron Foundries; 331111 Iron and Steel Mills; 331528 Other Nonferrous Foundries; 332313 Plate Work Manufacturing; 332911 Industrial Valve Manufacturing; 332919 Other Metal Valve and Pipe Fitting Manufacturing

American Cast Iron Pipe Company (ACIPCO), with 242,000 square meters of roofed production space and a daily production of 1,800 metric tons, is the largest individual iron pipe casting plant in the world. One of Birmingham's biggest companies and largest employers, a major presence in the city's business community, and the only pipe manufacturing company ever to be named by *Fortune* magazine as one of the 100 best companies to work for in America, ACIPCO is clearly exceptional in a number of ways. Unlike most industrial companies, ACIPCO is privately held; in 1922, the company placed all of its stock into a beneficial trust for its employees. And, the company's tradition of putting its employees first has been maintained to the present day: four elected company employees serve on the board of directors; ACIPCO boasts one of the oldest employee suggestion systems in the U.S.; the company provides on-site training for its employees, as well as a tuition reimbursement program; and ACIPCO's health benefits program, which includes on-site medical and dental care, is one of the most progressive in the country.

ACIPCO is also known for innovation and for diversity in its product lines. The company was instrumental in developing ductile iron and was the first to introduce it commercially in 1955.

Although the company name reflects its initial product—cast iron pipe—ACIPCO has progressed well beyond its initial product line and has boasted an international customer base since it began exporting its products in 1915. Today, its products include steel and iron pipe of various kinds for a variety of applications, fire hydrants, valves, pumps, and fabricated castings. In 2002, for the fifth year in a row, the company was named to *Fortune* magazine's list of 100 Best Companies to Work For in America.

Steeltown, Alabama

Founded in 1905, American Cast Iron Pipe Company held its principles of good employer-employee relations and team cooperation from the very beginning, making it an unusual example among industrial companies. John J. Eagan, company founder and ACIPCO's first president, founded his company on the then-novel principle that because employees make up a company, a company should take good care of its employees. In 1917, for instance, ACIPCO instituted a pension fund for its employees, a highly unusual practice at the time. Eagan is quoted in the 1993 book *The 100 Best Companies to Work for in America* as saying, "Industry has no right to take a man, use the best years of his life, and as old age approaches, to throw him out and employ young men in his place. It is one of the real joys to see men who otherwise would be dependent on their families receiving monthly through this fund their own money which they have earned and which has been set aside in this fund."

Likewise, ACIPCO was from the beginning a privately held company—and, upon Eagan's death in 1924 remained so, in the hands of its employees. All of the company stock had been placed in a trust in 1922, and ever after the trust has paid dividends to all employees based on company profitability. Eagan also left behind a corporate hierarchy that was unique to the pipe-casting industry, including a 12-employee elected board of operatives designed to facilitate communication between workers and management. Frequent meetings with managers helped to ensure that worker concerns were addressed promptly.

A Tradition of Innovation

From its inception, ACIPCO was at the forefront of the pipe-casting industry, an industry that dates back to the early 14th century with the introduction of cast iron cannons in Europe. In the 1920s, the company helped pioneer the development of centrifugal pipe casting, where a mold is spun about its horizontal axis while the metal is poured into the mold. The rotation generates centrifugal force, which causes the liquid metal to distribute evenly, forming a pipe of uniform thickness. Centrifugal casting remained a major element in ACIPCO's pipe manufacturing process 80 years later, incorporating new developments in pipe design and production along the way. Centrifugal casting was invented in 1918 by Dimitri Sensaud deLavaud, a Brazilian after whom the process was named. DeLavaud's invention eliminated the need for a central core in the pipe mold, and the mold was water-cooled, allowing for a high rate of repeated use. The deLavaud process is still used today by ACIPCO and other casting companies.

The invention of ductile iron in 1948 revolutionized the pipe-casting industry, and once again ACIPCO adopted the new technology early, having played a continuing role in its development and possible applications. The term "ductile" as applied to metal refers to a metal's capacity for being hammered or drawn to extreme thinness. Ductile iron combined the strength and durability of steel with cast iron's resistance to corrosion, making for a metal that was suitable for a wide variety of applications, especially the movement of water and sewage. Ductile iron is annealed, a process that softens the metal and makes it less brittle, to increase its strength and flexibility. Over the years, ACIPCO applied these manufacturing principles to steel pipe, fire hydrants, valves, and spiralweld pipe.

The 1960s ushered in an era of prosperity for the foundry industry in general, and ACIPCO was no exception, despite the social turbulence in the U.S. in general and Birmingham in particular. Although the country experienced a net loss of metal-casting facilities, those facilities that remained or that were newly built tended to remain open. This was partly due to increased demand from the U.S. military for cast-metal products, especially ammunition. It was also a period of general advancement in areas of technology and production; ACIPCO's steel pipe division began operations in 1963. William G. Gude, the editor of *Foundry* magazine, commented in a 1966 issue, "The most modern foundry built today is likely to be obsolete to a large extent 20 years from now, if not sooner. Conventional materials and production methods can be superseded almost overnight, and if the newer developments offer a major economic advantage, the implications are obvious." Additional pressure was brought to

bear in the 1970s by increasing environmental concerns related to industrial production. *Foundry* magazine noted in February 1970: "It's becoming rapidly evident that control of air and water pollution is going to be the big social (and political) issue of the '70s, surpassing Vietnam and civil rights." In 1971, Birmingham was the first U.S. city to shut down its industrial plants in response to the mounting pollution crisis.

ACIPCO was also an early adopter of computer-numerically-controlled (CNC) technology in its manufacturing process, a technology that allows for extremely precise work. Jerry Edwards, the president and owner of the highly-reputed Jordan Machine Company in Alabama from 1979 until his retirement, first encountered CNC technology during his 26-year tenure at ACIPCO, and applied it at his new company. He also brought to Jordan a couple of other innovations from ACIPCO: upon his retirement in the mid-1990s, 85 percent of the company stock was transferred to employee ownership, an arrangement similar to that at Edwards' former employer.

ACIPCO continued to develop and take advantage of new technologies as the century closed. In 1999, the company announced the formation of a new division, American SpiralWeld Pipe Company. The purpose of the new division was to manufacture spiral-welded steel pipe for water, wastewater, and other applications. ACIPCO began construction of a new facility in South Carolina, with production equipment by Pacific Roller Die, a leading manufacturer of pipe-production technology. Production at the brand-new 289,000-square-foot facility began in September of 2000. Vice President of Operations Don Gray, quoted in a company press release, stated: "As the U.S. population increases, we're seeing a rise in demand for larger diameter pipe to serve the water, wastewater, hydroelectric, and power generation industries. Our spiral-welded steel pipe, which can be manufactured up to 12 feet in diameter, will meet that demand." The process, where long strips of steel are coiled in a spiral formation, then welded together, can produce larger-diameter pipes than older methods.

However, ACIPCO did not neglect its older industries. It created a lining for ductile iron sewer pipe that incorporated epoxy and polythylene, two materials that were previously incompatible. The Water Environment Federation awarded ACIPCO an Innovative Technology Award in 2001 for this development. The company also built a Contiarc demonstration furnace at its Birmingham plant in the 1990s. The Contiarc furnace allows more efficient cast-iron production. As it entered the new millennium and neared its centennial anniversary, ACIPCO continued a tradition of close association between its research and development staff and its production, engineering, and sales teams to stay at the forefront of the industry.

Environmental Concerns

At the turn of the millennium, three major concerns faced the metalworking industry, and ACIPCO was no exception: the acquisition and retention of qualified employees, the impact of the industry on the environment, and the increasingly global state of the industry itself.

ACIPCO had the distinction of being the only pipe-casting company ever to be named to *Fortune* magazine's list of the

Key Dates:

1905: American Cast Iron Pipe Company (ACIPCO) founded by John J. Eagan in Birmingham, Alabama.
1915: ACIPCO begins exporting pipe products.
1917: ACIPCO institutes pension plan.
1922: Company places all of its stock into a beneficial trust for ACIPCO employees.
1924: Founder and company president John J. Eagan dies.
1948: Inception of ductile iron.
1955: Commercial introduction of ductile iron pipe by ACIPCO.
1963: American Steel Pipe division founded.
1971: Birmingham is the first U.S. city in which industrial plants are closed due to air pollution.
1990: Company wins AFS Environmental Affairs Service award.
1999: Company begins installation of new furnace to meet pollution standards. American SpiralWeld division founded.
2000: President and CEO Van L. Richey named National Management Association Executive of the Year.
2001: Company wins Innovative Technology Award from Water Environment Foundation.
2002: For the fifth year in a row, the company is named to *Fortune* magazine's list of 100 Best Companies to Work For in America.

''Best 100 Companies to Work For,'' let alone making the list five years in a row. In the 1993 book of the same title, authors Levering and Moskowitz observed that the company's on-site medical facility, which treated retirees and relatives as well as current employees, was one of the best in the city of Birmingham. The facility was part of one of the most comprehensive— as well as expensive—health-care plans in the U.S., and was designed by company employees. ACIPCO also preserved the open-relationship principles of its corporate hierarchy; as CEO Van L. Richey put it in a June 9, 2000 article in the *Birmingham Business Journal*, ''In manufacturing, [the slogan] is communication, communication, communication.'' He went on to describe the many points of contact between himself and all levels of the company that he had maintained or introduced. In 2000, Richey was named Executive of the Year by the National Management Association; in an interview with *Manage* magazine, published in August 2000, he cited some of the reasons for his company's success and discussed the importance of hiring and retaining qualified employees: ''With an employee turnover of less than one-half of 1%, we have to struggle to get the right employee proper training.'' He also said, ''We know there is a direct relationship between successful companies and those that emphasize training. Therefore, ACIPCO has eight classrooms teaching a number of skills, including English, math, and computer labs.'' *Fortune*'s 2002 report on the 100 best companies to work for in the U.S. found that ACIPCO employees averaged 76 hours of training per year.

The emphasis on communication manifested in sometimes surprising ways. In 1997, ACIPCO created the Threat Response Team, the purpose of which was to prevent violence in the workplace. The team's method involved the employees themselves, who were taught to recognize the indicators of potentially violent behavior, and to alert the team. ACIPCO human resources director Leann Barr told the *Birmingham Business Journal* in April 2000 that ''Safety is an essential part of the workplace. Just as we would not allow an employee melting iron to work without safety glasses, a hard hat and flame-retardant clothing, today our Threat Response Team also works to ensure that we have a safer place to work.'' And in 2001, ACPICO paid a $5 million settlement to 346 male employees who filed a discrimination suit in 1986. The suit claimed that the company's health insurance policy did not cover employees' children who did not live with employees. The company changed its policy in 1994 in response to a change in federal regulations.

ACIPCO was also responsive to outside influences on its industry, particularly in the areas of environmentalism and globalization. In 1999, the company began an expansion at its main facility in Birmingham with a price tag of $70 million. The purpose of the expansion was to provide space for an electrically fired furnace that would help the ACIPCO comply with new antipollution legislation. The company's older, coke-fired furnace had been installed in the 1970s and would, within another decade, require modifications to stay compliant with the law. CEO Van Richey told the *Birmingham Business Journal* in December 1999: ''When you have equipment that old, it starts costing a lot more in maintenance. But we also wanted to get ahead of the power curve on pollution control.'' Vice president and chief engineer James Woods added: ''We see coke being less available in the future. Plus, the new furnace will be more versatile.''

Another challenge the company had to face was increasing competition from foreign manufacturers. In 2001, the American Steel Pipe Division of ACIPCO joined Berg Steel Pipe Corporation and Stupp Corporation in petitioning the U.S. International Trade Commission (ITC) regarding Japanese and Mexican imports of steel pipe. The allegation was that, by selling at less than fair market value, the imports had damaged the domestic industry. The low prices of the imports stemmed in part from the 1997 economic crisis in southeast Asia; over the following three years, 25 American companies filed for bankruptcy protection and more than 27,000 steel workers lost their jobs. Early in 2002, the ITC approved new import tariffs on Japanese large-diameter steel pipe; an article in the January 2002 issue of *Underground Construction* predicted a subsequent rise in prices.

Despite the general economic downturn in the U.S. at the turn of the millennium, ACIPCO was well positioned to weather whatever storms might lie ahead. In 2001, the company enjoyed revenues of over $600 million and remained one of the Birmingham area's largest employers. As Vice President and Works Manager Arthur Edge commented at an American Foundrymen's Society conference in May 2000, ''Driving the cost down—that's the name of the game. Not so much expansion, but remaining competitive.''

Principal Divisions

American Ductile Iron Pipe; American Flow Control; American Steel Pipe; American Centrifugal; American SpiralWeld Pipe.

Principal Competitors

AK Steel Holding Corporation; McWane; Oregon Steel Mills.

Further Reading

"ACIPCO Named to *Fortune* List," *Foundry Management & Technology*, March 2000, p. 11.

Bailey, K. Stephen, "Executive Soundings," *Manage*, August 2000, p. 15.

Barlas, Stephen, "Pipe Cost Increases Expected," *Underground Construction*, January 2002, p. 16.

"Birmingham," *Encyclopedia Britannica*, accessed February 23, 2002, http://www.britannica.com.

Bourge, Christian, "Pipe Import Probe Continues," *American Metal Market*, February 26, 2001, p. 20.

"Briefs," *American & County*, February 2001, p. 58.

Carter, Sam F., "Ductile Iron Answers the Pipe Maker's Dream," *Ductile Iron News*, 2001, accessed February 22, 2002, http://www.ductile.org.

Clark, Lita A., "Workplace Violence: Here's a Wake-Up Call," *Birmingham Business Journal*, April 14, 2000, p. 19.

"The Explosive 60's," *Foundry Management & Technology*, April 1992, p. 17.

Foti, Ross, "Southeastern Foundrymen Discuss the State of the Region," *Modern Casting*, May 2000, p. 48.

Hatch, D. Diane, and James E. Hall, "Health Insurance Policy Was Discriminatory," *Workforce*, July 2001, p. 57.

Levering, Robert, and Milton Moskowitz, "The 100 Best Companies to Work For: In a Tough Year These Companies Tried to Do Right by Their Employees," *Fortune*, February 4, 2002, p. 72.

Levering, Robert, and Milton Moskowitz, *The 100 Best Companies to Work for in America*, New York: Doubleday, 1993.

"Melting/Refractories," *Foundry Management & Technology*, January 2001, p. B3.

Milazzo, Don, "ACIPCO Invests $70M Downtown to Meet Pollution Standards," *Birmingham Business Journal*, December 31, 1999, p. 17.

Milazzo, Don, "ACIPCO's Richey Named 2000 Exec of the Year," *Birmingham Business Journal*, September 1, 2000, p. 2.

Milazzo, Don, "Best in Business Winners Revealed," *Birmingham Business Journal*, June 9, 2000, p. 1.

Milazzo, Don, "Birmingham's 100 Buck the National Downturn," *Birmingham Business Journal*, November 2, 2001, p. 3.

Nicholson, Gilbert, "Jordan Machine is a Hot Job Shop," *Birmingham Business Journal*, June 29, 2001, p. 11.

Shott, Chris, "Bachus Urges 'Strong and Effective' Action Against Foreign Steel," *States News Service*, November 10, 2001.

Shunnarah, Nabella, "ACIPCO's Reputation is World-Renowned," *Birmingham Business Journal*, June 9, 2000, p. 10.

Shunnarah, Nabella, "Richey Carries on ACIPCO's Founding Legacy," *Birmingham Business Journal*, June 9, 2000, p. 6.

"Spiral Weldseam Plant Commissioned," *Metallurgia*, May 2001, p. 8.

"U.S. Steelmakers File Petition Against Japan," *Jiji Press English News Service*, January 11, 2001, p. 1.

—Genevieve Williams

∴ Amersham

Amersham PLC

Little Chalfont
Buckinghamshire HP7 7NA
United Kingdom
Phone: (44) 1494-544-000
Fax: (44) 1494-542-266
Web site: http://www.amersham.com

Public Company
Incorporated: 1982
Employees: 9,000
Sales: £1.4 billion (2001)
Stock Exchanges: London New York Oslo
Ticker Symbol: AHM
NAIC: 541710 Research and Development in the
    Physical, Engineering, and Life Sciences; 325411
    Medicinal and Botanical Manufacturing; 325412
    Pharmaceutical Preparation Manufacturing; 325413
    In-Vitro Diagnostic Substance Manufacturing; 325414
    Biological Product (Except Diagnostic) Manufacturing

Initially known as Amersham International PLC, Amersham PLC was formed in 1997 through the merger of Amersham International (U.K.), Pharmacia Biotech (Sweden), and Nycomed (Norway). The company took on the new name of Amersham PLC in July 2001, with its two businesses taking on new names on October 15, 2001: Nycomed Amersham Imaging became Amersham Health, and Amersham Pharmacia Biotech became Amersham Biosciences. The customer base for Amersham's products and technology are pharmaceutical and biotechnology companies and leading research and academic institutions in the United States, Europe, Latin America, and Asia.

Amersham has participated in a cross-licensing arrangement for the joint development, supply, and commercialization of some new DNA technologies, and has been the leader in protein sciences. The DNA agreement may give the company greater access to the DNA sequencing market. At the time of the 2001 annual report, Amersham was working toward expanding its imaging capabilities from the visualization of tissue structure and anatomy to the visualization of disease-related changes in the cells and molecules of the human body.

A Complex History

Amersham PLC was the product of three medical technology and research companies: Pharmacia based in Peapack, New Jersey; Nycomed headquartered in Roskilde, Denmark; and Amersham PLC, based in Little Chalfont, Buckinghamshire, the United Kingdom. All three were powerful and productive companies in their own right.

As these companies matured and evolved into the manufacturing of diagnostic tools and pharmaceuticals in the 1950s and 1960s, their developments and operations were frequently intertwined through joint ventures, partnerships, sales agreements, or buyouts among the companies. They were dealing with some of the same cutting-edge products, such as several iterations of X-ray contrast media used in medical diagnostic imaging. Although Nycomed remained an independent company with 2,500 employees and Pharmacia has likewise been hearty and independent with 59,000 employees worldwide, the areas in which they had joint ventures or common research and development were pivotal to Amersham's success.

Early Beginnings: Mid-1800s

Nycomed was founded in 1874 in Oslo, Norway, as an agency for imported pharmaceutical products by Morten Nyegaard, a pharmacist. By 1900, the business had expanded to encompass wholesale distribution of pharmaceuticals and chemicals. The company began to manufacture its own brand of pharmaceuticals in 1913, expanding to research and development in 1925. One of its first major products was aspirin. The company was known as Nyegaard & Co. from 1890 to 1986, when its name was changed to Nycomed.

Pharmacia dates back to 1853, when Carlo Erba, an Italian pharmacist, started his own company, which later became Farmitalia Carlo Erba. This company later merged with Kabi Pharmacia and Pharmacia Aktiebolag to create Pharmacia AB, a Swedish-based company. The Upjohn Company, which began as The Upjohn Pill and Granule Company of Kalamazoo, Mich-

Company Perspectives:

Amersham is about visualising life at all levels within the human body—from the molecules and biochemicals that make our genetic structure, to cells, tissues, and organs.

Our strategy is to build our position as a leading provider of products and technologies to enable the molecular medicine revolution, in which disease will be better understood, diagnosed sooner, and treated more effectively.

igan in 1886, grew throughout the 19th century to become an international company. In 1995, Pharmacia and Upjohn was created through the merger of Pharmacia AB and the Upjohn Company, a provider of healthcare products, animal health products, as well as diagnostics and specialty products. In 1998, the company relocated its global headquarters to Peapack, New Jersey, which is now the management and pharmaceutical headquarters for Pharmacia Corporation.

Pharmacia also encompassed Monsanto, which was founded in St. Louis, Missouri in 1901, and produced artificial sweetener. Monsanto expanded into one of the largest chemical companies in the United States, making saccharin, aspirin, caffeine, and vanilla. Another pharmaceutical company, which was formed in 1888 by a young druggist named Gideon Daniel Searle, manufactured bulk laxative, the first motion sickness drug, the first oral contraceptive, and other innovative products. Searle was headquartered in Skokie, Illinois, and became the pharmaceutical unit of Monsanto in 1985. In 1999, Monsanto and Pharmacia & Upjohn agreed to create a new company, Pharmacia Corporation.

Amersham was founded in 1940 wartime Britain when Dr. Patrick Grove, a 26-year-old organic chemist established a facility, Chilcote House, at the village of Amersham for extracting radium. This research was made possible following the confiscation of a shipment of radium ore. The radium was vital during the war for the production of luminous dials for ships and planes. By the war's end, the facility had produced approximately 35 grams of radium and 500 kilos of luminous compound.

Following the important discovery of dextran by Björn Ingelman of Pharmacia that put the company in the front ranks of international industry, Pharmacia moved from Stockholm to Uppsala in 1950 and made Ingelman research director. At about this same time, 1949, Amersham was doing pioneering work in producing radioactive isotope tracers, which were initially carbon-14, and were later tritium-labeled compounds. This work gave Amersham an international name, as radioactive tracers made major advances in molecular biology and initial work on sequencing DNA possible.

Ingenuity Flourishes in the 1950s and 1960s

In 1957, Pharmacia invented Sephadex, a filtration medium used in chromatography to separate biomolecules by size, and established Separations as a new business area. The discovery was made by Jerker-Porath of Uppsala and Per Flodin of Pharmacia, and was a gel-like substance based on cross-linked dextran that Björn Ingelman had developed during the war, thinking that

it might serve as a pectin substitute. The product was launched in 1960, with the name Sephadex drawn from SEparation PHArmacia DEXtran, and became a staple in large-scale manufacture of early pharmaceuticals, such as insulin, paving the way for other drug combinations. Since that time, more than 50 products based on Sephadex have been developed. Pharmacia established a Separations facility at Piscataway, New Jersey in 1963, which is now the headquarters for Amersham Biosciences. Likewise, Sephadex became a product of Amersham Biosciences following the merger with Pharmacia in 1997.

This very productive period in the 1950s and 1960s found the three companies producing watershed medical diagnostic tools. Under the direction of R&D Director Dr. Hugo Holtermann, Nycomed discovered the Isopaque X-ray contrast medium, leading to the company's serious involvement in medical diagnostic imaging. Amersham began marketing the first commercial RIA (radioimmunoassay) kit in 1965, to be used in measuring insulin levels in the blood of diabetics.

A radioimmunoassay is the immunoassay—a laboratory technique that makes use of the binding between an antigen and its corresponding antibody to identify and quantify the specific antigen or antibody in a sample—of a radiolabeled substance, such as a hormone or an enzyme. Radiolabeling is the tagging of an enzyme, hormone, or other substance with a radioactive tracer. An antigen is a substance that stimulates the production of antibodies when introduced into the body. During this time, Amersham also began making isotopes—atoms having the same atomic numbers but different mass numbers—for use in nuclear medicine.

A scientific breakthrough occurred in 1969 when Nycomed collaborated with Professor Torsten Almén of Lund University, Sweden in developing Amipaque, the first nonionic X-ray contrast medium. The new contrast medium greatly enhanced the field of diagnostic imaging in that it created far superior images under safer and more comfortable conditions for the patient.

Expansion and Product Development

After this wave of development, it is not surprising that Amersham Searle was established at Arlington Heights near Chicago to market Amersham's many products in the United States. Three years later, in 1971, Amersham expanded into Germany through an Amersham Buchler joint venture.

Nycomed continued to develop new products, with Omnipaque, a new nonionic X-ray diagnostic medium that went on the market in 1982, leading Nycomed to unprecedented growth. Omnipaque was a sterile solution that was ready to use, and was one of the top ten pharmaceutical products sold for several years. It continued to be a best-selling X-ray contrast agent worldwide, and, through a merger in 1997, became an Amersham product.

In 1982, Amersham International became the first company to be privatized under Margaret Thatcher. A flurry of acquisitions followed, with Pharmacia Biotech acquiring LKB Produkter AB, a Swedish company known for its laboratory equipment and its leadership in mass spectrometry and electrophoresis. Amersham International purchased Medi-Physics in Arlington Heights, Illinois in 1992, providing a facility for

Key Dates:

1874: Nycomed is founded in Oslo, Norway by Morten Nyegaard, a pharmacist.

1911: Pharmacia is established in Sweden.

1940: Amersham is founded by Dr. Patrick Grove in the village of Amersham in Britain, in Chilcote House, a facility to extract radium.

1946: Amersham becomes a national center for the development of radioactive materials.

1949: Amersham develops its first radioisotope tracers used in sequencing DNA.

1960: Pharmacia launches Sephadex, a filtration medium that is used in chromatography to separate biomolecules by size.

1963: The first Separations facility at Piscataway, New Jersey, is established by Pharmacia.

1965: Amersham's develops its first RIA (radioimmunoassay) kit for detecting insulin levels in the blood of diabetics.

1966: Amersham begins making isotopes for nuclear medicine.

1968: Amersham Searle is established at Arlington Heights near Chicago.

1969: Nycomed develops Amipaque, the first nonionic X-ray contrast medium.

1971: Amersham expands in Germany through an Amersham Buchler joint venture.

1975: Nycomed discovers Omnipaque, the top-selling X-ray contrast agent worldwide. 1982: Amersham International is the first company privatized under the Margaret Thatcher government.

1993: Amersham acquires United States Biochemical (USB), a major innovator in DNA sequencing technology.

1994: Amersham launches OncoSeed treatment for prostate cancer in the United States and also launches Myoview, a commercially successful heart imaging agent.

1997: Amersham merges with Pharmacia Biotech in a 55:45 joint venture to form Amersham Pharmacia Biotech; and Amersham International also merges with Nycomed to form Nycomed Amersham PLC and the Nycomed Amersham Imaging business.

1998: Amersham Pharmacia Biotech acquires Molecular Dynamics, one year after Molecular Dynamics launches MegaBACE the DNA sequencer

2000: The initial sequencing of the human genome is complete; and Amersham Health launches Datscan which is used in testing for Parkinson's.

2001: Amersham PLC, Amersham Health, and Amersham Biosciences launch new names.

2002: Amersham Biosciences acquires AG Technology and InnovaSep, two membrane filtration technology companies; and Amersham PLC purchases a 45 percent stake of Pharmacia's share of Amersham Biosciences.

manufacture of radioisotopes and iodine seeds, and purchased United States Biochemical (USB) in 1993, which led to the company becoming a major innovator in DNA sequencing technology.

Amersham further demonstrated its global reach and interest in nuclear medicine by acquiring a 50 percent stake in Nihon Medi-Physics in Japan in 1994. In the same year, Nycomed paid $450 million for Sterling Winthrop's diagnostic imaging business, becoming the largest supplier of contrast media. In 1994, Amersham launched Myoview heart imaging agent, which was an immediate commercial success, becoming Amersham's leading heart diagnostic. By 2000, sales worldwide were over £80 million.

Amersham International acquired United States Biochemical in Cleveland, Ohio in 1993, a leader in manual sequencing with its product Sequenase DNA polymerase, an enzyme that catalyzes the formation of polynucleotides of DNA or RNA using an existing strand of DNA or RNA as a template. ThermoSequenase DNA sequencing enzyme and DYEnamic ET primer sequencing kits were developed and marketed in 1995, both of which proved instrumental in the subsequent success of the MegaBACE DNA Analysis System launched in 1997 and the Human Genome Project.

"MegaBACE was the first capillary sequencer on the market that allowed sequencing to be performed much faster than it had been done before," explained Tracy Cheung, vice-president of Corporate Affairs. "Tasks could be accomplished in two hours that had previously taken ten hours. It was the MegaBACE that allowed the human genome to be sequenced more quickly."

Key Mergers

The race for both acquisition and development continued into the late 1990s, pausing for joint ventures, then wound up in a merger. Pharmacia Biotech acquired Hoefer Scientific Instruments in San Francisco, a supplier of instruments for electrophoresis and protein separation in 1995. In 1997, Amersham International's Life Science business merged with Pharmacia Biotech in a 55:45 joint venture to form Amersham Pharmacia Biotech. Amersham International also merged with Nycomed to form Nycomed Amersham PLC and the Nycomed Amersham Imaging business.

As Nycomed Amersham, the company also developed and marketed brachytherapy products in the late 1990s for treatment of prostate cancer, to be used with its OncoSeed brand seeds. The brachytherapy ("brachy" means short) products can be used in place of surgery by implanting radioactive I-125 prostate brachytherapy seeds into the prostate where they irradiate the tumor. The process has about the same survival rate as surgery and is a minimally invasive outpatient procedure for prostate cancer in the early stages. In 2001, the company developed a new generation of brachytherapy seed, EchoSeed, which utilizes conventional ultrasound imaging to assist physicians in placement of the seeds during an implant procedure.

Another product, Myoview, can be used with pharmacological stress agents for coronary artery disease patients who are unable to exercise. Visipaque, used to assist doctors in diagnosing coronary artery stenosis, is an X-ray product designed to be comfortable and safe for the patient who is considered to be at high risk because of other health issues. Yet another product, Optison, can be used in imaging heart wall abnormalities. Omniscan, Amersham's leading MRI (magnetic resonance imaging) product, has been used in neurology for detecting stroke and cancers of the brain, but has also been used in cardiology. However, an X-ray diagnostic, Omnipaque, that was developed 20 years ago, is still the best-selling product on the market.

"LEADseeker was launched in 1998 as a high-throughput drug screening system," Cheung stated. "There are biopharma companies that have thousands of chemical compounds that may not be good drugs, and they need to get these into their protein targets as quickly as possible to see which ones bind. LEADseeker is one of the quickest on the market."

In 1998, one year after Molecular Dynamics launched MegaBACE, the DNA sequencer used to sequence the first chromosome that was completely mapped in the course of the Human Genome Project, Amersham Pharmacia Biotech acquired the company. Molecular Dynamics had been the company's alliance partner since 1994. In 1999, Amersham sold Nycomed Pharma, which was a pharmaceutical business that was acquired through the merger with Nycomed, but was never a core business for Amersham.

Amersham Pharmacia Biotech's relentless research and acquisition positioned the company strategically when a high-production DNA sequencer was needed. *Regulatory Intelligence Data* stated in a 1999 issue, "The U.S. Department of Energy's Joint Genome Institute has tripled its capacity to decode human DNA with the purchase of 24 MegaBACE DNA sequencers form Amersham Pharmacia Biotech valued at nearly $5 million."

In 2000, Amersham Health launched a product called Datscan which is used in testing for Parkinson's disease. "This was the world's first objective test for Parkinson's," Cheung explained. "Prior to that, the only objective test for Parkinson's was post-mortem. You could not find out if you absolutely had it unless you were dead, which wasn't helpful."

Amersham also launched a range of products under the name Ettan that are used in protein analysis. "Having mapped the human genome, we now have a pretty good idea of genes," Cheung noted, "but genes are really only the recipe for the code for making the proteins that cause the disease. When proteins stop working, that's when you get disease, so we really need to understand proteins and how they work."

The Impact of the Human Genome Project on Health

The Human Genome Project (HGP) grew out of an initiative in the U.S. Department of Energy (DOE), which launched the 1986 Human Genome Initiative in search of a reference human genome sequence. The U.S. Human Genome Project was a 13-year project, with an expected completion date of 2003. Its goals included identifying all 30,000 genes in human DNA, and determining the sequences of the 3 billion chemical base pairs that make up human DNA. This information will then be stored in databases, providing improved tools for data analysis.

A working draft sequence of the entire human genome was generated in June 2000 that provided a scaffold for the finished version, becoming a road map to roughly 90 percent of genes on every chromosome. Since that time, genes associated with more than 30 disorders have been pinpointed, leading to a boom in spinoff sequencing programs on the human and other genomes in the public and private sectors.

These new genetic discoveries have led to medical applications of DNA-based tests that can be used to diagnose disease or confirm a diagnosis, and provide a prognosis about the course of a disease. The tests can also confirm the presence of a disease in people who do not show the symptoms of a disease, and may predict the risk of future disease in healthy people and their offspring. Because genomic data and technologies lead to new drugs that are targeted at specific sites in the body and at particular biochemical events leading to disease with fewer side effects, drug development can be cheaper, faster, and more effective.

Branding Identity: 2001

Tracy Cheung explained that Amersham PLC's most important success since the renaming of the company in 2001 was the developing of a clear brand with a unified identity that signified one company with two businesses.

"This helped improve understanding of the company," Cheung stated. "After the merger, we had three companies: Nycomed Amersham, Nycomed Amersham Imaging, and Amersham Pharmacia Biotech, all of which were sort of connected in some way, but it wasn't very clear how. Amersham PLC was two businesses, Amersham Health and Amersham Biosciences—very clear brand with unified identity. The logos that look very similar really demonstrated our commitment to using technologies from across both businesses to meet the needs of our customers."

Still Looking Ahead

In 2002, Amersham Biosciences acquired two separation companies, AG Technology and InnovaSep Technology, both in the Boston. AG Technology was an established supplier of hollow-fiber membrane filtration technology used in biopharmaceuticals manufacturing, while InnovaSep Technology was a new company that held several patent-pending membrane filtration technologies. Because bioprocessing, the separation of proteins used in the manufacture of biopharmaceuticals, such as insulin and monoclonal antibodies, is accomplished by using a series of filtration and chromatography steps, these were important purchases for Amersham Biosciences.

Amersham also became the sole owner of one of its own businesses. "In March 2002, we purchased the 45 percent of Amersham Biosciences that we did not own from Pharmacia," Tracy Cheung explained. "Amersham had already owned 55 percent from the merger in 1997." Amersham Biosciences paid £704 million (US $1 billion) for the Pharmacia side of the business.

Peter Ehrenheim, executive vice-president of Separations, stated that Amersham's chromatography "systems and media are used in the production of over 90 percent of all biopharmaceuticals on the market." The company continues to be a major supplier worldwide. In the meantime, Amersham Health was selected as the sole source supplier for the Mayo Foundation for Medical Education and Research in Rochester, Minnesota, for Amersham Health's line of X-ray and MRI products.

Principal Subsidiaries

Amersham Biosciences: Japan, Sweden, United Kingdom, United States, Sweden; Amersham Health: China, Japan, Norway, United Kingdom, United States.

Principal Competitors

Bracco; Shearing; du Pont; Mallinckrodt; Millipore; Bio-Rad Laboratories; Discovery Systems; Applied Biosystems; PerkinElmer.

Further Reading

"Amersham Acquires AG, InnovaSep," *High Tech Separations News*, March 1, 2002.

"Amersham Health Announces Sole Source, Five-Year Supply Agreement with Mayo Foundation for Medical Education and Research," *PR Newswire*, November 14, 2001, http://prnewswire.com.

"Amersham Health's OncoSeed Web Site Recognized as a Top Health Web Resource in 2001 by Med Ad News," *PR Newswire*, March 6, 2002, http://prnewswire.com.

"Amersham Pharmacia Biotech Adds to Its Integrated Proteomics," *PR Newswire*, December 7, 2000, http://prnewswire.com.

"Amersham to Take Over Pharmacia Stake," *Africa News Service*, March 13, 2002, http://comtexnews.com.

"Chinese Institute Initiates Major Sequencing Projects Using Amersham Pharmacia Biotech's DNA Sequencing Technology," *PR Newswire*, May 11, 2000, http://prnewswire.com.

"Energy Department's Joint Genome Institute Triples Its DNA Sequencing Capacity State-of-the Art Machines Will Help Decode Genes," *Regulatory Intelligence Data*, June 14, 1999.

"Marine Genomics Researchers Discover New Ocean Protein," *PR Newswire*, September 14, 2000, http://prnewswire.com.

"Nycomed Amersham—FDA Clearance and Launch of EchoSeed," *Market News Publishing*, June 4, 2001, http://comtexnews.com.

"Nycomed Amersham Imaging Awarded Sole-Source Agreement for BrachytherapyProstate Product—TheraSeed—From Premier Inc.," *PR Newswire*, May 9, 2001, http://prnewswire.com.

"Nycomed Amersham Imaging Launches National Education Initiative for OncoSeed Treatment for Prostate Cancer," *PR Newswire*, June 29, 2000, http://prnewswire.com.

"Nycomed Amersham and Mallinckrodt Agree on Ultrasound Patent Settlement and Announce Joint Development of Existing Ultrasound Products," *PR Newswire*, May 8, 2000, http://prnewswire.com.

"Nycomed Amersham and Theragenics Corporation Announce Distribution Agreement for TheraSeed," *PR Newswire*, September 19, 2000, p. 1956, http://prnewswire.com.

"Scientists from University of Delaware's 'Extreme 2001' Project and Amersham Biosciences Succeed at First-Ever Attempt to Sequence DNA at Sea," *Business Wire*, October 31, 2001, p. 2094, http://businesswire.com.

"Screening: Next Generation MegaBACE Sequencer" *Drug Discovery/Technology News*, February 1, 2000.

"Windber Research Institute Establishes State-of-the-Art Research Organization Using Amersham Biosciences Technology," *Business Wire*, December 19, 2001, p. 2189.

—Annette Dennis McCully

Amnesty International

Press Office, International Secretariat
Peter Benenson House
1 Easton Street
London WC1X 0DW
United Kingdom
Telephone: (44) 0 207 413 5566
Fax: (44) 0 207 413 5835
Web site: http://www.amnesty.org

Non-Profit Organization
Established: 1961
Employees: 350
Operating Revenues: £20.9 million (2001–2002)
NAIC: 813311 Human Rights Organizations

Two students in Portugal raise their glasses and toast, "To freedom." Akin to the butterfly whose wings were reputed to have started a hurricane, this simple act launched a worldwide organization that has changed the way people think about human rights. Winner of the Nobel Peace Prize in 1977, Amnesty International (AI) is a force to be reckoned with. With a membership of more than 1 million worldwide and originator and sponsor of countless campaigns for a host of human rights issues, AI is, in the words of Jean-Pierre Hocke, former United Nations High Commissioner for Refugees, "simply unique."

Amnesty International founder, Peter Benenson, was a wealthy British lawyer with a social conscious when he read about the Portuguese students in the fall of 1960. At the time, Portugal was under the dictatorial rule of António Salazar. The two students who toasted to freedom were arrested and sentenced to seven years in jail for this offense.

Benenson had been involved in human rights issues for nearly 20 years prior to 1960. He founded "Justice," a British lawyers' organization working to further the cause of the UN's Declaration of Human Rights. After reading the article about the students, he approached Louis Blom-Cooper, the legal correspondent at the London *Observer*. Benenson had an idea for an amnesty campaign for political prisoners. Blom-Cooper sug-

gested an article in the *Observer* to launch the campaign. Benenson and his friend Eric Baker, and several of Benenson's colleagues, spent the next several months outlining a strategy for their "Appeal for Amnesty, 1961" campaign. Along the way, Baker and Benenson collected material for a book on political prisoners' cases, called *Persecution '61*.

According to Linda Rabben's *Fierce Legion of Friends: A History of Human Rights Campaigns and Campaigners,* "The Appeal for Amnesty had four aims: to work impartially for the release of those imprisoned for their opinions; to seek for them a fair and public trial; to enlarge the right of asylum for political refugees; and to advocate for effective international machinery to guarantee freedom of opinion."

The *Observer*'s editor, David Astor, who knew Benenson, gave him free space in the newspaper. On May 28, 1961, "The Forgotten Prisoners" was published. The piece highlighted eight such prisoners, from various countries around the world. The response to the article was swift and tremendous. Newspapers around the world picked up the piece and ran it. Letters, donations, and information on other prisoners of conscience flooded to the *Observer* and the Appeals Office. Benenson and his colleagues put responders who lived close to each other in touch and encouraged the formation of local groups. Benenson came up with the "Threes" idea: each local group would be given three names of prisoners from the three different political blocs (Communist, West, and Developing World), and the group would be responsible for the campaign to release these prisoners and assist their families.

Diana Redhouse, a British artist who also founded what may be the first AI local group, was asked by Benenson to design AI's logo, a candle surrounded by barbed wire. Benenson said the image was inspired by an ancient proverb: "Better to light a candle than curse the darkness." The first Amnesty Candle was lit in December 1961. By that time, Benenson and representatives of groups working outside Britain had met and decided that the work was too important to last for only one year. The organization's name was changed to Amnesty International. By mid-1962, AI groups were in place or forming all over the globe, including West Germany, Belgium, Switzerland, the Netherlands, Canada, Ceylon, Greece, the United States, New

Zealand, Ghana, Israel, Mexico, Argentina, Jamaica, Malaya, Congo, Ethiopia, and India.

A New Model for Objective Advocacy

Benenson and his colleagues set up AI as a nonpolitical, nonreligious organization. The group established that it would not accept money from governments or governmental organizations and thus would be able to remain objective, not subject to political pressure. The organization set out to follow Voltaire's famous philosophy: "I may detest your ideas, but I am prepared to die for your right to express them." AI decided never to engage in comparisons between countries nor flag any political system as inferior or superior to another. The *London Times* pointed out AI's truly impressive impartiality, when AI was announced as the recipient of the Nobel Prize for Peace in 1977: "[Amnesty International] is disliked equally by Chile and the Soviet Union, by the Philippines and South Africa."

Before taking on a case or publishing a country report, AI practice has been to appoint a Research team to verify the facts of the case. The organization's accuracy has been widely recognized and its credibility has helped it remain influential. AI policy established that members would not work on their own country's research or on behalf of prisoners in their own country. Nor would members be responsible in any way for any of AI's work in their own country. Members could, however, lobby their government to implement human rights measures.

Prisoners of conscience adopted by AI, become the subjects of a global campaign. Members write letters on the prisoners' behalf, support the prisoners' families, arrange vigils, and more. AI also issues Urgent Action appeals for prisoners who are in imminent danger due to factors such as ill health or prolonged poor prison conditions. The first Urgent Action appeal, issued on behalf of Professor Luiz Basilio Rossi of Brazil, was issued on March 19, 1973. "I knew that my case had become public, I knew they could no longer kill me. Then the pressure on me decreased and conditions improved," he said.

In addition to its research and publicity campaigns, AI has routinely sent missions into hot spots around the world. The missions' delegates are carefully selected based on the proposed delegates' qualifications, experience, and gender in countries where the latter might be an issue. Missions always enter a country with permission. Missions often (but not always) have presented their report to the host country's government. At times a mission would be refused entry into a country and in some cases delegates have been harassed and imprisoned.

A nine-member International Executive Committee (IEC), whose members are elected every two years, governs AI. The IEC consists of seven members, each representing a different area of the world in which AI is active. Other members of the IEC are a treasurer and a member from the International Secretariat, AI's London headquarters. With the exception of the International Secretariat representative, the International Council elects all IEC members. The IEC meets at least twice a year. Its members can serve up to three consecutive two-year terms.

The International Council consists of IEC members and representatives of AI's sections. It is, according to AI's statue, the "ultimate authority for the conduct of the Affairs of Amnesty International." The International Council determines AI's strategic plan, and its "vision, mission, and core values." The Council is also responsible for accountability among AI's sections, and for evaluating performance against goals in the organization at large. The Office of the International Secretariat in London, handles the daily operations of AI. The secretary general is the head of the Office of the International Secretariat.

AI's "mandate" is the set of rules that has established the organization's action parameters—what the organization and its individual groups can and cannot do—and goals. The early mandate was simple, focusing on articles 18 and 19 of the Universal Declaration of Human Rights and the Prisoners of Conscience Campaign. In the mid-1970s, AI added a rule, forbidding members from taking on cases in their own country. Over the years the mandate expanded to include many social issues, such as women's rights and the rights of asylum seekers in the country to which they flee. In a controversial decision, AI added to their list of prisoners of conscience, people imprisoned solely due to their sexual orientation. Many members worried, over the years, that with each expansion of its mandate the organization was spreading itself too thin, and its work would suffer. So far, it appears that has not been the case.

The Crisis Years: 1962–1967

In 1962, AI decided to take on the case of Nelson Mandela, who was charged with trying to organize a strike and leave the country without a passport. At the time, he was leading peaceful antiapartheid activities. In 1964, Mandela was charged with sabotage and sentenced to life in prison. His turn to violence meant that, according to AI's mandate, he could no longer be considered a prisoner of conscience. But the British group that had adopted him continued campaigning for his release. Their actions resulted in a crisis that led to a membership poll. The overwhelming majority felt that AI should stick to its mandate and drop Mandela as a prisoner of conscience. However, many people felt it was wrong to abandon him at the time he was sentenced to a life term. The compromise that was reached, and used many times later for other cases, was that Mandela would be dropped as a prisoner of conscience. However, AI would petition the court on his behalf if it found out that the prison conditions were inhumane, if torture was used, or if the trial was deemed unfair.

In 1966, a far worse crisis erupted that threatened to destroy the organization. It resulted in Peter Benenson's resignation as president, and his severing his ties with AI for a few years. The crisis began with AI's decision to investigate British conduct against suspected terrorists in Aden, a British colony. The Swedish section of AI was given the task of investigating the allegations. Once the highly critical report was written, Benenson was convinced the London office was suppressing it under pressure from the British Foreign Office. After investigating the report in person, Benenson published it himself in Sweden. And he became convinced that the British government was unduly pressuring someone at AI, probably then Director General Robert Swann. Benenson began a campaign to move AI's headquarters to Switzerland, known for its neutrality. He could not convince anyone else at the organization of this need. Eventually, Benenson contacted famed human rights activist and AI member Sean MacBride, and together they decided to appoint an impartial investigator to look at Benenson's allegations. While the report was being compiled, proof that Benenson himself took money from the British government to finance a fact-finding mission in Rhodesia came to light.

In March 1967, with AI on the brink of self-destruction, the executive board held an emergency meeting, in which Benenson's resignation was accepted. The position of president was abolished, and Eric Baker was chosen as interim director general.

Building A Strong Organization: 1968–1992

Eric Baker faced a formidable task—with morale at its lowest and distrust in the London office running high, Baker had to reestablish AI's stability and sense of purpose. His leadership skills proved equal to the task. By July 1968, when Martin Ennals was appointed secretary general, the number of

AI groups was growing again, and more than a tenth of the prisoners of conscience the group adopted were freed.

Ennals headed AI for 12 years, and the highlight of his administration was the Nobel Peace Price awarded to the organization in 1977. He was known as a warmhearted individual, eager to help in every situation. These characteristics helped reduce the tension and mistrust that still lingered in the wake of the 1966 crisis. Under Ennals' direction, AI formalized its stand against the death penalty, and formalized its methods of work.

Thomas Hammarberg was chosen as secretary general in July 1980. He was more of a stickler for rules, compared to Ennals. He strode to streamline the organization, and placed emphasis on clarity and consistency in AI's global communication. In the first two years of his administration, AI doubled its membership.

Ian Martin, Hammarberg's successor, saw AI through the changes in Eastern Europe that started in 1989. In addition, as part of his campaign to attract younger members, he came up with the *Human Rights Now!* Rock Tour, a tour that swept through 19 countries featuring the likes of Peter Gabriel and Sting. Martin initiated sweeping organizational changes in the Secretariat, and introduced management training to the people in charge.

In 1992, AI saw its first secretary general from outside Europe—Pierre Sané from Senegal. Sané brought AI into the campaign for a human rights commissioner inside the United Nations, a position that was established and grew into a prominent and visible human rights advocate. As AI entered the new millennium, it recorded another first in Secretary General Irene Khan, the first woman, first Muslim, and first one from Asia to serve in that position.

The Nobel Peace Prize: 1977

When AI was selected to receive the 1977 Nobel Peace Prize, it was only fitting that it won the award on the Prisoners of Conscience Year. AI designated the award money to promote the organization in the Third World, where its presence was traditionally weak.

The Nobel Committee based its selection on a number of factors, not the least of which was AI's apolitical stance. In the presentation speech, Aase Lionas, chairman of the Norwegian Nobel Committee, also cited the impressive results AI achieved in its prisoners of conscience campaign. Of 6,000 prisoners AI adopted between 1972 and 1975, more than 3,000 had been released.

AI's secretary general, Martin Ennals, remained true to form and elected to keep a prior commitment—AI's first anti-death-penalty conference—instead of going to Oslo to receive the prize. In its place he sent a delegation headed by IEC chair Thomas Hammarberg. Mümtaz Soysal, a former Turkish prisoner of conscience and the IEC's vice-chair, delivered the Nobel lecture for AI.

The award was considered by many to be the second recognition of the organization by the Nobel Committee. Sean MacBride had won the award in 1974, for a peace activism career that included many leadership years at AI.

The New Millennium: Changing Times and a Youthful Image

AI, known for creative campaigns, proved itself capable once again in October 2000. A pilot Web site for AI campaigns, www.StopTorture.org, took AI's letter-writing campaigns into cyberspace. Winner of The Revolution Awards 2001 for "best use of e-mail," StopTorture allows registered users to launch an e-mail avalanche as soon as they are alerted to a case AI wants to take on. In Lebanon, the government found itself pleading with AI to stop the e-mails just one day after a petition for the rights of asylum seekers in Lebanon went up on the site. The Web site idea stemmed from a research done by AI that showed, according to the Web site developers, that "the chances of an individual being tortured are greatly reduced if awareness can be raised within the first 48 hours of someone being arrested or abducted."

Another creative new campaign for AI began in 1998, with the creation of a fund marked toward the purchase of stock in corporations that can be subject to shareholders' actions. The fund's most prominent purchase was stock in Exxon Mobil Inc. AI planned to introduce a shareholders' resolution during the May 29, 2002, Exxon Mobil annual meeting, calling on the company to promote human rights in some of the volatile areas the company does business in, such as Chad and Nigeria.

A member survey in 1999 revealed a disquieting fact about AI. Members were getting older, and for an organization wholly dependent on member support, this was a problem. In the spring of 2000, AI hired Bonnie Abaunza to head a new national office of artist relations. Abaunza started Artists for Amnesty, a campaign aimed to enlist young, popular, Hollywood luminaries who would lend their "star appeal" to the aging organization. AI hoped to start attracting high school and college students in order to continue building "a culture of human rights," as Dennis R. Palmieri, spokesman for Amnesty International USA, said in January, 2002. Palmieri continued: "And in order for us to do that, we have to be at the epicenter of pop culture." In 2002, AI was planning its first post-Oscar party, and a film festival in West Hollywood, with a human rights theme, of course.

On its Web site, AI quotes a former torturer from El Salvador ". . . if there's lots of pressure—like from Amnesty International or some foreign countries—we might pass them on to a judge. But if there's no pressure, then they're dead." Since 1961, the organization has proved that individuals coming together can wield enough power to sway countries and affect real change. With the changing times AI has to modify some of its tactics, but has remained true to its philosophy and ethics to make the world a better place for all people.

Principal Subsidiaries

The Children's Network; The Company Approaches Network; The Lawyers' Network; The Medical Network; The Military Security and Police (MSP) Network; The Women's Network; The Lesbian, Gay, Bisexual and Transgender (LGBT) Network.

Principal Competitors

UN Human Rights Commission; Médcins Sans Frontières; Human Rights Watch.

Further Reading

"Amnesty International Awarded the Nobel Peace Prize, December 10, 1977," *DISCovering World History*, Detroit: Gale Research, 1997, http://galenet.galegroup.com/servlet/dc.

"Amnesty International Is Founded, May 28, 1961," *DISCovering World History*, Detroit: Gale Research, 1997, http://galenet.galegroup.com/servlet/dc.

Calvo, Dana, "Amnesty Makeover: Human Rights Group Seeks Younger Members by Reworking Image," *Houston Chronicle*, January 9, 2002, p. 1.

Dougherty, Carter, "Amnesty to Use Oil Stake for Lobbying," *Washington Times*, April 4, 2002, p. C11.

"Human Rights Breakthrough," *Internet Magazine*, January 2001, p.12.

Power, Jonathan, *Like Water on Stone: The Story of Amnesty International*, Boston: Northeastern University Press, 2001, 331 p.

Rabben, Linda, *Fierce Legion of Friends: A History of Human Rights Campaigns and Campaigners*, Brentwood, Maryland: The Quixote Center, 2002, 272 p.

—Adi R. Ferrara

Anglo American PLC

20 Carlton House Terrace
London SW1Y 5AN
United Kingdom
Telephone: (44) 0 20 7698 8888
Fax: (44) 0 20 7698 8500
Web site: http://www.angloamerican.co.uk

Public Company
Incorporated: 1999
Employees: 204,000
Sales: $19.3 billion (2002)
Stock Exchanges: Botswana Johannesburg London
  Namibia Switzerland
Ticker Symbol: AAL
NAIC: 212111 Bituminous Coal and Lignite Surface
  Mining; 212112 Bituminous Coal Underground
  Mining; 212221 Gold Ore Mining; 421840 Diamonds
  Wholesaling (Except Industrial); 212299 All Other
  Metal Ore Mining

Anglo American PLC is considered the world's largest gold-mining organization. Through its 45-percent share in De Beers, the company has a major interest in the distribution of 80 percent of the world's rough-diamond production. The company was formed in 1917 as South Africa's first home-based public limited company, called the Anglo American Corporation of South Africa (AAC), and has since become a unique multinational group, headquartered in London, England. The company dominates South Africa's domestic economy, with interests in an estimated 1,300 South African companies and control of at least one-quarter (and possibly as much as two-fifths) of the South African stock market. The group's corporate structure is based only in part on majority share ownership of subsidiary, associate, and other companies. Much of its control and influence lies in a complex web of connections based on family ties, friendships, and mutual business interests, although that interest is not infrequently accompanied by various forms of financial or commercial pressure.

The corporation—or what might be referred to as the "Oppenheimer empire"—has become in many respects a holding company, with diversified interests, such as gold-mining, being the formal responsibility of a group of associate companies. During the long period of apartheid, the Oppenheimers and the group itself were critical of various aspects of the apartheid system, while at the same time many of apartheid's opponents attacked AAC on the grounds that it was profiting greatly from the system, and in practice was doing very little to change, or to mitigate, its effects. With apartheid's collapse in the early 1990s, AAC has been preoccupied with protecting the empire it built in the face of the pressures to nationalize some of its assets and to lessen its stranglehold on the South African economy.

Early History Beginning in 1902

The roots of AAC's history can be traced back to 1902, when Ernest Oppenheimer arrived in Kimberley representing diamond merchants A. Dunkelsbuhler & Co., a member of the Diamond Syndicate, the cartel that attempted to maintain prices for South African diamonds by regulating production. Working for Dunkelsbuhler and on his own account, Oppenheimer also became interested in gold- and coal-mining, and in 1905 acquired the Consolidated Mines Selection Company (CMS), originally formed in 1887, with properties on the Far East Rand gold field. By 1916, when that field's true value was more widely appreciated, Oppenheimer/CMS was in a stronger position there than any of the other Transvaal mining-finance groups.

CMS had a large number of German shareholders and directors, causing it to be rather unpopular during World War I. Oppenheimer was a naturalized British subject who identified strongly throughout his life with South Africa's British, against its Dutch Afrikaner community. Oppenheimer was nevertheless attacked because of his German origins. These points, coupled with the war-imposed restrictions on British capital exports, led him to seek U.S. financing to develop the field. An American connection in CMS introduced him to Herbert Hoover, through whom Newmont Mining Corporation, J.P. Morgan & Co., and Guaranty Trust became involved. With their support, AAC was formed on December 25, 1917, with £2 million of authorized capital, half of which was issued. Various political reasons have

Company Perspectives:

Anglo American PLC, with its subsidiaries, joint ventures and associates, is a global leader in the mining and natural resources sectors. It has significant and focused interests in gold, platinum, diamonds, coal, base and ferrous metals, industrial minerals and forest products, as well as financial and technological strength. The Group is geographically diverse, with operations and developments in Africa, Europe, South and North America, and Australia. Anglo American represents a powerful world of resources.

been advanced for the decision to locate the company in South Africa rather than Britain, but the primary reason was to avoid the possibility of double taxation problems.

AAC joined the ranks of the mining-finance groups characteristic of South African mining. Cecil Rhodes and other early financiers concentrated ownership of individual mines in the hands of a few holding companies that provided basic financial, administrative, and technical services for the mines they owned. This process of concentration had begun with the diamond mines, initially because some claimholders had insufficient capital to continue exploitation as workings went deeper, and ultimately because ownership concentration meant more efficient production control. Gold-mining did not face oversupply problems, but given gold's fixed price and the highly speculative nature of mining investment, concentration of ownership meant more efficient use of technical and administrative resources. It also focused wealth and power in the hands of the relative few who sought it and were able to command the necessary capital. A system of interlocking directorships developed, creating a close, interdependent network. A relative latecomer to the field, Oppenheimer soon showed that he was more than a match for his predecessors, as he set out to absorb much of what they had built, and took the concept of group control much further.

With a strong base in gold and access to U.S. capital, Oppenheimer was able to challenge the Diamond Syndicate and De Beers, the dominant producer. He was helped by influential British and German connections, and by contacts between AAC Director H.C. Hull, former finance minister of the Union of South Africa, and his former political colleague, Prime Minister Jan Smuts. Oppenheimer acquired most of the diamond mines in Namibia—then known as South West Africa—when the German companies operating them were encouraged to sell out to British interests. By the time De Beers and others learned of the negotiations, it was too late to prevent the sale to AAC, and they initially welcomed the stability these acquisitions implied.

AAC's Namibian mines were quickly brought under centralized control in Consolidated Diamond Mines of South West Africa (CDM). Initially CDM cooperated with the Diamond Syndicate, but in 1922, AAC and Barnato Bros. reached a separate agreement for the purchase of the Belgian Congo's diamond output. In 1923 they acquired major interests in the Companhia de Diamantes de Angola, diamond mines in West Africa, and a share in British Guiana's diamond production. CDM subsequently became part of the De Beers group in 1930.

(More recently, CDM and AAC have been cooperating with the Namibian government in developing the country's gold resources.)

In 1924, AAC was given an 8 percent share in the Diamond Syndicate. The purchasing agreements AAC had with non-South African producers, including the right to take all of CDM's production, gave AAC apparent control over such producers. This control was more apparent than real, but led smaller South African producers to look to AAC as an alternative to the syndicate, with whom they were increasingly dissatisfied, owing to the prices they were offered. The principle of selling all of South Africa's diamonds through a single channel was seriously weakened. AAC was asked to leave the syndicate, and established a rival organization joined by Dunkelsbuhler, Barnato Bros., and Johannesburg Consolidated Investments Ltd. (JCI), a group originally established by Barnato, and subsequently absorbed into AAC's ambit.

The South African government was concerned about the implications for revenue of limited diamond production and a potentially disastrous price-cutting war between the two syndicates. The Diamond Control Act of 1925 gave the government sweeping powers to take over diamond production and distribution, and to prevent extreme behavior, namely price-cutting. As a member of Parliament, Oppenheimer had been able to introduce an amendment that required the government, if it enforced any provisions of the law, to give preference to South African-registered diamond purchasers; AAC was the only one—while all the others were registered in London.

With AAC continuing to grow financially stronger in the face of declining world diamond demand, the new syndicate was able to outbid the old in an offer to South African producers. On July 30, 1925, the new syndicate's offer was accepted and the old syndicate collapsed. Having gained effective control of distribution, Oppenheimer moved to control production as well. He became a De Beers director, while AAC further strengthened its position by buying properties in two new South African fields and by consolidating and expanding its links with outside producers. Resistance was strong. Oppenheimer's bid, first made in May 1927, to take control of De Beers, only succeeded in December 1929 with the support of the Rothschilds, introduced through Morgan Grenfell. Oppenheimer became chairman of De Beers, clearing the way for the consolidation of production and distribution functions in one organization, the Diamond Corporation, formed in February 1930 under De Beers' and Oppenheimer's effective control.

Negotiations with Sir Chester Beatty and Sir Edmund Davis, which had led to agreements for purchasing west African, Angolan, and Congolese diamonds, also led Oppenheimer to participate in the development of the Northern Rhodesian—now Zambian—copperbelt and that country's lead and zinc mines. Although these rich deposits had been known to exist for several decades at least, technological difficulties had prevented exploitation. Progress in the use of flotation techniques opened up new possibilities after World War I. AAC acted as engineering consultant to several companies formed to exploit these deposits, bringing some of them together in Rhodesian Anglo American Limited (Rhoanglo), formed in December 1928. American capital was also involved in this venture, as it was in

Key Dates:

1917: Sir Ernest Oppenheimer founds Anglo American Corporation of South Africa (AAC).

1926: AAC becomes the largest single shareholder in De Beers.

1942: AAC's involvement in coal becomes significant through SA Coal Estates.

1963: The major industrial and commercial interests of AAC are incorporated into Anglo American Industrial Corporation (Amic); Scaw Metals is acquired as a prologue to entering the steel industry on a large scale.

1967: AAC creates the Mondi group and gains entry into the paper/timber industry.

1975: Anglo American Coal Corporation (Amcoal) is formed and acquires Greenfield's Collieries, becoming one of the world's largest private sector coal exporters; the company acquires its first offshore expansion through Minorco's acquisition of Hudson Bay Mining & Smelting.

1981: AAC becomes the first South African mining house to encourage the recognition of black trade unions.

1982: Jwaneng Diamond Mine in Botswana opens and becomes one of the world's chief gem producers.

1993: Minorco acquires the non-African assets of AAC, excluding diamonds, while AAC acquires all the African assets of Minorco.

1998: AAC combines with Minorco to establish Anglo American PLC.

1999: Anglo American PLC lists on the London Stock Exchange and enters the FTSE 100.

2001: Anglo American PLC eliminates its cross-holding with De Beers, increasing its interest in De Beers from 32 percent to 45 percent.

the other group operating on the copperbelt, Beatty's Rhodesian Selection Trust.

Oppenheimer wanted to combine Morgan Grenfell, Beatty, and others in a syndicate to develop the Mount Isa lead mine in northwest Queensland, Australia. Initial surveys were not promising, and AAC withdrew. AAC subsequently became involved in various Australian undertakings, ultimately establishing an Australian subsidiary. Overall, however, the group's direct involvement in Australia has been rather limited.

The 1930s Through the 1980s

The 1930s saw further expansion of AAC's holdings in the Far East Rand, in some cases in conjunction with New Consolidated Gold Fields. AAC also began to move into the Orange Free State gold fields. The areas it acquired initially were generally unpromising. It was only by purchasing a stake in European and African Investments Ltd. in 1943, and subsequently gaining full ownership by acquiring most of the shares of its parent company, Lewis and Marks, in 1945, that AAC laid the foundation for its subsequent domination of Free State gold-mining.

The 1930s and 1940s also saw the establishment of several subsidiary holding companies and the extension of the administration decentralization that characterizes AAC. The precise extent to which effective Oppenheimer family control was maintained through E. Oppenheimer Sons, which absorbed A. Dunkelsbuhler & Co. in 1935, is unclear, but it is clear that personal influence remained strong. Anglo American Investment Trust (ANAMINT) took over AAC's diamond interests in 1936, while West Rand Investment Trust (WRITS) took responsibility for gold mines in the Far West Rand field that were opening up at this time.

The decentralized structure was intended to allow, indeed to stimulate, on-the-spot decision-making, and to enable ideas to filter up from the people most directly involved in day-to-day operations. However, decentralization made it extremely difficult to trace the details of financial connections within the group as the constituent companies remained separately incorporated. Effective control, or at least coordination by central management, had not been sacrificed; information was constantly exchanged, both formally and informally. Interlocking directorships, and the power to appoint directors, were augmented by personal contacts based on friendship and, more importantly, by family connections. Members of the Oppenheimer family held important positions in many of the companies. On another level, AAC recruited people considered potentially high-powered, including a substantial number of former Rhodes scholars.

As the group developed, acquiring or establishing companies in various fields, the decentralized structure remained. Some companies became subsidiaries, with at least 50 percent of their shares held by AAC. In other cases control mechanisms were more flexible, but just as effective. These included holding a greater number of shares than anyone else; the control of essential supplies, markets, or technology; and various financial links.

Between 1945 and 1960, AAC became the world's largest gold-mining group, owing to expansion in the Orange Free State as well as the richer mines in the Far West Rand and Klerksdorp fields. Capital requirements were high, in part because the Free State gold deposits lay at considerably deeper levels than the Rand's. The 1946 African miners' strike, although rapidly repressed, was evidence of considerable upward pressure on African wages. AAC decided to base Free State development on more capital-intensive techniques.

Building on its original financial concept, AAC went farther afield in its search for capital, securing about 27 percent of the £370 million raised from British sources; 23 percent from Switzerland, Germany, elsewhere in Europe, and the United States; and 43 percent from within the AAC group itself. Most innovative, and significant in the longer term, was AAC's drawing on surplus capital and non-mining savings generated within South Africa itself for 7 percent. The greater availability of domestic capital was a particularly important development after World War II, forming the basis for a measure of domestic financing of development, which was associated in part with the expansion of Afrikaner, as opposed to British, capitalism. As internal savings increased over the following decades, they also laid the foundation for South Africa's ability to absorb a substantial portion of shares disposed of through disinvestment by foreign firms, although heavy reliance on foreign investment remained.

By 1960, AAC had taken over the leadership of the gold-mining industry. It was also making heavy inroads into the country's industrial and service sectors. The difficulties of importing manufactured goods from Europe during World War I had stimulated interest in domestic industrialization. Increasingly powerful Afrikaner politicians were wary of mining interests prepared to finance industrial development, partly because of an underlying antipathy to capitalists, and partly because of the politicians' foreign, particularly British, identity. This led in 1928 to the formation of the Iron and Steel Corporation (ISCOR) as a nationalized basis for the country's iron and steel industry. As post-World War II mining developments generated more capital, pressure to create domestic investment opportunities led to increased, though often reluctant, cooperation between the government and the private sector which was increasingly dominated by AAC.

Social and political considerations also became important, particularly after 1948 when the rationale for the apartheid system included the expectation that industries would be established along the borders of homeland territories, providing employment for the Africans increasingly forced to inhabit them. While that hope was never fulfilled, antagonism between the British and Afrikaners began to diminish in the face of a perceived common threat from black Africans, and by the growth of Afrikaner involvement in business. The importance of Oppenheimer's and AAC's financial strength also diminished some of the specific antagonism toward them. Despite the fact that Harry Oppenheimer, who succeeded his father as head of the group after World War II, often criticized the apartheid regime, it was widely accepted that he did not intend to attempt to destroy it, was prepared to work within it, and was pressing for changes that would improve the position of Africans primarily because it made good business sense.

In 1942 the government established the Industrial Development Corporation to promote and finance—through war taxes imposed on the mining industry—the expansion of ISCOR and a range of private industrial concerns. This was in some measure an attempt to create a counterweight to AAC. Its ability to draw on foreign capital sources, as well as foreign technology and other expertise, meant that the counterweight soon fell.

Initially, most of AAC's industrial activity was directly related to mining. It had acquired African Explosive and Chemical Industries through its earlier investments in diamond interests. Its acquisition of Lewis and Marks brought it Union Steel and Vereeniging Refractories. In 1936, AAC established Boart and Hard Metals, concerned with the use of industrial diamonds in mining and other drilling applications. In 1961 it created the Highveld Steel and Vanadium Corporation which, along with Steel Ceilings and Aluminum Works (SCAW), acquired in 1964, formed the basis of AAC's control of South African specialized steel production, as well as created a strong foundation for heavy engineering. The merging of three construction companies—Lewis Construction, James Thompson, and Anglo American Construction—into LTA Ltd. created a construction giant.

Diversification also led AAC into paper manufacturing (Mondi Paper Co., formed in 1967) and, through its 1960 takeover of Johannesburg Consolidated Investments, newspaper publishing (the Argus group and Times Media Limited).

Building on motor vehicle distribution in the McCarthy group, it moved—by combining with Chrysler and then Ford—into automobile production as well. In freight services, in conjunction with Safmarine, it led the growth of containerized shipping in the country. Retail stores and large property holdings have also been acquired.

An important merger involving AAC in the 1970s was between Rand Mines and Thomas Barlow. Rand Mines was a mining group that had not acquired interests in the Far West Rand and Orange Free State as its older Witwatersrand mines reached depletion. Seriously ailing, it came under AAC control in the 1960s, but AAC did little to revive it. Thomas Barlow had been a small engineering supply importer, which by 1970 controlled more than 70 companies manufacturing a wide variety of products. Barlow acquired all Rand Mines' issued shares in 1971. AAC held 10 percent of Barlow Rand's shares directly. By 1972, after reorganization and expansion, the merged group controlled 131 subsidiaries and associates in nine countries. Although executive control remained in the Barlow family hands, AAC was not without influence in the firm.

At least as important as its industrial links was AAC's involvement in the financial sector. In 1949, the South African government set up the National Finance Corporation (NFC) to receive large deposits—minimum £50,000—to be used for investment. Much of the NFC's funds came from and went back into mining. AAC, for its part, formed a private merchant bank, Union Acceptances Ltd. (UAL), in 1955, supported by Lazard Freres and Barclays Bank. Offshoots and mergers followed, the most important mergers being those in the 1970s which brought UAL, Syfrets Trust Co., Old Mutual, and Nedbank together as Nedsual, providing commercial banking, insurance, and other financial services. AAC went on to increase its holdings in insurance and other financial services institutions. Although AAC disposed of its Nedbank holdings by the late 1970s, the merger with Nedbank was only one of the moves made that contributed strongly to the destruction of the barrier between British and Afrikaner capital.

AAC did not merely compete with Barclays. The 1970s expansion saw AAC's holdings in Barclays National Bank reach 17.5 percent of the total shares issued. In 1986, when Barclays International was forced by public pressure to complete its disinvestment in South Africa, AAC acquired the greater part of the shares divested.

On the international scene, using many of the channels it had opened to bring capital into South Africa, AAC also expanded its own holdings, primarily in mining, throughout the world. In London, Charter Consolidated, a 1965 merger of the British South Africa Company, Central Mining, and CMS, gave AAC considerable investment opportunities in Africa, Europe, and Australasia.

Although diamonds replaced gold as AAC's single most important source of profit in the 1980s, and despite wide-ranging diversification, gold remained at the heart of the group's activities. A substantial holding in the U.S. precious metals refiners Engelhard Corporation, along with a stake in the U.K.'s Johnson Matthey, gave AAC access to important sources of highly profitable information about the world's gold trade.

AAC's share in Engelhard was held by its subsidiary Minerals and Resources Corporation (Minorco), officially renamed Minorco in 1974. Minorco grew out of Rhoanglo. It was through Minorco that AAC attempted to take over Consolidated Gold Fields (Consgold) in 1988. AAC and Consgold had been closely associated—directly and indirectly—in many enterprises over the years, but relations between them were based at least as much on rivalry as on common interest, and the attempted takeover came as no surprise. AAC acquired about 25 percent of Consgold. This attempt came up against U.S. antitrust legislation and Consgold was bought by Hanson Trust instead.

AAC was at the center of political controversy in South Africa in the 1980s, not merely because of its economic strength, but because the Oppenheimers and the group itself took a public stand on the apartheid question. Politically active Ernest Oppenheimer and his son Harry were not in favor of black majority rule, but they did press for relaxation of certain aspects of the apartheid regime. Not surprisingly, they were particularly interested in decreasing dependence on migrant labor. A more settled, stable labor force was considered more productive and efficient. Although some stabilization of labor did occur, relatively little could be done in the face of government opposition. In 1987, along with some other mining groups, AAC began to replace migrant workers' hostels with low-cost family accommodations. Like several other changes, this was seen by many as too little too late, and by others as merely a new method of social control. AAC was not prepared to raise African wages sufficiently to allow workers effective freedom of housing choice.

In 1985, AAC's chairman, Gavin Relly, and other senior AAC personnel met representatives of the African National Congress (ANC) in exile. In April 1990, AAC's Scenario Planning team published proposals for South Africa's constitutional development. These placed great emphasis on federalism and devolution of power. More dispersed state power, AAC argued, would facilitate accommodation of divergent interest groups. This, along with a massive image-building campaign in the U.K. press had been part of AAC's campaign to remain a major economic force in the country as its political structure changed inexorably.

A Decade of Change: The 1990s

The rapid unraveling of the apartheid system in the early 1990s quickly changed forever the environment in which AAC operated and gave rise to much speculation about AAC's future, as well as a great deal of maneuvering by AAC to protect its interests. The major political events followed one after another: in 1990 the ban on the ANC was lifted and Nelson Mandela was released from prison; in 1991 the remaining apartheid laws were repealed; in 1992, an all-white referendum approved a new constitution that would lead to eventual free elections; and in 1994 the first nationwide free elections were held and were won by the ANC, with Mandela elected president.

Meanwhile, the 1990s started for AAC with a change in leadership, as Julian Ogilvie Thompson, who at one time was Harry Oppenheimer's personal assistant, took over the chairmanship from the retiring Relly in 1990. At the same time, it was widely known that Oppenheimer's son Nicholas, then deputy chairman of AAC and the head of De Beers' London-based diamond sales operation, was being groomed as the next chairman. The new leadership faced the consequences of AAC's years of dealing with apartheid and the international boycotts and sanctions the system engendered. The company had been forced to reinvest its earnings within South Africa where it had no choice but to diversify in order to use all its excess cash. By the early 1990s, AAC had created, no doubt aided by the apartheid system itself, a powerfully diversified company with admitted control of 25 percent of the South African stock market, a figure that outside observers have placed as high as 40.5 percent. Threats to nationalize certain AAC assets, notably its mines, and to break up the AAC empire seemed quite real, although it eventually became apparent that Mandela had no intention of seizing the company's assets without compensation.

As part of a two-pronged defensive strategy, AAC first moved to protect some of its assets from nationalization by increasing its overseas investments and by transferring assets into the control of subsidiaries and affiliated companies located outside South Africa, with Luxembourg-based Minorco the key affiliate. Minorco expanded its North American mining operations by acquiring the American firm Freeport-McMoRan Gold Company in 1990 (it was later renamed Independence Mining) and the Canadian-based Hudson Bay Mining & Smelting in 1991. In a 1993 $1.4 billion stock and asset swap, Minorco took over the South American, European, and Australian operations of both AAC and De Beers, which meant that all of AAC's non-African, non-diamond assets were now consolidated within Minorco and out of the reach of nationalization.

AAC's second strategy was a longer term plan of making small concessions to the new political order over the course of several years, thus heading off the possibility that the country's new government of national unity would force AAC to make more dramatic changes. Essentially, this represented a revival of AAC's strategy of co-option, previously used successfully with the Afrikaners, now being employed with the new group in power. AAC sought to spin off some of its vast holdings to black South Africans, such as in the 1994 deal in which African Life was bought by a group of black businesspeople.

A more ambitious divestment began in 1995 when AAC divided its Johannesburg Consolidated Investment Company, Limited (Johnnies) subsidiary into three separate companies: AAC American Platinum Corporation Ltd. (Amplats), a trader of platinum and diamonds; JCI Ltd., an operator of gold, coal, ferro-chrome, and base metal mines; and Johnnies Industrial Corporation Ltd. (Johnnic), a holding company with industrial and real estate assets. AAC intended to hold onto its minority stake in Amplats, but to sell its stakes in JCI and Johnnic to black South Africans. As of mid-1996 neither of the stakes had been sold, but a serious bid was developing for Johnnic, whose lucrative holdings included a 13.7 percent stake in South Africa's largest brewing company, South African Breweries; 27.8 percent of a beverages group, Premier; 26.4 percent in an automobile maker, Toyota SA Marketing; and 43.2 percent of a newspaper and magazine publisher, Omni Media. Little interest had been apparent for the JCI stake, with the *Economist* speculating that black South Africans' business inexperience made running a holding company more attractive than the messy business of mining.

By the mid-1990s, ACC was slowly beginning to unbundle itself of its diverse and massive holdings in South Africa. The company's future was still clouded given the question of whether it was moving fast enough to suit those in the country wishing to see economic power transferred from white to black hands nearly as fast as political power had been transferred. And while Mandela's government seemed content with a go-slow approach, the political situation was still unstable in the country, especially given Mandela's advanced age. Nevertheless, AAC's moves to shelter more of its assets offshore made it much less likely that possible future government intervention in its affairs would prove devastating.

Major Changes in 1998

AAC undertook a major change in October 1998, when it announced a significant reorganization that would result in a company name change and moving company headquarters to London. It was a complicated restructuring. AAC held considerable cross-holdings with De Beers, the South African company best known for its status in the world diamond industry. AAC also held 43 percent of Minorco, a Luxembourg-listed company that held assets outside South Africa with interests in similar industry sectors; and De Beers also owned 23 percent of Minorco.

AAC made a successful offer for the shares it did not already own in Minorco, priced at $2.3 billion; a bid for the minorities of Amcoal, South Africa's largest coal company, valued at $1.6 billion; the acquisition of Amic, another of South Africa's largest industrial companies; and the acquisition of several of De Beers' investments. Cross-holdings would remain between the two companies, but the result was one company, named Anglo American PLC. The company now held all the previous interests in gold, platinum, coal, and so on, and De Beers retained only diamond interests.

The combining of companies created several benefits. Anglo American became one of the world's largest mining and natural resources companies, with an array of interests in gold, platinum, and diamonds, and an central presence in coal, base and ferrous metals, industrial minerals, and forest products. The formation of Anglo American allowed the group to compete more effectively around the world and to exploit new business and growth opportunities, supported by improved access to international capital markets.

Before the closing of the public offer, Minorco divested itself of its gold interests and interests in Engelhard Corporation and Terra Industries. Based on the closing share price of AAC on October 14, 1998, and reflecting the terms of the share offer for Minorco, Anglo American had a market capitalization of nearly £6.1 billion, enough to be included in the FTSE 100 index. The company commenced trading shares on the London Stock Exchange in May 1999, with secondary listings on the Johannesburg Stock Exchange and Swiss Exchange SWX.

Focusing on Core Business: 2001 and Beyond

At the time of its listing, Anglo American announced shareholder value enhancement as its key objective. The company focused its efforts on enhancing its core portfolio of businesses and holdings. To that end, by early 2001, it had successfully accomplished a number of steps in this process, including significant expansionary growth in many divisions; major acquisitions in its Industrial Minerals, Coal and Forest Products divisions; the accelerated disposal of non-core industrial interests, which led to the sale of US$840 million of assets in 2000; and the exchange of the major portion of its non-core holding in FirstRand in return for certain listed mining assets valued at around US$730 million.

Rumors began to swirl in January 2001 that the longstanding marriage between Anglo American and De Beers was about to dissolve. The following month, Anglo American announced the creation of DB Investments(DBI), in conjunction with Central Holdings Limited and Debswana Diamond Company (Proprietary) Limited. The result of this deal was the elimination of the complicated cross-holding between De Beers and Anglo American, which had dampened the share price of both groups for some time. Anglo American's interest in De Beers rose from 32.2 percent to 45 percent.

The results of this move were overwhelmingly positive for Anglo American. It greatly simplified Anglo American's structure and with the removal of the cross-holding it brought an immediate cash inflow of US$1,072 million and US$701 million on redemption of preference shares in DBI. It also increased the free float of Anglo American shares to approximately 90 percent.

Anglo American made financial news pages in March 2002 with the announcement by the mining group that it had taken a US$488 million charge in 2001 to cover the cost of restructuring its base metals operations. Amidst an extremely disappointing year for base metals, most of the exceptional costs resulted from the company's miscalculations of the dollar costs of its copper investments in Zambia. This led to the proposed closure of Konkola Copper Mines, which accounted for nearly two-thirds of Zambia's copper production. Anglo American had acquired the assumed low-cost assets two years prior, but its withdrawal from Zambia alone resulted in an exceptional charge of US$353 million. Operating profits fell 5 percent to US$3.3 billion before the exceptional costs of US$513 million.

Base metals were severely hit in 2001 by the worst prices in 30 years, while steel and stainless-steel prices also waned. But by early 2002, analysts were predicting an upturn for base metals and platinum, while coal was not expected to see a change for the better.

Principal Subsidiaries

Anglo Platinum: Amandelbul UG2; Bafokeng Rasimone; Lebowa Platinum; Maandagshoek; Pandora Joint Venture (50%); Polokwane Smelter; Potgietersrust Platinums; Precious Metals Refinery; Rustenburg Base Metals; Rustenburg Platinum; Twickenham Mine; Union Section UG2 Expansion Project; Waterval UG2 Project. AngloGold: Boddington (Australia; 33%); Cerro Vanguardia (Argentia; 46%); Cripple Creek & Victor (USA; 67%); Ergo; Geita (Tanzania; 50%); Great Noligwa; Jerritt Canyon (USA; 70%); Kopanang; Moab Khotsong; Morila (Mali; 40%); Morro Velho (Brazil); Mponeng; Navachab (Namibia); Sadiola (Mali; 38%); Savuka; Serra Grande (Brazil; 50%); Sunrise Dam (Australia); Tanami

(Australia; 40%); Tau Lekoa; TauTona; Union Reefs (Australia); Yatela (Mali; 40%). De Beers: De Beers Marine Namibia (Namibia; 85%); Debswana (Botswana; 50%); Finsch; Kimberley Mines; Koffiefontein; Namaqualand Mines; Namdeb (Namibia; 50%); Premier; Snap Lake (Canada); The Oaks; Venetia; Williamson Diamonds (Tanzania; 75%). Anglo Coal: Callide (Australia); Carbones del Cerrejón (Colombia; 33%); Carbones del Guasare (Venezuela; 25%); Cerrejón Zona Norte (Colombia; 33%); Dartbrook (Australia; 78%); Drayton (Australia; 88%); Eyesizwe Coal (11%); German Creek (Australia); Goedehoop; Greenside; Kleinkopje; Kriel; Landau; Moranbah North (Australia; 88%); New Denmark; New Vaal; Richards Bay Coal Terminal (27%). Anglo Forest Products: Aylesford Newsprint (United Kingdom; 50%); Cartonboard and Corrugating Paper; Europapier (Austria; 70%); Fibre Supply Forests; Frantschach Packaging (Austria; 70%); Frantschach Swiecie (Poland; 61%); Global Forest Products (49%); Merebank; Mining Timber; Mondi Packaging (Europe); Mondipak; Neusiedler (Austria); Richards Bay; Sawmilling; SiyaQhubeka Forests (65%); Anglo Industrial Minerals: Botswana Ash (Botswana; 21%); Cleveland Potash (United Kingdom); Copebrás (Brazil; 73%); Steetley Iberia (Spain); Tarmac Central Europe (Germany, Poland and Czech Republic); Tarmac France (France and Belgium); Tarmac Group (UK); Tarmac International Holdings (Far East and Middle East). Anglo Ferrous Metals: Australian Manganese (40%); Boart Longyear; Columbus Stainless (14%); Highveld Steel (78%); Samancor (40%); Anglo Base Metals: Anaconda Nickel (Australia; 24%); Barro Alto (Brazil); BCL (Botswana; 23%); Bindura (Zimbabwe; 53%); Black Mountain; Catalao (Brazil); Codemin (Brazil; 90%); Collahuasi (Chile; 44%); Gamsberg; Hudson Bay (Canada); Kolwezi Tailings (Congo; 30%); Konkola Copper Mines (Zambia; 33%); Lisheen (Ireland; 59%); Loma de Níquel (Venezuela; 91%); Mantos Blancos (Chile); Namakwa Sands; Nkomati (25%); Palabora (29%); Quellaveco (Peru; 80%); Salobo (Brazil; 50%); Skorpion (Namibia); Tati (Botswana; 43%).

Principal Competitors

BHP Billiton Ltd; Rio Tinto PLC.

Further Reading

Ball, Deborah, "Funds Will Reject Oppenheimer, Anglo American Bid for De Beers," *Wall Street Journal*, April 23, 2001, p. A16.

Block, Robert, "An $18.7 Billion Buyout of De Beers Appears Imminent," *Wall Street Journal*, May 18, 2001, p. A17.

——, "De Beers Owners Weigh Plan to Delist Diamond Giant," *Wall Street Journal*, February 2, 2001, p. A8.

"Dancing Partners: Business in South Africa," *Economist*, April 27, 1996, pp. 70–71.

Fuhrman, Peter, "Harry Oppenheimer, African Empire Builder, Is Smiling Again," *Forbes*, September 16, 1991, pp. 130–37.

Gregory, Theodore, *Ernest Oppenheimer and the Economic Development of Southern Africa*, Cape Town: Oxford University Press, 1962.

Hocking, Anthony, *Oppenheimer and Son*, New York: McGraw-Hill, 1973.

Innes, Duncan, *Anglo American and the Rise of Modern South Africa*, London: Heinemann Educational Books, 1984.

Jessop, Edward, *Ernest Oppenheimer: A Study in Power*, London: Rex Collings, 1979.

Kanfer, Stefan, *The Last Empire: De Beers, Diamonds, and the World*, New York: Farrar Straus Giroux, 1993.

Nevin, Tom, "Anglo, De Beers to Split?" *African Business*, January 2001, p. 30.

——, " 'Think Again, Anglo,' Says Anderson Mazoka," *African Business*, March 2002, p. 40.

"A New Scramble," *Economist*, August 12, 1995, pp. 17–19.

"Not a Golden Titan, More Like a Pig in a Poke," *Economist*, October 7, 1995, pp. 67–68.

Pallister, David, Sarah Stewart, and Ian Lepper, *South Africa Inc.: The Oppenheimer Empire*, London: Simon & Schuster, rev. ed., 1987.

Stein, Nicholas, "The De Beers Story: A New Cut on an Old Monopoly," *Fortune*, February 19, 2001, pp. 186–206.

Williams, Stephen, "Shock as Anglo Pulls Out of Konkola," *African Business*, March 2002, p. 41.

Wright, Chris, "Now Anglo American Migrates to London," *Corporate Finance*, January 1999, p. 4.

—Simon Katzenellenbogen
—updates: David E. Salamie, Stacee Sledge

Aquila

Aquila, Inc.

20 West Ninth Street
Kansas City, Missouri 64105
U.S.A.
Telephone: (816) 421-6600
Toll Free: (800) 487-6661
Fax: (816) 467-3591
Web site: http://www.aquila.com

Public Company
Incorporated: 1926 as Missouri Public Service Company
Employees: 7,377 (2001)
Sales: $40.4 billion (2001)
Stock Exchanges: New York
Ticker Symbol: ILA
NAIC: 221122 Electric Power Distribution; 221210
   Natural Gas Distribution; 422720 Petroleum and
   Petroleum Products Wholesalers (except Bulk Stations
   and Terminals); 541330 Engineering Services; 541511
   Custom Computer Programming Services

Aquila, Inc. is an international electricity and natural gas utility. It operates power generation facilities, distribution networks, and trading ventures in seven U.S. states and in Canada, the United Kingdom, New Zealand, and Australia. With more than six million customers throughout the world, Aquila ranks 33 on the *Fortune* 500.

1902–40: From a Single Generator to a Major Utility

Aquila's history began at the turn of the century in rural Kansas, where a farmer and miller named Lemuel K. Green began dabbling in property and banking transactions. In the waning years of the 1890s, he traded a collection of homestead and timber claims in Graham County for a flour mill in Lenora, Kansas. Within three years, Green had amassed sufficient capital to purchase the water-powered Alton Roller Mills that had employed him some years before, and turn over the Lenora flour mill to his father and uncle.

In 1902 Green sold the Alton mill, using the proceeds to establish a modern, steam-powered milling complex called the Solomon Valley Milling Company in the more populous locale of Osborne, Kansas. This new mill was equipped with an electric power generator, which enabled Green to produce and sell electricity, an enterprise that had long fascinated him.

By 1908, at the age of 48, Green decided to pursue the rapidly growing power generation business. He sold the Solomon mill and purchased the H.M. Spalding Electric Light Plant, a poorly run power company in nearby Concordia, Kansas, for $21,500.

At the time it was purchased, the Spalding company operated only from dawn to midnight—the power supply was flickered at 11:45 to warn customers of the impending blackout—and remained closed on Sundays. In order to provide electricity around the clock, Green negotiated a deal to buy power from a nearby flour mill that was equipped with an electrical generator. Meanwhile, Green put his sons, Ralph and Lawrence, to work in the company, setting utility poles and stringing power lines.

At this time an important advance was made in electrical lighting equipment. The traditional carbon filament light bulb, fragile and inefficient, was replaced by a new kind of bulb with a filament made of tungsten. As these bulbs became widely available to customers, the demand for electricity greatly increased.

Soon, dozens of towns near Concordia were asking for electric service. Green organized the community leaders and offered to string transmission lines to their towns if they would fund the construction. The communities issued bonds to cover these costs and before long the Spalding plant was serving 22 communities throughout northern Kansas. In addition, Green's success in securing large supplies of water required for running the generating facilities enabled him to sell the surplus in the city of Concordia. Still, with plenty of excess generating capacity, Green began a series of publicity campaigns to increase customer purchases of electrical appliances.

In 1916, sensing an opportunity to capitalize on his investment, Green sold the Spalding plant to a New York investment group headed by A.E. Fitkin & Company for $550,000. A short time later, during a visit to Pleasant Hill, Missouri, about 20 miles southeast of Kansas City, Green discovered yet another untapped market for electricity.

Company Perspectives:

We're committed to achieving a winning combination for our customers, shareholders and associates. While our core values define the rules of the game, we believe success is ensured when our associates possess the following characteristics: accountable, taking full ownership of what they do; best in class, performing at the highest possible level; creative in their efforts to arrive at win-win-win solutions; and driven in a relentless pursuit of results for our clients.

The local power company, the Reeder Light, Ice & Fuel Company, served Pleasant Hill, but had not yet penetrated the areas surrounding the growing town. Green purchased the company, naming it the Green Power & Light Company, and set out to expand the operation.

Adding generators and stringing new power lines were elementary problems. An expanded plant, however, would require vast quantities of water. Not wishing to use the low-grade, iron-rich well water prevalent in the area, Green purchased a tract of land that included a small river and dammed it to create Lake Baldwin. The lake not only fed the plant, it also provided surplus quantities of water to the residents of Pleasant Hill.

In 1922, searching for new opportunities to expand, Green constructed a second generating station near Clinton, about 50 miles south of Pleasant Hill. Additional expansion, however, would require financial resources that were not only beyond the means of the family, but also the local banks, and even the Kansas City loan company they had retained. The only alternative was to take the company public. Green Power & Light became the West Missouri Power Company in 1922, with shares sold to the public and a variety of other interests.

The company and its rival in the area, Kansas City Power & Light, settled on service boundaries in 1922. This arrangement cleared the way for additional acquisitions by West Missouri Power Company, including a franchise to serve the city of Nevada, Missouri, and its electric street railway in 1924. Within the next few years, the company was serving 56 communities south and east of Kansas City, and had an interest in the Ozark Utility Company, itself serving 35 towns in southwestern Missouri. In addition to generating electric power, the company now also provided manufactured gas.

In a dramatic move in late 1926, however, Lemuel Green negotiated the sale once again to the Fitkin group of West Missouri Power Company, which was to be merged with the Missouri Public Service Company (MPS). During this same time period, Green purchased 2,000 acres of orange grove property near Escondido, California.

Green died in 1930, at the beginning of the Great Depression. Ralph Green, principal inheritor of the family business, sold the family interest in the Ozark Utility Company that year to focus on the citrus business his father had started. However, he remained deeply interested in the companies the family had built in Missouri. It was with much disappointment that he watched them deteriorate under increasingly difficult circumstances.

1940–92: Expansion Domestically and Internationally

In 1940 Ralph Green saw an opportunity to take back the Missouri Public Service Company, which had absorbed the West Missouri Power Company. The Public Utilities Act of 1935 mandated that the enormous holding companies that owned all U.S. utilities divest them. Green, whose assets remained well protected during the Depression, was able to acquire a controlling interest in MPS, which was serving 100 communities in Western Missouri from the Middle West Corporation.

In 1943 Green also gained control of the Missouri Gas & Electric Service Company, which served about 40 communities. Two years later, he added the City Light and Traction Company of Sedalia, Missouri, to his growing system of utility companies. With service levels restored and the company once again financially sound, MPS absorbed Missouri Gas & Electric in 1952. Also, after several years of providing manufactured gas at a substantial loss to only two communities, MPS converted to natural gas and expanded its gas business into 12 new communities.

During the 1950s, the company faced nearly threefold population growth in its service territory, fueled by suburban growth, new industrial parks, the baby boom, and the development of the new Mid-Continent International Airport. New demand for gas and electricity was easily met through an ambitious and carefully researched expansion plan that more than doubled the company's capacity.

Ralph Green died in 1962, passing leadership of the corporation to his son Richard Green, who was named chairman of MPS in April 1963. Under his leadership the company saw somewhat slower, but steady growth, remaining a primarily suburban and rural power utility. During the 1960s MPS as well as other utility companies became increasingly encumbered by mounting state and federal regulations. In what would become a fortunate strategic move, MPS steered clear of adding the nuclear-powered facilities that promised such tremendous returns on investment despite high start-up and regulatory costs.

MPS entered a turbulent period beginning in the early 1970s. Battered by high interest rates and inflation and an adversarial, if not hostile, relationship with regulators, MPS found itself unable to exercise control over its markets or effectively manage its risks. The virtual end of OPEC control over world energy markets in 1979, however, brought about more favorable economic conditions, while the 1980s heralded an era of probusiness regulation under the administration of President Ronald Reagan.

In 1982 Green's son, Richard, Jr., assumed the position of chief executive officer. Demonstrating a fiery entrepreneurial spirit, the younger Green made an unsuccessful bid to acquire the Kansas-based Gas Service Company in 1983. Deciding to postpone his acquisition plans, Green instead formulated a business strategy that clearly identified the company's regulatory, weather, and general economic risks. Rick Green also asserted that MPS would concentrate solely on energy generation and related businesses; diversification into nonenergy assets was to be strictly avoided. By 1985, a reorganization was in order. The Missouri Public Service Company shed its geographically specific name and was reborn as UtiliCorp United Inc.

Key Dates:

1902: Lemuel K. Green establishes the Solomon Valley Milling Company, equipped with an electric power generator.

1908: Green uses proceeds from the sale of the Milling Company to buy the H.M. Spaulding Electric Light Plant in Concordia, Kansas.

1916: Green sells the Spaulding Plant and buys the Reeder Light, Ice & Fuel Company in Pleasant Hill, Missouri; renames it the Green Power & Light Company.

1922: Green builds a second generating plant in Clinton, Missouri; Green Power & Light is renamed the West Missouri Power Company, and it goes public.

1926: Green sells West Missouri Power, and it is merged into the Missouri Public Service Company.

1940: Ralph Green buys a controlling interest in the Missouri Public Service Company.

1943: Green gains control of the City Light and Traction Company of Sedalia, Missouri.

1952: Missouri Public Service merges with Missouri Gas & Electric.

1983: Missouri Public Service reorganizes and adopts the name UtiliCorp United Inc.

1985: UtiliCorp buys People's Natural Gas.

1986: UtiliCorp buys Northern Minnesota Utilities.

1987: UtiliCorp buys West Virginia Power and West Kootenay Power and Light in British Columbia.

1989: UtiliCorp buys Michigan Gas Utilities; Aquila Energy Corporation subsidiary is created to manage the company's unregulated gas operations.

1992: UtiliCorp enters a joint venture to distribute and market natural gas in the United Kingdom.

1993: UtiliCorp buys a minority interest in a New Zealand utility.

1995: UtiliCorp buys an interest in a second New Zealand utility; UtiliCorp buys 49.9 percent of an Australian utility.

1999: UtiliCorp buys an interest in an Australian gas business.

2000: UtiliCorp buys electrical distribution assets in Alberta, Canada.

2002: UtiliCorp buys an interest in another United Kingdom utility; UtiliCorp changes its name to Aquila, Inc.

While he was opposed to diversifying UtiliCorp's business, Green did, however, seek to diversify the company's regulatory risks and boost its winter sales. In 1985, UtiliCorp purchased People's Natural Gas with operations in five states. In 1986, it bought the gas distribution company Northern Minnesota Utilities. In 1987, it purchased West Virginia Power and West Kootenay Power and Light in British Columbia. In 1989, it acquired Michigan Gas Utilities, and in 1990, the company bought a West Virginia gas distribution network.

Thus, in five years UtiliCorp expanded its operations into eight states and British Columbia. Moreover, these properties diversified UtiliCorp's operations into natural gas distribution and marketing, as well as its traditional electricity generation and distribution businesses.

In 1989, the company assigned its unregulated gas operations to a newly created subsidiary, Aquila Energy Corp. In addition to its marketing functions, Aquila was responsible for such related, but unregulated, areas as natural gas storage and transmission. By 1990 Aquila was responsible for 21 percent of UtiliCorp's earnings.

UtiliCorp achieved its expansion while avoiding a substantial increase in debt or customer rates by continually offering shares of stock for sale, although it did reduce the Green family's stake in the company. Initially the offerings were made through local markets because the company was considered too small to interest Wall Street investors. As the company expanded, however, it also developed greater financial clout that enabled its shares to be traded on the New York Stock Exchange and allowed it to more easily secure backing for new projects. UtiliCorp also began an effort to increase employee ownership of the company to 25 percent, in the belief that it would increase employees' stake in the success of the company.

In 1991 UtiliCorp made its largest acquisition to date. Further pursuing its expansion strategy, the company engineered the takeover of additional electrical utility operations in Kansas and Colorado from Centel, a local telephone company that sought to concentrate on its core business. The addition of these operations boosted the number of UtiliCorp customers to nearly a million and increased the company's assets by almost $260 million. Other areas of growth included entrance into European markets. In 1992, UtiliCorp entered into a joint venture to distribute and market natural gas in the United Kingdom.

1992–2002: Deregulation Presents Opportunities and Perils

Congress had begun to deregulate the electrical industry in 1978. In 1992, it enacted the Energy Policy Act. This legislation allowed utilities and other entities to build electric generators and to sell the power produced at unregulated prices on the wholesale market. In doing so, it unleashed a series of changes in the previously staid utility industry unmatched since its birth about a century previously.

Many utilities, comfortable with the traditional regulatory regime that allowed them to collect guaranteed, if modest, profits yet saddled with large investments that might never be fully paid for under a competitive pricing regime, opposed this change. UtiliCorp, in contrast, adapted enthusiastically to the new rules. Its gas acquisitions gave it experience in that industry, which had successfully deregulated during the preceding decade. Its acquisition of utility operations in other states and in Canada and Great Britain gave it the kind of geographic diversification that deregulation encouraged. The company was free of the kinds of past investments that might inhibit its competitiveness.

During the 1990s, UtiliCorp aggressively pursued the business opportunities that deregulation permitted. It continued its international expansion. In 1993, UtiliCorp acquired a minority interest in a rural New Zealand utility. In 1995, it bought an interest in another New Zealand utility. In that same year, it purchased a 49.9 percent interest in an Australian electric distribution utility. In 1999, the company added gas businesses to its Australian portfolio. The year 2000 saw the company's Canadian operations expand with the acquisition of power distribution assets in Alberta. The company expanded its British operations in 2002.

At the same time, UtiliCorp diversified functionally, testing the new business opportunities opened by deregulation. The company's Aquila Energy unit expanded from managing the company's unregulated gas business to managing its unregulated wholesale power sales. It became one of the nation's major traders of electricity, arranging with other producers to deliver power to wholesale customers.

In 1996, UtiliCorp sold the first weather risk-hedging product, which allowed a customer to collect a premium if a specified weather event occurred that would have adverse consequences for its business. The company developed additional hedging products to help businesses manage financial risks resulting from such factors as the volatility in crop yields, inaccurate weather forecasts, and power supply blackouts.

UtiliCorp undertook a failed initiative to bundle power supply, telephone, and home security services into a package with a single bill. It also initiated telecommunications services in Australia and Kansas City.

In 2001, UtiliCorp spun off part of its Aquila unit, stating that it would divest the rest of the unit sometime in the future. The market for shares of unregulated power marketers, however, deteriorated. In 2002, less than a year later, UtiliCorp purchased all the shares it had sold. It then renamed the entire company Aquila, Inc.

By the beginning of the 21st century, the massive changes that had affected the utility industry during the preceding decade came into question. The deregulation of the California retail market in 1998, the large price increases and blackouts that followed, and the bankruptcy of one California utility and near-bankruptcy of another brought electrical utility deregulation into question. The fall of the nation's largest electricity trader, Enron, amid questions about the appropriateness and legality of its accounting practices, and subsequent suggestions that Enron may have engaged in fraudulent trading practices that contributed to California's power woes, raised additional questions about the wisdom of electricity deregulation. This occurred in a broader context of stock market decline and economic recession.

Aquila was not immune to these pressures. In May 2001, UtiliCorp/Aquila's stock price peaked at $37.55. By July 2002, it had declined to $6.75. Its debt ratings were reexamined. Management initiated a program including asset sales, a dividend reduction, and the sale of debt and equity securities aimed at improving the company's financial condition. Time would tell whether Aquila and many other electric utilities would regain financial health.

Principal Subsidiaries

Aquila Merchant Services, Inc. (100%); MEP Holdings, Inc. (100%); UtiliCorp Asia Pacific, Inc. (100%); UtiliCorp Asia Pacific Pty Ltd (100%); UtiliCorp Australia, Inc. (100%); UtilCo Group, Inc. (100%); UtiliCorp South Pacific, Inc. (100%); UtiliCorp Networks Canada Ltd. (100%); UtiliCorp Networks Canada (Alberta) Ltd. (100%).

Principal Competitors

AEP; Reliant Energy; Duke Energy; Mirant; Dynergy.

Further Reading

"Business Brief—UtiliCorp United Inc.," *The Wall Street Journal*, November 16, 1998, p. A2.

Butkus, Al, "Spreading the Weather Word," *Electric Perspectives*, September/October 1998, p.5.

Byrne, Harlan S., "Power Plays," *Barron's*, January 29, 1996, p. 17.

——, "Power Surge," *Barron's*, September 13, 1999, p. 22.

Cheddar, Christina, "UtiliCorp Hitches Future to Aquila Unit," *The Wall Street Journal*, March 6, 2002, p. B5A.

Cook, James, "Big Is Better," *Forbes*, January 21, 1991.

——, "UtiliCorp United: Diversification Succeeds Beyond Its Architect's Dreams," *Barron's*, June 10, 1991.

Goff, Sue, and Mark Golden, "Aquila Moves to Balance Its Books," *The Wall Street Journal*, June 18, 2002, p. C13.

Green, Richard C., *The Missouri Public Service Company: A Saga of Free Enterprise*, Princeton, N. J.: Newcomen Society in North America, 1967.

Grzanka, Len, "Energy One Provides a Lesson," *Public Utilities Fortnightly*, Fall 1998, p. 16.

Holden, Benjamin A., "Bid by UtiliCorp, Partners for Utility in Australia Wins," *The Wall Street Journal*, August 7, 1995, p. A14.

——, "UtiliCorp and Peco, Aided by AT&T, to Launch One-Stop Utility Service," *The Wall Street Journal*, June 24, 1997, p. A3.

Kohn, Bernie, "Utility Firm's Transformation Could be Model for DQE," *Pittsburgh Press*, July 3, 1991.

McGee, Suzanne, and Raymond Hennessey, "Deals and Deal Makers," *The Wall Street Journal*, April 25, 2001, p. C16.

O'Toole, Patrick, "Bundling Fizzles for Now," *SDM*, June 1998, p. 29.

Rosenberg, Martin, "UtiliCorp Looks to Europe for Expansion Possibilities," *Kansas City Star*, May 7, 1992.

Smith, Rebecca, "Shock Waves," *The Wall Street Journal*, November 30, 2001, p. A1.

"UtiliCorp Charges into New Zealand and Australia," *Utility Business*, April 1999, p. 32.

"UtiliCorp Expands Further into Canada," *Utility Business*, March 2000, p. 56.

"UtiliCorp Gains Power in New Zealand," *Utility Business*, October 1998, p. 18.

"UtiliCorp Proposes Doubling Its Stake in Power New Zealand," *The Wall Street Journal*, September 11, 1998, p. B4.

"UtiliCorp United Inc. Builds New Zealand Electricity Business," *The Wall Street Journal*, February 1, 1999, p. B2.

—John Simley
—update: Anne L. Potter

ARROW ELECTRONICS, INC.

Arrow Electronics, Inc.

25 Hub Drive
Melville, New York 11727
U.S.A.
Telephone: (516) 391-1300
Fax: (516) 391-1640
Web site: http://www.arrow.com

Public Company
Incorporated: 1935 as Arrow Radio
Employees: 12,400 (2001)
Sales: $10.1 billion (2001)
Stock Exchanges: New York
Ticker Symbol: ARW
NAIC: 421430 Computer and Computer Peripheral
  Equipment and Software Wholesalers; 421690 Other
  Electronic Parts and Equipment Wholesalers

Arrow Electronics, Inc., is the world's largest distributor of electronic components and computer products and a leading provider of services to the electronics industry. Arrow distributes these products and provides services to more than 175,000 customers through more than 200 sales facilities and 23 distribution centers in 40 countries and territories on six continents.

1935–80: From Seller of Used Radio Products to Major Electronics Distributor

Arrow Electronics was founded in 1935 as Arrow Radio, a retail outlet in New York City selling used radio equipment. However, Arrow's emergence as a major distributor of electronic components dates from 1968, when the company was purchased by three recent graduates of the Harvard School of Business.

By the mid-1960s, Arrow was selling a variety of home entertainment products and also had moved into electronic parts distribution. In 1968, B. Duke Glenn, Jr., Roger E. Green, and John C. Waddell, then working for an investment banking firm in New York, recognized the potential for growth in electronic parts distribution, and bought the company for $1 million in borrowed capital. They also purchased a company that reclaimed lead from old car batteries.

Using cash from the profitable lead reclamation business, the new owners began expanding Arrow's inventory of electronic parts, which allowed them to service their customers better. They also sacrificed profits, through aggressive pricing, in order to build volume. By 1971, Arrow had become the tenth largest electronic parts distributor in the United States, although still far behind Avnet Inc., the leading electronic parts distributor.

During the 1970s, Arrow continued its climb up the ranks of the largest distributors of electronic parts in the United States—to number nine in 1972, number five in 1976, and number four in 1977—primarily through internal growth. In 1974, Arrow also became the first distributor of electronic parts to introduce an online computerized inventory system to speed up delivery. Then in 1979, Arrow acquired West Coast-based Cramer Electronics, the country's second largest distributor of electronic parts at that time, with $150 million in annual sales. Although the acquisition, financed with junk bonds, left Arrow heavily in debt, it more than doubled the company's revenues. Its chief rival, Avnet, was still three times as big, but for the first time, Arrow could claim a national presence. Arrow was listed on the New York Stock Exchange in 1979.

With the takeover of Cramer Electronics, Arrow appeared to have fulfilled the vision of its 1969 annual report, which had predicted: "Significant opportunities exist for us in the electronics distribution business owing mainly to the fragmented competitive environment. . . . It appears likely that the future will belong increasingly to those few substantial distribution companies with the financial resources, the professional managements, and the modern control systems necessary to participate fully in the industry's current consolidation phase." Arrow would close 1980 with $350 million in sales.

1980–84: Tragedy and Rebuilding

But in December of 1980, a blistering fire raced through the conference center of a hotel in Harrison, New York, killing 13 senior executives from Arrow who had gathered for the company's annual budget meetings. Among the dead were Glenn,

then chairman of the company; Green, then an executive vice-
president, and all the department heads from the electronics
distribution division. Only Waddell, then an executive vice-
president, who had stayed behind at company headquarters to
answer questions about a two-for-one stock split announced
earlier that day, survived from the senior management team.

In a remarkable display of courage, Lynn Glenn, the widow of
the company's chief executive, addressed employees at company
headquarters the day after the fire. "I don't know your faces,"
she said, "but I'd know your names, because Duke always talked
about you. The company will go on. It won't be sold. You'll be
getting calls from competitors, but don't be spooked. Keep the
faith." According to *Fortune,* she then "fled into an adjoining
office and burst into tears." Despite her resolve, Arrow's stock
fell 19 percent on the first day of trading after the fire, and fell
another 14 percent before the month was out.

Waddell, who was named acting chief executive officer,
embarked on what *Fortune* described as "a one-man campaign
to assure security analysts, money managers, and journalists
that the company was stable and recovery was underway."
However, although sales held steady and none of the remaining
managers were lured away to the competition, Arrow's stock
continued to fall. That spring, the electronics industry was
plunged into a recession, further crippling Arrow's recovery.
By the time Arrow's stock bottomed out early in 1982, it had
lost 60 percent of its value.

Meanwhile, Waddell also was trying to rebuild Arrow's
senior management team. One of his first decisions was to go
outside the company to recruit senior executives, rather than
promote from within. That included finding someone to become
chief executive officer. "If I'd had my druthers," Waddell later
told *Fortune,* "I would have said to the board, there's only one
person who can be CEO of this company for the time being,
because nobody understands this child the way Waddell understands it."

However, the board did not have the same opinion of
Waddell, whom *Fortune* described as "slender and elegant . . .
a figure from a bygone era, an apparition out of F. Scott
Fitzgerald or *The Thin Man*," and in July of 1981, Arrow lured
Alfred J. Stein away from Motorola to be president and chief
executive officer. Waddell remained as chairman. "Stein was
clearly the biggest management coup in the history of distribu-

tion," Waddell told *Fortune* three years later. "You should
have seen the congratulatory letters and telegrams."

Unfortunately, Stein, who also had worked at Texas Instruments, did not mesh well at Arrow. Rob Klatell, then company
attorney, later told *Fortune* that with Stein's background in
manufacturing, he "kept looking for a facility to manage, and
all he had were these crazy salesmen running around." The
board fired Stein early in 1982, and named Waddell to the
position he felt he deserved. Six months later, Waddell recruited
Stephen Kaufman, a former partner with McKinsey & Co., to be
president of Arrow's electronics division.

In 1982, sales held steady at about $550 million and Arrow
lost $1.19 a share. But in 1983, with the recession in the
electronics industry over, sales reached $1.4 billion and Arrow
earned 85 cents per share. In 1984, *Fortune* declared that
"Kaufman's arrival marks the moment at which Arrow's
cruelly unconventional problem came to an end."

In 1983, with Arrow celebrating its financial and emotional
recovery, Waddell told *Forbes:* "Our strategic exercise for a
decade has been to get position. It cost us a lot of time, money
and aggravation. [After the fire] the overwhelming reality in my
life was that I had a job to do. Now it's time to turn our attention
to cashing in on a ten year investment."

1984–2002: Rapid Growth, Worldwide Expansion

The company made a major move in 1985 when Arrow
purchased a 40-percent interest in Spoerle Electronic, which
was already the largest distributor of electronic components in
Germany. As *Forbes* later reported, Kaufman, who spent several years in Europe as a consultant with McKinsey & Co., was
"a confirmed internationalist. At the time, no other American
electronics distributor had invested consistently in the fragmented European market, but Kaufman was convinced that
Europe's internal trade barriers would fall and that Arrow could
score big." Since then, Arrow has increased its share in Spoerle
to 70 percent, and has acquired 14 more European companies to
become the largest electronics distributor in Europe.

Arrow resumed its growth strategy in 1988 by acquiring
Kierulff Electronics, then the fourth largest electronics distributor in the United States, for $125 million. *Financial World*
noted, "Although economies of scale in electronics distribution
are notoriously hard to come by, the . . . purchase complements
Arrow's network nicely—and gives Arrow the $1 billion heft it
has been looking for." Arrow shut down all four Kierulff
warehouses and, as *Forbes* reported, "As if by a miracle, within
a year Arrow's bottom line went from a $16 million operating
loss in 1987 to operating profits of $10 million." To reduce its
debt, Arrow also sold its lead reclamation business in 1988.

In 1991, Arrow acquired Lex Electronics, formerly
Schweber Electronics and the third largest distributor in the
United States, and Almac Electronics Corporation, from their
British-based parent Lex Service, Plc. The company also ac-
quired a 50-percent interest in Silverstar Ltd. S.p.A., the largest
electronics distributor in Italy. A year later, Arrow purchased
Lex Service's distribution businesses in France and the United
Kingdom. Arrow affiliate Spoerle acquired Lex Electronics in
Germany.

Key Dates:

1935: Founded as Arrow Radio.
1968: Roger E. Green, John C. Waddell, and B. Duke Glenn, Jr., pay $1 million for the company.
1971: Arrow becomes the tenth largest electronic parts distributor in the United States.
1974: Arrow is the first electronic parts distributor to introduce a computerized inventory system.
1979: Arrow acquires Cramer Electronics, the nation's second largest electronic parts distributor.
1980: A fire kills 13 of Arrow's senior executives.
1985: Arrow buys 40 percent of Spoerle Electronic, Germany's largest electronic parts distributor.
1988: Arrow purchases Kierulff Electronics, the fourth largest electronics distributor in the United States.
1991: Arrow buys Lex Electronics and Almac Electronics Corporation. It buys 50 percent of Silverstar Ltd., an Italian distributor.
1992: Arrow buys distribution businesses in France and the United Kingdom. Spoerle buys a distributor in Germany.
1993: Arrow buys Component Agents Ltd., a Pacific Rim distributor; Zeus Components, Inc., a distributor specializing in supplying the U.S. military; CCI Electronique, a French distributor; and majority interests in Amitron S.A. and the ATD Group, distributors in Spain and Portugal.
1994: Arrow buys Field Oy of Finland, TH:s Group of Norway, Exatec A/S of Denmark, and two Australian distributors. It also buys Gates/FA Distributing, Inc. and Anthem Electronics in the United States.
1995: Arrow buys Components + Instrumentation (NZ) Ltd. of New Zealand.
1997: Arrow buys a United Kingdom distribution business and Conson Partners of the United States. It buys 51 percent of Support Net and forms a joint venture in South Africa.
1998: Arrow buys U.S. distributor Scientific and Business Minicomputers and Unitronics Componentes, a distributor in Spain and Portugal. It joins Marubun of Japan in a joint venture.
1999: Arrow buys Richey Electronics and the distribution group of Bell Industries in the United States. It buys majority stakes in Brazilian and Argentine distributors. It buys a Swiss distributor.
2000: Arrow buys Wyle Electronics and MOCA of the United States. It adds French, Israeli, Scandinavian, and Mexican distributors to its operations.
2002: Arrow sells its Gates/Arrow unit.

In 1993, Arrow became the first electronics distributor to claim a global reach when it acquired Components Agents Ltd., the largest multinational Pacific Rim distributor with operations in Hong Kong, Singapore, Malaysia, China, and South Korea. The same year, Arrow purchased the distribution division of Zeus Components, Inc., a distributor of high-reliability electronic components for the U.S. military; CCI Electronique, a French distributor; and majority interest in Amitron S.A. and the ATD Group, electronics distributors in Spain and Portugal.

Arrow moved into Scandinavia in 1994 by acquiring Field Oy, a Finnish company, and the TH:s Group, the leading distributor in Norway. The company also acquired Exatec A/S, one of the largest electronics distributors in Denmark, and increased its stake in Silverstar to a majority share. Also in 1994, Kaufman became chairman and Waddell took on the role of vice-chairman.

Later that same year, Arrow exchanged about $142 million in stock to acquire Gates/FA Distributing, Inc., a networking and DOS-based PC business. In October, Arrow purchased semiconductor and computer products distributor, Anthem Electronics for $390.6 million in stock. It also acquired two closely held Australian distributors.

In 1995, Arrow bought Components + Instrumentation (NZ) Ltd., a New Zealand distributor. It also reorganized itself into two marketing groups—one for its commodity PC business and one for the more technical and profitable midrange systems market. By 1996, Arrow was the world's largest distributor measured by sales.

In 1997, Arrow bought the electronic components distribution business of U.K.-based Premier Farnell PLC. It also purchased Conson, Inc., a distributor of mass storage products, and 51 percent of Support Net, Inc., one of IBM's largest distributors of midrange servers and networking products. It formed a joint venture to distribute electronic products in South Africa. Its most important action that year, however, was a major reorganization of its operations into seven business groups, each focused on a particular class of customer rather than on specific products.

With the slump in the PC market caused by the Asian financial crisis, the decline of PC prices, and the dearth of new products to attract customers, Arrow's sales grew by seven percent but its profits declined by 11 percent in 1998. Nevertheless, Arrow bought a majority interest in Scientific and Business Minicomputers, Inc., a leading technical distributor of mass storage products in the United States. It expanded its European operations with the purchase of Unitronics Componentes, S.A., a leading distributor in Spain and Portugal. Arrow also entered a joint venture with Marubun, Inc. of Tokyo to facilitate selling to Japanese-owned manufacturing operations in North America and the Pacific Rim.

Business recovered during the next two years. In 1999, Arrow bought Richey Electronics, Inc. and the electronics distribution group of Bell Industries, Inc. The company purchased majority interests in a Brazilian and an Argentine distributor and added a distributor to its Swiss operations. It also made its initial venture into online services.

In 2000, the company purchased Wyle Electronics, a distributor, and the Sun Microsystems distributor, MOCA, to expand its North American operations. Arrow acquired all or part of distributors in France, Israel, Scandinavia, and Mexico. It further developed several online initiatives, and it began to create various value-added services for which it planned to charge its customers added fees.

The beginning of the decline in the U.S. stock markets in 2000 signaled potential difficulties for Arrow's continued expansion. By 2001, the company faced significant declines in its revenues and profits. Demand for computers of all kinds declined as businesses and consumers significantly reduced purchases. The new Internet commerce industry shrank, as many enterprises went out of business. The rapidly expanding telecommunications industry found itself saddled with massive debt and severe overcapacity.

In response to these developments, the company reduced its inventory by 50 percent and eliminated 1,700 employees worldwide. Nevertheless, Arrow's sales declined 22 percent from $13 billion in 2000 to $10.1 billion in 2001. It recorded a profit of $357.9 million in 2000, but a loss of $73.8 million in 2001.

Sales continued their decline during 2002's first half. Sales declined 32 percent from $5.5 billion during the first half of 2001 to $3.7 billion during the same period of 2002. Profit declined from a $700 thousand gain to a $607 million loss. Arrow responded by selling its Gates/Arrow unit, which sold PCs, printers, other peripherals, and software, for $44.7 million in cash.

Principal Subsidiaries

Arrow Electronics International, Inc. (100%); Arrow Electronics Canada Ltd. (100%); Schweber Electronics Corporation (100%); 10556 Newfoundland Ltd. (100%); Schuylkill Metals of Plant City, Inc. (100%); Hi-Tech Ad, Inc. (100%); Consan, Inc. (100%); Arrow Electronics (Delaware), Inc. (100%); Arrow Electronics Funding Corp., (100%); Arrow Electronics Real Estate, Inc. (100%); Arrow Electronics (U.K.), Inc. (100%); Arrow Electronics South Africa, LLP (99%); Arrow Altech Holdings (Pty) Ltd. (50.1%); Panamericana Comercial Importadora, S.A. (66.67%); Elko C.E., S.A. (70%); Eurocomponentes, S.A. (99.99%); Macom, S.A. (70%); Compania de Semiconductores y Componentes, S.A. (70%); Arrow Electronics Asia Pacific, Inc. (100%); Arrow Electronics, Holdings Pty Ltd. (100%); Components Agent (BVI) Ltd. (90%); Texny (Holdings) Ltd. (100%); Arrow Strong Elkectronics Co. Ltd. (100%); Arrow Asia Distribution Ltd. (100%); AE Logistics Sdn Bhd (100%); Arrow/Ally, Inc. (75%); Arrow Components (NZ) Ltd. (75%); Arrow Electronics (CI) Ltd. (100%); Marubun-Arrow USA, LLC (50%); VCE Virtual Chip Canada, Inc. (49%); Technologies Interactives Mediagrif, Inc. (10%); Arrow Electronics Mexico, S. de R.L. de C.V. (100%); Dicopel, Inc. (60%); Dicopel S.A. de C.V. (60%); The Performance Consortium, LLC (50%); Wyle Electronics, Inc. (100%); Wyle Electronics de Mexico, S. de R.L. de C.V. (100%); Wyle Electronics Caribbean Corp. (100%); Marubun Corp. (5.2%).

Principal Competitors

Avnet; Pioneer-Standard Electronics; Rexel; Premier Farnel; Ingram Micro; Graybar Electric; WESCO International; Advanced MP Technology; All American Semiconductor; Future Electronics; Bell Microproducts; Tech Data.

Further Reading

Alster, Norm, "I Am a Growth Guy," *Forbes,* February 15, 1993, p. 118.
"Arrow Closes Support Net Deal," *The Wall Street Journal,* December 3, 1997.
"Arrow Completes Wyle Acquisition," *Electronic Buyers' News,* October 30, 2000, p. 90.
"Arrow Electronics' Acquisitions," *The Wall Street Journal,* November 17, 1994, p. A26.
"Arrow Electronics to Buy Anthem," *Corporate Growth Report Weekly,* October 3, 1994, p. 7473.
"Arrow to Acquire Bell Group, Richey," *Canadian Electronics,* November 1998, p. 1.
Bernstein, James, "Unrivaled Rivals," *Newsday,* June 13, 1994, p. C1.
"Business Brief—Arrow Electronics Inc.," *The Wall Street Journal,* November 29, 1994, p. 1.
"Business Brief—Arrow Electronics Inc.," *The Wall Street Journal,* September 19, 2000, p. C15.
Jorgensen, Barbara, "Arrow Acquisition Pointing to More Gains in Pacific Rim," *Electronic Buyers' News,* November 20, 1995, p. 8.
——, "Arrow Bolsters Partnerships in Japan," *Computer Reseller News,* September 14, 1998, p. 69.
——, "Arrow Buys Swiss Distributor," *Electronics Buyers News,* February 15, 1999, p. 36.
——, "Arrow Digests Most Recent Purchases," *Computer Reseller News,* October 19, 1998, p. 88.
——, "Arrow Moves into Argentina," *Electronic Buyers News,* October 11, 1999, p. 42.
——, "Arrow Realignment Targets Customer," *Electronic Buyers News,* October 27, 1997, p. 1.
——, "Arrow Solidifies French Connection via Tekelec," *Electronic Buyers' News,* February 14, 2000, p. 77.
Longwell, John, "Technical/Specialty Distributors," *Computer Reseller News,* June 4, 1996, p. 110.
Magnet, Myron, "Arrow Electronics Struggles Back," *Fortune,* April 30, 1984, p. 77.
Markowitz, Elliot, "Arrow Joins Big League," *Computer Reseller News,* August 1, 1994, p. 198.
McGough, Robert, "Phoenix," *Forbes,* June 6, 1983, p. 82.
O'Heir, Jeff, "Gates/Arrow Acquires Support Net for Midrange Capability," *Computer Reseller News,* October 20, 1997, p. 310.
Ojo, Bolaji, "Arrow Buys Stake in Israeli Distributor," *Electronic Buyers' News,* January 24, 2000, p. 25.
Pedriera, Pedro, "Current Market Slump Could Send the Channel Reeling," *Computer Reseller News,* August 3, 1998, pp. 53, 55.
Rayner, Bruce C. P., "Arrow's Kaufman: Planning a Profitable Path," *Electronic Business,* May 1, 1987, p. 47.
Sheerin, Matthew, "Arrow, Avnet Enter Brazil," *Electronic Buyers' News,* May 24, 1999, p. 5.
Souza, Christa, "Arrow Deepens Presence in Europe," *Electronic Buyers' News,* April 17, 2000, p. 8.
Sullivan, Laurie, "Arrow at Critical Phase as CEO Resigns," *EBN,* June 17, 2002, p. 1.
——, "Arrow Launches Fee-Bearing Web Site," *EBN,* May 14, 2001, p. 3.
——, "Arrow Targets Mexico with Dicopel Deal," *Electronic Buyers' News,* July 10, 2000, p. 6.
Walter, Clarke L., "More Mega-Mergers to Come?," *Electronic Business Today,* April 1997, p. 38.

—Dean Boyer
—update: Anne L. Potter

Ashland Inc.

50 E. River Center Boulevard
Covington, Kentucky 41012-0391
U.S.A.
Telephone: (859) 815-3333
Fax: (859) 815-5053
Web site: http://www.ashland.com

Public Company
Incorporated: 1924 as Ashland Refining Company
Employees: 25,100 (2001)
Sales: $7.72 billion (2001)
Stock Exchanges: New York
Ticker Symbol: ASH
NAIC: 325211 Plastics Material & Resin Manufacturing;
   325199 All Other Basic Organic Chemical
   Manufacturing; 32411 Petroleum Refineries

Ashland Inc. is a leading provider of goods and services to basic industrial and consumer markets, primarily those related to transportation and construction sectors. With approximately 25,000 employees and annual sales and operating revenues approaching $8 billion, Ashland has come a long way since its beginnings in 1924 as a regional petroleum refiner. The Covington, Kentucky-based company is now a Fortune 250 company with sales in more than 140 countries. Ashland brings superior product and service solutions to industries and consumers around the world—in highway construction, chemical and thermoplastic distribution, specialty chemicals, motor oil and car-care products.

Company Origins

The history of Ashland Inc. began with J. Fred Miles and the founding in 1910 of Swiss Drilling Company, an Oklahoma corporation. Miles had been raised in Oklahoma and worked in the oil business from his youth. After gathering a store of capital, he created Swiss Drilling with two other men to explore and operate new wells.

During this period, Standard Oil had an overwhelming presence in the industry, and, as a result, the U.S. government ordered a breakup of the company in 1911. The years immediately following the breakup, Standard Oil's near-monopoly was challenging the oil business, and Miles found that he could not survive on the low prices offered for Oklahoma crude. In 1916, he moved his operations to the new fields then opening in eastern Kentucky, where, with the help of some powerful financiers in Chicago and in Cleveland, Ohio, he obtained control of nearly 200,000 acres of oil land. Two years later the energetic Miles incorporated Swiss Oil Company in Lexington, Kentucky, with a group of backers that included the Insulls and the Armours of Chicago, with Miles serving as general manager and J.I. Lamprecht of Cleveland as president. Swiss Oil was soon one of the leading oil concerns in the state of Kentucky.

By the early 1920s, a postwar depression and the early exhaustion of key oil wells had thrust Swiss Oil into a precarious financial condition. Despite the company's difficulties, Fred Miles was eager to expand its operations into refining, and, in 1923, he hired the services of young Paul Blazer to select, buy, and operate the most advantageously located and outfitted refinery obtainable in the area. Blazer had gone into the oil-trading business after college and then picked up valuable experience as a partner in a Lexington refinery, from which he had just resigned when Miles made him the head of Swiss Oil's new division, Ashland Refining Company, in 1924. Blazer selected for his refinery an existing facility at Cattletsburg, Kentucky, on the Ohio River near the West Virginia border and just upstream from Ashland, where Blazer set up his modest offices. The Cattletsburg refinery had a capacity of 1,000 barrels per day and, after a program of extensive repairs, was soon operating profitably.

Blazer's choice of Cattletsburg was excellent because of several factors that would prove critical in the company's long-term success. In general, a refining operation that had access to its own local crude-oil supplies would do well in the eastern Kentucky region. Swiss Oil, though not a terribly successful company, did own a substantial amount of the region's crude and could therefore supply its new subsidiary with most of its needs. Ashland was thus able to sell regionally refined petroleum products, such as gasoline and motor oil, more cheaply than competitors who were forced to transport their crude or finished products from the Atlantic seaboard, the Mississippi River, or the Gulf of Mexico. The Cattletsburg site promised ready access to hundreds of miles of navigable rivers, by means of which Ashland could both receive crude and deliver product to the greater Ohio River basin. Until the introduction of pipelines, river freight was unmatched as an economic carrier of oil, and Ashland remained dependent on its river barges and terminals for the delivery of much of its refined product. These factors gave Ashland an early advantage over its much larger rivals and allowed the company to achieve a firm and lasting position as regional leader.

Success During the Depression and World War II

By 1926, Ashland's gross sales were $3 million a year, and Paul Blazer had confirmed his reputation as an outstanding refinery manager. J. Fred Miles had been eased out of Swiss Oil when the company required a bailout by one of its investors, and it was not long before the Ashland subsidiary was outperforming its parent company. Blazer steadily improved the refinery's operation and expanded sales of its products, and in 1929 he convinced Swiss Oil's board of directors to authorize Ashland's purchase of $400,000 worth of marketing companies in the area. Despite the onset of the Great Depression, this was followed by the 1930 acquisition of Tri-State Refining Company over the West Virginia border. Tri-State had a sizable refinery and its own team of gas stations and trucks, giving Ashland the makings of an integrated refining and marketing organization in the eastern Kentucky region. While inexpensive, river transport was continually threatened with the imposition of federal tolls that would largely negate its economy. Thus, in 1931, Ashland took the first in a long series of steps intended to lessen its dependence on river transportation of its crude supplies. When Ashland bought the Cumberland Pipeline Company for $420,000 in 1931, it facilitated shipment of crude from the Atlantic seaboard, as well as from its Kentucky fields. This opening to the sea would become vital when Ashland grew dependent upon Middle Eastern oil arriving by tanker.

So skilled an operator was Blazer that Ashland continued to turn a profit in the worst Depression years. Ashland was now the staff upon which leaned the ailing Swiss Oil, and in 1936, when it became apparent that the latter could not sustain the two companies, they were merged and Blazer elected president and chief executive officer of the new Ashland Oil & Refining Company. The combined companies showed a 1936 net profit

of $677,583 on sales of $4.8 million, good results at any time but remarkable in the Depression era. Blazer forged ahead with new investments, joining Standard Oil Company (Ohio) in a pipeline from fields in southern Illinois and adding a costly new unit to the Cattletsburg refinery. By the time the United States entered World War II in 1941, Ashland had nearly doubled its sales to $8 million.

During World War II, the petroleum industry came under fairly tight government control. Like all the other oil companies, big and small, Ashland benefited mightily from the rapid increase in demand for the entire spectrum of petroleum products, which were needed for everything from gasoline to rubber boots to explosives. With government assistance Ashland built a new facility at Cattletsburg for the refining of 100-octane aviation fuel, and within four years it had doubled and redoubled company revenues to $35 million in 1945. The following years saw an inevitable recession as the war machine was dismantled, but it soon became apparent that postwar America was about to indulge its love affair with the automobile as never before. From the remote mountain towns of West Virginia to the streets of Cincinnati, Ohio, the postwar economy moved on wheels powered by oil, and Ashland remained the region's most economical supplier of that oil.

Postwar Growth

In 1948, Ashland took a major step when it merged with Cleveland-based Allied Oil Company, a fuel-oil broker with sales slightly in excess of Ashland's. Allied had been started in 1925 by Floyd R. Newman and W.W. Vandeveer with the support of Blazer. The combined companies had revenue in that year of $100 million. Ashland's new Allied division was directed by Rex Blazer, nephew of Ashland's president and a former marketing executive at Allied. The merger extended Ashland's marketing area to Cleveland and as far west as Chicago, and, to make use of its new sales opportunities, Ashland soon added a trio of other acquisitions—Aetna Oil Company, a Louisville, Kentucky, refiner and distributor; Frontier Oil Company, of Buffalo, New York; and Freedom-Valvoline Oil Company, the Pennsylvania maker of Valvoline motor oil. The latter was already a well-known brand name and under Ashland's ownership has since become one of the most widely distributed motor oils in the world. By the time these purchases were completed in 1950, Ashland was the 19th-largest oil company in the United States and for the first time was listed on the New York Stock Exchange.

Sales in 1955 topped $250 million, though net income was only $10 million. In contrast to its early years, Ashland as a mature company tended to earn rather low levels of net income, which Blazer attributed to two basic factors. First, the company had far outstripped its limited sources of crude oil and never had much success as a prospector. This meant that it would never enjoy the extraordinary profits brought in by big oil strikes and that its crude-oil expense would always be somewhat higher than for a fully integrated oil concern. Second, Ashland also sold more refined products than it made, supplementing its own production with purchases of refined goods for resale, which necessarily resulted in a diminished margin. Such a policy also meant that Ashland's refineries were kept running at or near capacity, a clear gain in efficiency over plants forced to cut back

Key Dates:

1910: Swiss Drilling Company is founded by J. Fred Miles.
1916: Miles moves his operations to Kentucky.
1918: Swiss Oil Company is incorporated in Lexington, Kentucky.
1923: Paul Blazer is hired to head up Ashland Refining Company.
1930: Ashland acquires Tri-State Refining Company.
1931: Ashland buys Cumberland Pipeline Company.
1936: Swiss Oil and Ashland Refining Company merge to create Ashland Oil and Refining Company; Blazer is elected president and CEO of the new company.
1948: Ashland merges with Cleveland-based Allied Oil Company; acquires Aetna Oil Company, Frontier Oil Company, and Freedom-Valvoline Oil Company.
1956: Ashland acquires R.J. Brown Company.
1957: Blazer retires as CEO. His nephew Rex Blazer takes over the top management spot, with Everett Wells becoming the new president.
1962: Ashland acquires United Carbon Company and Humble Oil & Refining Company.
1965: Orin Atkins becomes CEO.

1966: Ashland acquires Archer Daniels Midland Chemicals Company; Ashland forms a new operating subsidiary, Ashland Chemical Company.
1970: Shareholders approve changing the company's name to Ashland Oil, Inc. Acquisitions include Union Carbide Petroleum Company and Empire State Petroleum; Ashland Oil Canada Limited is formed.
1975: Ashland Coal, Inc. is formed.
1981: Ashland acquires United States Filter Corporation and Integon Corporation; Atkins resigns his position of CEO and is replaced by John R. Hall.
1982: Scurlock Oil Company is acquired; Ashland Services Company is formed.
1994: Ashland's Valvoline division purchases Zerex; Ashland acquires Eurobase (Italy) and ACT Inc. (Pennsylvania).
1995: Company name is changed to Ashland Oil, Inc.
1996: Paul W. Chellgren succeeds Hall as chairman and CEO.
1997: Ashland consolidates operations of Arch Mineral and Ashland Coal.
1998: Marathon Oil Company and Ashland Inc. merge to form Marathon Ashland Petroleum LLC.

or work on shorter, more costly runs. Added to its advantageous system of waterway transport and freedom from the advertising expense associated with operation of a high-profile, branded chain of gas stations, Ashland's refining efficiency offset its lack of crude and enabled the company to earn a steady if unspectacular return on investment.

In 1957, after heading Ashland Oil for 22 years, Blazer retired as the chief executive. His nephew Rex Blazer took over the top management spot, while Everett Wells, a longtime associate of the senior Blazer, became the new president. The year before these changes, Ashland entered a new field with the purchase of the R.J. Brown Company of St. Louis, Missouri, a diversified manufacturer of petrochemicals. A great number of useful chemicals are derived from petroleum, and the oil industry as a whole was expanding rapidly into this new and largely unexplored area. Ashland steadily increased its petrochemical holdings, in 1962 buying United Carbon Company of Houston, Texas, makers of carbon black, and in 1966 adding Archer Daniels Midland Chemicals Company for $65 million. At that point Ashland formed a new operating subsidiary, Ashland Chemical Company, to oversee the workings of its manifold chemical interests.

The early 1960s were also notable for Ashland's 1962 purchase of the Central Louisiana pipeline system from Humble Oil & Refining. Central Louisiana was a major pipeline, gathering most of the oil produced in greater Louisiana and the Gulf of Mexico fields, and its acquisition by Ashland largely relieved the company of its worries about a steady supply of crude oil, made worse by the intermittent threat of new user tolls on the waterways. The net effect of these acquisitions was to boost Ashland's sales sharply, from $490 million in 1963 to $723 million three years later, elevating the company from the status of an independent to what might be called a "mini-major" oil

firm. The robust U.S. economy had much to do with Ashland's prosperity, of course, as more citizens relied on the automobile.

Changes in the 1970s and 1980s

In 1969, Ashland had entered the coal business and soon became one of the top-ten coal producers in the country. It also took advantage of its refineries' asphalt by-products to gain a leading place among the nation's road-construction firms. The result of such diversification was a gradual lessening of Ashland's dependence on oil refining for its sales dollar. By 1971, refining and marketing of oil accounted for only 57 percent of Ashland's $1.4 billion in revenue, with Ashland Chemical providing another 25 percent and its other holdings chipping in the remainder. This apparent balance was somewhat misleading, however; Ashland continued to rely on its refining and marketing divisions for the bulk of its net income, as the growing chemical business proved to be a sluggish moneymaker. Refining capacity reached 350,000 barrels per day in 1973, and, as always, Ashland's crude production was less than 20 percent of that figure, forcing the company to join the mounting number of U.S. oil refiners dependent upon Middle Eastern crude for their survival.

In 1970, shareholders approved changing the company's name from Ashland Oil & Refining to Ashland Oil, Inc. That same year Ashland consolidated most of its Canadian interests with those of Canadian Gridoil Limited to form Ashland Oil Canada Limited. Domestically, Ashland acquired Union Carbide Petroleum Company and Empire State Petroleum, and these were consolidated with other exploration and production activities into Ashland Exploration, Inc.

In the mid-1970s, Ashland became entangled in its first of a series of legal controversies. In 1976 chief executive officer Orin Atkins, a lawyer who had served in that position since

1965, agreed in response to a shareholder suit to repay Ashland some $175,000 in funds he was said to have spent improperly. The previous year, 1975, Ashland had been fined by the Securities and Exchange Commission for illegally contributing more than $700,000 to several political campaigns.

Ashland's problems with meeting its own needs for crude oil became increasingly pronounced as the company continued to expand its refining and marketing operations. The 1973 OPEC embargo and ensuing energy crisis had effectively raised the stakes in the oil-exploration game. After the early 1970s, only those companies willing and able to mount massive drilling campaigns would be likely to reap the benefits of crude-oil supplies. Ashland was simply not big enough to join the majors in their exorbitant outlays, and Ashland therefore got out of the production business entirely. Sale of most of its oil leases, equipment, and reserves netted Ashland about $1.5 billion by 1980, but it also left the company wholly dependent upon outside sources of crude, primarily in the Middle East. In 1975 all construction activities were consolidated, and Ashland Coal, Inc., was formed in anticipation of the increasing potential of coal in the national energy market. Ashland took a comprehensive review of all segments of its operations to determine necessary changes. As an initial step in this strategy to maximize return on existing assets, the company sold its 79 percent interest in Ashland Oil Canada.

In 1981, Atkins was forced out as chairman and chief executive officer by a group of executives who brought to light illegal payments Atkins had made to government officials in Middle East countries, most notably Oman. He was replaced in both positions by John R. Hall. In June 1988, two former Ashland employees won a wrongful-discharge suit against the company. The employees, a former vice-president for oil supply and a former vice-president for government relations, had accused Ashland of firing them in 1983 for refusing to cover up the illegal payments. The jury awarded the plaintiffs $70.85 million, $1.25 million of which was to be paid by Hall personally. The plaintiffs ultimately settled out of court for $25 million.

On July 13, 1988, Atkins was arrested by customs agents at John F. Kennedy International Airport and accused of selling company documents to the National Iranian Oil Company (NIOC). Atkins denied the charges. The papers Atkins allegedly peddled related to an ongoing, $283 million billing dispute between Ashland and NIOC. In 1989, Ashland settled the case with a $325 million payment to NIOC. The company's public image was not helped by a 1988 spill of four million gallons of diesel fuel into the Ohio River, although Ashland was credited with a prompt, candid response.

In the meantime, Ashland sales skyrocketed along with the price of oil. Hall watched revenue hit an all-time peak of $9.5 billion in 1981, but Ashland found itself squeezed by the high cost of crude, and net income actually dropped into a net loss during the first part of 1982, when a spreading recession only made matters worse. Atkins had also saddled Ashland with an unusually high debt ratio when, in 1981, he used the receipts from the oil-drilling asset sale to buy United States Filter Corporation and Integon Corporation for $661 million. Integon, an insurance holding company, hardly matched the range of Ashland's other interests and in due time was sold to reduce

debt. Once the recession had eased by 1983, Ashland's earnings again picked up, and the company's future brightened.

Scurlock Oil Company, a crude-oil gathering, transporting, and marketing firm, was acquired in 1982, thereby aiding Ashland in a shift from foreign to domestic crude-oil sources. In 1982, more than 20 corporate staff departments were brought together to form Ashland Services Company, a division that would cut overhead and also provide cost-effective services to the corporation and to its divisions and subsidiaries.

Restructuring and Acquisitions: Ashland in the 1990s

Ashland began the 1990s with a strong financial position. In 1992, Ashland surpassed $10 billion in sales for the first time, and it also established itself as the leading distributor of chemicals and solvents in North America by acquiring the majority of Unocal's chemical distribution business. Though refining profits were largely disappointing during the early 1990s, Ashland's chemical profits remained a boon for the company. Operating income from chemicals increased to $47 million in the last three months of 1994 compared to $28 million the year before.

Several important developments occurred in 1994. Ashland's Valvoline division purchased Zerex, the nation's number two antifreeze. Ashland also acquired Eurobase (Italy) and ACT Inc. (Pennsylvania), both companies that produced chemicals used in the creation of semiconductors. Also that year, Ashland began a new multi-well oil exploration in Nigeria and made a promising discovery in the first well sunk.

In an effort to have the name of the company reflect Ashland's increasingly diversified business, shareholders approved the name change from Ashland Oil, Inc., to Ashland Inc. in 1995. At the same time, the company began to shore up its nonrefining business segments to minimize the effect of its weak refining margins. According to Paul W. Chellgren, the company's president and chief operating officer, Ashland's strategy was to become an "integrated, but diversified company" by adding value to its petroleum products rather than by increasing volume. In 1996, Ashland chairman and chief executive officer John Hall announced his retirement, and Chellgren succeeded him in both positions.

In early 1997, Ashland announced plans to consolidate operations of Arch Mineral and Ashland Coal, thus creating the fifth-largest coal producer in the United States. Also in early 1997 Ashland was the first to be granted foreign trade subzone status at Akron-Canton Regional Airport in Ohio (known as "Foreign Trade Zone 181"). This status allowed Ashland to import crude oil to its Canton refinery and Lima storage facility without paying duties and tariffs. The subzone status was designed to protect those companies who imported oil not in its finished state (such as crude oil) and that diminished in volume once the oil had been processed into products such as asphalt, diesel fuel, or home heating oil. Tariffs on foreign crude were 2.5 cents a barrel in 1997. Not having to pay the fee saved Ashland more than $250,000 a year at its Canton facility. To further enhance efficiency and increase profitability, Ashland Inc. and Marathon Oil Co. announced in May 1997 a plan to merge their refining and marketing operations, with Marathon holding 62 percent of ownership and Ashland 38 percent. Ashland Chemical was expected to be the largest customer of the joint venture. On January 1, 1998, the merger was completed and Marathon Ashland Petroleum LLC (MAP) was formed, combining the major elements of the refining, marketing and transportation operations of the two companies.

In the late 1990s, Ashland was a highly diversified energy company, with extensive coal and petrochemical holdings to complement its core of oil refining and marketing. It was the nation's leading designer and builder of roadways through its APAC subsidiaries, which laid more than 13 million tons of asphalt in fiscal 1996. Oil remained the centerpiece of Ashland's corporate structure, however. Still relying on cheap river transport for much of its outgoing freight, Ashland delivered gasoline and related petroleum products to a large network of wholesalers and Ashland-affiliated gas stations. Ashland itself operated 742 SuperAmerica retail gasoline-grocery outlets in 1996 (SuperAmerica Group's 1996 sales were $1.9 billion). Added to these was the $1.2 billion in sales generated by the Valvoline, Inc., subsidiary, Ashland's nationally recognized brand name. Combined oil activities thus still provided well over half of the company's revenue and earnings, as Ashland continued to fill a narrow niche between international oil giant and regional independent.

In 1998, Ashland purchased 20 companies, including Eagle One Industries, a maker of car-care products; and Masters-Jackson, a group of highway construction companies. Ashland exited the coal mining business by spinning off Arch Coal, resulting in a reduction of its company holdings from 58 percent to 12 percent. Ashland would later sell its remaining holdings. In 2000, Ashland acquired Copenhagen-based Superfos, whose principal assets included a U.S. road construction business serving the Ashland operating area. The company was later sold, except for its road construction operations. Other acquisitions included Winyah Concrete & Block, a South Carolina-based full-service concrete and masonry supply organization; and Oklahoma's Vinita Rock Company. The purchase of Micro-Clean Inc., a semiconductor process parts cleaning operation, enhanced Ashland's position as a leading provider to the microelectronics industry through its Specialty Chemical's division. In the area of e-commerce, Ashland and e-Chemicals, Inc., the leading online chemical marketplace, created the chemical industry's first e-commerce alliance, enabling customers to purchase an array of 2,500 Ashland-distributed products through www.e-chemicals.com.

CEO Chellgren reported an "outstanding year" in 2000: "We dramatically improved our financial performance, continued to narrow our business focus while expanding key businesses, and adopted a new identity that boldly declares who we are and how we work." Operating income, net income and earnings per share all reached record highs. MAP continued to be their most important cash generator, and was described by Chellgren as "one of the best performing refining and marketing operations in the United States."

Ashland Strives to Change Its Image

For 34 years the Ashland logo represented a gas station sign. To better portray the new image of a "can-do" company for the twenty-first Century, Ashland adopted a new logo and tag line,

"The Who In How Things Work." Through this new identity, Ashland hoped to project the diversity and innovative mentality that define Ashland and its people, the people who know how to ask the right questions and deliver the right answers.

Chellgren reported another record year for Ashland in 2001: new records were set in earnings per share, net income, and operating income. He described 2001 as "the year of MAP." Ashland's thirty-eight percent interest in Marathon Ashland Petroleum LLC yielded operating income from refining and marketing that was nearly double that of any prior year in the company's history. As a result, operating profit from refining and marketing accounted for 76 percent of the operating income before corporate expenses.

The Valvoline division produced near-record results, with sales of premium motors oils climbing 27 percent. Their Eagle One line of automotive appearance products increased sales by 16 percent.

Other divisions performed less than remarkably. Ashland's chemical operations reported significant reductions in sales. Operating income fell in the APAC highway construction businesses, due to compressed construction margins, a severe winter in APAC's market area and special charges associated with improper recognition of construction contract earnings in the Manassas, Virginia, unit.

Ashland was optimistic for 2002 although doubtful that they would match the record results of 2001. Their optimism was based on the strength of refining and marketing operations of MAP. In 2001, MAP launched or completed several initiatives that would add considerably to their future operating income, including retail expansion in the Midwest, a new nationwide network of travel centers, and the startup of a heavy crude oil conversion unit at the Garyville, Lousiana, refinery. In an attempt to consolidate operations, Ashland Distribution closed nine facilities and conducted a "quality of business" review to focus on its most profitable accounts. E-commerce efforts accounted for 15 percent of Ashland Distribution revenues.

Ashland Specialty Chemical remained a worldwide market and technology leader supplying high-performance products and services. A leading European producer of gelcoats and polyester resins was acquired more than doubling the size of Ashland's unsaturated polyester resins business in Europe. Research and development efforts focused on new products and aggressively seeking to build new geographic markets and applications for existing product lines.

Valvoline continued to develop new products, including MaxLife motor oil, the first oil specifically formulated for higher mileage engines, and MaxLife transmission fluids and antifreeze.

Chellgren's vision for the future of Ashland is to provide solutions for customers; provide opportunity for employees to achieve and grow; provide value for shareholders; and provide commitment to shareholders. To achieve these goals, Ashland commits to the "delivery of products and services that are differentiated by our knowledge of customers' needs as well as our technical expertise. We will attract, develop and retain talented and diverse people and provide an environment that encourages innovation, demands accountability and rewards performance. We will achieve high returns on investment that result in high returns for our shareholders.'' Through a combination of people, technology, and customer focus, Ashland strives to be ''The Who In How Things Work.''

Principal Subsidiaries

Ashland International Ltd.; Ashland Petroleum Company; APAC, Inc; Ashland Distribution Company; Ashland Specialty Chemical Company; The Valvoline Company; Ashland Services B. V.; Marathon Ashland Petroleum LLC; Speedway SuperAmerica LLC.

Principal Competitors

Honeywell, Inc.; Pennzoil-Quaker State Company; Safety-Kleen Corp.; ATMI, Inc.; American International Petroleum Corporation.

Further Reading

''Ashland Considers Selling Its Big Stake in Arch Coal,'' *New York Times*, June 23, 1999, p. 4.

''Ashland Inc.,'' *Hoover's Handbook of American Business 2002*, 2001, pp. 200–201.

Butters, Jamie, ''Kentucky Merger Threatens to Subordinate One Company to the Other,'' *Knight-Ridder/Tribune Business News*, May 19, 1997, p. 519B1012.

''Environmental Accident Ushers in NovAlert,'' *Occupational Hazards*, March 1994, p. 99.

Fan, Aliza, ''Ashland to Stay True to Solid Reputation,'' *The Oil Daily*, January 30, 1995, p. 1.

Kovski, Alan, ''Ashland, Lyondell Gain on Chemicals, Slip Back on Poor Results in Refining,'' *The Oil Daily*, January 24, 1995, p. 3.

——, ''Marathon, Ashland Put Proposal in Writing to Combine Refining, Marketing Operations,'' *The Oil Daily*, May 16, 1997, p. 1.

Sachdev, Ameet, ''Ashland Inc. to Sell Shares in Exploration Unit,'' *Knight-Ridder/Tribune Business News*, January 31, 1997, p. 131B1290.

——, ''Ashland Oil to Seek a Partner for Refinery Business,'' *Knight-Ridder/Tribune Business News*, December 10, 1996, p. 1210B0939.

Scott, Otto, *Buried Treasure: The Story of Arch Mineral*, Washington, D. C.: Braddock Communications, 1989.

——, *The Exception: The Story of Ashland Oil & Refining Company*, New York: McGraw-Hill Book Company, 1968.

—Jonathan Martin
—updates: Terry Bain, Carol D. Beavers

ASML Holding N.V.

De Run 1110
5503 LA Veldhoven
The Netherlands
Telephone: (31) 40 268 3208
Fax: (31) 40 268 3655
Web site: http://www.asml.com

Public Company
Incorporated: 1984 as ASM Lithography Holding
Employees: 7,070 (2001)
Sales: EUR $1.84 billion (US $1.80 billion) (2001)
Stock Exchanges: Amsterdam N.V. Euronext NASDAQ
Ticker Symbol: ASML (NASDAQ), ASML (Amsterdam)
NAIC: 333295 Semiconductor Machinery Manufacturing

ASML Holding N.V. strives to be the world's largest manufacturer of semiconductor equipment in an industry that has seen many ups and downs. A global leader in advanced lithography (or imaging) systems, and one of the top five manufacturers of sophisticated technology systems for the semiconductor industry, ASML (originally called ASM Lithography Holding) offers an integrated portfolio of lithography, track and thermal systems, primarily for developing complex integrated circuits. Competing head-to-head with Canon Inc. and Nikon Corporation for domination in the semiconductor lithography equipment arena, ASML has placed fifth two years running on VLSI Research's top-ten list of semiconductor equipment manufacturers. Nikon finished third place in 2001, while Canon ranked sixth.

ASML grabbed market share not by thinking big, but rather by thinking small. The company is built on the concept of creating smaller and faster microchips for use in nearly all electronic goods. The stepper is the crucial and costly piece of equipment used in creating microchips by photographically imprinting circuit patterns on large silicon wafers that are later cut into dozens or hundreds of chips. Analysts maintain that ASML's steppers are of higher quality than competitors' products because they use a modular architecture rather than the more costly and problematic build-disassemble-ship-reassemble production process of other semiconductor manufacturers.

The Foundation of ASML

Established in The Netherlands in 1984, ASML was originally a shared venture between Dutch companies Royal Philips Electronics and Advanced Semiconductor Materials (now ASM International). The original target customer base was European and American companies. ASM International had already begun selling its wafer stepper when the joint venture was declared.

Initially focused on front-end thermal-chemical tools, ASM International was founded in 1968. The company began by manufacturing semiconductor process equipment, grew exponentially in both front- and back-end product lines, and opened a back-end operation in Hong Kong in 1975, where it still has an engineering and manufacturing site. An initial public offering (IPO) was made in 1981, and stock continues to trade on NASDAQ and the Euronext Stock Exchange in Amsterdam.

Financial pressures created by a mid-1980s chip industry downturn led ASM to sell its 50 percent ownership of ASML to Philips in 1988, the same year ASML entered the Asian market. This opened the door to competition between the two companies. Since, ASML has consistently ranked significantly higher than ASM International in VLSI Research studies of semiconductor equipment manufacturers.

Royal Philips Electronics has a long, illustrious history. The groundwork was built in The Netherlands in 1891 for what would become one of the world's largest electronics companies. Philips originally made its name developing carbon-filament lamps at the dawn of the 20th century, then created a research laboratory in 1914 to study physical and chemical occurrences to further encourage product advancements. The company introduced the medical X-ray tube, electric shavers, and the television camera tube. Philips is now a global leader in digital technologies for televisions and displays, wireless communication, speech recognition, video compression, storage and optical products, and the underlying semiconductor technology making future technological breakthroughs possible. Its partnership with ASM International in 1984 to create ASML helped push Philips into the semiconductor industry.

Divesting to Invest in the Future

Philips divested ASML in 1993 as part of a general plan for Philips to focus more on its core electronic activities. By then, ASML was primed to grow and expand on its own. It became a publicly traded company in February 1995 in a US$170 million transaction. Two years later, high demand for new stock pushed Philips to complete a US$266 million secondary offering of ASML shares. This brought the company down to its declared target of 25 percent ownership. In June 2000, Philips further reduced its interest in ASML to 6.7 percent.

The number of ASML employees had grown from 84 in 1984 to 4,377 in 2000. After the successful 2001 merger with Silicon Valley Group (SVG), company size nearly doubled. Global headquarters remained in Veldhoven, The Netherlands, while manufacturing sites and research and development facilities were located in Connecticut and California in the United States, and the Netherlands. Training facilities and development centers existed in Japan, Korea, The Netherlands, Taiwan, and the United States. The company had over 50 sales and service organizations throughout 16 countries.

Overview of ASML Technology

Semiconductors—the integrated-circuit chips that control everything from cellular phones and computers to aircraft navigational systems and elevators—are increasingly appearing in every conceivable electronic consumer goods, from appliances to greeting cards. This escalating need for integrated-circuit chips does not, however, guarantee smooth economic waters for the semiconductor industry. Partly because semiconductor manufacture is extremely capital-intensive—stepper machines cost as much as US$8 million each—the industry regularly faces temporary softening and shakeouts.

ASML has four distinct product divisions and one subsidiary: their Lithography division is based in Veldhoven, The Netherlands, and Wilton, Connecticut; the Track division works out of San Jose, California; the Thermal division is based in Scotts Valley, California; Special Applications Division is also located in Veldhoven; and MaskTools, the subsidiary, is in Santa Clara, California.

The company's Lithography division designs, develops, and manufactures equipment used to transfer circuit patterns onto wafers. The focus of the division has been to continually shrink the size of the integrated chip through smaller line widths, reducing resolution or feature size. This focus has greatly enhanced performance by allowing electricity to move more quickly across the chip. A smaller feature size also boosts the number of chips that can be imprinted on the wafer. ASML's Lithography division products include the TWINSCAN and Micrascan advanced lithography systems.

The Track division presents wafer track systems that complete the repetitive procedures of the wafer before and after lithographic exposure. These systems coat, develop, and bake light-sensitive material (or photoresist) on the wafer's surface. ASML has created an integrated-photoresist system, offering both service and support. Combined solutions such as this are increasingly important for each new generation of integrated chips. Product lines include the ProCell 90-SE and 88-Series photoresist processing systems.

ASML's Thermal Division builds large-batch and single-wafer thermal processing furnaces, as well as atmospheric pressure chemical-vapor deposition systems. This division creates proven thermal technology and expands new technologies to meet the growing need for highly productive, cost-effective, integrated-thermal systems. Thermal products include the APNext Vertical Cluster system, Xcelerate single-wafer furnace-RTP system, vertical processors, and thermal reactors.

The Special Applications division of ASML works on solutions for application markets by incorporating products and services from all company divisions for customers with unique requirements. It also offers a variety of system upgrade programs for clients using older technology. This division was formed in March 1998 to pursue lithography market opportunities for custom imaging solutions outside the area of the company's mainstream markets. Special Applications products include the PAS 5500, PAS 5000, and Micralign lithography systems.

ASML MaskTools is a wholly owned subsidiary of ASML. Its focus has been to advance improvements to the photomask, essential for printing integrated-circuit patterns when the line width of the integrated circuit is shorter than the wavelength of light used to print the circuit. ASML MaskTools has worked to expand the limits of lithography by creating design simulation software that acts as a conduit between semiconductor design and development.

Semiconductor Industry Ups and Downs in the 1990s

The semiconductor industry has historically seen demand booms and busts. During the rapid growth of the personal computer market in the early- to mid-1990s, chip manufacturers invested heavily in plant facilities, which led to oversupply in many key chip markets. The industry was then hit hard by a slowdown in demand for personal computers.

The industry saw a decline after 1995. Global chip sales were at US$50 billion in 1990; by 1995 that figure had grown to US$144 billion, but dropped to US$132 billion in 1996. That same year, ASML introduced its step-and-scan system, which outpaced competitors by making 100 wafers per hour as opposed to the standard 60.

A minor surge in 1997 brought sales up to US$137 billion, according to the Semiconductor Industry Association. A slowdown occurred in 1998, but the industry rebounded and growth continued through 1999. The year-end results were a sign of both the recovery and ASML's strong standing in leading-edge products. The industry experienced another successful year in 2000, as revenues soared to nearly US$204 billion, a 37 percent increase over 1999 sales of US$149 billion. In the first half of 2000, orders were placed for 217 systems, compared to 133 orders in the first half of 1999.

Further Inroads in the Late 1990s

In February 1999, ASML joined with Applied Materials to develop the SCALPEL electron-beam projection lithography (EPL) technology. According to Bill Brinkman, Bell Labs' physical sciences research vice-president, this would be "a tremendous breakthrough for semiconductor manufacturers building the next generations of powerful chips." Partnering with rival company Applied Materials gave an important boost to ASML's future advanced technology plans and spoke to ASML's practice of competing, yet cooperating when necessary to assist its customer base.

The following month, the U.S. Department of Energy and ASML came to an agreement that allowed ASML to participate in the Extreme Ultraviolet LLC program, developing extreme-ultraviolet (EUV) lithography technology. Under agreement conditions, ASML promised to construct a plant in the United States. equivalent to its facility in Veldhoven, using primarily American-made parts. ASML was concurrently involved in a European plan to develop EUV lithography, called the Euclides program. Two years later, as key ASML customers declared a preference for the EUV solution, ASML withdrew from the SCALPEL EPL venture.

In June 1999, ASML acquired MaskTools, a business unit of MicroUnity Systems Engineering Inc. of Sunnyvale, California. Declaring the need "to bring more than hardware to the customer," ASML Vice-Ppresident of U.S. Technology Development Doug Marsh said the capabilities of MaskTool's MaskRigger to ASML equipment was one of the values the company was looking to add to its product line.

ASML CEO of ten years Willem D. Maris, retired in January 2000 and was replaced by former Philips executive Doug Dunn. Maris had built ASML into the number two supplier in the world, for a time surpassing Canon and second only to Nikon. Severe softening of the industry in 2001 would scramble the top ten rankings of chip manufacturers, but ASML would remain steady during tumultuous times at number five. Dunn had been with Philips since 1993, as the head of Philips Semiconductors, and became the CEO of their Consumer Electronics division.

In July 2000, the chip business made an important move to larger wafers. A watershed event for the industry, makers stepped up from the standard 8-inch wafer to a much more cost-efficient 12-inch wafer (which the industry calls 300-millimeter wafers). ASML offered its own 300-millimeter product, TWINSCAN, a harbinger of a new chapter in the expansion of the company, incorporating new concepts and features. This seismic change allowed chipmakers to put twice as many chips on a single wafer, saving up to 30 percent in total costs. ASML, now the world's second largest maker of scanners and steppers, reported higher than expected first-half profits and expected gains in the second half of the year.

ASML broke into the Japanese semiconductor market in December 2000, marking a considerable coup for the company whose chief competitors had always been Japan's Nikon and Canon. But tough times were just ahead, and all of the rival semiconductor creators were going to feel the sting.

2001: Worst Slump in Industry History

The year 2000 started out strong for ASML and its competitors. ASML shipped a record 368 systems. But historically, slowdowns follow every boom in the chip industry. Market analysts had been predicting strong chip sales through 2001 and into 2002, but high-tech profits plunged in 2001, bringing with it the worst deceleration in semiconductor industry history.

In March 2001, ASML announced that it expected its financial results to be impacted by continued softening in the demand for lithography tools. While the company had previously predicted that it would ship a number of systems equal to production, it had become evident that 2001 sales would not equal those of 2000. A hiring freeze was put in place.

At the same time, ASML moved to acquire Silicon Valley Group (SVG), the only U.S. player in the lithography arena, and a company with an attractive business history with Intel. The road to acquisition was littered with potholes—most notably an argument by members of the House Armed Services Committee, who charged that the deal's implication for U.S. national security necessitated further study because SVG's technology was used in spy satellites. Powerful lobbying by U.S. lawmakers and the semiconductor industry persuaded the Bush administration to take a softer line, and in May 2001, the US$1.6 billion transaction was complete. But there were strings attached to the deal. ASML and SVG were given six months to sell SVG's Tinsley division, makers of optical equipment for military and aerospace applications. Tinsley was sold by year's end to SSG Precision Optronics. The acquisition put ASML in a position to claim the top spot of lithographic equipment manufacturers. Rival Nikon shipped 270 lithography systems in 1999, while ASML/SVG combined sold 245 units.

After a stellar year came a profit warning in July 2001, as ASML reported a loss of US$422.4 million. Hit hard by the industry downturn, ASML actually had slightly better than expected results, according to industry analysts. In response to the slowdown, ASML closed factories, discontinued product lines, and cut its workforce by 13 percent. A month later, ASML was hit hard with the cancellation of a US$100 million order by Intel, which pulled out after ASML failed to deliver equipment due to technical issues. ASML would announce net sales of EUR $1.84 billion for the year ending December 31, 2001, compared to net sales of EUR $3.1 billion for the previous year.

Despite the steep fall in revenue, results exceeded expectations of analysts and raised some hopes that the chip industry was beginning to emerge from its worst slowdown. Profits industry-wide were much lower than the previous year, but they represented a rise compared to the preceding three months. ASML remained pessimistic that the semiconductor market would bounce back before the end of the year. Unlike some of its competitors, it dismissed hopes of a recovery in late 2001, instead cautiously predicted a turnaround in the second half of 2002.

As a result of the continuing downturn in the semiconductor industry, ASML announced in October 2001 that it would further cut its global workforce by nearly 1,400 positions in an effort to speed up the assimilation of Silicon Valley Group. The move brought total job losses to 2,000—23 percent of ASML's workforce.

2002 Patent Infringement Lawsuit

Adding further frustration was a lawsuit brought on by Nikon in January 2002. The suit sought to halt all ASML sales in the United States. Specifically, Nikon asked the U.S. International Trade Commission to prevent sales of ASML's leading-edge lithography tools, claiming that ASML was infringing on seven of its patents. ASML responded publicly the following month, asserting that all seven Nikon patents were invalid; the official response was to be filed in Federal District Court in San Jose, California, in March.

The Future of ASML

If past performance is any indication, ASML will likely work through any tough times ahead. The semiconductor industry has a governing law, predicted by Intel cofounder Gordon Moore, that the power of microprocessors doubles every 18 months. Historically, this has largely held true. By virtue of this regular increase in the need for ever-efficient semiconductors, the industry has bounced back from intermittent slumps and ultimately thrived.

Principal Divisions

ASML Lithography; ASML Special Applications; ASML Thermal; ASML Track.

Principal Subsidiaries

MaskTools.

Principal Competitors

Applied Materials; Canon Inc.; Nikon Corporation; KLA-Tencor.

Further Reading

Alleyne, Matthew, "ASML Cuts Scalpel Deal," *Electronic Times*, February 1, 1999, p. 3.

"ASML Fact Sheet," Veldhoven: AMSL, 2000.

"ASML Press Backgrounder," Veldhoven: AMSL, 2000.

Cameron, Ian, "ASML Nearing the Next Step in Chips," *Electronic Engineering Times*, January 21, 2002, p. 3.

——, "The Contenders in the NGL Race," *Electronic News*, February 25, 2002, p. 22.

——, "Litho Merger Has Strings Attached," *Electronic Times*, May 14, 2001, p. 6.

Chappell, Jeff, "ASML Joins Mask Pattern Biz," *Electronic News*, July 2, 2001, p. 32.

——, "MaskTools, Numerical Make Nice," *Electronic News*, January 21, 2002, p. 2.

——, "Politics Hamper SVG-ASML Merger," *Electronic News*, March 12, 2001, p. 12.

Dorsch, Jeff, "ASML to Acquire MaskTools," *Electronic News*, June 7, 1999, p. 54.

——, "NeXt-Gen Lithography Crapshoot," *Electronic Business*, July 1998, pp. 45–48.

——, "U.S. Okays ASML Role in EUV Group," *Electronic News*, March 1, 1999, p. 13.

Jones-Bey, Hassaun, "Micronic and ASML Form Strategic Alliance," *Laser Focus World*, August 2001, p. 71.

Kallender, Paul, "ASML Acquires SVG for $1.6B," *Electronic News*, October 9, 2000, p. 14.

LaPedus, Mark, "Critics of ASML-SVG Merger Get It All on Tape," *Electronic Engineering Times*, April 23, 2001, p. 45.

Lowengard, Mary, "Home-Run Hitters of 1997," *Institutional Investor*, March 1998, pp. 95–102.

Ristelhueber, Robert, "Congressmen Boldly Seeking to Protect U.S. Interests Against.The Dreaded Dutch?" *EBN*, March 19, 2001, p. 46.

—Stacee Sledge

AstraZeneca PLC

15 Stanhope Gate
London W1Y 1LN
United Kingdom
Telephone: (44) 20-7304-5000
Fax: (44) 20-7304-5151
Web site: http://www.astrazeneca.com

Public Company
Incorporated: 1999
Employees: 50,000 (2000 est.)
Sales: US$16.48 billion (2001)
Stock Exchanges: New York London Stockholm
Ticker Symbol: AZN
NAIC: 325412 Pharmaceutical Preparation
Manufacturing; 325998 All Other Miscellaneous
Chemical Product and Preparation Manufacturing;
325131 Inorganic Dye and Pigment Manufacturing

AstraZeneca PLC is one of the world's leading pharmaceutical companies. Its corporate headquarters are in London, its research and development headquarters are in Södertälje, Sweden, and it has manufacturing facilities in 19 different countries. The company operates nine research and development sites and has sales in over 100 countries worldwide. AstraZeneca focuses its drug business on seven medical areas: anesthesia and pain control, cardiovascular, central nervous system, gastrointestinal (in which it is the world leader), infection, oncology, and respiratory. Its product range includes Losec—marketed in the United States as Prilosec—the world's top selling prescription drug, and Seloken, the world's leading cardioselective beta-blocker. The company is the result of the 1999 merger of two European pharmaceuticals companies: Astra AB of Sweden, which made pharmaceutical products and medical devices, and Zeneca PLC of the United Kingdom, a bioscience company that focused on pharmaceuticals, agricultural and specialty chemicals, and disease-specific healthcare services. One year after its merger, the company achieved sales of US$15.8 billion, with an operating profit of US$4 billion.

Astra: Early Development

Astra AB was formed in Sweden in 1913 by the initiative of more than 400 doctors and apothecaries who joined together to establish the company and to become its first shareholders. Two products—Digitotal, a heart medication, and Glukofos, a nutritional supplement—emerged from Astra's facilities in 1914, and the company began to prosper. When the apothecary Hjalmar Andersson Tesch joined Astra in 1915 as the company's new president he brought with him a number of his own pharmaceuticals; Astra's product line now comprised a variety of medicines and chemical compounds. Government wartime restrictions on imports created a demand for Astra's products, and the company bought new factory buildings to meet that demand. By the end of World War I, Astra was reporting handsome profits.

Astra: Interwar Difficulties

The years following the war proved less successful. In an attempt to create a company of international stature, the Swedish chemical company AB Svensk Färgämnesindustri acquired Astra's entire capital stock. The directors of Svensk incorrectly assumed that the shortage of raw materials during the war would persist in the postwar years. But, prices for raw materials dropped as war shortages disappeared. The company faced imminent bankruptcy, as its manufacturing costs grew larger than the prices its products could command in the marketplace.

A solution seemed possible when Sweden's first socialist government announced plans to create a nationalized pharmaceutical monopoly and authorized the state liquor monopoly to purchase Svensk Färgämnesindustri. However, within months, the socialist government fell, and its successor was staunchly opposed to the new monopoly. From 1921 until 1925, the government sought a private buyer who would release the state from its responsibilities. A purchaser was finally found in the form of a private consortium, and Astra became an independent company once again.

The company's new hierarchy, which included board members Erik Kistner and Richard Julin and company President Bafirje Gabrielsson, reorganized many of Astra's operations. The most

55

important of these changes allowed for the formation of the company's own distribution network. In just a few years, the company was again profitable. With the establishment of research and development facilities in the 1930s, Astra began to create more innovative products such as Hepaforte, a treatment for pernicious anemia and Nitropent, a medication for angina pectoris.

Astra's growth during the years prior to World War II resulted not only from its development of new products but also from its aggressive expansion and acquisition strategy. By 1940, company subsidiaries were operating in Finland, Latvia, Stockholm, and Hässleholm.

Restricted imports and shortages of raw materials during World War II placed Astra's products at a premium, and once again profits increased. The company constructed a new modern central laboratory and established a subsidiary to supervise the management of, and distribution to, Astra's numerous branch offices. The company established new subsidiaries in Denmark, Argentina, and the United States.

Astra: Development of Xylocaine Spurs Post-World War II Growth

In the postwar years, a number of successful pharmaceuticals emerged from Astra's laboratories such as Ferrigen, an iron preparation, and Sulfadital, a sulfa medication. The most important of all Astra's products developed during this period was Xylocaine, a local anesthetic developed in 1943. Xylocaine remained one of Astra's most popular products for years: by 1984, local anesthetics constituted 24 percent of Astra's total group sales and Xylocaine alone contributed SKr696 million.

The worldwide production of Xylocaine began in earnest during the 1950s, along with a significant increase in research and development spending. The company produced a number of successful new products throughout the 1950s, including Secergan (an anti-ulcer medication), Ascoxal (a treatment for oral infections), Jectofer (an injectable iron preparation), and Citanest (another local anesthetic). Throughout the 1960s, Astra continued to expand both at home and abroad. The company acquired a manufacturer of nutritional products and a distributor of medical supplies. It created and built new operations in Western Europe, South and Central America, and Australia. It joined with England's Beecham Research Laboratories in an attempt to develop synthetic penicillins.

By the 1970s, Astra formed separate divisions for its diverse activities: a pharmaceutical division for its array of drugs, a chemical products division produced agricultural products, nutritional products, cleansers, and recreational items, and a division was responsible for medical equipment and rust prevention products. By the end of the decade, however, Astra announced that it would concentrate solely on the production of pharmaceuticals, and the company sold all of its other holdings.

Astra: Re-Emphasis on Pharmaceuticals in 1980s

With a renewed commitment to the manufacture of pharmaceuticals, Astra's unique and highly efficient research units emerged as the company's strongest assets. By 1984, Astra's three most important products—Seloken (a heart disease medication), Xylocaine, and Bricanyl (a bronchodilator)—grew to generate over half the company's revenues; specifically, Seloken would become Astra's best-selling drug as well as one of the best-selling medications in the world.

The development of several new drugs to treat viral infections, gastrointestinal agents, and the central nervous system helped propel Astra's pre-tax earnings over the one billion kroner mark in 1985. Sales of the asthma drug Pulmicort helped propel total revenues to over SKr6.2 billion in 1988, by which time pre-tax earnings had risen to SKr1.5 billion.

Though Astra's financial performance was beginning to attract the attention of investors around the world, a core group of stockholders remained dissatisfied. Sweden's well-to-do Wallenberg family, which owned a ten percent stake in Astra, launched a search for a replacement for CEO and President Ulf Widengren. In 1988, they hired an unlikely candidate: 44-year-old chocolatier Hanakan Mogren. Mogren turned the company's former marketing program on its head, rescinding licenses and instead beefing up Astra's own distribution and sales organization. He established subsidiaries where there had previously been licensees and added nearly 1,000 sales representatives worldwide by the end of 1990. Mogren chose a tough market for his first outing, launching the anti-ulcer drug Losec in competition with Glaxo Pharmaceuticals's best-selling Zantac. Fortunately, Astra enjoyed a close relationship with longtime U.S. distributor Merck, which became an important ally in the competition, playing an especially vital role in convincing the U.S. Food and Drug Administration to approve Losec as a first-tier ulcer treatment. Astra formed a 50/50 joint venture with Merck, Astra Merck, Inc., which marketed the drug under the name Priosec in the United States. In his first two years at the helm, Mogren boosted sales by nearly 50 percent, from SKr6.3 billion to SKr9.4 billion, and increased pretax earnings by SKr1 billion.

Astra: Transformation Under Mogren in Early 1990s

The new leader intensified his transformation of Astra in the early 1990s, propelling the company into the ranks of the pharmaceutical industry's fastest growth vehicles. Mogren more than doubled the sales force from about 3,000 in 1990 to nearly 7,000 by mid-decade and boosted the company's roster of subsidiaries to 40 nations worldwide. These assertive moves succeeded in increasing the company's sales and income at a truly astonishing rate. Total sales quadrupled, from SKr9.4 billion in 1990 to nearly SKr39 billion in 1996, while pre-tax net mushroomed fivefold, from SKr2.5 billion to over SKr13 billion. Losec be-

Key Dates:

1913: Astra AB formed in Sweden.
1926: Imperial Chemical Industries (ICI, parent company of Zeneca PLC) founded in the UK.
1943: Astra develops Xylocane, which becomes the world's largest-selling local anesthetic.
1988: Hanakan Mogren appointed CEO of Astra AB.
1993: Zeneca PLC demerged from ICI.
1996: Astra's Losec becomes world's best-selling prescription drug.
1999: Astra AB and Zeneca PLC merge to form AztraZeneca PLC.

came the world's top-selling drug in 1996, with an estimated 200 million prescriptions and US$3.5 billion revenues.

Mogren's reign was not without its problems, however. In 1995, the company suffered from an embarrassing scandal when Lars Bildman, head of Astra's North American operations was fired and faced criminal charges for defrauding the company of over US$1 million. Additionally, Bildman's alleged sexual harassment of female employees resulted in several lawsuits. The company settled the suits, but its reputation suffered. Analysts also began to worry about Astra's fate in face of the fact that Losec's patents were due to begin expiring in 1999 and expressed concern over the vagueness of the company's strategy to handle the patent losses. Some criticized Astra's venture with Merck, saying that Astra Merck, Inc. missed important sales opportunities because of an inexperience sales staff. Most troubling to analysts was the paucity of Astra's drug ''pipeline''—since drugs can take years to test and find approval, their development must begin years before their launch. Astra's criticizers felt that the company had far too few promising new drugs in development. Beginning in 1997, the company's shares began to underperform compared to the rest of the industry. Rumors of a merger or acquisition in Astra's future began to circulate, and, in fact, the company had held extensive merger talks with British pharmaceuticals company Zeneca PLC in 1996. Those talks foundered because Zeneca felt that Astra's relationship with Merck was a barrier. In 1998, however, Astra and Merck dissolved their venture, and in December of that year, Astra and Zeneca announced that they would merge into a new company called AstraZeneca PLC. In freeing itself from its obligations to Merck, Astra made a deal wherein it would pay Merck between US$675 million and US$1 billion upon completion of the merger, US$950 million the following year, and continue to pay royalties to Merck for products sold in the United States at least through 2008.

Zeneca: Roots in ICI

Zeneca Group PLC was the result of a demerger from Imperial Chemical Industries (ICI). Formed in 1926, ICI was one of the United Kingdom's oldest and most renowned chemical corporations. By the end of the 1980s, ICI's pharmaceutical division was the company's most profitable business. Yet, with many different product lines and operations in widely diverse geographical regions, and as the chemical industry matured and

others such as pharmaceuticals and agrochemicals grew rapidly, ICI was ill prepared to meet the challenges of managing the complexities of its own businesses.

The prospects of a fully mature chemicals market, which meant intense competition, lower growth, and overcapacity in many regions throughout the world, convinced management at ICI that a comprehensive restructuring of the company was necessary. This realization was brought to a head when Hanson PLC acquired a small amount of stock in ICI, thus fueling speculation that executives at Hanson were preparing for a hostile takeover. The result was a series of meetings and consultations with Warburgs, ICI's merchant bank advisors, that established a strategy to separate the company into two new groupings, New ICI and ICI Bioscience, which was named Zeneca.

During its 65-year history, ICI had developed into an extremely complex and fully integrated organization with more than 120,000 employees working in 130 countries around the globe. Management decided to continue operating ICI as a chemical company in traditional markets, while the demerger gave Zeneca all of ICI's former pharmaceutical, agrochemical, and specialty products. When Zeneca was formed, it took approximately 30,000 employees from ICI.

Zeneca: Independence

Zeneca Ltd. was established as a 100 percent wholly owned subsidiary of ICI on January 1, 1993. By June of the same year, however, Zeneca existed as a totally separate company from ICI. Zeneca's market capitalization was actually more than that of ICI and placed the newly established company in the top 25 firms listed with the highest capitalization in the United Kingdom. A new headquarters was set up for Zeneca at 15 Stanhope Gate, having been custom-designed to meet the specific needs of the new organization. By the end of fiscal 1993, the first full year of Zeneca's operation, sales had increased approximately 12 percent to an impressive total amount of £4.44 billion, and the company's profit margin increased by an astounding 42 percent to £647 million. Zeneca's pharmaceutical operation immediately catapulted it into the ranks of the top 20 pharmaceutical companies worldwide.

By 1995, Zeneca was operating at full capacity. The company's group sales, comprised of pharmaceutical, agrochemical, and specialty products, amounted to £4.8 billion, and operating profit increased to £894 million. The company was ranked number two in worldwide sales of anticancer drugs, and it ranked as one of the top six agro-chemical firms around the globe. Zeneca had expanded to include facilities in more than 25 countries and sales of its products in more than 100 nations.

Zeneca Pharmaceuticals provided the largest amount of the company's sales with more than £2 billion in 1995. Its research and development efforts focused on providing treatment for a wide variety of cancers and disorders of the respiratory, cardiovascular, and central nervous systems. Casodex, an oral prostate cancer drug, Arimidex, for use by breast cancer patients, as well as Zoladex, Tomudex, the first cell-killing agent for advanced stages of colorectal cancer developed in nearly 30 years, and Accolate, an anti-asthma tablet developed to prevent asthma attacks. To expand its presence overseas, Zeneca also purchased a 50 percent share in Salick Health Care, Inc., one of the leading providers of comprehensive cancer and chronic disease care in the United States.

Herbicide products made up approximately two-thirds of Zeneca Agrochemicals' £1.6 billion in sales for 1995. Innovative herbicides such as Touchdown, Falcon, and Surpass, the latter specifically developed for use in maize, were extremely successful in the marketplace. The company's leading herbicide, Gramoxone, was adopted by farmers the world over. Zeneca Plant Sciences (ZPS), part of the company's agrochemical operation, concentrates on developing vegetables, fruits, and fiber crops with enhanced characteristics. In 1995, ZPS began working closely with Mippon Paper, a Japanese firm, and Shell Forestry, an American subsidiary of Shell Oil, to develop trees with modified lignin, which results in the tree pulp needing less chemical treatment and thereby producing a higher quality of paper.

Zeneca Specialties made and sold high performance pigments that put the color in plastics and paints for cars; developed smudge-resistant ink jet dyes used in the printing of magazines and in color photocopying equipment; supplied products to control contamination caused by unwanted bacteria such as the fungi and algae in swimming pools; manufactured a host of leather finishes, including those that liven up the color and sheen of handbags and leather coats; designed water-based resins that were ingredients to adhesives, paints, and inks used around the world; and even developed a low-fat alternative to meat that had no cholesterol and was high in fiber.

Beginning in 1995, Zeneca focused on a unique approach to the treatment of cancer. The company was one of the first pharmaceutical firms in the world that approached cancer not as a disease ultimately to be cured, but as a chronic disease with which patients could learn to live. Zeneca was so successful in its approach and in developing breast cancer and prostate cancer drugs that the direction of cancer research changed within the pharmaceutical industry as a whole, and many companies began to follow Zeneca's lead in cancer research.

Zeneca: Rumors of a Takeover

Almost from the moment Zeneca demerged from ICI, rumors that it was ripe for acquisition began to circulate. The company was certainly an attractive prospect for interested buyers: between its spinoff and 1996, the company doubled its pretax profits, and its stock value more than tripled. In 1997, the company was the second largest seller of cancer drugs. Additionally, the overall trend in the pharmaceuticals industry at that time was for small-to-medium-sized companies such as Zeneca to be taken over by industry giants. Further, 1997 saw the beginnings of a downturn for the company: patents on its most successful drugs Zestril (a heart medication) and Nolvadex (a cancer drug) were due to expire at the beginning of the 21st century, and some analysts were concerned that Zeneca did not have enough drugs in late-stage trials to compensate for the loss. Other analysts felt that Zeneca hadn't made alliances with biotechnology companies fast enough.

Still, the company was determined to maintain its independence. Sir David Barnes, Zeneca's CEO held a hard line, saying that any competitor had to be willing to pay a substantial premium for control of Zeneca. "I object to the idea that 'everyone's merging, and therefore you have to,' " he said in 1998, "In most mergers, one of the parties has embedded difficulties, and merging is really not the cure. It must be something that is in addition to growth and never a substitute for it. It isn't a valid long-term strategy." Nevertheless, the company was ruling out no possibilities, and it conducted talks with several suitors. Zeneca rejected merger talks with Astra AB in 1996 because of that company's close relationship with Merck, and 1998 negotiations with Glaxo Wellcome and SmithKline Beecham were scuttled when the two larger companies balked at Zeneca's premium. Finally, in December of 1998, the company announced its impending merger with Astra, who had recently disentangled itself from its obligations to Merck.

AstraZeneca: A Marriage of Equals

Investors greeted the news of the merger warmly: the day after the union was announced, Astra's share price increased 13 percent, and Zeneca's rose 7.5 percent. The new company, AstraZeneca PLC, would be the number three pharmaceuticals firm in the industry. The US$37 billion merger was completed on April 6, 1999, 80 days after its announcement, and the new company's stock was listed on the London, Stockholm, and New York stock exchanges. AstraZeneca was headed by Tom McKillop (formerly the CEO of Zeneca) as Chief Executive, and Percy Barnevik (of Astra) as Chairman. In many ways, the two companies seemed a perfect match for one another. They were of comparable size to each other (valued at over US$30 billion each), so they entered the merger on equal footing. "This merger is genuinely equal because we are bringing together two companies that have huge respect for each other," McKillop said in June of 1999, "It is not one company taking over the other.we are creating a new company." One of the first steps AstraZeneca took as a "new company" was to streamline its operations and focus solely on its pharmaceuticals business by spinning off the agricultural and chemical holdings Zeneca had brought to the merger. The company merged its agrochemical business with that of Novartis (another drug company) in 2000.

The new company faced challenges. While the combined drug portfolios created a stronger pipeline than the companies had held independently, AstraZeneca still faced patent loss on some of its major drugs, Losec in particular, which accounted for nearly 40 percent of the company's total sales. Once Losec's patent expired in 2001, other companies would be able to produce it generically at a significantly lowered price. AstraZeneca immediately put in place a strategy to offset the losses by defending secondary patents on the drug while simultaneously bringing replacement products to the market, namely Nexium, which was launched on March 19, 2001. In the early years of the decade, the strategy looked successful: within 17 weeks of its release, Nexium was ranked third in the market for new prescriptions in the class in the United States, and the company was optimistic about the release of Crestor, a cholesterol-lowering drug slated for release in the second half of 2002. "I believe AstraZeneca is well positioned for continued growth," said Tom McKillop in 2001, "We have the strategy, products, people, and skills to make a real difference in the world of healthcare."

Principal Subsidiaries

Astra Tech; Salick Health Care; Marlow Foods.

Principal Competitors

GlaxoSmithKline; Merck; Novartis.

Further Reading

Agovino, Theresa, "Drug Industry under Fire over Business Practices Consumers, Lawsuits Claim Firms Colluding to Squelch Competition," *Seattle Times*, May 25, 2001, p. A8.

"Agrochemical Merger Advances," *New York Times*, July 27, 2000, p. 4.

Ahmad, Sameena, "Zeneca Suffering from a Serious Shortage of New Drugs, Says Report," *Independent*, December 02, 1997, p. 24.

"Astra Adds Muscle in the U.S.," *Business Week*, November 14, 1994, p. 47.

"AstraZeneca Faces Losec Investigation," *Managing Intellectual Property*, June 2000, p. 6.

"AstraZeneca Latest Launches," *Chemist & Druggist*, July 10, 1999, p. 10.

"AstraZeneca Sees Challenging Times Ahead," *Chemist & Druggist*, February 17, 2001, p. 24.

"AstraZeneca's Poor Performance in UK," *Chemist & Druggist*, August 5, 2000, p. 24.

Barrett, Amy and Kerry Capell, "Prilosec Time Is Just About Up," *Business Week*, January 8, 2001, p. 47.

Bennett, Neil, "City: Just Add Astra," *The Sunday Telegraph*, December 13, 1998, p. 6.

Blackledge, Cath, "Glaxo/Astra Plot Courses for Success," *ECN-European Chemical News*, November 20, 1995, pp. 26–27.

Blanton, Kimberly, "New Astra CEO Makes Changes," *Boston Globe*, May 14, 1996, p. 39.

Brierley, David, "Keeping Zeneca on Side of the Gods," *The European*, December 12, 1996, p. 32.

"Corporate Profile: The Arranged Marriage," *Independent*, February 24, 1999, p. 5.

Cowell, Alan, "A Drop at AstraZeneca," *New York Times*, February 25, 2000, p. 4.

Davis, Wendy, "When Patents Expire," *Brandweek*, July 16, 2001, pp. 40–42.

"Drug Industry: European Unions," *The Economist*, December 12, 1998, p. 62.

"Economic Growth Rate is Still Impressive," *Northern Echo*, January 30, 2002, p. 12.

Flynn, Julia, "Astra Investors Breathe a Sigh of Relief," *Business Week*, December 21, 1998, p. 37.

Griffiths, Ian, "Zeneca Bidders May as Well Stay in Bed," *Independent on Sunday*, October 27, 1996, p. 2.

Grimond, Magnus, "The Investment Column: Zeneca Keeps Pace with Rivals," *Independent*, August 08, 1997, p. 23.

——, "Zeneca Sees Shares Dip Despite Surge in Sales," *Independent*, October 30, 1996, p. 19.

"Harassment Suit Against Astra Chief Is Dismissed," *New York Times*, May 29, 1997, p. D3.

Held-Warmkessel, Jeanne, *Pocket Guide to Prostate Cancer: (AstraZeneca)*, Sudbury, MA: Jones & Bartlett Publishers, Incorporated, December, 2000.

Icon Group International, Inc. Staff, *AstraZeneca PLC: International Competitive Benchmarks and Financial Gap Analysis*, San Diego: Icon Group International, Incorporated, October, 2000.

——, *AstraZeneca PLC: Labor Productivity Benchmarks and International Gap Analysis*, San Diego: Icon Group International, Incorporated, October, 2000.

Jarvis, Lisa, "AstraZeneca Introduces Next Generation Prilosec," *Chemical Market Reporter*, September 18, 2000, pp. 5, 12.

Jury, Jennifer, "European Tandem Wins GBP1.3B AstraZeneca Unit," *Buyouts*, June 21, 1999, p. 1.

Kirby, R. (Editor), *The Challenge of Rising PSA. Can We Delay Prostate Cancer Progression?: AstraZeneca-Sponsored Satellite Symposium, EAU, Geneva, April 2001*, Farmington, CT: S. Karger AG, October, 2001.

Koberstein, Wayne, "Executive Profile: Celebration & Labor: A New Company's Birthday," *Pharmaceutical Executive*, June 01, 1999, pp. 44–48, 50.

Langreth, Robert, "Approval of Zeneca Unit's Asthma Drug May Open Door for Other Treatments," *The Wall Street Journal*, September 30, 1996, p. B4D(E).

Mirasol, Feliza, "Astra and Zeneca Await Benefits from Their Merger," *Chemical Market Reporter*, January 11, 1999, p. 5.

Moore, Stephen D., "Astra's Successful Ulcer Drug May Become Bellyache," *The Wall Street Journal*, November 26, 1996, p. B4.

——, "Zeneca's Cancer Approach Catches On," *The Wall Street Journal*, June 10, 1997, p. B8(E).

Morais, Richard S. "The Confidence Man," *Forbes*, May 5, 1997, pp. 116–17.

Morrow, David J. and Andrew Ross Sorkin, "2 Drug Companies to Combine Troubled Agricultural Units," *New York Times*, December 2, 1999, p. C, 1:2.

Mullin, Rick, "A New Culture for Zeneca AG Products," *Chemical Week*, June 7, 1995, p. 40.

Mullin, Rick, "Zeneca Specialties' Global Stewardship," *Chemical Week*, July 5, 1995, p. 70.

Napoli, Maryann, "Misleading Claims for Popular Heartburn/Ulcer Drug," *Healthfacts*, August 2000, p. 3.

O'Brien, Liam, "Healthy Returns," *Supply Management*, April 26, 2001, pp. 30–31.

"Outlook: Zeneca Has Been," *Independent*, December 02, 1997, p. 25.

Owen, Geoffrey, and Harrison, Trevor, "Why ICI Chose to Demerge," *Harvard Business Review*, March-April 1995, pp. 133–140.

Pierson, Ransdell, "Prilosec Ousts Zantac on U.S. Top 10 Drug List," *Reuters Business Report*, August 22, 1997, http://www.elibrary.com.

Reier, Sharon, " 'The Last Rat': In the Fast Changing Drug Business, Management Has Become More Important than Pipeline," *Financial World*, November 22, 1994, pp. 38–41.

Schmelz, Abigail, "Astra Posts Mixed First-Half Results," *Reuters Business Report*, August 08, 1997, http://www.elibrary.com.

Seely, Robert, "European Drug Makers Zeneca and Astra Merging in Bid to Stay Competitive," *AP Online*, December 10, 1998, http://www.elibrary.com.

Stahl, Jason, "Merger Forms Largest Ag-Chem Business in World," *Landscape Management*, January 2000, p. 22.

Stevenson, Richard W., "A Certain Glow on Sweden's Astra," *New York Times*, November 22, 1992, pp. 3–13.

Stevenson, Tom, "Zeneca Shows Its Quality: The Investment Column," *Independent*, October 30, 1996, p. 21.

Stewart, Thomas, A., "How to Lead a Revolution," *Fortune*, November 28, 1994, pp. 48–50.

"Too Much Acid," *The Economist*, March 30, 1991, pp. 82–83.

"Too Much Sex, Not Enough Drugs," *The Economist*, February 14, 1998, p. 70.

Valdmanis, Thor, "Roche: Will It Swallow Zeneca?," *Financial World*, May 20, 1996, p. 24.

"When Big Pharma Chases Mega Pharma," *Chief Executive*, April, 2000, pp. 40–44.

Wood, Andrew, "Zeneca Stays Independent Counting on Internal Growth," *Chemical Week*, April 15, 1998, p. 24.

Yates, Andrew, "Drugs Chief Appointed New Head of Zeneca," *Independent*, May 23, 1998, p. 24.

——, ''Zeneca Stands up for Independence,'' *Independent*, March 06, 1998, p. 26.

Young, Ian, ''AstraZeneca Splits in Two,'' *Chemical Week*, October 20, 1999, p. 9.

''Zeneca Asthma Drug, First of a New Class, Gets FDA Approval,'' *The Wall Street Journal*, September 27, 1996, p. B2(E).

''Zeneca Pharmaceuticals Invests in SEQ Ltd, Developer of Breakthrough DNA Sequencing Technology,'' *Business Wire*, September 23, 1997, http://www.elibrary.com.

''Zeneca Reports 15 Percent Rise in Pre-Tax Profit,'' *Reuters Business Report*, May 23, 1997, http://www.elibrary.com.

—Thomas Derdak (Zeneca)
—updates: April D. Gasbarre (Astra);
Lisa Whipple (AstraZeneca)

AutoNation.

AutoNation, Inc.

AutoNation Tower
110 S.E. Sixth Street
Ft. Lauderdale, Florida 33301
U.S.A.
Telephone: (954) 769-7000
Web site: http://corp.autonation.com

Public Company
Incorporated: 1998
Employees: 30,000 (2001 est.)
Sales: $20 billion (2001)
Stock Exchanges: NYSE
Ticker Symbol: AN
NAIC: 441110 New Car Dealers; 441120 Used Car
Dealers; 522220 Automobile Financing; 524210
Insurance Agencies and Brokerages; 811111 General
Automotive Repair

AutoNation, Inc. is the largest automotive retailer in the United States. The company sells vehicles off of their more than 371 vehicle franchises in 17 states, as well as on AutoNation.com, the largest vehicle sales retailer on the Internet. The physical dealerships commonly offer products and services beyond automobile sales, including vehicle maintenance and repair services, vehicle parts, extended service contracts, and insurance products. The dealerships can also arrange financing for vehicle purchases through third-party sources. In addition to running the AutoNation.com Web site, the AutoNation Retail Group also manages the operation of approximately 270 Web sites for the company's franchised automotive dealerships. The company also includes AutoNation Financial Services, a finance arm, which has securities assets of more than $1 billion in 2000. Recent deals with AOL and Microsoft have strengthened AutoNation.com's customer referral power.

From Waste Disposal to Automotive Retail

Wayne Huizenga was one of the best-known entrepreneurs in the United States due to his wild success in creating two mammoth companies: Waste Management and Blockbuster Video. In 1995, Huizenga and a partner began a new foray into business with the purchase of Republic Industries, a U.S. waste-disposal company. Mr. Huizenga hoped to build Republic Industries into a group with interests in security, rubbish collection, and used-car superstores (large used-car supermarkets). After a failed attempt at purchasing the ADT group in 1996, a Bermuda-based security and car auction company, Republic succeeded in purchasing National Car Rental for $600 million in stock. The car rental company had 800 outlets in the United States and Canada, with a fleet of 100,000 vehicles. This purchase, and the purchase in the previous year of Alamo (another car rental company) firmly placed Mr. Huizenga's dream for supplying his used-car superstores with quality rental cars in reality.

At the same time that Republic was purchasing rental car companies to build a rental segment of Republic, they were also building AutoNation, a chain of used-car superstores. Mr. Huizenga merged AutoNation into Republic in April 1996. The used-car superstores offered customers a way to purchase used cars without the stress of bargaining or haggling; automobile's prices were set in advance to make a more customer-friendly atmosphere. By December 1996, Republic had begun acquiring new-car dealerships in addition to building the AutoNation chain of used-car mega stores.

Taking Out the Trash

Almost as soon as Huizenga's automobile chain was off the ground, he spun off the company's original business, the waste business, as Republic Services Inc. Huizenga sold all of the remaining interest in Republic Services in a public stock offering during the second quarter of 1997. The company continued to operate under the name Republic, but company officials began to take steps to make AutoNation the company's predominant national brand. The brand AutoNation began to be used at some of Republic's new-car dealerships. The first market the company tried the AutoNation brand in was Denver, Colorado, where the company consolidated its 17 dealerships under the name "John Elway AutoNation." Soon after, in 1998, the company took the definitive leap toward establishing AutoNation as a national brand when they changed the company's name from Republic Industries Inc. to AutoNation, Inc.

Company Perspectives:

AutoNation's Driven to Be the Best *vision is based on a foundation of operational excellence that drives an uncompromising focus on the customer. This vision shapes a company that's continuously improving and setting industry standards in all that it seeks to achieve, from superior shopping experiences to market-leading brands, to unmatched scale advantages and productivity-boosting best practices.*

Following the name change, the company was split into two operating groups: the AutoNation Retail Group and AutoNation Rental Group. The Retail Group oversaw the company's used-and-new car superstores and franchise, while the Rental Group oversaw the company's three automotive rental brands—National Car Rental Systems, Alamo Rent-A-Car Inc., and CarTemps USA. Each of the rental companies adopted AutoNation as their sub-brand, and the new-car franchises added the label "An AutoNation Company" to their dealerships.

Low Profits at Used-Car Mega Stores Trigger Big Changes in 1999

AutoNation's used-car mega stores did not turn the profits that the company had hoped for. The mega stores fell victim to an increase in new-car sales and with that increase, the devaluation of used cars. When the company's stock started slipping, AutoNation decided to open new-car dealerships inside the used-car superstores. Four of the used-new combination stores were AutoNation Dodge in Grand Prairie, Texas; Seminole Ford and AutoNation USA in Sanford, Florida; AutoNation Chrysler-Plymouth in Douglasville, Georgia; and AutoNation Nissan in Perrine, Florida. Regardless of AutoNation's positive outlook and statements surrounding the launching of the new-used stores, the integrated stores did not work the magic that AutoNation hoped they would.

The company's drooping profits and management's inability to turn those profits around caused AutoNation's founder and co-CEOs to step down from their positions to make room for fresh ideas in the form of a new chief executive. The new executive was Michael Jackson, who came to AutoNation with many years of automobile dealership experience. To take the chief executive position at AutoNation, it was necessary for Jackson to resign as president of Mercedes-Benz of North America. Only four months after Mr. Jackson had taken up the reins at AutoNation he faced the task of deciding what to do with the company's unprofitable 29 used-car mega stores. His decision was quick, on December 19, 1999, Mr. Jackson announced the closure of 23 of the company's 29 used-car mega stores and the integration of the remaining mega stores into new-car franchise outlets. In an interview with *Knight Ridder/Tribune Business News*, Jackson said, "I knew when I joined AutoNation of their announced plan to integrate used-car stores into our new-car stores, but after looking at it closer realized it would be difficult to do, would require that we invest an inordinate amount of capital into those stores and at the end of the day still end up losing money, which made no sense." He continued, "We decided to simply close the stores." In the same interview, Jackson went on to say, "Our focus now is on improving our operating margins and on creating a unique and branded customer experience in our new-vehicle franchises, which are now AutoNation's sole business focus. By closing the megastores, we have taken the necessary steps to ensure the long-term success of AutoNation."

Success on the World Wide Web: 1999

When AutoNation decided to take their business online to expand their customer reach and generate sales leads, they did not waste years developing the idea and Web site. AutoNationDirect.com and Web sites for 270 of AutoNation's dealers were developed in a quick 18 months, by a four-person information technology team and several vendors. The AutoNationDirect.com Web site enabled customers to buy vehicles from all of AutoNation's 400 new-and-used car stores without ever needing to visit the dealership. The Web sites for individual dealers were connected to the main Web site (www.autonationdirect.com) so that all leads that came onto any of the sites could be logged and tracked. If a customer visited the main umbrella site, AutoNationdirect.com, they were referred to the dealership geographically closest to them. AutoNationdirect.com was designed with a slew of features that the individual dealer's Web sites did not offer in order to establish AutoNationdirect.com as the focal point for the network of dealership sites. For example, at AutoNationdirect.com customers could apply for online financing, insurance procurement, and could utilize a chat line that allowed them to ask questions and get answers from a call center agent in real time.

Although AutoNation's Web site was slated to be used as a marketing platform, the company did not expect the Web site itself to generate a large amount of profits because they believed that few customers would be willing to buy a vehicle sight unseen. Instead, the company used the Web sites to build traffic to send out to its dealerships. In May 1999, AutoNation president John Costello discussed with *Automotive News'* Donna Harris the Web advantage as AutoNation saw it. He explained that promoting a Web site could expand a dealership's territory from the typical ten-mile radius to a 30-mile radius. He said, "The Internet provides an opportunity to generate greater traffic and revenue. The physical dealership will play an important role in the sales and ownership experience."

Because of the nature of the link between the Web sites and physical vehicle dealerships, it was important that AutoNation devise a strategy to contact salespeople at the dealerships and supply them with information about interested customers in a quick manner. The company used pagers to alert salespeople in the dealerships about incoming Internet leads, and some dealerships experimented with even more complicated technology to shorten the wait-time for possible customers. AutoNation's used-vehicle Cleveland store used the Merchant Notification System developed by NetSearch LLC of Scottsdale, Arizona. The system was a two-inch-by-three-inch wireless handheld computer terminal with a keyboard. This system allowed for salespeople to respond immediately to leads.

AutoNation Spins Off ANC Rental Corp.: 2000

On April 4, 2000, AutoNation announced that it expected to launch the spinoff of ANC Rental Corp. ANC Rental Corp.

included Alamo, National, and CarTemps rental operations. The announcement was long-awaited, due to the fact that ANC Rental lost $71 million in 1999. AutoNation reasoned that they were spinning ANC off in order to focus more completely on their new-car dealerships. On June 3, 2000, AutoNation completed the tax-free spinoff of ANC.

AutoNation Reports Big Loss: 2000

Due to the upheaval that AutoNation underwent in 1999 and the beginning months of 2000, it came as no surprise that the company announced a large loss for the first quarter of 2000. The spinoff of ANC and the closure of the company's 23 used-vehicle mega stores contributed to the reported $403 million loss. CEO Michael Jackson told *Automotive News*, in January 2000, that AutoNation intended to concentrate on becoming a new-vehicle retailer now that they were free of their rental business.

Following their first-quarter loss, the company forged ahead focusing all their energies on becoming a successful new-vehicle retailer. In July 2000, AutoNation decided to capitalize on brand recognition by changing the names of 28 of their 30 car dealerships in Florida to Maroone. The strategy of capitalizing on brand recognition was not a new one for AutoNation, they had consolidated a host of dealerships in Denver years before under the well-known name John Elway. Although they renamed existing dealerships, the AutoNation name was displayed underneath the Maroone and automaker names.

Exciting Internet Partnerships

Developing the online AutoNation brand and partnering up with well-known and well-connected Internet companies was an important next step in AutoNation's reach for new-vehicle sales success. On May 15, 2000, AutoNation and AOL announced their intention to ally and build the world's largest "virtual auto dealership." The companies built a co-branded Web site called, "AOL AutosDirect, Powered by AutoNation.com." The deal allowed AutoNation to be the exclusive retailer of new-and-used vehicles to AOL members who purchased a car or truck through

the new co-branded site. AOL members who purchased vehicles through this site were eligible to receive a slew of exclusive benefits.

Another important announcement, along the same lines as the AOL announcement, made on May 15, 2000, was that AutoNation acquired AutoVantage, a car-buying service from Cendant Corporation. AutoVantage was ranked by J.D. Power & Associates as one the most popular automotive lead providers, and had a network of approximately 900 dealers throughout the country. The purchase of AutoVantage gave AutoNation the reach they would need to serve AOL's geographically diverse customer base.

AutoVantage and AOL were not the only two exciting Internet partnerships that AutoNation had in the works. In October 2000, the company reached an agreement with Autoweb.com to allow AutoNation to use their content and technology platform of the Autoweb Web site. Autoweb.com technology allowed Web users to configure a vehicle by manufacturer, make, model, trim specifications, and other options, and then to perform comparison shopping with similar vehicles.

AutoNation did not limit Internet partnerships to the year 2000. In February 2001, the company entered into a three-year partnership with MSN CarPoint. Under their agreement, CarPoint would send Internet sales leads to AutoNation's dealerships and affiliated dealerships.

Stock Prices Soar: 2001

AutoNation's low stock price was affected by the success of their many high-profile Internet deals and the company's focus on new-car sales. Since 1997, AutoNation's stock had sunk steadily (more or less). The stock had traveled from more than $40 a share in January 1997 to $6.875 per share in 2000. Since January 1, 2001, share prices roughly doubled for AutoNation— the company's market capitalization had jumped to $3.6 billion.

New Developments in Successful Times

In order to continue serving their customers in the most friendly and responsible way, AutoNation created a managers' training program patterned after the successful programs developed by Burger King and The Walt Disney Co. The school aimed at establishing operating standards throughout its car dealership network. The education program was taught by ten AutoNation trainers and company executives and lasted 2½ days.

In October 2001, AutoNation announced that it had built an online dealer network of 2,928 franchises, called "e-Tail Network, Powered by AutoNation." Senior Vice-President of Operations Allan Stejskal, told *Automotive News*' Donna Harris that, "We expect to handle 2 million leads a year."

ANC Causes Trouble for AutoNation

Just months after AutoNation spun off ANC Rental (June 2000), ANC filed for Chapter 11 bankruptcy (November 13, 2001). When AutoNation spun off ANC, the company continued to guarantee its former unit's credit, as well as the six- to nine-month leases of a large amount of vehicles from Mitsubishi Motor Sales of America Inc. The bankruptcy filing caused

AutoNation to come to terms with the fact that they were not free from the woes of ANC's failing business. In an AutoNation filing with the U.S. Securities and Exchange Commission (SEC), the company reported that the Mitsubishi leases held AutoNation obligated for $4 million to $5 million a month, with the possibility of the obligation rising to $8 million a month. AutoNation feared that it could end up paying upward of $150 million if it had to cover ANC's credit obligations.

Exit from Lending Operations

To boost automotive sales, post-September 11, 2001, after the terrorist attacks in the United States, many loan companies offered low-no-interest loans (subvention loans). Loans like this, although they did boost new-car sales, usurped market share from AutoNation's finance business. AutoNation refused to offer loss-leading loans stating in the *Asset Securitization Report* in December 2001, "As an independent finance company, we are not in business strictly to move metal, and you have to profit from your loans. We absolutely refuse to compete with subverting zero-percent loans." AutoNation decided to exit the loan-origination aspect of the auto business in December 2001. The company's exit from the loan business had little impact on outstanding loan deals, due to the fact that World Omni Financial had long been contracted by AutoNation to do the actual financial work of the loans AutoNation was listed as the master servicer on.

New-and-Used Car Sales up for AutoNation: 2002

Automotive News reported in May 2002 that AutoNation topped both the used-vehicle sales and new-vehicle sales tallies for 2001. In addition to their selling success, AutoNation officials reported (in a conference call with *Daily Business Review* in April 2002) first-quarter earnings of $91.7 million, or 28 cents a share, compared with the earlier year's $59 million, or 17 cents a share. The company's streamlined focus on selling new-and-used cars is proving to be a successful business choice.

Principal Subsidiaries

AutoNation Financial Services; House of Imports, Inc.

Principal Competitors

Group 1 Automotive, Inc.; Sonic Automotive, Inc.; United Auto Group, Inc.

Further Reading

Altaner, David, "South Florida AutoNation Car Dealerships to Change Their Name," *Knight-Ridder/Tribune Business News*, May 8, 2000, Item 00130001.

"AutoNation, Autoweb.com Make a Deal," *Automotive News*, October 23, 2000, p. 4.

"AutoNation Beats the Street Earnings up 53%: Lower Interest Rates, Accounting Rules Change Help Figures," *Daily Business Review* (Miami, FL), April 24, 2002, p. A3.

"AutoNation Outlets Close," *The Business Journal*," December 17, 1999, p. 68.

Donovan, Kevin, "Feeling Pressure, AutoNation Debates Potential Exit from Lending Operation," *Asset Securitization Report*, December 10, 2001, item 00344004.

Gale, Kevin, "AutoNation Drives into Future with Tighter Operational Focus," *South Florida Business Journal*, June 16, 2000, p. 1.

Harris, Donna, "AutoNation Overpowers Its Web Buying-Service Rivals," *Automotive News*, October 29, 2001, p. 33.

——, "AutoNation Puts Checkbook Away," *Automotive News,* November 22, 1999, p. 4.

——, "AutoNation Sees Big Net Sales," *Automotive News*, May 10, 1999, p. 8.

——, "Chain Sees Megastore Rebound: New-Used Combos Fuel Comeback," *Automotive News*, October 18, 1999, p. 26.

——, "Pager Speeds Up Response to Internet Leads," *Automotive News,* May 10, 1999, p. 20.

——, "School Bell Chimes at AutoNation," *Automotive News*, August 27, 2001, p. 4.

Henry, Jim, "AutoNation to Get Sales Leads from CarPoint," *Automotive News*, February 3, 2001, p. 1.

Johnson, Greg, "ANC's Woes Could Harm AutoNation," *The Deal.com*, November 19, 2001, http://www.deal.com.

Mateja, Jim, "Its out with Old, in with New at Florida-Based AutoNation," *Knight-Ridder/Tribune Business News*, December 19, 1999, item 99355011.

May, Tony, "Pounds 700m Lost as ADT Deal Collapses," *The Guardian*, October 1, 1996, p. 20.

Miller, Joe, "Fresh Phase: Republic Becomes AutoNation," *Automotive News*, April 12, 1998, p. 4.

Sawyers, Arlene, "Top 100 Groups Add Sales in 2001; 10 Biggest Win More than 50 Percent of Used-Vehicle Volume," *Automotive News*, May 20, 2002, p. 32.

——, "AutoNation Reports $403.1 Million Loss for Quarter," *Automotive News*, January 31, 2000, p. 8.

——, "AutoNation to Sell New Nissans," *Automotive News*, April 26, 1999, p. 4.

Wallace, Bob, "Car Retailer Builds Site the Fast Way," *Computerworld*, July 12, 1999, p. 62.

Waters, Richard, "The Americas: Republic Industries Acquires Car Rental Concern," *Financial Times*, January 7, 1997, p. 17.

—Tammy Weisberger

AVIVA™

Aviva PLC

St Helen's
1 Undershaft
London, EC3P 3DQ
United Kingdom
Telephone: (44) 20-7283-2000
Fax: (44) 20-7662-8182
Web site: http://www.aviva.com

Public Company
Incorporated: 2000
Employees: 68,107
Sales: $43 billion (£28 billion)
Stock Exchanges: Euronext Dublin London Paris
Ticker Symbol: AV (London)
NAIC: 523120 Securities Brokerage; 523920 Portfolio
   Management; 524113 Direct Life Insurance Carriers;
   524126 Direct Property and Casualty Insurance
   Carriers

The product of multiple mergers, Aviva PLC is the United Kingdom's largest insurance and financial services group and the seventh largest insurer in the world. The London-based insurer has 25 million customers, more than £200 billion (US $306.5 billion) under management, and premium income and investment sales of £28 billion (US $43 billion) for 2001. It derives revenues from a trio of business platforms: life and savings products, general insurance, and fund management. Long-term life and savings has become the key focus and principal source of growth for the company. Targeting the needs of the aging and affluent populations in the United Kingdom and Europe, Aviva offers life insurance, annuities, unit trusts, pensions plans, and financial and investment services. The company's longstanding general insurance business focuses on home and auto coverage for individuals and the insurance needs of small businesses. Aviva is one of the top ten fund managers in Europe and the second largest U.K-based fund manager. The fund management business invests the group's funds held for policyholders.

Commercial Union Rises from London Fire

Aviva attained prominence with a pair of dawn-of-the-century mergers. In 1998, U.K. insurance giants Commercial Union and General Accident combined to form CGU. Two years later, in 2000, CGU merged with U.K. life insurance rival Norwich Union to form CGNU. In 2002, shareholders approved renaming the company Aviva.

Commercial Union (CU) was the largest of the insurance trio that combined to form Aviva, and also was first on the scene. CU emerged in 1861 in the aftermath of London's Great Tooley Street Fire, which raged for two days along the south bank of the Thames River. High claims from the destruction prompted insurance companies to more than double their rates for waterside warehouse fire coverage. Leading import and export merchants protested by forming the Commercial Union Fire Insurance Company, an insurer that would fix rates on a more precise evaluation of risks.

CU soon attracted a large volume of fire business as Britain's cities and industries were growing fast during the 1860s. Within a few years it had opened branches in major cities and appointed agents throughout Britain, as well as one in Hamburg, Germany. At the same time, CU began selling other products, becoming a "composite" insurer. Its first life policies were issued in 1862, and its first marine underwriter was appointed in 1863. Profits from life and marine business helped keep it going when fire claims were high.

With trading connections through their import and export businesses, CU directors were particularly alert to overseas opportunities. By the end of the 1860s the company had agencies in India, South Africa, the Caribbean and other foreign ports used by British merchants. In the United States, CU appointed agents in San Francisco and New York. The company was doing business in Chicago and Boston in 1871 to 1872 when both cities suffered disastrous fires. Unlike some local companies, CU met the resulting claims in full. By the 1880s its U.S. business was providing more than one-third of the company's fire premium income. By the end of the century, CU had expanded in Europe, Canada, and Australia and was drawing three-quarters of its premium income from abroad. The company ranked second only to the British company, Royal Insurance, in total worldwide fire income.

CU Grows Via Takeovers

At the start of the 20th century, CU appointed its first general manager, Evan Roger Owen, then looked to expand by buying existing insurance operations rather than opening new offices. The first strategic takeover came in 1900 when it bought Britain's Palatine Insurance Company of Manchester. Palatine had a strong fire business and had also achieved success in the relatively new field of accident insurance. The Palatine purchase made CU the first British company to handle all four classes of insurance: fire, life, marine, and accident. Acquisition of a half dozen other companies followed. In the United Kingdom, these included specialist accident company Ocean; composite insurer Union Assurance; and the oldest of all British insurance operations, Hand-in-Hand Fire and Life Insurance Society. In the United States, it purchased two companies—Philadelphia-based American and the California Insurance Company. Acquisition of Union Assurance and American were rescue buyouts as a result of the companies' severe losses from the 1906 San Francisco fire. By 1914, CU was the largest of the British composite companies, with a premium income of £7.5 million—almost four times what it had been in 1901. CU's business continued to grow throughout World War I despite disruption in Europe. After the war, in 1919, it lost its top position in the British insurance industry when two of its major rivals Royal and Liverpool & London & Globe merged.

In the postwar period, CU became more dependent on industry trends and economic conditions. The 1921 depression caused the first drop in CU's income since 1908, and the arrival of the Great Depression in 1929 brought a more lasting setback. Management switched from emphasizing expansion to cutting costs. Nevertheless, CU continued to grow, aided by the growth of automobile ownership and a huge new market for accident insurers. CU also continued to make acquisitions. It took over another small composite, British General, in 1926.

Post-World War II Challenges for CU

World War II and its long aftermath of austerity in Britain halted CU's growth in Europe through the 1940s. And the 1950s brought other challenges for the company. Fierce competition was driving rates down at a time when claims were rising and government regulations were imposing new burdens on insurers. As a result, all insurance companies found it more difficult to make profits, especially in the U.S markets. CU responded in 1959 with the friendly takeover of struggling North British and Mercantile Insurance Company, a longstanding U.K. insurer with a large proportion of its business in the United States. The merger boosted CU's assets from £192 million to £319 million. With mergers seen as the way to reduce costs and spread out risk, CU went shopping again in 1968, buying Northern and Employers Assurance. Ranking as the fourth largest U.K. insurer, Northern and Employers had a substantial life business, which complemented CU's comparative weakness in the area. The Northern and Employers acquisition restored CU for a time to the position of top U.K. composite and enabled the company to reduce its workforce. The U.K. staff, after rising to 11,800 in 1968, dropped to 8,400 in 1972, while premium income continued to grow. As a result, profits rose rapidly in the early 1970s.

In 1975, however, the company suffered its first loss in many years, mainly due to underwriting losses in the United States. Conditions were proving difficult for all insurers, partly because of increasing state control of premium rates. Profitability was restored in the following few years by reducing the company's less successful business in the United States. Meanwhile, the United Kingdom had entered the European Economic Community (EEC), and CU moved to strengthen its position in that market. It made two important acquisitions in the early 1970s: the Belgian company Les Provinces Réunies and Dutch composite Delta Lloyd, which operated a strong life business.

In the 1980s, CU further reduced its U.S. business, following bad losses in 1984 to 1985, but made more acquisitions in Continental Europe. Europe now accounted for 30 percent of CU's worldwide premium income. The company's profits reached a new peak of £202 million in 1988, but fell back to £150 million in 1989. In 1990, a new holding company, Commercial Union PLC, was formed to facilitate expansion into financial services activities, including unit trusts and investment management, stockbrokerage, and individual savings accounts. In 1992, CU began operations in Poland, and in 1996 opened offices in South Africa and Vietnam.

General Accident Covers Employers

General Accident (GA) emerged out of the same British industrial fervor as Commercial Union and paralleled its development in many ways. But rather than offering a solution to high fire premiums, GA filled the need for employer liability coverage. With trade unions alarmed about unsafe factory machines and hazardous working conditions, the British government introduced the Employers' Liability Act of 1880. The legislation made employers liable to workers involved in certain on-the-job accidents. In 1885, a group of entrepreneurs in Perth, Scotland, saw the insurance potential of this new legislation and formed General Accident & Employers Liability Assurance Association, Ltd. In return for an annual premium, the group would safeguard employers against any liability arising from employee accidents. Beyond the Perth office, GA assigned representatives to London and to Aberdeen and Edinburgh, Scotland.

The company received a boost in 1887. GA entered into an arrangement with Malcolm's Diary & Time-Table of Glasgow to insure for £100 any passengers killed in railway accidents on the

ance markets, the company was renamed General Accident Fire and Life Assurance Corporation in 1906.

GA Makes Inroads in Auto Coverage

Improvement in British living standards followed World War I, including an increase in automobile ownership. In 1924, Norie-Miller introduced a scheme that boosted GA's auto insurance income dramatically. In collaboration with Morris Motors, GA arranged that each car sold by that company would have free insurance coverage for one year; the premium to be paid by Morris. This plan had a high-claims cost because premiums were not tied to individual risks, but it introduced GA to a large section of the automotive community, and many motorists retained GA for auto and other types of insurance. The resulting business served GA well in the years that followed, especially after the introduction of the Road Traffic Act in 1930, which made third-party motor insurance compulsory for all drivers. By 1937, General Accident had already issued one million auto policies in Britain.

Throughout the 1930s, GA expanded in the United States as well as in Britain. The Potomac Insurance Company of Washington, D.C., GA's U.S. subsidiary, increased the firm's involvement in fire insurance. Other subsidiaries were added after World War II. In the United States, GA formed Pennsylvania General Fire Insurance Association in 1963. In Britain, GA took over The Yorkshire Insurance Company in 1967. A prolonged period of steady growth enabled GA's assets to reach £1 billion in 1975. By the early 1980s assets were over £3 billion and total premium income was more than £1.5 billion. U.S. operations continued to generate one-third of premium income.

During the 1980s, deregulation of the financial services industry led to a blurring of boundaries between insurance brokers and insurance companies in the complex British insurance market. These measures, and the proposed integration of the European Economic Community in 1992, created an opportunity for enormous growth. But competition among insurers also intensified. In response, General Accident committed to a stronger acquisition strategy. By the end of the 1980s, GA had acquired over 500 real estate brokerage agencies to market its home and life insurance.

The real estate business was not initially successful: the depressed British mortgage market during the late 1980s and early 1990s subjected GA to considerable losses. GA also assumed a heavy financial burden when in 1988 it bought out NZI Corporation, a New Zealand-based insurance and banking firm. The company viewed NZI as the platform from which it would launch an expansion into the Pacific market, especially Korea and Taiwan. But the takeover resulted in substantial and embarrassing losses for GA. During the late 1980s, the once-profitable U.S. insurance market also developed problems. Large awards against drivers and regulation of premium rates by many state governments led to severe losses in the auto market. GA's pre-tax losses in Massachusetts grew from US$4.5 million in 1984 to US$13 million in 1986. In 1988, GA withdrew entirely from Massachusetts. Harsh weather conditions worldwide caused massive losses through damage claims in the late 1980s. Life assurance premiums also rose due to the scare caused by acquired immune deficiency syndrome (AIDS).

condition that the victim possessed a copy of a Malcolm's timetable or diary. Malcolm's paid a 1 cent premium to GA for every 25 items sold. This GA insurance innovation was the beginning of a lucrative coupon insurance scheme. And 1887 was also the year that 27-year-old Francis Norie-Miller became chief executive of GA. An insurance innovator with enormous energy, he dominated the management of GA for many years and remained highly influential until retiring as chairman in 1944.

GA quickly pursued new product lines and new markets. In 1896, GA produced its first prospectus for automobile coverage. In 1899, it merged with Scottish General Fire Assurance Corporation and began offering both fire and accident coverage. Norie-Miller established a U.S. office in 1899, and soon after overseas branches in Australia, Canada, South Africa, Belgium, France, and Holland. Because of diversification into new insur-

In 1990, General Accident PLC was formed as the holding company for General Accident Fire and Life Assurance Corporation and new cost-cutting measures and market strategies were implemented. As a result, the company posted the largest profits among U.K. composite insurers in 1993. GA also added to its holdings by acquiring nonstandard auto insurer Sabre, in 1995, followed by life insurer and pension specialist Provident Mutual in 1996, and Canada's General Insurance Group Ltd. in 1997.

CU and GA Merge: 1998

Faced with unrelenting competition and falling premium rates in Europe, Commercial Union and General Accident announced in early 1998 that they would merge, joining in the consolidation trend among insurers. In creating a new company, CGU PLC, the two companies expected to capture greater market share, cut operating costs by 10 percent through job losses and integrating information technology systems. Completed in June, the transaction left CGU with £100 billion (US $165 billion), in assets under management, and a stock market value of £14.8 billion, making it the second largest British insurer behind Prudential. Analysts believed the merger bolstered the life insurance business potential of the new company, and gave it a more powerful presence in Continental Europe and the United States.

The merger indeed marked a shift toward building a stronger life and savings business, including financial and investment management services. CGU management had witnessed the rise in *bancassurance,* a service model for financial institutions that fulfilled both banking and insurance needs. CGU saw opportunity in this area as well, especially with the competition and difficulty in profitable growth from general insurance. At the time of the merger, the CGU business was 60 percent general insurance (auto, fire, and health coverage) and 40 percent life and savings products (life insurance, personal pensions, annuities, units trusts and financial services). A year later, in 1999, life and savings business had grown to over 50 percent of CGU's total business. The company solidified its relationships with French bank partner Société Générale that year, investing £490 to help it deflect a hostile takeover. It also entered into an agreement to buy 50 percent of The Royal Bank of Scotland Life Insurance Company, and entered into a *bancassurance* agreement with banks in Italy and Portugal.

Norwich Union Added to the Fold: 2000

In early 2000, CGU made another headline-grabbing move in line with its new strategy. The company announced plans to merge with giant life group Norwich Union, forming yet another new company, CGNU PLC. Norwich's roots dated back to 1797 when it was founded as a fire insurance company. In 1997, it had de-mutualized and became a public limited company on the London Stock Exchange. With the merger, CGNU became the U.K.'s largest multiline insurer and among the top five insurance companies in Europe. Norwich Union continued to operate its life and pensions, retail fund management, and general insurance businesses under its own name in the United Kingdom.

CGNU continued to reposition itself as a European-based financial services group focused on long-term savings. And following the Norwich merger management began to divest the company of businesses that conflicted with that strategy. It exited general insurance markets in South Africa, Germany, and the United States. White Mountain Insurance Group purchased the U.S. general insurance operations for £1.3 billion (US $1.9 billion) in 2001. Over the next year the company also sold off life businesses in Canada; general insurance businesses in France, Portugal, Belgium, and Brazil; and mortgage indemnity operations in Australia. Meanwhile, it created new *bancassurance* relationships in Spain, Singapore, and Hong Kong.

By the end of 2001, about 50 percent of CGNU's business was in the United Kingdom, and it held major market positions also in France, the Netherlands, Spain, Italy, Ireland, Poland, Turkey, Canada, Singapore, Australia, and New Zealand. Acquisitions and divestitures had significantly realigned CGNU's business mix. Life and savings accounted for 70 percent of its premium income, and 90 percent of that income was generated from its European operations. In 2002, the company changed its name to Aviva.

Principal Subsidiaries

CGNU Corporation (USA); CGNU Life Assurance; CGU Insurance; Commercial Union (Poland); Delta Lloyd (Netherlands); General Accident; Hibernian Group (Ireland); Morley Fund Management; Norwich Union; NZI (New Zealand); Scottish General Insurance Company.

Principal Competitors

Prudential PLC; Royal & Sun Alliance Insurance; Allianz; Legal & General Group; Zurich Financial Services; AXA.

Further Reading

Adams, Christopher, "Comment & Analysis: Not a Commercial Accident," *Financial Times* (London), February 26, 1998, p.17.

Cowell, Alan, "Two Large Insurers in Britain to Merge in $12 Billion Deal," *New York Times,* February 22, 2000, p. C4.

The First Hundred Years, Perth: General Accident, 1985.

Gray, Irvine, *A Business Epic 1835–1935: General Accident, Fire & Life Assurance Co. Ltd,* Perth: General Accident, 1935.

"History," *Aviva PLC,* accessed June 29, 2002, http//:www.aviva.com.

Knight, Alice W., *The Yorkshire Story,* York, 1975.

Liveing, Edward, *A Century of Insurance: The Commercial Union Group of Companies, 1861-1961,* London: Commercial Union, 1961.

Romance of a Business: Forty Years Work 1885–1924, Perth: General Accident, 1924.

Taylor, Roger, "Technological Advance Drives Union of GA and CU," *Financial Times* (London), February 26, 1998, p. 22.

"Two Big British Insurers Agree to Merge in $11.5 Billion Deal," *New York Times,* February 26, 1998, p. D4.

—update: Douglas Cooley

Banco Comercial Português, SA

Praça D. Joao I, 28
4000-295 Porto
Portugal
Telephone: (351) 21-321-1000
Fax: (351) 21-321-1759
Web site: http://www.bcp.pt

Public Company
Incorporated: 1985
Employees: 16,990 (2000)
Total Assets: EUR 62.961 billion (2001)
Stock Exchanges: Lisbon New York
Ticker Symbol: BPC
NAIC: 522110 Commercial Banking; 523920 Portfolio
    Management; 523120 Securities Brokerage; 523110
    Investment Banking and Securities Dealing

Banco Comercial Português, SA (BCP) is Portugal's largest financial institution. In the years since 1985, when it was founded, BCP has risen from a small upstart with a questionable future to the largest and most diverse private bank in Portugal. BCP and its subsidiaries offer a wide variety of services. The bank's major activities include individual and corporate customer fund-taking, credit granting, custody of securities, treasury services, foreign-exchange transactions, and money-market operations. Through the BCP Group's subsidiaries, the company is involved in insurance, asset management, investment and pension fund management, medium- and long-term credit, mortgage loans, corporate finance, company valuations, venture capital financing, brokerage and property management. BCP has risen to its success through a host of strategic acquisitions, successful international ventures as Portugal's growth market slowed, and through the vision of its well-regarded management team. In 2001, *Euromoney* named BCP the Best Bank in Portugal, and their investment arm, BCP Investimento, was named Portugal's Best Debt House and Best Equity House.

A Good Time to Start a Bank: 1980s

One year after Portugal's authorities opened up the country's banking system to private initiative in 1984, a group of 200 investors founded Banco Comercial de Portuguêes. One particularly notable member of the founding team was Americo Ferreira de Amorim. Amorim was one of Portugal's wealthiest and most important businesspeople at the time. Amorim owned and ran Corticeira Amorim, which controlled 35 percent of the world's cork market. He also owned and ran multiple other companies in financial services, real estate, and tourism through his investment company, Amorim Investimentos e Particpacoes. Before Amorim founded BCP, he and 20 other investors founded Banco Português de Investimento.

With Amorim's experience behind them, the founders established and incorporated BCP with an initial share capital of Esc 3.5 billion, and with the knowledge that they had wooed one of the country's leading bankers, Jardim Goncalves, from his high-level position at Banco Português do Atlantico (BPA) to the chairmanship of BCP. Banco Comercial Português promised Goncalves the opportunity to develop his own management team free of the usual familial and shareholder obligations that existed in many Portuguese banks. The extremely productive and active first years of BCP's operation caused the Portuguese banking market to sit up and take notice. From 1986 through 1998, BCP launched a wide variety of banking networks catering to individual retail, small business, private banking, large company, and institutional customers.

In 1987, the company was listed on the Lisbon Stock Exchange and implemented the first of many cross-selling strategies designed to bring BCP lasting success. BCP added the NovaRede network to their offering in 1989, which serviced the needs of middle-income clientele, and simultaneously opened 21 small branches using the latest technology to offer quick over-the-counter banking services. Soon after, BCP's net assets had grown to Esc 375 billion with Esc 244 billion in customer funds. This growth was partly due to BCP's strategy of opening bank branches across the country. State banks did not have the capital to expand and open new branches in order to compete with private banks like BCP. Private banks could fund their expansion from retained earnings and equity issues, while state banks did not have that freedom.

In 1990 their recent successes allowed BCP to announce the acquisition of the majority of the equity in Banco CISF, which became BCP's investment banking arm. After this, BCP

Company Perspectives:

To contribute to the modernisation and development of the Portuguese financial system and economy through the marketing of innovative, personalised financial products and services conceived to satisfy the overall financial needs and expectations of the various market segments, with very high quality and specialisation standards, playing an active role in the domestic consolidation process and in the strategic cross-border partnership trend involving European institutions, while preserving the autonomy of strategic decision and the national identity and vocation, and at the same time exploiting the business opportunities created by the "New Economy."

---

charged full-speed ahead founding banks that would meet the diverse needs of their customers. BCP opened subsidiary banks that gave their customers 24-hour, 365-day-a-year access to their accounts in supermarkets, from cellular phones, from their home telephones, and via the Internet.

Multi-Brand Strategy Pays Off

When BCP was founded, Goncalves introduced a banking technique that became BCP's hallmark: the segmentation of banking services by customer profile. The bank separated its core group of services into six branded segments: individual retail banking, commercial retail banking, private banking, the mass-market branch network, small banking, and telephone banking. After completing an in-depth analysis of each segment, BCP created a full range of products and services to meet all the financial needs that customers using the branded segments would need. The bank then marketed the different banking segments to their customers, each customer fit neatly into one or more of the branded offerings. Care was taken to differentiate between the segments, and BCP was thrilled when the individual brands began to inspire customer loyalty; the bank customers were proud to be a member of whichever banking segment they fit into. BCP's Namorado de Rosa said that the multi-brand strategy allows BCP to "reach out to customers who might be intimidated by one large brand." BCP kept their branded segments separate from each other; the services targeted at individuals and those designed for firms were kept physically separate from each other in the bank buildings as well as in their organized offerings. A manifestation of this was that private customers were served on a different floor of the bank building from commercial customers. This banking strategy aimed and succeeded at giving the customer the impression that they were being served personally, rather than by a large international banking institution.

International Expansion

BCP's philosophy of internationalization had been that the bank would, rather than attempt to move independently into foreign countries, seek out foreign partnerships that enabled them to set up a financial venture with a local face. In 1990, BCP's first international agreement was developed with Cariplo (Italy). In 1991 alliances with two European insurance groups, Friends Provident and Avero Central Beheer, were established. In 1992, BCP was listed on the New York Stock Exchange. Internationali-

zation continued with the 1993 cooperation agreement with Banco Central Hispanoamericano (BCH), which gave BCP access to the Spanish market. Through this agreement, BCH came to own 20 percent of BCP and gained access to Portugal, however BCP insisted on a statute that allowed BCH to vote with only 10 percent of its shares. In this same deal, BCP purchased a 2 percent stake in BCH and 50 percent of the share capital of the private banking subsidiary of BCH, Banco Banif de Gestion Privada. In 1995, BCP inaugurated Banco International de Macambique (BIM) in Mozambique. In 1998, BCP ventured into Poland with the launch of Millennium BIG Bank SA (Banco Millennium) in a joint venture with BIG Bank Gdanski (BBG).

In 2000, BCP also invested in Greece with the launch of NovaBank, and struck a partnership with Spain's Banco Sabadell. The year 2000 also brought an agreement between Achmea NV (a Dutch financial services group) and BCP to merge their insurance operations into Eureko NV. This agreement rose out of an alliance of eight European financial services companies and was designed to allow its members to sell insurance independently in their own markets, but to collaborate internationally. Achmea and BCP would own 72.2 percent and 15.1 percent of the new company, while the remaining alliance members would split the remainder.

BCP's partnership with Sabadell resulted in the launch of ActivoBank in 2001—an Internet bank that offered fund management, stock market trading, and deposit products offered in both Spain and Portugal. BCP also made its way to the United States in 2001, with the opening of four branches in New Jersey.

Acquisitions, Mergers, and Joint Ventures

Acquisition was imperative to BCP's success, and the company set out acquiring and merging soon after their inception. BCP began its tradition of acquisition with Banco CISF. Banco CISF was acquired by BCP in 1990, and was redesigned to become Banco Comercial Português de Investimento (BCP Investimento), BCP's investment banking arm.

In August 1994, BCP announced their first attempt to acquire Banco Português do Atlantico (BPA). BCP offered Esc 132 billion (US $837 million) bid for 40 percent of Banco Português do Atlantico's (BPA's)' equity. At that time, BPA was Portugal's second biggest bank with assets of Esc 3.4 trillion (US $19 billion). A group of BPA's shareholders were not happy with the prospect of BCP's hostile takeover and fought against the bid. Although the Portuguese government had originally intended to remain neutral, in September 1994 they blocked BCP's bid. Many people were suspicious of the government's action, believing that the government was influenced into blocking the bid by a group of companies that held a combined stake of almost 29 percent in BPA. Banco Português do Atlantico reportedly lent heavily to these companies, and they might have feared that BCP would not look as favorably on their businesses as BPA had.

This setback did not slow BCP down, nor did it diminish the bank's intent to acquire BPA. Less than year later, in March 1995, BCP, in a joint offer with Companhia de Seguros Imperio, acquired BPA. This acquisition allowed BCP to take over BPA's spot as the second biggest bank in Portugal.

Key Dates:

1985: A group of investors incorporates Banco Comercial Português (BCP).
1987: BCP lists on the Lisbon Stock Exchange.
1990: BCP acquires a majority equity of Banco CISF.
1992: BCP lists on the New York Stock Exchange.
1993: The company reaches a cooperation agreement with Banco Central Hispanoamericano (BCH).
1995: BCP acquires the majority of Banco Português do Atlantico (BPA), making BCP the second largest bank in Portugal.
1996: The company incorporates ServiBanca.
1998: The company launches Millennium BIG Bank SA (Banco Millennium) in Poland, in a joint venture with BIG Bank Gdanski (BBG).
1999: BCP acquires 30 percent of Achmea Bank's equity and 50 percent of Interbanco.
2000: BCP acquires Banco Pinto & Sotto Mayor (BPSM), Banco Mellow, and Imperio; forms a strategic partnership with Banco Sabadell; and launches NovaBank in Greece.
2001: Euromoney names BCP the Best Bank in Portugal, and their investment arm, BCP Investimento, is named Best Debt House and Best Equity House.
2001: The company partners with Sabadell to launch ActivoBank, an Internet bank, and opens its first branches in the United States in New Jersey.

Additional important BCP acquisitions included, in 1999, the acquisition of 30 percent of Achmea Bank's equity, 50 percent of Interbanco; in 2000, the acquisition of Banco Mello and Imperio, and the extremely important acquisition of Champlimaud's Banco Pinto & Sotto Mayor (BPSM). Following these acquisitions, Carolos Pertejo of J.P. Morgan estimated that BCP had 29 percent of Portuguese bank loans, controlled 37 percent of mutual fund assets and 36 percent of the life insurance market.

An important aspect of BCP's acquisition strategy was the successful merging of the banks they acquired into BCP's business model. BCP's strategy of merging BPA into BCP was a good example of the company's practice of approaching each new acquisition as an individual project. With BPA, BCP decided not to change the bank's name as it had extremely strong brand recognition in Portugal. "The decision has been not to merge the two banks [BCP and BPA] but rather operate them as two different franchises and produce cost synergies," said Salomon Brothers' Lecubarri. BCP reduced BPA's employees by 200 in the first half of 1996, and shifted 400 employees into different areas. The company planned to finish assimilation of BPA by 1997. BCP believed in looking at each acquisition and merger with fresh eyes, and planning the acquisition strategy accordingly.

In 1996, BCP entered into an innovative joint initiative with Jerónimo Martins Group to bring banks to grocery stores. The two companies came together to found expresso!Atlântico—Portugal's first in-store bank. The bank offered customers the

opportunity to access their bank accounts from Jerónimo Martins Group's large chain of food stores. Another joint venture that BCP participated in was with GE Capital, it was a joint venture that involved operational vehicle renting.

Banks, Beautiful Banks

From its inception in 1985, BCP placed importance on the physical appearance of their banks. The bank has paid special attention to both the architecture that they built, restored, and created and to the refurbishment of some of the banks that they acquired. BCP approached the project of constructing bank and headquarter buildings as an opportunity to demonstrate the company's character. The bank strove to create buildings that reflected their modernity, conservatism, innovation, prestige, and ecologic-mindedness.

When BCP began refurbishment of their downtown Lisbon headquarters in 1995, they broke ground on an interesting discovery. They found that there was a succession of landfills and underlying structures stretching down as far as the water table. These findings constituted a repository of the many civilizations that had inhabited Lisbon in the past. The bank undertook preservation of these artifacts, and conceived of a way to preserve the artifacts. BCP created a museum at the rear of its headquarters, called the Rua dos Correeiros Archaeological Centre.

The New Millennium: Trouble Coming?

Although advisors continued to believe BCP was a good bet for investors in Portuguese banking, in 2002 analysts were generally advising against any investment in the Portuguese banking sector. Portuguese banks had been weathering the same plummeting brokerage commissions' problems as global banks were, but they also had their own unique problems to contend with. Gross domestic product (GDP) growth had slowed since mid-2001 and consumer loans had been in a decrease pattern for longer. BCP remained confident throughout this period, and continued to feel secure that the new European unity would work in their favor rather than to their detriment. The bank's rapid international expansion in 2000 and 2001 placed them in a strategic position—with solid standing in Greece and Poland. The biggest risk that BCP took, becoming involved in the European Eureko alliance, had turned out to be the bank's least successful decision. The Eureko performed below BCP's expectations and failed in a EUR 20 million Internet venture. Perhaps as a result, Joao Ramalho Talone, the director responsible for Eureko, left BCP's executive board and was not replaced. Following Talone's departure, three additional executive board members resigned. The BCP executive board shrank to nine members.

The resignation of its board members did nothing to hamper BCP's desire to continue its process of expansion. In February 2002, BCP (along with its main competitor Caixa Geral de Depositos), announced their long-term intention to expand into Spain. BCP acknowledged that it was not yet large enough to plan large-scale activity in Spain, but they were working toward it. In April 2002, BCP reached an agreement with Banco Santander Central Hispono SA for the purchase of Grupo Financiero Bital SA of Mexico. The purchase would expand BCP's capital base.

BCP's need to expand to continue international expansion has lapped over into more areas than its retail banking arm. The bank's Head of Custody Paulo Guia, raised the question of what will happen in the future to BCP's custody operation. He, in 2001, discussed the fact that if BCP hopes to stay in the custody business, "We cannot remain independent for much longer. BCP cannot go it alone in the Euronext countries. The only way that we can retain the clients that we currently have is to enter into a joint venture or merge with a larger provider." In this case, rather than work to expand their base independently, BCP will need to look for a new partner. Although the times seem difficult, BCP has weathered tough times in the past and the stated intent to expand its base, seek out strategic partnerships, and acquire additional companies is nothing new to the dynamic bank.

Principal Subsidiaries

AF Investimentos; Atlantico; BII; BCP Investimento; Credibanco; LeaseFactor; Seguros e Pensoes; Servibanca; SottoMayor.

Principal Competitors

Caixa Geral de Depositos; Banco Totta & Acores; Banco Bilbao Vizcaya Argentaria, SA; Espírito Santo Financial Group SA.

Further Reading

"BCP's Positive Disturbance," *Euromoney*, June 1996, p. 220.

Blum, Patrick, "Energising the Nucleus," *The Banker*, December 1999, pp. 51–53.
"European Banking, It's a Knockout," *The Economist*, August 20, 1994, p. 61.
"Finance and Economics: Beautifying Branches," *The Economist*, March 24, 2001, p. 89.
Humphreys, Gary, "Private Banks Go for Blanket Coverage," *Euromoney*, March 1992, p. 11.
"Iberia: Foes and Friends," *The Banker*, January 1994, p. 24.
Kripalani, Manject, "The King of Cork," *Forbes*, October 26, 1992, p. 230.
McCurry, Patrick, "Portuguese Banks Expand," *Acquisitions Monthly*, February 2002, p. 77.
McGinley, Jo, "No Holiday for Club Med," *Global Investor*, September 2001, pp. 34, 40.
"Portuguese Banking: Dead End," *The Economist*, September 17, 1994, p. 85.
Rutter, James, "Bigger Should Be Better," *Euromoney*, June 1999, pp. 244–252.
Stewart, Jules, "Problems Loom as Loan Growth Slows," *Euromoney*, June 2001, pp. 44–52.
——, "Time for Family Planning," *Euromoney*, June 1997, pp. 143–151.
"Survey: Portugal—Big Fish in Small Ponds," *The Economist*, December 2, 2000, pp. S12–S14.
Unsworth, Edwin, "Eureko Outlines Expansion Plans," *Business Insurance*, July 10, 2000, p. 34.
Warner, Alison, "Spreading Their Wings," *The Banker*, November 1997, pp. 51–54.
——, "Then There Were Three," *The Banker*, November 1996, pp. 58–63.

—Tammy Weisberger

Bank of Ireland

Lower Baggot Street
Dublin 2
Ireland
Telephone: (353) 1 661 5933
Fax: (353) 1 661 5671
Web site: http://www.bankofireland.ie

Public Company
Incorporated: 1783
Employees: 17,356 (2001)
Sales: £4.6 billion (2002)
Stock Exchanges: New York
Ticker Symbol: IRE
NAIC: 522110 Commercial Banking; 523930 Investment
    Advice; 523920 Portfolio Management Companies

The Bank of Ireland is the oldest bank in Ireland. Throughout the turbulent Irish history, the bank has demonstrated remarkable entrepreneurship by taking innovative risks and making them work—from opening a commercial branch in a tiny agricultural community in the 18th century to offering remote offshore banking over the Internet in the 21st century. Their corporate agility and strength has earned them the nickname "the Celtic Tiger" and established them as leaders in the international banking industry and global economy.

A Strong Beginning: 1783–1800

The Bank of Ireland opened for business on June 25, 1783, in Dublin, a day that marked a turning point in the financial history of Ireland. Until that point, banking had been handled by private institutions and individuals. The economy had been unstable and money scarce: a combination that devastated many small banks trying to establish themselves. One bank that survived was David La Touche and Son. The founder's grandson, also David La Touche, was elected the first Governor of the Bank of Ireland. Several members of the wealthy La Touche family were the bank's first clients and opened large accounts. Ireland was under British rule, and La Touche was a member of

the Irish Parliament. His position helped the Bank of Ireland become appointed as the Official Government Bank. It became their duty to handle all funds coming into or going out of the Treasury Department.

Being the Official Government Bank gave the Bank of Ireland an economic edge over its competitors and helped create an image of security. This was important because the public had not forgotten the banking disasters of the earlier decades. The economy was bad and the majority of people were poor. The small group that did have money, mainly landowners, was very protective of their money and skeptical of banks. The promise of security helped attract some of this public sector. Checkbooks were issued from the bank's beginning; and in 1796, the bank issued personal passbooks to customers. Although the bank's main focus was securing larger commercial accounts, the number of private individual accounts was growing.

In 1784, the Bank of Ireland printed and issued its own paper currency in Irish pound and guinea denominations. The British government had decided to allow six Irish banks to issue their own currency under strict government regulations; the six included the Bank of Ireland, the National Bank, the Ulster Bank, the Northern Bank, the Provincial Bank of Ireland, and the Belfast Banking Company. The Bank of Ireland was the first to take advantage of this opportunity. Soon the other banks followed, and there were six different Irish banknotes as well as English currency being circulated in Ireland. By 1800, circulation of the Bank of Ireland's banknotes was £1.7 million (US $2.1 million).

Branching Out and Surviving the Great Potato Famine: 1880s

The bank quickly outgrew its Mary's Abbey location and purchased several small adjoining properties in 1790. It soon outgrew this expansion as well and purchased the Parliament House in College Green in 1803. The Parliament House Building had been vacated when the Irish Parliament was abolished according to the Act of the Union in 1801. This act declared Ireland part of "The United Kingdom of Great Britain." The Irish would no longer have their own Parliament; instead, they

Key Dates:

1783: Bank of Ireland is incorporated and opens at Mary's Abbey in Dublin.

1784: The company prints and issues its own bank notes.

1808: The company purchases the Parliament House as its new headquarters.

1825: The company opens seven branch offices in Ireland.

1922: Bank of Ireland is appointed as the official bank of the Irish Free State.

1926: The company acquires the National Land Bank and renames it National City Bank, Ltd.

1942: The Central Bank Act is passed, and the Bank of Ireland is no longer the official bank of Ireland.

1958: Bank of Ireland acquires the Hibernian Bank, Ltd.

1965: The company acquires Irish interests of National Bank, Ltd. and renames it National Bank of Ireland.

1970: The company opens an office in London.

1996: The company acquires the British building society Bristol & West and New Ireland Assurance, a life insurance company.

2000: The company initiates online banking.

2001: Bank of Ireland introduces Fsharp, an online banking service for customers living and working abroad.

2002: Ireland and the Bank of Ireland convert to the Euro.

would have a member represent them in the English Parliament. The architect Francis Johnson was hired to remodel the building in a manner that would suit banking needs. The result was a very impressive and prestigious headquarters.

Ireland was a country of agriculture. The majority of its people were farmers living in the outskirts and rural areas of the country; and there were no banks in these outlying areas. In 1825, the Bank of Ireland opened seven branch offices for these customers. The new branches, referred to as "agencies," opened in Cork, Waterford, Clonmel, Newry, Belfast, Londonderry, and Westport. Banking was a new approach to money handling for most of these people, and they were apprehensive. But they eventually recognized the value and convenience, and by 1881, the Bank of Ireland had 58 branches in operation.

The 19th century brought disaster to Ireland in the form of the Great Potato Famine (1845–1849). At that time, potatoes were the main, sometimes only, food source for the majority of Irish people. When a potato blight completely destroyed potato crops during those years, the Irish people and the economy suffered enormously. It was estimated that nearly 1 million people died from starvation and disease while another million emigrated in search of a better life. Landowners were left with fields of useless rotting potatoes. Resentment was building toward the English government because while Ireland's people were starving, large amounts of food were being exported untaxed to England. Landowners were left with huge farms they couldn't farm, and farmers did not have the money to buy land. The Encumbered Estates Act in 1849 was created to allow landowners to sell their land even if they did not own it free and clear. This money was collected by the courts and distributed among creditors.

This was an extremely difficult time for banks in Ireland because there was very little money. The Bank of Ireland was fortunate. Because they handled all government financial transactions, they had enough capital to function. The Bank of Ireland made many loans to other banks during the recovery period to help them survive. They also made loans to businesses, including the Dublin Corporation, to help them become reestablished. They could not do much to help the landowners due to a restriction that had been placed on them by the government: they were not allowed to lend money based on the security of land. When this restriction was lifted in 1860, they were in a position to make loans that would help revitalize the agricultural industry. The bank began paying interest on deposits as an incentive. By 1920, their deposit base was at £28 million (US $35.5 million) and loans to customers were £16 million (US $20.3 million).

20thCentury: Enduring the Troubles and Political Change

The beginning of the 20th century was a period of political turbulence. Ireland was still under English rule. Southern Ireland was fighting against both England and Northern Ireland for liberation. Northern Ireland did not want independence from the United Kingdom. The fighting took its toll on the barely recovering Irish economy. The *New York Times* reported a plunge in the Bank of Ireland's stock from 330 to 302 points in just ten days. There was civil unrest and crime. The Bank of Ireland suffered a loss of £4,000 in two branch robberies. The money was never recovered.

In 1922, Ireland split into the Irish Free State and Northern Ireland. The Irish Free State was given dominion status from England. Northern Ireland was still under English rule. The Bank of Ireland loaned the new Irish Free State government £1 million to help the fledgling organization. Soon after, the Bank of Ireland was appointed the official bank of the Irish Free State government. On February 7, 1922, an historical event marked the new Irish independence: Irish guards replaced the British guards who had guarded the Bank of Ireland's Parliament Building for over a century. In 1923, the Land Commission was established for making property loans. This caused the National Land Bank to suffer great financial difficulties since this had been their main business. In 1926, the Bank of Ireland purchased the failing National Land Bank and renamed it the National City Bank, Ltd.

In 1927, the new Irish Parliament, known as the Dail, passed the Currency Act. This act created the Currency Commission of Ireland whose responsibility was to oversee the issue of a new currency in the Irish Free State. The Currency Commission opened their office in the Armoury Building, which was part of the Bank of Ireland's Parliament Building headquarters. In 1928, the six different banknote series that had been circulated, were abandoned in favor of a single series of legal tender notes appearing in seven denominations and known as the Consolidated Banknote Issue. The Currency Commission also issued a new legal tender series for Northern Ireland known as the Belfast Issue. In Northern Ireland, all six of the earlier banknote series were still being circulated, as well as the new Belfast Issue and English currency. These multiple banknotes were confusing. The Bank of Ireland's banknote issue was greatly decreased during this time. This worked in the bank's favor because people began writing more checks in order to avoid the confusion.

In 1937, The Irish Free State became Eire under a new constitution. Eire declared an economic war against England and continued to strive for complete separation. They took a neutral status during World War II and refused to let England use Irish ports. They focused inward on ways to secure their independence and strengthen their government and economy.

In 1942, the Irish Parliament passed the Central Bank Act. According to this new act, the Central Bank of Ireland replaced the Currency Commission. In 1943, the Central Bank became the official bank of the Irish Government replacing the Bank of Ireland. The Central Bank became the only bank that could issue currency in Eire.

Ireland was once again undergoing political changes. In 1948, John A. Costello was elected Eire's prime minister. A new constitution ensued, and on April 18, 1949, Eire declared complete independence from England and became The Republic of Ireland.

End of the 20th Century: Growth and Diversity

No longer the official bank of the Irish government, the Bank of Ireland worked to expand and strengthen their position in the newly formed republic. They began acquiring interests in other banks and enterprises. In 1958, they acquired the Hibernian Bank Ltd. In 1965, they purchased the Irish shares of National Land Bank Ltd. and renamed it the National Bank of Ireland. This was a significant event. Daniel O'Conner established the National Bank in 1835 as a joint-stock venture. The bank's head office was in London, but its banking activities were mainly in Ireland. The majority of the bank's backers were English, and it was one of England's larger banks. This made it difficult to function considering the animosity and division between The Republic of Ireland and England. Since it was officially an English company, the tax on profits went to Britain, even though most of those profits came from transactions in Ireland. When the Bank of Ireland bought the Irish shares, the tax profits went to the Republic of Ireland's Treasury department. The National Commercial Bank of Scotland purchased the British shares.

The Bank of Ireland also focused on globalization. In 1970, the Bank of Ireland opened an office in London soon to be followed by offices throughout the United Kingdom. In 1997, they acquired Bristol & West, a large U.K. building society (equivalent to a savings and loan), and the New Ireland Assurance, one of Ireland's largest life insurance companies. By 2002, the bank operated over 250 retail branches in the Republic of Ireland and the United Kingdom. The Bank of Ireland also had businesses in Australia, Canada, Germany, Japan, and the United States.

In order to handle the rapid growth, the Bank of Ireland went through a radical restructuring and became The Bank of Ireland Group. This group was divided into four major divisions: Asset and Wealth Management, Corporate and Treasury, Retail, and Other.

The Asset and Wealth Management division was also called Bank of Ireland Asset Management (BIAM). It provided fund management services concerning pension funds for large institutions on a global level in the United States, Canada, Japan, Australia, and Germany. They also managed investments and global securities at home and internationally. The Corporate and Treasury division was subdivided into three business units: Treasury, International Financing, and Corporate Banking. The Treasury unit's main function was to manage the group's Irish government securities portfolio, as well as any trading in Irish gilts, foreign exchange, and interest rate markets. They also offered foreign exchange, deposit, loan, and bond services to wholesale, corporate, and financial institutions. The International Finance unit offered international asset financing, provision of structured financial transactions, and loans to multinational companies. The Corporate Banking unit made loans to large corporations on a global level.

The Retail division was subdivided into five units: Branch Banking, Building Society, Business and International Banking, Insurance and Retail Business, and Northern Ireland. Branch Banking provided traditional banking services such as deposits, loans, and checking accounts. The Building Society specialized in mortgages, savings, and investments. Business and International Banking consisted of four subunits: International Banking, Current Asset Financing, Bureau de Change, and International Consultancy. International Banking dealt with international trade and currency. Current Asset Financing provided loans secured by various assets. Bureau de Change offered foreign exchange services in major tourist areas. International Consultancy provided support and training to overseas financial institutions.

The Insurance and Retail Business unit was divided into eight subunits: Life Assurance, General Insurance, Installment Credit Leasing, Credit Cards, Direct Banking, Consumer Lending, E-business and Payments, and Payments and Electronic Banking. Life Assurance offered life and pension products while General Insurance offered a more general range of insurance products. Installment Credit Leasing dealt in industrial banking, installment credit, and commercial mortgages. Credit Cards provided merchant services and issued MasterCards and Visa cards. Direct Banking provided telephone-banking services. Consumer Lending, E-business and Payments, and Payments and Electronic Banking dealt with those specific services. Northern Ireland focused on the banking products and services.

The Other Group division contained five units: BOIe, Security Services, Trust Services, Corporate Finance, and Stockbrokering. BOIe was the e-commerce unit and consisted of six subunits: Business On Line, Clikpay, BOInet Internet Training, Banking 365 Online, Fsharp, and Set Up Online. Business On Line offered online banking for business customers. Clikpay was an online credit-card payment service. BOInet Internet Training taught courses in using the online services. Banking 365 Online offered online banking to retail customers in Great Britain. Fsharp provided online services to customers living and working abroad. Set Up Online was an e-commerce service education provider. The Security Services unit specialized in safekeeping of domestic and international involvements. Trust Services provided management of trust accounts. Corporate Finance advised companies on mergers, takeovers, restructurings, and other financial matters. Stockbrokering provided investment strategies and services to institutional and private investors.

Converting to the Euro: 2002

In January 2002, Ireland saw yet another change in its currency. The long-anticipated switch to the new standard currency known as the Euro became official. The change was made to simplify the European currency system and promote commerce between European countries. The 12-state members that converted to the Euro were Belgium, Germany, Luxembourg, Greece, Spain, France, Ireland, Italy, Finland, Portugal, Austria, and the Netherlands. The Bank of Ireland and its customers were well prepared when the changeover took place.

The success of e-banking and e-commerce made virtual banking a viable way for individuals and businesses to conduct banking. A connection between countries was just a click away. The use of different currency systems made this type of commerce and trade confusing. The Euro implementation was viewed as a major step toward globalization. In order to continue as a strong force in the banking industry, the Bank of Ireland had to keep current on the new technologies and be able to implement them in a manner that would service their individual customers as well as their large corporate accounts, not only in Ireland but throughout the rest of the world as well.

Principal Divisions

Banking 365; Bank of Ireland Asset Management (BIAM); Bank of Ireland (BOI) Treasury; BIAM Ltd.; BOI Commercial Finance Ltd.; BOI Corporate Banking; BOI Credit Card Services; BOIe, Business On Line; BOI Finance; BOI International Services Ltd.; BOI Internet Training; BOI Trust Services; Bristol & West, International Banking; Clikpay; Fsharp; IBI Corporate Finance Ltd.; ICS Building Society; First Rate Bureau de Change; International Finance Services; J&E Davy Holdings Ltd.; Lifetime Assurance Co. Ltd.; New Ireland Assurance Co. PIC.

Principal Competitors

Allied Irish Bank; Anglo Irish Bank; Royal Bank of Scotland.

Further Reading

"Banking in Ireland. Business, Bank Deposits, Loan and Harvests during a Civil War," *New York Times*, February 25, 1921, p. 24.

Blanden, Michael, "Celtic Tiger on the Prowl," *The Banker*, February 1995, p. 35.

"Building Societies in Turmoil," *The Banker*, May 1996, p. 10.

"The Central Bank," *Central Bank of Ireland*, accessed March 15, 2002, http://www.centralbank.ie.

"Chapter 9: Bank of Ireland," *Tithe an Oireachtas*, accessed April 3, 2002, http://www.irigov.ie.

"Debate on the Treaty between Great Britain and Ireland, signed in London on the 6th December 1921:Sessions 14 December 1921 to 10 January 1922," *CELT*, accessed April 6, 2002, http://imbolc.ucc.ie.

Dougherty, Joseph, "Central Bank of Ireland," *New York University School of Law* Web site, accessed March 15, 2002, http://www.law.nyu.edu.

"Due to Fear of Home Rule," *New York Times*, September 20, 1906, p.1.

"Encumbered Estates Act 1849," *Public Record Office of Nothern Irleand*, accessed April 4, 2002, http://proni.nics.gov.uk.

"The Great Famine in Ireland, 1845–1849," *Ireland*, accessed April 6, 2002, http://www.ireland-information.com.

"Ireland," *Irish Paper Money*, accessed March 28, 2002, http://irishpapermoney.com.

"Irish Dail Meets Today for Budget," *New York Times*, February 28, 1922, p. 2.

"Irish State Gets Loan of 1,000,000," *New York Times*, January 19, 1922, p. 17.

"The National Bank Ltd.," *The Royal Bank of Scotland*, accessed April 8, 2002, http://www.royalbankscot.co.uk.

"National Bank of Ireland Limited," *Debates of the Houses of Oireachtas*, accessed April 6,2002, http://www.oireachtas-debates.gov.ie.

"Welcome to Bristol & West," *Bristol & West*, accessed April 10, 2002, http://www.bristol-west.co.uk.

—Peggi Swan Skjelset

Barilla G. e R. Fratelli S.p.A.

Via Mantova 166
Parma, I-43100
Italy
Telephone: (39) 0521-2621
Fax: (39) 0521-270-621
Web site: http://www.barilla.com

Private Company
Founded: 1877
Employees: 7,033 (2001)
Sales: Euro 2.2 billion ($1.92 billion) (2001)
NAIC: 311823 Dry Pasta Manufacturing; 311812
Commercial Bakeries; 311821 Cookie and Cracker
Manufacturing; 422490 Other Grocery and Related
Products Wholesalers; 422410 General Line Grocery
Wholesalers; 551112 Offices of Other Holding
Companies

One of the world's largest food marketers, Barilla G. e R. Fratelli S.p.A. is a holding company that produces pasta, sauces, and packaged baked goods (including cookies, cakes, snacks, wafers, biscuits, and crisp breads) under the brand names Barilla, Mulino Bianco, Pavesi, Voiello, Wasa, Misko, and Filiz. The company is the world's largest pasta producer, holding leading shares of the world's top two pasta markets, Italy (35 percent) and the United States (13 percent). Barilla sells its products in about 100 countries, running 25 plants and marketing operations throughout Europe, and in the United States, South America, Australia, and Mexico. Family-owned throughout most of its long history, Barilla is 85 percent-owned by fourth-generation Barilla brothers, Paulo, Luca, and Guido.

Company Origins and Development

Barilla was founded in 1877 by Pietro Barilla as a bakery and pasta shop in Parma, a northern Italian city famed for its pasta and cheese. The company specialized in egg pasta, as opposed to flour and water (glutinous) pasta. In an attempt to increase his income, the patriarch nominally handed over his original shop to his wife and launched a second outlet in 1891. Within just three years, however, he was forced to declare bankruptcy and sell both operations. Barilla made a new start soon thereafter but didn't achieve consistent profitability until 1898, when he added extruded pasta to his small line of hand-made noodles and fresh-baked breads.

Production grew exponentially in the late 1800s and early 1900s, fueled by a combination of ever-increasing mechanization and customer-winning quality. Pietro's sons Riccardo and Gualtiero succeeded the founder in 1905. Riccardo oversaw the day-to-day operations of the factory, while Gualtiero focused on sales and promotion. In 1910, they built a new pasta factory closer to railroad and warehouse facilities and installed the region's first continuous bread-baking oven. The Barilla brothers launched the company's first trademark, featuring a "bakery boy" cracking a giant egg into a cart of flour, in 1910. This graphic representation symbolized the simple, yet high-quality ingredients used in Barilla's products.

In these early years Barilla pastas were sold in Parma through company stores and in other cities under exclusive contracts with grocers. Since all the pasta was sold in bulk, these outlets promoted the brand via in-store posters and displays. Barilla's frequent participation in international trade fairs won it awards for quality and wider recognition. By the early 1920s, Barilla pasta was exported (albeit in extremely limited quantities) to France and the United States.

After both Pietro and Gualtiero died in the 1910s, Riccardo's wife Virginia played an important role in the management of the business. Riccardo has been praised for his emphasis on capital investment of profits in plant, process, and promotion. During World War I, G. & R. Barilla Company supported its enlisted employees with care packages. The firm was buoyed in the early 1920s by Italy's strong economy, employing 300 in its pasta plant alone by mid-decade. In 1926, Barilla launched a new trademark featuring a "winged chef" carrying a plate of pasta.

Despite the challenges of the Great Depression—including a call for the outlaw of pasta because it was too fattening—Barilla managed to progress on several fronts. Riccardo's son Pietro, who joined Barilla as head of sales in 1936, was the chief architect of these changes. He exchanged the company's traditional horse-drawn carts for bright yellow Fiat autos and launched Barilla's first full-fledged advertising campaigns. His "Bonaventura" trading card promotion coordinated newspaper, point-of-sale, radio, and outdoor media and gradually began to broaden the brand's customer base to include much of Northern Italy. However, as Pietro confided to a friend in 1938, he would not be satisfied with part of Italy—he wanted to make Barilla the country's top brand of pasta. Unfortunately, his plan to achieve that goal was interrupted by World War II.

World War II Brings Corporate Crisis

Barilla's mid-century degeneration began when Pietro was drafted into military service in 1939. Wartime rationing and a government-controlled distribution system that funneled much of the company's production to the army eroded the consumer market Barilla had so carefully nurtured in the interwar period. Parma suffered a devastating air raid near the end of the war, and the Barilla plant in particular was sabotaged and fell into disarray. In 1943, the company lost L14 million, and in 1947 Riccardo, who had struggled with poor health throughout the war years, passed away.

Though they were discouraged by the events of the war and the soaring unemployment and inflation left in its wake, Pietro and his brother Gianni resolved to revive their birthright. Led primarily by Pietro, the company shed certain elements of its business and developed a strategy that focused on the consumer pasta market. After the government ended its rationing policy in 1947, Barilla exited its military contracts. During the latter years of the decade, the company sold its bulk retail outlets and divested the breadmaking facilities.

Barilla's postwar plan coalesced in the early 1950s, just as the Italian economy began to gear up for the "Economic Miracle" of the 1960s. During this period, the Italian economy was transformed from one of Europe's weakest, most agrarian economies to an industrial and consumer powerhouse. Over the course of the 1950s, Barilla became a shining example of this trend. In 1952, Pietro Barilla traveled to New York to observe packaging, advertising, production, and distribution methods used in the world's largest consumer-driven economy. He returned home resolved to build Barilla into Italy's premier pasta brand.

He accomplished this through heavy investments in advertising. Well-known graphic designer Erberto Carboni was charged with creating Barilla's new image, encompassing everything from the corporate logo to delivery vehicles, packaging, and advertising campaigns. His new trademark, a stylized egg lying on its side with the Barilla name in the yolk, would continue to be used (with revisions) throughout the next four decades. Carboni also made the now-famous "Barilla blue" background the standard for all packaging. His first tagline, "It's always Sunday with Barilla," won a national advertising prize. Having captured the leading share of the egg segment of the Italian pasta industry in the early 1950s, Barilla's new strategy moved it ahead of Buitoni to lead the flour-and-water sector as well by the end of the decade.

Having established its dominance of the pasta market, Barilla rediversified in the 1960s. However, instead of making fresh bread, the company capitalized on its existing production and distribution network by adding such nonperishables as breadsticks, cake mixes, sauces, and pizza.

National Economic Woes Trigger Early 1970s Sell-Off

This prosperous period came to a halt in the late 1960s, when rampant inflation compelled governmental price freezes on many staples, including pasta. After nearly 100 years under family control, Gianni Barilla decided that he wanted to sell his share of the business. Unable to buy his sibling's stake, then 61-year-old Pietro Barilla sold the family business to America's W.R. Grace & Co. in 1971 for more than US$70 million.

With pasta prices and profits locked in by federal fiat, Grace turned to new products for growth. Mid-decade the new parent introduced Mulino Bianco ("White Mill"), a premium line of breadsticks, cookies, cakes, biscuits, and bread. Grace supported the new brand with a highly successful promotional campaign that encompassed premiums ranging from tableware to toys. Nevertheless, as the Italian economy continued its tailspin in the 1970s, Barilla's new parent grew disenchanted with its foray into food. After owning the struggling pasta maker for eight years, Grace sold it back to Pietro Barilla for US$65 million. Pietro had financial help from Bührle, a Swiss company that continued to own 49 percent of Barilla into the mid-1990s.

Pietro Barilla maintained support of the Mulino Bianco division in the ensuing years. In fact, Barilla relaunched the brand in 1983, increasing the brand's annual sales from US$222 million to US$740 million by 1989. By 1987, Mulino Bianco contributed 50 percent of Barilla's total annual sales and had captured five percent of the European baked goods market. By that time, the brand enjoyed a 26 percent share of Italy's baked goods market.

The return of family management—not to mention the repeal of fixed pasta prices in 1978—revived Barilla's growth. Sales increased from US$288 million in 1979 to almost US$1 billion by 1986. Pietro Barilla also renewed the company's emphasis on marketing after retaking control. In 1984, he hired filmmaker Federico Fellini to direct "one of Barilla Pasta's most famous campaigns." Called "High Society," the ad portrayed pasta not as a mundane dish, but as a sexily simple entree. Advertisements featuring such diverse international celebrities as Paul Newman, Gerard Depardieu, and Cindy Crawford helped make Barilla one of the best-known brands in Italy by the early 1990s.

Challenges in the Mid-1990s

After guiding Barilla for a "second term" of 14 years, octogenarian Pietro Barilla died in 1993. His sons Guido, Luca,

Key Dates:

1877: Pietro Barilla opens a bread-and-pasta shop in Parma.
1910: Barilla opens its first factory and introduces its first trademark logo.
1936: Production ramps up on the eve of World War II.
1947: With the war over, Barilla moves to expand beyond Parma with a network of trucks throughout Italy.
1960: Barilla's employee count reaches 1,500.
1971: U.S-based multinational company W.R. Grace buys the majority holding of the Barilla family's shares.
1975: The Mulino Bianco product line is created.
1979: The Barilla family reacquires controlling interest in the company.
1987: Mulino Bianco accounts for 50 percent of Barilla's total sales and enjoys a 26 percent share of Italy's baked goods market.
1998: Barilla opens its first plant in the United States, in Ames, Iowa.
2001: Barilla reorganizes into two main business units, with one focusing on pasta and sauces, and the other on baked goods.

and Paolo took charge as chairman and joint vice-chairmen, respectively. Competition from private labels and cheaper brands combined with the relative inexperience of the new management troika to bruise Barilla's bottom line. By 1996, inexpensive own-label pastas had captured 15 percent of the Italian pasta market and 12 percent of cookies and baked goods. Barilla's revenues flattened at about US$2 billion, and its profits were halved from $73 million in 1993 to $37.5 million in 1995. The company was forced to close three plants, furlough 1,000 employees, and trim prices by 10 percent.

In 1995, the executive committee asked 66-year-old former Procter & Gamble Co. CEO Edwin L. Artzt to come out of his scant two-month retirement to help Barilla out of its tailspin. Artzt had held the top spot at Procter & Gamble from 1990 to 1995 and had led its battle against no-name brands. His turn-around scheme included several strategies that he had applied at Procter & Gamble, including Everyday Low Prices (EDLP) and an intensified global push. Under his guidance, Barilla cut the prices of products accounting for 70 percent of total sales by an average of 12 percent. He also encouraged more hard-edged advertisements focusing on Barilla's superior quality. The company expected to maintain its traditional high quality by investing US$26 million in a pasta research and development facility.

Another aspect of the strategy was an increased emphasis on global expansion to increase Barilla's proportion of international sales from less than 10 percent in 1994 to 50 percent by 2000. It targeted Asia, Latin America, and especially the United States, which had surpassed Italy as the world's largest pasta consumer in 1990. Although the company only had $10 million in United States pasta sales by 1995, it had captured .6 percent of that nation's pasta market after only one year of limited distribution.

Barilla also began a unique project in the Middle East, revealing a socially conscious aspect to its business. In 1997,

one of Barilla's subsidiaries, Barilla Alimentare S.p.A., established a cooperative business venture with Egypt, Jordan, the Palestinian Authority, and Israel's Peres Center for Peace. As Alessandra Sulzer describes in the July 2001 issue of *Harvard International Review*, "This venture will create a new strain of wheat that will be used to make pasta for local consumption and export, providing employment and technology to local producers and fostering links between Israel and Arab states."

Late 1990s and Beyond: Growth and Success Overseas

Although Barilla faced several formidable competitive challenges in the mid-1990s, the company had faced far greater hazards over the course of its long history. With the benefit of a young, well-educated management team and sound strategies, Barilla regained consistent, strong profit growth. By the decade's end, Barilla's expansion efforts established the company in several new countries, including the United States, Japan, Australia, Brazil, Mexico, Turkey, France, Austria, Germany, Sweden, Switzerland, Britain, and Greece. In 1999, Barilla's share of the U.S. market had grown to nine percent, with Barilla-brand products available in about 90 percent of U.S. grocery outlets. And by 2000, the company's U.S. market share continued to steadily climb to 11 percent. By the close of 2000, 60 percent of total sales for the company came from nonpasta products, while pasta accounted for 35 percent of sales.

The year 2001 was an exciting year for Barilla. The company had captured about 22 percent of the world pasta market. It also became the market leader in branded pasta sales in the United States, capturing 13 percent of the market. The company's net debt was cut down more than half, profits went up 16 percent, and overall overseas sales increased 10 percent. This was also the year for a major reorganization, whereby the company evolved into two main business units: one would focus on pasta and sauces, while the other would handle baked goods. Barilla bought Italian ice-cream maker Sanson, shed its cold meats subsidiary, Parmamec, announced plans to launch a series of fast-food operations throughout the world, and bought Kraft Foods' Mexican pasta business.

Barilla moved to boost its brand appeal and continued to establish itself abroad. In early 2002, the company struck a deal with Hollywood's DreamWorks studios to use the popular computer-animated character Shrek to help sell its Mulino Bianco products. By mid-year, the company bought Germany's largest baking group, Kamps AG. Barilla's U.S. market share already grew to 15 percent. With its savvy, Italy-based management and new investments abroad, Barilla appeared to be well on its way to many more successive years of steady growth and profits throughout the world.

Principal Subsidiaries

Barilla Alimentare S.p.A.; Barilla Dolciaria S.p.A.; Barilla Alimentare Dolciaria S.p.A.; Giovanni Voiello Antico Pastificio S.p.A.; Barilla Alimentare Sud S.r.l.; Molino e Pastificio F.lli Quinto e Manfredi S.p.A.; Barilla Alimentare Mediterranea S.p.A.; Forneria Meridionale S.p.A.; Forneria Lucana S.p.A.; Unione Laboratori S.r.l.; Barilla Dolciaria Industriale S.r.l.; Forneria Padana S.r.l.; Pavesi Societa per

Azioni; Panifici Italiani S.p.A.; Panem S.r.l.; Barilla Diversificazione S.p.A.; Nuova Forneria Adriatica S.p.A.; Barilla Servizi Finanziari S.p.A.; CO.RI.AL; Barilla France Sarl; Moulin Blanc Sarl (France); Barilla Deutschland GmbH; Misko AE (Greece); Banta EPE (Greece); Barilla International N.V. (Netherlands); Barilla Espana S.A.; Barilla America Inc. (United States); Barilla Luxembourg S.A. Holding (Luxembourg); Italest S.R.l. (63%); Polinvest Societé Anonyme (France) (56.15%); Barilla Suisse S.A.; Kamps AG.; Panificio S. Antonio Biagio Lecce S.p.A. (30%); Pragma S.r.l. (30%); Pragma 2 S.r.l. (30%); Pragma 3 S.r.l. (30%); Consorzio Politecnico Agroalimentare (33.33%); Filiz Gida Food Industry (Turkey) (35%); Daputa Sp.Zo.o (Poland) (30%).

Principal Competitors

American Italian Pasta; De Cecco; Goodman Fielder; Nestlé; New World Pasta; Spigadoro; Maple Leaf Foods.

Further Reading

Bannon, Lisa, "Italians Do Eat Oodles of Noodles, but Trend Is Limp," *Wall Street Journal,* May 10, 1994, pp. A1, A11.

Barone, Amy, and Laurel Wentz, "Artzt Steering Barilla into EDLP Strategy," *Advertising Age,* February 26, 1996, p. 10.

——, "Barilla Spends 10 Years Cooking Up Pasta," *Advertising Age,* January 13, 1997, p. 21.

"Barilla Changes Management Structure Again," *La Repubblica,* January 30, 2001, p. 32.

"Barilla Has Sold 100% of Parmamec," *La Repubblica,* April 10, 2001, p. 42.

"Barilla to Launch 'Fast-Pasta' Chain," *Il Sole 24 Ore,* November 8, 2001, p. 18.

"Barilla Looks for Growth Abroad," *Eurofood,* March 14, 2002, p. 8.

"Barilla Profits Grow 40%," *Eurofood,* May 11, 2001, p. 11.

"Barilla's Relaunch Spurs Grocery Sales," *Retail World,* April 6–12, 1998, p. 16.

Bentley, Stephanie, "Former Kraft Chief Quits Barilla Post After a Week," *Marketing Week,* October 4, 1996, p. 10.

Devine, Nora, "Kraft Foods Sells Mexican Pasta Business to Barilla," *Dow Jones News Service,* December 18, 2001.

Fabiana, Giacomotti, "Mulino Bianco Ads Reconstruct Italy," *Adweek,* October 24, 1994, p. 16.

Ganapini, Albino Ivardi, and Giancarlo Gonizzi, eds., *Barilla: A Hundred Years of Advertising and Corporate Communications,* Parma, Italy: Archivio Storico Barilla, 1994.

Giacomotti, Fabiana, "Milan: Y&R Cooks up Pasta Advertisements," *ADWEEK Eastern Edition,* January 16, 1995, p. 39.

Irvine, Steven, and Jules Stewart, "Selling the Family Silver," *Euromoney,* January 1996, p. 57.

Javetski, Bill, Gail Edmondson, and William Echikson, "Believing in Europe," *Business Week,* October 7, 1996, p. 22.

Johnson, Millard, "Iowa: Pasta and Steel," *Plants, Sites and Parks,* October/November 1998, pp. 138–39.

Lyman, Eric J., "Barilla Cooks Up First Global Ads: Italian Pasta Manufacturer Launches Worldwide Marketing Campaign," *Euromarketing Via E-Mail,* July 6, 2001.

——, "Hollywood Characters to Front Barilla's Global Ads: Barilla Group Signs Character Licensing Deals with DreamWorks," *Euromarketing Via E-Mail,* February 8, 2002.

Masera, Anna, "Barilla Puts Newman into Santa Claus Suit," *Advertising Age,* November 11, 1991, p. 39.

McCarter, Michelle, "Italian Loss May Mean Gain for Y&R," *Advertising Age,* November 27, 1989, p. 108.

Ono, Umiko, "U.S. Market for Pasta Is Bubbling with Italian Makers' Campaigns," *Wall Street Journal,* April 23, 1996, p. B7.

"Pasta, Present and Future," *Euromoney,* January 1996, pp. 64–66.

"Pile-Up at Spaghetti Junction," *The Economist,* December 3, 1994, p. 78.

Pouschine, Tatiana, "Mangia, Mangia," *Forbes,* November 20, 1987, p. 232.

Reeves, Scott, "Offerings in the Offing: No Fireworks, Just Pasta," *Barron's,* October 6, 1997, p. 39.

Reich, Ingo, and Axel Granzow, "Companies: Barilla to Acquire Germany's Kamps with Higher Offer," *The Wall Street Journal Europe,* April 24, 2002, p. A5.

Sansoni, Silvia, and Zachary Schiller, "Is That Ed Artzt Pushing Pasta?" *Business Week,* April 15, 1996, p. 102.

"Santista and Barilla End Association," *Gazeta Mercantil Online,* February 13, 1998, http://www.gazetamercantil.com.

Sulzer, Alessandra, "The Business of Cooperation: Peace and Profit through Joint Ventures," *Harvard International Review,* July 1, 2001, pp. 34–36.

Tagliabue, John, "Family Business (Extended): In Italy, New Generation of Leaders Looks Abroad," *Wall Street Journal,* November 7, 1995, pp. D1, D6.

——, "International Business: To Avoid Tariffs, Pasta Makers Come to U.S.," *The New York Times,* March 5, 1998, p. D4.

Tassi, Roberto, and Giorgio Soavi, "The Barilla Collection," *FMR: The Magazine of Franco Maria Ricci,* April 1993, p. 6.

Thompson, Stephanie, "Barilla Links Redesign to Ad Imagery," *Brandweek,* January 5, 1998.

Turcsik, Richard, "Barilla Sauces It Up in U.S. Market," *Brand Marketing,* February 1999, p. 10.

Wellman, David, "Westward Ho!" *Food & Beverage Marketing,* January 1996, p. 33.

—April Dougal Gasbarre
—update: Heidi Wrightsman

The Baseball Club of Seattle, LP

Safeco Field
1250 First Avenue South
Seattle, Washington 98134
U.S.A.
Telephone: (206) 346-4000
Fax: (206) 346-4100
Web site: http://www.seattlemariners.com

Private Company
Incorporated: 1976
Employees: 1,500
Sales: $202 million (2001)
NAIC: 711211 Sports Teams and Clubs

The Baseball Club of Seattle, LP, has become one of the most profitable franchises in Major League Baseball. Created in 1976 out of the ashes of the 1969 Seattle Pilots, who lasted one season, the Seattle Mariners in 2001 set a host of Major League records and tied the record for most wins in a season with a record of 116–46.

The Early Years: 1970s

When Seattle was awarded a baseball franchise in 1976, an investor group made up of Stanley Golub, Danny Kaye, Walter Schoenfeld, Lester Smith, James Stillwell, and James Walsh financed the team for $6.5 million. Dick Vertlieb was named the club's first executive director, and Lou Gorman became director of baseball operations. The Seattle Mariners played their first game on April 6, 1977. The team's inaugural game was played in Seattle's Kingdome—the American League's first domed-stadium—against the California Angels, before a crowd of 57,762. A possible harbinger of things to come, the team lost that first outing, 7-0, and went on to finish the season with a disappointing 64–98 record.

The young Seattle Mariners continued to struggle under manager Darrell Johnson, finishing seventh in the A.L. West in 1978 with a 56–104 record—which still stands as the team's worst season record. Lou Gorman was promoted to general manager in May 1978 and Dan O'Brien became president and chief executive officer the following January.

The Mariners hosted the Major League Baseball All-Star game in 1979 with only one Mariner, Bruce Bochte, making the All-Star team. Unfortunately, the excitement surrounding the All-Star game did little to polish the Mariners' season performance, as they closed the year with another disappointing record of 67–95.

Getting into the Swing of Things

The Mariners made their first managerial change in 1980 when Maury Wills replaced Darrell Johnson on August 4. The shake-up did not improve the team's fortunes and they ended the season with a 59–103 record. Perhaps more disappointingly, the team failed for a third straight season to draw 1 million fans to the Kingdome.

Ownership changed hands in 1981 when George Argyros purchased a majority interest in the club for $10.2 million in a sale approved by the League on January 29. Argyros would pay an additional $2.9 million in 1983 to become full owner. During his tenure as owner, he threatened several times to move the team to another city. He eventually forced a renegotiation of the team's lease on the Kingdome Stadium that dropped the annual cost from $3.5 million to $1.2 million, with two-years' worth of free rent between 1985 and 1987.

Maury Wills' reign as manager proved to be short-lived as he was replaced 24 games into the 1981 season by Rene Lachemann. The season was marred by a strike and the team finished the first half with a record of 21–36 and the second half at 23–29. Average attendance for the season was 14,000 in a facility that held more than 60,000.

The team achieved its first significant milestone in 1982 when veteran pitcher Gaylord Perry triumphed 7-3 over the New York Yankees to become just the 15th pitcher in baseball history to win 300 career games. Perry had been brought aboard in an attempt to boost attendance, and it worked. A crowd of 27,369 watched him win the historic game on May 6. Perry would go on to become the first Mariner to grace the cover of

Key Dates:

1976: The city of Seattle is awarded a new Major League Baseball franchise.

1977: The Seattle Mariners play their first game.

1981: The team is sold to George Argyros for $13 million.

1982: Veteran Gaylord Perry becomes the 15th pitcher in baseball history to win 300 career games; and the Mariners finish in fourth place in the A.L. West.

1990: Jeff Smulyan buys the team for $77.5 million.

1992: The team is sold for $125 million and The Baseball Club of Seattle, LP is incorporated.

1993: Lou Piniella is hired as team manager.

1995: The team wins its division for the first time.

1997: The Mariners win a second division title.

1999: The Mariners move into their new ballpark at Safeco Field.

2001: The team wins its third division title and ties the all-time record for most wins in a single season; and the All-Star game plays in Seattle with eight Mariners named to the team.

Sports Illustrated on its May 17, 1982, issue. In July 1991, Perry was the first one-time Mariner to be elected into the Baseball Hall of Fame in Cooperstown, New York.

That would not be the only highlight for the Mariners in 1982, as the team approached the .500 winning mark for the first time, finishing in fourth place in the A.L. West with a 78–84 record. A key force for the Mariners that year was pitcher Floyd Bannister, who led the American League in strikeouts and became the first Mariner to lead the League in a major category.

On June 25, 1983, in what would become known as the "Saturday Massacre," a plethora of unpopular team changes angered fans. First, manager Rene Lachemann was replaced with Del Crandall. Then, popular second baseman Julio Cruz was traded to the Chicago White Sox, and Gaylord Perry and starting shortstop Todd Cruz were let go. In response, attendance continued its downward spiral, with attendance averaging barely 10,000 fans per game. The team ended the year with a 60–102 record, a notable retreat from the previous year's flirtation with the .500 mark. In October, Hal Keller was promoted from director of Player Development to vice-president of Baseball Operations and general manager, while Chuck Armstrong was named president, a title he would retain until 1989.

The First Mariner Star

In 1984, Seattle's first genuine star arrived in the form of first baseman Alvin Davis, who would go on to play in the All-Star game and be voted 1984 Rookie of the Year. Also that season, first-year pitcher Mark Langston led the American League in strikeouts with 204 and posted a final record of 17–10 with a 3.40 ERA. The duo gave fans hope that the Mariners could finally build a successful franchise around a solid foundation, but the team finished in fifth place with a 74–88 record.

Attendance levels remained low at 870,372 for the year, but 1984 would be the last year that Mariners' attendance numbers dipped below one million. In September 1984, the Mariners changed managers and brought Chuck Cottier aboard for the 1985 season. The team finished 1985 with another 74–88 record. Phil Bradley led the club with a .300 batting average and made the All-Star team. Dick Balderson was named vice-president of Baseball Operations after the close of the season.

The team greeted another challenging year in 1986. Management changes persisted with the replacement of Cottier, the lightning-quick hiring and firing of Marty Martinez, the hiring of Dick Williams, and the team's dead-last finish in the A.L. West with a dismal record of 67–95.

Finishing last in 1986 became an advantage for the team when they were awarded first pick in the baseball draft. For their first pick, the Mariners chose 17-year-old Ken Griffey, Jr., who entered Seattle's Minor League system. During the 1987 season, the Mariners reached a high point with a club-record 78 wins and with pitcher Mark Langston and infielder Harold Reynolds playing in the All-Star game. The year would be important in another way, too, as Minor League third baseman Edgar Martinez stepped up to the Majors in September. Martinez made his mark with five doubles and a seven-game hitting streak that month, batting .372. Both Griffey and Martinez would go on to become Mariners superstars.

While the Mariners dropped to the bottom of the A.L. West again in 1988, another future Mariner luminary came to Seattle via the New York Yankees: slugger Jay Buhner. Buhner's addition to the team continued the trend of building for the future. Another manager change took place in June when Jim Snyder took the reins from Dick Williams. The following month, Woody Woodward stepped in as vice-president of Baseball Operations.

Rookie Griffey Hits the Ground Running

Opening day 1989 saw Ken Griffey, Jr., on the roster in center field, having impressed new manager Jim Lefebvre during spring training. No one could know it that day, but a new era in Mariners baseball had begun. Junior, as he was quickly dubbed, reached second base in his first Major League plate appearance, and a week later, in the Mariners' home opener at the Kingdome, hit a home run off the first pitch thrown to him at his new ballpark. The 19-year-old player was well on his way to Rookie-of-the-Year honors when a broken bone in his left hand sidelined him for six weeks. In the end, the award would not be his. Although the Mariners won 16 of 25 games without Junior, it wasn't enough to earn them their first winning season.

Another sea change came for the Mariners on May 25, 1989, when the team traded ace Mark Langston to the Montreal Expos for three players—one of which was 6'10" pitcher Randy Johnson. Quickly nicknamed "The Big Unit," Johnson would go on to become one of modern-day baseball's most dominant pitchers.

In October 1989, Mariners ownership changed hands again when radio mogul Jeff Smulyan purchased the team for $77.5 million. Smulyan assumed the role of chairman, and Gary Kaseff was named president. After Smulyan's first year, rumors began to circulate that he wanted to move the team to a different city.

The Early 1990s

Randy Johnson brought the franchise its first no-hitter on June 2, 1990, and went on to win 14 games over the course of the season. Junior made the All-Star team for the first time, hitting .300 for the season, and logging 22 home runs and 80 runs batted in. Junior also helped make baseball history on August 31, when he and his father—former Cincinnati Reds outfielder Ken Griffey, Sr., who was signed to the Mariners on August 29—became the first father and son to play in a game together on the same Major League team. Seattle would finish the season with a 77–85 record.

It was a modest margin, but the Mariners had a winning season in 1991 with an 83–79 record. Junior brought home the club's first Silver Slugger Award and was named to his second All-Star team. Despite posting a winning record, Lefebvre was fired at the end of the season and replaced by Bill Plummer.

In 1992, Edgar Martinez joined Most Valuable Player Ken Griffey, Jr., on the All-Star roster, earned a Silver Slugger Award, and brought Seattle its first batting crown. Fan-favorite Martinez ended the season with a .343 average. Unfortunately, under Plummer's tutelage, the team fell well under .500, ending the season at 64–98.

One distraction during the 1992 season was continuing volatility in team ownership. For the fourth time in their 16-year history, the Mariners changed ownership hands. On the brink of leaving the Northwest under Smulyan's ownership, the Mariners received an offer from Japanese Nintendo CEO Hiroshi Yamauchi to contribute $75 million toward the purchase of the team as a gift to Seattle, corporate home of Nintendo of America. Controversy ensued when some baseball traditionalists raised their voices against what they saw as selling out America's pastime to the Japanese. Major League Baseball ultimately agreed to a 60 percent acquisition by Yamauchi, with the condition that he limit his voting interest to 49 percent. Local investors contributed the remaining 51 percent of the $125 million total sale price. Yamauchi would do Seattle another enormous favor five years later, when he suggested the club pursue Japanese baseball superstar Ichiro Suzuki.

In 1992, under the restrictions set forth by Major League Baseball, The Baseball Club of Seattle, LP, assumed control of the Mariners. Chuck Armstrong returned as president and chief operating officer, while the board of directors included John Ellis (chairman), Minoru Arakawa (son-in-law, president of Nintendo, and representative of Hiroshi Yamauchi, whose reluctance to fly has kept him from attending a single Mariners game), Chris Larson, Howard Lincoln, John McCaw, Frank Shrontz, and Craig Watjen. Rumblings also began about the need for the Mariners to have a new ballpark to truly attain long-term success in Seattle.

This unusual ownership group would burn through $77 million in losses during their first seven seasons and received criticism from the media and some sectors of the public over the fight to get a new stadium approved and constructed. But the singular goal of this management team was to keep the Mariners in Seattle and ultimately they would achieve that—and more. The Mariners would grow into one of the most successful teams in baseball history, judged by both outstanding performance and overwhelming community support.

Baseball great Lou Piniella came aboard as manager in 1993. Having led the 1990 Cincinnati Reds to a World Series Championship, Piniella was hired to take the team to a new level of success. Pitcher Chris Bosio threw the team's second no-hitter on April 22, 1993, in just his fourth start as a Mariner pitcher. Mariner superstar Ken Griffey, Jr., was also inked into the history books after hitting home runs in eight straight games in July, tying the record held by 1956 Pittsburgh Pirate Dale Long and 1987 New York Yankee Don Mattingly.

With Piniella as the new skipper, the team quickly improved, finishing fourth in the A.L. West with 82 wins—a number they were happy to reach at the time but that would eventually be dwarfed by a historical Piniella-helmed 2001 season. Total attendance during Piniella's first year rose from 1,651,367 the previous year to 2,052,638.

The 1994 season proved a strange one. The season was shortened by a players' strike and the Mariners' home schedule was curtailed when, just three hours before game time on July 19, the first of four 15-pound Kingdome ceiling tiles crashed to the ground. The game was called off and the team played the rest of their season on the road. They finished third in the division for the first time, with a 49–63 record. Despite the shortened and odd season, Junior racked up 40 home runs.

A Crowning Achievement: 1995

The Mariners enjoyed their most successful year as an organization in 1995. On May 22, Piniella became the team's most winning manager with his 234th triumph in a Mariner uniform, this one over the Boston Red Sox. The team went on to earn their first American League West title, and then, appearing in the playoffs for the first time in their 18-year history, narrowly won a nail-biting Division Series against the New York Yankees. Down two games to none in a best-of-five series, including a 15-inning loss in game two at Yankee Stadium, the Mariners tied the series and then battled back in the fifth and deciding game from a 5–4 deficit in the 11th inning by scoring two runs off an Edgar Martinez double to win 6–5.

Piniella was crowned Manager of the Year and Randy Johnson took home the Cy Young Award for Most Valuable Pitcher in the Majors. The Mariners' Cinderella story, its likable roster of popular players, and the edge-of-your-seat playoff series with the Yankees was credited by many sports writers and fans around the country with polishing the tarnished image of America's favorite pastime after the previous season's bitter strike. The team's marketing motto for the following year already rang true: "Ya gotta love these guys!"

Although the magical 1995 Mariners did not make it past the Cleveland Indians in the American League Championship Series, the team struck while the baseball iron was hot. Building on the momentum of the dramatic Yankees' playoff series, the Mariners and their supporters in the community were able to pressure the Seattle City Council into a special session in which they devised a new stadium plan that sidestepped the results of the previous year's failed stadium ballot initiative and approved construction of a state-of-the-art, retractable-roof baseball park in downtown Seattle.

The club earned a record 85 wins in 1996, but fell behind the Texas Rangers for the division title. Impressive rookie Alex Rodriguez joined Jay Buhner, Ken Griffey, Jr., Edgar Martinez, and catcher Dan Wilson on the American League All-Star team. Rodriguez also claimed his first Silver Slugger Award and the A.L. batting crown, finishing the season with a .358 batting average, 36 home runs, and 123 RBIs.

The team returned to the playoffs in 1997, winning the A.L. West with yet another club record of 90 wins. And another handful of talented Mariners participated in the All-Star game, including Randy Johnson, Ken Griffey, Jr., Jay Buhner, Dan Wilson, and second baseman Joey Cora. Junior would go on to be named American League MVP, while Martinez earned Designated Hitter of the Year. Another important milestone was reached as the team topped 3 million in attendance for the first time. In addition, construction started on the new stadium across the street from the Kingdome. But the playoff magic from 1995 could not be conjured and the Mariners lost the Division Series to the Baltimore Orioles.

The team had a disappointing season in 1998, finishing 11½ games out of first place in the A.L. West. Although individual players continued to post impressive, record-breaking numbers, it seemed that longstanding pitching problems had finally caught up with the talented offensive team and they struggled to achieve the previous years' successes. In an unpopular move, singular pitching standout Randy Johnson was traded to the Arizona Diamondbacks and the Mariners subsequently fell out of the playoff race in July.

Changes abounded for the team in 1999. Some were positive and some decidedly were not. The team moved into its impressive new ballpark in July, with its retractable roof and $517 million price tag. Lou Piniella became the 14th Major Leaguer to amass 1,000 career wins as a manager and 1,000 career hits as a player. Ken Griffey, Jr., earned his ninth Gold Glove and seventh Silver Slugger, and Alex Rodriguez claimed his third Silver Slugger. Pitcher Freddy Garcia threw a club rookie record of 17 wins. Still, the team finished third in the A.L. West with a record of 79–83.

In September 1999, Howard Lincoln was selected chairman and CEO, and John Ellis was appointed chairman emeritus. The following month Pat Gillick was named executive vice-president and general manager of Baseball Operations.

But by far most devastating to the team in 1999 was the trade of Ken Griffey, Jr. Throughout the second half of the season there had been much media attention paid to the star player's alleged displeasure with his offensive numbers in the new park, which featured longer home run fences than the Kingdome's. After weeks of speculation, the Mariners' original franchise player was traded to the Cincinnati Reds, and after ten years, an era in Mariners baseball came to a close.

The end of a Seattle era arrived on the morning of March 26, 2000, when the 24-year-old Kingdome was demolished with the use of 4,461 pounds of explosives. Rising 250 feet into the Seattle skyline and weighing 130,000 tons, the Kingdome took fewer than 20 seconds to collapse into a heaping, dusty mound of twisted iron and cement.

The loss of superstar Griffey cast a pall on the proceedings in early 2000, but it soon became apparent that the team would be okay. With a fresh roster that included pitchers Aaron Sele and Kazuhiro Sasaki, outfielder Mike Cameron, and first baseman John Olerud, the team claimed a wild-card berth, then swept the Chicago White Sox in the Division Series and came close to surpassing the Yankees in the ALCS. Olerud collected a Gold Glove and Alex Rodriguez claimed his forth Silver Slugger. The revamped bullpen saw Sasaki named Rookie of the Year. Attendance numbers remained steady and totaled 2,914,624, despite the absence of Griffey. Unbelievably, the team suffered yet another superstar loss at the close of the season when Alex Rodriguez signed with the Texas Rangers in a record-breaking 10-year deal worth $252 million.

Best Record in Baseball History: 2001

After having lost three of baseball's biggest names and most skilled players in just two years—Johnson, Griffey, and Rodriquez, the 2001 Mariners would stun the baseball world and, without reaching the World Series, rise to heights no one thought possible.

New players added to the roster to help fill the Alex Rodriguez void, known as the "A-Rod" void, included the virtually unknown right-fielder Ichiro Suzuki (unknown in the United States, that is) and veteran second baseman Bret Boone. Both players helped the unsung 2001 Seattle Mariners bust open the A.L. record for wins in a season and tie the all-time highest-winning record in the 130-year history of Major League Baseball, finishing the season at a remarkable and historic 116 wins and 46 losses, including 59 victories on the road (an American League record) and 20 wins in April (a Major League record).

In fact, it was a Mariners season filled with records. The team was in first place from the start of the regular season until the finish—162 games—which tied the Major League record. Ichiro Suzuki made a name for himself in the United States after years of notoriety in Japan. He tied the Major League record for hitting safely in a game with 135 and set a new record for hits by a rookie with 242. He was crowned Rookie of the Year and the League's Most Valuable Player. Bret Boone had the best season by a second baseman in A.L. history, crushing 36 home runs and driving in 141 runs. Veteran pitcher Jamie Moyer became the Mariners' second 20-game winner and closing pitcher Kazuhiro Sasaki set a Major League record with 13 saves in April. Lou Piniella was voted A.L. Manager of the Year and General Manager Pat Gillick was named Executive of the Year. The All-Star game was played in Seattle, with eight Mariners named to the team. Attendance reached an all-time high of 3,507,326 for the year.

The Mariners went on to grab handily their third A.L. West title, and then barely avoided elimination in the Division Series against the Cleveland Indians. But the ALCS crown was not to be theirs as they faced the New York Yankees, who would go on to win their third straight World Series.

The Mariners poured $18.8 million into the Major League Baseball revenue pool in 2001, an amount that matched what the Florida Marlins siphoned. The team reported a league-high profit of $14.8 million, making them one of baseball's most successful franchises.

With the opening of the 2002 season, the Seattle Mariners were perched for another run at the pennant. Their mix of ownership, management, players, and a beautiful new ballpark was expected to keep attracting fans and achieving success.

Principal Subsidiaries

Everett Aqua Sox (A); Peoria Mariners (Rookie); San Antonio Missions (AA); San Bernardino Stampede (A); Tacoma Rainiers (AAA); Wisconsin Timber Rattlers (A).

Principal Competitors

Texas Rangers; Oakland Athletics; New York Yankees; Cleveland Indians.

Further Reading

Carpenter, Les, "KIRO's Outta There: M's Switch to KOMO," *Seattle Times Online*, April 24, 2002, http://www.seattletimes.com.

Finnigan, Bob, "M's Bankruptcy Not Discussed Yet, Despite Losses," *Seattle Times*, February 3, 1985, p. C1.

Flynn, Mike, "A Salute to Mariners Ownership," *Puget Sound Business Journal*, accessed June 26, 2002, http://www.seattle.bizjournals.com.

Greene, Jay, "The Mariners Catch a Tsunami," *BusinessWeek Online*, June 25, 2001, http://www.businessweek.com.

Hodson, Jeff, "Kingdome Collapses in Cloud of Dust," *Seattle Times Online*, March 26, 2000, http://www.seattletimes.com.

Kuhn, Bowie, *Hardball: The Education of a Baseball Commissioner*, New York: Times Books, 1987.

"Seattle Mariners History," *Seattle Mariners Online*, accessed June 10, 2002, http://www.seattlemarines.com.

Seattle Post Intelligencer, *Mariners 2002: A Joy Ride into the Record Books*, Seattle: Seattle Post Intelligencer, 2001, 96 p.

Smith, Craig, "Mariners Confirm $6.1 Million Loss in 1984," *Seattle Times*, April 5, 1985, p. E1.

Van Lindt, Carson, *The Seattle Pilots Story*, Marabou Publishing, 1993.

Zumsteg, Derek, "Baseball in Seattle," *Baseball Prospectus*, March 28, 2002, http://www.baseballprospectus.com.

—Stacee Sledge

BASF

BASF Aktiengesellschaft

Carl-Bosch-Strasse 38
67056 Ludwigshafen
Germany
Telephone: (49) 621-60-4-32-63
Fax: (49) 621-60-42525
Web site: http://www.basf.com

Public Company
Incorporated: 1952 as Badische Anilin- und Soda-Fabrik AG
Employees: 92,545 (2001)
Sales: DM 32,500 billion (US $29 billion) (2001)
Stock Exchanges: Frankfurt London New York Paris Zurich
Ticker Symbol: BA (Paris), BAS (Frankfurt), BAS (Zurich), BF (New York), BFA (London)
NAIC: 325000 Chemical Manufacturing, 325411 Medicinal and Botanical Manufacturing, 325320 Pesticide and Other Agricultural Chemical Manufacturing, 325131 Inorganic Dye and Pigment Manufacturing, 325110 Paint and Coating Manufacturing, 325110 Petrochemical Manufacturing, 325188 All Other Basic Inorganic Chemical Manufacturing, 325311 Nitrogenous Fertilizer Manufacturing, 325190 Other Basic Organic Chemical Manufacturing, 325200 Resin, Synthetic Rubber and Artificial and Synthetic and Filaments Manufacturing, 334613 Magnetic and Optical Recording Media Manufacturing, 211111 Crude Petroleum and Natural Gas Extraction, 324191 Petroleum Lubricating Oil and Grease Manufacturing

Since the company's founding in 1865, Badische Anilin- und Soda-Fabrik AG (now known as BASF Aktiengesellschaft) has been a major influence in the world chemical industry. As one of the three largest German chemical companies, BASF exerted an influence from 1924 to 1947 that extended far beyond dyes and nylons. When the company joined with Bayer and Hoechst to form the world's largest chemical cartel—one of the most powerful cartels in history—BASF was instrumental in helping to secretly rearm Germany.

For its role during these years, the chemical cartel, known as the I.G. Farbenindustrie AG (I.G. Farben) consisting of the merger of companies such as BASF AG, Bayer AG, and Hoechst AG, was broken up by the Allies, and BASF again existed as an independent company. Despite the fact that almost half of its plant in Ludwigshafen, Germany, was reduced to rubble during World War II, BASF was able to reestablish its presence in the chemical industry. It is now the world's largest chemical maker, just ahead of du Pont and Bayer. In addition to its flagship production facilities in Ludwigshafen (the world's largest chemical site), BASF operates major facilities in Caojing, China; Geismar, Louisiana; Yeosu, Korea; Altamira, Mexico; Singapore; Antwerp, Belgium, Schwarzheide, Germany; and Tudela, Spain. BASF holds a significant share of the international market in chemicals, natural gas, plastics, pharmaceuticals, crop protection agents, and its original product, dyes.

Early History in the Late 19th Century

BASF was founded in 1865 by Friedrich Engelhorn, a jeweler, along the banks of the Rhine River at Mannheim. Using the discoveries of the English scientist William Perkins, BASF became one of the first companies to manufacture dyes from coal tar. Its specialty was the bright bluish-purple known as indigo. The attraction of BASF's process lay in the fact that it took coal tar, a messy byproduct of gas distillation, and transformed it into something that replaced a more expensive and unreliable organic substance.

BASF's synthetic dyes were less expensive, brighter, and easier to use than organic dyes. Profits from these dyes were used to finance BASF's diversification into inorganic chemicals later in the century as well as new production facilities across the river in Ludwigshafen.

By the early 20th century, journalists were calling BASF "The World's Greatest Chemical Works." In 1910 the company employed over 8,000 people and by 1926 this number had grown to 42,000. Its production facilities in Ludwigshafen alone covered 2,787 acres. American journalists were im-

Company Perspectives:

BASF is the world's leading chemical company. We aim to increase and sustain our corporate value through growth and innovation. We offer our customers a range of high-performance products, including chemicals, plastics, coating systems, dispersions, agricultural products, fine chemicals as well as crude oil and natural gas. Our distinctive approach to integration, known in German as Verbund, *is our strength. It enables us to achieve cost leadership and gives us a decisive competitive advantage in the long term. We act in accordance with the principles of sustainable development.*

pressed by BASF's charity and reported, "The company has given a great deal of attention to welfare work; especially to housing, hygiene and the care of the sick."

BASF's sanatoriums and dispensaries, along with its main production facilities, were financed in part by business arrangements that would be illegal today in either Germany or the United States. Beginning around 1900 leaders of the German chemical industry began to dream of what was, in effect, the merger of most German chemical companies. Should this cartel be formed, said Carl Duisberg, the man who eventually set up the I.G. Farben, ". . . the now existing domination of the German chemical industry, especially the dye industry, over the rest of the world would then, in my opinion, be assured."

Cartels Formed in Early 20th Century

By 1904 two major cartels had been formed. The first of these cartels included Bayer and BASF; the second cartel was anchored by Hoechst. Not only did these firms avoid competition and fix prices, but they also set up a quota system and even shared their profits. For instance, a marketing agreement was reached for the sale of indigo, which was one of the most profitable dyes.

Both cartels played an important role during World War I. Not only was dye necessary for garments, the basic chemical formulas for dyes could be altered slightly to make mustard gas and munitions. Companies such as BASF provided gas and explosives for German troops and, previous to the United States' entry into the war, they initiated economic activities that stunted the growth of the chemical companies important to the U.S. war effort. For instance, BASF had sold aniline at below market prices to U.S. firms in order to discourage aniline production by U.S. companies. As part of the dye cartel it had also engaged in a practice called "full-line forcing." If a dealer wanted to purchase item A for example, available only from BASF, the dealer was forced to purchase the whole product line, effectively eliminating U.S. producers.

After the war the German government recognized the importance of the chemical industry, especially the dye industry. Not only did the chemical industry bring in needed foreign currency, it was critical to defense. Since the buildup of the chemical industry was so important to Germany, the cartels were granted government loans as well as a ten-year tax deferment. The

cartels also received a special allotment of coal, which was scarce at the time.

I.G. Farben Formed in 1925

In 1925 the top executives in the chemical industry decided that the duplication of product lines and the maintenance of separate sales forces was wasteful. As a result, hundreds of German chemical companies (including Bayer and Hoechst) formally merged with BASF. This new corporation, headquartered at Ludwigshafen, was renamed the Interessengemeinschaft Farbenindustrie, or I.G. Farben. BASF ceased to exist as a legal entity; it operated for the next 26 years as "Betriebsgemeinschaft Oberrhein," or the upper Rhine operating unit of I.G. Farben.

The I.G. Farben set quotas and pooled profits. But this large trust was more than an economic entity—it was a political one. I.G. Farben's executives feared that leftists might triumph in Germany's unstable political climate and that I.G. Farben itself would be nationalized. This led to the I.G. Farben's support for Adolf Hitler. As early as 1931 its directors made secret contributions to the Nazi Party.

Notorious World War II Years

The I.G. Farben profited handsomely from its support of Hitler and his foreign policy, and it grew tremendously during World War II. By 1942 the cartel was making a yearly profit that was 800 million marks more than its entire combined capitalization in 1925, the year of its founding. Not only was the I.G. Farben given possession of chemical companies in foreign lands (the I.G. Farben had control of Czechoslovakian dye works a week after the Nazi invasion), but the captured lands also provided its factories in Germany with slave labor. In order to take advantage of slave labor, I.G. Farben plants were built next to Maidanek and Auschwitz.

At its peak, the I.G. Farben had controlling interest in 379 German firms and 400 foreign companies. It has been noted that one of the historic restraints on Germany was its lack of colonies to supply necessary products, such as rubber. During this time, the I.G. Farben, synthesizing many of the country's chemical needs with a native product, provided Germany with the self-sufficiency it lacked during World War I.

Near the end of the war, the BASF production facilities at Ludwigshafen were bombed extensively. While factories built during the war were often camouflaged, the old BASF factories were more visible to American bombers, which often flew over Ludwigshafen on the way back from other bombing raids and dropped any leftover bombs on the ammonia and nitrogen works. During the war BASF factories sustained the heaviest damage in the I.G. Farben with 45 percent of BASF buildings destroyed.

Postwar Rebuilding of BASF

With the surrender of Germany, I.G. Farben's problems had only just begun. Immediately after the war many members of the Vorstand, or board of directors of the I.G. Farben, were arrested and indicted for war crimes. There was a large amount

---

Key Dates:

1865: Badische Anilin- und Soda-Fabrik AG (BASF) is founded by Friedrich Engelhorn in Ludwigshafen, Germany, for the production of coal tar dyestuffs.

1897: Indigo dye is first synthesized by BASF.

1908: Development of the Haber-Bosch process revolutionizes the production of nitrogen fertilizers.

1913: BASF's first ammonia synthesis plant starts operation at Oppau.

1925: I.G. Farbenindustrie AG (I.G. Farben) is founded in Frankfurt with the merger of BASF and other chemical and pharmaceutical companies, including Bayer AG (Bayer) & Farbwerke Hoechst Aktiengesellschaft vormals Meister Lucius & Bruning (Hoechst).

1939: I.G. Farben joins the war effort in Germany.

1945: Allied Control Council orders the dissolution of I.G. Farben. BASF's Ludwigshafen plant continues to operate independently.

1951: Under the name Badische Anilin- und Soda-Fabrik AG, BASF develops Styropor, a white rigid foam used as an insulating and packaging material.

1952: Company is incorporated under the name of Badische Anilin- und Soda-Fabrik AG.

1958: BASF establishes a join venture with The Dow Chemical Company, United States.

1965: BASF begins acquiring other companies to produce surface coatings, drugs, crop protection agents, and fertilizers.

1969: BASF acquires Wyandotte Chemicals Corporation, United States, and Wintershall AG, the German oil company.

1972: Company changes its name to BASF Aktiengesellschaft.

1975: BASF acquires Boots Pharmaceutical (United Kingdom), and a majority interest in Knoll AG. (The remaining interests in Knoll AG are purchased in 1982.)

1990: BASF takes over a united Germany's Synthesewerk Schwarzheide.

1991: BASF Ecology Laboratory begins work.

1993: BASF & Gazprom (Russia's leading natural gas producer) establish WINGAS to market and distribute gas in Central and Eastern Europe.

1995: BASF opens its first plant in Nanjing, China.

1998: With PetroFina, BASF constructs the world's largest steamcracker plant at Port Arthur, Texas; the company founds BASF Plant Science, a worldwide research platform, with sites in Germany, Sweden, Canada, and the United States.

2000: BASF is listed on the New York Stock Exchange (NYSE) under the listing BF and the company's worldwide pharmaceutical business is sold to Abbott Laboratories, Inc.

2001: The company begins transacting business via Elemica, a neutral electronic marketplace and sets up a global extranet platform, WorldAccount.

---

of written evidence incriminating the Vorstand, most of it written by the directors themselves. I.G. Farben executives were in the habit of keeping copious records, not only of meetings and phone calls, but also of their private thoughts on the I.G. Farben's dealings with the government. Despite the quantity of written evidence and testimony from concentration camp survivors, the judges at Nuremberg dealt with the Vorstand leniently. Journalists covering the 1947 proceedings attributed the light sentences, none of which was longer than four years, to the fact that all the sentences in the trials were becoming less severe toward the end, and to the judges' unwillingness to lower the standards for active participation in war crimes to include businessmen.

The Potsdam Agreement referred to the necessity of dismantling the I.G. Farben in the interests of "peace and democracy." But from the very beginning the Allies disagreed over the fate of the I.G. Farben. The British and French favored a breakup of the company into large separate companies, while many U.S. officials advocated that the company be divided into smaller and therefore less influential firms. Negotiations over the cartel's fate lasted for several years. The French and British plan eventually prevailed.

After operating under Allied supervision from 1947 to 1952, the I.G. Farben was divided in 1952 into three large firms—Bayer, Hoechst, and BASF—and nine smaller firms. After this reorganization BASF was once again a small corporation lo-

cated on its original Ludwigshafen site. Its share of the 30,000 I.G. Farben patents had been taken away; some of its trade secrets had been sold for as little as $1.00. It was isolated from its previous suppliers in Eastern Europe and, in fact, most of its basic supplies, such as coal, were insufficient. The 55 percent of its buildings that had not been destroyed were filled with outdated equipment. Leading BASF from its refounding until 1965 was Board Chairman Carl Wurster, who started at the company as a chemist.

West Germany, lacking money to import chemicals from abroad, was in dire need for chemicals produced at home. By 1957, BASF's sales of nitrogen and ammonia products were approaching their wartime levels. BASF initially lagged behind both Bayer and Hoechst in profits, in part because its product line included such items as fertilizers, plastics, and synthetics which were easily challenged on the market by competitors. Between 1957 and 1962 sales grew 59 percent, less than either Bayer or Hoechst. As prices for plastics and fertilizers stabilized in 1963, however, sales for the company increased 19 percent in one year.

BASF's growth during the postwar period was impressive. In the ten years after the dissolution of the I.G. Farben, the company increased its capital from DM 81 million to DM 200 million. Employing only 800 workers in the late 1940s, it employed 45,000 by 1963. Although BASF had lost all of its patents in 1952, within ten years it had recovered a large number of them.

Impressive Growth in the 1960s and 1970s

BASF began its second decade of independence from the I.G. Farben with a switch to oil as a base for most of its old, coal-based formulas. With the purchase of Rheinisch Olefinwerke, BASF added petroleum to the long list of raw materials it was able to provide. The company soon became the world's largest producer of plastic, and provided an astonishing 10 percent of the international requirement for synthetic fibers.

Despite these gains, BASF was still faced with problems. It was the possessor of the old I.G. Farben soda and nitrogen works, but these products were often in oversupply. BASF competed with other European producers who were not burdened with this product and who were situated in more petroleum-rich countries. Nevertheless, the company reached DM 1 billion in sales during 1965. Bernard Timm, the newly appointed board chairman with a background as a physicist, attributed the company's performance in 1965 to a judicious mix of plastics, farm chemicals, raw materials for coatings, dyes, and fibers.

In 1969, another significant year for the company, BASF purchased Wintershall, which had half of the German potash market and produced a quarter of the country's natural gas. This acquisition was the largest in German history, and with it BASF jumped over Bayer to become the nation's second largest chemical company. A large new plastics plant at Antwerp made PVC, polyethylene, and caprolactam (a nylon intermediary) at an accelerated rate.

Following the impressive growth of BASF during the 1960s, the 1970s started slowly. After much encouragement by the state of South Carolina in the United States to build a $200 million dye and plastics plant in an impoverished area near Hilton Head, the company's plans were thwarted by an unlikely coalition of outside agitators, local residents, and Southern gentry who feared damage to the beautiful Carolina coastline. In 1971 large investments in fibers and plastics were lost due to overcapacity. Synthetic fibers, whose prices were low in relation to the petroleum used in their manufacture, continued to plague BASF throughout the decade.

Despite the problems with fibers, however, the company continued to grow. The growth plan favored by Timm, who served as board chairman until 1974, and Matthias Seefelder, chairman from 1974 to 1983 and a chemist by trade, featured vertical integration, expansion abroad, and emphasis on consumer products. Of the three successors to the I.G. Farben, BASF was the one left with the least attractive product line.

In order to remedy this situation, BASF marketed its line of magnetic cassette tapes (a product it claims to have invented) and then ventured into videotapes. As for vertical integration, the company had ample access to raw materials and chose to modify existing raw materials rather than diversify into unfamiliar fields.

U.S. Expansion in the 1980s

Since there was little room to grow in Germany, the expansion into foreign markets was a cornerstone of BASF's strategy for growth. And the 1980s were a decade of significant growth for BASF in the United States. In order to avoid U.S. tariffs BASF formed numerous partnerships with American companies and acquired others. Wyandotte Chemicals Corporation of Wyandotte, Michigan, had been a major acquisition in 1969. The 1980s began with the purchase of Fritzsche Dodge and Olcott, Inc., the third largest U.S. producer of flavors and fragrances, not to mention Cook Industrial Coatings and Allegheny Ludlums. This last acquisition put BASF among the top 15 pigment manufacturers in the United States. The 1985 purchase of American Enka doubled BASF's fiber capacity. Although BASF's 1980s foreign ventures were by no means limited to the United States, its emphasis on U.S. expansion was understandable. At the time, the United States consumed one-third of the world's chemical production. The company's holdings in the United States also cushioned BASF against fluctuations in the value of the deutschemark and the dollar.

In 1986 the increasing importance of its U.S. operations was highlighted when BASF consolidated all North American operations under a new subsidiary called BASF Corporation. Within the entire BASF Group, the new company ranked second in size only to the flagship BASF AG, and generated 20 percent of overall group sales. Nearly all—90 percent—of the BASF Corporation's sales were generated from products it produced in North America.

The very year of its consolidation, BASF Corporation was in the news when the Oil, Chemical and Atomic Worker's Union decided to strike at a plant located in Geismar, Louisiana. Union allegations of unsafe working conditions prompted the U.S. Congress to investigate conditions at the plant. The union announced a campaign of negative publicity directed against the company. The strike surprised the management at BASF, which with the exception of World War II, generally treated workers well. Asked about the labor difficulties, a highly ranked BASF executive said, "We haven't had a strike since 1924, except a work stoppage in 1947 to protest our president being tried for war crimes." The strike—which evolved into a lockout—dragged on and on until it was finally settled with a union victory in 1989.

Transformation of BASF in the 1990s

After Hans Albers had served as board chairman from 1983 to 1990, he was succeeded by Jürgen F. Strube. The year 1990 was a fitting one for a change in leadership; it was the 125th anniversary of the company's founding, and represented the beginning of one of the most remarkable periods in BASF history, a period of furious activity—restructurings, acquisitions, divestments, joint ventures, and immense capital expenditures, all on a scale unprecedented in BASF history. Strube took over BASF after it had posted one of its strongest years ever in 1989, with sales of DM 46.16 billion and net income after taxes of DM 20.2 billion. Sales would then fall for each of the next four years, while net income fell for the next three. The levels of 1989 would not be surpassed until 1995.

The reasons for BASF's struggles were many: a cyclical downturn in the chemical industry in the early 1990s, to which the company was still highly vulnerable; a serious recession in Germany, brought on in part by the cost of German reunification; healthcare reform efforts in Europe, which led to the increasing use of generic drugs to contain costs, with BASF's proprietary drug sales suffering as a result; and the Common Agricultural Policy reform effort, which reduced the amount of farmed land and the amount of chemicals used in farming it, thus hurting the sale of BASF agricultural products. The German reunification also affected BASF in a more direct way when it took over—for nothing—Synthesewerk Schwarzheide, one of the largest chemical businesses in the former East Germany. BASF converted it into BASF Schwarzheide GmbH, but then had to spend DM 1.4 billion to modernize and expand its facilities.

Strube quickly responded to the crisis by initiating a serious cost-cutting program and by identifying businesses BASF should divest. Cost-cutting efforts included the closure of a number of plants and a gradual workforce reduction that saw BASF's employee numbers fall from a high of 136,990 in 1989 to 106,266 in 1994, a reduction of more than 22 percent. Divested operations were identified as businesses in which BASF was not competitive. These included the Auguste Victoria coal mine, which BASF had used to supply itself with coal since 1907, sold in 1990 to Ruhrkohle AG; the flavors and fragrances business of Fritzsche Dodge and Olcott, which was no longer viewed as a good fit; and the advanced materials division, which was not profitable enough to retain.

Strube also wanted to make BASF less susceptible to the cyclical downturns of the chemical industry by bolstering the company's noncyclical businesses. The company's consumer products area was beefed up with the 1991 acquisition of AGFA-Gevaert's magnetic tape operations, which were reorganized with BASF's existing magnetic tape business to form BASF Magnetics GmbH, producer of tapes, videocassettes, and diskettes. A more important and daring venture began in 1990 when Wintershall, BASF's oil and gas subsidiary, entered into an agreement with Gazprom—the world's largest natural gas producer, based in Russia—to build and operate pipelines for distributing Gazprom natural gas to the German market, directly challenging Ruhrgas, Germany's near-monopoly natural gas supplier. After committing itself to invest more than DM 4.5 billion over the next decade in what was described as the largest project in company history, BASF could boast of already attaining 10 percent market share in its first year of operation (1995), and aimed to reach 15 percent by 2000.

The natural gas venture was perceived by BASF as a long-term investment, as were the company's large expenditures in China. Although other countries were also targeted by BASF for significant investment in the 1990s—including Japan, Russia, India, Malaysia, and Korea—it was China that saw astounding expenditure levels. BASF's first plant in China opened in 1992 in Nanjing, a production facility for unsaturated polyester resins. By 1995 the company had committed DM 600 million to various Chinese ventures, including plants for making pigments, textile dyes, polystyrene, and vitamins, all through various joint ventures. In 1996 another joint venture was formed, this one to build a US$4-billion petrochemical facility, also in Nanjing, in what was the single biggest investment in China yet by a chemical company.

Meanwhile, acquisitions bolstered BASF's plastics operations. In 1992 the polystyrene-resins operation of Mobil was acquired for US$300 million. Then, two years later, BASF paid

US$90 million for Imperial Chemical's polypropylene operations in Europe. Also in 1994, a new steamcracker plant located in Antwerp became operational after an outlay of DM 1.5 billion, the largest single capital expenditure in BASF history. Further moves in plastics came in 1996 when two joint ventures were formed, one with Hoechst in polypropylene and one with Shell in polyethylene. Because of German antitrust laws, these had to be set up as separate businesses, with joint venture partners allowed to have only limited control over their operations.

Early in 1994, BASF reached the important decision to retain its struggling pharmaceuticals business as a core business and to pour money into its growth. The next three years saw a flurry of activity in this area. In 1994 a new biotechnology and genetic engineering research center was opened by BASF Bioresearch Corporation in Worcester, Massachusetts, to develop drugs for fighting cancer and immune system diseases. BASF gained a foothold in generic drugs that same year by acquiring the German generic drugmaker Sagitta Arzneimittel, and by entering into a 50–50 joint venture with IVAX to market generic drugs. The following year BASF's Pharmaceuticals sector received a huge boost with the acquisition of Boots Pharmaceuticals, based in England, for US$1.3 billion. Boots was merged into BASF's existing drug operations, forming the new Knoll Pharmaceuticals.

Following the Boots acquisition, BASF created a new Health and Nutrition sector to highlight the importance of both pharmaceuticals and agricultural products to the company's future. Included in this sector were pharmaceuticals, fine chemicals (notably vitamins), crop protection agents (herbicides, fungicides, etc.), and fertilizers. In 1996, crop protection expanded when BASF paid US$780 million for the North American corn herbicides business of Sandoz, which was ordered divested as part of the merger of Sandoz and Ciba to form Novartis. Another joint venture was also initiated that year in an agreement with Lynx Therapeutics, based in California, to form BASF-Lynx Bioscience AG, for research in biotechnology and genetic engineering for the development of new pesticides and drugs. BASF planned to invest more than DM 100 million (US $66 million) in this venture, in which it held a 51 percent stake. Also in 1996, the Food and Drug Administration (FDA) approved the antiobesity drug sibutramine—developed by Boots—from which the company expected annual worldwide sales of DM 800 million (US $525 million).

As part of the restructuring that created the Health and Nutrition sector, BASF in 1995 also created an Information Systems sector. This was short-lived, as magnetic tape products were identified as a non-core business and sold early in 1997 to KOHAP of Korea. Another non-core business was potash and in 1996 BASF's holding in Kali und Salz was sold to Potash Corporation of Saskatchewan. Also in 1996, BASF purchased Zeneca's textile dye operations for US$208 million, making BASF third worldwide in textile dyes, trailing only DyStar (the merger of Bayer and Hoechst textile dye businesses) and Ciba's spinoff specialty Chemical division.

By 1997, BASF was operating five main sectors: Plastics and Fibers, Colorants and Finishing Products, Health and Nutrition, Chemicals, and Oil and Gas. The company had plans to spend more than DM 20 billion (US $13 billion) on acquisitions in the coming years, concentrating on businesses that will counter the cyclical chemical area—notably its Health and Nutrition sector—and on strengthening itself outside Europe. These goals were met by the following acquisitions: Punch Printing Inks, Ltd. (Ireland) and Schou Trykfarver A/S (Denmark); the U.S. surfactant businesses of Olin Corporation and PPG; and a portion of Dow Benelus N.V. (Terneuzen). In a joint venture, BASF acquired 50 percent holding of Hanwha Chemical Corporation in Korea. Another long-term goal was to set up a more streamlined structure in Europe (where the conglomerate had more than 100 separate companies), one similar to the integrated BASF Corporation in the United States. To this end, the following companies were consolidated: BASF Singapore (Pte.) Ltd.; BASF South Africa (Pty.) Ltd., Polioles S.A. de C.V., Wintershall Exploration (United Kingdom) Ltd. and Wintershall (United Kingdom) Ltd.

Developing markets in Southeast Asia and the Far East had been a goal of BASF since the 1980s. Through joint ventures with local partners, BASF opened the first production plants in China, at Shanghai and Nanjing, the location of an integrated petrochemical site, BASF's largest investment in China.

At the heart of the BASF's integrated-production strategy in North America was the construction of the world's largest steamcracker plant, begun in 1998 with PetroFina, in Port Arthur, Texas. The Port Arthur plant was one of the largest single investments made by BASF outside Europe; other steamcracker plants were located in Ludwigshafen (since 1965) and Antwerp, Belgium. The steamcracking process involves the "cracking" of naphtha by adding steam at a temperature of 800°C to form ethylene and propylene, used to make plastics, surface coatings, solvents, raw materials, crop protection agents, and vitamins.

Through joint ventures in 1998, BASF broadened their plant biotechnology operations with research sites in Germany, Sweden, the United States, and Canada. BASF Plant Science, a worldwide research platform, was founded with Svalöf Weibull, Sweden's seed producer.

Shell partnered with BASF in 1999 to establish one of the world's largest polyolefin manufacturing plants. Through a joint venture with European companies Montell, Elenac, and Targor, BAFS began manufacturing polyethylene and polypropylene. This paved the way for the creation of Bassell N.V. in 2000.

From the mid-1970s BASF expanded into pharmaceuticals through the acquisition of Knoll AG and Boots Pharmaceutical (United Kingdom). Although strengthening its presence in the North American market, its worldwide pharmaceutical business was sold to Abbott Laboratories, Inc. in late 2000, following settlement of legal action alleging "a conspiracy among vitamin manufacturers to fix prices, allocate markets and engage in other practices in violation of the Sherman Act and the antitrust, consumer protection and/or common laws of the various states" against BASF and other codefendants.

Record Sales in 2000 and Expanded E-Commerce Capabilities

In the first and second quarters of 2000, BASF achieved record sales. Chairman of the Board of Executive Directors, Dr. Jürgen F. Strube, attributed this milestone to a strategy of continuous change, the strength of their integrated approach to manufacturing (*Verbund*), their global presence and spirit of innovation. To further enhance their global position, BASF took strategic positions in several ventures, including new Internet marketplaces for chemicals and thermoplastics. In February, BASF acquired a stake in ChemConnect, the leading U.S. online chemicals and plastics marketplace.

In June 2000, BASF shares were listed on the New York Stock Exchange (NYSE) under the trading symbol BF. Another milestone was reached in the United States in July when BASF made its largest acquisition, American Home Products, a crop protection program. This acquisition made BASF the world's third largest supplier of agricultural products. The first *Verbund* site in Asia was opened as BASF Petronas Chemicals. The joint venture with the Malaysian state enterprise in Kauntan produced acrylic monomers. Other operations included the merger of its textile dye activities in DyStar as a result of a joint venture with Bayer and Hoechst. The end of 2000 recognized BASF as "number one among world chemical companies and among German businesses" in *Fortune magazine's* "Global Most Admired Companies."

Business Units Reorganized in 2001

BASF reorganized its core business units into five segments to optimize value-adding chains by bundling product groups. These business segments were Chemicals, Plastics and Fibers; Performance Products; Agricultural Products and Nutrition; and Oil and Gas. These segments were further divided into 12 operating divisions.

BASF's Chemical segment, comprising Inorganics, Petrochemicals, and Intermediates divisions, produced a range of products from basic petrochemicals and inorganic chemicals to specialty intermediates and related products. Based on sales in 2001, this division was one of the largest chemical producers in the world, meeting the needs of many industries, including chemical, construction, automotive, electrical, electronics, detergents, colorants, coatings, and health and nutrition industries.

The Plastics and Fibers segment produced not only plastics but also fiber products. Styrenic plastics, engineering and high-performance plastics, thermoplastics, foams, nylon fibers, nylon intermediates, and polyurethanes were products made for construction, packaging, automotive, household appliances, electrical and electronics, consumer products, textile, and carpet industries. To retain its large European market, BASF's Plastics and Fibers segment spent approximately EUR 146 million on research and development activities in 2001.

High-value chemicals such as surfactants, pigments, automotive and industrial coatings, dispersions, and adhesive raw materials were produced by the Performance Products segment. BASF also produced acrylic acid and its derivatives, as well as polymers, like superabsorbents, which were used to manufacture sanitary care products. These products were sold throughout the world in the automotive, paper, packaging, textile, sanitary care, construction, coatings, printing, and leather industries.

The Agricultural Products and Fine Chemicals divisions, functioning under the Agriculture Products and Nutrition segment, produced a variety of agricultural products, including herbicides, fungicides, and insecticides. The Agricultural Products division was based in Mount Olive, New Jersey. Fine Chemicals produced in this segment included vitamins, carotenoids, pharmaceutical active ingredients; polymers for pharmaceuticals, cosmetics and human nutrition, aroma chemicals UV filters, amino acids, and feed enzymes. This segment was previously named Health and Nutrition, prior to the 2001 selling of Abbot Laboratories, Inc. (United States).

Activities of the Oil and Gas segment, operated through BASF's subsidiary Wintershall AG and its corresponding subsidiaries and affiliates, included the exploration and production of crude oil and natural gas. Throughout Central and Eastern Europe, natural gas marketing, distribution, and trading were handled in partnership with Gazprom of Russia. Oil and Gas operations were conducted in North Africa, the Middle East, Germany, and Argentina.

In 2001 BASF began transacting business in Europe and the United States via Elemica, a company-neutral electronic marketplace, allowing electronic transactions supplying neopentyl glycol between BASF, The Dow Chemical Company, and DSM in The Netherlands. These transactions provided the necessary infrastructure to link BASF's Enterprise Resource Planning (ERP) system with customers with suppliers. Another important e-commerce advance was WorldAccount, an integrated-global extranet platform for customer product information resources. In early 2002, BASF joined with Dell Computer Corporation, in the United States, to introduce a worldwide corporate PC standard in an effort to streamline company communications and business processes.

BASF continued to make important advances in pharmaceuticals in 2002 with the introduction of Kollicoat IR, a water-soluble tablet coating designed to improve tablet strength and protect active ingredients. With other brands launched previously, BASF remained one of the leading producers of pharmaceutical excipients and active ingredients.

At the release of the 2001 Annual Report, BASF Chairman Dr. Jürgen F. Strube stated that the goal of BASF remains to increase corporate value through growth and innovation in 2002. Based on restructuring and improving efficiency, BASF hoped in the future to generate significantly higher earnings from ongoing business with the same level of sales.

Principal Subsidiaries

BASF Antwerpen N.V. (Antwerp, Belgium); BASF Coatings AG (Münster-Hiltrup, Germany); BASF Corporation (New Jersey, USA); BASF Español S.A. (Tarragona, Spain); BASF S.A. (Säo Bernardo do Campo, Brazil); BASF Schwarzheide GmbH (Schwarzheide, Germany); Elastogran GmbH (Lemförde, Germany); Wintershall AG (Kassell, Germany).

Principal Divisions

Business Segments: Agricultural Products and Nutrition; Chemicals; Coatings; Functional Polymers; Oil and Gas; Performance Products; Plastics and Fibers; Operating Divisions: Agricultural Products; Fine Chemicals; Inorganics; Intermediates; Oil and Gas; Performance Chemicals; Performance Polymers; Petrochemicals; Polyurethanes; Styrenics; Regional Divisions: Africa; Asia; Europe; North America; Pacific Area; South America.

Principal Competitors

Bayer AG; The Dow Chemical Company; du Pont.

Further Reading

Alperowicz, Natasha, "BASF to Idle Production in Europe," *Chemical Week*, November 21, 2001, pp. 15–16.

Alperowicz, Natasha, Lyn Tattum, and Emma Chynoweth, "Managing the Business Cycle at BASF: Gas Deal Provides Hope for Improving Results," *Chemical Week*, December 16, 1992, pp. 22–26.

Alperowicz, Natasha, Michael Roberts, and Debbie Jackson, "Domestic Pressures Turn the Screw on German Chemical Firms," *Chemical Week*, March 31, 1993, pp. 34–35.

Baker, John, "BASF Invests in Chinese Future," *ECN-European Chemical News*, October 7, 1996, p. 25.

"BASF AG," *Mergent Industrial Manual*, New York: Moody's Investor Service, 2001, pp. 912–916.

"BASF: Change, Focus, Speed," supplement to *ECN-European Chemical News*, November 1995.

"BASF Claims Top Spot among Investors in Korea," *Chemical Marketing Reporter*, September 23, 1996, p. 5.

BASF Milestones in Its History, Ludwigshafen, Germany: BASF Aktiengesellschaft, 1995.

"BASF Targets Acquisitions That Cut Cycles: The Company Also Wants to Structure European Business Like That of U.S.," *Chemical Marketing Reporter*, November 18, 1996, pp. 7, 41.

Chandler, Jr., Alfred D., "The Enduring Logic of Industrial Success," *Harvard Business Review*, March/April 1990, p. 130.

Gibson, Paul, "How the Germans Dominate the World Chemical Industry," *Forbes*, October 13, 1980, p. 155.

Hayes, Peter, *Industry and Ideology: I.G. Farben in the Nazi Era*, London: Cambridge University Press, 1987.

Layman, Patricia L., "For BASF, Big Is Still Better," *Chemical and Engineering News*, September 16, 1996, pp. 13–15, 18.

Milmo, Sean, "BASF, Lynx Form Biotech Collaboration," *Chemical Marketing Reporter*, October 28, 1996, p. 7.

"The Money Pit: Investing in Eastern Europe," *Economist*, June 22, 1991, pp. 74–75.

Reier, Sharon, "Hundred Years War: How BASF Allied Itself with the Russians to Battle Germany's Gas Monopoly," *Financial World*, September 14, 1993, pp. 28–30.

Richman, Louis S., "Hans Albers: BASF," *Fortune*, August 3, 1987, p. 50.

Schroter, Harm G., "The German Question, the Unification of Europe, and the European Market Strategies of Germany's Chemical and Electrical Industries, 1990–1992," *Business History Review*, Autumn 1993, p. 369.

Sheridan, Mike, "BASF Atofina Cracker Is Finally Up and Running," *Chemical Marketing Reporter*, February 18, 2002, p. 4.

—updates: David E. Salamie, Carol D. Beavers

The Basketball Club of Seattle, LLC

351 Elliot Avenue West, Suite 500
Seattle, Washington 98119
U.S.A.
Telephone: (206) 281-5800
Fax: (206) 281-5828
Web site: http://www.nba.com/sonics

Private Company
Incorporated: 1966
Employees: 70 (est.)
Sales: $80.0 million (2001 est.)
NAIC: 711211 Sports Teams and Clubs

Professional basketball in Seattle, Washington, had its beginnings on December 20, 1966, when the city was awarded a National Basketball Association (NBA) franchise, with the club beginning play at the Seattle Center Coliseum in the 1967/68 season. With only two West Coast teams at the time, team owner Sam Schulman was optimistic, ''I have a dream for this great city. I intend to pull together some of the most talented men in this country. Together, we will bring the world championship to Seattle.'' Basketball fans in the area submitted names for the club that would reflect the Indian lore of Seattle. Others suggested names that reflected Seattle's oldest industries, including Miners, Loggers, Captains, and Stevedores. Finally, it was decided the team should have a soaring, uplifting name—the Seattle SuperSonics—to remind the rest of the country that Seattle was home of the world's largest manufacturer of jet aircraft.

Owner Schulman and team management, under the direction of the first General Manager Don Richman, selected Al Tucker of Oklahoma Baptist as the team's first ever college draft pick. In the NBA expansion draft, Seattle picked up Tom Meschery from the San Francisco Warriors, Walt Hazzard from the Los Angeles Lakers, Bob Weiss from Philadelphia, and Rod Thorn from St. Louis. Al Bianchi, who in 1966 had ended a ten-year career as a former reserve guard with the NBA's Syracuse Nationals and Philadelphia 76ers, became the SuperSonics' first head coach.

SuperSonics Begin First Season at the Seattle Center Coliseum

The Seattle SuperSonics' first game was played on September 19, 1967, a preseason game in San Diego, California, against the San Diego Rockets. The NBA newcomers' first season ended with 23 wins and 59 losses, fifth in the their Western Division and the second worst in the league. In the regular season, their first game against San Francisco ended in a disappointing loss of 144–116. Other high-scoring losses were to Philadelphia (160–122) and four other opponents who racked up 150 points or more against the SuperSonics. The Sonics' biggest offensive night was on February 11, when they beat San Francisco 146–118. For the season, opponents averaged 125.1 points per game, while Seattle averaged 118.7 points. Seattle played thirty-one games their first season, entertaining 202,263 fans in the Seattle Center Coliseum, with attendance averaging 6,524 per game.

Walt Hazzard was selected to play on the West All-Star Team and finished the season ranked seventh in the NBA in scoring with an average of 23.9 points per game (ppg) and fifth in assists with an average of 6.2 assists per game (apg). Bob Rule and Al Tucker were selected for the NBA All-Rookie Team.

Sonics Acquire Lenny Wilkins

Bianchi retained the head-coach job for a second year and guided the Sonics to a 30–52 season, inching up seven wins. At the beginning of the 1968/69 season, the Sonics acquired Lenny Wilkins in a trade with the St. Louis Hawks for Walt Hazzard. Wilkins, a 6' 1'' point guard, was an All-Star in his first season in Seattle, finishing ninth in the NBA in scoring (22.4 ppg) and second in the league in assists (8.2 apg). Known for his flash ball handling and acrobatic shots, he became a driving force on the court and off.

The 1969/70 season saw Wilkins take over the coaching reins from Bianchi, while continuing to play his regular position. Under his leadership the Sonics continued to improve their game ending the season with a 36–46 record, and averaging 115 points per game. Wilkins lead the league in assists, averaging 9.1 per game. The Sonics' record improved again to 38–44 in 1970/71. Wilkins continued to shine as a Sonic, finishing sec-

---

Key Dates:

1966: Seattle is awarded an NBA franchise.

1967: The Seattle SuperSonics play their first game on September 19, 1967.

1968: The Sonics acquire guard Lenny Wilkins.

1969: Lenny Wilkins becomes a player/coach.

1973: Bill Russell takes over as Sonics head coach.

1974: The Sonics host the NBA All-Star Game.

1975: The Sonics qualify for the NBA finals.

1977: Lenny Wilkins returns to the Sonics as head coach.

1979: The Sonics become NBA champions.

1980: Seattle's Freddie Brown becomes the league's first three-point percentage leader.

1983: Barry Ackerley of Ackerley Communications purchases the Sonics.

1985: Bernie Bickerstaff replaces Wilkins as head coach.

1986: Two firsts for the NBA and Seattle Center Coliseum: an NBA game is cancelled due to rain and Freddie Brown's No. 32 jersey is retired.

1987: Seattle hosts the NBA All-Star Game for a second time.

1990: Assistant coach K.C. Jones becomes head coach.

1992: George Carl takes over as head coach; Jack Sikma's No. 43 jersey is retired.

1994: Wally Walker assumes post as Sonics' president.

1995: The Sonics make KeyArena their new home.

1998: Paul Westphal replaces George Karl as head coach.

2000: Nate McMillan replaces Paul Westphal as Sonics head coach.

2001: The Sonics are purchased by The Basketball Club of Seattle, LLC.

---

ond in the league in assists with an average of 9.2 per game and was named the All-Star Game's Most Valuable Player (MVP).

The team's first winning season came in 1971/72, when they finished with a record 47 wins and 35 losses. That season they came close to making the NBA playoffs, thanks not only to Wilkins' on- and off-court guidance, but to the acquisition of Spencer Haywood, a superstar from the American Basketball Association (ABA).

Sonics Challenge NBA Rule

Based on the NBA's rule prohibiting the signing of a player until his college class had graduated, Haywood had left the University of Detroit after his sophomore year in 1969 to sign as a free agent with the ABA's Denver Rockets. The Sonics, however, challenged the NBA rule, and following a landmark ruling, Haywood became the first undergraduate player ever to enter the NBA. As a first-time Sonic, Haywood made the All-NBA First Team, started in the All-Star Game, and finished fourth in the league in scoring, averaging 26.2 points per game.

Wilkins Makes Way for Bill Russell at the Helm

The Lenny Wilkins era came to a close at the end of the 1971/72 season, when he left the Sonics organization for Cleve-

land. Under the leadership of Tom Nissalke and Bucky Buckwalter, who both coached during the next year, the Sonics ended the season with a disappointing 26–56 record, reflecting the loss of Wilkins on and off the court.

In an effort to turn things around for the Sonics, owner Sam Schulman named Bill Russell as the new head coach for the 1973/74 season. Russell, a 13-year veteran of the NBA, with eleven NBA championships with the Boston Celtics, had been a player/coach at Boston for three seasons. A good match for the Sonics, Russell helped the Sonics improve their win-record by ten games, finishing in third place in the Pacific Division. Individual players made outstanding contributions as well. Jim Fox, acquired in the 1972/73 season, recorded thirty rebounds against the Los Angeles Lakers; Fred "Downtown" Brown, acquired in 1971, scored 58 points against the Golden State Warriors; and Spencer Haywood finished ninth in the NBA in scoring, sixth in rebounding, and ninth in blocked shots. In mid-season Seattle hosted its first All-Star Game.

Sonics Make the Playoffs

The 1974/75 season marked another milestone for the Sonics. Not only did the team compile a winning season of 43 wins and 39 losses, they also qualified for the NBA playoffs for the first time in their eight-year history. After disposing of the Detroit Pistons in a best-of-three series, they lost to the Golden State Warriors in the Western Conference Semifinals. The Warriors went on to win the NBA championship.

The Sonics returned to the NBA finals after another winning season in 1975–76, again posting a 43–39 record. This time they were beaten out of the Western Conference Semifinals by the Phoenix Suns.

The 1976/77 season witnessed the Sonics slipping to a 40–42 season. In the off-season, the club underwent major restructuring with Assistant Coach Bob Hopkins replacing Bill Russell as head coach for the 1977/78 season. To the fans' dismay, a number of players were traded or benched. New faces to the lineup included Paul Silas, rookie Jack Sikma, Marvin Webster, Gus Williams and John Johnson. Owner Sam Schulman persuaded Lenny Wilkins, the club's new general manager, to return to his old coaching post. After implementing personnel changes, Coach Wilkins did, in fact, turn the team around to finish the season with a 42–18 record, and took them to the finals. The Sonics dispatched the Los Angeles Lakers, Portland, and Denver, to face the Washington Bullets in the finals. After trading victories through the series, Washington prevailed in Game 7 with a 105–99 victory.

Sonics Win the NBA Championship

Once again Coach Wilkins guided the Sonics to the NBA playoffs in 1978/79. The club posted their first 50-win season with a 52–30 record. In the post-season, they defeated the Lakers for the Western Conference title, and went on to face the Washington Bullets in the finals for the second time. After losing the first game to the Bullets, Seattle went on to win the next four games, clinching the NBA championship. Although the NBA-champion Sonics featured no big-name superstars,

Wilkins was credited by a Seattle sportswriter with "putting all the necessary ingredients into the pot at the right time."

The following season posted another first for Seattle. With the advent of the three-point shot in the NBA, Seattle's "Downtown" Freddie Brown became the league's first ever three-point percentage leader (0.443). They were off to the conference finals again after a 56–26 season, but lost the Western Conference title to the Los Angeles Lakers.

The 1980/81 season saw Seattle slip to 34 wins and 48 losses. Prior to the season opener, Paul Westphal came to Seattle in a trade with Phoenix for Dennis Johnson. Free agent Gus Williams failed to sign a contract with the Sonics and sat out the entire season. Paul Westphal and Jack Sikma were selected to represent the Sonics in the All-Star Game.

The club regained their footing in the conference with the 1981/82 season. Their 52–30 season record marked the third time in franchise history the team won over 50 games. Once again they were off to the finals, beating Houston in the first round of the playoffs, only to lose to the San Antonio Spurs in the Western Conference finals.

The following season, Seattle finished third in the Pacific Division with a 34–48 record.

League stars were Gus Williams, who finished sixth in assists and seventh in steals, and Jack Sikma who in his fifth season with Seattle, finished fifth in rebounding and tenth in free throw shooting. Sikma, Williams and David Thompson represented the Sonics in the All-Star Game.

Ackerley Communications Purchases Team

The Sonics franchise changed hands before the 1983/84 season, when owner Sam Schulman sold the team to Barry Ackerley of Seattle's Ackerley Communications, a diversified media and entertainment company. This acquisition fell under the newly established Sport and Entertainment segment of the company. This year also marked the end of Fred Brown's thirteen-season career with the Sonics when he retired. He left as the team's career leader in games played (963), scoring (14,018 points), field goals (6,006) and steals (1,149). His uniform, No. 32, was retired in 1986. Although finishing third in the NBA in defense, Seattle earned the fewest wins since the 1972/73 season, finishing with a 31–51 record. Jack Sikma continued to shine, making his seventh straight All-Star appearance.

Wilkens Era Comes to an End

Prior to the 1985/86 seasoning opening, Coach Lenny Wilkins was bumped up to the front office, after compiling a 478–402 record as coach of the Sonics. Bernie Bickerstaff replaced Wilkins as head coach on June 20, 1985. This season the Sonics achieved another NBA milestone: the first NBA game ever postponed due to rain when a leaky roof at the Seattle Center Coliseum halted a game against the Suns in the second quarter. The game was concluded the following day. Six foot, seven inch rookie Xavier McDaniel, who lead NCAA in both scoring and rebounding his senior season at Wichita State, played his first season in Seattle and earned NBA All-Rookie Team honors.

During the off-season, longtime center Jack Sikma was sent to Milwaukee for Alton Lister, a move that signaled a change in Seattle's style of defense. When Sikma left the Sonics he had accumulated more rebounds (7,729) blocked shots (705) and free throws made (3,044) than any player in team history. His No. 43 jersey was raised to the Seattle Center Coliseum rafters in 1992.

Big Three Make NBA History

On May 28, 1986, Bob Whitsitt was hired as President of the Sonics. Dale Ellis was acquired from Dallas and began his first season with Seattle. Ellis turned out to be one of the most prolific three-point shooters in NBA history. With Tom Chambers and Xavier McDaniel, Ellis was part of a trio that made league history—the first time three players from one team averaged 23 points or better in a season. All three were ranked among the league's top fifteen scorers. Ellis was also recognized as the NBA's Most Improved Player. Chambers was voted the All-Star Game MVP, as Seattle once again hosted the All-Star Game in February 1987. Newcomer Nate McMillan set a franchise record with 25 assists on February 23, 1987. Despite finishing with a 39–43 season, Seattle made the playoffs and reached the Conference Finals for the third time in team history. They lost in four straight games to the Lakers. Coach Bickerstaff was named Sporting News NBA Coach of the Year.

The Big Three (Ellis, McDaniel, and Chambers) provided most of the scoring again in the 1987/88 season. Another player contributing to the winning 44–38 season was Nate McMillan, finishing sixth in the league in assists and eighth in steals.

In July 1988, the Sonics let Chambers go to Phoenix and brought in rebounding champ Michael Cage from the Los Angeles Lakers. On November 9, the Sonics played Milwaukee in a seemingly endless five-overtime game which was eventually won by the Bucks by a single point, 155–154. In spite of losing the game, the Sonics' total points matched their all-time high. Dale Ellis continued his reign on the court finishing third in the NBA in scoring and second in three-point shooting and represented Seattle in the All-Star Game.

The most intriguing player on the roster in 1989 was 6-foot, 10-inch Shawn Kemp, drafted right out of high school. Known for earth-shaking dunks, he earned the nickname "Reign Man" and would go on to earn many honors in a Sonics uniform.

Coaching Changes Begin Team Restructuring

Coach Bickerstaff lead the team to a 41–41 finish in 1990, an ending repeated in 1991 under the leadership of K.C. Jones. Jones had coached the Boston Celtics to two championships in the 1980's and had won eight championships as a player. But, on November 18, Seattle scored only 65 points in a loss to the Clippers, marking the weakest offensive performance of the team in franchise history.

Other team changes in midseason saw Xavier McDaniel go to the Phoenix Suns on December 7 in exchange for long-distance threat Eddie Johnson and a couple of draft picks. Dale Ellis left for Milwaukee in a trade for Ricky Pierce; and Olden Polynice went to the Los Angeles Clippers for Benoit Benjamin. Shawn Kemp set a Sonics' single-game record for blocked shots by snuffing ten Lakers' attempts on January 18. First-round draft pick Gary Payton, who had been *Sports Illustrated's* College Player of the Year at Oregon State, took over point guard duties from Nate McMillan and led the team in assists.

The team remained in transition during the 1991/92 season. Coach K.C. Jones was fired on January 15, and was succeeded by George Karl. Karl, who played five years with the San Antonio Spurs in the mid-70's, had coached two-year stints with the Cleveland Cavaliers and the Golden State Warriors. He had also coached Albany of the Continental Basketball Association and Real Madrid in Europe.

The team appeared headed for a major turnaround under Karl and finished the season winning 27 of their last 42 games. On March 3, the Sonics won their 1000th game with a victory over Denver. They advanced to the Western Conference Semifinals over Golden State, but fell to Utah in five games.

Fans of the Sonics' 1992/93 season experienced an exciting, unconventional brand of basketball. The team ended in second place in the Pacific Division with a 55–27 record, the second best in club history. Power forward Shawn Kemp continued to entertain with spectacular offensive moves and dramatic slam dunks. Point guard Gary Payton developed a jump shot to augment his offensive repertoire and gained a reputation as a tenacious defender. The entire Sonics team seemed to thrive on an innovative defensive strategy devised by Assistant Coach Bob Kloppenburg. Midseason dealt center Benoit Benjamin and unsigned draft choice Doug Christie to the Lakers for Sam Perkins. The Sonics set a team record with twenty-three steals (two short of an NBA record) in a victory over Sacramento. Coach Karl recorded his 200th career win on April 22 against the Los Angeles Clippers. The team set a franchise record by selling out 26 home games. Another playoff run saw the Sonics beating Utah in the first round, and Houston in the Conference Semifinals, but the Charles Barkley-led Phoenix Suns were too much for the Sonics as they fell in the Western Conference Finals in seven games.

In 1993–94 the club picked up Detlef Schrempf from the Indiana Pacers and Kendall Gill from the Charlotte Hornets in preseason trades. The team went from being the NBA's best team in the regular season, with a 63–19 record, and winning the Pacific Division for the second time in NBA playoff history, to becoming the first No. 1 seed ever to lose to a No. 8 seed with a loss to the Denver Nuggets. Their sixty-three wins, however, included the team record for most home wins (37) and most road wins (26). McMillan lead the league in steals and the team set a team record with 1,053 steals, second highest total in NBA history. Kemp finished in the top 25 in scoring. The team sold out all forty-one home games, a franchise first.

Following the off season, Sonic President Bob Whitsitt, who had won NBA Executive of the Year honors the previous year, resigned in an apparent dispute with ownership. During the summer Wally Walker, a former NBA player and the Sonics' part-time broadcast analyst, was hired to fill his spot. One of his first moves was to trade Ricky Pierce and the draft rights to Carlos Rogers to the Golden State Warrior for Sarunas Marciulionis and Byron Houston.

The 1994/95 season was reminiscent of the year before, although the Sonics played the entire season in the Tacoma Dome while a new stadium was being built. The Sonics started out as one of the league's best teams and ended with a 57–25 record. Schrempf finished second in the league in three-point percentage, shooting a team record of 51.4 percent. For the third straight year, the Sonics lead the league in steals. Karl won his 300th career NBA game. Shawn Kemp, Gary Payton, and Detlef Schrempf all made the All-Star Team, giving Seattle more representatives in the midseason classic than any other NBA club. Other key players were second year Ervin Johnson and Bill Cartwright. Once again, however, their playoff hopes were dashed by the Lakers in the first round.

KeyArena, located on the campus of The Seattle Center, opened its doors as the new 17,072-seat home of the Seattle SuperSonics on October 26, 1995. The Sonics' first game in their new venue was a win on November 4, 1995, against the Los Angeles Lakers. The team fit comfortably in the new arena and set a club record of 38 home game wins. Away from home, they beat the Chicago Bulls in one of only ten losses the Bulls suffered all season. In February and March, the Sonics posted a team-record 14-game wining streak, and later became the first team in NBA history to lead the league in steals for four straight seasons. Shawn Kemp, Gary Payton and the Sonics coaching staff represented the team in this year's All-Star Game. Kemp lead the team in scoring; Payton led the NBA in steals, was named the NBA Defensive Player of the Year, and won a berth on the U.S. Olympic basketball team. At the end of the season, the Sonics had posted a record of 64 wins and eighteen losses, the tenth best in NBA history. In the playoffs, they marched over the Sacramento Kings, the Houston Rockets, and the Utah Jazz to advance to the finals—the first time since their 1979 championship series. Facing the Bulls, the Sonics lost the first three games, but rebounded with back-to-back wins in games four and five, before the Bulls ended Seattle's championship run in the sixth game.

For the fifth straight season, Seattle won at least 55 games in 1996/97, and became the first team to lead the NBA in steals for five consecutive seasons (11.02 a game). In post-season play, they edged out the Lakers for their third Pacific Division title in four years. After defeating the Phoenix Suns, they faced the Houston Rockets who won in the final seconds of game seven of the Western Conference Semifinals. Kemp, Payton and Schrempf once again represented the Sonics on the All-Star Team. Payton was named First Team All-Defense for the fourth straight season. Seattle led the NBA in steals-to-turnover ratio with 0.73, and forced more turnovers (18.7) than any other team in the league.

Having been termed the team that couldn't win games when it counted, namely the playoffs, Seattle began the 1997/98 season looking toward the finals. With seven new players, the Sonics found themselves once again on top of the Pacific Division for the fourth time in five seasons, and posted another winning season with 61 wins and 21 losses. In a key move by Sonics President Wally Walker, a three-way trade was negotiated with Milwaukee and Cleveland to bring three-time All-Star Vin Baker to Seattle. In his first season as a Sonic, Baker did not disappoint his teammates and coach: he averaged 19.2 points per game, 8 rebounds per game, and finished fifth in the NBA in field goal percentage. Other key contributors to the team were Jerome Kersey, Greg Anthony, Aaron Williams and Dale Ellis. In the post-season, Seattle overcame Minnesota in the first round, but were beaten by the Lakers in five games, in no small way due to the phenomenal play of Shaquille O'Neal.

Coach Karl Leaves the Sonics

Although the 1998/99 season was another stellar season for Gary Payton, the Sonics finished 25–25 in the lockout-shortened season and missed the playoffs for the first time in nine years. Payton became the Sonics' all-time steals leader, scored his 10,000th NBA point and recorded his eighth triple-double (double digits in points, rebounds, and assists). In May 1998, Coach Karl left the Sonics to be replaced by former player Paul Westphal. Nate McMillan ended his 12-year career as Seattle's all-time steals and assists leader, but remained with the Sonics coaching staff as an assistant.

In the 1999/2000 season, Seattle's three-season home-sell-out record was broken at 114 on November 4, 1999. Gary Payton continued to lead the team in scoring, steals, and assists, and ended the season with 315 consecutive starts, the longest currently in the league. He was named First Team All-NBA for the second time, and was the second leading vote getter behind Shaquille O'Neal. Brent Barry was acquired from the Chicago Bulls and Ruben Patterson signed a three-year contract with the Sonics. Their playoffs hopes were dashed for the ninth time in ten years when they lost to the Utah Jazz in the first round.

Paul Westphal was replaced as head coach at the beginning of the 2000/2001 season by Nate McMillan, who was named interim coach on November 27, and later signed a four-year contract with the Sonics. He recorded his first career coaching victory on November 28 against the neighboring Trail Blazers in Portland, and went on to finish the season with a 38–29 record. Desmond Mason was signed as a first-round draft pick; and Patrick Ewing was acquired from the New York Knicks. Gary Payton passed Fred Brown as the team's all-time leading scorer with 14,018 points and became the eighth player in NBA history to compile 15,000 points, 6,000 assists, and 1,000 steals. He was named NBA Hometown Hero of the Month in April. As

the first Sonics to ever do so, Desmond Mason won the NBA Slam Dunk contest during the NBA All-Star weekend.

Starbuck's Founder Purchases the Seattle SuperSonics

In 2001, The Basketball Club of Seattle LLC purchased the Seattle SuperSonics from Barry Ackerley for $200 million. The Basketball Club of Seattle LLC, a group of private investors, was headed by Howard Schultz, founder of Starbucks Coffee Company. Schultz, an avid sports fan, hoped by acquiring ownership of the team to make outstanding sporting events accessible to the entire community and is committed to bringing an NBA championship to the city of Seattle, not unlike the aspirations of original owner Sam Schulman.

Principal Competitors

Los Angeles Lakers, Portland Trail Blazers, Phoenix Suns.

Further Reading

Aretha, David, *The Seattle Supersonics Basketball Team*, Springfield, N.J.: Enslow Publishers, Inc., 1999, 48 p.

Flynn, Mike, "Schultz Has Confidence in Game Plan," *Puget Sound Business Journal*, October 12, 2001, p. 54.

Goodman, Michael, *Seattle SuperSonics*, Mankato, Minn.: Creative Education, Inc., 1998, 32 p.

Italia, Bob, *Inside the NBA: Seattle SuperSonics*, Minneapolis: ABDO Consulting Group, 1997, 32 p.

Newman, Elizabeth, "Jack Sikma, Sonics Center May 3, 1982," *Sports Illustrated*, September 17, 2001, p.20.

O'Donnell, Chuck, "Xavier McDaniel: Anything Can Happen," *Basketball Digest*, February 2002, p. 74.

Peterson, Tom, *Seattle Supersonics*, Mankato, Minn.: Creative Education, Inc., 1989, 28 p.

Seattle SuperSonics, *2001–02 Seattle SuperSonics Media Guide*, 2002, 320 p.

Shields, David, "The Capitalist Communitarian," *The New York Times Magazine*, March 24, 2002, p. 28.

Taylor, Phil, "Seattle SuperSonics: As Preparations Are Made for the Rashard Lewis Era," *Sports Illustrated*, October 29, 2001, p 180.

—Carol D. Beavers

Big Lots, Inc.

300 Phillipi Road
Columbus, Ohio 43228-0512
U.S.A.
Telephone: (614) 278-6800
Fax: (614) 278-6676
Web site: http://www.biglots.com

Public Company
Incorporated: 1967 as Consolidated Stores Corporation
Employees: 46,246 (2002)
Sales: $3.433 billion (2001)
Stock Exchanges: New York
Ticker Symbol: BLI
NAIC: 452990 All Other General Merchandise Stores;
   421990 Other Miscellaneous Durable Goods
   Wholesalers

Big Lots, Inc., the nation's largest closeout retailer, sells everything from consumables, seasonal products and furniture to housewares, toys and gifts. The company operates over 1,300 closeout stores in 45 states. The stores operate under the names Big Lots, Big Lots Furniture, Pic 'n' Save and Mac Frugal's Bargains. The company's wholesale operations are conducted through Big Lots Wholesale, Consolidated International, and Wisconson Toy, and online shopping is available at http://www.biglotswholesale.com. Big Lots differentiates itself from the dollar stores and large-scale discount retailers by offering a wide range of products and prices in their 25,000 to 50,000-square-foot stores. Big Lots acquires leftover, discontinued, and otherwise unwanted products from approximately 3,000 vendors located around the world. Some of the vendors include Proctor & Gamble, Mattel, and small-scale manufacturers in China and the Philippines.

Consolidated Stores Corporation

When Consolidated Stores Corporation (CSC) went public in 1985, just three years after opening their first closeout store, with a $33.4 million stock offering, the majority of the funds raised went to pay off debt incurred during the purchase of CSC from its main stockholders, the Shenk and Schottenstein families, who also happened to be key stockholders and executives in the new CSC. Only $1.9 million of the money raised was earmarked for the opening of 40–45 new stores. The new CSC, upon acquiring the old CSC, switched the company's fiscal year to the traditional retail fiscal period and divested two of CSC's subsidiaries, AMT and Covairs Auto Parts store, in order to focus the company's operations on one market: the retail and closeout business.

CSC hit the jackpot when they opted to expand their closeout wholesale business into retail. Since that first store opened, in 1982, CSC opened more than 300 additional stores and became the nation's largest closeout chain. In the wake of an excellent fiscal year, CSC targeted 1988 as a year to catch its management and management systems up to its explosive growth. Sol Shenk, Chairman and founder of CSC told *Discount Store News* in 1998, "We knew how to secure merchandise, but were lacking in installing procedures and people. The bottom line was that sales were down, the warehouse was a mess." Shenk added, "We were not able to meet projections. We didn't have the attributes and professional skills of a company our size." James Guinan, president of CSC's retail operations, explained that another problem the company faced was that the buying lines simply couldn't absorb the number of stores they were opening in early 1987. "... As a result, [we] filled the shelves with a lot of low-end goods ...[that were] great for the consumer, but the margins weren't there." CSC's solutions for the problems Shenk and Guinan discussed were to bring in a "whole new layer of top management people," to improve operations by developing new systems including a computerized truck routing system, an electronic mail system, and a centralized training system to help standardize store operation. To increase CSC's margins, they planned to venture into market unfamiliar to them—the soft goods market—and also, into the import market.

When CSC was named, by *Discount Store News*, one of the ten most profitable chains in 1994 it seemed that the changes and improvements that the company had instituted had indeed improved operations and margins. CSC continued to open retail stores across the United States, stores in the Midwest were

Company Perspectives:

We are the nation's largest broadline closeout retailer. The Company's goal is to build upon its leadership position in closeout retailing, a growing segment of the retailing indus- try, by expanding its market presence in both existing and new markets. The Company believes that the combination of its strengths in merchandising, purchasing, site selection, distribution and cost-containment has made it a low-cost, value retailer well-positioned for future growth.

routinely called Consolidated Stores, while stores opened in other regions of the United States were called either Big Lots, Odd Lots, Itzadeal, or All For One.

Consolidated Stores Expands Further

CSC expanded its retail toy business, which included its operation of 115 Toy Liquidators, the Wisconsin Toy wholesale operation, and sixteen The Amazing Toy Store retail outlets, with the $315 million purchase of Kay-Bee Toys in 1996. CSC purchased Kay-Bee Toys with high hopes. "Toys is the best closeout business we have. We think we will be the true value player in toys," said Michael Potter, Senior Vice President and Chief Financial Officer of CSC, at the time. However, it wouldn't be long before CSC opted out of the retail toy market altogether.

CSC's expansion was not complete with its latest purchase; the company needed more distribution capacity. In 1997, CSC purchased a 665,000 square-foot distribution center in Mont-gomery, Alabama in order to cut distribution costs to its south-ern stores. The company also set its sights on improving its furniture business. In 1998, CSC operated 171-furniture depart-ments within its Big Lots general discount stores and had 26 freestanding Big Lots furniture stores. The company planned on opening 50 additional freestanding furniture and 100 additional furniture departments in the coming year.

Consolidated Stores Rethinks Business Plan

The first sign that long-time closeout store Consolidated Stores Corporation was thinking about drastically altering their business structure appeared when the Board retained the invest-ment banking firm Credit Suisse First Boston to help the com-pany pursue strategic repositioning alternatives. The company's intent to refocus their business became crystal clear when, on June 27, 2000, Consolidated Stores announced that its Board of Directors had decided to divest its toy operation, Kay-Bee Toys Division—separating the toy division irrevocably from the company's closeout business. Kay-Bee Toys (and Toy Liquida-tors), purchased by CSC in the mid-1990s for $329 million, had been a disaster from the get-go as they were purchased just as the toy market was experiencing over-expansion. After the purchase, however, CSC continued to sink money into Kay-Bee Toys when they put $80 million into KBKids.com.

The divesture was orchestrated quickly, and on December 8, 2000 the company announced that the $305 million sale of Kay-Bee Toys was complete. An affiliate of Bain Capital, Inc.

purchased the Toy division in conjunction with Kay-Bee Toys management, who were retained to lead Kay-Bee Toys.

In a press release announcing the finalization of the sale of Kay-Bee Toys, Michael J. Potter, Chairman and Chief Executive Officer of Consolidated Stores said, "This sale is an important step forward in the strategic repositioning of our company. With the divestiture of Kay-Bee, we are now able to focus on a single closeout business model, which represents our core competency. As the country's largest closeout retailer, we believe we are uniquely positioned to grow our business well into the future."

Big Changes

Upon scaling the company's interests down to focus solely on their closeout retail business, Consolidated Stores launched a wide-reaching plan to improve their overall business. On May 15, 2001, the first step of the process, changing the company's name from Consolidated Stores Corporation to Big Lots, Inc, took place. "The name change is a step toward building a strong brand," said Michael J. Potter in an article written for Business First-Columbus. The name change brought Big Lots, Inc.'s more than 1,300 stores together under the Big Lots name. 856 stores already operated under the Big Lots name and the remaining stores who operated as Odd Lots, Mac Frugal's and Pic 'n' Save were slated to have their names changed by the end of 2002.

Along with the name change, the company planned to spruce up the brand's image in order to attract a more affluent group of bargain shoppers. Al Bell, Vice Chairman of Big Lots told *HFN Weekly* in May 2001, "We want to appeal to a broader demo-graphic, to appeal to the customer who wants a bargain but doesn't necessarily need a bargain." Some of the superficial changes that Big Lots made to win over these customers included improved lighting, restrooms and floors. Big lots invested $80,000 per store to repaint and otherwise improve the stores. Changes to the company's stock of products included plans to expand their home furnishings and seasonal items. The basic plan for upgrading the stores was to make them brighter, friendly and to offer better service. In addition to rebranding many stores, Big Lots intended to open approximately 80 new Big Lots stores in 2001 and launched a customer-service training program.

Big Budget Advertising

By bringing all of their stores together under the Big Lots name, the company afforded themselves a simpler task in adver-tising. Rather than launching multiple advertising campaigns for multiple stores, Big Lots could now focus their entire adver-tising budget on the Big Lots brand. The company pledged $27 million to the Big Lots advertising effort, well more than double the company's marketing budgets for the previous years. SBC Advertising, the firm that handled the company's advertising for the past 3 years, managed the campaign. Upon taking control of the Company, Mr. Potter decided to cancel multiple advertising circulars (that the company had relied upon to bring in busi-ness). The circular advertising strategy was streamlined, to allow the company to invest more time and money on their new, big budget advertising campaign.

The campaign included 3 new television spots featuring the company's 3-year spokesman, Jerry Van Dyke. The spots fol-

---

Key Dates:

1967: Sol Shenk opens his first discount wholesale and retail store, focusing on auto parts.

1967–1971: Shenk's stores grow into a small chain of Corvair Auto Stores.

1982: Consolidated Stores Corporation opens its first Odd Lots closeout store.

1985: Consolidated Stores goes public with a $33.4 million stock offering.

1994: Consolidated Stores named one of the ten most profitable chains in 1994.

1996: The company purchases of Kay-Bee Toys for $315 million.

1999: Internet retail site KBkids.com LLC is launched as a joint venture with BrainPlay.com.

2000: Consolidated Stores divests Kay-Bee Toys Division in a $305 million sale, focusing the company's attention on its closeout business.

2001: Consolidated Stores changes its name to Big Lots, Inc. and launches a $27 million campaign to re-brand its McFrugal's, Pic 'N' Save, and Odd Lots stores; the company launches a business-to-business Web site, www.Biglotswholesale.com and begins construction of a 1.2 million square-foot distribution center in Durant, Ohio.

---

lowed an introductory TV, print, and radio campaign that focused on the markets where the Big Lots name was new. The TV spots were designed to help cast Big Lots as "a meaningful and acceptable alternative for consumers," said David Dennis to *ADWEEK* in July 2001, SBC Advertising's president, he continued, noting that the perception to overcome is "that you have to hide in the closet and be ashamed to shop" at closeout stores. Comedian Mr. Van Dyke had been an effective spokesman as he was known by all generations for his work on both *The Dick Van Dyke Show,* and *Coach* which many people watch in re-runs.

The advertisements aimed to convey the message that not only was shopping at Big Lots nothing to be ashamed of, but that it was the smart way to shop. Additionally, the advertisements strove to convey the message that people who wanted to save the most money and get the best products needed to shop at Big Lots every week because the products in the stores are changed frequently.

Continuing Change in 2001

Big Lots faced a $10.7 million loss, in August 2001, caused by slow sales, lowered profit margins and the company's continued investment in converting its multiple non-Big Lots-named stores into Big Lots. In response to the dwindling share price (the share price fell 9 cents) the Company slashed prices countrywide.

Other major changes Big Lots underwent during the fall of 2001 included an upgrade of the company's merchandising systems. Previously the stores had been disorganized; products were displayed on shelves with little reason and the distribution infra-

structure needed attention. Big Lots invested in a 300,000-foot expansion of its Montgomery, Alabama distribution center, enabling it to serve over 300 stores in the southeast. Enlarging and expanding upon the number of distribution centers allowed Big Lots to stock their stores with more items, which offered customers a deal-hunting shopping experience that the company hoped would inspire weekly visits to the store. Each store received a new truckload of merchandise weekly, which made it possible for the same customer to return once a week and find new deals, new brands and different items. The advertising campaigns stressed the fun and savings potential of shopping at Big Lots on a weekly basis.

While this type of treasure hunt shopping experience was integral to the Big Lots concept, the Company found that their customers also needed a predictable element to their shopping; customers needed to have certain products delivered consistently. By expanding the size of the Big Lots distribution centers, Big Lots was able to supply customers with both new, unexpected products and a host of standards (like diapers and other household products). All of the company's stock was tracked by a renovated data processing system that let buyers track Big Lots stock in order to learn which products were moving and which were not. The renovated data processing system eventually allowed Big Lots managers to get a more complete picture of what they needed to stock in their particular store for each coming week.

Big Lots also invested in educating and training their store-level employees in order to supply customers not only with more and better-organized products but with an improved customer service experience. Joe Cooper, vice president and treasurer of Big Lots, told *Home Furnishing Network* in January 2002, "In today's competitive environment, we can no longer allow basic customer service to be a limiting factor in our success. Through a new customer service program, stores are focusing on operating initiatives that come directly from what customers have told us they value. We are measuring our progress from our customers' perspective and provide incentives that encourage associate involvement and improvement." Another effort to boost customer service was tied to customer's responses on random customer service polls (some customers would receive a survey on the back of their sales receipt, that if they completed they received $3). The surveys allowed employees to earn bonuses for positive customer feedback, further motivating staff to focus on customer service.

The large amounts of money and attention put into rebranding and improvement did not immediately show a positive financial effect. Despite low sales for 2001, Michael Potter took a long-term and optimistic view when speaking with *MMR*, "[We] remain enthusiastic about our key strategic initiatives. . . . The 204 stores we've converted to the Big Lots name this year have delivered strong initial sales increases. Those strong results combined with ongoing store and merchandising initiatives reinforce our view that this year's investment in repositioning will drive positive results over the coming years."

Big Lots on the World Wide Web

While the stores were undergoing rebranding and new distribution centers were being built, Big Lots expanded its business to include an online, business-to-business store. Big Lots launched its website, www.Biglotswholesale.com in November 2001. The website enabled businesses to shop 16 product categories, sell seasonal specials, and $1 clearance items. Because there was no membership fee to shop the site, it was possible for non-business customers to make use of the site also.

Continued Expansion

In the beginning months of 2002, the advertising campaign and a particular commercial entitled ''Closeout Moment,'' beat out approximately 700 entrants to receive honors as a finalist at the Retail Advertising Conference's Awards. Although the advertisement didn't win first place it, in the words of Kent Lasen, Executive Vice-President of Merchandising, ''claimed the people's choice'' (as reported in *Retail Merchandiser*, April 2002). Financially, the advertising campaign and overall company facelift has begun to work wonderfully—the average number of transactions increased 4.3 percent and the size of the average transaction increased by 9.7 percent. Consumables, a long-time cash cow for Big Lots, continued to post double-digit sales gains (they already made up 30 percent of Big Lots' sales).

With the unification strategy and rebranding efforts working as planned, Big Lots set its sights on continued expansion. Furniture departments were added to many Big Lots stores, and, in 2002, owned 62 free-standing furniture outlets. Big Lots furniture departments and stores were instant successes as they consistently carried furniture with brands like Pier-1 and sold the stock at 30 percent-50 percent off what customers would pay in the name-brand store. When customers became familiar with Big Lots' possible inventory, the furniture segment of Big Lots grew at least 35 percent, becoming one of Big Lots most profitable sectors.

As Big Lots saw their TV commercials making a difference in the markets they were broadcast to, the company began drafting plans to open 53 new stores in 2002, all in Big Lots current 45-state market. The Company also tested another upgraded design for the Big Lots stores in May 2002; the design included even cleaner and brighter specifications, improved merchandise layouts and new signs.

2002: Big Lots Reports First Quarter Growth

On May 21, 2002, Big Lots reported first quarter net income of $12.2 million, compared to earnings of $0.3 million in the first quarter of 2001. Michael Potter attributed the successful

quarter to all of the restructuring and strategic initiatives that the company had undergone since the divesture of Kay-Bee Toys. Customer traffic rose every month since November 2001 after falling for three straight years. There is no doubt that much of Big Lots success is due to the leadership of Michael Potter, who took over the company as Kay-Bee Toys was divested. The company predicted that the coming years will see a rise in sales and stock shares.

Principal Divisions

Big Lots Wholesale; Closeout Division.

Principal Competitors

99 Cents Only Stores; Kmart Corporation; Target Corporation; Wal-Mart Stores, Inc.; Tuesday Morning.

Further Reading

''Big Lots,'' *DSN Retail Fax*, November 5, 2001, p. 2.

''Big Lots, Inc.,'' *Business First-Columbus*, August 24, 2001, p. A32.

''Big Lots Is in the of Midst Major Transition,'' *MMR*, October 29, 2001, p. 46.

''Big Lots Reports First Quarter EPS of $0.11, Compared to Flat Earnings Last Year, Company Raises Second Quarter Guidance,'' *PR Newswire*, May 21, 2002, http://www.prnewswire.com.

Buchanan, Lee, ''Big Changes at Big Lots Under Way,'' *HFN: The Weekly Newspaper for the Home Furnishing Network*, May 28, 2001, p. 13.

''Charge Results in Loss at Big Lots,'' *MMR*, March 25, 2002, p. 8.

Howell, Debbie, ''Big Lots Starts to See Dividends of Single-Banner, Closeout-only Plan,'' *DSN Retailing Today*, April 8, 2002, p. 17.

Jensen, Trevor, ''Bigger Budge Backs Big Lots Rebranding Moves,'' *ADWEEK*, June 2, 2001, p. 6.

Kroll, Louisa, ''Out of the Discard Bin,'' *Forbes*, May 27, 2002, p. 104.

''Making a Big Deal Over Big Lots,'' *Retail Merchandiser*, April 2002, p. 12.

Prior, Molly, ''Big Lots Launches Ad Campaign Touting Market Leader Status,'' *DSN Retailing Today*, July 23, 2001, p. 3.

Showalter, Kathy, ''Big Lots Hopes to Benefit from Economic Downturn,'' *Business First-Columbus*, May 18, 2001, p. A13.

Sloan, Carol, ''Big Lots Speeds Up Name Shift,'' *Home Textiles Today*, June 4, 2001, p. 8.

——, ''Big Lots Has Big Plans for Textiles,'' *Home Textiles Today*, June 18, 2001, p. 2.

Zaczkiewicz, Arthur, ''Big Lots Find Niche Between Dollar Stores, Big Boxes,'' *HFN: The Weekly Newspaper for the Home Furnishing Network*, January 21, 2002, p. 44.

—Tammy Weisberger

Bonneville Power Administration

905 NE 11th Avenue
Portland, Oregon 97232
U.S.A.
Telephone: (503) 230-3000
Toll Free: (800) 282-3713
Web site: http://www.bpa.gov

Government-Owned Agency
Established: 1937
Employees: 2,878 (2001)
Sales: $4,278.7 million (2001)
NAIC: 221111 Hydroelectric Power Generation; 234920
Power and Communication Transmission Line
Construction; 221113 Nuclear Electric Power
Generation; 221119 Other Electric Power Generation

Bonneville Power Administration (BPA), a United States federal agency created in 1937 by the Roosevelt administration and Congress, markets wholesale electricity and transmission to public and private utilities as well as some large industries in the Pacific Northwest region of the United States. The bulk of the energy that BPA sells comes from the Columbia River and its tributaries. BPA is part of the United States Department of Energy. The agency supplies approximately half the electricity used in the Northwest and operates many of the region's high-voltage transmissions. Conservation plays an important role in BPA's practices; BPA invests in research and development of alternate energy sources regularly and works with salmon conservation groups to secure the safety of the Northwest's salmon population. BPA is not tax-supported and recovers all of its costs through the sales of electricity and transmission.

Late 1930s and Early 1940s:
Developments During the New Deal

Faced with the reality of insufficient rainfall, a sore need for work, and the possibility of producing a large amount of electricity, on July 16, 1933, President Roosevelt authorized the $60-million Grand Coulee Dam project that would bring elec-

tricity to 11 states and distribute much-needed water to farming communities. Another dam, the Bonneville Dam that passes through the Cascade Mountains between Oregon and Washington, was also under construction during this time period. Before the two projects were completed, Congress and President Roosevelt wisely anticipated the need to market and regulate the power that these new power sources would generate. The Bonneville Power Administration (BPA) was created in 1937 to address this need. Some of BPA's early goals were to bring electricity to small farms, rural areas, and small communities that were not being served by private utilities.

These two dams produced an extremely large amount of electricity; the Grand Coulee Dam itself is the third largest producer of electricity in the world. The large amount of electricity in BPA's control allowed them to carry out the job assigned to them by the Roosevelt administration—to sell affordable electricity to the small communities and to extend their service territory over all of Washington, Oregon, Idaho, and western Montana. Eventually, BPA's service territory increased to include small portions of California, Nevada, Utah, Wyoming, and eastern Montana.

1950s–1960s: Organized Distribution of Power

While the dams were under construction, BPA built a network of transmission lines that would distribute the electricity the dams produced. The first line built connected the Bonneville Dam to Cascade Locks, which was three miles from the dam. Throughout the 1940s, 1950s, and 1960s, BPA constructed interconnected networks and loops of high-voltage wire that reached out to connect BPA's service territory.

Dispatchers who coordinated and monitored the power flowing through these lines oversaw electricity distribution. Eventually BPA constructed transmission lines that ran far south into California and the Southwest, and north to connect with lines in Canada.

1970s–1980s: Nuclear Power Plants

During the 1970s, BPA joined forces with the Washington Public Power Supply System (WPPSS) and four private utilities—Puget Sound Power & Light Co, Washington Water Power Co., Portland General Electric, and Pacific Power & Light Co.—to finance the construction of three nuclear plants to generate additional energy for the Pacific Northwest. All of the nuclear plants being constructed during this time period (not just the three guaranteed by BPA) were plagued by high construction costs and declining demand for power. These factors caused BPA, in September 1984, to recommend delaying the construction of two of the nuclear plants they were tied to. A spokesman for BPA told the *Wall Street Journal* in 1984, "We anticipate a delay of at least 27 months. We're not going to need the power as soon as we thought. If we bring those two plants on line too soon, we'll have power we can't sell. And that's a good way to lose money."

The private utilities affected by the delay of construction reacted to this announcement, and others like it, in outrage. The four private utilities quickly filed suit, claiming that the closing down of these nuclear power projects caused their companies considerable loss. BPA strove to find a settlement with the four companies; one proposal discussed was that the private utilities would be guaranteed by BPA the same amount of electricity they would have gotten from the stalled nuclear plants. In exchange, the lawsuit the utilities launched would be dropped.

BPA and the four private utilities signed an agreement on September 19, 1985, to settle the $2-billion suit. The agreement allowed that BPA would supply the private utilities with the same amount of power (roughly) for the same estimated price that they would have paid for the operating of a nuclear power plant if it had been finished as scheduled. In exchange, BPA received the option to purchase the private utilities share of the nuclear project and the suit brought against them was dropped. Many public utilities were dismayed by this settlement, arguing that the four private utilities were let off the hook for their nuclear obligations and that they received cheap power at the expense of public utilities.

The high price of the botched nuclear project added to the factors that forced BPA to raise electricity rates. Aluminum plants, lumber, and plywood industries were particularly hard hit by the raised electricity prices as their industries were already in decline.

1980s and Early 1990s: Electricity Bills Rise as Conservationism Grows

The federal Northwest Electric Power Planning and Conservation Act of 1980 insisted that BPA assess conservation and renewable energy resources. BPA, in response, took into consideration many studies in conservation. One study, launched in

1983 by the Hood River Conservation Project (HRCP), retrofitted 2,989 homes. The result showed an averaged energy saving of 15 percent. Groups studying the Pacific Northwest's salmon species announced in November 1991 that sockeye salmon were an endangered species. This finding affected BPA in a major way, as the announcement of an endangered species in one of the BPA's primary hydroelectricity generating waterways caused them to allow for more water to remain in the waterways, cutting the amount of power that was produced. BPA announced, soon after the endangered species announcement, that electricity rates would rise five to 15 percent and that they intended to replace the lost energy with conservation measures and the purchase of power from regions outside of the Pacific Northwest.

Not surprisingly, the announcement that BPA would raise electricity rates was met with extreme dissatisfaction from both industrial and private customers. Customers complained that BPA was too free spending with rate payers' money and that the power authority was overstaffed. BPA responded by shaving a few percentage points off the expected increase and explained, more in detail, why the rates needed to be raised. The explanation included a discussion of the lack of rainfall the region had seen in the past six years, the fact that BPA charged aluminum companies variable rates depending on the price of the metal (the metal price was set extremely low), and finally the Endangered Species Act, which caused BPA, according to executive assistant administrator Steven Hickcock, to "operate the system differently. We're flowing the river more for the convenience of fish than for the needs of energy users."

In response to their customers' outrage at the increasing electricity rate, BPA froze hiring and launched an efficiency study aimed at reorganizing the agency. The study was scheduled to take place over two years. The agency also found it necessary to slash expenses to balance BPA's sluggish revenue stream. The cuts took place in three areas: a 50-percent reduction in administrative expenses, travel, and training; a 25-percent cut to programs including salmon recovery and energy conservation; and the termination of the two WPPSS nuclear plants that BPA had delayed construction on earlier. *Puget Sound Business Journal* reported that, "although the cuts sound dramatic, they affect only a small percentage of the agency's costs." The *Journal* went on to state that, "Only 23 percent of BPA's annual expenses—about $500 million a year—are for daily operations. The remaining third of the agency's annual expenses go to payments on its debt to the U.S. Treasury, depreciation and rate supports for residential and farm customers."

Mid- to Late 1990s: More Rate Hikes

Chief administrator at BPA, Randy Hardy, announced that he would seek special legislation to help make large-scale changes in the way the BPA was run, aiming to turn the bureaucratic agency into an efficient organization modeled after corporate America. Hardy also announced BPA's plan for tiered rates beginning in 1995. In the past, BPA offered virtually the same rates to customers no matter what the agency's actual cost of delivering the power to a specific location was. With the new plan, BPA proposed to empower the agency to charge according to its own costs. The tiered rates system also allowed BPA to charge different rates depending on how the electricity was

Key Dates:

1933: Construction begins on Grand Coulee and Bonneville Dams.

1937: Congress and Roosevelt Administration create Bonneville Power Administration to market the energy produced by the Grand Coulee and Bonneville Dams.

1940s–1960s: BPA constructs networks and loops of high-voltage wire to connect BPA's service territory.

1980: The passage of the Northwest Electric Power Planning and Conservation Act forces BPA to assess and implement conservation and renewable energy resources.

1991: Sockeye salmon species are declared an endangered species, causing BPA to drastically alter its hydroelectricity practices, which results in the production of less power and forces BPA to raise electricity rates.

1992: BPA enters into a power-swap agreement with Southern California.

2000: BPA's investments and research into renewable energy resources begin to show results.

2001: BPA launches education and marketing programs and offers incentives to urge customers to conserve energy.

2002: BPA's wind power facilities show positive results in the Northwest.

generated. However, due to a variety of factors, the tiered rate structure was shelved soon after it was announced. BPA continued to scrutinize all of their projects and facilities in an effort to trim off any extra fat.

Aluminum and other manufacturers received welcome news when BPA proposed in July 1995 a wholesale power rate cut that would reduce electric bills by 12.7 percent. BPA was moved to propose this radical shift in pricing when Kaiser Aluminum & Chemical Corp. proposed shifting some of its business away from BPA to Washington Water Power Co.. Another surprising move by BPA occurred when they agreed to allow their industrial customers to purchase 250 megawatts of electricity from other sources. In October 1996, the customers were able to purchase even more of their electricity (up to 25 percent) from other sources. By allowing their industrial customers to do this, BPA bought itself a little more flexibility with their dwindling energy resources. BPA was strapped to generate and purchase enough power to supply their industrial and private customers, pay off their debt, and conserve enough water to assure the Pacific Northwest's endangered species a chance at recuperation. Something in BPA's supply cycle had to give, and the industrial customers were the most logical first choice, due to the rates that BPA was contractually obliged to give them.

1990s: Is Sharing a Good Thing?

When BPA agreed to swap power with California in 1992 they believed that the agreement was a win-win situation. A one-year swap was made with four California utilities for more than

600 megawatts of energy to be sent south during the summer, air-conditioning season. California would return the energy later in the year to heat the Northwest's homes during the colder winter season. However, BPA came under fire for this arrangement. Pacific Northwest customers feared that they would find themselves short on power when the need arose. Californians worried that BPA was profiting unduly from their need.

In fact, the supply of power that BPA shared with California contributed to the drain of the Pacific Northwest's hydroelectric reserves. Nine years after the arrangement, in 2001, BPA had not yet received any power from California to hold up their end of the agreement, which contributed to the Pacific Northwest's energy deficiencies during the 1990s and into 2001. The deal turned completely sour when, in 2001, California found themselves in dire need of power. BPA refused to supply power to the ailing state unless California prepaid for the electricity.

2000: Fiber Optics and Other Inventive Technologies

When BPA was founded in 1937, one of its original missions was to bring utility services to rural areas. By joining with Washington Public Utility Districts (PUD) Association to bring fiber optic cables to the communities they serve, BPA kept the original spirit of their agency alive.

Like many corporations during the 1990s, the agency saw an opportunity to capitalize on the growing environmental awareness of many of its customers while at the same time advancing the viability of sustainable energy technologies. BPA sold its first "green power" to Tacoma Power in April 2000. Green power is generated from renewable sources and costs more than other electricity. A portion of the sale of "environmentally preferred power" was designated to the Bonneville Environmental Foundation to help restore Northwest watersheds and develop additional renewable energy projects. One source of environmentally preferred power BPA is researching is solar power. In May 2000, BPA pledged $900,000 over five years to the Regional Solar Radiation Data Center. BPA has been funding research projects around solar data since the early 1980s with the hope that solar energy might someday be as successful as hydropower. Wind energy is another alternate energy source on which the BPA has set their sights. BPA planned to invest in multiple wind power projects; the power administration hoped that wind power would prove to be one of their most important power solutions.

Another alternative energy technology that BPA has been involved with is fuel cells. A fuel cell is a device that converts the energy of a fuel—hydrogen, natural gas, methanol, gasoline, etc.—and an oxidant—air or oxygen—into useable electricity. BPA entered into an agreement with IdaTech, a developer of fuel cell systems and fuel processing technology, to purchase 110 fuel cell systems. In June 2000, IdaTech delivered the first batch of ten of the fuel cell system units that BPA agreed to purchase. This initial delivery was part of a testing phase, aimed at introducing fuel cell systems to home and small commercial applications by 2003.

BPA showed that their interest in technology wasn't limited to new electricity advances when they launched an Internet auction site aimed at providing incentives to high-volume customers to conserve energy during periods of short-capacity and high price.

2001: Rates Rise as Supply Dwindles

After watching the mistakes that California made in their energy market, BPA felt it necessary to take decisive action in securing enough power for the Northwest. In January 2001, they made the announcement that, "BPA is on a path to wholesale rate increases averaging 60 percent over the next five years unless the region can find a way to cut costs." The region jumped to action and an agreement on a new five-year rate structure was reached in February with BPA's utility customers. The dwindling power supply also reinvigorated BPA's conservation-education efforts. The agency announced in June 2001 that wholesale customers had to commit to reduce their power demand by another 1,000 megawatts if they wanted to avoid a 150-percent rate hike.

Despite BPA's rate increase and conservation efforts, the power administration declared a power emergency in April 2001, a move that allowed the company to bypass the Endangered Species Act and forgo spilling water over dams to help salmon. Instead, BPA sent the water through turbines to generate electricity. There was an immediate backlash by conservationists and fish and wildlife rights agencies against BPA's decision. In June 2001 BPA responded with a promise to fund 11 high-priority projects designed to provide immediate aid to endangered fish in the Columbia Basin.

All of the efforts that the BPA put into conservation worked to reduce the amount that the power administration would have to raise rates—the agency found that it was only necessary to raise the rates 46 percent, instead of the expected 250-percent increase.

2001–02: Signs of Recovery

With the aid of increasing rainfall, the closure of several aluminum plants that had demanded large amounts of electricity from BPA, successful conservation efforts, wind-generated power, and new power plants, the Northwest's power supply began to recover in 2001. Throughout the ups and downs of the energy industry in the 1990s and early 2000s, consumers in the Pacific Northwest have remained highly conservation conscious, putting pressure on BPA and other organizations, and BPA has continued to research and invest in renewable energy.

Principal Competitors

The AES Corporation; Dynegy Inc.; Reliant Energy, Inc.

Further Reading

"Bonneville Power Administration," *Business Journal-Portland*, November 3, 2000, p. 5.

"Bonneville Power Administration," *Power Engineering*, June 2001, p. 18.

"BPA: More Demand Cuts Needed to Avoid Huge Price Spikes," *Energy Daily*, June 7, 2001, p. 2.

"BPA: Northwest Faces 60 Percent Rate Hikes," *Energy Daily*, January 29, 2001, p. 4.

"BPA Proposes Power Rate Cut," *American Metal Market*, July 12, 1995, p. 2.

"BPA to Raise Rates 46 Percent," *Energy Daily*, July 2, 2001, p. 3.

Brinkman, Jonathon, "Northwest Utility Declares Power Emergency," *Knight-Ridder/Tribune Business News*, April 5, 2001.

"Conservation is 'In' Again," *Northwest Public Power Association Bulletin*, April 2001, p. 26.

Davis, Tina, "California Crunch Intensifies: BPA Threatens to Cut Power to SCE," *Energy Daily*, June 1, 2001, p. 1.

Ernst, Steve, "New Power Plants Ready to Feed Northwest Needs," *Puget Sound Business Journal*, August 10, 2001, p. 5.

Evans, Chris, "Power Crisis Showing Signs of Easing in NW," *American Metal Market*, August 9, 2001, p. 1.

"Fuel Cell Generators Delivered to BPA," *Energy Conservation News*, June 2000.

Holly, Chris, "BPA Tackles High Power Prices," *Energy Daily*, February 22, 2001, p. 1.

Marks, Anita, "BPA Allows Customers to Shop for Some Power Elsewhere," *Business Journal-Portland*, April 21, 1995, p. 2.

——, "BPA Considering Unplugging Plants," *Business Journal-Portland*, March 17, 1995, p. 1.

——, "BPA Exec Plans More Staff Cuts, '95 Rate Hike," *Business Journal-Portland*, July 12, 1993, p. 1.

——, "BPA Freezes Hiring, Launches Efficiency Study to Cut Costs," *Business Journal-Portland*, November 9, 1992, p. 1.

——, "BPA Reducing Size of Rate Increase after Big Customers Grouse," *Business Journal-Portland*, September 14, 1992, p. 1.

——, "BPA Swaps Power with S. California," *Business Journal-Portland*, May 11, 1992, p. 1.

——, "BPA's Tiered Rate Scheme Making Big Customers Nervous," *Business Journal-Portland*, July 8, 1994, p. 6.

——, "Cash-Strapped BPA Feels Nukes' Financial Fallout," *Puget Sound Business Journal*, April 23, 1993, p. 15.

McNamara, Will, "BPA Plans to Supply the Most Wind Power," *Northwest Public Power Association Bulletin*, August 2001, p. 18.

Nichols, Christina, "Conservation Pays: Insulating the Future," *Technology Review*, July 1987, p. 14.

"NW States Propose Power Allocation Plan," *Northwest Public Power Association Bulletin*, October 1999, p. 17.

Ohrenschall, Mark, "Conservation Update: Calls for Conservation Still Urgent," *Northwest Public Power Bulletin*, April 2002, p. 23.

"Pacific Northwest Struggles to Balance Concerns for Fish vs. Electricity," *Knight-Ridder/Tribune Business News*, May 20, 2001.

"RESOURCES: BPA Funds Solar Data Center," *Energy Conservation News*, May 2000.

Sliz, Deborah, and M. Lindsay, "Northwest Energy Restructuring Moving Along in Washington," *Northwest Public Power Association Bulletin*, July 1999.

"Tacoma Buys 'Green Power'," *Puget Sound Business Journal*, April 28, 2000, p. 17.

Walters, Dennis, "Washington," *The Bond Buyer*, November 19, 1991, p. 1008.

"Washington PUD Association, BPA Sign Historic Agreement," *Northwest Public Power Association Bulletin*, December 1999, p. 24.

—Tammy Weisberger

THE BON·TON
We've Got What You Want

The Bon-Ton Stores, Inc.

2801 East Market Street
York, Pennsylvania 17402
U.S.A.
Telephone: (717) 757-7660
Fax: (717) 751-3198
Web site: http://bonton.com

Public Company
Incorporated: 1929 as S. Grumbacher & Son
Employees: 9,000 (2001)
Sales: $749.8 million (2001)
Stock Exchanges: NASDAQ
Ticker Symbol: BONT
NAIC: 452110 Department Stores

The Bon Ton Stores, Inc. is a leading regional department store chain with sales in fiscal year 2001 of $749.8 million. The company concentrates on serving medium-sized communities, and at the start of 2002, operated 73 stores in Pennsylvania, Maryland, New York, New Jersey, Georgia, Massachusetts, and West Virginia. Bon-Ton stores are typically anchor stores in shopping malls and the primary department stores in their communities. They offer a wide assortment of moderately priced name brand and private label clothing, cosmetics, shoes, accessories, and home furnishings. The Grumbacher family controls 94 percent of the company's stock.

Early History

Bon-Ton was started in 1898, when Max Grumbacher and his father, Samuel, opened S. Grumbacher & Son, a one-room millinery and dry goods store on Market Street in York, Pennsylvania. From the beginning, according to company material, the Grumbachers operated their business "with a close attention to detail and a conviction that business success would come to those who offered customers quality merchandise at a fair price with careful attention to their individual needs and wants."

As automobiles replaced horses and the country became more industrialized, through World War I and the Roaring Twenties, the Grumbachers continued to meet their customers' needs. The store grew bigger and, in 1929, the company was incorporated as S. Grumbacher & Son, Inc. In 1931, Max's son, Max Samuel (M.S.), joined the company. When Max the elder died in 1933, his widow, Daisy, and their two sons, M.S. and Richard, continued the business, forming a partnership in 1936. Following World War II, the family decided to expand operations. In 1946 a second Bon-Ton was opened, in Hanover, Pennsylvania. Two years later, the company moved outside Pennsylvania, acquiring Eyerly's in Hagerstown, Maryland, and in 1957 purchasing McMeen's in Lewistown, Pennsylvania. These early moves set Bon-Ton's policy of growing into adjacent areas by opening new stores and acquiring existing businesses.

The 1960s, 1970s, and 1980s: Years of Growth

During the next three decades, The Bon-Ton Stores continued to expand. In 1961, M.S.'s son, M. Thomas "Tim," entered the business, representing the fourth generation of Grumbachers. During the 1960s, the company opened new Eyerly's and Bon-Ton stores in several Pennsylvania communities and one in West Virginia. They also started a discount chain, Mailman's, and, in 1969, retired the McMeen's name. During the 1970s, as the popularity of shopping centers began to grow, Bon-Ton opened 11 new stores in Pennsylvania and West Virginia.

The 1980s formed a period of rapid consolidation in the retail department store industry as major chains bought their competitors. The Bon-Ton Stores began the decade by opening more stores, establishing a new division, Maxwell's, and acquiring Fowler's department store in New York. When Tim Grumbacher was made CEO in 1985, the company operated 18 stores in four states. Two years later the company made a major move, buying the 11-store Pomeroy's chain from Allied Department Stores. That purchase made it possible for the company to move into seven new markets in Pennsylvania.

It also marked the beginning of a major shift in the company's marketing strategy and operations to concentrate on moderate-priced merchandise. The company discontinued the Mailman's discount chain, closed those stores, and eliminated the low-margin product lines such as appliances and electronics

106

at the Pomeroy's stores. It renamed all the remaining Eyerly's and Maxwell's to either Bon-Ton or Pomeroy's and placed emphasis on providing a deep selection of brand-name merchandise, such as Liz Claiborne, Levi Strauss, Alfred Dunner, Esprit, and Esteé Lauder. The company also instituted its "Certified Value" program, which maintained value prices on a limited number of key items within each of its major product groups, such as turtlenecks, fleece, and denims.

With the increased income being generated from the Pomeroy acquisition, the company hired senior executives from national chains to strengthen its management and made significant investments to improve its operating and information management systems. In 1989, E. Herbert Ross, who had been with Federated Department Stores for 24 years, was named president and COO.

The Early 1990s

The company began the decade by changing its logo in 1990 and completing the integration of the Pomeroy units. As those stores achieved the level of quality and style of the core stores, their name was changed to Bon-Ton. All stores carried apparel for the whole family, and offered cosmetics and accessories. Twenty-eight stores also carried home furnishings, such as china, linens, housewares, and gifts. Four offered bedding and furniture. All stores contained leased shoe departments, and many also had leased fine jewelry departments and leased beauty salons. Women's clothing was the largest merchandise category, representing 30.5 percent of net sales in fiscal year 1990. Net sales for 1990 increased 6.4 percent over 1989, with stores that had been open for 12 months or more (a common retail industry measurement) increasing their net sales by 7.8 percent.

In 1991, the company, S. Grumbacher & Son, changed its own name to The Bon-Ton Stores, Inc. and went public, selling four and a half million shares on the NASDAQ market. At that time, Bon-Ton operated 33 stores, varying in size from approximately 30,000 to 160,000 square feet. Most were one of several anchor tenants in shopping malls in secondary markets; the others were located in or adjacent to strip shopping centers.

Prior to the initial public offering (IPO), the company developed a strategic real estate, identifying markets with similar demographic and competitive characteristics within or contiguous to its existing markets. Based on this plan, and despite the 1990–1992 recession that battered the department store industry, Bon-Ton continued to grow. It opened four new stores in New York and Pennsylvania and acquired the two-store Watt & Shand chain in Lancaster, Pennsylvania. In September 1992, President E. Herb Ross resigned and was replaced by Terrance Jarvis. In 1993 the company closed more stores than it opened

and comparable store sales had a loss, a first for the company. However, net sales increased slightly, to $336.7 million from $333.7 million the year before.

Acquisitions Continue to Add to Company's Growth

The Bon-Ton Stores saw tremendous activity in 1994. In July, it acquired the Adam, Meldrum & Anderson Company (AM&A) for $2.1 million and the assumption of $40.6 million in AM&A's debt. The transaction added ten stores in and around Buffalo, New York. In September it purchased 19 Hess Department Stores (Hess's), one of its major competitors in Pennsylvania, for $60 million. And in October it acquired certain assets of C.E. Chappell & Sons, Inc. (Chappell's), a six-unit department store company based in Syracuse, New York. These transactions doubled the company's size to 70, added 3.1 million square feet of retail space, and opened up three new markets—Buffalo and Syracuse, New York, and Allentown, Pennsylvania.

As Bon-Ton grew in the region, outlet stores for brand names such as Liz Claiborne and London Fog, and discount stores such as Kmart and Wal-Mart, were becoming more popular. These stores offered customers, particularly those in suburban and secondary markets, shopping alternatives and low prices. The Bon-Ton Stores competed by concentrating on customer service, investing in its workforce to provide personal shopping skills when working with customers. Sales associates received training in selling, customer service, and product knowledge. The company offered a liberal exchange and return policy, free gift-wrapping, free shopping bags, and special order capabilities. Selected stores also offered a personal shopper service. Associates were encouraged to keep notebooks of customers' names, clothing sizes, birthdays, and major purchases. In 1994 customers opened 250,000 new Bon-Ton credit card accounts, providing a customer database with over two million names.

The company also competed with its merchandise. To accomplish its goal of fashion leadership, Bon-Ton emerged as the first in its markets to identify fashion trends: to advertise and stock new merchandise and to carry a full complement of sizes and colors of the items it sold. During 1994 the company added more name brands to its inventory, including Nautica, Tommy Hilfiger, Ralph Lauren Home, and Susan Bristol, and expanded its private-label brands to 10 percent of its sales.

The company ended the leasing of its shoe department and made it a company-owned business. This allowed Bon-Ton to offer footwear more in line with its apparel merchandise and resulted in a sales increase of 20 percent. The company also developed a Big and Tall Men's area. The concentration on customer service, more upscale fashion lines, and internal niche marketing led to an increase in comparable store sales of 6.1 percent for the year. Combined with the business from the 35 newly acquired stores, Bon-Ton's net sales for 1994 rose 47 percent to $494.9 million, and earnings soared to $1.23 per share or 55.3 percent.

1995 and Beyond

The year 1995 proved to be a difficult year for The Bon-Ton Stores as it integrated the AM&A, Hess's, and Chappell's stores into its operations. The company had net losses of 19 cents per

Key Dates:

1898: Max Grumbacher opens Grumbacher & Sons dry goods store.
1929: The company is incorporated as S. Grumbacher & Son, Inc.
1946: The company's second store opens in Hanover, Pennsylvania.
1961: Bon-Ton begins an era of rapid expansion.
1990: The company changes their logo and applies the Bon-Ton name to all stores.
1991: S. Grumbacher & Son, Inc. changes its name to The Bon-Ton Stores, Inc and the company goes public.
1994: The company competes with outlet stores by offering improved customer service.
1995: Bon-Ton adds more home furnishings to its apparel mix.
1998: Bon-Ton offers a second public stock offering.
1998: The company creates the charitable Bon-Ton Stores Foundation (BTSF).
2002: Bon-Ton's growth comprises 73 stores in nine states.

share in the first quarter and 18 cents per share in the second quarter, but Wall Street analysts did not appear worried, since comparable-store sales increased 4.8 percent for the first half compared with 1994. As Peter Schaeffer, a stock analyst with Dillon, Read, & Co. told Susan Reda in an October 1995 *Stores* article, "Bon-Ton is a substantial company and this year's weak earnings do not connote a disaster in the making. The potential for this chain is great. I'm looking for a rebound next year."

The losses in the first half were due largely to poor sales performance at the AM&A and Chappell's stores. To bring the AM&A units in Buffalo into line with The Bon-Ton Stores' moderate-priced apparel, the company had to eliminate the budget store business, which accounted for 10 percent of AM&A's sales. In Syracuse, the company had to reduce Chappell's heavy emphasis on clothing and introduce other merchandise offerings. Because the merchandise mix in the Hess's stores in Allentown was comparable with that of Bon-Ton, the changeover was less difficult, and sales performance was in line with expectations. During the year Bon-Ton acquired four vacant stores in Rochester, New York, giving the company locations in each of the four dominant malls serving that market. Late in 1995, Bon-Ton opened a 75,000-square-foot store in Elmira, New York.

Leadership Changes in the Company

Another factor in the company's financial picture was the cost of its leadership change. In January, Terrance Jarvis resigned as president, and a search began for his successor. In August the company named Heywood Wilansky president and CEO. Wilansky had held those positions at the Foley's division of The May Department Stores Company, and May Company filed a breach of contract suit against him and The Bon-Ton Stores. Although the suit was settled in October, the litigation charges contributed to losses in the third quarter.

In addition, 1995 brought the company increased home furnishing business, including china, linens, housewares, and gifts. Ken McCartney was hired from Horne's to become Bon-Ton's first general merchandise manager. He added furniture in 19 stores and saw home furnishings sales increase from 10 percent to 14 percent of the company's merchandise mix.

In January 1996, the end of its fourth quarter, the company closed three stores and announced plans to close five to seven underperforming stores, eliminating 700 positions. That restructuring represented the final steps in "digesting" its acquisitions. For its fiscal year 1995, The Bon-Ton Stores reported net sales of $607.4 million, a 22.7 percent increase from 1994. Because of fourth-quarter restructuring charges of approximately $6 million, along with nonrecurring charges in the third quarter of $3.5 million, Bon-Ton had a net loss of $9.2 million for the year. Excluding those charges, net income for 1995 was $200,000 or $0.02 per share. Comparable-store sales for the year increased 0.2 percent.

By the mid-1990s the outlook for the department store industry was much brighter than it had been a few years earlier. "The shock and surprise of the mid-1990s is department stores' viability. Their bottom lines are a lot healthier than anyone would have forecast," retail consultant Alan Millstein said in a November 1995 *Business Week* article. Department stores were expected to slowly regain market share from outlet stores and discount retailers, according to a January 1996 *Business Week* article. As it entered the last half of the decade, however, The Bon-Ton Stores faced national competition (from The May Department Stores) in 13 of its 44 markets. In addition, Bon-Ton dealt with problems because it catered to the economically stretched middle-class customer. Ed Dravo, an investment analyst in San Francisco, recommended selling Bon-Ton shares in his column in the September 12, 1995, issue of *Financial World*. "Not only does Bon-Ton have economics playing against it, it is also in the retailing category that Wal-Mart likes to extinguish. Revenues are flat and earnings have disappeared."

The restructuring at the end of 1995, merchandise changes (including private brands and home furnishings), continued customer services, and centralized functions able to support a large store base appeared to place the company in a good position. Sales for February and March totaled $84.8 million, a 3.8 percent increase from the year before, despite the Blizzard of 1996. Comparable-store sales increased 4.4 percent. Although Heywood Wilansky assumed the position of CEO, the Grumbacher family continued to be represented on the board of directors, with M. Thomas Grumbacher serving as chairman. Since the family held 94 percent of the stock and remained involved with the company, there appeared little likelihood of a takeover by a national department store chain.

Struggles for the Company Continue

But by the third quarter of 1996, the company was continuing to struggle with more losses. Although the third-quarter reported loss was less than the same quarter a year prior, this was due to the opening of the four stores in New York that period. For the third quarter in 1996, the company reported a net loss of $242,000. Talk began to surface, suggesting the possible closing of another five stores in early 1997.

The beginning of 1997, however, reflected a company that was in a much better position. Changes in merchandising started off the year with the company focusing on the higher-end brands introduced earlier. A previous introduction of Lauren for Women was successful enough to invoke Bon-Ton to continue the ''better'' offerings, a plan they hoped would distinguish them from competitors J.C. Penney and Sears. Earnings for the fiscal year 1997 increased to 36 percent. ''We are very pleased with our results for the year, particularly the significant increase in net income,'' said COO Michel Gleim in March of 1998. He credited the restructuring initiatives of the year before and the introduction of the new lines. Also contributing to the gain was the reduction in the number of vendors the company used and the elimination of a pension plan offered by one of the acquired companies. An additional store opening in New York went ahead as planned.

In May 1998 the company announced another stock offering of 4,600,000 shares. The proceeds were to be used for further expansion and upgrading of existing sites. Part of this expansion included a new store in Westfield, Massachusetts, making it the Bon-Ton Stores' first entry into the New England area. The move was part of the company's plan to move into smaller markets. Other expansion moves that year included upgrading existing stores, establishing stores as cornerstones of shopping malls, and general improvements. During this year the company also introduced a corporate philanthropy sector called the Bon-Ton Stores Foundation (BTSF). The foundation allocated funds to each store to be used for charitable donations and involvement. Funds were also issued to each store for local community projects.

Looking ahead to 1999 and the end of the century, the company planned more growth in the form of new stores, expansions, and yet more remodels. The plans would increase The Bon-Ton Stores' total square footage by 300,000 square feet and continue to focus on smaller markets. The overall desire for Bon-Ton was to expand to one million square feet in the next five years. Frank Tworecke was named vice chairman and chief merchandising officer at the end of 1999.

Economic Challenges Confront Bon-Ton Stores in New Era

The new century continued to bring challenges to Bon-Ton as it coped with less-than-desired sales profits. When the economy declined at the beginning of 2001, so did consumers' spending habits. Low cost and high value dominated consumers' interests during this period; low-priced retailers such as Wal-Mart reported increased sales during this time. To achieve the target net income for the year, the company had to eliminate 187 positions, resulting in 137 layoffs. Further trouble lay in the charges made by the New York State Attorney General that the company engaged in dishonest advertising practices. The Attorney General's Office alleged that ''discounted'' prices on some of the higher-end items such as jewelry and appliances were no lower than ''regular'' prices for these items. The company refuted the charges.

Despite a year of disappointing figures in 2001, Bon-Ton was able to report an increase in sales for the month of October. However, the terrorist attacks in the United States on September 11 troubled the economy and thus affected the retail clothing business. While October had looked good and November promising, the Christmas season slowed in sales so much that the company dropped their sales expectations to an all-time low. Still, while their competitors announced layoffs, Bon-Ton had no such plans.

Future Challenges

As the economy continued to struggle into 2002, Bon-Ton kept its focus on quality merchandising, expansion, and growth. The company had expanded to 73 stores in nine states. A new line of clothing, by Madison & Max, forged a new partnership with Federated Merchandising Group and was a hopeful prospect for the company. In January, Bon-Ton agreed to pay New York state a $100,000 fine to settle the misleading advertising charge; though they did not admit to any wrongdoing, the company agreed to restructure its advertising practices.

The company's plans for 2002 and beyond included balancing its merchandise between moderate and better goods; evangelizing the company's private brand; improving inventory management; increasing customer services; improving its technological infrastructure; and matching merchandise to each market. Because economic conditions had made it difficult to guess where consumers' dollars lay, Bon-Ton changed its strategy from an aggressive expansion plan to a focus on current merchandising and operations, while continuing to establish footholds in secondary markets.

Principal Subsidiaries

Adam, Meldrum & Anderson Co., Inc; The Bon-Ton National Corp.; The Bon-Ton Receivables Corp.; The Bon-Ton Stores of Lancaster, Inc.; The Bon-Ton Trade Corp.

Principal Competitors

Boscov's Stores; Federated Department Stores, Inc.; J.C. Penney; Elder-Beerman Stores Corporation; The May Department Stores Company; Kohl's Corporation; Sears, Roebuck and Co.

Further Reading

Adkins, Sean, ''The Bon-Ton Breaks Ahead,'' *The York Daily Record*, November 10, 2001, http://www.ydr.com.
''Bon-Ton Pays $100,000 Advertising Fine,'' *York Dispatch Online*, January 9, 2002, http://www.yorkdispatch.com.
''Bon-Ton Same-Store Sales Drop,'' *Wall Street Journal*, January 11, 2002, p. B2.
''Bon-Ton Shifts Execs,'' *Home Textiles Today*, July 31, 2000, p.2.
''Bon-Ton Stores Inc: Loss of $484,000 Is Posted after Charge for Staff Cuts,'' *Wall Street Journal*, November 23, 2001, p. B5.
''The Bon-Ton Stores, Inc. Said It Expects a Net Loss for the Fourth Quarter,'' *Reuters*, February 5, 1996.
''Bon-Ton Stores Sales Decline,'' *Wall Street Journal*, May 11, 2001, p. B2.
''Bon-Ton Stores Sales Fall 1.7%,'' *Wall Street Journal*, September 7, 2001, p. B2.
''Bon-Ton to Buy Steinbach Locations,'' *Home Textiles Today*, April 5, 1999, p. 8.
''The Bon-Ton to Expand or Renovate Stores in Three Shopping Malls,'' December 12, 1998, *http://www.reji.com.*

Brownlee, Lisa, "Bon-Ton Stores Says Profit Estimate of Analysts Is 'A Little Aggressive,' " *Wall Street Journal*, August 29, 1997, p. A7.

Chandler, Susan, "An Endangered Species Makes a Comeback," *Business Week*, November 27, 1995, p. 96.

——, "Gloomy Days Are Here Again," (Industry Outlook 1996: Services—Retailing), *Business Week*, January 8, 1996, p. 103.

"Charge Is Planned in Period for Expenses from Layoffs," *Wall Street Journal*, June 12, 2000, p. B4.

"Charges Dip Bon-Ton Stores Deeper into Red," *Women's Wear Daily*, November 17, 1995, p. 9.

Cohen, Nancy E., *Doing a Good Business: 100 Years at the Bon-Ton*, Greenwich Publishing Group, 1998.

Dravo, Ed, "Short Takes," *Financial World*, September 12, 1995, p. 77.

Erlick, June Carolyn, "Bon-Ton Expands Home Goods," *HFN: The Weekly Newspaper for the Home Furnishing Network*, October 9, 1995, p. 11.

"Fiscal Period Loss Narrows; Firm May Shut Five Stores," *Wall Street Journal*, November 22, 1996, p. B4.

Kurtz, Mary, et al., "Reinventing the Store: How Smart Retailers Are Changing the Way We Shop," *Business Week*, November 27, 1995, pp. 84–91.

"Measuring the Business of Corporate Philanthropy: The Bon-Ton Stores Foundation," Summer 2001, *http://www.measuringphilanthropy.com/casestudies*.

Pogoda, Dianne, "Bon-Ton Pumps Up Its Base," *Women's Wear Daily*, September 29, 1994, p. 3.

Pressler, Margaret Webb, and Steven Pearlstein, "Growing Out of Business: The Shakeout Has Just Begun in the Overbuilt Retail Industry," *The Washington Post*, February 22, 1996, pp. A1, A8.

Reda, Susan, "The Bon-Ton Presses Regional Growth Plan," *Stores*, October 1995, pp. 22–23.

Ross, Julie Ritzer, "Routing Software Helps Retailers Curb Transportation Costs," *Stores*, August 1998, pp. 98–99.

Short History of the Company, York, Penn.: The Bon-Ton Stores, Inc., 1995.

"Strong Sales Help Retailer Swing to $573,000 Profit," *Wall Street Journal*, November 21, 1997 p. B4.

"Tworecke Is Bon-Ton Vice Chair," *Home Textiles Today*, November 29, 1999, p. 18.

"Young, Charlie, "Holiday Sales down for the Bon-Ton," *York Dispatch Online*, January 11, 2002, http://www.yorkdispatch.com.

—Ellen D. Wernick
—update: Kerri DeVault

The Boston Beer Company, Inc.

75 Arlington Street
Boston, Massachusetts 02116
U.S.A.
Telephone: (617) 368-5000
Fax: (617) 368-5500
Web site: http://www.samadams.com

Public Company
Incorporated: 1984
Employees: 355 (2000)
Sales: $190.6 million (2000)
Stock Exchanges: New York
Ticker Symbol: SAM
NAIC: 312120 Breweries

As America's leading microbrewer, The Boston Beer Company, Inc. has made Samuel Adams known for being more than a signatory of the Declaration of Independence or a rebellious participant in the Boston Tea Party. Boston Beer's pivotal role in sparking the microbrewery boom of the 1990s has become the seed of business legend. The company is the seventh largest brewer in the United States and claims the leading position in the craft beer market. Although technically, Boston Beer's success has propelled its production level over the top—the annual production of other microbreweries remains under 15,000 barrels—the company remains the yardstick by which industry success is measured.

Headquartered in Boston, Massachusetts, Boston Beer brews and markets about 18 seasonal and year-round beers, including its flagship Samuel Adams Boston Lager, an all-malt Pilsner-style beer based on a 100-year-old formulation. The company sells about 1.2 million barrels of beer nationwide, based out of its two breweries, and contracts with three breweries across the United States to produce beers using its ingredients and recipes. The company also sells HardCore-brand cider and its BoDean's Twisted Tea malt beverage. Its beers have won many international awards and are available in international markets such as Australia, Canada, Finland, Germany, Hong Kong, Ireland, Japan, Sweden, and the United Kingdom.

Original founder, Chairman James Koch owns about 33 percent of the company.

1984: Founded on Life Savings and Hard Work

Boston Beer Company was founded by C. James Koch (pronounced Cook), a Cincinnati native who moved to Boston to study at Harvard's Law and Business schools. In the early 1980s, Koch (descended from five generations of brewmasters) noticed an increase in the sales of imported beers. In April 1984, with $100,000 of his own savings, $140,000 from supportive family and friends, and the sales savvy of Rhonda L. Kallman (his former secretary and, eventually, company marketing vice president), 33-year-old Koch quit his well-paying job as management consultant to Boston Consulting Group. Armed with a recipe formulated by his great-great-grandfather, St. Louis-based brewer Louis Koch, the young James Koch derived a beer that was more full-bodied than typical U.S. brews. Koch's recipe adhered to rigorous German beer purity laws that demanded top-quality ingredients and long brewing and fermentation periods.

After cooking up the first few batches on his kitchen stove, Koch contracted with 30-year-veteran Pittsburgh Brewing Co. to manufacture his brown-bottled, premium lager in their modern plant. Door-to-door marketing of the new beer began in downtown Boston in 1985, netting Koch a customer base of 25 restaurants and bars. Shipments of Samuel Adams Boston Lager were under way by April. Ironically, Koch was unable to find a distributor willing to carry his product, so he was forced to buy a truck and do it himself.

Because of the brew's high retail cost—$20 per case, against Heineken's $17—these first sales were the hardest. Koch and Kallman used a personal approach by encouraging bartenders to sample their product and explaining why Samuel Adams was a higher-quality brew from a better company. Their dogged persistence eventually won over the New England market. By 1987 the company was poised to enter the finicky Manhattan market where, Koch contended in the *Wall Street Journal*, "New Yorkers are well behind other cities in accepting quality American beers." He added, "But we've done so well elsewhere, we're ready to invest the time and money in educating New York.'' By 1988, Koch and Kallman had such a strong sales base that they were able to acquire $3 million from an investment banking firm for the purchase of an old brewery within Boston's Jamaica Plain section. Although efforts to establish a full-scale brewing operation there were quickly nixed because of the prohibitive costs associated with outfitting a brewery, the location would serve as a research and development facility, as well as a tourist attraction.

1990–92: Boston Beer Goes National

Boston Beer soon saw its distribution networks grow to include Washington, D.C. and Chicago. In 1990, as part of its controlled, targeted expansion strategy, the company further expanded its market by reaching an agreement with Portland, Oregon-based Blitz-Weinhart Brewing to brew and distribute its product in the western United States. It also opened the Samuel Adams Brew House in Philadelphia, where the Samuel Adams flagship brand is still brewed. Distribution increased in 1992, when California's Pacific Wine Co. agreed to distribute Boston Beer products on the West Coast. With distribution now encompassing the 48 contiguous states, Koch watched 1992 sales increase 63 percent to $48.2 million, resulting in net income of $1.6 million.

Since upscale U.S. beer drinkers' tastes ran strongly to imports, marketing a new high-end brew required some creativity. As early as 1986, Koch earmarked a large portion of the company budget for marketing. He composed some quirky radio advertisements promoting the quality of his product. And he did some flag-waving, touting Samuel Adams as a Made-in-the-U.S.A. alternative to pricey foreign brews. But, more important, Koch recognized the value in focusing his efforts on a specific market segment, rather than the general beer-drinking public. In addition to catchy slogans like ''Declare Your Independence from Foreign Beer,'' his ads were also an impassioned attempt to educate listeners about beer in general and about what made Samuel Adams unique.

But Samuel Adams's rise to the top had stronger foundations than the flurry of interest generated by a clever ad campaign. Boston Beer made a quality product. The company used only four age-old ingredients—hops, malt, yeast, and water—a time-honored four-vessel, all-malt process, and a secondary fermentation process called krausening to create a smoother brew. Use of relatively rare European-grown Hallertau Mittelfrueh, Spalt Spalt, Saaz, and Tettnang hops provided a distinctive aroma and spicy edge. Boston Beer watched its flagship brand win numerous awards at Denver's annual Great American Beer Festival and more medals at the 1994 World Beer Championship than any other brew. Tellingly, Koch's 1993 advertising campaign, which claimed his product as the best beer in the United States ''four years running,'' unleashed

arguments and threats of litigation by rival microbrewers in an increasingly competitive beer industry. Similarly, ads claiming that Samuel Adams was the sole American beer imported into Germany ruffled feathers of more than one competitor who maintained a European market for their product. Ultimately, the hue and cry over Koch's jealous advertising strengthened the name recognition of his company's product as consumers went to the bar to find out what all the fuss was about.

Due to both clever ad strategies and quality products, Boston Beer watched its production increase from 294,000 barrels in 1992 to 714,000 by 1994. From 1992 to 1993 the company expanded its employee base from 87 to 110; and the following year 170 people worked to produce and promote Boston Beer products. These increases in production and staff were the result of increased sales; and the company's sales staff, which numbered more than 90 people by the end of 1994, personally contacted customers whose collective beer tab earned the brewer a net income of more than $9 million. Well trained in brewing techniques—all company employees were required to spend a day brewing beer in Boston—company salespeople continually educated retailers about the quality of their products.

As sales and profits increased, so did the money the company allotted to advertising. Boston Beer sponsored bar beer nights that featured Samuel Adams giveaways including T-shirts and caps, distributed coasters, table cards, restaurant umbrellas, and menu boards. To increase public exposure, the company also donated their product to charity events. Samuel Adams was served at each of the social balls and dinners that accompanied President Clinton's ascension to the presidency in 1993. By 1995, along with other microbreweries like Mistik Beverages, Boston Beer began to consider the benefits of a television advertising campaign to promote its product; television testing was still under way through 1996.

1995–1996: Going Public

Prompted by its forward momentum, Boston Beer made the decision to go public in 1995, offering 3.1 million shares in November. Of those, it held back 990,000 shares, directing these toward its loyal customers. These customers included not only the bar owners, shop owners, and wholesalers who distributed company products; every six-pack of Samuel Adams sold at retail came with a mail-in coupon for discounted shares in Boston Beer's growing operation. More than 130,000 customers were quick to invest in a piece of their favorite brew. By the close of the year, the company reported net income of $5.9 million on revenues of $151.3 million. Production was a record 961,000 barrels divided among an increasing array of products that included Samuel Adams Brand Ale, Boston Lager, Cream Stout, Honey Porter, and Triple Bock, as well as such tempting seasonal variations as Cranberry Iambic and Winter Lager. In addition, the company produced and marketed beers under the Boston Lightship brand. The Oregon Original brands, brewed by the company-owned Oregon Ale and Beer Company, had also been introduced to most major markets by 1995.

Not surprisingly, Boston Beer's success spawned a host of imitators. In fact, throughout the early 1990s, approximately 55 new breweries were established each year. Of these, the company perceived a real threat in the similarly named Boston Beer

Works. Although Boston Beer would sue the coattail brewery, it lost the suit in 1994.

Much of the success of Boston Beer was its ability to foster and stay on top of a niche market for the second-most popular beverage in the world (the first being tea). Unlike other microbrewers—skilled craftspeople who pride themselves on small-batch production and local distribution, often eschewing the "business" side of the business by leaving advertising to word of mouth—Boston Beer was ambitious. A tiger in the industry, it went for the jugular, directly challenging high-priced imports like Heineken, St. Pauli Girl, and Beck's. Strategically avoiding head-to-head combat with domestic giants like Miller Brewery, Anheuser-Busch, and Budweiser, whose highly financed promotional "lifestyle" campaigns featured frogs, dogs, and buxom, bikini-clad beach babes, Boston Beer aimed for a share of the import market. Instead of gearing its product toward twentysomething middle-class males, Samuel Adams targeted connoisseurs, beer aficionados with an eye for quality and a taste for an exceptional product. Advertising the weaknesses of imported beers, namely, that foreign brews headed for the United States have fewer premium ingredients, a "lighter" taste, and are less fresh because of long shipping times (like other perishable foodstuffs, beer "goes sour" and loses its flavor and quality after as little as four months), the company prided itself on the quality of ingredients and brewing skill it brought to its products. By directly tackling the premium imports, Boston Beer created a new marketing niche, domestically brewed premium beer, and assumed a leadership position within the growing specialty beer market.

In addition to encouraging other beer-brewing entrepreneurs, the major U.S. breweries did not respond to the advances made by Boston-based upstart Koch by lying down. Watching a segment of a relentlessly sluggish beer market mushroom almost overnight would tantalize any businessperson. Beer giants Anheuser-Busch, Coors, and the Philip Morris-owned Miller Brewery used their leverage to try to restrict the supply of raw materials and national distribution network of the entire microbrewery industry, a $400 million market divided among almost 500 brewers by 1994. Their efforts forced many craft brewers to confine their distribution within regional markets, with a select few becoming the targets of takeovers as the giants maneuvered for a piece of the growing microbrew pie.

The "if you can't beat 'em, join 'em" strategy proved to be increasingly popular. Adopting an increasing array of small-scale guises, such as Miller's nonexistent Plank Road Brewery (Miller's original name in 1855), the major breweries attempted to cash in on the micro movement by introducing a battery of so-called "craft" beers into the high-end marketplace. Aesthetically appealing labels proclaiming brands like Red Dog, Killian, Blue Moon, Elk Mountain, Eisbock, Leinenkugel, Red Wolf House, and Augsburger filled retail beer shelves and popped up in point-of-sale tavern displays. Even importers responded to the competition by distributing "micros" of their own, such as Heineken's Tarwebok and Labatt's Moretti La Rossa.

In its position as microbrewery industry leader, Boston Beer encouraged cultivation of the brewmeister's art. In 1995 it organized the first annual World Homebrew Championships, a summer gathering of 60 judges entrusted with the task of choosing the best among brews from around the world. Three category winners were announced in 1996 and their brews successfully marketed by the company under the names LongShot American Pale Ale, LongShot Hazelnut Brown Ale, and LongShot Black Lager. Meanwhile, Koch continued to indulge in the brewer's art, deriving new brews for the discerning palate. During 1995 he introduced three new products—Scotch Ale, Cherry Wheat Ale, and Old Fezziwig Ale—increasing the company's product line to 14. Triple Bock, first introduced in 1994, is a dark, sherry-like barley beer that is aged in oak casks. An acquired taste, it is a sipping beer that boasts a 17 percent alcohol level. Boston Beer's spicy Cherry Wheat Ale, introduced as a seasonal brew, became an annual product due to customer demand. The second World Homebrew Contest generated a second series of LongShot beers, which were available in limited quantities in select markets, but in 1997, the contest itself was put on hiatus.

Despite its ranking as one of the top ten brewers in the United States, Boston Brewery prided itself on being a small fish in an ocean containing a few large sharks; in the mid-1990s, the combined sales of the entire U.S. microbrewery industry accounted for less revenue than the total sales of Michelob Light in any one year. In a market dominated by a handful of giants, tenth-ranked Boston Brewery is, in the words of Koch, "like being the 12th largest car company." Anheuser-Busch's production had reached the millionth barrel by the first week of the year, Koch explained to writer Greg W. Prince in the December 1994 issue of *Beverage World*. "When I tell people we're one five-hundredth of the beer business ... [they] are surprised at how small we really are."

1996–1997: The Market Slides, from Peak to Soggy

Although Boston Beer's third-quarter 1996 results once again showed record results, the 294,000 barrels sold were fewer than the company had expected for its product line, sending mini-shockwaves throughout the microbrewery industry. Other small-scale brewers, many of which were fledgling operations, wondered if the wave they had been riding had crested. Even as the overall beer market continued to stagnate because of the increasing influence of health-conscious consumers, the market for upscale craft beers remained on an ascent—albeit one not quite as steep—because these same consumers expressed a clear preference for quality malt liquor products when they chose to indulge. On the strength of third-quarter net sales of $46.1 million, the company went ahead with the planned purchase of Cincinnati's historic Hudepohl-Schoenling Brewing Co., its Midwest contract brewery. Also in 1997, HardCore Cider Company, an affiliate of Boston Beer, launched HardCore Crisp Hard Cider and HardCore Apple Cranberry Cider in 11 cities nationwide.

Throughout 1996, beer sales began to level off across the board, with both micros and large brewers alike posting more moderate increases in sales. Feeling an especially acute pinch due to lackluster Budweiser earnings, Anheuser-Busch fronted a group complaint to the Bureau of Alcohol, Tobacco and Firearms (BATF) leveled against Boston Beer, Pete's Brewing Co. (makers of Pete's Wicked Ale), and fellow top-gun brewer Miller. Accusing the two micros of false advertising in their reported claims to brew "in small batches" instead of through large-scale contracted breweries, Busch and associates also demanded that Miller's parentage of both Icehouse and Red Dog be legitimized on the label rather than cloaked by its fictitious alter-ego, the Plank Road Brewery.

In retaliation, in March 1996 Boston Beer petitioned the BATF to request "full disclosure" on all beer labels. This would end the widespread use of encoded freshness dates and require point-of-product origin to be clearly identified. Boston Beer had been among only a handful of brewers to print encoded freshness dates on their products, so that consumers could evaluate their products, a practice it initiated in 1989. The brewer also accepted product returns after expiration dates had been reached. Boston Beer's move to raise industry accountability to its own standards quickly received the nod from *Consumer Reports*, which praised both the company's packaging and product by voting Samuel Adams the best in the United States in its 1996 craft-brewed ale taste test.

Furthermore, in April 1997, an advertising-industry watchdog resolved a dispute between Anheuser-Busch and Boston Beer. The Budweiser brewer protested the Samuel Adams claim that their beer comes from New England, when it is also produced by contract brewers in the Midwest. The National Advertising Division, an arm of the Council of Better Business Bureaus, decided that Busch's ads, questioning the brand's New England heritage and high price, were not accurate.

Around this time, Boston Beer also began efforts to bring its brew home to Boston, purchasing an abandoned brewery that it slated for renovation and planned for operation by January 1997. Meanwhile, the regional distribution of company-contracted brewing sites—which included Pittsburgh Brewing Co., upstate New York's F.X. Matt Brewing Co. and Genesee Brewing Co., Cincinnati's Hudepohl-Schoenling Brewing Co., and the Stroh-owned Blitz-Weinhart—continued to ensure the freshness of its products to its large customer base outside the greater Boston area. However, Boston Beer pulled out of its contract with Pittsburgh Brewing Co. after 1988, and in July 2001, Boston Beer and Hudepohl-Schoenling Brewing Company announced that they were not renewing their contract brewing agreement. But in Feb. 1999, Pabst Brewing Company assured Boston Beer that it would continue Boston's brewing contract with Stroh upon completion of the proposed sale of Stroh brands and brewing assets to Pabst.

Boston Beer also entered into a working relationship with Seagram Beverage Company. Under the terms of the agreement, in exchange for ownership of both trademark and trade name and future royalties on sales, the company agreed to aid the liquor giant in 1997 with the development and marketing, of its new Devil Mountain craft beer line. Commanding a sales force of 115 people by 1996, Boston Beer began to introduce its product line internationally in Germany, Ireland, Japan, and Hong Kong. In May 1996 the company signed an agreement with England's Whitbread PLC to aid the United Kingdom's fourth largest brewery in the development of a craft brew that catered to British tastes. The company also literally took to the skies, as Samuel Adams became American Airlines' in-flight beer on transcontinental flights beginning in mid-1996. Although pleased to have acquired an international profile, the company's efforts remained concentrated upon its domestic market. Its goals continued to be educating the consumer and developing a taste for a top-quality beer while maintaining profitability.

1998–2002: Fighting Flat Sales

In 1997, the tide began to turn for the industry. Boston Beer was still experiencing growth but not the 30 to 40 percent increases the company had seen over the past five years. And smaller brewers were consolidating. In February 1998, Koch predicted on CNN that the next few years would be difficult for the smaller craft brewers. Although the healthiest of microbreweries, even Boston Beer was seeing sales and earnings fall. Looking at the saturated high-end beer market, industry analysts predicted that Boston Beer would survive because it was the only microbrewer with a national franchise. Also in 1998, as the company celebrated its 10-year anniversary since Boston Beer Company started brewing in its Jamaica Plain brewery, it introduced Samuel Adams Boston IPA, a traditional British India Pale Ale.

On January 28, 1999, addressing the bust that had hit the industry for the past two years, with Boston Beer's stock at less than half its $20 initial public offering (IPO) price, Steven Syre wrote in the *Boston Globe*, "Boston Beer has taken no disastrous wrong turns or missed any great opportunities on the way to this predicament. It is stuck in a consumer category that lost some of its cachet and may be fighting an uphill demographic battle." The market for specialty beers in the 1990s had expanded to include not only yuppie businesspeople but twentysomething drinkers as well. These younger drinkers had gained their more sophisticated taste for malt liquors on the strength of the craft beer renaissance, a phenomenon directly attributable to Koch and Boston Beer. Industry analysts attributed Boston Beer's flat performance to competition from high-end imports such as Heineken and Corona. "Imports stole their thunder," trade newsletter editor Benj Steinman told the *Boston Globe* in the aforementioned article. "The core user base was never that large. So once they weren't expanding the experimental customer base it was tough to grow. A lot of their growth had come from trial customers." That year, Boston Beer expanded its sports marketing tie-ins, such as a March basketball promotion with ESPN.

The company posted an 8 percent volume increase in the first quarter of 2000. A contributing factor was the early 2000 launch of BoDean's Twisted Tea, a malt- and tea-based beverage. Also that year, Boston Beer and craft brewer Sleeman Breweries of Canada joined forces; Sleeman would represent the flagship Samuel Adams brand in Canada, and Boston Beer would conduct market research in the States to uncover possible markets for Sleeman brand products. In 2000, the company also undertook an effort to assure freshness by buying back all out-of-code Samuel Adams for the month of March, an expenditure of about $2 million. (The distributor usually absorbs this cost.) Everything was recycled—the glass, the packaging, and even the beer, which was fermented into ethanol, an environmentally friendly additive for gasoline.

In January 2001, Martin Roper was named CEO, replacing Koch, who retained the title of chairman. In the second quarter of that year, the company saw an increase in gross profit margin, which it attributed to factors such as increased pricing and changes to the product mix. In July that year, the company kicked off test-marketing for a Samuel Adams Light product in Providence, Rhode Island. and Portland, Maine, with the tagline, "Taste the revolution." On July 24, 2001, beer newsletter editor Steinman told *the Boston Globe*'s Chris Reidy, "There's a bit of a disconnect, but it's sort of a necessity" for full-bodied Samuel Adams to pursue the light beer category; it's sensible given the lower-calorie/lower-alcohol sector's potential for growth.

By January 2002, after test-market success, Samuel Adams Light arrived in New England bars and restaurants, and would land in stores that March. The new brew set a record in the Reduced Calorie Lager Category in December 2001 at Chicago's World Beer Championships. "We've worked for years to develop a recipe that offers the flavor and drinkability that beer lovers want," Koch said, describing the beer's two-row malt and Noble hops. "The world's best ingredients give Sam Light a flavor and complexity never before found in light beer." The hops used in the brew, which weighs in at 128 calories, 4.2 percent alcohol by volume, are among the world's most expensive and are grown in the Spalt region of Germany. The newest addition to the Samuel Adams portfolio gives Boston Beer a channel for growth in an otherwise soft market.

Principal Divisions

Oregon Original (India Pale Ale); Samuel Adams (Boston Ale, Boston Lager, Cherry Wheat, Cream Stout, Golden Pilsner, I.P.A., Pale Ale, Triple Bock); Samuel Adams (Double Bock, Octoberfest, Spring Ale, Summer Ale, Winter Lager); HardCore (Golden Cider, Hard Crisp Cider); Twisted Tea.

Principal Competitors

Anheuser-Busch; Gambrinus; Heineken; Pyramid Breweries; Redhook Ale.

Further Reading

Asimov, Eric, "Beer from Boston Brewery Makes Its Way to New York," *Wall Street Journal*, June 24, 1987.

"Boston Beer Appoints CEO to Replace Koch," *Boston Globe*, February 2, 2001, C4.

"Boston Beer Sees the Light," *Beverage Aisle*, September 2001, p.8.

"Busch to Bottle Up Ads Targeting Rival," *Newsday*, April 1, 1997, p. A43.

Hill, Sam and Rifkin, Glenn, *Radical Marketing: From Harvard to Harley, Lessons from Ten That Broke the Rules and Made It Big*, New York: HarperBusiness, 2000, 304 p.

Holson, Laura M., "Private Sector; The Shows Must Go On," *New York Times*, August 12, 2001, Money and Business p. 2.

Karolefski, John, "Boston Brewin'," *BrandMarketing* (Supplement to *Supermarket News*), April 7, 1997, p.1.

Krass, Peter, ed. *Industry Leaders Speak Their Minds: The Conference Board Challenge to Business*, John Wiley & Sons, 2000.

Mamis, Robert A., "Market Maker," *Inc.*, December 1995.

McCarthy, Michael, "Oops!" *USA Today*, August 28, 2001, p.3B.

McCune, Jenny C., "Finding Your Niche," *Small Business Reports*, January 1994.

Melcher, Richard A., "Those New Brews Have the Blues," *Business Week*, March 9, 1998, p. 40.

Morris, Valerie, "Brewer of Samuel Adams Beer," *CNN*, Transcript #97081502FN-L17, August 15, 1997.

Prince, Greg W., "Solid Ground," *Beverage Aisle*, June 15, 2001, p. 52.

——, "Little Giants," *Beverage World*, December 1994.

Reidy, Chris, "Anheuser-Busch Agrees to Modify Ads Targeting Sam Adams," *Boston Globe*, April 1, 1997, p. C2.

——, "Boston Beer Chooses New Advertising Agency," *Boston Globe*, August 4, 1998, p. C9.

——, "Boston Beer Company Tests Product in Maine," *Boston Globe*, July 24, 2001.

Rosenberg, Ronald, "IPO, Entrepreneur Hopes to Brew Interest on 'Net," *Boston Globe*, March 18, 1998, p. D4.

Syre, Steven, "Fighting Flat Sales," *Boston Globe*, January 28, 1999, p. D1.

Thierry, Lauren, "CEO of Boston Beer," *CNN*, Transcript # 98022618FN-L03, February 26, 1998.

Turcsik, Richard, "Boston Beer, ESPN Team Up," *BrandMarketing*, March 1999, p. 8.

—Pamela L. Shelton
—update: Michelle Feder

British American Tobacco PLC

Windsor House
50 Victoria Street
London SW1H 0NL
United Kingdom
Telephone: (44) 20 7845 1000
Fax: (44) 20 7845 2127
Web site: http://www.bat.com

Public Company
Incorporated: September 29, 1902, as British American
  Tobacco Company Ltd.
Employees: 87,000
Sales: £24,831 million
Stock Exchanges: London AMEX
Symbol: BATS (London), BTI (AMEX)
NAIC: 312229 Other Tobacco Product Manufacturing;
  111910 Tobacco Farming; 551112 Offices of Other
  Holding Companies

British American Tobacco PLC is the second largest international tobacco holding company in the world. It sells 300 tobacco brands in 180 markets, has a 15% global market share, and manufactures and processes tobacco products in more than 66 nations.

Origins in Anglo-American Trade War

British American Tobacco originated from a compromise between two rival tobacco manufacturers: one American and one British. James Buchanan (''Buck'') Duke, head of the highly successful American Tobacco Company, decided in 1901 to make a bid for the U.K. market. In response, several smaller independent British tobacco companies banded together to form the Imperial Tobacco Company Ltd. It was from these two tobacco companies that British American Tobacco was born.

Imperial Tobacco was able to resist American Tobacco's attempt to capture its native market but only after a prolonged trade war that proved expensive for both companies. After American Tobacco withdrew from the English marketplace, Imperial was in a stronger position and decided to press its advantage.

When Imperial started to make moves toward the American market, Chairman Duke saw the need for a compromise. A truce was called, and the two rival merchants agreed not to conduct business in each other's domestic markets. Each company also assigned brand rights to the other so that consumers who had grown accustomed to a given brand would not be lost. This deal also initiated the creation of a new company, British American Tobacco (BAT), of which American Tobacco owned two-thirds and Duke was the first chairman.

This new company, registered in London in 1902, acquired the recipes and trademarks of both originating companies. It also acquired all the export business and overseas production operations of each company. The new company's sales and growth potential seemed limited compared to the successes of Imperial and American. Nevertheless, the company grew slowly but steadily during the first decade of the century.

In 1911 the American government sued many U.S. tobacco companies in an early application of antitrust law. Both British American Tobacco and American Tobacco were among the defendants. On appeal, the Supreme Court ruled that much of the domestic tobacco industry engaged in illegal practices in restraint of trade. The Court sent the case back to a special four-judge panel appointed to hear the case in the first instance to devise a remedy. The panel's disposition of the case harmed neither of Duke's companies. In an arrangement approved by the panel, American Tobacco canceled most of its covenants with British American Tobacco and Imperial and sold all of its shares in British American. Most of the sold shares were bought by British investors, and subsequently British American Tobacco was listed on the London Stock Exchange.

This left British American Tobacco, still chaired by Duke, able to sell its product independently all over the world, except in the United Kingdom where it was still bound by its covenant with Imperial. Imperial at this time also retained a one-third share of British American, but this did little to impair the company's success. Duke's operation began rapid expansion of

Company Perspectives:

Our companies are committed to providing consumers with pleasure through excellent products, and to demonstrating that we are meeting our commercial goals in ways that are consistent with reasonable societal expectations of a responsible tobacco group in the 21st century.

British exports and overseas operations. Many new subsidiaries were established around the world during the brief period between the disentanglement from American Tobacco and World War I. Local sources of raw materials were discovered and developed, and international sales grew steadily.

The war brought large numbers of women into the company for the first time. The women were employed primarily in the distribution of cigarettes to the troops abroad, most of whom had switched to cigarettes from the less convenient pipe. The switch, although initiated by soldiers during wartime, caught on with civilians internationally, and British American began selling cigarettes in increasing numbers.

The end of the war brought even greater fortunes to British American Tobacco. Historically, no commercial enterprise had been able to penetrate the huge Chinese market beyond the coastal government trading stations. British American, under Duke's leadership, was able to exploit this untapped interior market, achieved record growth in the years immediately following this breakthrough, and maintained impressive sales levels throughout the rest of Duke's chairmanship. While chairman, Duke was the pioneer of British American's growth, the company's next chairman, Sir Hugo Cunliffe-Owen, was its pioneer of decentralization.

Decentralization and Growth: 1923–1962

Sir Hugo had been involved with British American Tobacco since its inception. Early involvement in the negotiations between American Tobacco and Imperial endeared him to Duke, who appointed Sir Hugo as director and secretary. Sir Hugo held those positions until Duke retired in 1923 (and died two years later) and then succeeded him as chairman. When Sir Hugo inherited the chair, British American's capitalization had quadrupled since 1902, and its sales had grown by nearly a factor of 40. By 1923 the company's world sales had grown to 50 billion cigarettes per year.

Sir Hugo visited China in 1923 to decentralize one of British American's biggest operations. Chinese cigarette consumption had grown from 0.3 trillion in 1902 to 25 trillion in 1920 and to nearly 40 trillion by the time of his visit. Sir Hugo's plan was to restructure BAT China Ltd. into independent regional units that could continue to operate if local conditions deteriorated. Sir Hugo also spent a great deal of time and energy over the next two decades lobbying the Chinese government to minimize the taxation of tobacco.

Sir Hugo's decentralizing efforts spread from China to many of British American's other international operations. The chairman felt that increased local autonomy would lead to

better decisions and improved group performance. This proved true despite skepticism that too much decentralization could produce an unwieldy corporate structure. In 1927, British American had the resources to enter the U.S. market, monopolized at one time by American Tobacco. Sir Hugo acquired Brown and Williamson, a small tobacco producer in North Carolina. With British American's help, this modest company has grown to become a major cigarette manufacturer in the United States. This pattern of rapid growth from modest beginnings was maintained through the Depression and steadily through World War II. At the end of the war, in 1945, Sir Hugo stepped down from the chairmanship and became simply titular president of the company.

Without Sir Hugo's active participation, the management of British American did little other than maintain the company's steady growth through the late 1940s and 1950s. Profitability remained undiminished and the company successfully weathered the storm of the Communist Revolution in China, at which time all of BAT China Ltd.'s assets were nationalized.

Diversification: 1962–1988

By 1962, British American Tobacco's capitalization was such that it was able to begin major moves toward diversification. During that year, British American acquired minority interest in two companies, neither of which was involved in tobacco production or sales. Mardon Packaging International handled cigarette packaging and was thus a logical choice for acquisition. Wiggins Teape Ltd., on the other hand, was a large specialty paper manufacturer. Mardon was not highly successful at first. It was formed from five smaller packaging companies in cooperation with Imperial Tobacco and its first-year turnover was modest. It grew steadily, however, and by the end of the 1970s was advancing turnover at a rate of 15% per annum.

The success of these two enterprises, which later became wholly owned subsidiaries of British American Tobacco, paved the way for further and greater acquisitions. The groundwork was now laid for British American's transformation from a large tobacco company to an even larger conglomerate. While other major tobacco companies attempted to diversify into other packaged goods, British American wasted little time in moving into unrelated but profitable fields. During the 1960s and early 1970s, several major international fragrance and perfume houses were brought in to create a third segment of British American Tobacco's group. These companies included such internationally known concerns as Lentheric, Yardley, and Germaine Monteil.

Once these companies were thoroughly absorbed into British American's operations, the company turned its eye toward a West German department store chain called Horten. It first bought a minority share. Later it acquired the entire company. This led almost immediately to further department store chain acquisitions. Gimbels and Saks Fifth Avenue were acquired in the United States, Kohl's and Department Stores International in the United Kingdom, and Argos, the British catalog store, joined in 1979. Patrick Sheehy, before becoming British American's chairman, was involved in one more such acquisition. Marshall Field's department stores were the unwilling subject of a takeover bid conducted by the controversial team of Carl

Icahn and Alan Clone. Sheehy was able to convince BAT to make a friendly bid for the chain and managed to prevent Icahn from succeeding.

Many of these investments gave British American a good deal of trouble at first, just as Mardon had previously. While Saks Fifth Avenue, which appealed to the upper-middle-class consumer, maintained high profitability, Gimbels, despite efforts to bring in wealthier clientele, has had a consistently poor showing. With the exception of Gimbels, the company absorbed and made a success of its retailing leg as well as its earlier expansion into paper.

In 1972 the treaty of Rome brought the United Kingdom into the European Economic Community (EEC) and terminated the agreements between British American Tobacco and Imperial Tobacco. New restraint of trade laws prohibited their arrangement. The companies exchanged brand rights once again, each retaining full ownership of its original brands in the United Kingdom and Western Europe only. British American kept its brand and trademark ownership in the rest of the world and in the duty-free trade outside Western Europe. Ties with Imperial Tobacco were finally severed in 1980 when that company sold

its remaining few shares in BAT after having made major reductions over the preceding decade.

Due to the increasingly diversified nature of British American's interests, the name of the company was officially changed to BAT Industries Limited in 1976, and management was restructured for tighter control. BAT Industries became a holding company for several smaller operating companies organized according to industry. These operating companies in turn controlled the individual manufacturing and retailing enterprises.

Appleton Papers was added to the BAT operation in 1978. This American company established BAT as the world leader in the manufacture of carbonless paper. That year BAT also acquired Pegulan, a large home-improvements company in West Germany, as well as two fruit juice companies in Brazil. Other purchases followed in pulp production in Brazil and Portugal.

Within two years of his 1982 accession to BAT's chairmanship, Patrick Sheehy decided to add a fourth leg to BAT's existing three supports. Eagle Star, a British insurance group, was involved in an unfriendly takeover struggle with the West German firm Allianz when Sheehy contacted its chairman, Sir Denis Mountain, with a friendly proposal. Eagle Star, which had rejected a low bid from Allianz as "grossly inadequate," accepted a similar bid from BAT as Sir Denis felt the two companies could work together well. In fact, BAT Industries saw a 26 percent rise in pre-tax profit during the first half of 1987, 45 percent of which was due to Eagle Star. Hambro Life Assurance, another large British firm, became Allied Dunbar when it was acquired by BAT in 1985. In 1988, BAT expanded its financial services group into the United States, with the acquisition of the insurance enterprise, Farmer's Group Inc.

After the addition of financial services to BAT's portfolio, Sheehy implemented a policy of "focusing and reshaping the business" rather than continuing to move into new areas. Sheehy believed that BAT should only be involved in companies able to maintain a leadership position in their markets. This led to some significant divestitures for BAT. In 1984, British American Cosmetics, International Stores, and Kohl's Food Stores were all sold. Mardon Packaging was sold to its own management in 1985, and in 1986, Gimbels and Kohl's (U.S.) department stores were put up for sale. That year 88 Batus retail stores were also divested in the United States along with the West German Pegulan.

With the increasing uncertainty of a long-term market in tobacco, Sheehy also took steps to decrease BAT's dependence on that industry. In 1986, only 50 percent of BAT's pre-tax profit came from its tobacco group. This was down from 57 percent in 1985 and 71 percent in 1982. This change did not result from a decrease in tobacco sales, however, but to overall growth in the other groups, most notably Eagle Star, which increased its contribution to BAT's profits from 11 percent in 1985 to 19 percent in 1986.

Return to Tobacco: 1988–2002

In July 1988, Sir James Goldsmith brought BAT's diversification strategy into question. A British billionaire, who had previously participated in a number of leveraged buyouts of U.S. companies, Sir James launched a hostile takeover of BAT. He proposed a buyout financed entirely by debt. Of the $21 billion Sir James offered for the company, $6.4 billion would have been raised through high-yield junk bonds and the remainder by a consortium of banks assembled by Bankers Trust. Current BAT shareholders would receive no cash for their shares. They would instead receive shares of Sir James' investment company, Hoylake Investments, and bonds from the loans.

Sir James planned to pay the loans with the proceeds from selling BAT's non-tobacco holdings. Sir James' proposed buyout failed in May 1990, when California insurance regulators refused to approve his acquisition of the insurance company, Farmer's Group. Nevertheless, this attempted buyout caused BAT to begin to reconsider its diversification strategy.

In the United States and, to some extent in Europe, the 1990s were not good years for cigarette sales. The U.S. courts awarded multimillion-dollar verdicts to smokers who sued tobacco companies for severe illnesses that they claimed to be tobacco-related and to relatives of smokers who died from such illnesses. Governments at both the federal, state, and local levels discouraged smoking through such means as bans on advertising, bans on smoking in public places, the imposition of significant taxes on tobacco products, and other measures. These initiatives substantially reduced tobacco consumption in the United States and, to a lesser extent, in Europe.

From a worldwide perspective, however, demand for tobacco products remained strong. Asia comprised many tobacco customers and offered even more potential customers. The end of the Soviet Union's domination of the nations of Eastern Europe in 1989–1990 opened promising new markets for tobacco products. Thus, BAT was in a good position to move its business back to the exclusive sale of tobacco. The company began to do so in 1990 when it sold or spun off parts or all of numerous non-tobacco properties. These included Wiggins Teape Appleton, PLC; Breuners; Ivey; Marshall Field's; Saks Fifth Avenue; and 50 percent of Horten. In 1993 the company sold one of its financial properties, Eagle Star Levin N.V.

Using the cash proceeds from these sales, BAT began in 1994 to purchase numerous tobacco properties throughout the world. In that year, it acquired major interests in several Eastern European and Asian tobacco processors. It also bought 100 percent of American Tobacco. Between 1995 and 1997, BAT continued disposing of non-tobacco properties and acquiring tobacco properties throughout the world.

In 1998 the company spun off its remaining non-tobacco enterprises and consolidated its tobacco operations into the renamed British American Tobacco. At the time, CEO Martin Broughton expressed the company's determination to regain ''world leadership in tobacco.'' This move was followed in 1999 by the acquisition of Rothman's, a significant player in tobacco markets in Asia and Africa. This purchase made British American second only to Philip Morris in global market share. In 2000, the company acquired Canada's dominant tobacco company, Imasco.

Thus, after spending about a third of the past century moving away from the tobacco business, British American Tobacco used the last decade of the century to position itself as the kind of tobacco company it was during its first decades of existence.

Principal Subsidiaries

B.A.T. Capital Corporation; B.A.T. International Finance PLC; BATMark Ltd.; British American Racing (Holdings) Ltd.; British American Tobacco (1998) Ltd.; Ciberion Ltd.; ITC Ltd. (32%); Skandinavisk Tobaskcompagni AS (26%); VST Industries Ltd. (32%).

Principal Competitors

Philip Morris; Japan Tobacco; Gallaher.

Further Reading

Cochran, Sherman, *Encountering Chinese Networks: Western, Japanese, and Chinese Corporations in China, 1880–1937*, Berkeley: University of California Press, 2000, p. 257.

Cox, Howard, *The Global Cigarette: Origins and Evolution of British American Tobacco, 1880–1945*, New York: Oxford University Press, 2000, p. 401.

——, ''Learning to Do Business in China: The Evolution of BAT's Cigarette Distribution Network, 1902–41,'' *Business History*, July 1997, pp. 30–65.

—update: Anne L. Potter

Cardinal Health, Inc.

7000 Cardinal Place
Dublin, Ohio 43017
U.S.A.
Telephone: (614) 757-5000
Toll Free: (800) 234-8701
Fax: (614) 757-8871
Web site: http://www.cardinal.com

Public Company
Incorporated: 1971
Employees: 48,900 (est.)
Sales: $44.4 billion (2002)
Stock Exchanges: NYSE
Ticker Symbol: CAH
NAIC: 422210 Drugs, Drug Proprietaries, and Druggists'
Sundries Wholesalers; 421450 Medical, Dental and
Hospital Equipment and Supplies Wholesalers;
551112 Offices of Other Holding Companies

Named for Ohio's crimson state bird, Cardinal Health, Inc., ranks among America's top wholesale drug distributors, with 50 principal pharmaceutical distribution facilities and 78 medical-surgical distribution facilities in the United States. Under the direction of Robert Walter since 1971, the company has evolved from a rather inconsequential Ohio food distributor into a trend-setting leader of the pharmaceutical industry. A steady stream of acquisitions—50 since its inception—has helped to multiply Cardinal Health's sales from $429 million in 1986 to nearly $48 billion in 2001. By the mid-1990s, Cardinal came within about $1 billion in annual sales of breaking into the top spot among wholesale drug distributors, having an estimated 18 percent of the $57 billion wholesale market compared to the 19 percent stakes held by leading competitors McKesson Corporation and AmerisourceBergen Corporation.

During the course of its growth spurt, Cardinal diversified from its core wholesale drug distribution business into specialty laboratory and pharmaceutical supplies, computer software, and retail drugstores. While it was not the country's largest drug distributor in terms of sales in the mid-1990s, Cardinal Health did rank highest in terms of market capitalization and profitability. A.G. Edwards investment analyst Donald Spindel asserted that "Cardinal has been the most innovative and the fastest growing. To me, they're really the top company in the industry." By the end of 2000, three companies—Cardinal, AmerisourceBergena, and McKesson—controlled 90 percent of drug wholesaling.

1971 LBO Presages Transformation of Mid-Ohio Distributor

In 1971, just six months after his graduation from Harvard's MBA program, 26-year-old Robert Walter acquired Monarch Foods through a leveraged buyout. Walter hoped to build this small central Ohio grocery distribution company—which he renamed Cardinal Foods—into an industry leader through acquisitions, but soon discovered that he was too late: the market had already begun to consolidate. To make matters worse, Cardinal was compelled to withdraw ten tons of salmonella-infected, prepackaged roast beef mid-decade.

Since consolidation within the wholesale segment of the grocery business was out of the question, Walter attempted to shift his growth strategy, launching Mr. Moneysworth warehouse supermarkets. By the mid-1980s, Cardinal had three Mr. Moneysworth outlets and plans to open stores in Ohio, West Virginia, and Kentucky.

But, Walter did not abandon the distribution industry. Rather, he turned to a business segment that was more profitable, more fragmented, and ripe for consolidation: pharmaceuticals. The company made its first foray into pharmaceutical distribution in 1980, when it acquired a drug distributor in Zanesville, Ohio, 60 miles from Columbus, and became known as Cardinal Distribution. Walter used the proceeds of a 1983 initial public offering to launch an acquisition spree that would gain steam over the next decade. During the 1980s, he targeted relatively small, privately-held distributors in adjacent states and regions for his friendly acquisitions. Reasoning that these local managers knew their markets and would work hard to maintain growth, Walter focused on successful companies with

Company Perspectives:

Cardinal Health, Inc., is the leading provider of products and services supporting the health care industry. Cardinal Health companies develop; manufacture, package, and market products for patient care; develop drug-delivery technologies; distribute pharmaceuticals, medical-surgical and laboratory supplies; and offer consulting and other services that improve quality and efficiency in health care. Headquartered in Dublin, Ohio, Cardinal Health employs more than 49,000 people on five continents and produces annual revenues of more than $40 billion. Cardinal is ranked #23 on the current Fortune *50 list and was named as one of "The World's Best" companies by* Forbes *magazines in 2002.*

managers he characterized as "the kings in our company" in a 1993 interview with *Forbes* magazine's Reed Abelson. Walter operated Cardinal as a holding company, allowing affiliated companies to continue relatively autonomously. The new subsidiaries brought the parent company geographic growth and economies of scale. He told Abelson, "Knowing what I know now, I didn't know what I was doing. But it worked." Key acquisitions—focused in the eastern United States—included Ellicott Drug Co. (1984); James W. Daly, Inc. (1986); and John L. Thompson Sons & Co. (1986).

Late 1980s Exit from Grocery Business

Walter gave up on the marginally profitable grocery business in 1988, when he sold the Cardinal Foods, Inc., Midland Grocery Co., and Mr. Moneysworth subsidiaries to Roundy's Inc., a cooperative wholesaler, for $27 million. Instead of declining, Cardinal's annual revenues actually increased by one-third that year, and its net income more than doubled.

In contrast with his entry into the grocery distribution business, Walter's foray into drug distribution proved well timed, for retail drugstores and hospitals were increasing their purchases from distributors. Cardinal's acquisitions, while relatively small, were indicative of a budding trend toward consolidation in the distribution industry. Mergers and acquisitions shrunk the number of participants in this market by more than half, from 135 in 1984 to 80 in 1989 and less than 60 by 1995. By the end of the decade, Cardinal had accumulated a four-percent stake in the $22 billion wholesale drug business. Sales mounted from $429 million in 1986 to $700 million in 1989, while net income grew from $6 million to $9 million during the same period.

Cardinal's profitable growth did not come exclusively from acquisitions. From 1986 to 1989, in fact, the company was able to increase productivity in nearly 80 percent of its operations. Computer automation was an important factor in this program. Cardinal employees developed IBM-compatible software to increase purchasing, inventorying, and distribution efficiency. A company executive told *Financial World*'s Jagannath Dubashi that the AccuNet system "can reduce the administrative costs of [a hospital's] pharmacy operations by as much as 80 percent." AccuNet not only helped Cardinal cut its own operating margins by 20 percent from 1988 to 1991, but also

increased its level of customer service, offering its clients automated inventory management and up-to-date drug pricing information. Computer links with customers enabled Cardinal to fill and ship orders within 24 hours of receipt.

Ever Larger Acquisitions Mark 1990s

Cardinal moved steadily up the ranks of the country's largest drug distributors with revenues exceeding $1 billion for the first time in 1991. It simultaneously increased its geographic reach in the early 1990s via significantly larger acquisitions. Purchase or perish was the theme in the market that by 1993 was dominated by seven major companies which monopolized 78 percent of the industry's estimated $40 billion sales. The addition of four new subsidiaries moved Cardinal from its bulkhead in the Northeast United States into the Mid-Atlantic and Southeastern states. Acquisitions included Ohio Valley-Clarksburg (1990, the Mid-Atlantic); Chapman Drug Co. (1991, Tennessee); PRN Services (1993, Michigan); and Solomons Co. (1993, Georgia).

By the end of 1993, the company was ready to turn westward, but its rapid growth had caught the attention of well-established industry leaders McKesson Corp. and Bergen Brunswig Corp. When Walter made a move to acquire Alabama's Durr-Fillauer Medical, Bergen Brunswig quickly launched a bidding war with the upstart Ohio company. Under pressure from Bergen Brunswig, the price tag shot up from $250 million to $450 million in just four months. Although Walter lost the battle for Durr-Fillauer, he did not leave the contest empty-handed; Cardinal drew five of the target company's top managers to its ranks. Moreover, some industry observers criticized Bergen Brunswig for overpaying and praised Walter's self-control throughout the ego-charged competition.

Walter more than made up for this minor setback with several major acquisitions from 1994 to 1996. The merger of Cardinal and Whitmire Distribution in 1994 added over $2.25 billion in annual sales and made Cardinal America's third-largest drug distributor. With its strong distribution network in the western and central United States, Whitmire was a long-sought piece of Cardinal's nationwide puzzle. The parent company's geographic scope—32 distribution centers across the country—enabled it to compete for bigger business. In 1994, the company signed a $900 million contract to supply mass merchandiser Kmart's nearly 1,700 pharmacies. And, in 1995, it earned the right to supply pharmaceutical goods to the 175-store Wakefern grocers' cooperative.

The acquisition of Medical Strategies in 1994 added Healthtouch computerized kiosks to Cardinal's repertoire. These electronic point-of-purchase machines offered pharmacy customers access to up-to-date data on illnesses and treatment options. The kiosks generated income via advertising and promoted featured products with coupons; Cardinal claimed that its more than 1,000 Healthtouch machines "increase incremental sales of the featured products by 20 percent on average."

Cardinal entered the retail drug industry late in 1995, when the parent company traded $348 million worth of its stock for full ownership of St. Louis-based Medicine Shoppe International, a pharmacy franchiser with over 1,000 stores. Less than six months later, Cardinal announced its $870-million stock swap for Pyxis, the nation's leading manufacturer of automatic drug dispensing machines used in hospitals. Pyxis subsidiary Allied Pharmacy Management Inc. gave Cardinal entree into the health care information network business. PCI Services, Inc., a pharmaceutical packager, was acquired in July 1996 for $145 million in cash and $56 million of borrowed money. Reflecting on his company's recent activities, Walter noted, "Cardinal has been progressively expanding its business beyond the purely logistical side of drug distribution to providing a full range of value-added information, marketing and educational services to our customers."

These acquisitions helped make Cardinal virtually impervious to the recession that gripped the country in the early years of the decade. For while customers like hospitals and drugstores—themselves under pressure from managed health care plans and other cost-conscious insurers—whittled away at drug distributors' gross profit margins, reducing them from over 17.5 percent in 1960 to 6.5 percent by 1992, Cardinal's increasing share of the market and high level of efficiency helped it maintain consistent growth in sales and profit.

Cardinal also maintained healthy margins by focusing on the most profitable segments of its business. In the 1980s, for example, the company targeted independent drugstores that could not demand the volume discounts sought by larger chains. But, as these retailers began to disappear from the pharmaceutical landscape, Cardinal sought out new profit centers: Pyxis' groundbreaking dispensers, Medicine Shoppe's retail pharmacies, and Healthtouch information systems, for example. Nevertheless, Cardinal was not completely impervious to the cost-cutting pressures that plagued the industry; its gross margins declined from 7 percent in 1992 to about 5.8 percent in 1996.

Fueled by its record-setting acquisitions, Cardinal's sales and net income multiplied rapidly in the early 1990s. Revenues

doubled from $874 million in 1990 to almost $2 billion by 1993, then nearly quadrupled to $7.8 billion by 1995. Net income made similar advances, growing from $13 million in 1990 to $34 million in 1993 and $85 million in 1995. Employment more than tripled during this period and Cardinal's distribution centers nationwide increased from 6 to 32. In an early 1995 profile, *Financial World*'s Jennifer Reingold characterized Cardinal as "by far the healthiest" of the drug distribution industry's five largest companies. Although it was not the sales leader at that time, Cardinal topped the industry in profits and market capitalization. Cardinal Health stockholders—CEO Walter among the largest with about 8 percent of its stock—were well rewarded. According to *Forbes* magazine's 1996 analysis of U.S. companies' 10-year total return, Cardinal ranked 25th.

Cardinal evolved beyond drug distribution into total health care by acquiring companies that serve health care manufacturers and providers of patient care. In 1997, Cardinal acquired Owen Healthcare, of Houston, Texas, a leading provider of pharmacy management and information services for hospitals. In 1998, the Federal Trade Commission blocked Cardinal's attempt to buy competitor Bergen Brunswig and McKesson's attempt to acquire AmeriSource Health. The decision was upheld by a federal judge. Cardinal did acquire R.P. Scherer, the world's largest maker of soft-gels and other drug-delivery solutions, located in Basking Ridge, New Jersey. The following year, Cardinal bought Allegiance, the largest medical-surgical products distributor in the United States. Also acquired in 1999 was Automatic Liquid Packaging, a Woodstock, Illinois-based custom manufacturer of sterile liquid pharmaceuticals and other health care products.

Another record-breaking year followed for Cardinal in 2000. Operating revenues reached an all-time high of more than $25 billion. Net earnings grew 24 percent to $730 million. Contributing to the success were enhanced operations resulting in an improved market position and increased productivity, as well as the continuing implementation of a focused acquisition strategy. In August, Cardinal completed the acquisition of Bergen Brunswig's medical supply distribution business, a distributor of medical, surgical and laboratory supplies to doctors' offices, long-term care and nursing centers, hospitals and other providers of care. Bergen Brunswig Medical Corporation was acquired for approximately $180 million. Other 2000 acquisitions included Rexam Cartons, Inc.; Enhanced Derm Technologies, Inc.; ENDOlap, Inc.; Ni-Med kit manufacturing; CurranCare, LLC; VegiCaps Division (from American Home Products Corporation); and a manufacturing facility in Humacao, Puerto Rico. Cardinal also established a two-pronged Internet strategy with the launch of cardinal.com, a comprehensive, web-enabled site for health care product procurement, fulfillment, support and information; and NewHealthExhange.com, an independent, Internet-based business-to-business electronic health care exchange with McKesson, AmerisourceBergen, Fisher Scientific, and Owens & Minor.

In January 2001, Cardinal celebrated its 30th anniversary and began another banner year in financial records and value to customers. Stock prices rose 40.2 percent and sales rose 28 percent to $38.7 billion. Chairman Walter credited the company's success to "strong internal growth combined with meaningful acquisitions and significant partnerships.'' For the year, nearly $30 billion was spent on 13 acquisitions, with each company meeting the company's standard of being ''outstanding by itself, fitting closely into our strategy, and making Cardinal collectively stronger for the future.'' Bindley Western Industries, Inc., an Indianapolis, Indiana-based wholesale distributor of pharmaceuticals and provider of nuclear pharmacy services, was acquired in February. Other acquisitions included International Processing Corporation; Critical Care Concepts; American Threshold; FutureCare; SP Pharmaceuticals, LLC; Professional Health-Care Resources; and a manufacturing facility in Raleigh, North Carolina. To foster long-term partnerships with providers and manufacturers, Cardinal formed ArcLight Systems, LLC, a venture between Cardinal and several retail chain pharmacies to provide real-time pharmaceutical sales data to pharmaceutical manufacturers.

As of August 2001, Cardinal had 48,900 employees in twenty-two countries on five continents. Forty-two percent of Cardinal employees lived outside the United States. The company's U.S. facilities were located in 41 states and Puerto Rico. Cardinals' operations were organized based on the products and services offered, comprising four reporting segments: Pharmaceutical Distribution and Provider Services, Medical-Surgical Products and Services, Pharmaceutical Technologies and Services, and Automation and Information Services. Through innovative products and services to tens of thousands of customers in the health care industry, Cardinal has more than adequately survived in its highly competitive industry. It received such accolades as number 23 on *Business Week's* list of ''50 Best Companies,'' and among the top 100 of *Internet Week*'s top commercial web innovators.

A Look to the Future

In his ''10 Reasons for Our Optimism,'' Chairman Walter sees a bright future for Cardinal that starts with ''a favorable health care environment and includes some of Cardinal's strengths that enable us to be particularly successful, like market-leading positions, superior scale and resources, and propriety offerings.'' Coupled with past investments, a diversified business model, a seasoned management team, and risk and ownership orientation, the tradition and culture continue as Cardinal's blueprint for success.

Principal Subsidiaries

Allegiance Healthcare; ALP (Allied Liquid Packaging); Bergen Brunswig Medical Corporation; Cardinal Distribution; Medicine Shoppe International, Inc.; Pyxis Corporation; R.P. Scherer.

Principal Competitors

AmerisourceBergen Corporation; McKesson Corporation.

Further Reading

Abelson, Reed, ''It's My Money,'' *Forbes*, March 29, 1993, pp. 56–57.
''America's Largest Corporations,'' *Fortune*, April 15, 2002.
Appleby, Chuck, ''Betting Against Health Care,'' *Hospitals & Health Networks*, June 20, 1996, pp. 34–37.
Autry, Ret, ''Cardinal Distribution,'' *Fortune*, June 3, 1991, p. 104.
Byrne, Harlan S., ''Cardinal Distribution Co.: Acquisitions Carry Drug Wholesaler South and West,'' *Barron's*, November 11, 1991, pp. 47–48.
''Cardinal Health Inc.,'' *Hoover's Handbook of American Business 2002*, 2001, pp. 320–321.
''Cardinal Health Plans to Buy Drugstore Franchiser,'' *New York Times*, August 29, 1995, p. C3.
''Cardinal to Buy Daly, Drug Wholesaler,'' *Supermarket News*, September 30, 1985, p. 14.
''Cardinal to Buy PCI in Stock Transaction Valued at $201 Million,'' *Wall Street Journal*, July 25, 1996, p. C20.
Dubashi, Jagannath, ''The Tie that Binds,'' *Financial World*, April 30, 1991, p. 66.
Freudenheim, Milt, ''Cardinal Health to Buy Pyxis in Stock Swap,'' *New York Times*, February 8, 1996, p. C1.
Heun, Christopher T., ''Pharmacies Band Together to Share and Sell Drug Data,'' *Company Business and Marketing*, 2001.
Jereski, Laura, ''Cardinal Health, Its Red-Hot Growth Slowing, Defends Its Flighty Price with Wider Margins,'' *Wall Street Journal*, January 16, 1996, p. C2.
Marsh, Barbara, ''Bergen Brunswig to Take 'Goodwill' Charge of $87 Million,'' *Los Angeles Times*, October 8, 1998, p. C2.
Maturi, Richard, and Melynda Dovel Wilcox, ''Small Stocks with Big Ideas,'' *Changing Times*, March 1990, pp. 59–61.
Mehlman, William, ''Cardinal on Cutting Edge of Wholesale Drug Boom,'' *Insiders' Chronicle*, June 11, 1990, pp. 1–4.
Murray, Matt, ''Cardinal Health Takes Pulse of New Arenas for Growth,'' *Wall Street Journal*, February 28, 1996, p. B4.
Pearlman, Andrew, ''Cardinal Distribution: Popping Pills,'' *Financial World*, July 24, 1990, p. 18.
Reingold, Jennifer, ''Cardinal Rule,'' *Financial World*, January 31, 1995, pp. 36–38.
Reitman, Valerie, ''Cardinal Sets Whitmire Deal for $303 Million,'' *Wall Street Journal*, October 12, 1993, p. A2.
Rose, Frederick, ''Bergen Brunswig's Shares Jump 10 Percent on Rumors Cardinal Health May Bid,'' *Wall Street Journal*, February 27, 1995, p. B6.
Siwolop, Sana, ''Cardinal Doesn't Need Any Medicine,'' *Financial World*, September 19, 1989, p. 18.
Speer, Tibbett L. ''Just Say Grow,'' *Hospitals & Health Networks*, August 5, 1996, pp. 34–35.
''The Best Performers,'' *Business Week*, Spring 2002.
Ukens, Carol, ''Wholesalers Push Inventory Consignment for Cost Efficiencies,'' *Drug Topics*, July 8, 1996, p. 108.
Vecchione, Anthony, ''Cardinal Health Signing Merger Deal with Pyxis,'' *Drug Topics*, February 19, 1996, p. 25.
Wright, J. Nils, ''Whitmire to Merge with Cardinal,'' *Business Journal Serving Greater Sacramento*, January 31, 1994, pp. 2–3.
Zimmerman, Susan, ''Roundy's to Buy Cardinal Food Unit,'' *Supermarket News*, March 28, 1988, p. 1.

—April Dougal Gasbarre
—update: Carol D. Beavers

Carlton Communications PLC

Carlton Communications PLC
25 Knightsbridge
London SW1X 7RZ
United Kingdom
Telephone: (44) 020 7663 6363
Fax: (44) 020 7663 6300
Web site: http://www.carltonplc.co.uk and
 http://www2.carlton.com

Public Company
Incorporated: 1983
Employees: 14,000 (est.)
Sales: £1,702 billion (2001)
Stock Exchanges: London NASDAQ
Ticker Symbol: CCM (London), CCTVY (NASDAQ)
NAIC: 512110 Motion Picture and Video Production;
 334220 Radio and Television Broadcasting and
 Wireless Communications Equipment Manufacturing;
 334612 Prerecorded Compact Disc (except Software),
 Tape, and Record Reproducing; 512199 Other Motion
 Picture and Video Industries; 514110 News
 Syndicates

Carlton Communications PLC has thrived for more than a decade in the cramped, highly regulated waters of the British market. During the 1990s, it began buying companies, both smaller and larger than itself. Besides owning U.K. television networks, the company provides production facilities, tape duplicating services, and electronic video equipment, which are marketed primarily in Europe and the United States. In the new millennium, when faced with the challenge of securing advertising dollars, the company has focused its interests on free and pay television, content creation, and media services.

Rising from Obscurity During the 1980s

Michael Green, the man who brought Carlton Communications from obscurity into the league of $1 billion companies, grew up in a business-oriented family. Rather than relying on higher education (he left public school at age 17), Green benefited from contacts through the family of his wife, Janet Wolfson, whom he married in 1972. Those contacts included Janet's brother David, with whom Green established a printing and photo-processing company dubbed Tangent Industries, and Lord Wolfson, Green's father-in-law, who owned Great Universal Stores, which hired Tangent to reproduce its catalogs.

After 15 years with Tangent, Green bought Transvideo (renamed Carlton Television Studios) in 1982. Fleet Street Letter soon became part of the fold, and the group of companies went public as Carlton Communications. The Moving Picture Company (MPC), Europe's largest video facilities provider, joined Carlton in a joint venture soon thereafter, acquiring the U.K. subsidiary of California's International Video Corporation for £400,000. Carlton acquired MPC itself in July 1983 for £13 million. MPC's Mike Luckwell remained as managing director in the new company and became Carlton's largest single shareholder.

Carlton acquired more than a dozen companies (at a cost of over £600 million) in the remainder of the decade, all related to either television and film or electronics. Importantly, Green valued cash flow and strict financial controls. When companies were acquired, existing managers were trained to practice strict accounting practices. The result was profits and success. By 1985, Carlton was producing projects as diverse as commercials, rock music videos, and corporate videos. The purchase (worth £30 million) of Abekas Video Systems in 1985 made Carlton a manufacturer of video editing gadgets (the division was sold ten years later to Scitex Corporation for $52 million). Carlton grossed £38.1 million in 1985.

The goal of acquiring a broadcasting station took several years to realize and divided the partnership of Green and Luckwell. The two had differing strategies for acquiring Thames after Britain's Independent Broadcasting Authority (IBA) thwarted Carlton's attempts to gain a controlling interest (Luckwell preferred to defy the IBA), and Luckwell left the company in 1986, selling his shares for £25 million. The IBA interfered with Green's bid for his next target, London Weekend Television, allowing him only a 10 percent share. In response, Green sold his existing 5 percent share for £1 million.

After failing in a group bid for a direct satellite broadcasting service, Green finally succeeded in acquiring a stake in a broadcast network, gaining 20 percent of Central Television in exchange for £18 million and stock. D.C. Thomson and Pergamon Holdings owned equal 20 percent shares. Green had previously hired Bob Phillis away from Central Television to replace Luckwell as Carlton's managing director; Phillis was able to return to his seat on the Central Television board of directors after the deal. Soon afterward, Carlton moved into film production with the £7.3 million acquisition of Zenith Productions; Carlton later had to sell much of Zenith so the company could stay independent.

Sometimes Carlton seemed a bit ahead of its time, as in the 1986 purchase of satellite dish manufacturer Skyscan, which was sold in 1988 due to poor sales. Carlton's biggest buy of the decade proved more fortuitous. The company paid $780 million for Ronald Perleman's U.S.-based Technicolor, the world market leader in videocassette duplication and motion picture film processing. Despite the 1987 stock market crash, Green was able to raise the necessary funds. In five brisk years, Green transformed Carlton from a relatively obscure company into an international corporation that garnered half its revenues (since the Technicolor purchase) from U.S. operations.

Into the Living Room 1991–1996

In 1989, Carlton's stock took a serious fall, from a high of £9.60 a share to a low of £2.98 in the course of a year. Pre-tax profits grew just 13 percent in 1990, a lackluster performance for Carlton, and the market shuddered. Carlton won a 1991 bid for a London weekday broadcasting license, in spite of competition from Thames and a David Frost/Richard Branson coalition (CPV-TV), which outbid Carlton by £2 million but were denied the license as the Independent Television Commission (ITC) were unconvinced about the quality of their programming (Branson's Virgin Group later did outbid Carlton for MGM's British cinemas). The deal signaled a recovery for Carlton.

Besides the annual license fee, Carlton agreed to pay 15 percent of advertising revenue (estimated to be approximately £50 million per year) to the British government for the ten-year duration of the contract. *The Daily Telegraph* and Italian publishers Rizzoli Corriere della Sera each bought five percent of Carlton's stock prior to the bid, worth £43.2 million. The Daybreak consortium, in which Carlton held a 20 percent share, lost the bid for the breakfast television license to the Sunrise consortium of LWT, Scottish Television, *The Guardian* newspaper company, and Walt Disney. Carlton, optimistic about the future of morning television, promptly bought a 20 percent share in Sunrise for £5.4 million.

At the end of 1993, Carlton announced it would buy Central Independent Television for £624 million ($925 million), thereby combining the first and third largest independent television companies in Britain. The timing could have helped both of them escape being consumed by European companies when ownership restrictions were relaxed in 1994. In 1995, Carlton was Britain's largest broadcaster, controlling 30 percent of ITV (channel three, the U.K.'s first commercial channel) advertising revenues through its London and Midlands stations. *The Economist* reported Carlton's biggest challenge would be expanding into foreign broadcasting markets, in which Green expressed interest, as well as into newspapers and other types of media.

Although Carlton aborted a venture with the German station Vox, it invested in two other overseas ventures in 1995. France Télé Films, a cable channel launched in cooperation with France Télévision, would rely on programming from Carlton's CTE library (stocked with 4,000 hours as of 1995, including 200 films) as well as that of France Télévision. Carlton also entered a partnership with Singapore's Channel KTV, also cable-based, which prepared to add two karaoke channels to its existing services.

Almost half of Carlton's profits came from broadcast television in 1995. In spite of the growth of satellite and cable services, Carlton remained optimistic about the importance of free-to-air broadcasting. Nigel Walmsley, Carlton's director for Broadcasting, told shareholders in a 1995 annual report that only terrestrial broadcasting reached mass audiences since cable and satellite channels "tend to take audience share from existing minority channels, thus fragmenting the total cable and satellite audience."

A 1 percent increase in turnover (to £169.1 million) boosted operating profits for the Video and Sound Products division by 43 percent in 1995 to £32.5 million. Its primary components, Quantel and Solid State Logic, produced equipment for making special effects. Both companies were market leaders based on such state-of-the-art technologies as Quantel's digital visual effects editing systems ("Henry" for television and "Domino" for film) and Solid State Logic's "Axiom" and "9000-J Series" digital audio consoles. Quantel supplied the printing industry with its Graphics Paintbox system.

Notably, the acquisition of Cinema Media extended Carlton's advertising sales capability from television onto the big screen. Cinema Media, renamed Carlton Screen Advertising, quickly became a market leader distributing promotional materials to cinemas throughout the United Kingdom. Carlton's acquisition of Westcountry Television expanded their coverage to 39 percent of the U.K. population. And the acquisition of Action Time brought one of Europe's most successful producers of entertainment programs into the Carlton fold.

Moving into the Millennium:
Focus on Interactive and Digital Media

In 1997, Carlton formed a partnership, British Digital Broadcasting, with longtime competitor Granada. British Digital Broadcasting was awarded three principal digital terrestrial

---

Key Dates:

1983:   Carlton Communications PLC is incorporated and listed on the London Stock Exchange.
1985:   Carlton acquires Abekas Video Systems, a manufacturer of video editing gadgets.
1986:   Carlton acquires Skyscan, a satellite dish manufacturer.
1987:   Carlton acquires 20 percent of Central Television.
1988:   Carlton acquires Technicolor and is listed on NASDAQ.
1993:   The company produces its first broadcast of Carlton Television.
1994:   The company acquires the remaining 80 percent of Central Independent Television.
1996:   The company makes several key acquisitions and launches the Carlton Food Network.
1997:   Carlton forms a partnership with competitor Granada named British Digital Broadcasting.
1998:   Carlton expands Technicolor internationally and launches Carlton Interactive, ITV2, and ONdigital.
1999:   The company continues to make large acquisitions and forms an alliance with TF1, a venture to operate European Internet businesses.
2000:   Carlton Interactive partners with several major Internet businesses.
2001:   Carlton sells Technicolor to Thomson Multimedia.

---

television licenses. These licenses allowed British Digital Broadcasting one half of the digital terrestrial capacity in the United Kingdom, and in November of 1998, the partnership launched ONdigital, the world's first multichannel service through an aerial. ONdigital moved Carlton into the lucrative pay-television market.

In 1998, Carlton launched ITV2, to complement ITV1, their mainstay terrestrial channel. ITV2 allowed their viewers to see rebroadcasts of the ITV1 program and also broadcasted a range of original programs. Carlton also invested in television program and film libraries. By the end of 1999, Carlton was the world's largest distributor of classic British films television programs, offering 18,000 hours of television programs and 2,000 films to over 100 countries.

Technicolor benefited in the 1990s as Hollywood studios issued large-scale releases (for example, *Batman Forever* opened simultaneously on 4,500 screens), which required many duplicates. Declining currency values brought Film and Television Services turnover down to £251.8 million in 1995, although operating profit increased 9 percent to £41.6 million. Beside Technicolor, the division boasted some of the largest postproduction facilities in the world, such as The Moving Picture Company in London and Complete Post in Los Angeles. In 1995 when sales for the Video Production and Duplication division (including Technicolor and Carlton Home Entertainment) were £474.2 million (profits down 9 percent to £60.7 million), a new one-million-unit-per-day videocassette facility was under construction in Michigan. Beginning in 1996, digital video discs offered Technicolor a new format to master. The

company also produced CDs and CD-ROMs through Technicolor Optical Media Services. In 1999, Technicolor continued its expansion internationally and started the development of digital cinema. Carlton sold Technicolor to Thomson Multimedia in 2001.

Principal Divisions

Channels (Broadcast Television, Advertising Sales); Content (Film and Television Services, Production, and Distribution); Digital Media (Digital Terrestrial and Interactive Television Services, Internet).

Principal Competitors

BBC; Granada PLC; RTL Group SA; British Sky Broadcasting Group PLC; NTL Incorporated.

Further Reading

Amdur, Meredith, "Battle Lines Drawn in Asian Satellite TV," *Broadcasting & Cable*, June 28, 1993, p. 21.

Baldo, Anthony, "Bonanza: American Reruns Dominate European Television, but Changes Are Coming," *Financial World*, April 16, 1991, pp. 44–45.

——, "Media: The Enemy Within," *Financial World*, April 16, 1991, pp. 24–32.

"Britain: And the Winners Are. . . .," *The Economist*, October 19, 1991, pp. 67–68.

Burton, Patrick, "C5 and the Threat of London TV Monopoly," *Marketing*, January 14, 1993, p. 15.

"Carlton Links with LWT Sales," *Marketing*, January 21, 1993, p. 10.

"Carlton Revs Up Motor Show," Advertorial, *Marketing*, July 15, 1993, p. 5.

Carter, Meg, "ITV Takes Seats for the Big Fight," *Marketing Week*, July 9, 1993, pp. 20–21.

——, "Keeping and MAI on the Big Time," *Marketing Week*, January 28, 1994, pp. 16–17.

Clarke, Steve, "Brits Venture Beyond Isles," *Variety*, January 22, 2001, p 53.

——, "Merger Hold-off Taunts U.K. Biz," *Variety*, October 1, 2001, p. 62.

Crawford, Anne-Marie, "Digital TV's Formative Year," *Marketing*, October 7, 1999, p. 30.

Dawtrey, Adam, "Regulators Prodded by U.K. Mega-Merger," *Variety*, Nov 29, 1999.

Douglas, Torin, "Big Bills in the New Year," *Marketing Week*, January 8, 1993, p. 15.

DuBois, Peter C., "Worth the Trip," *Barron's*, February 20, 1995.

Fisher, Liz, "Set on Broadcasting Its Ambitions," *Accountancy*, January, 1992, pp. 17–19.

Foster, Anna, "Behind the Carlton Screen," *Management Today*, April 1989, pp. 52–56.

Fry, Andy, "TV Franchises: Who Loses Out?" *Marketing*, April 4, 1991, pp. 18–19.

"Greenland," *The Economist*, December 4, 1993, pp. 68–69.

"Granada Profits Rise but Takeover Talk Hits Shares," *Irish Times*, posted November 25, 1999, http://www.ireland.com.

Guyon, Janet, "UK Broadcaster Carlton Makes Bid for Rest of Central," *Wall Street Journal*, November 30, 1993, p. 12.

Higham, Nick, "Green Shoots of Discovery?" *Marketing Week*, April 29, 1994, p. 19.

Hudson, Richard L, "British Telecommunications Stirs Rush to Test Europe's Multimedia Market," *Wall Street Journal*, November 18, 1994, p. 7D.

Lipin, Steven, ''Bankers Trust Woes Spread to Money Unit,'' *Wall Street Journal*, December 8, 1993, p. 3.

''London Cable Hitch,'' *Marketing*, May 20, 1993, p. 10.

Marcom, John, Jr., ''Is This One for Real?'' *Forbes*, July 24, 1994, p. 252.

Mistry, Tina, ''Shock as Unilever Dumps Carlton TV,'' *Campaign-London*, January 7, 1994, p. 1.

Pratt, Tom, ''Merrill Limps to Market with Two Big UK Preferred Deals,'' *Investment Dealers Digest*, October 4, 1993, pp. 14–15.

Robinson, Jeffrey, ''The Modest Media Magnate,'' *Business-London*, October, 1990, pp. 100–104.

Sorkin, Andrew Ross, ''British Media Merger,'' *New York Times*, November 27, 1999, p. B3(N).

''UK Consumers Blissfully Unaware of Digital TV Revolution,'' *Marketing Magazine*, February 8, 1999, p. 6.

''The Wearing of the Green,'' *The Economist*, July 8, 1995, p. 68.

Wilkinson, Amanda, ''ITV Roadshow to Woo Top Clients,'' *Marketing Week*, January 24, 2002, p. 13.

—Frederick C. Ingram
—update: C.J. Gussoff

China Telecom

33, Er Long Lu, Xicheng District
Beijing 100032
China
Telephone: (86) 10-6602-7043
Fax: (86) 10-6602-7254
Web site: http://www.ct1000.com

Established: 1994
Employees: 500,000
Sales: US$21.9 billion (2001)
NAIC: 513310 Telecommunications Networks, Wired;
513322 Telecommunications Carriers, Cellular
Telephone

China Telecom dominates China's largest fixed-line telephone services with 95 percent of the services for 1.2 billion people in 31 provinces. In addition to these 165 million fixed-line accounts, China Telecom has the world's largest wireless market, with about 120 million subscribers, and a history of poor service. Effective May 16, 2002, China Telecom is separated into China Netcom Communication Group Corporation in the North and China Telecom Corporation in territories in the West and South to generate competition and greater efficiency. The northern operations cover ten provinces, and merged with former rivals Netcom and Jitong Communications. The southern and western operations include 21 provinces that comprise China Telecom.

China Telecom operations consist of four major components: fixed-line telephony, which is basic telephone service; Internet telephony, a category of hardware and software required to transmit Internet submissions over phone lines; VPN (virtual private network), a network system construed to submit data using telephony technology; and CDMA (code division multiple access), the technology behind cell-phone usage.

China is considered to be the last gold mine of telecommunications because of its vast and rapidly growing market. *Xinhua News Agency* reports that the total assets of China's telecommunications sector topped 1 trillion yuan (US $120 billion) at the end of 2001. Investment in fixed assets (tangible property used in the operation of a business) for the industry came to 243 billion yuan (US $29.2 billion). The number of telephone users in China increased by 94 million in 2001 after the installation fee was removed, resulting in a total of 145 million mobile-phone users—the largest number of any country in the world—and 179 million fixed-telephone subscribers, the second highest worldwide.

Company Beginnings and Overview

China Telecom got its start in 1994 as an independent company, owning and controlling all public telecommunications, including mobile, fixed-line, and postal services. It was heavily regulated and influenced by the Ministry of Posts and Telecommunications (MPT).

By 1998, 1.2 billion people in China relied on telecommunications services. A countrywide modernization effort meant more focus on this sector of the economy was necessary. The people needed improved services and better quality telecommunications services. These two points were foremost in the minds of China Telecom executives when they attended the country's PT/Expo telecommunications show in October of that year.

China Telecom planned to invest US$18 billion in telecommunications services that year and the next, with 80 percent slated for public telecom infrastructure. Business was good, with revenues for the first three quarters of 1998 at US$20 billion. Subscribers totaled 104.4 million and the number was going up rapidly. More than 20.8 million new customers joined in 1998, including 7.7 million cellular-phone customers. By contrast, China Telecom's only competitor, China Unicom, had only 1 million customers at that time.

Company director Ni Yifeng had plans to increase the number of telephone exchanges by 20 million lines each year. Part of the company's goal was to enhance the nationwide transmission network as well, as the actual number of telephone users for the year 2000 turned out to be more than twice the projected number. The company also wanted to develop products for VPNs (virtual private networks—private networks that are built atop a public network); frame relays (an interface used for WANs—wide area networks); Internet; and ISDN (integrated service digital network) lines.

To get help with these plans China Telecom called on an old ally, Nippon Telegraph and Telephone Corporation (NTT) for help, requesting management lessons as well as technical assistance. The relationship between NTT and the Chinese government dated back to 1980.

Telecom Restructuring 1998

In March 1998, the government had passed a telecommunications law that changed the regulatory structure and allowed more competition in the industry. China wished to enter the World Trade Organization (WTO). However, entry into the WTO required proof of a competitive atmosphere and a demonstrated customer-centered market environment. Up to this point, China's telecom industry was dominated by China Telecom, which was a mammoth entity.

At this same time, a competitor, China United Telecommunications Corporation (China Unicom), tried to gain a foothold in the industry. However, the MPT (Ministry of Posts and Telecommunications) used its power and China Telecom used its dominance to successfully prevent China Unicom from becoming a significant competitor. China Unicom struggled to create new business, but its lack of government backing and a substantial customer base limited its ability to grow and compete.

The first item on the restructuring list was to break down the powerful ministry alliance between the MPT and China Telecom. The government absorbed the MPT into the Ministry of Information Industry (MII). This new body was given the responsibility of governing all telecommunications operators. It was also assigned the task of establishing telecommunications policy, freeing up the market, and assisting with the planning for the prospective WTO bid. In being given responsibility for all telecommunications operators, it was hoped that the MII would be forced to govern fairly, separate government from business, and promote competition.

While China Telecom made plans for the future, the government was hard at work influencing these plans. In early December 1998 the government announced it was considering breaking up the China Telecom monopoly by breaking up the company itself. The MII submitted plans to China's Cabinet that proposed breaking up the company either along geographical lines or by services. Another possibility on the horizon was to privatize the company, although recent new rules restricting foreign company involvement into China suggested this would not be a viable solution.

On December 17, 1998, the MII announced breakup plans would be put on hold. The government ruled that operation of foreign companies in China was illegal, so the MII had to compensate the foreign companies for their loss of business.

The MII had submitted a plan that broke China Telecom into smaller companies along business lines, but the State Council had rejected that plan. The Council instructed the MII to come up with a plan that fostered more competition. In response, the MII first separated the postal services into their own entity, then began breaking up China Telecom.

The First Breakup: 1999

Much speculation surrounded the proposed breakup plans at the end of 1998, but the MII refused to divulge its intentions. "The main idea is to separate the government function from the business function and to let the enterprises enter a market economy," said Cheng Guanghui, then spokesperson for the MII, without further elaboration.

The breaking up of the company finally began in 1999 and took more than two years to complete. China Telecom was offering essentially four services at this point: fixed-telephone lines, mobile communications, paging, and satellite transmissions. Each of these parts was broken into separate companies. While waiting for the government's breakup decisions, the company forged ahead with company growth.

Plans for investing in 12 provinces were designed to boost China Telecom's presence in the Western provinces. One official deemed the investments "important because of their political significance." China Telecom also purchased ATM (asynchronous transfer mode that allows dynamic allocation of bandwidth) network equipment to carry digital data. In May 1999, China Telecom's paging division, Guoxin Paging, was handed over to China Unicom. Guoxin Paging had an annual revenue of US$1 billion. Once absorbed into China Unicom, it boosted the company's share of the paging market to 80 percent.

In 2000, the mobile operations were spun into a separate company called China Mobile, and soon became the second largest mobile network in the world. By the end of 2000, China Mobile served 78 percent of China's mobile subscribers. The Satellite division also became its own company called ChinaSat. In May, the newly revamped China Telecom once again began operations with 98 percent of all fixed-line subscribers. However, by the end of 2000, this number had dropped to 95 percent.

Emerging Competitors

The desire for increased competition did not end with the breakup of China Telecom. China Unicom was still struggling to emerge despite being the recipient of China Telecom's paging business. As the sole holder of operational licenses in China, the company forged ahead and offered an initial public offering (IPO) of US$6.9 billion in June 2000. It was permitted to charge 10 to 20 percent less in mobile fees than its only competitor, China Mobile.

China Railway Telecom, or Railcom, which offered all telecom services except mobile, first established a national fixed-line network that spanned 120,000 km. In March 2001, it gained permission to offer rates 10 to 20 percent cheaper than China Telecom. However, in June of the same year, a connection

Key Dates:

1994: China Telecom and China Unicom are established as independent, non-government-backed companies.

1997: China Telecom's network becomes the world's second largest fixed-line telephone network, with more than 100 million lines.

1998: The government forms the regulatory Ministry of Information Industry (MII); and postal services are separated from China Telecom and absorbed into the MII.

1999: The government begins to restructure China Telecom into four separate companies; and China Unicom is granted an exclusive permit for Internet and ISP (Internet service provider) services.

2000: As part of restructuring, China Mobile and China Satcom are spun off as separate companies; fixed-line competitor China Railways Communications Limited (Railcom) is established; and telephone users in China surpass the 200 million mark.

2001: China becomes a member of the World Trade Organization (WTO).

2002: China Telecom is reorganized into China Netcom Communication Group Corporation in the Northern provinces and China Telecom Corporation in the Southern provinces.

agreement allowing both companies to offer nationwide services was signed.

China Netcom, which had data, VOIP (voice over Internet protocol), and Internet operations, was considered to be a future competitor to China Telecom and held the fastest fiber-optic network in the country. As data services were more in demand, the company's responsiveness to the market positioned them as a potential major player.

By June 2001, the seven licensed public telecom operators included China Telecom and its two break-off companies (China Mobile and ChinaSat), China Unicom, Jitong (data and Internet operations), China Netcom, and China Railway Telecom.

Competitive Fee Reductions

The reduction of fees was a common practice during this time of restructuring. In June 1999, MII had awarded China Telecom, Unicom, Jitong, and Netcom the licenses to offer IP telephony services for 50 percent less for long-distance and international calls. For other reasons as well, China Telecom was merely moderately profitable by 2000, with only 11 of 31 regional branches reporting profits. Part of this was due to its employee structure; when mobile, satellite, and paging operations were divested, the employees stayed with the fixed-line operations.

Several of China Telecom's subsidiaries also ran schools, hotels, shops, and other businesses, which added up to high-company operating costs. In May of 2000, the company's IPO plans hit another snag when investors opted for the competitor,

China Unicom, over China Telecom. By the end of 2000, it became obvious that China Telecom's monopoly was slowly being chiseled away by discounts awarded to other telecoms and its own inefficiencies.

The MII also reduced fixed-line and IP telephone charges (including Internet connection fees) by more than 50 percent in January 2001. China Telecom still had 95 percent of the market and was more seriously undermined by this move than other MII changes. The company lost about US$3.6 billion that year.

China Telecom Embraces High-Tech Opportunities

The year 2000 brought new changes in telecommunications regulations. Designed to clarify some vague definitions, the rules were welcomed by telecom operators. Foreign companies showed interest even though no specifics were included for their involvement. The basic tenet of the rules was to allow the telecoms to focus on upgrading services rather than to continue to engage in price wars.

This meant that China Telecom could forge ahead with more plans to upgrade services and engage in technical progress as well. In October of that year they teamed with Hutchinson Global Crossing, a Hong Kong-based network operator to create the Shenzhen-Hong Kong fiber-optic transmission system (SDH). The SDH extended China Telecom's fiber-optics offerings to a total of 80 kilometers from Guangzhou to the border of Hong Kong, and made a direct connection to the system found there.

Four months later, China Telecom began 2001 with a shaky start when an undersea cable broke, leaving China's Internet users with no connections for ten days in February. However, the company forged ahead with more technology dreams—specifically, broadband plans. Broadband networks not only allowed more data to transmit but could run video and voice signals through at the same time.

Physically, broadband meant elimination of copper cables that were notorious for inefficient transmissions. Having broadband technology could mean more business opportunity for China Telecom as evidenced in their US$101 million deal with Canada-based Nortel Networks to construct a 15,000-kilometer network. By providing high-speed devices such as ISDN (integrated service digital network) through this network, the company could switch China's 22.5 million Internet users from dial-up to digital. China Telecom estimated that by 2005, they would have 20 million broadband users.

China Telecom remained dominant in its position at this time, despite the earlier divestment of several of its businesses. Their Internet (data communications) branch, ChinaNet, was the leading data center and Internet access provider in China. Fixed-line telephony still accounted for 90 percent of consumers' needs; however, increased demand for more technology and better service began to put pressure on China Telecom.

Dreams of an IPO

In December 2000, China Telecom had begun to prepare for an initial public offering to raise US$10 to US$15 billion on the New York and Hong Kong stock exchanges. Scheduled for July 2001, it was to be one of Asia's biggest IPOs. Merrill Lynch and

Morgan Stanley were hired to underwrite the IPO. However, in May of that year, the company placed all its plans on hold indefinitely. The investment climate was bad, and global interest in telecom stocks was down. Industry analysts also blamed China Telecom's reform process, which was supposed to have been completed by then.

The reform program was planned to prepare China Telecom for an overseas listing, which would involve major structural reform to be completed by March 2001 when the company went public. However, by May 2001, the plan had still not been approved. Discouraged about their future when the reforms had not materialized, some employees jumped to better-paid jobs at China Mobile and China Unicom later in the year.

The reform program consisted of returning the company to its core business of telecom operations. The company was to rid itself of all activities not directly related to telecom operations, laying off 200,000 workers in the process and focusing on the parts of the company that were profitable.

Another part of China Telecom's IPO process was an application for a mobile license. Unfortunately, the MII announced in March 2001, that it would not grant another mobile license that year. China Telecom wanted the government to expedite its breakup plans, as the delay was holding back the company's desire for a successful initial public offering (IPO). The company had originally wanted to list on the Hong Kong and U.S. markets and raise US\$8 to US\$10 billion in 2001. These plans were put on hold when talk of another restructure began. China Telecom needed government approval to list. When China Telecom went public it would be the first telecom company in China to go public and to list funds in an international market.

Expanded Internet Services

Formerly only the northern-based Jitong was offering Internet access besides ChinaNet. By June 2001, China Netcom, China Unicom, and China Railway all began to enter the Internet market. Independent providers began to spring up as well. And network upgrades allowed cable providers to offer Internet services for the first time. Contributing to the growing competitive landscape were the MII's goals of fostering competition by becoming a more independent entity.

In an effort to compete with these newcomers and their lower rates, China Telecom cut its Internet Protocol (IP, meaning long-distance connections made using Internet technology, not to be confused with Internet access) fees by 50 percent in March 2001. The company had already increased charges for its fixed-line operations by about 60 percent the year before, possibly contributing for the loss of customers to less expensive operators.

Other preemptive moves by China Telecom included waiving installation fees and giving gifts to new subscribers. The new policies confirmed that China Telecom could no longer deny the looming competition ahead.

Price Wars Continue

The price wars of early 2001 were only the start of the emerging competitive telecom market. By now, China Telecom was still the dominating player but the others were becoming increasingly competitive.

One such company was China Railcom, the country's second-biggest fixed-line telecom operator that was established at the end of 2000. It initiated price wars by setting rates at half the rate that China Telecom charged, and targeted completion of a long-distance call network by June, mere months after the company was established.

China Telecom had to face yet another new obstacle, the loss of its monopoly on Internet bandwidth. China Unicom was awarded permits to build and operate its own international landing station, allowing the company to use undersea cable operations without having to negotiate prices with China Telecom. Local start-up ISPs could work with China Unicom as well, continuing to chisel away at China Telecom's dominance.

However, China Telecom continued to prosper and grow. In 2001, the company's number of digital communications increased by 17.61 million units over 2000, for a total of 33.22 million units, and an increase of 31.6 percent over 2000. The total browsing time of Internet users reached 143 billion minutes, an increase of 140.3 percent over 2000. China Telecom's total digital communication income in 2001 came to 9.65 billion yuan (US \$1.17 billion).

Restructuring Redux 2002

China's entry into the World Trade Organization (WTO) triggered more change for China Telecom, which still held 95 percent of the market and was considered a monopoly. Because of the WTO pressures, another restructuring was on the horizon.

In the summer of 2001, the Chinese government began to plan another breakup of China Telecom. In December, the government approved a plan to split the company into two separate companies. One would take the ten Northern provinces, and the other the Southern provinces. The northern group would combine with two smaller companies to form a new company called China Netcom. The southern half would remain China Telecom, with 21 provinces.

Much later than initially planned, on May 16, 2002, the split became official when the Northern provinces became China Netcom Communication Group Corporation, and the Southern and Western provinces became China Telecom Corporation. These two regional companies, divided by the Yellow River, would be allowed to build more networks and to compete with each other, although this would likely take years as the local phone services would not immediately overlap.

The newly structured China Telecom would retain 70 percent of its long-distance network, with the remaining network handed over to China Netcom. "Reform is the direction and competition is the goal," stated Wu Jichuan, head of China's Ministry of Information Industry (MII) during a ceremony honoring the split. Minister Wu, as reported in the *Reuters Business Report* for May 16, 2002, further noted that the goal in dividing China Telecom, which had a longstanding reputation for poor service and high prices, was to "break the monopoly and improve the quality of telecom services."

Competition was further enhanced by plans to issue both new companies wireless operating licenses. Next on the drawing board were plans for an expected US$3 to US$5 billion initial public offering (IPO) by China Telecom in Hong Kong and New York later in 2002. As of May 2002, the telecom market in China was shared by China Telecom Corporation, China Netcom Communication Group Corporation, China Mobile, China Unicom, China Satcom, and China Railcom.

It is hoped that China Telecom can step up to real competition. On December 11, 2001, when China joined the World Trade Organization, it promised, as a condition of membership, to allow foreigners to own up to 50 percent of telecoms ventures in China after two years, and 49 percent of mobile-phone companies after five years. Telecommunications investors are unlikely to pass the opportunity for a parcel of this last gold mine.

Principal Competitors

China Mobile; China Netcom; China Unicom.

Further Reading

"Breakup of China Telecom Is Not Imminent," *Telenews Asia*, December 17, 1998. "Breakup of China Telecom, U.S. Department of Commerce," *National Trade Data Bank*, November 3, 2000.
"China Breaks Up China Telecom in Hopes of Spurring Industry," *AP Worldstream*, May 16, 2002.
"China Telecom Confirms Digital Communication Target," *AsiaInfo Services*, March 15, 2002.
"China Telecom Expects Hong Kong Stock Exchange Listing Later This Year," *Xinhua News Agency*, February 26, 2002.
"China Telecom Faces Price War," *ChinaBiz*, March 4, 2001, http://www.chinabiz.org.
"China Telecom Monopoly Split, Division on North-South Basis," *BBC Monitoring Newsfile*, May 16, 2002.
"China to Open Its Telecom Market," *China Business Information Network*, December 2, 1998.
"The Chinese Telecom Rush Is On," *Business Week Online*, July 16, 2001.
"Chinese Telecommunication Reform Ended Up," *AsiaInfo Services*, May 22, 2002.
Einhorn, Bruce, *Business Week International Editions*, "The Telecom Rush Is On," *Business Week International*, July 16, 2001, p. 16.
Greenberg, Jonah, "China Pushes Telecoms Reform on WTO Entry," *Reuters*, December 11, 2001.
——, "China Splits Phone Giant, Paving Way for Big IPOs," *Reuters Business Report*, May 16, 2002.
Pappas, Leslie, "The Last Emperor Exits," *Newsweek International*, May 17, 1999, p. 57.
"Telecom Splitting Decision Vital," *China Daily*, August 20, 2001.
"Telecoms Split Plan under Fire," *China Daily*, October 23, 2001.
Zerega, Blaise, "China Braces for a Breakup," *RedHerring*, September 15, 2001.

—Annette Dennis McCully

SECURITY SERVICES

Chubb, PLC

Chubb House
Stains Road West
Sunbury-on-Thames
Middlesex TW16-7AR
United Kingdom
Telephone: (44) 1932-785588
Fax: (44) 1932-779481
Web site: http://www.chubbplc.com

Public Company
Incorporated: 2000
Employees: 52,000 (2001)
Sales: £1.5 billion (2001)
Stock Exchanges: London
Ticker Symbol: CHB
NAIC: 541330 Engineering Services; 922160 Fire
Protection; 561621 Security System Services (except
Locksmiths)

Chubb, PLC is among the world's five largest providers of security services to businesses and governments. The company is active in electronic security systems, including the design, installation, and monitoring of intrusion detection and alarm systems, of access control systems, and of closed circuit TV systems and appropriate alarms. It designs fire protection and suppression systems, trains firefighting personnel, services fire protection installations, advises on compliance with fire safety laws and regulations, and helps to maintain mandatory fire systems service records. It also provides security personnel to serve as guards, patrol and response agents, and security officers for major events and similar functions. Chubb has offices in 20 nations on five continents.

Chubb has been a name associated with security since 1818 when the Chubb business, a lock and safes manufacturer, was founded in the United Kingdom. Today's Chubb, PLC, however, is the direct product of the 2000 spin off of it and Kidde, PLC, as independent companies from Williams, PLC. At the same time Williams, which had changed its name from Wil-

liams Holdings in 1998, dissolved itself. Nigel Rudd and Brian McGowan founded Williams Holdings in 1982 with a total capital of £400,000.

1982–90: Williams Holdings Grows Rapidly

Williams Holdings acquired diverse businesses—engineering concerns, foundries, manufacturers of household fixtures and building materials, makers of fire protection equipment, virtually any low-tech concern that had a large market share and showed signs of inefficient management. Williams' managers then examined the newly purchased company closely, eliminated redundant or wasteful assets, invested in new equipment and made the subsidiary the lowest cost producer among its competitors. They then had the choice of selling the enterprise at a profit or keeping it as a contributor to Williams Holdings' revenues.

In the early 1980s, several British companies had adopted similar business models. It was relatively easy for a small and unknown company to find, acquire, and improve poorly managed companies, and Williams was quite successful at it. Rudd identified takeover targets. McGowan handled relations with the City (London's Wall Street) and company administration. A third associate, Roger Carr, headed the teams that performed the hands-on restructuring of each newly acquired company.

Williams Holdings made its first acquisition of Ley's, a successful, but less than optimally efficient, foundry in 1982. From this start, it required only two years for the company to establish a reputation for acquiring troubled businesses and making them profitable. Nevertheless, by 1984, the company was in financial difficulty, having assets of £10 million and debts of £11 million. At that time, Rudd discovered a depressed forging, metals, and plastics company, J and HB Jackson. It was cash rich, with £26 million in assets and £11 million in cash. In 1985, Williams bought the firm for £30 million financed by a stock sale. Immediately, the £11 million in cash extinguished Williams Holdings' debt, and the company became debt free with assets of about £30 million.

With that transaction, Williams' stock rose, providing it with a means of financing new acquisitions without taking on major

Company Perspectives:

Chubb is a leading worldwide security services provider, differentiated from its international competitors by the breadth of its security services offering and its ability to integrate these services for the benefit of customers.

debt. By 1991, the company had acquired another dozen companies, turned their businesses around and accumulated assets worth about £1 billion.

The 1990s: A New Strategy

Although this takeover strategy had been successful during the 1980s, by the 1990s it had become problematic. A decade of takeovers, not only by Williams but also by conglomerates such as Hanson, BTR, and Tomkins, reduced the population of inefficient companies. Williams Holdings itself had grown large and famous enough that it was harder for the company to target an acquisition without attracting the attention of potential competitors.

By the early 1990s, too, the market had lost confidence in Williams. In 1991, a £764 million bid for the defense electronics, communications equipment, and security firm Racal failed. Moreover, the *Economist* magazine, probably reflecting City opinion, questioned the benefit of the proposed acquisition for Williams. At about the same time, analysts expressed their discomfort with the complexity, even the opacity, of the company's financial statements. Consequently, the company's stock price fell and it remained out of favor for a time.

The early 1990s also saw the kind of disenchantment with conglomerates composed of unrelated companies that had afflicted Wall Street a decade earlier come to the City. A number of British conglomerates produced poor financial results at the time. The City's response was to lower the premium accorded their shares and to adopt the view that it was not possible for a management to run a number of unrelated businesses effectively.

To confront these problems, Williams altered its strategy. It maintained its focus on growth through acquisition, but decided to concentrate on fire protection, security, and building products. As Carr described the decision in a 1997 interview, "We looked at where growth was greatest, where barriers to entry were higher, and where our brands were strongest, where the businesses were international and had products that wouldn't go out of fashion. Fire and security fitted that bill very well." He added that home improvement products seemed too good to sell.

To implement this strategy, the company began to divest holdings that did not fit those categories, often by helping current managers to acquire the businesses through management buyouts. With the cash produced by these sales, Williams acquired companies that fit the new criteria. By 1994, these changes and a general economic recovery had revived Williams' fortunes. Financially its profits, cash flow, earnings per share and dividend had increased noticeably from the previous year's less than satisfactory results. Organizationally, it owned a variety of well-respected brands. Its share price again rose.

Even before its strategy shift, Williams had made significant acquisitions in both the fire protection and security businesses. In 1988, it bought Pilgrim House Group, an acquisition that included Kidde, a major fire protection business. The purchase of Yale and Valor, PLC in 1991 brought with it the Yale lock brand, one of Williams' first major security related businesses. Between 1991 and its dissolution in 2000, Williams acquired about 130 businesses, most of them in the fire control and security businesses. It also disposed of all businesses that did not contribute to Williams' strengths in these areas.

Particularly important to the development of Williams' strength in security systems was the company's purchase of Chubb Security, PLC, in 1997 for about £1.2 billion. Until 1992, Chubb had been Racal-Chubb Security, the security arm of the same Racal Electronics, PLC that Williams had attempted and failed to buy in 1991. When Williams made its bid, Racal had just spun off its enormously successful cellular phone unit as Vodafone. The expectation was that without Vodafone, Racal's strengths in defense, communications equipment, and security would be more visible and command a better share price.

Some observers questioned this logic. They noted that without the contribution of Vodafone, Racal's financial performance left much to be desired. Moreover, the Racal-Chubb security group bankrolled the rest of the company, accounting for about a third of sales and most of the company's profits. These analysts suggested that Racal, which had postponed plans to spin off Chubb soon after the divestiture of Vodafone, had to keep the profitable security business until it had either sold or revived its other businesses. Moreover, the spin off of Vodafone greatly reduced Racal's capitalization, making it quite susceptible to a hostile takeover attempt, at least until the company strengthened its weak segments.

This takeover attempt happened much sooner than anyone expected. The day after Vodafone's official spinoff, Williams Holdings made an unexpected hostile bid for the remainder of Racal. Williams' motivation for this bid was unclear. Williams' chairman, Nigel Rudd, told at least one interviewer that the company wanted Racal's security business. The company's financial advisors and Britain's Monopolies and Mergers Commission, on the other hand, indicated that Williams would have to sell the security business to avoid U.K. antitrust restrictions. Moreover, there was little to suggest that Williams had any experience in the operation of high-tech companies like Racal's nonsecurity subsidiaries, which included defense electronics, telecommunications and data communications equipment, and specialized software.

To induce shareholders not to commit their shares to Williams, Racal promised to divest the profitable Chubb subsidiary and distribute its shares to Racal shareholders. This commitment and doubts about Williams' plans for and ability to run the company gave Racal the advantage in this struggle. After a three-month clash, Williams' takeover bid failed. Williams owned or had valid acceptances for only 35.8 percent of Racal.

In September 1992, Chubb Security PLC was spun off to Racal shareholders as an independent company. The new company provided security products, primarily hardware, such as locks and safes, but also some electronic products. Observers

Key Dates:

1818: Chubb founded as a lock and safes company.
1982: Williams Holdings founded and acquires Ley's foundry.
1985: Williams Holdings acquires J and HB Jackson.
1988: Williams Holdings acquires Pilgrim House and its Kidde unit.
1991: Williams Holdings acquires Yale and Valor PLC, attains assets of £1 billion, and makes an unsuccessful attempt to acquire Racal PLC.
1992: Chubb Security PLC spins off from Racal and becomes an independent company.
1997: Williams Holdings acquires Chubb Security PLC.
1998: Williams Holdings changes its name to Williams PLC.
1999: Negotiations with Tyco International to take over Williams fail.
2000: Chubb PLC spins off as an independent company; Williams PLC dissolves.
2001: Chubb's first full year as an independent company.

recognized that independence made the smaller company more susceptible to a takeover by another company. This possibility became reality in February 1997, when Williams purchased Chubb for about £1.3 billion.

Analysts saw the deal as a logical one: Chubb and Williams were engaged in similar security businesses, but they were each active in different geographic areas. Williams was strong in the Americas and continental Europe; Chubb had a presence in the United Kingdom and the Asian-Pacific region. Thus, the buyout created a global subsidiary. Williams' CEO, Roger Carr, suggested that the deal would also produce financial savings resulting from the consolidation of purchasing, distribution, and production plants. Some analysts, though, thought Williams had paid too much for the company.

Despite this cavil, the Chubb deal was a further step in Williams' long-term strategy to convert itself from a conglomerate of unrelated businesses to an enterprise focused on security and fire protection products and services. It united major world security brands, including Yale, Kidde, and Chubb, into a company with total (including its building products subsidiaries) annual sales of about £2.7 billion in 1997.

Even after the completion of this deal, Williams continued to restructure. Of the approximately 130 acquisitions the company made between 1991 and its dissolution in 2000, about 90 of them were made after the Chubb acquisition, and these were exclusively of security and fire protection businesses. At the same time, the company disposed of its building products businesses.

The costs of this restructuring hurt Williams' financial performance. Its share price languished. In response to this weakness, Williams began a series of on-and-off negotiations with the Bermuda-based, U.S.-managed conglomerate Tyco International, Ltd.. Tyco had been very active in making acquisitions and was interested in Williams' security and fire protection

businesses. Both would be a good fit for Tyco's fire and security unit, which had 1998 sales of $4.7 billion because it would add to its meager European presence. In 1999, these negotiations failed, mostly because the companies could not agree to an appropriate price for Williams.

These negotiations did not slow Williams' independent restructuring efforts, however. Among other major dispositions, it sold its home improvement unit, a major component of its building products business to Britain's Imperial Chemical Industries, PLC in 1998. The company continued its active program of acquisitions.

Despite these efforts, however, the company could not re-ignite its business. In 1999, the company's pretax profit declined 49 percent despite a 17 percent increase in sales. This decline resulted from "exceptional charges" related to the company's ongoing restructuring activities. Williams' executives decided to take decisive action to try to improve shareholder value.

A New Company Faces a New Century

In March 2000, Williams announced plans to split into two separate businesses: Chubb, focused on security products and services and on those aspects of fire protection most directly related to security, and Kidde, focused on the remainder of Williams' fire protection activities, much of it aviation related. At the same time, the company announced the sale of its hardware-based Yale lock unit to Sweden's Assay Abloy for £825 million. Soon thereafter it sold the last of its building products units, its North American paints units, to Masco Corporation.

When Chubb debuted on the London Stock Exchange in November 2000, it was a fully developed business, with six-month pro forma revenues of £672.4 million, current assets of £1,751.7 million, liabilities of £1,423 million, and 44,223 employees throughout the world. (The cited figures are pro forma and unaudited because they reflect the results of the business units that would be combined into Chubb when they were still part of Williams. It is not possible to produce financial statements comparable in every way for the units' results as part of Williams and their results as part of Chubb.)

Chubb's stated growth strategy consisted of five prongs: increasing its international presence through internal growth and through acquisitions; consolidating the highly fragmented industry by acquisition and by expanding existing operations; targeting specific sectors that had rapidly growing and specific security needs; introducing innovative products and services to the market; and consolidating its worldwide service under the Chubb brand so that it could become increasingly recognized.

In conformance with these goals, Chubb made significant acquisitions after becoming independent. The company spent £27.6 million on acquisitions in 2000. These strengthened its position in Germany, the Netherlands, Spain, Canada, and Australia. The £203.6 million it devoted to acquisitions in 2001 was focused on South Africa, Taiwan, the United States, and Korea.

When the new company reported on 2001, its first full year of independent operations, it was too soon to make a judgment about its prospects for success. On one hand, Chubb reported a nine percent increase in sales, profit growth of nine percent and dividend growth of seven percent. On the other hand, these results were comparisons to the pro forma results of 2000. Chubb's share price had declined from about 255p at its debut to a range of about 130p to 190p between December 2000 and April 2002. (It must be noted, however, that stock markets throughout the Western world were undergoing significant corrections at this time.) And the company was still coping with substantial restructuring costs. At the beginning of the 21st century, it was, therefore, too soon to speculate about the eventual success of Chubb in its new incarnation.

Principal Subsidiaries

ATSE; Chubb China Holdings Ltd.; Chubb Electronic Security Ltd.; Chubb Fire Limited; Chubb Ireland Ltd.; Chubb New Zealand Ltd.; Chubb Security Australia Pty Ltd.; Chubb Guarding Services Ltd.; Compagnie Centrale Sicli; CSG Security Inc.; FFE Building Services Ltd.; Firm Security Ltd.; General Incendie SA; Guardforce Ltd.

Principal Competitors

Tyco; Securitas; Secom; Falck/Group 4.

Further Reading

"Big Test Ahead as Williams' Jumbo Comes under Scrutiny," *Euroweek*, June 6, 1997, p. 23.

Blackhurst, Chris, "Metal Detection Pays Dividends," *Management Today*, April 1991. p. 108.

"Britain's Boring New Bosses," *The Economist* (London), September 2, 1995, p. 64.

Brown, Curtis, "New Chubb Marketing Chief Plans Direct Boost for Expansion Drive," *Precision Marketing*, January 25, 2002, p. 6.

Clifford, Leon, "Back to Roots for Racal," *Electronics Weekly*, April 15, 1992, p. 24.

——, "A Tough Act to Follow for Elsbury," *Electronics Weekly*, June 24, 1992, pp. 12–13.

——, "What Future for Racal after Vodafone Split," *Electronics Weekly*, September 11, 1991, pp. 14–15.

Collier, Andrew, "Racal to Spin Off Telecom Units," *Chilton's Electronic News*, November 19, 1990, p. 15.

"Corporate Report: Williams Holdings PLC," *The Wall Street Journal*, Eastern Edition, October 11, 1988, p. 1.

Davidson, Andrew, "Roger Carr," *Management Today*, December 1997, pp. 46–50.

"Divide and Lose: British Takeovers," *The Economist* (U.S.), September 21, 1991, p. 82.

Fallon, James, "Hostile Bid for Racal Threatens Data Com," *Chilton's Electronic News*, September 23, 1991, pp. 1–2.

Hailstone, Laura, "Mergers," *Flight International*, October 31, 2000, p. 2001.

Hooper, Laurence, "Racal Sought by Williams Holdings PLC," *The Wall Street Journal*, Eastern Edition, September 18, 1991, p. A11.

"International Brief," *The Wall Street Journal*, Eastern Edition, December 24, 1991, p. C14.

Kaye, Jon, "Racal Electronics PLC," *Datamation*, July 1, 1992, p. 79.

Maremont, Mark, "Tyco and Williams Revive Merger Talks," *The Wall Street Journal*, Eastern Edition, June 8, 1999, p. A3.

——, "Tyco's Talks to Acquire Williams PLC Stall," *The Wall Street Journal*, Eastern Edition, June 29, 1999, p. A4.

"Nigel Rudd," *Management Today*, December 1994, pp. 58–62.

Orlebar, Edward, "Williams Looks for a Buy-Back," *The Independent Sunday* (London), September 7, 1997, p. 5.

Oyama, David I., "World Watch," *The Wall Street Journal*, Eastern Edition, March 8, 2000, p. A14.

"Racal Electronics to Consolidate Shares on Chubb Demerger," *Computergram International*, September 17, 1992, p. 19.

"Racal Plans Spinoff of Unit Next Spring," *The Wall Street Journal*, Eastern Edition, November 22, 1991, p. B4A.

"Racal Sets Chubb Spin-Off for October," *Computergram International*, June 11, 1992, p. 17.

"Sir Ernest Harrison Defends His Plan," *Computergram International*, December 13, 1990, p. 18.

Streetly, Martin, "Williams Stalks Racal With Predatory Bid," *Flight International*, September 25, 1991, p. 13.

"Williams Holdings Offers to Pay $2.11 Billion for Chubb Security," *The Wall Street Journal*, Eastern Edition, February 18, 1997, p. A18.

—Anne L. Potter

CHUGAI

Chugai Pharmaceutical Co., Ltd.

1-9, Kyobashi 2-chome, Chuo-ku
Tokyo 104-8301
Japan
Telephone: (81) 3-3281-6611
Fax: (81) 3-3281-2828
Web site: http://www.chugai-pharm.co.jp

Majority-Owned Subsidiary of Roche Group
Incorporated: 1943
Employees: 4,931 (2001 est.)
Sales: $122.7 million (est.)
Stock Exchanges: Tokyo Nagoya Osaka Fukuoka
Ticker Symbol: 4519
NAIC: 325412 Pharmaceutical Preparation
   Manufacturing; 325411 Medicinal and Botanical
   Manufacturing

Chugai Pharmaceutical Co., Ltd. is the fifth largest pharmaceutical company in Japan, with branch offices, plants, research laboratories, affiliates, and subsidiaries located worldwide. The company's main business, accounting for 76.2 percent of net sales in 2001, is in the discovery, development, and marketing of prescription drugs for cancer and infectious diseases, blood disorders, bone disorders, and heart and vascular disorders. Chugai also develops nonprescription products (over-the-counter drugs and insecticide products), diagnostics products (enzyme-immunoassay kits and DNA probes), and implant-related products (artificial bone implants and internal fixation devices). Chugai consistently invests nearly 20 percent of its net sales in R&D, one of the highest levels among Japanese pharmaceutical companies and consistent with the highest levels in the industry. As a result of a unique merger in late 2001, Chugai is now a subsidiary of the Switzerland-based Roche Group.

1925 to 1979: The Early Years

Originally named Chugai Shinyaku Shokai, the company was founded in 1925 as a pharmaceutical trading company. The company was incorporated in 1943 and changed its name to Chugai Pharmaceutical Co., Ltd. In 1944 the company acquired Matsunaga Pharmaceutical Co., Ltd. By 1951, Chugai began to establish the foundation for its future growth, with the successful commercial production of glucuronic acid and its launch under the brand name Guronsan. Guronsan was a popular line of health tonics and continued to be a successful product into the 21st century. Even after more than 40 years, Guronsan still commands a large share of Japan's liquid health tonics market.

Another successful Chugai product, Varsan, was launched during the 1950s and has been heavily marketed ever since. Synonymous with pest-control in Japan, Varsan has grown into a successful line of home-use insecticide products, including Japan's most popular smoke-type fumigators. Further innovative development led Chugai to bring to market such highly competitive, original new drugs as Ulcerlmin (sucralfate), an antiulcer agent in 1968, and Picibanil, an immunotherapeautic anticancer agent in 1975. The company also introduced Rythmodan (disopyramide phosphate) in 1978, and Glyceol (glycerin plus fructose) in 1979.

The 1980s: Outgrowing the Japanese Market

The 1980s marked a time when Chugai, along with other Japanese pharmaceutical companies, began to establish strong research and co-marketing ties with other countries and their respective markets. Such a widespread industry shift was not arbitrary. By the mid-1980s, Japan's pharmaceutical companies as a group sold only about 3 percent of their drug output abroad. And the industry's bread and butter for years, Japan's national health insurance plan, which had been generously paying for antibiotics and other drugs, began to decrease that coverage. According to Joel Dreyfuss in his story for *Fortune* magazine in July 1987, prescription drug coverage had decreased by as much as 40 percent during the previous six years. Dreyfuss quotes a Chugai executive at the time, Katsuaki Asano, for his plain honesty about the company's new strategy: "We are forced to go abroad. If you're confined to the domestic market, it doesn't pay at all."

In an effort to overcome the limitations of an increasingly limited Japanese market, Chugai began to set up subsidiaries

Company Perspectives:

Our mission is the discovery, development, and successful commercialization of innovative therapeutic products that satisfy unmet medical needs. We will become a profitable leader in our areas of therapeutic focus by applying state-of-the-art technologies, fostering creativity, and developing our people.

and joint ventures overseas, as well as new branch offices in The United States (New York in 1982), Europe (London in 1986), and another part of Asia (Taipei in 1988). In 1989, Chugai acquired the United States-based Gen-Probe, Inc., for about $110 million, or almost double the market price for Gen-Probe's stock. Gen-Probe had already been working with Chugai to help the Japanese company market diagnostics products in Japan for infectious diseases and cancer. A leader in the industry for its development of genetic probes, a new, promising technology used in diagnostics tests, Gen-Probe was an attractive fetch for Chugai, which was looking to expand its diagnostics offerings.

Another way Chugai helped ensure that it could compete in the world markets was to invest heavily in R&D, so that it could develop new, competitive drugs. Chugai's pre-1980s record of innovation continued with the 1981 release of Alfarol (alfacalcidol), an agent for bone metabolic disorders, and the launch in 1984 of Nicorandil, an antianginal agent now marketed under the name Sigmart. Later, in 1989, the company introduced Amoban (zopiclone), a drug to help address sleep disorders.

Throughout the 1980s, Chugai focused a substantial portion of its R&D capabilities into using genes as drug discovery tools. Chugai began research into drugs that target specific genes, which enabled the company to equip itself with an array of advanced genetic engineering technologies.

Such technologies include transgenic technologies for the functional analysis of genes and antibody engineering technologies for the design and production of target antibodies. One of the world leaders in antibody engineering, Chugai utilized genetic engineering to create recombinant antibodies and altered their functions. Antibodies from mice and other mammals, for example, were altered structurally to conform to the shape of human antibodies and then further reduced in antigenicity for therapeutic use in a process called "humanization." Such advanced genetic engineering technologies would later, in the 1990s, allow Chugai to help lead the development of antibody drugs and to launch two major biotechnology drugs.

Chugai also distinguished itself as one of the few companies in the world to be investigating more than 500 vitamin D derivatives. Alfarol (alfacalcidol), an activated vitamin D_3 preparation for treating osteoporosis, was well received in Japan since its initial marketing in 1981. The product became a cornerstone of Japanese research on treatments for bone metabolic disorders. Later, in 2000, Chugai's vitamin B derivative R&D led to the launch of Oxarol (injection), which is the first agent approved in Japan for treating secondary hyperparathyroidism in hemodialysis patients.

Chugai's aggressive moves during the early 1980s initially showed mixed results. Even though Chugai's sales were steadily increasing, earnings were not as impressive. For example, sales rose 4.4 percent, from $387.4 million in 1983 to $404.3 million in 1984, while earnings fell 7.4 percent, from $19.8 million in 1983 to $18.3 million in 1984. However, toward the end of the decade, Chugai's financials were much more impressive. By 1988, for example, the company had a net income of $60 million on revenue of $991 million.

The 1990s: Greater Breakthroughs and Overseas Investments

Chugai's commitment to R&D has paid off in a number of ways, including the launch of two breakthrough biotechnology drugs in the early 1990s: Epogin (recombinant human erythropoietin, EPOCH, epoetin beta), an agent for the treatment of anemia associated with chronic renal failure, and Neutrogin (recombinant human granulocyte-colony stimulating factor, rG-CSF, lenograstim)—marketed as Granocyte in Europe—for the treatment of neutropenia associated with immuno-depleting cancer treatment.

Launched in 1990, Epogin quickly became one of Chugai's principal products. The product was used to alleviate anemia and improve the quality of life (QOL) of patients who were undergoing or preparing for hemodialysis due to renal insufficiency. By 2001, Epogin had more than 60 percent share of the Japanese market for comparable products. That same year, Chugai introduced Epogin S, the same product in convenient, sterile, prefilled syringes. Neutrogin, another one of Chugai's principal products, was launched in 1991. The product was used to treat neutropenia resulting from aplastic/hypoplastic anemia or from chemotherapy treatment for leukemia and other cancers, as well as to treat neutropenia in bone marrow transplant patients. By 2001, Neutrogin had a 39 percent share of the Japanese market for comparable products. Chugai introduced other drugs later during the 1990s: Keiten (cefpirome sulfate) in 1993, Preran (trandolapril) in 1996, and Taxotere (docetaxel hydrate) in 1997.

Chugai continued to improve its presence abroad during the 1990s, by establishing additional offices, labs and joint ventures around the world. In 1990, Chugai and Rhône-Poulenc Santé (later known as Aventis) established Chugai-Rhône-Poulenc (later known as Chugai-Aventis), a joint venture to carry out development and marketing of Granocyte in Europe. Later, in 1993, Chugai established Chugai Pharma Europe, Ltd. in London. In 1995, Gen-Probe, Inc. spun off its pharmaceutical assets and licenses to the newly created therapeutics company, Chugai Biopharmaceuticals, Inc. in San Diego. During that same year, Chugai established Chugai Research Institute for Molecular Medicine, Inc.

In 1996, Chugai formed a joint venture, Chugai MSD Co., Ltd., with Merck & Co., Inc., to develop, manufacture, and market over-the-counter medicines in Japan. Chugai MSD launched its first product line in 1997: Chugai Ichoyaku, which contains a switch-OTC gastrointestinal agent, sucralfate. The joint venture followed up with successful introductions of an antidiarrhetic, and Efeel, a gastrointestinal remedy based on the H2 antagonist famotidine. The joint venture did not last for long, however; Merck left in mid-1999, citing low returns on the over-the-counter business. According to the *Financial Times* report on the separation, "The U.S. company, the world's biggest drugs group by sales, said it had misread the direction Japan's regulatory environment would take. When it set up the joint venture in 1996 it had expected the government to encourage self-prescription as a way of controlling healthcare costs. That never materialized."

In March 1997, Chugai established Chugai Shindan Kagaku Co., Ltd., Chugai Diagnostics Science Co., Ltd., and Chugai Pharma Marketing Ltd. (CPM) in London. In 1999, Chugai entered a joint venture with Eli Lilly and Company, enabling Lilly to accelerate drug development of compounds targeted for the Japanese market and Chugai to co-promote and co-market products developed through the collaboration that are sold in Japan. The collaboration initially set out to manage clinical trials of the antidepressant Prozac and other drugs to treat impotence and attention-deficit disorder. Later, in 2001, Lilly announced that it would leave the joint venture and transfer the management of the clinical trials to Lilly's Japanese unit. Chugai, in exchange for giving up the rights to co-promote and co-market Prozac and other drugs associated with the joint venture, would gain an unspecified improvement to an existing agreement to market Lilly's osteoporosis drug, Evista, in Japan. Also in 1999, Chugai strengthened its platform in Europe. It established CPM marketing branches in Germany and France and worked with Aventis' subsidiaries throughout Europe to co-promote products.

Even though Chugai's sales in Japan still made up 90 percent of the company's sales, the company's efforts to emerge globally were promising. With all of the expansions, joint ventures and drug discoveries throughout the 1990s, Chugai's business continued to grow at a healthy pace. Boosted by sales growth and efforts to streamline production, Chugai reported in June of 1994 that sales that year had already climbed 35 percent to $84.9 million when compared to the previous year. In 1998, overseas sales increased 22.4 percent to ¥20.1 billion. Although net profits in 1999 were expected to fall 25 percent, overall sales were expected to rise 2.3 percent that same year.

A New Millennium, A New Chugai

In 2000, Chugai had introduced two new drugs: Suvenyl (sodium hyaluronate) and Oxarol (Maxacacitol). During 2001, Chugai's sales had grown another 13.1 percent to $1.67 billion. The company's net income had jumped 47.8 percent to $122.7 million. Of Chugai's 2001 sales, prescription pharmaceuticals accounted for 76 percent; and nonprescription products accounted for 13 percent; while diagnostics products and other products accounted for 9 percent and 2 percent respectively.

In early 2001, Chugai's CEO and chairman, Osamu Nagayama, began to talk about how Chugai would consider a partnership with a foreign group to strengthen its research and marketing capabilities, extending well beyond Japan into new markets. In February, the *Financial Times* quotes Mr. Nagayama: "We need a partner who can create synergies in terms of R&D, in our budget and in technology." Coming from a top executive of one of Japan's fiercely independent pharmaceutical companies, this was certainly news. But the conditions were ripe: Japan's prescription drug market was shrinking, few of Japan's pharmaceutical companies had the ability to market their own medicines abroad, and deregulation had allowed foreign drug companies to take hold in Japan.

In December 2001, the Swiss pharmaceutical giant, Roche Group, announced with Chugai that they had entered into a new, shattering business-model alliance to turn Chugai into a leading research-driven pharmaceutical company. Chugai would first have to sell its Gen-Probe subsidiary, which competed with certain diagnostics businesses of Roche. Roche would then merge its Japanese subsidiary, Nippon Roche, into Chugai at a ratio of 39 to 61 percent. And then after that, Roche would acquire a controlling 50.1 percent stake in Chugai, for a minimum of US$1.23 billion cash in one of the biggest mergers between a foreign and Japanese company. The newly formed group moved Chugai from the tenth largest to the fifth largest pharmaceutical company in Japan.

Although the new enterprise represented a major shake-up in the Japanese pharmaceutical industry, Chugai benefited from a major boost in R&D resources and distribution. The company name did not change and chairman and CEO, Osamu Nagayama, remained in position. Also, according to the complex agreement, Chugai continued to function as an autonomously managed company, closely coordinating its operations with Roche. Chugai became Roche's exclusive pharmaceuticals representative in Japan with rights to develop and market all pharmaceutical products which the Roche Group chose to commercialize in Japan. And for all Chugai products outside Japan and South Korea for which Chugai sought a partner, Roche had the right to license-in. Newly merged with Roche in the new millennium, Chugai was well positioned to secure itself as a global pharmaceutical and medical products company in each of the major markets.

Principal Subsidiaries

C&C Research Laboratories (Affiliate); Chugai Aventis S.N.C.; Chugai Biopharmaceuticals, Inc.; Chugai Business Support Co., Ltd.; Chugai Diagnostics Science Co., Ltd.; Chugai Distribution Co., Ltd.; Chugai Pharma Europe Ltd.; Chugai Pharma France S.A.S.; Chugai Pharma Marketing Ltd.; Chugai Pharma Marketing Ltd. (Germany); Chugai Pharma Taiwan Ltd.; Chugai Pharma U.K. Ltd.; Chugai Pharma U.S.A., Inc.; Chugai Pharma U.S.A., Inc. (New York); Chugai Research Institute for Molecular Medicine, Inc.; Chugai Shoji Co., Ltd.; Chugai Transportation Co., Ltd.; CSK Research Park Co., Ltd.; Eiko Kasei Co., Ltd.; Gotemba Chugai Service Co., Ltd.; Hiroshima Chugai Pharmaceutical Co., Ltd.; Koei Pharma Co., Ltd.; Medical Culture Inc.; Shanghai Chugai Pharma Co., Ltd.; Takaoka Chugai Pharmaceutical Co., Ltd.; Tohoku Chugai Pharmaceutical Co., Ltd.

Principal Competitors

Amgen; Aquila Biopharmaceuticals; Atlantic Technology Ventures; Corixa; Dainippon Pharmaceutical; Immunex; Nippon Kayaku; Sankyo Co.; Shire BioChem; Takeda Chemical Industries; Targeted Genetics; Vical.

Further Reading

Borrus, Amy, "Japan's Next Battleground: The Medicine Chest," *Business Week*, March 12, 1990, p. 68.

"Chugai Identifies Three R&D Fields," *Biotechnology Newswatch*, November 2, 1992, p. 15.

"Chugai Moving into France and Germany," *Marketletter*, March 1, 1999.

"Chugai Pharmaceutical Co.: Pretax Profit Jumped 35%, Helped by Sales for First Half," *Wall Street Journal*, August 11, 1994, p. A6.

"Chugai Pharmaceutical Enjoying Good Performance," *Japan Chemical Week*, May 7, 1999.

"Chugai Restructures for the 21st Century," *Marketletter*, September 7, 1998.

Dreyfuss, Joel, "Japan's Push in Pharmaceuticals," *Fortune*, July 20, 1987, p. 85.

"Exclusive Marketing of Granocyte to Be Commenced in France," *Chugai Discovery: Chugai Pharmaceutical Newsletter*, November 2001.

"Firm Posts 71% Decline in Pretax Profit for Half," *Wall Street Journal*, August 10, 1990, p. A7.

"Gen-Probe Deal Could Herald More Japanese Biotechnology Takeovers," *BioBusiness Daily*, November 6, 1989, p. 7.

Hall, William, and Michiyo Nakamoto, "Roche Seals Dollars 1.2bn Merger with Japanese Drugs Group: Deal Highlights Country's Willingness to Take Part in Global Restructuring," *Financial Times*, December 11, 2001, p. 1.

——, "Roche Takes Control of Chugai: Merger Is One of the Biggest Between a Foreign and Japanese Company," *Financial Times*, December 11, 2001, p. 25.

Hamilton, David P., "Medicine & Health (A Special Report): The Bottom Line—False Alarm: Remember All That Talk about the Japanese Taking Over Biotech? Never Mind," *Wall Street Journal*, May 20, 1994, p. R14.

"International Corporate Report," *Wall Street Journal*, April 23, 1985, p. 1.

Johnstone, Bob, "Bucks from Bugs," *Far Eastern Economic Review*, April 26, 1990, p. 78.

Leung, James, "Japan's Drug Firms Are Moving to Raise Their Sales Overseas—Research on New Products Also Seen Likely to Boost Stock Prices of Concerns," *Wall Street Journal*, July 20, 1987, p. 1.

Lieber, Tammy, "Lilly Leaves Joint Venture," *Indianapolis Business Journal*, December 10, 2001, p. A4.

"Lilly in Drug Discovery Pacts," *Chemical Market Reporter*, March 29, 1999, p. 12.

"Marketing Rights Granted for Granocyte in 39 Additional Countries," *AIDS Weekly Plus*, May 12, 1997, p. 15.

"Merck, Chugai in a Joint Venture," *Wall Street Journal*, September 19, 1996, p. B7.

Nakamoto, Michiyo, and David Pilling, "Chugai Mulls Foreign Partnership," *Financial Times*, February 5, 2001, p. 18.

Nazario, Sonia L., "Chugai to Buy Gen-Probe Inc., Stirring More Fear in U.S. of Biotechnology Loss," *Wall Street Journal*, October 31, 1989, p. 1.

O'Donnell, Peter, "Invasion Alarms in Japan," *Pharmaceutical Executive*, May 1996, p. 40.

Pilling, David, "Merck Quits Joint Venture," *Financial Times*, July 19, 1999, p. 21.

"Roche/Chugai," *Financial Times*, December 11, 2001, p. 24.

—Heidi Wrightsman

Clif Bar Inc.

1610 Fifth Street
Berkeley, California 94710
U.S.A.
Telephone: (510) 558-7855
Toll Free: (800) 884-5254
Fax: (510) 558-7872
Web site: http://www.clifbar.com

Private Company
Incorporated: 1997
Employees: 100 (2001)
Sales: $68 million (2001)
NAIC: 311999 All Other Miscellaneous Food
    Manufacturing; 311423 Dried and Dehydrated Food
    Manufacturing

Based in Berkeley, California, Clif Bar Inc. is a leading maker of natural energy and nutrition foods. The company's products include the Clif Bar energy bar, the Clif Bar Ice Series, the Luna energy bar specifically for women, and Clif Shot energy-boosting gel for endurance activities. The story of Clif Bar Inc. is the story of Gary Erickson, founder and CEO, who turns his passion for the outdoors and his love of cooking into a multimillion-dollar business. An avid cyclist, skier, climber, baker, and visionary, Erickson conceives the idea of the Clif Bar while on a 175-mile bike ride in 1986.

An Entrepreneur in the Making

Gary Erickson, founder and CEO of Clif Bar Inc., graduated from Cal Poly San Luis Obispo with a business degree, and set out on an around-the-world trip that would reveal to him his love of the outdoors and his entrepreneurial bug. He returned to California and began his professional career with Avocet, a Palo Alto company that made bicycle seats. As head of the company's saddle research and development and manufacturing division, he invented the gel saddle, the world's first truly comfortable bicycle seat, which was later displayed at the Museum of Modern Art in New York City. In 1986, Erickson left

Avocet to become a professional baker and proprietor of Kali's Bakery, named for his grandmother, in Emeryville, California, specializing in all-natural calzones and gourmet cookies.

According to Erickson, his inspiration for the Clif Bar came during a 175-mile bike ride, the 12-hour ride he termed his "Epiphany Ride." He had packed his usual energy bars, but during the trek found them to be unappetizing, sticky, and hard to digest, "After miles of riding and a number of those energy bars, I wanted a bar that actually tasted good." So, using his skills as a baker, he created an energy bar that tasted great and used only all-natural ingredients. Originally named Kali's Bar, Erickson's tasty new bar debuted in 1992. In 1997, the year the company was incorporated, the name was changed to Clif Bar after Erickson's father, Clifford. The Clif Bar was originally distributed by Avocet and was an immediate hit with athletes and active people for its great taste, wholesome ingredients, innovative flavors, and the sustained energy it delivered.

Erickson envisioned his product as more "down home," and without the typical "power" or hard-core image of other energy bars. Its consumers obviously agreed. The Clif Bar quickly became one of the top-selling energy bars in the country. Distributed originally in bike and outdoor stores and natural foods markets, its popularity led to increased distribution in other markets, including grocery and convenience stores, health clubs and spas. Clif Bar came in the following flavors: Apricot, Chocolate Almond Fudge, Chocolate Chip, Cookies 'N Cream, Carrot Cake, Chocolate Brownie, Chocolate Chip Peanut Crunch, Cranberry Apple Cherry, and Crunchy Peanut Butter.

The company was recognized for its phenomenal growth, when in 1997 it was included in *Inc.* magazine's annual list of the 500 fastest-growing private companies in America. The following year it increased 101 spots to land at 152 on the *Inc.* 500 list. Company sales of $5 million in 1995, jumped to $22 million in 1997, as a result of wider distribution in convenience stores, supermarkets, and European markets.

Clif Bar Introduces Luna

In March 1999, Clif Bar Inc. introduced a new product especially for women. Recognizing the unique nutritional needs of women, the Luna bar was named after the moon and was created as a result of consumer input. Luna's original four flavors—LemonZest, Chocolate Pecan Pie, Nutz Over Chocolate, and Toasted Nuts 'N Cranberry—quickly joined ranks with the Clif Bar in popularity and sales. Within a year, Luna bars became the No. 1 energy bar with a 17 percent market share of the more than 700 types of energy bars sold in natural foods stores nationwide. Clif Bar became the No. 2 brand, with a 13 percent market share. In the first half of 2000, Clif Bar sales grew 17 percent and accounted for seven of the top 25 best-selling energy bar flavors. In January 2001, the first TV spots and print ads in *Self, Shape* and *InStyle* magazines appeared for Luna Bars.

Other Clif Bar products have enjoyed equal popularity. In March 2002, the MOJO Bar, the first snack bar to combine salty snack flavors and sound nutrition, was unveiled at the 22nd Annual Natural Products Expo West in California. As an alternative to sweet-tasting bars, MOJO Bars came in flavors like Honey Roasted Peanut, Mixed Nuts, Honey BBQ Almond, Spicy Salsa Peanut and Curry Cashew. Mojo Bars joined The Clif Bar Ice Series, the first energy bar with a shot of caffeine and chocolate drizzle icing; and the Clif Shot, an energy-boosting gel for endurance activities.

A study conducted in 2001 by the Human Performance Laboratory at St. Cloud State University, Minnesota, upheld Clif Bar's nutritional claims. The study indicated that Clif Bar energy bars do "provide a sustained, moderate increase in blood sugar levels, crucial for enhancing athletic performance. The findings also suggested that nonathletes who eat Clif Bars can expect a sustained energy boost during hectic workdays and busy weekends." The results of this study were presented at the annual conference of the American College of Sports Medicine in Baltimore, Maryland.

It's about the Journey, Not the Destination

Erickson's philosophy of "doing good things for life" was evident in all phases of his very successful business. He made it a priority to provide a healthy work environment for his employees, enabling them to maintain balance in all aspects of their lives and get paid for keeping in shape. He provided indoor climbing walls, a complete workout facility, personal trainers, camping and skiing trips, and volunteer opportunities on company time. In 2001, Clif Bar Inc. employees committed to work over 2,000 volunteer hours of community service, approximately the number of hours worked by one full-time employee.

Erickson was quoted as saying, "I don't have plans to sell this company or go public. I'd like to keep it privately held while really taking care of our employees and sharing in the profits."

Erickson spread his humanitarian spirit to other causes outside the work arena. From trail maintenance and educational reading programs to Habitat for Humanity and Meals on Wheels, the influences of Clif Bar have been felt. Clif Bar has sponsored hundreds of nonprofit organizations and charitable events annually. A portion of the proceeds from the sale of Luna Bars has supported the Breast Cancer Fund and the American Dietetic Association. The Breast Cancer Fund logo has appeared on every Luna bar wrapper in an effort to raise awareness of breast cancer through each purchase. In November 2000, Erickson recreated his "Epiphany Ride" by leading a 175-mile, cancer fund-raising bike ride. A donation of $10,000 was made to the Lance Armstrong Foundation, which helps people manage and survive cancer. Erickson was joined on the trip by employees and members of the United States Postal Service Pro Cycling Team.

Following the terrorist attacks of September 11, 2001 in the United States, Clif Bar Inc. shipped 26,000 Clif and Luna bars to rescue and relief workers in New York, donated $6,000 to the American Red Cross and committed a further $100,000 to victims and families of the tragedy. Also in 2001, ten bicycle groups were each awarded $500 grants under the auspices of Clif Bar's and the International Mountain Biking Association's IMBA/Clif Bar Trail Preservation Grants. The intent of the grants was to support projects that preserve and enhance trail access, promote environmental education, and inspire conservation in the mountain bicycling community. Since 1995, Clif Bar Inc. has been an IMBA corporate member and donated more than 50,000 Clif Bars to fuel IMBA's trail-building and maintenance projects. The IMBA logo has appeared on the back of every Clif Bar wrapper.

Another nonprofit organization benefiting from Clif Bar Inc. has been Access Fund, a national nonprofit organization dedicated to keeping climbing areas open and to conserving the climbing environment. The Access Fund logo has also appeared on every Clif Bar wrapper. Also supported by Clif Bar Inc. were Leave No Trace, an organization founded in the 1970s in response to the increasing numbers of visitors to public lands, and the 2080 Program, which was developed to encourage and make easy volunteer opportunities for Clif Bar Inc. employees.

Clif Bar Inc. Sponsors Winners

Since its inception, Clif Bar Inc. has supported athletes and their events—from weekend warriors to professional athletes. Clif Bar and Clif Shot were official sponsors in 2000 of the United States Postal Service Pro Cycling Team, one of the sport's premier teams and Tours de France winner, with cyclist Lance Armstrong. The United States Postal Service Pro Cycling Team also competed in the Tour of Spain, the Word Cup, and the Classics events, as well as major domestic races. In 2002, an agreement was signed extending sponsorship until 2004. In 2001, Clif Bar Inc. and Luna Bars announced the formation of Luna Chix, an all-women's professional mountain bike team whose mission included fund-raising, awareness, and support for women's issues, like breast cancer and The Breast Cancer Fund.

Key Dates:

1986: Gary Erickson experiences his "Epiphany Ride," a 175-mile bike ride; and opens Kali's Bakery.
1992: Debut of the Kali's Bar, an all-natural energy bar.
1999: *Inc.* magazine names Clif Bar Inc. one of the country's fastest-growing private companies.
1997: The name of Kali's Bar is changed to Clif Bar and the company incorporates as Clif Bar Inc.
1999: Clif Bar Inc. introduces the Luna bar, an energy bar for women.
2000: Clif Bar Inc. sponsors the U.S. Postal Service Pro Cycling Team.
2001: Clif Bar Inc. receives Market Engineering Entrepreneurial Award from Frost & Sullivan; and the company ships products and donations to rescue and relief workers in New York following the terrorist attacks of September 11, 2001.
2002: Clif Bar Inc. introduces the Mojo bar, a snack bar that combines salty flavors and sound nutrition.

Participants in major events that Clif Bar Inc. supported have included the Sea Otter Classic, Lamisil AT Escape From Alcatraz Triathlon, U.S. Open Snowboard Championships, U.S. Extreme Boardfest & U.S. Extreme Freeskiing Championships, the LaSalle Bank Chicago Marathon, the city of Los Angeles Marathon, and the Marine Corps Marathon. Not only has Clif Bar Inc. provided Clif products and financial support to these events, the company has also offered training tips via the Web and race-day pace teams to help marathoners achieve their individual race goals.

Clif Bar Inc. Products Receive Honors and Awards

The 1999 *Inc.* magazine honored Clif Bar Inc. by selecting the company's Web site as one of the 20 best small-business Web sites in the country. In 2000, *Inc.* magazine named Clif Bar Inc. one of the country's fastest-growing private companies (#387) for the fourth straight year. In June 2001, consulting firm Frost & Sullivan presented Clif Bar Inc. with its Market Engineering Entrepreneurial Award for superior entrepreneurial ability. Also in 2001, the *San Francisco Business Times* selected Clif Bar Inc. as one of the fastest-growing private companies within the San Francisco Bay area.

Awards honoring the Clif Bar have included the Editor's Choice award by *Mountain Bike* and *Better Nutrition's* favorite brand. In 2001, *Outside* magazine honored Cookies 'N Cream as one of the "Best Things for the Good Life." In July 2001, the Clif Bar Ice Series was selected as a "Hot New Product" by *Distribution Channels*; its Chocolate Java Avalanche was presented with *Bicycling's* "Best Overall Energy Bar" designation. Luna captured first place in the "Healthy Snacks Category" of Taste Test 2000, a competition sponsored by the American Wholesale Marketers Association. *Prepared Foods*

magazine described the Luna Bar as "conceived with a purpose" and "finding almost immediate success" and selected it as one of the Top 10 New Food Products in 2001. The *Better Nutrition* reader advisory panel chose Luna and Clif Bar as a favorite health-food brand.

Gary Erickson Remains Committed to Product Quality

Gary Erickson has been committed to growing a private, independent, value-driven organization. *Inc.* magazine's recognition of Clif Bar Inc. as one of America's fastest-growing private companies for four straight years, reflects the success of this commitment. Many benefits have been derived from the production of these nutritional products—from everyday consumers to world-class athletes, from employees to nationally competing racing teams, from reading tutors to breast cancer researchers. The success of Clif Bar Inc. is a true reflection of Erickson's commitment to making the world "a better place to live, work, and eat."

Principal Competitors

PowerBar, Inc.; Balance Bar Company.

Further Reading

"Clif Bar Climbs to Top of Energy Bar Sales in Stores," *Health Products Business*, October 2000, p. 10.
"Clif Bar Inc.," *Inc.*, November 15, 1999, p. 99.
"Clif Bar Inc. Announces Luna Chix Mountain Bike Team Roster and Sponsors," *Business Wire*, December 18, 2001, p. 357.
"Clif Bar Inc. Brings on Mojo: The First Snack Bar of Its Kind," *Business Wire*, March 8, 2002, p. 104.
"Clif Bar Inc. Donates $5000 to IMBA Clubs for Mountain Bike Trail Preservation," *Business Wire*, November 16, 2001, p. 168.
"Clif Bar Inc. Extends Sponsorship Agreement with U.S. Postal Service Pro Cycling Team through 2004," *Business Wire*, November 5, 2001, p. 556.
"Clif Bar Inc. Honored for Entrepreneurial Excellence," *Business Wire*, April 10, 2001, p. 737.
"Clif Bar Inc. Named to *Inc.* 500 List 4th Year in a Row," *Business Wire*, October 13, 2000, p. 266.
"Famous Cyclists Join Clif Bar Inc. CEO and Employees on Commemorative Cancer Fundraising Ride," *Business Wire*, November 8, 2000, p. 389.
Frankel, Mark, "Letting Go," *Working Woman*, June 2001, pp. 50–53.
"An Historic First for the Category," *Business Wire*, November 29, 2001, p. 218.
"Maker of the Clif Bar Introduces Luna," *Business Wire*, March 12, 1999, p. 96.
"Muscling In: Clif Bar Pumps First TV," *Brandweek*, December 4, 2000, p. 7.
Reyes, Sonya, "Marketers of the Next Generation," *Brandweek*, March 26, 2001, p. 33.
"University Study Indicates Clif Bar Energy Bars Deliver on Promise of Providing Sustained Energy," *Business Wire*, May 31, 2001, p. 2,075.

—Carol D. Beavers

Compagnie Financière Richemont AG

Rigistrasse 2
6300 Zug
Switzerland
Telephone: +41 (0) 41-710-3322
Fax: +41 (0) 41-711-7102
Web site: http://www.richemont.com

Public Company
Incorporated:
Employees: 10385 (2002)
Sales: $3.75 billion (2002)
Stock Exchanges: London Switzerland
Ticker Symbol: RIT (London), CFR (Switzerland)
NAIC: 551112 Offices of Other Holding Companies;
 316993 Personal Leather Goods (Except Women's
 Handbag and Purse Manufacturing); 334518 Watch,
 Clock, and Part Manufacturing; 339911 Jewelry
 (Except Costume) Manufacturing; 448310 Jewelry
 Stores; 316992 Women's Handbag and Purse
 Manufacturing; 312221 Cigarette Manufacturing

Created as a holding company for the Rupert family's international interests, Compagnie Financière Richemont AG (Richemont) has grown into a world-famous global luxury goods company. The company owns many of the brands that do much to define the word luxury: Cartier, Jaeger Le Coultre, Piaget, Baume & Mercier, Vacheron Constantin, A. Lange Sohne, Officine Panerai, Chloé and Lancel. Richemont also owns 80 percent of the jewelry maker Van Cleef & Arpels. When Richemont merged Rothmans International, its tobacco unit, with British American Tobacco (BAT) in 1999, they received 35 percent ownership of BAT. Richemont is controlled by the Rupert family, with Johann Rupert directing the family's interests. The company has also dabbled in businesses outside of the luxury sphere, including stakes in French television company Canal+ and U.S. catalog company Hanover Direct, but continues to focus its attention on the luxury market.

A South African Family Business

Richemont was created in 1988 when the Rupert family decided to spin off the international assets from their core company, Rembrandt Group Ltd. The Rembrandt Group was founded by Anton Rupert to manufacture cigarettes in South Africa. Shortly after World War II, the Rembrandt Group began licensing cigarette brands from the Rothmans, the long-established English tobacconist. During the 1950s, Rupert built upon his relationship with Rothmans and began investing in the company. Over time, Rothmans gained additional footholds in the cigarette market by taking stakes in Dunhill and Cartier.

Anton Rupert's son, Johann Rupert, was handed the reins to the newly formed Richemont after he had gained professional experience outside of the family business. After college Johann Rupert worked in New York at Chase Manhattan and Lazard Feres before returning to South Africa to run his own merchant bank. Johann Rupert ran Richemont with a hands-off style. He believed strongly in allowing his luxury brands the money and time that they would need to develop and blossom into money-makers, rather than expecting them to perform immediately. In order to support Johann Rupert's approach, it was necessary for Richemont to carry a large amount of cash on hand. In 1989, Richemont's purchase of Philip Morris Company's 24-percent stake in Rothmans, secured control of Rothmans International for the Rupert family. At the time of Richemont's investment into Rothmans, the company cash reserves were listed at $750 million, with the annual flow estimated at approximately $500 million a year.

Early 1990s: Divide, Merge, and Acquire

In 1992, Richemont announced losses attributed to a variety of currency fluctuations, including a decline in interest income and the fluctuation of the pound. Johann Rupert was not concerned by these losses of profits; instead he reiterated the importance of fiscal patience, stating, ''Richemont's strength, however, lies in its ability to take a long-term view, as demonstrated by its recent investment in new businesses, notwithstanding their adverse effect on short-term profitability.'' Johann Rupert focused his attention on a short-term view of his own when, in 1993, he announced his intention to split Richemont's tobacco

Company Perspectives:

In the luxury world more than elsewhere, the ultimate condition for success lies in a company's capability to reinvent itself and to entrust new generations with its own heritage. A luxury brand is an expression of a lifestyle, in line with its time while anticipating trends. Like an artist, a strong luxury brand is a living being, which must create and innovate to become eternal. Today, the luxury way of life has become an integral part of the modern society, conveying a feeling of exclusivity.

In the fine watch sector, jewelry, accessories and fashion, Richemont has compelled recognition by the targeting of its portfolio brands. Whether they are linked to privilege and patrimony or associated with the idea of elegance and distinction, our brands impose themselves as essential brands in their respective field of expertise.

At the very heart of the beauty of each of our products, a whole array of know-how is apparent, each the outcome of dreams and creativity. As history and traditions nourish our brands' identities, our strength is that we do not live for only the moment.

and luxury goods interests into two separate companies, merging Cartier and Dunhill Holdings PLC to create a luxury goods group called Vendome. The company said in a statement, "The reorganization would produce two focused groups. The separate managements would be able to respond more effectively to the major changes facing the tobacco and luxury goods industries by concentrating exclusively on their field of business expertise." The company also said, "The new group [Vendome] will be in a strong position to make the additional investment necessary to maximize brand control and further improve profitability, develop new markets, and make acquisitions as the industry is rationalized and consolidated."

After a short period of time, during which there was a question of whether the Dunhill's minority shareholders would block the proposed merger because of the higher valuation that the merger placed on Cartier over Dunhill, the merger was approved and the new entity was named Vendome Luxury Group. In addition to Cartier and Dunhill, Vendome included many of the world's most well-known luxury brands: Chloé, Karl Lagerfeld, Piaget, Baume & Mercier, and Mont Blanc. Joseph Kanoi, who had been head of Cartier, became chairman and chief executive of Vendome; while Lord Charles Duoro, longtime chairman of Dunhill became deputy chairman. Richemont hoped that by merging these two groups, Vendome management could cut costs by developing an integrated system for distribution and purchasing.

Vendome's operations were organized into two independently managed groups, Vendome SA and Vendome PLC. Vendome SA was based in Paris and included Cartier, Chloé, Karl Lagerfeld, Sulka men's wear, Mont Blanc, Baume & Mercier, and Piaget. Vendome PLC was based in London and included Alfred Dunhill and Hackett men's wear. Richemont emerged from the merger as the owner of 70 percent of Vendome. Existing public Rothmans' shareholders owned 18 percent of Vendome, while existing shareholders of Dunhill

owned 8 percent. The remainder of the Vendome shares was held by companies associated with Luxco (Vendome's holding company). In 1995, Richemont's desire to operate Vendome with complete control became reality when Richemont bought out Rothmans International's minority shareholders. In 1996, the company's interests continued to expand when Richemont's television subsidiary NetHold (which was formed the year before) merged with France's Canal + .

Late 1990s: Stock Buyback and BAT Merger

Joahnn Rupert's theory that luxury brands need the freedom to operate on a long-term schedule was the impetus behind Richemont's plan to buy back the 30 percent of Vendome Luxury Group that it did not already own. "When we had total family control of Cartier we were able to give management a much longer time horizon for brand support," Johann Rupert said. "By taking Vendome private it means that over the next three, five or 10 years it will be easier for management to be less concerned with earnings per share on a six-month basis and more concerned with three- or five-year plans." Richemont offered to buy the 30 percent at a premium, but warned that the company may not proceed with their bid "in the event of any further collapse in the world markets, which would be likely to have a material adverse impact on the business of Vendome." In 1997, the board of Vendome agreed to Richemont's bid. Upon completion of the buyout in 1998, Richmont followed through with plans to take Vendome private. Vendome, valued at $5.74 billion, became free of stock market pressures.

In the same year, Vendome experienced an 8.5 percent drop in profits. The company chalked up the low sales of luxury products to Asia's economic turmoil. Richemont's tobacco interests continued to perform well, however, as they managed to avoid the bulk of the legal problems that cigarette companies in America underwent during this same time period. Richemont's tobacco interests accounted for 75 percent of the company's $1.7 billion in fiscal profits.

Rothmans International and British American Tobacco—the world's fourth and second largest international global cigarette companies—announced in 1999 that they intended to come together in a $21 billion merger. The two companies had a combined sales volume of 900 billion cigarettes in 1997. The merged group resulted in the two companies retaining the BAT name, and with Richemont and Rembrandt owning a 35 percent share. BAT Chairman Martin Broughton said, "This merger represents a major step forward in the achievement of our vision to become the world's leading international tobacco company." He added that the merger would enable them [BAT] "to play to our proven strengths in maintaining a portfolio of brands, while shifting resources to the premium international brands sector, which enjoys higher margins." The merged group owned many popular cigarette brands, including Lucky Strike, Peter Stuyvesant, Benson & Hedges, Dunhill, and Rothmans.

Van Cleef Acquisition and Company Reorganization

In 1999, in addition to merging Rothmans with BAT, Richemont acquired a 60 percent interest in Van Cleef & Arpels, the prestige jewelry house. Arpel family members held onto 20 percent of the remaining interest, while the remaining 20 percent belonged to Fingen SpA, a holding company owned by Marcello and Corrado Fratini. The Fratinis had announced their intention to purchase all of Van Cleef in 1998. When asked why they chose to bring in partners, Fabio Cavana, a general manager of Fingen, said, "It was a golden opportunity. Originally, the takeover was going to be leveraged. Then Richemont approached us with money and management skills that we could not turn down. We could not have asked for better partners." Richemont kept Van Cleef operations separate from its Vendome Luxury Group, continuing with the company practice of keeping their many brands separate and distinct.

After the company had completed its round of acquisitions and mergers it became necessary, during 1999 and 2000, for Richemont and Vendome to undergo staff reorganization to account for new responsibilities. Joseph Kanoi, who spent more than 25 years as chairman and chief executive of Vendome Luxury Group, retired on January 1, 2000 and was replaced with Johann Rupert. Alain Dominique Perrin was appointed senior executive director of Richemont, removing him from his position at Vendome, where he had similar responsibilities to those he undertook at Vendome. Perrin was made responsible for the development and implementation of all of Richemont's marketing, manufacturing, and strategic operations. Along with Johann Rupert's move to Vendome's Geneva offices came many of his past responsibilities, including the responsibility for providing and coordinating several central functions across all of Richemont's companies. Callum Barton, who had been the director of Alfred Dunhill, was moved from London to Geneva to be operations director of Richemont.

The New Millennium: Additional Acquisitions

Richemont continued its practice of acquiring luxury brands when the company joined forces with Audemars Piguet in 2000

in order to purchase the much sought-after Stern Group. The Stern Group was the leading manufacturer and supplied much of the world's luxury watch brands with watch dials. Prominent luxury brands The Swatch Group, LVMH Moët Hennessy Louis Vuitton, the Gucci Group, and Waterford Wedgwood PLC had competed with Richemont for the purchase of the Stern Group.

Another important Richemont acquisition that occurred in 2000 was the purchase of Les Manufactures Hologeres (LMH). LMH was the watch-making division of Mannesmann AG. The $1.57 billion purchase included 60 percent of Jaeger LeCoultre, 100 percent of IWC and 90 percent of A. Lange Sohne. The acquirement of the remaining 60 percent of Jaeger LeCoultre rounded Richemont up to 100 percent ownership of the company. The acquisition of Stern Group and LMH bolstered Richemont's manufacturing capabilities. Richemont also acquired Montegrappa of Italy, a niche watch brand, in early 2000.

The Richemont brands did well in 2000. The company announced a 69 percent growth in after-tax profits, and a 32.1 percent rise in sales in the first half of the year. This same year, Richemont exited the pay-television and electronic media market with the disposal of their holdings in Vivendi (which they acquired in 1999 when they exchanged their Canal+ interest for a 2.9 percent interest in Vivendi), the satellite television company.

The Highs and Lows of 2001

Throughout the beginning months of 2001, Richemont was flying high. The company underwent another management restructuring due to influx of new management from their recent acquisitions. In keeping with Richemont's desire to keep its brands separate and independent from each other, the company released a statement asserting, "The structure will insure that the various 'Maisons' maintain their separate, vertical autonomy and produce integrity whilst obtaining maximum synergistic benefits from this important strategic acquisition." The company also increased their ownership stake in Van Cleef & Arpels when it purchased Fingen SpA's 20 percent share.

In June of 2001, Richemont announced another large profit leap, and focused much of their enthusiasm for the coming year's success around the growing market for luxury goods in the United States. While Rupert made hopeful statements celebrating the leap in the U.S. market, he maintained his characteristic speculation about the future of the world's economic health. "We run this group as if something bad is going to happen," Rupert said. "If it doesn't we will do very, very well. But if its does, we will survive." Rupert was wise to have maintained a skeptical attitude about the world's financial future, as the terrorist attack of September 11, 2001 in the United States shook the global market and Richemont's profits plummeted 78 percent.

Immediately after September 11, Richemont issued a warning that its first-half operating profits, stating that the tragedy in New York could exacerbate the company's profit downturn. "The tragic events of recent days have clearly thrown the world into turmoil," Johann Rupert said. "This will increase the uncertainties already prevailing in economies worldwide such that short-term forecasting has become difficult.'' Richemont followed their initial profit warning, with a statement issued in late October stating, ''The positive sales trend seen over the first 10 days of the month was reversed such that, on a like-for-like basis, sales for the month of September as a whole decreased by some 13 percent.'' Richemont was not the only luxury goods company issuing dire statements; similar statements were issued by LVMH and Gucci.

At the end of 2001, Richemont released figures that supported the company's prediction that sales would not be as glorious as they had been previous to September 11. The company reported that their net profits plummeted 78 percent. However, the company's stake in BAT continued to work its magic, keeping the company awash in funds. Johann Rupert noted that the company had a ''good cash flow'' from its interest in BAT and that in the first six months of 2001, that investment generated $200 million in dividends. This ''good cash flow'' allowed Johann Rupert to continue with his practice of taking the pressure off of his luxury brands to allow them to creatively develop in their own time.

Principal Subsidiaries

Cartier SA (France); Chloé International SA (France); Lancel SA (France); Van Cleef & Arpels France SA (80%); Richemont Northern Europe GmbH (Germany); Lange Uhren GmbH (Germany; 90%); Richemont (Asia Pacific) Limited (Hong Kong); Richemont Italia SpA (Italy); Alfred Dunhill Japan Limited; Mont Blanc Japan Limited; Richemont Japan Limited; Cartier Monde SA (Luxembourg); Richemont Finance SA (Luxembourg); Richemont Luxury Group SA (Luxembourg); R&R Holdings SA (Luxembourg; 66.7%); Cartier International BV (Netherlands); Mont Blanc International BV (Netherlands); Van Cleef & Arpels BV (Netherlands); Baume & Mercier SA (Switzerland); Cartier International SA (Switzerland); Cartier SA (Switzerland); CTL Horlogerie SA (Switzerland); Interdica SA (Switzerland); IWC International Watch Co. AG (Switzerland); Manufacture Jaeger-LeCoultre SA (Switzerland); Piaget (International) SA (Switzerland); Richemont Securities AG (Switzerland); Vacheron & Constantin SA (Switzerland); Van Cleef & Arpels Logistic SA (Switzerland; 80%); Alfred Dunhill Limited (UK); Cartier Limited (UK); Hackett Limited (UK); James Purdey & Sons Limited (UK); Richemont International Limited (UK); Cartier, Incorporated (US); Mont Blanc Inc. (US); Richemont North America Inc. (US); Van Cleef & Arpels Inc. (US; 80%); British American Tobacco (21%).

Principal Competitors

Gucci Group NV; LVMH Moët Hennessy Louis Vuitton SA; Tiffany & Co.; Chanel SA.

Further Reading

Conti, Samantha, ''Richemont Buys 60% of Van Cleef,'' *WWD*, May 13, 1999, p. 16.

Hall, William, ''When Time Is a Business's Ultimate Luxury,'' *Financial Times*, June 9, 2000, p. 34.

Fallon, James, ''Profits Decline for Parent of Dunhill and Cartier,'' *WWD*, December 7, 1992, p. 6.

——, ''Richemont's Restructuring Plan Halts Dunhill, Rothmans Trading,'' *WWD*, June 24, 1993, p. 3.

——, ''Dunhill Shareholders May Block Merger of Cartier and Dunhill,'' *Daily News Record*, June 29, 1993, p. 10.

——, ''Richemont AG Merges Cartier, Dunhill Holdings,'' *WWD*, June 28, 1993, pp. 1–2.

——, ''Richemont Warns,'' *WWD*, September 14, 2001, p. 2.

——, ''Vendome Stock Buyback Eyed by Richemont,'' *WWD*, December 1, 1997, p. 2.

Kroll, Luisa, ''Smoke This,'' *Forbes*, July 6, 1998, p. 272.

Marcom, Jr., John, ''The Quiet Afrikaner behind Cartier,'' *Forbes*, April 2, 1990, p. 114.

—Tammy Weisberger

Danske Bank Aktieselskab

2-12 Holmens Kanal
DK-1092
Copenhagen K
Denmark
Telephone: Phone: +45 33-44-00-00
Fax: +45 39-18-58-73
Web site: http://www.danskebank.com

Public Company
Incorporated: 1990 as Den Danske Bank
Employees: 18,958 (2001)
Total Assets: DKr 1,539 billion (2001)
Stock Exchanges: Copenhagen OTC
Ticker Symbol: DNK (Copenhagen), DEAFY (OTC)
NAIC: 522110 Commercial Banking; 524113 Direct Life
   Insurance Carriers; 524126 Direct Property and
   Casualty Insurance Carriers; 524114 Direct Health
   and Medical Insurance Carriers

Danske Bank Aktieselskab is the largest banking group in Denmark and among the three largest in Scandinavia. It has branch networks in Denmark, Norway, and Sweden; subsidiaries in Norway and Luxembourg; foreign branches in Finland, Germany, the United Kingdom, and the United States; and representative offices in France, Japan, Poland, and Spain. The bank offers a wide range of financial services, including insurance, mortgage finance, asset management, brokerage, credit card, real estate, and leasing services.

Historical Background

The result of a surprise merger among three of Denmark's six largest banks, the current Danske Bank Aktieselskab incorporated on January 1, 1990, as Den Danske Bank. The second private bank established in Denmark was incorporated in 1871 as Den Danske Landmandsbank, Hypothek-og Vexelbank i Kjobenhavn (The Danish Farmer's Bank, Mortgage and Exchange Bank of Copenhagen). Its founder was Hartvig Abrahamsson Gedalia, a saddle maker who traded bonds and shares as a sideline and later became a full-time broker at the Copenhagen Stock Exchange. At its

founding, the bank's objective was "to make farmers' spare capital profitable and to supply them, on completely adequate security, with the capital that their enterprises stood in need of." The bank also facilitated trade, to the extent that its original name was inadequate to describe its full activities.

By 1910, Den Danske Landmandsbank had become the largest bank in Scandinavia. By 1922, however, the post-World War I economic crisis pushed the bank to near-failure from which the state bailed it out. After the rescue, the bank quickly recovered and regained its status as Denmark's largest bank. Over the years, the bank developed from a farmers' bank to a commercial bank serving all segments of Danish society. To reflect this change, the bank shortened its name to "Den Danske Bank" in 1976.

Kjobenhavns Handelsbank ranked as Denmark's second largest bank at the time of the 1990 merger. Founded by the merchant D.B. Adler, Aktieselskabet Kjobenhavns Handelsbank began transacting business on April 18, 1873. In 1920 when southern Schleswig reunited with Denmark after World War I, Handelsbank took over the branches of Schleswig-Holsteinische Bank in the region recovered. This development gave the bank a strong presence in southern Denmark that endures to this day.

Handelsbanken also felt the effects of post-World War I economic crisis. Unfounded rumors of major losses culminated in a 1931 run on the bank. When the Danish central bank issued a liquidity guarantee and a declaration of confidence in the bank, the crisis soon passed.

Provinsbanken, Denmark's fifth largest bank in 1990, was founded in 1846 by the name "Fyens Disconto Kasse" by a group of merchants led by Lorentz Bierfreund. It was the nation's oldest private bank. In 1967 it merged with Aarhus Privatbank under the name "Den Danske Provinsbank." Subsequently, it merged with a number of provincial banks.

Danish Consolidation: 1900–1995

The 1990 merger came as a surprise because Den Danske and Handelsbanken had been aggressive competitors for first place among Danish banks. Several economic and financial developments, both internal to Denmark and in the general European context, impelled the merger. Most immediately, Denmark had experienced a period of stagnant growth since about 1986. This stagnation slowed or reversed lending and deposit growth and caused a 45 percent increase in Danish bankruptcies. Bank returns suffered as a result. These developments contributed to a search for ways to rationalize banking operations and cut costs. The merger partners expected that the greater size of the combination would make the pursuit of these ends easier.

Systemically, the Danish banking sector was highly fragmented in two senses. About 70 commercial banks and 140 savings banks served a population of 5.1 million. Very few large banks with a national presence competed with 15 to 20 regional banks and a plethora of banks that operated in a single town or village; and 18 banks and 10 savings banks accounted for a 90 percent market share.

Moreover, Denmark's strong cooperative history had left financial functions divided among four kinds of institutions. Until banking deregulation in 1975, savings banks were owned by their depositors and were prohibited from entering commercial banking activities. The 1975 deregulation removed these restrictions, placing savings banks and commercial banks under the same banking act. Despite this change, the new law still prohibited savings banks from converting to public companies and raising money through the issuance of stock. A 1989 law eliminated this restriction. Savings banks became equal in all respects to the private commercial banks and became candidates for mergers or acquisitions by other banks.

Denmark's large mortgage credit associations also grew out of the cooperative movement. By law "self-owning associations of borrowers," these associations issue bonds, secured by the mortgaged property, to finance the construction and acquisition of residential property. Before the Den Danske merger, the two largest mortgage associations each had assets of about DKr 300 billion compared to the premerger Den Danske's assets of about DKr 176 billion. By 1990 these institutions had begun to compete directly with the banks. Their mortgage businesses could neither undertake other banking functions nor raise equity through the issue of shares, but they circumvented these restrictions by forming holding companies with separate subsidiaries that could do both.

Insurance companies, prohibited from conducting any business except insurance, also created holding companies to overcome that restriction. By 1990, they too, had begun to invade the territory of the commercial banks by forming separate banking subsidiaries.

Denmark's membership in the European Union (EU) added to the pressures on the banks. EU policies eliminating restric-

tions on cross-border ownership of businesses threatened the relatively small Danish institutions with takeovers by larger banks in other European nations. European economic integration also encouraged growth in the size of businesses, as they expanded to operate beyond the borders of their countries of origin. Larger businesses required larger banks with access to more capital to meet their financial needs.

The merger of Denmark's fourth, fifth, and eighth largest banks into Unibank, which became the nation's second-ranked bank, immediately after the Den Danske merger confirmed that Danish banks felt themselves endangered.

Having established a substantial asset base of about DKr 350 billion, the new Den Danske Bank proceeded on a course of rationalization of existing operations and expansion into new lines of business. It moved quickly to reduce its branch network and announced plans to cut its staff by 10 percent over two to three years. By 1992 the bank was well along in reducing its branch network from 750 to approximately 550. By the end of that year, it had achieved its staff reduction goal.

Soon after the merger, Den Danske's Chief Executive, Knud Sorensen, stated that the bank was not interested in growing via mergers and acquisitions. It expected to expand "organically," by expansion of its existing organization. Den Danske began such growth in 1991 when it established its own life insurance and pensions subsidiary and announced its intention to make mortgage credit, backed by bank-issued bonds, available to its customers. By early 1995, the bank's "organically" grown subsidiaries controlled only a 7 percent share of the life insurance market. Its mortgage operations were more successful. By January 1995, Den Danske captured 15 percent of Danish gross new mortgage lending.

Den Danske's first major departure from the path of organic growth was not entirely voluntary. It resulted from the Danish tradition whereby strong financial institutions rescued other financial organizations that faced disaster. In 1992, Baltica Holdings, which controlled the country's largest insurance group, faced a severe liquidity crisis resulting from its attempts to join the trend among Danish financial institutions to diversify beyond their core businesses. In Baltica's case, this diversification included investments in real estate. In the difficult economic environment of the late 1980s and early 1990s, these investments lost value and endangered the survival of the company. At that point, Den Danske, the only financial institution strong enough to rescue Baltica, purchased a 32 percent stake in the company and held an option to acquire another 23 percent.

Den Danske planned to dispose of the company, but the Supreme Court ruled in 1993 that Baltica's life insurance subsidiary, Danica, could not pay a dividend for 25 years. This made it impossible to sell the company. The bank then decided to acquire all of Baltica. In 1995, Den Danske sold many of Baltica's assets, keeping Danica, which brought Den Danske's life insurance market share to about 30 percent.

Post-1995 Pan-Nordic Expansion

By 1995 the Scandinavian economic crisis of the late 1980s and early 1990s had resolved itself. This elimination of excess economic risk freed all Nordic financial institutions, relatively small by European standards, to pursue Pan-Nordic expansion.

Den Danske was no exception. Partly in response to incursions by banks based in other Scandinavian nations into Denmark, Den Danske established a full branch in Stockholm and representative offices in Helsinki and Oslo in 1995.

Some questioned the advantages of cross-border mergers and acquisitions. They suggested that such combinations did not reduce the duplication of services, staff, and operations that within-border mergers did. Therefore, minimal or no cost savings and rationalization could be realized. Nevertheless, most Nordic financial institutions, Den Danske among them, pursued increases in their customer base, revenues, and assets beyond their national boundaries. A major reason behind this strategy was a desire to grow so that they could maintain their independence from the expansionistic designs of other Nordic and European financial institutions. Thus, Den Danske, along with many Nordic banks, came to view all of Scandinavia as its home market and began to pursue business throughout the region.

This pressure toward within- and cross-border expansion increased substantially by the mid-1990s as the previously settled Danish financial scene became highly competitive. Den Danske and Unibank held about 60 percent of banking assets between them, but in 1995, a third potential competitor formed. Bikuben, the flagship of the savings bank movement, and GiroBank, originally formed an alliance to facilitate cash transfers within the postal system, becoming an independent full-service bank with a contract to continue management of postal transfers. Later Bikuben and GiroBank merged to form BG Bank. The new institution immediately became Denmark's third-ranked bank. It also had significant cross-holdings in one of the nation's large mortgage credit associations and a major insurance company.

By 1998, BG Bank remained a distant third in both size and profitability. To protect itself from potential acquisition by Den Danske or Unibank or by a foreign financial institution, BG Bank merged, under a holding company, with Realkredit Danmark, one the nation's major mortgage credit associations.

At about the same time, foreign banks continued to make incursions into Denmark and other, less traditional, financial service groups emerged. These included the Norwegian group Finax, which entered the consumer credit market with the Accept credit card. The FDB cooperative retail group, with 1,200 stores in Denmark, also threatened to launch its own financial services in the near future.

In the face of this increasing competition, Den Danske significantly advanced its Pan-Nordic strategy. In 1997, Den Danske made its first major cross-border purchase. It bought Ostgota Enskilda Bank, Sweden's only remaining provincial bank after a wave of banking consolidation had swept the country. This move gave Den Danske an existing network of 29 branch offices in southern Sweden and an established brand under which to conduct business. Chief Executive Knud Sorensen stated that the acquisition was a "unique opportunity to break into the Swedish market" at a relatively low cost of both money and time. The combination also came at an opportune time because a bridge was due to connect Denmark and southern Sweden in 2000. Den Danske would have a good base of operations to serve the region when it inevitably evolved into a single market.

The bank followed this move with several smaller cross-border acquisitions. To expand its securities trading, corporate finance and asset management businesses, it purchased brokerage firms in Norway, Sweden, and Finland. It also bought a mortgage credit business in Sweden.

By 1999, Den Danske had digested these acquisitions. It faced continued consolidation among banks in other Scandinavian countries, especially Sweden, and incursions into the Danish markets by these same banks. It also saw speculation that larger European banks outside of Scandinavia might be interested in acquiring Nordic banks. To meet this competition and to try to defend itself from a takeover, Den Danske made its next Pan-Nordic deal, acquiring Fokus Bank, Norway's third largest bank. This move extended the bank's presence from Denmark and Sweden to Norway.

In the same year, MeritaNordbanken, the result of a 1998 merger between a Finnish and Swedish bank, first signaled its desire to acquire Unibank as a means of establishing itself in Denmark. The bank made the purchase in March 2000, immediately making itself Den Danske's most significant competitor, and placing pressure on Den Danske to respond. This, however, was difficult because few major acquisition targets had survived the consolidation wave of the preceding several years.

Den Danske, now officially named Danske Bank Aktieselskab, merged with RealDanmark, the holding company that owned both the mortgage credit association Realkredit Danmark and BG Bank. With this move, Danske Bank solidified its position as Denmark's leading financial institution. It became the nation's largest bank and biggest mortgage credit bank. It ranked among the country's top life insurance and pension providers and controlled the largest Danish mutual fund.

The Future of Danske Bank

The beginning of the 21st Century saw a Danish banking and financial environment very different from that of only a decade before. The nation's largest banks had merged, made acquisitions, and been acquired. The second largest bank, Unibank, was a subsidiary of a foreign bank, and the largest, Danske, owned significant branch networks and other assets in the other Scandinavian countries. Although Denmark still had numerous small banks, its three largest banks—Danske, Unibank and Jyske—accounted for 70 percent of the market.

In Scandinavia, too, waves of mergers and acquisitions had cut the population of major banks to about five. Observers speculated about the next trend to affect Nordic banks. Little potential for combinations among the region's banks remained. The Baltic nations and Poland presented some opportunity for continued expansion, but the Baltics had relatively small populations, and larger German, French, and Irish banks had already established themselves in Poland. Acquisitions by larger European banks to the south were also possible, but observers questioned the desirability of the relatively small Nordic banks to the much larger major European banks.

Principal Subsidiaries

Danske Bank International S.A. (100%); Danske Bank Polska S.A. (91%); Danske Capital Finland Oy (100%); Danske Corporation (100%); Danske Finance, Asia, Ltd. (100%); Danske Kredit Realkredit Aktieselskab (100%); Danske Private Equity A/S (100%); DDB Fokus Invest AS (100%); DDB Invest AB (100%); Forsikringsselskabet Danica Skadeforsikringsaktieselskab af 1999 (100%); RealDanmark A/S (96%); Realkredit Danmark A/S (100%).

Principal Competitors

Nordic Baltic Holdings; Svenska Handelsbanken; SEB; Swedbank; Jyske Bank.

Further Reading

Adams, Richard, "Bonds," *Financial Times* (London), April 9, 1997, Survey-Danish Banking and Finance, p. 3.
Barnes, Hilary, "Subjected to a Barrage of Reforms," *Financial Times* (London), January 13, 1986, Section III, p. 7.
Barnes, Hilary, "Bikuben and GiroBank in Merger Negotiations," *Financial Times* (London), September 26, 1995, p. 24.
——, "A Bright Patch in the Nordic Gloom," *Financial Times* (London), November 19, 1991, Survey, p. 2.
——, "Danish Megabanks . . . And Then There Were Two," *Financial Times* (London), April 25, 1990, Survey, p. 40.
——, "Denmark 5: Giants Begin to Stir," *Financial Times* (London), April 5, 1989, Survey, p. 5.
——, "Denmark 4: Banks Reduce Branches in Streamlining Move," *Financial Times* (London), September 21, 1990, Survey, p. 4.
——, "Denmark's Top Banks to Merge," *Financial Times* (London), November 15, 1989, p. 29.
——, "Ill Winds Bypass Danish Banks," *Financial Times* (London), October 23, 1991, p. 28.
——, "Insurance," *Financial Times* (London), April 9, 1997, Survey-Danish Banking and Finance, p. 5.
——, "The Leaders," *Financial Times* (London), April 8, 1998, Survey-Danish Banking, p. 3.
——, "Motive for the Mergers," *Financial Times* (London), March 25, 1991, Survey, p. 32.
——, "Nordic Banking 5; 'Attitude' Has Been a Success Factor," *Financial Times* (London), January 11, 1988, Survey, p. 5.
——, "Nordic Banking Integration," *Financial Times* (London), April 9, 1997, Survey-Danish Banking and Finance, p. 6.
——, "Riding for a Fall: Denmark," *Financial Times* (London), October 27, 1998, Survey-Nordic Banking and Finance, p. 3.
——, "Rivals Accentuate the Positive," *Financial Times* (London), November 24, 1989, p. 32.
——, "Sound, Despite Losses—Danish Banks," *Financial Times* (London), March 25, 1991, Survey, p. 32.
——, "Subjected to a Barrage of Reforms," *Financial Times* (London), January 13, 1986, Section III, p. 7.
——, "Survey of Danish Banking and Finance," *Financial Times* (London), April 7, 1994, pp. 2, 5.
——, "Survey of Danish Banking and Finance," *Financial Times* (London), March 21, 1996, pp. 3, 4.
——, "Survey of Danish Banking and Finance: In Leaner and Meaner Shape," *Financial Times* (London), March 21, 1996, p. 1.
——, "Survey of Denmark," *Financial Times* (London), November 29, 1993, p. 12.
——, "Survey of European Finance and Investment: Nordic Countries," *Financial Times* (London), March 23, 1992, p. 4.
——, "Survey of Nordic Banking and Finance," *Financial Times* (London), June 21, 1993, p. 12.
Brown-Humes, Christopher, "Companies and Finance Europe," *Financial Times* (London), February 23, 2001, p. 28.
——, "Handelsbanken Eyes Nordic Buys," *Financial Times* (London), October 25, 2000, Companies and Finance Europe, p. 34.
——, "Institutions Head for Cross-Border Expansion," *Financial Times* (London), October 13, 1999, Survey-Nordic Banking and Finance, p. 1.
——, "Rivals Play Down Nordic Bank Buy," *Financial Times* (London), March 7, 2000, Companies and Finance Europe, p. 28.
——, "Survey of Danish Banking and Finance," *Financial Times* (London), March 29, 1995, pp. 6, 7
Burt, Tim, "Big Institutions Buy Up Their Smaller Rivals," *Financial Times* (London), April 15, 1999, Survey-Danish Banking and Finance, p. 3.
Criscione, Valeria, et al., "Bank Completes Quest for Regional Identity," *Financial Times* (London), October 17, 2000, Companies and Finance Europe, p. 40.
Evans, Garry, "Pinstripes Versus the Trinity," *Euromoney*, February 1991, pp. 63–66.
Evans, John, "Nordic Banks Combine to Repel EC Invasion," *The American Banker,* December 19, 1989, p. 6.
Fossli, Karen, "Survey of Danish Banking and Finance," *Financial Times* (London), April 7, 1994, p. 4.
George, Nicholas, "Dynamic Growth Region: Baltic Banks," *Financial Times* (London), October 13, 1999, Survey-Nordic Banking and Finance, p. 3.
——, "Expanding Network of Financial Services: Banking," *Financial Times* (London), June 11, 1999, Survey-Baltic Sea Region, p. 6.
Graham, George, "Banks," *Financial Times* (London), April 9, 1997, Survey-Danish Banking and Finance, p. 2.
"Growth Formula Is Business as Usual," *Financial Times* (London), October 13, 1999, Survey-Nordic Banking and Finance, p. 5.
MacCarthy, Clare, "Banks Maintain Strong Profitability: Denmark," *Financial Times* (London), November 12, 2001, Survey-Nordic Banking and Finance, p. 4.
——, "Merger Creates a National Champion: Denmark," *Financial Times* (London), October 31, 2000, Survey-Nordic Banking, p. 6.
——"Ripe for Takeovers from Abroad," *Financial Times* (London), October 13, 1999, Survey-Nordic Banking and Finance, p. 5.

—Anne L. Potter

Delicato Vineyards, Inc.

455 Devlin Road, Suite 201
Napa, California 94558
U.S.A
Telephone: (707) 265-1700
Fax: (707) 265-7837
Toll Free Fax: (877) 824-3600
Web site: http://www.delicato.com

Private Company
Incorporated: 1973
Employees: 220
Sales: $110 million (est.)
NAIC: 111332 Grape Vineyards; 312130 Wineries

Delicato Vineyards, Inc. is one of the largest family-owned and operated winemakers in California, where 90 percent of the U.S. wine is produced. The privately held company cultivates over 10,000 acres of vineyards in the state's central valley and coastal regions and, between its two wineries, it turns out about 20 million gallons of wine each year. Annual sales are estimated at $110 million. Starting as a Prohibition-era farm that grew grapes for home winemakers, Delicato has grown successful as a "winemaker's winemaker," contracting to make and sell bulk wine for other brands to bottle under their own labels. The practice continues to be the mainstay of Delicato's business. Starting in the mid-1990s, however, the winery began an earnest push toward producing and selling wine under three of its own brands, and a number of its releases have won awards. Among Delicato's vineyard holdings is the 8,100-acre San Bernabe Vineyard in Monterey County, which claims the distinction of being the largest single grape-growing property in the world.

Gaspare Indelicato Plants First Delicato Vines

Gaspare "Nono" Indelicato, founder and patriarch of Delicato Vineyards, arrived in central California in 1912 from Sicily. The 18-year-old immigrant heralded from generations of farmers who planted grapes among their crops and enjoyed making their own wine. While picking grapes in a Lodi, California vineyard, Indelicato met Italian-born Catherine, or "Caterina." They mar-

ried in 1921. Two years later, Indelicato borrowed money from a bank in order to buy and farm a 68-acre onetime dairy ranch in nearby Manteca, impressed by how the landscape resembled his Sicilian homeland. Caterina's twin sister and her husband Sebastiano Luppino lived on the farm with them and, in 1924, Indelicato and Luppino planted small plots of Carignane, Mission, and Zinfandel vines for making their own wine. The poor farmers soon discovered that their grapes could also bring in cash. Home winemakers, plentiful after Prohibition was enacted in 1919, were allowed to produce up to 200 gallons yearly for personal use, and Indelicato sold and shipped grapes to winemaking families in Chicago and on the East Coast, helping him to keep current on his loan payments.

Like many, Indelicato's fortunes dipped in 1929 with the Depression. But the repeal of Prohibition in 1933 hurt even more. Demand for wine grapes fell and prices plummeted to under $5 per ton as home winemaking dropped off. Some area farmers plowed under their vines or lost their land. A friend of Indelicato had to plead with the bank to keep it from foreclosing on the Manteca farm. Rather than give up on grapes, Indelicato and Luppino in 1935 decided to try their hand at large-scale winemaking. Working in an old hay barn, the men and their wives took turns working the hand-operated wine press to squeeze their fruit, then fermented the juice in wooden vats borrowed from neighbors. Their first vintage yielded 3,451 gallons of red wine. For marketing purposes, the winemakers Americanized their names—Gaspare became "Jasper" and Sebastiano became "Sam"—and launched Sam Jasper Winery, using road signs to advertise.

The winemaking business took off. Local families—mostly Italians—bought Sam Jasper wine for 50 cents a gallon, which Indelicato often delivered in his truck. The partners opened a cellar to age their wine, added vineyards to maintain a consistent supply of grapes, and continued with wholesale and retail wine trade. Gradually the winery gained a reputation as a reliable producer of good everyday table wines, and began making bulk wine that other winemakers used to blend with their own wines, or simply bottled and sold as their own wine. Functioning as a "vintner's vintner" became the foundation of the Indelicato business. By 1940, Sam Jasper Winery was making and selling about 15,000 gallons a year and charging 95

Company Perspectives:

For more than 75 years, the Indelicato family has been crafting fine wines while assembling a portfolio of world-class estate vineyards. Today, Delicato harvests more than 10,000 acres of vineyards across the top grape-growing regions of California. These range from the coastal cool of the legendary San Bernabe Vineyard in Monterey, one of California's oldest grape-growing regions, to the rolling foothills of Lodi.

A celebrated team of highly experienced winemakers has brought decades of expertise to bear on these remarkable grapes, to create Delicato wines of distinctive character, memorable quality, and exceptional value at a variety of price points.

Our vision is to establish Delicato as a leading Coastal winery and perpetuate our name in California winemaking by participating in its foremost grape-growing regions: the Central Coast, North Coast, and Central Valley; and developing a range of well-respected, well-recognized wine brands that are the best in their class.

cents a gallon. By 1944 the price jumped to $1.90 a gallon. Profits from the business enabled Indelicato to build a new brick house and he and Caterina took their only trip back to Italy.

Three Sons Expand Business: 1950–1987

In the 1950s, Indelicato's three sons—Frank, Anthony, and Vincent— joined the business. The winery also introduced and experimented with new wines under the Sam Jasper label. Among them were Green Hungarian, Sauternes, and Pink Tingle, a lemon-flavored white wine aperitif and forerunner of the wine cooler. The company bought grapes to supplement its own vineyard harvests and, by 1955, bulk wine production had reached 74,107 gallons and continued to climb in the following years. Yet, when Gaspare Indelicato passed away in 1962, the winemaking operation was still a small, struggling family affair. Anthony served as winemaker, Vincent as a sales representative, and Frank as cellar manager. The business took a significant leap forward two years later. In 1964, the Indelicatos had six giant, glass-lined concrete fermentation tanks shipped in on railcars from Texas, expanding the family's winemaking capacity to 403,000 gallons—triple the volume produced the previous year.

In 1973 the Indelicato brothers incorporated the business and renamed it Delicato Vineyards. Around the same time wine consumption began to accelerate in the United States. Smaller, well-known California coastal wineries that did not have the production capacity to keep up with the demand turned to Delicato. The company supplemented grapes from its own 120 acres of Zinfandel vines at Manteca, and 300 acres of varietals near Lodi, by purchasing fruit from the Napa, Sonoma, and Santa Barbara Counties. Delicato production soon surpassed the 1 million gallon mark. In 1975 the winery built a tasting room and corporate offices at the Manteca Vineyard.

The third generation of Indelicatos began working at the winery at the start of the 1980s. Delicato also raised its visibility in the local community. In 1983, the winery began its annual Delicato Charity Grape Stomp Festival during Labor Day weekend. Over time the tradition came to draw thousands who sampled wine, ate pasta, and participated in grape stomping, a time-honored grape-crushing technique. Meanwhile, the winery continued producing bulk wine sold under other labels with some limited bottling of varietal wines under a Delicato label. Several of its wines collected medals in wine-judging competitions. For its 50th anniversary in 1985, the winery brought in a winemaking consultant to help develop its 1983 Carneros-Napa Valley Cabernet Sauvignon.

San Bernabe Vineyard Purchase: 1988

By the mid-1980s the Indelicato family saw the market moving from generic, blended wine to varietals. Wine consumers wanted Chardonnay instead of "white wine" or Cabernet Sauvignon rather then "red wine." Delicato began to shift from growing and crushing grapes for generic-wine production to growing and processing grapes for the premium-varietal market. The first step came in 1987 when the company purchased 110 acres in the middle of a vast, 20-square-mile vineyard and ranch in Monterey County near King City. Delicato began building a winery there with a capacity to crush 40,000 tons of grapes. Then the following year it bought the entire 12,640-acre estate for an undisclosed amount.

Known as the San Bernabe Vineyard, the historic grape-growing property was developed according to a master plan and laid out in 212 vine blocks for efficient planting, watering, and harvesting. Wine industry experts believed the property's 8,100-acre vineyard was the largest contiguous vineyard in the world and estimated it contained more than a quarter of all Monterey Country grapevines. The previous owners, the Prudential Insurance and the Southdown Companies, had hired an independent farm management company to grow grapes and market them. Between 15 and 25 of California's leading varietal wine brands—including many boutique wineries in the Monterey area—had purchased their grapes from San Bernabe.

The Indelicato family believed the San Bernabe had the potential to produce varietal grapes and wines that could challenge the acclaimed offerings from the Napa and Sonoma Counties to the north. A year after the acquisition, Delicato began a gradual replanting of the vast vineyard. With its 13 soil types, 22 microclimates and extensive wells, reservoirs and canals, viticulturists had the luxury of matching grape varieties with environments that brought out the most desirable characteristic in the fruit and wine. Delicato eventually cultivated 27 grape varieties at the vineyard, most for commercial sale, and a few for experimental purposes. San Bernabe brought Delicato considerable attention and praise. In a *Business Wire* article, San Francisco-based wine industry analyst Jon Fredrikson called the purchase "a bold and brilliant move" and "quantum leap forward" for Delicato. "It follows the Indelicato family's strategy of shrewd, conservative management that controls production costs, allowing it to fit efficiently into the structure of today's wine industry and benefiting future generations as well," Fredrikson said.

Soon after, Delicato garnered some unwanted publicity. In the late 1980s, California's supply of Chardonnay and Zinfan-

Key Dates:

1924: Gaspare Indelicato plants grape vines on his Manteca, California, farm; later he sells the fruit to home winemakers.

1935: Indelicato and his brother-in-law, Sebastiano Luppino, open Jasper and Sam's Winery.

1940: Sam Jasper Winery makes and sells about 15,000 gallons of wine a year and charges 95 cents a gallon.

1964: The Indelicato family purchases six large fermenters and triples their winery-production capacity.

1973: Delicato Family Vineyards is incorporated.

1975: The winery builds a tasting room and corporate offices at the Manteca Vineyard.

1983: The winery begins its traditional annual Delicato Charity Grape Stomp Festival during Labor Day weekend.

1988: Delicato buys the 12,000-acre San Bernabe Vineyard estate.

1994: Chief winemaker Tom Smith is hired.

1995: The company purchases 800 acres of vineyards near Lodi, California.

1997: Delicato releases 5,000 cases of its own premium-brand wine under the Monterra label.

2000: The company opens an executive office and retains a public relations firm in the California wine capital, Napa.

2001: Delicato is named "Best USA Wine Producer" at the International Wine and Spirit Competition and wins six individual medals including a gold for its Monterra 1998 Merlot.

2002: The winery's 2000 Shiraz wins two awards at the California State Fair Wine Competition.

del grapes began to shrink due a small harvest and growing consumer demand. With prices rising spectacularly, state authorities suspected that some grape-growers and brokers might exploit the situation by selling cheaper grapes and passing them off as more costly varieties. Delicato was among the wineries that unknowingly bought grapes in 1988 from a broker who misrepresented them. Delicato recalled and replaced the Zinfandel wine it produced, and cooperated with a U.S. Attorney's investigation. But federal authorities charged the winery with not keeping required records of the purchase after learning of the deception. In 1992, three Delicato employees pleaded guilty to record-keeping charges and the winery agreed to pay a $1 million fine. In the wake of the grape-swapping scandal, the winery also began including a controversial clause in its paperwork that required grape-growers and brokers to promise "under penalty of perjury" that the fruit they delivered was 100 percent consistent with a variety shown on delivery tags.

Developing Premium Wine: 1990s

Delicato entered the 1990s with Vincent Indelicato as new company president and ranked as the nation's 12th largest vintner. The winery located within the San Bernabe Vineyard had a capacity to produce 2 million gallons of wine. The Manteca Winery had been enlarged to produce up to 44 million gallons, and had an 11,000-barrel computerized aging warehouse adjacent to it. And Delicato's vineyard holdings continued to grow. In 1995 the company expanded its 1,250-acre Lodi vineyard—dubbed Clay Station—by buying 800 acres of the defunct Borden Ranch residential development for $2.7 million.

The Indelicato family had produced and marketed wine bearing the Delicato label since the early 1980s, but it was not until the 1990s that the winery made a serious push to move from bulk wine to its own brands of bottled varietals. In 1994, Delicato hired veteran California vintner Tom Smith as its chief winemaker. Two years later, in 1996, it introduced the Delicato Family Vineyards brand, an inexpensive, everyday table wine bearing a distinctive blue label. Eager to overcome its image as a bulk wine producer, Delicato also began developing an even higher-quality product, a brand featuring the distinct attributes of Monterey County fruit that could compete with North Coast wines. Made with San Bernabe grapes, the Monterra label debuted in 1993 in Delicato's tasting room. Wider distribution commenced in 1997, when the winery produced 5,000 cases of wine predominantly sold in the U.S. restaurants and wine shops, and select international markets.

By the end of the decade Delicato had become the fifth largest winery in California. It sent about 12 percent of its production to overseas markets such as the United Kingdom, Sweden, and the Benelux countries, and stood 10th among California wine exporters. About 90 percent of its total production volume still consisted of processing bulk wine for other wineries. Over 40 wineries bought Delicato grapes; its wineries crushed and processed about 12 million cases per year for vintners such as Beringer, Canandaigua, Robert Mondavi, and Sutter Home. Another 1 million cases appeared under the inexpensive Delicato Family label. Monterra production had risen to around 60,000 cases. At San Bernabe, Delicato sold about 80 percent of the crop on contract or custom-crushed the fruit for wineries such as Bonny Doon, Estancia, Kendall-Jackson, J. Lohr and Joseph Phelps. Smith reserved the rest of his prized San Bernabe grapes for the Monterra and Delicato lines. Meanwhile, Vincent Indelicato stepped down as company president and Eric Morham, the first nonfamily executive, filled president and CEO roles in 1999. And, signaling its intentions to compete in the premium-wine market, Delicato in 2000 opened an executive office in the California wine capital Napa, and retained a public relations firm there to help promote its brands.

Reaping the Awards

Delicato's efforts to become a source of premium-wine grapes and its own premium wines paid dividends in July 2001 when it was named winner of the "Best USA Wine Producer" at the International Wine and Spirit Competition. Smith and third-generation family member Chris Indelicato, received the trophy at a black-tie event in London. The winery also won a total of six individual wine medals, including a gold for its Monterra 1998 Merlot. Afterward, the *San Francisco Chronicle* singled out Smith as one of its "winemakers to watch."

The same year the winery debuted a third brand. During the late 1990s, Delicato embarked on what became known as the Halo Project, an effort to create world-class, ultra-premium wine. The result was released in 2001 when 5,000 cases under the Delicato Monterey Vine Select label, retailing for around $40 a bottle, were released.

More good news followed during the early 2000s. An A.C. Nielsen market research report identified the Delicato Family Vineyards brand Shiraz (Syrah) as the top domestic Shiraz brand in the United States and number three behind imported Australian brands Rosemount and Lindermans. The winery's 2000 Shiraz also won two awards at the California State Fair Wine Competition. Later that year *Beverage Dynamics*, a leading beverage merchandising publication, recognized both Delicato Family Vineyards and Monterra brands in its annual survey of beverage industry sales leaders. The publication noted that Delicato Family Vineyards had shown 27.6 percent sales growth over the last four years, establishing it as one of the three fastest-growing premium-wine brands in the United States. The Monterra brand, it reported, had shown 25.7 percent growth since it was introduced in 1998. *Wine & Spirits* magazine, a popular national consumer wine publication, also named Monterra and Delicato Family Vineyards "Value Brands of the Year" in their June 2001 issue. The recognition continued into the next year when the Indelicato family was honored at the 2002 Legends of California annual fund-raising wine auction and dinner for contributions to the state's wine and grape-growing industries. The award had previously been won by such heralded California wine producers as the Mondavi and Sebastiani families.

Principal Subsidiaries

Delicato Monterey Winery; Delicato Vineyards (LLC).

Principal Competitors

Golden State Vineyards; Bronco Wine Company; Arroyo Secco Vineyards.

Further Reading

Boyd, Gerald D., "Delicato Family Vineyards," *Vineyard and Winery Management*, May 1999.
Boyd, Gerald D., and Karola Saekel, "Winemaker of the Year," *San Francisco Chronicle*, posted November 4, 2001, http://www.sfgate.com.
"Delicato Named Best U.S. Winery," *Business Wire*, posted June 26, 2001, http://www.lexis-nexis.com.
"Delicato Vineyards Admits Record-Keeping Violations, Winery to Pay $1 Million Fine," *Business Wire*, December 31, 1991, accessed April 23, 2002, http://www.lexis-nexis.com.
"Delicato, Prudential Announce Deal for 'Largest Vineyard in the Free World'," *Business Wire*, August 18, 1988, http://www.lexis-nexis.com.
Dunne, Mike, "Delicato Launches a More Refined Wine," *Fresno Bee*, May 16, 2001, p. E4.
Indelicato, Dorothy, and Arlene Mueller, *Wine, Food & the Good Life*, San Francisco: The Wine Appreciation Guild, 1993.
Laube, James, "California's Delicato Vineyards Expands from Bulk to Boutique," *Wine Spectator*, November 15, 1999.
Moran, Tim, "Delicato to Bottle Its Own Vintage," *Fresno Bee*, December 27, 1999, p. C1.
"San Joaquin County, Calif., Family Honored with Wine Award," *Knight-Ridder/Tribune Business News*, posted May 21, 2002, http://www.infotract.galegroup.com.
Sinton, Peter, "California Wines Quenching in the World," *San Francisco Chronicle*, posted January 23, 1999, http://www.sfgate.com.
——, "Growing Grapes for other Companies' Products," *San Francisco Chronicle*, July 31, 2001, p. E1.
Walker, Larry, "Affordable, Quality Wine for Troubled Times," *Business Wire*, posted October 26, 2001, http://www.lexis-nexis.com.
——, "The World's Biggest Little Vineyard Delicato/San Bernabe," *Wines & Vines*, January 2001, p. 16.

—Douglas Cooley

Digital River, Inc.

9625 W. 76th Street, Suite 150
Eden Prairie, Minnesota 55344
U.S.A.
Telephone: (952) 253-1234
Fax: (925) 253-8497
Web site: http://www.digitalriver.com

Public Company
Incorporated: 1994
Employees: 450
Sales: $57.8 million (2001)
Stock Exchanges: NASDAQ
Ticker Symbol: DRIV
NAIC: 454110 Electronic Shopping and Mail-Order
Houses; 541511 Custom Computer Programming
Services; 514210 Data Processing Services

Digital River, Inc. is helping to define its entire industry. It builds, hosts, and manages e-commerce Web sites and Internet marketing solutions that enable business-to-business and business-to-consumer clients to cut costs and grow revenue. Digital River supplies full-service e-commerce solutions that include site hosting and development, system integration, order management, e-marketing, fulfillment, and customer service. The company takes over buying, processing, payment and product delivery for clients' systems. Incorporated in Minnesota in February 1994 and reincorporated in Delaware in December 1997, Digital River has acquired many other companies—several at bottom-barrel prices—to build one of the most successful e-commerce service provider pioneers in the industry's relatively short history. The company has 450 employees with global operations headquartered in Eden Prairie, Minnesota, and offices in Chicago, Los Angeles, San Jose, and London. Currently counting 13,000 clients in its portfolio, Digital River has grown exponentially, even when similar companies have crashed and burned, and has succeeded by focusing on operations and costs, while many of its competitors pile up debt and burn through cash reserves.

By serving as a marketing intermediary and connecting software publishers and retailers to their online clients, Digital River has been likened by some to an online vending machine, but unlike the traditional vending machine, the services sold by Digital River do not end with the sale. The company also provides its retail clients with encryption software, high-speed Internet connections, marketing, and database management. All of these services are difficult for e-retailers to manage on their own, as they eat up time, money, and labor. With the aid of a central server and multiple software protections, Digital River takes the reins in providing thousands of clients with multiple ongoing e-services.

The Beginnings of Digital River

CEO and founder Joel Ronning had more than 20 years of experience developing computer technology before he came up with the idea behind Digital River. He founded Mirror Technologies, a manufacturer of Macintosh peripherals and components, in 1983, only to be pushed out by investors two years later. Rather than coddle a bruised ego, Ronning caught the competitive spirit and created a similar company in MacUSA—which eventually became Tech Squared, Inc.—and aggressively went after Mirror Technologies. Within three years, Ronning had acquired Mirror Technologies at a fire-sale price, and Tech Squared went on to reach sales of more than $46 million.

An epiphany struck Ronning in 1993 that eventually led to the creation of Digital River. He wondered why software was being sent in expensive packaging when it could more easily and affordably be transported directly to a person's computer via the Internet. Doing away with the cost of traditional packaging provided software publishers with a financial incentive to try digital delivery, while the electronic solution also appealed to Ronning's environmentally conscious interests.

A New Way of Acquiring Software

In August 1994, with $1 million in start-up funds—$800,000 from Fujitsu Ltd. of Japan, one of Tech Squared's primary suppliers—Ronning amassed a group of programmers to develop a system that would distribute software digitally. The company eventually took out 12 patents for the encryption model developed by these employees. At the time, the Internet was being used primarily as a tool for the government and academics; Ronning's plan was to distribute software via bulletin board servers, the most feasible technology. But by 1996, the Internet had exploded in popularity and reach, offering a far better opportunity to realize Digital River's objective of delivering software swiftly and efficiently throughout the world. Utilizing the Internet as its core technology, Digital River grew rapidly, with sales soaring from $2 million in 1997 to $21 million in 1998. Although the company posted a net loss of $13.8 million in 1998, it was on the right track, with a company-wide profit safely projected for 2001.

One key to Digital River's success was its capability to allow retailers to sell software to customers in such a way that the client never knew they had left the retailer's Web page. For example, when customers of Major League Baseball, who teamed up with Digital River in May 2001, wanted to make a purchase through any of the 30 Major League Baseball franchise Web sites, they automatically moved electronically to Digital River for completion of the transaction. But all signs—including logos—made the purchase appear to be taking place through Major League Baseball. A proprietary Digital River security code, called the Software Defense Mechanism, shielded the system from hackers and offered security to users making credit card purchases.

Digital River's technology was not limited to software. Any digital information could be purchased online, including music and movies. E-commerce had become one of the purest ways of conducting business and Digital River was quickly becoming an important player in the arena. In July 1999, Digital River added to its downloadable software the capability to deliver Internet music.

In 1996 the company created an innovative digital commerce model and established its Software and Digital Commerce Services Division. Specializing in software, retail, education and shareware, this division offered digital tools for volume licensing and flexible e-catalogs to help clients design, manage, and grow Web commerce.

Digital River Goes Public and Experiences Exponential Growth

A few months before going public in the summer of 1998, Digital River signed an agreement with *USA Today* to enable software to be sold via the *USA Today* Web site. Digital River already held similar arrangements with 90 other Web sites, but *USA Today* was an especially sweet deal, as its site was one of

the most popular on the Internet at the time. Digital River was claiming 5 million online visitors each month via all of its affiliate Web sites and expected to grow to 25 million visitors by the following year, with the help of acquisitions like the *USA Today* account.

Digital River went public on August 10, 1998, selling 3 million shares at $8.50 and garnering roughly $23 million after fees. At the time of the initial public offering (IPO), Digital River held contracts with 1,222 software publishers and 346 online retailers, including Corel, Lotus Development, Micro Warehouse, Network Associates and Symantec, among many others. The company maintained a database of roughly 123,000 software products from a variety of software publishers, including 18,000 titles and over 105,000 digital images, such as photos, clip art and typeface fonts.

Fourth-quarter earnings in 1998 were up 600 percent over 1997. The stock price rose 354 percent in its first year, with a second offering in December netting another $47 million and bringing the company's year-end total cash and investments to nearly $74 million.

In April 1999, Digital River reinforced its already strong industry position by acquiring Public Software Library and Maagnum Internet Group, two privately held companies that distributed software programs via the Web for some 2,500 shareware publishers. The company paid $6.5 million in stock and $2.5 million cash for Public Software Library and $5.2 million in stock for Maagnum. Both companies had been two of the largest distributors of registration codes, required to make downloaded software products work after trial periods expired. The acquisitions gave Digital River even further-reaching access to more shareware publishers.

Video game king Sega signed on with Digital River in July 1999, utilizing the e-commerce outsource provider's flagship platform offering, CommerceBridge. This partnership was Digital River's first foray into the lucrative gaming market, helping to significantly build the company's customer base.

CommerceBridge consisted of ten e-commerce modules from which a client could choose those that best fit their needs. The modules offered Web store hosting, transaction processing, security, data center management, fraud prevention, order tracking, online reporting, marketing and merchandising, customer and distribution fulfillment, and customer service. This plethora of services appealed to IT managers looking for the advantages of an e-commerce Web site, but not the negative aspects of internally maintaining such a challenging, expensive and time-consuming infrastructure. The average cost of developing and launching an e-commerce site was reaching $1 million with a timeline between five and 12 months; Digital River was able to charge $100,000 for comparable sites, with a deployment timeline of two to four weeks.

Building on Success

Many of the most popular computer utilities were now available for download directly from the Internet. Primarily freeware or shareware, these programs cost next to nothing to procure. Directly related to their low or nonexistent price tags, personal computer users downloaded these programs in droves.

One negative aspect of such nondiscriminate downloading was that people often forgot which programs they had added to their machine.

Enter a new Digital River service, eBot. Introduced in September 1999, eBot scanned hard drives and automatically offered to update software with the latest versions, a benefit to the average PC user who did not know how to locate upgrades and fixes for their software. This approach to downloaded software maintenance was hardly new, as Symantec had been offering a similar product for some time, but eBot hoped to lure customers with improvements such as a sophisticated download manager that would let users schedule, monitor and control various software transfers. If a download was stopped or interrupted for any reason, the manager knew exactly how to continue where it left off. eBot not only fixed problems, as similar programs had done, but it actively sought the problems out, as well. More than 95 percent of the products offered via eBot were free, making it a relatively low-revenue venture for Digital River, but the company believed the product would bring much-needed visibility. In March 2000, *The Business Journal* recognized Digital River as Electronic Distributor of the Year, for continuing to blaze a trail for electronic software distribution.

Ronning had the foresight to bet his business on the assumption that traditional channel models would evolve into electronic delivery. As online sales grew, he again had the wherewithal to think ahead of the curve and branch out into marketing, launching the E-Marketing Services Division. The purpose of this new, separate division was to use strategic planning to plan, execute, track and evaluate clients' online businesses to capture yet another piece of the e-commerce pie. By using direct mailing, campaign management, e-mail list servers and merchandising programs, Digital River was poised to create integrated online marketing plans to help clients grow their online businesses.

In early 2000, Digital River launched two new services calculated to facilitate returns for e-commerce purchases and create a managed Web presence for new distribution channels. The E-Returns Management System and E-Reseller Network System resolved possible conflicts around channel management by helping manufacturers uphold sell-side dealer and distributor relationships while increasing direct distribution channels.

August 2000 saw Digital River expand its business-to-business services to encompass more sophisticated and integrated e-commerce systems. The company was evolving into a full-service commerce service provider, leasing software and entire services on the Internet. Digital River announced a $2.75 million customer service center upgrade that included the integration of Siebel Systems' Siebel Call Center 2000 and Siebel

eService. This move was made in hope that it would double response capability by the end of 2000, with the ultimate goal of achieving 100 percent customer satisfaction.

A Change of Strategy in 2001

Digital River had originally focused on the software industry because they were the early adopters of the Internet, but seeing a shift back to the traditional business-to-business model, the company moved to the e-business model to support manufacturers. The company took a step away from its software distribution roots and embraced high-end non-software clients such as corporate giants Coors, Nabisco, and 3M. Grasping the business adage to embrace change or die, Digital River watched the e-business stock crash and its successful, reasonably secure business formula be knocked around by a swiftly changing, unforgiving marketplace. Unlike many of their competitors, Digital River struck out for different ground, offering its e-services to the traditional corporate market.

Acquisitions had become a key component of Digital River's long-term growth strategy. To that end, the company moved to obtain struggling e-commerce outsourcers that were weighing exit strategies, with established client bases and viable platforms. Digital River's E-Rescue Program was launched to assist companies left behind by e-commerce service providers that were failing or no longer in business. The E-Rescue Program was created to help victims smoothly move operations from their current, failing providers to Digital River.

Third-quarter numbers for Digital River had shot up, representing a year-over-year increase of 84 percent. This solid performance marked two noteworthy company milestones. For the first time since becoming a public company, Digital River recorded positive earnings before interest, taxes, depreciation and amortization. Secondly, September was the first month that Digital River achieved profitability on a company-wide basis, before goodwill amortization and acquisition-related costs.

Digital River and its CEO Joel Ronning have been recognized for many prestigious industry awards. Ronning was named Ernst & Young's Entrepreneur of the Year in 2000 and Digital River was lauded as one of the top 100 Internet companies by *Internet World* in the same year. The company made *Interactive Week*'s 2001 Interactive 500 in 2001, while Ronning was named of one *VARBusiness* magazine's 2001 Top 20 Visionaries and *CRN* magazine's 2001 Top 25 Executives.

Principal Divisions

E-Business Services; E-Marketing Services; E-Products; Software & Digital Commerce Services.

Principal Competitors

CyberSource; Network Commerce; Scient.

Further Reading

Black, Jason, "Baseball's E-Commerce Pitch," *Internet World*, September 15, 2001, p. 14.
Blank, Dennis, "Fraud Problems Take High-Tech Priority," *Bank Technology News*, September 2001, p. 12.

Claburn, Thomas, "Take Me to the River: Joel Ronning Rides the E-Commerce Rapids," *Ziff David Smart Business for the New Economy*, May 1, 2001, p. 46.

Clancy, Heather, "First Step: Better Management of Businesses' Software Assets: Digital River Looks at Electronic Licensing," *Computer Reseller News*, December 6, 1999, p. 89.

Dalton, Gregory, "Oversees Fraud Finder," *Information Week*, September 27, 1999, pp. 382–383.

Gilyard, Burl, "The Entrepreneur," *Corporate Report-Minnesota*, October 1998, p. 40.

Hibbard, Justin, "Top Retailers to Sell Software Via Internet," *Information Week*, January 4, 1999, p. 26.

Jaleshgari, Ramin, P., "On the Fast Track: These Hot Integrators Broke Growth Records—and the VAR Mold," *VARBusiness*, July 5, 1999, p. 39.

Kindley, Mark, "Feel the Power: The Channel Still Rules," *VARBusiness*, June 14, 1999, p. 5.

Kutler, Jeffrey, "Joel Ronning of Digital River: Turning the E-Corner," *Institutional Investor*, February 2002, pp. 22–24.

Madden, John, "Digital River to Manage Sega's Online Game Store," *PC Week*, July 19, 1999, p. 58.

Moriarity, Michelle, "Assisting the Online Gold Rush," *Computer User*, February 1999, p. 50.

Nelson, Matthew, "E-Commerce Companies Get Help with Returns," *Information Week*, February 7, 2000, p. 101.

Senia, Al, "Nabisco Enters the Internet Age: A Reinvented Digital River Takes Retailer into Digital Space," *VARBusiness*, January 22, 2001, p. 34.

——, "The New Science of Selling: As IT Loses Its Grasp on Corporate Decision-Making, Solution Providers Engage a New Breed of Tech-Savvy Business Manager," *VARBusiness*, March 5, 2001, p. 8.

——, "Service after the Sale: Inside E-Marketing," *VARBusiness*, January 22, 2001, p. 36.

Stone, Adam, "Midwest Company Contradicts Rumor That E-Commerce Has Died," *Silicon Valley/San Jose Business Journal*, November 16, 2001, p. 19.

Stone, Elaine Ellis, "Growth Spurt: Digital River Impresses the Industry and Investors," *Corporate Report-Minnesota*, June 1999, p. 32.

——, "Rapid Run," *Corporate Report-Minnesota*, May 1999, p. 20.

Torode, Christina, "Computer Reseller News' Top 25 Executives of 2001," *CRN*, November 12, 2001, p. 133.

Vizard, Michael, "Digital River CTO Advocates CSP Model," *InfoWorld*, September 18, 2000, p. 36.

Vogel, Andrew, "From the Research Desk: Bigger than the 500," *VARBusiness*, June 14, 1999, p. 46.

—Stacee Sledge

The Dow Chemical Company

2030 Willard H. Dow Center
Midland, Michigan 48674
U.S.A.
Telephone: (989) 636-1000
Toll Free: (800) 422 -8193
Fax: (989) 636-1830
Web site: http://www.dow.com

Public Company
Incorporated: 1947
Employees: 50,000
Sales: $27.8 billion (2001)
Stock Exchanges: Amsterdam Bavarian Berlin Brussels
Chicago Düsseldorf Germany Hamburg Hanover
London New York Pacific Paris Stuttgart
Switzerland Tokyo
Ticker Symbol: DOW (New York)
NAIC: 325131 Inorganic Dye and Pigment
Manufacturing; 325188 All Other Basic Inorganic
Chemical Manufacturing; 325211 Plastics Material
and Resin Manufacturing; 325611 Soap and Other
Detergent Manufacturing; 325612 Polish and Other
Sanitation Goods Manufacturing; 326122 Plastics Pipe
and Pipe Fitting Manufacturing; 326130 Laminated
Plastics Plate, Sheet, and Shape Manufacturing;
326150 Urethane and Other Foam Product (Except
Polystyrene) Manufacturing

To say that The Dow Chemical Company is a very large chemical company is an understatement. At the end of 2001, Dow took over du Pont as the largest chemicals company in the United States. At last count the company offered more than 2,000 different products. Approximately half of Dow's income comes from basic chemicals, but plastics, specialty chemicals, consumer products, and pharmaceuticals are also important to the company.

The Early Years

Herbert Dow began his career around 1890, when he convinced three Cleveland businessmen to back his latest project, which involved the extraction of bromide from brine. Dow's idea was to extract the huge underground reservoirs of brine, souvenirs of prehistoric times when Lake Michigan had been a sea. This brine was being used for salt, but Dow was determined to distill bromides and other chemicals from it. His first venture, called Canton Chemical, failed and was superseded by Dow Chemical.

Dow's use of an electric current to separate bromides from the brine was revolutionary. He was experimenting with electrolysis at a time when the electric light bulb was still viewed with suspicion. (At the time, President Harrison refused to touch the newly installed light switches in the White House for fear of electrocution.) However, Dow constructed primitive cells from wood and tar paper, and began producing bromides, as well as bleaching agents, for another fledgling company by the name of Kodak.

In the first years of this century, Dow began to sell his bromides abroad, but the Deutsche Bromkonvention, a powerful group of German bromide producers, declared an all-out price war against Dow Chemical. German and British bleach makers (bromide is used in bleach) reduced the price of their product from $1.65 to $.88 a pound in the United States, which was less than cost. Dow's plants depended on a price of $1.65 in order to make a profit. While other American bleach makers closed for the duration of the price war, Dow went deeper into debt and fought for his share of the domestic and foreign markets. One of his successful tactics was to purchase the imported bromide that the Germans were selling in New York at a price below cost, and then resell it in Europe where the price of bromide was still $1.65 per pound.

Resilience through War and Depression

After the bromide war came World War I, which, among other things, ended German domination of the world chemical industry. The German naval blockade forced American industry to turn to American chemical makers for essential supplies.

160

Company Perspectives:

To constantly improve what is essential to human progress by mastering science and technology.

Dow was pressed into the manufacture of phenol, used in explosives, and magnesium, used in incendiary devices. At the time these two substances had limited use outside of munitions, but they were later to play an important role in the development of Dow Chemical and the chemical industry in general. Phenol would become a key ingredient required for the manufacture of plastics, and magnesium would make aviation history.

After the war, Congress protected the fledgling American chemical industry by imposing tariffs, so that the country would not become dependent on foreign chemical manufacturers again. By 1920 Dow Chemical was selling $4 million worth of bulk chemicals like chlorine, calcium chloride, salt, and aspirin every year. By 1930 sales had climbed to $15 million and the company stock had split four times. Before the stock market crashed in 1929 the price per share had climbed to $500.

Dow's success drew the attention of du Pont, which wished to acquire the Midwestern bromide manufacturer until Herbert Dow threatened to leave the company and take his engineers with him. Without Herbert Dow's leadership and ingenuity the company was not regarded as worth the price of purchase and du Pont subsequently withdrew its offer.

Herbert Dow died just as the Depression began and was replaced by his son Willard. Willard Dow, like his father, considered research, as opposed to production or sales, the key to the company's future. Despite the state of the economy, Willard Dow approved expenditures for research into petrochemicals and plastics. The company's product line expanded to include iodine, ethylene, and materials to flush out oil from the ground. A new plant was constructed that would extract bromine from seawater. There was also a rumor on Wall Street that Dow's new method could extract gold from the seawater. The rumor turned out to be true. However, for every $300 worth of gold, $6,000 worth of bromine could be recovered.

World War II: Depression-Era Strategies Pay Off

During World War II, Dow Chemical's new research resulted in handsome rewards. Even before America's entrance into the war, Dow had started to expand in preparation for future hostilities. One of its first wartime contracts was with the British, who desperately needed magnesium. Dow produced some of this metal at its new plant in Freeport, Texas, which extracted magnesium from seawater. Dow later supplied the metal to the United States and even shared its patented process with other companies. In 1943, Dow and Corning Glass formed Dow Corning, a company that manufactured silicone products for the army. The company later expanded into civilian markets.

Before World War II the potential value of magnesium in the manufacture of airplanes had gone unnoticed, and during this time Dow Chemical was the only U.S. magnesium producer. Yet even with a monopoly on the metal, the company lost money on its production. This was typical of Dow Chemical at that time; it often invented a product and then patiently waited for a market. During the war, Dow produced over 80 percent of the magnesium used by the United States, which later led to federal investigations into whether or not Dow had conspired to monopolize magnesium production in the country. The U.S. press, however, sided with Dow and eventually the charges, which had included accusations of a conspiracy with German magnesium manufacturers, were dropped.

Besides manufacturing magnesium the company also made styrene and butadiene for synthetic rubber. During World War II the Japanese had conquered the rubber plantations of the Far East and soon this commodity was in short supply. Due to the fact that Dow had persisted in plastics research during the Depression, it was at the forefront of manufacturing synthetic products, including rubber. Besides making styrene and butadiene, it molded Saran plastic, now known as a food wrap, into pipes, or had it woven into insect screens to protect soldiers fighting in the tropics.

Postwar Expansion

After the war the company had to adapt to the postwar economy. One of management's concerns was that Dow Chemical had placed such a strong emphasis on research and development in the past that it sometimes ignored the fact that it was supposed to be making profits. The Marketing and Sales departments were reluctantly increased. Said one man employed at the time, "You got the feeling that Willard looked on sales as a necessary evil."

Despite the fact that Dow had to share trade secrets with its competitors during the war, it ranked as the sixth largest chemical company in the country and was well positioned to take advantage of the increasing peacetime demand for chemicals. Its product line was extensive and included chemicals used in almost every conceivable industry. Bulk chemicals accounted for 50 percent of sales and plastics accounted for 20 percent of sales, while magnesium, pharmaceuticals, and agricultural chemicals each accounted for 10 percent of sales.

Dow expanded significantly during the postwar period, going heavily into debt in order to finance its growth. The man who presided over this expansion was Willard Dow's brother-in-law, Lee Doan (Willard Dow had been killed in a plane crash). One of Doan's first tasks was to reorganize the company and make it more customer-oriented. Willard's and Herbert Dow's tenures had been previously described by insiders as "capricious." The emphasis now was on long-range planning.

In the year of Willard's death, 1949, sales were $200 million, but ten years later they had nearly quadrupled. Products such as Saran Wrap began to make Dow a high-profile company. Dow's growth surpassed that of its competitors, and the company was soon ranked fourth in the industry. The company's plants had previously been located in Texas and Michigan, but during the 1950s important production centers were built elsewhere. Foreign partnerships like Ashai Dow in Japan were formed, and the company expanded its presence in the European market.

Key Dates:

1897: Herbert Dow founds The Dow Chemical Company.
1900: Dow and Midland Chemical Company merge.
1906: The company produces their first agricultural product.
1933: Dow begins extracting bromine from seawater.
1935: Dow enters the plastics business.
1937: Dow is listed on the NYSE on June 26.
1942: Dow's first international expansion begins with Dow Chemical Canada, Ltd.
1943: Dow and Corning Glass merge to form the Dow Corning Company, specializing in silicone products.
1952: Dow establishes Ashai-Dow in Japan, its first subsidiary outside North America.
1953: Saran Wrap becomes a household product.
1964: Dow exceeds $1 billion in annual sales.
1968: Ziploc bags are test-marketed.
1970: The company introduces an automotive product line.
1972: Dow introduces the insecticide Lorsban.
1973: Dow becomes the first foreign industrial company listed on the Tokyo Stock Exchange.
1989: Dow and Eli Lilly form DowElanco, a joint venture to produce agricultural products.
1996: Du Pont Dow Elastomers, a Dow-du Pont joint venture, begins operations.
1997: Dow buys Eli Lilly's share in DowElanco.
1998: DowElanco is renamed Dow AgroSciences, and the DowBrands unit is sold to S.C. Johnson & Son.
1999: Dow announces plans to merge with Union Carbide.
2001: The Dow-Union Carbide merger is finalized.

Restructuring, Growth, and Controversy

Dow began the 1960s with a change of leadership. Ted Doan succeeded his father and, with Ben Branch and Carl Gerstacker, reorganized the company. Communication had become a problem because of Dow's vast size, so the company was broken into more manageable units that could be run like small businesses. Marketing, however, became more centralized. The management liked to think of their company as democratic, with overlapping lines of responsibility. The structure of the company was deliberately arranged so that employees would use their own initiative to invent new products and to manufacture existing products at a lower cost. The strategy worked.

In 1960, Dow purchased Allied Labs, thus entering the world of pharmaceuticals. Also in the early 1960s, Dow Corning began collaborating with two Texas plastic surgeons, Frank Gerow and Thomas Cronin, on silicone breast implants. This venture would spell trouble for Dow Corning and its parent companies, some 30 years later.

Throughout the 1960s, Dow's earnings increased approximately 10 percent each year. Among the company's hundreds of products, however, one began to receive an inordinate amount of publicity—napalm. Beginning in 1966 the company became the target of anti-Vietnam War protests. Company recruiters were overrun on college campuses by large numbers of placard-waving students. Dow defended its manufacture of the

searing chemical by saying that it was not responsible for U.S. policy in Indochina and that it should not deprive American fighting men of a weapon that the Pentagon thought was necessary. Critics charged that the gruesomeness of the weapon made it imperative for the company not to cooperate with the government. Right or wrong, the public outcry against Dow demoralized a company that wanted to be associated with Handi Wrap rather than with civilian Vietnamese casualties.

The Troubled 1970s

At the beginning of the 1970s, *Forbes* magazine predicted that Dow would have trouble growing because of its indebtedness. In 1974, however, the same *Forbes* reporter was subjected to criticism by CEO Carl Gerstacker because Dow had a record year. The oil embargo benefited Dow since it had its own petroleum feedstock with which to manufacture its various specialty chemicals; its competitors could not find the necessary petroleum. Noted Gerstacker: "Price wasn't the problem in '74; it was availability." Dow increased the price of many of its chemicals and its earnings increased, despite a strike in its hometown of Midland, Michigan. After the six-month strike, Dow gave the strikers a 10 percent bonus and gave each pensioner $2,000 worth of bonds. Company stockholders did not mind management's sudden display of generosity; that year they received a 30 percent return on equity.

The year 1975 was followed by an oversupply of petrochemicals and a business slowdown, and the company's earnings began to slide. Since the company was doing almost half of its business overseas, an unfavorable rate of exchange added to the above problems.

By 1978 a change of leadership was deemed necessary; Gerstacker's retirement from the board of directors was the end of an era. Carl Gerstacker's management strategy was, "you should have as much debt as you can carry." During recessions and slowdowns, borrowed money was used for research and development as well as plant expansion. He was an administrator in the tradition of Herbert Dow, but the moves that had catapulted Dow to a position of leadership in the chemical industry seemed unwise in the business climate of the late 1970s. P.F. Oreffice, who Gerstacker had referred to as "a little old lady in tennis shoes" because of his conservative fiscal policy, became president and CEO.

Recession and Recovery: The 1980s

Soon after his promotion, Oreffice reorganized Dow as most of his predecessors had done after their appointment. These frequent reorganizations were less a testimony to the inadequacy of the previous organization than an admission that the company was outgrowing previously successful arrangements. This time management was reorganized on a geographical basis, since Dow had plants all over the world. In 1980, the year of the reorganization, sales exceeded $10 billion for the first time.

In the early 1980s a pattern of write-offs that depressed earnings began to emerge. In 1983 the write-off of two ethylene plants and a caustic soda plant caused earnings to drop 16 percent. Ethylene, a lead additive that prevents knocking in automobile engines, had been an important product for Dow at one time. In 1985 earnings fell 90 percent from the previous year as additional ethylene plants were closed.

Another factor that depressed 1985 products was the decrease in price and demand for basic chemicals. Dow derived 50 percent of its income from commodity chemicals that are sold by the ton. Foreign competitors, Arab chemical companies in particular, invaded the American market in the same way that Dow once invaded the European bromide market. To make matters worse, the market for commodity chemicals is sensitive to world economic conditions. Dow's position as an American company complicated matters further. When the dollar was strong, as it was in 1984 and part of 1985, the company's exports were harder to sell and its foreign earnings, when converted to dollars, were smaller.

In 1981, Dow purchased Merrell Drug, thus expanding its Pharmaceutical division. With the purchase Dow assumed liability for Bendectin, an antinausea drug that was blamed for birth defects. Despite the fact that Dow won practically all law suits (independent studies proved no connection between the drug and birth defects), the cost of continuing litigation forced the company to take Bendectin off the market.

In 1984, Dow purchased Texize, which boasted a strong line of detergent products, from Morton Thiokol. Research spending remained at almost 90 percent of cash flow. Extra-strong ceramics and plastics for the electronics industry are among the numerous specialty chemicals that Dow hoped would account for two-thirds of its sales in the 1990s. The company still placed a premium on innovation, however, and stated that it anticipated placing 15 to 25 new products on the market each year. However, some felt that the expansion into pharmaceuticals, specialty chemicals, and household products, required a new approach to management. According to an analyst with Kidder and Peabody, "If you're running a monolithic chemical business, management is the same across all products. Now they're going to have hundreds of small businesses to manage."

The company appointed a new chairman of the board, Robert Lundeen, and launched a new ad campaign, in which working for Dow was equated with "doing something for the world." Eager to rid itself of the adverse publicity surrounding topics such as Vietnam and alleged environmental abuse, Dow actually supported an increase in the Environmental Protection Agency's budget and a strengthening of rules regarding hazardous waste. This marked a significant philosophical turnaround for a company that had argued against a ban on dioxin in the 1970s.

Despite its changes in management, however, Dow was hurting in 1985, as it failed to recapture market share lost during the 1980 to 1982 recession. Profits tumbled from $805 million in 1980 to $58 million in 1985. Frank Popoff was promoted to president and CEO from his position as head of Dow Chemical/ Europe. Largely on the strength of Popoff's decisions, the firm improved marketing and sales of value-added products, which commanded higher prices. Dow began to win market share in this higher-margin area as it increasingly concentrated on finding new applications for existing products.

The company's efforts found a ready-made market in the auto industry, which was in the midst of a campaign to increase efficiency and cut costs. Dow concentrated on other durable

sectors as well, like appliances, housewares, and electronics. It also looked into packaging and the recreation and healthcare industries. Since Dow already made so many plastics, chemicals, and hydrocarbons cheaply, increased sales of these products at higher margins offered an immediate hike in profits. This strategy was immediately successful, and the company received a further boost when the U.S. dollar began to fall, making it easier for Dow to sell against German companies and other competitors.

Oil prices fell in 1986, further feeding Dow's recovery. With the dollar continuing to fall and the world economy humming, the spread between raw material costs and final prices expanded until the firm's plastics business was making a record 25 to 30 percent on sales during mid-1987.

Dow continued to diversify through acquisition, but tried to concentrate on firms with a base in chemicals, paying special heed to firms with technologies or distribution systems deemed not practical for Dow to develop internally. A joint venture in agricultural chemicals, called DowElanco, was begun with Eli Lilly. Dow acquired 39 percent of Marion Laboratories, a pharmaceuticals firm, for $2.2 billion, then joined it with Dow Merrell, making it a public company with a 67 percent Dow stake.

By 1988 commodity chemicals accounted for just 53 percent of the firm's $13.3 billion in sales. Its move into pharmaceuticals was proving to be a success, with $1.1 billion in sales a year. Its star drug was Seldane, an antihistamine with sales that were reaching hundreds of millions of dollars. In 1989, Merrel Dow's Pharmaceutical division merged with Marion Labs to form Marion Merrel Dow, in which Dow had a 71 percent stake. Total Dow sales for 1989 reached $17.6 billion, an increase of $7 billion over five years earlier, with profits up to $2.5 billion.

The 1990s and Beyond

In 1990 the world economy headed into recession. As in past recessions, the chemical industry, plagued by overcapacity, began a price war and began cutting output. Dow was the leading low-cost producer of commodity chemicals, hydrocarbons, and plastics. Rather than cut capacity, Dow continued to produce chemicals at a lower profit margin in the hopes of keeping its market share and driving out weaker competitors. Profits fell, but the company maintained its position in the marketplace; even du Pont was forced to cut production of polymers.

The Persian Gulf War temporarily caused the price of oil to rise, further hurting Dow. When the war ended, the slowdown in the chemical industry continued. Many in the industry believed that it was just another cycle in a cyclical industry. Frank Popoff, however, maintained that the slowdown represented a more fundamental shift in the industry, one that was eroding the advantages of bigger firms. The strategy, Popoff felt, was now to be as lean and fast as small firms while maintaining an R&D advantage.

Despite these beliefs, Dow was forced to build new plants for commodity chemicals when a Canadian supplier decided to become a competitor. Dow began building ethylene plants in Alberta, Canada, and Freeport, Texas. Even after 40 years in Asia, sales there still accounted for less than 10 percent, while

European sales accounted for 31 percent of total sales. But with Europe mired in recession and European sales slowing, Dow began pushing into Asia again, building a petrochemicals plant in China, where it enjoyed an expanding polyurethane business. Though its growth had been slowed by the downturn in chemicals, Dow had nevertheless reduced its dependence on commodity chemicals from 80 percent of sales in 1980 to 45 percent in 1992, making it one of the world's most diversified chemical firms.

With success came growing controversy. Starting in the early 1980s, Dow Corning faced questions and lawsuits regarding the safety of its silicone breast implants. Many women claimed to have developed autoimmune diseases as a result of silicone leakage from the implants. Faced with many individual lawsuits, as well as class action suits, Dow Corning filed for Chapter 11 bankruptcy protection in 1995, and settled with breast implant recipients for $3.2 billion. Dow, however, as a 50 percent shareholder in Dow Corning, was named in many individual lawsuits. Both Dow and Corning (the other 50 percent shareholder) were still attempting to reach a settlement of these suits in 2002. Interestingly, as of 2001, with over 20 independent studies done, no causal relationship between silicone breast implants and autoimmune diseases (or cancer) has been established.

Another controversy erupted on August 4, 1999, when Dow announced plans to merge with Union Carbide, one of the world's leading manufacturers of polyethylene plastics, and a pioneer in the petrochemical industry. The announcement drew fire from various groups, including Dow shareholders. At issue was Union Carbide's reputation, and possible continuing liability, following the Bhopal gas leak disaster in India ("The world's worst industrial accident"). Plans for the $11.6 billion merger nevertheless moved on. To receive clearance from the Federal Trade Commission (FTC) and international regulators, Dow agreed to divest itself of a number of polyethylene plants worldwide. The FTC granted approval for the merger on February 5, 2001. Union Carbide became a wholly owned subsidiary of Dow.

Throughout the 1990s and into the new millennium, Dow continued to reinvent itself through sales and acquisitions of various assets. In 1995 Dow sold its stake in Marion Merrel Dow to Hoechst for $7.1 billion. In 1998 its consumer products subsidiary, known as DowBrands, was sold to S.C. Johnson & Son. DowBrands included the Home Food Management unit, responsible for familiar names such as Ziploc and Saran Wrap. The second DowBrands unit, Home Care Products, made products such as Spray 'N Wash and Fantastik. Dow purchased ANGUS Chemical from TransCanada Pipelines in 1999. In 2000 it acquired General Latex Chemical Corporation and Flexible Products Company, both manufacturers of foam products. Another foam business, Celotex Corporation (makers of foam

insulation) was purchased in 2001. The same year Dow expanded its agricultural product line by acquiring the agricultural chemicals arm of Rohm and Haas.

The recession that began in late 2001 did not spare the chemical giant, and Dow announced a workforce reduction of 8 percent. Dow seemed to bounce back with stronger earnings at the start of 2002. In June 2002, Dow was awarded the National Medal of Technology "for the vision to create great science and innovative technology in the chemical industry and the positive impact that commercialization of this technology has had on society," according to the official citation.

Principal Subsidiaries

Compañía Mega SA (28%); Dow AgroScience; Dow Automotive; Dow Corning Corporation (50%); du Pont Dow Elastomers LLC (50%); EQUATE Petrochemical Company K.S.C. (45%); Mycogen Corporation; Nippon Unicar Company Limited (50%); Petromont and Company, Limited Partnership (50%); Total Raffinaderij Nederland NV (45%); UCAR Emulsion Systems; Union Carbide; UOP LLC (50%).

Principal Competitors

BASF AG; Bayer AG; du Pont; BP Chemicals; BP; Eastman Chemical; Novartis.

Further Reading

"Chronology of Silicone Breast Implants," *Frontline: Breast Implants on Trial*, program transcript, accessed August 10, 2002, http://www.pbs.org.

Cimons, Marlene, "Long Shunned, Morning Sickness Drug May Be Staging a Comeback," *Los Angeles Times*, December 7, 2000.

Donnelly, Francis X., "Dow-Carbide Merger Assailed," *Detroit News*, May 12, 2000, http://detnews.com.

"DowBrands Sells Business to S.C. Johnson & Son, Inc.," *PR Newswire*, October 28, 1998, http://prnewswire.com.

"The Dow Chemical Company Wins the National Medal of Technology," *PR Newswire*, May 9, 2002, http://prnewswire.com.

Duerksen, Christopher J., *Dow vs. California: A Turning Point in the Envirobusiness Struggle*, Washington, DC: Conservation Foundation, 1982.

Harman, Adrienne, "Metamorphosis," *Financial World*, February 2, 1993.

"International Company News Richardson," *The Globe and Mail*, March 19, 1981.

Meyer, Richard, "Avoiding the Fifth," *Financial World*, November 15, 1988.

Poland, Alan Blair, *A History of the Dow Chemical Company*, Ann Arbor: University Microfilms, 1980.

Quickel, Stephen, "Uncle!," *Financial World*, May 15, 1990.

—updates: Scott M. Lewis, Adi R. Ferrara

E.On AG

E.On AG
E.On-Platz 1
40479 Düsseldorf
Germany
Telephone: +49 (211) 4579-0
Fax: +49 (211) 4579-501
Web site: http://www.eon-ag.com

Public Company
Incorporated: 2000
Employees: 151,953 (2001)
Sales: EUR 80 billion (US $78.2 billion) (2001)
Stock Exchanges: Frankfurt New York
Ticker Symbol: EOA, EON
NAIC: 221111 Hydroelectric Power Generation; 221112 Fossil Fuel Electric Power Generation; 221113 Nuclear Electric Power Generation; 221119 Other Electric Power Generation; 422690 Other Chemical and Allied Products Wholesalers; 211111 Crude Petroleum and Natural Gas Extraction; 221121 Electric Bulk Power Transmission and Control; 213111 Drilling Oil and Gas Wells; 213112 Support for Oil and Gas Operations; 324110 Petroleum Refineries; 211112 Natural Gas Liquid Extraction; 221210 Natural Gas Distribution; 325120 Industrial Gas Manufacturing; 422720 Petroleum and Petroleum Products Wholesalers (Except Bulk Stations and Terminals); 562211 Hazardous Waste Treatment and Disposal; 562112 Hazardous Waste Collection; 924110 Administration of Air and Water Resource and Solid Waste Management Programs; 523110 Investment Banking and Securities Dealing; 234930 Industrial Non-Building Structure Construction

E.On AG is the largest listed power generation company in Europe. The company was formed through the 2000 merger of VIAG AG and VEBA AG, companies that were initially founded in the 1920s. In their early years, VIAG had specialized in aluminum, electricity, and nitrogen, while VEBA had focused on coal and petroleum exploration and production. Both companies grew rapidly and prospered during the armament years before World War II and during the war as companies operated by the German Reich. They struggled financially during the post-war years of occupation by the Allies and oil crises of the 1970s. However, in the 1980s, the two companies privatized and diversified along similar timelines to emerge as prosperous conglomerates encompassing aluminum, energy production, telecommunications, chemicals, and upstream and downstream oil industry. By the late 1990s, it was no longer profitable to compete in so many areas, so VIAG and VEBA merged to become E.On in 2000, focusing on the core industries of energy and chemicals, and selling aluminum, oil, and telecommunications interests to corporations that specialized in these areas.

VIAG's Origins

The beginnings of VIAG (Vereinigte Industrie-Unternehmungen Aktiengesellschaft) date back to World War I. Soon after the beginning of World War I, it became clear that a free enterprise economy would not be able to satisfy wartime production requirements, and that for many sectors a state-run economy was necessary. As early as August 13, 1914, the Kriegsrohstoff-Abteilung (KRA—War Commodities Department) of the Prussian War Ministry was founded, to guarantee the supply of raw materials needed for military purposes. In other words, these were materials for the arms industry, for clothing, and for other military equipment.

The KRA used new Kriegsgesellschaften (war companies) to procure the required products or to arrange for their procurement or manufacture. Kriegsmetall AG, Kriegschemikalien AG, and Kriegswollbedarfs AG were only a few of these large-scale organizations. As a consequence of the economic measures connected with the Hindenburg Program—a plan developed in 1916 to strengthen the adaptation of German industry for armaments production—the Prussian War Ministry combined under one organization all the military raw materials businesses and the procurement of substitutes by establishing the Kriegsamt (KA—War Office) for the entire Reich in November 1916.

The German aluminum industry received a significant impetus from the war, with the Hindenburg Program in particular providing further stimulus for its expansion. The company Vereinigte Aluminium Werke AG (VAW), based in Berlin, was founded on April 21, 1917, to manufacture the aluminum needed for the war. All of the country's aluminum interests were gradually collected in this company. Initially owned half by the Reich and half by a consortium made up of Chemische Fabrik Friesheim-Elektron AG, Metallbank, and Metallurgische Gesellschaft AG, the Reich took over full ownership at the end of the war.

The Lauta plant, which began operation in October 1918, consisted not only of an aluminum works but also of an aluminum oxide factory and a large power station connected to the brown coal or lignite mine Erika, owned by Ilse-Bergbau AG. However, the power station was sold in 1920 to Mitteldeutsches Kraftwerk AG. The high energy requirements of the aluminum industry meant that electricity from brown coal and from water power were particularly important. After the war, Erftwerk AG, running an aluminum works at Grevenbroich, and, like VAW, half-owned by the Reich until the end of the war, when it assumed full ownership, and the aluminum works at Töging am Inn were incorporated into VAW.

The Aluminum/Energy Link

The locations of these production sites were primarily determined by the need for a constant energy supply offered by neighboring electricity plants. Only a few days after the foundation of VAW, on April 27, 1917, the Innwerk Bayerische Aluminium AG—known as Innwerk AG from 1938—was established at Munich-Töging to provide a constant energy supply for the operation of the aluminum works.

Like VAW, the Reich's nitrogen works owed their creation to the shortage of raw materials that arose during World War I. Before the war, the production of explosives and of fertilizers containing nitrogen was based principally on the processing of Chilean saltpeter, imports of which to Germany could be cut off in the event of war. For this reason, Bayerische Stickstoff-Werke AG (BStW) was founded at Trostberg in early 1908, basing its production on the Frank Caro method and partly-owned by the Deutsche Bank. In 1915, commissioned by the Reich, BStW began to construct two calcium cyanide factories, at Piesteritz near Wittenberg and at Chorzow in Upper Silesia.

The Oberschlesische Stickstoff-Werke AG (OStW), to which the Chorzow factory was sold, was founded in December 1916, and was later appropriated by the Polish state. The Piesteritz factory remained under the Reich's ownership. It was incorporated into Mitteldeutsche Stickstoff-Werke Ag (MStW) on February 24, 1920, and all the company's shares—60 million marks—were acquired by the Reich. Finally, on May 28, 1920, Bayerische Kraftwerke AG—BKW, from 1939 known as Süddeutsche Kalkstickstoffwerke (SKW) AG—was formally incorporated, with its headquarters in Munich.

Germany's Interests in Electric Power

Apart from aluminum and nitrogen, the country's industrial interests were directed toward the electric power industry, as the production processes of both the aluminum and calcium cyanide industries were dependent on a sufficient supply of energy. On February 9, 1915, the BG-JAG brown coal works undertook to establish a large power plant for the production of nitrogen at Piesteritz.

As brown coal was used only to produce electrical current, the company changed its name to Electrowerke AG (EWAG). The large Zschornewitz power station had begun operation by the end of 1915. In 1918, EWAG began to develop grid electricity supply as its core activity. Deutsche Werke Aktiengesellschaft (DW) was founded at Berlin on December 4, 1919, with the object of converting about 20 armaments workshops and war shipyards owned by the Reich and the states of Prussia, Bavaria, and Saxony to peace-time production.

Another important company that was later to form the basis of VIAG was the Reichs—Kredit-Gesellschaft, which dated from 1919. To regulate the financial management of the Kriegsgesellschaften, founded during the economic control of World War I, the Imperial Treasury established a Statistical Office for War Companies. After the end of World War I, this office was gradually extended, producing the Reichs-Kredit und Krontrollstelle GmbH, based in Berlin and founded on July 20, 1919, which was transformed into the Reichs—Kredit-Gesellschaft mbH (ERKA) in September 1922. After the foundation of VIAG, ERKA, which remained stock-owned, became the company's bank.

VIAG Created to Manage the Reich's Industrial Interests

At the end of March 1923, the National Treasury Ministry that administered and supervised the Reich's industrial interests was dissolved in connection with the government's cost-cutting plans. Efforts were also made to find a means of managing the Reich's wide-ranging industrial interests, hitherto assigned to the Industry Department, in a non-bureaucratic way, organizing them on consistent, purely commercial principles. The two functions of the Industry Department were separated: the actual management of the companies was to be transferred to a specially created holding company, while the pure financial custody and management were transferred to the National Finance Ministry.

The holding company, based in Berlin, was founded on March 7, 1923, under the name Vereinigte Industrie-Unternehmungen Aktiengesellschaft (VIAG). The objects of the company were as follows: the holding of shares in commercial enterprises of every type; the operation, administration and financing of companies, as well as the undertaking of related

Key Dates:

1923: VIAG AG (Vereingte Industrie-Unternehmungen Aktiengesellschaft) founded by the German Reich.

1929: VEBA AG (Bereinigte Elektrizitäts und Bergwerke AG) established.

1935: VEBA expands into petroleum industry, develops coal-derived gasoline and synthetic rubber; VEBA is a major participant in the Third Reich's Four Year Plan for armaments manufacturing and chemical refineries.

1941: Stinnes' family's share in Hugo Stinnes Corp. is seized by the United States as assets of the enemy.

1945: VEBA turned over to Federal Republic of Germany by Allies.

1965: VEBA acquires 95 percent of Hugo Stinnes AG.

1986: VIAG partially privatized.

1987: VEBA becomes a public company.

1988: VIAG fully privatized.

1994: VEBA enters telecommunications market in joint venture with British Cable & Wireless.

1995: VIAG Interkom founded, a joint venture with British Telecom.

1999: Following a public offering, VEBA sells a 34.5 percent stake in Stinnes AG.

2000: VIAG and VEBA merge to become E.On AG.

2001: E.On sells VIAG Interkom for EUR 11.4 billion (US $11 billion).

2002: E.On sells VAW Aluminium to Norsk Hydro for EUR 3.1 billion (US $3 billion), completes acquisition of British utility Powergen PLC for EUR 8.1 billion (US $7.9 billion), becomes full owner of Ruhrgas, and sells its remaining 65.4 percent stake in Stinnes AG.

banking transactions; and, in general, the adoption of any measures which seemed appropriate to the management board in order to attain or further the aims of the company. The company was entitled to establish branches both in Germany and abroad and to enter into cooperation agreements. Thus VIAG was defined purely as a stock holding company, which was not directly involved in production.

The founder of VIAG was the German Reich. In the foundation proceedings of March 7, 1923, the share capital was set at 600 million marks, divided into 600,000 shares at 1,000 marks apiece. The Reich was shareholder. Subsidiaries were the Reichs—Kredit-Gesellschaft mbH, Elektrowerke AG, Vereinigte Aluminium-Werke AG, and Duetsche Werke AG. Shareholdings in Elektrowerke AG and the Württembergische Landes-Elektrizitäts AG, in Vereinigte Aluminum-Werke AG and Innwerk, in Bayerische Aluminium AG and Deutsche Werke AG were among the most important of the assets transferred.

In the years following its foundation, VIAG concentrated on its core activities of aluminum, nitrogen, and electricity and strengthened the economic integration of these areas. The geographical centers of the group's activities emerged as central Germany and upper Bavaria. In central Germany, the company

had EWAG, operating the Lauta power station using brown coal from Ilse-Bergbau AG, the aluminum works of VAW, and the calcium cyanide works at Peisteritz, supplied with electricity by the Mitteldeutsche Stickstoffwerke. Similarly, in upper Bavaria the hydroelectric power stations of Innwerk, Bayerische Aluminium AG, and Alzwerke GmbH worked together with the Töging aluminum factory—acquired by VAW in 1925, and the carbide factory of Bayerische Kraftwerk AG. Most of VIAG's shareholdings that did not fit with the core group activities were disposed of in the following years.

VIAG's First Profit

Before the beginning of the 1930s, the management of VIAG restructured its individual factories to attain profitability. The only income earned by VIAG was the dividends from its group companies. VIAG's net profits rose by 42 percent to 12 million reichsmarks between 1925 and 1929. In the financial year 1924–1925, a dividend of 5 percent was paid out for the first time. In the following years the dividend rose to 8 percent. A significant initial undertaking by the group was the conversion in 1925 of the separate factories of Deutsche Werke AG into independent companies better able to acquire production requirements for themselves, such as the factory at Spandau, which was converted into Deutsche Industriewerke AG (DIW), and was the only one of these companies to remain in the VIAG group.

VEBA's Beginnings

Founded as Vereinigte Elektrizitäts und Bergwerke AG (VEBA) in 1929, VEBA traces its roots to the mid-nineteenth century, when William Thomas Mulvaney emigrated from London to Germany. Mulvaney was born in Northern Ireland in 1806 and began his working life as a surveyor in London. When the British Civil Service was restructured in the 1850s, Mulvaney was among the many who were made redundant. Upon moving to Germany in 1855, he used his surveying skills to select for purchase a number of coal fields in Westphalia. He employed new procedures for the construction of extremely efficient mine shafts, which put his mines ahead of others in production.

By 1865, his 1,230 miners were mining 330,000 tons of coal per year, much more than others with the same number of miners. After the war of 1870–1872, coal prices fell and Mulvaney's Irish shareholders sold out. In 1873 he formed, with two German banks, the Hibernia & Shamrock-Bergwerksgesellschaft zu Berlin, with 5.6 million marks as capital. Mulvaney served as the chairman of the board until his death in 1885.

Beginning in 1889, the company went through a period of expansion, attracting the unwanted attention of the Prussian government, which accumulated a 46 percent stake in the energy company by 1904. In spite of opposition from privately held banks and mining companies, the state acquired full control of Hibernia in 1917.

Hibernia formed the core of a state-owned energy cartel created through the 1929 amalgamation of the coal company with Preussischen Elektrizitäts-G.G. (PreussenElektra), the federal electric utility formed in 1927, and Preussichen Bergwerks- und Hütten AG (Preussag). The purpose of the formation of VEBA was to entice international financing for the companies.

No foreign capital was invested, though some internal investments were obtained.

VEBA survived as a state owned business into the early 1930s. In 1933, VEBA became a major participant in the Third Reich's Four Year Plan, converting some of its works into armaments factories, and expanded into the petroleum industry in 1935, when it created a chemical refinery called Hüls. Intense wartime research led to the development of coal-derived gasoline and synthetic rubber. VEBA managed to avoid being bombed by the Allies until 1944, and by the end of 1945, the works were all repaired and in full operation again. After the War, most of the members of the board were arrested; one managed to disappear.

The Stinnes Link to VEBA

A businessman named Hugo Stinnes was creating what would become the biggest business concern in German history. His namesake company, Hugo Stinnes AG, would become part of the VEBA group in 1965. Born in 1870, Stinnes was the grandson of the successful coal merchant Mathias Stinnes; he founded Hugo Stinnes AG at 23 with a capital of 50,000 marks.

Initially, Hugo Stinnes followed his grandfather's formula for success, acquiring mines, building ships, and setting up coal depots throughout the North, Baltic, and Mediterranean seas. He was also involved in the massive expansion by amalgamation of the gas and electricity supplier Rheinisch-Westfälische Elektrizitätswerk AG. In 1909, he began to build up a trading center for his businesses in Hamburg, where he was most active during World War I.

In 1916, Stinnes bought out Eduard Woermann, and acquired the Hamburg-Amerika and the Norddeutscher-Lloyd, as well as shares in the Woermann and German East African lines, and he bought the entire business of coal merchants H.W. Heidmann and two hotels, one of which became offices for his empire. Having wiped out his competitors at home, he moved toward those in the occupied countries of Belgium and France, amalgamating and incorporating at will, and encouraging the German government to deport Belgian workers.

Stinnes continued after the war as before. His Deutsch-Luxemburg concern had been most seriously damaged, so in 1920 Stinnes arranged for its merger with the Gelsenkirchener Bergwerks AG, founded in 1873 by Emil and Adolf Kirdorf, to form the Rheinelbe Union, linking it with the Siemens-Konzern, which dealt in electrical appliances, instruments, automobiles, and trucks. The huge Siemens—Rheinelbe—Schuckert-Union had absolute control of both supply and market. With a capital of 615 million marks, it made Stinnes the most powerful businessman in Germany, if not in Europe.

He tried to earn popularity with the press by purchasing book publishers, paper mills, bookbinders, printers, and, finally, a few newspapers. For variety, he bought an automobile factory, the Esplanade Hotel in Berlin, and a few other hotels in Thüringen. Lastly, he began to move into banking, where he met his greatest opposition.

Stinnes once said that he had worked hard in order to make money for his children. Alas, within a year after his death in 1924, his sons had argued with the directors of the empire and with the banks their father had offended, and the banks sold sections of the company. Hugo Stinnes, Jr. got some American backing to form the Hugo Stinnes Corporation in New York. However, the family's share of the corporation was seized by the United States in 1941 as assets of the enemy. In 1947, Dr. Heinz Kemper was appointed by the Allies as trustee of Stinnes assets, which were transferred to the newly founded Hugo Stinnes AG in 1956. In 1965, VEBA acquired 95 percent of Hugo Stinnes AG, then in 1992, acquired the remaining 5 percent of the newly renamed Stinnes AG and took it off the stock exchange.

Armament and VIAG's Burgeoning Profits

The armament process, which began in 1933, brought an upturn in business for VIAG as for other companies. The number of employees rose by 66 percent over 1932–1933 to 30,387, with the number increasing to 70,000 in the years immediately prior to the war. VIAG and its companies, as a group owned directly or indirectly by the Reich, were harnessed into the armament program of the National Socialist government, especially after 1936. By 1935, the production capacities of group subsidiaries were already being used to the full, causing VIAG's businesses to extend their plants. VAW built a new aluminum oxide plant, Nabwerk, at Schwandorf, for example, and nitrogen production was increased considerably.

The annexation of Austria to the German Reich in March 1938 brought a significant increase in VIAG's sphere of activity, including looking after electro-industrial interests in the territories which had been adjoined to the German Reich. To meet this objective, VIAG founded the Österreichische Elektrowerke in Vienna on April 22, 1938; the company was renamed Alpen-Elektrowerke Aktiengesellschaft (AEW) one month later. In connection with the takeover of the Austrian National Bank by the Reichsbank and the transfer of the Österreichische Industriekredit AG to the Österreichische Creditanstalt-Wiener Bankverein (CA), VIAG received 76 percent of the bank's converted share capital of 70.7 million reichmarks as a contribution to an increase in its own capital base.

Expansion in the 1930s and 1940s

VIAG's expanded activities during the War included increasing its shareholding in Ilse-Bergbau AG to more than 60 percent by acquiring further ordinary shares worth 10 million reichsmarks. It also acquired further shares in Innwerk AG from the state of Bavaria, as well as 50 percent of the share capital the electricity company Bayernwerk Aktiengesellschaft (BAG) in Munich. Together with the state of Bavaria and the electricity company Rheinisch-Westfälisches Elektrizitätswerke AG (RWE), VIAG founded the Bayerische Wasserkraftwerke Aktiengesellschaft (BAWAG), based in Munich on January 26, 1940.

When the war ended, VIAG was sequestrated and administered, at first, by trustees. VIAG's situation between May 1945 and July 1951 was determined by the military rule in the four zones of occupation. Ludger Westrick, the general trustee appointed by the Bavarian state authorities and previously a director of VAW, is largely to be credited with extricating VIAG from military law through his attempts to restructure the business in cooperation with the Allies. This was made all the more difficult as dismantling of works under the Allied war repatriations program and the shortage of raw materials that dominated the day-to-day business. When the relevant Allied authorities lifted all bans, restrictions, and controls in 1951, complete reorganization of VIAG began with the election of a management board and the formation of a supervisory board. Bonn became the base of the new company, which in its first deutschmark (DM) accounts recorded a share capital that had dwindled to DM160 million.

VIAG's Post-War Profits Increase

After the financial year 1949–1950, net profits increased every year, reaching DM1.45 million in 1951–1952. In 1952–1953, a dividend, of 3 percent, was paid for the first time. VIAG had created a solid foundation for further progress. Share-holdings of VIAG totaled DM 254.06 million making up 95.9 percent of total group assets.

From 1953 to 1960, processes of consolidation, rationalization, and modernization dominated the business activities of the separate VIAG works. Dividends were raised by 1 percent each year, so that by 1959–1960 VIAG was able to pay out dividends of 10 percent. Bayernwerk AG raised its capital by DM 50 million to DM 150 million to increase its utilization of primary energy sources in Bavaria, such as brown coal, which were cheap at the time.

This strategy led to a decisive change in VIAG's energy supply base in subsequent years. In 1956, two-thirds of the electricity was produced by hydroelectric power and only one-third by steam power, but by 1960, thermal electricity generation from brown coal had already overtaken hydroelectric power. VIAG and its subsidiaries now formed a modern, stable group. In the following years the company devoted itself to expanding its subsidiaries to meet the continually growing markets for electricity, aluminum, and chemical products. Between 1960 and 1972, VIAG invested over DM 5 billion in its subsidiaries.

Post-War Changes for VEBA

The Allies turned VEBA over to the Federal Republic of Germany (West Germany) at the war's end. The government formed a new 21-member board of directors in 1952 and inaugurated a period of expansion. There were major extensions to chemical works and power plants. In 1956, because of the high cost of coal production, VEBA turned to oil production. Initially, share prices were high, but when they dropped VEBA bought quite a few of its own shares. Soon afterward, another VEBA subsidiary built the first nuclear power plant in West Germany. By the early 1990s, nuclear generators would provide nearly half of VEBA's power.

Struggling Toward Capitalization

In the 1970s, two issues were at the center of public interest: capital-raising for investments and privatization. The government's privatization plans—after its successes with Preussag and the Volkswagen works—aroused heated public debate and dominated the headlines in press articles on VIAG from the end of the 1950s until the actual privatization in 1986. In 1968–1969, the

plans to privatize VIAG escalated to become an electoral issue and a subject of dispute between the parties. Another significant problem for VIAG was the fact that the company could not go to the capital markets to raise funds for financing and investment. The group could only obtain the funds needed for investment through bank loans, that is, by incurring debt.

VIAG could not develop freely in the market, and so could only work with restricted resources; in spite of its successful evolution, the group faced a serious obstacle to growth. Expansion through acquisition, indispensable for the effective development of an industrial group, was impossible. Internal expansion also proved extremely difficult. The consequences of these problems could be seen in high reserves, depreciation, and dividends, which were disproportionately low in relation to the company's success.

Although the federal government, as sole shareholder, had received DM124 million in dividends since 1953, it could not make funds available for any increase in capital. Because of this, VIAG was forced to increase its own reserves by drawing on current profits. In 1968, the share capital of DM 254 million was raised by DM50 million to DM304 million at a rate of 220 percent. The Kreditanstalt für Wiederaufbau—a bank for reconstruction founded in 1948 offering middle to long-term loans from the Marshall Plan as well as its own funds—took up the new shares. In this way VIAG acquired new funds amounting to DM 110 million. From this time onwards, the Kreditanstalt für Wiederaufbau held around 16 percent of the increased share capital.

The Aluminum and Electricity Production Mix

Associate companies continued to form the basis of VIAG's success in the 1970s. Growing industrialization and the progressive mechanization of work processes led to an increase in electricity consumption in VIAG's aluminum and calcium cyanide business. The aluminum works in particular, with the expansion and increased use of their capacity, needed significantly more electricity. Electrochemical production, with electricity consumption of just over four billion kilowatt hours (kWh), had a correspondingly high share of the total. Through the continuing expansion of electricity production, especially in the field production from steam power, VIAG's need for externally generated electricity was steadily reduced. VIAG's share of total electricity production in the federal republic stood at around 8 percent in 1965; by 1970 it had sunk to about 7 percent.

Aluminum had long been regarded as the principal business of VIAG. Although electric power production grew faster after World War II, VAW remained the group's largest business in terms both of turnover and of work force. VAW—with its subsidiaries, Vereinigte Leichtmetall-Werke GmbH (known from 1971 as VAW Leichtmetall GmbH), Aluminium Norf GmbH, Aluminium-Oxid Stade GmbH, and VAW of America Inc.—dominated VIAG's business activities throughout the 1970s and until the beginning of the 1980s. In 1960, VAW had a 70-percent share of aluminum production in the federal republic and met 30percent of the country's aluminum requirements. In 1971 VAW produced 248,000 tons of primary aluminum in total.

The aluminum crisis dominated the whole of the 1970s and the first years of the 1980s. The crisis had begun as early as

1968, when the federal republic placed high taxes on exports but reduced taxes on imports, a measure equivalent to a revaluation of the deutschmark by 4 percent. In 1969, the federal government raised the value of the deutschmark by 8.5 percent making US$1 equivalent to DM 3.66. As the aluminum price was largely dependent on the dollar, any speculation on the currency exchange market involving an upward valuation of the deutschmark or a devaluation of the dollar had catastrophic results for the aluminum market.

The oil crises of 1973 and 1976, and the accompanying increased price of oil required for electricity production, exacerbated the situation. In 1975, production declined significantly, leading to a reduction in working hours for VIAG's employees; the company lost DM120 million. Only in 1983 was the crisis successfully overcome. SKW at Trostberg was restructured during this period. While the share of the main product, calcium cyanide, declined to around a third of the total output, acrylic nitril production increased substantially. In 1981–1982, Hoechst AG sold its 50 percent share in SKW to VIAG, which now owned 100 percent of the company.

In the 1970s, electrical power production acquired increasing importance. Of the total profits of over DM 47.5 million produced by subsidiaries in 1973, DM 42 million came from the electrical sector. In particular, Bayernwerk AG, in which VIAG had a 38.86 percent shareholding—it had to hand over some of its BAG shares to the Bavarian state after the war—was operating with great success. Electricity production by VIAG companies in this sector amounted to 22.6 billion kWh in 1973. Gradually nuclear energy came to play an increasingly important role.

The share of electricity produced by nuclear power, which had amounted to only 4 percent in 1978, had risen to 70 percent by 1988, after the incorporation into the grid system of the nuclear power, which had amounted to only 4 percent in 1978, had risen to 70 percent by 1988, after the incorporation into the grid system of the nuclear power station Von Isar II in Bavaria. Hydroelectric power now only played a minor role. By the mid-1980s, VIAG had managed to overcome the crisis in the aluminum sector and had successfully completed the restructuring of its activities. At the beginning of 1981, VIAG acquired 50 percent of Thyssengas GmbH—an important step on the path of acquisition.

VEBA Restructures

In 1971, VEBA embarked upon a grand reorganization scheme, disbanding Hibernia and putting nearly all of its shares into VEBA Chemie AG. VEBA was restructured along four main lines of operation: the supply of energy, chemicals, glass, and trade-transport services. In 1973 and again in 1979, the Federal Antitrust Commission ruled against VEBA's share dealings, although the Commission's ruling was ignored and the deals permitted by means of "ministerial permission." By this time, VEBA had some 900,000 shareholders, and was the biggest joint stock company in Europe.

VEBA encountered difficulties in the 1970s, when overcapacity and the global oil shortage combined to put the squeeze on the energy company's oil business. In 1981, VEBA added the U.S.-based exploration firm Mark Producing to its oil-seeking arms in Libya and Syria. When oil prices started to decline, VEBA again found itself on the wrong end of the energy industry's cycle. While the purchase and eventual divestment of Mark Producing was judged a "disaster" by Sharon Reier of Financial World, VEBA's subsequent affiliation with the state-owned Petroleos de Venezuela (PDVSA) helped build VEBA Oel into the largest German-owned oil company, supplying 60 percent of its own petroleum needs.

Privatization for VIAG at Last

After a partial privatization in 1986, the group was fully privatized in 1988. From May 3, 1988, onward, the federal government and the Kreditanstalt für Wiederaufbau sold their remaining shares in VIAG at a rate of DM210. In the second stage of the privatization, 6.96 million shares of DM50 each, with a nominal value of DM348 million were placed with a consortium of 51 banks under the leadership of Deutsche Bank AG.

Apart from the privatization, the period from 1984 to 1990 was marked by the sale and purchase of new shareholdings and by the restructuring of subsidiaries. Freed from state restrictions, VIAG was now able to be active on the capital markets, and could plan further acquisitions. At the beginning of 1986, VIAG acquired 15 percent of the share capital of Didier-Werke AG, at Wiesbaden. On January 1, 1990, VIAG took over Klöckner & Co. (KlöCo), at Duisburg-Hamborn, a company that had gotten into difficulties, together with Bayernwerk AG. Steel accounted for about half of the KlöCo's turnover amounting to nearly DM 12 billion; one-third of turnover came from energy, building products, heating technology, machine tools, transport, and textile importing; 14 percent of turnover came from raw materials, chemicals, and environmental technology; and 4 percent from trading in industrial plant.

Bayernwerk AG, a Munich utility, and VIAG established a joint industrial holding company, based in Berlin and named VBB Viag-Bayernwerk-Beteiligungs-Gesellschaft mbH, with each company having a 50 percent share. On January 1990, VBB acquired a 24.99 percent stake in Gerresheimer Glas AG at Düsseldorf. VIAG also acquired a series of other shareholdings between 1985 and 1990 through its subsidiaries, especially VAW, SKW-Trostberg AG, and Bayernwerk AG. The reunification of Germany offered VIAG possibilities for a new field of activity, especially in the central German factories that were lost at the end of World War II.

VEBA's Struggles in the Early 1990s

Rudolf von Benningsen-Foerder remained at the helm of VEBA through 1989, occasionally selling off a company or two or buying a few others. In 1987, the government's last 25.55 percent was sold and VEBA became a public company. Chief Financial Officer Ulrich Hartmann advanced to CEO and led the company through the mid-1990s.

VEBA's sales fell by 6.8 percent from 1992 to 1993 as declining chemical prices contributed to a 47.3 percent drop in net income. In 1991, when British investment bank S.G. Warburg's report that VEBA's constituent parts were more valuable than the whole, the company instituted a reorganization, selling several divisions and restructuring those that remained. The program included the elimination of 10,000 jobs. Hüls was the hardest hit, with a 27 percent work force reduction by the end of 1994. According to The Economist, Hartmann hinted that VEBA could shed its petrochemical core in the years to come.

The criticism, combined with a general downturn in the petrochemicals market, helped prompt an early 1990s diversification. In 1991, VEBA formed Baltic Cable, a joint venture with Swedish utility Sydkraft, to provide cable services in the two countries. VEBA also acquired Lion, a small software company, in the early 1990s, and faced wider competition in the energy business, as Germany opened that industry to international competition.

These measures helped fuel a seven percent rise in sales, from DM66.3 billion in 1993 to DM71.0 billion in 1994, and a healthy 51-percent rebound in profits, from DM1.01 billion to DM1.53 billion over the same period. With interests in electricity, oil, chemicals and transportation, VEBA AG was Germany's fourth-largest conglomerate in 1995. While over two-thirds of its annual revenues were generated in the European Community, the business also had operations in North America, Latin America, the Asia/Pacific region, and Africa.

The Scramble for Germany's Telecommunications Market

In 1995, there was a rush of competition as companies geared up for the liberalization of the telecommunications industry, due in 1998 with the end of the Duetsche Telekom AG (DT) voice services monopoly. VIAG joined the fray with British Telecommunications PLC to offer telecommunications services in Germany. DT had been serving over 95 percent of Germany's DM 70 billion ($45 billion) telecom market. On the heels of VIAG's announcement, VEBA, parent to Vebacom GmbH, negotiated with Cable & Wireless PLC to form a joint venture for telecommunications services in Germany that would be in direct competition with Duetsche Telekom.

Of these leaps into telecommunications, The Economist quips, "One of the more fashionable things to do if you are a slightly stodgy but rich European utility is to branch out into telecoms of one sort or another. It is not just that the phone market seems to be growing whilst most other public services look a little sluggish. It is also a question of sex appeal: who wants to be in the boring old business of delivering electricity, pumping water, or bringing commuters to work when there are things like satellite telephony and multimedia in the air?"

As it happened, Britain's Cable & Wireless pulled out of its joint venture with VEBA and RWE in 1997, one year before liberalization of Germany's telecom industry, demonstrating the frenetic rate of change in telecommunications. VEBA then made an offer to C&W to gain its 45 percent stake in Vebacom and, in the following year, made a deal with BellSouth Corporation in the United States for a joint venture to provide fixed and mobile communications services in Germany.

In 1998, VIAG, partnering with Orange PLC, won one of two very competitive licenses from the Swiss Communications Commission for mobile communications in Switzerland. Swis-

scom had had the mobile communications market to itself. The 1.8 GHz license was awarded to a consortia in which Orange and VIAG owned significant minority stakes. Orange and VIAG partnered on GSM-1800 licenses in three European countries, the others being Germany and Austria.

In spring 1999, VEBA and RWE AG agreed to sell the wireless assets of their telecommunications subsidiary to Mannesmann Arcor for $1.23 billion, a transaction that included a 6,600-mile fiber optic network, the customer base, trade name, and 2,800 employees. VEBA said it would focus on wireless telecommunications in the future.

Merging of VEBA and VIAG

VEBA and VIAG, both massive energy and chemicals conglomerates, announced in the press in September 1999 their planned merger, worth EUR 13.4 billion (US $14.0 billion). The companies had a combined annual turnover of 150 billion marks (US $80 billion) and 200,000 employees. The logic given was that the merged company could then become a global player, with its headquarters in Düesseldorf, co-led by Ulrich Hartmann, chairman of VEBA, and Wilhelm Simsom, chairman of VIAG. The key areas of the companies, chemicals and power supply, were to be launched in January 2000. Hartman noted that other major units of VEBA and VIAG would merge over the next few years.

According to the Xinhua News Agency, analysts stated that the "two main reasons for the merger are the fierce competition in a liberalized German domestic energy market, and, more important, the tougher pressure facing German companies in the European and world stage since the European common currency has been launched." It was estimated that the two companies would save about 1.6 billion marks per year by 2002. About 2,500 jobs, primarily in the energy unit, would be cut.

The Oil Daily further stated that the consolidation of European gas and electricity markets was accelerating because of the speed with which barriers were being knocked down by major U.S. companies, such as Enron Corporation and Southern Company. The combined new company, which would be owned 64.5 percent by VEBA and 35.5 percent by VIAG (VEBA was more than twice the size of VIAG), would focus on core products of energy and specialty chemicals, using the sale of non-core assets to fund acquisitions. VEBA also bought 10 percent of VIAG from the Bavarian government for about EUR 1.6 billion (US $1.59 billion), while Bavaria held 15 percent of VIAG. The newly merged VEBA and VIAG, the second and third largest energy companies respectively, would then be Europe's largest listed energy company.

The non-core businesses that would be divested were worth about $29 billion, and included all telecommunications holdings, aluminum, packaging, electronics, and logistics. The merged company would hold on to its oil interests, all of which came from VEBA. Although the new group would be based in VEBA's Düsseldorf headquarters, the energy division, focused on newly merged PreussenElektra and Bayernwerk, would be based in Munich. The specialty chemicals would include VEBA's Degussa-Huls division and VIAG's SKW Trostberg, and would also be based in Munich.

As noted in Chemical Week, the mega-merger "combined VEBA subsidiary Degussa-Huls with VIAG's SKW arm, creating the third largest German chemical company, after BASF and Bayer, with sales of EUR 16.34 billion (US $16 billion) per year." The restructuring launched by the new company included the divestment of businesses with combined sales of EUR 28.2 billion per year, approximately half its sales. Businesses that were up for sale included MEMC Microelectronic Materials and VEBA's 65.5-percent share of logistics group Stinnes, parent company of the world's largest chemical distributor Brenntag. Others included VAW Aluminium, mobile phone company E-Plus, packaging group Schmalback-Lubeca, glass maker Gerresheimer Glas, Cable television firm Cablecom, and trading company Kloeckner.

One of the more complex divestitures was that of VEBA Electronics Group, based in Santa Clara, California, made up of four member companies: MEMEC, EBV Elektronik, Raab Karcher Electronic Systems, and Wylie Electronics. In North America, Insight Electronics, Unique Technologies, and Impact technologies covered the semiconductor specialist market for MEMEC. VEBA Electronics had sales of $5.47 billion in 1999, a 33 percent increase over 1998.

In April 2000, VEBA and VIAG announced that their new company's name would be E.On AG, with the merger scheduled for June 2000. E.On would have 40 departments in 18 business areas, with the chemicals subsidiaries merger of Degussa-Huls and SKW Trostberg taking place later in the year. VIAG agreed to sell its 72.9 percent stake in glass packaging producer Gerresheimer Glas to private equity company Investcorp. The combined companies of Degussa-Huls and SKW Trostberg, with sales of EUR 5 billion (US $4.7 billion), were to become Degussa. E.On planned to double the sales of its remaining businesses to EUR 18 billion (US $17.5 billion) by 2004.

Let the Acquisitions Begin!

E.On, as Germany's second largest power company, announced its acquisition of the British utility Powergen for US$7.3 billion in May 2001, a deal that was approved by regulators later in the year, ultimately closing in spring 2002. This was E.On's opportunity to break into the U.S. market, as Powergen-owned LG&E, a Kentucky electricity supplier. The deal was the most recent in a series of mergers and acquisitions that had restructured Europe's deregulating energy markets in a two-year period. The acquisition made E.On the second largest electricity supplier in the world, with Electricité de France being the first. It was reported in Europe that E.On stated that it had another US$35.2 billion to finance acquisitions.

In July of 2001, BP acquired 51 percent of E.On's VEBA Oel's downstream business in an effort to compete with Royal Dutch/Shell, making BP the largest downstream company in Germany. VEBA Oel had interests in five refineries at the time. E.On received in return a 51-percent stake in BP's Gelsenberg subsidiary that held the British company's 25.5 percent interest in Germany's leading gas distributor Ruhrgas. In addition, BP paid E.On US$1.63 billion in cash, and assumed US$950 million in debt. According to the *Oil Daily*, the acquisition was the first step toward BP's full ownership of VEBA Oel in June 2002, when it acquired the remaining 49-percent in return for its

remaining interest in Ruhrgas and a further US$2.4 billion. BP's acquisition of VEBA Oel and its Aral chain of gas stations gave it a 25-percent share of the German retail market and the leader in all of Europe, with the exception of Italy and the Balkans, with an average of 16-percent market share. The deal between also enhanced E.On's emerging profile as an international multi-utility.

The international operations of VEBA Oil and Gas were acquired by Petro-Canada in January 2002, a deal valued at C $3.2 billion (US $2 billion) in cash, and involving production of 175,000 barrels of oil equivalent per day (boe) and gas reserves of 600 million boe. The acquisition was a significant expansion for Petro-Canada, which moved the company more deeply into the North Sea, North Africa, and Latin America, and increased the company's holdings in Libya, Venezuela, and Syria. The expansion increased daily production by 78 percent for Petro-Canada production.

The New World of Energy Markets

By May 2002, Europe's major power utilities were positioned for takeovers in the United States, but found the number of targets depleted at home by the takeover frenzy of US$100 billion, while the valuations of American energy firms were halved by the collapse of Enron. Europe reported that European utilities had spent about US$25 billion on U.S. power companies in the previous four years, but still want a bigger presence in the world's largest power market. E.On Chairman Ulrich Hartmann stated that he planned to make two acquisitions in the U.S. midwest, using funds from planned asset sales and potential bank loans for expansions.

In July 2002, E.On acquired a 40-percent stake in Ruhrgas, a company that is held publicly by ExxonMobil, Shell, and Preussag for EUR 4.1billion (US $3.98 billion). In its completion of the acquisitions of Gelsenberg, Bergemann, and the ExxonMobil, Shell, Pruessag shares, E.On became the full owner of Ruhrgas. Conversely, E.On sold its 65.4-percent stake in Stinnes AG to Deutsche Bahn AG for cash in August 2002 for EUR 32.75 per Stinnes share, or 24.5-percent premium over the stock's closing price on June 26, 2002. In this continued shifting from a diversified conglomerate to an international energy presence, only time will tell what paths E.On will take to reinvent itself in the future.

Principal Subsidiaries

E.On Energie AG, Munich, Germany; Viterra AG, Essen, Germany; Degussa AG, Düsseldorf, Germany; Stinnes AG, Mülheim/Ruhr, Germany; Schleswag AG, Rendsburg, Germany; EWE Aktiengesellschaft, Oldenburg, Germany; EMR GmbH, Herford, Germany; e.dis Energie Nord AG, Fürstenwalde, German; Avacon AG, Helmstedt, Germany; Wesertal GmbH, Hameln, Germany; PESG Aktiengesellschaft, Paderborn, Germany; TEAG Thüringer, Erfurt, Germany; Energie-Aktiengesellschaft Mitteldeutschland EAM, Kassel, Germany; E.On Bayern AG, Regersburg, Germany; Thüga Aktiengesellschaft, Munich, Germany; E.On Kerndraft GmbH and E.On Kraftwerke GmbH, Hanover, Germany; Ruhr Energie GmbH, Gelsenkirchen, Germany; E.On Netz GmbH, Bayreuth, Germany, E.On Wasserdraft GmbH, Landshut, Germany; E.On

Sales & Trading GmbH, Munich, Germany; Espoon Sähkö Oyj, Espoo, Finland; E.On Scandinavia AB and Sydkraft AB, Malmö, Sweden; Powergen PLC, Coventry, UK; E.On Benelux B.V., Rotterdam, The Netherlands; E.On Bohemia s.r.o., Prague, Czech Republic; E.On Polska Sp. Z o.o., Warsaw, Poland; E.On Italia S.p.A., Milan, Italy; E.On Hungária Rt, Budapest, Hungary, LG&E Energy, Louisville, Kentucky, United States.

Principal Competitors

BASF AG; RWE.

Further Reading

Alperowicz, Natasha. "SKW Bulks Up in the U.S. Acquiring a Specialties Presence," *Chemical Week*, August 4, 1999, p. 28.

Breskin, Ira, "VEBA to Streamline Chemical Operations after 'Marked' Loss," *Journal of Commerce and Commercial*, December 11, 1992, p. 7A.

"BP Boosts German Presence with Veba Deal," *The Oil Daily*, July 17, 2001.

"Consortia Led by SBC, Orange Gain Hotly Contested Swiss GSM Licenses," *Communications Today*, April 21, 1998.

"Die Doppelganger: German Utilities," *The Economist*, July 8, 1995, p. 64.

"Falling Chemical Prices Tip VEBA Into the Red," *ECN-European Chemical News*, August 23, 1993, p. 15.

"German Company VEBA A.G. to Lay Off 10,000 by 1995," *The Oil and Gas Journal*, September 13, 1993, p. 40.

"Germany's Herr Handy," *The Economist*, December 7, 1996, p. 66.

"Klaus Pilts, VEBA Director, Dies in Avalanche," *Journal of Commerce and Commercial*, April 16, 1993, p. 7A.

Reier, Sharon, "At the Crossroads," *Financial World*, July 7, 1992, p. 27.

Treue, Wilhelm, *Die Geschichte der Ilseder Hütte*, Peine, 1960.

"VEBA Results Held Back by Chemical Prospects," *ECN-European Chemical News*, April 4, 1994, p. 21.

Vollmer, Alfred. "New Venture to Tackle Deutsche Telekom Monopoly," *Electronics*, January 23, 1995, p. 1.

"Why West Germany is Selling Two Gems in the Crown Jewels," *The Economist*, July 5, 1986, p. 57.

—Manfred Pohl (trans. by Susan Mackervoy) (VIAG);
April Dougal Gasbarre (VEBA)
—update: Annette Dennis McCully

Electrocomponents PLC

5000 Oxford Business Park South
Oxford OX4 2BH
United Kingdom
Telephone: +44 (0) 1865-204000
Fax: +44 (0) 1865-207400
Web site: http://www.electrocomponents.com

Public Company
Incorporated: 1937 as Radiospares
Employees: 4,900 (2002)
Sales: £824 million (2001)
Stock Exchanges: London
Ticker Symbol: ECM
NAIC: 444190 Other Building Material Dealers; 421690
   Other Electronic Parts and Equipment Wholesalers;
   421610 Electrical Apparatus and Equipment, Wiring
   Supplies, and Construction Material Wholesalers

Electrocomponents PLC sits in the top tier of U.K. companies. Electrocomponents has joined the FTSE 100 index of the United Kingdom's largest companies and was recently noted in a *Management Today* survey as Britain's eighth most admired company. The international company sells a wide array of electronic products to engineers, technical users, small electronic companies, and other business clients through paper, online, and CD-Rom catalogues. Almost all of the products found in an Electrocomponents' group catalog, and there are approximately 300,000 products offered group-wide, can be delivered to the customer overnight. Electrocomponents has expanded out of its original U.K. market to service many countries in Europe, Asia, and most recently, with the purchase of Allied Electronics in 1999, the United States and Canada. In addition to purchasing Allied Electronics from Avnet Corporation, Electrocomponents has formed a strategic alliance with Avnet, giving Electrocomponents an opportunity to expand its business capabilities and service more high-volume orders.

Small Beginnings

Electrocomponents was founded in 1937 by two Jewish émigrés who had fled to London to escape Hitler. The two men, J.H. Waring and P.M. Sebestyen, found themselves in London with the prospect of supporting themselves weighing heavily on them. Their gaze settled on a niche they'd uncovered, supplying parts for the radios that were quickly becoming an integral part of many Londoners' daily lives. The men saw opportunity because they observed that the radios' parts broke often, the valves in particular, and the parts needed to repair them were difficult to come by. The two men took advantage of these machines' unreliability and began distributing the scarce parts to local radio repair shops. The company, called Radiospares Limited and located in northwest London, grew rapidly, and within a year, six sales representative were added to the Radiospares staff.

The founders' objective was to provide a replacement part for every job, so they were always open to adding additional products to their offerings. When televisions became popular (and proved as unreliable as radios), television parts were added to Radiospares' product list. In 1947, the same year that the company began to sell television parts, Radiospares established its first export link with Radionics in Dublin, Ireland. By the end of the war, the small, local distribution company had evolved into a much larger national distribution company. In 1954, the founders of Radiospares decided to expand the company's focus from distributing solely to fix-it shops and home users to include distribution to the industrial sector. In the early 1960s, the work of manufacturing radios and TVs had shifted from English to Japanese manufacturers. Radiospares understood that when the new products were released, they would not need as much repair as the old products had required because the new manufacturers were focusing efforts on creating products that worked more reliably. Radiospares saw that their market would drop off drastically in the coming years, so the company shifted its business strategy more completely into supplying components to the industrial sector.

The shift away from home users was a good one, and in 1967 Radiospares was "floated" on the London Stock Exchange as

Electrocomponents PLC. Soon after the company's successful stock exchange listing, the company was valued at £2.75 million. The founders decided that it was time for them to leave the company.

Continued Success

The founders' departures did nothing to affect the continued growth and success of the original company. In 1971, the company changed its name from Radiospares to RS Components. RS Components' success as a distributor of electronic components to small businesses was based on the company's dedication to offering a large variety of products, and having all of those products available for quick delivery. RS Components supplied product primarily to small electronics companies, and by 1974 the RS catalogue offered over 2,500 products and had opened distribution centers in both Birmingham and Manchester. RS Components continued to grow and succeed through the 1970s, and in 1976 RS Components' sales exceeded £1 million per month. As the company succeeded in its niche, the executives had to continually reassess the company's focus in order to decide which direction to allow the company to grow.

Diversification during the 1980s

The direction that the company decided to take in the 1980s was toward diversification. The company built up a subsidiary called Electrolighting that was designed to sell lights to retail outlets, and purchased other companies involved in computers and in the distribution of office supplies. The only long-term division that Electrocomponents held onto was called Pact. Pact was a distributor of electrical appliances and audio accessories complete with its own Panda and Wellco brands, and its own label and packaging facilities. Pact continued to operate until its closure in March 2001, when Electrocomponents announced, "[Pact's] operations were not core to the Group's strategy."

In 1981, the company's market value had risen to £60 million, and in 1984 they made a move out of London to a newly built warehouse in Corby. The warehouse had been built to become the company's main warehouse and it would hold and distribute the bulk of the company's product. By 1995, the warehouse stocked 58,000 different product lines, and any

product on its shelves could be shipped on the same day the order was placed-which meant that customers could receive their product the next day. The bulk of the orders came in during the last few hours of the workday (the warehouse was open from 8:00 a.m. to 8:00 p.m.); as soon as the order was logged into the computer, the warehouse staff could begin the process of locating, packaging, and sending it out to the customer. In 1995, it was reported that the Corby warehouse alone serviced the bulk of the company's average 16,000 orders a day. This next-day service was a major aspect of RS Components' success. The company's ability to stock a large array and quantity of products and their dedication to quick turnaround won them the loyalty of a large customer base.

Changing of the Guard: Diversification Gives Way to Expansion

In 1990, the longtime leading executive of Electrocomponents, John Robinson, resigned from his position of managing director of the company and was quickly replaced by Sir Keith Bright. There was speculation about whether Robinson had been strong-armed out of the company. Robinson said of his departure, "It was not an amicable parting. But it was more to do with personalities than questions of strategy." Bright, who had worked at London Regional Transport, was given the titles of deputy chairman and chief executive. In 1991, the same year that the company's profits fell by six percent, Bright brought in a new chief executive, Bob Lawson.

Lawson made some substantive changes upon taking office—he closed or disposed of most of the newer businesses that the company had taken on during their diversification phase, and turned his attention toward expanding the company's reach. In the first year that he was in office, the company expanded, opening RS Germany. The following year (1992), the company acquired and merged Radio Parts in Denmark into RS Denmark, an RSCC joint venture was begun in India, and RS's former New Zealand distributor was acquired in order to form RS New Zealand. The expansion continued, and in 1995 and 1996, RS acquired three more companies—its former distributor in Singapore to open RS Singapore; the company's Spanish distributor Amidata to form RS Amidata; and RS Component's South African distributor. In 1996, RS Chile opened as a start-up.

One of the largest and most important moves that Lawson made was to expand upon RS Components' business in the Far East. The initial moves he made toward the East developed into hubs in Singapore and Hong Kong. RS Singapore was opened to service the ASEAN region in South Asia, and RS Hong Kong to service China and North Asia. In April 2000, the company published its first Chinese language catalogue (60,000 products), CD-Rom, and Web site, and in September 2000, the company opened a fulfillment center in Shanghai. In 1998, Electrocomponents committed around £30 million toward developing a centralized distribution center in Japan. The RS form of distribution was not available to Japan before RS Components launched their business there.

Another major change that the company underwent during Lawson's first few years in office was to alter one of the company's fundamental business practices. Lawson said in 1995, ''Historically, the business was always product-driven. In the past five years, I believe we have made it service-driven.'' Some aspects of the service-driven elements of Electrocomponents are: next-day delivery, catalogues in three formats (paper, CD-Rom, and Internet), teams of engineers in constant search for new and better products that fit the company's quality standards, and another team of engineers who answer customers' questions about the company's products. In 1998, Lawson discussed customer care, ''We get very upset if any of our competitors outserve us with a customer. It's a personal affront if anyone else serves them better. We have three ground rules for customer service: (1) we will be the provider of innovation to our customers; (2) always provide the customer with an innovative solution; (3) always be their first choice.''

Taking Advantage of Technology

In 1995, the company introduced a new way for their customers to flip through their catalog—on CD-Rom. The CD-Rom was offered to Electrocomponents customers for free, and the drive that the customers would need to run it was sold below cost to encourage customers to make use of the new offering. The CD-Rom catalog was expensive to design and build, but once Electrocomponents' customers caught on, the company was sure that both they and their customer would uncover benefits. The CD-Rom catalog allowed customers access to all of the same products that the paper catalogue offered, but with more ease. Customers could perform searches, access more photos, and even order their products online if their computers were hooked up to a modem.

In 1998, Electrocomponents jumped onto the Internet bandwagon and published an RS Components Web site and catalogue. The catalogue offered 100,000 products, and cost more than $1 million to produce. Electrocomponents hoped and expected that the Internet catalogues would eventually make both their CD-Rom and paper catalogues obsolete. The RS Components Web site contains at least 10,000 documents, most of which are technical manuals that customers can use for reference. If customers cannot find an answer to their question in the documents provided, they are given the opportunity to ask technical questions while online. In 2001, the company reported, ''The site is

well appreciated by customers and came in second only to Dell in the Forrester awards for European business-to-business Web sites. E-Purchasing is an innovative development to help our customers trade over the Web in a controlled manner and to save transaction costs . . . on an £80 order!''

A Major Deal

In 1999, Electrocomponents gained its first successful foothold in the United States and Canada with the $380 million purchase of Allied Electronics from one of Electrocomponents' major competitors, Avnet Corporation. Allied had been a catalogue business very similar to RS Components, but Allied operated primarily in the United States and Canada. Lawson said that Avnet and Electrocomponents had been discussing various alliances for years, ''But to make it work, the Allied business had to be outside the Avnet group. Allied became a threat to us [Electrocomponents] because we would be sharing trade secrets with Avnet, and they had a potential competitor in their back pocket.'' In addition to the purchase of Allied, the two companies agreed to ally themselves in a variety of ways. Through their allegiance, Avnet gained electronic access to point-of-sale data on Electrocomponents' worldwide customers, and Electrocomponents would rely on Avnet to help them fill volume orders that the company would not have been able to fill without aid. In addition, Avnet became Electrocomponents' primary supplier of electronic components.

In 2000, soon after Electrocomponents' purchase of Allied, the company was valued at £3,000 million and joined the FTSE 100 index of the United Kingdom's largest companies.

Making the Most of Technology

In 2002, keeping with their practice of embracing technology and developing with it, Electrocomponents launched a free e-procurement service called PurchasingManager. The service was designed to allow an unlimited number of employees to place low-value orders on the RS Components Web site from their Internet-capable computers. Purchasing managers at the individual company level were enabled to set allowable spending levels for employees and received e-mail notification if an employee exceeded his or her spending limit. The service was designed to be customizable and Electrocomponents hoped that it would free purchasing managers' time to work on more strategic tasks.

Principal Subsidiaries

RS Components (operating in 24 countries); Allied Electronics (United States and Canada); Radiospares (France); Radionics (Ireland); RS Amidata (Spain); RS Chile; RS Japan.

Principal Competitors

Avnet Corporation; Arrow Electronics, Inc.; Pioneer-Standard Electronics, Inc.; Future Electronics Catalog Sales Corp.

Further Reading

''Allied to be Sold: Newark Reorganizes,'' *Purchasing,* July 15, 1999.

Bowen, David, "WWW + Flair = New Business," *Management Today,* May 1998, pp. 84–88.

Clutterbuck, David, and Walter Goldsmith, "Customer Care Versus Customer Count," *Managing Service Quality,* 1998, p. 327.

Cocks, Phil, "Partnership in Pursuit of Lean Supply," *Purchasing & Supply Management,* February 1996, p. 32.

Jorgensen, Barbara, "Why Avnet Is Selling Its Catalog Business," *Electronic Buyers' News,* June 14, 1999, p. 5.

Lynn, Matthew, "Where Now Cash Cow?" *Management Today,* March 1995, p. 46.

Odell, Patricia, "U.K.'s Parent's Plans for Allied," *Catalog Age,* September 1999, p. 16.

Page, Nigel, and Rick Marsland, "A World to the Wise," *Director,* September 1998, pp. 53–55.

Parker, Robin, "RS Launches Free Service for Unlimited Number of Users," *Supply Management,* February 28, 2002, p. 13.

—Tammy Weisberger

Enterprise Oil PLC

Grand Buildings
Trafalgar Square
London WC2N 5EJ
United Kingdom
Telephone: +44 (0) 20 7925-4000
Fax: +44 (0) 20 7925-4643
Web site: http://www.entoil.com

Public Company
Incorporated: 1983
Employees: 650 (2001)
Sales: £274.4 million (2001)
Stock Exchanges: London New York
Ticker Symbol: ETP.LN (London), ETP (New York)
NAIC: 211111 Crude Petroleum and Natural Gas
Extraction; 213112 Support Activities for Oil and Gas
Operations

Enterprise Oil PLC is the largest independent oil exploration and production company in the United Kingdom, competing against much larger companies, such as British Petroleum and Shell. Its core areas of oil and gas production areas (major finds of 100,000 barrels of oil equivalent per day or more) are the United Kingdom and Ireland, Norway and Denmark, and Italy, with growing operations in the U.S. Gulf of Mexico and Brazil. Other international joint ventures are in Australia, Greece, Iran, Western Siberia, Morocco, Kazakhstan, Cambodia, and Peru. The company has produced 242,000 boe/d (barrels of oil and gas equivalent per day) in 2001 and has 1.49 billion barrels of oil and gas in reserve worldwide.

Enterprise Oil was formed in 1983 (although it was officially incorporated at the end of 1982) as a government initiative by the Secretary of State for energy to take on the oil-producing activities of the British Gas Corporation just prior to that state-owned organization's privatization. The fledgling company was given a good start by its government parent, launched free of debt and protected by tax breaks in the 1983 budget, allowing it to write off over 80 percent of its exploration costs against taxes on existing production. Floated on the London Stock Exchange in 1984, Enterprise was the inheritor of several interests in the North Sea, including five commercial oil fields, a stake in 11 fields where oil had already been found, and a share in 14 other possible sites. In the next decade, Enterprise substantially widened its inherited interests in the North Sea and created an increasing portfolio of international interests.

Enterprise's Operations in the North Sea

The United Kingdom Continental Shelf (UKCS) in the North Sea remained the company's strongest area; at the end of 1993, Enterprise held interests in 113 blocks in the region, equating to a net acreage of 4,704 square kilometers, from which the company drew 72.8 percent of its total production. Almost from its inception, Enterprise concentrated on strengthening its U.K. interests through acquisition and exploration.

In 1985 during its first full year of operations, the company purchased Tanks Oil and Gas, and agreed to a farm-in deal with Conoco, and acquired Saxon Oil. Two years later the company enhanced its international oil and gas interests and position considerably with the acquisition of Imperial Chemical Industries (ICI). This coup, however, was to be overshadowed by another venture Enterprise was simultaneously—and secretively—planning: the Nelson project.

Convinced by a combination of seismic data and sheer intuition of the great potential of one of the blocks it had acquired an interest through its earlier deal with Conoco, Enterprise completed a complicated series of swaps with other oil companies—all unsuspecting of Enterprise's objective—to achieve 100 percent ownership of the block, some 180 kilometers to the east of Aberdeen. The company's maneuvers, described in retrospect by the *Independent* as "little short of brilliant," were vindicated when in 1988 Enterprise announced its discovery of one of the largest oil finds of the decade. (The project was named after the famous British admiral Horatio Nelson, with whom Enterprise, with its head office in London's Trafalgar Square, claims an affinity.) Enterprise subsequently reduced its stake in the Nelson field to a 31.57 percent interest. However, it retained its position as operator of the £1.1 billion project, becoming the first indepen-

Company Perspectives:

Enterprise Oil aspires to be the world's leading independent exploration and production company. Our vision is to deliver a superior combination of growth in value and financial returns by harnessing the power of our creativity and knowledge with integrity and passion.

dent U.K. company to operate a major North Sea oil field. The operation came on stream in February 1994.

Expanding Core Operations to Norway

In 1989, Enterprise further consolidated its position in the UKCS by acquiring the non-U.S. interests of Texas Eastern. In 1991, through a joint arrangement with the French company Elf Aquitaine, Enterprise acquired all of Occidental Overseas Ltd.'s North Sea license interests; as a result, the company also obtained a one-third interest in Elf Enterprise Petroleum Ltd. (EEP), the holding company of Occidental's former U.K. assets. Another important UKCS interest was Enterprise's stake in the Scott oil field, which began production in 1993.

Enterprise's activities in the North Sea include projects in Norway as well. The company's operations on the Norwegian Continental Shelf began in 1989, when it formed Enterprise Oil Norge Ltd. with the Norwegian interests it had acquired from Texas Eastern. Over the next four years, Enterprise built up its presence in the area. At of the end of 1993, it held interests in 24 blocks totaling 1,201 square kilometers. Early in 1994 the company clinched a deal to finance a three-year Norwegian North Sea exploration in exchange for the right to farm into three licenses held by Esso Norge—thus increasing its net acreage on the Norwegian Continental Shelf (NCS) by 25 percent.

By March 2001, Enterprise had interests in ten producing fields on the Norwegian Continental Shelf and one in Denmark, exceeding 100,000 barrels per day for the first time in 2000. Six out of seven wells drilled in the area were successfully producing. The Jotun field alone produced 130,000 barrels per day during 2000.

Another Core Production Area in Italy

The North Sea has historically been and still remains Enterprise's primary area of operations, but the company is increasingly developing international interests as well. It first targeted Italy for exploration in 1985, with successful results. Enterprise opened a Rome office in 1988 and within four years had discovered three promising sites for exploitation: Monte Alpi, Tempa Rossa, and Cerro Falcone. With Enterprise's later partnership with Eni, the Italian state oil company, in the lucrative Val d'Agri development, Italy became one of the company's three core areas of exploration and production.

Enterprise's enviable success with the Nelson field coincided, ironically, with a slump in industry prices, which, in 1993 and 1994 reached their lowest level in 20 years. In response, the company instituted cost-cutting measures in equipment and procedures and restricted its activities to newer fields where

modern, cost-efficient production facilities were in place and thus operating costs were lower. In this effort Enterprise was in line with the industry as a whole, which, it was reported in 1994, had formed a government-supported initiative, Cost Reduction in the New Era (CRINE). Some 36 U.K. offshore operators are members of CRINE, which aims to reduce the capital costs of new North Sea developments by standardizing equipment and procedures. In the past each project was developed with its own individually tailored—and thus highly expensive—engineering plan; oil companies, including Enterprise, are now recognizing that a more standardized approach to development can be much less costly and just as effective. The standardization of procedures and an increasing use of automation wherever possible also help to reduce costs, as does increasing cooperation among offshore operators.

A Model for Inspired Leadership

Enterprise Oil has established a solid and favorable reputation over the years: the *Independent* claimed in 1994 that Enterprise "has been a showcase of inspired management and leadership in a difficult market," and *The Financial Times* agreed, saying Enterprise "has built a reputation for strong management and far-sightedness." It was thus quite surprising and unexpected that the company became embroiled in an almost farcical—and ultimately unsuccessful—takeover bid for a rival independent oil and gas company, London and Scottish Marine Oil (Lasmo).

The two companies "started out as the Tweedledum and Tweedledee of the U.K. oil industry," according to *The Financial Times*, but their fortunes soon diverged dramatically. At one time Lasmo was the more successful and enjoyed the status of the United Kingdom's leading independent oil and gas company; indeed, in 1986 the company actually owned a substantial stake of Enterprise (some 30 percent), and speculation was rife that Lasmo would attempt a takeover. Enterprise, however, greatly strengthened its position, first through its acquisition of ICI's worldwide interests and then with the great leap forward of the Nelson coup, and thus became clearly too powerful for takeover.

Lasmo, on the other hand, found its fortunes declining, reaching the nadir following a disastrous 1991 takeover of another oil and gas company, Ultramar. Financial pundits delighted in repeating the joke of Lasmo's strange arithmetics: how to add a £1 billion company to another £1 billion company and end up with—a £1 billion company. Losing money, seriously strapped for cash, and staggering under a backlog of debt, Lasmo appeared ripe for takeover—or so Enterprise thought.

Its bid got off to an unfortunate start when Enterprise was forced to show its hand before it was ready; leaked information had caused Lasmo's share price to rise dramatically, prompting the watchdog Takeover Panel, in an unusual move, to require Enterprise to publicly clarify its intentions. Over the next few months, a media battle ensued. Enterprise was accused of megalomania, Lasmo of monumental incompetence. Enterprise was charged with dubious accounting practices, Lasmo with staggering incompetence. Enterprise was denounced for offering Lasmo shareholders a poor deal, mere "junk paper," Lasmo for really quite astonishing incompetence. Gleeful city commentators speculated that the only reason the mudslinging was

Key Dates:

1983: Enterprise Oil PLC is established in the United Kingdom.
1984: Enterprise Oil shares are listed on the London Stock Exchange.
1985: Company acquires Saxon Oil.
1988: Rome office opens.
1989: Company forms Enterprise Oil Norge Ltd. in Norway.
1991: Sir Graham Hearne is appointed Chairman.
1992: Enterprise Oil shares are listed on the New York Stock Exchange; Pierre Jungels is appointed chief executive.
1995: Company opens office in Peru.
1998: Company opens Brazil office.
1999: Enterprise Oil and London and Scottish Marine Oil (Lasmo) decide not to merge and exploration begins in Western Siberia.
2000: Company realizes a 30 percent increase in production with new fields in Norway.
2001: Sam Laidlaw is appointed chief executive and natural gas activities are expanded.
2002: Enterprise Oil board accepts $6.2 billion purchase bid from Royal Dutch Shell, subject to regulatory review and shareholder approval.

not worse was that the chairmen of the two companies were socially friendly, often hunting wildfowl together. In July 1994, Enterprise's bid for Lasmo failed.

Enterprise wanted Lasmo because it believed that the two companies would dovetail together resourcefully. Simply put, Enterprise had significant cash reserves but relatively poor long-term development prospects, whereas Lasmo enjoyed potentially profitable assets but, debt-ridden as it was, had little cash to exploit them. The two companies to some extent overlapped geographically, but Enterprise was stronger on the oil side whereas Lasmo had more gas reserves. Acquiring Lasmo would have roughly doubled Enterprise's size, but Enterprise's assertion that the company needed to be one of the ''big boys'' to compete in the oil business was widely ridiculed; even if the Lasmo takeover had been accomplished, it could not have brought Enterprise into the league of the real big boys, such as Shell and Esso.

Enterprise suffered some damage to its reputation during the course of its failed bid, but the harm would probably be short-lived for a company that enjoyed a reputation for making good, solid deals prior to that fiasco. More importantly, the media spotlight trained on the company during the bid process highlighted questions about Enterprise's future. Riding high in 1994, thanks particularly to the handsome payoffs of the Nelson and Scott developments, Enterprise faced potential difficulties as the decade progressed. In the oil industry a company is only as good as its last discovery. The production of Enterprise's star players, Nelson and Scott, would have peaked by 1995 or 1996, and industry commentators stressed that the challenge for Enterprise would be to discover or acquire new profitable sources. With oil prices so low, however, it was risky to invest significant capital in exploration, even for the financially healthy En-

terprise; in 1993 drilling levels had fallen to their lowest in the company's history.

Prudent management and disciplined control of costs placed Enterprise in a strong position in the mid-1990s. Satisfying revenue from its high-profile projects left the company financially robust, despite falling oil prices. Its healthy cash base, however, needed to be invested wisely. Financial analysts were divided over whether Enterprise's takeover of Lasmo would have been a good thing or not, but clearly the company had to acquire or discover new oil-producing assets in the near future.

Headed in the Right Direction

The *Oil and Gas Journal* reported in 1995 that Enterprise Oil had added several fields in the North Sea for exploration and production of forties blend crude (an important crude consisting of oil and gas liquids), to reach a production level of 400,000 barrels per day. Later that year, the company ''took a 40 percent interest in block 50 in the sub-Andean Santiago basin from Argentina's YPF SA and Quintana Minerals Corporation, Houston.'' At this same time, Enterprise also opened an office in Lima, Peru.

Enterprise lived up to its vision of applying creativity for growth in financial returns in 1996. As stated in *Hart's Petroleum Finance Week*, Elf Enterprise Petroleum (EEP) sold its 63.7 million shares amounting to 12.9 percent of Enterprise Oil PLC following reorganization. *Hart's* states, ''Enterprise estimates that it will assume £118 million (US $177 million) of net debt in return for mature oil and gas assets provisionally valued at £219 million (US $328.5 million) as a result of what amounts to a reverse merger.''

Enterprise continued to be pursued by possible suitors, reported *The Oil Daily* in 1996. The company's ''value has been pegged at US$2.5 billion to US$3 billion.'' Unsurprised, Enterprise Oil Finance Director Andrew Shilton said that the numerous takeover battles ''have piqued interest in independents such as his firm.''

Lucrative Gas Exploration

In 1998, Enterprise and EEX, an independent based in Houston, Texas, encountered hydrocarbon-bearing sands in two blocks in deep water in the Gulf of Mexico, *The Oil Daily* reported. In fact, Enterprise set a record for the deepest well in the area at 27,864 feet.

''People think that the Gulf of Mexico is played out, or overcompetitive,'' said Chief Executive of Enterprise Jungles Pierre. ''But even in the shallow waters, Chevron announced recently the discovery of 1 tcf (trillion cubic feet) of gas'' off the coastline of New Orleans. ''The market possibly does not realize that 1 tcf of gas in the shallow waters of the Gulf of Mexico is worth around $1.5 billion, whereas 1 tcf in the Caspian is worth nothing.''

More Expansion

The Financial Times reported that Enterprise and Lasmo again struggled over whether to merge in 1999, hoping to integrate their operations. The companies ultimately decided against the merger because of differing visions and strategies. Lasmo and British-Borneo were later acquired by Eni.

Later in the year, Enterprise took a 7.5 percent stake in Khanty Mansiysk Oil in Western Siberia. By 2002, this interest rose to 46 percent. The year 1999 also saw the beginnings of a joint venture in Brazil with Petrobras, Elf, and Shell to explore for hydrocarbons in the deep waters of the Campos Basin, covering 2,600 square kilometers. *The Financial Times* explained in July 2000 that the company also gained a 100 percent interest in the offshore Gyrfalcon field near Louisiana, along with interests in 19 other deep-water exploration blocks. Enterprise expanded its gas exploration and production, entering into an agreement with Iran to develop six offshore fields, the *Weekly Petroleum Argus* reported in 2001.

Because of technical problems in the North Sea and delays on sites in Italy, Enterprise's share price fell when it could not meet its reduced production target of 255,000 boe/d for the year, about 8 percent below expectations. This setback did not keep the company from targeting an output of 350,000 to 360,000 beo/d by mid-decade.

In late 2001, Enterprise apparently received another takeover bid, but turned it down after lengthy negotiations, refusing to identify the potential buyer. However, the *Weekly Petroleum Argus* speculates that the much larger Italian Eni may have been the bidder. The *Knight-Ridder/Tribune Business News* suggests that Eni was prepared to pay £3.4 billion for the company.

In January 2002, *Petroleum Intelligence Weekly* interviewed U.K. Energy minister Brian Wilson who said, "The demise of Enterprise would be bad news for the U.K. North Sea, which, as a mature province, has become increasingly dependent on smaller players with low-cost bases squeezing value out of smaller fields." He said the government policy of encouraging independents such as Enterprise in the North Sea was producing 'great results.' " He added that there was no guarantee that those projects deemed attractive to independents would appeal to a state-owned oil giant like Eni.

The End of the Struggle for Independence

Although Enterprise had given every indication of staying independent, its board accepted a bid of US$6.2 billion (£4.3 billion sterling, including debt) in April 2002 from Royal Dutch Shell. The deal was subject to acceptance from shareholders. Patrick d'Ancona, head of public relations at Enterprise said that the deal was a good price from Shell and that the transaction reflected the central plank of Sam Laidlaw's strategy that he announced in February of 2002, which was about delivering shareholder value. "At that time, our independence was seen as a tool with which to best pursue that," d'Ancona explained, "but, in the light of this offer, clearly we could accelerate the process of delivering value to shareholders. The board recognized the value of this bid."

Principal Subsidiaries

Enterprise Energy Ireland Ltd. (Ireland); Enterprise Oil do Brasil Ltda. (Brazil); Enterprise Oil Exploration Ltd. (Greece); Enterprise Oil Exploration PLC (Scotland); Enterprise Oil Ital-

iana SpA (Italy); Enterprise Oil Middle East Ltd. (Iran); Enterprise Oil Norge Ltd. (Norway); Enterprise Oil Services Inc. (USA).

Principal Competitors

British Petroleum (BP); Shell Oil Company; Kerr-McGee.

Further Reading

Barker, Thorold; Corzine, Robert, "A Slow and Tortuous Dance Followed by a Final Stumble over Strategy and Culture," *The Financial Times*, April 1, 1999, p. 32.

"A Bid Too Far for the Starship Enterprise," *The Times (London)*, May 21, 1994.

"Britain's Enterprise Oil Shapes Up to Do Battle with Italian Bidder," *Knight-Ridder/Tribune Business News*, January 16, 2002.

"Cash Flow Booms for Enterprise," *The Times (London)*, March 11, 1994.

Davidson, Andrew, "Graham Hearne," *Management Today*, July 1996, pp. 50–54.

"A Decade-Long Dance Draws towards a Close," *Independent*, April 29, 1994.

"Defiant Enterprise Vows to Go It Alone," *International Petroleum Finance*, April 2001, p. 8.

Durgin, Hillary, "International: Enterprise Oil in Gulf of Mexico Acquisition," *The Financial Times*, July 17, 2000, p. 26.

"Elf Enterprise Finance Sells Its 12.9% Stake in Enterprise Oil Following Reorganization," *Hart's Petroleum Finance Week*, Potomac; February 5, 1996, p. 1.

"Enterprise: Active in the Southern Appennines," *Petroleum Economist*, November 1997, p.16.

"Enterprise, but Not Enough to Get Lasmo," *Guardian*, June 25, 1994.

"Enterprise Flushed Out as Lasmo Stalker," *Guardian*, April 28, 1994.

"Enterprise Oil Ready to Spend War Chest," *Lloyds List*, January 10, 1994.

"Enterprise Recommended," *The Financial Times*, April 22, 1999, p. 50.

"Enterprise Stake in Siberian Fields," *The Financial Times*, October 20, 1999, p. 32.

"Exploration and Development Action Still Percolating in Peru," *Oil & Gas Journal*, December 4, 1995, p. 78.

Fan, Aliza, "Strong Performance by Enterprise Places Company at Center of Takeover Speculation," *The Oil Daily*, June 10, 1996, p. 1.

"Gas Is Golden for UK Oil Firms," *Weekly Petroleum Argus*, August 6, 2001, p. 2.

"Gloves Off in Pounds 1.4bn Battle for Lasmo," *Observer*, June 12, 1994.

Gorman, Brian, "UK's Enterprise Plans to Make Big Splash in Gulf of Mexico Despite Its Late Arrival," *The Oil Daily*, July 16, 1998.

Hobday, Nicola, "Shell Buys Enterprise Oil for $6.2B," *The Daily Deal*, April 2, 2002.

"The Independent: Enterprise Oil Results 2001," *Chemical Business Newsbase*, April 24, 2001.

Key Facts 1994, London: Enterprise Oil, 1994.

Key Facts 2002, London: Enterprise Oil PLC, 2002.

Kroenwetter, Eric, "EEX, Enterprise Announce Discovery in Gulf, Compare Prospects with Shell's Auger Field," *The Oil Daily*, June 23, 1998.

Lascelles, David, and Peggy Hollinger, "Analysts Fear the Errors of Over-Ambition," *The Financial Times*, April 28, 1994.

"Lasmo, the Perfect Fit for Enterprise," *Independent*, April 28, 1994.

Mortished, Carl, "Enterprise's 1.5bn Bid for Lasmo Flops," *The Times (London)*, July 2, 1994, p. 21.

"Mystery Bidder Puts UK Enterprise in Play," *The Oil Daily*, January 9, 2002.

"National Sentiment Creates Complications for Energy," *The Oil Daily*, January 23, 2002.

"Nelson's New Success Is the Result of Enterprise," *Daily Telegraph*, February 19, 1994.

"New Financial Mind-Set Required for Further British Offshore Projects," *Hart's Petroleum Finance Week*, Potomac; September 11, 1995, p. 1.

"North Sea Turns Rough for Britain's Oil Industry," *The Times (London)*, March 8, 1994.

"Oil Wars," *Daily Telegraph*, May 21, 1994.

"Reserve Judgment," *Economist*, June 23, 1983, pp. 79–80.

Rhodes, Anne K, "UK North Sea's Forties Blend Crude Assayed," *Oil & Gas Journal*, January 23, 1995, p. 48.

"Takeover Targets Enterprise (Corporate)," *Weekly Petroleum Argus*, January 14, 2002, p. 2.

"UK Independents: Last of a Dying Breed," *Weekly Petroleum Argus*, March 19, 2001, p. 6.

"United Kingdom—UK Energy Minister Brian Wilson Has Had His Say in the Enterprise Oil Takeover Debate, Although It Remains Unlikely He Will Ultimately Do Anything to Protect the Company from the Advances of Italy's Eni or Any Other Suitor," *Petroleum Intelligence Weekly*, January 28, 2002, p. 7.

Washer, Jim, "Sam's Plan Fails to Convince Enterprise Investors," *Energy Intelligence Briefing*, February 5, 2002, p. 1.

—Robin DuBlanc
—update: Annette Dennis McCully

Evergreen Marine Corporation (Taiwan) Ltd.

Evergreen Marine Building
166, Minsheng East Road, Sec2
Taipei, 104
Taiwan
Telephone: +886 (2) 3312 3126
Fax: +886 (2) 3312 3525
Web site: http://www.evergreen-marine.com

Public Company
Incorporated: 1987
Employees: 1,438
Sales: NT $3.5 billion (US$101.9 million) (2001)
Stock Exchanges: Taiwan
Ticker Symbol: EMC
NAIC: 483111 Deep Sea Freight Transportation; 483211 Inland Water Freight Transportation; 488310 Port and Harbor Operations; 488320 Marine Cargo Handling (All but Dock and Pier Operations); 488510 Freight Transportation Arrangement; 484110 General Freight Trucking, Local; 484121 General Freight Trucking, Long-Distance; 488490 Other Support Activities for Road Transportation; 493110 General Warehousing and Storage; 493190 Other Warehousing and Storage; 493120 Refrigerated Warehousing and Storage; 234990 All Other Heavy Construction

With more than 130 owned and long-term chartered ships, Evergreen Marine Corporation (Taiwan) Ltd. is the third largest container-shipping firm in the world. As a corporation that is part of the Evergreen Group, Evergreen Marine and its affiliates serve Asia, Europe, the Americas, Australia, Africa, and the Mediterranean. The parent corporation is responsible for directing worldwide operations, planning service routes, and assigning personnel.

Evergreen is a regularly scheduled global marine and intermodal shipping carrier that transports containerized cargo between ports and destinations in more than 80 countries through its worldwide service network. The company is not a part of the conference system—a group of shipping companies of different ownerships and nationalities servicing the same ports that agree to use the same rate structure. In addition to feeder services that expand the reach of Evergreen into hundreds of minor ports, intermodal road, rail, and river barge services carry the company's containers far inland, directly to its customers. The company is certified to ISO 9002, the international voluntary standard for quality, and complies with the standard at all locations.

Evergreen's Origins

On September 1, 1968, Dr. Chang Yung-fa, from the Taiwan port of Keelung, founded the Evergreen Group by beginning a shipping business with one secondhand, 20-year old cargo vessel named the Central Trust to provide "go-anywhere" service. Chang garnered the funds to launch his business through a loan from Japan's Marubeni trading house. He was intent on building up his business to a scheduled shipping service, and established the company's first liner service for the previously neglected Middle East trade route less than a year later.

Chang's success has made him one of the wealthiest entrepreneurs in the world and a celebrity in his home country. The son of a ship's carpenter, he grew up in the shipping industry. Before he started Evergreen in 1968, the 41-year-old Chang had worked his way up from a lowly shipping clerk, to sailor, and eventually to captain of a ship. The hard work and leadership skills that had helped him attain that position would prove to be essential to the future success of his fledgling company. Chang started Evergreen with 50 employees, 32 of whom worked at sea.

During his first year of business, one of Chang's customers paid him handsomely to make a delivery to the Persian Gulf. The opportunistic Chang realized that this potentially lucrative shipping route between East Asia and the Persian Gulf was being neglected by his competitors, many of whom were focusing on the giant North American market. At the time, several oil-rich Middle Eastern countries were just becoming familiar with 20th century technology and modern culture, and were spending billions of dollars on massive modernization projects, such as the construction of schools, communication infrastructure, hospitals, airports, and power plants. Chang quickly zeroed in on that route. He purchased a second ship in 1969, and initiated regularly scheduled service to the Middle East. Despite early losses, Chang was able to secure enough capital to purchase several more vessels during the early 1970s.

As his Middle East service expanded, Chang searched for other untapped market niches. In 1972, he began offering service between East Asia and Central America, a region that most shipping companies had dismissed as highly unprofitable. Evergreen Marine Corporation (Japan) Ltd. was established in Tokyo, and realized rapid growth. Then, in 1974, Evergreen began offering service between East Asia and the U.S. East Coast—Evergreen opened a New York office in cooperation with a U.S. company and purchased four new vessels from a Japanese shipbuilder. Evergreen Marine Corporation (New York) was established, followed by Evergreen Marine Corporation (California) in 1976.

The new ships were relatively small S-class vessels, and many observers believed that they were too small to be profitable considering the extreme competition in the U.S. East Coast market. Despite these predictions, Evergreen succeeded in carving out a market. Chang further developed the company's American market opportunities, ordering more ships and launching new service routes to California in 1976 and then to Seattle in 1977. Due to these heavy investments, Evergreen posted a string of early losses throughout the late 1960s and early 1970s; further, the company was affected along with the rest of the shipping industry by the energy crises of 1974 and 1975. Eventually, though, business improved in the late 1970s and Evergreen began to show profits.

Containerized Shipping Sweeps the Industry

Evergreen's survival and growth during the industry downturn of the mid-1970s was the result of savvy business management, sheer tenacity, and Chang's willingness to take risks. Chang's gains were particularly impressive considering that his competition largely comprised containerized shippers. Indeed, prior to the late 1960s, most freight was shipped loose on bulk carriers. Goods were trucked or sent by rail to a port, unloaded, and then reloaded onto a ship. The system was slow and inefficient, and the open goods were vulnerable to spoilage and pilferage. In 1956, American Malcolm McLean, the operator of a trucking company, conceived the idea of containerized shipping, in which goods were loaded into a container at the factory, taken to port, and loaded directly onto a ship. By the late 1960s, established shipping companies had either converted to the new system or had been trammeled by their competitors.

Unfortunately for Chang, Evergreen lacked the resources necessary to convert older ships to containerized haulers. It was largely because of that disadvantage that he attacked the smaller,

neglected routes during the late 1960s and early 1970s, and concentrated on efficiency and customer satisfaction. When Evergreen finally did convert to containerized shipping, the company took the industry by storm, offering containerized shipping in its U.S. markets on the East Coast in 1975. In spite of the fact that this new venture took place during the oil crisis and a subsequent downturn in marine transportation, the effort was a success. This same year also saw the establishment of Evergreen Group Incorporated S.A. in Panama, which was renamed Evergreen International S.A. in 1981. In 1979, Evergreen Marine Corporation (U.K.) was established as Evergreen's European headquarters for operations and business development, a function that was later transferred to Hamburg, Germany. When this change occurred, the U.K. office became the company's exclusive agent in the United Kingdom and Ireland.

Throughout the late 1970s, Chang aggressively invested in Evergreen to update existing ships and expand its line of freighters. As part of Chang's plan to develop a worldwide network of containerized shipping routes, Evergreen initiated new routes serving Europe, the Red Sea, and the East Mediterranean. At the same time, he augmented the expansion effort with Evergreen Transport Corporation, a trucking company that he started in 1973 to support Evergreen Marine's shipping operations.

Evergreen's willingness and ability to penetrate competitive global markets was evidenced by its North European initiative. At the time, this lucrative market was primarily managed by the well-established Far Eastern Freight Conference (FEFC). The FEFC was predominantly made up of established shipping companies, and outsiders like Evergreen were not encouraged to compete. Nevertheless, Evergreen executives began an in-depth analysis of the North Europe market, as they did for all of the regions that they considered servicing. Although they were hesitant to tap the market because of the entrenched competition, Evergreen officials commenced service in Northern Europe in 1979. The gamble paid off, and Evergreen quickly developed a profitable operation in the region.

Evergreen's Global Profile

To showcase its global expansion, the Evergreen Group was renamed Evergreen International S.A. (EIS) in 1981. Not surprisingly, more extensive routes were developed, and a massive worldwide company headquarters was constructed in Taipei, Taiwan in 1986. That same year, Evergreen Marine Corporation (New York) and Evergreen Marine Corporation (California) merged to form Evergreen International (USA), and, in 1987, Evergreen International (Deutschland) GmbH in Hamburg, Germany was established as the company's new European headquarters, with all responsibilities being transferred from the London office.

Evergreen had established itself as an emerging force in the global shipping industry at this time. The company's green shipping containers were an increasingly common sight in ports throughout the world, and Evergreen was aggressively investing for future growth. Importantly, Evergreen launched its prosperous ''round-the-world'' service in 1984. This ambitious scheme linked Evergreen's fleet of vessels, as well as some ships owned by other carriers, to offer through service around

Key Dates:

1968: Evergreen Marine is established with one second-hand cargo vessel.

1969: First liner service begins on Middle East trade route.

1972: Evergreen Marine Corporation (Japan) Ltd. is established in Tokyo.

1974: Evergreen Marine Corporation (New York) Ltd. is established.

1975: Evergreen Group Incorporated S.A. is established in Panama.

1976: Evergreen Marine Corporation (California) is established.

1979: Evergreen Marine Corporation (U.K.) is established in London, later becoming the exclusive agent of Evergreen for the United Kingdom and Ireland.

1981: The company is renamed Evergreen International S.A. (EIS) to highlight the global expansion of the Evergreen Group.

1984: The company initiates two-way around the world container service, eastbound and westbound.

1986: Headquarters offices are built in Taipei, Taiwan; Evergreen Marine Corporation (New York) and Evergreen Marine Corporation (California) merge to form Evergreen International (USA).

1992: Evergreen Marine International (USA) is renamed Evergreen America Corporation.

1993: Evergreen Star Hong Kong Ltd. is established, replacing its agent for Evergreen Marine Corporation and Uniglory Marine Corporation.

1995: Evergreen International (Deutschland) GmbH becomes certified to ISO 9002.

1997: Evergreen Philippines Corporation (EGP) is established in Manila to handle operation of Evergreen and Uniglory services.

2002: Evergreen Group fleet numbers 61 full container vessels. Owned ships and those chartered long term total 130 over 400,000 TEU (twenty-foot equivalent units).

the globe. Evergreen began regularly sending eastbound ships from Singapore to Pusan and Tokyo, through the Panama Canal, to New York, across the Atlantic, through the Suez Canal, and back to Singapore. A similar westbound service departed regularly from Tokyo, and made stops in Korea, Singapore, Europe, and New York, among other ports. The round-the-world voyages typically required about 75 days and were coordinated with the help of satellite systems.

Investing in Growth and Employees

Partly to help finance the round-the-world service, Evergreen invested more than US$1.5 billion in new ships, terminals, trucks, and containers between 1983 and 1986. The heavy investments surprised other members of the shipping industry, most of which were suffering from a severe industry downturn. They watched curiously as Evergreen expanded, while at the same time excess shipping capacity was suppressing prices and reducing industry profits. Furthermore, competitors wondered

where the tight-lipped Chang found the money to expand; some analysts speculated that Japanese trading house Marubeni was financing Evergreen under the table, while others suspected various Japanese or American banks.

Regardless of who fronted the investment capital, Evergreen's operations swelled during the mid-1980s as its reach stretched to every corner of the globe. While many of its competitors reduced services or failed, Evergreen's share of major east-west shipping routes ballooned to a dominating 10 percent. Amazingly, Evergreen was still a private company—75 percent owned by Chang and 25 percent owned by his employees.

Evergreen's stunning gains during the shipping industry recession of the mid-1980s were largely attributable to the company's innovative and disciplined workers. The company's philosophy was reflected by its name, Evergreen, which symbolized Chang's goal of constant growth. That growth was achieved by an incessant preoccupation with customer service, which drove the company to become constantly more proficient and productive. Evergreen's heavy investments in cutting edge technology, for example, had made it the most cost-effective carrier in the world.

Evergreen ships were outfitted with microcomputers and satellite tracking systems that allowed the company to pinpoint the exact location of each of its containers at all times. As a result, Evergreen's large ships were staffed by just 17 crew-members in comparison to an industry average of about 30. A 1986 study showed that Evergreen's cost of delivering a 20-foot container was only US$835, compared to US$1320 for the average major U.S. carrier. Furthermore, Evergreen was generating a profit of about US$80 per container while the industry average was less than $10.

Chang gave the credit for Evergreen's success to its top-notch employees. In contrast to most other shipping lines, Evergreen staffed its ships with highly trained crew members, many of whom had college degrees. Chang personally interviewed every employee that joined the Taiwan office, and once applicants were invited to join Evergreen they were treated well. The company paid higher salaries than most of its competitors and fringe benefits were plentiful. For example, Chang motivated workers by compensating them with ownership shares in the company. The result was an intense loyalty toward, and respect for, the company, which translated indirectly into customer loyalty. Evergreen's Taiwan headquarters was quiet and efficient. The highly dedicated employees arrived early and departed late, and their desks were devoid of personal effects. Furthermore, no one smoked, sipped tea, read newspapers, or used telephones for personal calls during business hours.

By late 1986, Evergreen was operating 52 ships and managing 160,000 containers. Moreover, in addition to Evergreen Marine, Chang's privately held enterprise had branched out to include 14 different companies, most of which were engaged in the manufacturer, storage, and transportation of containers. All of the divisions had names beginning with "Ever." For example, Chang owned Everlaurel, a Japanese trading company, and Evergenius, a software supplier. Those two companies mirrored Chang's intent to diversify out of the shipping industry into a range of new businesses.

Indeed, Chang felt that he had achieved his goal of permeating the shipping industry and that the only challenge remaining was to increase Evergreen's market share. To raise expansion capital for more growth, Chang took Evergreen public in September 1987 with a listing on the Taiwan Stock Exchange. Financials released in that year showed that Evergreen's diversified operations had garnered $1.2 billion in revenues in 1986, $50 million of which was netted as profit.

Beginning in 1988, Evergreen Marine Corp. entered a period of consolidation. During that time, the company worked to reorganize its existing operations, cut unnecessary overhead, and reevaluate its presence in foreign markets. Meanwhile, Chang pursued new ventures through Evergreen Marine Corp.'s parent company, the Evergreen Group.

Evergreen Takes to the Skies

Chang Yung-fa, still at the helm of Evergreen at 62 in 1989, the world's largest container-shipper at that time, stuck his neck out to buy eight Boeing 747-400 jumbo jets, and four extended range twin engine Boeing 767-300s for a grant total of US$1.7 billion. He also completed an order for 14 new MD-11s with McDonnell Douglas. Barring complications, the planes would be in use by 1992, partnering for passenger and freight service with Cathay Pacific, Lufthansa, Japan Air Lines, and Singapore Airlines. The aircraft purchases followed the formation of Evergreen Airways in March, just after the government decided to allow local, privately owned companies to establish international passenger and cargo airlines.

The founding of the new air service "clearly has the support of the Taiwanese government," *The Economist* stated. Chang Yung-fa was helping reduce Taiwan's "embarrassingly stubborn trade surplus with the United States," which reached US$9.1 billion in the first nine months of 1989—a 23 percent rise on the same period the previous year and higher than the government's US$8.1 billion target for the whole of 1989. Interestingly, Taiwan had a population of 20 million at that time but was the 13th largest trading nation. The government wanted to reduce the island's reliance on trade with America, and would need efficient transportation links around the world.

EVA's planes reflected the technology focus of Evergreen's ships. Televisions were mounted on the backs of seats, for example, and satellite telephones were available. Furthermore, EVA's technologically advanced planes averaged less than one year in age by 1994, giving the company a significant long-term advantage over competitors with aging fleets. By 1994, EVA was operating 20 aircraft and serving cities in Asia, North America, Europe, and Australia.

Rate Struggles and Expansion

With the goal of increased trade in mind, Evergreen offered a US$200 per container discount in 1990 over the previous year, which flew in the face of a rate stabilization pact discussed with ten other large North Atlantic carriers. Several other shipping firms had increased their rates by 8 percent. Evergreen later accused North Atlantic lines of conducting a smear campaign by leaking misleading reports that blamed Evergreen for undermining collective attempts to increase rates. The contracts involved included Beck's and Heineken for shipping beer from Europe to the United States. *International Freighting Weekly* stated that Evergreen's unusual outburst blamed other members of the Eurocorde Discussion Agreement for "leaking biased reports, claiming it was an attempt to discredit the line."

Another of Evergreen Group's major ventures in the early 1990s was its hotel business, which represented Chang's efforts to become active in travel and leisure industries. Evergreen's first hotel was the Evergreen Plaza Hotel, which opened in Hong Kong in 1991. The hotel featured 22 floors with 360 rooms and offered a full range of amenities for business travelers. Evergreen opened a second hotel, the 400-room Evergreen Laurel Hotel, in Taiwan in 1992. In 1993, moreover, the company began operating a second Evergreen Laurel Hotel in Bangkok. Other Evergreen hotels were slated to open during the mid-1990s. Evergreen's hotels offered luxury accommodations, Western cuisine, and full recreational and conference amenities.

Along with this expansion went a flurry of renaming for the subsidiaries. The Hamburg office was renamed Evergreen Deutschland GmbH in 1992, and Evergreen Marine International (USA) was renamed Evergreen America Corporation in the same year, with its headquarters in Jersey City, New Jersey. The new American headquarters was responsible for all operations in the United States, Canada, and the Caribbean area. By 2002, Evergreen America had 26 local offices, all reporting to the Jersey City office. Evergreen Marine Corporation (Japan) Ltd. was also renamed that year as Evergreen Japan Corporation, with branch offices in Osaka, Nagoya, Fukuoka, and Sendai. The London office was also renamed Evergreen U.K. Ltd.

At about this time, Evergreen began to provide refrigerated containers in response to customer demand, and ordered three new container vessels to be delivered in 1993. The new ships, each 3,399 TEU, would be used on the westbound around the world routes, along with the 11 3,428 TEU vessels. In 1993, Evergreen Star Hong Kong Ltd. was established, replacing the company's agent for Evergreen Marine Corporation and Uniglory Marine Corporation. Having a presence in Hong Kong was viewed by Evergreen as a means to pave the way for better business relations in Hong Kong and Mainland China.

While the Evergreen Group expanded, Evergreen Marine Corporation was renamed Evergreen Marine Corporation (Taiwan) Ltd., and renewed its global expansion effort. It was aided by its smaller sister company Uniglory, which was started in 1984 and was 50 percent owned by Evergreen in early 1995. The number of ships operated by Evergreen Marine declined between 1986 and 1993, but Evergreen's shipping capacity increased. Indeed, in 1993 Evergreen Marine launched its first ship with more than 4,000 TEUs (twenty-foot equivalent units—an indicator of carrying capacity). In 1994, moreover, Evergreen ordered 10 new giant ships; five with 4,229 TEU capacity and five with 4,900 TEU capacity. That brought the total number of ships operating in Evergreen Marine's fleet to 56 by 1995.

On Evergreen's 25th anniversary in 1993, the company was displaying healthy revenues of $1.2 billion and profits of $106 million. During that short time, Chang had built the largest shipping company in the world and had become a world-renowned entrepreneur with companies involved in a vast array of industries. Furthermore, at the age of 66 and still firmly in control of the company he started, Chang showed no signs of slowing down. When asked to give advice to shipping industry newcomers in the 1994 *Journal of Commerce and Commercial*, Chang suggested: "they must better themselves with all-round shipping experience and a strong willingness to serve customers' needs. There also has to be a commitment to taking some risks in life because not everything turns out successful. And finally, one must possess a spirit of adventure."

Still Pursuing Quality

In 1994, Evergreen Marine Corporation received a quality award for service performance from several customers, including Olin Corporation, Toyota Motor Sales, Venture Stores, and Target Stores. Olin, a chemical firm that is based in Stamford, Connecticut, praised Evergreen for its service and safety record. The company had not applauded the performance of any ocean carrier before. In 1995, the company's headquarters in Hamburg became certified to ISO 9002, the voluntary international standard for quality that had become a prerequisite for international trade in Europe.

In 1997, to meet the growing needs of customers in the Philippines, Evergreen Philippines Corporation (EGP) was established in Manila. The new company handled the operation of Evergreen and Uniglory services, working independently with the departments and sections as a team. By 2002, the Philippines office had branch offices in Cebu, Davao, and General Santos.

Evergreen's ability to offer good rates and stay outside the conference system came to fruition in 1998, according to *Traffic World*. "The line is one of the biggest carriers in the world—second in TEU counts in U.S. trade lanes with about 1.2 million in 1997, according to PIERS [*PIERS Trade Monitor*, a publication that deals with maritime research]. It also has a reputation for offering good service at discount prices—just below those of conference carriers. Indeed, Evergreen often has been the carrier of choice in major trade lanes, such as the trans-Atlantic, where it has been offering rates only a tad below those of the Trans-Atlantic Conference Agreement."

Evergreen Marine Corporation and COSCO agreed to launch ESA in 1999, a joint service linking major ports in Asia with Mauritius, South Africa and the east coast of South America. The carriers anticipated lower operating costs through the new partnership. Evergreen contributed eight ships capable of carrying 2.728 containers, while COSCO committed one vessel of 1,960 TEU (20 foot equivalent unit) and one chartered ship. The route would be Hong Kong, Kaohsiung, Singapore, Port Louis, Durban, Cape Town, Buenos Aires, Montevideo, and Santos.

Fledgling Airline Profitable

In spite of a region-wide recession for Asian airlines, EVA Air posted an after tax profit of NT$62.59 million (US$1.94 million) in 1998. *China News* reported that the company had a target of NT$46 billion (US$1.34 billion) for the end of 1999, nine percent higher than its profit for 1998. A shift in main focus from passenger to cargo service mid-year took the carrier from a deficit to a profit for the year. Tony Chou, head of EVA Air's operations division, explained, "The next two to three years will still be very lean years for the civil aviation industry. Our confidence, however, has been built up by our first quarter performance this year. We got better than expected results, and we are hopeful we will be able to hold this up."

EVA Air has developed some appealing services to attract passengers, such as providing deluxe service, a cross between the business and economy class, which was a major hit. The airline also made arrangements with hotels and resorts to capture the tourist market. Chou noted, "We look at our customers' behavior first, and later introduce innovations that meet their demands. We present EVA Air as a new airline that is aggressive and energetic. We are not afraid to make changes provided they would satisfy our customers."

This gung-ho approach carried over to the freight business, a good idea since it amounted to 41 percent of EVA's business. Evergreen estimated that cargo would account for 50 percent of EVA's business the following year, as the cargo business was growing at a rate of 14 percent a year. The company purchased three more aircraft to accommodate the new business, and anticipated expansion from its fleet of 40 planes serving 32 destinations to between 60 and 70 wide-bodied aircraft by 2008. In addition to new services to Atlanta, and between Taiwan and India, the airline entered into alliances with leading domestic carriers who provided connections between Mumbai and Bangalore and Madras and Delhi to increase services in India. The company also launched passenger services to Canada after flights booked in the Canada-bound Taipei route exceeded 300,000 in the first nine months of 1998.

Burgeoning Growth and Mergers

In August 1999, Evergreen Marine Corporation and China Ocean Shipping Company (COSCO) jointly launched a service linking South Africa and South America, providing 10 vessels on a weekly route. Evergreen contributed eight ships from its 20 2,728 TEU G-type fleet while COSCO provided the 1,960 TEU Sky River and one chartered vessel. The service, the ESA, linked the main ports in the Far East with Mauritius, South Africa, and the east coast of South America, with a port rotation of Hong Kong, Kaohsiung, Singapore, Port Louis, Durban, Cape Town, Buenos Aires, Montevideo, and Santos.

In October 1999, the Evergreen Group announced that it would be building 25 new container ships, half of which would be managed by Lloyd Triestino Company, the Italian shipping company acquired by Evergreen the year before. As reported in the *Central News Agency (Taiwan)*, President Chang Jung-fa stated that the ships were to be used to build up the Triestino fleet with its 42 Panamanian-registered container ships. Evergreen acquired Lloyd Triestino for US$35 million and took on its US$100 million in debt, but allowed the company to keep its name and to operate as a sister company to Evergreen. Triestino would develop new services, including expanded service to Mainland China. Evergreen had just launched weekly service linking Mainland China, the Mediterranean, and Northern Europe.

Chang also stated that Evergreen Group would merge Evergreen Marine Corporation (Taiwan) Ltd., the world's second largest container carrier, with Uniglory Marine Corporation, an

Evergreen subsidiary. Uniglory would then become an intra-Asia trade department within Evergreen Marine. Along these same lines, Evergreen Marine Corporation (Taiwan) Ltd. joined the Crowley/APL/Lykes alliance in the trade between the east coasts of North and South America, withdrawing its small charter vessels. The combined service would use six vessels with an average 2,300 TEU capacity in a weekly rotation, and would cover New York, Norfolk, Charleston, Miami, Rio de Janeiro, Santos, Paranagua, and Buenos Aires. In addition, Evergreen and its Panamanian affiliate Unigreen Marine improved services between the United States, The Caribbean, and Venezuelan markets, using three B-type vessels. The companies also planned to offer transshipment at Panama to and from Evergreen's eastbound and westbound around the world services.

In March 2001, The New World Alliance (TNWA) announced expansion of its trans-Pacific services with a creative slot exchange partnership with Evergreen Marine Corporation over a two year period. The exchange of container space marked the first time that APL, Hyundai Merchant Marine (HMM) and Mitsui O.S.K. Lines (MOL), as members of The New World Alliance and Evergreen had worked together. Evergreen purchased space on TNWA's weekly service between the U.S. Pacific Northwest and major Asia ports—the Pacific Northwest Express (ONX)—and TNWA purchased space from Evergreen on its services linking Asia and the U.S. east coast. An article in *PR Newswire* stated that the deal was a win for customers and carriers alike, as existing services would be enhanced and more transportation options would be provided for customers.

A new container terminal built by Evergreen Marine Corporation at Taranto in southeastern Italy opened for business in early July 2001, replacing the Gioia Tauro terminal to become the company's maritime freight transition center in the Mediterranean. The new terminal, which could handle two million TEU containers per year, had a one-kilometer pier that can berth three large container ships at a time. The pier could be expanded to 2.5 kilometers long, capable of berthing seven ships.

Evergreen's rapid and innovation expansion paid off. *Traffic World* reported in May 2001 that the company's operating profits were up from US$28.9 million in 1999 to US$40.1 million, a 39 percent increase over the previous year. Revenue increased 15 percent to US$1.9 billion. Just to make sure it could keep up, however, Evergreen was putting larger and faster ships into service, and was developing slot exchange relationships with other carriers. Unfortunately, the latter part of the year reflected what much of the rest of the shipping industry was experiencing—a significant slowing of business for Evergreen Marine Corporation and Greencompass Marine, both of which reported August revenues of about 8.55 percent less than the previous year. These losses continued after the September 11, 2001, terrorist attacks on the Twin Towers in New York City, but most of the major shipping firms remained optimistic because of their diversity of services and destinations.

Adieu, Singapore

In early 2002, Evergreen Marine Corporation announced plans to move its transshipment hub from the Port of Singapore Authority (PSA) to the Malaysian southern Port of Tanjung Pelepas (PTP) because of significantly cheaper container handling charges. Chang Yung-fa was quoted in Bernama: The Malaysian National News Agency as stating, "Charges for Tanjung Pelepas are more than 50 percent lower than those in Singapore. Our company has annually handled about 1.2 million TEUs on container cargoes in Singapore, so the difference between the two ports amounts to as much as NT$200 million ($584,000) or so."

The shift was a major loss for the state-owned PSA, which had lost 10 percent of its container volume the year before due to economic slowdown and the Danish global container liner Maersk Sealand's shift to PTP. Maersk, the largest container shipping company in the world, moved 1.8 million TEUs through Singapore annually. Evergreen Marine and its Uniglory Marine Corporation had been moving nearly 1.2 million TEUs through Singapore annually, which came to about 7 percent of the total number of containers handled by PSA. The change would take place in August 2002 when Evergreen's contract with PSA expired. PTP essentially performed a major coup in landing Maersk and Evergreen, as the port had just been established in 1999.

Still More Frontiers to Conquer

Evergreen Marine also announced in *IPR Strategic Business Information Database* that it would begin new operations from Mainland China in March 2002. The expansion to China business must overcome longstanding political hurdles that blocked direct transport to the mainland. Fortunately, Evergreen's decision was in response to China's Vice Minister of Foreign Trade and Economic Cooperation, An Min, who called for Taiwan to take measure to open direct trade and transport. The company's acquisition of Lloyd Triestino a year earlier allowed Taiwanese companies direct shipping lines with China. Evergreen established representative offices in Dalian, Tianjin, and Qingdao as part of its primary strategy to further develop the market, planning to secure a strong market share of China's potentially significant trade growth after it joined the World Trade Organization.

In March 2002, Evergreen announced that it would launch regular container service from Taiwan to the west coast of South America, providing a weekly container service between Taiwan and Panama, Colombia, Ecuador, Peru, and Chile. An Evergreen spokesman stated in *AsiaPulse News* that the cargo travel time between southern Taiwan's Kaohsiung Port and destinations in Chile and Colombia would be shortened by 31 to 26 days respectively.

Evergreen planned to pick up on the total logistics trend by increasing its investment in forwarding operations, container depots, warehousing, and trucking in China, Southeast Asia, the Indian subcontinent, and South America. Given Evergreen's savvy moves historically and the fact that it reported a profit of NT$1.7 billion (US$50.3 million) in 2001, up 35 percent from 2000, it seemed likely that its cautious but strategic approach to the China markets and logistics business would pay off.

Principal Subsidiaries

Evergreen America Corporation (select U.S. and Canadian cities); Evergreen International S.A. (Panama); Evergreen Japan

Corporation; Evergreen Deutschland GmbH; Evergreen U.K. Ltd.; Evergreen Star Hong Kong Ltd.; Evergreen Philippines; Evergreen Poland Sp.Zo.O.

Principal Competitors

Maersk Sealand (Denmark); Hanjin Shipping (Korea); Hyundai Merchant Marine Ltd. (Korea).

Further Reading

Bangsberg, P.T. "Evergreen Eyes China Market," *JoC Online*, June 25, 2002, http://www.joc.com.

Bray, Julian. "Evergreen Sees Red Over Rate Reports: Taiwanese Attack North Atlantic Lines," *International Freighting Weekly*, April 30, 1990, p. 14.

"Business Briefs," *South China Morning Post*, May 17, 1999.

Canna, Elizabeth, "What's Next for Evergreen?" *American Shipper*, October 1994, p. 38.

"Chairman Chang's Vision," *Journal of Commerce and Commercial*, September 22, 1993, p. S3.

"Eva Airlines Gets Results Despite Crisis," *China News*, June 7, 1999.

"Evergreen Celebrates 25 Years of Service and Success," *Journal of Commerce and Commercial*, September 22, 1993, pp. S1–S2.

"Evergreen Group to Build 25 Container Ships," *Central News Agency (Taiwan)*, October 28, 1999.

"Evergreen Seals Plan to Move to PTP," *Business Times*, April 4, 2002.

"An Evergreen Tug-of-War Between PTP and PSA," *Business Times*, January 10, 2002.

Fabey, Michael. "Elbows Out," *Traffic World*, March 30, 1998, p. 22.

"Hotels and Resorts Prove Natural Extension," *Journal of Commerce and Commercial*, September 22, 1993, p. S9.

Kilgore, Margaret A., "Evergreen Marine Sails into Leadership," *Southern California*, May 1986, Section 1, p. 7.

"Leading Asia Lines See Losses," *South China Morning Post*, October 17, 2001.

"Malaysian Port Nabs Evergreen from Singapore," *Business Recorder*, April 4, 2002.

Moskowitz, Milton, *The Global Marketplace*, New York: Macmillan, 1987.

Parker, John. "Floating on Black Ink," *Traffic World*, May 7, 2001, p. 40.

Sauder, Rick, "Quiet Event Will Have Port Shaking with Four-year-long Repercussions," *Richmond Times-Dispatch*, March 1993.

"The Secret to Evergreen's Success," *Journal of Commerce and Commercial*, September 22, 1993, p. S2 (2).

"Ship," *Encyclopedia Britannica*, accessed August 27, 2002, http://search.eb.com/eb/article.

"TNWA Announces Slot Exchange with Evergreen," *PR Newswire*, March 29, 2001, http://www.prnewswire.com.

Stoner, Leigh. "Evergreen Rocks Atlantic Rate Boat," *International Freighting Weekly*, March 26, 1990, p. 3.

"Worldwide Aviation Success Built on Transportation Heritage," *Journal of Commerce and Commercial*, September 22, 1993, p. S10.

—Dave Mote
—update: Annette Dennis McCully

F. Hoffmann-La Roche Ltd.

Grenzarcherstrausse 124
CH-4070 Basel
Switzerland
Telephone: +41 (61) 688-1111
Fax: +41 (61) 691-9391
Web site: http://www.roche.com

Public Company
Incorporated: 1919
Employees: 63,717 (2001)
Sales: CHF 29.16 billion (US$19.53 million) (2001)
Stock Exchanges: London New York
Ticker Symbol: ROG (London), RHHBY (New York)
NAIC: 325412 Pharmaceutical Preparation
Manufacturing; 339112 Surgical and Medical
Instrument Manufacturing; 325320 Pesticide and
Other Agricultural Chemical Manufacturing; 325411
Medicinal and Botanical Manufacturing; 551112
Offices of Other Holding Companies

Founded in 1896 in Basel, Switzerland, F. Hoffmann-La Roche Ltd. has grown from a small drug laboratory into one of the world's leading research-based healthcare companies active in more than 130 countries. Roche is involved in the discovery, development, and manufacture of pharmaceuticals and diagnostic systems, and is a producer of vitamins and carotenoids. It has research centers in Switzerland, Japan, the United States, and Germany.

The company's Pharmaceutical division engages in the research and development, manufacture and distribution of pharmaceuticals for the treatment of infectious diseases, cardiovascular diseases, inflammatory and autoimmune diseases, bronchopulmonary diseases, metabolic disorders, and in the fields of virology, oncology, hematology, dermatology, and neurology.

The Diagnostics division engages in developing and marketing tools for research in genomics and proteomics, test methods for viruses such as HIV and HCV, integrated laboratory work-

stations, and devices for patients' own use. Its products are delivered through its affiliates all over the world.

Roche Vitamins and Fine Chemicals division is a bulk supplier of vitamins and carotenoids to the feed, food, pharmaceutical, and cosmetic industries. Its products include medicinal feed additives, amino acids, polyunsaturated fatty acids, feed enzymes, sunscreens, and emulsifiers.

The Early Years Under Fritz Hoffmann-La Roche

At the beginning of the 20th century, Fritz Hoffmann-La Roche's family had hoped that he would become a scientist, but when he showed no interest in a scientific career, his father, a wealthy Basel silk merchant, founded F. Hoffmann-La Roche & Co. for his son.

Hoffmann-La Roche was a talented entrepreneur who soon proved a success in his own right—and ahead of his time. He was committed to standardized packaging and to maintaining product quality and was convinced that the future belonged to branded pharmaceuticals. He recognized the importance of forming ties between the pharmaceutical industry and the community of academic scientists. Hoffmann-La Roche instituted the company's commitment to research, generously funding the company's facilities around the world to offer scientists a freedom in experimentation usually associated only with university laboratories.

Despite such well-intentioned policies, the young company experienced hardship in its early years; after only a few years in business, Hoffmann-La Roche faced bankruptcy. Disregarding his father's dying wish that he abandon the pharmaceutical business, Hoffmann-La Roche arranged for recapitalization (mainly from his own family). This time, the company enjoyed almost immediate success. Dr. Emil Barell, a young employee, developed several successful drugs: Thiocal, a cough medicine, and Digalen, an extract from the digitalis plant used in the treatment of heart disease. Other new products included Pantopon, a painkiller, and Sirolin, a cough syrup.

The revived company's future looked promising. By the eve of World War I, Hoffmann-La Roche's products sold on four continents. To standardize the marketing of products, the com-

190

Company Perspectives:

We want to be innovative, and see change as an opportunity. Being active in high-technology fields, we must recognize new trends at a very early stage and be open to unconventional ideas. We see complacency as a threat. It is therefore our policy to encourage everywhere in the company the curiosity needed to be open to the world and to welcome change.

pany adopted the name Roche (Hoffmann-La Roche's wife's maiden name) as its world trademark. Yet World War I created complications that threatened the success of its recent past.

The company's new factory in Germany, at Grenzach, produced a major share of Roche pharmaceuticals. But the Germans boycotted the company because they suspected it was supplying France; meanwhile, French doctors accused the company of being pro-German. In Britain, Roche products were blacklisted when the rumor spread that the company was producing poison gas for the German Army. Most devastating of all, the company lost more than 1 million francs in uncollected receivables in Russia during the Revolution.

This series of disasters forced the company to go public in 1919. Of the 4 million francs of paid-in capital used to reorganize the company, Fritz Hoffmann-La Roche supplied 3 million; the remainder came from his brother-in-law, two associates, and Dr. Barell. The following year, 1920, the company asked shareholders to double their subscriptions.

A Second Era of Growth and Expansion: 1920–1945

The year 1920 also marked the death of Fritz Hoffmann-La Roche. Barell assumed the role of president and ushered in a new era of growth and expansion. At the same time, an American, Elmer H. Bobst, became general manager of the company's U.S. subsidiary. The U.S. branch had been established in 1905, and Bobst's regime had been a resounding success: Under his leadership the company introduced Allonal, a pain reliever, which became the company's first million-dollar product.

Then a tragedy occurred in the Hoffmann-La Roche family that changed the course of company leadership: Emanuel, Fritz' eldest son, died in a car accident. In the late 1930s, Emanuel's widow married Paul Sacher, founder and conductor of the Basel Chamber Orchestra. Sacher assumed control of 49 percent of company shares—the interests of his wife, his stepson, Lukas Hoffmann, and his stepson-in-law, Jakob Oeri, a Basel surgeon. All three men filled seats on the board of directors. Sacher remained active in company decisions into the late 1980s.

In the years preceding World War II, the company's strategy shifted; it gradually moved from extracting medicines from natural sources to synthesizing them, and its most important breakthrough came in the large-scale production of synthetic bulk vitamins. Barell obtained a process for synthesizing vitamin C as early as 1933. Later successes included vitamins A and E. In 1971 the company enjoyed between 50 and 70 percent of the world market for vitamins, and production continued to grow.

As World War II approached, the company's American subsidiary assumed greater importance. In 1928, Nutley, New Jersey had become the site of the company's U.S. headquarters; when war and possible Nazi invasion of Switzerland threatened, the company prepared to expand the Nutley site. Company interests were also transferred to a Canadian holding company called Sapac. American operations in Nutley came under the administration of Sapac, whose vast production and research operations soon made it virtually an independent company.

Not only were assets transferred in the early 1940s, but Emil Barell himself moved to Nutley until the end of the war. Differences in their personalities and their approaches to business caused Bobst and Barell to disagree constantly, and, in 1944, Bobst resigned. He went on to assume control of the struggling Warner-Lambert Company and directed one of the most impressive comebacks in the pharmaceutical industry. Barell hired Lawrence Barney, recruited from the prestigious Wisconsin Alumni Research Foundation, to be president of the U.S. branch. Barney remained at Roche for the next 20 years. Emil Barell died in 1953 at the age of 79. His successor, Albert Caflisch, served until 1965.

Innovations in Research and Development: 1945–1965

The years between 1945 and 1965 were important to the company not only in terms of changes in executives, but also because of innovations in research and development. During this period, Roche released its line of phenomenally successful benzodiazepines, Valium and Librium, developed after years of research by scientist Leo Sternbach.

Librium was introduced in 1960. This new tranquilizer was revolutionary in its ability to relieve tension without simultaneously causing apathy. Before long, the company was barely able to keep up with demand; it now held the patent to the one of the best-selling prescription drugs in the world—*the* best-selling drug in the United States. In 1963, Roche introduced Valium to the market, and, by 1969, Valium exceeded Librium in popularity. Never before had a pharmaceutical company introduced two significant market successes in so short a time. By 1971, some 500 million patients had used one or the other of the drugs, generating an estimated US$2 billion in sales. With several years to go before patents expired, the two drugs continued to break sales records.

Difficulties in the 1970s

The company's success in developing benzodiazepine tranquilizers, however, was no protection from the vicissitudes of the daily operations of a large multinational company. Hoffmann-La Roche's pricing policy came under attack when the British Monopolies Commission discovered that Roche Products Ltd., the U.K. subsidiary of Hoffmann-La Roche, was paying the parent company the sums of US$925 a kilo for Librium and US$2,300 a kilo for Valium. In Italy, a country in which there are no drug patents, the costs per kilo were US$22.50 and US$50 respectively. Based on these findings, the Monopolies Commission ordered the company to reduce its prices 50 to 60 percent in the United Kingdom and to repay excess profit estimated at US$30 million.

Key Dates:

1896: F. Hoffmann-La Roche & Co. is founded in Basel, Switzerland.

1919: The company goes public.

1920: Fritz Hoffmann-La Roche dies and Emil Barell assumes the role of president; and Elmer Bobst becomes head of the company's U.S. subsidiary.

1928: Nutley, New Jersey, becomes the site of the company's U.S. headquarters; and company interests are transferred to Sapac, a Canadian holding company.

1944: Elmer Bobst resigns.

1953: Emil Barell dies and Albert Caflisch replaces him.

1960: The company introduces Librium, a benzodiazepine tranquilizer that relieves tension without causing apathy.

1963: The company introduces Valium and it exceeds Librium in popularity.

1965: Caflisch dies and Adolf Jann assumes control of the company.

1978: Fritz Gerber becomes chairman of the board.

1986: The company releases Roferon-A, a treatment for rare forms of cancer.

1990: The company restructures into divisions; Roche purchases a majority shareholding in California's leading biotech company, Genentech, Inc.

1994: The company acquires Syntex Corporation, which becomes Roche Bioscience, a major R&D development site.

1995: Fritz Gerber becomes chief executive officer.

1998: Franz Humer becomes chief executive officer.

1999: Roche inaugurates a new R&D facility in Basel.

2000: Roche spins off its Fragrances and Flavors division as a new company, called Givaudan.

2001: Roche acquires Amira Medical, a corporation active in diabetes monitoring.

In response, the company petitioned the House of Lords to overturn the government's order. Adolf Jann, head of Hoffmann-La Roche since Caflisch's death in 1965, vigorously defended the company's pricing policies. Formerly known for its unwillingness to disclose financial information, the company now put its financial cards on the table, running full-page newspaper advertisements defending its prices on the basis of its traditionally high costs for research and development. Information about company sales and profits were made public for the first time. In 1973, US$500 million of the US$1.2 billion volume at Roche was attributable to the sale of Valium and Librium.

Among consumers increasingly alarmed about the escalating costs of drugs, the company's arguments were generally ignored, and Germany, the Netherlands, Australia, Sweden, and South Africa began investigations of their own. By 1980, after years of litigation, Roche had emerged from the controversy virtually unscathed, having agreed to adhere thereafter to a system of voluntary price restraints.

The tumultuous price wars of the 1970s were not the only source of difficulties for the company. In 1976 a poison cloud of TCDD, a dioxin found in Agent Orange, escaped from Icmesa, an Italian chemical factory owned by Roche. TCDD is an unwanted byproduct of trichloropenol, a drug produced by Icmesa. Although the cause of the poison cloud remains speculative, experts believe that on the day of the accident the temperature in the reactor was accidentally allowed to rise to 300 degrees centigrade, 125 degrees greater than the safe temperature for production.

Nearly 80,000 domestic fowl and half the pigs in the area died as a result of the accident. Six days after the blast, the first case of chloracne, a human skin disease caused by TCDD, was reported. The company alerted the authorities by supplying a map of the area that they believed to be contaminated and advising that the area be evacuated. The Italian government, with the full assistance of the company, initiated investigative procedures and decided to evacuate 267 acres on which some 700 people lived. An additional 5,000 people, living in the periphery of the area, were instructed about preventive measures. Despite these precautions, there were finally 136 confirmed cases of chloracne. Roche paid more than US$17 million in 1978 to cover the costs of decontamination and the relocation and settlement of displaced people; in 1980, the company paid Italian authorities a further US$114 million in compensation.

The 1980s–1990s: Reorganization and Acquisition

In 1978 there was another change of the guard at Roche, with Fritz Gerber becoming head of the company. Gerber led Roche into a joint venture to market Zantac, an antiulcer drug with GlaxoSmithKline, the British pharmaceutical company, in the 1980s. Using 750 Roche salespeople, the two companies challenged GlaxoSmithKline's popular drug Tagamet, and their aggressive marketing strategies led Zantac to capture 25 percent of the market in little more than six months. Roche also moved to the forefront of genetic engineering, particularly in its production of interferons. Roferon-A, released on the market in June 1986, was marketed as a treatment for rare forms of cancer.

The late 1980s and early 1990s were also a time of reorganization at Roche. In the spring of 1986, the heads of all Roche companies met to discuss the company's structure and, as a result, individuals business units were strengthened and made increasingly autonomous. Accounting and reporting practices were standardized and modernization measures were implemented in all areas. In 1989, the company transformed its businesses into true divisions, which began to operate like independent companies. The spin off of Givaudan (formerly the Fragrances and Flavors division) in 2000 left Roche with three divisions: Pharmaceuticals, Diagnostics, and Vitamins and Fine Chemicals.

Roche also made some major acquisitions in the 1990s. In a move that attracted widespread attention, Roche purchased a majority shareholding in California's leading biotech company, Genentech, Inc. in 1990. Further strengthening its position in the worldwide healthcare market, in 1991, it purchased Nicholas, a European-based producer of nonprescription medicines. In 1994 it took over Syntex Corporation, which became Roche Bioscience, one of the company's major research and development sites, and led to staff cuts in research, production, and marketing totaling 5,000 jobs. The acquisitions in the late 1990s of Boehringer Mannheim and the Corange Group, strengthened the Diagnostics division and made Roche the world leader in the area of diagnostics products.

Roche continued to launch new products throughout the 1990s: Inhibace, an antihypertensive, in 1990; Mabthera, for cancer therapy; and Zenapex, to prevent organ rejection after transplant, in 1997. Inhibace was the first Roche product designed with the aid of computer modeling techniques and won the 1999 Prix Galien, Roche's fourth such award. Other landmarks in the 1990s included the 1991 acquisition of worldwide marketing rights to the polymerase chain reaction from Cetus Corporation, which opened the way to developing better diagnostic tests, and the 1995 discovery of a new class of therapeutics, protease inhibitors, for treatment of AIDS.

In the mid- to late 1990s, the company again changed leadership. Franz Humer, who had been head of the Pharmaceuticals division since 1995, was elected chief executive officer in 1998, replacing Fritz Gerber, who remained president of the board. Humer also replaced Gerber as president in 2001. The era of Franz Humer promised to be as eventful as those of his predecessors. In 1999, Roche inaugurated its new R&D facility in Basel. It also acquired the rest of Genentech and, in 2001, acquired Amira Medical, a corporation active in the diabetes monitoring business. During the early years of the 21st century, the company formed an alliance with Chugai of Japan in 2001, establishing its footing in the world's second largest healthcare market. Other 2001 partnerships included those forged with the Mayo Clinic, Combinatrix Corporation, and Millenium Pharmaceuticals, Inc. in the United States; deCODE genetics in Iceland; Prionics Inc. in Switzerland; and Innogenetics NV in Belgium. The decision to separate the company's vitamins business marked its commitment to concentrate on its core pharmaceuticals and diagnostics businesses.

Principal Subsidiaries

F. Hoffmann-La Roche Ltd.; Genentech, Inc.; Givaudan-Roure SA; Hoffmann-La Roche Inc.; Roche AG; Roche Consumer Health (Worldwide) SA; Hoffmann Roche Diagnostics Corporation; Roche Molecular Biochemicals; Tegimenta AG; Teranol Ltd.

Principal Competitors

Abbott Laboratories; AstraZeneca PLC; Aventis; Bristol-Myers Squibb Company; GlaxoSmithKline PLC; Merck and Company, Inc.; Pfizer Inc.

Further Reading

"1896–1996: Highlights in the History of an International Basel Company," *Roche Magazine*, January 1996.

"AIDS Treatement to Be Reduced in Price," *Guardian*, May 12, 2000, p. 1.

Banks, Howard, "How Roche Got an Edge on Its Competitors," *Forbes*, November 2, 1998, p. 100.

Bilefsky, Dan and Vanessa Fuhrmans, "DSM to Buy Roche Holding's Vitamins Business," *Wall Street Journal*, September 4, 2002, p. A.6.

Fikes, Bradley J., "The Biggest Biotech IPO in History," *BioVenture View*, September 1999, p. 14.

Hill, George, "Building a War Chest, " *Med Ad News*, December 1999, p. 34.

Landau, Peter, "Roche Holdings to Spin Off Givaudan-Roure F&F Entity," *Chemical Market Reporter*, December 13, 1999, p. 28.

Moore, Samuel K. "Vitamins Makers Settle U.S. Civil Suit for $1.17 Billion," *Chemical Week*, November 10, 1999, p. 15.

Moore, Stephen D., "Roche, Decode Claim They Located Gene Linked to Alzheimer Disease," *Wall Street Journal*, August 21, 2000 p. 4.

Reeve, Simon, "Unhealthy Roche Looks For a Cure," *European*, April 13, 1998, p. 24.

"Roche Buys Controlling Stake in Chugai," *Economist*, December 15, 2001, p. 7.

"Roche Creates Doubts About Future," *Pharmaceutical Business News*, June 6, 2001, p. 1.

"Roche Earnings Hit New Heights: Humer Defends Development Pipeline," *Marketletter*, August 21, 2000.

"Roche Maps Strategy While Awaiting Fate of Vitamins Biz," *Chemical Market Reporter*, March 11, 2002, p. 21.

"Roche Upbeat on Pipeline Despite Problems with Trocade and Bonviva," *Marketletter*, April 17, 2000.

"UK: First Effective Pill for Influenza," *Daily Telegraph*, May 26, 2000, p. 13.

—update: Carrie Rothburd

Fiat SpA

250 Via Nizza
10135 Turin
Italy
Telephone: +39 (011) 683-1111
Fax: +39 (011) 683-7591
Web site: http://www.fiatgroup.com

Public Company
Incorporated: 1906 as Societa Anonima Fabbrica Italiana di Automobili
Employees: 223,953 (2001)
Sales: EUR 58 billion (2001)
Stock Exchanges: New York
Ticker Symbol: FIA
NAIC: 336111 Automobile Manufacturing; 336211 Motor Vehicle Body Manufacturing; 336412 Aircraft Engines and Engine Parts Manufacturing; 336510 Railroad Equipment (Rolling Stock) Manufacturing; 333111 Farm Machinery and Equipment Manufacturing; 551112 Offices of Other Holding Companies

Fiat SpA, one of Europe's largest companies, is perhaps best known as a manufacturer of automobiles. However, the company also produces commercial vehicles, construction machinery, thermomechanics and telecommunications equipment, metallurgical products, engine components, railroad stock, tractors, and airplanes. Fiat has interests in bioengineering, transportation, and financial services companies and also owns one of Italy's leading newspapers, *La Stampa*.

Fiat's Turin Becomes "Italy's Little Detroit"

Fiat was founded in 1899 by Giovanni Agnelli, an ex-cavalry officer, and a few other Turin businesspeople. The city of Turin, often known as "Italy's Little Detroit," was developed with Fiat money; in the 1990s, half of its population, either directly or indirectly, remained dependent on Fiat for its livelihood.

The company (Fabbrica Italiana Automobili Torino) began manufacturing automobiles and engine parts for the automotive

industry early in the 20th century. With the advent of World War I, however, Fiat significantly expanded its production line, and as the years passed, the company became a conglomeration of various manufacturing enterprises. By the early postwar years, Fiat was manufacturing so many products that Giovanni Agnelli felt it was time to improve central administration.

To help him in his reorganization efforts, Giovanni Agnelli hired Vittorio Valletta, a university professor and former consulting engineer, in 1921. Their aim was to control all of the manufacturing processes as completely as possible, thus reducing their dependence on foreign suppliers. Soon the company became more diverse by pouring its own steel and producing its own plastics and paints. In a further reorganization, Agnelli formed a holding company, the IFI (Industrial Fiduciary Institute), in 1927. In the 1990s, IFI remained one of the wealthiest and most influential holding companies in Europe. It also remained a closed company, owned and operated by Giovanni Agnelli's heirs.

Fiat's Early Automobiles

In its first two decades, Fiat produced only two types of automobile: the basic, limited options model and the deluxe model. The company had little incentive to offer other models since it was protected by the Italian government's high-tariff policy (known as "kept capitalism"); as a result, imported cars were far beyond the reach of the average Italian. Indeed, more than 80 percent of all the cars sold in Italy were Fiats, and much of the remaining 20 percent of the country's car sales consisted of expensive Italian-made Lancias and Alfa Romeos.

Finally sensitive to Italian complaints that Fiat's "cheap" car was too expensive, the company developed the Topolino, or "Little Mouse," a four-cylinder, 16-horsepower two-seater that averaged 47 miles per gallon. It was an immediate success and accounted for 60 percent of the Fiats sold in Italy up until the mid-1950s.

Fiat's Plants Targeted by Allied Forces

Fiat flourished in World War II as it had in World War I, and profits increased significantly under Benito Mussolini's much heralded modernization program. But the company's production of planes, cars, trucks, and armored vehicles for the European and African campaigns of the Axis forces made its plants prime targets for Allied bombing raids.

Fiat faced the postwar era with war-torn plants and antiquated production facilities, and at the height of its disarray, in 1945, Giovanni Agnelli died. Valletta was named president and managing director and immediately set about reviving the company's fortunes, aided by Agnelli's grandson, Giovanni Agnelli II, who became a senior vice-president.

Once the Allied effort to rebuild postwar Europe was under way, Vittorio Valletta applied to the U.S. government for a loan to renovate and modernize company facilities. He reasoned that Fiat was crucial to Italy's recovery and should therefore be entitled to special help. Well aware of the political benefits of a strong Italy, the Americans granted Fiat a US$10 million, six-month revolving loan. Other loans soon followed, and the company was back in business, gearing up for full production ahead of most of its West European competitors. By 1948, Fiat's holdings represented 6 percent of Italy's industrial capital.

But fewer people were able to buy cars than before the war, and Fiat, like other car manufacturers, felt the effects of a smaller market. In response, to reduce its production costs substantially, Fiat built a plant for its 600 and 1300 models in Yugoslavia that was able to produce about 40,000 automobiles yearly. Other foreign expansion followed rapidly. Additionally, the company managed to secure a lucrative manufacturing contract from NATO.

Fiat's foreign forays were a mixed blessing; its Italian workers began to fear for their jobs and worker agitation became a severe problem. On a few occasions Vittorio Valletta was held prisoner in Communist-led worker uprisings in Turin. The political situation did not cease until the mid-1950s when the U.S. government tied an anti-communist clause to its US$50 million offshore procurement contracts with Fiat. This resulted in the firing, relocation, and political reeducation of many Fiat employees, as well as improvements in the company's already elaborate (by U.S. standards) social welfare program. The Italian workers formed three unions, the largest of which cooperated closely with company management.

Vittorio Valletta spent US$800 million in expansion and modernization in the 15 years following World War II and built the most impressive steelworks in Italy. By 1959, Fiat sales reached US$644 million, representing one-third of its country's mechanical production and one-tenth of its total industrial out-

put. The price of Fiat's stock quintupled between 1958 and 1960; even so, Fiat did not reduce the relative price of its cars.

Fiat Joins EEC

Still running the company in 1960 at the age of 76, Vittorio Valletta was a keen supporter of Italy's membership in the European Economic Community (EEC). He was sure that Italian companies were strong enough to survive direct competition from the other five members. Fiat itself had the advantage of a highly trained staff, the swiftest production lines in Europe, and listed assets of US$1.25 billion. But Italy's organization of manufacturers, Confindustria, opposed EEC membership, believing that France and Germany would quickly dominate the market. Nevertheless, by the end of the first year of membership, Italian companies made 283 deals with companies in other EEC countries; the only deal involving the giant Fiat was a sales arrangement with the French automaker Simca.

Vittorio Valletta's confidence in his company's competitiveness within the EEC was seriously questioned when, in 1961, intra-community tariffs were lowered and import quotas were dropped. At the same time, American automakers such as General Motors, Ford, and Chrysler were significantly expanding their European operations. It quickly became apparent that Fiat had underestimated the potential sales of foreign-made cars in Italy. Unwilling to wait months for delivery of a Fiat, or simply tired of its models, Italians were more than ready to consider the increasing array of foreign vehicles. Moreover, Fiat misjudged its domestic market and failed to introduce a model that might appeal to the many Italians moving from the lower- to the middle-income bracket. In three years, from 1960 to 1963, Fiat's domestic sales dropped a massive 20 percent, from 83 to 63 percent.

The company filled the gap in its product line with its 850 sedan, and by 1965, Italian car imports had dropped to 11 percent. But part of the revival in Fiat's domestic sales was effected by less positive means: the company launched a vigorous campaign against car imports enlisting the aid of its newspaper, *La Stampa*. This campaign was aided and abetted by the Italian government, which angered car-exporting countries by imposing a supposedly nondiscriminatory anti-inflation tax on automobiles.

Meanwhile, Fiat's exports improved and sales to underdeveloped nations flourished. In addition to its assembly plants in Germany and Austria, the company built plants in numerous other countries, including India, Morocco, Egypt, South Africa, Spain, and Argentina. Fiat also signed an agreement with the Soviet Union in 1965 for a facility capable of producing 600,000 units a year by 1970.

Giovanni Agnelli Succeeds Valletta

After running Fiat for 21 years, Vittorio Valletta was succeeded in 1966 by Giovanni Agnelli II, the founder's grandson. Under Agnelli's leadership, the company's annual sales came close to US$2 billion by 1968, and for a short time Fiat edged out Volkswagen as the world's fourth largest automaker. At that time, Fiat's cooperative arrangement with the French carmaker Citroen made it the world's sixth largest non-American firm; the company operated 30 plants and employed 150,000 work-

Key Dates:

1899: Fabbrica Italiana Automobili Torino (FIAT) is founded in Turin, Italy, by Giovanni Agnelli and a few other Turin businesspeople.

1906: Fiat is incorporated as Societa Anonima Fabbrica Italiana di Automobili.

1908: Fiat manufactures its first aircraft engine.

1909: The company's first U.S. site is inaugurated at Poughkeepsie, New York.

1914: Fiat produces their first trucks for freight haulage.

1915: Fiat's first airplane comes off the line.

1917: The company's steel manufacturing and railroad industry begins.

1919: Fiat produces their first wheeled tractor, the ''earth machine.''

1922: The Lingotto Project goes on stream, as the first automobile manufacturing plant designed for mass production and the largest automotive complex in Europe; Fiat produces the world's first electric diesel locomotive.

1927: The holding company, IFI (Industrial Fiduciary Institute) is formed.

1953: The Fiat 1400 is produced as the first Italian vehicle offered in a diesel version.

1965: Fiat signs an agreement with the Soviet Untion for the construction of an automotive complex in Togliattigrad.

1969: Fiat acquires Ferrari and Lancia.

1976: Fiat's Brazilian plant becomes operational; and Libya acquires a 10 percent interest in Fiat under an arrangement with Colonel Khadafi.

1983: The company introduces the innovative Uno.

1986: Fiat Auto acquires Alfa Romeo.

1991: Fiat acquires New Holland.

1993: Fiat acquires Maserati and introduces the Punto.

1999: Fiat acquires Case Corporation and New Holland NV, to expand its agricultural business.

2000: The company's railroad activities are sold to Alstom.

2001: Global Value is launched, a joint venture with IBM to manage technological infrastructure and software applications.

---

ers. Giovanni Agnelli II candidly credited Fiat's success to the company's near monopoly of its domestic market for half a century, but he warned that more sophisticated production methods were required if Fiat was to survive in the international market. He imposed a schedule for new models of two years from drawing board to assembly line and standardized many car parts to allow more interchange between models.

Giovanni Agnelli II also sought to further diversify Fiat's products to lessen its dependence on autos and trucks, which accounted for 86 percent of its revenue. At the same time, he set about improving the company's flagging sales performance in underdeveloped countries, and in 1969 he made two notable acquisitions. Fiat took full control of the Italian car manufacturer Lancia and announced a merger with Ferrari, the famous Italian racing car company. When Ferrari's problems had surfaced in 1962, owner Enzo Ferrari had turned down the Ford Motor Company, but accepted financial backing from Fiat. Further losses forced Ferrari to sell, and his company was reconstructed as Fiat's Racing Car division.

While the Ferrari and Lancia acquisitions were good for Fiat's image both at home and abroad, its domestic situation worsened. The company had to contend with Italy's 7.3 percent inflation rate and a series of strikes; 1972 production fell short by 200,000 vehicles. For the first time in its history, Fiat failed to show a profit or pay an interim dividend. Fortunately, news from abroad was good. Agnelli's younger brother, Umberto Agnelli, who had doubled sales at Fiat France in 1965 to 1970 and constructed successful plants in Argentina and Poland, had gone on to direct American sales. The number of Fiats sold there doubled between 1970 and 1972 and Fiat cars became the fourth largest selling import in the United States. Umberto returned to Italy as second-in-command to help his brother with the pressing problems at home.

Fiat Thrives in Foreign Markets

However, Fiat's domestic fortunes deteriorated to the point where the company seemed a likely candidate for partial state ownership. In 1973, Fiat slipped US$30 million into the red, and after a three-month strike in 1974, Italy's Socialist Labor minister granted the union a monthly pay increase significantly higher than Fiat's final offer. Amidst Fiat's loud protests, the government also imposed ceilings on the prices the company could charge for its automobiles—and this at a time when sales were down 45 percent because of worldwide apprehension over the energy crisis. Finally, it seemed, the days of government protection for Fiat were over; the politicians now had to listen to their constituents, many of whom, at that time, viewed the industrial bosses as enemies of the people. Fiat's case was not helped by the Agnelli brothers' refusal to reveal the value of IFI, the family-owned holding company whose funds—in Swiss banks—were beyond Italian government scrutiny.

However, Fiat's foreign holdings continued to offset its severe troubles on the home front, and the company thrived in the less saturated markets of Eastern Europe, Turkey, and South America. Its largest overseas investment was an US$86 million plant in Brazil, which became operational in 1976. Other foreign ventures included a project with the American Allis Chalmers company, an important manufacturer of earth-moving equipment with units in the United States, Italy, and Brazil, and under an arrangement with Colonel Khadafi in 1976, Libya acquired a 10 percent interest in Fiat. This purchase cost Moammar Khadafi US$415 million, and Fiat shares immediately rocketed on the Milan Exchange. Since Libya paid almost three times the market price, serious questions were raised about Khadafi's long-term motives. But Fiat had no such qualms; Khadafi's purchase eased its cash flow at a time when the company earned less than US$200,000 on sales of about US$4 million and had dipped into reserves in order to pay shareholders.

Meanwhile, the company's domestic woes continued. In 1974, with a heavy backlog of unsold cars to keep it going, Fiat fired all of its Italian workers with violent records. A year later, the company laid off a massive 15 percent of its Italian work force and was able to weather the ensuing strike.

Fiat's management was convinced that it could beat its powerful competitors by producing cars at the lowest-possible price. Through its subsidiary Comau, a leader in the automation field, Fiat retooled and partially robotized its factories and standardized yet more Fiat car parts. The assembly robots provided the company with much greater flexibility on production lines, since the machines could easily be programmed to perform a variety of tasks on a variety of models. Further worker layoffs were justified by Fiat by the rise in production rates. The annual output per worker in 1979 was 14.8 units; in 1983 the output was up to 25 units per worker.

Fiat's bold and successful moves to modernize were matched by major changes abroad. The company entirely removed itself from the U.S. market, choosing not to compete against General Motors, Ford, Chrysler, and Japanese imports. In South America, the company closed operations in Uruguay, Chile, Colombia, and Argentina, retaining only its facility in Brazil. Fiat's international operations were also brought under the aegis of a new holding company, the Fiat Group.

Although it had retreated from several large international markets, conceding in part its role as an export-oriented company, Fiat had led the way in Europe toward factory automation during the early 1980s, a move that several of Europe's other volume carmakers—Volkswagen, General Motors, Renault, Peugeot—copied. In 1986, Fiat purchased Alfa Romeo, paying state-owned Finmeccanica US$1.75 billion to acquire the luxury car manufacturer. The following year, the first Alfa Romeo car, the 164, to appear under Fiat ownership made its debut, selling strongly in Italy but recording disappointing sales elsewhere. The dismal sales performance of the 164 was the first of many difficulties Fiat would experience with Alfa Romeo, as sales and production volume dipped throughout the remainder of the 1980s and into the early 1990s. By 1993, the number of cars manufactured under the Alfa Romeo name had slipped to slightly over 100,000, roughly the same number produced in 1970 and considerably less than the number of cars manufactured before Fiat's takeover.

Fiat Acquires Maserati

In 1989, Fiat acquired part of another luxury car manufacturer, paying US$120 million for a 49 percent interest in Maserati SpA, then four years later purchased the remaining 51 percent from De Tomaso Industries for US$51.2 million. The addition of Alfa Romeo and Maserati to Fiat's automobile operations broadened the company's collection of automobile lines, bringing two luxury brand names to the company's established Ferrari, Innocenti, and Lancia-Autobianchi models. Despite the less-than-robust sales performance of Fiat's Alfa Romeo unit, annual sales grew prodigiously throughout the latter half of the 1980s, more than doubling between 1985, a year in which merger discussions with Ford Motor Company collapsed, and 1990. Fiat's ability to generate additional income from the increase in its revenues also met with considerable success, providing resounding evidence that the company had recovered from the financial malaise that characterized its operations during the early 1980s. In 1981, Fiat's income as a percentage of sales was a miserable 0.4 percent; by 1986 the company was realizing 7.2 percent of its annual sales as profit

and its pioneering move into factory automation appeared to be paying dividends.

In 1990, however, Fiat's growth came to a stop. A global recession that crippled the economies of many countries hit the European car market particularly hard, exacerbating the traditional problems—high labor costs and industry overcapacity—that plagued European carmakers. Fiat's profits plummeted 51 percent in 1990, and its income as a percentage of sales slipped to 2.8 percent. The recession continued to hamper sales throughout the early 1990s as Fiat struggled to withstand the debilitative effects of the dwindling demand for automobiles. By the mid-1990s, the European car market was showing some signs of recovery but continued to be stifled by depressed economic conditions, inhibiting Fiat's ability to reap the rewards that, under more favorable conditions, would be derived from its enviable share of the European car market.

In an effort to expand its global productivity, Fiat developed new automobile models designed for a broader and more competitive market. The result of this strategy was the introduction in 1993 of the Punto, an intermediate car designed specifically to meet the needs of European drivers. In 2000, Fiat entered into an alliance with General Motors, which created joint ventures in purchasing and power-train production. Following this agreement, Fiat Auto Holdings BV was created and became Fiat's main automotive sector, including automobile and light commercial vehicles, with the exception of Ferrari and Maserati.

In further attempts toward diversification, Fiat continued to make their other products more marketable. Agricultural and construction products made way for aviation equipment, commercial vehicles and production systems. Innovations in the mass transit area produced light transport vans and quarry and construction vehicles, as well as long-distance highway trucks. Although active in the railroad industry from its early beginnings, in 2000, Fiat sold its railroad activities to Alstom.

Fiat's Ten Operating Sectors Aim at Globalization

The year 2000 witnessed the development of Fiat's ten operating sectors: Automobiles, Agricultural and Construction, Machinery, Commercial Vehicles, Metallurgical Products, Components, Production Systems, Aviation Publishing and Communications, Insurance and Services. The Agricultural sector, under the auspices of CNH Global in 1999, acquired New Holland NV and American Case Corporation, and excelled in the production of tractors, harvesting and baling equipment, and loaders. Growth in this sector remained positive in 2001 due to a favorable dollar conversion rate and strong demand for farm equipment in North America.

Iveco (Industrial Vehicles Corporation), the Commercial Vehicles sector of Fiat, came about in 1974 as the result of an agreement between Fiat and Germany's Klockner-Humboldt-Deutz. This sector has been active in the transport industry, producing light to heavy commercial vehicles. Assisting in the developing momentum in this sector, the EuroCargo Tector (intermediate vehicle) was introduced in September 2000. In the following year Iveco acquired a 50 percent share in Irisbus from Renault and began establishing markets in South America, Eastern Europe, and Asia.

Teksid, headed up the Metallurgical Products sector with headquarters in Avigliana, near Turin. This sector specialized in the production of metal components for the automotive industry, including cast iron, aluminum and magnesium, and established Fiat as the world leader in the production of engine blocks (cast iron), cylinder heads (aluminum), and instrument panels (magnesium). New plants during 2001 were in various stages of development in Sylacauga, Alabama in the United States; Hua Dong, China; Mexico; and Strathroy, Canada.

Magneti Marelli, created in 1919, designed, developed, and produced high-tech automotive components, systems and modules. In 2000 this sector established itself as the world leader in the field of car lights, second in Europe for instrument panels, and third for petrol injections systems.

The Production Systems sector, or Comau, began machine tool production in 1935, and continued to expand its product range. In 1999, Fiat acquired Pico (American bodyworks systems) and Renault Automation and Sciaky, strengthening its position as a major supplier. New branches were established in Australia, China, Romania, and Germany.

FiatAvio, the Aviation sector, began in 1908 and continued in 2001 to develop, produce, and distribute components and systems for airplanes and helicopter engines, as well as assemble turbines for marine propulsion. It produced propulsion systems for launchers and satellites in space operations, and was the world leader in power transmission technology for aircraft engines. It participated in programs with General Electric, Pratt & Whitney, and Rolls-Royce.

The Fiat Group created Editrice La Stampa in 1926 to publish Turin's daily newspaper, *La Stampa Itedi*. Italiana Edizioni SpA was created in 1980 to further develop Fiat's Publishing and Communications sectors through a single entity. In 1999 an Internet portal was created in partnership with CiaoWeb (www.ciaonordovest.it).

In 1998, the Fiat Group created Toro Targa Assicurazioni as part of a joint venture with Targa Services to distribute insurance products through the Fiat car dealer network. Toro Assicurazioni, created in 1833, remained one of the largest insurance groups in Italy.

The Business Solutions sector was created in 2000 and grouped together service companies operating in the field of shared services for businesses, especially information technology. Global Value was launched in 2001, the result of a joint venture with IBM to manage technological infrastructure and software applications.

In 2001, Fiat operated in 61 countries; ran 242 manufacturing plants and 131 research and development centers. Forty-six percent of their production was generated outside Italy; exports accounted for over 67 percent of total sales. The success of Fiat's globalization strategy continues to depend on diversification. A presence in markets around the globe will be an integral part of the group's strategy as it focuses not only in its present markets, but also on emerging countries such as India, China, Brazil, and Argentina. According to a press release delivered by the Group in February 2002, "In order to operate with greater agility and flexibility in this challenging environment, the Group is implementing decisive measures throughout its industrial organization, from the redefinition of its processes, to the structural reduction of its inventories, from the restructuring and streamlining of its manufacturing facilities to the reorganization of the entire Automobile Sector." Fiat which began as one of the founders of the European motor industry, will continue to follow its original growth strategy—penetration of foreign markets and focus on innovation.

Principal Subsidiaries

Bioengineering International BV; Business Solutions SpA; CNH Global NV; Comau Pico Holding Corp.; Comau Service SpA; Comau System SpA; Deutsch Fiat GmbH; Ferrari SpA; Fiat Acquisition Corporation; Fiat-Allis BV; Fiat Automoveis, s.a.; Fiat Auto SpA; FiatAvio SpA; Fiat Concord SA; Fiat do Brazil SA; Fiat Financing Holding BV; Fiat France SA; Fiat USA, Inc.; IHF SA; Itedi SpA; Iveco N.V.; Magneti Marelli SpA; Maserati SpA; Teksid S.p.A.; Toro Assicurazioni SpA.

Principal Competitors

BMW; The Ford Motor Company; Volkswagen.

Further Reading

Biagi, Enzo, *Il signor Fiat: Una biografia*, Milan: Rizzolii, 1976.
Castronovo, Valerio, *Giovanni Agnelli: La Fiat dal 1899 al 1945*, Turin: Einaudii, 1977.
"Fiat Auto Buys All of Maserati," *Automotive News*, May 24, 1993, p. 2.
"Fiat Performs CPR to Revive Alfa Romeo," *Automotive News*, May 16, 1994, p. 26.
"Honorary Chairman Says Fiat Betting on Growth of Auto Sector," *Xinhua News Agency*, April 29, 2002, p. 1008119.
Kurylko, Diane T., "Mercedes, Fiat Discuss Joint Venture," *Automotive News*, April 18, 1994, p. 45.
"Who'll Take Over from the Patriarchs?" *Business Week*, May 13, 2002, Is. 3,782, p. 60.
Wielgat, Andrea, "Fiat Optimistic about Sales," *Automotive Industries*, April 2002, Vol. 182, Is. 4, p. 4.

—updates: Jeffrey L. Covell, Carol D. Beavers

FOSTER'S
GROUP

Foster's Group Limited

77 Southbank Boulevard
Southbank, Victoria 3006
Australia
Telephone: +61 (3) 9633-2000
Fax: +61 (3) 9633-2002
Web site: http://www.fostersgroup.com

Public Company
Incorporated: 1962 as Elder Smith Goldsbrough Mort Ltd.
Employees: 14,000 (2001)
Sales: A$5.164 billion (US$2.82 billion) (2002)
Stock Exchanges: Australia London
Ticker Symbol: FGL
NAIC: 312120 Breweries; 312130 Wineries; 312140
   Distilleries

Foster's Group Limited, whose beer commercials once taught drinkers to speak Australian, has also developed a taste for fine wine. With its purchase of California leader Beringer Wine Estates, Foster's has evolved into a "global premium beverage company." The Group's Beringer Blass division sells about 15 million cases of wine per year in more than 67 wine markets.

The company produces and markets the most famous beer of the land Down Under, Foster's Lager, as well as the country's other leading beer brands, such as Victoria's Bitter and Crown Lager. One of the world's largest brewers, Foster's has brewing operations in Australia, Fiji, Vietnam, India, and China, plus wine operations in Australia, Chile, the United States, the Netherlands, France, and Germany.

The company has four main divisions: Carlton & United Breweries (CUB), Beringer Blass Wine Estates, Foster's Brewing International, and The Lensworth Group. CUB is the company's Australian beer and leisure arm, and of the four main divisions, the company's biggest profit driver. Managed by Foster's Brewing International, Foster's Lager is sold in more than 150 countries. The Lensworth Group, the company's property division, is developing communities in Queensland, New South Wales, and South Australia.

Origins: From Jam to Beer

Though Foster's predecessors date to the late 19th century, many sources trace the company's emergence as a major force in Australian business to the activities of one man, John Elliott. Through an astonishing series of acquisitions over the course of more than a decade, Elliott assembled a major conglomerate using a moderately sized jam company as its nucleus. At about the age of 30, Elliott returned to Australia after a brief stay in the United States, where he had worked as a consultant. Beginning in the early 1970s, with his only significant business experience consisting of a short stint at Australia's largest corporation, Broken Hill Proprietary Co. (BHP), and a six-year engagement at the American consulting firm of McKinsey & Co. (two of those years in Chicago, and four in Australia), Elliott set out to conquer the business world from the top, running his own company rather than working his way up from within one. After rounding up about A$30 million in backing from a collection of Australian business leaders, Elliott purchased Henry Jones (IXL) Ltd., a Tasmanian company whose main businesses were making jam and canning fruit. (IXL was the food company's lead brand of jam. Its name was a phonetic spelling of "I excel.") Henry Jones grew during the rest of the 1970s through a series of acquisitions of companies that could provide necessary auxiliary services, including canning, packing, milling, and freezing operations.

One of the companies that had helped finance Elliott's takeover of Henry Jones was Elder Smith Goldsbrough Mort Ltd. Australia's leading stock and station agency business. In operation since 1839, this company provided a wide range of agricultural services, including livestock and wool auctioning, real estate services, and farming supply merchandising. In 1981, Elder Smith became the target of a takeover attempt by the Bell Group, a company controlled by one of the richest men in Australia, Robert Holmes à Court. Elder Smith's management asked Elliott to act as a "white knight" and rescue it from the hostile raider through a merger. What took place was essentially a reverse takeover, with the larger Elder Smith buying out Henry Jones (IXL), to create Elders IXL Ltd. The Jones management team assumed the new company's leadership positions.

One important asset that Elder Smith brought into the merged company was its fledgling banking operation, in which

199

it provided farmers with a variety of financial services that
included advances, acceptance of deposits, and mortgages. The
company's work in the world of finance was expanded in 1982,
when, a mere month after the merger's official completion, the
company acquired the Wood Hall Trust, a British company with
financial interests throughout the Far East and Australia. Elders
also diversified into the oil business in 1982, with the purchase
of a 19.9 percent interest in Bridge Oil Limited, a large publicly
held company.

The next event of great importance for Elders was the 1983
takeover of Carlton & United Breweries Ltd. (CUB), best
known as the makers of Foster's Lager. CUB was founded in
1888 by W.M. and R.R. Foster, American immigrants to the
''land Down Under.'' Before their arrival on the Australian
brewing scene, virtually all the country's beer was imported
from Great Britain. The Foster brothers introduced lager beer—
a lighter brew that was better suited to Australia's harsh climate
than heavy British ales—as well as refrigeration to the island.
CUB began its long evolution into an international brewing
powerhouse in 1901, when it shipped Foster's Lager to Aussies
serving in the Boer War in Africa. In the early 1980s, CUB used
Foster's growing worldwide reputation to overcome the Australian brewing industry's notorious provincialism. By the
mid-1980s, Foster's Lager was the nation's top brand.

CUB's relationship with Henry Jones had started in 1980,
when the brewery purchased Elder Smith's premerger, 33 percent stake in that company. CUB had also acted as something of
a matchmaker during the formation of Elders IXL by buying
Holmes à Court's share of Elder Smith, and thereby eliminating
the specter of further takeover attempts by him. Between these
two actions, CUB had become Elders IXL's major shareholder
at over 49 percent by 1983. Toward the end of that year, New
Zealander Ron Brierley, head of investment holding company
Industrial Equity Ltd., launched a bid to take over CUB. Once
again Elliott responded quickly, raising US$720 million in two
days with which to start buying CUB stock. Within a couple of
weeks, Elliott had taken control of over half of the brewery's
stock, and by the middle of 1984, he had gained full ownership.

Evolution of Elders IXL in the 1980s

The rest of the 1980s was marked by a nonstop series of
acquisitions in a variety of industries, including mining operations and more beer companies. One result of this period was
Elliott's reputation as one of a rising breed of Australian takeover artists, a group whose members included Holmes à Court,

media mogul Rupert Murdoch, and Alan Bond (also known as
the man who took America's Cup out of America). The takeover of CUB, the largest in Australia up to that time, also
created a substantial debt for Elders. The strategy for reducing
the debt was to sell off the unprofitable parts of the various
acquired companies at the same time new ones were being
sought. For example, by the middle of the decade, there was no
longer a Food division at Elders, whereas food was once the
company's core industry. By 1986 the old jam factory in the
suburbs of Melbourne, now housing the company's headquarters, was nearly the only remnant of the old version of Elders.
Also dumped were the 350 pubs once controlled by Carlton &
United. Among the company's purchases during the mid-1980s
was a 40 percent stake in Roach Tilley Grice & Co., a major
Australian stockbrokerage, and a 20 percent interest in Kidston
Gold Mines Ltd., both in 1984.

In 1985, Elliott launched a takeover bid for Allied-Lyons
PLC, a company four times the size of Elders. Elliott's initial bid
for Allied, a British brewery and food conglomerate in which he
already held a 6 percent share, totaled A$2.3 billion, the money
coming from a multinational banking syndicate led by Citicorp.
The move for Allied reflected a desire on the part of Elders'
management to expand substantially into European markets,
prompted by the limitations of Australia's population of only 15
million. The bid for Allied eventually reached A$2.7 billion, but
it was allowed to lapse without achieving its goal. One reason for
the failure of the takeover attempt was Allied's merger with the
Canadian liquor company Hiram Walker, which was itself fend-
ing off a takeover bid. Meanwhile, Elliott once again became
involved in a raid orchestrated by Holmes à Court, this time
saving Broken Hill Proprietary Co. (BHP), Australia's largest
corporation, from a hostile takeover. With Holmes à Court's Bell
Resources in control of 18 percent of BHP in the midst of its
unfriendly bid, Elliott suddenly came up with about 19 percent of
that company over the course of just a few hours and was invited
to join BHP's board. Though grateful for Elliott's assistance in
warding off the raid, BHP in turn purchased 19 percent of Elders
in order to preclude the possibility of that company launching a
BHP takeover attempt of its own. Before 1986 was over, Elders
became the first foreign company to own a major British brewery
when it acquired not Allied-Lyons, but Courage Brewing Ltd.,
England's sixth largest brewer. Elders paid A$2.1 billion for the
brewery and the 5,000 pubs the company also controlled. This
purchase greatly expanded the presence of Foster's beer in Europe. Previously there had been a licensing agreement with
London brewing giant Watney's.

By the end of 1985, Elders was selling beer in about 80
countries around the world. The company's profit for that year
was A$112 million, a 73 percent increase over the previous
year, on revenues of A$5.4 billion. In 1987, Elders made its first
North American beer acquisition, purchasing Carling O'Keefe
Breweries, the third largest brewer in Canada, for about A$300
million. By that year, Elders was the world's number six beer
maker. It was a heady time for Elliott in other ways as well. He
was a rising star in Australia's Liberal Party, and his Carlton
Football Club won the Australian equivalent of the Super Bowl.

In 1988, Elders bought the remaining 60 percent of Roach &
Co. Ltd., the stock brokerage into which it had bought five years
earlier. That year there was widespread speculation that Elders

Key Dates:

1888: W.M. and R.R. Foster build a large brewery near Melbourne.

1907: Carlton and United Breweries Proprietary (CUB) is formed when the Foster brothers merge operations with five other breweries.

1981: Elder Smith is merged into Henry Jones, forming Elders IXL Ltd.

1986: The company acquires Courage Brewing Ltd., followed by Canada's Carling O'Keefe Breweries in 1987.

1989: Carling O'Keefe and Molson form a joint venture, Molson Breweries of Canada.

1990: John Elliott resigns as chairman and CEO, and Elders IXL changes its name to Foster's Brewing Group Limited.

1992: Molson Breweries chief Ted Kunkel becomes CEO.

1996: Foster's acquires Mildara Blass, one of Australia's leading premium wine companies, and Rothbury.

1998: Foster's acquires the Austotel hotel chain, making it Australia's largest operator of hotels.

2000: Foster's acquires Beringer Wine Estates for about A$2.9 billion (US $1.2 billion).

2001: Foster's merges the Beringer and Mildara Blass wine businesses, renaming the division Beringer Blass Wine Estates; the company removes ''Brewing'' from its formal name, becoming Foster's Group Limited.

would mount a takeover bid for Anheuser-Busch, which controlled about 40 percent of the beer market in the United States. These rumors were fueled in part by the fact that the Bond Group, the company's chief rival in its home country, with whom it virtually split in half the Australian beer market, had recently purchased G. Heileman Brewing Co. of Milwaukee, establishing a strong American base of operations. Although Elders held about one percent interest in Anheuser-Busch, no action was taken toward a takeover at that time. Acquisitions had expanded the company substantially over the last half of the decade, from A$7 billion in 1985 to A$17.6 billion in 1989. Net worth multiplied rapidly as well, from A$112 million to a peak of A$795 million in 1988 before ending the decade at A$630 million. In 1989, Elders IXL was Australia's largest conglomerate, but the strains of a decade-long, debt-funded acquisition spree were beginning to show.

Foster's as Primary Business in 1990

In 1989, Elders merged its North American beer operations (Carling O'Keefe) with Toronto's Molson Breweries. (In 1998, Foster's sold its 50 percent interest in Canadian Molson Breweries for A$1.1 billion.) At the time of its creation, the joint venture controlled 53 percent of the beer market in Canada. Other events of 1989 reshaped the company's future and ultimately led to Elliott's departure from the company he had built into an international empire. Harlin Holdings Group, a private investing firm owned mainly by Elders managers and led by Elliott, bought a 17 percent stake in Elders to secure the com-

pany from bids for control by outsiders. Australian regulators ruled that Harlin had to extend its offer of A$3 per share to all shareholders. As a result of this decision, Harlin embarked on what amounted to a takeover campaign for Elders, and ended up with a 56 percent holding in the company. This was a far greater share than the group had intended to purchase, and the Harlin Holdings Group found itself A$2.8 billion in debt.

The solution to this situation, proposed by Elliott, was to spin off the company's agricultural business as a public company, carry on strictly as a beer operation, and sell off everything else, with proceeds going to the shareholders, the largest of which was Harlin. In addition, Harlin would also sell a portion of its holdings in both the remaining and spun-off corporations. In 1990, Elders began actively disposing of its non-beer enterprises. The company's paper, mineral, oil, and gas investments were divested in June of that year with the sale of Elders Resources NZFP to Carter Holt Harvey. Other properties that were sold off included the company's stockbrokerage and investment banking businesses, its North American grain operations, and its holdings in Scottish & Newcastle Breweries PLC. In addition, over 80 subsidiaries were liquidated that year.

While this streamlining process was taking place, Peter Bartels replaced Elliott as chief executive officer of Elders in May 1990. Elliott retained his chairmanship of the company's board. For the fiscal year ending in June 1990, Elders reported the largest loss in the history of Australian business, A$1.3 billion. Much of the loss was attributable to huge write-offs associated with the company's ongoing structural overhaul. The losses were particularly disastrous for Elliott's Harlin Holdings, which had come to rely entirely on dividends from its shares of Elders to make the interest payments on its huge bank debts. Harlin moved to alleviate some of its financial pressure by selling about 20 percent of its holdings in Elders for A$960 million to Japan's Asahi Breweries Ltd..

In December 1990, the name of Elders IXL was changed to Foster's Brewing Group Ltd., which better reflected the company's increasing focus on the beer part of its business. Throughout 1991, the divestment of non-brewing properties continued. Elliott was succeeded as chairman by Neil Clark. Elliott continued as a board member, holding one of the three seats controlled by International Brewing Holdings Pty., the new name for the Harlin Group. International Brewing was still the Foster's largest shareholder at 38 percent in the early part of 1992, but its dependence on dividends from these shares as its sole source of revenue proved problematic. In March 1992, Peter Bartels resigned as chief executive of Foster's. His resignation, according to the March 3 issue of the *Wall Street Journal*, came about because of his opposition to increased dividends, for which Elliott and Clark had been lobbying. Bartels was replaced by Edward T. ''Ted'' Kunkel, formerly head of the company's joint venture with Molson.

In June 1992, International Brewing was put into receivership by BHP, to whom it owed over A$1 billion. In September of that year BHP became the largest shareholder in Foster's, with a 32 percent stake in the company. BHP acquired this share from two sources, the security on its own defaulted loans to International Brewing, and by buying the shares controlled by the Vextin syndicate, a group of banks to whom International Brewing had also owed in excess of A\$1 billion. Elliott, along with the other representatives of International Brewing, made his final exit from the Foster's board of directors in that month as well. Foster's reported a net loss for the third year in a row in the fiscal year ending in June 1992. The company lost A\$951 million in that year, once again due largely to substantial write-downs, many of which were the results of unsound property loans made by the company's defunct investment banking branch.

Concentration on Brewing in Mid-1990s

By the mid-1990s Foster's was a pared-down version of its former self, with sales whittled from a high of A\$17.6 billion in 1989 to A\$7.2 billion in 1994. Under the direction of CEO Kunkel, who had earned a reputation as a skilled brewer and manager while at Foster's Carling O'Keefe subsidiary in Canada, the company turned its attention from the 1980s upheaval to concentrate on the business of brewing and selling beer.

Kunkel soon found that his work was cut out for him. Although his company controlled enough brands to give it leading shares of the Australian and Canadian markets as well as a number two rank in the United Kingdom, its namesake brand, Foster's, was struggling at home. Inextricably linked to the conspicuous consumption of the 1980s, the brand quickly fell out of favor in the recession-battered 1990s. In spite of (some analysts claimed because of) expensive marketing campaigns, and as budget-conscious Aussies traded down to cheaper brews, the market share for Foster's Lager was halved from about 16 percent in 1987 to seven percent by 1993. Perhaps more ominously, Australia's already-small domestic market was shrinking at an alarming rate due to a combination of demographic, social, and economic factors. Kunkel refused to sacrifice Foster's profit margin, telling *Forbes* magazine's Subrata Chakravarty, "I'm not a discounter, I'm a brand builder." Fortunately for the company, many of the beer drinkers who remained, opted for another Foster's brew, Victoria Bitter, making that label the nation's leading brand by 1993.

Though the company continued to shepherd its namesake brand in the domestic market, it had become clear that Foster's best opportunities for future growth lay overseas. In 1993 the company launched a concerted effort to gain market share on the United Kingdom's leading lager, Carling's Black Label. It was an ambitious goal; at 14 percent of the lager market, Foster's was a fairly distant second to Black Label's 19 percent. On the other side of the globe, Foster's was forging ties to the Chinese beer industry, which was expected to grow at double-digit rates in the mid- to late 1990s. In 1993, Foster's took a 60 percent stake in the government-owned Huaguang Brewery and created a second joint venture with the Princess Brewery. By 1996 the Australian company had acquired a third Chinese interest, the Tianjin Bohai Brewing Company, as well. However in 1998, to curtail losses and focus on building the Foster's brand in the Shanghai beer market, Foster's made public its intention to sell two of its three China breweries.

Foster's ongoing rationalization program saw the divestment of the U.K. Courage Brewing interests. In 1997, Molson Breweries made moves to begin repurchasing the equity stakes held by Miller Brewing Co. and Foster's. (The following year, Foster's sold its 50 percent interest in Canadian Molson Brew-

eries for A\$1.1 billion. More recently, in 2001, Foster's and Miller Brewing formed an arrangement called the Foster's USA partnership, in which Foster's has a 49.9 percent interest.) Also in 1997, major stakeholders Asahi Breweries and Broken Hill Proprietary announced the impending sale of their stakes in Foster's. Meanwhile, in 1997, Foster's became the first foreign brewer to announce plans to establish operations in India. Stepping toward its objective of pursuing high-growth emerging markets in Asia, the company also invested in the Vietnam beer market, purchasing two breweries in that country.

Around this time, Foster's decided to enter the wine industry and build a significant wine business. The process started with the 1996 acquisition of two Australian winemakers, Mildara Blass and Rothbury. The following year, to fulfill the company's objective of launching an international wine club business, Mildara Blass acquired the Australian company Cellarmaster Wines, one of the world's largest wine club operators. The company later purchased wine clubs in the Netherlands and Germany.

A Millennial Move into Wine

The year 2000 heralded an era of dramatic change for Foster's. That year, Foster's acquired Beringer Wine Estates, a leading U.S. wine company, in a transaction valued at A\$2.9 billion. As a result, Foster's transformed itself from a beer business with a Wine division into "a global premium-branded beverage company." Building on its 1996 purchase of Mildara Blass, the Beringer acquisition gave Foster's access to more than 10,000 acres of vineyard in California, high-end brands such as Meridian and Stag's Leap, and in the context of slow growth in the company's core beer business, a chance to expand Beringer brands into Asia and Europe while marketing Mildara brands in the U.S. through Beringer distribution networks. The acquisition significantly affected the company's composition. Beringer doubled the size of the company's wine business and increased the portion of its profits from overseas. The acquisition prompted a flurry of discussion about merger activity and global consolidation of the wine industry, as producers sought lower costs and larger, high-growth markets such as Asia. The purchase sealed the Foster's Group's drive to build a well-balanced business with strong cash flows, growth prospects, and diversity of investment risk.

In 2001 the company announced the new name and focus of its Wine division: Mildara Blass and Beringer Wine Estates merged to become Beringer Blass Wine Estates. By the fall of 2001 wine was being sold in three channels: the traditional wine trade, clubs, and wine services. In 2000, Foster's pursued an e-commerce initiative to target the U.S., British, and European markets. The company purchased the U.S. direct-wine marketer Windsor Vineyards and a 25 percent share in Australian e-tailer Wine Planet. The following year, to stem further losses, Foster's acquired the remaining shares of Wine Planet, and folded the operation into its existing group of wine clubs. In 2001, Beringer Blass added International Wine Accessories to its portfolio.

In April 2001, Foster's announced its intention to change its name from Foster's Brewing Group to Foster's Group Limited. Removing the "Brewing" reflected the company's composition of businesses—beer, wine, and leisure property. At the time, Australian companies were making news by expressing interest in U.S. wineries; for instance, Foster's rival Lion Nathan expanded into wine and the Australian conglomerate Southcorp revealed interest in the U.S. market. On June 5, 2001, Becky Gaylord of the *New York Times* linked the trend of Australian acquisitions with Foster's name change, and noted that the company puts US$6.00 of every US$10.00 it invests into wine. In the latter half of 2001, Foster's pursued ''bolt-on'' acquisitions that could add immediate value, including Etude Wines in Napa Valley. Meanwhile, Foster's planned to sell up to 50 hotels over the next three years to improve returns in its Australian Leisure and Hospitality division.

At the company's 2001 General Meeting in October of that year, Kunkel described the company as ''battle ready'' to address uncertain times. Kunkel warned that Foster's might not be immune from the economic fallout in the United States after the events of September 11. But, he said, the company's strategy of achieving product and geographic diversity would spread business risk. Looking at the state of the company, Kunkel said Foster's had achieved a better split between its beer, wine, and leisure businesses, and a better mix of strong cash and growth businesses. Beringer Blass was producing more than 15 million cases of premium wine a year, and was at that point the world's third largest premium wine company by earnings. Meanwhile in Asia, the company had reached a break-even cash position for the first time, and the region would remain a key part of the company's goal to establish Foster's as a global brand. At the meeting, Kunkel emphasized, ''What we are about is inspiring global enjoyment.'' Fittingly, in the beginning of 2002, Foster's was on the cusp of launching its signature beer in Paris, a market it had been eyeing for several years.

Principal Subsidiaries

Australian Leisure and Hospitality (Liquor Shops and Hotels); Beringer Blass Wine Estates; Bourse du Vin International (Wine Club, the Netherlands); Cellarmaster Wines Pty. Ltd. (Wine Club); Carlton and United Breweries Limited; The Continental Spirits Company; Foster's USA (U.S.; 49.9%, Beer Distribution); Heinrich Maximillian Pallhuber (Wine Club, Germany); The Lensworth Group Limited (Investments); Windsor Vineyards (Direct-Wine Marketer, U.S.).

Principal Competitors

Lion Nathan; Kendall-Jackson; Anheuser-Busch.

Further Reading

Abrams, Paul, and Shawn Donnan, ''Foster's to Double Wine Operations with Beringer Deal,'' *Financial Times* (London), August 30, 2000, p. 25.

Abrams, Paul, and John Thornhill, ''A Fine Wine with a Hint of Marketing,'' *Financial Times* (London), September 2, 2000, p. 11.

''The Brewers' Fight for Survival,'' *Euromoney*, May 1990.

''Can Foster's Become the Real Thing?,'' *Economist*, September 12, 1987.

Chakravarty, Subrata N., ''Soap Opera Down Under,'' *Forbes*, February 15, 1993, pp. 140–42.

Crabbe, Mathew, ''The Beer Baron Goes Banking,'' *Euromoney*, November 1988.

Daniusis, Paul G., ''What's Brewing Down Under?,'' *Beverage World*, September 1993, pp. 52–5.

Debes, Cheryl, ''An Aussie Raider's Heady Bid to Buy a British Brewer,'' *Business Week*, September 23, 1985.

——, ''An Unquenchable Thirst for Breweries,'' *Business Week*, October 19, 1987.

Drury, Barbara, ''Foster's Acquires Taste for Wine,'' *Sunday Business*, September 3, 2000, p. 18.

''Elders IXL Acquires over Half of Shares of Australian Brewer,'' *Wall Street Journal*, December 13, 1983.

''Foreign Beers Raised Highly into China Market,'' *Xinhua News Agency*, June 27, 1996.

Gaylord, Becky, ''In Australia, Even Foster's Is Turning to Wine,'' *New York Times*, June 5, 2001, p. W1.

Hemp, Paul, ''Elders Cleared to Again Seek Allied-Lyons,'' *Wall Street Journal*, September 4, 1986.

Hewat, Tim, *The Elders Explosion: One Hundred and Fifty Years of Progress from Elder to Elliott*, Sydney: Bay Books, 1988.

Karp, Johnathan, ''Cheers: Wheelock and Foster's Plan China Beer Ventures,'' *Far Eastern Economic Review*, July 7, 1994, p. 63.

Kilgore, A. *A Globalisation of Fosters: A Case Study of Elders IXL*, Nepean, Australia: University of Western Sydney, School of Business, 1990.

Kraar, Louis, ''John Elliott: Australia's Apostle of Beer and Business,'' *Fortune*, January 5, 1987.

Lowenstein, Jack, ''The Brewer's Fight for Survival,'' *Euromoney*, May 1990, pp. 97–101.

Maher, Tani, ''Molson-Elders: A Case of Deja Vu,'' *Financial World*, March 7, 1989.

Maremont, Mark, ''Foreign Beermakers Go Pub-Crawling,'' *Business Week*, October 6, 1986.

McMurray, Scott, ''Elders IXL Has 1% of Anheuser-Busch,'' *Wall Street Journal*, September 28, 1988.

''Our Turn Now,'' *Economist*, April 19, 1986.

''Pabst, Foster's Target China,'' *Beverage World*, July 1993, p. 18.

Schnitt, Paul, ''Californias Booming Wineries Tempt Global Companies,'' *Sacramento Bee*, September 6, 2000, p. A1.

Schoolman, Judith, ''How to Spell Wine in Napa Valley: Foster's,'' *New York Daily News*, Aug. 30, 2000, p. 33.

——, ''Australia Brewing Group to Buy California Wine Company for $1.5 Billion,'' *New York Daily News*, August 31, 2000.

''Sell, Sell, Sell,'' *Economist*, May 5, 1990.

Witcher, S., ''Australia's Foster's Brewing Posts Loss for Third Consecutive Year,'' *Wall Street Journal*, September 16, 1992.

——, ''Elders IXL Posts $1.08 Billion Loss for Fiscal Year,'' *Wall Street Journal*, September 26, 1990.

——, ''Era Ends at Foster's,'' *Asian Wall Street Journal Weekly*, June 8, 1992.

——, ''Foster's Brewing of Australia Names New Chief,'' *Wall Street Journal*, March 11, 1992.

—Robert R. Jacobson

—updates: April Dougal Gasbarre, Michelle Feder

Google™

Google, Inc.

2400 Bayshore Parkway
Mountain View, California 94043
U.S.A.
Telephone: (650) 330-0100
Fax: (650) 618-1499
Web site: http://www.google.com

Private Company
Incorporated: 1998
Employees: 400 (2001)
Sales: $65 million (est.)
NAIC: 541512 Computer Systems Design Services;
    514191 Online Information Services

Chances are, if you've ever searched for anything on the Internet, you've discovered Google.com. Chances are also, once you've discovered Google.com, yours is one of over 150 million Internet searches that Google.com handles a day. With reliable and almost instantaneous results (the life span of a Google query normally lasts less than half a second), Google claims one of the widest audiences among Web sites, with 3 billion searchable documents and more than 21 million unique users per month. A dot-com company that made it, Google Inc. has not only survived, but is making a profit. Credit is given to top-rate technology, a rare sales model and an aggressive vision for what's ahead.

Google Conceived at Stanford

Google, Inc., the developer of the award-winning Google search engine, was conceived in 1995 by Stanford University computer science graduate students, Larry Page and Sergey Brin. Their meeting at a spring gathering of new Ph. D. computer science candidates launched a friendship and later a collaboration to find a unique approach to solving one of computing's biggest challenges: retrieving relevant information from a massive set of data.

By 1996 this collaboration had produced a search engine called BackRub, named for its unique ability to analyze the "back links" that point to a given Web site. Continuing to perfect the technology in 1998, Page and Brin built their own

computer housing in Larry's dorm room, a business office in Sergey's room, and Google had a new home. The next step was to find potential partners who might want to license their search technology, a technology that worked better than any available at the time. Among the contacts was David Filo, a friend and Yahoo! founder. Filo encouraged the two to grow the service themselves by starting a search engine company.

BackRub Becomes Google

The name "Google" was chosen from the word "googol," a mathematical term coined by Milton Sirotta, nephew of American mathematician Edward Kasner, for the number represented by 1 followed by 100 zeros. A googol, or google, represented a very large number and reflected the company's mission to organize the immense, seemingly infinite, amount of information available on the World Wide Web.

Unable to secure the financial support of the major portal players of the day, cofounders Page and Brin decided to make a go of it on their own. They wrote a business plan, put their graduate studies on hold, and searched for an investor. They first approached Andy Bechtolsheim, founder of Sun Microsystems, and friend of a Stanford faculty member. Impressed with their plans, Bechtolsheim wrote a check to Google Inc. for $100,000. The check, however, preceded the incorporation of the company, which followed in 1998.

Shortly after its incorporation, Google Inc. opened its new headquarters in the garage of a friend in Menlo Park, California. Their first employee was hired—Craig Silverstein, who later became Google's Director of Technology. By this time, Google.com was answering 10,000 search queries a day. Articles about the new Web site with relevant search results appeared in *USA Today* and *Le Monde*. In December, *PC Magazine* named Google to its list of Top 100 Web Sites and Search Engines for 1998.

Google Signs Its First Commercial Search Customer

With the number of queries growing to 500,000 a day, and the number of employees growing to eight, Google moved its offices to University Avenue in Palo Alto in February 1999. With interest in the company growing as well and Google's commitment to running its servers on the Linux open source

204

Company Perspectives:

Google's founders have often stated that the company is not serious about anything but search. They built a company around the idea that work should be challenging and the challenge should be fun. To that end, Google's culture is unlike any in corporate America, and it's not because of the ubiquitous lava lamps and large rubber balls, or the fact that the company's chef used to cook for the Grateful Dead. In the same way Google puts users first when it comes to our online service, Google Inc. puts employees first when it comes to daily life in our Googleplex headquarters. There is an emphasis on team achievements and pride in individual accomplishments that contribute to the company's overall success. Ideas are traded, tested and put into practice with an alacrity that can be dizzying. Meetings that would take hours elsewhere are frequently little more than a conversation in line for lunch and few walls separate those who write the code from those who write the checks. This highly communicative environment fosters a productivity and camaraderie fueled by the realization that millions of people rely on Google results. Give the proper tools to a group of people who like to make a difference, and they will.

operating system, Google signed on with RedHat, its first commercial customer.

By early June, Google had secured $25 million in equity funding from two leading venture capital firms in Silicon Valley: Sequoia Capital and Kleiner Perkins Caulfield & Buyers. Staff members from the two investors joined Google's board of directors. Joining as new employees were Omid Kordestani from Netscape, who became Google's Vice President of Business Development and Sales; and UC Santa Barbara's Urs Hölzle, who became Google's Vice President of Engineering. Having again outgrown their work space, the company moved to the Googleplex, their current headquarters in Mountain View, California.

Google continued to expand in many ways. AOL/Netscape selected Google as its Web search service, helping push daily traffic levels to over 3 million. The Italian portal Virgilio and the UK's leading online entertainment guide, Virgin Net, signed on as well. *PC Magazine* awarded Google its Technical Excellence Award for Innovation in Web Application Development and included it in several of its "Best of" lists. *Time* magazine named Google to its Top Ten Best Cybertech list for 1999.

The Google Culture Evolves

Although the company grew rapidly, it still maintained a small company feel. The Googleplex helped nurture an atmosphere of innovation and collegiality with its exercise balls, lava lamps, workout room, grand pianos and visiting dogs. Sophisticated computer equipment was originally set up on wooden doors supported by sawhorses. Charlie Ayers, former cook for the Grateful Dead was hired as company chef. Twice-weekly street hockey games were held in roped off areas of the parking lot and weekly staff meetings were held in the open space among employees' desks.

Improvements to the search engine itself came in the introduction of the Google Directory, which was based on Netscape's Open Directory Project, and the ability to search via wireless devices. Thinking globally, Google also introduced ten language versions for search users.

In May 2000 Google received a Webby award for Best Technical Achievement for 2000 and a People's Voice Award for Technical Achievement. The following month, Google introduced its billion-page index and, with 18 million search queries per day, officially became the world's largest search engine.

Google Launches Keyword-Target Advertising Program

A number of clients in the United States, Europe and Asia began signing up to use Google's search technology on their own Web sites. By launching a keyword-targeted advertising program, Google added another source of revenue. On June 26, the company's reputation was further solidified with the announcement of a partnership with Yahoo! Other partners adding Google to their sites were China's leading portal NetEast and NEC's BIGLOBE in Japan. In an effort to extend its keyword-advertising to smaller businesses, Google introduced AdWords, a self-service advertising program that could be activated with a credit card. Google Number Search was launched, making wireless data entry easy and faster. Other awards received included the addition to *Forbes'* Best of the Web Round-Up, *PC World*'s recognition as "the Best Bet Search Engine" and the *WIRED* Readers Raves award for Most Intelligent Agent on the Internet. *PC Magazine UK* honored Google with their Best Internet Innovation award.

By December, Google was answering more than 60 million searches per day. The Google Toolbar, a highly popular innovative browser plug-in, was introduced in late 2000. Searches could be generated from a Google search box and by right-clicking on text within a Web page and highlighting keywords in results.

Reaching the 100-million search mark per day in 2001, Google acquired the assets of Deja.com and integrated all the data in Deja's Usenet archive dating back to 1995 into a searchable format. Google PhoneBook was launched, providing publicly available phone numbers and addresses search results. By early 2001 Google was powering search services at Yahoo! Japan, Fujitsu NIFTY and NEC BIGLOBE, the top three portals in Japan, as well as U.S. corporate sites, Procter & Gamble, IDG.net, Vodaphone, and MarthaStewart.com. Dr. Eric Schmidt joined Google in May as chairman of the board of directors and would eventually become CEO. Schmidt had previously served as chairman and CEO of Novell and CTO of Sun Microsystems.

The list of search services customers continued to grow throughout 2001 with the addition of Sprint and Handspring. By midyear, Google powered 130 portal and destination sites in 30 countries, with advertising programs attracting more than 350 Premium Sponsorship advertisers and thousands of AdWords advertisers. Click-through rates were delivered four to five times higher than click-through rates for traditional banner ads.

Key Dates:

1995: Google founders Sergey Brin and Larry Page meet at Stanford University.
1997: BackRub, the precursor to the Google search engine, is founded.
1998: Google is incorporated and moves into its first office in a Menlo Park, California, garage.
1999: Google moves its headquarters to Palo Alto, California, and later to Mountain View, California; Red Hat becomes Google's first commercial customer.
2000: *Yahoo! Internet Life* magazine names Google the Best Search Engine on the Internet; Google becomes the largest search engine on the Web and launches the Google Toolbar.
2001: Google acquires Deja.com's Usenet archive and launches Google PhoneBook; Dr. Eric Schmidt joins Google as chairman of the board of directors and is later appointed CEO.
2002: Google launches the Google Search Appliance, AdWords Select, the 2001 Search Engine Awards, and Google Compute.

Country domains were offered in the U.K., Germany, France, Italy, Switzerland, Canada, Japan, and Korea, with users selecting Google's interface in nearly 40 non-English languages.

By the beginning of the fourth quarter of 2001, Google announced an achievement that had eluded many other online companies: profitability. With the appointment of Schmidt as new CEO, co-founders Larry Page and Sergey Brin became President, Products and President, Technology, respectively. Google was awarded another Webby, this time for the new Best Practices category.

Cingular Wireless and more than 300 of Sony's corporate Web sites were linked to Google by mid-2001. The new Google Image Search index was launched with 250 million images. Google Zeitgeist, from the German Zeit (time) + Geist (spirit), meaning the general intellectual, moral, and cultural climate of an era, published results of search patterns, trends and surprises. On a monthly, weekly, and sometimes daily basis, the Google Zeitgeist page was introduced to reflect lists, graphs, and other tidbits of information related to Google user search behavior.

In September, Google purchased the technology assets of Outride, Inc., and partnered with Universo Online (UOL) to provide access to millions of UOL users throughout Brazil and Latin America. On the global scene, Google launched a new tabbed home page interface on Google.com and 25 international sites. The Arabic and Turkish languages were added and the Google Toolbar launched versions in five new languages. Lycos Korea came onboard as well.

By the end of 2001, Google had increased the size and scope of searchable information available through the Google search engine to 3 billion Web documents, including an archive of Usenet messages dating back to 1981. Google News Headlines was added and Google Catalog Search enabled users to search and browse more than 1,100 mail-order catalogs. New sales offices were opened in Hamburg, Germany, and Tokyo, Japan.

With 2002 Comes the Google Search Appliance

In January 2002, Google announced the availability of the Google Search Appliance, an integrated hardware/software solution that extended the power of Google to corporate intranets and Web servers. AdWords Select was launched, an updated version of the AdWords self-service advertising system with new enhancements, including cost-per-click-based pricing.

More honors were received in 2002, including "Outstanding Search Service," "Best Image Search Engine," "Best Design," "Most Webmaster Friendly Search Engine," and "Best Search Feature" in the 2001 Search Engine Watch Awards. Expansion of global capabilities continued with the launching of interface translation for Belarusian, Javanese, Occitan, Thai, Urdu, Klingon, Bihari, and Gujaratie, bringing the total number of interface language options to 74. Google Compute offered a new toolbar feature to access idle cycles on Google users' computers for working on complex scientific problems. Folding@home, a non-profit research project at Stanford University aimed at understanding the structure of proteins in order to develop better treatments for certain illnesses, was the first beneficiary of this effort. Google Web APIs service enabled programmers and researchers to develop software that accessed billions of Web documents as a resource in their applications. Awards in mid-2002 included Google's founders, Brin and Page, being named to *InfoWorld's* list of "Top Ten Technology Innovators" and an M.I.T. Sloan eBusiness award as the "Student's Choice."

A multi-year agreement with AOL was announced to provide results to AOL's 34 million members and millions of visitors to AOL.com. Under the agreement, Google's search technology began powering the search areas of AOL, CompuServce, AOL.com and Netscape. Google Labs was launched, enabling users access to Google's latest and evolving search technologies. Seven new interface languages were introduced, including traditional and simplified Chinese, Catalan, Polish, Swedish, Russian and Romanian. Global expansion continued with a new office opening in Paris to complement existing international offices in London, Toronto, Hamburg and Tokyo. The 2002 Google Programming Contest, launched in early 2002, announced its first winner of $10,000 for the creation of a geographic search program that enables users to search for Web pages within a specified geographic area.

Plans for the remainder of 2002 at Google include efforts to intensify its global push—half the company's search queries come from aboard—and to expand its corporate search services, which power the Web sites for other corporations. So far Google has amassed 130 clients worldwide including Martha Stewart Omnimedia, Cisco Systems, Sony and Cingular Wireless. As Google continues to grow, some wonder whether it can maintain the culture and focus that has propelled it so far. To Brin and Page, the company's cautious start has forced it to enter the search services arena with a deeper understanding of the market. At present, it is truly the dot.com engine that could.

Principal Competitors

AltaVista; Ask Jeeves; Inktomi.

Further Reading

Blumenstein, Rebecca and Geoffrey Fowler, Jared Sandberg, Rebecca Buckman, Kris Maher, ''Beyond Global,'' *The Wall Street Journal*, March 21, 2002, p. B6.

Cummings, Betsy, ''Beating the Odds,'' *Sales & Marketing Management*, March 2002, pp. 24–29.

Swisher, Kara, ''Beneath Google's Dot-Com Shell,'' *The Wall Street Journal*, January 21, 2002, p. B1.

—Carol D. Beavers

Grupo TMM, S.A. de C.V.

Avenida de la Cuspide 4755
Mexico City, D.F. 14010
Mexico
Telephone: +52 (55) 5629-8866
Fax: +52 (55) 5629-8899
Web site: http://www.tmm.com.mx

Public Company
Incorporated: 1958 as Transportacion Maritima
    Mexicana, S.A.
Employees: 10,213
Sales: 9.18 billion pesos ($1 billion) (2001)
Stock Exchanges: Mexico City New York
Ticker Symbols: TMM A and TMM L (Mexico City)
    TMM and TMM/L (New York)
NAIC: 482110 Line-Haul Railroads; 494230 Specialized
    Freight Trucking, Long Distance; 488310 Port &
    Harbor Operations; 488320 Marine Cargo Handling;
    488991 Packaging and Crating; 511120 Offices of
    Other Holding Companies

Grupo TMM, S.A. de C.V., formerly Transportacion Maritima Mexicana, S.A. de C.V. (TMM) is the holding company for the largest multimodal and logistics shipping company in Latin America. The company manages some Mexican ports and has established alliances with U.S. shipping and trucking firms. Its most valuable holding is its majority stake in Grupo TFM, S.A. de C.V., a joint venture with Kansas City Southern Industries Inc. that operates Mexico's most important railway.

Maritime Powerhouse: 1960–90

The enterprise founded in 1955 became Transportacion Maritima Mexicana, S.A. in 1958. It was founded by Enrique Rojas, who became its president and chairman of the board, and the enterprise was backed by a group of private investors, including the Serrano Segovia family. The federal government, by means of the Bank of Mexico, the National Bank of Foreign Commerce, and Nacional Financiera—its development

agency—acquired 30 percent of the firm's equity in 1962, with the rest remaining in private hands. TMM began operations on the Atlantic and Gulf of Mexico coasts in 1960 by acquiring Linea Mexicana. Pacific Coast liner service to Central and South America began in 1961, transatlantic services on a regular basis to Northern Europe in 1963, and regular services to the Far East and Mediterranean in 1968.

By 1970 TMM was Mexico's most important shipping line, although it represented only 10 percent of the nation's total seaborne commerce. Some 33 ships with combined 250,000 metric tons of deadweight were visiting 54 foreign ports in 21 American, European, and Asian countries. In 1969 these ships traveled 1.09 million nautical miles and transported 1.58 million metric tons of cargo. Some 11 of these ships were practically new and included specialized vessels to carry coal, cereals, minerals, and other bulk cargos. In 1971 TMM took possession of two container ships, built for the firm in Yugoslav shipyards. These were the first two container ships to fly under a Latin American flag and had the capacity to carry 417 containers, of which 60 percent could be refrigerated.

TMM began trading shares of its common stock on Mexico City's stock exchange in 1981. The company, which had established storage capacity for bulk liquids in 1973, branched out further in 1982 by purchasing the Texas-Mexican Railway, a line running from the Mexican border with Texas to the port of Corpus Christi, Texas, a port used by many Mexican shippers. The following year it began transporting automobiles and auto parts in specialized ships from Japan to Long Beach, California. By 1985 it also had added an air-freight subsidiary and an interoceanic container transport service that crossed the Isthmus of Tehuantepec by road and rail as an alternative to the Panama Canal for shipping between the Atlantic and Pacific oceans. With a wholly owned fleet of 29 ships in 1985 and chartered ships as well, it was offering service to more than 100 ports in 26 countries. The company was a major beneficiary of new government regulations directing public-sector shippers to use Mexican-flag merchant vessels whenever possible.

In 1990 TMM added Ensanada, Baja California, as its first Mexican port of call after leaving Long Beach. This made it the only carrier offering direct service to Ensanada, which was located only about 65 miles from the many maquiladoras, or assembly plants, on the Mexican side of the border with California. Although most of these plants were owned by U.S. companies, in recent years Japanese and other Asian countries had stepped up their investments in maquiladora plants, thereby generating an increasing flow of electronic components, textiles, and consumer items from East Asia to Mexico. TMM's revenues in 1990 came to $402 million. Its fleet of 35 ships transported more than 200,000 containers and about four million tons of bulk cargo. Specialized TMM ships carried about 100,000 automobiles that year. About one-fifth of company revenues were coming from a single client, Nissan Motor Co.

Jose Serrano Segovia became chairman of TMM following the 1991 purchase by Grupo Servia, S.A. de C.V., a family corporation, of about one-third of TMM's common stock. Later that year TMM made its first equity offering in the United States, selling American depositary receipts—the equivalent of shares—and the next year it raised $91 million with an international public offering of shares. The shares held by government bodies were put on the market in 1992.

Rail and Road Links Eclipse Shipping: 1992–2000

TMM, in 1992, began a tanker-vessel operation and launched a $650-million investment program to upgrade its fleet and to expand its operations in surface transportation. As part of this endeavor it established a joint venture with J.B. Hunt Transport, Inc. (terminated in 2002) to transport goods over the Mexico-Texas border by means of rail or truck. In 1993 TMM and a smaller Mexican shipping line that it later acquired, Tecomar S.A., joined together to begin a vessel-sharing venture offering weekly service between three Mexican ports, two Texas ports, and seven European ones. TMM had been using five ships that sailed at about eight-day intervals between some of these destinations. Under the new agreement, it replaced the ships with three larger ones. By this time TMM was hauling more than half of all Mexican imports and exports. Also in 1993, TMM signed a seven-year contract to carry petrochemical products of Petroleos Mexicanos (Pemex) within Mexico and a five-year contract to move the giant firm's oil within Mexico. In 1994 TMM and J.B. Hunt began transporting goods for Cifra, S.A. de C.V., which owned the Aurrora department store chain and was a partner of Wal-Mart Stores Inc. in its Mexican operations.

TMM lost money in 1994, when a sudden peso devaluation resulted in an economic crisis. The crisis struck Mexico's banks most of all, and TMM lost much of its 43-million-peso ($14 million) investment in shares of failed Grupo Financiero Cremi. However, since 92 percent of TMM's revenues were in dollars, not pesos, the company was not as hard hit as most, and it returned to profitability in 1995. By 1996 TMM was planning to

replace its seven trans-Pacific vessels with six faster, 22-knot ones. The company in 1995 had won-in partnership with Stevedore Services of America, Inc. (SSA)—a 20-year concession from the Mexican government to operate the container terminal at Manzanillo, Mexico's most important Pacific port. In 1996 TMM paid $7.9 million for a 25-year concession, again with SSA, to operate the international cruise and cargo terminals, plus a multipurpose terminal, at Acapulco, including the right to open duty-free shops to serve tourists from passenger ships. Also in 1996, the company won a 20-year concession for $7.1 million to operate the international cruise terminal at Cozumel Island and announced a ten-year distribution contract with Allied Domecq Group, a large dealer of wines and spirits such as tequila, rum, and brandy. Port facilities at Tuxpan, Veracruz, were opened in 1996 in collaboration with Tecomar.

TMM and Kansas City Southern Industries submitted, in December 1996, a successful bid of 11.07 billion pesos (about $1.4 billion) to the Mexican government for a 50-year concession to operate Ferrocarril del Noreste, S.A. de C.V., Mexico's most important railway line. The joint-venture partners established a new company, Transportacion Ferroviaria Mexicana (TFM), to operate the rail line, with Serrano Segovia as president and chief executive officer. By 2002 TFM was hauling 60 percent of all rail traffic crossing the border between the United States and Mexico.

TMM joined with CP Ships Holding, Inc., a subsidiary of Canadian Pacific Ltd., in 1998 to establish a joint venture named Americana Ships Ltd., with 40 ships and combined sales volume of $1.2 billion a year. This arrangement brought the shipping lines of TMM and CP Ships' Lykes Lines and Ivaran Lines together, but the lines maintained their separate brand names and continued to compete against one another for cargo contracts. (Ivaran was soon merged into Lykes, however.) The main benefit was the savings expected to result from combining the purchasing power of the carriers in negotiating with stevedoring and other terminal services, inland transportation, warehousing services, and insurance coverage.

In 1997 TMM had revenues of $477.3 million but it lost money that year, and again in 1998. In 1999 it lost an alarming $62.6 million on revenues of $844.7 million, even though the company's share of Grupo TFM had net earnings of $82.5 million. The maritime segment of its business fell by nine percent in revenue while its rail revenue grew by more than 40 percent, thanks to TFM. Javier Serrano Segovia, nephew of TMM's chairman, became chief executive officer early in the year.

TMM renegotiated its trans-Pacific shipping arrangements in 1999, when it began a direct service between Mexico and East Asia, without stops in California. The Mexican port of call was Ensenada, and the company used smaller vessels that could enter this shallow-draft harbor. The advantage of docking at Ensenada for Korean and Japanese manufacturers was its close proximity to Tijuana, which had become the television manufacturing corridor for North America and the location for many Japanese and Korean television and electronics maquiladora operations. From Ensanada these ships continued south to TMM's container terminal at Manzanillo and its intermodal link to Mexico City, where most of the double-stack cargo was electronics, toys, and other consumer goods.

Key Dates:

1960: TMM begins shipping operations on the Atlantic and Gulf of Mexico coasts.
1970: TMM is Mexico's biggest line, with 33 ships.
1992: The company forms a joint venture to truck goods to the United States.
1995: TMM wins the first of several concessions to operate Mexican port facilities.
1997: Through a joint venture, TMM begins operating Mexico's leading railway.
1999: TMM withdraws from its original business of general maritime shipping.
2001: TMM merges into Grupo Servia, which then becomes Grupo TMM.

TMM sold nine containerships in 1999 that had formerly been chartered to Americana Ships and were no longer needed because of overcapacity and low rates in its key trans-Atlantic market. Later in the year it sold for $68.5 million its 50-percent stake in Americana Ships to its partner, Canadian Pacific, and Canadian Pacific's shipping division, CP Ships Holdings, Inc., plus its entire division of scheduled worldwide liner services. It also received $46.1 million from SSA by increasing SSA's share of the ports-and-terminal venture to 49 percent and sold its share of a joint venture to market bulk supplies of liquid chemicals in four ports for $27.8 million. From these and other asset sales in 1999 and 2000 TMM raised $277.3 million. The decision to sell its stake in Americana Ships came soon after Standard & Poor's downgraded the company's credit rating. ''We were too small a carrier to remain in international shipping,'' Brad Skinner, a TMM officer, told Maja Wallengren of *Latin Trade* in 2002. ''We could not compete, so what we did was shift the company to where the country is going.'' The sale reduced TMM's debt from $600 million to less than $400 million.

TMM continued specialized marine transport, winning, for example, a contract to ship a million tons of liquid petrochemicals for Celanese Mexicana, S.A. from its La Cangrejera complex near Coatzacoalcos, Veracruz, to Houston. Ford Motor Co. hired TMM to manage the logistics, transportation, and distribution of after-market auto parts in Mexico, and DaimlerChrysler Corp. named the company its ''Best Transporter of the Year'' in 1999. General Motors Corp. made a $20-million investment in TFM's multimodal subsidiary. A concession to manage the port of Progreso, Yucutan, was purchased for $4.5 million. TMM also was running 13 Mexican logistics centers within Mexico. Railroad revenues now accounted for about 70 percent of company revenues.

TMM in 2001 and 2002

TMM's division for specialized marine transport had 32 ships, owned or rented, in 2002, with a total of 223,100 deadweight tons. It was deploying supply ships and tankers to serve the petroleum industry, parcel boats to transport liquid chemicals, automobile-transport boats, and, in Manzanillo, tugboats. The ports and terminals division was managing (with SSA) four ports under concessions from the federal government and was also operating facilities in the ports of Veracruz and Tuxpan. The logistics division was providing intermodal services, including packaging, by sea and rail with offices in 13 Mexican cities and strategic alliances as a maritime agent in Chile, Costa Rica, Ecuador, and Venezuela. Its customers, besides the Big Three U.S. auto manufacturers and Nissan Corp., included such U.S. firms as Procter & Gamble and Costco. This division was operating 420 trucks and 200 road-rail semitrailers. The railroad division represented TMM's share of Grupo TFM, which included the Texas-Mexican Railway, a subsidiary of Mexrail, Inc. (Mexrail, in which, as well as TFM, TMM held a 51-percent share, was sold to TFM in 2002 for $64 million.) TMM was merged into Grupo Servia, which then became Grupo TMM, in 2001. Members of the Serrano Segovia family retained a majority of the voting shares of common stock and, in 2001, held 46.5 percent of the total shares.

Of TMM's revenues of $1 billion in 2001, the rail division accounted for 66 percent; specialized maritime, 17 percent; ports and terminals, nine percent; and logistics, seven percent. Of the company's operating income of $189.1 million, rail accounted for 81 percent; ports and terminals, 16 percent, specialized maritime, two percent; and logistics, one percent. Net income came to $8.9 million. The long-term debt at the end of 2001 was $953.2 million and the total debt about $1.29 billion.

Principal Divisions

Logistics; Ports and Terminals; Railway; Specialized Marine Transport.

Principal Subsidiaries

Administracion Portuaria Integral de Acapulco, S.A. de C.,V. (51%); Autotransportacion y Distribucion Logistica, S.A. de C.V. (51%); Comercializadora Internacional de Carga, S.A. de C.V.; Grupo Transportacion Ferroviaria Mexicana, S.A. de C.V. (38%); Lactocomercial Organizada, S.A. de C.V.; Maritima Mexicana, S.A. de C.V. (60%); Naviera del Pacifico, S.A. de C.V.; Seglo, S.A. de C.V. (39%); Servicios Mexicanos en Remolcadores, S.A. de C.V. (60%); Terminal Maritima de Tuxpan, S.A. de C.V.; TFM, S.A. de C.V. (31%); TMM Logistics, S.A. de C.V.; TMM Multimodal, S.A. de C.V. (97%); TMM Puertos y Terminales, S.A. de C.V. (51%).

Principal Competitors

Allied Holdings, Inc.; C.H. Robinson Worldwide, Inc.; Grupo Ferroviario Mexico, S.A. de C.V.; Union Pacific Corp.

Further Reading

Bonney, Joseph, ''First Class, Business and Coach,'' *American Shipper,* April 1999, pp. 77–78.
Freudmann, Aviva, ''CP Ships, TMM Form Shipping Venture,'' *Journal of Commerce,* July 30, 1998, p. 1A.
Gonzalez, Miryam, ''Hacia puerto seguro,'' *Expansion,* November 27, 1991, pp. 63, 65, 67.
Hall, Kevin G., ''Mexican Carrier Aims to Boost Global Presence,'' *Journal of Commerce,* February 9, 1996, p. B1.
——, ''TMM Plans to Increase Diversification, Seek Revenue from Non-Maritime Sector,'' *Journal of Commerce,* March 9, 1999, pp. 1A, 12A.

Kelton, Peter, "Mexico's Transport Giant Expands Far and Wide," *American Metal Market,* January 14, 1994, p. 6.

McCosh, Daniel J., "TMM Refocuses Core Mission," *Journal of Commerce,* April 6, 2000, pp. 12–13.

Moffett, Matt, "Mexican Companies Face Stark Choices in Adapting to Free Trade Agreement," *Wall Street Journal,* October 5, 1992, p. A7A.

Nagel, John M., "Mexican Ship Line TMM Takes Steps to Increase Overland Transport Links," *Traffic World,* October 17, 1994, pp. 19, 21.

"La nueva ola del transporte maritimo," *Expansion,* December 30, 1970, pp. 17, 20, 22, 24–25.

Olguin, Claudia, "Doble travesia," *Expansion,* June 7, 1995, pp. 48–49.

Orme, William A., Jr., "Government Selling Stock in Mexican Line," *Journal of Commerce,* February 20, 1985, p. 12A.

Perez Moreno, Lucia, "La tempestad de TMM," *Expansion,* February 2, 2000, pp. 12–13.

Plume, Janet, "U.S., European Groups to Benefit From Mexican Companies' Linkage," *Journal of Commerce,* January 8, 1992, p. 8B.

Torres, Craig, "Financial Manager Gutierrez Returns to Steer Expansion of Mexico's TMM," *Wall Street Journal,* March 21, 1995, p. B8.

Wallengren, Maja, "From Sail to Rail," *Latin Trade,* September 2001, p. 66.

Wostler, Allen R., and Kevin G. Hall, "Mexico Ship Line Struggles to Escape Peso's Undertow," *Journal of Commerce,* March 6, 1995, pp. 1A, 7A.

—Robert Halasz

Gucci Group N.V.

Rembrandt Tower, 1 Amstelplein
1096 HA Amsterdam
The Netherlands
Telephone: +31 (20) 462-1700
Fax: +31 (20) 465-3569
Web site: http://www.guccigroup.com

Public Company
Incorporated: 1923
Employees: 9,223 (2001)
Sales: $2.285 billion (2001)
Stock Exchanges: Amsterdam Euronext New York
Ticker Symbol: GUC (New York)
NAIC: 316992 Women's Handbag and Purse
  Manufacturing; 316999 All Other Leather Goods
  Manufacturing; 315999 Other Apparel and Other
  Apparel Manufacturing

Gucci Group N.V.'s designs and clothing have become one of the most-recognized labels in the retail industry. Along with Karl Lagerfeld, Cartier, Alfred Dunhill, and Ralph Lauren, Gucci offers wealthier clientele from around the world an acknowledged badge: the "GG" on its leather products that symbolizes membership in an elite club. During the late 1920s and throughout the 1930s, Gucci was the first company to establish a label in the retail industry that is regarded by the general public as synonymous with wealth, status, power, and luxury. However, due to family feuding in the 1980s and mismanagement of the Gucci's image and resources, by the early 1990s, the company was almost bankrupt. As a result, shares in the firm were sold to InvestCorp International, which eventually won full control in 1993 and took Gucci public. A new management team and a revamped image, coupled with excess capital, soon enabled Gucci to reach unprecedented financial success, and the company then began a series of strategic acquisitions, which includes the French fashion house Yves Saint Laurent, Boucheron, Sergio Rossi, and Balenciaga. Gucci now has over 200 franchised and company-owed stores worldwide.

Creating a Mythical Exclusive Brand: Early Roots 1923–1950

The founder of the famous retail empire was Guccio Gucci. Born in Florence, Italy, in 1881, Gucci was forced to leave the country when his father's hat-making company went bankrupt. Driven out of the house by his embittered father, Gucci traveled to London and landed a job as a dishwasher at the Savoy Hotel. The Savoy Hotel was quickly becoming one of the most notable gathering places for the American and European upper classes. The reason for its popularity was Cezar Ritz, the most famous chef in the world at the time. Ritz knew how to lure the wealthy elite by appealing to the sensibilities of their taste buds, and Gucci soon learned that the key to attracting moneyed customers was the perception of quality and exclusiveness.

Gucci worked his way up from dishwasher to waiter, all the while observing the lifestyles and habits of the highest levels of international society. One of his most important lessons involved the way the hotel's affluent guests transported their personal possessions from one grand luxury palace to another. Gucci noticed that all the dwellers in the Savoy Hotel used quality-leather luggage, made by craftsmen from all over Europe. Gucci also discovered that it was the notion of "quality" that obsessed people like Lilly Langtry and Sir Henry Irving. Items that were most fashionable and of the best quality had to be possessed, and people with good taste cared little about the cost. For three years, Gucci worked and learned about what was needed to secure the patronage of the gilded class. After saving enough money, Gucci returned home to Florence to begin a new life.

Gucci married a young seamstress, Aida Calvelli, and had four sons and one daughter; he also adopted a boy that Aida bore out of wedlock. He first worked in an antique store and then at a leather firm. With so many mouths to feed, money was always in short supply. When World War I started, Gucci was drafted to fight for the Italian army, and he served as a transport driver. After the war ended, he returned home to a city with an economy that had been destroyed. But Gucci recognized an opportunity to use the experience he had gained in London, and so he started working at a leather firm that specialized in quality-leather products. The owner of the firm, a man named Franzi, taught him all the elements of leatherwork, including the selection of hides, the tanning processes, and how to work with different types of leather. An ambitious and able man, Gucci was chosen to open Franzi's new store in Rome.

By 1922, Guccio Gucci had dreams of opening his own shop, and, encouraged by his wife Aida (who also helped find an investor by the name of Calzoni), a Gucci leather business started operations in Florence one year later. The little store made leather goods for the wealthy tourists who visited Florence in record numbers during the 1920s. Soon he had made enough money to buy out his partner, Calzoni. As the business grew, reputation of Gucci's sturdy, quality luggage began to spread in European social circles. During this time, he also began a repair operation for luggage. This unexpected source of work helped increase the reputation of Gucci's store for quick, careful, first-class workmanship. The sense of quality he had learned from his time at the Savoy Hotel, and the perception that expensive products were more valued than inexpensive ones, convinced him to raise his prices. By the end of 1923, the Gucci store had become widely known for its distinctive craftsmanship, and it was frequented not only by wealthy tourists but by the local elite as well.

During the 1920s, Benito Mussolini rose to power as Italy's dictator, and many nations imposed harsh sanctions on the country. As a result, Guccio Gucci was no longer able to purchase all the leather needed for his shop. This apparent misfortune, however, turned to Gucci's favor. Without the needed leather, Gucci was forced to design and make handbags and luggage of both canvas and leather. Leather was employed only on the most-used parts of the luggage, such as corners, clasps, and straps. In addition, new items including belts, wallets, and various ornamental designs were becoming more fashionable, and Gucci capitalized on their popularity. By the end of the decade, the Gucci store had become one of the most important shopping places for wealthy customers from Italy and abroad. Flocking to his business in order to buy beautiful and highly innovative leather creations, people were willing to pay premium prices for quality goods made by expert craftsmen. The Gucci mystique had been born. Some of these early Gucci creations are displayed at the Museum of Modern Art in New York City.

The war clouds that grew over Europe during the 1930s did not affect the Gucci store. Tourists from around the world, especially the United States, traveled to Florence not only to view famous works of art such as Michelangelo's *David* but to

purchase a piece of Gucci luggage. Business boomed and the family grew in wealth and prominence. With the onset of World War II in 1939, however, life changed suddenly for everyone in Italy, including the Gucci family. The war between Gucci's customers—British, German, French, American, Italian— almost destroyed the company. Sales dropped precipitously, and plans for expanding into other major Italian cities were indefinitely delayed. The family shop that already had been opened in Rome kept the family in business since the ancient metropolis had been declared an "open city" by the Allies and was not bombed during the early part of the war.

Unfortunately, by the end of the war Italy was in ruins as a result of the fighting between German and Allied forces, and the tumult and chaos left behind did not contribute to the sale of Gucci's premium-priced leather goods. Almost every person in Italy suffered from deprivation and impoverishment, and the Gucci family was not immune from the postwar hardships. Yet Guccio Gucci was able to arrange loan money from a number of Italian banks, and immediately he began to revitalize his shops in Florence and Rome. Guccio Gucci's son, Aldo Gucci, was in charge of the shop in Rome and achieved new heights of success during the occupation by Allied soldiers. American soldiers thronged the shop and purchased anything that Gucci had made to send to mothers, wives, and girlfriends back home. Within one year after the end of the war, both Gucci shops in Florence and Rome had achieved sales figures near prewar levels.

During the postwar period, Guccio Gucci and oldest son Aldo began to create a myth to surround the company's products. An exclusive design—back-to-back linked stirrups in the founder's initials "GG"—was printed on all the firm's luggage and handbags, and hunting and stable yard colors were used to give the Gucci shops an aristocratic air. The legend that the Gucci family had been saddle makers to the great Florentine families also started at this time. All of this history was contrived, of course, but it helped place the Gucci family on a level more equal to the people who bought their wares.

The early 1950s brought many celebrities to Gucci's store in Florence, including Princess Elizabeth of England, Eleanor Roosevelt, Elizabeth Taylor, and Grace Kelly. Grace Kelly once appeared at the store in a panic, explaining that she was in desperate need of a gift for a friend's wedding. When she asked if the store had a floral scarf, Gucci replied that he did not but that he would be happy to make her one. This incident gave rise to the Gucci floral scarf that soon thereafter became world famous. In spite of the worldwide interest in the purchase of his products, Guccio Gucci was reluctant to expand his operations. However, when Guccio died in the summer of 1953, son Aldo Gucci immediately arranged for a Gucci company to open stores in the United States.

The Rapid Expansion of a Legend: 1950s–1980s

After the death of the founder, three of Guccio Gucci's sons, Rodolfo Gucci, Vasco Gucci, and Aldo Gucci, became equal shareholders in the company. Rodolfo acted as the general manager, Vasco as the supervisor of operations at the manufacturing plant in Florence, and Aldo as the director of foreign operations. Under Aldo's direction, new Gucci stores were opened in Philadelphia, San Francisco, Beverly Hills, Palm Beach, and

Chicago. The factory in Florence located on the Via Caldaie was expanded, and land was purchased in the Sandicci area outside the city for a new production plant. Demand for luxury items was growing by leaps and bounds in the late 1950s, and Gucci was at the forefront of companies that were frequented by the rich and famous.

The Gucci stores were most successful during the 1960s. Anyone who had the money sought the Gucci name on shoes, luggage, handbags, and scarves. The Gucci moccasin was worn by John Wayne and Jerry Lewis. Princess Margaret of England, Audrey Hepburn, and Imelda Marcos purchased Gucci shoes—a lot of them. Revenues were at an all-time high, and profits were pouring in. Although there were minor disagreements, the Gucci brothers and indeed the entire family lived and worked in peace and harmony.

When Vasco Gucci died in 1975, everything at the company began to change. Over 9,000 customers per day were buying products from the Gucci stores in the United States, over 600 employees were on payroll, and the business had increased 25 times over the previous decade. Gucci shoes were "the" item to buy and wear, along with Gucci belts, luggage, and accessories. Gucci products had achieved world status. Yet employees in the New York store, as well as in the other U.S. stores, developed a reputation for rude behavior toward customers. Discourteous treatment, icy stares, and put-downs were widely known to occur at Gucci, and rumor had it that Aldo did nothing to discourage the way his employees treated customers. Although this report was not good news, a more important problem had arisen. In 1978, Gucci Shops Incorporated, Aldo's U.S. branch of the family firm, had recorded revenues of over $48 million—but no profits. According to Aldo, the costs of opening up new stores across the United States had soaked up the firm's hefty profit margin.

Family Breakdown and the Loss of an Empire: 1980s

As the company grew during the early 1980s, family feuds and disgruntled employees marred the aristocratic image the Guccis had carefully nurtured since the 1920s. Paolo Gucci, the son of Aldo, was bitter since he had been left out of the major decisions made during the board of directors' meetings. He began to inquire into his father's record-keeping procedures and informed the Internal Revenue Service about certain discrepancies. Rodolfo died in May 1983, and his son, Maurizio, also began to take a keener interest in the company since he was now one of the major shareholders. A consummate businessman with a charming personality and ruthless disposition, Maurizio arranged for his cousin Paolo to sign over his shares in the company and forced his uncle Aldo to relinquish the position of president.

By 1985, despite what the world press had termed the "Gucci Wars," the company itself was still growing. The family squabbles and power plays had hurt the firm's reputation, but its long history and its pervasive trademark contributed to Gucci's continuing financial success. In the United States, Gucci Shops Incorporated reported profits of over $5 million on revenues of $62 million. In Italy, company shops reported revenues of over $200 million and profits approximating 8 percent of the total. The Gucci operation in London made over £10 million, with profits running at 10 percent. By 1986, 153 Gucci stores around the globe were selling over $500 million worth of merchandise.

The late 1980s were terrible times for the Gucci family and their luxury retail empire. In the United States, Aldo Gucci was charged with tax evasion and misappropriate use of company funds. Over $7 million worth of taxes had been evaded while Aldo was head of Gucci's U.S. operation, with approximately $11 million spirited out of the country. Aldo was sentenced to a year and a day in jail and was fined $30,000. He had already paid back over $1 million to the U.S. Treasury. At the age of 81, Aldo began serving his prison time in the "country club," the Eglin Penitentiary in Florida, where many of the convicted Watergate defendants had been incarcerated.

The conviction of Aldo was just the beginning of more to come; by the early 1990s the Gucci operation was in disarray. Sales dropped precipitously, and debts began to accumulate. Now in complete control of the organization, Maurizio brought in an outside investor group from Bahrain, InvestCorp International, to help revive the firm. Yet even the influx of cash from InvestCorp did not help. In 1992, the renamed Gucci America Inc. had lost over $30 million, not counting past debts of over $100 million. As a result, InvestCorp brought suit against Maurizio for withholding information about the state of Gucci's U.S. operation. In attempting to force Maurizio to sell his remaining 50 percent ownership to InvestCorp, the Bahrain group said that additional money would be forthcoming only if Maurizio left the company. Maurizio fought back with counter suits, but finally he gave in and sold his remaining interest to InvestCorp in September of 1993. This transaction marked the first time that control of the firm was not in family hands. Yet, the Gucci family's problems did not cease with the loss of the company. As it reeled from the chaos it had created, an assassin shot Maurizio Gucci on a street in Milan on March 27, 1995. Although, at the time, Italian investigators speculated that he had been killed because of personal debts, in 1998 Maurizio's widow was charged and eventually convicted for his murder; she was sentenced to 29 years in prison.

Rebuilding Gucci to Become a World Leader in Luxury Goods: 1990s

During the mid-1990s, InvestCorp appointed its own management team and began the arduous task of rebuilding the company. In 1994, it promoted several key staff members, including Tom Ford, who was given the title of creative director, and Domenico De Sole, the head of Gucci America, who became Gucci's CEO in 1995. De Sole immediately started work on reclaiming Gucci's image as a luxury brand, which had been cheapened in the 1980s by plastic and canvas products bearing the trademark of the intertwined "G"s. To this aim, he continued a process he had started in the United States of cutting back franchise and duty-free outlets and began spending heavily on advertising. In a further effort to bring the company back to profitability, De Sole closed the extravagant new headquarters opened in Milan by Maurizio four years earlier and relocated the management to the company's native city of Florence. He also increased the budget for staff development, thus improving the atmosphere in Gucci shops as employees began to treat customers more respectfully. These management decisions, along with Tom Ford's bold and updated Gucci designs, which boasted a flashy, 1960s style, helped sales and profits to increase dramatically in both Europe and the United States. By late 1995, projected figures were very promising and the outlook for Gucci and its U.S. operation improved substantially.

After several years of reshaping Gucci and finally returning it to profitability, InvestCorp decided to capitalize on its investment in 1995, making an initial public offering (IPO) in October and selling a 30 percent stake in the company. At the time, Gucci was valued at about $135 billion. Due to a delay in filing by the Italian stock market authority, the company did not offer its shares in Milan, but instead traded shares on the New York and Amsterdam Stock Exchanges and London's SEAQ International market—a mistake the Italian stock market authority would come to regret deeply. The offering was 16 times over-subscribed and the $22-per-share opening price was immediately shattered due to the stock's high demand. And this demand did not decrease. By March of 1996, less than six months after the initial offering, InvestCorp's remaining 51 percent stake had more than doubled in value. Encouraged by the unprecedented value in its shares and an excellent economy, InvestCorp sold the rest of its shares. At the end of the 1997 fiscal year, Gucci's sales were $975 million with an 18 percent profit margin. Since the IPO, shares had risen 323 percent. Gucci had finally completed its move from a troubled money-losing company to one of Wall Street's most popular stocks.

However, this tremendous success did not mean that Gucci was without its problems. Competitors had noticed the company's quick ascendancy to the top, and by 1998 Gucci was watching several of its investors for indications of a hostile takeover. One of its archrivals, Prada, had secretly amassed a 9.5 percent stake in the company. Although Gucci had based its operations in the Netherlands for its favorable tax laws, the country's lack of business regulation left the company vulnerable. Under Dutch law, investors that wanted to buy a controlling interest in the company were not compelled to make a bid for all the stocks.

By 1999, this vulnerability became a serious threat when Louis Vuitton Moet Hennessey (LVMH), a French luxury goods group, bought Prada's shares and combined them with its own, giving itself a 34.4 percent interest in the company and—Gucci executives feared—enough power to claim controlling interest. A bitter battle ensued to secure Gucci's future. Eventually, Pinault-Printemps-Redoute (PPR), an LVMH competitor, made a controversial deal with Gucci to increase the company's capital and purchase a 40 percent stake in the company. The capital PPR invested effectively reduced the value of LVMH's stock to 20 percent. LVMH challenged the legality of the move and over for the next two years fought the issue both in the courts and in the press. Finally, in 2001, with the pending investigation of its business practices, PPR made an offer to LVMH for 100 percent of its shares. The deal was accepted and Gucci's management was secured.

PPR's investment in Gucci gave the company tremendous influence and capital, which enabled it to purchase Yves Saint Laurent at the end of 1999. This acquisition turned out to be the start of a string of strategic acquisitions that helped Gucci branch out into other industries, expand its lines, and dramatically increase its profits. By 2000, its revenue reached $2.25 billion, with a profit margin of 47 percent. Although the world economy soon slowed down, by 2002 Gucci was relatively financially undamaged and announced in March its intention to open 70 new stores around the globe.

Principal Subsidiaries

Alexander McQueen (51%); Balenciaga (91%); Bédat & Co. (85%); Bottega Veneta (78.5%); Boucheron; Gucci America Inc.; Gucci; Luxury Timepieces Design; Luxury Timepieces International; Sergio Rossi (70%); Stella McCartney (50%); YSL Beauté; Yves Saint Laurent.

Principal Competitors

Chanel SA; LVMH Moët Hennessy Louis Vuitton SA; Compagnie Financière Richemont AG.

Further Reading

Auerbach, Jonathan, "Gucci Sues U.S. Unit for $63.9 Million," *Women's Wear Daily*, June 23, 1993, p. 2.

Bachrach, Judy, "A Gucci Knockoff," *Vanity Fair*, July 1995, p. 86.

Barone, Amy B., "Gucci: Domenico De Sole," *Advertising Age*, December 1996, p. I16.

Burton, Jonathan, "Dressed for Success," *Chief Executive*, January/February 1997, p. 19.

Forden, Sara Gay, "Banks Putting Big Squeeze on Gucci Chief," *Women's Wear Daily*, April 26, 1993, p. 1.

——, "Bringing Back Gucci," *Women's Wear Daily*, December 12, 1994, p. 24.

——, "InvestCorp Buys All of Gucci," *Daily News Record*, September 28, 1993, p. 2.

——, "Maurizio Gucci and InvestCorp: A Total Buyout," *Women's Wear Daily*, September 28, 1993, p. 1.

——, "Maurizio Gucci Asks Court Help on InvestCorp," *Women's Wear Daily*, July 30, 1993, p. 2.

——, "Maurizio Gucci Slain Outside Milan Office by Unknown Assailant," *Women's Wear Daily*, March 28, 1995, p. 1.

——, *The House of Gucci: A Sensational Story of Murder, Madness, Glamour, and Greed*, New York: William Morrow & Company, 2000.

Hansen, James, "Death of a Dynasty," *Director*, April 1997, p. 42.

McKnight, Gerald, *Gucci: A House Divided*, New York: Donald I. Fine, 1987.

Marcial, Gene G., "Scuffed-up Gucci May Get a Shine," *Business Week*, August 4, 1997, p. 65.

Reda, Susan, "The Perils of Going Public," *Stores*, October 1996, p. 48.

Rice, Faye, "The Turnaround Champ of Haute Couture," *Fortune*, November 24, 1997, p. 305.

Thurston, Charles, "The Globalization of the Good Life," *Global Finance*, October 1998, p. 27.

—Thomas Derdak
—update: Arianna Dogil

Hanjin Shipping Co., Ltd.

Hanjin Shipping Building
25-11, Yoido-Dong
Youngdeungpo-Ku
Seoul
South Korea
Telephone: +82 (2) 3770-6114
Fax: +82 (2) 3770-6748
Web site: http://www.hanjin.com

Public Company
Incorporated: 1977
Employees: 3,673 (1999)
Sales: W 4.61 billion (US$3.57 billion) (2001)
Stock Exchanges: Seoul
Ticker Symbol: HJS
NAIC: 483111 Deep Sea Freight Transportation; 483113
    Coastal and Great Lakes Freight Transportation;
    483211 Inland Water Freight Transportation

Hanjin Shipping Co., Ltd., a Korean global carrier, was established in 1977 by its family-run parent conglomerate, the Hanjin Group. In an industry that requires significant investment and industry knowledge to compete successfully, Hanjin Shipping surpasses expectations and proves to be an adaptable operation when it is faced with a variety of political and economic challenges. Leading a fleet of 123 vessels transporting containers, bulk cargo, liquefied natural gas, and oil, Hanjin Shipping serves 70 ports in 35 nations. Since its inception, the company has carefully weaved its way through influential industry conferences and powerful strategic partnerships while maintaining an independent focus on corporate priorities.

In the Beginning: The Hanjin Group and Hanjin Container Lines, Ltd.

The Hanjin Group is one of Korea's influential *chaebol*—large conglomerates that are generally family-run and active in a variety of industries. In 1945, Choong-hoon Cho founded Hanjin Transportation Co., Ltd., now one of Korea's largest transportation and logistics companies and the mother firm of the Hanjin Group. The diversified affiliates that currently comprise the Hanjin Group cover the spectrum of air, land, and sea transportation; information and communication; heavy industry and construction; banking; and social welfare operations. In addition to Hanjin Shipping, the group's 20 other companies include Korean Air Lines, Hanjin Heavy Industries and Construction Co., and Hanjin Information System & Telecommunications Co.

In the early 1970s, developing nations, Korea among them, controlled just 8 percent of the total world shipping fleet. And compared to traditional categories of cargo, very few companies operated container vessels, the area in which Hanjin Shipping would make an impact, due to the significant investment and industry knowledge required. Containers are truck trailer bodies that can be detached from the chassis for loading onto a vessel or railcar.

In 1972, the Hanjin Group introduced its first container liner operation, Daejin Shipping Co., but it was only a regional feedering service that transferred containers to a larger ship, which conducted the ocean voyage. The Hanjin Group and Sealand Service of the United States established a joint-feedering venture in 1977. Later that year, Daejin and Sealand created a new company to compete in the international container liner market—Hanjin Container Lines, Ltd. The new company established a trans-Pacific service in 1979.

Korean Government Subsidies and Consolidation Policies in the 1980s

Korean operators overcame the high investment and know-how requirements of container shipping by functioning as low-cost competitors and gaining knowledge through cooperative agreements. For five years beginning in 1979, the Korean government provided its container vessel operators, Hanjin Container Lines included, with annual grants supporting their efforts. This assistance was critical as an international shipping recession developed in the early 1980s.

In 1984, the Korean government aimed to improve its world position further through its Shipping Industry Rationalization Policy. Continuing over the next two years through government pressure and, in some cases, demands for consolidation, the

Key Dates:

1945: Choong-hoon Cho founds Hanjin Transportation Co., Ltd., the first firm of the Hanjin Group.

1977: Hanjin Container Lines, Ltd. is established by the Hanjin Group.

1979: Hanjin Container Lines, Ltd. introduces a trans-Pacific service.

1986: The company opens its first exclusive container terminal in Seattle, Washington.

1988: Hanjin Shipping Co., Ltd. is created through a merger with Korea Shipping Corporation.

1994: Soo-ho Cho, third son of Choong-hoon Cho is elected president of Hanjin Shipping.

1995: The company introduces a new trans-Atlantic service.

1997: The company acquires a majority interest in DSR-Senator Lines of Germany.

1998: The company launches the United Alliance, an around-the-world service with DSR-Senator, Cho Yang Shipping Co., and United Arab Shipping Company.

1999: Hanjin Group is charged by Korea's National Tax Serivce (NTS), US$445 million for tax evasion due to Hanjin Shipping's involvement.

2000: Chan-gil Kim becomes president; and CyberLogitec is established to provide logistics services through advanced technology.

2001: CKYH, the world's largest alliance, is formed with Cosco Container Lines, Yang Ming, 'K' Line, and Senator Lines.

policy resulted in the reduction of the number of Korean shipping firms from 70 to 12—helping the remaining companies benefit from greater economies of scale through larger operations. Hanjin Container Lines was excluded from this government program due to the minority ownership interest held by the U.S. firm Sealand. By 1985, Korean container vessels neared 2 percent of the total world fleet. In 1986, Hanjin Container Lines opened an exclusive container terminal in Seattle, Washington. This facility was the first of what would eventually become a series of ten dedicated terminals in strategic port locations around the world for the company's fleet.

In November 1986, Hanjin Container Lines announced its resignation from the Asia North America Eastbound Rate Agreement (ANERA). The conference was about to restrict its 16 members from entering into individual service contracts separate from ANERA, so Hanjin Container Lines decided it should function independently to be as competitive as possible. The company reduced the size of its fleet slightly, as well as the number of port calls, allowing it to target high quality of service for its core customers. The Korean government, as a debt reduction measure, offered a new financial assistance package to five leading Korean operators, with Hanjin Container Lines excluded as before.

Hanjin Shipping Co., Ltd. Established in 1988

While Hanjin Container Lines was not included in the government's initial consolidation efforts, it did acquire Korea Shipping Corporation, which was suffering from almost US$1 billion of debt in December 1988, to become Korea's largest shipping company under the new name of Hanjin Shipping Co., Ltd. The company began to compete based on service through its expanded operations, rather than focusing mostly on price as it had done in the past. Hanjin Shipping's net profit for 1988 was W 1.5 billion Korean (US$18.3 million), a recovery from the previous year's loss of W 800 billion.

At the beginning of the 1990s, Hanjin ranked 12th in the world's container carrier industry. Having separated from other industry conferences in the past, Hanjin Shipping again exerted its independence by leaving the TransPacific Westbound Rate Agreement in October 1990. Hanjin Shipping's total fleet had grown to 25 container liners and 14 bulk vessels.

A variety of new routes were added by Hanjin Shipping in the early 1990s to continue its rise as a major player in shipping. Due to growing demand in the Asia-Europe shipping market, a "pendulum service" was introduced in 1991, with vessels coming from the U.S. West Coast, stopping in Asia, continuing to Europe, and then returning to the Far East. And to strengthen the link between Asia and the U.S. East Coast, Hanjin Shipping and Yang Ming Marine Transport of Taiwan established a joint operation for an Atlantic all-water route in April 1991. With partner companies, Hanjin Shipping added container service in Mexico, a Singapore-Australia route, and a new around-the-world route.

During 1991 and 1992, new container terminals opened in Long Beach, California and Osaka, Japan. And the company's market share grew an impressive 13 percent during 1993 due to competitive pricing and large new vessels in its fleet. Mr. Soo-ho Cho, third son of Choong-hoon Cho, was elected as president of Hanjin Shipping in 1994, and the company opened an exclusive container terminal in Tokyo, Japan.

Global Expansion in the Mid-1990s

Hanjin Shipping moved toward its goal of offering comprehensive worldwide service through the introduction of a new trans-Atlantic route between the U.S. East Coast and Northern Europe in January 1995. The service operated through a slot-charter agreement under Tricontinental Group's DSR-Senator Lines of Germany and Cho Yang Shipping Co. of Korea. In June, the three carriers announced an agreement to form a worldwide carrier service network which was phased in starting in January 1996 and fully operational two years later, covering major east-west routes supported by north-south feedering services. The global shipping alliance broadened the companies' scope of service significantly, helping them reduce the cost-per-container through the greater economies of scale in the partnership.

New sea routes were launched by Hanjin Shipping to Thailand and Vietnam, as well as a China-Europe express service—a first for a foreign carrier. Hanjin Shipping also began to transport liquefied natural gas (LNG) between Korea and Indonesia via the first Korean vessel specialized for that purpose. Two additional LNG ships were introduced over the next five years. Container operations generally made up 75 percent of the company's cargo, but its fleet also provided sophisticated wet and dry bulk service.

Hanjin Shipping became the world's eighth largest container carrier by 1996, with approximately 60 percent of its revenue from the U.S. market. And while conferences for particular routes ruled the shipping industry in the late 1980s, the creation of several strategic alliances in the 1990s became the new guiding force consolidating the industry in order to compete globally.

In February 1997, Hanjin Shipping purchased 75 percent of DSR-Senator Lines, a company with strengths in each of Hanjin's sensitive areas. DSR-Senator Lines still managed itself independently, though this transaction marked the first foreign acquisition of a majority interest in a German shipping company. With the purchase, Hanjin Shipping became the fourth largest container carrier in the world based on cargo volume, after Sealand Service of the CSX Corporation, Evergreen Line of Taiwan, and Maersk Line of the A.P. Moller Group (Sealand and Maersk, members of one of the first worldwide alliances, would later merge in 1999). Hanjin Shipping continued its growth by adding new routes and investing W 550 billion in new ships and the creation of new logistics infrastructure. By August, the company reached an important benchmark in the shipping industry by becoming the first Korean corporation having transported a cumulative of 10 million, 20-foot equivalent units, or TEUs. During the fall of 1997 at the Port of Long Beach, California, Hanjin Shipping opened a new US$300 million exclusive container terminal with a rail-yard—a 170-acre complex with an extra 30 acres available for expansion—making it the largest U.S. marine terminal and on-dock rail-yard at the time and tripling the company's existing space in Long Beach.

Mergers, Alliances, and the Asian Economic Crisis during the Late 1990s

A currency crisis soon developed in Asia, with the value of the Korean won falling dramatically in October 1997, leaving Asian markets in poor condition. In 1998, Hanjin Shipping left the Trans-Atlantic Conference Agreement (TACA), which it had joined in 1994, freeing the company from the conference's price controls. The company planned to pursue a larger share of the trans-Atlantic market through lower prices in high-volume areas. In response, TACA cut shipping prices by nearly 18 percent for its members. Outgoing DSR-Senator Lines' Chief Executive Karl-Heinz Sager considered industry prices to be dangerously low, and the competition only intensified.

In February, Hanjin Shipping and its partners began replacing its costly bidirectional around-the-world service with three pendulum services for North America, Europe, and the Far East. The partnership of Hanjin Shipping with DSR-Senator Lines, Cho Yang Shipping, and United Arab Shipping Company was then officially named the United Alliance.

To improve its cash flow during the Asian economic crisis, Hanjin Shipping sold 17 container ships and laid off employees to produce an additional US$350 million. The company also began to manage DSR-Senator Lines directly, though they did not merge despite Hanjin Shipping's 80 percent interest. New exclusive container terminals opened in Hamburg, Germany; Kaohsiung, Taiwan; and in Korea. Despite poor expectations from the start of 1998, Hanjin Shipping survived the Korean economic downturn over the previous year. And considering the

industry as a whole between 1990 and 1998, container vessels' share of world trade had increased from 9 percent to 13 percent.

Effective May 1, 1999, the U.S. Ocean Shipping Reform Act aided the industry's long-term recovery by permitting confidential negotiations and contracts between individual shipping lines and importers or exporters. And the Trans-Pacific Stabilization Agreement, in which Hanjin Shipping was a member, raised container fees by 50 percent once the partial deregulation began. The shipping industry continued to enjoy immunity, granted in 1916, from U.S. antitrust laws.

Reform and New Leadership at the Dawn of the 21st Century

The Korean government turned its focus to reforming the *chaebol*, blamed for nearly bankrupting the nation through questionable business practices and expansion funded by extraordinary amounts of debt. In October 1999, the Hanjin Group, Korea's sixth largest *chaebol*, was hit with a W 541.6 billion fine (US$445 million) by Korea's National Tax Service (NTS) for tax evasion due to W 1.08 trillion of unreported income—some of which was diverted for personal use. Included in the group's violations, Hanjin Shipping directed 3.8 billion won into foreign bank accounts 16 times. The Hanjin Group apologized to the public for its behavior and promised to "renew itself as a company that will contribute to the economic and social growth of the country."

With such scrutiny of its financial management over the previous year, the Hanjin Group replaced four of its affiliate companies' presidents, including Hanjin Shipping's Soo-ho Cho, who became the company's vice chairman in 2000 after six years as president. Mr. Cho was replaced by Chan-gil Kim, who had been serving as vice president. Hanjin Shipping and Yang Ming, developing a partnership that began in 1991, announced that they would ship between Asia and the U.S. East Coast together.

To enhance the company's logistics efforts while embracing e-commerce, Hanjin Shipping launched CyberLogitec in May. The information and telecommunications operation provided logistics services enhanced by Internet technology, while also raising venture capital to invest in logistics-related companies.

In October, Hanjin Shipping signed a 25-year lease, valued at more than US$1 billion, with the Port of Long Beach to move from the company's existing container terminal to a new 375-acre facility, with the first phase of 260 acres to be constructed by summer of 2002, and the remaining 115 acres to be completed in 2003. By the end of the year, Hanjin Shipping had transported 2 million TEUs—a record for the company in a single year. Despite the record cargo volume, the company suffered a net loss of US$58.8 million for the year (compared to a net profit of US$32.2 million for 1999).

Cross-Alliances, New Technology, and Logistics in Early 2001

In January 2001, Hanjin Shipping joined an existing partnership for a Gulf-Asia Express route reaching the Middle East, India, Pakistan, and Asia. During the following month, Hanjin

Shipping established Atlantic Gulf Europe, its first direct South Atlantic route, complementing its North Atlantic service through the United Alliance. The company, along with fellow members of the new Independent Carriers Alliance, began to provide service from the U.S. East Coast to eastern South America. Hanjin Shipping also entered into space-sharing agreements on various routes with 'K' Line of Japan in order to fill excess capacity and cut costs. This arrangement was notable as the partners were members of competing alliances. In 2001 there were more than 150 space-sharing agreements filed with the Federal Maritime Commission, compared to 87 in 1997.

A shipping Web site partnership, GT Nexus, was launched by Hyundai Merchant Marine in 2001 with Hanjin Shipping and other carriers. The comprehensive service allows carriers and importers or exporters to communicate with each other confidentially, managing pricing, contracting, and tracking processes through the site. Hanjin Shipping then established Hanjin Logistics in Chicago, Illinois, as an inland operation focusing initially on transporting cargo by train, east-to-west, while planning expansion across the country and into Canada. After a difficult period experienced by Cho Yang, its ships in the United Alliance's two major pendulum routes were replaced in April by Hanjin Shipping and Senator Lines.

With an economic downturn in the United States, container rate negotiations in spring of 2001 did not continue the trend of higher rates enjoyed by shipping companies for the two previous years, although Hanjin Shipping was able to retain most of its customer base. Worldwide rankings in 2001 placed Hanjin Shipping fourth, its same ranking for a number of years, behind Maersk Sealand; APL Limited, a U.S. cargo carrier; and Evergreen. Hanjin Shipping opened its tenth exclusive container terminal, a 120-acre facility, in Oakland, California in June 2001.

Ailing Global Markets and Uncertainty in 2002

The year of 2001 became a mix of extreme highs and lows. For the first six months of 2001, Hanjin Shipping earned operating profits of W 232 billion, a 60 percent increase over the same period of the previous year, and a company record due to cost reduction measures and oil price stability. However, high foreign exchange rates resulted in a net loss of W 15.9 billion, compared to a net profit of W 60.7 billion for the same period of the previous year.

The terrorist attacks in the United States on September 11, 2001, beyond the immeasurable human impact, had a devastating effect on the shipping industry as well. Many U.S. ports were immediately closed for security reasons. London's Wartime Insurance Council quadrupled carriers' insurance premiums. And the U.S. economy, in a major downturn already, fell into an even worse position with a similar effect on the global economy which sent shipping prices down as well. Hanjin Shipping's service to the Port of Portland, Oregon, was suspended at the end of the year, though it was restored by the following summer. Continuing cost reduction and garnering new customers became even more important to carriers during such unpredictable economic times.

In November 2001, Hanjin Shipping signed a global alliance agreement with Cosco Container Lines, Yang Ming, 'K' Line,

and Senator Lines—forming the world's largest alliance in the shipping industry with gradual implementation expected to be complete in 2003. The alliance was named CKYH (CYK was the name of Cosco, 'K' Line, and Yang Ming's existing venture). Participating carriers in the alliance planned the sharing of ships, terminals, and equipment—enabling them to cut costs while improving overall service to secure new customers. Other competing alliances smaller than CKYH include the Grand Alliance led by P & O Nedlloyd of the United Kingdom, Maersk Sealand of the A.P. Moller Group, and the New World Alliance headed by APL of the United States. For 2001, Hanjin Shipping posted a W 230.4 billion operating profit, although after taxes, charges, and exchange rates are considered, the company had a net loss of W 78.3 billion.

Cargo volume began to show signs of recovery along with the U.S. economy during the spring of 2002. In May, the business media reported that the debt-burdened Hanjin Group would break itself into four independent affiliate operations. Hanjin Shipping responded to the speculation in June by explaining that the Hanjin Group remained intact, although the company admitted that events over the next year or two may result in the group's split as reported. Such a move would likely affect shareholding arrangements of the group's affiliates without altering the operations of Hanjin Shipping and its 123 vessels, as the company has run independently of the Hanjin Group for years in its service of 70 ports in 35 countries.

Rather than focusing on becoming the biggest in the business, Hanjin Shipping now aimed to provide customer-centered shipping service that is safe, punctual, and seamless through integrated logistics. Despite signs of recovery, great uncertainty lingered in the world markets during 2002. In the early stages of the largest global shipping alliance, and with an impressive record of adapting to and surviving challenges over its relatively short history, Hanjin Shipping is in a reasonably strong position to continue its mission to become the world's most reliable and trusted name in the industry.

Principal Subsidiaries

CyberLogitec; Hanjin Logistics, Inc. (U.S.); Keoyang Shipping (48.6%); Senator Lines GmbH (Germany; 80%).

Principal Competitors

The A.P. Moller Group; CSX; Neptune Orient.

Further Reading

Bangsberg, P. T., "South Korea Lines to Get New Aid," *Journal of Commerce*, February 20, 1987, http://www.joc.com.

Carding, Tony, "Hanjin Finds Round-the-World Service in Two Directions," *Traffic World*, October 24, 1997, http://www.trafficworld .com.

Dupin, Chris, "The Gray Ship Approaches," *Journal of Commerce*, March 5, 2001, http://www.joc.com.

——, "A Tricky Course," *Journal of Commerce*, January 7, 2002, http://www.joc.com.

Joseph, Gloria, "Hanjin Shifts its Focus," *Journal of Commerce*, October 22, 1986, http://www.joc.com.

Lee, B. J., "Hanjin Group Family Fined for Tax Evasion," *South China Morning Post*, October 5, 1999, http://www.scmp.com.

Mongelluzzo, Bill, "Hanjin Soon to Be Biggest Korean Carrier," *Journal of Commerce*, November 30, 1988, http://www.joc.com.

Ralph, Bill, "Right Size, Right Service," *Journal of Commerce*, August 7, 2000, http://www.joc.com.

Richardson, Paul, "Korean Lines Do Better than Expected Amid Regional Woes," *Journal of Commerce*, November 30, 1998, http://www.joc.com.

"Taxing the Tycoons," *Economist*, November 23, 1991, p. 88.

"The Top 25 Ocean Carriers," *World Trade*, April 1997, p. 52.

Thanopoulou, Helen A., Dong-Keun Ryoo Masts, and Tae-Woo Lee, "Korean Liner Shipping in the Era of Global Alliances," *Maritime Political Management*, Vol. 26, No. 3, 1999, pp. 209–229.

Wastler, Allen R., "Container Carriers' Options Include Global Reach or Specialized Services, and Little Else," *Journal of Commerce*, January 6, 1997, http://www.joc.com.

—Christopher W. Frerichs

i n v e n t

Hewlett-Packard Company

3000 Hanover Street
Palo Alto, California 94304
U.S.A.
Telephone: (650) 857-1501
Toll Free: (800) 752-0900
Fax: (650) 857-7299
Web site: http://www.hp.com

Public Company
Incorporated: 1947
Employees: 86,200 (2001)
Sales: $45.2 billion (2001)
Stock Exchanges: New York Pacific Frankfurt London
    Paris Tokyo Zürich
Ticker Symbols: HWP (2001); HPQ (2002)
NAIC: 334111 Electronic Computer Manufacturing;
    334112 Computer Storage Device Manufacturing;
    334119 Other Computer Peripheral Equipment
    Manufacturing; 333313 Office Machinery
    Manufacturing; 334413 Semiconductors & Related
    Device Manufacturing; 334613 Magnetic & Optical
    Recording Media Manufacturing; 334519 Other
    Measuring & Controlling Device Manufacturing;
    334510 Electromedical & Electrotherapeutic
    Apparatus Manufacturing; 511210 Software
    Publishers; 541512 Computer Systems Design
    Services; 811212 Computer & Office Machine Repair
    & Maintenance

Since merging in 2002, Hewlett-Packard (HP) and Compaq have created the new HP (Hewlett-Packard Company), serving more than one billion customers in more than 160 countries on five continents. The new HP is a market leader in all the essential components of business infrastructure—servers, storage, management software, imaging and printing, personal computers, and personal access devices. The new HP is the leading consumer technology company in the world, offering a range of technology tools—from digital cameras to PCs to handheld devices.

HP Began As Maker of Test and Measurement Products

Hewlett-Packard had its beginnings with Stanford University graduates, William Hewlett and David Packard, who were encouraged by Professor Frederick Terman to start their own business. With only $538 and workspace in a garage behind Packard's rented house in Palo Alto, California, the two men began working on a resistance-capacity audio oscillator, a machine used for testing sound equipment. After assembling several models—baking paint for the instrument panel in Packard's oven—they won their first big order, for eight oscillators, from Walt Disney Studios, which used them to develop and test a new sound system for the animated film Fantasia.

On January 1, 1939, Hewlett and Packard formalized their venture as a partnership, tossing a coin to decide the order of their names. Hewlett won. In 1940, with a product line of eight items, the two men moved their company and its three employees to a building in downtown Palo Alto.

During World War II, Terman, who was then in charge of antiradar projects at Harvard, contracted his former students to manufacture microwave signal generators for his research. When the war ended, HP took full advantage of the growth in the electronics sector, particularly in the defense and industrial areas. The founders also defined their respective roles in the company: Hewlett would lead technological development, and Packard would be in charge of management. Hewlett-Packard Company was incorporated in 1947, and by 1950 had 70 products, 143 employees, and revenues of $2 million.

HP introduced a revolutionary high-speed frequency counter, the HP524A, in 1951. This device, which reduced the time required to measure radio frequencies from ten minutes to about two seconds, was used by radio stations to maintain accurate broadcast frequencies, particularly on the newly established FM band.

The company maintained stable and impressive growth through the end of the decade. In November 1957, Hewlett-Packard offered shares to the public for the first time and moved into a larger complex in the Stanford Research Park.

In 1958, with revenues of $30 million, HP made its first corporate acquisition: the F.L. Moseley Company of Pasadena, California, a manufacturer of graphic recorders. The company's expansion continued in 1959, with the establishment of a marketing office in Geneva, and a manufacturing facility in Boeblingen, West Germany. After adding another factory in Loveland, Colorado, in 1960, Hewlett-Packard purchased the Sanborn Company, a medical instruments manufacturer based in Waltham, Massachusetts, in 1961.

The company gained wider public recognition when it was listed on the Pacific and New York stock exchanges in 1961 and in the Fortune 500 a year later. In 1964, Hewlett-Packard developed a cesium-beam "flying clock," accurate to within one-millionth of a second. Company engineers embarked on a 35-day, 35,000-mile world tour to coordinate standard times.

In 1963, Hewlett-Packard expanded its presence in Japan through a joint venture with the Yokogawa Electric Works; and in 1965 it acquired the F & M Scientific Corporation, an analytical-instruments manufacturer, based in Avondale, Pennsylvania. In 1966, the company opened its central research laboratory, which became one of the world's leading electronic research centers.

HP Moves into Calculators and Computers in the Late 1960s and 1970s

Although primarily a manufacturer of instruments for analysis and measurement, Hewlett-Packard developed a computer in 1966, specifically for its own production control, the HP-2116A, and had no plans to enter the computer market. Two years later, however, HP introduced the HP-9100A, the first desktop calculator capable of performing scientific functions. In 1969, David Packard was appointed deputy secretary of defense in President Richard Nixon's administration, and returned to HP as a director in 1972.

A handheld scientific calculator, the HP-35, was partially designed by Bill Hewlett in 1972. It was known as the "electronic slide rule." When Texas Instruments entered the market in 1973, Hewlett-Packard's device, which retailed at $395, was forced into the high end of the market.

Signaling a change in company strategy, in 1972, Hewlett-Packard made its first decisive move into business computing, a field dominated by IBM and Digital Equipment Corporation, with the HP3000 minicomputer. In spring 1974, despite record earnings and escalating growth, the company refocused on product leadership, and established a new, highly decentralized structure, allowing each of the company's divisions conduct its own research and development.

In 1977, Bill Hewlett relinquished the presidency and later his role as chief executive to John Young, a career HP man determined to make the company successful in the computer market. Although he was chosen by Hewlett and Packard, Young was virtually unknown to the company's customers and 37,000 employees.

HP Introduces Personal Computers and Printers in the 1980s

Hewlett-Packard introduced its first personal computer, the HP-85, in 1980, to a cool reception. Its move into information processing, however, proved successful and the company quickly established itself as a leading computer vendor. A six-year program began to develop architecture and software that would be compatible with existing programs. In the meantime, HP introduced a number of other products, including the HP9000 technical workstation (1982), the HP150 touchscreen PC, the HP ThinkJet inkjet printer (1984), and the HP LaserJet printer—a phenomenally successful product that came to dominate the printer market soon after its 1984 debut.

Compaq Beginnings: Making IBM Clones

When International Business Machines Corporation (IBM) introduced its first personal computer (PC) in 1982, Compaq was among dozens of other companies, including HP, entering the market with IBM clones—computers that looked and performed like IBM PCs, but were often less expensive. Compaq set itself apart from other clone manufacturers by producing IBM-compatible PCs that were faster, superior in quality, and offered additional user features. Its unique management team was made up of seasoned professionals from Texas Instruments (TI) and IBM. Compaq's staff also had the technical and business grounding to establish new industry standards on its own—without following IBM.

Compaq had come to be in the summer of 1981, when Joseph R. "Rod" Canion, James M. Harris, and William H. Murto, three senior managers from TI, decided to start their own company, but had not decided on a product. The entrepreneurs eventually decided to build a portable PC that met industry standards set by IBM. With only $1,000 each to invest, Canion, Harris, and Murto approached Ben Rosen, president of Sevin-Rosen Partners, a high-technology venture capital firm in Houston. Rosen, who became Compaq's chairman, offered an initial investment of $2.5 million.

When Compaq arrived on the scene, venture capitalists were beginning to force many entrepreneurs to turn over control of their companies to more experienced management professionals. As Rosen—who had lost a $400,000 investment in another PC start-up—explained in *Management Today* in 1985, "In the early days, it was an area for flamboyant people . . . who transformed their personalities into companies. Now the busi-

Key Dates:

1939: William Hewlett and David Packard enter into a partnership; Hewlett-Packard (HP) is born.
1940: HP operations begin in Palo Alto, California.
1947: HP is incorporated.
1951: HP introduces the HP524A high-speed counter.
1957: HP shares are offered to the public.
1958: HP acquires F.L. Moseley Company, manufacturer of graphic recorders.
1959: HP establishes a marketing office in Geneva and a manufacturing facility in Boeblingen, West Germany.
1960: HP opens factory in Loveland, Colorado.
1961: HP purchases the Sanborn Company, a medical instruments manufacturer and is listed on the New York Stock Exchange.
1966: HP develops its first computer.
1969: David Packard is appointed deputy secretary of defense under U.S. President Nixon.
1972: HP introduces a handheld scientific calculator, the HP-35; HP introduces the HP3000 microcomputer.
1977: Bill Hewlett relinquishes his role as president of HP to John Young.
1980: HP introduces its first personal computer, the HP-85.
1982: Compaq Computer Corporation is founded.
1983: Compaq initial public offering raises $67 million; securities are traded on NASDAQ.
1984: HP's LaserJet printer makes its debut; Compaq computers are introduced in Europe; Compaq introduces the first Compaq desktop, the Compaq Deskpro.
1985: Compaq securities begin trading on the New York Stock Exchange.
1986: Compaq ships its 500,000th personal computer and completes construction of Compaq Main Campus in Houston.
1987: Compaq manufactures its one-millionth personal computer and opens manufacturing facility in Scotland.
1988: HP's stock begins trading on the Tokyo stock exchange.
1989: HP purchases Apollo Computer; Compaq purchases Wang facility in Stirling, Scotland; Compaq introduces Compaq Systempro and the first Compaq notebook PC, the Compaq LTE.
1990: Compaq establishes East European sales organization and opens office in Berlin.
1991: HP introduces the 95LX palmtop personal computer; Eckhard Pfeiffer is named CEO of Compaq; Compaq announces its first billion-dollar quarter; Compaq enters the Japanese marketplace and introduces its first modular PC, the Compaq Deskpro/M family.
1992: Lewis E. Platt replaces Young as head of HP; Compaq introduces its first printer product, the Compaq

Pagemarq; Compaq computer training center is established in China.
1993: Packard retires and Platt is named chairman, president and CEO of HP; Compaq introduces Compaq DirectPlus and delivers first Pentium processor-based products; Compaq's PC Division is split into Desktop and Notebook PC divisions; Presario family is launched; Compaq's printer business is discontinued.
1994: Compaq surpasses IBM as the number one seller of PCs worldwide; Compaq introduces first sub-notebook, Compaq Aero; Compaq opens a manufacturing facility in Brazil.
1995: HP launches the Pavilion line of home computers. Compaq is awarded Europe's largest-ever PC contract with British Telecom; HP opens manufacturing facility in China; HP acquires Thomas-Conrad and NetWorth.
1996: HP co-founder, David Packard dies on March 26, 1996; Compaq introduces its handheld PC, the PC companion, and its Armada family of value-priced, flexible notebooks.
1997: HP acquires Verifone, Inc., maker of in-store terminals for verifying credit card transactions; Compaq announces the new Presario 2000 series and introduces the TFT 500, flat-panel monitor; Compaq acquires Microcom and Tandem Computer Inc.
1998: *Forbes* magazine names Compaq its 1997 Company of the Year; the U.S. Environmental Protection Agency names Compaq the "Green Lights Corporate Partner of the Year"; Compaq is also awarded Novell's Service Excellence Award; Compaq acquires Digital Equipment Corporation.
1999: HP president Platt retires and Lucent-executive Carly Fiorina is appointed president and CEO.
2000: Compaq acquires assets of Inacom and creates Custom Edge, Inc.; Compaq announces 10-year corporate alliance with The Walt Disney Company; Compaq unveils iPAQ Pocket PC.
2001: HP co-founder Bill Hewlett dies on January 12, 2001; HP acquires application server specialist Bluestone Software; Compaq creates the AltaVista Company and acquires Shopping.com; Michael D. Capellas is appointed president and chief executive officer of Compaq; Compaq and Yahoo! announce a comprehensive global technology and marketing alliance; Compaq unveils "Evo" notebooks and workstations; Hewlett-Packard and Compaq announce their planned merger.
2002: HP and Compaq merge on May 3, 2002; HPQ is unveiled as new stock ticker for combined company.

ness requires a very different kind of manager. It has become a very unforgiving industry.''

In 1983, Compaq's consensus management approach, which allowed every division of the company a say in product development, proved valuable. Canion, Compaq's chief executive

officer, strongly supported the idea of producing a briefcase-size, or laptop, computer. The marketing research director, however, concluded that the market for such a computer did not exist. Canion relented, and Compaq waited while other companies, including Gavilan Computer Corporation and Data General Corporation, attempted to market such a product and failed.

Meanwhile, Compaq shipped its first two products, the Compaq Portable and the Compaq Plus, and set the standard for portable—although larger than a briefcase—full-function PCs. In 1983, Compaq shipped more than 53,000 portable PCs throughout the United States and Canada; increased their workforce from 100 to 600; and increased production from 200 machines in January to 9,000 in December. The company recorded $111.2 million in revenues, the most successful first year of sales for a U.S. company.

A key factor in Compaq's growth was a strong cooperative relationship with its dealers. With nearly 90 PCs on the market aimed at business professionals, shelf space was very competitive. Compaq did not have a direct sales force of its own, and, thus, did not compete with its authorized dealers. This arrangement gave dealers more incentive to carry Compaq computers. Compaq also motivated its authorized dealers through what was called "Salespaq," through which Compaq paid a percentage of the dealer's cost of advertising, sales training, or incentives.

Compaq's ability to develop, produce, and market new products in a very short time period was another key ingredient in its success. Once a product was approved, Compaq undertook all aspects of its development simultaneously; factories were built, marketing and distribution arrangements were made, and engineers refined the product design. The product cycle in the PC industry was typically 12 to 18 months; Compaq delivered in six to nine months. This fast turnaround in product development enabled Compaq to introduce the latest technology before its competitors. In 1984, for example, IBM announced a new version of its PC that experts felt would set back other PC manufacturers. Compaq pulled its resources from every branch of the company, and within six months introduced and shipped its DESKPRO line of desktop PCs. Fifteen months later IBM shipped its portable PC, which was two pounds heavier and offered fewer features than Compaq's portable model. From the first quarter of 1983 to the last quarter of 1984, Compaq's production increased from 2,200 computers to 48,000. Despite the 1984 industry shakeout, Compaq reported an increase in sales to over $500 million. In March 1985, Rosen's original investment of $2.5 million increased in value to $30 million.

Compaq in the Late 1980s: New Products and Markets

Expediency in product development also led to a turning point in Compaq's history. In 1985, Intel, a leading manufacturer of microprocessors, wanted to market its powerful new microprocessor, the 80386, as soon as possible. Intel felt confident that a Compaq product based on the new microprocessor would see a quick entry into the market. Their collaboration resulted in Compaq's 1987 introduction of the DESKPRO 386. Based on Intel's new chip, this new PC performed over three times faster than IBM's fastest PC, and nearly twice as fast as Compaq's closest competitor. It took IBM nine months to introduce a comparable machine using Intel's 80386. By then, Compaq was developing a portable version of its new PC.

In 1986, Compaq became the first company to achieve Fortune 500 status in fewer than four years. From 1986 through 1989, Compaq's revenues increased fivefold to $3 billion, while other PC manufacturers—including Apple Computer and Sun

Microsystems—had setbacks. Much of this growth was due to Compaq's successful marketing efforts in Europe. Led by Eckhard Pfeiffer, former head of TI's European consumer electronics operation, Compaq began its European campaign in 1984, before most other U.S. vendors. In 1989, Compaq became the number two supplier of business PCs to the European market, achieving $1.3 billion in international sales. With the PC market in Europe growing about 33 percent faster than the U.S. market, Compaq had an edge on other PC manufacturers.

Meanwhile, in 1986, HP introduced its new family of Spectrum computer systems, developed at a cost of $250 million. The project was based on a concept called RISC (Reduced-Instruction-Set Computing), which enabled programs to run at double or triple conventional speed by eliminating many routine instructions. In spite of critics' claims that the stripped-down instruction set made the program less flexible and overspecialized, other computer companies soon began developing their own RISC chips.

While market projections for Spectrum were good, and the system itself was state of the art, HP initially failed to capitalize on its technology because of the company's strategy of focusing on markets rather than product lines. Sales efforts, however, were soon redoubled on every level. The company even began joint marketing with telecommunications and peripherals companies previously regarded as competitors.

John Young's leadership of Hewlett-Packard was highly regarded. The Precision Architecture line gained wider acceptance after a problematic introduction, and came to be seen as a bold gamble. By 1988, Young had restored the company's momentum, with net earnings rising 27 percent during that year. Directors Hewlett and Packard were no longer involved in the day-to-day running of the business, and, in 1987, Walter B. Hewlett and David Woodley Packard, the sons of the founders, were elected to the board. In 1988, the company's stock began trading on the Tokyo stock exchange—its first listing outside the United States. The following year, HP gained listings on four European exchanges: London, Zürich, Paris, and Frankfurt.

In April 1989, Hewlett-Packard paid $500 million for Apollo Computer, a pioneer in the design, manufacture, and sale of engineering workstations. Integrating the two companies and eliminating unnecessary engineers and salespeople proved more time-consuming than anticipated, and as sales dropped, Hewlett-Packard slipped back to second position in late 1989. The company faced a further setback when Motorola Inc. delayed introduction of the advanced microprocessor chip it had promised HP for a new line of workstations.

In November 1989, Compaq introduced the Compaq SYSTEMPRO personal computer and the Compaq DESKPRO 486, utilizing technology known as Extended Industry Standard Architecture (EISA), a hardware design that Compaq developed to challenge IBM's Microchannel hardware design for its PS/2 PCs. These technologies increased the speed of PCs, enabling them to perform such complex operations as networking and multitasking. An added advantage of EISA was its ability to attract customers accustomed to using more powerful minicomputers and mainframe computers. By incorporating EISA into its new products, Compaq began to set industry standards. While IBM was producing computers based on the Microchannel technology, many other manufacturers were using EISA technology. Initial sales of the SYSTEMPRO were slow but, as CEO Canion told a Business Week correspondent, "We realized we were opening up a whole new market. . . . We knew it would take some time."

Company sales for Compaq for 1990 reached $3.6 billion, with net income of $455 million, record figures for the eighth consecutive year. During that year, Compaq opened new subsidiaries in Austria, Finland, and Hong Kong, and authorizing dealers in the former East Germany, Hungary, Yugoslavia, Argentina, Mexico, and Trinidad. International sales accounted for over half of Compaq's total revenue in 1990, eclipsing North American sales for the first time. Nine new products were introduced during that year, including updated versions of the DESKPRO 386 desktop PC and a high-performance notebook PC, the Compaq LTE 386s/20. By the end of 1990, Compaq had 3,872 authorized dealers throughout the world, over 2,000 of them in North America.

Following a trend that developed in the information processing industry in the late 1980s and early 1990s, HP forged alliances with a number of companies that had previously been competitors. These included Hitachi, a microchip company; Canon, which provided the engines for HP's best-selling laser printer line; and 3Com, with which HP had a marketing and research agreement. Purchases during this period included Eon Systems, a manufacturer of equipment that monitored computer networks; and Hilco Technologies, a maker of factory software in which HP obtained a 25 percent stake.

Early 1990's Difficulties Led to Restructuring at HP

In spite of the new focus on workstation technology and cooperative trade agreements, HP began 1990 with sagging profits and a lackluster consumer response to its new product line. In 1990, earnings fell 11 percent to $739 million, down from $829 million in 1989. David Packard, the retired co-founder of the company, returned to his office to take a more active role in running the business.

John Young, president and CEO, undertook a thorough restructuring of Hewlett-Packard. By eliminating excess layers of management and dividing computer products into two main groups: those sold directly to big customers (workstations and minicomputers) and those sold through discount dealers (printers and PCs). In a move away from the consensus style of management, he set up a virtually autonomous design group within the computer division, and put it in charge of developing a new workstation based on the RISC technology that Digital had helped pioneer. The results were impressive. After only a year of development, the Series 700 workstations were introduced in 1991 to universally favorable reviews. The machines were considered several years ahead of their time, a crucial advantage in an industry where the constant development of new technologies makes products obsolete almost as soon as they reach the market.

HP's 95LX palmtop personal computer, also introduced in 1991, established an important new market in information devices. The 95LX, which retailed for $699, contained built-in

Lotus 1-2-3 spreadsheet software, and immediately became a hot seller.

The resurgence of the company was not achieved without a price. HP cut 3,000 positions in 1990 and a further 2,000 positions in 1991. While executives agreed that downsizing was a necessary evil, the staff reductions, together with a more aggressive advertising stance, changed the company's image. When John Young announced his retirement in July 1992, he presided over a dynamic, if less paternalistic, company. His successor, Lewis E. Platt, an executive vice-president and head of the company's computer systems organization, took over in November 1992. Following Packard's retirement as chairman in 1993, Platt was named chairman, president, and CEO of HP.

1991 also Brings a Slump to Compaq

For reasons ranging from economic recession and price competition to problems with the flow of distribution, Compaq's sales and earnings fell in 1991 for the first time in the company's history. The DESKPRO 386 PC series continued to be a bestseller, with desktop PCs accounting for close to three-fourths of Compaq's total revenue. In September 1991, a new line of Compaq computers was introduced with "Intelligent Modularity." This system, the DESKPRO/M, enabled users to more readily upgrade key components as their needs and the available technology changed, by organizing components into five easy-to-access modules: memory, input/output, EISA/ISA expansion cards, processor, and video graphics controller.

Compaq was forced to alter its established distribution strategy somewhat in 1991; eight of the company's ten most important dealer chains had merged into four. This led Compaq to gradually start authorizing computer consultants and discount chains to sell its products. Direct sales techniques of its own, such as a toll-free hotline, were stepped up as well.

In late 1991, a dramatic management shake-up took place. Following a gloomy board meeting at which a $70 million third-quarter loss was announced, company founder and CEO Canion was forced to resign. Pfeiffer, who had been promoted to executive vice-president and chief operating officer, replaced Canion. A major reorganization of the corporate structure ensued. The company was realigned into desktop and systems divisions. As part of a 1,440-person staff reduction program, about 12 percent of the company's entire work force was laid off. In addition, five high-ranking executives left the organization, including senior vice-president of engineering James C. Harris, the last remaining company founder.

In June 1992, Compaq introduced 16 new products, including the company's first low-cost desktop PCs (COMPAQ ProLinea), low-cost notebook PCs (Contura), and upgradeable desktop PCs with advanced graphics and audio capabilities. The same month, Compaq announced the initiation of a new Peripherals Division, a worldwide arm whose mission would be to develop printers and printer-related items. The division's initial line of products, including the August 1992 debut of the Compaq Pagem printer, launched Compaq into the rapidly growing market for network printers. The printer line was a failure, however, and was abandoned in 1993.

Compaq's Presario Leads a Consumer Push in the Mid-1990s

Under the leadership of Eckhardt, Compaq began a major push into the consumer and home office markets with an effort centered around the Presario line of home computers launched in August 1993. The company's hottest new PC, the Presario line, included models selling for less than $1,500. Compaq sold more than 100,000 Presarios in the first 60 days after introduction, with sales fueled by a $12 million television advertising blitz, the company's first such campaign in three years. In 1993 alone, Compaq sold $500 million worth of Presarios. By 1994, the company managed not only to fend off its low-price competitors, it also surpassed IBM as the number one seller of PCs worldwide.

Not content with its PC dominance, Compaq in the mid-1990s aimed to capture a much wider market. Following the introduction of the Proliant server PCs as its entry into the market for servers (powerful computers used for corporate networks and Internet web sites), the company went after the corporate mainframe and minicomputer market with the launch of the Armada mainframe-class server, the top-of-the-line model which sold for upwards of $100,000. On the lower-end server front, in 1994 Compaq launched the ProSignia VS server, which cost only about five to ten percent more than a desktop PC.

Also in 1994, Compaq revamped its logistics system in order to begin building its PCs to order from a huge stockpile of parts. With a build-to-order system, Compaq would realize significant inventory and manufacturing cost savings.

Other Compaq initiatives of this period included moves into high-speed networking equipment and Internet services/products, as well as the October 1996 launch of a successful line of engineering workstations. Compaq realized astounding growth: revenues increased from $5.79 billion in 1992 to $20.01 billion in 1996; and net income, which had peaked in 1990 at $577 million, registered at $988 million in 1994, $893 million in 1995, and $1.32 billion in 1996. With a wider range of products, Compaq generated about 15 percent of its revenues from the consumer PC market, 48 percent from corporate desktop PCs, and 35 percent from servers and workstations in 1997.

HP Aggressively Expands in PCs in the Mid-1990s

When Platt took over as CEO of Hewlett-Packard in 1992, its share of the personal computer market was a mere one percent. Moreover, PCs accounted for only 5.7 percent of the company's overall revenues of $16.4 billion. By 1995, HP was the fastest-growing maker of PCs in the world, having initially targeted corporate customers. In August 1995, HP went after the home PC market with the launch of the Pavilion line. Throughout this revitalization of the company's PC lines, HP adopted a much more aggressive pricing policy. Its market share soared, with the company leaping to third place in mid-1997, edging out Dell Computer and trailing only Compaq Computer Corporation and IBM. By 1998, Hewlett-Packard derived 19.1 percent of its total revenues of $47.06 billion from the sale of personal computers.

HP's pursuit of personal computer prominence was problematic given that sector's relatively low margins, but Platt felt the company had to be a major player in PCs in order to remain one of the top computer companies in the world. Although Platt did not want HP to be ''just'' a peripherals company, the firm continued to churn out successful products in that area: the HP Color LaserJet printer and the HP OfficeJet multifunction machine (a combined printer, fax machine, and copier), both introduced in 1994; and the HP OmniGo 100 handheld organizer, which debuted in 1995. With the Internet and electronic commerce burgeoning, HP in mid-1997 paid nearly $1.2 billion to acquire VeriFone, Inc., a maker of in-store terminals used to verify credit card transactions. HP hoped to combine a personal computer or other electronic device with a VeriFone-derived card reader and appropriate software to create a system with additional payment options for electronic commerce purchases. Also in 1997, HP was added to the companies that comprise the prestigious Dow Jones Industrial Average. Meantime, co-founder David Packard died on March 26, 1996.

HP's revenues had been growing at an annual 20-percent-plus clip from 1993 through 1996, but, in 1997, these increases began to shrink. Sales increased from $38.42 billion in 1996 to $42.9 billion in 1997, or 11.6 percent, then to 47.06 billion in 1998, an increase of 9.7 percent. Net income fell from $3.12 billion in 1997 to $2.95 billion in 1998. Among the reasons for the decline were the Asian economic crisis; HP's slow response to opportunities presented by the explosion of the Internet; and falling prices for personal computers and computer peripherals. In addition, HP's printer lines, especially in the inkjet area, were being buffeted by competition from new, low-cost rivals and declining margins in the PC and printer areas were dragging down the profitability of HP as a whole.

Compaq Acquisitions in the Late 1990s

In February 1997, Compaq released a $999 PC, the Presario 2000, in another aggressive, low-price move aimed at attracting the 60 percent of U.S. households without a PC. Later in 1997 the company acquired, through a stock-for-stock transaction valued at about $4 billion, Tandem Computers Incorporated, a leader in fail-safe high-end servers with annual sales of $2 billion and a sales force 4,000 strong. Compaq also spent $280 million for Microcom, Inc., a provider of devices for remote access to networks.

Moreover, Compaq had its eye on an even bigger deal. In June 1998 the company completed its $9.1 billion acquisition of Digital Equipment Corporation, the number four computer maker in the United States. Digital, which became a subsidiary of Compaq, was a leading maker of high-end workstations and servers, giving Compaq an even greater presence in those markets. Digital also brought to Compaq a 22,000-person service operation for large companies—computer services having been one of Compaq's weakest areas. The deal increased Compaq's annual revenues to more than $37 billion and vaulted the company into the number two position among all the computer firms in the world (behind only $78.5 million-in-revenues IBM), it also positioned Compaq as one of the world leaders in just about every computer sector. The company was number one worldwide in desktop computers, number three in portable computers, number three in workstations, number one in both PC servers (costing less than $25,000) and entry servers (less than $100,000), and number six in midrange servers ($100,000 to $1 million). In computer services, Compaq was suddenly number three, behind IBM and EDS.

Compaq took a $3.6 billion charge against earnings in 1998 related to the acquisition of Digital and announced plans to cut 15,000 Digital jobs and 2,000 at Compaq. Areas of overlap began to be addressed, such as the folding of Digital's PC production into that of Compaq and the scaling back of Compaq's network equipment unit. However, it would take some time before the full impact of this combination—at the time the largest merger in the relatively short history of computers—could be assessed.

Compaq's transformation from a PC company to a global IT—and Internet—leader accelerated during 1998, based on the vision of President Pfeiffer, "At Compaq, we envision a world where virtually all information is online and people can communicate, conduct commerce and securely access the information they need from anywhere at any time." Through the acquisition of Digital, Compaq acquired AltaVista, the world's fastest Internet search and navigation guide, and the following year created a separate company, The AltaVista Company, to extend Compaq's Internet leadership position. Compaq also announced that year the formation of Compaq.com, a business division to drive Internet sales of Compaq products and services, and the acquisition of online retailer Shopping.com.

Compaq President Pfeiffer Resigns; Michael D. Capellas Takes Charge

In the wake of disappointing earnings and shareholder suits, President Pfeiffer resigned and was replaced as President and CEO by Michael D. Capellas, who had joined the company in 1998. Capellas issued more layoffs and organized the company around three global businesses groups-Enterprise Solutions and Services, Commercial Personal Computing, and Consumer. A restructuring plan was implemented to drive down costs and operating expenses. During the second half of the year, Compaq returned to profitability, reduced operating expenses and began to focus on increasing growth and stockholder value. Strategic alliances with Microsoft and Oracle were re-energized and a strategic partnership was formed with CMGI, by which CMGI would acquire control of Compaq's Alta Vista business and its related properties (Shopping.com and Zip2). Innovative products and services were introduced, including the Aero 8000, the world's most secure, mobile and easy-to-use Handheld PC Professional device; and the light-weight portable projector, MP1600.

Capellas saw Compaq "guided by a single, focused vision: Everything to the Internet." At the end of 1999, Compaq joined forces with Cable & Wireless to deliver global e-business solutions; in 2000 acquired PC reseller Inacom; and created Custom Edge, Inc., a direct sales unit. In April, a 10-year corporate alliance was announced with The Walt Disney Company. In technology, the iPAQ Pocket PC was introduced and earned the first ZDNet "tech Trendsetter Award."

By mid-year, the Compaq started showing significant progress and by the end of the year, revenue was up 10 percent, gross margin was up almost one percentage point, operating expenses were down, operating profit was up more than threefold, and earnings per share more than tripled from 1999. Capellas credited the success to Compaq's enterprise business, particularly the high-end storage and server businesses. Compaq was the number one provider of Web servers, number one in the highest measure of system availability and number one in high-performance technical computing.

1999 HP Plans to Spin Off Noncomputing Lines

In late 1998, HP launched a comprehensive review of its operations and announced in early 1999 its intention to spin off into a separate firm, Agilent Technologies, its noncomputing segments: test and measurement products and service, medical electronic products and service, electronic components, and chemical analysis and service. These segments generated about $7.6 billion in revenues during 1998, or 16 percent of the total. Hewlett-Packard hoped this major divestment—which included the company's original lines of business—would sharpen the firm's competitive instincts, energize its workforce, and enable it to become a more aggressive player in the increasingly important sphere of the Internet. The company also announced that upon completion of the spinoff, Platt would step down as chairman and CEO.

In July 1999, HP named the 20-year veteran of AT&T and Lucent Technologies, Carleton (Carly) S. Fiorina as President and CEO. Fiorina was responsible for HP's reinvention as a company that makes the Internet work for businesses and consumers. According to Fiorina, the reinvention of the company resulted from the goal "to restructure and revitalize ourselves to recapture the spirit of invention that is our birthright and apply it to meeting customer needs." Under her leadership, HP returned to its roots of innovation and inventiveness and focused on delivering the best total customer experience.

HP revealed a new strategy designed for the Internet, based on Web services to people and businesses through the use of information appliances over infrastructure solutions. HP positioned itself to deliver Web services, intelligent devices and servers and infrastructure of servers and software. By the end of the year, HP had introduced a new brand campaign focusing on the company's history of invention and innovation and introducing a new company logo. Under Fiorina's direction, HP also realigned its businesses into two customer-facing organizations and three product-generation organizations.

In 2000, HP introduced the high-end Superdome server line and announced that it would acquire Bluestone Software, resulting in the further expansion of its Internet software portfolio. A new business initiative, HP e-Inclusion, was introduced. This program addressed the digital divide by fostering sustainable, profitable businesses in developing countries.

Two new software families were introduced in early 2001—HP Netaction Software Suite and HP Open View Software Suite—thus, uniting its software offerings into a comprehensive platform for developing, implementing and maintaining Internet-based services. A new business organization, HP Services, was announced in March, with responsibilities in consulting, outsourcing, support, education and solutions deployment.

In 2001, Compaq continued to shift its emphasis from hardware to services, comprising 24 percent of Compaq's revenue in 2001. The Global Services unit of the company continued to be the company's strongest segment. Compaq's Alpha microprocessor operations were sold to Intel and a comprehensive global technology and marketing alliance was announced with Yahoo!. Computing on Demand was introduced which would allow customers to purchase a variety of computing resources.

Acquisitions and a Merger of Worldwide Importance

In September HP acquired StorageApps, manufacturer of storage virtualization appliances, and Indigo, a leading commercial and industrial printing systems company. Perhaps the biggest news to the industry occurred on September 3, 2001, when HP and Compaq Computer Corporation announced a definitive agreement to merge, creating a new $87 billion global technology leader.

On May 3, 2002, Hewlett-Packard officially closed its $19 billion acquisition of Compaq Computer Corporation. Compaq investors received 0.6325 shares of Hewlett-Packard for every Compaq share they owned, and Compaq stock ceased being traded. HPQ became the new stock ticker for the combined company. Ms. Fiorina retained her position as Chairman and CEO of the new HP. Former Compaq president and merger coauthor, Michael Capellas, became president of the new HP, with responsibilities for the new company's global business groups, worldwide sales, supply chain management and e-commerce operations. According to Chairman Fiorina, "We merged Compaq and HP to create a stronger company to serve our customers—a company with a richer portfolio of products and solutions and a deeper services team." The new HP was officially launched on May 7, 2002, with an ad titled "We Are Ready."

Principal Subsidiaries

HEWLETT-PACKARD: Hewlett-Packard Puerto Rico; Hewlett-Packard World Trade, Inc.; Heartstream, Inc.; Microsensor Technology, Inc.; VeriFone, Inc.; Hewlett-Packard Asia Pacific Ltd. (Hong Kong); Hewlett-Packard Caribe Ltd. (Cayman Islands); HP Computadores (Brazil); Hewlett-Packard Computer Products (Shanghai) Co., Ltd. (China); Hewlett-Packard de Mexico S.A. de C. V.; Hewlett-Packard Espanola, S.A. (Spain); Hewlett-Packard Europe B.V. (The Netherlands); Hewlett-Packard France; Hewlett-Packard GmbH (Germany); Hewlett-Packard Holding GmbH (Germany); Hewlett-Packard (India) Software Operation Pte. Ltd.; Hewlett-Packard Italiana S.p.A. (Italy); Hewlett-Packard Japan, Ltd.; Hewlett-Packard Korea Ltd.; Hewlett-Packard Ltd. (U. K.); Hewlett-Packard (Malaysia) Sdn. Bhd.; Hewlett-Packard Malaysia Technology Sdn. Bhd.; Hewlett-Packard (Manufacturing) Ltd. (Ireland); Hewlett-Packard Medical Products (Qingdao) Ltd. (China); Hewlett-Packard Microwave Products (M) Sdn. Bhd. (Malaysia); Hewlett-Packard Penang Sdn. Bhd. (Malaysia); Hewlett-Packard S.A. (Switzerland); Hewlett-Packard Shanghai Analytical Products Co., Ltd. (China); Hewlett-Packard Singapore Pte. Ltd.; Hewlett-Packard Singapore Vision Operation Pte. Ltd.; BT&D Technologies Ltd. (U. K.); CoCreate Software GmbH (Germany); Shanghai Hewlett-Packard Company (China); Technologies et Participations S.A. (France). COMPAQ: Digital Equipment Corporation; Microcom, Inc.; Tandem Computers Incorporated; Compaq Computer Australia Pty. Limited; Compaq Computer GesmbH (Austria); Compaq Computer N.V./S.A. (Belgium); Compaq Canada Inc.; Compaq Computer A/S (Denmark); Compaq Computer OY (Finland); Compaq Computer S.A.R.L. (France); Compaq Computer GmbH (Germany); Compaq Computer Hong Kong Limited; Compaq Computer S.p.A. (Italy); Compaq K.K. (Japan); Compaq Computer B.V. (Netherlands); Compaq Computer New Zealand Limited; Compaq Computer Norway A.S.; Compaq Computer Asia Pte. Ltd. (Singapore); Compaq Computer S.A. (Spain); Compaq Computer AB (Sweden); Compaq Computer AG (Switzerland); Compaq Computer Taiwan Limited; Compaq Computer Limited (U. K.).

Principal Operating Units

Chemical Analysis Group; Components Group; Consumer Products Group; Enterprise Computing Solutions Organization; HP Labs; Information Storage Group; LaserJet Solutions Group; Medical Products Group; Personal Systems Group; Test and Measurement Organization.

Principal Competitors

Canon; Dell Computer; IBM; Apple Computer; eMachines; Gateway; NCR; NEC; Siemens; Sony; Sun Microsystems.

Further Reading

Arnst, Catherine, "Now, HP Stands for Hot Products," *Business Week*, June 14, 1993, p. 36.

Arnst, Catherine, et. al, "Compaq: How It Made Its Impressive Move Out of the Doldrums," *Business Week*, November 2, 1992, pp. 146+.

Bank, David, and Leslie Cauley, "Microsoft, Compaq Make Net-Access Bet," *Wall Street Journal*, June 16, 1998, pp. A3, A8.

Buell, Barbara, "Hewlett-Packard Rethinks Itself," *Business Week*, April 1, 1991.

Burrows, Peter, "Compaq Stretches for the Crown," *Business Week*, July 11, 1994, pp. 140–42.

——, "Lew Platt's Fix-It Plan for Hewlett-Packard," *Business Week*, July 13, 1998, pp. 128–31.

——, "The Printer King Invades Home PCs," *Business Week*, August 21, 1995, pp. 74–75.

——, "Where Compaq's Kingdom Is Weak," *Business Week*, May 8, 1995, pp. 98, 102.

Clark, Don, and George Anders, "After Split, Outsider May Be Hired As Next CEO, Breaking Tradition," *Wall Street Journal*, March 3, 1999, pp. A3+.

"Compaq Computer Corporation," *Hoover's Handbook of American Business 2002*, Austin: Hoover's, Inc., 2001, pp. 398–399.

"Compaq's Compact," *Management Today*, May 1985.

Connor, Deni and Denise Dubie, "HP Shores Up Storage, Management Wares," *Network World*, Nov 5, 2001, p. 10+.

Depke, Deidre A., "A Comeback at Compaq?," *Business Week*, September 23, 1991.

Gannes, Stuart, "America's Fastest-Growing Companies," *Fortune*, May 23, 1988.

Heller, Robert, "The Compaq Comeback," *Management Today*, December 1994, pp. 66–70.

Goldgaber, Arthur, "The Teflon Tech Company: How Long Will Wall Street Give Hewlett-Packard the Benefit of the Doubt?," *Financial World*, July/August 1997, pp. 90–93.

Hamilton, David P., and Scott Thurm, "H-P to Spin Off Its Measurement Operations: Sharper Focus on Computing Will Emerge," *Wall Street Journal*, March 3, 1999, pp. A3+.

"Hewlett-Packard," *Hoover's Handbook of American Business 2002*, Austin: Hoover's, Inc., 2001, pp. 712–713.

Hof, Robert, "Hewlett-Packard Digs Deep for a Digital Future," *Business Week*, October 18, 1993, pp. 72–75.

——, "Suddenly Hewlett-Packard Is Doing Everything Right," *Business Week*, March 23, 1992.

Hof, Robert, and Peter Burrows, "Hewlett-Packard Heads for the Home," *Business Week*, May 8, 1995, p. 102.

"HP Closes Compaq Merger," *HP.com*, posted May 3, 2002, http://www.hp.com.

"HP Fact Sheet," Palo Alto, Calif.: Hewlett-Packard Company, 1998.

Hutheesing, Nikhil, "HP's Giant ATM," *Forbes*, February 9, 1998, pp. 96+.

"HP to Change NYSE Trading Symbol from HWP to HPQ," *HP.com*, posted May 2, 2002, http://ww.thenew.hp.com.

Kirkpatrick, David, "Fast Times at Compaq," *Fortune*, April 1, 1996, pp. 120+.

——, "The Revolution at Compaq Computer," *Fortune*, December 14, 1992, pp. 80+.

Klein, Alec, "As Cheap Printers Score, H-P Plays Catch-Up," *Wall Street Journal*, April 21, 1999, pp. B1+.

Kotkin, Joel, "The Hottest Entrepreneur in America Is . . . the 'Smart Team' at Compaq Computer," *Inc.*, February 1986.

Linden, Dana Wechsler, and Bruce Upbin, "Top Corporate Performance of 1995: 'Boy Scouts on a Rampage,' " *Forbes*, January 1, 1996, pp. 66+.

Loeb, Marshall, "Leadership Lost—and Regained," *Fortune*, April 17, 1995, pp. 217+.

Losee, Stephanie, "How Compaq Keeps the Magic Going," *Fortune*, February 21, 1994, pp. 90+.

McWilliams, Gary, "Compaq at the Crossroads," *Business Week*, July 22, 1996, pp. 70–72.

——, "Compaq-Digital: Let the Slimming Begin," *Business Week*, June 22, 1998, p. 44.

——, "Compaq: There's No End to Its Drive," *Business Week*, February 17, 1997, pp. 72, 74.

——, "Mimicking Dell, Compaq to Sell Its PCs Directly," *Wall Street Journal*, November 11, 1998, pp. B1, B4.

McWilliams, Gary, et. al, "Power Play: How the Compaq-Digital Deal Will Reshape the Entire World of Computers," *Business Week*, February 9, 1998, pp. 90–94, 96–97.

Nee, Eric, "Compaq Computer Corp.," *Forbes*, January 12, 1998, pp. 90+.

——, "Defending the Desktop," *Forbes*, December 28, 1998, p. 53.

——, "Lew Platt: Why I Dismembered HP," *Fortune*, March 29, 1999, p. 167.

——, "What Have You Invented for Me Lately?," *Forbes*, July 28, 1997, pp. 76+.

Packard, David, *The HP Way: How Bill Hewlett and I Built Our Company*, edited by David Kirby with Karen Lewis, New York: HarperBusiness, 1995.

Palmer, Jay, "Still Shining: Growth in PC Demand Abroad, Networking Make Compaq's Prospects Bright," *Barron's*, December 11, 1995, pp. 15–16.

Pitta, Julie, "Identity Crisis," *Forbes*, May 25, 1992.

——, "It Had to Be Done and We Did It," *Forbes*, April 26, 1993, pp. 148–52.

Ramstad, Evan, "Compaq's CEO Takes Tricky Curves at High Speed," *Wall Street Journal*, January 5, 1998, p. B4.

Ramstad, Evan, and Jon G. Auerbach, "Compaq Buys Digital, an Unthinkable Event Just a Few Years Ago," *Wall Street Journal*, January 27, 1998, pp. A1, A14.

Stross, Randall E., "What's a High-Class Company Like Hewlett-Packard Doing in a Lowbrow Business Like PCs?," *Fortune*, September 29, 1997, pp. 129+.

Uttal, Bro, "Compaq Bids for PC Leadership," *Fortune*, September 29, 1986.

Ward, Judy, "The Endless Wave: Eckhard Pfeiffer Has Turned Compaq Around—Only to Face New Competition," *Financial World*, July 4, 1995, pp. 32–35.

Webber, Alan M., "Consensus, Continuity, and Commonsense: An Interview with Compaq's Rod Canion," *Harvard Business Review*, July/August 1990.

Whiting, Rick, "Compaq Stays the Course," *Electronic Business*, October 20, 1989.

Wiegner, Kathleen K., "Good-Bye to the HP Way?," *Forbes*, November 26, 1990.

Zell, Deone, *Changing by Design: Organizational Innovation at Hewlett-Packard*, Ithaca, NY: ILR Press, 1997.

Zipper, Stuart, "Compaq—Life After Canon?," *Electronic News*, November 4, 1991.

—John Simley (Hewlett-Packard);
Lynn Hall and Robert R. Jacobson (Compaq)
—updates: David E. Salamie; Carol D. Beavers

Honeywell Inc.

Honeywell Plaza
101 Columbia Road
P.O. Box 4000
Morristown, New Jersey 07962-2497
U.S.A.
Telephone: (973) 455-2000
Toll Free: (800) 707-4555
Fax: (973) 455-4807
Web site: http://www.honeywell.com

Public Company
Incorporated: 1927 as Minneapolis-Honeywell Regulator
   Co.
Employees: 115,000 (2001)
Sales: $23.65 billion (2001)
Stock Exchanges: New York London Paris Amsterdam
   Brussels Geneva Zurich Basel
Ticker Symbol: HON
NAIC: 334512 Automatic Environmental Control Manu-
   facturing for Residential, Commercial, and Appliance
   Use; 334511 Search, Detection, Navigation, Guidance,
   Aeronautical, and Nautical System and Instrument
   Manufacturing; 334513 Instruments and Related
   Products Manufacturing for Measuring, Displaying, and
   Controlling Industrial Process Variables; 334290 Other
   Communications Equipment Manufacturing

Honeywell Inc. traces its beginnings to 1885, the year that Al Butz invented the "damper flapper." The damper flapper started a business that would become the backbone of Honeywell Inc. Honeywell is most familiar to the public for its low-tech thermostats, especially the "Honeywell Round," Model T86, known in the 1950s for its snap-off plastic cover that could be painted to match the interior of a home. Today, Honeywell is a multinational corporation that is not only a leading supplier of home, office, and industrial control systems, but also a major defense contractor and an integral part of America's space exploration program. Honeywell products include turboprop engines, flight safety and landing systems, automation and controls, heating, ventilation, materials used in semiconductors, polymers for electronics, fibers, friction materials, and consumer car products.

Honeywell Beginnings in the Thermostat Business

In 1883, when delivery men still toted coal into American basements, Albert Butz created a device to lift a furnace's damper when a home became too cold, letting fresh air fan the flames and warm the house. In 1886, the device was patented and the Butz Thermo-Electric Regulator Company formed to manufacture it. Butz, from Minneapolis, Minnesota, was more an idea man than a man of business, and the company does not seem to have prospered. In 1888, Butz sold the patent for the damper flapper to his patent attorneys, who founded the Consolidated Temperature Controlling Company the same year.

During its first years, the company went through financial difficulties and several name changes. It became the Electric Thermostat Company in 1892, the Electric Heat Regulator Company in 1893. In 1898, William Sweatt, a businessman who had joined the company in 1891, took over the company. He took charge of marketing the damper flapper, increasing advertising and even going door-to-door with his salesmen. This firsthand contact with customers prompted Sweatt to sell the wheelbarrow company he owned at the time and cast his entire future into the Electric Heat Regulator Company.

The damper flappers Sweatt sold remained basically the same until 1907, when a clock was added. The thermostat could automatically let a house cool at night and warm it in the morning. The clock also gave the thermostat a new look that would survive well into the 1930s. When consumers responding to his ads began to request the "Minneapolis" regulator, Sweatt changed the name of his product. He began calling the thermostat "The Minneapolis Regulator" in 1905; in 1909, "The Minneapolis" was put on the face of the thermostats and on the motors, and in 1912 Sweatt officially changed the name of the company to the Minneapolis Heat Regulator Company.

One year later, in 1913, Sweatt's son, Harold R. Sweatt, who had been elected to the board in 1909 at the age of 18, was elected vice-president. At the time, the company had 50 people and a motorcycle whose engine powered several machines. Sales hit $200,000 in 1914, the year that Sweatt's second son, Charles, joined the company. Sweatt stressed to his sons the importance of manufacturing thermostats, saying that it made no sense competing with their best customers by making furnaces.

As coal furnaces began to be replaced by sometimes dangerous oil burners, Minneapolis Heat Regulator made a circuit that stopped and started the burners. Early attempts failed to eliminate "puffs," as these explosions were called, but modifications on the circuit soon made it possible for the regulator to shut down the burner in case of a malfunction, and the Series 10 was born.

As the home heating market continued to expand, many companies began to manufacture products to compete with the Minneapolis Regulator. In the face of this competition, the company merged with the Wabash, Indiana-based Honeywell Heating Specialties Company in 1927. The two companies had been making complementary and competing products, including oil burner controls, clock thermostats, and regulators, and had even been involved in a legal suit over patents at the time of the merger.

Acquisitions and Company Buyouts Contribute to Honeywell's Growth

The combination surprised the industry, and even the corporate heads themselves. But, the merger made a lot of sense. Minneapolis Heat Regulator doubled its business and became a publicly held company, under yet another name: the Minneapolis-Honeywell Regulator Company. William Sweatt became chairman of the board in the new Minneapolis headquarters; Mark Honeywell, president; Harold Sweatt, vice-president and general manager; and Charles Sweatt, vice-president. The merger gave the business the resources to expand even after the 1929 stock market crash, and marked the start of a decade of acquisition and growth.

In 1931, Minneapolis-Honeywell bought Time-O-Stat Controls Corporation through an exchange of stock. Time-O-Stat was the result of a 1929 merger between four Wisconsin heating controls companies. The purchase brought the company several mercury switch patents and other controls technology. Minneapolis-Honeywell's next big acquisition marked a move to industrial accounts. In a chance train meeting, Willard Huff, Minneapolis-Honeywell treasurer, and Richard Brown, president of Brown Instrument Company, began discussing the similarities of their businesses. Brown's products measured the high temperatures inside industrial machines, while Minneapolis-Honeywell was a low temperature controls company. Within weeks, the firms were negotiating, and by the end of 1934, Minneapolis-Honeywell had purchased Brown's assets for $2.3 million.

Finally, in 1937, dissatisfied with the high costs of its own pneumatic control devices for larger buildings like schools and offices, Minneapolis-Honeywell bought the only two competing companies in the field: National Regulator Company and Bishop & Babcock Manufacturing Company. In the ten years from the 1927 merger with Honeywell, Minneapolis-Honeywell had tripled its employee ranks and its sales. Despite the Depression, the company had $16 million in sales and 3,000 employees.

Honeywell Branches Out to Help Military

Harold Sweatt had become president in 1934, following Mark Honeywell, who had succeeded William Sweatt. At the start of World War II, Sweatt headed a company with the experience and resources needed to develop precision instruments and controls for the military. In 1941, the army called upon a group of Minneapolis-Honeywell engineers who had worked on heat regulating systems to develop an automatic bomber pilot that gave precise readings of high-altitude coordinates. The company also produced a turbo regulator and an intricate fire control system. By war's end, Minneapolis-Honeywell was well on its way to becoming a major defense contractor.

After the war, Harold Sweatt held fast to his father's rule and kept moving in the direction of controls. He purchased two planes and turned them into flying laboratories for his aviation and research staffs. He also began buying companies related to the manufacture of control instruments. One such purchase came in 1950, when Sweatt bought the Micro Switch Division of the First Industrial Corporation of Freeport, Illinois. Micro switches are used in vending machines, industrial equipment, and even tanks and guided missile systems. Generally they need a small amount of physical force to activate the electronics. Two years after the purchase, Minneapolis-Honeywell was making 5,000 variations of micro switches.

Entering the Computer and Aerospace Business

About this time, Raytheon, a Massachusetts electronics firm, approached Minneapolis-Honeywell about teaming up to enter the computer business. After studying the issue for months, Minneapolis-Honeywell accepted Raytheon's offer in April of 1955. The companies formed Datamatic Corporation, a subsidiary owned jointly by the two companies. In 1957, the company installed its first line of mainframe computers. The Datamatic 1000 filled several rooms and weighed some 25 tons, and the first unit sold for $2 million. But, Datamatic lacked the customer base that gave competitors like IBM an early edge. Raytheon wanted out, and that year the operation became Minneapolis-Honeywell's Datamatic division.

The company's aerospace divisions were also developing quickly. From the development of its first autopilot in 1941,

Key Dates:

1883: Damper Flapper is created by Albert Butz.
1909: First controlled thermostat is created.
1927: Company incorporated as Minneapolis-Honeywell Regulator Company.
1941: Honeywell becomes a major defense contractor during WWII.
1950–1959: Honeywell's advancements in microswitches lead the company to enter the computer market.
1967: The computer division shows a profit for the first time.
1988: The company focuses on its aerospace divisions to boost company profits.
1999: AlliedSignal and Honeywell merge.
2000: Honeywell's acquisition by General Electric is rejected by the European Union.

Minneapolis-Honeywell was at the forefront of technology. By 1964, Minneapolis-Honeywell won a bid to make space vehicles designed to carry a variety of NASA equipment. Two were eventually launched, but the company decided expenses were too great to enter into the prime contract field. Still, the company was involved in every American space mission, and supplied digital flight control systems and display and performance monitors for the space shuttle. Also in 1964, the stockholders approved yet another name change, to Honeywell Inc.

While Honeywell ventured further into computers and aerospace technology, its international operations were also expanding. Between 1945 and 1965, Honeywell's overseas business in Great Britain, Canada, Japan, and the Netherlands had grown from almost nothing to account for 23 percent of sales and 20 percent of its work force; these percentages stayed roughly the same into the 1980s. In 1965, Honeywell's overseas operations consisted of 17 subsidiaries with 12,000 employees and revenues of more than $160 million.

Meanwhile, the computer division finally showed a profit in 1967, 12 years after it was established. But research and development costs continued to be enormous. In 1970, Honeywell shocked the business world by purchasing the large systems computer segment of General Electric. The purchase doubled its business and added 25,000 employees in a new subsidiary called Honeywell Information Systems (HIS). The move put Honeywell in second place in computers, behind only IBM. But in the end, the merger only pitted Honeywell against IBM, leading to a long, hard struggle and, eventually, disillusionment.

Turbulent Times for Honeywell

The early 1970s were a bumpy time for Honeywell. The company received a lot of negative publicity for its involvement with the war in Southeast Asia and for its investments in South Africa. One of the most vocal demonstrators was Charles Pillsbury, a dissident stockholder and heir to the flour empire, who in 1970 shouted the memorable question to Honeywell president James H. Binger, "How does it feel to be the Krupp of Minneapolis?," referring to the German industrialist who had

helped re-arm Germany following World War I. But Binger, an outspoken and controversial leader, declared in 1971 that as long as the conflict in Southeast Asia continued, Honeywell would furnish support.

Within the corporation, the 1970s were marked by efforts to streamline business and cut out nonproductive assets. One of the divisions that dwindled during this period was the home smoke alarm business, which was finally cut in 1980. The market had become increasingly competitive; though well known for its fire protection products, the company discontinued its line. Honeywell's entry into microcomputers did turn a profit, doubling sales every year between 1976 and 1980. Unfortunately, however, HIS suffered nearly a 50 percent decline in operating profits between 1981 and 1982. Compounding the company's financial difficulties, anti-apartheid activists protested against the company's South African interests, and Native Americans claimed that land Honeywell held for defense experiments was sacred, and demanded Honeywell stop all activities there.

In 1982, Honeywell began a major corporate restructuring. James Renier, a Honeywell executive who had climbed the ranks, became president of the computer division. A total of 3,500 jobs were eliminated through layoffs, retirements, and transfers, earning Renier the nickname "Neutron Jim": "[All] the buildings were still there," one survivor explained to the *Wall Street Journal*, "it's just the people who were gone." Renier became president and CEO of Honeywell in 1986. Renier also redefined the corporate attitude toward IBM, resolving to live in an IBM world and begin marketing products that would work alongside IBM computers.

Once the computer division was whipped into some kind of shape, Honeywell decided in 1986 to sell the majority of it to Group Bull of France and Japan's NEC Corporation, creating a three-way joint venture. Honeywell retained 42.5 percent of the stock, but intended to sell all but 20 percent to its partners. The divestiture of its computer unit left Honeywell to concentrate on sales of thermostat systems, automation products, and aerospace and defense equipment.

By the latter decades of the twentieth century, Honeywell was a powerful force in the public and private sectors. In the mid-1980s, the company had more than 35 divisions, 80 subsidiaries, and offices in all 50 states and around the world. In 1986, the company purchased the Sperry Aerospace Group, now incorporated into Honeywell's aerospace division. Honeywell consistently won military contracts in the millions of dollars, making torpedoes, guidance systems, and ammunition for the nation's defense; meanwhile, sales of its home, building, and industrial controls divisions reached $3 billion in 1987.

Beefing Up the Aerospace Division Boosts Honeywell's Business

In 1988, Honeywell suffered from a series of unusual charges related to the company's defense unit. Serious cost overruns in a number of contracts, many of them carryovers from the days when Unisys owned the unit, had to be absorbed by the company, resulting in a net loss of $434.9 million for the year. As a general slowdown in defense contracts combined with the Pentagon's waste-reduction measures created a tougher business climate for defense contractors, James Renier looked to the company's commercial aerospace business to pick up the slack. By 1989, defense and aerospace accounted for almost half of Honeywell's sales and were contributing significantly to the bottom line. At the same time, automation systems were getting a boost from an upswing in capital investment.

The streamlined and focused Honeywell looked forward to reaping the rewards of its high-margin units. Honeywell had a solid foothold in the automation-systems market and continued to be a leader in heating controls and alarm systems. Buoyed by the 1987 acquisition of Sperry Aerospace Group for $1 billion, sales in its space and aviation unit leapt by 21 percent a year, despite a $435 million loss posted for the unit in 1988. Renier also streamlined operations, cutting 5,000 jobs, improving inventory turnaround time, and accelerating receivables collection. By 1991, although a recession had hit the company's major markets, operating margins had grown to 11 percent, and net income was about $331 million.

The recession continued through 1992, especially in the airline industry. But, losses in Honeywell's Space and Aviation Unit were offset by record sales in its automation-systems unit. From a marketing perspective, the company began to successfully exploit growing societal concerns about environmental protection. Its most successful controls and automation systems were designed to help industries conserve energy, improve productivity, and meet emission standards set by the U.S. Clean Air Act.

Renier resigned as chairman and CEO in 1993, succeeded by Michael R. Bonsignore, who had been president and chief operating officer of the company. Despite its improved marketing focus and successful new line of building controls, Honeywell's 1993 sales were about $6 billion—$1 billion less than they were in 1988. Profits had declined dramatically, and a lawsuit further threatened the company's profitability, when a jury awarded Litton Industries a $1.2 billion judgment against Honeywell for patent infringement.

Under Bonsignore the company met its projected financial goals for 1994. Nevertheless, investor confidence began to erode, as the company's long-term restructuring plan was perceived as a failure. Competitors Emerson Electric Co. and Rockwell International Corp. had nearly twice the operating margins of Honeywell, even in a sluggish market. Net income declined in 1994 to $279 million, although sales had increased 1.7 percent to $6.06 billion. Honeywell's stock prices slid as analysts complained that the company should have been more aggressive in trimming costs and accused management of supporting a "clubby, paternalistic culture that avoids tough decisions." Even a reversal of the $1.2 billion Litton judgment and a $600 million stock buyback did little to reverse Honeywell's slipping stock prices.

Despite these difficulties, Honeywell management remained confident in its restructuring plans and predicted double-digit growth in the near future. Their confidence was based on the fact that Honeywell remained a leader in technological development and continued to hold a respectable market share in both of its key divisions. But, the company's future was tied to

management's ability to deliver profits. Based on Honeywell's inconsistent financial record of the late 1980s and early 1990s, Bonsignore had a difficult task in front of him.

Honeywell and AlliedSignal Merge

In 1999, Honeywell merged with AlliedSignal, Inc., resulting in a big reformation for Honeywell and adding to its business ventures. AlliedSignal bought Honeywell for $13.8 billion in stock, taking the Honeywell name and closing its Morristown, New Jersey headquarters.

AlliedSignal formed in 1920 when five chemical companies combined, creating Allied Chemical and Dye Corporation. In 1985 this company merged with Signal Companies, Inc., and grew to become one of the leading technology and manufacturing companies in the Dow Jones Industrial Average. AlliedSignal manufactured aircraft equipment such as engines, brakes, flight data recorders, warning systems, collision-avoidance systems, and cockpit voice recorders.

At the time of the merger with Honeywell, AlliedSignal had established a strong presence in the aircraft equipment industries. The merger would complement Honeywell's aircraft control system division and boost its aerospace operations. A Prudential Securities analyst called the new company an "aerospace powerhouse."

Six Sigma: Success Builds on Quality Control Standard

Another result of the Honeywell-AlliedSignal merger was the beneficial Six Sigma program, which Honeywell revamped and renamed "Six Sigma Plus." Used as a measuring practice, Six Sigma refers to a strategy in enhancing function within an organization to produce savings. For instance, a company might employ Six Sigma concepts to a customer service department to ensure that they are achieving high-quality standards with positive economic results as well. The term Six Sigma in engineering refers to the smallest acceptable margin of error; in Honeywell, the term Six Sigma Plus referred to its commitment to keeping the business running effectively in all aspects.

The Six Sigma Plus system worked well for the company; applying these standards saved Honeywell $2.2 billion by 1999. Though the Six Sigma program had started at AlliedSignal, it proved to be key in keeping the merger between the two companies running smoothly.

Bouncing Back after Failed GE Merger

The early part of the 21st century brought troubles to Honeywell when the European Commission rejected General Electric's purchase of Honeywell. The purchase would have been a real boon to Honeywell; but the failed merger caused the company morale problems, initiated a tumble in stock price, and cost CEO Michael Bonsignore his job. The company subsequently split into four operating segments and earnings plunged 92 percent. The European Union (EU) had rejected the merger fearing the company would have too much power in the aircraft industry. Honeywell in turn appealed the rejection, not to overturn the ruling so much as to ensure that they would not be held accountable for any potential findings of abuse of power by the EU.

Despite the setback the company was quick to rebound and move forward with grace. Though the GE buyout failure was a real blow, Honeywell used the experience to strengthen its core businesses. CEO Bonsignore was replaced by veteran AlliedSignal executive Larry Bossidy. Honeywell continued to roll out new products, including its 900-series jet engines. The company started an aggressive acquisition strategy with the goal to increase revenues to $12–13 billion (a few billions' increase). They divested small, underperforming operations, reduced the number of suppliers, and streamlined operations in small ways elsewhere. On the public relations front, Honeywell executives worked to boost morale, retain their best managers, make it clear that the company was not for sale, and assure their customers that, in the words of President and CEO Robert Johnson, "all that merger stuff is behind us."

Results were promising. Honeywell continued to win 86 percent of its contract bids, sales were ahead of budget, and the rate of turnover among middle and senior managers were not significantly greater than the same period a year prior. Customer satisfaction was also up. By making some changes after the GE fiasco, the company actually had learned some tough lessons.

Honeywell Continues Worldwide Presence and Future Growth

Thermostats are still a major part of Honeywell's business; today home and commercial accounts together make up a quarter of Honeywell sales. In the commercial arena, Honeywell designs computerized control systems that regulate heat and electricity flow for large buildings, and also manufactures its own switches, electronic parts, and motors for these systems. The company has also ventured into "smart" buildings that regulate themselves with packages that can link together a building's phone lines, control devices, and information systems.

When David M. Cote took over as Chairman and CEO in 2002, global operations and company growth were continuing to thrive at Honeywell. By 2002 the company had customers and products in more than 95 countries and employed 43,000 people worldwide. Its footprint included the Asian Pacific, Europe, Middle East, Africa, and Latin American regions, and incorporated all aspects of the Honeywell business—manufacturing, aerospace, control technologies, turbocharging systems, chemical, power generation, electronics, and others. On the home front, Honeywell worked with the Federal Avia-

tion Administration on air safety initiatives in the wake of the September 11, 2001, terrorist attacks. For the near future, the company also outlined commitments to employee learning and satisfaction, superior customer service and product quality, and desires to continue building up the businesses.

Principal Subsidiaries

Honeywell Aerospace; Honeywell Automation & Control; Honeywell Industrial Control; Honeywell Mesurex Corp.; Honeywell Transportation & Power; Honeywell Consumer Products; Honeywell Sensing and Control; Honeywell DMC SVC Inc., Honeywell Friction Materials; Honeywell Federal Systems Inc.; Honeywell Finance Inc.; Honeywell Asia Pacific Inc. (Hong Kong); Honeywell Ltd. (Canada); Honeywell Europe S.A.; Tata Honeywell Ltd. (India, 50%); GoldStar-Honeywell Co., Ltd. (South Korea, 50%).

Principal Competitors

Eaton; General Electric; Pratt & Whitney.

Further Reading

"AlliedSignal, Honeywell in Big Aerospace Merger," *The Seattle Times*, June 7, 1999 p.B1.
"AlliedSignal, Honeywell Unite," *Electrical World*, July/August 1999, p. 5.
Berss, Marcia, "Under Control," *Forbes*, January 31, 1994, pp. 50–54.
Bossidy, Larry, *Execution: The Discipline of Getting Things Done*, New York: Crown, 2002.
——, and Ram Charan, "How Did Honeywell Chairman Larry Bossidy Turn the Company Around?" *Fortune*, June 10, 2002, pp. 149–152.
Catlin, Gill, "A Marriage Made in Hell," Minnesota Public Radio, broadcast July 3, 2001.
The First 100 Years, Minneapolis: Honeywell Inc., 1985.
"GE and Honeywell Appeal Deal Rejection," *Mergers and Acquisitions*, November 2001, pp. 15–17.
Kelly, Kevin, "Not So Sweet Times at Honeywell," *Business Week*, February 20, 1995, p. 66.
"Northrop Grumman Has Reached a $440-million Settlement with Honeywell," *Aviation Week & Space Technology*, January 7, 2002, p. 19.
Sikora, Martin, "Why All Buyers Should Care About the GE/Honeywell Misfire," *Mergers and Acquisitions*, September 2001, pp. 6–12.
Therrien, Lois, "Honeywell Is Finally Tasting the Sweet Life," *Business Week*, June 3, 1991, p. 34.
Velocci, Jr., Anthony L., "Honeywell on Acquisition Trail," *Aviation Week & Space Technology*, July 30, 2001, p. 39.

—updates: Maura Troester; Kerri DeVault

IKON Office Solutions, Inc.

70 Valley Stream Parkway
Malvern, Pennsylvania 19355
U.S.A.
Telephone: (610) 296-8000
Fax: (610) 408-7025
Web site: http://www.ikon.com

Public Company
Incorporated: 1952
Employees: 37,600 (2001)
Sales: $5.274 billion (2001)
Stock Exchanges: NYSE
Ticker Symbol: IKN
NAIC: 421420 Office Equipment Wholesalers; 323119
Other Commercial Printing; 541511 Custom
Computer Programming Services; 541512 Computer
Systems Design Services; 421690 Other Electronic
Parts and Equipment Wholesalers; 532420 Office
Machinery and Equipment Rental and Leasing;
422120 Stationery and Office Supply Wholesalers;
561439 Business Service Centers

IKON Office Solutions, Inc. remains one of the world's leading providers of products and services that help businesses communicate. IKON provides total business solutions, including copiers and printers, color solutions, distributed print, facilities management, imaging and legal document solutions, as well as network design and consulting, and e-business development. IKON has approximately 600 locations worldwide including the United States, Canada, Mexico, the United Kingdom, France, Germany, Ireland, and Denmark and earned more than $5 billion during revenue in fiscal year 2001.

Tinkham Veale II and the Alco Oil and Chemical Company

IKON Office Solutions, Inc., can trace its heritage to Tinkham Veale II, founder of Alco Standard Corporation. Veale was born in Topeka, Kansas, on December 26, 1914, and earned a Bachelor of Science degree in Mechanical Engineering from Case Institute of Technology, Cleveland, Ohio, in 1937. Four years later, he married Harriett Alice Ernst, the daughter of A.C. Ernst of the accounting firm Ernst & Ernst. With the help of his father-in-law, Veale bought a stake in an engineered goods manufacturer, which prospered during World War II, and made Veale a millionaire by age 37. With his youth and newly found wealth, Veale retired to breed and race horses and invest his money. After a short-lived retirement, Veale admitted, "I retired when I was young and after I was finished being retired, I went back to work. I was very bad at being a retired man."

In 1951, Veale joined the board of Alco Oil and Chemical Company in Pennsylvania, and was named director and president of the company in 1954. In 1960, Veale and his associates formed a holding company, V & V Associates, and bought a large minority share in Alco Oil and Chemical, which in 1962 was renamed Alco Chemical. Three years later, Alco merged with V & V Associates, setting into motion a partnership strategy that would witness the birth of the Valley Forge, Pennsylvania-based conglomerate, Alco Standard Corporation. Veale served as president of Alco Chemical until 1954 and director until 1986. The success of Veale's strategy was based on buying small, privately owned companies with cash and Alco Standard stock, and making the proprietors his partners. By 1968 52 companies had been acquired.

Alco Standard Focuses on Office Products and Paper Distribution

Alco Standard branched out into a variety of industries, including electrical, metallurgical, and distribution businesses; coal-mining; and paper distribution. From the success of their national paper distributor, Unisource, the company entered into other distribution fields, including pharmaceuticals, steel products, auto parts, foodservice equipment and liquor, and in 1981 witnessed the growth of their distribution to 75 percent of sales.

As manufacturing ventures in plastics, machinery, rubber, and chemicals had not grown as rapidly as the distribution units, the manufacturers were merged into Alco Industries in 1984 and sold to its managers, with Veale keeping a minority stake. In

1986, Ray Mundt succeeded Veale as chairman of Alco Standard, and switched the company's focus to two main business groups: office products and paper distribution.

In 1987, IOS Capital in Macon, Georgia, was formed to provide lease financing primarily for office equipment marketed in U.S. marketplaces. IOS Capital would later become one of the largest captive finance companies in North America.

In 1992, Alco Standard entered into a joint venture with Europe's IMM Office Systems. Although this venture did not work out, the dissolution agreement gave Alco two subsidiaries: Denmark's Eskofot and France's STR. Another restructuring came about in 1993 when John Stuart succeeded Mundt as CEO (and chairman in 1995). Alco's largest purchase came in 1995 with the acquisition of the Southern Business Group PLC, a UK-based copier distribution and service company, which was renamed A:Copy (UK) PLC. In 1996, Alco acquired 97 businesses, and the following year spun off Unisource. During the second quarter of 1996, Alco completed two mergers: Legal Copies International, Inc. and JMM Enterprises. The Office Products group advanced rapidly due to strong cash flows and other strategic divestitures. By the end of September 1996, revenues had reached $4.1 billion. The paper distribution business was spun off to shareholders in December 1996 as a separate, publicly owned company.

Alco Standard Becomes IKON Office Solutions

Alco Standard officially changed its name to IKON Office Solutions, Inc., on January 23, 1997, reflecting the company's intention to focus solely on their office technology business. The New York Stock Exchange listing became IKN. Another 123 companies were purchased during fiscal years 1997 and 1998, but profits dropped. As a result, James Forese, newly elected president and CEO, cut IKON's workforce by about 3,000 between 1998 and 2000 to reduce expenses.

With a more streamlined workforce and centralized focus, IKON Office Solutions entered the new century as one of the world's leading providers of products and services that help businesses communicate. The main goals of CEO Forese in 1999 were cutting costs, improving productivity, and strengthening discipline throughout the company. Through an international distribution and services network, IKON concentrated not on manufacturing, but on providing customers with products and services, including copying, printing and scanning, network design, and Internet-based document repositories, through vendors like Canon, Ricoh, Oce', Hewlett-Packard, Adobe, EFI, IBM, Microsoft, and T/R systems. IKON office locations could be found worldwide in the United States, Canada, Mexico, the United Kingdom, France, Germany, Ireland, and Denmark.

IKON Integrates Operations into Three Major Business Sectors

In 1996, IKON began an acquisition strategy that was focused on supporting IKON's total office solutions strategy announced in early 1996. The company's acquisitive period ended in the second quarter of 1998, and at that time, the Company was structured into three divisions—Business Services, Document Services, and Technology Services. Business Services concentrated on providing office equipment; Document Services concentrated on the production of large quantities of legal and business documents; and Technology Services concentrated on furnishing networking and systems analysts expertise.

In 1999, though, IKON began to change the structure of its operations in order to function more effectively as a "one-stop" provider of integrated solutions matched to customer's business communications needs. First, IKON North America was created by integrating the company's largest businesses: Business Services and Management Services of the Document Services division. IKON North America now provided copier and printer equipment and facilities management services throughout North America and included the Company's captive financing subsidiaries in North America.

The remaining business units of Document Services—Business Document Services, Legal Document Services, and Business Imaging Services—as well as Technology Services, which had received several awards in 1999 for industry leadership, were now included in the Other operating segment. These focused on print-on-demand services, electronic file conversion, and providing information system expertise and education and training.

At this time, IKON Europe was fully integrated and providing customers with total office solutions including copiers and printer systems, computer networking, print-on-demand services, facilities management, hardware and software product interfaces and electronic file conversion throughout Europe as well as financing through the Company's captive financing subsidiary in Europe. In 1999, Marconi, PLC (U.K. General Electric) awarded IKON a multi-million dollar contract to provide all document production for Marconi locations worldwide. IKON was named "preferred vendor" for Marconi and its affiliates, evidencing the successful application of the integrated services concept in Europe.

In 2000, Business Document Services and Legal Document Services were integrated into IKON North America along with the network integration capabilities of Technology Services to support the shift toward providing higher-end, networked digital equipment and related services. In addition, separate units were established for e-Business development, named Sysinct, as well as Education and Telecommunications. These units (and Business Imaging Systems) remained part of the Other segment.

Key Dates:

1951: Millionaire Tinkham Veale II joins the board of Alco Oil and Chemical Company.

1952: Alco Oil and Chemical Company is incorporated.

1954: Veale is named director and president.

1960: Veale and his associates form the holding company V & V Associates and buy a large minority share of Alco Oil and Chemical Company.

1962: Alco Oil and Chemical Company is renamed Alco Chemical.

1965: Alco Chemical merges with V & V Associates and is renamed Alco Standard Corporation.

1968: The company has acquired 52 other companies.

1969: Alco Standard is listed on the New York Stock Exchange under the symbol ASN.

1984: Alco Industries is formed and sold to its managers; Veale keeps a minority stake.

1986: Ray Mundt succeeds Veale as chairman and refocuses the company to two business groups: office products and paper distribution.

1987: IOS Capital, Inc., is formed in Macon, Georgia.

1993: John Stuart succeeds Mundt as CEO.

1995: The company's largest purchase occurs with the acquistion of the Southern Business Group PLC, a U.K.-based copier distribution and service company which is renamed A:Copy (UK) PLC.

1996: Alco Standard Corporation spins off a paper distribution business to shareholders; and acquires 97 businesses.

1997: Alco Standard Corporation changes its name to IKON Office Solutions and focuses solely on the office technology business; and the NYSE listing becomes IKN.

1998: James J. Forese becomes president and CEO of IKON.

1999: The company is awarded a multimillion-dollar contract by Marconi PLC (U.S. General Electric).

2001: IKON introduces IKON Online, an equipment-ordering and customer service Web site.

2002: James J. Forese retires as President and CEO, but remains as chairman; Matthew J. Espe succeeds Forese as President and CEO.

In the last quarter of 2001, IKON exited the telephony business in the U.S. and Europe, and in the first quarter of 2002, the company sold technology education. These actions were taken as a result of IKON's plans to eliminate or downsize certain business lines in 2002 that did not present long-term potential or fit strategically with IKON's core offerings, namely equipment sales, outsourcing, equipment service and supplies, and leasing.

IKON Positions Itself to Meet Digital Technology Needs

In 2001, IKON introduced a customized e-catalog, IKON Online, a Web-based means of ordering contracted equipment and supplies, placing service calls, and submitting meter readings. IKONSupplies.com was implemented as a public site which would allow customers to order low-end equipment and supplies via the Web. IKON also offered print e-procurement and online document-repository capabilities through Digital Express, a Web-based document management system.

IOS Capital became one of the largest captive financing companies in North America, with a lease portfolio of $3 billion. In 2001, it financed more than 75 percent of all IKON North America's equipment sales, a percentage that has increased steadily from 67% in 1999.

Other resources developed in 2001 by IKON to assist their customers, included the Solution Center and the Proposal Response Center. The Solution Center provided a single point of contact for critical information to sales personnel; the Proposal Response Center offered assistance in managing large bids and proposals. IKON University was implemented to provide programs in sales, management and leadership, project management, and technology training. The International Technical Olympics was held to challenge and reward service technicians by competing in events to test their skills in areas such as digital knowledge and problem solving.

IKON earned the designation as the largest independent distributor of office equipment in North America and the leading direct distributor for both Canon and Ricoh products. IKON's outsourcing business offered complete facilities management services, and was the leading provider to the legal community, providing onsite and offsite production and distribution of specialty legal documents, enhanced by digital scan-to-file services and document-coding. IKON also provided imaging services through its Business Imaging Services segment and it provided e-business strategy and solutions design through Sysinct.

Revenues for 2001 totaled $5.273 billion, down from $5.446 billion in 2000. Although a leader in its field, IKON experienced a 3.2 percent loss in revenues in 2001 due to decisions to de-emphasize or close down certain hardware and service offerings and the impact of a slowing economy. Overall decreases resulted from decreases in net sales, and service and rentals revenue. Revenues of IKON North America decreased by 3.6 percent, primarily due to a decline in revenue from sales of network integration, technology hardware, low-end copier/printer and facsimile equipment, as well as growing economic pressures. IKON Europe revenues decreased by 6.9 percent in fiscal 2001, due mainly to the impact of foreign currency translation and a decrease in sales of technology hardware, offset by an increase in revenue from the sale of office and production equipment. Other revenues decreased by 9.6 percent. The decreased revenues related to the telephony and education operations, from which the company exited in the fourth quarter of 2001. In addition, IKON planned to downsize the digital print production network and reduce the number of regional print centers.

IKON emphasized their customer-focused, value-driven approach by being profitable, generating strong cash flow, and building shareholder value, according to CEO Forese. Plans for the future included leveraging the size and scope of the company through centralized processes to streamline infrastructure, as well as investments to provide a competitive edge in the digital marketplace.

Principal Operating Units

IKON Europe Other; IKON North America.

Principal Competitors

Canon; Danka; Global Imaging Systems; Hewlett-Packard; Kinko's; Lanier Worldwide; Lexmark International; Oce'; Sharp; Tech Data; Xerox.

Further Reading

Albright, Brian, "I Think IKON," *Frontline Solutions*, February 2002, pp. 10–12.

Damore, Kelly, "Video, Telephony Work Gets Noticed," *The News-weekly for Builders of Technology Solutions*, May 6, 2002, p. 20.

"Gold for IKON," *Printing World*, April 22, 2002, p. 10.

"IKON Launches Web-based Meter Read Submission Service," *Electronic Commerce News*, May 13, 2002, p. 1.

"IKON Office Solutions," *Hoover's Handbook of American Business 2002*, Austin: Hoover's Inc., 2001, pp. 746–747.

Simon, Ruth, "Thou Shalt Not Waste Deals," *Forbes*, December 2, 1985, p. 62.

—Carol D. Beavers

illycaffè SpA

Via Flavia 110-34147
Trieste
Italy
Telephone: +39 (040) 38-90-111
Fax: +39 (040) 38-90-490
Web site: http://www.illy.com

Private Company
Incorporated: 1933
Employees: 500 (2001 est.)
Sales: US$113.1 million (1999 est.)
NAIC: 311920 Coffee and Tea Manufacturing; 333311
     Automatic Vending Machine Manufacturing

The second largest espresso manufacturer in Italy (Luigi Lavazza is the largest), illycaffè SpA annually produces over 12 million pounds of a single premium blend of gourmet coffee for both brewed and espresso preparation. Considered to be one of the finest coffees in the entire industry, illy coffee is a blend of 100% high-quality Arabica beans, meticulously selected through a unique system perfected over decades and overseen by three generations of the entrepreneurial Illy family. According to *Coffee and Cocoa International*, "illycaffè's entire ethos is built on quality." Illy is the leading brand in Italy's hotel, restaurant, and bar segment and is sold in over 70 countries through a network of subsidiaries and distributors. About 40 percent of illycaffè's sales come from outside Italy. The company estimates that its coffee is sold in more than 40,000 restaurants and coffee bars, serving over five million cups of illy coffee a day.

The Early Years

In 1933, the industrious and analytical Francesco Illy founded illycaffè in Trieste, Italy. Originally an accountant who had been drafted into World War I and stationed in Trieste, Mr. Illy decided to stay on in Trieste after the war ended, to marry his sweetheart and begin a coffee business. As a roaster of what is arguably the world's finest coffee, illycaffè fittingly finds its home in a city rich with coffee history. Since the 17th century, shipments of coffee beans from Africa, Brazil and other places have been delivered to Trieste and conveniently transferred to other coffee-drinking cities such as nearby Vienna. Coffee production and a café culture thrived in Trieste, already a well-established tradition by the time Mr. Illy began his coffee business.

By 1935, within only two years of founding his company, Mr. Illy made some major developments in espresso coffee. Most notably, he developed the modern espresso machine, the "illetta." His was the first automatic espresso machine to measure water automatically and to use compressed air instead of steam (the standard at the time). The compressed air made it possible to have espresso without the tendency to burn, a side effect easily caused by steam. In the same year, Mr. Illy also developed a method of packaging roasted coffee in airtight containers with nitrogen gas to help prevent oxidation. This method of packaging made it possible to maintain the coffee's freshness for years while actually enhancing the complexity of the coffee's flavor. As illycaffè explained it, the aroma of the coffee improves with this unique packaging, because the coffee's volatile aroma compounds are allowed to bind with the oils inside the beans. The company likens the flavor-enhancing effect of its special packaging to the aging process of wine.

It was not long before Mr. Illy's company officially became a big family business. By 1948, Mr. Illy's son, Ernesto, fresh with a Ph.D. in Chemistry, began his coffee career inspecting espresso machine parts for his father's company and the Swiss sister company which manufactured them. By 1956, Ernesto assumed some control within the company as co-owner and manager of the Trieste illycaffè. Then, in 1963, he was appointed president, managing director, and general manager of the entire company. Nicknamed the "espresso evangelist" by many coffee connoisseurs, Ernesto was recognized by the entire coffee industry and governments throughout the world for his expertise in coffee science.

As a passionate advocate, lecturer, and founder of many coffee industry conventions, associations and seminars, Ernesto immediately established himself and his family business as a world-class coffee industry presence. Illycaffè's rise to

Company Perspectives:

The illy Mission: to provide the ultimate coffee experience by offering coffee lovers and connoisseurs the finest products, service, education, and innovation. To partner with our customers whose clientele demand the very best quality and value. To carry on the tradition of excellence which has been a family passion for well over 60 years.

imminence began in the 1960s, when Ernesto founded the ASIC (Association Scientifique Internationale du Café) in 1965. He remained a leader in the group in subsequent decades, most recently as vice president. From 1966 into the mid-seventies, he served as an advisor and president to the AIIPA (Italian Association for Food Products) and the CIC (Italian Coffee Committee). In 1967 he founded EUCA (European Union of Coffee Associations), also serving as president for several years into the mid-1970s. It was clear that Ernesto's scientific expertise and political savvy would help illycaffè distinguish itself as a premium roaster and marketer of espresso coffee throughout the world.

Espresso Science and Quality Control

Illycaffè recognized that premium coffee would have to come from premium production methods. From bean to cup, the company managed a level of quality control that was the envy of the industry. The standard first began close to home for the Illy family, as early as when founder Francesco tinkered with espresso machines and coffee packaging. His legacy of innovation and quality control remains fully embraced by the illycaffè of today. For decades, the company was known for always applying the strictest and technologically advanced scientific method possible to quality improvement. In fact, its program is a model for coffee research and development, collaborating with notable experts from the academic world as well as within the field.

Soon after taking control of the company in the 1960s, Ernesto Illy established a research laboratory that became a breeding ground for inventions and patents, furthering illycaffè's mission for espresso quality. He came to hold 17 patents on various aspects of coffee processing and preparation methods. As R.W. Apple, Jr., personally observed for the *New York Times*, illycaffè "maintains a laboratory equipped with sophisticated instruments like gas chromatographs, infrared emission pyrometers and flame ionization detectors. Coffee beans are cut into slices eight microns thick for analysis in an electron microscope. Every step of the manufacturing process is monitored by computers, and there are 114 quality-control checks between the time bags of raw beans arrive on the loading docks to the time roasted beans are shipped in sealed cans."

In another fascinating account, Chris Partridge, for *The Times (London)*, reported in 1995 that Ernesto "put together a group of mathematicians and software scientists to use the massive Cray supercomputer recently installed at the University of Bologna to work out exactly how hot water flows through ground coffee in an espresso machine." One of the devices illycaffè likes to boast about is a patented machine—similar to a bean sorter—that typically rejects 1.5 percent of the beans based on color, mottling, and other aspects detectable by the machine's red and green wavelength scanning. The rejects are sold to other roasters. Once canned, the beans are randomly selected for Ernesto and a specially trained team to taste-test. And beyond the company plant's walls, the shipments are rigorously tested by an outside laboratory for hints of any contaminants such as insects, lead, cadmium, and biological toxins.

While illycaffè had always consistently held an enviable amount of quality control at the roasting level, it was not always easy for the company to find high-quality green beans to start with. Ernesto Illy asserts that it takes 55 beans to make one cup of espresso, and only one bad bean to ruin it. To help ensure that its coffee bean sources offered consistently high-quality beans, the company led some key initiatives to extend its quality standards beyond the company itself. For example, the company began an annual coffee bean competition in Brazil in 1990, considered to be a kind of Oscars for the coffee industry. Each year, illycaffè closely studies the beans of Brazil's top growers and awards the producer of the highest-quality beans a cash prize of US US$30,000 and a 30 percent premium over market for the winning coffee lot. Second and third prizes are US$20,000 and US$10,000, respectively. More than 500 Brazilian producers participate in the competition, working with illycaffè year-round to produce better coffee.

Also, in 1997, Illycaffè moved to invest US$250 million annually in efforts to improve Brazilian coffee, including after-harvest treatment methods, research, and genetic improvements. Illycaffè also directly educates growers on planting and production methods, conducts field trials of new coffee varieties, and works with the University of Sao Paolo through Pensa to conduct coffee production development studies. In 1999, illycaffè published a pocket manual of coffee growing guidelines, and opened a coffee university in Naples, Italy. Then, in early 2000, in association with the University of Sao Paolo, illycaffè inaugurated the illy University of Coffee in Sao Paolo. Suddenly, people could earn a degree in the business of coffee, covering everything from coffee planting to production to marketing. According to Miriam Jordan of the *Wall Street Journal* in February 2001, "Italian espresso maker illycaffè SpA, arguably the most fastidious coffee buyer in the world, has tripled imports from Brazil in the past decade after it started helping growers improve their crops." Brazil's quality of coffee has made such a turnaround since the days when the country's growers were set up for quantity, not quality. The turnaround, thanks in large part to illycaffè, is even more significant as it comes at a time when coffee prices overall are at a seven-year low. Illycaffè claims that growers who work closely with illy to produce quality beans turn out better profits, substantiating the company's firm belief that better coffee is better business.

The Art of illycaffè Espresso

Since 1992, illycaffè has shrewdly established a strong relationship with the art world. The company began to successfully associate its fine coffee with other fine tastes for the "good life." The company sponsors art exhibitions and contests, and commissions famous artists to contribute to illycaffè's ever-

242   **illycaffè SpA**

Key Dates:

1933: illycaffè is founded.

1935: Francesco Illy develops the modern espresso machine and coffee packaging that maintains freshness for years.

1948: Francesco's son, Ernesto, joins the company as an espresso machine inspector.

1956: Ernesto Illy becomes co-owner and manager of the company.

1963: Ernesto Illy becomes company chairman.

1981: illycaffè introduces the Illypod, premeasured and wrapped servings of espresso grounds.

1990: The company sponsors the first annual coffee grower's competition in Brazil.

1992: The company receives the Qualité France certification for its espresso.

1996: illycaffè licenses its E.S.E. (Easy Serving Espresso) system to other manufacturers and becomes the first European agro-industrial company to receive ISO 9001 certification for its production process.

1997: Ernesto Illy is awarded a "Lifetime Achievement Award" by the Specialty Coffee Association of America.

1999: illycaffè founds the first coffee university in Naples, Italy.

2000: The company cofounds a second coffee university, in Sao Paolo, Brazil.

---

growing line of fashionable cup-and-saucer sets. Some of the exhibitions the company has supported include "James Rosenquist: The Nineties," an exhibit of the American pop artist (1995); "Robert Rauschenberg at San Lazzaro," a showcase of the modernist master (1996); and the 47th Venice Biennale, one of the world's oldest and most prestigious international visual arts exhibitions (1997). Ultramodern and fanciful designs distinguish illycaffè's limited edition of cup-and-saucer sets, from Jeff Koons's colorful near-abstract animals to David Byrne's monochrome space alien visages to Norma J.'s surrealistic washing machines suspended in a clear blue sky. The company also supports emerging artists, offering a special award, the Premio illycaffè, at the Venice Biennale.

Illycaffè's association with the arts also helped to keep its product quite visible. The company's foray into the film arts in 1999, for example, was extremely successful. Illycaffè spent over US$4 million to air a commercial created by Francis Ford Coppola. Coppola was asked to create a standard one-minute spot, and then a special "cinematic" two-minute version to be shown at a special movie-like premiere in Rome. Also planned was a 15-minute, behind-the-scenes movie about Coppola's work for the company. Although these were Hollywood-like production plans, the project was new territory for the filmmaker, as it was his very first television commercial. After some awkward co-concepting between the filmmaker and the coffee company, the tiny film successfully evolved into a dreamy homage to the Italian barista, or coffee bar operator. Distributors from the United States and other markets clamored to air this exciting collaborative commercial.

Premium Espresso throughout the World

As part of its strategy to appeal to more at-home coffee drinkers as well as the usual restaurant or coffee bar clientele, illycaffè developed a way to make preparation of espresso much easier than by using the traditional, tricky, "tamp and pull" method. In 1981 the company introduced a line of premeasured servings of illy coffee, also known as "pods." With these pods, and a pod-compatible espresso machine, espresso could be easily and consistently made within 30 seconds—without the fuss of measuring and dealing with messy coffee grains. The company boasted that the system was so easy, even Ernesto Illy's granddaughter was able to prepare her grandfather a perfect cup of espresso at the age of four. Unfortunately, the specialized, pod-compatible machines were expensive and only practical investments for businesses such as restaurants and coffee bars.

Even though illycaffè's contributions to espresso-making was widely embraced by the professional espresso-making sectors, espresso-making remained relatively unpopular in consumers' homes. According to *The Economist*, "In the early 1990s, only one in every five household with an espresso machine used it regularly, because the results were so unreliable." Even though this is well after illycaffè introduced its easy-to-use, tea-baglike espresso pod, this is well before illycaffè made strides breaking into markets beyond its home country. Italy was easily the market leader in espresso-making, for both the home and professional sectors. Other countries were still far behind in espresso consumption. Although an espresso craze gripped the United States during the 1990s—powered in large part by the promotional efforts of the ubiquitous Starbucks chain—it was some time before illy coffee was available to the U.S. home market. Until then, illy coffee was only available in fine U.S. restaurants and a select few specialty food stores.

By the mid-1990s, coffee consumption in the United States soared, especially in the espresso sector. Research by the Special Coffee Association of the United States found that 40 percent of young people (up to age 29), consumed espresso, coffee, or cappuccino. Illycaffè's business was doing quite well by then: Its sales in 1992 rose by 53 percent, and in 1993 rose another 45 percent, and was expected to rise 38 percent in 1994. Exports had been growing by about 35 to 40 percent annually. The company was in a good position to make another bold move to try to capture a bigger share of the growing espresso market. In 1993 the company began to slowly introduce its espresso to select retailers, most notably Williams-Sonoma. By 1995 a full-scale distribution system was in place for the United States.

Illycaffè also made a move to help make espresso-making much more appealing and affordable to the U.S. home market. It partnered with several espresso roasters and machine makers—including Gevalia, Lavazza, Starbucks, Alessi, Ariete, Electrolux-Zanussi, Gaggia, Mulinex-Krups, and Saeco, among others—to develop standardized pods and pod-compatible machines. Illycaffè also headed an industry-wide effort to develop comprehensive guidelines for the standard so that other coffee companies could also develop the products. The standardized machine and pod, together as a system, was dubbed E.S.E (Easy Serving Espresso). The E.S.E. partners represented 80 percent of the worldwide espresso machine market share, so there was much hope that E.S.E. would take off and appeal to more at-home espresso drinkers. It was not until 1998 that the standardized system would debut in markets. By then, already one in ten American households had an espresso maker, according to a survey conducted by the National Coffee Association. Also by then, sales were up another 10 percent for illycaffè. During 1999, sales of E.S.E. units grew by 7.5 percent, compared to E.S.E.'s debut year. Overall, illycaffè sales were up 16 percent in 1999, and up 17 percent in 2000.

Illycaffè in the New Millennium

Illycaffè's goal was to become the first global brand of coffee. If family commitment is any indication of illycaffè's singular drive for success in the new millennium, then the future looked bright for the espresso company. Chemist, author, and CEO Andrea Illy led the company, supported by other family members: his father, Ernesto Illy, as chairman of illycaffè; his mother Anna, a board member; and siblings Anna, a board member, and Riccardo, as vice president and current mayor of Trieste. Another son of Ernesto, who was also named Francesco, served as the corporate image director and author of several books, including one on coffee history and lore. So far, under Andrea's leadership in the last five years, the company's sales have doubled, despite a generally ailing coffee market.

In 2001, overall coffee prices sunk to record lows, an effect of the glut of cheap robusta coffee coming from new coffee-producing countries such as Vietnam. This cheap coffee, however, had not prevented premium growers; they managed to continue to thrive. Optimistic about illycaffè's future, Andrea Illy boldly predicted that in a few decades, the company's sales will be as much as four or five times what they are now. Although espresso is a mere 2 percent of the world market for roasted coffee, illycaffè's commitment to quality, and its unique influence on premium Arabica coffee-growers (most notably Brazilian, and potentially those of other countries), promised to secure the company great returns for some time to come.

Principal Competitors

Lavazza; Nestlé; Starbucks.

Further Reading

"A Brewing Success," *Food Research & Development*, November 1994, p. 6.
"Americans Are Consuming More Coffee," *Gazeta Mercantil Online*, December 9, 1996, http://www.gazetamercantil.com.
Apple, Jr., R. W., "Discovering La Dolce Vita in a Cup," *New York Times*, October 24, 2001, p. F1.
Barrett, Amy, "Italian Coffee Roaster Illycaffè Moves at Full Steam into U.S. Home Market," *Wall Street Journal*, November 8, 1999, p. A47.
Beaven, Debbie, "Java-Loving Net Users Hit the Refresh Button," *Courier-Mail (Australia)*, February 14, 2002, p. 7.
Bell, Jonathan, "Espresso: Where the Leaders Stand," *Tea & Coffee Trade Journal*, November 1, 1998.
Betts, Paul, "It Adds Up to a Heap of Beans: Paul Betts Travels to Trieste to Meet a Family Dedicated to Good Espresso," *Financial Times (London)*, March 29, 1997, p. 13.
"Brazilian Coffee Provokes Enthusiasm in Illycaffè," *Gazeta Mercantil Online*, November 28, 1997, http://www.gazetamercantil.com.
Catchpole, Andrew, "Calling the Shots: Who Would Have Thought That a Cup of Coffee Could Be So Complicated?" *The Daily Telegraph (London)*, October 20, 2001, p. 6.
Cheney, Glenn, "Tropical Depression: Brazil at the Worst of Times," *Tea & Coffee Trade Journal*, December 20, 2001.
Collins, Alf, "Fresh Today," *Seattle Times*, June 4, 1986, p. C9.
Earle, John, "Special Report on Italian Food and Wine: Why We Ask for a Cappuccino," *Times (London)*, June 30, 1987.
Ferretti, Fred, "A Gourmet at Large: Espresso Evangelist, Ernesto Illy," *Gourmet*, December 1998, pp. 100–102.
"Get Your Masters in Cappuccino," *Business Week*, June 21, 1999, p. 8.
Gugino, Sam, "The Perfect Cup," *Cigar Aficionado*, December 1999.
Hamlin, Suzanne, "Test Kitchen; Espresso (and Cappuccino) Artistry at Home," *New York Times*, February 25, 1998, p. F3.
Hunter, Catherine, "Illycaffè Says 2000 Sales Unaffected by Green Coffee Woes," *Dow Jones Newswires*, July 19, 2001, http://www.dowjonesnews.com.
——, "Interview: Coffee Should Copy Wine Industry to Up Returns," *Dow Jones Newswires*, May 23, 2001, http://www.dowjonesnews.com.
——, "Interview: Illycaffè CEO Says Coffee Price Outlook Grim," *Dow Jones Newswires*, September 11, 2000, http://www.dowjonesnews.com.
——, "Interview: Top Coffee Roasters Want in on Quality Talks," *Dow Jones Newswires*, November 16, 2001, http://www.dowjonesnews.com.
Illy, Andrea, "I'm a Coffee Doctor," *New York Times*, March 28, 2001, p. C10.
——, and R. Viani, eds., The Chemistry & Technology of Espresso Coffee: The Chemistry of Quality, *San Diego: Academic Press*, 1995, p. 288.
"Illycaffè Increases Capital Fivefold," *Il Sole 24 Ore*, July 8, 1999.
"Illycaffè' Plan Begins in Trieste," *Il Sole 24 Ore*, September 7, 2000.
"Illycaffè Sales Rise on Foreign Growth," *Eurofood*, June 8, 2000, p.9.
"Illycaffè Sponsors Exhibition of Twentieth Century Italian Art at P.S.1 Contemporary Art Center," *Antiques & The Arts Weekly*, December 17, 1999.
Illy, Ernesto, "A Beautiful Experience," *Coffee and Cuisine*, November, 1998.
"Illy Gives Incentives to Brazilian Coffee," *Gazeta Mercantil Online*, November 28, 1997, http://www.gazetamercantil.com.
Illy, Riccardo, The Book of Coffee: A Gourmet's Guide, New York: Abbeville Press, 1992, p. 192.
"Illy, Un Business Espresso Expects Turnover to Rise to L 150bn in 1994," *Il Sole 24 Ore*, September 8, 1994.
"Increasing At-Home Espresso Consumption with E.S.E. Technology," *The Coffee Reporter: A Publication of the National Coffee Association of U.S.A., Inc.*, May 2000.
"In Search of a Perfect Cup," *Economist*, December 20, 2001.
Jordan, Miriam, "Brazil Cultivates a Spot in Gourmet-Coffee Market," *Wall Street Journal*, February 2, 2001, p. B1.
Lisovicz, Susan, "Illycaffè Pres. & Chairman," [interview transcript], *CNN: Business Unusual*, May 3, 2001.
Medintz, Scott, "Grinders, Keepers," *Money*, September 1998, p. 9.
Mitchener, Brandon, "A 'Tea Bag' for Espresso: Illycaffè Aims to Perk Up Global Market for Coffee," *Asian Wall Street Journal*, October 24, 1996.
"New Standard Simplifies Restaurant Espresso Preparation," *Hotel Online*, May 6, 1998, http://www.hotel-online.com.
Partridge, Chris, "The Quest for Great Espresso," *The Times (London)*, May 26, 1995.
Perry, Charles, "Profile: A Quick Espresso with a Coffee Chemist," *Los Angeles Times*, March 14, 1996, p. 11.
"Premium Coffee Makes Inroads," *Food Industry Week*, October 31, 1997, p. 2.

''Rare Gourmet Espresso Blend Now Available Nationally,'' *PR News-wire*, October 14, 1993.

Regan, Gary, ''Espresso without the Mess: Single-Serve Pods Help Deliver a Consistently Good Brew,'' *Nation's Restaurant News*, November 23, 1998, p. 37.

''Tea & Coffee Men of the Year,'' *Tea & Coffee Trade Journal*, December 1990, p. 8.

''University Illy Do Café,'' *Tea and Coffee Trade Online*, June/July 2000, http://www.teaandcoffee.net.

Wentz, Laurel, '' 'Godfather' Director Films TV Ad for Italy's Illycaffè,'' *Advertising Age International*, June 1, 1999.

''. . . While Illy Reports 10% Growth,'' *Eurofood*, May 20, 1999, p. 13.

Wolf, Burt, ''Magic Beans: How the Trieste Dukes Got the Dough and We Got Espresso,'' *Salon.com*, April 6, 2000, http://www.salon.com.

—Heidi Wrightsman

Imagine Foods, Inc.

1245 San Carlos Avenue
San Carlos, California 94070
U.S.A.
Telephone: (650) 595-6300
Fax: (650) 327-1459
Web site: http://www.imaginefoods.com

Private Company
Incorporated: 1982
Employees: 60
Sales: $100 million (2000)
NAIC: 311412 Frozen Specialty Food Manufacturing;
    311423 Dried and Dehydrated Food Manufacturing

Imagine Foods, Inc. is a multimillion-dollar producer of organic and natural foods products that are sold in more than 25 countries around the world. The company's nondairy beverages, frozen desserts, and organic soups and broths are category leaders and are sold under the popular Rice Dream, Soy Dream, and Imagine Foods product lines. In 20 years, company founder Robert Nissenbaum has taken Imagine Foods from humble regional beginnings to international success.

A Personal Passion: Imagine Foods' Beginnings

Robert Nissenbaum had an interest in natural foods, organic gardening, macrobiotic diet, and yoga, and in 1971, at just 20 years of age, he opened the Morning Dew Organic Food Market in St. Louis, Missouri. The Morning Dew Organic Food Market is often considered among the earliest modern natural/organic food stores in the United States. At the time the market opened, Nissenbaum's interests in healthy living and vegetarian diet were also being explored by a small, but active percentage of the population who were growing concerned with links between diet, health, well-being, and the environment. The Morning Dew Organic Food Market became a central meeting place for people cultivating these interests. The small store offered a place where organic and vegetarian foods—as well as ideas on healthy, sustainable lifestyles—were readily available.

With the small success of the Morning Dew Organic Food Market under his belt, Nissenbaum helped found the Sunshine Inn just three years later. Also located in St. Louis, the Sunshine Inn was another breakthrough in the early health foods market. The Inn was one the earliest and longest-lasting natural foods restaurants, serving customers for nearly 25 years before it closed. At the Sunshine Inn, Nissenbaum began experimenting with creating nondairy foods, many of which would eventually form the basis of Imagine Foods' product line. Aside from enjoying numerous vegetarian dishes, diners at the Sunshine Inn had the opportunity to sample Nissenbaum's creations, which included vegan shakes made with combinations of nuts and fruits.

In 1982, Nissenbaum and a partner formed Imagine Foods. Nissenbaum's nondairy concoctions, made popular at the Sunshine Inn, had led him to develop several flavors of rice-based milk. He also worked on perfecting an ice cream alternative, also based on rice, to give people who wanted to follow a dairy-free diet a delicious frozen dessert without milk or added sugar. Nissenbaum tested his frozen dessert, called Rice Dream, on friends and family, and began selling it in local co-ops and natural foods stores. Two years later, he brought the dessert to an Atlanta natural foods trade show, where it garnered significant interest. Several major American natural foods wholesalers wanted to place immediate orders for Nissenbaum's Rice Dream frozen dessert.

This quick success strained the small factory that had been producing Rice Dream, and Nissenbaum determined that for Imagine Foods to thrive, it would have to leave its Midwestern roots behind. Nissenbaum decided to move Imagine Foods to Northern California, where the company would be geographically closer to its sources of organic rice and other agricultural ingredients, as well as to the exploding natural foods movement on the West Coast, where vegetarian and organic eating was a major part of the culture. Nissenbaum rented a small house in Palo Alto, California, in close proximity to a small, family-owned ice-cream plant. The house became Imagine Foods' corporate headquarters and Nissenbaum convinced the plant to manufacture Rice Dream.

By 1994, Imagine Foods faced growing competition from such notable companies as White Wave and Tofutti Brands.

Company Perspectives:

Imagine Foods' President and CEO, Robert Nissenbaum, says of his company: "Having experienced the benefits of a natural foods diet on my quality of life as well as the environment, I wanted to make great-tasting natural foods products that would make it easier for people to adopt a healthier lifestyle. It takes more time and effort to prepare healthy food and eat well, so our products help with that. Additionally I wanted to foster a work environment where people are encouraged to thrive—professionally, creatively and spiritually. I also wanted to give back to the community. People enjoy working at Imagine Foods for these reasons and it plays a big part in our success."

Key Dates:

1971: Robert Nissenbaum opens the Morning Dew Organic Food Market in St. Louis, Missouri.
1982: Nissenbaum and a partner start Imagine Foods in St. Louis.
1984: Imagine Foods moves operations to Palo Alto, California.
1989: The company introduces a frozen line of Stuffed Veggie Pocket sandwiches.
1994: Rice Dream beverages become the number one selling product line across all product categories in the natural foods industry.
1998: The company launches Power Dream, a soy-based sports beverage.
1999: The company undertakes major product recalls due to undeclared ingredients.
2001: The company launches Soy Dream, a line of soy-based products.
2002: Imagine Foods celebrates 20th anniversary.

But, the company continued to enjoy major success. In 1994, Imagine Foods' line of Rice Dream beverages became the number one selling product line across all product categories in the natural foods industry, a distinction they would hold for the rest of the decade.

As the 1990s progressed, Imagine Foods continued to expand their product line. In 1998, they introduced Power Dream, a soy-based, shelf-stable, meal-replacement energy drink, which quickly became popular among high-performance athletes. In 1999, the Food and Drug Administration (FDA) published a final rule in the Federal Register, authorizing foods that contained at least 6.25 grams of soy protein per serving, that were low in saturated fat and cholesterol, and that met the nutrient content for a "low fat" food, could legally make claims about the foods' role in reducing the risk of heart disease. Under these regulations, both the Power Dream drink line and the Soy Dream beverages qualified for this FDA heart-healthy claim. In 2001, Imagine Foods relaunched their Power Dream line and established a promotional relationship with Dave Scott, a six-time winner of the Hawaii Ironman and first inductee into the Triathlete Hall of Fame. The choice of Scott as a spokesperson for the beverage allowed Power Dream to gain additional legitimacy among athletes, and to secure its place in the competitive energy food market, which has traditionally been dominated by products in bar or cookie form.

In 1998 and 1999, Imagine Foods suffered a series of product recalls stemming from undeclared ingredients. In 1998, the company recalled 6,050 cases of Creamy Mushroom Soup because the packaging did not declare that the soup contained soybeans. The next year, the company had to recall a large quantity of Vanilla Swiss Almond flavor Rice Dream frozen desserts because they may have contained peanuts, which was undeclared on the package. The latter was a serious situation due to the strong, sometimes fatal allergies individuals can have to peanuts.

Moving into the Millennium: Becoming a Household Name

In 2000, Imagine Foods faced a packaging infringement claim brought against it by competitor Amy's Kitchen. Amy's Kitchen attempted to prohibit the company from shipping or selling any more of their Stuffed Veggie sandwich products. Amy's claim was that the Imagine package imitated a design and image that was proprietary to Amy's Kitchen. However, the United States District Court for the Northern District of California absolved Imagine Foods of the charges, and Imagine continued to sell the line. That same year, Imagine Foods voluntarily recalled 32 oz. packages of its Rice Dream Original Enriched beverages in 14 states. The product was suspected of being contaminated with *Bacillus cereus*, a bacterium that can cause diarrhea, nausea, and other harmful symptoms when consumed.

Ever since the 1999 ruling by the FDA regarding the potential health benefits of soy, soy foods had been attracting growing interest. Because of this, foods previously unknown to most North Americans—including the types of organic and vegetarian foods produced by Imagine Foods since its inception—were finding an audience and an increasing demand. Whereas many of their competitors had already introduced soy-based frozen desserts, which had begun to drive the sales and growth of that segment of the industry, in 2001 Imagine Foods introduced a soy-based companion line to their frozen Rice Dream desserts. Soy Dream frozen desserts and novelties hit the market, and again, like its rice-based predecessor, were followed by a line of soy beverages, called Soy Dream. The Soy Dream line also included an enriched series, which made the beverage nutritionally comparable to cow's milk.

Late in 2001 the company suffered another recall bump when it had to recall several thousand Rice Dream and Soy Dream frozen dessert containers because they may have contained undeclared milk protein, which posed an extreme health hazard for consumers with severe sensitivities or allergies to milk protein. Yet, despite these recalls and in the face of ever-growing competition, Imagine Foods has continued to produce some of the industry's top-selling products.

While its products have continued to gain in popularity, finding their way onto the shelves of traditional grocery stores as well as remaining a staple of the natural foods markets, Imagine Foods has continued to make community service an important part of its tradition, donating thousands of cases of food to nonprofit organizations, charities, and health-based organizations.

In 2002 the company celebrated its 20th anniversary. At the occasion, Robert Nissenbaum reflected on the success of his company, ''Lots of things have changed since 1982, but our company goals haven't changed much since the early days.'' Bucking the trend of smaller natural foods companies merging with larger organizations, Imagine Foods has remained private, with Nissenbaum remaining the company's owner and main product developer. However, since its beginning, this small company *has* changed, moving beyond its humble local beginnings to become a multimillion-dollar producer of organic and natural foods products that are sold in more than 25 countries around the world.

Further Reading

''A Dairy-Free World,'' *Washington Post*, January 1, 2002, p. F4.

Havala, Suzanne, ''*Vegetarian Journal*'s Guide to Non-Dairy Frozen Novelties,'' *Vegetarian Journal*, June 30, 1994, pp. 23–24.

''Healthy Fare,'' *Frozen Food Age*, May 1996, pp. 61–64.

''Just Imagine . . .'' *Nutrition Action Healthletter*, April 1, 2001, p. 1.

Mangels, Reed, ''Nutrition Hotline: Fortification of Soy Milk,'' *Vegetarian Journal*, October 31, 1995, p. 2.

McMath, Robert, '' 'Tis the season for Indulgence: It Can Be Both Jolly and Healthy,'' *Brandweek*, November 29, 1993, pp. 30–32.

''Rice Dream Beverages,'' *Vegetarian Journal*, June 30, 1991, p. 24.

Roberts, William A., ''Meatless in the Mainstream, '' *Prepared Foods*, March 1, 2002, p. 2.

Sagon, Candy, ''What It's Like to Dwell Among the Meat Eaters,'' *Washington Post*, March 13, 2002. p. F1.

Schmelzer, Paul, .''Label Loophole: When Organic Isn't,'' *The Progressive*, May 1, 1998.

—C. J. Gussoff

Immunex Corporation

51 University Street
Seattle, Washington 98101-2936
U.S.A.
Telephone: (206) 587-0430
Fax: (206) 587-0606
Web sites: http://www.immunex.com;
        http://www.amgen.com

Wholly Owned Subsidiary of Amgen Inc.
Incorporated: 1981
Employees: 1,618
Sales: $986.8 million (2001)
NAIC: 325414 Biological Product (Except Diagnostic)
    Manufacturing; 325412 Pharmaceutical Preparation
    Manufacturing; 533110 Owners & Lessors of Other
    Non-financial Assets

Immunex Corporation is a biopharmaceutical company that develops, manufacturers, and markets therapeutic products for the treatment of cancer, infectious diseases, and autoimmune disorders. The company more than doubled its revenue base between 1992 and 1993 as a result of a merger with Lederle pharmaceutical units of American Cyanamid Company. However, in the mid-1990s, Immunex was still trying to achieve profitability after investing heavily in research and development since its inception in 1981. Immunex is best associated with the development of products such as Enbrel, used in the treatment of rheumatoid arthritis; Novantrone, used to treat acute nonlymphocytic leukemia and pain associated with prostate cancer; and Leukine, for use in bone marrow transplant patients. In July 2002, Immunex was bought by Amgen Inc., the world's largest biotechnology company.

Immunex Founded by Scientists Gillis and Henney

Immunex was formed during the start of the biotechnology craze of the early 1980s. Biotechnology, as it was known in the mid-1990s, was born in the early 1950s, when the structure of DNA was discovered; that revelation lead to the understanding of the process by which proteins are formed. Subsequent breakthroughs, particularly in the early 1970s, showed that it was possible to genetically alter microorganisms and, importantly, produce mass amounts of proteins that naturally occurred only in small quantities. A handful of companies pioneered the commercial biotechnology industry during the middle and late 1970s, but it was not until the early 1980s that a horde of competitors jumped into the game. The pivotal turning point came when the U.S. Supreme Court ruled that genetically engineered bacterium could be patented. For many, that ruling suggested the possibility of fantastic profits for biotech innovators.

Eager to make their mark in the burgeoning commercial biotechnology industry were scientists Steven Gillis and Christopher Henney. Henney, a Ph. D., was internationally recognized for his research in immunology. Gillis also had a doctorate—in biological sciences from Dartmouth College—and was recognized for his contributions related to immunology research. Gillis and Henney believed that they possessed the expertise to develop a method of producing large quantities of certain hormones that showed promise in fighting infection. At the urging of Seattle patent attorney Jim Uhlir, they formed Immunex as a means of developing and commercializing their techniques and drugs.

Joining the duo was Steve Duzan, an entrepreneur who owned an industrial ice-making machine business at the time. Duzan had become intrigued by the emerging biotechnology industry after being introduced to Gillis and Henney. Although prior to joining their startup effort, Duzan had virtually no experience in medical-related industries and did know how to raise investment capital. He was, however, known as a tenacious, hard-driving manager. At the age of 34, Duzan had arranged the leveraged buyout of the Washington-based Cello Bag Co. Inc. Then, in 1980, he engineered the sale of the company to ARCO Chemicals, Inc. He used cash from that deal to purchase North Star Ice Equipment Corp., a small manufacturer of ice-making machines that exported much of its output to the Middle East. Duzan overhauled that company's manufacturing operations and managed to improve its profitability.

Duzan was looking for another company to buy when he met Gillis and Henney. Instead, he helped them to form a completely

Company Perspectives:

Immunex is a leading biopharmaceutical company dedicated to developing immune system science to protect human health. Applying our scientific expertise in the field of immunology, cytokine biology, vascular biology, antibody-based therapeutics and small molecule research, we work to discover new targets and new therapeutics for treating rheumatoid arthritis, or RA, asthma, and other inflammatory diseases, as well as cancer and cardiovascular diseases.

new company called Immunex. Gillis and Henney, naturally, managed the scientific side of the business, while Duzan went to work finding capital to fund Immunex's cash-hungry research and development operations. As it turned out, many of the entrepreneurial skills that Duzan had learned in his previous business exploits were well suited to the seat-of-the-pants biotechnology sector. For the first six months, Duzan worked without a salary while he scrambled to secure investors. "Immunex was the penniless new kid on the block going up against these giants like Hoffman-LaRoche and Kodak," recalled Stephen Graham, an attorney at Immunex's law firm, in a July 21, 1991 *Business Journal-Portland* article. "But time and time again," he added, "when Steve looked at a transaction with those people, he would decide what a relatively little guy had a right to expect. And then he would double it. And then he would go out and get it."

While Duzan labored to find cash to fuel Immunex's product development engine, Gillis and Henney oversaw an ambitious research effort to generate various immune system stimulants and related technologies. Their goal was to develop a breakthrough drug, or drugs, that would allow Immunex to become a full-fledged pharmaceutical company that developed and manufactured its own products. But, that pivotal product proved elusive for Immunex's research team. The company's pursuits did succeed, however, in producing a number of valuable technologies and products that earned the company respect in the biotechnology industry. Specifically, Immunex discovered and cloned a long list of genes producing substances that could work in the human body to stimulate various blood cells to fight cancer, heal wounds, and prevent auto-immune diseases like arthritis and diabetes.

Immunex Introduces Leukine

Among Immunex's most important products during the mid-1980s were its Interleukin drugs and GM-CSF (Granulocyte Macrophage Colony Stimulating Factor). Those products were essentially immune system proteins that acted as hormones in the body, with each hormone commanding only specific types of cells. Each class of cells could be stimulated to respond with antibodies, enzymes, and other substances that multiplied and attacked infection. For example, Immunex's centerpiece drug, GM-CSF (marketed as Leukine), was a blood-growth stimulator that enhanced the body's production of white blood cells. Leukine could fight infection in cancer patients whose white blood cells had been destroyed during bone marrow transplants. It also had potential applications related to chemotherapy.

Although Immunex was at the technological forefront in its niche, the company faced numerous roadblocks to success. Chief among its hurdles was the Food and Drug Administration (FDA) drug approval process. To shepherd a drug through the intimidating FDA gamut, a company typically had to invest millions of dollars completing its own tests and striving to comply with Federal regulations. The obvious risk was that the drug would fail to meet FDA approval and the company would be stuck with the loss. For a smaller company like Immunex, failure could be virtually devastating. To help bring their drugs and technologies to market, therefore, many biotech startups sought other avenues to profit. Common routes included selling or licensing proprietary technology to large pharmaceutical companies, or partnering with bigger competitors to develop and market new drugs.

Immunex managed to stay solvent and continued to fund its research and development arm during the 1980s, in essence by selling its technology to companies that had the financial backing to take it to market. Some analysts criticized the strategy because it effectively turned Immunex into a "research boutique" and represented a diversion from the company's goal of becoming a true pharmaceutical company that marketed its own drugs. But, the tactic was necessary to keep the company afloat given the volatile environment of the biotechnology industry. A critical juncture for the company came in 1983, shortly after the company had gone public to raise cash through an initial public stock offering. For no apparent reason related to Immunex's performance, the company's stock price plunged from $11 to $4. The price remained suppressed while biotech investors questioned the viability of the entire industry.

Unable to generate acceptable proceeds from the sale of more stock, Duzan arranged a number of deals that benefited Immunex. He negotiated with some large American and European drug companies, selling marketing and manufacturing rights to most of the major immune-system stimulants that it had cloned. Those agreements included high-profile products like GM-CSF and its Interleukin drugs. Although forfeiting company rights to some of that technology, Duzan was credited with swinging deals that, in the long term, worked in Immunex's favor. For example, in selling marketing rights for GM-CSF to German pharmaceutical manufacturer Behringwerke AG, Duzan won a concession to oversee clinical trials for Leukine. That move later made it possible for Immunex to become a true pharmaceutical company, rather than just a research lab that collected royalties from its inventions.

Throughout the 1980s, Immunex developed a number of promising technologies, most of which it sold or licensed to other companies. As fees and royalties income increased, revenues rose steadily to about $2.4 million in 1985, $11.3 million in 1987, and $23.3 million by 1989. Profits remained elusive, however, as the company continued to pour millions into research and development. Investors had generally been patient with Immunex because the company had been so successful at developing new products. Investor patience gradually wore thin, as they watched the company spend millions without ever successfully taking a drug to market. Immunex managed to post meager profits in 1988 and 1991, but those surpluses were insignificant compared to big losses in other years. Indeed, between 1985 and 1990 Immunex lost nearly $30 million.

Despite ongoing losses, it seemed as though Immunex had turned the corner toward profitability going into the early 1990s. In a series of bold and complex deals initiated in 1989, Duzan reacquired, sold, and swapped the rights to a number of its drugs. The end result was that Immunex, by 1990, was in a position to possibly begin marketing its own technology. ''In this business you've got to become a marketing organization,'' Duzan said in a April 15, 1990, *Seattle Times* article. ''Because that's the only way you can get enough cash flow to sustain your research.'' The most significant result of Duzan's wheeling and dealing was that Immunex managed to reacquire the U.S. co-marketing rights to GM-CSF and certain Interleukin drugs from its German partner Behringwerke AG. The move was risky because GM-CSF had not been approved for use in the United States by the FDA.

Immunex Receives FDA Approval for Leukine

Investors finally had something to cheer about when, in March 1991, Immunex won FDA approval to market Leukine (GM-CSF) in the United States to treat bone marrow transplant patients. The company's shares rocketed to a record high of $59

following the announcement, and Immunex initiated an aggressive marketing program to sell the product. Shortly after the approval, Immunex was selling Leukine through a 50-member sales team organized to market the product to oncology specialists. At the same time, Immunex continued to invest millions of dollars into new drugs. Chief among its research projects in the early 1990s was Pixie 321, a synthetic molecule that was designed to incorporate the properties of Leukine and Immunex's Interleukin 3 (a cancer-fighting compound). Duzan hoped to sell that and other drugs through its own sales force.

Despite notable successes during the late 1980s and early 1990s, Immunex continued to disappoint some analysts and investors. The company chalked up heavy losses, largely related to research expenses, totaling $78 million in 1992. The company had hoped to offset that deficit with increased sales of Leukine, but its marketing effort failed to live up to some analysts' hopes. The problem was partially attributable to a product similar to Leukine that was introduced by competitor Amgen. Amgen received approval for its drug, Neupogen, in 1992. Whereas Leukine had been approved for the bone marrow transplant market, Neupogen was approved for use in the much larger chemotherapy market. The result was that shipments of Neupogen bolted to $290 million in 1993, while revenues from Leukine topped out at less than $23 million. ''One company operates in an ocean, the other in a pond,'' surmised Deborah Wardwell, a Seattle stock analyst, in the August 8, 1994, *Seattle Times*.

Immunex Bought Out by American Cyanamid

Encountering a fate similar to that experienced by many other biotech companies, Immunex was bought out. In June 1993, American Cyanamid purchased the company and merged it with its Lederle Oncology unit to form a new, publicly traded company still known as Immunex, and headquartered in Seattle. Lederle Oncology was a leader in the immunology industry and had about a half dozen proprietary products in its drug portfolio. Lederle, with its more established marketing network, seemed like a natural complement to Immunex's powerful research operations. The merger initially failed to produce the desired results, however, because Lederle's products did not sell as well as expected. That problem, combined with less-than-stellar gains with Leukine, created investor disappointment with Immunex. The stock price slipped to $30 before dropping to less than $15 per share in 1994.

Frustrated, American Cyanamid brought in a new chief executive to replace Duzan, who had been accused of alienating Wall Street with his brusque nature and questionable management decisions regarding Leukine. Specifically, he had been criticized for allowing Amgen to steal more than 90 percent of the market for Leukine. Gillis, who was an Immunex cofounder and heading up Immunex's research operations at the time, stepped in as a temporary president and CEO for a few months until American Cyanamid appointed Edward Fritzky to the position. (Cofounder Henney had left Immunex in 1989 to start his own consulting company.) Fritzky came to Immunex from American Cyanmid's Lederle Laboratories division where had overseen the launch of six new products in that division and, at the age of 45, was considered a seasoned veteran in the pharmaceutical industry.

American Cyanamid Bought Out by American Home Products

Interestingly, American Cyanamid was bought out by American Home Products (AHP) in mid-1994, making the latter company the majority owner of Immunex. Fritzky remained president and CEO of the company, however, and sustained his efforts to turn Immunex into a development and marketing powerhouse in its pharmaceutical niche. Unfortunately, profits continued to evade Immunex going into the mid-1990s, amidst a string of setbacks. In September 1994, for example, cofounder Steve Gillis resigned his post to pursue other research goals. More importantly, the FDA refused to approve Leukine for use in the $500 million chemotherapy market that was dominated by Amgen. The stunning news sent Immunex's stock price tumbling 20 percent to less than $13 per share by May 1995. Nevertheless, management remained optimistic, given the company's proven research capabilities, pipeline of high-potential drugs, and ongoing efforts to get FDA approval to use Leukine in chemotherapy applications.

Despite setbacks, Immunex continued to strengthen its oncology franchise operations and apply understanding of immune system science beyond cancer care and into infectious and inflammatory diseases. Studies continued on new indications for Leukine and the chemotherapeutic Novantrone, shown to benefit men with hormone refractory prostate cancer. Also in 1995, Immunex marked a milestone in the battle against rheumatoid arthritis, with a clinical study of a recombinant TNF (tumor necrosis factor) receptor that proved to neutralize TNF's ability to promote inflammation, resulting in improvement in swollen and painful joints.

Immunex Introduces Enbrel

The company's financial outlook improved in 1995 and 1996 through research efforts, the franchising of existing products, and development of a broader marketing focus. In 1996, the FDA approved a new claim for Novantrone for relieving pain in late-stage prostate cancer patients, and Leukine Liquid, a white blood cell stimulant available in a multidose vial. With revenue growth from the increased sales of these products, research continued on the TNF receptor, brand named Enbrel. Other products in the development pipeline included FLT-3 ligand, affecting transplant patients; CD40 ligand, a potential candidate for the treatment of cancer and infection; and other cancer and inflammation fighting products, including TRAIL and TACE, respectively. Wyeth-Ayerst, a division of AHP, and a leader in the anti-inflammatory market, came on board to assist with investing in and marketing Enbrel. The research agreement with AHP was restructured which allowed Immunex fewer investment concerns in discovery research, and a new senior vice president position of marketing was added. These developments enabled Immunex to "transition from a biotechnology research firm with a few pharmaceutical products into a pharmaceutical enterprise dedicated to the research and development of innovative new therapeutics." The company hoped to profit from a strong market awareness and aggressive commercialization of its products.

The year 1997 was seen as a breakthrough year for Immunex. In its race to become the first to market a successful rheumatoid arthritis therapy, Immunex continued clinical trials on Enbrel. A new indication for Novantrone was also launched for treating patients suffering from prostate cancer. Record sales of Novantrone and Leukine were reached. In the area of research, promising biological therapeutic candidates, Nuvance for asthma sufferers and Mobist, an anti-tumor therapy, were introduced. As a result of increased pressure for faster development of emerging technologies and intense competition in the pharmaceutical business, Immunex formed alliances with Digital Gene Technologies, Inc., a genomics company, and American Oncology Resources, a network of U.S. oncologists.

Enbrel Receives FDA Approval

Another breakthrough year followed in 1998, with the FDA's approval of Enbrel for treatment of moderate to severe rheumatoid arthritis in patients with inadequate response to existing therapies, thus making Enbrel the first in a new class of rheumatoid arthritis drugs. Sales of Enbrel alone reached nearly $13 million in the first weeks of marketing. Expanding the potential uses for other drugs, Immunex introduced research describing the potential for Novantrone for treating patients with progressive multiple sclerosis (MS). Leukine was being evaluated for its ability to treat patients with HIV/AIDS; and Enbrel was being studied for treatment of chronic heart failure. Studies continued on Nuvance, for asthma sufferers; and Mobist and CD40 ligand, for use in cancer treatment.

With product success came financial success: total product sales reached a record $170 million for the year; sales of cancer products grew to record levels as well, lead by Leukine with a 21 percent increase over the previous year. Cash reserves at year-end reached $145 million. Immunex restructured a strategic alliance with AHP, giving AHP options to select and develop certain products and returning to Immunex worldwide rights to certain cancer products. A new consumer campaign was launched, called Enliven, to assist new patients through their initial therapy on Enbrel. A new Web site was launched, www.enbrelinfolcom, providing reimbursement assistance and customer service for patients and providers. Through alliances with ArQule, Genetics Institute, Digital Gene Technologies, and Medarex, Immunex enhanced their product growth and development capabilities.

Enbrel continued to spell success in 1999, with $367 million in U.S. sales. Two stock splits were declared in 1999: two-for-one splits in March and August. Having previously been accepted in the adult rheumatoid arthritis market, Enbrel became the first FDA-approved therapy for juvenile rheumatoid arthritis as well. Additional research was conducted in expanding the uses of Enbrel for the treatment of psoriatic arthritis and chronic heart failure. In oncology treatments, studies continued on Leukine, Mobista, and CD40 ligand, brand-named Avrend. An alliance was announced with Genentech, Inc., to jointly develop TRAIL, found to suppress and reverse tumor growth.

Construction began on a new 50,000-square-foot process development facility located in Bothell, Washington. In partnership with Wyeth-Ayerst, renovations began on a commercial-scale biologics manufacturing plant in Rhode Island; and plans were underway for a new research and technology center in

Seattle, called the Helix Project, to house a world-class collaborative team in the field of immune system science.

Marketed products in 2000 included two major therapeutic classes: anti-inflammatory (Enbrel) and specialty therapeutics (Leukine, Novantrone, Thioplex, Amicar, Methotrexate sodium injectable, and Leucovorin calcium). Revenues from sales of Enbrel reached $652.4 million, approximately 76 percent of the company's total revenue for the year. In anticipation of increasing demands for Enbrel, a program was initiated to help insure uninterrupted therapy for U.S. patients. The Enbrel enrollment program called for patients who were prescribed Enbrel before January 1, 2001, to register with Immunex and receive an enrollment number, thus insuring their continued supply of the drug.

As of 2001, Leukine had received FDA approval for use in bone marrow transplant therapies for the treatment of leukemia, lymphoma and Hodgkin's disease and for use in peripheral blood progenitor cell mobilization and post-transplantation support. Novantrone was approved for treatment of certain cancers, including acute nonlymphocytic leukemia; for treating patients with pain associated with hormone refractory prostate cancer; and for treatment in MS.

In the areas of research and development, Immunex continued to focus not only on producing new biological therapeutic candidates, but building pharmaceutical franchises and expanding the commercial usefulness and revenue-producing ability of key products. These included new indications of Enbrel to include therapies for congestive heart failure, psoriatic arthritis, and psoriasis. Leukine was investigated for treatment of malignant melanoma, mucositis, anti-tumor adjuvancy, and HIV/AIDS. Clinical trials continued on Nuvance in asthma therapy; Mobista as an anti-tumor agent; and Avrend in cancer treatment.

The marketing relationship continued with AHP, with Immunex owning the rights to Enbrel in the United States and Canada, and AHP owning the rights to Enbrel in all other countries. As a result, Immunex did not receive royalties or shares of gross profits from sales of Enbrel outside the United States and Canada. Leukine was available to patients only in the United States and marketed through a specialty sales force within Immunex. In June 2000, Immuntex entered into a five-year comprehensive genomics agreement with Celera Genomics. The following month, Immunex entered into a joint development and commercialization agreement for ABX-EGF, a fully human antibody created by Abgenix, Inc., for treatment of tumors, including lung, prostate, pancreatic, colorectal, renal cell, and esophageal. In December, a five-year agreement was reached with Cambridge Antibody Technology (CAT) for the use of CAT's proprietary antibody phage display library for the discovery, development and potential commercialization of human monoclonal antibodies. Other research and development arrangements continued with Genentec and Digital Gene Technologies.

Immunex Sets Records for
Sales, Profit and Cash Flow

The business of biotechnology continued to be lucrative for Immunex in 2000. Records for product sales, profit and cash flow were broken from the previous year, and a new record in the financial world was set with the largest healthcare secondary

stock offering ever. On March 20, 2000, Immunex effected a three-for-one stock split.

Product sales for 2001 reached $960 million, a 16-percent increase over the previous year's sales. New records were set for sales of Enbrel, with plans to expand manufacturing capacity to keep up with growing demand. For the first time, sales of Leukine exceeded $100 million. In its first full year of sales, Novantrone increased 19 percent from the previous year. Immunex was added to the S&P 500, and *Fortune* magazine recognized the company as the eighth "Fastest Growing Company in America" and one of the "100 Best Companies to Work for in America."

In expanding technologies, Enbrel received FDA approval for psoriatic arthritis and trials continued for the treatment of psoriasis; ankylosing spondylitis, an inflammatory disease of the spine; and Wegener's granulomatosis, an inflammatory disease of blood vessels. Biotechnology manufacturing capabilities were expanded through the acquisition of the Rhode Island manufacturing plant from AHP, with FDA approval expected in 2002.

Three new product candidates entered "transition" status, the stage in which clinical development commences within 12 to 18 months: RANK, a bone resorption inhibitor for use in cancer and osteoporosis treatment; TEK, an anti-angiogenesis factor for use in cancer treatment, and Anti-IL-4R, an antibody for asthma therapy. Two new products in clinical development included IL-1 for treatment of inflammatory disease and ABX-EGF, codeveloped with Abgenix for inhibiting the growth of cancerous tumors.

Immunex Announces Plans to Merge with Amgen

On December 17, 2001, Immunex announced an agreement and plan to merge with Amgen Inc. and AMS Acquisition, Inc., a wholly owned subsidiary of Amgen. The total Immunex price tag would be $16 billion. Under terms of the agreement, AMS Acquistion Inc. would be merged with and into Immunex, with Immunex becoming a wholly owned subsidiary of Amgen. Each share of Immunex common stock would be exchanged for a fixed ration of 0.44 shares of Amgen common stock and cash of $4.50. Amgen would also acquire AHP's 41 percent stake in Immunex for the same purchase price per share. The price would give AHP an 8 percent stake in the new company. According to Immunex Chairman Fritzky, "The proposed integration of Immunex into Amgen would unite two biotech industry pioneers, both of which have delivered on the promise of biotechnology with leading products. The product portfolio, scientific leadership, commercial expertise, and drive for results would create a strong foundation for the new Amgen in its aspiration to become the world's best human therapeutics company."

Representing a key step in accelerating Amgen's long-term growth, on July 16, 2002, the acquisition of Immunex Corporation was complete. According to Kevin Sharer, Amgen's chairman and CEO, "Amgen will now have an enhanced position as the biotechnology leader, with a wide range of important drugs, including proven blockbusters Epogen, Neupogen, and Enbrel." Amgen also acquired key Immunex personnel in the merger. Ed Fritzky, former chairman and CEO of Immunex, became a member of Amgen's board of directors, and Doug

Williams, previously Immunex executive vice president and chief technology officer, will lead the Seattle research site. Peggy Phillips, Immunex executive vice president and chief operating officer was expected to serve as a special advisor to Amgen. The integration of Amgen and Immunex produced a new Amgen, the world's largest biotechnology company with an unrivaled portfolio of primo drugs and the marketing muscle to successfully commercialize its products.

Principal Competitors

AstraZeneca; Centocor; Genentech; GlaxoSmithKline; Merck; Roche; Wyeth.

Further Reading

"Amgen Snags Immunex in $16 Billion Deal," *Chemical Market Reporter*, December 2001, p. 2.

Cushing, William G., "Immunex Founder Stephen A. Duzan Named High-Tech Entrepreneur of the Year," *Business Wire*, February 10, 1989.

Dowell, Valoree, "Immunex Appoints Steven Gillis Acting Chairman and Chief Executive Officer," *PR Newswire*, September 17, 1993.

——, "Immunex Founder Resigns, Continues as Consultant," *PR Newswire*, September 29, 1994.

"Drug Helps Delay Progression of Multiple Sclerosis" *FDA Consumer*, January-February 2001, p. 4.

Grunbaum, Rami, "Energetic CEO's Goal: Deliver on Immunex Promise," *Puget Sound Business Journal*, April 22, 1994, p. 1.

——, "Stephen Duzan: Immunex Chairman Puts Young Company in the Big Leagues," *Business Journal-Portland*, July 22, 1991, p. 12.

Gupta, Himanee, "Immunex's 1st Product Brings Profit," *Seattle Times*, July 26, 1991, p. C10.

Harrison, Joan, "Amgen/Immunex Acts as a Carrot for Firms with Big Growth Aspirations," *Mergers and Acquisitions*, March 2002, p. 23.

Heberlein, Greg, "Immunex Chief Rolls with the Punches," *Seattle Times*, August 8, 1994, p. E1.

——, "Merger Boosts Immunex Stock," *Seattle Times*, August 18, 1994, p. D1.

Lalonde, James E., "Betting On a Blockbuster: Wall Street Now See 'Transformed' Immunex," *Seattle Times*, April 15, 1990, p. E1.

——, "Immunex Founder Resigns," *Seattle Times*, August 2, 1989, p. G10.

"Leukemia Drug Approved for Prostate Cancer," *FDA Consumer*, March 1997, pp. 2–4.

Lim, Paul J., "Immunex Reassures Investors," *Seattle Times*, April 27, 1995, p. D3.

Milburn, Karen, "Immunex Cools Expectations," *Puget Sound Journal*, April 24, 1989, p. 10.

Price, Margaret, "Immunex: Tempest in a Test Tube?" *Financial World*, November 17, 1987, p. 18.

—Dave Mote
—update: Carol D. Beavers

Imperial Chemical Industries PLC

20 Manchester Square
London W1U 3AN
United Kingdom
Telephone: +44 (0) 207-834-4444
Fax: +44 (0) 207-834-2042
Web site: http://www.ici.com

Public Company
Incorporated: 1926
Employees: 38,596 (2001)
Sales: £6.425 billion (2001)
Stock Exchanges: New York London
Ticker Symbol: ICI

Imperial Chemical Industries PLC (ICI) has gone from being the premier chemical-manufacturing company of Great Britain to being one of the most innovative companies in the world. In more than 70 years, ICI has sought patents on more than 33,000 inventions, resulting in more than 150,000 patents worldwide for products ranging from chemotherapy drugs for cancer patients to insulating materials and polymers. Half of the most significant inventions since World War II are thought to have originated in Great Britain, where ICI has dominated the industry since its inception in 1926.

In 1993 the company reinvented itself as two new industrial giants: ICI, a continuing world leader in paint and explosives, expanding on the ICI tradition of developing heavy chemicals; and Zeneca Group, comprising specialty pharmaceuticals and other biotechnology businesses. The new ICI offers a group of world businesses with leading positions in explosives, paints, titanium dioxide, and other versatile materials such as polyurethane, polyester film, and acrylics.

Nobel Beginnings: Four Chemical Companies Become One

Imperial Chemical Industries (ICI) was formed by the 1926 merger of Great Britain's four major chemical companies: Nobel Industries Ltd.; Brunner, Mond and Company Ltd.; United Alkali Company; and British Dyestuffs Corporation. The birth of ICI coincided with the rise of the two other great chemical cartels: du Pont and I.G. Farben. Unlike its foreign competitors, however, ICI was never dismantled by the government.

Perhaps the most famous of the four companies that merged into ICI was the dynamite business founded by Alfred Nobel. The chemical industry of the late 19th century was largely shaped by Nobel's inventions. Before Nobel invented dynamite, blasting for engineering purposes was done with gunpowder and previous experiments with the more powerful nitroglycerine had ended disastrously. Nobel's contribution to explosives was twofold: He first mixed nitroglycerine with porous clay so that the nitroglycerine became relatively safe to handle, and then invented a detonating device that controlled the blast. More powerful and predictable than gunpowder, Nobel's dynamite made ambitious civil engineering projects such as the Suez Canal possible.

By 1883, a mere 12 years after its founding, British Dynamite Company (soon changed to Nobel's Explosives Ltd.) had grown into a company with significant annual sales. Due to the dangers associated with making dynamite, Nobel's first large plant was located in a rural area of Scotland. Transportation was a problem for the company because Parliament had passed stringent laws concerning the transport of nitroglycerine. Many shipments of the explosive liquid had to be smuggled to factories—sometimes even in hatboxes.

Like the Swede Alfred Nobel, the founder of Brunner, Mond and Company was also a foreigner. Ludwig Mond was a university-educated German Jew who emigrated to England, first of all, because the alkali industry was there and, secondly, because anti-Semitism was on the rise in Germany. Despite an inauspicious beginning, in 1871 Mond and his partner John Brunner were able to build a strong alkali business on the grounds of a former girls' school. Mond and Brunner's contribution was to produce alkalis using the Solvay, rather than the Leblanc process.

The third alkali manufacturer that would become a part of ICI was the United Alkali Company. Capitalized at more than £8 million, the company at the time of its conception was the largest chemical business in the world. The United Alkali Com-

Company Perspectives:

ICI's vision is to be the industry leader in creating value for customers and shareholders. ICI will succeed by operating at the highest levels of excellence, acquiring unrivalled knowledge of key markets and using technology creatively. The result will be products which deliver greater benefits for the company's customers, higher returns for shareholders and increased rewards for employees.

pany (UAC) began as an association of Lancashire producers who engaged in price-fixing and also set production quotas. Like its rival, Brunner, Mond, the UAC conducted a large business in China and Japan in the mid-19th century. Unlike Brunner, Mond, UAC failed to quickly realize certain technological advances (such as using electrolysis in the production of chlorine), and soon lost its position as a powerful entity.

The fourth segment of ICI, the British Dyestuffs Corporation, was formed much later than its three fellow companies. The BDC was formed as a response to the embargo of German dyes during World War I, which had seriously depressed some segments of British industry. In comparison with their American and German peers, British dye makers were not technologically advanced. This was in part due to the large English textile industry, which used its political and economic resources to keep dye prices low and thereby discouraged research into more sophisticated production methods.

Industrial Products, Imperial Horizons

At the beginning of World War I, Nobel's dynamite company was a major ammunition supplier. As the war progressed, however, there was less open warfare than predicted. Instead, the war developed into an extended siege and, as a result, came to rely more on high explosives than bullets. These high explosives were very different in composition from Nobel's gunpowder. The TNT and lyddite that English troops needed to blast their way through German defenses included coal-tar derivatives, and these, forming the basis of aniline and anthracene dyes, came from the dye industry. So the British Dyestuffs Corporation, to its surprise, found itself a manufacturer of armaments. Since TNT could be used more economically when mixed with ammonium nitrate, Brunner, Mond and Company (by then a major supplier of ammonia) was also pressed into service, along with the United Alkali Company.

By 1926, Nobel Industries Ltd. and Brunner, Mond were the two largest companies in the otherwise enervated British chemical industry. Both had been shaken by the 1925 merger of many German chemical firms into I.G. Farben—the largest cartel in the world. Since I.G. Farben was in direct competition with British companies for exports, it was feared more than the du Pont cartel, which operated primarily in the United States.

Both Nobel and Brunner, Mond initially considered joining I.G. Farben, but were unable to reach a satisfactory agreement with the Germans. After months of negotiations, they decided to form a British cartel, led by Sir Harry McGowen of Nobel Industries and Sir Alfred Mond. British Dyestuffs and the

United Alkali, weakened by a worldwide depression, were in no position to withstand pressure from their more powerful competitors and also agreed to the merger. The newly formed British cartel was soon in contact with du Pont, Allied Chemical and I.G. Farben. The name "Imperial," was chosen with careful consideration, intended to represent the company's ongoing importance to the British Empire and beyond. According to Sir Harry McGowen, in a note to a du Pont competitor, the formation of the Imperial Chemical Industries was "the first step in a comprehensive scheme . . . to rationalize the chemical manufacture of the world."

Reinventing Itself: Imperial Chemical Industries Is Born

ICI began doing business on January 1, 1927, with 33,000 employees. The newly formed company was divided into main product areas for alkalis, dyestuffs, explosives, general chemicals (including chlorine, acids, and synthetic ammonia), and metals. It also concentrated on producing cellulose products, fertilizers, lime, and a rubberized fabric known as "leathercloth." By 1928, staff had occupied the newly built, monumental headquarters on Millbank, facing the Houses of Parliament in London.

Early in ICI's history, the company chose fertilizers as its main growth area, and 10 percent of its capital was concentrated in a £20 million fertilizer plant in Billingham, England. By 1929, the onset of the Depression in the United States caused the demand for fertilizer to fall and the native demand was not large enough to support the huge Billingham plant. To partially protect its investment, ICI signed an agreement with I.G. Farben, which established production quotas for nitrogen, the main ingredient in fertilizer. In 1935 the companies agreed that I.G. Farben would sell nitrogen in all of Europe, except for Spain and Portugal, as well as South and Central America, while ICI would control the markets in the United Kingdom, Spain, Portugal, Indonesia, and the Canary Islands. And they agreed to share the Asian market.

Despite the agreement with I.G. Farben, nitrogen sales for ICI decreased and the Billingham plant was eventually closed. ICI's return on equity dropped to 4 percent in the early 1930s. The company then tried to produce oil from coal; however, despite government subsidies, the oil produced by ICI could not compete with regular oil. In the mid-1930s, with two failed plans behind it, ICI finally began to give more attention to its neglected Dyestuffs division.

Plastics: A New Line of Versatile Products

In the 1930s the word "plastic" began to be used to describe the wide variety of synthetic substitutes used for materials such as wood, leather, and metal. Unlike American and German dye makers, British dye makers had never used their knowledge of chemistry to diversify into plastics, specialty chemicals or pharmaceuticals.

ICI's Dyestuffs division, with only a small research budget, was able to begin production of agricultural and rubber chemicals around 1929; however, it was the Alkali division and not the Dyestuffs division that discovered polyethylene.

Key Dates:

1926: Four major chemical companies in Great Britain merge to become Imperial Chemical Industries (ICI): Nobel Industries Ltd.; Brunner, Mond and Company Ltd.; United Alkali Company; and British Dyestuffs Corporation.

1927: ICI opens for business with 33,000 employees in five main product areas: alkali products, explosives, metals, general chemicals, and dyestuffs.

1929: ICI signs a deal with I.G. Farben, establishing production quotas for nitrogen, the main ingredient in fertilizer.

1933: ICI researchers "discover" polyethylene, which is later patented and sold as an insulating material.

1935: Due to declining demand for fertilizer, ICI agrees to let I.G. Farben exclusively sell nitrogen in parts of Asia, Europe, and South and Central America.

1948: The result of a U.S. antitrust suit, ICI and du Pont end the exchange of technical information and cooperation on prices and markets.

1952: ICI opens a huge chemical complex in Wilton, England.

1965: ICI begins an ambitious building plan in Britain, Germany, and the United States.

1972: Britain joins the Common Market, focusing its attention on the United States.

1977: ICI continues its American investment, with acquisitions that include a paraquat plant in Bayport, Texas.

1982: Sir John Harvey-Jones assumes the role of chief executive, changing the company's focus from outdated products to drugs and specialty chemicals.

1986: ICI turns its focus to paint and specialty products with the purchase of Beatrice's Chemical division and Glidden Paint.

1993: ICI "demerges" its bioscience businesses, splitting into two companies: ICI and the separate, publicly listed Zeneca Group, which later merges into Astra-Zeneca.

1997: ICI makes its biggest-ever acquisition of four businesses from Unilever: National Starch, Quest, Unichema, and Crosfield—and moves into specialty products and begins the divestment of its bulk commodity businesses.

1999: ICI forms Uniqema, a health and personal care products company, with the merger of five ICI businesses.

Polyethylene is a versatile plastic produced when ethylene is subjected to extreme pressure. Reginald Gibson and Eric William Fawcett made the first recorded observation of the new polymer in an ICI laboratory on March 25, 1933. However, polyethylene experiments had exploded and ICI forbade its scientists to pressurize ethylene, restricting work to new safety cubicles. Then in 1935, however, ICI Researchers Michael Perrin, John Paton, and Edmond Williams and Equipment Engineer Dermot Manning tried again, producing 8.5 grams of the polymer. Despite infighting over which division would develop polyethylene, ICI patented and sold it as an insulating material. In June 1937, it was agreed that the newly formed Plastics division would take over development in its use as a moulding material, while the Dyestuffs division considered its textile uses and the Alkali division considered using polyethylene for electrical and other, unspecified uses.

ICI's work with polyethylene changed with the advent of World War II. Although production of the accidental invention had languished for five years, polyethylene actually found another important usage in radar. By the time the war broke out in 1939, scientists had found a way to use it to provide electrical insulation to radar masts.

War Brings Profits . . . and Loss

When Britain's rearmament began in 1936, ICI became a major producer for the British government. Although ICI dominated the British chemical industry, prewar production raised a problem in that the new plants built for the war effort might stand idle after hostilities ended and, consequently, lead the company to bankruptcy. ICI was reluctant to imitate du Pont's policy and charge higher prices for their products in order to pay

for the new construction. Fortunately ICI and the British government reached an agreement whereby the government paid for the construction of new plants and ICI managed them for a reasonable fee.

Almost every industry in Britain required ICI chemicals: 25 plants produced materials ranging from light metals and guns, to mustard gas, detonators, and alloys. During this time, ICI unsuccessfully attempted to make an atomic bomb. As a result of a disagreement with the director of the Manhattan Project (the U.S. war effort to produce the atomic bomb), ICI company researchers were not allowed to work with American scientists on atomic research.

A New Era: ICI Struggles to Move Ahead

The end of the war brought two major changes for ICI. The first was a result of the antitrust suit brought by the United States against the 800 various agreements ICI had signed with du Pont to regulate competition. Although the legal decision against ICI-du Pont partnership was not rendered until 1952, the exchange of technical information and cooperation on prices and markets ended in 1948. The second important postwar event was the 1952 opening of a huge chemical complex in Wilton, England. The Wilton plant included a 4,000-ton nylon polymer unit, as well as ammonia and hydrogen plants, and production facilities for phenol and organic chemicals. Despite this new complex, however, most of ICI's productive capacity was obsolete.

Unlike the largest German and American chemical companies, ICI did not prosper during the 1950s. There were two reasons why this happened. The first reason was that the company had lost its monopoly over the chemical markets of Britain and its colonies. The second reason was its outmoded productive capacity and old-fashioned managerial style. ICI was not in a position to either defend its old territory or take advantage of the opportunities that "decartelization" offered.

Until the mid-1960s, ICI continued on its same course. It was a small company in relation to its product line and rather than specializing in a few products that it could have efficiently manufactured in large plants, ICI manufactured hundreds of products inefficiently. *Forbes* magazine, in describing this stage in ICI's history, said that, "Nothing short of a full-scale industrial revolution could have saved ICI."

Increased exports and larger and more efficient plants saved the company from bankruptcy. Beginning in 1965, ICI initiated an ambitious building plan that included an ethylene cracker (facilities used in chemical manufacturing) in Britain, fiber spinning operations in Germany, and a huge PVC plant in Bayonne, New Jersey. The course pursued by ICI had some inherent risks, and most important of these was overcapacity. Nonetheless, the expansion permitted ICI to produce chemicals at a more competitive price. After the building plan was underway in 1967, sales in Europe increased an average of 33 percent a year until the end of the decade.

While ICI expanded externally in the late 1960s, internal changes also took place; most important was a change in labor relations. Shop employees began to be paid weekly rather than hourly wages, and most enjoyed substantial raises. In return for higher wages, these workers began to assume duties and responsibilities that had previously been the concern of supervisors. By the early 1970s, productivity had climbed 11 percent, although ICI remained behind its competitors in this respect.

The 1970s did not begin well for ICI. Between 1970 and 1972, ICI's profits declined 13 percent while profits for the largest U.S. chemical manufacturers increased 18 percent to 26 percent. Throughout the decade, ICI's profits were erratic. For example, profits climbed to £568.6 million in 1974, but then they dropped 33 percent in 1975. Despite inexpensive natural gas from the North Sea, plastics and fibers depressed profits in 1975 and subsequent years.

Joining Europe, Rejoining the World

Although Britain had joined the Common Market in 1972, ICI focused its attention not on Europe but on the United States. In 1971, ICI purchased Atlas Chemical Industries and was almost immediately issued a restraint of trade judgment. As a result, ICI had to sell the Atlas Explosives division. Perhaps it was this experience that led management to concentrate more on American investments than on further acquisitions. ICI's U.S. investment in 1977 included a paraquat plant in Bayport, Texas and a new laboratory for ICI Stuart Pharmaceuticals division.

In Britain the company's fertilizer division proved to be a consolation. After the discovery of natural gas in the North Sea during the previous decade, ICI had signed a long-term contract for inexpensive gas. ICI's feedstock for its ammonium nitrate-fertilizer was so inexpensive that it would sell fertilizer for £60 a ton when the market price was £80. By 1975, ICI controlled over one half of the British market for ammonium nitrate. Prices

fell so low that other fertilizer producers requested that the British government raise ICI's prices. The government, mindful of ICI's price-cutting escapades during the 1920s, threatened to introduce a pool-price system unless ICI increased its prices and refrained from keeping competitors out of the market.

All in all, the chemical company did not perform substantially better in the 1970s than it had in the previous two decades. It remained a large, but often inefficient company committed to many unprofitable products. The future began to look more promising in 1982, however, when Sir John Harvey-Jones took over the reins of ICI.

Out of the Laboratory and into the Marketplace

Known as the charismatic leader of ICI for the next five years, Harvey-Jones cut costs ruthlessly, laying off thousands of workers and closing dozens of plants in an effort to improve the company. Among his accomplishments, he ended ICI's dependence on bulk chemicals, which had accounted for 40 percent of profits in 1979 but dropped to just 16 percent after three years under his stewardship. He also de-emphasized polyethylene and concentrated on higher margin products such as drugs and specialty chemicals instead. The results were impressive; by 1983, profits had climbed to US$939 million—more than double that of the previous year.

As part of ICI's revitalization program, Harvey-Jones began to look for additions to the company's product line. One of the more interesting products at that time was polyester produced by genetically engineered bacteria fed on starch and water. This bacteria-produced polyester had some initial success as a surgical stitching.

In 1984, still under the direction of the flamboyant Harvey-Jones, ICI launched a major acquisition campaign, expanding investments in its North American division. One of the first steps was the 1986 purchase of Beatrice's Chemical division for US$750 million, followed by many smaller purchases and then the purchase of Glidden Paint, also in 1986. It proved to be a good move: In the next two years, the acquisition of Glidden ICI's paint shipments increased at a healthy rate of 7 percent, twice the industry average.

An ICI executive was quoted in 1986 as saying that ICI had enough cash to acquire two more companies the size of Glidden. Although it seemed poised for such acquisitions (asking to extend its borrowing limit to US$10 billion), the company still had problems. During 1985, profits slipped 12 percent. While ICI blamed the decline on the strength of the pound, *The Economist* magazine cited a continuing problem with bulk chemicals and decreased fertilizer sales. Additionally, the plastics market was plagued by overcapacity, and ICI had to adapt to become less dependent on its former staples.

Theorists say that ICI originated to dominate the British Empire, but when that dissolved, the company found itself laden with slow-moving products and unable to compete internationally. It wasn't until the 1980s, under the leadership of Harvey-Jones (before his retirement in 1987) that ICI finally began to reorient itself toward more profitable goods. By the 1990s, most Western chemical companies had reached the conclusion that bulk chemicals were no longer profitable.

Changes Again: One Company Becomes Two

It was in 1993 that ICI made the move to separate its bioscience businesses—including agricultural chemicals, pharmaceuticals, seeds, and biological products—into a publicly listed company, known as Zeneca Group (which later merged to become AstraZeneca). This "demerger" resulted in a substantial increase in company profitability, most notably four years later when ICI made its biggest acquisition to date with the US$8 billion purchase of four businesses from Unilever: National Starch, Quest, Unichema, and Crosfield. ICI officials called it "a journey of change and transformation," explaining that the acquisition marked the company's first move into the modern age by focusing on specialty products and paints on a global scale.

By the end of 2000, under the direction of Chief Executive Charles Miller Smith, ICI completed that restructuring, enabling it to concentrate on growing the business and improving its performance and margins worldwide. Smith stated, "In just over three years ICI has transformed itself into one of the world's leading providers of specialty products, including food, flavor, and fragrance ingredients, as well as remaining a world leader in paints."

Since that acquisition, ICI sold off other entities in order to improve its focus on paint-related products. Between 1997 and 2001, ICI claimed to make more than £6.1 billion in divestments, selling its polyester businesses primarily to du Pont, acrylics to Ineos Acrylics, and other product lines and holdings to PPG and Hunstman. It also spent more than £5.7 billion in acquisitions, investing in entities such as the catalyst science company Systenix and the specialty chemical company Uniqema.

Focus and Refocus

By early 2002, ICI had ranked among the world's largest producers of specialty products and paints, which it sold under a range of leading brand names, such as Dulux, Glidden, Valentine, Coral, Hammerite, and Cuprinol. In the past year, more than 45,000 employees produced in excess of 50,000 products at more than 200 locations in 55 countries. ICI also continued to be involved in the production of synthetic resins and polymers, silica-based and alumina-based chemicals, surfactants, and catalysts. In addition to paint, products that the company continued to produce included industrial adhesives, refrigerants, and specialty starch, fragrances, flavors and food ingredients.

Despite its refocus on paint, in its more than 75-year history to date, ICI had patented more than 33,000 inventions, ranging from plastics to pharmaceuticals. On the plastics side, ICI developed polyester and its derivative terylene (the most widely used synthetic fabric in the world at the dawn of the 21st century), as well as perspex, a recyclable material used in a

wide range of items, from lighting and signage to furniture. Well-used pharmaceuticals developed by company scientists included beta-blocker heart drugs and the antimalaria drug Paludrine.

Carol Kennedy, in the book, *ICI: The Company That Changed Our Lives*, (a follow-up to the two out-of-print historical volumes written by the late company historian, Dr. W.J. Reader), credits ICI laboratories with many life-changing inventions and discoveries. Kennedy called the company's decision in 1993 to rebirth itself as two new industrial giants pioneering—similar to that of the work of the company's founding fathers, Alfred Nobel and Ludwig Mond, in bringing the company together years ago. The charismatic Sir John Harvey-Jones, who will later become a writer and lecturer, summarizes an industrial career as "not just inventing some new product; it is creating something which wasn't there before."

Principal Subsidiaries

ICI Paints; National Starch and Chemical Company; Performance Specialties (Uniqema and Synetix); Quest International.

Principal Competitors

Ciba Specialty Chemicals; Clariant International Ltd.; Degussa AG; Akzo Nobel; Sherwin-Williams; PPG; IFF; Givaudan; Firmenich.

Further Reading

"British Industry Today: Chemicals," pamphlet prepared for British Information Services by the Central Office of Information, London: 1978, p. 76.

Clarke, Ian M., *The Spatial Organization of Multinational Corporation*, London: Croom Helm, 1985, New York: St. Martin's Press, 1986, p. 287.

Kennedy, Carol, *ICI: The Company That Changed Our Lives*, 2nd ed., London: Paul Chapman, 1993, p. 240.

Mattera, Phillip, *World Class Business: A Guide to the 100 Most Powerful Global Corporations*, New York: Henry Holt and Company, 1992, pp. 378–384.

Pettigrew, Andrew, *The Awakening Giant: Continuity and Change in Imperial Chemical Industries*, Malden, Mass: 1985, p. 536.

Reader, W.J., *Imperial Chemical Industries: A History: The First Quarter Century, 1926–1952, Vol. 2*, London: Oxford University Press, 1975, p. 569.

——, W.J., *Imperial Chemical Industries: A History:: The Forerunners 1870–1926, Vol. 1*, London: Oxford University Press, 1970, p. 563.

"Stauffer Chemical to Be Sold to Parent of ICI Americas," *Washington Post*, June 8, 1987, p. F34.

Warren, Kenneth, *Chemical Foundations: The Alkali Industry in Britain to 1926*, London: Oxford University Press, 1980, p. 208.

—update: Melissa London

Imperial Tobacco Group PLC

P.O. Box 244
Upton Road
Bristol BS99 7UJ
United Kingdom
Telephone: 44 (117) 963-6636
Fax: 44 (117) 966-7405
Web site: http://www.imperial-tobacco.com

Public Company
Incorporated: 1901
Employees: 7,500 (2001)
Sales: £5.918 billion (2001)
Stock Exchanges: London New York
Ticker Symbol: ITY
NAIC: 312221 Cigarette Manufacturing; 312229 Other
    Tobacco Product Manufacturing; 111910 Tobacco
    Farming

Imperial Tobacco Group PLC is the United Kingdom's leading tobacco company, with extensive international operations: making and marketing cigarettes, cigars, pipes, roll-your-own and pipe tobacco, and cigarette papers in more than 110 markets worldwide. In the United Kingdom, it is the brand leader in cigarettes, cigarette papers, and roll-your-own and pipe tobacco; and the company is number two in cigars. Imperial is the world leader in the roll-your-own tobacco market with Drum, Van Nelle Tabak, and Golden Virginia; and in the cigarette papers market with Rizla. The company has 13 manufacturing sites around the world. Imperial's cigarette brands include Lambert & Butler, Regal, Embassy, John Player (Ireland's market leader), and Superkings; manufacturing takes place in the company's factory in Nottingham, England. Cigars are produced under the Castella, Classic, and Panama names at the company's factory in Bristol, England. In 2001, Imperial Tobacco begins to distribute and market Philip Morris International's Marlboro cigarettes in the United Kingdom.

Early 20th Century: Protectionist Beginnings

At the dawn of the 20th century, the British tobacco industry was thriving, with about 500 tobacco manufacturers and more than 300,000 retail stores specializing in tobacco products and related wares. Operating as individual entities, the manufacturers attracted the attention of James Buchanan (Buck) Duke, head of the American Tobacco Company (ATC). Duke undercut rivals to the point of working at a loss, to persuade smaller competitors to agree with him. In this way, American Tobacco had achieved dominance in the United States and had set its sights on the European continent. The British tobacco industry was aware that ATC had allocated an enormous cash reserve of $30 million toward snatching up individual competitors in the united Kingdom.

Duke arrived on the British tobacco scene in late summer 1901 and promptly bought Ogden's, a factory that made nationally popular pipe tobaccos and cigarettes. Ogden's chairman said, "For every £1 of capital issued by us they have £100, so the contest in a cutting competition, whenever it came, would be unequal." In this context, Duke then approached other companies, including John Player and Sons, Gallaher, and Cope's. Reportedly, he even burst upon the Player brothers (the company's namesake "sons") and said, "Hello, boys. I'm Duke from New York come to take over your business." The ATC chief was rebuffed there and at other companies, but the British tobacco industry was worried. By December 1901, 13 U.K. tobacco firms had answered the challenge by registering as "The Imperial Tobacco Company (of Great Britain and Ireland), Limited." The largest of the 13 contributors was Wills, whose business dated back to 1786. Fittingly, the first chairman of the board was Sir William Henry Wills, Britain's second wealthiest man of the era. Although the 12 other businesses might have had concerns about Wills' dominant position, the new company's structure might have appeased them: When the operations joined Imperial, they ceased to be separate entities and became parts of a single business. However, each firm continued to trade under its own name and was responsible for its own sales and manufacturing.

The battle for the British market began, and predictably, ATC cut prices. Imperial gained a key weapon when it acquired the retail business of Salmon & Cluckstein, which ran a chain of tobacconist shops throughout the country. Imperial also launched a ''bonus to customers'' plan, by which a slice of the company's profits was allocated to wholesale and retail dealers who signed an agreement. ATC replied to this with a bonus agreement of its own, offering dealers all of Ogden's net profit for four years, plus £200,000 a year for the same time frame.

Imperial was not only holding its ground, but gained the upper hand, and decided to continue the fight on ATC's home turf. Surprisingly, Imperial was welcomed in America. Meanwhile, ATC experienced huge losses in the United Kingdom—in just ten months, Ogden's had lost more than £350,000 on sales totaling £7.5 million, versus Imperial's profit of £5 million in its first year.

In September 1902, ATC raised the white flag: The company turned over Ogden's to Imperial and stopped operations in Great Britain and Ireland. In turn, Imperial halted its U.S. expansion plans, except for buying tobacco leaf. Imperial gained rights to sell American Tobacco's brands in the United Kingdom, and the American company gained rights to sell Imperial brands in its native market. A new company was registered in the U.K., the British-American Tobacco Company Limited, to market both firms' products overseas. But in 1911, after a United States Supreme Court antitrust ruling, American Tobacco split into four companies and sold its interest in BAT. At that point, the 1902 agreement was changed to let Imperial sell some of its brands in the United States. Imperial retained a share in British-American Tobacco for many years.

1920s–1950s: Consolidation

The first 20 years of the 20th century were an era of consolidation for Imperial. Until the end of World War I, the structure of the company remained largely unchanged, with the exception of establishing the American Leaf Buying Organization in 1902, the purchase of the J & F Bell tobacco business in 1904, and two years later, the formation of a firm to process waste products for agricultural use. A look at the numbers of employees at John Player & Sons between the wars gives a sense of the firm's rapid growth: 2,500 in 1914; 5,000 in 1928; and 7,500 by 1939.

During World War I, cigarette consumption rose dramatically, and brands such as Woodbine, known as the ''soldier's smoke,'' were popular in the trenches. In 1918, Imperial explored new areas such as manufacturing cigarette paper, which until then had been nearly a French monopoly. In 1920, Canon's Marsh Tobacco Bonds was established to store bonded tobacco leaf. In 1923 and 1924, Wills' and Players' manufacturing plants were

established in Ireland. In 1926 a leaf buying and processing operation was launched in Africa, as was the British Leaf Tobacco Company of Canada. In 1927, Imperial gained a share in the Finlay chain of tobacconist shops (becoming a wholly owned subsidiary in 1963), and in 1930, a controlling interest was bought in Robert Sinclair Ltd., a tobacco wholesaler. Tobacco acquisitions continued throughout the late 1930s, 1940s, and 1950s. As time went on, rationalization gradually whittled the smaller producers into larger units, eventually molding Imperial's 22 constituent companies to three by the end of 1980: W D & H O Wills, John Player & Sons and Ogden's.

Meanwhile, in the 1920s and 1930s, Imperial was waging a different kind of war: the battle of cigarette coupons, which first appeared in the 1920s. Although in 1930, Imperial's chairman spoke out against these promotions, other companies pursued them, and thus ate into Imperial's market share. In the summer of 1932, Imperial launched the Wills Four Aces coupon brand, and by the end of the next year, the brand gained more than one-sixth of the coupon market. More than 320 million coupons were issued, and were redeemed for more than 3 million gifts, but it cost the company almost three-quarters of a million pounds. The vicious competition hurt the industry, and in October 1933, Imperial achieved an agreement with the six largest manufacturers to end coupon trading starting at the end of that year.

During World War II, cigarette sales continued their upward swing, and despite a reduced labor force and limited supplies, Imperial still shipped nearly 12 billion cigarettes and 1,750,000 pounds of pipe tobacco to troops overseas. In the late 1950s, the number of U.K. smokers hit a peak of 23 million.

1960s–1970s: Diversification and Difficulties

By the 1950s, Imperial controlled more than 80 percent of the U.K. tobacco market, but its market share decreased during the next decade because of competition from the Gallaher Group, maker of Benson & Hedges cigarettes. Meanwhile, the first Royal College of Physicians report about the health effects of tobacco was published in 1962. The report recommended restrictions on tobacco advertising, increased taxation on cigarettes, limiting the sale of cigarettes to young people, and providing more information on the tar and nicotine content of cigarettes. Cigarette sales fell for the first time in a decade. In 1964 the government banned cigarette advertising on television, ending a period since 1955, when the first commercials for the Capstan and Woodbine brands were broadcast.

In this cooling climate, Imperial's management sought ways to reduce the company's risk. In the 1960s and 1970s, Imperial began to diversify from its almost complete dependence on tobacco, with somewhat haphazard diversification into food, drink, and leisure operations with acquisitions such as the snack-food company Golden Wonder Crisps (1961), and the Courage & Barclay brewery (1972). To signify this broadened portfolio, the company was renamed Imperial Group in 1973, and Imperial Tobacco Limited was formed as a unit to oversee its tobacco business. By 1979, Imperial Group employed about 100,000 people.

With the oil crisis and recession, the 1970s was Imperial's most challenging decade. The United Kingdom joined the European Economic Community (EEC) in 1973, and by 1978, the resulting changes in the tax system weakened the company's market position. Before joining the EEC, Britain had a system in which the weight of tobacco determined the amount of tax, which favored the market for smaller cigarettes, which Imperial dominated. But the new "end-product" taxation system treated all cigarettes the same, regardless of weight, so that king-size cigarettes were taxed at the same rate as standard-size cigarettes. Gaining more puff for the buck, smokers switched in droves to king-size cigarettes. Before this time, less than one out of every ten cigarettes sold in the United Kingdom was king-size. By 1984 that number jumped to almost eight out of every ten. The impact on Imperial was huge. About two-thirds of cigarettes sold in the United Kingdom before 1976 were Imperial brands, but, as David Churchill wrote in the *Financial Times* (London), "Imperial was slow to react to these changes." And as a result, other tobacco vendors entered into the fray.

Through the 1970s, Imperial still held a stake in BAT, which focused on exports and the duty-free market, while Imperial's business was limited almost entirely to the United Kingdom and Ireland. In 1973, Imperial and BAT agreed that each would control its own brands in the United Kingdom and Continental Europe. In 1980, Imperial sold off the last of its financial holdings in BAT. Also that year, in a move to lessen Imperial's dependence on U.K. earnings, the company bought the U.S. hotel and restaurant chain Howard Johnson (but sold it to Marriott Hotels in 1985).

Despite the difficulties of the 1970s, that time period did see an achievement: the opening of what the company calls the two most modern tobacco manufacturing centers in the world: the Player's Horizon factory in Nottingham in 1972, followed by the Wills Hartcliffe factory in Bristol in 1974.

1986–1996: The Hanson Era

Imperial Tobacco began the 1980s with a major reorganization, from which the company surfaced as a leaner, more efficient operation. Amid the decline in the tobacco market and the need for greater cost-effectiveness, the company closed four factories and centralized the administrative functions of Wills, Player's, Ogden's, and Imperial Tobacco (Imports). But according to Gareth Davis, who became Imperial's chief executive in 1996, Imperial still was saddled with excessive costs by 1986 when conglomerate Hanson Trust acquired it in a US$4.3 billion hostile takeover. Davis told *The Independent*'s Roger Trapp in a December 6, 2000 article, "Hanson was very good for us. It knocked us into shape."

Right away, Hanson set to work by divesting the patchwork of branded-consumer goods Imperial had assembled, and reshaped the company as a streamlined, low-cost manufacturer of high-quality tobacco—a mission that remains in place. Hanson cut Imperial's tobacco brands from more than 100 to five brand families, a move that decreased its U.K. market share to 33 percent by 1990. It sold Imperial's brewing businesses to Elders IXL (now Foster's Group Limited), and divested the restaurant and food businesses. Between 1986 and 1993, it cut tobacco operations from five factories and 7,500 employees to three factories and 2,600 employees. Faced with a mature market and declining U.K. cigarette consumption, Imperial began expanding overseas in 1994, and by 1996, exports had risen to 15 percent of sales. In light of the founding of the Single European Market in 1993, Imperial's actions were not unusual. The company needed to enhance efficiency and cut production expenses to compete against its Continental counterparts.

In 1990, in an historic ruling, a judge criticized Imperial for its treatment of pensioners. The case arose when participants in the 26,000-member fund were faced with a choice: staying in their plan, which was closed to new members, or switching to another open plan within the group. In the *Financial Times* of December 6, 1990, Eric Short reported that in 1985, when it became clear that Hanson was pursuing the Imperial Group, the latter had created rules in the plans to prevent the new employer from gaining access to assets of the Imperial Tobacco pension fund. However, in denying access to the acquiring company, the new rules also restricted access to the plan's beneficiaries. The judge ruled that proposals affecting the future of pension plan members have to be made in good faith. The ruling was regarded as a victory for employees.

In 1996, striving to improve its share price, Hanson announced that it was "demerging" its diverse businesses into four independent companies. Imperial would remain committed to its cigarette, cigar, and tobacco business, but it would focus on the U.K., Irish, Continental European, and Asia-Pacific markets. The demerger of Imperial Tobacco took place on October 1, 1996, and Imperial began trading on the London Stock Exchange. Meanwhile, five days before trading was to begin, a group of former smokers came forward with a class-action lawsuit against Imperial Tobacco and Gallaher, who together accounted for 80 percent of cigarette sales in the united Kingdom. The claimants, who suffered from lung cancer, asserted that the tobacco companies failed to fulfill their duty to decrease health risks by reducing tar levels in cigarettes when the link between tar and cancer became clear in the late 1950s.

During the Hanson era, many of Imperial's businesses were sold off and the core tobacco operations were completely reorganized to enhance efficiency and cost-effectiveness. Between 1987 and 1995, productivity nearly tripled, the brand portfolio was streamlined, and market share increased. In 1996, the market capitalization of the newly independent Imperial was £2 billion.

1996–2000: Independent and Thriving

The post-Hanson period began on a roll. Under the direction of new CEO Davis, who apparently never is photographed knowingly without an Imperial product in his fingers, the company acquired Rizla, the world's leading brand of hand-rolling cigarette papers and one of the tobacco industry's oldest players, for £185 million. The deal enhanced Imperial's stance in the hand-rolling market, where Golden Virginia commanded 60 percent of legitimate tobacco sales. Based in the Netherlands, Rizla claimed two-thirds of the world market for hand-rolling tobacco paper, thus broadening Imperial's European presence. Davis told Magnus Grimond of *The Independent* in a January 29, 1997 article that the company had its eye on Rizla for about five years but had been preoccupied with the demerger.

The following year, Imperial acquired hand-rolling tobacco manufacturer Douwe Egberts Van Nelle from Sara Lee for £652 million. The purchase added the Drum brand to the existing Golden Virginia brand in hand-rolling tobacco. Imperial renamed the operation Van Nelle Tabak. After the two acquisitions, the composition of Imperial's income changed, with one-quarter of profits now coming from outside the United Kingdom. Thanks to these two highly regarded deals, Imperial was admitted to the FTSE 100 Index in December 1998. Imperial also gained a listing on the New York Stock Exchange.

The results for 1998 were positive, with a 12 percent increase in the group's operating profit. Rizla had been integrated, and Van Nelle Tabak had widened the company's international presence. Chairman Tom Kyte said that the profits came in spite of punitive tax increases, which he said contributed to the U.K.'s declining cigarette market, made worse by goods smuggled from EEC countries with lower cigarette taxes. Also that year, Lambert & Butler became the U.K.'s leading cigarette brand family. Meanwhile, Imperial widened its presence in Europe and select emerging markets.

In early 1999, the company revealed plans to close one of three Van Nelle Tabak plants as part of an 18-month project to streamline and control costs in the hand-rolling tobacco operations. Imperial invested in new technology, such as expanding the factory in Nottingham with a £330-million expenditure over the next two and a half years. In 1999, Imperial acquired a portfolio of brands in Australia and New Zealand. Also that year, Imperial launched the lower-priced Richmond King Size, followed by Richmond Superkings in 2000. The company has heralded this brand family as one the most successful introductions by any tobacco manufacturer in recent years.

In February 1999, the biggest legal action ever brought against the U.K. tobacco industry fell apart. In a significant win for the companies, the group of lung cancer victims withdrew their High Court case against Imperial and Gallaher. The tobacco companies agreed not to pursue the claimants for legal costs approaching £14 million as long as they agreed never to sue again. The outcome has been heralded as a legal landmark.

At the end of a decade in which smokers fell out of favor, Imperial came to be rated as one of the U.K.'s largest and most successful companies. At the same time, U.S. investors responded more quickly than their British counterparts to appreciate that Imperial had no exposure to the U.S. market—and U.S. litigation. In a *Times* (London) article published May 24, 1999, Gareth Davis told Robert Lea there are two things the company will never do: "We will not go into anything outside of tobacco or tobacco-related products—the company has been there, done that and thrown away the T-shirt. And we will not, ever, be going into the U.S.—for the obvious reason." The obvious reason being potential litigation and the possibility of billions of dollars in healthcare settlements as a result.

The Next Century: Going Global

Although born amid British protectionism, Imperial approached its centennial with a cosmopolitan world view. By December 2000, 44 percent of the business was international. And the overseas portion of the workforce had dramatically shifted—from 5 percent at the time of the demerger to almost 50 percent at this juncture. In 2000, the company acquired the Baelen Group, a Belgian manufacturer of roll-your-own tobacco; EFKA, a German manufacturer of cigarette papers and tubes; and Mayfair Vending, a U.K.-based operation that tripled Imperial's cigarette vending business.

The following year transformed the company's stature. In early 2001, Imperial had increased prices across all products in the United Kingdom to offset the impact of market declines, estimated at about 10 percent a year. But with a contract to start distributing Marlboro cigarettes in the United Kingdom for Philip Morris International in September 2001, Imperial overtook its rival Gallaher as the U.K. market leader. By February 2002, Imperial saw its U.K. cigarette market share increase to 48.7 percent. Davis estimated that the Marlboro contract was worth about £10 million a year to Imperial. In 2001, the company also gained a market presence in Africa and Vietnam with its purchase of a 75 percent stake in France's Tobaccor SA, the second largest cigarette manufacturer and distributor in sub-Saharan Africa. In November 2001, Imperial said its full year after-tax profit was up 10 percent, even with cigarette consumption shrinking in its home market. In addition, Imperial's international sales surpassed domestic sales for the first time.

By the end of 2001, Imperial's fifth consecutive year as a public company, the company had made strides in its strategy of generating sustainable profit growth, both by investment in new markets and brands and through acquisitions, supported by a low-cost manufacturing base. In October of that year, the company announced a planned restructuring of its manufacturing and supply chain operations, which would take place over the next 18 months and consume an investment of about £16 million. Meanwhile, Davis praised the British government for its efforts toward ending the illicit cigarette trade, such as the increased number of customs officers scouting out illegal tobacco imports. Looking forward, as with all tobacco companies, Imperial faces continued pressures from regulatory authorities and governments.

Principal Operating Units

Imperial Tobacco International Limited; Imperial Tobacco Limited; John Player & Sons Limited (Ireland); Rizla International BV (The Netherlands); Sinclair Collis Limited.

Principal Competitors

British American Tobacco; Gallaher; Philip Morris International.

Further Reading

Baker, Lucy, "Smuggling Crack-Down Pays Off for Imperial," *The Independent* (London), May 10, 2001, p. 21.

Blackwell, David, "Cigars All Round as Imperial Finds Itself on a Roll," *Financial Times* (London), May 8, 1999, p. 2.

——, "Imperial Tobacco Raises Overseas Sales by 24%," *Financial Times* (London), November 27, 2001, p. 29.

Churchill, David, "BAT Succumbs to Pressures of Rising Duty and Falling Demand," *Financial Times* (London), February 4, 1984, p. 3.

"Cigarette Producers Dabble in Dual Pricing," *Business Week*, March 29, 1976, p. 33.

Clausen, Sven, "UK Groups in Battle for Reemtsma," *Financial Times* (London), January 11, 2002, p. 27.

Cole, Robert, "Imperial's Advantages Could Go Up in Smoke," *The Times* (London), November 27, 2001, p. 23.

Cowell, Alan, "Profit up at Tobacco Concern," *New York Times*, November 27, 2001, p. W1.

Doran, James, "Imperial Knocks Gallaher off Top UK Tobacco Slot," *The Times* (London), November 27, 2001, p. 25.

Foley, Stephen, "The Investment Column: Imperial Tobacco Looking High," *The Independent* (London), November 27, 2001, p. 19.

France, Mike, "Insurers Hear a Smoke Alarm," *Business Week*, May 13, 1996, p. 102.

Gilbert, Nick, "Profile Martyn Day: Smoking Out the Tobacco Giants," *The Independent* (London), May 11, 1997, p. 5.

Griffiths, Lucy, "Tobacco Company Slammed over Environmental Reporting," *Accountancy Age*, March 29, 2001, p. 3.

Grimond, Magnus, "Imperial Tobacco Rolls Out Pounds 185m Offer for Rizla," *The Independent* (London), January 29, 1997, p. 21.

Guerrera, Francesco, " 'Safe Haven' Status Puts Tobacco Groups in Footsie," *The Independent* (London), December 7, 1998, p.17.

"Hanson Leads the Way down Demerger Road," *Corporate Money Quarterly*, July 10, 1996, pp. ii–iii.

Hasell, Nick, "Imperial Tobacco," *The Times* (London), May 8, 2001, p. 21.

——, "Imperial to Highlight Worldwide Strength," *The Times* (London), November 26, 2001, p. 21.

The Imperial Story 1901–2001, Bristol, U.K, 2002.

"Imperial to Distribute Marlboro," *Financial Times* (London), August 15, 2001, p. 15.

"Imperial Wins Marlboro's UK Rights," *The Independent* (London), August 15, 2001, p. 15.

Kapner, Suzanne, "Bids in for German Tobacco Company," *New York Times*, December 6, 2001, p. W1.

Lacoursiere, Catherine, "Spinoffs Start to Sputter," *Treasury & Risk Management*, January 1997, pp. 28–31.

Lea, Robert, "Corporate Profile: Imperial Tobacco," *The Times* (London), May 24, 1999, p. 48.

Mason, John, "Lawyers Heartened by Tobacco Settlement in US," *Financial Times* (London), March 22, 1997, p. 4.

Mcintosh, Bill, "Imperial Tobacco Africa Buy Looks Good," *The Independent* (London), April 3, 2001, p. 19.

"Outlook: Yield Gap Carries Ominous Message," *The Independent* (London), October 20, 1998, p. 17.

"A Pension Fund Maverick Who Advocated the 'Cult of the Equity,' " *Financial Times* (London), March 22, 1999, p. 6.

Pretzlik, Charles, "Imperial Tobacco's Income Attractions Make It a Difficult Habit to Kick," *Financial Times* (London), November 10, 1998, p. 27.

Rice, Robert, "Judge to Decide Whether Lung Cancer Court Fight Is Too Late," *Financial Times* (London), December 7, 1998, p. 24.

Rice, Robert, and Ross Tieman, "Tobacco Groups Sued in UK Legal Landmark," *Financial Times* (London), September 28, 1996, p.1.

Riley, Barry, "The Long View: Imperial Preference Shared," *Financial Times* (London), May 25, 1991, "Weekend" magazine, p. 1.

Short, Eric, "Judge Attacks Pension Fund Move," *Financial Times* (London), December 4, 1990, p. 22.

——, "Judge Smokes Out Predators," *Financial Times* (London), December 6, 1990, p. 10.

Tieman, Ross, "Evolution Plays Its Part in Hanson's Big Bang," *Financial Times* (London), February 21, 1997, p. 21.

——, "Tobacco Sector Set to Light Up at Gallaher's Return," *Financial Times* (London), May 15, 1997, p. 25.

Trapp, Roger, "Corporate Profile: Imperial Tobacco—Rolling in It," *The Independent* (London), December 6, 2000, p. 3.

Urry, Maggie, "A Continuing Stately Dance to the Music of Money," *Financial Times* (London), January 2, 1999, p.16.

Wood, Lisa, "Imperial Tobacco to Cut 350 Jobs," *Financial Times* (London), December 10, 1986, p. 8.

Yates, Andrew, "Gallaher Allegations Hit UK Tobacco Firms," *The Independent* (London), March 17, 1998, p. 24.

—Michelle Feder

Inchcape PLC

22a St. James's Square
London SW1Y 5LP
United Kingdom
Telephone: +44 (0) 20 7546 0022
Fax: +44 (0) 20 7533 9117
Web site: http://www.inchcape.com

Public Company
Incorporated: 1958 as Inchcape & Co. Ltd.
Employees: 11,000
Sales: £3.2 billion (2001)
Stock Exchanges: London
Ticker Symbol: INCH
NAIC: 441110 New Car Dealers; 551112 Offices or
Other Holding Companies

Inchcape PLC, a company with more than a 150-year history—starting as a shipping and trading firm and evolving into a diversified conglomerate—has reinvented itself at the end of the 20th century. The company now describes itself as the world's largest independent automotive distribution group, operating in more than 20 international markets, including the United Kingdom, Greece, Australia, Hong Kong, and Singapore. Inchcape has relationships with many of the world's leading car manufacturers, including Mazda, Ferrari, Jaguar, BMW, Peugeot, and Subaru, but has a particularly strong partnership with Toyota Motor Corporation, representing that company in 11 markets, including Belguim, Greece, Hong Kong, and Singapore. With its entry into the e-commerce market with its new and used car-purchasing retail Web site Autobytel UK, Inchcape continues to reinvent itself for the future.

19th Century Origins

Inchcape PLC was launched as an overseas trading company in 1958, yet the origins of its constituent companies date back to the late 18th and early 19th centuries. Thus, the creation of Inchcape dates back to the early expansion of commerce with India by a group of Scottish merchants. In 1847 a meeting took place in Calcutta between William Mackinnon and Robert Mackenzie, two merchants from Campbeltown, which led to the formation of their general merchanting partnership, Mackinnon Mackenzie & Company. Realizing the benefits of combining trading with ocean transport, especially with the gold rush to Australia in 1851, the business expanded and diversified. In 1856, Mackinnon at age 34 founded the Calcutta & Burmah Steam Navigation Company (C&B), secured from the East India Company the contract for carrying the mails between Calcutta and Rangoon, and incorporated the company in London with a capital of £35,000, of which Mackinnon Mackenzie & Company invested £7,000, becoming agents for the new shipping line. As a result of their success in carrying troops from Ceylon (now Sri Lanka) to India during the Indian Mutiny of 1857 to 1859, and through Mackinnon's contacts with the influential civil servant Sir Henry Bartle Frere, the partners obtained further contracts to support a fleet of coastal steamers carrying mails around the Indian coast with extensions to the Persian Gulf and Singapore. In 1862, C&B raised sufficient additional capital—a total of £400,000—to float the company under the new name of the British India Steam Navigation Company (BI). Mackinnon Mackenzie & Company continued to act as agents for the BI for nearly 100 years.

Sir William Mackinnon also promoted steamer traffic to the Dutch East Indies, establishing a Dutch-registered shipping line around Java, and forming the Netherlands India Steam Navigation Company in 1868. With the opening of the Suez Canal in 1869, BI ships entered the Mediterranean Sea, establishing a trunk line between London and India via the Suez Canal in 1876. In the process, Mackinnon Mackenzie & Company became one of the greatest Eastern agency houses, and the BI posed a mighty challenge to all other shipping lines operating between the United Kingdom and the East, including the giant Peninsular & Oriental Steam Navigation Company (P&O).

These events were the backdrop to the formative years of James Lyle Mackay, named Lord Inchcape in 1911. Born in 1852, the son of an Arbroath shipmaster, Mackay left Scotland at the age of 20 and worked in the customs department of Gellatly, Hankey and Sewell. Mackay, who joined Mackinnon Mackenzie & Company's Calcutta office in 1874, was to be-

Company Perspectives:

Inchcape, as an international automotive services group, provides quality representation for its manufacturer partners, a choice of channels to market and products for its retail customers and a range of business services for its corporate customers. Operating primarily in the U.K., Greece, Belgium, Australia, Hong Kong and Singapore, its key partners are Toyota, Subaru, Ferrari, Jaguar and Land Rover. Inchcape's activities include exclusive Import, Distribution and Retail, Business Services, automotive E-commerce and Financial Services.

come the heir to the Mackinnon businesses after the death of Mackinnon in 1893. Mackay first became a partner after saving the BI's Bombay office from bankruptcy, and was to become president of the prestigious Bengal Chamber of Commerce a record three times between 1890 and 1893. A member of the Viceregal Council and a close friend and confidant of Lord Lansdowne, Viceroy of India, Mackay gained a knighthood for his contribution to the solution of India's currency problems and the ultimate adoption of the gold standard in India. Mackay returned to the United Kingdom in 1894 as a director of the BI, replacing William Mackinnon's nephew, Duncan Mackinnon, as chairman in 1913. Continuing his work on the Council of India, Mackay's growing reputation as an outstanding public servant led to his being offered the viceroyalty of India in 1909. Prime Minister Herbert Asquith opposed Mackay's nomination, however, on the grounds of his commercial interests in the subcontinent, and Mackay was offered a peerage in 1911 by way of compensation. He chose the name of Baron Inchcape of Strathnaver, commemorating the Inchcape Rock, located 12 miles from Arbroath, and expressing his loyalty to the clan Mackay, whose home is in Strathnaver. Between 1913 and 1932, Lord Inchcape personified Britain's shipping industry as chairman of the BI and the P&O, after effecting a merger between the two lines in 1914.

Less well known than Lord Inchcape's shipping activities is his consolidation of an extensive group of commercial interests in India and beyond. These began with his accumulation of shares in Mackinnon Mackenzie & Company. Sir William Mackinnon had no son, his nephew Duncan died in 1914, and his great-nephews were killed in World War I, so Inchcape became the sole-surviving senior partner of the Mackinnon enterprise, and by 1950 the Inchcape family held a controlling interest. Inchcape's chairmanship of the BI and P&O resulted in a very close connection between Mackinnon Mackenzie & Company and the shipping line, to the extent that many observers came to believe that they were one company.

Mackinnon Mackenzie & Company spawned a variety of other enterprises to serve the BI routes. The BI originally employed small private firms in local ports of call as agents, but eventually replaced them with firms within the Mackinnon complex. These all came under the control of the senior partners and ultimately under Lord Inchcape himself. To separate the trading businesses from the shipping line, the Macneill & Barry partnership was developed to take over the extensive tea and

merchanting operations that Lord Inchcape had acquired in 1915. Amalgamated in 1949, Macneill & Barry Ltd. comprised three merchant partnerships formed in the second half of the 19th century: Barry & Company, Macneill & Company, and Kilburn & Company, involved in tea, coal, jute, river steamers, and various trading enterprises. Their principals included the Assam Company, the oldest tea company in India; the River Steam Navigation Company; and the India General Steam Navigation and Railway Company. Between 1951 and 1956, Macneill & Barry took over Kilburn & Company, and the three groups set up Pakistan-based companies. In 1965 the two river steamer businesses were sold to the government of India.

In 1906, Mackay made a successful strategic acquisition, of Binny's, a South India-based textile business. Founded in 1799, Binny's originally carried out banking and general merchanting, diversifying in the 1840s into agriculture and textiles. Indian production of textiles boomed in the 1860s, when the U.S. Civil War interrupted cotton supplies, and by the late 19th century Binny's mills managed 70,000 spindles with over 1,500 looms. Yet in 1906, with the crash of the great Arbuthnot & Company banking house with whom it was closely involved, Binny's faced bankruptcy. Its greatly undervalued assets were acquired by Mackay and a consortium of Mackinnon partners for £53,000. Binny & Company Ltd., as it had become in 1906, made record profits in World War I with the production of khaki cloth, and by 1917 was supplying over a million yards per month. Binny & Company was subsequently restructured, setting up an Engineering department, and rose to greater prominence during World War II, producing one billion yards of cloth a year by 1942.

Owing to the need to supply shipping-agency services to the BI, Mackinnon group enterprises were established in East Africa, the Persian Gulf, Australia, and London. In East Africa, as Sir William Mackinnon began to open up the region to British influence, the BI operated a steam shipping service. In 1872, Archibald Smith, a member of the staff of William Mackinnon & Company in Glasgow, Scotland, together with a Mackenzie man from Calcutta, established an agency to operate as BI agents and general traders. In 1887, Sir William Mackinnon won from the sultan of Zanzibar in East Africa, the right to administer a coastal strip of land in return for customs revenue, which led to the founding of the Imperial British East Africa Company (IBEA), partly in response to the buildup of German interests in this area. Smith Mackenzie & Company took a stake in IBEA and acted as its agents, until the charter was surrendered in 1897. Smith Mackenzie & Company and the agency for Shell in East Africa became joint coaling agents to the admiralty during World War I and in the 1930s gained the agencies for British American Tobacco, Imperial Chemical Industries, and British Overseas Airways Corporation.

In 1862, when a contract was won to carry mail eight times a year up and down the Persian Gulf, the merchant partnership that became Gray Mackenzie & Company was formed, helping to develop navigation on the Euphrates and Tigris Rivers, and establishing a diversified trading business in an area that was also facing German expansionism. In World War II, Gray Mackenzie & Company acted as agents for the British government in unloading military cargoes; the growth of its business was helped by the spectacular development of the oil industry and

Key Dates:

1847: Two Scottish merchants, William Mackinnon and Robert Mackenzie form their general merchanting partnership Mackinnon Mackenzie & Company.

1874: James Lyle Mackay, later the first Lord of Inchcape, starts working in the Calcutta, India office of Mackinnon Mackenzie & Company, and eventually runs the organization.

1906: Mackay and a consortium of Mackinnon partners purchase Binny & Company Ltd., producers of khaki cloth.

1958: The diverse Mackinnon group interests are consolidated to form Inchcape & Company, Ltd., run by Mackay's grandson, the third Lord Inchcape. The company goes public and is listed on the London Stock Exchange.

1967: The company acquires the Borneo Company entering the motor vehicle distribution and timber and construction business.

1969: The company acquires Gilman & Company, a trading group in Hong Kong.

1981: Company is reincorporated as Inchcape PLC.

1982: Lord Inchcape relinquishes his title of executive chairman, becoming life president of the Inchcape group.

1994: Lord Inchcape dies, severing the last business link between Inchcape group and the Inchcape family.

1998: Inchcape announces its restructuring plan to focus solely on its international motors operations, the largest and most successful part of the company.

1999: Inchcape is reborn as a motors-only company.

the rapidly growing need to service the expanding ports of the Middle East.

The Mackinnon complex also branched into Australia, with BI services at first managed by the British India and Queensland Agency Company Ltd. The Mackinnon partners invested in the formation of a major Australian shipping conglomerate in 1887, the Australasian United Steam Navigation Company (AUSN), formed with a capital of £600,000. In 1894, Mackay was appointed to the board of the AUSN and, in 1900, spent several months in Australia successfully restructuring the business. In 1915 he created a new merchant partnership, Macdonald Hamilton & Company, formed by two trusted Mackinnon appointees, B.W. Macdonald and David Hamilton. The AUSN, which had once owned 42 steamers, declined in the face of increasing competition from railways in the 1920s, and Macdonald Hamilton & Company diversified its activities into mining, pastoral management, and operating the P&O agencies in Australia. The P&O acquired Macdonald Hamilton's P&O-related activities in 1959 and 1960.

The London partnership of Gray Dawes & Company was set up to serve the BI as a shipping and brokering agency, and eventually became a bank and a travel agency. It represented the interests of Smith Mackenzie & Company and Binny & Company in London, and set up a Secretarial department to administer the estate of James Mackay, the first Lord of Inchcape, after his death in 1932.

Consolidation and Expansion: Late 1950s through 1970s

These diverse Mackinnon group interests were consolidated and reorganized during the 1950s, coming together as Inchcape & Company Ltd. in 1958 at the initiative of the third Lord of Inchcape. Tax considerations necessitated the conversion of these companies into private limited companies—whose former partners became the principal shareholders—controlled through London-based subsidiaries. Also in 1958, Inchcape & Company became a public company through a public offering of 25 percent of its equity, and starting in 1958 embarked on a program of growth and diversification, principally through acquisitions. The group today reflects the merger and acquisition activities of the last quarter of the 20th century, rather than the original companies that came together in 1958.

During the 1960s and 1970s, under the leadership of the third Lord of Inchcape, the company expanded to over 150 times its previous capitalization, due principally to a series of successful acquisitions, especially those of the Borneo Company in 1967; Gilman & Company in 1969; Dodwell & Company in 1972; Mann Egerton & Company in 1973; Anglo-Thai Corporation in 1975; A.W. Bain Holdings in 1976; and Pride & Clarke, which held the Toyota agency for the United Kingdom, in 1978. In this period, through several capitalization issues, 64 original shares costing £80 in total in 1958 were worth nearly £2,000 by 1975.

The merger with the Borneo Company almost doubled the size of Inchcape overnight, bringing in new interests in Canada, the Caribbean, Hong Kong, Malaysia, Singapore, Brunei, and Thailand. The Borneo Company operated jointly with Inchcape in the United Kingdom and Australia, but introduced two new activities into the group's portfolio: motor vehicle distribution and timber and construction business. This merger, in which Inchcape entered new geographical regions in familiar businesses and entered new businesses in regions that it knew well, established a pattern for subsequent acquisitions and allowed considerable local autonomy to exist among local staff.

Through Peter Heath, originally a director of the Borneo Company, Inchcape acquired Gilman & Company, one of the great trading groups of Hong Kong. Gilman & Company was seeking an acquirer but did not wish to be taken over by an existing Hong Kong business. The acquisition of Dodwell & Company gave the group further interests in this region, which it maintained as quasi-independent companies, rather than forming one large entity. Dodwell & Company was founded in Shanghai in 1858, and by the 1970s had established extensive businesses in shipping, motors, and business-machine trading in Hong Kong, Japan, and many other Far Eastern ports and cities.

Mann Egerton & Company, acquired in 1973, laid the foundations for Inchcape's motor-distribution business. Founded at the end of the 19th century in Norwich by an electrical engineer and an early motoring pioneer, Mann Egerton sold cars manufactured by de Dion, Renault, and Daimler for between £200 and £300 per car, at the turn of the century initially from branches in the eastern counties of England. By the 1970s, Mann Egerton distributed British Leyland cars, as well as an extensive range of luxury cars, but faced a possible takeover bid from an unwanted source, and felt increasingly vulnerable as a result of a wave of oil shocks.

The acquisition of Anglo-Thai Corporation involved the issue of nearly nine million Inchcape £1 ordinary shares, three times the number issued before, increasing Inchcape's market value by about 90 percent, and adding to group assets in the Far East and Southeast Asia. In one of the group's few predatory bids, valuable businesses such as Caldbeck Macgregor & Company, a well-known importer and distributor of wines and spirits, were included. In 1976, with A.W. Bain Holdings, Inchcape developed an important insurance business through a share issue second only to that involved in acquisition of the Anglo-Thai Corporation. With Pride & Clarke, the group gained the valuable concession of exclusive Toyota distribution in the United Kingdom after an issue of £1 million in £1 ordinary shares and £6.9 million in cash, in what some observers called the biggest bargain of the century. By 1989, the Motors segment was contributing two-thirds of group turnover and 53.6 percent of group profits, the greater part contributed by Toyota.

Reorganization in a Modern Era: 1980s, 1990s, and Beyond

Inchcape—reincorporated as Inchcape PLC in 1981—under the chairmanship of George Turnbull in the 1980s reinforced its concentration on its core businesses. Inchcape's key businesses at that time were organized into three main areas: services, marketing and distribution, and resources. The service businesses consisted of buying, insurance, inspection and testing, and shipping. The marketing and distribution businesses covered business machines, consumer and industrial services, and motors. The resource-based businesses covered tea and timber.

In April 1990, Toyota paid Inchcape £110 million in cash for a 50 percent stake in Inchcape's United Kingdom-based distributing business known as Toyota (GB). With this acquisition, Toyota also acquired a holding of nearly 5 percent in Inchcape itself.

Inchcape had a difficult time in the early 1990s during CEO Charles Mackay's tenure in part because it had in prior decades overdiversified into areas not related to its core distribution business. The company continued to expand during this period, in particular in the shipping services and insurance areas. Through a variety of acquisitions from 1990 through 1993, Inchcape expanded into or expanded its shipping businesses in China, Korea, Vietnam, Indonesia, Canada, Turkey, Ecuador, and the United States. The U.S. acquisitions were seen as particularly strategic as Inchcape was able to secure operations for the Pacific, Atlantic, and Gulf coasts of the United States, with the goal of operating a broad shipping agency covering all three coasts.

In insurance, Inchcape's Bain Clarkson Ltd. insurance broker was bolstered through the 1994 acquisition of Hogg Group PLC for £176.6 million (US $264.9 million). The newly named Bain Hogg Group instantly joined the ranks of the world's ten largest brokers, and Inchcape had gained a presence in the U.S. insurance market for the first time through Hogg Robinson Inc. Meanwhile, Inchcape's marketing operation was bolstered in a smaller way with the 1992 acquisition of the Spinneys group of companies, which ran a chain of supermarkets in the Middle East, from Bricom Group Ltd. for £32.1 million (US $57.9 million).

A combination of factors plunged Inchcape into its two most difficult years ever, 1994 and 1995. Difficult economic conditions in some of the company's key markets—particularly in Western Europe and Hong Kong—dampened consumer spending, while the strength of the yen made Inchcape's Japanese products, notably the Toyota automobiles, less attractive than those of competitors based outside Japan. In certain areas such as marketing, Inchcape had also become a more bureaucratic organization than in the past, and had lost touch with some of the local markets it served. As a result, pretax profits fell 15.8 percent from 1993 to 1994 and 92.4 percent from 1994 to 1995. The resulting plunge in Inchcape stock caused the company to be dropped from the prestigious PT-SE 100 index in late 1995. First, David Plastow retired as chairman of Inchcape at the end of 1995 and was replaced by Colin Marshall, who at the same time was chairman of British Airways PLC and deputy chairman of British Telecommunications PLC. Then in March 1996 Mackay stepped aside as CEO, and Philip Cushing, who was managing director, took his place.

The new management team determined that Inchcape had to focus on its core international distribution businesses in order to turn things around and began making significant business divestments, including selling the Bain Hogg insurance brokerage subsidiary to the Aon Corporation in the United States for £160 million in 1996. The company began to jettison unprofitable businesses, and significantly reduce the workforce.

In March 1998 spurred by the fact that the Asian economic crisis had more than split in half Inchcape's shares between October and January, Inchcape made a major announcement. The diversified company was to undergo a complete restructuring to focus exclusively on worldwide car distribution, the most successful part of the group. One of the first major sectors to go was the company's Russian soft-drink bottling business, whose losses skyrocketed from £7.1 million to £21 million between June and September 1998. Inchcape sold that part of their operations to The Coca-Cola Company for US$87 million in October (US $100 million less than the price agreed on in principle just two months earlier). The sales of bottling businesses in South America, marketing services in Asia and the Middle East, the global shipping business, and the Asia-Pacific Office Automation business were some of the wide range of divestments that quickly followed. In July 1999 another management shuffle had Peter Johnson succeeding Philip Cushing as CEO, and that same month the new motors-only Inchcape was officially born. The appointment of Sir John Egan as Chairman in June 2000 (replacing Marshall) rounded out the new leadership, reflecting the newly refocused Inchcape.

The transition to a motors-only focus was not entirely smooth. The automobile industry in the United Kingdom was thrown into controversy in 2000 when the Competition Commission issued report findings showing that new car prices in the United Kingdom were between 10 percent and 12 percent higher than in other countries. Consumer confidence plummeted, and the industry suffered. Inchcape's operating profit in the U.K. fell from £25 million in 1999 to £0.7 million in 2000. The auto industry scrambled to respond to the report, offering lower interest rates and price reductions. The consumers came back, and in 2001, the U.K. new car market soared by 10.7 percent. This helped Inchcape's U.K. operating profit to improve to £13.7 million in 2001.

The year 2000 found Inchcape selling its 49 percent share of Toyota (GB) to Toyota Motor Corporation for £42.1 million, which provided Inchcape with additional funds for investments in other ventures, plus gave Toyota 100 percent ownership in one of its key markets. The partnership between Inchcape and Toyota remained strong, as Toyota's largest independent distributor, Inchcape continued to represent the company in markets including Greece, Belgium, Hong Kong, and Singapore.

Inchcape's Asian investments steadfastly rebounded from the region's economic crisis of the mid- to late 1990s. The Hong Kong market profits posted an exceptional spike in 2001, due mainly to the strength of taxi sales. Due to a government incentive campaign that encouraged taxi drivers to switch from diesel to Liquified Petroleum Gas (LPG) cars, taxi sales surged 130 percent. With Toyota dominating 90 percent of the taxi market, Inchcape saw its Hong Kong operating profit leap from £40.7 million to £48.9 million between 2000 and 2001.

In 1999, Inchcape expanded into the rapidly developing market of e-commerce with the launch of Autobytel UK, the result of a partnership with the U.S.-based Autobytel.com, an Internet-based new and used car purchasing service. Though by 2001, the wholly owned U.K. subsidiary still posted losses, Inchcape had high hopes for future growth in expanding this market of e-commerce. By taking a chance in a financially unproven medium, Inchcape continued its quest to anticipate market changes and remain at the forefront of the industry.

Principal Subsidiaries

Autobytel Ltd. (U.K.); Bates Motor Group Ltd. (U.K.); Borneo Motors (Singapore) Pte. Ltd. (63%); Crown Motors Ltd. (Hong Kong); Eurofleet Ltd. (U.K.); Inchcape Automotive Australia Pty. Ltd.; Inchcape Automotive Ltd. (U.K.); Inchcape Fleet Solutions Ltd. (U.K.); Inchcape Motors Ltd. (Singapore; 63%); Inchcape Overseas Ltd. (U.K.); Inchcape Retail Ltd. (U.K.); Inchcape Vehicle Contracts Ltd. (U.K.); Maranello Concessionaires Ltd. (U.K.); Mazda Motors (Hong Kong) Ltd.; The Motor & Engineering Company of Ethiopia Ltd. S.C. (94%); Subaru (Australia) Pty. Ltd. (90%); Toyota Hellas S.A. (Greece); Toyota Belgium N.V./S.A.

Principal Competitors

Hyundai; Mitsui O.S. K. Lines; Pendragon.

Further Reading

Burt, Tim, and Flested, Andrea, "Inchcape Works on Restructuring Drive," *Financial Times*, January 21, 2002, http://www.ft.com.
Canna, Elizabeth, "More Acquisitions for Inchcape," *American Shipper*, December 1991, p. 79.
"Car Firms under Pressure," *BBC News Online*, April 10, 2000, http://news.bbc.co.uk.
Foster, Geoffrey, "Inchcape's Less Perilous Passage," *Management Today*, January 1988, p. 46.
Gillis, Chris, "Inchcape's Open Door to China," *American Shipper*, January 1996, p. 50.
Griffiths, Percival Joseph, *A History of the Inchcape Group*, London: Inchcape & Company Ltd., 1977, p. 211.
——, *A History of the Joint Steamer Companies*, London: Inchcape & Co. Ltd.
Jones, Stephanie, *Trade and Shipping: Lord Inchcape 1852–1952*, Manchester, England: Manchester University Press, 1989, 222 p.
——, *Two Centuries of Overseas Trading: The Origins and Growth of the Inchcape Group*, London: Macmillan, 1986.
Ladbury, Adrian, "Bain Hogg Group," *Business Insurance*, July 18, 1994, pp. 35–36.
Lindberg, Ole, et al., "Companies That Made Their Mark," *International Management*, January/February 1993, p. 60.
Magnier, Mark, "Inchcape Plans Expansion into 3 Asian Nations," *Journal of Commerce and Commercial*, March 19, 1992, p. 8B.
Porter, Janet, "Inchcape Grows with Purchase of Three Shipping Businesses," *Journal of Commerce and Commercial*, February 23, 1993, p. 8B.
Souter, Gavin, "Global Broker Merger: Bain Clarkson, Hogg Combination to Break into Top 10," *Business Insurance*, May 2, 1994, pp. 1, 61.
Taylor, Roger, "Inchcape Plans Three-Way Split," *Financial Times* (London), March 3, 1998.
Tieman, Ross, "Inchcape sells Bain Hogg to Aon for £160m," *Financial Times* (London), October 16, 1996.
Vincent, Lindsay, "Inchcape's True Brit," *Observer*, April 4, 1993, p. 40.
Wighton, David, "Inchcape to Focus on Distribution Business," *Financial Times*, March 26, 1996, p. 24.
William, John, "Inchcape's Sales Loses Sparkle," *Financial Times* (London), October 6, 1998.

—Stephanie Jones
—updates: David E. Salamie; Linda M. Gwilym

Infineon Technologies AG

St.-Martin-Strasse 53
81669 Munich
Germany
Telephone: +49 (89) 2-34-2-5649
Fax: +49 (89) 2-34-2-6155
Web site: http://www.infineon.com

Public Company
Incorporated: 2000
Employees: 33,800 (2001)
Sales: EUR 5.671 billion (2001)
Stock Exchanges: Frankfurt New York
Ticker Symbol: IFX (Franfurt), IFX (New York)
NAIC: 334413 Semiconductor and Related Device
Manufacturing

During Infineon Technologies AG's short life as an independent company, it has become the fourth largest DRAM manufacturer in the world, the second largest semiconductor manufacturer in Europe, and one of the top ten semiconductor manufacturers in the world. With 33,800 employees, Infineon has 16 manufacturing sites and 29 research and development sites in Europe, Asia, and the United States. The company's three major areas of work include communications; memory; and automotive, which includes semiconductors that go into cars. Infineon's communications products and services encompass fixed-line communications, wireless communications, and security and chip card integrated circuits (ICs). The company stated earnings of nearly EUR 5.7 billion (US$5.2 billion) for the fiscal year ending September 30, 2001.

Infineon's Leap to Independence

Infineon Technologies AG, the former Siemens Semiconductor, was founded on April 1, 1999, as a wholly owned spinoff of Siemens AG. The split followed the harsh price erosion in DRAMs, with Siemens Semiconductor posting a US$674 million pre-tax income loss for its 1998 fiscal year. As reported in the March 22, 1999 issue of *Electronic News*,

Siemens Chairman Heinrich von Pierer, stated in November 1998 that the DRAM downturn "entails losses we simply cannot sustain. It is not fair to our stockholders."

The *Electronic Buyers' News* on May 24, 1999 reported, "Infineon's operating losses amounted to approximately US$56.7 million in the six months ended March 31, 1999. The German company also reported that its semiconductor division lost about US$464.6 million for the full fiscal year ended September." The need to reduce the risks associated with such dramatic earnings charts is understandable when following the market trends for semiconductors. By the end of 2001, Siemens had reduced its ownership of Infineon shares to 41.3 percent.

As explained to potential investors in Infineon's annual report, the semiconductor industry is cyclical, with recurring bouts of "economic downturns that involve periods of production overcapacity, oversupply, lower prices, and lower revenue." The outlining of risk factors explained that sales for semiconductor products grew more than 40 percent in 1995, decreased by 9 percent in 1996, increased by 4 percent in 1997, and increased by 8 percent in 1998. In 1999, the increase was 19 percent that leapt to 37 percent in 2000, during which time Infineon posted a revenue growth of 72 percent. Unfortunately, the semiconductor market came to "the most far-reaching collapse in the semiconductor industry" in the fiscal year 2001.

Volatile nature aside, one of the immediate advantages of becoming independent was that Infineon could gain many new customers outside of Siemens, although the parent company remained a major customer. This expansion of the customer base was Infineon's first major success as an independent company. The president and CEO of Siemens Semiconductors, Ulrich Schumacher, retained his position at the new company.

A Harrowing Ride

During Infineon's first year as a public company, it led the world market in producing chips for chip cards, with a 34 percent share, and was cited by *Electronics Weekly* on November 10, 1999, as "one of the most impressive performers in a strong year for its parent Siemens." In fact, *Electronic Engineering Times* on January 24, 2000 noted, "The chipmaker posted profits totaling US$70 million in its first fiscal year after a loss of US$800 million for the former Siemens AG unit the previous year.''

Other markets that were established in 2000 included mobile communications, Internet access, electronic banking, electronic and mobile commerce, as well as innovative security and authentication systems, including biometric systems, such as fingertip sensors. Other sophisticated products were emerging with advanced encryption technologies and state-of-the-art security memory products and controllers, along with Infineon's first Bluetooth chipset. An international consortium of computer and communications companies for delivery was developing the Bluetooth open system standard over short-range wireless modems. However, this unbelievably profitable ride up the charts came to a screeching halt at the end of 2000 before beginning its lurching descent down the other side.

In a letter to shareholders on the company Web site, CEO and President, Ulrich Schumacher, stated that the market collapse for semiconductors in 2001 had to do with the significant decline in price and demand for memory products and communications markets that usually drive growth. Because of slow growth in the communications market, demand for security and chip card ICs were also down. The end result was that Infineon's total revenues dropped 22 percent to EUR 5.7 billion in the 2001 fiscal year, compared to record revenues of EUR 7.3 billion in the 2000 fiscal year. The loss per share in 2001 was EUR 0.92, in stark contrast to the profit per share in 2000 of EUR 1.83.

Schumacher explained that intensive price wars among memory products manufacturers led to ''a shakeout among DRAM manufacturers,'' which was accompanied by increased pressure on prices for communications products in the second half of the year. The reduced demand for mobile communications alone resulted in an 18 percent drop in revenues for the Infineon's Wireless Communications. Fortunately, the security and chip card ICs had an increase in revenues of 57 percent, the automotive and industrial revenues increased 25 percent, and the wireline communications increased by 15 percent.

Infineon wisely developed a set of measures called ''Impact'' to streamline the business and cut costs to maintain the strength and productivity of the company during downtimes. The goal of the program was to gain cash savings, including capital expenditures, of more than 1.5 billion Euro by the end of

the 2002 fiscal year. About 70 percent of the savings were not related to personnel, although the streamlined work environment made it necessary to cut 2,400 jobs by the end of 2001. A second public offering in July 2001 netted Infineon EUR 1.5 billion, and the company received more than EUR 650 million by divesting its infrared components business and selling its interest in an opto-semiconductor joint venture. Having stabilized somewhat financially, the company has expanded its role in the less volatile markets for specialty-developed memory products and high-performance chips.

Infineon's Strategic Objective

As stated in the company's annual report, Infineon planned to achieve profitable growth by targeting fast-growing areas of the semiconductor industry and build upon its position as a leading innovator in the semiconductor industry. The company planned to attain this objective by focusing its diverse technologies—in particular its strengths in mixed-signal, radio-frequency, embedded digital signal processing, embedded control, power, DRAM and embedded DRAM—on key applications in communications systems for wireless and wireline transmission of speech and data, as well as in automotive and industrial electronic systems. Its aim was to provide innovative products and services and to fully exploit and, as appropriate, expand its world-class manufacturing facilities. By doing so, the company aimed to enable its customers to be successful in their own markets. By working with industry leaders among its customers, Infineon believed it developed the knowledge and experience required to continue to be at the forefront of the semiconductor industry.

Memory Products

The DRAM (Dynamic Random Access Memory) manufacturing accounted for 30 percent to 40 percent of the company's revenue. ''Besides the standard DRAMs that are used in PCs, we focus on high performance DRAMs,'' explained Joachim W. Binder, Infineon's senior manager of Investor Relations and Financial Communications. ''These are special DRAMs for graphics applications, workstations, and networking, and focus more on performance than on cost, and have a higher clock frequency.''

Infineon was the first company to use 300-millimeter (mm) wafers for DRAM production instead of the standard 200mm. This bigger wafer size is more efficient, and requires a new fabrication process to produce. Binder notes that while the larger wafers are not faster, they have 2.5 times the area, so are able to process more chips per wafer. ''Since we are the first to do this for DRAM,'' Binder states, ''we claim to be the leader here.''

This shift to larger wafers required new equipment and new plants. The company has built up its 300mm fabrication plants while continuing to run its 200mm fabrication plants, but will eventually convert the 200mm DRAM fabs to logic products. New plants being built have been 300mm fabs.

Rambus Patent Suit

In the midst of Infineon's early prosperity in 2000, Rambus, Inc. filed suit against the company in Virginia and Germany, alleging that Infineon's SDRAM (Synchronous Dynamic Ran-

Key Dates:

1999:   Infineon Technologies AG splits from Siemens AG.
2000:   Infineon is listed as an IPO on the Frankfurt and New York Stock Exchanges; Rambus, Inc. files suit against Infineon for patent rights infringement.
2001:   U.S. District Court dismisses Rambus' case against Infineon, and a secondary public offering nets EUR 1.5 billion.

dom Access Memory) infringed upon its patent rights. An important part of Infineon's DRAM portfolio, SDRAM is a type of DRAM IC, along with DDR DRAM. Rambus sought an injunction against Infineon's production of SDRAM and DDR DRAM. Infineon denied the claims and filed counterclaims, stating that the patents relied on by Rambus were invalid. Court proceedings began in December 2000 in Germany and early 2001 in the United States.

The district court in the U.S. proceedings dismissed Rambus' claims against Infineon in two separate decisions in April and May 2001, awarding Infineon US$3.5 million, which was later reduced to US$350,000, according to Virginia state law. After post-trial motions, the judge awarded Infineon another US$7.1 million for attorney fees and legal costs and granted an injunction to bar Rambus from asserting against Infineon's SDRAM and DDR DRAM products that comply with JEDEC (the Solid State Technology Association standards for the semiconductor industry) or any current or future U.S. patent directed to specific technologies described in the standards.

In 2002 the case was still active in German courts and unbound by the decision of the U.S. trial court. If Infineon were barred from producing SDRAM and DDR DRAM, it would be greatly affected financially, as the company would have to stop producing these products or enter into licensing agreements with Rambus. Groups that would be affected include all of the memory products. Infineon licenses RDRAM from Rambus, which was not in dispute.

Wireless Communications

Infineon Wireless Communications have designed, developed, manufactured, and marketed semiconductors and system solutions for wireless applications, including cellular telephone systems, short-range wireless systems, such as cordless telephone systems and Bluetooth radios, and devices used with global positioning systems (GPS). (Bluetooth is an open-systems standard for the delivery of data over a short-range wireless modem.) Infineon calculated that GPS would be an important market for ICs, as U.S. regulations will require that all mobile telephones users in the United States be able to pinpoint their locations via GPS.

The world market for semiconductors used in digital cellular telephone systems and pagers was about US$6.5 billion in 2000 with about a 40 percent reduction in production and sales in 2001. The worldwide market for radio frequency and baseband semiconductors for digital cordless telephone systems has grown steadily and was estimated to be about US$450 million in 2000.

Wireline Communications

Infineon Wireline Communications have designed, developed, manufactured, and marketed semiconductors and fiberoptic components for communication access, such as WANs (Wide Area Networks), MANs (Metropolitan Area Networks), and LANs (Local Area Networks). The company had a 6 percent share of the worldwide sales of wireline communications ICs in 2000. These products included ISDN (Integrated Services Digital Network) chipsets, coders/decoders (known as codecs), and subscriber line interface circuits (SLICs) used in telephony-based products.

Other important Infineon products are high-speed optical network components and modules. Infineon specializes in 10- to 40-gigabit-per-second optical networking for fiber-optic networks. Infineon also has held a leading position in the broadband access technologies market and has said it plans to develop products using advanced versions of DSL (Digital Subscriber Line) technology. The demand for ever-increasing bandwidth has focused Infineon's research and development on the convergence of voice and data networks in a single infrastructure, increased investment in network access and WAN/MAN infrastructure, and the emergence of the optical transponder that allows integrated opto-electrical conversion. (Opto-electrical components function by reacting to or creating light signals.)

Security and Chip Card ICs

Infineon has also been the market leader worldwide in the manufacturing of chip card and security integrated circuits (ICs) that go into plastic cards, as well as manufactured and marketed security controllers, security memories, and other semiconductor and system solutions used in specific security features. The company's 2001 annual report stated that it was the world's largest manufacturer of chip card ICs, with 43 percent of the market share in 1999 and 34 percent in 2000. The company's market is driven by the trend toward increased security in telecommunications, banking, health services, electronic commerce, and Internet communications.

The use of chip cards and security ICs has been more prevalent in Europe than in Asia and the United States. The bulk of the market has been comprised of security controllers, which were complete computer systems on a chip that can be used for access control, encryption, and copy protection. The rest of the market was made up of security memories that combine memory with security logic functions to provide secure data storage, access, and communication.

Infineon's security and chip card IC products encompass chip card ICs including security controllers and security memory ICs for cards and the terminals that read them, and key applications that include mobile communication, credit/debit cards, prepaid telephone cards, and health insurance cards. Infineon's MultiMediaCard is a solid-state secure storage device that combines high-capacity memories with small size. This card can provide data storage for mobile telephones, personal digital assistants, digital cameras, and music players.

Infineon makes security ICs for use in security systems, secure data communications, and electronic commerce, and developed FingerTIP IC, a biometric sensor that can register and identify fingerprints, and can replace personal identification numbers and passwords for mobile telephones and notebook computers. A recent development used in tracking parcels and baggage are the identification system ICs that use standard and security ICs, permitting convenient, contactless identification of goods through radio-frequency devices. However, the biggest revenue from the chip card and security IC business has come from thin SIM cards (Subscriber Identification Modules) that go into cellular handsets.

Automotive and Industrial

Infineon's Automotive and Industrial group has developed, manufactured, and marketed semiconductors and systems solutions for automobiles and industry. Automotive applications comprised about 55 percent of this group's sales in 2000, with the balance serving industrial applications. Infineon had 7 percent of the automotive market in 2000—not including radio—that made the company the largest supplier of automotive electronics in Europe and the second largest worldwide. In industrial applications, the company focused on power management and supply, and drives and power distribution.

The five basic product classes included in automotive and industrial are: (1) automotive sensors, (2) microcontrollers, (3) automotive power ICs, (4) power management and supply, and (5) industrial ICs. Infineon's primary automotive products include semiconductors for power train applications that perform functions, such as engine and transmission control, and safety and vehicle dynamics that manage the operation of airbags, antilock braking systems, electronic stability, and power steering systems. Other automotive applications include body and convenience systems used in light modules (door locks, power windows, mirror control), and electrical power distribution systems, and infotainment, such as those used in dashboards, navigation/telematics, and car radios.

The industrial applications for semiconductors has been fragmented in terms of suppliers and customers, and characterized by many standardized and application-specific products. These products have been applied in many industries, such as factory automation, power supply, and consumer products. The range of semiconductor products has been based on about 1,500 different chip types to about 1,100 customers for use in industrial automation and control systems. These products encompassed power modules, discrete semiconductors, and controllers.

Some of the industrial product applications include uninterruptible power supplies, such as power backbones used for Internet servers, and switched-mode power supplies for PCs. Other industrial uses are battery chargers for mobile phones, notebook computers, and other handheld devices, as well as drives for machine tools motor controls, pumps, fans and heating, ventilation, air-conditioning systems, and transportation. Infineon also supplies semiconductors for Industrial automation, meters, and sensors, and other industrial applications, such as power distribution systems and medical equipment.

Growth through Partnerships

Infineon has had major partnerships with IBM and Toshiba for memory products, and with Cisco, JDS Uniphase, and Nortel for fiber optics. The company partnered with Nokia in the development of radio frequency (RF) transceivers, and with Motorola and Hitachi in the development of automotive electronics. Sony has also been a partner with Infineon in the area of contactless security applications. Infineon has stakes of 20 percent or more in 60 to 80 subsidiaries worldwide.

With IBM, Infineon developed the first 1-megabit and 4-megabit DRAMs, and has since issued the first 512-megabit DRAMs. Infineon was the first company to bring 256- and 512-megabit DRAM to the market. Infineon also worked with Toshiba on nonvolatile memories.

Binder has said that these partnerships are beneficial. In the fall of 2001, one publication suggested that Infineon was seeking a DRAM partner and cited examples of semiconductor companies that have found acquisitions to be advantageous. Talks with Toshiba about joining Infineon in a joint venture did not come to fruition. However, *Electronics Weekly* on March 13, 2002 reported that Infineon "has completed talks with two Taiwanese DRAM manufacturers, Mosel Vitelic and Winbond, who signed agreements to help the company in the upcoming market recovery."

Dr. Ulrich Schumacher, president and CEO of Infineon stated, "Infineon considers these co-operations as a major step to prepare for the upcoming market recovery, and will pave the way for further augmenting of our position in the consolidating DRAM industry." Infineon will lease its DRAM technology to Winbond in 2003, thereby gaining exclusive access to standard DRAM chips that were manufactured using this technology.

"Infineon has benefited from the increased demand for memory for PCs and mobile devices, as well as the use of cellular handsets," Binder explained, "as well as the increase in bandwidth for optical networks." As the semiconductor markets become ever more diverse, Infineon plans to continue to provide innovative solutions through its products.

Principal Competitors

Philips Semiconductors; Samsung Electronics; STMicroelectronics; Motorola; Micron Technology; Applied Micro Circuits Corporation; Broadcom Corporation; PMC-Sierra; GlobeSpanVirata; Toshiba; Texas Instruments.

Further Reading

Ascierto, Jerry, "Siemens Names New Semi Division Infineon Technologies: Spin-off Moves toward Its Own Goal of Going Public in Near Future," *Electronic News*, March 22, 1999, p. 16.

Clarke, Peter, "IBM Gives Logic Partner Infineon Access to Copper," *Electronic Engineering Times*, May 3, 1999, p. 26.

Druce, Chris, and Melanie Reynolds, "Downturn Hits Infineon," *Electronic News*, November 19, 2001, p. 14.

Dunn, Darrell, "TI, Infineon Edge into Bluetooth—Two Chipsets Said to Offer Improved Reception Sensitivity," *Electronic Buyers' News*, September 18, 2000, p. 39.

Hachman, Mark, "NeoMagic Adds Infineon as Third Foundry," *Electronic Buyers' News*, May 3, 1999, p. 8.

"Infineon Turnaround Impresses Siemens," *Electronics Weekly*, November 10, 1999, p. 8.

Liu, Sunray, "Sales in Region Climbed to $838 Million in 1999—Infineon Gets Added Strength from Asia Pacific," *Electronic Engineering Times*, January 24, 2000, p. 40.

MacLellan, Andrew, "In The Highly Volatile DRAM World, Infineon Must Choose a Partner Wisely," *EBN*, November 19, 2001, p. 32.

Manners, David, "Infineon Signs DRAM Deals for 20,000 Wafers a Month," *Electronics Weekly*, March 13, 2002, p. 2.

——, "Silicon Gladiator," *Electronics Weekly*, September 8, 1999, p.12.

Robertson, Jack, "Infineon Posts Six-Month Operating Loss of $57M," *Electronic Buyers' News*, May 24, 1999, p. 20.

——, "Infineon, Toshiba Resume Talks on DRAM Merger," *EBN*, November 26, 2001, p. 8.

Robertson, Jack, and Corinne Bernstein, "Infineon Off to a New Start," *Electronic Buyers' News*, November. 1, 1999, p. 72.

—Annette Dennis McCully

Interbrew S.A.

Vaartstraat 94
B-3000 Leuven
Belgium
Telephone: +32 (16) 24-71-11
Fax: +32 (16) 24-74-07
Web site: http://www.interbrew.com

Public Company
Incorporated: 1988
Employees: 25,500 (2000 est.)
Sales: EUR 7.303 billion (2001)
Stock Exchanges: Brussels Euronext
Ticker Symbol: INTB
NAIC: 312120 Breweries; 312111 Soft Drink
    Manufacturing

With operations on every continent on the globe, Belgium's Interbrew S.A. ranks second among the world's brewing companies behind only Anheuser-Busch and first in its home country, with brewing operations in 26 countries and sales in over 120. The company emerged as a top European brewer in the late 1980s, when two Belgian brewing families merged their closely held, centuries-old interests to form Interbrew. Under the direction of a succession of CEOs, the firm advanced from the middle ranks of the global beer hierarchy to the upper echelon via the US$2.7 billion acquisition of Canada's John Labatt Ltd. in 1995. This was followed by other acquisitions, notably major U.K. brewers Bass and Whitbread in 2000, and major German brewer Beck's in 2001. Also in 2000, the company issued an initial public offering (IPO) and began trading on the Euronext Stock Exchange in Brussels.

Interbrew's strategy for growth has contrasted sharply with that of the beer industry's "Big Three." Anheuser-Busch, Heineken NV, and Miller Brewing Co. all focus on pushing their flagship brands throughout the world, while Interbrew has grown by acquiring leading national and regional brands, then investing in production and promotion to increase those beers' sales. In 2002, the company's stable of brands included Hungary's Borsodi Sör, Mexico's Dos Equis, the U.S.'s Rolling Rock, Canada's Labatt's Blue, the U.K.'s Bass and Whitbread, and Germany's Beck's, as well as a host of smaller brands from countries all over the world. Interbrew has been cashing in on this cadre of specialty beers by exporting select brews, including its own Stella Artois, from one region to another.

Origins and Development

Interbrew was formed through the 1987 union of the Artois Brewery, owned by the de Spoelberch clan, with the Van Damme family's Piedboeuf Brewery. Artois traced its history to the late 14th century, when the Den Horen Brewery was established in Louvain, Belgium. This business was acquired and renamed by master brewer Sébastien Artois in 1717. It is not clear when the de Spoelberchs assumed ownership of the company, which retained the Artois moniker throughout the remainder of the 20th century. The Piedboeuf family brewery, on the other hand, was established in 1853 and acquired by Albert Van Damme in 1920.

Both companies undertook programs of European expansion through acquisition in the late 1960s, and even joined forces in 1971 to effect the joint purchase of a third Belgian brewery. The multi-brand strategy developed over the course of three decades, as both companies bought competitors in the Netherlands, France, Italy, and Belgium, yet retained these new affiliates' disparate brewing heritages and brands. This policy fostered the development of two families of truly distinctive beers. Stella Artois enjoyed a legacy that extended back to 1366, Leffe Blond was brewed in a tradition that could be traced to a mid-13th-century Belgian monastery, and Hoegaarden was a white beer with more than 500 years of history behind it.

When Artois and Piedboeuf merged in 1987, the joint owners hired José Dedeurwaerder to rationalize operations. A citizen of both Belgium and the United States, the new CEO shed inefficient plants, won concessions from organized labor, and invested heavily in the newest brewing technology. His efforts nearly tripled overall productivity, from 2.5 hectoliters (66 gallons) per hour in 1990 to 6.5 hectoliters (172 gallons) in 1995. In spite of these apparent successes, Dedeurwaerder abruptly resigned in early 1993. He was succeeded by Hans Meerloo.

Company Perspectives:

We consider our brand portfolio to be our key asset. Brand image is a critical factor in a consumer's choice of beer. Brand promotion and advertising are essential tools to build brand image, market share, and turnover. We strive to grow and maintain our market share by positioning and promoting our brands clearly and consistently as core, premium, or specialty brands across all their markets; although internationally we may position a brand that is a core brand in its home market as premium or specialty. Our main marketing objectives are to promote a domestic lager brand to be our primary brand in each market, to support this primary brand with at least one other brand in our portfolio, and to enhance Stella Artois' status as an international brand. Brand cycles are very long with beer brands being built over the course of many years and brand strength often lasting for decades. We intend to continue to invest heavily to maintain and enhance our brands.

Interbrew continued to pursue its strategy of growth through acquisitions in the early 1990s. The company achieved full ownership of Belgium's Belle-Vue Brewery and Hungary's Borsodi Sör brand beer in 1991. These acquisitions provided insight about Interbrew's multi-brand strategy. The firm groomed Belle-Vue for export to the French market, targeting this cherry-flavored wheat beer at women. A reinvigorated advertising campaign helped sell 8 percent more Borsodi Sör in its first year under new management. Interbrew continued to penetrate Eastern Europe with the 1994 acquisitions of Rumania's Bergenbier and Croatia's Ozujsko. Although some analysts viewed Interbrew's burgeoning cadre of international beers as a liability, others noted that the company's "connoisseur" brands accounted for over one-fourth of its net income and only 13 percent of sales. While vital to Interbrew's overall strategy, all the company's late 1980s and early 1990s acquisitions paled in comparison to the events to come.

Interbrew Emerges as a Global Brewing Powerhouse in the 1990s

By the early 1990s, Interbrew was Europe's fourth largest brewer, with US$2 million in sales and distribution throughout 80 countries. While impressive, the company's owners and executives realized that its status as a middling brewer on the global stage threatened its profitability and competitiveness. Furthermore, the company's core European market was showing signs of decline. Specifically, per capita beer consumption on the continent slid 6 percent in the early 1990s as the result of health concerns and more stringent drunk driving legislation. Interbrew's erratic fiscal results reflected this troublesome trend, as annual sales vacillated from a high of BFr 59.1 million in 1991 to 1992 to a low of BFr 48.7 million in 1993 to 1994. As a result, Interbrew started seeking a way to penetrate the all-important North American beer market. This was not an easy task: Anheuser-Busch and Miller commanded a combined total of two-thirds of the U.S. market, leaving the rest of the industry's competitors to fight over the dregs.

But Interbrew got a couple of very important breaks in the mid-1990s. First was a market trend that saw craft beers and imports chalking up double-digit sales increases as consumers sought out unique tastes. But even more importantly for Interbrew, an overall consolidation of the global beer industry put Canada's John Labatt Ltd. into play in 1995. Gerald Schwartz's Onex Corp. soon launched an uninvited attempt to take over Toronto's John Labatt Ltd. for US$2.3 billion. Labatt CEO George Taylor put out a summons for a "white knight" that was answered with a personal response from Interbrew CEO Hans Meerloo. By midyear, Interbrew was able to bring a successful C$2.7 billion (US$2 billion) offer for Labatt, with particular interest in Labatt's international holdings. The deal was also structured so that Labatt's non-brewing enterprises, including broadcasting interests, could be sold off afterward; company spokesman Gerard Fauchey told *Mclean's* in June 1995: "We're brewers, not managers of hockey or baseball teams or television stations."

Although some industry observers thought the price, at 14 times cash flow, was steep, Interbrew CEO Meerloo perceived several valuable factors in the deal. Chief among these was Labatt's extensive North American distribution system, which could be used to peddle the parent company's trendy European brands throughout the United States and Canada, particularly the flagship Stella Artois brand. Labatt's patented process for making "ice beer" held out the potential for increased brand differentiation, global licensing revenues, and cost reductions, not to mention the fact that Labatt's flagship brand ranked second among Canada's beer labels, with a 45 percent market share. Significantly, Labatt was also Canada's most profitable brewer. Finally, the new subsidiary's multi-brand strategy ("50 beers exported to 40 countries") meshed well with Interbrew's own program. As then President Hugo Powell of Labatt's told *Mclean's* in June of 1995: "Right from our first two-hour meeting, we saw that our companies shared many values. We realized we had a chance to get a committed, patient owner who could provide great growth potential." The acquisition brought with it a 22 percent stake in Mexico's Dos Equis brand, which boasted a 45 percent share of that country's market, as well as America's Rolling Rock brand. The merger nearly doubled Interbrew's annual revenues and advanced it from 15th among the world's brewers to fourth.

Interbrew maximized the purchase of Labatt by spinning off what it considered extraneous activities that were significantly less profitable than the core brewery operation. These included Labatt Communications Inc., which encompassed a francophile sports network, the Discovery Channel, and BCL Entertainment (involved in concert promotion). The company also sold its 20 percent share of Canada Malting Co. to ConAgra Inc. and expected to divest itself of the Toronto Argonauts football team, the Toronto Blue Jays major league baseball club, and its 42 percent stake in the Toronto SkyDome. These sales of these assets was expected to net US$1 billion and helped reduce the US$1.6 billion debt accumulated in the friendly takeover. However, it was not until 2000 that Interbrew was able to sell the Toronto Blue Jays, when Canadian cable company Rogers Communications made a bid in July of that year. The deal closed with Rogers acquiring an 80 percent stake in the team, with Interbrew retaining 20 percent.

It seemed that CEO Meerloo's two-year term in office had been highly successful. Not only did he elevate Interbrew to the

Key Dates:

1717: Sébastien Artois acquires and renames the Den Horen Brewery.

1853: The Piedboeuf Brewery is founded.

1920: The Piedboeuf Brewery is acquired by the Van Damme family.

1987: The Artois Brewery and Piedboeuf Brewery combine to form Interbrew.

1991: Interbrew acquires Belle-Vue Brewery in Belgium and Borsodi Sör beer brand in Hungary.

1993: The company disposes of Coca-Cola Bottling SA subsidiary.

1994: The company ceases operations in Africa, and makes several key international acquisitions; begins to sell Stella Artois in China.

1995: The company acquires John Labatt Ltd.; CEO Hans Meerloo resigns.

1996: Interbrew sells Moretti SpA to Heineken and Labatt Brewing U.K. to Whitbread Beer Company; forms joint venture with Femsa Cerveza SA de CV (Mexico).

1999: The company acquires interests in Bosnia and Russia; Hugo Powell becomes CEO; Beer.com, a promotional web site, is launched.

2000: The company acquires brewing operations of Whitbread PLC and Bass PLC; issues an IPO and begins trading on the Euronext Brussels exchange; is raided by the European Commission along with several other breweries in a cartel investigation.

2001: Interbrew is fined for participating in a secret cartel from 1993 to 1998.

2002: The company sells the Carling portion of Bass to Adolph Coors Company and closes the deal to acquire Beck's.

---

upper echelon of the brewing industry, but he was also credited with more than doubling the corporation's net margins via an early 1990s reorganization. The BFr 20 billion program cut costs and reinvigorated marketing across the board, thereby doubling profits from BFr 1.3 million in fiscal 1992 to BFr 2.7 million in fiscal 1994, despite a 17 percent reduction in annual revenues over the same period.

Notwithstanding these achievements, the Van Dammes and the de Spoelberchs were apparently unhappy with the Labatt price tag. Represented by board members Viscount Philippe de Spoelberch and Alexandre Van Damme, the families apparently blamed Meerloo, who resigned in the fall of 1995. A 1995 *Forbes* article asserted that ''Interbrew is now without a clear leader. Johnny Thijs in Europe and Hugo Powell in Canada are chief operating officers who report to Chairman Paul De Keersmaeker . . . a crony of the owners.'' Some analysts have cited dissension among the de Spoelberch and Van Damme factions for the high turnover in the chief executive office.

Following the Labatt acquisition, Interbrew was reorganized into two primary divisions. One focused on Europe, Asia, and Africa, while the other concentrated on the Americas. Interbrew

began importing its Stella Artois to the People's Republic of China via joint ventures formed in 1994 and 1996. The company hoped to establish a strong foothold in what was expected to be the world's fastest-growing consumer market of the 21st century. The continuing decline of European beer consumption and subsequent price wars not only encouraged Interbrew's expansion outside the Continent, but also fueled the divestment of some European interests. In 1995, for example, Interbrew sold its Italian affiliate, Moretti, to Heineken NV. The company also revealed its plan to divest its limited mineral water and soft drink interests and use the proceeds to reduce debt. In 1999, Interbrew revamped operations into one global structure.

Dominated by Labatt, the Americas division focused on rationalizing the newest operations into Interbrew's global beer family. In his first annual report, Hugo Powell, now division COO, emphasized globalization, cost-cutting, fortification of brands, and capital investment as keys to this business' future.

The Labatt purchase began an ongoing period of expansion through acquisition for Interbrew, as over the next seven years the company began buying breweries large and small, always with an eye toward that brewery's market share in its home country. These included a 67 percent stake in Bulgaria's Bourgasko Pivo, 80 percent of Bulgaria's Astika, 50.8 percent of Ukraine's DESNA, 62.5 percent of Bulgaria's Pleven Brewe, a merger with Russia's Sun Brewing Ltd. to create Sun Interbrew, a majority stake in Bosnia's Uniline, 81.4 percent of Ukraine's Rogan, 40.8 percent of Slovenia's Pivovarna Union, a full acquisition of Germany's Diebels, and several more. By the year 2000, the company had brewing operations in 23 countries, up from only four a decade before. Now Interbrew's chief executive since 1999, Hugo Powell told the London *Financial Times* in September 2000 that ''The beer industry is consolidating fairly rapidly and will continue to do so. By operating as a local brewer and achieving the scale of an international business we get the best of both worlds.'' Interbrew at this point ranked third worldwide, behind Anheuser-Busch and Heineken. Also in 2000, Interbrew made its entry into *Fortune* magazine's list of most admired companies in the beverages category, ranking at number 10.

During the same period, Interbrew turned its attentions to the North American market, introducing its Stella Artois brand in New York late in 1998. A subsequent rise in popularity in Belgian food and beer in general in New York City made conditions favorable for Interbrew to import its many specialty brands, encouraged at least in part by promotional efforts from the company itself, including one involving renown Belgian chef Herwig Van Hove in late 2000. Interbrew's move into North America came at an opportune time; a 1996 article in *Country Living* magazine noted that the U.S. craze for microbrews in the 1990s had opened the door for foreign imports, which U.S. beer drinkers were now ready to try. It seemed that Interbrew's strategy of buying specialty beers and shipping them around the world was perfect for such an environment.

Interbrew's two major acquisitions, however, were the U.K.'s Bass, and Germany's Beck's. In early 2000, Bass had 25 percent of the U.K. market while Whitbread, a competing brand, had 15.8 percent. Both companies were up for sale that year; at the same time, Interbrew announced its plans to go public before the end of the year. By June, Interbrew had acquired Whitbread's brewing business for £400 million (US$590.9 million) and Bass' brewing operations for £2.3 billion (US$3.5 billion). Both companies had elected to sell their brewing businesses in order to concentrate on leisure and hotel industries, leaving Interbrew with a controlling share in the U.K. beer market. For this very reason, however, the deal raised regulatory concerns, and the U.K. Competition Commission threatened to force the sale of Bass to a government-approved buyer in January 2001, not long after Interbrew issued its IPO. Interbrew sought a judicial review of the case, and was rewarded in May 2001 when the British High Court overturned the commission's decision, claiming that Interbrew had been treated unfairly. Nonetheless, Powell told the London *Financial Times* in June 2001 that "We have assumed from January that we would be faced with a disposition and that the disposition would be Bass in the UK." The situation was eventually resolved when Interbrew agreed to sell Bass' Carling brand to Coors, the U.S.'s third-largest brewer, for £1.2 billion (US$1.75 billion). At the end of the shakeout, Interbrew retained a 20.6 percent share of the British beer market.

Another threat to Interbrew's IPO plans was an investigation by the European Commission into alleged price-fixing by the company. In March 2000, inspectors from the European Commission raided the headquarters of several major European breweries, including Interbrew's Netherlands office. The purpose of the investigation was to determine the existence of a cartel in the European beer market because, as a spokesperson for the Commission stated in the London *Financial Times:* "There are a number of countries where the beer market is dominated by two or three big players, but it is not always the same players in each market." The move was part of a wave of new antitrust measures in various industries across Europe, prompted by the move to a single currency and, thus, a more unified market where price-fixing could have farther-reaching consequences. The Commission's antitrust commissioner, Mario Monti, was quoted in *Business Week* as saying, "We now have a single market and need a new competition policy." In October the Commission accused both Interbrew and Alken Maes of operating illegal cartels, and in December 2001 fined both companies, as well as two others, for their participation in secret cartels from 1993 to 1998. Interbrew's cooperation with the Commission, however, won it a reduced fine, from 10 percent of its turnover to EUR 46.5 million (US$30 million).

Despite these complications, Interbrew went through with its IPO, which allowed it to pursue a broader range of financing possibilities than would be available to a privately held company. The London *Financial Times* quoted CEO Powell in its April 26, 2000, edition: "The listing will be the start of a new era. Access to external funds is a major advantage which will optimise Interbrew's acquisition opportunities." In addition, proceeds from the IPO would help pay off the incurred debt from the Bass and Whitbread acquisitions. By November some details of the IPO were available: 88.2 million shares, or roughly 21 percent, would be made available in December. Chairman Paul De Keersmaeker was quoted in the November 9 edition of *The New York Times* as saying that "expansion on the international level is vital for our company," as Interbrew's strategy all along had involved the movement of local brews into other markets. The IPO, issued on December 1, 2000, was valued at US$2.5 billion.

Within six months, Interbrew had its eye on its next major acquisition: privately owned Beck's. As one of Germany's biggest breweries, with 2000 sales of around US$800 million and operations in 120 countries, Beck's represented an attractive opportunity for the rapidly expanding Interbrew. Although its Bass purchase was still in question, in July 2001 Interbrew emerged as the front-runner to acquire Beck's, and in August beat out competing offers from Scottish & Newcastle and Anheuser-Busch with a deal worth £1.1 billion (US$1.58 billion). Powell called the deal "a unique opportunity to buy a global brand" in the London *Financial Times*, adding, "We don't see any comparable brand being available for acquisition for the next three to five years." The deal met with criticism in the financial community where concerns were raised that as Stella Artois and Beck's brands competed with each other, the new acquisition meant that Interbrew would be competing against itself. The deal also raised competition concerns similar to those attending the Bass purchase, this time from the European Commission which was already investigating the company for illegal price-fixing. However, the Commission cleared the deal in October 2001, and it was finalized in early 2002.

While Interbrew focused on new acquisitions, it also concentrated on local operations worldwide, including the opening of themed Belgian Beer Café bars. By mid-2001, 31 such bars were in operation across Europe and in the United States, Australia, and New Zealand. In September of the same year Interbrew took over distribution of Guinness and Kilkenny beers in France with an eye toward increasing Guinness' market share in that country. At the same time, the company embraced a more global marketing strategy, including the launch of a non-brand-specific web site for beer lovers, Beer.com, in 1999. In 2001 the company announced its intentions to issue a compilation CD associated with the site with selections chosen from over 1,600 submissions received during that year's Rolling Rock Battle of the Bands contest.

Interbrew's strategy seemed to be working. In 2001 the company claimed a 63 percent rise in profits, to EUR 200.2 million (US$177.7 million), with a 56 percent rise in overall sales. Entering 2002, it looked very much as though Interbrew intended to continue its strategy of global acquisition and local branding as rumors circulated that its next purchase would be South African Breweries, an acquisition that, if completed, would make Interbrew the second largest brewer in the world behind Anheuser-Busch. By January 2002, *Business Week* had observed that Interbrew was now a serious contender with Heineken for the number two spot and was in second place in terms of volume.

Principal Subsidiaries

Astika (Bulgaria; 82%); Bass Beers Worldwide Italy; Bass Beers Worldwide Spain (34%); Bianca Interbrew Bergenbier (Romania; 51%); Borsodi Sörgyar (Hungary; 97%); Brasseries de Luxembourg (26.5%); Brasseries Stella Artois (France); Brauerei Diebels (Germany); Burgasko (Bulgaria; 74%); Cerveceria Cuauhtemoc Moctezuma (Mexico; minority share 30%); Chernigiv Brewery Desna (Ukraine; 51%); Guangzhou

Zhujiang (China; 45%); Industrija Piva I Sokova Trebjesa (Yugoslavia; 64.8%); Interbrew Asia Pacific (Singapore); Interbrew Belgium; Interbrew Efes Brewery (Romania; 50%); Interbrew Nederland; Interbrew U.K.; Jingling Breweries (China; 60%); Kamenitza (Bulgaria; 70%); Labatt Breweries of Canada; Labatt USA (70%); Marina Hemingway (Cuba; 50%); Nanjing Breweries (China; 80%); National Distribution Company (Romania; 56%); Oriental Brewery Company Ltd. (South Korea; 34%); Prazké pivovary a.s. (Czech Republic; 77%); Proberco (Romania; 77%); Sun Interbrew Russia (34%); Staropramen Slovakia (34%); Uniline export-import d.o.o. (Bosnia; 51%); Zagrebacka Pivovara (Croatia;66%).

Principal Competitors

Anheuser-Busch; Heineken; Molson.

Further Reading

"The Adventurous Life of the Belgians," *The Economist*, June 10, 1995, p. 56.

"And the Winners Are . . .," *Fortune*, October 2, 2000, p. 191+.

"Another Interbrew Purchase," *East European Markets*, February 16, 1996.

Barrington, Stephen, "Belgian Brewer Interbrew Supports Beer Lovers' Site," *Advertising Age*, November 1, 1999, p. 54.

Beirne, Mike, "Interbrew Sings Praises of Beer.com," *Brandweek*, August 13, 2001, p. 40.

"Belgian Blast," *Cheers*, November 2000, p. 14.

"Belgians Take Off out West," *Beverage World*, June 1992, p. 10.

"Big Brewer Comes Out of Shadows," *Wall Street Journal*, June 28, 2000, p. A14.

Bilefsky, Dan, "Belgian Brewers Accused of Operating Cartel," *Financial Times* (London), October 3, 2000, p. 9.

——, "Interbrew IPO Is Four Times Subscribed," *Financial Times* (London), November 30, 2000, p. 31.

——, "Interbrew Keeps a Clear Head: Regulatory Concerns Fail to Dent Brewer's IPO Confidence," *Financial Times* (London), October 30, 2000, p. 38.

"Brewer Wins Court Ruling," *New York Times*, May 24, 2001, p. W1.

Brooks, Christopher, *Country Living*, July 1996, pp. 128–9.

Buckley, Neil, "Interbrew to Fund Deals with Listing," *Financial Times* (London), April 26, 2000, p. 30.

"Bulgarian Beer Finds Buyers," *East European Markets*, June 9, 1995.

"Business This Week," *The Economist*, June 17, 2000, p. 5.

"Carling's Sale Signals the Start of Big Shake-Up for British Brewing," *Grocer*, February 9, 2002, p. 52.

Clarke, Hilary, "Belgium's Strong Drinks," *International Management*, June 1992, pp. 62–64.

"Commission Fines Belgian and Luxembourg Brewers for Market-Fixing," *European Report*, December 8, 2001, p. 345.

"Consolidation in Beer Industry Increasing," *Modern Brewery Age*, July 10, 2000, p. 28.

Daykin, Tom, "Miller Brewery Taps into Foreign Markets," *Milwaukee Journal Sentinel*, December 4, 2000.

Dombey, Daniel, "Interbrew Still Assumes Forced Disposal of Bass," *Financial Times* (London), June 13, 2001, p. 24.

Dombey, Daniel, Adam Jones, and Bettina Sener, "Interbrew Swallows Beck's for GBP1.1bn," *Financial Times* (London), August 7, 2001, p. 23.

"European Beer Market Consolidates," *Beverage Industry*, June 13, 2000, p. 6.

"Freddy Heineken's Recipe May Be Scrapped," *Business Week*, January 28, 2002, p. 56.

Gibbens, Robert, "Interbrew Sells Labatt Communications to Management-Led Group," *Financial Times* (London), July 18, 1995.

Gibbens, Robert, "John Labatt Agrees to $2 Bill Takeover by Interbrew," *Financial Times* (London), June 9, 1995.

Guerrera, Francesco, and Daniel Dombey, "Brussels Clears Interbrew to Swallow Beck's," *Financial Times* (London), October 27, 2001, p. 17.

——, "Brussels Raises Concerns Over Interbrew Deal," *Financial Times* (London), October 15, 2001, p. 29.

"Guinness Deal," *Marketing Week*, September 6, 2001, p. 35.

"Guinness Signs Distribution Agreement with Interbrew for France," *European Report*, September 5, 2001, p. 600.

Hargreaves, Deborah, "Inspectors Raid Large Breweries," *Financial Times* (USA), March 25, 2000, p. 2.

"Interbrew," *Liquid Foods International*, October 1999, p. 9.

"Interbrew Acquires 40.8% of Pivovarna Union (Slovenie) After IPA," *European Report*, January 30, 2002, p. 600.

"Interbrew Bags Ukrainian Brewer," *Corporate Money*, January 31, 2001, p. 4.

"Interbrew Buys Beck," *Beverage Industry*, September 2001, p. 11.

"Interbrew Buys 62.5% Stake in Bulgaria's Pleven Brewe," *European Report*, February 17, 1999.

"Interbrew Circles Over SAB," *Grocer*, December 1, 2001, p. 6.

"Interbrew Co-operation Wins It a Reduced Fine," *Grocer*, December 8, 2001, p. 12.

"Interbrew Develops Global Structure," *Duty-Free News International*, November 15, 1999, p. 13.

"Interbrew Finalises Acquisition of Diebels," *European Report*, September 12, 2000, p. 600.

"Interbrew Finalises Acquisition of German Brewers Beck," *European Report*, February 13, 2002, p. 600.

"Interbrew Programme," *Marketing Week*, August 23, 2001, p. 28.

"Interbrew Sells Carling to Coors for GPB1.2 Billion," *European Report*, January 9, 2002, p. 600.

"Interbrew Still Thirsting for Fresh Acquisitions in Its Quest to Consolidate the World's Beers," *Financial Times* (London), September 27, 2000.

"Interbrew to Take Counter Measures on British Ban," *Xinhua News Agency*, January 4, 2001.

"Interbrew to Use Acquisition to Build Brands in Ukraine," *Euromarketing*, September 17, 1996, p. 2.

"International Briefs: Interbrew to Invest in Russian Brewer," *New York Times*, April 6, 1999, p. C4.

"Invasion of the Cartel Cops," *Business Week*, May 8, 2000, p. 130.

Jones, Adam, "Interbrew Ordered to Sell Carling," *Financial Times* (London), September 19, 2001.

Kelly, Brendan, "Rogers Makes Pitch for Blue Jays," *Variety*, July 24, 2000, p. 21.

Khermouch, Gerry, "Interbrew's Star, Stella, Makes Quiet N.Y. Entry," *Brandweek*, October 12, 1998, p. 8.

——, "Labatt Shuffles U.S. as Interbrew Charges In," *Brandweek*, June 12, 1995, p. 3.

"Leaked SAB Bid Document Doctored," *Africa News Service*, December 3, 2001.

Macklem, Katherine, "The Blue Jay Play: In the Name of 'Convergence,' Ted Rogers Buys Toronto's Ailing Baseball Team," *Maclean's*, September 11, 2000, p. 34.

Meller, Paul, "Anonymous Interbrew Takes on the Kings of Beer," *New York Times*, August 12, 2001, sec. 3, p. 4.

——, "Big Belgian Beer Maker Posts 63% Rise in Profit," *New York Times*, September 6, 2001, p. W1.

Moreira, Peter, "Coors Grabs Carling from Interbrew," *The Daily Deal*, December 24, 2001.

Munk, Nina, "Make Mine Hoegaarden," *Forbes*, December 18, 1995, pp. 124–126.

Oram, Roderick, "International Company News: Heineken Confirms Moretti Purchase," *Financial Times* (International), February 27, 1996.

Parker-Pope, Tara, "Beer Consumption in Europe Wanes in Wake of a Widespread Recession," *Wall Street Journal*, February 21, 1995, p. A13.

Parry, Diane, "Bass Sale Closes Brewing Chapter," *Leisure Week*, June 29, 2000, p. 8.

Raabe, Steve, "Coors' Officials Tout Potential of $1.7 Billion British-Brewery Purchase," *Denver Post*, December 28, 2001.

Ratner, Juliana, Francesco Guerrera, and Charles Pretzlik, "Interbrew Eyes Whitbread and Bass," *Financial Times* (London), April 29, 2000.

Robertiello, Jack, "New York Goes Belgian," *Cheers*, July-August 1999, p. 20.

Saigol, Lina, and Peter Thal Larsen, "Interbrew Leads Race for Beck's," *Financial Times* (London), July 24, 2001, p. 21.

Swift, Melanie, "Whitbread Dumps Beer for Leisure," *Leisure Week*, June 1, 2000, p.1.

Symonds, William C., and Linda Bernier, "A Belgian Brewer's Plans Come to a Head," *Business Week*, June 19, 1995, p. 56.

Tagliabue, John, "Still Growing, Brewing Giant to Sell Shares," *New York Times*, November 9, 2000, p. W1.

Vlessing, Etan, "Rogers Catches Blue Jays in $122 Million Play," *Hollywood Reporter*, September 5, 2000, p. 32.

Voyle, Susanna, and Charles Pretzlik, "Decision Leaves Industry Shaken, Not Stirred," *Financial Times* (London), January 4, 2001.

——, "Interbrew Buys Bass Round for GPB2.3bn," *Financial Times* (London), June 15, 2000.

Whitehouse, Christine, and Simon Robinson, "Biz Watch," *Time International*, December 10, 2001, p. 16.

Whitfield, Bruce, "Timothy Wood: Global Market Report," *Africa News Service*, January 29, 2002.

Willis, Andrew, "The Winning Brew," *Maclean's*, June 19, 1995, pp. 44–45.

——, "A Bidding Battle: Labatt's Sale of Hot TV and Sports Assets Draws a Crowd," *Maclean's*, June 26, 1995, pp. 24–25.

—April Dougal Gasbarre
—update: Genevieve Williams

International Power PLC

Senator House
85 Queen Victoria Street
London EC4V 4DP
United Kingdom
Telephone: +44 (0) 20-7320-8600
Fax: +44 (0) 20-7320-8700
Web site: http://www.internationalpowerplc.com

Public Company
Incorporated: 2000
Employees: 2,300
Sales: £1.1 billion
Stock Exchanges: London New York
Ticker Symbol: IPR
NAIC: 221122 Electric Power Distribution; 221112 Fossil
    Fuel Power Generation; 221119 Other Electric Power
    Generation

International Power PLC is the largest of the three main electricity-generating companies created from the breakup of the nationalized electricity industry in England and Wales. Carved out as a separate division of the Central Electricity Generating Board in 1989 as privatization loomed, International Power was incorporated as a public limited company (PLC) in 1990 and the majority of its shares were sold to the public a year later. International Power, Nuclear Electric, and PowerGen became the big three electricity generators in England and Wales. By the mid-1990s, International Power's and PowerGen's market shares were decreasing and continued to decline as the industry became more competitive. While International Power is likely to continue to hold a significant niche in the home energy market, the company is also looking to allied ventures for new areas of growth, in particular the opportunities offered in international power markets.

Commercial Electricity, National Policy, and the Creation of National Power

Electricity was first harnessed for practical use in the United Kingdom in the late 19th century with the introduction of street lighting in 1881. By 1921, over 480 authorized but independent electricity suppliers had sprung up throughout England and Wales, creating a rather haphazard system operating at different voltages and frequencies. In recognition of the need for a more coherent, interlocking system, the Electricity (Supply) Act of 1926 created a central authority to encourage and facilitate a national transmission system. This objective of a national grid was achieved by the mid-1930s.

The state consolidated its control of the utility with the Electricity Act of 1947, which collapsed the distribution and supply activities of 505 separate bodies into 12 regional boards, at the same time assigning generating assets and liabilities to one government-controlled authority. A further Electricity Act in 1957 created a statutory body, the Central Electricity Generating Board (CEGB), which dominated the whole electricity system in England and Wales. Generator of virtually all the electricity in the two countries, the CEGB, as owner and operator of the transmission grid, supplied electricity to the area boards, which they in turn distributed and sold within their regions.

This situation continued for 30 years, until the government mooted the idea of privatizing the electricity industry in 1987. The proposal became the Electricity Act of 1989, and a new organizational scheme was unveiled. The CEGB was splintered into four divisions, destined to become successor companies: National Power, PowerGen, Nuclear Electric, and the National Grid Company (NGC). National Power and PowerGen were to share between them England and Wales' fossil-fueled power stations; Nuclear Electric was to take over nuclear power stations; and the NGC was to be awarded control of the national electricity distribution system. The 12 Area boards were converted, virtually unchanged, into 12 Regional Electricity Companies (RECs), and these were given joint ownership of the NGC. At the end of 1990 the shares of the RECs were the first to be sold to the public. The majority of National Power and PowerGen's shares were offered for sale the following year, though the government retained ownership of 40 percent of each of the new companies' shares.

National Power before and after Industry Privatization

In order to understand National Power's role within the electricity industry it is helpful to understand how the system

Company Perspectives:

International Power is a leading independent power producer that generates enough electricity to light millions of homes around the world. We have the resources and skills to play an active role in all phases of the power generation chain, including development, construction, operation, and trading and marketing.

operated until the extensive changes brought on by the Utilities Act of 2000. The provision of electricity consisted of four components: generation, transmission, distribution, and supply. In England and Wales, generation was the province of National Power, Powergen, and Nuclear Electric. Transmission is the transfer of electricity via the national grid through overhead lines, underground cables, and NGC substations. Distribution was the delivery of electricity from the national grid to local distribution systems operated by the Regional Electricity Companies. Supply, a term distinct from distribution in the electricity industry, refers to the transaction whereby electricity is purchased from the generators and transmitted to customers. Under the terms of its license, National Power had the right to supply electricity directly to consumers, but in the company's earlier years that right was little exercised. National Power's usual customers were the RECs, which in turn sold the electricity to the end users.

A new trading market was devised with the privatization scheme for bulk sales of electricity from generators to distributors—the pool. A rather complicated pricing procedure existed in the pool: each generating station offered a quote for each half hour of the day, based on an elaborate set of criteria including the operating costs of that particular plant, the time of day, the expected demand for electricity, and the available capacity of the station. The NGC arranged these quotes in a merit order and made the decisions regarding when to call each plant into operation. The pool system was not relied upon exclusively, however the generators frequently made contractual arrangements with distributors for a specified period of time as a means of mutual protection against fluctuations in the pool price.

National Power's position in the industry is a legacy of the comparative status it inherited with privatization. The undisputed leader of the industry, National Power provided nearly half the electricity supplied in England and Wales via its 40 power stations, boasting an aggregate Declared Net Capacity or Capability (DNC) of 29,486MW (a megawatt here is defined as the generating capacity of a power station in any given half hour). Its smaller rival PowerGen, in second place, had 18,764MW DNC. Nuclear Electric's figure was 8,357MW, the National Grid Company controlled 2,088MW, and British Nuclear Fuels PLC, the United Kingdom Atomic Energy Authority, and small independent generators together accounted for about 2,900MW. Another, though limited, source was provided by linkages with the Scottish and French electricity systems, with which import or export deals were sometimes agreed. National Power and PowerGen between them thus controlled 78 percent of the electricity market in England and Wales, of which about 46 percent was held by National Power, with the majority of the rest controlled by Nuclear Electric.

Privatization of the utility was designed to promote a beneficial result through the free play of market forces. The introduction of competition in power generation, it was argued, would lead both to greater efficiency within the industry and to lower prices for the consumer. Within a few short years, however, concerns had arisen, as some critics of the scheme had predicted from the start. The creation of three big players holding such a significant majority of the electricity-generating market was never likely to embody the purest form of free market operations.

In 1994, the industry watchdog, the Office of Electricity Regulation (Offer), became concerned about National Power and PowerGen's continuing dominance of the market. The market share of the big two had in fact declined since privatization, with National Power controlling some 33 percent and PowerGen holding less than 25 percent, but rumors were rife that Offer would refer them to the Monopolies and Mergers Commission (MMC). After six months of deliberation, Offer stopped short of that proceeding, but the regulator imposed strictures on the two generating companies, requiring that they should use all reasonable endeavors to sell a specified amount of generating capacity—in the case of National Power 3,000 to 4,000MW, or 15 percent, of its total power output—and submit to price capping for a period of two years.

The demand to sell a portion of its holdings was expected to cause little hardship to National Power. Moreover, the issue of which plant to sell when was left to the company's discretion, provided it complied with Offer's deadline of December 31, 1995. Thus the company would not be forced to make a disadvantageous sale. In preference to an outright sale, some speculated that National Power might arrange an asset exchange with a foreign power company. Another alternative under consideration was the demerger option, whereby a new company, designed to own and operate the capacity in question, could be created from a portion of National Power's capital holdings.

The required price caps, ironically, were likely to prove less burdensome to National Power and PowerGen than to the state-owned Nuclear Electric and to small independents, both existing and potential. While Offer's strictures caused the two largest players to lose around one-third of their market share, the companies retained their dominant position in the market. National Power and PowerGen had, in effect, continued to control the establishment of pool prices, and this was unlikely to change to any significant degree. Residential customers, who purchased their electricity through the RECs, saw little change in their electricity bills, while most major industrial customers, who purchased straight from the pool, saw their prices fall 20 percent. While the potential for price hikes existed in long-term forecasts, given the costs of an environmental cleanup, the company hoped to offset such increases with greater efficiency.

The government, apart from its concerns about fair competition and price, was especially eager to resolve any controversy or questions regarding National Power and PowerGen to clear the way for the sale of its remaining 40 percent share in each of the two companies. The sell-off to the public in February 1995 raised a welcome £4 billion for the government, some £2.5 billion of which was attributable to National Power. Controversy dogged the two generators right to the end, however, as spiraling prices in the electricity pool, albeit over a period of only a month, prompted Offer to delay publication of the share prospectus.

The Shift from Coal to Gas

The electricity industry was slowly but dramatically changing in the 1990s. While plans were being laid to modernize and improve power generation, coal- and oil-fired plants remained the mainstay of the utility. Most of the stations National Power inherited after privatization were products of the 1960s and 1970s (with the notable exception of the 1980s-vintage Drax). British-mined coal remained, in 1995, the overwhelmingly dominant fuel source, but National Power, like others in the industry, was exploring a more diversified fuel base.

The company was slowly reducing the stockpiles of coal accumulated in the days of government ownership when the CEGB bought more generously than necessary from the British Coal Corporation. Since privatization National Power had already shut down some coal-fired plants. Some capability was made redundant by excess generating capacity, and more was jettisoned in favor of the trend toward combined cycle gas turbine plant (CCGT) during the so-called dash for gas. National Power's first CCGT plant, at Killingholme, South Humberside, was completed in 1993. One in North Wales followed in 1994, with another in Bedfordshire expected in 1995, and yet another in Oxfordshire in 1996. Moreover, a fifth CCGT plant was in the early planning stages. More closures of coal-fired plants were likely as the new CCGT stations came online.

Linked economic and environmental factors motivated the move to gas. Environmental improvements were urgently needed in the energy industry—the issue was long ignored in the state sector. Regulations emanating from both London and Brussels were becoming increasingly stringent and were making coal increasingly unattractive. Despite the availability of technology designed to reduce sulfur-dioxide emissions from coal-fired stations (the primary cause of acid rain), for example, it was often more economically advantageous to simply replace these stations with CCGT plants. The exception during this time was Drax, National Power's massive North Yorkshire coal-fired power station, which supplied approximately 10 percent of England's and Wales' electricity. In the biggest project of its kind in the world, National Power was cleaning up the plant through the implementation of flue gas desulfurization (FGD) retrofits, designed to significantly reduce sulfur-dioxide emissions. The effort began even before privatization but was not expected to be completed until 1996. Costing an estimated £65.8 billion, the station was expected to result in a 90 percent reduction in harmful emissions.

To the dismay of the beleaguered British coal industry, National Power, like the other electricity generators, continued to look at the import of foreign coal for use in its stations. Foreign-mined coal was not only potentially cheaper but in general had a significantly lower-sulfur content than its British counterpart, thus obviating the need for expensive desulfurization equipment.

With gas as an increasingly popular and sensible option for the energy industry, National Power also took steps to ensure its own reliable and cost-effective supply; in 1991 alone the company arranged to buy the entire output from the Caister field in the North Sea, made a 15-year deal with Norwegian suppliers, and made another deal with Ranger Oil in the United Kingdom. The company was also involved in gas exploration, having a 25 percent stake in a consortium led by Total Oil Marine which was exploring a block in the southern North Sea. Even wind power was being investigated and employed, though on a very small scale as of the mid-1990s. The subsidiary National Wind Power Ltd. was established in 1991 and was expected to be producing 250MW by the end of the century.

National Power's Expanding Scope

National Power was also moving into the field of combined heat and power generation (CHP), another wave of the future for the energy industry. One of National Power's business units, National Power Cogen, was responsible for the development of schemes for such clients as Lancaster University, the chemical manufacturers Albright & Wilson Ltd., the paper manufacturers SCA, and Sterling Organics Ltd., makers of paracetemol.

National Power branched out into the industrial property business in 1993, leasing land at its Eggborough power station to an air separation plant, Air Gas Products. The mutually profitable idea behind the arrangement was that new factories, conveniently located, could tap directly into their power source, therefore rendering unnecessary the need for a middleman in the form of a regional electricity company.

National Power also looked to the international arena for its future growth. The CEGG's overseas activities in its state sector days were restricted almost exclusively to consulting projects carried out by the subsidiary British Electricity International

Ltd. After privatization, with its share of the home market dwindling, National Power substantially boosted its international profile. The creation of a full-fledged division within National Power devoted to researching and developing overseas business strategies and opportunities via a 1993 internal restructure is indicative of the company's vision of its future.

American National Power Established in the United States

In 1993 the company moved into the United States with the purchase of American National Power for £103 million. A well-established and successful enterprise, American National Power operated in Virginia, Georgia, and New Jersey. National Power's other major foreign ventures included Portugal's Pego power station, owned by a consortium led by National Power, and a £64 million investment in an oil-fired power station project in Pakistan. While National Power's international presence was still young, the company was confident of its prospects. Independent financial commentators tended to agree. Blessed as the company was with healthy cash reserves, and clearly aware of the tremendous potential of the international market, National Power could expect to be well compensated through such wise investments.

A look at National Power's 1995 sales figures showed a mixed but generally optimistic prospect. On one hand, the company's market share was much reduced and electricity prices were down, and capital expenditure was up due to investments in new plants and environmental improvements. Nevertheless, costs to the company were dramatically reduced due to a rigorous, some might say ruthless, cost-cutting program implemented since privatization. Under the plan, rationalization and increased efficiency measures decisively chopped operational costs, fuel supply expenses were pared, and staff costs were drastically slashed (the pre-privatization workforce of 17,000 was just over 5,000 in 1995). As a result National Power saw consistently rising profits despite continually falling market share.

Poised for Expansion

Controller of nearly half of Britain's electricity market at the end of 1990, National Power had only a third of that market four years later, and the company's share was expected to diminish still more as competition increased. Nonetheless, National Power would likely remain a significant force in U.K. power generation as the company continued to improve and adapt to meet changing conditions in the energy industry. Furthermore, with a strong cash base to support an avowed and active interest in overseas projects, National Power was poised for international expansion.

The first attempted expansion effort began within the United Kingdom when in 1996, National Power bid for Southern Electric at the same time that PowerGen bid on Midlands Electricity PLC. According to the *Economist*, these transactions were overruled by the British government after the Monopolies and Mergers Commission (MMC), Britain's antitrust watchdog, had approved the bid. The MMC apparently allowed the bid to proceed with some reservations, stating that the mergers "may be expected to operate against the public interest." As a result, the MMC came under fire in the media for failing to understand

that huge vertical mergers between generators and distributors would reduce rather than increase competition and keep prices high.

By 1998 National Power PLC had more than 10,000MW operating, along with 8,000MW of equity, and was listed among the top 25 developers in *Independent Energy*. The publication credited the company's early international acquisitions and greenfield developments as pivotal to its being a strong force in coming years. The company continued its expansion by taking a stake in Malaysian power generator Malakoff Bhd, and added another 18 percent stake to its 48 percent share in Czech power producer Elektrarny Opatovice. National Power also entered into a joint venture with EuroGas Inc. to develop a gas-fired combined heating plant (CHP) in western Poland.

In another attempt to expand within the United Kingdom, National Power bid for Midlands Electricity in 1999, and was given a conditional go-ahead by regulators. Because of competition concerns Secretary of State for Trade and Industry Stephen Beyers declared that National Power would have to sell its 4,000MW Drax coal-fired power station and create a new system of "earn out" payments from Texas Utilities' Eastern Group before the bid could proceed. (Eastern had bought 4,000MW of capacity from National Power in June 1996 for a down payment and continued payments over eight years that were calculated through a formula based on actual output.) Drax was the largest coal-fired plant in Europe and was estimated to be worth about £2 billion. With full approval from its shareholders, National Power divested Drax to the AES Corporation of Arlington, Virginia for US$3 billion. At that time, AES owned power plants or sold electricity in 23 countries and had had operations in the United Kingdom for ten years.

This same year found National Power involved in many other kinds of new business. Ground was broken in Blackstone, Massachusetts for a 589MW gas-fired merchant power plant and was reported by *Business Wire* to be among the world's cleanest power plants. Joseph Fitzpatrick, senior vice-president of American National Power, stated, "This will be the largest power plant investment in the state in 25 years and will meet state-of-the-art environmental compliance in the United States." National Power also delved into fuel cell technology with the SRT Group, Inc. and the U.S. Department of Energy. As reported in *Battery & EV Technology*, the technology "allowed the production of inexpensive hydrogen while co-providing a reduction in on-peak energy costs."

Fuel cell technology in the United Kingdom focused on "regenerative fuel cell electrical energy that can be converted into chemical potential energy by charging, and releasing the stored energy on discharge," as explained in *Modern Power Systems*. The publication further noted, "National Power has developed a new regenerative fuel cell system and a 15MW/120MWh (megawatt hours) utility scale storage energy plant based on the technology being built at Didcot. It is believed that this will be one of the largest energy storage plants of its kind in the world."

National Power's Decision to Demerge

By November of 1999, National Power was mired in financial woes brought about by unfortunate foreign investments and regulatory pressures. The company pulled out of its multibillion-dollar Malaysian power project, deciding not to buy a 20 percent stake in the 2,420MW Kapar power station, and sold two power stations to rival companies. Dividends to shareholders were also reduced. *Europe Energy* reported, "National Power ended months of speculation over its strategy by announcing a demerger of international business from its domestic operations and the return of up to 600 million pounds (Euro 973 million) of capital to its shareholders." The publication also quoted Chairman John Collins, "The board considers that the proposed demerger represents the best way forward for the company and for our shareholders. It is now the right time for them to be established as highly focused individual entities." Collins' announcement followed the departure of Chief Executive Graham Henry who resigned to take responsibility for a loss in investor confidence in the company. The demerger created International Power PLC and Innogy PLC—the United Kingdom generating assets, with International Power consisting of the international portfolio of emerging markets of the utility.

The new CEO of International Power (IP), Peter Giller, expressed his enthusiasm on taking over the new company by volunteering to become the first British corporate chief to be paid entirely in stock. As reported in *Energy Daily*, he received nearly US$2.9 million in stock as his base pay for his first three years. He was also due to be paid an additional US$1.44 million in shares for every 20 percent increase in the company's stock price, although he would not get the extra shares unless IP's stock price went up at least 52 percent and the company's earnings per share rose by at least 21 percent over the three-year period. If all these performance goals were met Giller was to receive another stock bonus worth US$2.9 million. The catch was that Giller could not cash in any stocks for a year and would have to go without salary and benefits during that time. Judging from the rapid acquisitions and climbing profit, this remuneration arrangement apparently demonstrated that Giller applied himself to building International Power's scope, profitability, and status.

Giller noted in *Energy Daily* that volatility in an energy market, such as the rapidly rising prices in California in 2000, is not alluring. "What we need is a decent average price," he said. "You can't survive just on needle-peaks." Giller was evaluating Chicago and the upper-Midwest areas as potential untapped markets, and was also interested in New England and New York.

By April 2001, IP was growing steadily more geographically diverse with 50 percent in the United States, 20 percent in Australia, 17 percent in Spain, and with potential developments in Malaysia, Quator, Oman, Turkey, the Czech Republic, Portugal, and South Africa. Two of the most important acquisitions took place shortly after the demerger. Through its Australian National Power subsidiary, the company paid £32.4 million (A $88 million) for a 19.9 percent stake from Scottish Power, which increased its stake in the Hazelwood power station in Australia from 71.9 percent to 91.8 percent. International Power also purchased the 1,000MW Staffordshire-based Rugeley power plant in the United Kingdom from TXU Europe for US$280 million. The *Africa News Service* reported in April 2001 that International Power had established an office in South Africa to evaluate investing in the state-owned electricity group Eskom or to establish an independent power producer. The publication further noted that Malcolm Wrigley, regional direc-

tor of International Power in Southern Africa, was interested in investing in South Africa because the country had a stable economy with independent courts and a reasonable rule of law. Following this flurry of investments, the company reported in June 2001 that its first quarter profits were up by 50 percent, and the *Wall Street Journal* reported that its pre-tax profits for the first quarter of 2001 rose to £98million (EUR 155.3 million).

As stated in *Power Economics*, "Sir Neville Sims, chairman, said the strong results were as a result of the commissioning of plants in the U.S., the strength of operations in Australia, and continuing opportunities in Europe." In July International Power sold its 25 percent equity interest in Union Fenosa Generation, a major Spanish power producer, to Union Electrica Fenosa, a major Spanish power company and the majority owner, for US$560 million in cash. International Power realized more than a US$45 million return on its investment made in 1999. The year 2001 also saw International Power involved with Abu Dhabi's largest independent power and water project through the Abu Dhabi Water and Electricity Authority for the 15,000MW and 100-million gallon-per-day Shuweihat plant. IP partnered with CMS of the United States for a 40 percent stake in the US$1.6 million project.

International Power's pre-tax profit for the first nine months of 2001 came to £186 million, up from the £80 million loss during the same period the year before as National Power. *Project Finance* pointed out, "International Power has stuck to its strategy of growth in the U.S., Europe and the Middle East and Australia, claiming that the geographical spread of its operations will protect it from any market downturn." The publication expressed hope that this geographically diverse approach would be effective, especially since IP was heavily involved with two power plants in Pakistan, yet reluctantly admitted that these were about to pay a dividend for the first time in three years. International Power had a 26 percent stake in the Hub River project, the 1,292MW residual fuel oil-fired plant 45km from Karachi, and a 36 percent stake in Kot Addu, a 1,600MW CCGT plant in the Punjab region. The dividends were small but relevant to IP as the resolution of power issues in Pakistan were International Power's first major success after the demerger according to IP's London Media Relations Officer, Aarti Singhal.

Peter Barlow, director of finance at International Power in London, stated in *Project Finance*, "We have assumed that we will get no income out of Pakistan and that is reflected in our credit rating. These dividends are too small to make a difference but they are a demonstration of our relationship with the Water and Power Development Agency (WAPDA)." In spite of tensions in the Middle East, International Power remained positive about its investments, including the US$1.6 billion Shuweihat IWPP power and desalination plant in Abu Dhabi, and has about US$100 million invested in the project. Barlow stated in *Project Finance*, "We still feel that there is substantial opportunity in new build in the Middle East. Abu Dhabi is stable politically and is the best credit risk in the region." However, the major focus of IP's investment has been in the United States where there are now five operating power plants at Hartwell, Oyster Creek, Milford, Bayonne, and Midlothian, with a further 2,790MW of gross capacity under construction. International Power is expected to have at least 50 percent of its assets in the United States, all of which will be merchant risk. However,

Barlow notes that future development will not be in Texas or Massachusetts where all other U.S. plants were established.

Principal Subsidiaries

American International Power PLC; Australian International Power PLC; Hub Power Company (HUBCO) (Pakistan; 26%); Kot Addu Power Company (KAPCO) (Pakistan; 36%); Malakoff (Malaysia; 20%); Uni-Mar (Turkey; 33%).

Principal Competitors

AES; Mirant; Tractebel.

Further Reading

"Bills Will Rise for Clean Electricity," *Guardian*, January 14, 1994.

Bowman, Louise, and Peter Barlow, "Low Fat Spread," *Project Finance*, November 2001, p. 36.

"Britain's Electricity Shocker," *Economist* (Editorial), April 13, 1996.

Burr, Michael, "Top Developers of 1998," *Independent Energy*, June 1998, pp. 24–27.

"Customers Set to Benefit by up to £500m," *Financial Times*, February 12, 1994.

Day, Kathleen, "AES to Buy British Power Plant," *Washington Post*, August 1, 1999.

"DTI: Ian Lang Accepts Undertakings from PowerGen and National Power in Follow-up to MMC Reports," *M2 PressWIRE*, March 6, 1997.

"EuroGas Enters into Agreement with National Power to Develop Power Plant in Western Poland," *PR Newswire*, June 10, 1998, http://www.prnewswire.com.

"Generators in Deal to Sell Plant and Reduce Prices," *Financial Times*, February 12, 1994.

"Global Utilities Are Set to Pounce In," *Africa News Service*, April 11, 2001.

Hamid, Jalil, "Update 1-British NatPower (NPR.L) Quits Malaysia Power Deal," *Reuters*, August 1, 2000.

"International Power Acquisitive—Again," *Power Economics*, June 2001, p.30.

"International Power Continues Australian Expansion," *Corporate Money*, November 22, 2000.

"International Power Sells Stake in Spanish Generator," *Energy Daily*, July 26, 2001, p. 3.

"Investors Chronicle Survey: Electricity," *Investors Chronicle*, April 22, 1994.

"The Lex Column: Power Play," *Financial Times*, February 12, 1994.

Lobsenz, George, "International Power CEO Places Big Bet on Global IPP—His Entire Salary," *Energy Daily*, October 24, 2000.

"Mideast Power Deals," *World Gas Intelligence*, August 22, 2001, p. 5.

Mortished, Carl, "Regulator Forces Power Prospectus Rewrite," *The Times* (London), January 28, 1995, p. 25.

"MPS Update: Energy Storage: Revelation of Regenesys," *Modern Power Systems*, August 1, 1999, pp. 28–29.

"National Power Beats Forecasts," *Lloyds List*, May 19, 1994.

"National Power Breathes Life into Factories," *Yorkshire Post*, March 11, 1994.

"National Power to Close Five Plants," *Independent*, April 1, 1994.

"National Power to Consider Job Cuts," *Independent*, May 19, 1994.

"No Stampede in Power Station Sale," *Financial Times*, February 12, 1994.

"Power Generators Meet Offer to Head off MMC Enquiry," *The Times* (London), January 24, 1994.

"Rugeley Sold for $282 Million, *Power Economics*, June 2001, p. 6.

Shahriman, Johari, "Nat Power Pulls Out of Kapar Plant Consortium," *Business Times* (Malaysia), August 1, 2000.

Shepherd, Nick, "Electricity; International Power Profit Ends U.S. Fears," *Utility Week*, November 23, 2001, p. 8.

"Special Report on Competitive Power," *Daily Telegraph*, March 11, 1994.

"SRT Plans Low-Cost Reversible Fuel Cell," *Battery & EV Technology*, August 1, 1999.

"Survey of Drax: The Big Clean-Up," *Financial Times*, January 14, 1994.

"Tough Package of Not Much," *Independent*, February 12, 1994.

"TXU Sells UK Plant to International Power," *Energy Daily*, June 12, 2001, p. 3.

"UK Generators Seen Stalking Regional Power Firms," *Reuters*, September 27, 1998.

"UK Government to Decide Nat Power Fate," *Reuters*, April 8, 1999.

"UK's National Power Buy Given Green Light," *Reuters*, April 9, 1999.

"UK's National Power in Malaysian Acquisition," *European Report*, May 6, 1998.

"UK's Nat Power to Demerge," *Europe Energy*, November 26, 1999.

Waller, Martin, "Options Row Mars Power Launch," *The Times* (London), February 7, 1995, p. 23.

—Robin DuBlanc
—update: Annette Dennis McCully

Invensys PLC

Carlisle Place
London SW1P 1BX
United Kingdom
Telephone: +44 (20) 7834-3848
Fax: +44 (20) 7834-3879
Web site: http://www.invensys.com

Public Company
Incorporated: 1819 as Siebe PLC
Employees: 70,000 (2002 est.)
Sales: £6.972 billion (2002)
Stock Exchanges: OTC
Ticker Symbol: IVNSY
NAIC: 541330 Engineering Services; 221122 Electric
    Power Distribution; 511210 Software Publishers;
    541511 Custom Computer Programming Services;
    551112 Offices of Other Holding Companies

Invensys PLC grew out of the merger in 1999 of Britain's Siebe PLC and the British manufacturing conglomerate BTR PLC. Already the worldwide leader in the design, manufacture, distribution, and installation of controls and control systems as Siebe, the company has positioned itself to become a diversified manufacturing giant after merging with BTR and changing the company name to Invensys. While analysts have questioned the wisdom of Invensys' move from a relatively "pure play" controls and controls systems group to a diversified engineering and manufacturing empire, there is little doubt that the emerging company will become one of the world's leading manufacturing concerns with industry dominance in the high value-added controls and automation industries. The merger, at a price of approximately £6 billion, represents only the latest in a long span of acquisitions that had enabled Invensys to grow from a company producing revenues of just £370 million in the mid-1980s to a giant with annual sales of nearly £7 billion in 2002.

Beginnings as Siebe

Invensys' beginnings as Siebe stemmed from the arrival of former Austrian cavalry officer Augustus Siebe in London in

1819. A natural inventor, Siebe would be credited with a number of innovative products, ranging from water pump and rifle component designs to the product that would come to define Siebe for much of the 20th century—the world's first diving suit. The success of the Siebe diving suit led the company to focus on this new market, and from the 1890s, the company developed into a specialized marine engineering company with an emphasis on safety and rescue systems. As such, Siebe became a supplier to the British Royal Navy, among others, developing breathing apparatus and submarine emergency escape equipment. As the world took to the skies in the early part of the 20th century, Siebe adapted its underwater breathing apparatus for use in high-altitude conditions. By then, Siebe's designs had also gone underground, as the company developed safety and rescue equipment for mining operations. Among noteworthy Siebe products were its Proto and Salvus rescue suits—the Proto name eventually would become synonymous with rescue stations in Britain's mining community.

Throughout this time, Siebe remained a small, barely profitable manufacturing company. Until the 1960s, the company's revenue hovered below the £1.5 million mark; the company's overhead, including an extended payroll, left little of its revenue for profits. By 1963, however, the company acquired new management in the person of Barrie Stephens, formerly with General Dynamics and later granted the royal British title "Sir." Assuming the managing director's position, Stephens spent the 1960s restructuring Siebe's operations, trimming staff by more than half, and expanding the company into new directions. At the end of the 1960s, Stephens led Siebe into the first of what would become a long string of acquisitions. By the end of the decade, while bringing the company's revenues past the £2 million mark, these moves also had quintupled Siebe's profits. Siebe's business, which remained primarily British-based, doubled to reach £4 million by 1972.

A Change of Strategy at Siebe during the 1970s

In the 1970s Stephens started the process of transforming Siebe from a small domestic safety products company to a global group, targeting the broader engineering controls category. In 1972 the company made its first significant acquisition, the purchase of leading safety product specialist James North &

Sons. This company, larger than Siebe itself, was the leading European manufacturer of safety products and systems and gave Siebe its first strong foothold on the European continent. The James North acquisition also marked another company trait: rather than place the Siebe name on North's operations, Siebe continued to market its new subsidiary's products under the North brand name. The result of this practice was that the Siebe name remained relatively unknown, even though its brands led their respective markets.

The North purchase gave a new impulse to Siebe's revenue growth. By the end of 1973, Siebe's sales topped £18 million and reached £20 million the following year. Steady and continued growth followed throughout the 1970s, despite an international recession caused by the Arab oil embargo. By the end of the decade, Siebe's sales topped £50 million.

Siebe Becomes a Controls Specialist during the 1990s

Siebe continued to build its U.K. and European businesses, while eyeing entry into the North American market. The company found an opening in 1982 with the acquisition of Tecalemit, one of the leading garage equipment and automotive tubing suppliers. This addition would help raise Siebe's sales to more than £156 million by 1984. The Tecalemit purchase also would lead the company into a new direction. Included in the Tecalemit acquisition were two subsidiaries producing electronic controls systems. These did not, however, fit together with Siebe's other businesses, and the company searched for a buyer for the two subsidiaries. The search was not successful, as a long slump in the computer and electronics industries had weakened the marketplace. Nonetheless, the controls subsidiaries remained profitable operations.

The Tecalemit controls subsidiaries also provided essential pieces of the Siebe puzzle. With the company undergoing rapid growth and strong profits, Stephens's war chest provided opportunities for still larger acquisitions. The next Siebe acquisition came in 1985, with the purchase of compressed air systems and equipment specialist CompAir. That acquisition proved doubly interesting: in addition to providing Siebe with a complement to its North American garage equipment and safety equipment markets, CompAir brought with it three subsidiaries specialized in hydraulic controls systems. The new controls category fit neatly with the Tecalemit controls subsidiaries, and a new Siebe division was born.

By the end of the decade the child had grown larger than the parent. The new subsidiaries had given Siebe a solid footing in the North American market. But they also would encourage the company to invest more heavily in what was still a fairly young

industry. The long-predicted reliance on computers and computer systems was becoming more and more of a reality in the 1980s, particularly with the widespread adoption of numeric control manufacturing systems and processes and the increasing use of automation and robotics in manufacturing.

In just five years Siebe would build a worldwide presence in the controls industry. The company's revenues would soar past £1.2 billion. Although the company continued its safety equipment and other manufacturing activities, controls would become its core focus. Three important acquisitions brought Siebe to this point. The first, made in 1986, added the U.S. company Robertshaw to the growing Siebe portfolio of subsidiaries. One of the leading controls manufacturers in the North American market, Robertshaw added its specialty category—appliances—to Siebe's list.

Siebe Solidifies Itself through Acquisitions

Siebe quickly reinforced its entry into appliance controls with the acquisitions of two more U.S. companies, Ranco and Barber-Colman, in 1987. These acquisitions also gave Siebe entry into industrial and commercial building control systems as well as into automotive control systems. In the appliance control segment, meanwhile, Siebe had achieved a worldwide leadership position. Ranco also added more than 75 years of experience in the heating and air-conditioning temperature control segment, as well as control systems for commercial and home refrigeration. The Ranco and Barber-Colman acquisitions pushed Siebe's turnover past the £1 billion mark in 1988.

Siebe's longstanding leader, Barrie Stephens, who had raised the company's revenues more than 1,000 times in less than 30 years, began moving toward retirement in the 1990s. At the start of the decade, Stephens named the American Allen Yurko as the group's managing director and COO. During the years to follow, Stephens would transfer the company's day-to-day leadership to Yurko, who was named CEO in 1994. In the meantime, Siebe had gained global leadership of the controls industry.

A significant acquisition came in 1990, with the purchase of the Foxboro Company, a world leading process controls automation company based in Foxboro, Massachusetts that had fallen on hard times in the 1980s. At a price of approximately US$650 million, Siebe added Foxboro's more than US$500 million in sales of its Unix-based control automation and other control systems products. Foxboro's specialty—that of implementation of large-scale control systems for oil refineries, chemical and pharmaceutical plants, nuclear and other power generation plants, and control systems adapted to the pulp and paper industries—placed Siebe firmly at the forefront of the world's control process industry. After restructuring Foxboro's operations, including trimming an oversized management and a vast private security staff, Siebe returned its new subsidiary to profitability by 1992.

Between 1992 and 1998, Siebe would conclude an impressive number of acquisitions, ranging from the 1993 purchase of Germany's Eberle, to the 1996 acquisition of Unitech PLC, the company's largest acquisition to that date. Unitech brought the company its electronic power controls, while adding significant reinforcement to Siebe's Asian-Pacific sales, which continued to lag behind its U.S. and European sales. Other acquisitions during this period include those of Eckardt AG and Schmidt Armaturen, both of Germany, Sweden's NAF Group, Triconex Corporation, Appliance Control Technology Inc., Eliwell SpA, LeROI International, Fabex Inc., and Satchwell Controls Systems Ltd., the U.K. leader in the building automation segment. The 1997 purchase of APV PLC marked Siebe's second bid for that leading food, beverage, dairy, and pharmaceutical process automation control specialist (the first takeover attempt having been fought and lost by Siebe in the mid-1980s).

Siebe's acquisition activity enabled the company to maintain its revenue and profit growth in the face of the difficult economic climate of the first half of the 1990s. By its year end 1996, the company neared £2.6 billion in revenues. The company, which, despite its worldwide dominance of the control systems market, remained in large part unknown to the public, nonetheless became known for its so-called "black belts," a staff of some 300

managers sent into newly acquired subsidiaries to assist in the restructuring and integration in the Siebe group.

Sir Barrie Stephens retired in 1998, passing on full leadership of Siebe to Allen Yurko in that year. The company's chairmanship was delegated to Lord Colin Marshall. Yurko would lead Siebe on its most aggressive acquisition year ever, one that would catch industry observers by surprise. Throughout 1998 the company made a number of acquisitions, including that of manufacturing process execution software designer Wonderware, which would be merged with the company's existing Foxboro operations. The company also added Electronic Measurement, a maker of power supply controls, and Eurotherm, which specialized in temperature controls. To accommodate these acquisitions, Siebe engaged on a restructuring drive, eliminating a number of jobs, a process that would continue through the end of the year and prepare the way for Siebe's largest-ever acquisition.

Siebe Merges and Becomes Invensys in 1999

In November 1998, Siebe announced that it had agreed to merge with British manufacturing conglomerate BTR to form BTR Siebe, which would change its name to Invensys in February 1999. The deal added BTR's £4.8 billion annual sales to Siebe's £3.9 billion and created one of the United Kingdom's largest manufacturing groups. The arrangement also left Siebe basically in control of the merged entity, with Yurko remaining in place at the new manufacturing giant's helm.

The portrait of the post-merger BTR Siebe suggested more of an acquisition than a partnership, as Siebe's management, including key figures CEO Allen Yurko and Chairman Lord Colin Marshall, retained the top positions. Nonetheless, BTR, which struggled through much of the 1990s, provided several of its own top figures, including its CEO Ian Strachan, who served as the merged group's deputy chairman, and Kathleen O'Donovan, who continued her previous position as the new group's CFO. After the merger, Siebe shareholders retained 55 percent of the company's shares.

Siebe's product line now numbered more than 10,000 individual products produced by more than 150 subsidiaries around the world and included such well-known brand names as Foxboro, Robertshaw, APV, Univam, ACL-Drayton, Eberle, and many others. Siebe manufactured controls and control systems ranging from components for small appliances to sophisticated turnkey control automation systems for such projects as nuclear power stations and offshore drilling platforms. In addition to its manufacturing, Siebe also produced the software to drive its control systems under various computer platforms.

BTR, which had its own history of rapid expansion through acquisition, brought its diversified range of products to Siebe, centered around four primary areas: process controls; specialized engineering systems; power drives for gear boxes and motors; and drivetrain and other systems for the automotive industry. At the same time, the company was expected to continue the process of shedding BTR's more diversified interests, which included subsidiary companies in the packaging, laminates, building products, sporting goods, and office furniture industries, among others.

The addition of BTR gave Siebe not only that company's Process Controls divisions, specializing in valves, meters, and batteries, but also its specialized engineering activities, principally in airplane repair, filtration and railroad signaling systems, and in automotive and power drive manufacturing. Although Siebe was criticized for abandoning its "pure play" status to take on a new role as a diversified manufacturing conglomerate, the BTR acquisition nonetheless presented a number of opportunities for synergy, while adding to Siebe's own manufacturing lines. Meanwhile, Siebe's long experience in integrating and restructuring subsidiaries, while sustaining its own steady growth, made the BTR acquisition seem less of a risk.

An Economic Downturn at Invensys

In 1999, however, that turned out not to be the case. Invensys was hit hard by the global recession. The slowdown in the U.S. economy, and in particular the downturn in the technology sector, forced Invensys to cut 11,000 jobs by June 1999. Yet between August and October 1999, Invensys purchased several companies with an eye toward increasing its interest in software and services. UK Data Collections Services Ltd. and Com-Trol were purchased for £52 million, while Marcam Solutions Inc. was purchased for US$60 million.

An even larger acquisition took place the following July, with the purchase of slumping Dutch software company Baan for US$802 million, which included US$90 million of debts. This step was taken to help move Invensys toward its goal of becoming a more integrated-software and systems provider, but ultimately it brought further turmoil, as share prices fell rapidly just days after the acquisition. September profit warnings chopped nearly a third off of share price.

Two months later Invensys moved to spin off its Power Systems division—its fastest-growing business, accounting for 20 percent of group sales—to increase profits and shareholder value. Analysts saw the move as a positive one, set to help improve operating cash flow. The proposed spinoff never happened and the company continued to be slammed by the economic slowdown.

In July 2001, after a third profit warning in ten months, increased pressure from shareholders, and heavy criticism for his handling of the company, CEO Allen Yurka announced his impending retirement. His resignation, coupled with the latest profit warning, indefinitely postponed the anticipated Invensys initial public offering (IPO) and gave way to rumors that Invensys could be facing a takeover bid. No takeover occurred, but the company continued to find itself on shaky ground.

A New CEO and a New Direction for the New Millennium

New CEO Rick Haythornwaite replaced Yurko in October 2001. Haythornwaite believed previous management had spent too much energy on excessive restructuring, and wanted to take Invensys in a different direction. Invensys had dropped 23,000 jobs during the previous three years and shares had fallen from 195p to 27p over a 12-month period. Haythornwaite's biggest immediate challenge was how to manage the high debts incurred by Invensys, which at the time of his taking over the position totaled more than £3 billion.

Haythornwaite moved quickly to sell Invensys's storage unit, the largest sell-off since the company sold more than a dozen businesses for £1.8 billion in 1999, at the time of the original merger. The European Commission would eventually approve the US$505 million acquisition by U.S. company EnerSys Holdings Inc. of Invensys's Energy Storage Business in March 2002.

Furthering Haythornwaite's desire to steer Invensys in a new direction, two investment consultants were hired in December 2001 to help the company sell two units. In February 2002, an aggressive regeneration master plan was announced that would thin the company and halve its debt to £1.5 billion. The biggest change involved selling its industrial components and systems units. This bold move carved out a more compact group, capable of rapid rebound and sustainable long-term growth. The plan detailed a wider reorganization of its other main businesses into two core divisions, Production Management and Energy Management. The Production Management division comprised Foxboro, Wonderware, Triconex, APV, Eurotherm, and Baan, with total estimated sales of £1.6 billion; the Energy Management division combined Energy Solutions, Metering Systems, Appliance and Climate Controls, and Power Systems, with total estimated sales of £2.4 billion.

After a rough couple of years during which Invensys withstood fundamental structural changes, the company took steps to streamline its organization and emphasize its strengths in anticipation of regaining market share, achieving sustainable growth, and once again becoming a leading player within its markets.

Principal Subsidiaries

APV Systems (U.K. and Denmark); Baan Company N.V. (The Netherlands); BAE Automated Systems (U.S.); Densei-Lambda KK (Japan); Eurotherm Holdings Ltd. (U.K.); Fasco Industries Inc. (U.S.); Foxboro Company (U.S.); Hawker (France and Germany); Lambda Electronics Inc. (U.S.); Maple Chase Company (U.S.); North America Water Inc. (U.S.); Powerware Corporation (U.S.); Ranco (U.S. and Japan); Rexnord Corporation (U.S.); Robertshaw Controls Company (U.S.); Safetran Systems Corporation (U.S.); Satchwell Controls Systems Ltd. (U.K.); Saturnia-Hawker Sistemas de Energia Ltda. (Brazil); Teccor Electronics Inc. (U.S.); Westinghouse Brake and Signal (U.K.); Wonderware Corporation (U.S.).

Principal Divisions

Energy Management; Production Management.

Principal Competitors

ABB; GE Industrial Products and Systems; Honeywell International.

Further Reading

Cowell, Alan, "Invensys Spinoff Planned," *New York Times*, November 23, 2000, p. 1.

Edgecliff-Johnson, Andrew, "Time for Siebe to Weave Its Magic at BTR," *Financial Times*, November 25, 1998.

Guyon, Janet, "Troubled Baan Drags Down Its Savior," *Fortune*, July 24, 2000, p. 56.

Holmes, David, "Siebe Merger Debate Hots Up," *Reuters Finance UK*, November 27, 1998.

Kapner, Suzanne, "Cost Cuts Help Invensys," *New York Times*, November 16, 2001, p. 1.

Konicki, Steve, "Invensys Sees Bright Future for Baan Software," *Informationweek*, November 27, 2000, pp. 114–16.

——, "Invensys Takes Control of Slumping Baan," *Informationweek*, July 31, 2000, p. 105.

Malkani, Gautam, "Invensys Set to Demerge Power Systems," *Financial Times*, November 22, 2000, p. 28.

Mazurkiewicz, Greg, "The Biggest Company You Never Knew Speaks Out," *Air Conditioning, Heating & Refrigeration News*, December 11, 2000, pp. 10–11.

——, "Strategic Alliance Formed by Invensys and Williams," *Air Conditioning, Heating & Refrigeration News*, December 11, 2000, p. 11.

Rogoski, Richard, "Invincible Invensys," *Communications News*, January 2001, pp. 16–18.

"Siebe Company History," London: Siebe PLC, 1998.

"Siebe's Driving Force Takes a Tighter Grip on the Controls," *Financial Times*, November 24, 1998.

—M. L. Cohen
—update: Stacee Sledge

Kellogg Company

One Kellogg Square
Battle Creek, Michigan 49016-3599
U.S.A.
Telephone: (616) 961-2000
Fax: (616) 961-2871
Web site: http://www.kelloggs.com

Public Company
Incorporated: 1906 as Battle Creek Toasted Corn Flake
Company
Stock Exchanges: New York
Ticker Symbol: K
NAIC: 311230 Breakfast Cereal Manufacturing; 311412
Frozen Specialty Food Manufacturing; 311812
Commercial Bakeries; 311999 All Other Food
Manufacturing

Will Keith Kellogg once estimated that 42 cereal companies were launched in the breakfast-food boom during the early years of the 20th century. His own venture, founded as the Battle Creek Toasted Corn Flake Company, was among the last, but it outlasted most of its early competitors and has dominated the ready-to-eat cereal industry. The Kellogg Company, as it was ultimately named, followed a straight and profitable path, avoiding takeovers and diversification, relying heavily on advertising and promotion, and posting profits nearly every year of its existence.

Kellogg's Corn Flakes Are Born

By the time Kellogg launched his cereal company in 1906, he had already been in the cereal business for more than ten years as an employee of the Adventist Battle Creek Sanitarium run by his brother, Dr. John Harvey Kellogg. Dr. Kellogg, a strict vegetarian and the sanitarium's internationally celebrated director, also invented and marketed various health foods. One of the foods sold by Dr. Kellogg's Sanitas Food Company was called Granose, a wheat flake the Kellogg brothers had stumbled upon while trying to develop a more digestible form of bread. The wheat flake was produced one night in 1894 follow-

ing a long series of unsuccessful experiments. The men were running boiled wheat dough through a pair of rollers in the sanitarium basement. The dough had always come out sticky and gummy, until by accident the experiments were interrupted long enough for the boiled dough to dry out. When the dry dough was run through the rollers, it broke into thin flakes, one for each wheat berry, and flaked cereals were born.

Commercial production of the Granose flakes began in 1895 with improvised machinery in a barn on the sanitarium grounds. The factory was soon in continuous production, turning out more than 100,000 pounds of flakes in its first year. A ten-ounce box sold for 15 cents, which meant that the Kelloggs collected $12 for each 60-cent bushel of wheat processed, a feat that did not go unnoticed around Battle Creek, Michigan.

In 1900 production was moved to a new $50,000 facility. When the new factory building was completed, Dr. Kellogg insisted that he had not authorized it, forcing W.K. to pay for it himself.

Meanwhile, other companies were growing quickly, but Dr. Kellogg refused to invest in the company's expansion. Its most notable competitor was the Postum Cereal Company, launched by a former sanitarium patient, C.W. Post. Post added Grape-Nuts to his line in 1898 and by 1900 was netting $3 million a year, an accomplishment that inspired dozens of imitators and turned Battle Creek into the cereal-making capital of the United States.

In 1902 Sanitas improved the corn flake it had first introduced in 1898. The new product had better flavor and a longer shelf life than the 1898 version. By the following year the company was advertising in newspapers and on billboards, sending salesmen into the wholesale market, and introducing an ambitious door-to-door sampling program. By late 1905, Sanitas was producing 150 cases of corn flakes a day with sales of $100,000 a year.

Battle Creek Toasted Corn Flake Company Is Launched

The next year W.K. Kellogg launched the Battle Creek Toasted Corn Flake Company with the help of another enthusiastic former sanitarium patient. Kellogg recognized that advertising and promotion were the keys to success in a market flooded with look-alike products—the company spent a third of its initial working capital on an ad in *Ladies Home Journal.*

Orders, fueled by early advertising efforts, continually out-stripped production, even after the company leased factory space at two additional locations. In 1907 output had reached 2,900 cases a day, with a net profit of about a dollar per case. In May 1907 the company became the Toasted Corn Flake Company. That July a fire destroyed the main factory building. On the spot, W.K. Kellogg began making plans for a new fireproof factory, and within a week he had purchased land at a site strategically located between two competing railroad lines. Kellogg had the new plant, with a capacity of 4,200 cases a day, in full operation six months after the fire. "That's all the business I ever want," he is said to have told his son, John L. Kellogg, at the time.

By the time of the fire, the company had already spent $300,000 on advertising but the advertising barrage continued. One anonymous campaign told newspaper readers to "wink at your grocer and see what your get." Winkers got a free sample of Kellogg's Corn Flakes. In New York City, the ad helped boost Corn Flake sales fifteen fold. In 1911 the advertising budget reached $1 million.

By that time, W.K. Kellogg had finally managed to buy out the last of his brother's share of the company, giving him more than 50 percent of its stock. W.K. Kellogg's company had become the Kellogg Toasted Corn Flake Company in 1909, but Dr. Kellogg's Sanitas Food Company had been renamed the Kellogg Food Company and used similar slogans and packaging. W.K. sued his brother for rights to the family name and was finally successful in 1921.

Company Is Reincorporated as the Kellogg Company

In 1922 the company reincorporated as the Kellogg Company because it had lost its trademark claim to the name "Toasted Corn Flakes," and had expanded its product line so much that the name no longer accurately described the company. Kellogg had introduced Krumbles in 1912, followed by 40% Bran Flakes in 1915, and All-Bran in 1916.

Kellogg also made other changes, improving his product, packaging, and processing methods. Many of those developments came from W.K.'s son John L. Kellogg, who began working for the company in its earliest days. J.L. Kellogg developed a malting process to give the corn flakes a more nut-like flavor, saved $250,000 a year by switching from a waxed paper wrapper on the outside of the box to a waxed paper liner inside, and invented All-Bran by adding a malt flavoring to the bran cereal. His father credited him with more than 200 patents and trademarks.

Kellogg Expands into Canada

Sales and profits continued to climb, financing several additions to the Battle Creek plant and the addition of a plant in Canada, opened in 1914, as well as an ever-increasing advertising budget. The one exception came just after World War I, when shortages of raw materials and railcars crippled the once-thriving business. W.K. Kellogg returned from a world tour and canceled advertising contracts and sampling operations, and, for six months, he and his son worked without pay. The company issued $500,000 in gold notes in 1919, and in 1920 posted the only loss in its history. Still, Kellogg rejected a competitor's buyout offer.

At that point the Battle Creek plant had 15 acres of floor space, production capacity of 30,000 cases a day, and a shipping capacity of 50 railcars a day. Each day it converted 15,000 bushels of white southern corn into Corn Flakes. The company had 20 branch offices and employed as many as 400 salesmen. During the next decade the Kellogg Company more than doubled the floor space at its Battle Creek factory and opened another overseas plant in Sydney, Australia, in 1924.

Also during that period, W.K. Kellogg began looking for a successor since in 1925 he had forced his son, who had served briefly as president, out of the company after J.L. had bought an oat-milling plant and divorced his wife to marry an office employee. W.K. Kellogg objected both to his son's moral lapse and to his preference for oats. Several other presidents followed, but none could manage well enough to keep W.K. Kellogg away. During the Great Depression the company's directors decided to cut advertising, premiums, and other expenses. When Kellogg heard of it, he returned from his California home, called a meeting, and told the officers to press ahead. They voted again, this time adding $1 million to the advertising budget. The company's upward sales curve continued right through the Depression, and profits improved from around $4.3 million a year in the late 1920s to $5.7 million in the early 1930s.

In 1930 W.K. Kellogg established the W.K. Kellogg Foundation to support agricultural, health, and educational institutions. Kellogg eventually gave the foundation his majority interest in Kellogg Company. The company, under W.K.'s control, also did its part to fight unemployment, hiring a crew to landscape a ten-acre park on the Battle Creek plant grounds and introducing a six-hour, four-shift day.

Vanderploeg is named President of Kellogg Company

In 1939 Kellogg finally found a permanent president, Watson H. Vanderploeg, who was hired away from a Chicago bank. Vanderploeg led the company from 1939 until his death in 1957. Vanderploeg expanded Kellogg's successful advertise-and-grow policy, adding new products and taking them into new markets. In 1941 the company began a $1 million modernization program, updating old steam-generation equipment and adding new bins and processing equipment. The company also added new plants in the United States and abroad. Domestic plants were established in Omaha, Nebraska; Lockport, Illinois; San Leandro, California; and Memphis, Tennessee. Additional foreign operations were established in Manchester, England, in 1938, followed by plants in South Africa, Mexico, Ireland, Sweden, the Netherlands, Denmark, New Zealand, Norway,

---

Key Dates:

1894: The wheat flake is first produced by Dr. John Harvey Kellogg and Will Keith Kellogg at the Sanitas Food Company.

1898: Kellogg's corn flake is introduced.

1905: Granose (corn) flakes begin commercial production.

1906: Battle Creek Toasted Corn Flake Company is founded in Battle Creek, Michigan, by Will Keith Kellogg.

1907: The company is renamed Toasted Corn Flake Company; the main factory building is destroyed by fire.

1909: Company is renamed the Kellogg Toasted Corn Flake Company.

1914: International expansion begins in Canada.

1915: Bran Flakes cereal is introduced.

1916: All-Bran cereal is introduced.

1922: Company is incorporated as the Kellogg Company.

1924: Kellogg opens overseas plant in Sydney, Australia.

1928: Rice Krispies are introduced.

1930: The W.K. Kellogg Foundation is established.

1938: International expansion begins in the United Kingdom.

1939: Watson H. Vanderploeg becomes president of Kellogg.

1964: The Pop-Tart is introduced.

1969: Kellogg acquires a tea company, Salada Foods.

1970: Kellogg acquires Fearn International.

1976: Kellogg acquires Mrs. Smith's Pie Company.

1977: Pure Packed Foods is acquired.

1979: William E. LaMothe becomes CEO.

1982: Nutri-Grain cereals are marketed.

1988: Kellogg sells its U.S. and Canadian tea operations.

1992: Arnold G. Langbo replaces LaMothe as chairman and CEO.

1993: Kellogg sells Mrs. Smith's Frozen Foods, Cereal Packaging, Ltd., and its Argentine shack food business; Kellogg opens a plant in Riga, Latvia.

1994: Kellogg teams with ConAgra to create a cereal line sold under the Healthy Choice label; Kellogg opens a plant in Taloja, India.

1995: Kellogg opens a plant in Guangzhou, China.

1999: Carlos Gutierrez becomes CEO; Kellogg sells the Lender's division to Aurora Foods and acquires Worthington Foods.

2000: Kellogg acquires convenience food maker Kashi Company; Kellogg reorganizes its operations into two divisions (USA and International).

2001: General Mills passes Kellogg as the number one cereal maker; Kellogg acquires Keebler Foods.

Venezuela, Colombia, Brazil, Switzerland, and Finland. During the five years after World War II, Kellogg expanded net fixed assets from $6.6 million to $20.6 million. As always, this expansion was financed entirely out of earnings.

The company also continued to add new products, but it never strayed far from the ready-to-eat cereal business. In 1952 more than 85 percent of sales came from ten breakfast cereals, although the company also sold a line of dog food, some poultry and animal feeds, and Gold Medal pasta. *Barron's* noted that Kellogg's profit margins, consistently between 6 and 7 percent of sales, were more than double those of other food companies. The company produced 35 percent of the nation's ready-to-eat cereal and was the world's largest manufacturer of cold cereal. Kellogg's success came from its emphasis on quality products; high-speed automated equipment, which kept labor costs to about 15 percent of sales; and substantial foreign earnings that were exempt from the excess-profits tax. Dividends tended to be generous and had been paid every year since 1908; sales, which had been $33 million in 1939, began to top $100 million in 1948. By the early 1950s an estimated one-third of those sales were outside the United States.

Kellogg's Begins Television Advertising

In the early 1950s Kellogg's continued success was tied to two outside developments: the postwar baby boom and television advertising. To appeal to the new younger market, Kellogg and other cereal makers brought out new lines of presweetened cereals and unabashedly made the key ingredient part of the name. Kellogg's entries included Sugar Frosted Flakes, Sugar Smacks, Sugar Corn Pops, Sugar All-Stars, and Cocoa Crispies. The company created cartoon pitchmen to sell the products on Saturday morning television. Tony the Tiger was introduced in 1953 following a contest to name the spokesperson for the new cereal, Kellogg's Sugar Frosted Flakes of Corn. Sales and profits doubled over the decade and in 1960 Kellogg earned $21.5 million on sales of $256.2 million and boosted its market share to 40 percent.

The company continued adding new cereals, aiming some at adolescent baby boomers and others, like Special K and Product 19, at their parents. Kellogg's Corn Flakes still led the cereal market and got more advertising support than any other cereal on grocers' shelves. Kellogg poured nearly $10 million into Corn Flakes advertising in both 1964 and 1965, putting more than two-thirds of those dollars into television.

In 1969 Kellogg finally made a significant move away from the ready-to-eat breakfast-food business, acquiring Salada Foods, a tea company. The following year Kellogg bought Fearn International, which sold soups, sauces, and desserts to restaurants. Kellogg added Mrs. Smith's Pie Company in 1976 and Pure Packed Foods, a maker of nondairy frozen foods for institutional customers, in 1977. Kellogg also bought several small foreign food companies.

The diversification may have been motivated in part by increasing attacks on Kellogg's cereal business. Criticism boiled over in 1972 when the Federal Trade Commission (FTC) accused Kellogg and its leading rivals General Mills and General Foods of holding a shared monopoly and overcharging consumers more than $1 billion during the previous 15 years. The FTC said the companies used massive advertising (12 percent of sales), brand proliferation, and allocation of shelf space to keep out competitors and maintain high prices and profit margins. There was no disputing the profit margins, but the companies argued that the advertising and product proliferation were the result of competition, not monopoly. The cereal companies won their point following a lengthy hearing. During the same period, the industry's presweetened cereals and related advertising also took a beating. The American Dental Association accused the industry of obscuring the sugar content of those cereals, and Action for Children's Television lodged a complaint with the FTC, saying that the mostly sugar cereals were equivalent to candy. Kellogg flooded consumer groups and the FTC with data playing down the sugar content by showing that only three percent of a child's sugar consumption comes from presweetened cereals. This publicity caused sugared-cereal sales to fall 5 percent in 1978, the first decline since their introduction in the 1950s.

The biggest threat to Kellogg's continued growth wasn't criticism, but rather the aging of its market. By the end of the 1970s growth slowed dramatically as the baby boom generation passed from the under-25 age group, which consumes an average of 11 pounds of cereal a year, to the 25 to 50 age group, which eats less than half as much cereal. Cereal-market growth dropped, and Kellogg lost the most. Its market share fell from 43 percent in 1972 to 37 percent in 1983.

New Chairman LaMothe Continues to Push Cereal Business

While Wall Street urged the company to shift its growth targets into anything but the stagnating cereal market, Kellogg continued to put its biggest efforts into its cereal business, emphasizing some of the same nutritional concepts that had given birth to the ready-to-eat breakfast business. And Kellogg was less unwilling than unable to diversify. It made three unsuccessful bids for the Tropicana Products orange juice company and another for Binney & Smith, makers of Crayola crayons. Despite its problems, Kellogg believed the cereal business still represented its best investment opportunity. "When you average 28 percent return on equity in your own business, it's pretty hard to find impressive acquisitions," said Chairman William E. LaMothe, a onetime salesman who became CEO in 1979.

In 1984 Kellogg bought about 20 percent of its own stock back from the W.K. Kellogg Foundation, a move that increased profits and helped defend the company against future takeover attempts, while satisfying a legal requirement limiting the holdings of foundations without giving potential raiders access to the stock.

Meanwhile, the company's response to generally sagging markets in the late 1970s was much like W.K. Kellogg's during the Depression: more advertising. Kellogg also boosted product research and stepped up new-product introductions. In 1979 the company rolled out five new products and had three more in test markets. By 1983 Kellogg's research-and-development budget was $20 million, triple the 1978 allotment. Targeting a more health-conscious market, Kellogg spent $50 million to bring three varieties of Nutri-Grain cereal to market in 1982. Kellogg added almost as many products in the next two years as it had in the previous four. And in 1984 Kellogg sparked a fiber fad when it began adding a health message from the National Cancer Institute to its All-Bran cereal.

By the mid-1980s the results of Kellogg's renewed assault on the cereal market were mixed. The company's hopes of raising per capita cereal consumption to 12 pounds by 1985 fell flat. But Kellogg did regain much of its lost market share, claiming 40 percent in 1985, and it continued to outperform itself year after year. In 1986 Kellogg posted its 30th consecutive dividend increase, its 35th consecutive earnings increase, and its 42nd consecutive sales increase.

Kellogg Sells Tea Companies

In 1988 the company sold its U.S. and Canadian tea operations, in a demonstration of Kellogg's renewed commitment to the cereal market. In the early 1990s, however, Kellogg failed to move fast enough to profit from the oat bran craze and lost market share in the United States, primarily to General Mills, Inc.'s oat-heavy brands such as Cheerios and Honey Nut Cheerios. Further erosion resulted from an upsurge in sales of private-label store brands, notably those produced by Ralston Purina Company spinoff Ralcorp Holdings Inc.. By developing knockoffs of such Kellogg standbys as Corn Flakes and Apple Jacks and selling them for as much as a dollar less per box, Ralcorp and other companies increased private-label cereal market share to 6 percent by 1994 at the expense of Kellogg and other makers of brand-name cereals. Sales of branded cereals increased only 3 percent in 1994 over 1993; in this flat market, Kellogg's U.S. market share fell to as low as 33.8 percent in 1994.

In order to hold on to as much of its market share as it could, Kellogg management once again turned to increased marketing and advertising in 1990. Even in the face of the pressure from lower-priced private-label products, the company also continued to raise its prices in the early 1990s to generate sufficient revenue. This trend was finally reversed in 1994, however, when General Mills lowered its prices, forcing Kellogg to do the same.

In the midst of these difficulties, LaMothe retired in 1992 and was replaced as chairman and CEO by the president of Kellogg, Arnold G. Langbo. Under Langbo's direction, the company underwent a reengineering effort in 1993 that committed the company to concentrate its efforts on its core business of breakfast cereal. That year and the next, Kellogg divested itself of such noncore assets as its Mrs. Smith's Frozen Foods pie business, Cereal Packaging, Ltd., based in England, and its Argentine snack food business.

Its emphasis on its core business was also extended to its operations outside the United States, where company officials saw the greatest potential for future growth. By 1991 Kellogg held 50 percent of the non-U.S. cereal market, and 34 percent of its profits were generated outside the United States. In most of the markets in which it operated, it had at least six of the top ten cereal brands. Looking to the future, Kellogg's primary target markets of Europe, Asia, and Latin America had not yet reached the more mature levels of the United States. While per capita cereal consumption in the United States was ten pounds per year, in most other markets it was less than two pounds. After expanding into Italy in the early 1990s, Kellogg became the first major cereal company to open plants in three markets: the former Soviet Union with a plant in Riga, Latvia, in 1993; India with a plant in Taloja, in 1994; and China with a plant in

Guangzhou, in 1995. With these new operations, Kellogg had 29 plants operating in 19 countries and could reach consumers in almost 160 countries.

Kellogg Competes with General Mills for Market Share

Although Kellogg had a commanding position internationally, it faced a new and more formidable international competitor starting in 1989. General Mills and the Swiss food titan Nestlé S.A. established a joint venture called Cereal Partners Worldwide (CPW), which essentially combined General Mills' cereal brands and cereal-making equipment with Nestlé's name recognition in numerous markets and vast experience with retailers there. By 1994, CPW was already beginning to eat into Kellogg's market share in various countries.

Overall, Kellogg's 1990s difficulties had only slowed—not stopped—the firm's tradition of continual growth. Net sales increased at the modest rates of 7 percent, 2 percent, and 4 percent in 1992, 1993, and 1994, respectively (1994 was Kellogg's 50th consecutive year of sales growth). With U.S. sales still accounting for 59 percent of the overall total, however, and competition heating up overseas, Kellogg faced its most challenging environment since the early 1920s. In addition to its aggressive expansion into overseas markets with huge potential for growth, another promising sign for a bright future for Kellogg was a revitalized new product development program. More disciplined than the scattershot approach of the 1980s, the program was beginning to produce such winners as Low Fat Granola, Rice Krispies Treats, and a line of cereal developed as a result of the 1994 partnership with ConAgra, Inc., under the food conglomerate's Healthy Choice brand.

In 1997 and 1998 operations were expanded in Australia, the United Kingdom, Asia, and Latin America, but extremely competitive market conditions resulted in declines in sales and earnings in 1998. The result was a refocusing in two key areas: new product development and the complete overhaul of corporate headquarters and the North American organization structure. Product development included the addition of new cereals, innovative convenience foods, and new grain-based products; product improvement measures added to the nutritional value of all products. The Ensemble line of heart-healthy foods was introduced in November 1998 and included frozen entrees, bread, dry pasta, baked potato crisps, frozen miniloaves, cookies, and a ready-to-eat cereal similar to General Mills' Cheerios line.

An increase in overall marketing investments was targeted for the seven largest cereal markets: the United States, the United Kingdom, Mexico, Canada, Australia, Germany, and France. In response to the growth of "on-the-go" convenience foods, geographic distribution was expanded for such products as Nutri-Grain bars, Rice Krispies Treats squares, and Pop-Tarts toaster pastries.

New Chairman Gutierrez Reorganizes Company

In an effort to reduce costs and create a more focused and accountable workforce, about 25 percent of its North American workforce was let go and steps were taken toward the reorganization of the corporate structure. As a result, several top officers

left in 1998 and 1999. In April 1999, Cuban-born and 25-year veteran of the company Carlos M. Gutierrez became CEO. Gutierrez's vision for Kellogg was "to begin a process of renewal designed to strengthen significantly the ability of the Kellogg Company to compete and prosper in the 21st century." His new team included eight new top executives, including four who joined the company in 1999 and 2000.

Gutierrez took many bolds steps to hold on to the company's position as the world's leading producer of ready-to-eat cereal in spite of declining stock value, including selling the Lender's bagel division to Aurora Foods and shutting down the Ensemble line of cholesterol-reducing foods. Despite protestations from the community and workforce, the historic hometown plant in Battle Creek was closed and 550 jobs were eliminated. In late 1999, Kellogg acquired Worthington Foods, Inc., manufacturer of meat alternatives, frozen egg substitutes, and other healthy food products, under the brands of Morningstar Farms, Natural Touch, Worthington, and Loma Linda.

As in 1999, Kellogg continued the process of renewal in 2000, with its second consecutive year of earnings growth. Sales, however, declined by 0.4 percent and share performance was again disappointing. With sales falling or remaining stagnant in the ready-to-eat cereal business, the strategy of the company involved allocating resources first to the United States' markets, and then to other core markets in the United Kingdom/Republic of Ireland, Mexico, Canada, and Australia/New Zealand; setting targets for long-term growth; and executing a sound business plan.

To strengthen their competitive position, in 2000 Kellogg acquired Kashi Company, a natural cereal company in the United States; two convenience food businesses in Australia; and the Mondo Baking Company, a manufacturer of convenience foods in Rome, Georgia. On October 26, the company announced that an agreement had been reached to acquire Keebler Foods Company, the largest acquisition in the 95-year history of the company. The acquisition, completed in March 2001, brought to Kellogg not only Keebler's cookie and cracker business, but also their direct store door (DSD) delivery system, which was expected to increase the growth potential of snack foods such as Kellogg's Nutri-Grain bars and Rice Krispies Treats squares.

In the fourth quarter of 2000, Kellogg's operations were restructured into two major divisions—USA and International—to streamline operations and reduce costs. Kellogg International was further delineated into Europe, Latin America, Canada, Australia, and Asia. In U.S. operations, Kellogg's Raisin Bran Crunch cereal remained the most successful new U.S. cereal product since the mid-1990s, with a 0.9 percent market share. Consumer promotions included American Airlines frequent flyer miles, and affiliations with NASCAR, the Olympics, and Major League Soccer. Other advertising connections were made with the movie *How the Grinch Stole Christmas* and Pokemon. Kellogg also launched Eet & Ern, an Internet-based consumer loyalty program.

The Kellogg International division had responsibility for all markets outside the United States, providing products to more than 160 countries on six continents worldwide. The four largest Kellogg International markets were the United Kingdom/ Republic of Ireland, Mexico, Canada, and Australia/New Zealand. The United Kingdom/Republic of Ireland remained Kellogg's largest market outside the United States, and experienced a 3 percent increase in cereal sales during 2000. The fastest growing international market was Mexico, where the direct store delivery system was effectively implemented.

Cereal competitor General Mills had closed the gap in the U.S. market share, and passed Kellogg in 2001 as the number one cereal maker. According to Kellogg CEO Gutierrez, "after a year of change, a stronger Kellogg is emerging." The change marked the building of a better business model in which "short-term sales and earnings growth were sacrificed to lay the foundation for great value creation in the future." In Kellogg USA, the acquisition of Keebler was completed in 2001 resulting in a more profitable sales mix. Advertising through brand-building was increased with tie-ins with Disney, American Airlines, and the Cartoon Network. In the cereal category, Special K Red Berries cereal was launched in March and proved to be the most successful new product in this category since the 1998 introduction of Raisin Bran Crunch. Pop-Tarts increased its sales and category share and benefited from the introduction of Chocolate Chip Pop-Tarts. A number of products in the snacks category benefited from the inclusion in Keebler's direct store delivery system. Growth was also evident in the natural and frozen foods category, with Kashi proving to be the fastest growing brand in the natural cereals category.

Like Kellogg USA, Kellogg International's focus on "volume to value" in 2001 was applied to sales, marketing, and new-product initiatives. In the United Kingdom, the most important brands and innovation projects were prioritized. Successful product campaigns were launched for Crunchy Nut Red cereal and Special K bars. Kellogg India Ltd. was permitted by the Foreign Investment Promotion Board to launch new products, Cheez-It Crackers, Keebler Cookiers, and Special K cereal. In other parts of Europe, Kellogg pulled back on investments in smaller markets and attempted to bring prices in line in preparation of the launch of the Euro currency.

By 2002 the Kellogg team, headed by Chairman Gutierrez, remained optimistic for the future of the Kellogg Company. After a year of significant changes, the company emerged "a stronger organization, (with) a tighter focus and revitalized employees whose determination is greater than ever." The year 2002 indicated progress in the form of sustainable, reliable sales and earnings growth. With products manufactured in 19 countries and marketed in more than 160 countries worldwide, Kellogg showed more focus than ever to regain and retain its position as the world's leading producer of cereal and a leading producer of convenience foods.

Principal Subsidiaries

Kellogg USA Inc.; Kellogg Company Argentina S.A.C.I.F.; Kellogg (Aust.) Proprietary Ltd. (Australia); Kellogg Brasil & CIA; Kellogg Canada Inc.; Kellogg de Colombia S.A.; Nordisk Kelloggs A/S (Denmark); Kellogg's Produits Alimentaires, S.A. (France); Kellogg (Deutschland) Gesellschaft mit beschrankter Haftung (GmbH); Kellogg de Centro America S.A. (Guatemala); Kellogg (Japan) K.K.; Nhong Shim Kellogg Co. Ltd. (Korea); Kellogg de Mexico S.A. de C.V.; Kellogg Company of South Africa (Proprietary) Limited; Kellogg Espana, S.A.; Kellogg Company of Great Britain, Ltd.; Alimentos Kellogg S.A. (Venezuela); Kellogg India Ltd.

Principal Competitors

General Mills; Kraft Foods; Quaker Oats.

Further Reading

Brown, Gerald, J.B. Keegan, and K. Wood Vigus, "The Kellogg Company Optimizes Production, Inventory, and Distribution," *Interfaces*, November/December 2001, pp. 1–15.

Carson, Gerald, *Cornflake Crusade*, Salem, N. H.: Ayer, 1976, 305 pp.

"Energy, Diet Bars Show High Growth," *National Petroleum News*, June 2002, p. 20.

Gould, William, *Kellogg's: The Greatest Name in Cereals (VGM's Business Portraits)*, Lincolnwood, Ill: VGM Career Horizons, 1997, 48 pp.

The History of Kellogg Company, Battle Creek, Mich.: Kellogg Company, 1986.

Hunnicutt, Benjamin Kline, *Kellogg's Six Hour Day*, Philadelphia: Temple University Press, 1996, 261 pp.

"Kellogg Company," *Frozen Food Age*, March 2001, p. 1.

"Kellogg Company," *Hoover's Handbook of American Business 2002*, 2001, pp. 816–17.

Knowlton, Christopher, "Europe Cooks Up a Cereal Brawl," *Fortune*, June 3, 1991, pp. 175–78.

Mukherjee, Abarish, "India: Kellogg Gets FIPB Nod for Four New Products," *Businessline*, December 27, 2001, p. 1.

Powell, Horace B., *The Original Has This Signature: W.K. Kellogg*, Englewood Cliffs, N. J.: Prentice-Hall, 1956, 358 p.

Serwer, Andrew E., "What Price Brand Loyalty?," *Fortune*, January 10, 1994, pp. 103–04.

Treece, James B., and Greg Burns, "The Nervous Faces around Kellogg's Breakfast Table," *Business Week*, July 18, 1994, p. 33.

Woodruff, David, "Winning the War of Battle Creek," *Business Week*, May 13, 1991, p. 80.

—updates: David E. Salamie, Carol D. Beavers

Koninklijke Philips Electronics N.V.

The Rembrandt Tower
The Netherlands
Telephone: +31 (20) 59-77-777
Fax: +31 (20) 59-77-070
Web site: http://www.philips.com

Public Company
Incorporated: 1912 as N.V. Philips Gloeilampenfabrieken
Employees: 189,000 (2001)
Sales: EUR 32,339 million (2001)
Stock Exchanges: Amsterdam London New York
Ticker Symbol: PHI (Amsterdam), PLE (London), PHG
  (New York)
NAIC: 334310 Audio and Video Equipment Manufac-
  turing; 333298 All Other Industrial Machinery
  Manufacturing; 551112 Offices of Other Holding
  Companies

Koninklijke Philips Electronics N.V. is the holding company for the Philips Electronics group, Europe's largest electronics company. The company is a world leader in color television sets, lighting, electric shavers, medical diagnostic imaging and patient monitoring, and one-chip TV products. It has offices and manufacturing facilities in more than 60 countries.

Foundation and Growth: 1891–1930

The early years of the company were very much a family affair. On May 15, 1891, Gerard Philips, a young engineer who saw commercial potential in newly developing electrical technology, formed Philips & Company, a partnership with his father, Frederik Philips, to manufacture incandescent lamps and other electrical products. The elder Philips, a wealthy tobacco merchant and banker from Zaltbommel, provided the financing while Gerard contributed the technical expertise.

Philips & Company began operations in a small factory in Eindhoven, in the Netherlands. Production started in 1892, but the fledgling company encountered problems from the very beginning. The firm could not produce as many lamps as Gerard had forecast, nor did the lamps fetch the price he had expected.

Father and son had underestimated the strength of international competition in the young industry, especially from the large German manufacturers who had entered the market in the early 1880s and were already well established.

The company suffered heavy financial losses in 1893, and by 1894 the two men decided to sell the business. That might have been the end of the family's venture into the electrical industry had it not been for the fact that the only offer they received was considered unacceptable by Frederik. After negotiations broke down with the prospective buyer, the Philipses decided to risk everything rather than sell at too low a price.

The company was clearly in need of someone with commercial skills and ambition to make it profitable. Frederik was preoccupied with his banking and commercial interests in Zaltbommel, and, while Gerard possessed the technical ability necessary to manufacture electric light bulbs and other innovative products, he was not by nature a businessperson. Frederik thus turned to his youngest son, Anton.

Anton Philips, who was 16 years younger than Gerard, joined the firm in early 1895. Anton had left school early to work in London for a brokerage firm. This brief training in business helped; once he assumed control, Anton began winning the company new customers both at home and abroad. In a few years, the company was growing at a healthy rate.

At the dawn of the century the company kept pace with constant innovations in the electrical industry by developing a skilled staff of technical and commercial specialists. When the carbon-filament lamp became obsolete after 1907, Philips and other companies pioneered the development of lamps that used tungsten wire, which produced three times as much light for the same amount of electricity. Philips was also at the forefront of revolutionary improvements in the manufacture of filament wire, which gave rise to the production of incandescent lamps of all types and sizes. In 1912, Philips & Company was incorporated as NV Philips Gloeilampenfabrieken and began offering its shares on the Amsterdam Stock Exchange.

As the company grew, it became increasingly evident to both Gerard and Anton that a strong R&D capability would be critical to its survival. Consequently, in 1914 Gerard appointed a young physicist, Gilles Holst, to lead the company's research effort. Dr. Holst and his staff worked as a separate organization, reporting directly to the Philips brothers; this laboratory eventually developed into the Philips Research Laboratories.

The Netherlands remained neutral in World War I, to the company's benefit. Shortages of coal for the production of gas resulted in gas rationing, which in turn stimulated the use of electricity. By 1915, Philips had succeeded in producing a small, economical argon-filled lamp that was immediately in great demand.

When Germany prohibited the export of argon gas, Philips avoided a production breakdown by completing its own argon-production facility. Similarly, the glass bulbs used in manufacturing its lamps, which had been obtained from factories in Germany and Austria before the war, suddenly fell into short supply. The brothers decided in 1915 that the supply problem could be solved only by constructing a glass works of their own. That factory opened in 1916, followed shortly by additional facilities for the production of hydrogen gas and corrugated cardboard. These moves were the first steps toward the vertical integration of the company's production processes.

After the war, Philips began to expand its overseas marketing efforts significantly. Before 1914, Philips had autonomous marketing companies in the United States and France. In 1919, La Lumiagere Economique was established in Belgium, followed by similar organizations set up in 13 other European countries as well as China, Brazil, and Australia.

Research conducted under the direction of Dr. Holst played a critical role in the development of new products during this time. Fields such as X-ray radiation and radio reception were given high priority, resulting a few years later in product-line additions such as X-ray tubes and radio valves.

In 1920 a holding company, N.V. Gemeenschappelijk Benzit van Aandeelen Philips Gloeilampenfabrieken, known as N.V. Benzit, was formed and assumed ownership of Philips. Gerard Philips retired in 1922 and was succeeded as company chairman by Anton, who was 48 years old.

Under Anton's management, the company began to manufacture complete radio sets; it displayed its first model at the Utrecht Trade Fair in September 1927. From then on, rather than manufacturing just electrical components, the company started to manufacture complete products whenever possible—a significant change in management strategy.

During the 1920s, the company's headquarters at Eindhoven underwent extensive renovation and expansion, with the construction of additional buildings for new and existing industrial products. Toward the end of the decade, Philips Lamp Works set up more overseas subsidiaries in Asia and Africa, as well as in Europe.

Depression and War: 1930–1946

The worldwide Depression of the 1930s, however, stalled the company's robust expansion, forcing employee layoffs and an administrative reorganization. As a result, new budgeting methods and an improved cost-price calculation were introduced to facilitate a faster response to changing market conditions. Research continued with considerable vigor, producing new products such as gas-discharge lamps, X-ray equipment, car radios, telecommunications equipment, welding rods, and electric shavers, all of which ultimately helped alleviate the company's financial difficulties. And, despite its problems, the company opened a number of new offices in South America.

The international trade barriers erected by many national governments during the 1930s in an attempt to protect domestic industries from foreign competition forced a major change in the structure of the company. As a result of the barriers, it became extremely difficult for Philips to supply its overseas marketing companies from its headquarters in Eindhoven. Management responded by establishing local production facilities in foreign countries.

Anton Philips retired in 1939 as president, though he remained active in a supervisory role. He was succeeded as president by his son-in-law, Frans Otten, while his son, Frits Philips, was made a director of the company.

The ominous political developments in Europe at the end of the 1930s prompted management to prepare for the worst. The North American Philips Corporation (NAPC) was founded in the United States in anticipation of the possible Nazi occupation of the Netherlands. When the Nazis invaded in May 1940, Dutch defenses crumbled and the country capitulated within a week. The management of Philips followed the Dutch government into exile in England. Eventually, the top management made its way to the United States, where NAPC managed operations in non-occupied countries for the duration of the war. Frits Philips, while attempting to maintain as much independence as possible from Nazi authorities, remained behind to manage operations in the Netherlands.

Philips' activities in the Netherlands suffered seriously as the war progressed. In 1942 and 1943 company factories were bombed by the Allies, and in 1944 the Nazis bombed them a final time as they withdrew. Thus the first order of business after the war ended was reconstruction. By the end of 1946, most of the buildings had been restored and production had returned to its prewar level.

Postwar Expansion: 1946–1971

The postwar years were a time of worldwide expansion for the company. The existing Eindhoven-centered management

Key Dates:

1891: Philips & Company is founded as a partnership between Gerard Philips and his father, Frederik Philips.

1892: Philips & Company begins producing electric lamps, in a small factory in Eindhoven.

1912: The company incorporates as N.V. Philips Gloeilampenfabrieken and offers its shares on the Amsterdam Stock Exchange.

1914: Philips establishes a research laboratory.

1920: N.V. Gemeenschappelijk Benzit van Aandeelen Philips Gloeilampenfabrieken (NV Benzit) is formed as a holding company for the Philips group.

1927: Philips displays its first complete radio set at the Utrecht Trade Fair.

1939: The North American Philips Corporation (NAPC) is formed as a base of operations in anticipation of the possible Nazi occupation of the Netherlands; and Anton Philips retires and his son-in-law Frans Otten becomes president.

1942: The Philips factories in the Netherlands are bombed by the Allies in 1942 and 1943, and in 1944 the Nazis bomb the factories as they withdraw.

1972: Philips brings its first videocassette recorder to market.

1986: Philips introduces the optical disk and the compact disc; and Cornelis van der Klugt becomes the president.

1989: Philips withdraws from the defense electronics market.

1991: N.V. Benzit is dissolved; the name of the holding company is changed to Philips Electronics N.V.; Philips introduces the CD-interactive player to the U.S. market.

1995: Philips Consumer Communications (PCC) is formed to manufacture and market digital cellular phones.

1997: Philips launches a successful DVD player into the market; and Lucent Technologies folds its retail phone operations into PCC.

1998: Lucent withdraws from PCC; and Philips sells its PolyGram record company.

1999: Philips changes its name to Koninklijke Philips Electronics NV.

2001: Philips launches a DVD recorder.

2002: Philips announces marketing and distribution deals with Nike, AOL Time Warner, and Dell Computers.

structure was revised to allow overseas operations more autonomy. National organizations, responsible for all financial, legal, and administrative matters, were created for each country in which Philips operated. Manufacturing policy, however, remained centralized, with various product divisions in Eindhoven responsible for overall development, production, and global distribution.

The research arm of the company remained a separate entity, expanding in the postwar years into an international organization with eight separate laboratories in Western Europe and the United States. Philips' laboratories also made major technological contributions in electronics, including the development of new magnetic materials, and work on transistors and integrated circuits.

The growth of the Common Market, established in 1958, presented the company with new opportunities. While factories had previously manufactured products solely for local markets, larger-scale production units encompassing the entire European Economic Community (EEC) were now possible. With export to Common Market countries made easier, a new approach to product development was also necessary. Philips' factories were gradually integrated and centralized into International Production Centers—the backbone of its product divisions—as it made the transition from a market-orientated to a product-oriented business.

The Japanese Challenge: 1971–1990

Frits Philips was named president in 1961 and managed the firm during a very prosperous decade, so that when, in 1971, Henk van Riemsdijk was appointed president, he took over a company riding the crest of 20 years of uninterrupted postwar success. The 1970s, however, were a difficult time, as competition from Asia cut into Philips' markets. Many of its smaller, less-profitable factories were closed as the company created larger, more efficient units. The company also continued its innovative efforts in recording, transmitting, and reproducing television pictures. In 1972, for example, the company introduced the first videocassette recorder to the market.

In 1977, Nico Rodenburg became president. Under Rodenburg sales grew steadily for most of the late 1970s and early 1980s, but increased profits did not follow. As Japanese companies, with their large, automated plants, flooded the market with inexpensive consumer electronics, Philips, with factories scattered throughout Europe and rising labor costs, saw its market share continue to decline.

The company's fortunes began to change with the appointment of Wisse Dekker as president and chairman of the board in January 1982. Dekker initiated an ambitious restructuring program intended to control Philips' unwieldy bureaucracy and increasingly haphazard productivity. After only a few months, Dekker had closed more than a quarter of the company's European plants and had significantly pared down its global workforce.

Dekker also began to seek acquisitions and joint ventures designed to help concentrate the company's resources on its most profitable and fastest-growing product lines. Philips bought the lighting business of the U.S. company Westinghouse outright, and acquired a 24.5 percent stake in Grundig, the largest West German consumer-electronics firm. In the United States, North American Philips consolidated the operations of its Magnavox Consumer-Electronics division with the Sylvania and Philco businesses it had already purchased from GTE Corporation, in 1981. Two years later, the company announced a 50–50 joint venture with AT&T to manufacture and market public-telephone equipment outside the United States, a deal it hoped would save millions in R&D costs.

When Cornelis van der Klugt assumed the presidency of Philips in 1986, he continued to seek acquisitions and joint ventures to improve the company's market position. Philips' research in solid-state lasers and microelectronics, resulting in advancements in the processing, storage, and transmission of images, sound, and data—also helped regain part of the market lost to the Japanese. This research produced innovative items such as the LaserVision optical disc, the compact disc, and optical telecommunications systems.

Van der Klugt reorganized the company, eliminating an entire layer of management and setting policy by committee. Van der Klugt also made an effort to globalize the company's structure, improving profitability; Philips' profits rose 29 percent in 1988. Rationalization of operations also played a role in this restructuring. In 1987, Philips geared up for a major international push into consumer electronics, and targeted U.S. markets hoping to broaden its market share in TVs, VCRs, and CD players.

In response to Japanese competition, van der Klugt also began to drop non-core activities in favor of development in electronics. In late 1989, for example, the company began a graceful withdrawal from the defense market, where it had maintained a leading stride since developing nuclear control instruments (chiefly for nuclear power generation) and fire control and radar instruments for missile systems in the 1950s. Philips sold its Dutch defense electronics subsidiary, Hollandse Signaalapparaten (HSA) to Thomson SA of France at the end of 1989 and put other European defense subsidiaries (and interests) up for sale shortly thereafter. Philips also began to share rising R&D costs with other large corporations such as AT&T, Siemens AG, and Whirlpool through joint ventures.

New and Continuing Challenges: 1990–2002

Despite these efforts, profits for the first quarter of 1990 plunged from Dfl 223 million in the first quarter of 1989 to a mere 6 million. Even worse, the plunge was announced only two months after Philips had released its 1989 annual results, forecast an improvement in 1990 profits, and gave no hint of pending problems. Eleven days later Cornelis van der Klugt resigned, and Jan Trimmer became chairman of the company.

Philips had designated Trimmer as van der Klugt's successor in March 1990, but his succession was slated for July 1991, on van der Klugt's scheduled retirement. Trimmer went to work immediately, using the special shareholder meeting called to ratify his appointment to announce plans to eliminate 10,000 jobs and to predict a 1990 full-year loss of Dfl 2 billion. Nevertheless, profits again plunged during the second quarter, this time by 84 percent to Dfl 37 million.

By October, Trimmer announced the initiation of "Operation Centurion," aimed at raising productivity, stimulating cost consciousness, decentralizing decision-making, and reducing employment levels to match those of the company's competitors. He also promised to sell or scale back operations that lacked the potential to make a reasonable profit. The first specific actions under the program were the imposition of an additional 35,000 to 45,000 reduction of jobs and the withholding of dividend payments in 1990. The company's final 1990 loss amounted to Dfl 4.24 billion. In addition, the company's debt reached 160 percent of its equity, and interest costs alone consumed 84 percent of operating profit.

In early 1991, Philips announced that it would simplify its legal structure and change its name. Gemeenschappelijk Benzit van Aandeelen (NV Benzit), Philips' holding company, would dissolve. Philips Gloeilampenfabrieken NV would change its name to Philips Electronics NV and would become the holding company for the entire group. In addition, the company sold its 47 percent interest in Whirlpool International, BV, its home appliance joint venture. It also sold most of its loss-making computer business. These actions, and the elimination of the dividends for another year, contributed to a net gain of Dfl 1.2 billion in 1991 compared to 1990's loss of Dfl 4.2 billion.

In June 1992, Philips announced that both its second-quarter and full-year earnings would fall sharply. The company attributed its problems to a declining market for consumer electronics. In July, Philips announced that it would sell several billion florin of real estate to raise funds to pay down its crushing debt and reduce annual financing costs. In September, Philips announced additional cost-cutting measures aimed at saving several million florin. These measures had little effect on the company's financing costs, however. By the third quarter, net financing costs had ballooned to Dfl 464 million from Dfl 199 million the previous year. Philips recorded a 1992 full-year loss of Dfl 900 million.

By 1993, Philips' cost-cutting measures, the sale of its interest in Japan's Matsushita Electronic Industrial Co., the liquidation of its debt, and improvements in results in its Consumer Electronics and Consumer Products divisions produced an annual profit of Dfl 856 million. Both 1994 and 1995 were also profitable.

This profit recovery, however, concealed some major marketing problems at Philips. The 1991 U.S. introduction of the CD-interactive player, a system that could be attached to a television and serve as a platform for game playing, teaching or entertainment software, illustrated these problems. Having invested more than US$1 billion in the system in the hope that it would become a major revenue producer and strengthen the Philips brand in the United States, the company saw the system fail in that market. The system lacked software that would appeal to the U.S. consumer. Its operation was too complex. And it was too expensive. In five years, only 400,000 units were sold in the United States. Similar fates met the company's Digital Compact Cassette and its high-definition television standard.

By 1996 a decline in the demand for semiconductors, poor performance at the company's PolyGram record company unit, Asian competition and declining European demand contributed to declining first-half results. In July, Philips announced the elimination of another 6,000 jobs. Nevertheless, the company recorded a Dfl 500 million full-year loss.

Cor Boonstra assumed the chairmanship in October 1996. He initiated yet another restructuring program. In the first five months of his tenure, he sold 18 companies and identified another 13 for future disposal. He made plans to outsource more production work to Asia. He also indicated an intention to change the company's traditional engineering orientation to a marketing one.

This marketing shift paid off when the company introduced its DVD recorder. It arranged to have Hollywood movies available for use with the system. It saved money by outsourcing production and it negotiated a standard for the system with other major manufacturers. The system's 1997 introduction was a success.

In 1995 the company formed Philips Consumer Communications (PCC) in an attempt to compete in the cellular equipment market. In 1997, Lucent Technologies folded its retail telephone equipment business into PCC. By the end of 1988, the venture had lost more than US$500 million, and Lucent withdrew from the venture.

The company sold its 75 percent owned PolyGram unit and announced the closure of about a quarter of its worldwide factories by 2002. Nevertheless the virtual meltdown of Asian financial markets and the consequent decline of Asian and Latin American demand for Philips products contributed to a 56 percent decline in operating income for 1998. By 1999, the company's income had increased substantially. Philips Electronics also changed its name to Koninklijke Philips Electronics NV.

By 2000, Philips was enjoying the boom in electronic products seen by other electronics and telecommunications companies. Its yearly results were outstanding. Sales rose by 20 percent and income increased from EUR 1.8 billion to EUR 9.6 billion. It appeared that Philips had finally overcome the problems that had afflicted it during the preceding decade.

By 2001, however, the bottom had dropped out of the Internet and the telecommunications markets. The September terrorist attacks on the United States, further worsened the environment for Philips' sales. The consequences for Philips were disastrous. Its full-year sales declined by 15 percent, and it recorded a record loss of EUR 2.6 billion.

Even before the end of the year, restructuring began again. An additional 10 percent of the workforce had been slashed by the end of 2001. The company indicated that job cuts and additional outsourcing would proceed in 2002. To increase revenues, Philips launched a DVD recorder in 2001. In 2002, it announced marketing and distribution deals with Nike, AOL Time Warner, and Dell Computers.

The company reported a EUR 9 million profit during the first quarter of 2002 and predicted a full-year profit. It was just possible that Philips was again on its way toward recovery.

Principal Subsidiaries

ADAC Laboratories, Inc. (100%); Atos Origin (49%); LG Philips LCD Co. (50%); MedQuist (71%); Origin BV (98%); Philips Electronics North America Corp. (100%); Philips Oral Healthcare, Inc. (100%); Taiwan Semiconductor Manufacturing Co. (23%); VLSI Technology, Inc. (100%).

Principal Competitors

Hitachi; Matsushita; Sony; Fujitsu; NEC; Siemens.

Further Reading

Baker, Stephen, et al., "Well, That Didn't Last Long," *Business Week*, February 5, 2001, p. 60.

Bilefsky, Dan, "Philips's 2nd Quarter Loss Overshadows Tech Sector," *Wall Street Journal*, July 18, 2001, p. A14.

——, "Philips Posts Record $2.3 Billion Loss," *Wall Street Journal*, February 8, 2002, p. B10.

——, "Philips Sees 2002 as a Turnaround Year," *Wall Street Journal*, January 8, 2002, p. A12.

——, "Philips Trims Its Mobil-Phone Business," *Wall Street Journal*, June 27, 2001, p. A10.

Bilefsky, Dan, and Arent Jan Hesselink, "Philips of Europe Records a Profit," *Wall Street Journal*, April 17, 2002, p. B3.

Bouman, P. J., *Anton Philips of Eindhoven*, London: Weidenfeld and Nicolson, 1956.

Carreyrou, John, and Toby Sterling, "Philips's Profit for 3rdQuarter Nearly Doubled," *Wall Street Journal*, October 22, 1999, p. A17.

Dorsey, James M., "Chip Sales Boost Profit at Philips," *Wall Street Journal*, July 19, 2000, p. A18.

——, "Philips President Boonstra to Retire," *Wall Street Journal*, August 31, 2000, p. B13.

Dorsey, James, and Edward Harris, "Philips Electronics Posts Sharp Drop in Net," *Wall Street Journal*, April 18, 2001, p. A19.

du Bois, Martin, "Electronics Giant Philips to Slash Sites," *Wall Street Journal*, November 3, 1998, p. A17.

——, "Philips Net Drops 77% as It Speeds Plans to Cut Costs," *Wall Street Journal*, October 25, 1996, p. A11.

——, "Recovery at Philips Stalls," *Wall Street Journal*, February 12, 1999, p. A12.

du Bois, Martin, et al., "Philips, Lucent Plan Their Venture's End," *Wall Street Journal*, October 16, 1998, p. B4.

du Bois, Martin, and Richard L. Hudson, "Philips Profit Plunged by 56% in 2nd Period," *Wall Street Journal*, August 7, 1992, p. A6.

Fisher, Lawrence M., "Gateway 2000 Backs Sony/Philips Disk Format," *New York Times*, June 16, 1995, p. D8.

Hagerty, Bob, "N.V. Philips Net Climbed by 30%," *Wall Street Journal*, March 2, 1990, p. A10.

——, "N.V. Philips Net Declined 84% In 2nd Quarter," *Wall Street Journal*, August 10, 1990, p. A7A.

——, "NV Philips Stock Falls on Comment Over '91 Prospects," *Wall Street Journal*, April 8, 1991.

——, "N.V. Philips To Eliminate 10,000 Jobs," *Wall Street Journal*, July 3, 1990, p. A3.

——, "Philips Electronics Profit Surged," *Wall Street Journal*, August 2, 1991, p. A6.

——, "Philip's Next Chairman Will Inherit Opportunities as Well as Headaches," *Wall Street Journal*, March 2, 1990, p. B4C.

——, "Philips's Timmer Faces Challenge," *Wall Street Journal*, June 29, 1990, p. A10.

——, "Philips to Eliminate 35,000 to 45,000 Jobs," *Wall Street Journal*, October 26, 1990. p. A12.

——, "Some Bulls See Philips Electronics as a Bargain," *Wall Street Journal*, December 16, 1991, p. C10.

Hagerty, Bob, et al., "Philips Electronics Stock Tumbles," *Wall Street Journal*, June 18, 1992, p. C13.

Heerding, A., *The History of N.V. Philips' Gloeilampenfabrieken*, translated by Derek S. Jordan, Cambridge: Cambridge University Press, 1980.

Hooper, Laurence, "Philips Reports Strong '91 Results," *Wall Street Journal*, February 28, 1992, p. A11.

Hudson, Richard L., "Philips Electronics Plans More Cuts," *Wall Street Journal*, September 4, 1992, p. A4.

——, "Philips Reports Big Loss for '92," *Wall Street Journal*, March 5, 1993, p. A6.

——, "Philips Reports Big Rise in Net," *Wall Street Journal*, August 6, 1993, p. A8.

——, "Philips Reports Loss For Quarter," *Wall Street Journal*, November 6, 1992, p. A11.

"International Brief—N.V. Philips," *Wall Street Journal*, November 29, 1990, p. A9.

Keller, John J., "Lucent, Philips to Produce Phones Jointly," *Wall Street Journal*, June 18, 1997, p. A3.

Levine, Jonathan B., "Has Philips Found Its Wizard?," *Business Week*, September 6, 1993, p. 82.

Nelson, Mark M., "Big Shakeup at N.V. Philips Is Likely Today," *Wall Street Journal*, May 14, 1990, p. A10.

Nelson, Mark M., and Martin du Bois, "N.V. Philips Shares Are Sold Off," *Wall Street Journal*, May 4, 1990, p. A8.

"N.V. Philips Plans to Simplify Structure," *Wall Street Journal*, February 28, 1991, p. A8.

"Philips Electronics to Sell Cable Stake," *Wall Street Journal*, February 26, 1997, p. B71.

"Philips Plans Sales of Assets to Reduce Debt," *Wall Street Journal*, July 21, 1992, p. A9.

"Philips Reports Profit of $267.6 Million for 4th Period," *Wall Street Journal*, March 4, 1994, p. A5E.

"Philips Signs $5 Billion Pact to Sell Parts to Dell," *Wall Street Journal*, March 28, 2002, p. B7.

Pringle, David, and Dan Bilefsky, "Philips Plans to Unveil Digital Videodisk Recorder," *Wall Street Journal*, August 24, 2001, p. B7.

"Profit at Philips More than Doubled in 1994," *Wall Street Journal*, February 23, 1995.

Sterling, Toby, "Philips Electronics Tops Expectations," *Wall Street Journal*, April 20, 2000, p. A20.

Trachtenberg, Jeffrey A., "Short Circuit: How Philips Flubbed Its US Introduction of Electronic Product," *Wall Street Journal*, June 28, 1996, p. A1.

—updates: Kerstan Cohen, Anne L. Potter

L. and J.G. Stickley, Inc.

1 Stickley Drive
Manlius, New York 13104-0480
U.S.A.
Telephone: (315) 682-5500
Fax: (315) 682-6306
Web site: http://www.stickley.com

Private Company
Incorporated: 1904
Employees: 1,255
Sales: $137 million (2001)
NAIC: 337122 Wood Household Furniture (except
    Upholstered) Manufacturing; 337121 Upholstered
    Household Furniture Manufacturing; 337211 Wood
    Office Furniture Manufacturing

Founded in 1900 by Leopold and John George Stickley, L. and J.G. Stickley, Inc. is a manufacturer and marketer of premium solid wood furniture. Privately owned by the Audi family since 1974, the company now operates a facility greater than 400,000 square feet in Manlius, New York, an upholstery plant in North Carolina, and six retail showrooms in New York and Connecticut.

1898–1916: The Stickley Brothers and the American Arts and Crafts Movement

The eldest of five brothers, Gustav Stickley started out making knockoffs of Victorian furniture; however, his aesthetic sensibilities lay with the clean, unadorned lines of the British Arts and Crafts movement. In 1898, Stickley visited England where followers of the new design philosophy were in revolt against the excessive ornamentation and shabby workmanship that they felt resulted from mass production techniques. Led chiefly by William Morris and fellow Britisher John Ruskin, Scotsman Rennie Mackintosh, and Austrian Josef Hoffman, supporters of the Arts and Crafts movement practiced a return to handcrafted styles and preached a simpler life.

Stickley, then 41, returned home to Eastwood, New York, where he set up his Craftsman Shops in 1898 and began to experiment with his own distinctive designs. He favored clean lines and emphasized the inherent beauty of natural wood and leather. Like Morris, he sought inspiration in the styles of the medieval period. He worked in natural white oak because of its strength and "honesty." Rejecting ornamentation and valuing craftsmanship, he based his designs on rectilinear forms; construction features, such as mortise and tenon and dovetail joints, doubled as decoration. He labeled his original pieces with his name and shopmark, which depicted a small joiner's compass inset with the slogan "Als ik kan," or "To the best of my ability," in Flemish.

Stickley's furniture—called Mission Oak because of the early 1900s popularity of California mission architecture and because it somewhat resembled the furniture used in the missions—soon found enthusiastic support. So, too, did Stickley's philosophy, which others embraced as visionary and reformist. Soon manufacturers across the country were creating their own versions of "mission" furniture. These included Stickley's own younger brothers: Leopold and John George, who incorporated in Fayetteville, New York, in 1904, and, in 1905, introduced their first furniture line alongside Gustav's Mission Oak at a Grand Rapids trade show; Albert Stickley, who made furniture under the label Stickley Brothers Co. in Grand Rapids, Michigan; and Charles Stickley, who shared ownership of Stickley and Brandt Chair Co. in Binghamton, New York.

All of the Stickleys were accomplished craftsmen, who, like their older brother, were not opposed to machines; they simply used machinery to get the manufacturing process to the point where the hand could efficiently take over and complete the joinery. It was not industrialization per se that they rejected, but the sloppy work practices encouraged by mass production. In fact, Leopold and John George Stickley introduced some cutting edge designs and innovative construction techniques of their own with their Handcraft line. However, only Gustav Stickley attempted to market a lifestyle.

Like his European counterparts, Gustav Stickley published on the subject of his philosophy of simplicity. He introduced his own magazine, *The Craftsman*, whose masthead announced its purpose as being "in the interest of better art, better work, and a better, more reasonable way of living," and filled it with trea-

Company Perspectives:

Our corporate mission is to offer honest craftsmanship, inherent value, and unmatched service. Our goal is to be recognized by the discerning customer as the finest solid wood furniture manufacturer in the world.

tises and illustrations of his furniture and interior design— every aspect of the designed environment, from tiles and pottery to gardens and landscape. He also developed and sold model house plans in *The Craftsman* and in his two books of home designs.

By 1907, the American Arts and Crafts movement had taken on a life of its own across the United States, becoming a popular statement against certain aspects of industrialization and a work ethic based on handicraft. Stickley had invented "the furniture of the American ideal," according to a 1983 *New York Times* article, "simple, sturdy, unpretentious; functional, natural—a homemade style that was an ethic to live by." The Greene Brothers in California and Frank Lloyd Wright in the Midwest became champions of the new style. In 1908, the Stickley family moved to a 650-acre farm in Parsippany, New Jersey, where Stickley envisioned opening a school for training craftsman. The farm also supplied produce for the Craftsman restaurant, owned and operated by Stickley at his business headquarters in New York City.

1918–1974: L. & J.G. Stickley, Inc.

Yet by the mid-1910s, furniture tastes were changing; by the end of World War I, the public desired more traditional designs once again. Despite Gustav Stickley's success, the Craftsman Shops went bankrupt in 1916, the victim of changing tastes and mass-produced versions of Stickley's own work. Stickley retired from the furniture business to the home of his granddaughter where he died in 1942. In 1918, Leopold and John George Stickley acquired Gustav's factory. John George died in 1921. Leopold traveled widely throughout Europe collecting trestle tables, corner cupboards, dressers, and Windsor chairs, and developed a successful line of American Colonial furniture called the Cherry Valley Collection, launched in response to market trends, in 1922.

In the following decades, Gustav Stickley's work was largely forgotten, his furniture retired to basements and attics. L. & J.G. Stickley continued to manufacture furniture for the next three decades in Fayetteville, New York. A savvy businessman, Leopold Stickley secured contracts to build desks and chairs for nearby colleges and high schools during the Depression when many furniture companies were going bankrupt. During World War II, he manufactured furniture for the Navy. In 1956, Leopold Stickley was honored as "The Revered Dean of Cabinet Makers" by magazines that included *Better Homes and Gardens*, *House Beautiful*, *House and Garden*, *Town and Country*, *Fortune*, *New Yorker*, and *National Geographic*, as a craftsman "whose Art & Craftsmanship has contributed mightily to American home life." Upon his death a year later, his widow, Louise Stickley, took over the business.

1974–2002: The Audis Lead the Company to New Success

During the 1960s, Louise Stickley let many of the company's craftsmen go without replacing them. She refused to hire women as furniture makers or men with long hair. By the early 1970s, after more than ten years of losses, L. & J.G. Stickley's remaining work force of about 20 men was almost completely demoralized, and sales had dropped to about $235,000. By the early 1970s, still out of fashion, Stickley Mission Oak pieces sold alongside mission-style knockoffs in antique shops for identical prices. In 1973, Stickley called Alfred Audi, son of E.J. Audi, Stickley's largest dealer and a close friend of Leopold, and told him that she was thinking of closing shop. Audi bought the ailing company.

Audi had graduated from Colgate University and served three years in the National Guard before becoming president of E.J. Audi, his family's long-established furniture distributorship in Manhattan, in 1968. He had grown up sleeping in a Stickley bed. Audi asked his wife, Aminy, a former schoolteacher at the United Nations School in New York City, to support him in selling their Brooklyn brownstone and moving to upstate New York so that they could buy and run L. & J.G. Stickley, Inc.

After securing a Small Business Administration loan for $200,000, the Audis bought the company along with the rights to Gustav Stickley's original designs and his name. Alfred Audi, in charge of production, hired new workers—including women and men with long hair—and invited Stickley retirees to return to work when they felt like it. Aminy Audi took charge of marketing. Together, the couple introduced new styles of furniture that he knew would sell—Queen Anne and Chippendale collections—and set about to mend the company's strained relationships with furniture dealers.

By 1975, the Audis first full year at the helm of L. & J.G. Stickley, the company's sales had more than tripled, but the business was still so undercapitalized that the Audis had to dip into sales and withholding taxes to meet payroll expenses. Banks refused to give the revived company loans despite the surge in demand for their product because the Audis were "too new to the business," according to a 1990 *Forbes* article. Finally, in the late 1970s, the tide began to turn, and with the help of a few small loans and the Audis' 90-hour work week, sales reached $7 million in 1983. In 1984, the Audis began construction on a new plant in Manlius, New York, two miles from the original Stickley factory, and introduced their 18th Century Mahogany line. The company moved to Manlius in 1985.

A change in decorating trends brought about the Audis next big break. Interest in Arts and Crafts Furniture had been growing on the part of collectors, antique dealers, art historians, and museums since the mid-1970s. Mission Oak was once again being featured in interior design publications and collectors— some of them famous—bid for Stickleys at auctions. After attending an Arts and Crafts auction at Christie's in 1988 at which Barbra Streisand bought a 1903 Gustav Stickley sideboard cabinet built for his Craftsman Farms home for $363,000, the Audis began to reproduce between 30 and 40 items from the original Mission Oak line.

In 1989, the Mission Oak line grew to 15 percent of the company's sales of $25 million, helping Stickley boost overall

Key Dates:

1898: Gustav Stickley opens Craftsman Shops in East-wood, New York.
1900: Leopold and John George Stickley purchase the Collins, Sisson & Pratt furniture company in Fay-etteville, New York.
1904: L. and J.G. Stickley incorporates.
1905: Both Craftsman Shops and L. and J.G. Stickley introduce Mission Oak at a trade show in Grand Rapids, Michigan.
1916: Gustav Stickley goes bankrupt.
1918: Leopold and J.G. Stickley purchase Craftsman Shops.
1921: J.G. Stickley dies.
1922: Leopold Stickley announces the introduction of the Cherry Valley Collection.
1942: Gustav Stickley dies.
1958: Leopold Stickley dies; Louise Stickley takes over management of the company.
1974: Alfred and Aminy Audi purchase L. & J.G. Stickley.
1985: The company moves into a new plant in Manlius, New York.
1995: Stickley acquires the former Heirloom upholstery factory.
1999: Stickley enlarges its upholstery facility.
2002: The company opens it new showroom in Fayette-ville, called Stickley, Audi & Co.

second generation of Audis, Carolyn and Edward, joined the company after completing college. Carolyn Audi focused on dealer relationships, including marketing, display, product development, and training. Edward Audi focused on equipment and computer upgrades to improve production processes.

By the turn of the century, Stickleys were sold throughout the world by more than one hundred independent dealers and through Stickley's own five-store chain. After close to ten expansions, the company operated a facility of more than 400,00 square feet in Manlius, New York. It expanded its High Point plant with a 65,000-square-foot addition in late 1999, and there were plans to move forward with a Craftsman Inn and a Craftsman House hotel and restaurant, capitalizing on Gustav Stickley's lifestyle philosophy. In 2002, the company added a 78,000-square-foot showroom in Fayetteville, New York, which replaced the 38,000-square foot-showroom at the Manlius plant. This showroom, which used the new retail name, Stickley, Audi & Co., also showcased furniture by other manufacturers, such as Baker, Century, Henredon, Hickory Chair, Vanguard, Ralph Lauren, Hancock & Moore, Leathercraft, Ekornes, Cibola, and Bradington-Young.

As the Audis embarked upon their second quarter of a century in business, others attributed their success to their personal patience, hard work, and sense of timing and risk. Aminy Audi herself credited the golden rule in a 1999 *Leaders* magazine interview: "Treat people as you would have them treat you. Be compassionate and caring. If you are compassionate and caring, people will become productive, and in productivity you reap the rewards that lead to a healthy bottom line."

sales 16 percent. The company was now comfortably profitable and expanding, and in 1992, the Audis introduced coordinating mission-style lamps and accessories, following Gustav Stickley's original designs. That same year, the Mission Oak line accounted for 48 percent of the company's overall sales of $37 million. By the early 1990s, the price of antique Stickleys had dropped; however, L. & J.G. Stickley continued to benefit from the resurgence in popularity of Arts and Crafts designs.

Annual sales growth for the decade from 1980 to 1990 was 19 percent. Between 1994 and 1999, the company doubled in size. In the second half of the 1990s, the company began to diversify and update its offerings, introducing more new lines than it had during the ten previous years. In 1995, Stickley added its Metropolitan line, a contemporary take on Mission Oak in solid cherry and acquired the Heirloom upholstery factory in High Point, North Carolina. A year later, it embarked on a second update with its 21st Century Mission line, also built from solid cherry. In 1999, it brought out its French collection, called Directoire. In spring 2000, the company introduced museum-quality reproductions of early Colonial designs under the label "Williamsburg Reserve Collection."

Stickley was by now operating a second shift to lower overhead and keep its machines going more than 90 hours a week. A

Principal Subsidiaries

Stickley Fine Upholstery; Stickley, Audi & Co.

Principal Competitors

Baker Furniture Co.; Henredon.

Further Reading

Brown, Christie, "The Stickley Crash," *Forbes*, April 26, 1993, p. 190.
Danial, Michael, "The Mission of the Stickley Brothers," *Wood & Wood Products*, December 1997, accessed via *ISW Online*, http://www.iswonline.com.
Garet, Barbara, "Against All Odds," *Wood & Wood Products*, October 1993, p. 41.
Giovannini, Joseph, "On Stickley Day, Houses and Furniture," *New York Times*, September 29, 1983, p. C8.
Machan, Dyan, "Rescuing a Proud Name," *Forbes*, February 5, 1990, p. 132.
Pelo, Marilyn, "Furniture with a Mission," *New York Times Magazine*, December 14, 1980, p. 170.
"What You Can Learn from a Family Business," *Leaders*, October-December 1999.

—Carrie Rothburd

Las Vegas Sands, Inc.

3355 Las Vegas Boulevard South, Room 1A
Las Vegas, Nevada 89109
U.S.A.
Telephone: (702) 414-1000
Toll Free: (877) 883-6423
Fax: (702) 414-1100
Web site: http://www.venetian.com

Private Company
Incorporated: 1988
Employees: 4,000
Sales: $523.9 million (2001)
NAIC: 72112 Casino Hotels

The Las Vegas Sands Hotel was a Vegas institution for 44 years. In its heyday, it was the center of entertainment in Las Vegas, with some of show business's biggest names performing there, most notably Frank Sinatra and the ''Rat Pack'' (Sinatra, Dean Martin, Sammy Davis, Jr., and Peter Lawford). For the last seven years of its existence, the Sands Hotel was run by Las Vegas Sands, Inc. (LVSI). When LVSI closed the Sands in 1996, a spectacular new resort, the Venetian Casino Resort Hotel, was built in its place. The Venetian, according to *The Gambler Magazine*, ''raised the bar of expectation of what is considered a world-class mega-resort.''

A Rocky Beginning: 1988

Chairman and sole owner of LVSI, Sheldon G. Adelson, made a name for himself as creator of COMDEX, the world's premier computer trade show, held in Las Vegas, that grew in size and prestige exponentially during the 1990s. COMDEX was produced by The Interface Group (TIG), a 21-employee trade show company that Adelson and his partners built into a vertically integrated organization that owned its own travel agency and airline. However, for convention-goers available hotel rooms in Las Vegas were often difficult to find. ''Comdex and (similar) shows were bringing a lot of people into there who didn't gamble,'' said Harold Vogel, at the time a vice-president at Merrill Lynch Capital Markets. Hotel-casino owners were

therefore reluctant to set rooms aside for convention guests. Also, as Adelson explained, ''If we generate the passengers and carry them to their destinations, it only makes sense to own the destination, too. It gives us quality control over the product we sell to the customer.'' So in 1988, TIG purchased the Las Vegas Sands Hotel. Adelson felt the TIG's choice of the Sands was natural: ''Las Vegas is something very special. There's only one Las Vegas, there's only one strip. And the Sands is the crown jewel of the strip,'' Adelson said.

Adelson and his partners incorporated LVSI in Nevada in 1988 for the purpose of buying and running the Sands. The hotel was purchased from financier Kirk Kerkorian, who earlier purchased the hotel from Howard Hughes' heirs, the Summa Corporation. In February 1989, the Nevada Gaming Control Board approved the sale. Adelson appointed Henri Lewin, a former Hilton executive, as the hotel's president.

Lewin was a colorful figure, and his style clashed with Adelson's, often publicly. Gaming revenues at the Sands were disappointing, and ten months after he was appointed president of the Sands, Lewin was fired from his job. He later sued LVSI and settled out of court. Management of the hotel was handed to a team headed by Al Benedict, a former executive at MGM Grand. Benedict's team resigned seven months later, and Steve Norton was appointed interim president of the Sands.

LVSI added the Sands Expo and Convention Center to the hotel, a 575,000-square-feet convention facility. The plan was to add another tower to the hotel, almost doubling its capacity. The initial architect for the expansion project, Nikita Zukov, was fired four months into the job. According to LVSI, he failed to develop the project on budget. He later sued for breach of contract and won a $1.3 million award. During the trial, Henri Lewin testified for Zukov, blasting Adelson and his management style. The convention facility opened and was making money, but the old Sands, with 750 rooms, could not compete with the new mega-resorts sprouting around it, especially the gilded Mirage that opened across the street.

In 1991, Adelson assumed leadership of the hotel, and in the ensuing years the convention center nearly doubled in size, to 1.15 million square feet. The casino area expanded as well. The

Company Perspectives:

The Company's primary business objective is to provide a premium destination casino resort experience in order to drive superior returns on invested capital and to increase asset value. To achieve this objective, the Company: operates a "must-see" destination resort at a premier location at the heart of the Strip; captures premium room rates through a differentiated superior all-suites product; drives hotel occupancy and casino utilization through the link to the Expo Center and the Congress Center; caters to a higher-budget customer mix by offering a unique combination of assets and facilities; leverages the Casino Resort's premium co-branding strategy to drive revenues; and targets premium gaming customers.

Key Dates:

1988: Financier Kirk Kerkorian buys the Las Vegas Sands Hotel, announces its sale to The Interface Group (TIG); and TIG forms Las Vegas Sands, Inc. (LVSI) to run the property.

1989: LVSI completes the Sands purchase and Henri Lewin is named hotel president.

1990: Lewin is fired; Al Benedict assumes leadership of the hotel, resigns in August; and Steve Norton is named interim president.

1991: LVSI Chairman Sheldon G. Adelson takes over the running of the hotel.

1995: TIG sells its Trade Show division to Japan's Softbank; and Adelson buys out his partners' share in LVSI.

1996: The Sands Hotel is closed and imploded.

1997: The Venetian Resort Hotel Casino breaks ground.

1999: The Venetian opens and is run by Venetian Casino Resort, LLC, owned by LVSI, with Robert Goldstein as president and COO.

2000–2001: The Venetian is featured in *Condé Nast Traveler* magazine's "Gold List of the World's Best Places to Stay" two years in a row.

new rooms, however, were never added, and despite a $20 million refurbishment, the hotel, in the words of one Mirage guest, still looked "seedy."

A New Resort and a Look Ahead: 1995

In 1995, TIG sold its Trade Show division to Japan's Softbank. Adelson used the proceeds from the $800 million cash sale to buy out his partners in LVSI, becoming sole owner of the company. William P. Weidner became LVSI's president and COO. Adelson had already expressed his interest in opening a mega-resort, and in early 1996 the news broke that the famed Sands Hotel would be closed and demolished, to make room for a new themed resort.

The Sands Hotel closed on June 30, 1996 and was imploded on November 26 of that same year. On April 14, 1997, the Venetian Resort-Hotel-Casino broke ground. The hotel was themed after renaissance Venice, down to the Grand Canal reproduction in the Grand Canal Shops area. Two historians checked the accuracy of details during the hotel's construction. The Venetian opened on May 3, 1999. At a cost of $1.5 billion, and with 500,000 square feet of retail space and suites averaging 700 square feet, the Venetian "raised the bar of expectation of what is considered a world-class mega-resort," according to *The Gambler Magazine*.

The hotel was run by Venetian Casino Resort, LLC, with Robert Goldstein as president and COO. Venetian Casino Resort, LLC was owned and managed by LVSI. The property was physically connected to the Sands Expo and Convention Center, making the entire complex one of the largest hotel and meeting complexes in the United States (the Sands Expo was run by The Interface Group Inc.—Nevada, a separate entity from LVSI, though both companies are owned by Sheldon Adelson). In 2001 and 2002, the Venetian was featured in *Condé Nast Traveler* magazine's "Gold List of the World's Best Places to Stay." The hotel strove to cater to both gamblers and business travelers in order to drive revenues. In the first quarter of 2002, the Venetian was one of only three Las Vegas hotels that showed increased cash flow compared with the same quarter the previous year.

LVSI planned to construct a second resort, of equal size to the Venetian, at a future unspecified date. Concrete plans for

this development were suspended in the wake of the September 11, 2001, attacks in New York City that severely impacted the tourism industry.

In early 2002, it looked as though the company was heading into global and virtual expansion. In February 2002, Galaxy Casino, Inc., a joint venture between Venetian Casino Resort, LLC and Macau and Hong Kong investors, had been granted a provisional concession for Macau Gaming License. Macau, a small territory that was controlled by Portugal for over 400 years, reverted back to China in 1999, but was allowed to retain its capitalist system for the following 50 years. The Macau gaming market was closed to competition for decades. Galaxy Casino and Stephen Wynn's Wynn Resorts (Macao) Ltd. were the first outside gaming companies to be granted concessions in Macau. Sheldon Adelson also announced plans for the Venetian to develop a convention center in China. LVSI announced it was looking into Internet gambling as an additional source of revenue. In May 2002 the company issued $850 million in second mortgage notes to refinance their debt and allow for these expansions.

Principal Subsidiaries

Grand Canal Shops Mall LLC; Venetian Casino Resort, LLC (100%).

Principal Competitors

Mandalay Resort Group; MGM Mirage; Park Place Entertainment.

Further Reading

Bates, Warren, "Hotel's History Full of Legends, Mystique, Wild Weekends," *Las Vegas Review-Journal*, May 17, 1996, p.2A.

Carton, Barbara, ''Needham Firm Wins Rights to Sands; Nevada Board Rejects Three Proposed Partners,'' *Boston Globe*, February 10, 1989, p. 21.

Coleman, Zach, ''U.S. Regulators are Expected to Scrutinize Macau Proposal—Venetian Awaits Nod from Nevada Authorities,'' *Wall Street Journal*, March 25, 2002, p. A12.

Harris, Kathryn, ''Kerkorian to Sell Sands Hotel for $110 Million,'' *Los Angeles Times*, April 26, 1988, HOME magazine, p. 2.

Kanigher, Steve, ''Resort Owner Has Much at Stake in Latest Gaming Industry Venture,'' *Las Vegas Sun*, April 29, 1999, http://www.lasvegassun.com.

Patterson, Gregory A., ''Taking a Gamble on Las Vegas: Dynamic Interface Owner Pushes Charter Company into the Big Time,'' *Boston Globe*, May 8, 1988, p. A1.

Strow, David, ''Adelson in Net Gaming Pact,'' *Las Vegas Sun*, April 1, 2002, http://www.lasvegassun.com.

Stutz, Howard, ''Adelson to Take Over Sands Operation,'' *Las Vegas Review-Journal*, April 30, 1991, p. 6e.

Szecsodi, Peter, ''Where Fantasies Come True,'' *The Gambler Magazine*, May 31, 2002, http://www.thegamblermagazine.com.

''Venetian Posts Increase in Cash Flow for First Quarter,'' *Associated Press Newswires*, April 24, 2002, http://www.djinteractive.com.

—Adi R. Ferrara

La-Z-Boy Incoporated

1284 North Telegraph Road
Monroe, Michigan 48162-3390
U.S.A.
Telephone: (734) 242-1444
Fax: (313) 241-4422
Web site: http://www.la-z-boy.com

Public Company
Incorporated: 1941
Employees: 19,700 (2001)
Sales: $2.154 billion (2002)
Stock Exchanges: New York
Ticker symbol: LZB
NAIC: 337121 Upholstered Household Furniture Manu-
   facturing; 337122 Nonupholstered Wood Household
   Furniture Manufacturing; 442110 Furniture Stores

La-Z-Boy Incorporated is the largest independent manufacturer of upholstered furniture in the United States and third
overall in the manufacture of residential furniture. La-Z-Boy
enjoys near-universal name recognition. In fact, its name has
become practically synonymous with the reclining chair.

Birth of the La-Z-Boy Recliner

La-Z-Boy originated in a love of carpentry shared by two
cousins, Edward Knabusch and Edwin Shoemaker, both of
Monroe, Michigan. In the early 1920s, Knabusch was a carpenter at the Weis Manufacturing Company and spent his evenings
repairing furniture as well as building novelty and custom furniture in a workshop set up in the family garage. Despite the fact
that Shoemaker was being groomed by his father to take over
the family farm, he was far more interested in carpentry and
spent his free time in his cousin's new workshop.

In 1925, Knabusch's hobby became a full-time business when
he left Weis Manufacturing to start his own business. His first
project was to invent a new bandsaw guide. Because of his
engineering aptitude, Shoemaker was hired by Knabusch and
together they completed the project. Afterward, business increased significantly, spurring Knabusch to purchase new equipment. By March 1927 the business had expanded far beyond any
expectations shared by the two cousins, and they decided to form
a partnership under the name Kna-Shoe Manufacturing Company. Meanwhile, business continued to expand and the partners
soon outgrew Knabusch's family garage. By the end of 1927,
with the financial support of friends and family, a new factory
was completed north of Monroe. Built in the middle of a cornfield
that fronted a cow path, the site led many to say the two men were
foolish to establish their factory so far from the city. However,
their gamble paid off as rumors of a state highway became reality
soon after; the old cow path became M-24 (Telegraph Road), a
major north-south Michigan artery.

As a rule, the partners preferred to develop new designs rather
than copying the products of other companies. One such design
was the Gossiper, which was a telephone stand with a built-in
seat. Although the Gossiper was an immediate success, a large
manufacturer soon copied the design and sold it more cheaply
than Knabusch and Shoemaker. Other products would follow, but
none were as successful as the simple wood-slat porch chair that
reclined to follow the body's contour, whether sitting up or
leaning back. Believing they had a winner, the two men sought to
market the new chair. However, when Arthur Richardson, a buyer
for the Lion Store, suggested that they upholster the new chair for
year-round use indoors, they changed their plans. Lacking any
upholstery knowledge, the partners called upon George Welker to
assist in upholstery decisions.

To protect their new invention the men incorporated in 1929
as the Floral City Furniture Company, abandoning the Kna-
Shoe name because people mistook the company for a shoe
manufacturer. Through friends and family, the men raised
$10,000 to secure the necessary patents and began production.
The men attended their first furniture show in May 1929 and
returned with more orders than they could fill.

As their innovative recliner became increasingly popular,
the need for a name became apparent. The partners held a public
contest to name the recliner, thus finding a name and generating
further interest in their product simultaneously. In November
1930, the winning name, La-Z-Boy, was trademarked, and the
patent for the new mechanism was issued in January 1931. Soon

thereafter, the partners licensed the right to manufacture the chair to existing companies. Floral City manufactured the metal recliner mechanism and retained the rights to manufacture and sell the chair in Monroe County. At the same time, Floral City Furniture returned to repairing furniture and manufacturing novelty/custom furniture.

An Emphasis on Retail Sales

Flourishing during the depths of the Great Depression, the men redoubled their efforts in retail sales. In 1933 the first floor of their factory was converted into a showroom. To celebrate the opening of the showroom, a circus tent was set up in front of the store to display furniture. Soon, the "Furniture Shows" were drawing people from Detroit and Toledo. With Edward Knabusch's keen marketing sense, the company's flamboyant shows helped to assuage the anxiety of a people caught in the grips of a horrible Depression. While other companies frantically worked for quick sales, Floral City provided entertainment in addition to their high-quality products. Knabusch and Shoemaker were able to sell their wares in ever-increasing numbers, while thousands of other businesses faltered and failed. Business was so successful that in 1935 the partners opened a new showroom.

By the late 1930s, problems with the licensing agreements and increasing costs to manufacture the reclining mechanism led Shoemaker to develop a new mechanism. Completed in June 1938, the new mechanism was so different from the original that all new patents were required. The licensing agreements came to an end in 1939, and all manufacturing operations returned to Floral City Furniture.

World War II Years

In order to separate the manufacturing and retailing functions, the La-Z-Boy Chair Company was incorporated in May 1941. A new factory designed by Knabusch and Shoemaker was completed on October 15, 1941, but the new facility would not produce La-Z-Boys until six years later due to America's entry into World War II. While Woodall Industries produced specialized plane parts in the new building, La-Z-Boy rented out garage space to produce seats for tanks, torpedo boats, turret guns, and armored cars.

At the war's end, the company reverted to civilian trade, and production of La-Z-Boy recliners began at the new building in 1947. La-Z-Boy rode their solid reputation and emerged as the

Baby Boom favorite into the 1950s. The platform rocker was introduced in 1951. The company's most unusual promotion took place late in the decade. In 1959 the company built a loveseat designed to look like a car seat. Upholstered in mink, the loveseat was fitted with lights, horns, fins, and tires. Unlike the imaginative promotions of the Depression era, which combined style with substance, and marketing with manufacturing, the loveseat was all style.

Innovation and Advertising

By the beginning of the 1960s, the company regained the balance of innovation and promotion that had marked the company's earlier successes. La-Z-Boy began a long-lived marketing campaign that used the support of such celebrities as Bing Crosby, Ed McMahon, Johnny Carson, Joe Nameth, Alex Karras, and most importantly, Jim Backus. Known for his role as the voice of the myopic cartoon character Mr. Magoo, Backus recorded more than 15,000 television and radio commercials for La-Z-Boy during the 1960s.

A burst of product innovation accompanied this successful advertising campaign. Late in 1960, the partners introduced the Reclina-Rocker. Unlike other recliners, this one formed an unbroken line of support from head to toe and utilized independent seat back and footrest mechanisms. The partners commented that "[the] chair was like magic. It sold well from the beginning. The problem was making enough of them." Other new products included the Reclina-Way wall chair, which allowed the chair to be placed very close to the wall while maintaining the ability to fully recline; the La-Z-Touch recliner, which featured a massage system to reduce muscle tension and stress; and the Reclina-Rest reclining chair. In order to keep up with increasing production and to help the company expand into the national market, La-Z-Boy opened its first factory outside of Michigan in Newton, Mississippi, in 1961.

The renewed marketing efforts, along with the introduction of the Reclina-Rocker, helped La-Z-Boy's sales increase from $1.1 million in 1960 to $52.7 million in 1970. In March 1972, the company went public, and, in the first year, 600 people bought over 320,000 shares in over-the-counter trading. The company enjoyed continued success throughout the 1970s, experiencing new sales records every year except for 1975, despite the shutdown of the partners' first company, Floral City Furniture, in 1974. By the end of the 1970s, La-Z-Boy operated nine manufacturing plants: two in Michigan, and one each in Arkansas, California, Mississippi, Missouri, South Carolina, Tennessee, and Utah. In addition, La-Z-Boy had established licensing agreements with plants in Canada, Germany, Italy, Japan, New Zealand, Great Britain, Mexico, and South Africa. In 1979, the company purchased Deluxe Upholstering Ltd., a company that had previously manufactured La-Z-Boy products under a licensing agreement, and formed La-Z-Boy Canada Ltd. as a subsidiary.

New products and improvements to old ones contributed to the company's continued success in the 1970s. The company introduced a sleeper sofa in 1977 that represented the first major departure from La-Z-Boy's popular recliners. Applying the same high quality and mechanical savvy to the new product, the sofa featured a removable back, allowing greater portability; an

Key Dates:

1928: Cousins Edward Knabusch and Edwin Shoemaker, ("the two Eds") create the first folding wood-slat porch recliner.

1929: The porch recliner is upholstered, allowing for indoor, year-round use; the La-Z-Boy name is chosen.

1931: The patent for La-Z-Boy is issued, and the partners license the right to manufacture the chair to existing companies.

1941: La-Z-Boy incorporates; and stops chair production to create plane parts for World War II.

1947: Production of recliners resumes; and matching ottomans are introduced.

1952: The first La-Z-Boy recliner with built-in footrest is introduced.

1960: La-Z-Boy begins making rocker recliners; and opens its first factory outside Michigan in Mississippi.

1970: The company offers recliners with electric controls.

1972: The company goes public; 600 people buy shares in over-the-counter trading.

1975: The company introduces recliners that move away from walls.

1986: The company introduces power recliners and power-assisted lifts.

1987: La-Z-Boy begins trading on the New York Stock Exchange.

1989: The company opens its first La-Z-Boy Furniture Gallery.

1993: The company's new line of recliners offers massage and heat; another line targets customers with smaller body types.

1999: The company offers recliners with built-in beverage coolers, phones, caller ID, and motorized-massage options.

2000: La-Z-Boy and Microsoft team up to offer the Explorer E-cliner, a recliner with built-in WebTV Internet access and tools.

2001: The company introduces chairs for children.

innerspring mattress unique to La-Z-Boy's sleeper sofa; a counterbalancing mechanism; and a patented weight distribution mechanism. At the same time, the company improved the immensely popular Reclina-Rocker by integrating the Reclina-Way's ability to be placed very close to the wall, thus creating the Wall Reclina-Rocker.

New Marketing Strategies and Aggressive Acquisitions

In 1982, the company reached a major turning point when Patrick Norton of Ethan Allen, renowned for its marketing savvy, was made senior vice-president of sales and marketing at La-Z-Boy. Norton recalled that upon arriving at La-Z-Boy he found "a company with great plants, a great name, and a great product but a bit short on marketing direction." Charles Knabusch, adopted son of cofounder Edward Knabusch, assumed the position of chairman of the board in 1985 and, with Norton's help, concentrated on improvements in five major areas.

First, they actively sought to attract women. The furniture was redesigned in the mid-1980s to attract female customers, and in the early 1990s ad campaigns began to target women. In 1991 the company launched the largest ad campaign in its history without using a single television spot. Instead, the campaign concentrated on magazines, especially upscale women's titles. Jim Krusinski, director of advertising and public relations, stated that "Women are our primary target audience," and when choosing home furnishings, "it's common knowledge that many women tend to go to the magazines for ideas." The new campaign was in stark contrast to past "television-oriented" campaigns featuring various celebrities. Krusinski added, "We won't go back."

Second, La-Z-Boy began diversifying product lines through acquisitions and internal product development. Beginning with Burris Industries in December 1985, a maker of high-end motion chairs, La-Z-Boy went on to acquire RoseJohnson Incorporated in January 1986; Hammary Furniture, a manufacturer of residential tables and upholstery manufacturer, in September 1986; and the Kincaid Furniture Company, a producer of solid-wood dining and bedroom furniture, in January 1988. In all, La-Z-Boy spent about $80 million on these acquisitions and not without criticism.

In 1989, the company became a target of a hostile takeover by its largest institutional investor, Prescott Investors, which owned 5.6 percent of the shares. Thomas Smith, Prescott's leading general partner, charged that earnings and share value had not grown at an acceptable rate and placed much of the blame on La-Z-Boy's acquisitions. However, in the end, Prescott backed off and La-Z-Boy stood by the new acquisitions. In addition to these acquisitions, La-Z-Boy created a new division, the La-Z-Boy Contract Group, composed of three entities: La-Z-Boy Business Furniture, La-Z-Boy Healthcare, and La-Z-Boy Hospitality. By 1993 these divisions and other subsidiaries amounted to 30 percent of La-Z-Boy sales.

In addition to acquisitions, new product development within the company signaled a broadening perspective. La-Z-Boy expanded into stationary and motion modular furniture and continued to support the sleeper sofas introduced in the late 1970s. In 1980, La-Z-Boy's sales of $160 million were derived almost exclusively from recliners. By 1993, recliner sales amounted to 57 percent of the company's nearly $700 million in total sales.

Third, La-Z-Boy reevaluated its retail system. In the 1970s and 1980s, independently owned La-Z-Boy Showcase Shoppes were opened across the country. In-Store Galleries within Independent General Furniture Dealers displayed La-Z-Boy furniture in separate dedicated settings. At the same time, ineffective dealers unwilling to push the product were eliminated. By the late 1980s, 42 percent of all the La-Z-Boy dealers in existence in 1980 had been eliminated. In 1989 the company reached a major turning point in its retail operations when it opened the first La-Z-Boy Furniture Gallery. These superstores facilitated the display of a much larger and more diverse selection of La-Z-Boy furniture. By 1993 the company was operating 63 La-Z-Boy Furniture Galleries and planned to transform many La-Z-Boy Showcase Shoppes into galleries. The La-Z-Boy proprietary retail system included 750 locations, accounting for about half of La-Z-Boy's upholstered furniture sales, and thousands of independent retail outlets, regional furniture chains, and a major nationwide retailer.

Fourth, technological innovations placed La-Z-Boy at the forefront of the furniture industry. In the late 1970s, the company automated its material requirements planning process, which greatly simplified the acquisition of materials, manufacturing processes, and distribution. By the late 1980s, La-Z-Boy had introduced computer-aided design (CAD) to expedite the research and development of products, enabling the company to cut the delivery time of new products by 60 percent. Additionally, La-Z-Boy adopted an Electronic Data Interchange to facilitate the electronic transmittal and tracking of orders. As a result, retail operations were able to reduce ordering time and to track the progress of an order more accurately. As of 1993, the company had implemented the La-Z-Boy Screen Test video catalog system that allowed customers to review every style, color, and fabric offered by La-Z-Boy at the touch of a button.

Finally, La-Z-Boy set its sights on globalization. Although La-Z-Boy had licensed its chairs internationally for 30 years, international sales amounted to only one-half of 1 percent of La-Z-Boy sales by the early 1990s. However, with the opening of markets in Eastern Europe and the former republics of the Soviet Union, La-Z-Boy redoubled its efforts to market its recliners in Europe. More importantly, La-Z-Boy made its most significant move toward globalization when it developed recliners designed for smaller Asian body types in 1993.

Beginning in 1987, La-Z-Boy began trading on the New York Stock Exchange, and in 1990 the company moved into the *Fortune* 500 at number 496, reaching number 460 by 1994. In spite of an economic downturn in furniture sales from 1989 to 1991, La-Z-Boy enjoyed continued success. La-Z-Boy sales rose 10 percent to $805 million in fiscal 1994, which represented the company's 12th straight year of record sales. La-Z-Boy continued to be the number one manufacturer of recliners with over 30 percent of the market.

A New CEO

When Charles Knabusch died in 1997, and Edwin Shoemaker a year later died (in his recliner), La-Z-Boy ceased to be family-owned. Gerald Kiser took over as president in 1997 and had big shoes to fill. Company sales had continued to increase for the past 17 years, and the company pulled in $1.2 billion in revenues. No longer a sole manufacturer of recliners, the company had acquired five furniture makers and sold dining room sets, tables, entertainments centers, and other furniture. But although recliners still constituted one third of the company's sales, it was getting more difficult for La-Z-Boy to generate more growth. They had to come up with new plans.

One move was to continue the company's growth with more acquisitions. La-Z-Boy bought LADD furniture in 1997, making themselves the largest residential furniture manufacturer in the United States. The deal was expected to increase La-Z-Boy sales to more than $2 billion.

Declining Sales and Company Consolidation

However in 1999 the economy began to sink and took the furniture market along with it. Bankruptcy filings by Montgomery Ward stores hurt La-Z-Boy, and sales dropped for the first time in 20 years. Foreseeing poor revenues for 2000, the company decided to try a new tactic. The La-Z-Boy name was one of the most recognized. They spent $50 million on advertising and for the first time targeted more affluent and younger buyers, a strategy none too easy considering La-Z-Boy's present "tacky" connotations. Up to then the company had catered to sports fans and basic armchair living styles. Still, the company thought it would be worth trying and began to roll out updated offerings, such as chairs covered in designer fabrics. Design, too, became all more important, especially with the company's desire to start catering to women. Smaller, more feminine chairs, updated styles, retro looks, and fabrics created by "painter of light" artist Thomas Kincaid, added to the La-Z-Boy lines. The company took care however, not to alienate its main consumer market and to and keep its chair franchise.

By the middle of 2000, La-Z-Boy had decided to start consolidating. They closed their Lea Industries and Pilliod plants, incorporating production into their other facilities. In addition, La-Z-Boy had to close its Chilhowie, Virginia plant and move production of the lodging line to American of Martinsville due to the September 11th terrorist attack aftermath and its impact on lodging furniture needs. While some employees transferred, 245 lost their jobs, bringing the total eliminated jobs to almost 3,000 since July 2000.

In September, La-Z-Boy streamlined at the top as well; their management and reporting structure broke into two groups, Casegoods and Upholstery. The Casegoods group comprised the dining room sets, hutches, and tables, while sofas and chairs fell under the Upholstery group. In addition they incorporated their LADD line into these two divisions and phased out the LADD name.

New Features and Innovations

By the new millennium the high-tech boom had not only taken over business but had infiltrated the La-Z-Boy Design teams as well. While they had already designed chairs with advanced features, nothing else showcased the Web-savvy world more than La-Z-Boy's newest recliner, created as a joint venture with Microsoft, Inc. Called the "Explorer E-cliner," this model featured a La-Z-Boy chair with built-in keyboard tray and an infrared beam that connected to a Sony WebTV receiver. Users could sit comfortably in their favorite recliner and surf the Web without leaving the chair.

For 2002, La-Z-Boy began to branch out its lines even more. They entered a joint venture with European household goods manufacturer Steinhoff Group to produce a line of chairs for the European market. The collection would be manufactured in Steinhoff's base in Germany. Later that year the company decided to showcase a new line of designer recliners featuring looks by top fashion designers such as Tommy Hilfiger, Nicole Miller, and Cynthia Rowley. The company felt these chairs would extend their "new look of comfort" concept. While the initial run was auctioned off for charity, La-Z-Boy had started to evaluate a mass-production option with a possible marketing target of professional women.

Principal Subsidiaries

England Corsair Furniture; Hammery Furniture Company; Kincaid Furniture Company; La-Z-Boy Canada Ltd.; La-Z-Boy Contract Furniture Group.

Principal Competitors

Ethan Allen Interiors Inc.; Furniture Brands International; The Natuzzi Group.

Further Reading

Bary, Andrew, "Comfy Again: After a Deep Slump, the Furniture Industry Is Bouncing Back," *Barron's*, November 8, 1993, pp. 14–15.

Cortez, John, "La-Z-Boy Cozies Up to Print," *Advertising Age*, July 22, 1991, p. 41.

"In Memory of Edward M. Knabusch, 1900–1988," *La-Z-News*, March 1988.

Jannsen, Albert B., *I Remember When . . .: A History of La-Z-Boy Chair Company*.

Kolebuck, Frank, "Automating to Streamline, Producing to Recline," *Manufacturing Systems*, November 1991, pp. 30–32.

Kupfer, Andrew, "Success Secrets of Tomorrow's Stars," *Fortune*, April 23, 1990, pp. 77–84.

Nulty, Peter, "What a Difference Owner-Bosses Make," *Fortune*, April 25, 1988, pp. 97–104.

Schifrin, Matthew, "Rocking the Recliners," *Forbes*, October 16, 1989, pp. 194–96.

Slat, Charles, "La-Z-Boy: Gradually Going Global," *Monroe Evening News*, December 5, 1993, pp. E1–E2.

"Sleeper Joins La-Z-Boy Line," *Monroe Evening News*, February 14, 1977, pp. A1, A14.

—Bradley T. Bernatek
—update: Kerri DeVault

Les Schwab Tire Centers

1250 East 3rd Street
Prineville, Oregon 97754
U.S.A.
Telephone: (541) 447-4136
Fax: (541) 416-5488
Web site: http://www.lesschwab.com

Private Company
Employees: 7000 (2001 est.)
Sales: $790 million (2001 est.)
NAIC: 441320 Tire Dealers; 421130 Tire and Tube
  Wholesalers; 441310 Automotive Parts and
  Accessories Stores

Les Schwab's first attempt at selling tires in Prineville, Oregon, has blossomed into one of America's largest and most successful independent tire chains, Les Schwab Tire Centers. Les Schwab Tires includes over 330 locations throughout Oregon, Washington, Idaho, Montana, California, Nevada, Alaska, and Utah. Les Schwab Tires prides itself on continued customer service—the practice of greeting customers as they drive into the shop's parking lot has long been a company trademark. In addition to selling tires and batteries and doing alignment, brake, and shock work, Les Schwab Tires produces truck tires, constructs new trucks and equipment, and operates five tire retread plants. Another major source of pride for Les Schwab Tires is the profit-sharing and retirement programs that Schwab began during the beginning stages of his career. When Les Schwab was recognized as *Modern Tire Dealers* magazine's Tire Dealer of the Year in December 2000, his policy of sharing more than 51 percent of his company's profits with employees was mentioned and applauded. This policy makes millionaires out of many Les Schwab employees by the time they retire.

Humble Beginnings

Les Schwab tried his hand at many trades before settling on the franchised tire business. Orphaned at a young age, Schwab was left to fend for himself when he was just 15 years old. He proved that he was extremely capable of taking care of himself and his brother when he convinced the principal of his school to let him out early to deliver newspapers. This job allowed him to earn the $8.00 a month he needed to pay his and his brother's rent. By the time he was 16, he had become circulation director of one of the newspapers he had been delivering. After serving in World War II and working once again as the circulation manager upon his return to Oregon, Schwab was anxious to open a business of his own. In 1952 he and his wife, Dorothy, sold their house, borrowed $1,100 from Dorothy's brother, and purchased OK Rubber Welders, a franchised tire shop in Prineville, Oregon. Although Schwab barely knew anything about tires, he was able to make a success of his store, grossing approximately $10,000 in sales a month, and $150,000 in the first year. In the next two years, Schwab expanded his business to include two more stores.

By 1955 when Schwab acquired his third OK Rubber Welders store in Redmond, Oregon, he knew that operating as a franchise was not going to work for him. It was not his own creation and he had too many ideas and theories that he wanted to test out. Soon after he acquired the third store, Schwab changed the name of his shops to Les Schwab Tire Centers, developed and began implementing an idea that is now called the "supermarket tire concept." The supermarket tire concept turned his tire warehouse into a showroom that customers could walk through in order to select the exact tires that they would like to purchase. Schwab also aimed to stock multiple brands of tire in each size to give customers more options. Schwab's idea was not popular with the major tire distributors but proved an incredibly successful business strategy for Les Schwab Tires.

Independent Thinking

As Schwab opened more stores, he became increasingly independent in his strategic business plans. In 1966, Schwab decided to take down all of the rubber company's signs that advertised particular brands of tires and replaced them with his own Les Schwab Tires sign. Many of the rubber companies were disgruntled at this change; one supplier who objected adamantly to Schwab's new practice found his brand dropped from Schwab's offerings altogether. In 1966, Schwab added six stores and a retread shop in Idaho to his empire, bringing the count of stores he owned up to 18. Retreading was a significant

Company Perspectives:

The Les Schwab Company's biggest challenge is to continue to offer opportunity for its employees and to build people. Its goal is to continue to provide the Les Schwab basics of customer service, to be original and innovative, and to stay independent. It's important to always remember we are in business for one thing, and that is to take care of our customers.

addition to the Les Schwab Tires business plan. Les Schwab Tires retreads worn tires and sells them with the same warranty that would come with a new tire. By 1972, Schwab had increased his number of stores to 35, and he had not stopped opening stores. Schwab was able to grow at such a fast rate, partly due to his sales success, that Les Schwab Tires redoubled its sales volume every five years.

Prineville, Oregon: The Perfect Spot for Headquarters?

Les Schwab's headquarters has been located in Prineville, Oregon, since the purchase of his first OK Rubber Welders store. The Prineville location has grown from the 1,400 square-foot shed with no running water that Schwab purchased in 1952, to a large cluster of buildings including a three-story administrative building with offices for 150 staffers, a large training-and-meeting facility, a computer center that keeps Les Schwab Tire Centers computers running in five states, and the largest retread shop in America. Within eyesight of the administrative headquarters, Schwab created a storage area for four million scrap tires that would be chopped up and buried. The Prineville compound also included a 450,000-square-foot warehouse that stores hundreds of thousands of new tires.

Although Prineville was significantly off the beaten track, Schwab opted to keep Les Schwab Tire Centers headquartered there for the long haul. In 1995 when word leaked out that Les Schwab Tires was considering moving its headquarters to be closer to the regions that the company was expanding into, Prineville's community rallied to keep Les Schwab Tires where it was. Phone calls streamed into Les Schwab Tire Centers headquarters, and a plan was concocted to help the company build the new warehouse it needed at the site of the Prineville Airport Industrial Park. Prineville was thrilled with Les Schwab Tires decision to stay and the town held the company responsible for its burgeoning growth.

Computers to the Rescue

The Les Schwab Tire Centers Prineville headquarters had been computerized since 1972, but it was not until 1982 when the company began considering the possibility of computerizing individual retail stores in order to speed up the invoice process. The company updated its computer system to IBM System/38 and dial-up modem technology and began the process of outfitting its stores with a computer network. When 80 stores were computerized, they finally saw a measurable difference from the previous system. The computerized-stores sent out invoice statements ten days earlier than before, and received payments earlier as a result. The system that Les Schwab Tires had chosen to use had many advantages: it was relatively inexpensive, it used a programming language in which the Les Schwab Tires programming staff was already fluent, and the system was programmed so that if a store had serious computer troubles, they could be dealt with remotely from headquarters.

In 1994 when Les Schwab Tires found that the POS (point of sale) terminals in their retail stores were not operating as well as they needed them to be, the company opted to look for a new solution. "The problem," explained Les Schwab Tires Telecommunications Manager Pam Ontko, "boiled down to transaction speed and memory capacity. During regular business times, transactions took about 30 seconds to process, but during our peak times the old terminals we had been using could take as long as three minutes to obtain a transaction authorization. This caused extensive queuing at checkout counters and caused anxiety for the customer waiting for their credit card to process." Les Schwab Tires opted to install the T7E terminals from Hypercom, Inc. in Phoenix, Arizona. The new terminals were significantly quicker than the previous ones, and featured considerably more memory capability. Ontko noted, "The T7E has separate, single, labeled keys to press to perform the most common functions, and so requires minimal training. In fact, after installing the initial 12 stores, we fine-tuned the instructions that include some special procedures for our stores. From this, our stores were able to install the equipment." The process for generating reports and other daily transactions was simplified with the new system, due to its user-friendly layout. The new computers also gave Les Schwab Tires some of the tools it needed to stay competitive in the near future, like the capability to support debit/ATM cards, check scanners, and other necessary business components.

Compassionate Company

Les Schwab Tires took advantage of many opportunities to raise and donate money to charity. Some of the community service activities that Les Schwab Tires was involved in were uniquely suited to them. The company donated tires/wheels to the Cottage Grove, Oregon, Police Department's D.A.R.E. (Drug Abuse Resistance Education) program. A police officer who is part of the D.A.R.E. program drives a fancily decorated and stereo-sound enhanced GEO Tracker, a car that was recovered from a drug dealer, when making rounds to the local elementary schools to teach the 7-part D.A.R.E. program. Les Schwab Tires contributed to the community when the company participated in the Society of Vintage Racing Enthusiasts (Sovren) Group's Northwest Vintage Races. In that event, for $10,000, a person could drive a vintage car, souped up with Toyo Tires and Les Schwab Tires decals. Ten executives from the Seattle area purchased rides. The event raised more than $300,000 for the Children's Hospital of Seattle. In addition, Les Schwab Tires became well known for its practice of sponsoring sports teams (commonly basketball teams) in towns where the company has shops.

Tire Troubles

In the early 1990s, a general concern about the growing piles of old vehicle tires grew into legislation. Many of the states that Les Schwab Tires operated in passed their own laws, and in 1991, an Idaho law went into effect that prohibited the disposal

---

Key Dates:

1952: Les Schwab purchases a small OK Rubber Welders tire store in Prineville, Oregon.

1954: Les Schwab starts his first profit-share program with the store manager of his Redmond, Oregon, OK Rubber Welders branch.

1966: Les Schwab decides to abandon the OK Rubber Welders franchise and operate them as an independent business. He changes the business name to Les Schwab Tire Centers and forms the Les Schwab Retirement Trust.

1972: Les Schwab opens his 35th Les Schwab Tire Centers store.

1982: Company computerizes individual retail stores.

2000: *Modern Tire Dealers* magazine recognizes Les Schwab as Tire Dealer of the Year.

---

of tires in landfills. In 1994, Idaho's Board of Health and Welfare voted to require a tracking system for used tires. These types of laws were passed because it was found that tire piles posed major fire risks. Les Schwab Tires noted that their company had a built-in $1.00 fee on all new tire sales that was slated to pay for tire cleanup. The company piled its tires and waited patiently for an economical solution to the problem of disposing of old tires. However, in 1996, Les Schwab Tires headquarters had more than four million tires stacked a few miles west of it, and still no economical and environmentally sound solution regarding the old tires was in sight.

Seizing Opportunities

When the Asian currency markets fell in 1998 and the Asian automobile market took a dive, Les Schwab Tires wasted no time taking advantage of the strong dollar-value in Korea. Les Schwab Tires quickly swooped into the Korean rubber market and scooped up the deals left behind when tire suppliers' customers began to bow out of orders.

Another example of Les Schwab Tires' ability to quickly turn a potentially harmful situation into a success for the company occurred in 2000, when Firestone tires, in a highly publicized tire recall, recalled tires that had been standard on the Ford Explorer. While Ford dealerships and Firestone tire stores were having trouble servicing all of the people that were flooding their shops, Les Schwab Tires was waiting patiently for car owners to find their way to their shops. Schwab's history of stocking Firestone-brand tires made them uniquely prepared to deal with the influx of people seeking tire replacements. In addition, when the tire recall went into effect, Schwab had begun to stock thousands of extra tires in its Prineville tire warehouse and hired additional truck drivers to distribute them. Les Schwab Tires replaced the tires for free as long as the $100-a-tire reimbursement Firestone was willing to pay was not exceeded.

Tire Dealer of the Year

In 2000 at the age of 83, Les Schwab received recognition as *Modern Tire Dealers* (*MTD*) magazine's Tire Dealer of the

Year. Les Schwab was the eighth person to be chosen as the recipient of this award. During the ceremony that took place at the Les Schwab headquarters in Prineville, Oregon, Les Schwab Tires was awarded an etched-glass plaque, a portrait of Les Schwab, and a $1,000 donation in his name to the Prineville Community Hospital. During a speech given by an old friend and former editor, Lloyd Stoyer of *MTD*, Les Schwab was honored for his business and personal successes. Stoyer talked of Schwab's policy of sharing 51 percent of the company's profits with employees, stating that, "Never in the history of the tire industry has one person been so generous to so many." Les Schwab's wife, Dorothy, was also honored for her role in the company's success. She was presented with a dozen roses while the crowd applauded her with a standing ovation.

Les Schwab Tires has been repeatedly selected in local polls as one of the public's favorite businesses. In 1990 the company was awarded one of Oregon State University's Family Business Awards; in 2002, the *Wenatchee Business Journal*'s Readers' Choice Awards announced Les Schwab the winner in their "Best Customer Service" category.

In recent years, President Tom Wick has been chosen to head up Les Schwab Tire Centers while Les Schwab continues to reduce his responsibilities at the company.

Principal Competitors

Discount Tire Co.; Sears, Roebuck & Co.; TBC Corporation; Wal-Mart Stores, Inc.

Further Reading

Helliwell, John, "Tire Chain Linked Via System-3x," *PC Week*, August 18, 1987, p. C6.

Marshall, John, "Northwest Chain Store Enhances Customer Service and Lowers Operational Costs by Replacing Outdated POS Terminals," *Chain Store Age Executive* and *Shopping Center Age*, June 1994, p. 92.

Maynard, Micheline, "Firestone's Crisis Is Other Dealers' Opportunity," *New York Times*, September 17, 2000.

"MTD's Tire Dealer of the Year: Family, Friends Honor Les Schwab," *Modern Tire Dealer*, December 2000, p. 10.

"OSU Makes Family Business Awards," *Oregon Business*, June 1990, p. 16.

Roesler, Rich, "Tire Plan Aims to Prevent Piles at Area Dealers, Already Careful about Where Their Used Tires Go, Foresee Little Change," *Spokesman Review*, November 11, 1994, p. B1.

Rose, Michael, "Les Schwab Hits Road with Korean Rubber," *Business Journal-Portland*, May 15, 1998, p. 1.

Schwab, Dorothy, "Early Days Weren't Easy," *Modern Tire Dealer*, March 1997, p. 28.

Schwab, Les, *Les Schwab Pride in Performance: Keep It Going*, Bend, Oregon: Maverick Publications, 1986, p. 228.

Stoyer, Lloyd, "King of the Northwest," *Modern Tire Dealer*, March 1997, p. 22.

"Tire Pile Not Going Anywhere as Firm Weighs What To Do," *Seattle Times*, September 15, 1996, p. B3.

"Wouldn't Leave for the World," *Oregon Business*, June 1995, p. S7.

—Tammy Weisberger

Liberty Media Corporation

12300 Liberty Boulevard
Englewood, Colorado 80112
U.S.A.
Telephone: (720) 875-5400
Fax: (720) 875-7469
Web site: http://www.libertymedia.com

Public Company
Incorporated: 2001
Employees: 7,455 (2001)
Sales: $2,059 million (2001)
Stock Exchanges: NYSE
Ticker Symbol: L, LMC.B
NAIC: 513210 Cable Networks; 513220 Cable and Other
    Program Distribution

Liberty Media Corporation is a holding company with a variety of subsidiaries and investments operating in the media, communications, and entertainment industries. Each of Liberty's businesses is separately managed. For the year ended December 31, 2001, Liberty had five operating segments: Starz Encore Group, Liberty Livewire, On Command, Telewest, and Other.

Liberty Media Is Born

John C. Malone, who would earn a reputation as the "king of cable programming," began his career in 1970 as president of Jerrold Communications, a subsidiary of New York-based General Instrument Corporation, and supplier of cable TV equipment. Robert Magness, a former Texas rancher, was a customer of Malone's who in the 1950's had started the company that became Denver-based cable operator Tele-Communications, Inc. (TCI). In an effort to provide sound leadership for a financially struggling TCI, Malone was named Chief Economic Officer (CEO) in 1973, at the age of 32. By restructuring TCI's debt in 1977, Malone paved the way for expansion into bigger cable markets after deregulation in 1984. He also began acquiring programming assets by buying stakes in Black Entertainment

Television (BET) in (33 percent in 1979), the Discovery Channel (15 percent in 1986) and American Movie Classics (50 percent in 1986). In 1987, he purchased 12 percent of Turner Broadcasting's stock. Entering the European markets in 1991, TCI merged with United Artists Cable International (formerly United Cable), a broadband service provider in the U.K. Prior to the merger, TCI was United Artists' largest shareholder. The joint venture company was renamed Telewest Communications.

In 1991, TCI spun off much of its programming assets and 14 cable systems, due in part to antitrust pressure from government regulators. The result was Liberty Media Corporation, with Malone as chairman and principal shareholder. During the first two years in operation, Liberty Media launched Court TV, introduced the film channel, Encore, and acquired an interest in the Home Shopping Network. Another home-shopping network and competitor of the Home Shopping Network, QVC, partnered with Liberty Media and the Comcast Corporation, giving Liberty Media an 80-percent voting stake in QVC.

In 1994, Liberty Media was reacquired by TCI. The following, year it joined forces with Rupert Murdoch's News Corporation to create FOX/Liberty Networks, a national sports network. When Turner Broadcasting was acquired by Time Warner in 1996, control of TCI's stake in Turner Broadcasting was passed on to Liberty Media, giving them a 9 percent holding in Time Warner. The same year John Malone became chairman of TCI following the death of Robert Magness.

In 1997, Robert R. Bennett was named President and CEO of Liberty Media, with John Malone serving as Chairman of the Board. Bennett had been employed by Liberty Media since 1990, serving as principal financial officer and in other officer capacities. Prior to joining Liberty Media, Bennett was Vice-President and Director of Finance at TCI where he had been employed since 1987, after leaving The Bank of New York's Communications Entertainment and Publishing Division.

The attractiveness of the Spanish-speaking market in the United States. prompted Liberty Media, Sony, and other investors to purchase Telemundo in 1998 for $780 million. In 1998, BET was bought out jointly by Liberty Media and BET's chairman, Robert Johnson.

AT&T Buys TCI

In 1999 the American Telephone and Telegraph Company, an integrated telecommunications services and equipment company known as AT&T, purchased TCI for $55 billion, folding TCI Ventures into Liberty Media, as well as parts of Sprint PCS, United Video Satellite Group (Gemstar-TV Guide), General Instrument, and TCI International. This combination known as Liberty Media Group and headed by Chairman Malone added assets in technology, wireless telephone and international cable and programming businesses. Liberty Media's interest in FOX/Liberty Networks was traded for an 8 percent interest in News Corporation. Purchased the same year were Associated Group, a wireless communication services and radio broadcasting company, and a stake in Teligent, a wireless communications company. In 2000, Liberty Media invested in Cendant Corporation, a worldwide provider of travel, real estate, vehicle, and financial services; PRIMEDIA, a magazine publisher and specialty video producer and distributor; and Corus Entertainment, a Canadian media group; Todd-AO, an Atlanta-based company specializing in motion picture and television post-production, renamed Liberty Livewire; and Denver's Ascent Entertainment Group, a multimedia distribution and entertainment service provider specializing in satellite distribution support services. Other transactions in 2000 included folding Liberty Media's European and Latin American broadband assets into UnitedGlobalCom (UGC) and merging Japan-based Jupiter Telecommunications, of which Liberty Media owned 50 percent, with Microsoft's Titus Communications. An 11 percent equity stake in France's UGC had been purchased in the fall of 1999, with additional interests acquired in 2002. UGC was the largest operator of cable television systems outside the United States.

AT&T Spins Off Liberty Media

In November 2000, AT&T announced that Liberty Media Group would be one of four planned spin-offs as the company was restructured into separate cable, wireless, corporate and consumer businesses. In February of the following year, Liberty Media filed a $38.4 initial public offering (IPO), the largest in IPO in history. The spin-off, completed on August 10, 2001, enabled Liberty Media to begin trading as an independent publicly-traded company, to raise capital on its own, and to use its stock as currency in acquiring, merging, or partnering with other companies. Each outstanding share of AT&T Class A Liberty Media Group tracking stock was redeemed for one share of Liberty Series A common stock and each outstanding share of AT&T Class B Liberty Media Group tracking stock was redeemed for one share of Liberty Series B common stock.

Common stock began trading on the New York Stock Exchange under the symbols LMC.A and LMC.B.

Prior to the spin off, BET Holdings was acquired by Viacom, Inc., in exchange for 15.2 million share of Viacom's common stock. In an effort to expand their European activities and control by ownership a large European cable television business on which to build other businesses, Liberty Media attempted to acquire six of the nine regional cable television companies in Germany. German anti-trust authorities turned down the proposed acquisition. The company did not appeal the decision.

In December 2001, Liberty Media exchanged their 21 percent interest in Gemstar-TV Guide International for News Corporation shares, making them a leading shareholder with an 18 percent interest in the company. Another agreement in 2001 allowed Liberty Media to exchange a portion of their interest in USA Networks Inc. and certain other assets for shares in Vivendi Universal as part of a larger transaction between USA and Vivendi. Liberty Media agreed to sell Telemundo to General Electric's NBC for $2.2 billion.

As of December 31, 2001, Liberty Media's most significant consolidated subsidiaries either wholly or majority owned and controlled were Starz Encore Group LLC (Starz Encore Group), Liberty Livewire Corporation, and On Command Corporation. Other operations were conducted through entities in which Liberty Media did not have a controlling financial interest, but did have significant influence over the operating and financial policies included USA Networks, Inc.; Discovery Communications, Inc.; QVC. Inc.; UnitedGlobalCom, Inc.; and Telewest Communications PLC. Ownership interests were held in companies in which Liberty Media had no significant influence, including AOL Time Warner, Inc., Sprint Corporation, the News Corporation Limited, and Motorola.

Effective January 2, 2002, the NYSE ticker symbol for the Series A common stock was changed to ''L.'' Liberty Series B common stock continued to be traded under LMC.B. The year 2002 also witnessed Liberty Media principally engaged in two fundamental areas of business: video programming and interactive television services, consisting of interests in video programming services; and communications, consisting of interests in cable television systems, telephone and satellite systems. Interests were held in numerous globally branded entertainment networks such as the Discovery Channel, USA, QVC, Encore, and STARZ! Successful non-public affiliates included Japan's Jupiter Telecommunications and Court TV. Liberty's assets included interests in international video distribution business; international telephony and domestic wireless telephony; plant and equipment manufacturers; and other businesses related to broadband services.

Starz Encore Group provided programming through cable, direct-to-home satellite and other distribution media throughout the U.S. Liberty Livewire provided sound, video and post-production and distribution services to the motion picture television industries in the United States., Europe, Asia and Mexico. On Command provided in-room, on-demand video entertainment and information services to hotels, motels, and resorts. Other consolidated subsidiaries included Liberty Digi-

Key Dates:

1970: John C. Malone becomes president of Jerrold Communications.
1973: Malone is named CEO of TCI.
1991: Liberty Media is spun off from TCI.
1994: Liberty Media is reacquired by TCI.
1997: Robert R. Bennett becomes President and CEO of Liberty Media, with John C. Malone serving as Chairman of the Board.
1999: AT&T purchases TCI.
2001: Liberty Media is split off from AT&T and its tracking stock recapitalized as common stock trading on the New York Stock Exchange.
2002: Liberty Media's Series A common stock symbol is changed to ''L.''

tal, Inc., Pramer S.C.A. and Liberty Cablevision of Puerto Rico. Liberty Digital was engaged in programming, distributing and marketing digital and analog music services to homes and businesses. Pramer was a distributor of video programming services in Argentina. Liberty Cablevision of Puerto Rico provided cable television and other broadband services in Puerto Rico.

Liberty Media Faces the Future

Liberty Media began 2002 committed to their strategy of opportunism and value-creation. Although the company continued to look into new areas for acquisition, they nurtured their operating businesses, as the company viewed these assets as likely to provide the greatest long-term value to the company. Looking forward, Liberty Media remained committed to producing, acquiring, and distributing entertainment and informational programming, as well as electronic retailing services through its subsidiaries and affiliates. Such programming would continue to be delivered to viewers in the United States and overseas via cable television and other distribution technologies. Major activities for the coming years were identified by the company to be in video programming and interactive television services, cable and telephony, and satellite communications services.

Principal Subsidiaries

Starz Encore Group LLC (100%); Liberty Digital, Inc. (84%); Liberty Livewire Corporation (85%); On Command Corporation (63%); Pramer S.C.A. (Argentina) (100%); Discovery Communications, Inc. (50%); QVC Inc. (42%); Jupiter Programming Co., Ltd. (Japan) (50%); USA Networks, Inc. (20%); Telewest Communications PLC (Content Division) (UK) (25%); Torneos y Competencias, S.A. (Argentina) (40%); Liberty Cablevision of Puerto Rico, Inc. (100%); Liberty Satellite & Technology, Inc. (27%); TruePosition, Inc. (89%); Telewest Communications PLC (Cable Division) (UK) (25%); Jupiter Telecommunications Co., Ltd. (Japan) (35%); UnitedGlobalCom, Inc. (72%); Cablevision S.A. (Argentina) (50%); Metropólis-Intercom, S.A. (Chile) (50%); Chorus Communication Limited (Ireland) (50%).

Principal Competitors

Bertelsmann; CANAL+; Carlton Communications; Comcast; Cox Communications; Fox Entertainment; Hearst; KirchGruppe; NBC; News Corporation; Rainbow Media; Turner Broadcasting; Universal Studios; Univision; ValueVision; Viacom; Disney.

Further Reading

''AT&T Subsidiary Liberty Media to Acquire Ascent Entertainment for 1.90 Times Revenue,'' *Weekly Corporate Growth Report*, November 1, 1999, p. 1.

''Chorus Looking to Buy Part of NTL's Irish Network, *Cable Europe*, January 24, 2001, p. 1.

''Executive Suite: Liberty Media Corporation and TCI Ventures Group Prepare for Merger and New Leadership Structure,'' *EDGE, on & about AT&T*, July 20, 1998, p. 1.

''Liberty Cablevision of Puerto Rico Tests IP Telephony,'' *Worldwide Telecom*, August 1, 2002.

''Liberty Media Corporation,'' *Hoover's Handbook of American Business 2002*, 2001, pp. 872–873.

''Liberty Media Group to Purchase the Todd-AO Corporation for 2.31 Times Revenue,'' *Weekly Corporate Growth Report*, December 20, 1999, p. 10535.

Meyer, Cheryl, ''Liberty Gives Nod to Wink Deal,'' *The Daily Deal*, June 25, 2002.

Minard, Lawrence, ''Europe's New King of Fiber,'' *Forbes*, August 7, 2000, pp. 92, 93.

Musero, Frank, ''Liberty Media Files $38B IPO,'' *The IPO Reporter*, February 26, 2001, p. 10.

O'Connor, Colleen, ''Liberty Media Shoots for Independence,'' *The IPO Reporter*, November 27, 2000, pp. 1–6.

Sims, Calvin, ''Diller Acquires QVC Stake,'' *The New York Times*, December 11, 1992, p D1.

Sormani, Angela, ''Deals Flood In,'' *European Venture Capital Journal*, September 1, 2001, p. 71.

Vittore, Vince, ''IP Telephony's Second Chance, *Telephony*, November 26, 2001, pp. 38–40.

—Carol D. Beavers

Lucasfilm Ltd.

P.O. Box 2009
San Rafael, California 94912-2009
U.S.A.
Telephone: (415) 662-1800
Fax: (415) 662-2437
Web site: http://www.lucasfilm.com

Private Company
Incorporated: 1971
Employees: 2,000 (est.)
Sales: $1,500 million (2001 est.)
NAIC: 512110 Motion Picture and Video Production;
  512120 Motion Picture and Video Distribution;
  512190 Postproduction Services and Other Motion
  Picture and Video Industries

The 16th largest motion picture producer in the United States, ranked by revenues, Lucasfilm Ltd. is an independent film and television production and distribution company developed by George Lucas, creator of the popular and profitable *Star Wars* and *Indiana Jones* film series. By 1995, Lucasfilm consisted of three entities: Lucasfilm Ltd., Lucas Digital Ltd., and LucasArts Entertainment Co. Lucasfilm Ltd. created Lucas's motion picture and television productions and administered the THX theater and the home theater licensing and certification procedures. Lucas Digital Ltd. oversaw operations of Industrial Light & Magic (ILM), the world's foremost visual effects production facility, and Skywalker Sound, one of the world's premier sound engineering facilities. Finally, LucasArts Entertainment Company produced multimedia and interactive computer entertainment and educational computer software, while also overseeing the licensing responsibilities for Lucasfilm stories and characters.

1970s: George Lucas Breaks into the Movie Business

Company founder George Lucas was born in 1945 in Modesto, California, and was educated at the University of Southern California's (USC) film school. Having won a scholarship to observe Francis Ford Coppola direct the film *Finian's Rainbow,*

Lucas would later recall in a *New York Times* interview, "Francis forced me to become a writer and to think about things other than abstract and documentary films." In 1971, Lucas wrote and directed his first feature film, *THX 1138,* the story of a future world in which people live in underground cities run by computers. Inspired by a short film he wrote while a student at USC, *THX 1138* was produced by Francis Ford Coppola's American Zoetrope studios. The following year, Lucas created his own film company, Lucasfilm Ltd., with offices in Hollywood, across the street from Universal Studios.

In 1973, Lucas experienced his first commercial success with the film *American Graffiti,* a humorous look at one evening in the lives of some recent high-school graduates in the early 1960s, which Lucas co-wrote and directed. In addition to receiving a Golden Globe award and awards from the New York Film Critics and the National Society of Film Critics, *American Graffiti* received five Academy Award nominations. Moreover, Lucas became known as one of the most popular directors in Hollywood, and his company began to expand. During this time, for example, Lucas founded Sprocket Systems, which later became Skywalker Sound, a full-service audio post-production facility. He also created Industrial Light & Magic (ILM) to develop the use of computer graphics in film, focusing particularly on the striking visual effects that would be used in the upcoming film *Star Wars.*

Late 1970s to Early 1980s: Star Wars *Is Born*

Lucas wrote and directed the first *Star Wars* film in 1977. Made by Lucas and Lucasfilm for Twentieth Century Fox, the film reportedly incurred production costs of around $6.5 million. A fantasy/science fiction (sci-fi) tale featuring a young hero, a princess, a pilot, a villain, and a host of robots and creatures, *Star Wars* became a number one box-office attraction as well as an important part of U.S. culture and film history. The film's characters also became the basis for a very profitable line of children's toy figures and other merchandise. In fact, profits from *Star Wars* allowed Lucas to fully finance subsequent films in the series and to retain a higher portion of the profits. Over the next six years, Lucas wrote and executive produced the *Star Wars* sequels *The Empire Strikes Back* (1980) and *The Return of the Jedi* (1983). Through 1995, all three films would maintain

Key Dates:

1971: Lucasfilm Ltd. Incorporates; George Lucas writes and directs his first feature film, *THX 1138.*

1973: George Lucas experiences commercial success with the film *American Graffiti.*

1975: Industrial Light & Magic is established to produce visual effects for the upcoming *Star Wars* film.

1977: *Star Wars* is released and received six Academy Awards.

1980: *The Empire Strikes Back* is released.

1981: *Raiders of the Lost Ark* is released.

1983: *Return of the Jedi* is released. The Computer Division reorganizes to form Pixar and Games.

1984: *Indiana Jones and the Temple of Doom* is released.

1986: Lucasfilm sells Pixar to Steven Jobs.

1989: LucasArts Entertainment Company is established, which includes the Games Division.

1995: The Library of Congress honors *American Graffiti* by naming it to the National Film Registry.

1997: *Star Wars Special Edition* premiers nationwide.

1999: *Star Wars Episode One: The Phantom Menace* is released. Trustees of the Presidio National Park in San Francisco select Lucasfilm as preferred developer of 23 acres for its proposed Letterman Digital Arts Center, pending an environmental review.

2002: *Star Wars Episode Two: Attack of the Clones* is released.

positions among the top 15 box-office attractions of all time and would continue to generate record toy sales.

Mid-1980s: The Empire Expands

In the early 1980s, a wholly owned subsidiary, LucasArts Entertainment Company, was added to Lucasfilm's holdings, providing, according to company literature, "an interactive element in George Lucas's vision of a state-of-the-art, multi-faceted entertainment company." LucasArts developed, in part, under the leadership of R. Douglas Norby, who joined Lucasfilm in 1985 after serving as chief financial officer at Syntex Corporation. As president and chief executive officer of Lucas-Arts until 1992, Norby helped the subsidiary become a leading developer of entertaining and interactive multimedia computer software for schools, homes, and arcades. Such products combined Lucas' storytelling and character development strengths with the newest, most advanced technologies available. Early game efforts included: "Maniac Mansion," "Battlehawks 1942," "Their Finest Hour: The Battle of Britain," "Secret Weapons of the Luftwaffe," "Loom," and "The Secret of Monkey Island." The company also produced software products based on the *Star Wars* and the *Indiana Jones* series. "X-Wing" would become the best selling CD-ROM entertainment title of 1993, and in 1994 "Rebel Assault" became one of the best selling CD-ROM software of all time. Educational products, developed by the LucasArts Learning sub-unit, included "GTV: American History from a Geographic Perspective," an interactive video disc and computer learning effort involving both the National Geographic Society and the California State Department of Education. Another program, "Life Story," was developed in partnership with Apple Multimedia Lab and the Smithsonian Institution.

LucasArts was also charged with overseeing the licensing and design of toys and other products based on Lucasfilm ideas and characters. Comic books and novels extending the *Star Wars* and *Indiana Jones* universes were successful ventures for LucasArts. In 1991 *The New York Times* indicated that Lucas-Arts licensed *Star Wars* toys had grossed over $2.6 billion dollars around the world.

George Lucas Breaks from Tradition

As Lucasfilm continued to profit, George Lucas gradually began to separate himself from traditional Hollywood. In 1981, he relinquished membership in the Academy of Motion Picture Arts and Sciences, the Writers Guild, and the Directors Guild and began moving his offices to Skywalker Ranch, a 3,000-acre secluded production facility located in San Rafael, 25 miles from San Francisco. Named for the *Star Wars* character Luke Skywalker, the ranch became the business and production hub of the Lucas financial empire. Discussing his intentions for the new ranch complex in an interview for the *New York Times,* Lucas said, "As opposed to Hollywood, where the film makers support the corporate entity, Lucasfilm will support the overhead of the ranch. We'll make money out of the money by buying real estate, cable, satellite, solar energy—without buying anything we're ashamed of, like pesticides—and then the corporation will give us the money to make films."

Despite their detachment from Hollywood, Lucas and Lucasfilm continued to create widely successful films, producing a popular series of Indiana Jones movies, which were directed by Lucas's friend and colleague Steven Spielberg. The three movies, *Raiders of the Lost Ark* (1981), *Indiana Jones and the Temple of Doom* (1984), and *Indiana Jones and the Last Crusade* (1989), featured the adventures of Indiana Jones, an heroic archaeologist whose work brings him into contact with villains, dangerous situations, and romance. All three films achieved wide financial success.

Not all Lucasfilm productions achieved commercial success. Such motion pictures as *More American Graffiti* (1979), *Howard the Duck* (1986), *Labyrinth* (1986), and *Radioland Murders* (1994) met with disappointing ticket sales and critical reviews. Nevertheless, George Lucas remained a leader in his field; in 1992, he received the Academy of Motion Picture Arts and Sciences' prestigious Irving G. Thalberg award for pioneering work in film technology. Moreover, any losses the company incurred by its few commercial disappointments were offset by Lucasfilm's involvement in all aspects of movie production; ILM in particular began to thrive and gradually became the company's most profitable division.

Described by Lucasfilm as "the largest and most advanced digital effects system in the entertainment industry," ILM not only mastered the traditional arts of blue screen photography, matte painting, and model construction, but also pioneered the development of motion control cameras, optical compositing, and other advances in special effects technology. Its use of computer graphics and digital imaging in feature films also involved developing such breakthrough techniques as "morphing," which allowed the seamless transformation of one object into another. ILM's film credits in the 1980s and 1990s included most of the *Star Trek* movies, *ET: The Extraterrestrial* (1982), *Cocoon* (1985), *Back to the Future* (1985), *Who Framed Roger Rabbit?* (1988), *Ghost* (1990), *Terminator 2: Judgment Day* (1991), *Jurassic Park* (1993), *Schindler's List* (1993), *Forrest Gump* (1994), and many others. In fact, by the end of 1994, ILM had handled special effects for over 100 feature films, several of which won Academy Awards for best visual effects and technical achievement.

ILM also began working with Walt Disney Productions in 1985, developing over the years such theme park attractions as Captain EO (1986) for Disneyland, Star Tours simulator ride for Disneyland, Body Wars (1989) for Disneyworld's EPCOT Center, and Space Race (1991) a simulator ride for Showscan.

Skywalker Sound was also thriving during this time, with sound post-production studios in Santa Monica, West Los Angeles, and at the Skywalker Ranch complex. At these facilities—which comprised sound and foley stages, mixing and editing studios, and screening rooms, all renowned for their technical sophistication and versatility—the sound was recorded for such popular films as *Jurassic Park*, *Mrs. Doubtfire*, and *Quiz Show*. Skywalker also undertook television commercial projects for such products as Pepsi, Listerine, the Jenny Craig diet plan, and Malaysian Air, among others.

1990s: The Empire Continues to Expand

In February 1993, Lucasfilm announced a reorganization, opting to spin off ILM and Skywalker Sound into units of a new company called Lucas Digital Ltd. Film producer Lindsley Parsons, Jr., a former manager of production at MGM/UA Entertainment, CBS Theatrical Films, and Paramount Pictures, was named president and CEO of Lucas Digital, while George Lucas served as the company's chairperson.

Two months later, Lucas Digital's ILM subunit teamed up with Silicon Graphics Inc., of Mountain View, California, to create The Joint Environment for Digital Imaging (the acronym JEDI referring to the heroic knights of the *Star Wars* trilogy). The joint effort was created to serve as a film production unit as well as a test lab for new technology in visual effects. The connection between Lucasfilm and Silicon Graphics was actually forged in the late 1980s, when Lucasfilm began using Silicon Graphics workstations to create their special effects. By working together, Lucasfilm gained greater access to Silicon Graphics's more advanced computer workstations, while Silicon Graphics gained access to Lucasfilm's proprietary software. The companies expected to revolutionize filmmaking through their use of computer graphics and reduce the costs of producing special effects by as much as 90 percent.

During this time, Lucasfilm also made a name for itself in the field of television production, performing its most notable work perhaps in 1993 through the television series *The Young Indiana Jones Chronicles*. Written and executive produced by George Lucas, the series won the Banff Award for Best Continuing Series, a Golden Globe nomination for best dramatic series, an Angel Award for Quality Programming, and ten Emmy Awards.

Another of Lucasfilm's activities involved its THX Group, which, according to Lucasfilm literature, was "dedicated to ensuring excellence in film presentation." The commercial portion of the certification program, developed in 1982, involved certifying the quality of the listening environment in commercial theaters. THX-certified theaters were required to meet Lucasfilm standards for such factors as speaker layout, acoustics, noise levels, and equalization of the signal. By 1995, Lucasfilm claimed over 770 certified installations in theaters and soundstages around the world.

Mid-1990s: A Pioneer in Fields of Technology and Workplace Satisfaction

The THX system also had applications in the home theater, a concept that was gaining popularity in the mid-1990s. Lucasfilm's home THX system certified equipment to ensure that it maintained the quality of film sound as it was transferred to the home. Specifically, home THX certification and licensing program controlled parameters that affected the clarity of dialogue, "soundstaging" (localizing sounds), surround sound diffusion, frequency response, and transparency. Such licensing was available to equipment manufacturers for certification of front and center speakers, surround speakers, subwoofers, amplifiers, preamplifiers, receivers, laser disc players, front video projection screens, and cords and interconnects.

In 1994, for the fourth year in a row, *Working Mother* magazine named Lucasfilm, Lucas Digital, and LucasArts Entertainment among the top 100 workplaces for working mothers. The magazine praised the companies' child-care centers, flexible working hours, and profit sharing plans, as well as their reputation for equal treatment in pay. Moreover, the companies subsidized 100 percent of health care costs for the employee and 75 percent for the family. Not surprisingly, the three companies enjoyed a low turnover rate.

In the mid-1990s, George Lucas remained very involved in the arts and education, serving as chairperson of the George Lucas Educational Foundation as well as on the board of directors of the National Geographic Society Education Foundation, the Artists Rights Foundation, The Joseph Campbell Foundation, and The Film Foundation. He was also a member of the USC School of Cinema-Television Board of Councilors. Moreover, Lucasfilm also remained poised for growth, announcing plans in 1994 to produce three more installments of the *Star Wars* series and one more installment of the Indiana Jones series. Plans were to film the three *Star Wars* films simultaneously and to released them biannually, beginning in 1998 or 1999. Steven Spielberg agreed at that time to direct the *fourth Indiana Jones* movie. With such projects underway, the companies that Lucas founded seemed well prepared for continued profitability.

Late 1990s: Deals, Re-releases, and Prequels

George Lucas's announcement that he would re-release the original *Star Wars* series remastered and enhanced, and that he would direct three additional *Star Wars* films ("prequels"), that would reveal the history behind the original trilogy, sparked a host of commercial deals. Companies clamored to negotiate for a piece of the *Star Wars* legacy. In 1996, Lucasfilm and PepsiCo aligned forces in an approximate $2 billion global marketing deal. PepsiCo gained rights to for the launch of the enhanced movies, while Lucasfilm retained the ability to search for additional partners for the new franchise coming in 1999. Random

House and Scholastic got a piece of the pie when they signed agreements with Lucasfilm to develop books based on the forthcoming prequels. The agreement allowed that Scholastic would publish three sets of *Star Wars* books for each new format, and a novelization of each new film. Fox also secured a deal; Fox agreed to distribute all three of the upcoming movies and received, for an undisclosed sum, the network broadcast rights to the first of the three films. Unity, a communications agency, was hired to mastermind the global marketing launch of the *Episode One*, in 1999. The much sought after multi-year, multi-million dollar toy rights went to Galoob and Hasbro, prompting Hasbro to purchase Galoob. Nintendo snagged another hot deal—the rights to *Star Wars* videogames.

The 1997 re-release of *Star Wars*, the first movie in the original trilogy, grossed more than $250 million domestically, a good start to the upcoming string of re-releases and prequels.

New Technologies and New Star Wars Movies

George Lucas stunned the movie industry in 1999 when he announced that Lucasfilm would bankroll the first digital projectors to be used in theaters. The projectors debut would be timed to show *Phantom Menace*, the title of the first of the three *Star Wars* prequels. The first movie in the prequel series, *Star Wars Episode One: Attack of the Clones*, was released on May 19, 1999.

Later in 1999, Lucasfilm was selected by the trustees of the new Presidio national park, intended to become a part of Golden Gate National Recreation Area in San Francisco, California, to develop a motion picture complex at the site.

Additional strides in technology were taken, over the years, by ILM, the largest f/x studio in the film business. The company supplied complex computer graphics for several computer graphic-rich films, including *A.I. Artificial Intelligence*, *Pearl Harbor*, *The Mummy*, and *Harry Potter and the Chamber of Secrets*.

2000s: Learning from His Mistakes

Although the release of *Star Wars Episode One: The Phantom Menace*, and *Star Wars Episode Two: Attack of the Clones*, (released in 2002) were successful, there were lessons to be learned. One of which was that although toys and games sold as forecast, apparel and some other products did not sell as anticipated. Howard Roffman, vice president of sales for Lucasfilm, told *Discount Store News* in August, 1999, that although apparel had never been a strong category for licensing, "Some retailers bought into it heavily, and in some channels there is too much merchandise." After a disappointing run of apparel sales after the *Episode One* release, retailers have vowed to be more cautious.

Lucasfilm also learned from the release of *Episode One*. Just days after releasing the movie in the United States, Lucasfilm found that hawkers in many foreign countries managed to procure bootleg copies of the film to sell on the streets. In order to avoid the same problem, Lucasfilm decided to release the second movie worldwide on the same day—May 16, 2002. Additionally, in order to scoop the unauthorized Internet sites, Lucasfilm created his own "underground" Web site, complete with fake news stories and features in order to keep ahead of the

game. *Episode Two*, released in 2002, was one of the top-grossing films of the year, and *Episode Three* is expected to perform at least as well. Lucasfilm is sure to have more gems up its sleeve, and is poised to continue its legacy.

Principal Subsidiaries

Lucas Digital Ltd.; LucasArts Entertainment Co.; Industrial Light & Magic (ILM); Skywalker Sound.

Principal Competitors

New Line Production Inc.; Paramount Pictures.

Further Reading

Carlton, Jim, "George Lucas Chosen To Develop Presidio Park in San Francisco," *Wall Street Journal*, June 16, 1999, p. 4.

Champlin, Charles, *George Lucas: The Creative Impulse*, New York: Harry A. Abrams, Inc., 1992.

"A Disturbance in the Force," *Discount Store News*, August 23, 1999, p. A6.

Fantel, Hans, "In the Action With Star Wars' Sound," *The New York Times*, May 3, 1992, p. 35.

Fisher, Lawrence M., "LucasArts and Mattel In Joint Toy Venture," *The New York Times*, April 26, 1991, p. D4.

——, "Lucasfilm and Silicon Graphics Team Up," *The New York Times*, April 8, 1993, p. D3.

——, "Lucasfilm Subsidiary Loses Chief Executive," *The New York Times*, April 9, 1992, p. D4.

Fisher, Sara, "Digital Movie Projectors are Coming Soon," *Los Angeles Business Journal*, March 22, 1999, p. 3.

Gill, Eric, "Camp THX," *Audio-Video Interiors*, September 1994, pp. 46–55.

Graser, Mark, "Lucas Empire Continues Growth at Light Speed," *Daily Variety*, April 11, 2002, p. A1.

Griffiths, Anna, "Unity Masterminds Promotion of New Star Wars Film Worldwide," *Campaign*, May 21, 1999, p. 2.

Grover, Ronald, "The Emperor Strikes Back; How Lucas is Maximizing the Take on Attack of the Clones," *Business Week*, May 6, 2002, p. 38.

Harmetz, Aljean, "But Can Hollywood Live Without George Lucas?," *The New York Times*, July 13, 1981, Sec. 3, p. 11.

Jensen, Jeff, "PepsiCo Beams into 'Star Wars': $2 Billion Deal Offers Model for Future Alliances Tied to Lucasfilm Franchise," *Advertising Age*, May 20, 1996, p. 62.

Longsdorf, Amy, "George Lucas Interview," *Laserviews*, January/February 1995, p. 15.

"LucasFilm Awards Star Wars Licenses to RH, Scholastic," *Publishers Weekly*, March 2, 1998, p. 12.

Moskowitz, Milton, and Carol Townsend, "Ninth Annual Survey of the 100 Best Companies for Working Mothers," *Working Mother Magazine*, October 1994, pp. 48+.

Petrikin, Chris, "Force is with Fox," *Variety*, April 6, 1998, p. 8.

Pollock, Dale, *Skywalking: The Life and Films of George Lucas*, New York: Harmony Books, 1983.

Poor, Alfred, "Star Wars Goes Digital," *PC Magazine*, June 22, 1999, p. 35.

Snyder, Beth, "Toy Fair Girds for 'Phantom Menace' Burst—Marketing to Kids: Demand for Star Wars Toys About to Explode," *Advertising Age*, February 8, 1999, p. 46.

Wilkinson, Scott, "The Force Is With Him," *Home Theater Technology*, October 1994, pp. 64–68.

—Terry W. Hughes
—update: Tammy Weisberger

M. Shanken Communications, Inc.

387 Park Avenue South
New York, New York 10016
U.S.A.
Telephone: (212) 684-4224
Toll Free: (800) 866-0775
Fax: (212) 684-5424
Web site: http://www.mshanken.com

Private Company
Incorporated: 1972
Employees: 150 (2000)
Sales: $31.2 million (2000 est.)
NAIC: 511120 Periodical Publishers; 511130 Book
  Publishers

M. Shanken Communications, Inc. is a diversified publishing and communications company founded by chairman Marvin R. Shanken. In 30 years, Shanken has transformed a beverage-industry newsletter he bought for $5,000 into a nifty publishing empire worth more than $31 million. M. Shanken Communications' publications include *Impact*, *Market Watch*, and *Food Arts* for the trade, as well as *Wine Spectator*, *Cigar Aficionado*, and *Cigar Insider* for the consumer. The company's annual reviews and forecasts covering the alcohol beverage industry are widely considered the most authoritative in their field. The company also produces books such as James Laube's *California Wine* and *Wine Spectator's Ultimate Guide to Buying Wine*. In addition, M. Shanken Communications produces the award-winning Web sites CigarAficionado.com and WineSpectator.com. The company also plays host to events held around the country, including the Impact Annual Marketing Seminar, *Market Watch*'s Annual Leaders Award Banquet, *Wine Spectator*'s Wine Experience, and *Cigar Aficionado*'s Big Smokes. The company also has raised millions of dollars for worthy charities and supported wine education and research through the *Wine Spectator* Scholarship Foundation.

Starting Up

Marvin Shanken, the founder of the company that bears his name, was not new to the entrepreneurial world, although it might have seemed that way when he bought a struggling beverage-industry newsletter for $5,000 in 1973. That newsletter, *Impact*, was a trade publication covering the spirits industry. It was a change of direction for Shanken, who had previously been an investment banker. Although he was not an outstanding student at the University of Miami, he went on to earn an M.B.A. from American University. As an investment banker, he specialized in real estate, which eventually took him to Northern California. There, he acquired a personal passion for wine. Shanken told *Forbes* magazine in January 1993, "I have two passions in life—wine and cigars." Combining this personal passion for what he has referred to as "the finer things in life" with a consumer's perspective, Shanken turned his personal interests into a successful business.

In 1979, Shanken purchased *Wine Spectator* for $40,000; hardly a princely sum, even then, for a publication destined to become the most widely read wine enthusiast's magazine in the world. The magazine debuted in 1976 in San Diego, under the leadership of a wine enthusiast named Bob Morrisey. In an interview with his own publication 17 years later, Shanken said, "It was a tabloid newspaper, and the first time I laid eyes on it I loved it . . . Wine publications then were either highly technical or elitist, a turnoff to consumers who were interested in learning more about wine." Thus began Shanken's enterprise of popularizing what had previously been considered an esoteric luxury, although, as he put it, "I think the only reason I agreed to do it is that I didn't want the *Wine Spectator* to die."

From the beginning, however, Shanken set his sights on improving the magazine. At the time his company purchased it, it was still primarily a regional publication, focused almost entirely on Northern California. "I wanted to cover the whole wide world," Shaken told *Wine Spectator* in 1996. He also concentrated on improving the overall quality of *Wine Spectator*'s content. "The idea was to upgrade the quality of our commentary and our research and our tasting reports to the journalistic level of non-wine publications I admired, such as

324

Key Dates:

1973: Marvin Shanken buys beverage-industry newsletter *Impact* for $5,000.

1976: *Wine Spectator* magazine launches in San Diego.

1979: Shanken buys *Wine Spectator* for $40,000.

1980: *Wine Spectator* begins panel-based scoring and tasting of wines.

1982: *Wine Spectator*'s editorial office moves from San Diego to San Francisco.

1989: *Wine Spectator*'s circulation reaches 65,000.

1990: M. Shanken purchases *Food Arts*; *Wine Spectator*'s circulation reaches 100,000.

1992: M. Shanken launches *Cigar Aficionado*, which reaches a circulation of 100,000 with its second issue.

1993: *Wine Spectator*'s circulation reaches 120,000; the magazine is extensively redesigned as a lifestyle publication.

1994: *Cigar Aficionado* interviews Fidel Castro.

1995: *Cigar Insider* launches.

1996: The company launches WineSpectator.com.

1997: M. Shanken acquires regional affluent-lifestyle magazine *Country*, and *Aspen Country*.

2000: *Cigar Aficionado* is revamped with a new logo and greater coverage of non-cigar-related topics.

2001: *Wine Spectator*'s circulation reaches 323,000.

2002: *Hamptons Country* suspends publication.

the *Wall Street Journal* and the *New York Times* . . . Today,'' he added, ''I believe that goal is achieved.''

The 1980s: Expansion and Complication

Taking over a struggling publication based on a personal passion may have seemed like a questionable business model, but M. Shanken had some good fortune along the way, chiefly in the form of the growing popularity and selection of wines. Although from the beginning Shanken wanted his magazine to be for wine consumers, in the late 1970s this was a less daunting proposition than it might be today. As Thomas Matthews commented in a 1996 editorial in the magazine, ''In 1976 . . . the wine world was a smaller, simpler place.''

Nonetheless, in 1980, *Wine Spectator* began panel-based tasting and scoring of wines. That same year, the magazine's circulation reached 35,000, up from its inaugural run of 3,000 copies in 1976, and a vast improvement from its circulation of 1,000 when M. Shanken purchased it. Already, it seemed, its orientation toward the consumer and broader focus were paying off. By 1986, the magazine was reviewing over 1,000 wines every year, and that number continued to grow into the next decade.

In 1990, M. Shanken purchased *Food Arts*, a specialty-interest publication for the fine food industry with a circulation of 50,000. Its readership, primarily chefs, restaurateurs, and caterers, was in line with the company's existing audience of wine enthusiasts and beverage-industry professionals; by this

time, M. Shanken had added *Market Watch*, an industry publication similar to *Impact*, to the fold. Shanken told *Folio* magazine at the time of the purchase that ''*Food Arts* represents a unique and compatible property in the context of my basic business.'' Like *Wine Spectator*, *Food Arts* made a business out of appealing to an under-explored niche, albeit a narrower one: ''What they [*Food Art*'s readership] want is not normally found in the major restaurant magazines.''

Food Arts, which was launched in 1989, had lost money its first year, but Shanken was determined to turn the magazine's performance around. ''We expect this book to be an important financial success within three years,'' Shanken told *Folio*. His goal at the outset was to triple the amount of advertising in the magazine; advertising had already been established as a major revenue source for M. Shanken's other publications.

By 1990, M. Shanken had expanded in other ways in addition to the growth of its flagship publication. Shanken told *Folio* that *Wine Spectator* had grown 40 percent in revenue yearly since his company purchased it, and the magazine's paid circulation in 1990 was 100,000—an increase of almost 200 percent from its circulation only ten years earlier. Meanwhile, although Shanken would not reveal circulation numbers for *Impact*, he claimed its distribution covered almost every company in its industry. Revenue was estimated at over $1.5 million by *Forbes* in 1989.

In the 1980s, M. Shanken also expanded into book publishing and catalog sales. Both of these areas were closely in line with the company's main industry; the books included yearly market reports from *Impact* magazine, and the mail-order catalogs offered Shanken products. Revenue from the catalogs alone was expected to exceed $4 million in 1989.

One of the secrets of M. Shanken's success was aggressive promotion on the part of its founder—which amounted, essentially, to promotion of personal tastes. Since 1979, Shanken had collected antique poster art, including works by artists such as Henri de Toulouse-Lautrec. As owner of these works, Shanken was entitled to use them for promotional purposes—and that is exactly what he did. Other products in M. Shanken's mail-order catalogs included merchandise featuring poster art Shanken owned. The images were also used to promote M. Shanken's magazines. ''Posters were the first important means of building brand names,'' Shanken told *Forbes* in October 1989. ''I'm just trying to expand my market.'' By using every means available to promote his publications and his company, Shanken had turned a few minor magazines into a small empire. As *Fortune* put it in 1994, ''[Shanken] markets his own tastes and passions to readers seeking guidance in theirs.''

A Tasteful Cigar

[sw2]In 1992, apparently against all common sense—''Most people thought I'd lost my mind,'' Shanken told *Folio* in 1996—M. Shanken took another plunge, launching *Cigar Aficionado*. Despite the growing intolerance of tobacco, plus the fact that cigars were not as popular as cigarettes, the magazine took off at a pace that surprised even Shanken. The original circulation goal for *Cigar Aficionado* was 20,000. By the second issue, it was 100,000. ''There will always be successful people

with dough who are only interested in living the good life—but even I can't believe this is possible,'' Shanken told *Forbes* in January 1993.

In fact, Shanken initially expected his new magazine to lose money. As he told *Fortune* in 1994, ''I figured we'd get maybe 15,000 to 25,000 readers, and I'd be running it at a loss for the rest of my life.'' Instead, it turned a profit immediately; of the 154 pages of the first issue, 53 were ads. By 1994, *Cigar Aficionado* had interviewed Fidel Castro and was drawing advertising from companies such as Mercedes, Cartier, and Rolex due to its upscale readership. Between this and a yearly charity event called the Big Smoke, *Cigar Aficionado*—and, by extension, Marvin Shanken—was credited with jump-starting the popularity of cigar smoking, which swelled in the early to mid-1990s.

By the end of 1995, the magazine's circulation had reached a quarter of a million, and other publications were reporting the growing popularity of cigar smoking. William Rusher of the *National Review* wrote in 1995, ''Cigars are making a comeback in the United States that deserves to be called historic . . . the immediate precipitating factor is a new quarterly magazine called *Cigar Aficionado*.'' The high profile of some cigar smokers, including business executives and celebrities, contributed to the upscale, individualistic image of the cigar, and cigar bars and cigar-related events sprouted across the United States. Other publishing companies launched cigar-related magazines, and M. Shanken introduced a monthly newsletter, *Cigar Insider*.

By 1997, *Cigar Aficionado* had become a bimonthly publication, with an estimated worldwide readership of 1.5 million. Four major cigar manufacturers had gone public, and cigar imports had soared to 297 million in 1996, from 100 million yearly from 1980 to 1992. The magazine had also become an award winner, picking up Temple University's ''Acres of Diamonds'' award, a 1999 National Magazine Award for General Excellence in New Media, and regularly winning *Folio* magazine's award in the men's lifestyle category. In fact, *Cigar Aficionado* had been positioned as a men's magazine, as opposed to specifically a cigar smoker's magazine, since its inception. An editorial written by Marvin Shanken for the company's debut issue in the fall of 1992 was titled ''A New Men's Lifestyle Magazine'' and noted, ''*Cigar Aficionado* is about taste. But it is not limited to the taste of a great smoke. This magazine intends to awaken and explore many of the pleasures that drive successful men.'' This included coverage of travel, fine liquor, restaurants, and other features only tangentially related to smoking.

As the popularity of cigars rose during the 1990s, the twin concerns of health and sales to children—emphasized by the massive litigation that took up much of the decade—were applied to cigar smoking. In 1995, 800 *Cigar Aficionado* readers marched in front of the White House in protest of anti-smoking laws, before adjourning to a local Big Smoke event. In 1998, the cigar industry responded to mounting concerns with an advertising campaign called Banding Together, which was reported in the March/April issue of *Cigar Aficionado*, emphasizing that cigars were for purchase by adults only. ''We . . . have said it repeatedly from the day the magazine was launched—cigars are an adult pleasure,'' the magazine said.

As with *Wine Spectator*, *Cigar Aficionado*'s editorial approach was as an advocate for consumers, even in 2001 challenging the conventional wisdom that the best cigars came from Cuba. Ironically, the cigar boom in the mid-1990s—itself attributed at least in part to *Cigar Aficionado*—was at least partly to blame, despite the Cuban embargo; as demand rose, production was forced to keep pace, leading to a decline in quality.

The 1990s: Generalization and Retraction

In general, M. Shanken's practice throughout the 1990s was to generalize. This not only involved shifting both of its flagship publications away from their specialized interests, but taking on other related projects as well.

In 1993, *Wine Spectator* had an audited circulation of 120,000 and, according to Shanken, revenues of $11 million. It was by far the largest moneymaker for the company, which reported overall revenues of $20 million for 1993. Despite these impressive numbers, that year the magazine underwent a substantial redesign. The magazine shifted emphasis from wine enthusiasts to lifestyles for people who loved wine, a subtle but significant difference that allowed *Wine Spectator* to expand its readership, its content, and its advertising. Shanken was quoted in an April, 1996 issue as saying, ''This was what was needed to sustain and increase the growth of the audience of *Wine Spectator* in the '90s and beyond.'' Nonetheless, Shanken maintained, ''The wine-makers and their wines are the stars of *Wine Spectator*.''

The year 1997 saw the acquisition of *Country* magazine. A lifestyle magazine for affluent New Yorkers, *Country*'s readership was perfectly aligned with M. Shanken's target audience. *Country* was launched in 1993 by editor and publisher Joseph DeCristofaro, and was a controlled-circulation, regional-oriented publication focusing on the Hamptons and published four times each year during the summer. *Aspen Country*, a similar magazine focusing on Aspen, was launched in 1996. In 1998, Shanken announced plans for a Napa edition as well, based on his long familiarity with the region and its particular attractions for *Country*'s upscale readership. This was intended to be merely the first of a series of regionally focused expansions, a different application of M. Shanken's niche-market appeal. ''This is a national brand that we are developing slowly,'' Shanken told *Mediaweek* in December 1998. ''We think of ourselves as niche marketers—we have a niche with cigars, we have a niche with wine. There's no reason not to have niches by market.''

However, in the January 2002 issue of *Circulation Management*, it was noted that *Country* had suspended publication the previous November. There were, however, plans to resume publication in 2003.

Another significant expansion for M. Shanken was a web presence. The company launched WineSpectator.com in 1996; a cigar site followed soon after. By 1999, the wine site had attracted over 15 million visits and had 300,000 registered users. It also provided content to WineShopper.com, linking reviews and other editorial content. M. Shanken also entered into partnerships with other online ventures; among the most significant was an agreement with eSkye.com, a business-to-business site for the alcohol beverage industry. The agreement gave eSkye.com users access to *Wine Spectator*'s extensive database of wine ratings, allowing users, which included restaurants, bars, and liquor stores, to make informed purchasing decisions.

As the new millennium began, M. Shanken seemed poised to adapt to changing market conditions that had led to a decline in circulation in 1999. Emphasizing its role as a general lifestyle magazine since its inception, *Cigar Aficionado* shifted even more in that direction as the popularity of cigar smoking began to wane. Quoted in *Folio* in February 2000, executive editor Gordon Mott said, "The magazine has never been just about cigars—it's been a men's lifestyle magazine." Marvin Shanken added, "Seventy-five percent of the editorial has nothing to do with cigars." By April of that year, *Cigar Aficionado* had undergone a substantial revamp, complete with a new logo, greater coverage of non-cigar-related topics, and the relegation of cigar content to the back pages. Shanken told *Advertising Age*, "This magazine's potential can be converted into a larger readership if non-smokers understand it to be a true lifestyle magazine for affluent men." And M. Shanken's Senior Vice-President Niki Singer was quoted in a June 1998 issue of *Advertising Age:* "Now that the cigar industry has leveled off, we're still seeing double-digit increases because of strong growth in luxury goods."

Principal Competitors

Condé Nast; Gruner + Jahr; Hearst Communications Inc.; Time Inc.; The Wine Advocate, Inc.

Further Reading

"11th Annual Editorial Excellence Awards," *Folio*, December 1, 2000, p. 40.

Bogardus, Tim, "Marvin's Minions," *Folio*, April 1, 1995, p. 50.

Brown, Christie, "Old Wine in New Bottles," *Forbes*, October 16, 1989, p. 279.

Donaton, Scott, " 'Cigar Aficionado' Lets Smoke Clear in Revamp," *Advertising Age*, April 17, 2000, p. 6.

——, "Where There's Smoke, There's Shanken's Star," *Advertising Age*, March 11, 1996, p. S2.

Endicott, R. Craig, "Ad Age 300: The Annual Countdown," *Advertising Age*, June 15, 1998, p. S1.

Farnham, Alan, "He Did It His Way," *Fortune*, May 2, 1994, p. 132.

Goldbogen, Jessica, "Magazine Aims to Put 'Style' into Living in the Big Apple," *HFN*, October 16, 2000, p. 89.

Granatstein, Lisa, "Scrambled Eggs," *Mediaweek*, May 3, 1999, p. 12.

Gremillion, Jeff, "Shanken Whets Palate for Wine Country," *Mediaweek*, December 14, 1995, p. 16.

"Hamptons Country (Folding)," *Circulation Management*, January 2002, p. 29.

Hart, Margaret Allison, "Smoking in the Boys Room," *Chief Executive*, November-December 1994, p. 72.

Lefton, Terry, and Mark Adams, "Philip Morris Plans Magazine," *Mediaweek*, January 8, 1996, p. 4.

Levine, Joshua, "The Good Life," *Forbes*, January 18, 1993, p. 103.

Manly, Lorne, "Publishers Smoke Out New Market," *Folio*, October 15, 1995, p. 35.

Matthews, Thomas, "The History of Wine Spectator," posted November 15, 2001, http://www.winespectator.com.

——, "Marvin Shanken Looks Back at 20 Years of Wine Spectator," posted April 30, 1996, http://www.winespectator.com.

——, "Twenty Years of Wine History," posted April 30, 1996, http://www.winespectator.com.

Motavalli, Jim, "Blowing Smoke: The Unhealthy Cigar's Glamorous Image Is a Lot of Hot Air," *E Magazine*, March 13, 1998, p. 42.

"M. Shanken Communications Signs Alliance with eSkye.com," posted May 1, 2000, http://www.winespectator.com.

Posnock, Susan Thea, "20 Power Launches for the 90s," *Folio*, February 2000, p. 35.

Rich, Cary Peyton, "Shanken Adds Food Arts to the Menu," *Folio*, February 1990, p. 47.

Rusher, William A., "The Cigar, Revisited," *National Review*, August 14, 1995, p. 57.

Savona, David, "Smoke and Mirrors," posted April 30, 1998, http://www.winespectator.com.

Shanken, Marvin R., "A Conversation with Fidel," accessed May 15 2002, http://www.cigaraficionado.com.

——, "The Decline of Cuban Cigars," posted May 2001, http://www.cigaraficionado.com.

——, "A New Men's Lifestyle Magazine," accessed May 15 2002, http://www.cigaraficionado.com.

Shanken, Marvin R., and Gordon Mott, "The Cigar Industry Launches an Aggressive Campaign," posted March 1998, http://www .cigaraficionado.com.

——, "Five Years of Pleasure," November 1997, http://www.cigar aficionado.com.

Sucov, Jennifer, "Shanken's Folly," *Folio*, February 1, 1996, p. 46.

"Thumbnail Facts," New York: M. Shanken Communications, 2002.

Vermeulen, Karla, "Wine Spectator Goes On-Line; 50,000 Wine Reviews Accessible," posted October 31, 1996, http://www .winespectator.com.

Wilson, Steve, and Rolf Maurer, "Editorial Excellence Awards," *Folio*, August 1, 1996, p. 42.

"Wine Spectator at 25 . . . and the Man Behind the Magazine," New York: M. Shanken Communications, 2002.

"Wine Spectator Becomes a Content Provider for WineShopper.com," posted November 15, 1999, http://www.winespectator.com.

—Genevieve Williams

Macromedia, Inc.

600 Townsend Street
San Francisco, California 94103-4945
U.S.A.
Telephone: (415) 252-2000
Toll Free: (800) 756-9603
Fax: (415) 626-0554
Web site: http://www.macromedia.com

Public Company
Incorporated: 1992
Employees: 1,880 (2002)
Sales: $75.6 million (2002)
Stock Exchanges: NASDAQ
Ticker Symbol: MACR
NAIC: 511210 Software Publishers

Anyone who uses the Internet knows Macromedia, Inc.'s products well, if not necessarily by name. Macromedia's Flash, Shockwave, FreeHand, Director, and other software have helped to define multimedia content, applications, and interactivity on the Web. AOL Time Warner (Netscape), Microsoft, and Apple have integrated Macromedia's technology into their products, ensuring widespread use. Web developers depend on Macromedia's suite of Web design, development, and media player products to design and deliver compelling, interactive content on the Internet. The company also strives to promote the Web as a premiere media content provider. To that end, the company's Shockwave.com Web site provides millions of users with media content, including games and films.

Emerging from the Primordial Multimedia Ooze

Macromedia formed in 1992 when Authorware and Macro-Mind/ParaComp merged. Authorware was a multimedia authoring software company started by Michael Allen in 1985, and MacroMind/ParaComp was a multimedia, design, and visualization software company created by the merger of ParaComp and MacroMind in 1991.

During its early years, Macromedia was establishing a foothold in the media-design authoring software field while stream-

lining the merger. They purchased Altsys Corp., maker of the then-popular FreeHand illustration and desktop publishing software. They also acquired Altsys' Fontographer program. The purchase marked the company's foray into illustration and design, though it worried some users who were accustomed to Macromedia's strong suit in multimedia software.

In 1995, Web-browser pioneer Netscape incorporated Macromedia software into its Web browser, creating a substantial user base. A year later Macromedia unveiled its Shockwave product, which would soon become the company's most successful creation and was synonymous with the Macromedia brand. Shockwave allowed Web users to view animation and movies through standard browser technology.

Despite the early success of Shockwave, Macromedia found itself in debt by 1997. CEO Robert Burgess, who joined the company in 1996, began shifting the focus of Macromedia from CD-ROM software to Web tools, and cut 10 percent of the workforce. However, the many acquisitions early on still meant debts. The company suffered further blows when shareholders filed class-action lawsuits accusing the company of insider trading.

In the latter part of the decade the company continued to focus on its Web and animation products while completing more acquisitions. In early 2001, they bought Seattle-based AtomFilms, creating AtomShockwave. AtomFilms promoted short films that were delivered on the Internet and to independent distributors. Later that year Macromedia also bought Allaire, a Web site development software firm, for about $360 million.

Macromedia Strives to Become "Darling of the Internet"

Macromedia's biggest strength in the beginning was its Director and Authorware tools, programs used by developers to create educational and entertainment CD-ROMs. They then focused on the illustration and design fields in 1994 when they bought FreeHand-maker Altsys Corp. Macromedia kept the Altsys headquarters in Richardson, Texas, but renamed the organization Digital Arts Group of Macromedia. CEO James Von Ehr became a Macromedia vice-president until 1997, when he left to start another venture. The purchase saved the print

328

Company Perspectives:

Macromedia enables the most effective user experiences. Our mission is to make the development of dynamic content more efficient, more affordable, and more accessible to millions of customers. With products that range from Web development and graphics creation to server software that powers innovative Internet businesses, Macromedia bridges the gap between Web design and development. With an open, integrated, and approachable product line, a customer base of over two million Web professionals, and a business defined by broad distribution of server, development, and player software, Macromedia enables its customers to realize what the Web can be.

page-layout FreeHand product, since an earlier acquisition of Altsys by Adobe (maker of the market leading PageMaker software) threatened its existence. Macromedia promised to promote FreeHand, despite some analysts' concerns that a graphics company could not adequately manage a print production product. Other analysts pointed out that a print production product rounded out Macromedia's offerings.

Moving on, Macromedia then began its focus on establishing itself as an Internet software company. This was a tough endeavor, as Macromedia was a strong player in desktop applications but would have to face stiff competition on the Web with powerhouses such as Oracle, Microsoft Inc., and Sun Microsystems, Inc. Still, the company planned to move away from CD-ROM-based applications to develop software that would both be distributed on and for the Internet.

Macromedia Establishes Itself on the Web

Shockwave was the company's answer to broadening multimedia for Web use. The new software would work with Macromedia's Director program to compress multimedia applications to be run over the Internet. This piece was significant because up to this point, multimedia was difficult to transmit over the Internet. Compression meant that Director file sizes could be reduced about 60 percent; this also added security to user downloads. Not only were the multimedia pieces themselves smaller, but Macromedia claimed that Web pages with Shockwave technology were smaller than Web pages without any multimedia files at all.

To get the word out, Macromedia planned to ship its new Shockwave software free of charge, hoping that it would boost other sales of Macromedia software. They also worked with both Sun Microsystems and CompuServe. CompuServe became the first company to integrate Macromedia software into its products; in the meantime, Sun worked with Macromedia to enhance its Java Internet programming language and tools to work with Macromedia's multimedia software. Under their agreement, Macromedia would license Java and incorporate it into their multimedia products.

The partnerships with Sun Microsystems and CompuServe were a boon for the company in establishing itself among the big players. Eric Schmidt of Sun said their deal gave Macromedia a "serious presence on the Web." The announcement of

a Sun alliance made Macromedia stock rise 6 points in October 1995. The company stock had more than doubled in less than six months during this time.

Despite the agreements, Sun Microsystems still remained a competitor, as did Netscape, with whom Macromedia had made a deal earlier. However, Sun felt they could still work together since multimedia technology and the Java programming language was complementary to each other. Java technology was better suited for large applications such as databases; Macromedia's software was designed for longer streams of media such as video clips. Under the Netscape deal, Netscape would also incorporate Macromedia's technology into their Web browser, further broadening Shockwave's Web presence.

But success did not quite come so fast for Macromedia with Shockwave. The stock jumped from $30 to $63 in October, but it had dropped back to $50 in December when brokers downgraded the shares. Microsoft's Net strategy announcements also hurt share sales.

A further setback was the delay in releasing Shockwave for the Macintosh public. The company demonstrated a version at the MacWorld trade show in San Francisco in January 1996, but announced that the product would not be available for Mac users for six more weeks. The product was released for Windows 3.1 and Windows 95 platforms as a plug-in with Netscape's Netscape Navigator 2.0. Users who were used to Macromedia's focus on Macintosh software development up to this point were disappointed that the company chose to release a Microsoft Windows version first.

But the Windows version was proving to be a real success since its debute in December 1995. Hundreds of Shockwave sites had popped up, offering multimedia games, animations, and user interfaces. The company admitted it failed in communicating the delays to Macintosh developers, but reiterated that they were trying to establish themselves as a cross-platform company.

They then got to work developing the next version of Shockwave, which was to include support for streaming audio, media-specific compression, and the ability to download large movies in pieces.

More New Products

Continuing their Web development software strategy, Macromedia unveiled a new product in 1997. Dreamweaver was the developers' bridge between high-end Web authoring tools and WYSIWYG (What You See Is What You Get) applications.

Web developers would not use WYSIWYG—an environment in which one can develop a Web page by creating it onscreen instead of by writing lines of computer code—because those editors lacked the ability to control the code. Most WYSIWYG editors at this point added unnecessary code to Web pages that, while helping people design Web sites with no programming knowledge, constricted Web gurus at the same time. Dreamweaver based its technology on both these offerings; its WYSIWYG editor did not add code and allowed developers to design in either environment.

What made Dreamweaver initially successful was that Macromedia did not try to position it against existing WYSIWYG editors (Microsoft's FrontPage was an example of one),

Key Dates:

1992: Macromedia forms from a merger of MacroMind/ ParaComp and Authorware.

1993: The company's revenues hit $37 million and an initial public offering (IPO) is made.

1994: Director4 is released; and the company grows to 155 employees.

1995: The company acquires Altsys and renames the organization Digital Arts Group of Macromedia; and FreeHand and Shockwave are released.

1996: Rob Burgess joins as CEO.

1997: Macromedia Flash, a product that streamlines multimedia Web use, is introduced; and Dreamweaver, a Web page development platform, debuts.

1998: Fireworks debuts; the company launches its Universal Media Initiative to increase the usability of its software in Web environments; Shockwave .com, featuring games, music, cartoons, and interactive media is launched.

1999: The company acquires Elemental Software; and introduces CourseBuilder.

2000: Macromedia University is founded.

2001: The company acquires Allaire, a Web site development software firm; acquires AtomFilms, a short films maker that creates AtomShockwave; HomeSite5 is introduced; and ColdFusion5 debuts.

2002: Flash MX, an expanded Web development program, and Flash Player 6 are released; the company launches a learning initiative with SmartForce to develop e-learning content based on Macromedia software.

but targeted it against bare bones HTML (hypertext markup language) editors. Dreamweaver offered the best of both worlds; developers could hard-code HTML and then see the results in the WYSIWYG window.

In addition to Dreamweaver, Macromedia found success in its Flash product. While Shockwave was proving successful in the more-advanced development applications, it was also too bulky and complicated for ordinary Web use. The company hoped its new Flash product would be the key to streamlining multimedia Web use. Flash was born from a product called FutureSplash Animator, made by FutureWave Software Inc. Macromedia bought the company in January 1997 and incorporated the FutureSplash product into its line, renaming it Macromedia Flash. By again utilizing Sun Microsystems' Java technology, Flash could be used to deliver multimedia on any machine regardless of platform. In 1997, Macromedia teamed up Flash with RealNetworks to produce RealFlash, a client-server streamlining product that enabled full-length presentations with synchronized audio and sound.

Trials and Tribulations

Macromedia was not without its trials during this intense growth period. By 1997, Macromedia was the creator or licenser of several products: the design and development tools Shockwave, Director, Dreamweaver, and Fontographer; the

print production platform FreeHand; media players Shockwave Player and Flash; and their learning development application Authorware. But while the stock had reached an all-time high of $63 in 1995, by March 1997 it had plunged 20 percent to $15 before steadily dropping to about $8 a share. The plunge was due to a much-publicized delayed release of Director6 and lagging sales of Macintosh computers. The company reported a loss of $15.3 million for the 1997 fiscal fourth quarter.

To combat the financial troubles the company shifted some executives around; Bob Colligan resigned as CEO but remained chairman; Rob Burgess then took over as president, phasing out the CEO position. Burgess had several plans. First, he reorganized its Products divisions and cut the workforce by 10 percent. Next, the company as a whole focused on eliminating any future financial surprises. Part of that plan was to reorganize into more focused market segments. The effort to move away from desktop software to Internet-based applications continued, as well as a shift from a focus on the Macintosh sector to the PC market. Macromedia did have several good things going for it at the time; it was the leader in developing desktop media tools; graphic artists coveted their applications; and the company had no debt on the books in early 1997. Based on these factors, though the stock was at an all-time low, analysts were starting to make noises that Macromedia might be a good buy.

But another snag hit the company when investors filed a class-action lawsuit in August 1997 accusing the company and five executives of insider trading. The suit claimed Macromedia misled the stockholders on products success and health while engaging in insider trading during the last half of 1996. Macromedia settled the suit in August 2001, paying $48 million and clearing itself of any admission of liability.

Adapting Multimedia for the Web Environment

Macromedia's Universal Media Initiative launched in October 1998 was designed to increase the usability of its software in Web environments. The Initiative's goal was to adapt the multimedia authoring tools such as Shockwave and Flash to Web standards such as Java and Dynamic HTML. In this way users would not need special plug-ins to view Shockwave and Flash animations, and could create Web-based animation using HTML.

This was important as it allowed Flash and Shockwave to proliferate even further in the Web environment. Designers had more freedom in their Web sites because their choice of design tools would work on any user's browser; likewise, users did not need special software to view any Web site.

In keeping with the Web application theme, Macromedia also launched the successful Shockwave.com Web site in early 1998. It featured games, music, cartoons, and interactive media and drew 60,000 daily visitors. By 1999 the Web site alone was generating $3.3 million in advertising on the site.

The focus on Internet product direction was attributed to Macromedia's success in 1998. In one year the company bounced back from an all-time stock low to almost its high again. Revenues in 1998 reached $114 million and then rose to $153 million in 1999. Flash3 and Dreamweaver accounted for 20 percent of the company's sales, and deals with both Microsoft and Netscape allowed Flash to be bundled with their respective Web browsers.

During this year Macromedia also decided to get out of the video editing business; it discontinued its weaker xRes and Extreme 3D products and then sold its never-released digital video technology to Apple.

Focus on Product Improvement

During the last part of the decade and into the new century Macromedia continued to build on the success of its products, especially its popular Flash products. Flash reached Version 5.0 by 2001 and was bundled on both Apple Macintoshes and PCs, ensuring that 98 percent of the public could view Web pages with Flash animation. Likewise marketers could build ad banners and Web sites using Flash; Jupiter Media Metrix reported that 54 percent of all deployed online advertising was created using it.

For 2002, Macromedia released Flash MX, an expanded Web development program that promised to increase usability for both developers and end users. This version of Flash was promoted to let users develop for the Internet as a business-oriented application rather than a static, content-oriented tool. Macromedia hoped that Web developers would use the newest version of Flash together with Macromedia's other Web development tools to create "rich Internet applications."

Branching out into the entertainment industry, Shockwave.com bought short films maker AtomFilms in 2001. The Seattle-based film company distributed digital films online. The combined company, named AtomShockwave, reached 15 million unique users every month and produced 2,000 game, film, and animation titles.

Despite another stock drop in early 2002 and the overall decline in the Internet economy, Macromedia was poised to continue driving the Web-based application movement and to keep their products at its forefront. The company also launched a learning initiative with SmartForce, who agreed to develop more than 100 hours of e-learning content based on Macromedia software. Worldwide, Macromedia was making a name for itself as well; in February, 2002 Finnish Telecom company Nokia decided to work with the company to integrate Flash into Nokia's Mediaterminal information/entertainment device. By 2002 Macromedia had more than 20 products and 30 offices in 13 different countries; and with the rapidly changing face of the Internet and general Web use, they could expect those numbers to only grow.

Principal Subsidiaries

Allaire Corporation; AtomShockwave Corp.; Macromedia Canada Ltd.; Macromedia Ireland (Pty.) Ltd.

Principal Competitors

Adobe; Microsoft; Quark; Accrue Software; Corel; iEntertainment Network; Loudeye Technologies; RealNetworks; SGI; Sonic Foundry; Viewpoint; ImaginOn; Aptas; Internet Pictures; Bitstream; Apple Computer.

Further Reading

Abes, Cathy, "Graphics Products Refocused," *Macworld*, September 1998, pp. 30–32.

Beale, Stephen, "Macromedia Unplugged," *Macworld*, January 1998, pp. 26–27.

Becker, David, "Flash: More than Just Eye Candy," *CNET.com*, posted March 3, 2002, http://www.news.com.com.

——, "Losses Mount for Macromedia," *CNET.com*, posted January 16, 2002, http://www.news.com.com.

Brigham, Joan-Carol, "Publishing's Future on the Web," *Computer Reseller News*, August 12, 1996, p. S42.

Clancy, Heather, "Macromedia Ponders Channel Expansion," *Computer Reseller News*, December 7, 1998, p. 77.

Dillon, Nancy, "Macromedia Reanimated," *Computerworld*, September 28, 1998, p. 96.

Einstein, David, "Macromedia Tries to Enliven the Net," *SF Gate*, posted October 31, 1995, http://www.sfgate.com.

Festa, Paul, "Investors Sue Macromedia Again," *CNET.com*, posted September 4, 1997, http://www.news.com.com.

——, "Macromedia Patching Shockwave Privacy Hole," *CNET.com*, posted March 11, 1999, http://www.news.com.com.

Hagendorf, Jennifer, "Macromedia Sets Agenda for Flash," *Computer Reseller News*, April 20, 1998, p. 30.

Janah, Monua, "Macromedia's Wild Ride," *Informationweek*, December 25, 1995, p. 87.

Karpinski, Richard, "Mac Shockwave Delayed," *Communicationsweek*, January 15, 1996, p. 31.

Kary, Tiffany, "Macromedia Sinks on Lack of Outlook, Downgrades," *CNET.com*, posted May 3, 2001, http://www.news.com.com.

Kozel, Kathy, "Macromedia's 'Ignite the Web' Conference Loses Its Spark," *E Media Professional*, January 1998, p. 11.

Levitt, Jason, "Web Tool Rivalries Intensify," *Informationweek*, March 24, 1997, p. 84.

"Macromedia," *Computer Reseller News*, November 3, 1997, p. 82.

"Macromedia Inc.: Profit of $1.9 Million Posted as Sales More than Double," *Wall Street Journal*, May 8, 1998, p. B4.

"Macromedia Inc.: Wider-than-Expected Loss of $15.3 Million Reported," *Wall Street Journal*, May 1, 1997, p. B6.

"Macromedia to Expand to Internet," *Computer Reseller News*, November 13, 1995, p. 85.

Malik, Om, "Macro-Makeover," *Forbes*, September 7, 1998, p. 248.

Markoff, John, "Macromedia Lays Out Strategy for More Uses for Flash Player," *New York Times*, posted April 29, 2002, http://www.nytimes.com.

"Nokia Integrates Macromedia's Software into Infotainment Device," *Telecomworldwire Coventry*, February 7, 2002.

"Shockwave Buys AtomFilms.com," *San Francisco Business Times*, posted December 18, 2000, http://www.bizjournals.com/sanfrancisco.

Singer, Michael, "Macromedia Settles 1997 Class Action," *Silicon valley.internet.com*, posted August 30, 2001, http://www.siliconvalley.internet.com.

Swartz, Jon, "Poor Mac Sales Hurt Developer," *SF Gate*, posted August 29, 1996, http://www.sfgate.com.

——, "Slow Mac Sales Hit Stocks," *SF Gate*, posted July 10, 1996, http://www.sfgate.com.

"Technology Pact Reached on Netscape Web Browser," *Wall Street Journal*, June 9, 1998, p. B4.

Vadlamundi, Pardhu, "Macromedia's Purchase of Altsys Raises Questions," *InfoWorld*, November 7, 1994, p. 24.

Veverka, Mark, "After a Steep Drop, Macromedia May Start to Lure Bottom Fishers," *Wall Street Journal*, March 26, 1997, p. CA2.

Walsh, Jeff, "Macromedia Eases Web-based Training," *InfoWorld*, September 14, 1998, p. 44.

——, "Macromedia Targets HTML Editors," *InfoWorld*, October 13, 1997, p. 77.

Yamada, Ken, "Macromedia Teams Up with Oracle to Target Internet Arena," *Computer Reseller News*, November 6, 1995, p. 281

—Kerri DeVault

Mediaset SpA

Via Paleocapa, 3
20121 Milan, Italy
Italy
Telephone: +39 (02) 854-142-83
Fax: +39 (02) 210-230-25
Web site: http://www.gruppomediaset.it

Private Company
Incorporated: 1993
Employees: 4,370 (2001)
Sales: EUR 2.371 billion (2002)
Stock Exchanges: Italian/ISE
Ticker Symbol: MS
NAIC: 513120 Television Broadcasting; 541890 Other
    Services Related to Advertising

Mediaset SpA is Italy's most important privately owned communications and broadcasting group and one of the largest in the world. Its success is based on the vision of the founder of the Fininvest Group, Silvio Berlucsoni, to create a totally integrated group able to control all aspects of the television business—signal broadcasting, in-house television production, the acquisition of film and drama rights, and the collection of advertising—to successfully challenge the monopoly of the state broadcaster Radio Televisione Italiana (RAI).

Mediaset is Born

The development of commercial television in Italy can be credited to Milan-born Silvio Berlusconi, who in 1975 set up a holding company, Fininvest, which provided direct competition to the public-sector broadcasting organization RAI (Radio Televisione Italiana). Over the next 25 years, Berlusconi built a communications conglomerate that would dominate Italian commercial television, become Europe's second largest media empire and Italy's third largest private company. Due to a Constitutional Court ruling in 1975 that legitimized private television operations, over 700 commercial stations sprang up around Italy. Berlusconi's first venture into television market-

ing was the result of the operations of Publitalia, a subsidiary that initially provided advertising for titles rented from his major film library to other local stations. Over the next ten years, television advertising increased from 15 percent to 50 percent, and to 70 percent by the end of 2000.

In 1978, Berlusconi became a television station owner himself when he founded TELEMILANO, which in 1980 became Canale 5, a broadcasting network owned by the Fininvest Group. By the mid-1980s, the Fininvest Group had acquired their major competitors, Italia 1 and Rete 4, thus breaking the state monopoly in television and advertising and dominating commercial television in Italy.

However, in October 1984, Italian magistrates ruled that this conglomeration itself was in breach of RAI's monopoly right to broadcast a simultaneous national service, and ordered them to shut down. Berlusconi appealed to powerful political associates, including the Prime Minister, Bettino Craxi, who signed a decree to reopen the Fininvest Group stations, thus establishing a duopoly in national television and giving the commercial networks and RAI's public channels an overall market share of between 40 and 45 percent each.

The fear of additional demands for the breakup of his company provoked Berlusconi to contest the forthcoming general election. Under the banner of a new party, Forza Italia, his coalition won 43 percent of the popular vote in March 1994 and formed a government seating Berlusconi as prime minister. Amid concerns of conflict-of-interest, Berlusconi resigned from all managerial positions and chairmanships of his company. Nonetheless, after nine months his administration fell. Berlusconi continued to divulge major interests in his company, including a 20 percent stake in Mediaset for EUR 1.1 billion to three outside investors, including Saudi Prince Al Waleed Bin Talaal, South African businessman Johann Rupert, and the Kirch Group of Germany. Over the next few years, he continued to sell shares to banks and other institutions, and eventually relinquished majority control.

In 1991, Canale 5, Italia 1, and Rete 4 began live broadcasting and obtained national broadcasting licenses the following year. Mediaset was born out of a reorganization project that

Key Dates:

1975: Fininvest Group is established by Silvio Berlusconi.
1978: TELEMILANO is founded and later becomes Canale 5, a network of broadcasters that is owned by the Fininvest Group.
1980: Canale 5 begins broadcasting in Italy.
1982: The Fininvest Group purchases Italy's privately owned Italia 1.
1984: The Fininvest Group purchases Italy's privately owned Rete 4.
1991: Canale 5, Italia 1, and Rete 4 begin live broadcasting.
1992: Canale 5, Italia 1, and Rete 4 obtain national broadcasting licenses.
1993: Mediaset is created from the consolidation of Canale 5, Italia 1, and Rete 4 to become Italy's major private television and communications network.
1995: Mediaset assumes control of Publitalia '80, the advertising arm of the Group's networks and takes over R.TI., the company which holds the broadcasting licenses for the company's three networks.
1996: Mediaset obtains a listing on the Milan Stock Exchange and partners with Albacom, the telephone-line transmission company.
1997: Mediaset acquires shares in Telecinco, Spain's second largest commercial broadcaster amd launches MEDIAVIDEO, a teletext service.
1998: Mediaset launches Happy Channel, a thematic satellite channel.
1999: Mediaset launches Mediaset Online (www.mediaset.it), a vertical television portal on the Internet and joins Blu SpA, the holder of Italy's fourth mobile telephone license.
2000: Mediaset consolidates all its digital activities into Mediadigit.
2001: Mediaset launches the digital platform MTChannel to promote programming of popular science issues; the company also launches TgCom (www.tgcom.it), an online general news service, and TgFin (www.tgfin.it) an online business and financial news service.

created an integrated group of these television and communications entities, which would grow independently, and secure strategic investors and financial partners.

By 1995, Mediaset had assumed control of Publitalia '80, the advertising collector for the Group's networks and R.TI., the holder of their respective broadcast licenses. In addition that year, the Group took over control of Videotime, TRI Music, and Elettronica Industriale, a countrywide signal distribution network.

Mediaset obtained a stock exchange listing (MS) on the Milan Stock Exchange in July 1996, and became a partner in Albacom, a fixed-line telephone company of British Telkecom and Banca Nazionale del Lavoro the same year.

Mediaset Acquires Spanish Broadcaster

To establish alliances with other world players in television, electronic media, and telecommunications, in 1997 Mediaset acquired shares in Telecinco, Spain's second largest commercial broadcaster. The same year, Mediaset launched MEDIAVIDEO, a teletext service generating 800-plus pages of constantly updated information. The Happy Channel was launched in 1998 as Mediaset's first thematic satellite channel dedicated to comedy and broadcast digitally by Italian broadcaster Telepiu.

Mediaset Online

The vertical portal MediasetOnline (www.mediaset.it) was launched January 1999. Germany's KirchMedia, the subholding for the Kirch Group's activities in commercial television and rights trading, reached an agreement with Mediaset to address the challenges of globalization. Also in 1999, Mediaset joined Blu SpA, Italy's fourth mobile telephone license holder. Other acquisitions included Gestevision Telecinco SA and Publiespana SA. Through a joint venture with the Kirch Group, Mediaset partnered in the creation of Epsilon, for the development of the production, acquisition, and distribution of films, TV movies, series and other content on a European scale.

In 2000, Mediaset consolidated all its digital activities into Mediadigit, which consequently acquired a stake in CFN (Class Financial Network), owned by Class Editori, a thematic channel focusing on digitally distributed economic and financial news. Other Internet activities led to an agreement with Jumpy, the Internet portal of the Fininvest Group. Two new channels were introduced in April and produced by Mediadigit: Comedy Life, a channel dedicated to women, and Duel, dedicated to action programming.

The following year, MTChannel was launched to promote programming of popular science issues; and Tgcom (www

.tgcom.it) was launched as the Group's new Internet news service. Mediaset Online (www.mediasetonline.com) was launched as the Group's new television vertical portal (vortal) to disseminate information and entertainment to a mass audience. Mediaset entered the online business and financial news sector with TgFin (www.tgfin.it), a Web portal that provided fast and reliable information for small investors and financial professionals.

Mediaset's operations were divided into the Commercial Television division and the Broadcasting and Content group. The Commercial Television division generated revenue from the sale of advertising on company television networks. The Broadcasting and Content group carried out the development and implementation of program schedules, the production of original programs, and the management of the television-signal broadcasting network. This group consisted of Italian TV, International Broadcasting, Telecommunications, and Finance. Mediaset also maintained operations with the recording industry through its subsidiaries and operations in the telecommunications sector through investments in subsidiaries operating in the fixed telephone market.

The 2001 consolidated net revenues of the Mediaset Group totaled EUR 2.351 billion, an increase from previous years as a result of the overall performance of television, and in particular, advertising revenues. With 4,370 full-time employees in 2001, Mediaset continues to direct control over all aspects of the television business, from scheduling to production, and from acquisition to broadcasting. Mediaset has developed economically, financially and productively into an independent, solid company. Originally a generalist television in Italy, Mediaset is embarking on expansion abroad through its strong alliance with Kirch Media, of Germany's Kirch Group and Spain's Telecinco, Europe's most profitable broadcaster.

Principal Subsidiaries

Albacom SpA; Electtronica Industriale SpA; Kirch Media Gmbh & Co.; Mediadigit SpA; Mediaset Investment S.a.r.l.; Mediatrade SpA; Publieurope International Ltd.; Publieuros Ltd.; Publitalia '80 S.p.A.; R.TI. SpA; Telecinco; Videotime SpA.

Principal Competitors

Bertelsmann; Radio Televisione Italiana (RAI); Vivendi Universal.

Further Reading

Boston, William, "Germany's Kirch Opens Gates to Investors in Drive to Grow," *Wall Street Journal*, January 5, 1999, p.17.

"Building Blocks: Mediaset and the Kirch Group Join Forces," *Variety*, December 20, 1999, Volume 377, Issue 6, p. 46.

Foreman, Liza, "TV Titans Go Euro, Global," *Variety*, May 29, 2000, Volume 379, Issue 2, p. 42.

"Future of Italian Free TV Giant Depends on Political Maneuvers," *Broadcasting & Cable's TV International*, May 14, 2001, Volume 9, Issue 10, p. 10.

"Gruppo Mediaset RTI," *Video Age International*, January 2000, Volume 20, Issue 1, p. S6.

"Kirch Plans to Unload Tele 5," *Broadcasting & Cable's TV International*, October 29, 2001, Volume 9, Issue 21, p. 4.

"Mediaset Takes Kirch Stake," *Broadcasting & Cable's TV International*, September 19, 2000, Volume 8, Issue 18, p. 5.

"Questions Surround Mediaset Stake," *Broadcasting & Cable's TV International*, September 17, 2001, Volume 9, Issue 18, p. 3.

Trofimov, Yaroslav, "Berlusconi Steams Ahead toward Italy's Vote on Sunday," *Wall Street Joiurnal*, May 9, 2001, p. A3.

"Who's Who in Italy's 3G/UMTS Auction," *Wireless Insider*, October 2, 2001, Volume 18, Issue 39, p. 1.

Zecchinell, Cecilia, "Evision Envisions $125 Million in Production," *Variety*, October 8, 2001, Volume 384, Issue 8, p. B8.

—Carol D. Beavers

METRO AG

Metro AG

Schluterstraße 41
40235 Düsseldorf
Germany
Telephone: +49 (211) 6886-2870
Fax: +49 (211) 6886-2000
Web site: http://www.metro.de

Public Company
Incorporated: 1996
Employees: 230,848 (2001)
Sales: EUR 52 billion (US$45.73 billion) (2002 est.)
Stock Exchanges: Düsseldorf Frankfurt Xetra
Ticker Symbol: MEOG.D (Düsseldorf), MEOG.F
   (Frankfurt), MEOG.DE (Xetra)
NAIC: 445110 Supermarkets and Other Grocery (except
   Convenience) Stores; 445120 Convenience Stores;
   452110 Department Stores; 551112 Offices of Other
   Holding Companies

One of the largest retailers in the world, Metro AG is a Düsseldorf-based holding company formed through the 1996 merger of four giant German retailing groups. It operates 2,250 stores in 25 countries, and competes with such notable conglomerates as U.S. retail king Wal-Mart, Carrefour of France, and German rival Tengelmann. The company employs almost a quarter-million people. Metro concentrates on four core businesses: cash-and-carry wholesale outlets, retail food markets, consumer electronic stores and home-improvement centers, and department stores. With strong retail and price competition in the German marketplace, the company has aggressively pursued growth in foreign markets. Between 1997 and 2001, international sales jumped from 5 percent of the group business to 45 percent. The cash-and carry business accounts for 75 percent of foreign sales and is the company's most profitable division overall.

Beisheim Founds Metro Cash & Carry: 1964–1995

Metro's global retail/wholesale empire began as Metro SB-Grossmarkte, a cash-and-carry business that German entrepre-

neur Otto Beisheim founded in 1964 in Mulheim. Popularized in the United States, cash-and-carry operations departed from traditional wholesale models by allowing commercial customers to pick and purchase goods at distribution centers, then haul them away in their own vehicles. Benefits included lower prices, larger product selection, extended business hours, and immediate possession of merchandise. Operating under the name Metro Cash & Carry, the company received financial backing in 1967 from the Franz Haniel & Cie. industrial dynasty and the Schmidt-Ruthenbeck family, also wholesalers. Beisheim and his new partners each controlled one-third of the shares in the company.

The infusion of capital enabled Beisheim and his partners to expand cash-and-carry outlets within and beyond German borders. In 1968, Metro joined with Dutch conglomerate Steenkolen Handelsvereniging NV (SHV) and established a company in the Netherlands operating as Makro Cash & Carry. Nine western European countries became home to Metro and Makro wholesale outlets by 1972. Expansion into retailing soon followed. In the early 1980s, Metro and Union Bank of Switzerland made a major acquisition, German department store chain Kaufhof AG. As Metro gained controlling interest in the company, it steered Kaufhof toward converting some stores into specialized fashion and shoe outlets, and investing in consumer electronics (Media Markt and Saturn) and computer businesses. In late 1992, the Metro added another retail conglomerate to its portfolio, buying a majority stake in the German holding company Asko Deutsche Kaufhaus. Asko's properties included retail and wholesale grocery networks, furniture stores, and Praktiker home-improvement centers.

By 1993, privately held Metro had controlling stakes in Kaufhof, Asko, and Asko's subsidiary Deutsche SB-Kauf—all companies listed on European stock exchanges. The holdings not only left Metro with a dominant market share in the German food-retailing sector, but elevated it to one of the largest retailing groups in the world. Indeed, Metro had an estimated 180 companies under its management, including brand-name businesses such as SB-Kauf supermarkets, Massa discount stores, computer chain Vobis, office supply group Pelikan, Adler clothing stores and AVA department stores. Along the way

Metro had become Metro Holding, with its headquarters and leader, Beisheim, locating in Baar, Switzerland. Entering his seventies, reclusive billionaire Beisheim retired from active management of the company in 1994. He turned over the reins to close associate Erwin Conradi, who had joined Metro in 1970. Conradi would dominate the company management over the next five years.

Becoming Europe's Largest Retail Group: 1995–1998

Conradi announced in October 1995 that Metro Holding planned to establish a new company—Metro AG—by merging its four largest German operations: Kaufhof, Asko, SB-Kauf, and Metro Cash & Carry. The merger was largely driven by Europe's sluggish consumer spending and crowded retail sector. "Consumer confidence over the coming years looks likely to remain weak," Conradi explained in a March 1996 interview with *The Daily Telegraph*. "Price will become even more important and for companies that means cost savings will be more vital than ever." Consolidation allowed the new group to cut costs while boosting sales and creating a platform for global expansion. Conradi estimated sales would rise to DM 76.4 billion (US$52 billion) in 1998, more than 22 percent above the group's 1995 total. He added that net profits would double over the period from DM 719 million to DM 1.47 billion.

In May 1996, shareholders for publicly traded Kaufhof, Asko, and SB-Kauf approved a share-swapping plan and merger backdated to the beginning of the year. With an estimated value of US$10 billion, Metro AG was headquartered in Düsseldorf / Cologne and overnight became the largest retailer in Europe and among the top five in the world. The company was listed on the German DAX stock index for the first time on July 25, 1996. Under a complex ownership arrangement, privately held Metro Holding retained a 60 percent stake in the company, a stake controlled by Beisheim and the Haniel and Schmidt-Ruthenbeck families via another holding company. First year net sales for the new company came in at DM 55 billion (US$35.4 billion) and net profit at DM 717 million (US$393 million). The company had just over 130,000 employees.

Following the consolidation, Metro embarked on a series of acquisitions and divestitures designed to strengthen core businesses and move ahead with expansion. In 1997 it added 59 Wirichs home-improvement centers to complement the Praktiker chain. It bought computer and restaurant holdings, and disposed of fashion, furniture, and some retail and wholesale grocery outlets. Foreign sales grew 50 percent as five chains—Real, Media Markt, Praktiker, Adler, and Vobis—launched operations in other European countries. Metro Cash & Carry, already in 15 countries, opened its first stores in Romania and China. But 1997 proved to a disappointing year for shareholders. Sales increased to DM 56.8 billion (US$31.7 billion), but net profit fell from DM 717 million (US$393 million) in 1996 to DM 623 million (US$309 million). Even with added expansion costs, the profit figures weighed in lower than management expected.

The buying and selling continued into 1998. Metro fortified its profitable European cash-and-carry operations by purchasing 196 Makro Cash & Carry stores from SHV Makro NV of the Netherlands for US$2.7 billion. Metro later bought out the remaining interest that the parent company Metro Holding held in SHV Makro, a move made to guarantee investors full profits from the businesses. Metro also added to its portfolio the well-known Allkauf and Kreigbaum "hypermarkets"—known as combination grocery/department stores.

Focusing on Core Businesses: 1998

Entering 1998, investors and industry analysts still lacked confidence Metro was on the right track. Many criticized the retail giant for being overly diversified, lacking a coherent strategy, and subject to mysterious ownership. Shareholders also had concerns about the company's low profit margins.

Metro was indeed diversified. It had 13 independent operating divisions at the end of 1997. The glut of companies included wholesale food outlets, three department store chains, hypermarkets, food stores, discount stores, consumer electronics centers, home-improvement centers, three computer centers, fashion centers, shoe stores, restaurant and catering services, and real estate and support companies. The concerns over the company's structure and strategy compelled Metro to embark on a DM 5 billion (US$2.7 billion) reorganization program in the fall of 1998. Hans-Joachim Korber replaced Klaus Wiegandt as management board chairman, and Korber pushed forward a plan to concentrate on just four core businesses.

The program also called for Metro systematically to shed non-core business chains through a new subsidiary Divaco (initially Divag). Metro invested DM 350 million in Divaco and retained a 49 percent stake. A group of investors led by Deutshe Bank managed it. In December, Metro transferred to Divaco companies generating sales of DM 16 billion (US$9.6 billion) and employing 34,000 workers. The banished businesses included 813 Vobis computer stores, 143 Kaufhalle and 25 unprofitable Kaufhof department stores, fashion and shoe stores, Tip discount stores, and Kaufhalle's real estate business. Divaco sold 165 Tip stores to Berman retailer Tenglemann for DM 375 million in late 1998. A year later, trying to raise cash for expansion, Metro disposed of additional assets by selling and leasing back its retail real estate. In a joint venture with

Key Dates:

1964: Otto Beisheim founds Metro SB-Grossmarkte, a wholesale business that becomes Metro Cash & Carry.
1967: Haniel and Schmidt-Ruthenbeck families become Beisheim's partners.
1968: Metro Cash & Carry expands to the Netherlands, opening Makro Cash & Carry stores.
1993: The company acquires a majority interest in Asko Deutsche Kaufhaus.
1994: Beisheim retires from active management of Metro and Erwin Conradi is appointed president of the Metro Holding Board.
1996: Metro Holding merges Asko, Metro Cash & Carry, Kaufhof and Deutsche SB-Kauf to create Metro AG.
1998: Metro purchases Makro Cash & Carry and Allkauf and Kreigbaum hypermarket chains; and establishes Divaco to sell non-core businesses.
1999: Rumors circulate that Wal-Mart will purchase all or part of Metro; and Hans-Joachim Korber is named CEO.
2000: The company's original partners deny rumors of the Metro merger; and Supervisory Board Chairman Erwin Conradi resigns.
2001: Cash-and-carry operations expand to Russia and Croatia; and the company purchases Primus-Online, an e-commerce business.
2002: The company's cash-and-carry operations expand to Vietnam.

Westdeutsche Landesbank that raised DM 5.4 billion, Metro sold the ground under 290 retail outlets in Germany, Turkey, Greece, Hungary, and Luxembourg.

Metro's financial numbers for 1998 finished strong. The Makro acquisition drove six months sales up 62 percent, with year-end figures hitting to DM 91.7 billion (US$54.7 billion, EUR 46.8 billion). Net income jumped 19 percent to DM 735 million(EUR 579 million). The company was one of the strongest performers on the German DAX. International expansion also moved smartly ahead, with foreign business contributing 35.2 percent to total sales in 1998 and company payroll climbed above 181,000.

Merger Speculation: 1999

Investor confidence was short-lived, however. From an all-time high of DM 153 marks (EUR 78.5) in January 1999, company stock dropped 20 points on the DAX by the end of March and hovered there the rest of the year. For the year, sales dipped to DM 85.7 billion (US$44.1 billion, EUR 43.8 billion) and net income dropped to DM 713 billion (EUR 305 billion). Metro added another 73 foreign outlets, and introduced a customer loyalty program "Payback" at the Real and Kaufhof chains. It also launched its first Internet business activities with the Kaufhof and Metro Cash & Carry units.

Merger and acquisition rumors dominated Metro's press coverage as stiff competition and stagnant growth in European retailing drove companies to look for partners to secure market share. The entrance of U.S.-based Wal-Mart onto the scene exacerbated the pressures. During 1998, Wal-Mart had acquired nearly 100 German hypermarkets with annual sales of US$3.1 billion. In early 1999 reports surfaced that the world's largest retailer had an interest in buying all or part of Metro. A Metro official responded by saying a merger "would not be a congenial get-together." Still, speculation persisted. Analysts identified the Netherlands' biggest retailer Ahold, and British retail group Tesco, as possible merger or acquisition candidates for Metro. And in January 2000 reports surfaced that management for Metro and the U.K.-based retailer Kingfisher were having preliminary discussions. Metro continued to deny any interest in merging. "Of course people call us, of course we talk to them," said Metro Supervisory Board Chairman Conradi in the January 26, 2000 *Financial Times*. "But we have not actively been pursing any deal and neither should we, as our competitive position is not at risk." Industry insiders thought otherwise. Several believed some or all of the three original partners wanted to sell their shares to Wal-Mart in order to invest in non-retail interests. The partners were bound to act together under agreement in effect until 2003.

Merger rumors peaked in July 2000 when German newspaper *Welt am Sonntag* reported that Metro would transfer its Real chain of hypermarkets and Extra grocery chain to Wal-Mart, which wanted to continue to expand in Germany. Metro would in turn acquire around 1,000 of Wal-Mart's Sam's Club warehouse outlets. Metro's original partners this time issued a formal statement denying an interest in selling the company. They also asserted that they planned to maintain their cooperation for an indefinite period and sustain their commitment to Metro. At the same time, the partners announced that Conradi would resign. Some industry observers viewed Conradi's resignation as a dismissal for the supervisory board chairman's failed negotiations with Wal-Mart and French retailer Carrefour, which later acquired the French group Promode and replaced Metro as Europe's largest retailer. Others contended that Metro Executive Board Chairman Korber had threatened to leave if Conradi stayed. Korber and management board members reportedly felt Conradi blocked management decisions, which in turn delayed restructuring and expansion, specifically the acquisition of SHV Makro's additional cash-and-carry stores in Asia and Latin America.

Korber Takes Charge in 2000

By September 2000, there were several new faces on the Metro management board. To streamline the strategic decision-making process, Metro had reduced seats on the board from five to four. Korber retained the chairmanship along with his CEO title. In charge of balancing the family members demands with increasing Metro shareholder value, Korber reaffirmed Metro's commitment to international expansion, especially with the cash-and-carry business in Europe and Asia. But he resisted recommendations that Metro attempt to boost its share price by divesting of poorly performing food retail and home-improvement chains and focusing on profitable cash-and-carry and electronics stores. The company's four-part divisional makeup consisting of cash-and-carry (Metro, Makro), food retail (Real, Extra), nonfood specialty (Media Markt, Saturn, Praktiker), and department stores (Galeria Kaufhof) was "optimal," according to Korber.

In an effort to become more visible to investors, the company began to draw up its consolidated annual financial statements according to the International Accounting Standards (IAS). To promote entrepreneurial thinking within Metro, Korber introduced the control and management tool EVA (Economic Value Added) and benchmarking. The company also instigated incentives ranging from stock options for managers to merit pay for shop employees. Metro continued its advance into e-commerce and in June 2000 Metro acquired controlling interest in Cologne-based Internet service company Primus-Online.

Pursuing Profitability: 2001–2002

Metro's 2000 sales numbers met most analysts' expectations for Europe's restrained retail market. Fueled by growth in the cash-and-carry business, sales for 2000 grew to EUR 46.9 billion (DM 91.8 billion, US$44.1 billion), up over 7 percent from EUR 43.8 billion the previous year. Pre-tax profit climbed 10.7 percent to 754 euros. Sales abroad climbed to 42.2 percent of all sales. Kaufhof, the struggling department store division Metro had considered selling, registered a pre-tax profit of 7.2 percent after adopting the "Galeria" concept that appealed to upper-income, ethnically diverse urban consumers.

Metro opened another 80 retail outlets in 2001, bringing the store count up to 2,249. Cash-and-carry stores were opened for the first time in Russia and Croatia. Metro continued to push retail operations to develop high-brand recognition and store concepts. Sales figures rose 5.5 percent to EUR 49.5 billion (US$44.2 billion) for 2001, slightly lower than the 6 percent predicted number. Foreign sales rose to 44.4 percent of total sales. However, pre-tax profits dropped 10.7 percent to EUR 673 million. Based on 2001 sales, Metro ranked first in Germany, third in Europe and fifth in the world among retailers. But Korber had little interest in rankings. "We do not build an empire but rather develop our company to be profitable in the long run," said Korber in a September interview in the German business magazine *Focus Money*.

At the end of the first quarter of 2002, Korber predicted Metro group sales would hurdle the 52 billion euro mark by year-end. By 2003 he expected sales figures for outlets outside Germany to exceed those within its borders. The company's ongoing expansion resulted in its first cash-and-carry store in Vietnam in March 2002. Openings were planned in India and Japan before year end. Metro also announced it would open a chain of Real hypermarkets in Moscow and sell its stake in Divaco by the end of the year.

Under Korber, Metro moved ahead on a strategy based on internationalizing core retail operations, enhancing shareholder value, and creating brand awareness among consumers for retail outlets. Expansion efforts continued to focus on developing new stores "organically" and without incurring the costs and risks of acquisitions. Cash-and-carry operations, with 384 stores in 22 countries, remained the largest revenue producer in the group, accounting for 45 percent of the group's sales, or EUR 22.7 billion in 2001. Metro management remained committed to setting profitability targets for each of its independent sales divi-

sions. While public talk of mergers and acquisitions largely died in 2000, the agreement among Metro's original owners to act in unison is set to expire in 2003, and could raise the issue again.

Principal Operating Units

Cash-and-Carry: Metro; Makro. *Food Retail:* Real; Extra. *Nonfood Specialty:* Media Markt; Saturn; Praktiker. *Department Stores:* Galeria Kaufhof. *Other:* Metro MGE Einkauf (Purchasing); Gemex Trading AG (Import Agent); Metro MGL Logistik (Merchandise Movement); Metro Distributions-Logistik (Warehouse Delivery); Metro Wertstoff-Circle Services (Waste Disposal); Metro MGI Informatick (IT Services); Metro Real Estate Management (Construction Services); Metro Werbegesellschaft (Advertising); Dinea Gastronomie (Restaurants/Catering); Primus-Online (Internet Services), Divaco (Investment).

Principal Competitors

Wal-Mart Stores, Inc.; Carrefour SA; REWE-Zentral AG; Royal Ahold NV; Tengelmann Warenhandelsgesellschaft OHG; Edeka Zentrale AG; AVA Allgemeine Handelsgesellschaft der Verbraucher AG; Karstadt Quelle AG.

Further Reading

"Analysts Continue to Regard Metro AG as Non-Seller," *Suddeutsche Zeitung*, January 5, 2000, *Lexis-Nexis Academic Universe*, posted March 5, 2001, http://www.lexis-nexis.com/universe.

Andrews, Edmund L., "German Giants Spinning Off Big Businesses," *New York Times,* November 17, 1998, p. C6.

Benoit, Bertrand, "Aiming for More Cash than Carry," *Financial Times* (London), December 20, 2000, p. 20.

——, "Price War Puts Metro Independence in Question," *Financial Times* (London), January 26, 2000, p. 30.

Benoit, Bertrand, Richard Rivlin, and Susanna Voyle, "Metro Must Win Family Holders," *Financial Times* (London), January 22, 2000, p.16.

Bowley, Graham, "Metro Casts Doubt on Makro Dakeover," *Financial Times* (London), August, 19, 1997, p.19.

——, "Metro Launches Structure Changes," *Financial Times* (London), September 17, 1998, p.42.

——, "Retailer Metro in Move to Head Off Its Rivals," *Financial Times* (London), November 13, 1998, p.19.

Brasier, Mary, "German Giant on Retail Stage," *The Daily Telegraph*, March 15, 1996, p. 26.

"Business Brief—Metro AG: Unadjusted Sales Soar 62%, Lifted by Marko Purchase," *Wall Street Journal* (Eastern edition), posted August 27, 1998, http://www.wsj.com.

Dempsey, Judy, "Metro Sees Sharp Rise after Merger," *Financial Times* (London), March 15, 1996, p.27.

Du Bois, Martin, and Matt Marshall, "German Retailer Metro's Shares Plunge 7.5% after It Announces Its Profit Will Decline 25%," *Wall Street Journal* (Eastern edition), December 19, 1997, p. A15.

Dunsch, Jurgen, and Joachim Herr, "Kaufhof Boosts Performance and Targets Niche Market," *Frankfurter Allgemeine Zeitung*, posted April 3, 2001, http://www.faz.com.

"Europe's Biggest Retailer Buys Warehouse Stores," *The New York Times*, December 19, 1997, p. D3.

Kock, Brigette, "Erwin Conradi: A Great Fighter Steps Down," *Frankfurter Allgemeine Zeitung*, posted July 14, 2000, http://www.faz.com.

——, "Ongoing Speculation Boosts Metro Share," *Frankfurter Allgemeine Zeitung*, posted July 14, 2000, http://www.faz.com.

Kock, Brigette, and Anna Mayer, "Hans-Joachim Korber: Fighting Spirit Pays Off," *Frankfurter Allgemeine Zeitung*, posted January 9,2002, http://www.faz.com.

Le Prioux, Celine, "A New German Distribution Empire Is Born," *Agence France Presse, Lexis-Nexis Academic Universe*, posted May 31, 1996, http://www.lexis-nexis.com/universe.

Machova, Alena, "Wal-Mart, Metro and the Others," *Moderni Obchod Online*, posted September 2000, http://www.con-praha.cz/en/mo.

"Metro AG Sells All Its Retail Property Operations," *Die Welt*, January 6,2000, *Lexis-Nexis Academic Universe*, posted March 5, 2001 http://www.lexis-nexis.com/universe.

"Metro AG: Weary of Food Fights," *Agri-Food News from Germany*, December 2000, http://www.atn-riae.agr.ca.

"Metro Confirms to Sell Divaco Stake by Year-End, Denies to List Real Estate Unit," *FT.com Financial Times*, posted March 19, 2002, http://www.news.ft.com.

"Metro Looks Abroad for 2001," *CNN*, posted May 10, 2000, http://www.cnn.com.

"Metro Plans to Set Up Real hypermarket Chain in Moscow," *FT.com Financial Times*, posted April 3, 2002, http://www.news.ft.com.

"Metro Sees 2002 Sales, Profit Growth," *CNN*, posted March 26, 2002, http://www.cnn.com.

"Metro Wants to Expand Abroad When Merger Complete," *Turkish Daily News*, posted May 27, 1996, http://www.turkishdailynews.com.

Mitchener, Brandon, "Analysts Embrace Metro's Merging of German Units," *Wall Street Journal* (Eastern edition), March 15, 1966, p. B5.

Peitsmeier, Henning, "Smaller Metro Board Presses On with Internationalization," *Frankfurter Allgemeine Zeitung*, posted September 21, 2000, http://www.faz.com.

Seckler, Valerie, "Wal-Mart Said Eyeing Deal for German Retailer Metro," *Women's Wear Daily*, February 10, 1999, p. 4.

"Shares in Metro Fall as Takeover Denied," *Die Welt*, September 14, 2000, p. 19.

"A Shopping Market Stacked with Difficulties," *Financial Times* (London), *Lexis-Nexis Academic Universe*, posted August 1, 2000, http://www.lexis-nexis.com/universe.

Waller, David, "German Retailer Plans Hive-off," *Financial Times* (London), January 3, 1993, p. 22.

——, "Secretive Retailer Extends Its Tangle Web of Interests," *Financial Times* (London), December 8, 1992, p. 21.

Zagelmeyer, Stefan, "METRO Social and Employment Standards to be Maintained in Transferred Companies," *European Industrial Relations Observatory Online*, posted February 28, 1999, http://www.eiro.eurofound.ie.

—Douglas Cooley

National Express Group PLC

75 Davies Street
London W1Y 1FA
United Kingdom
Telephone: +44 (20) 7529-2000
Fax: +44 (20) 7529-2100

Public Company
Incorporated: 1988
Employees: 39,302 (2000)
Sales: £2.5 billion (2001)
Stock Exchanges: London
Ticker Symbol: NEX.L
NAIC: 488999 All Other Support Activities for
      Transportation; 488119 Other Airport Operations;
      561110 Office Administrative Services; 485510
      Charter Bus Industry

If you have ever used public transportation in the United Kingdom or Australia, or ridden on a school bus in the United States, you probably have National Express Group PLC to thank for your arrival. National Express, one of the world's leading international public transport groups, moves over one billion passengers a year worldwide through its bus, train, and coach operations.

Since its privatization in 1988 and formation as a company in the early 1990s, National Express has grown from a small express coach operation to a huge multinational corporation that actively pursues new opportunities. The company maintains a reputation for efficiency and innovation, and is dedicated to changing the perception of public transportation from a last resort to an easy, affordable, quality-travel option.

Origins of National Express: The Rise of Public Transportation in Britain

The major piece of British legislation that changed the landscape of public transportation was the Transport Act of 1980. It altered the required-licensing restrictions and allowed for competition. Soon after its enactment, other companies began appearing, offering long-distance coach routes in the United Kingdom. National Express jumped into this newly competitive market, offering new services and low fares, and continued to maintain a strong customer base and major brand. In this growing spirit of competition, National Express was allowed to be fully privatized by the Government in 1988. The management performed a full buyout, which took place in March.

National Express Group PLC was formed and shares were first offered on the London Stock Exchange in December of 1992. The newly public company was valued at £60 million. The prospectus stated the objectives of the company were to refocus and improve the profitability of their core coach business, to develop new products and services within its existing operations, and to acquire new businesses as financially viable in the passenger transport market.

Rapid Growth: Acquisitions and Successes, 1993–1999

The company immediately began to keep its promises of acquiring new businesses and adding to its portfolio. In 1993, just one year after becoming a public company, National Express acquired several major new properties. It acquired Scottish Citylink, expanding its services across Scotland. A few months later, the Group acquired Eurolines, an express coach company with a Pan-European network, followed by the acquisition of East Midlands Airport. In April 1995, National Express acquired Bournemouth Airport.

In 1995, the company took over the operations of one of Europe's largest urban bus systems, West Midlands Travel. This, along with the 1997 acquisition of Taybus Holdings, a Dundee-based bus company, expanded National Express's bus interests in their home nation.

The mid-1990s also saw the privatization of the rail industry in the United Kingdom. National Express took this opportunity to expand into rail services, and it applied for and was awarded the franchises for the Gatwick Express and Midland Mainline in 1996. The next year, National Express acquired three more rail

Company Perspectives:

We operate local transport businesses which are run by local people to meet the needs of the communities we serve. We conduct our business to ensure that these communities receive both economic and social benefits. Our 40,000 employees are committed to improving the quality, value for money and the safety of all our services. We invest in all aspects of our services, to attract more passengers and maximise the use of public transport systems. We are committed to taking advantage of the many opportunities for growth which exist in the international public transport market.

Key Dates:

1988: National Express is privatized by the British government.
1992: The company's stock is first offered on the London Stock Exchange.
1993: The company acquires Scottish Citylink, expanding its services in Scotland, and Eurolines, an express coach company.
1995: The company acquires Travel West Midlands, one of Europe's largest urban bus systems.
1996: The company acquires its first train companies: Gatwick Express and Midland Mainline.
1997: The company acquires Taybus Holdings, a Dundee-based bus company, and three more rail companies: Northern London Railways (Silverlink), Central Trains, and ScotRail.
1998: The company acquires Crabtree-Harmon's school bus interests in the United States.
1999: The company becomes the single largest private transport operator in Australia.
1999: The company purchases other U.S. student transportation bus operators: Robinson Bus Service and Durham Transportation.
2000: The company acquires London's Prism Rail, WAGN, and c2c commuter train lines; and operates Stewart International Airport (north of New York City).

companies. North London Railways (also called Silverlink), Central Trains, and ScotRail, became part of the National Express network. These acquisitions made the company one of the largest rail operators in the United Kingdom. They continued to concentrate on their bus services as well, expanding their operations in December with the Belgian bus operator, Bronckaers.

In 1998 the company began to examine overseas acquisition opportunities. It entered the United States markets in September by becoming involved in student transportation. It acquired Crabtree-Harmon, the seventh largest student transportation bus company in the states, with 82 school bus contracts mainly in Missouri, but also in other Midwest states including Kansas, Iowa, Oklahoma, Utah, and Colorado. This gave National Express its first foothold in the U.S. bus system. One year later they added Robinson Bus Service and Durham Transportation, both also major student transportation bus operators. These acquisitions placed National Express as one of the top three largest U.S. school bus operators.

National Express also began acquiring properties in Australia, quickly becoming the single largest private transport operator within that country. In May of 1999, it acquired bus operations in Melbourne, Brisbane, Sydney, and Perth when it took over National Bus Company Pty. Limited (NBC), the largest privately owned bus company in Australia. In September, National Express was awarded three of the available five rail and tram franchises within Melbourne and the state of Victoria.

Times of Trial: 2000–2002

National Express made another major acquisition in the United States in 2000, expanding its presence in the states from student transportation to airport operations. On March 31, it took over a 99-year lease on the formerly commercial Stewart International Airport, located 55 miles north of New York City, making National Express the operator of one of the nation's privatized airport.

National Express, satisfied it had established a strong international presence, again began to concentrate on additional expansions in the United Kingdom. In 2000, National Express acquired Prism Rail. Prism Rail, made up of the busy London commuter train operating companies WAGN and c2c, was a major addition to National Express' local offerings. The

group also acquired the Wales and West and Valley Lines and began work on a nationwide, multi-modal smart card ticketing system for public transport services after it acquired Prepayment Cards Ltd. (PCL). The group's introduction of travel smart cards for bus and rail passengers was targeted to increase the network of public transport services, offering passengers wider-ticket availability, as well as ease and speed of use. An added benefit for the Group was the introduction of special programs using the technology that would work to improve passenger loyalty and would put into place frequent-user plans for bus and rail users.

However, the spirit of expansion would be short-lived. In July, the company announced that Atlantic Express Transportation Group Inc., a New York-based student transportation operator, had commenced legal proceedings in damages in excess of US$75 million. Atlantic claimed that National Express had used confidential information gained as part of a due diligence to assist with their acquisition of Crabtree-Harmon. The company decided to pay Atlantic the sum of US$24.5 million to settle the claim out of court while maintaining this was not any type of an admission of liability to the charges. In October, a major tragedy changed the face of the British transportation system. Major setbacks began with the catastrophic derailment of a high-speed train at Hatfield, England, between London and Leeds. In this crash, four people were killed and at least 24 were injured. This crash caused a crisis in the transportation market, and National Express saw an immediate drop in income at its franchises, resulting from disruption on the rail network and speed restrictions imposed after the crash. National Express' shares also fell 35 percent due to this disruption on the railways.

With all its expansion within its bus and rail markets early in the year, and the troubles the industry faced in 2000, the company decided in March 2001 to leave the British airport market. It sold both its East Midlands and Bournemouth Airports to Manchester Airport. They decided to refocus and concentrate again on revitalizing their core businesses in the wake of a declining market.

Before the industry had adequate time to recover, the transportation industry had to again contend with a major tragedy—the terrorist attacks on the United States on September 11, 2001. These attacks had a resounding effect on global travel, and National Express saw a significant decrease in already low levels of traffic and a downturn in leisure travel in the United Kingdom and in their global interests. The Group also had to manage a doubling of their insurance premiums to £60 million because of the attacks.

In 2002, help was needed for some of National Express's major lines, and two of National Express's railroad subsidiaries received assistance from the Strategic Rail Authority (SRA) in order to avoid potential reductions in service. Central Trains, which operated passenger services in the Midlands, East Anglia, and central and South Wales, received £22 million and £34 million went to bail out ScotRail. The year continued to be a difficult one for the Group, after a coach driver, en route from Plymouth to Scotland, was stabbed in the face and shoulder after confronting a passenger who activated a smoke alarm in the vehicle's toilet.

The Group continues to keep positive that the industry will normalize, and remains steadfast regarding National Express's position to take advantage of the impending recover. Chief Executive Phil White wrote in the company's annual letter to investors, "U.K. train patronage has recovered to pre-Hatfield levels but there is still no real evidence of growth returning. However, we intend to play an integral part in rebuilding consumer confidence in U.K. rail. Our bus businesses worldwide continue to perform well and we intend to grow these operations both organically and by acquisition."

Principal Subsidiaries

Altram LRT Limited (33%); Inter-Capital and Regional Rail Limited (40%); National Express Trains Limited (100%); West Midlands Travel Limited (100%).

Principal Competitors

FirstGroup; Go-Ahead Group; Stagecoach; Arriva PLC.

Further Reading

Bainton, Roy, "Travellers' Fare: The Privatization of British Railways," *New Statesman & Society*, November 17, 1995, p. 10.

"British Bus Company Expands with $174 Million Buyout," *New York Times*, January 5, 2000, p. C3.

"Britain's National Express Acquires U.S. Bus Firm," *Wall Street Journal*, August 17, 1999, p. A16(W).

"Coach Driver Stabbed by Passenger," *BBC News*, posted March 13, 2002, http://news.bbc.co.uk.

Deveney, Paul J., "British Airways Ponders Joint Bid for Eurostar Train," *Wall Street Journal*, March 16, 1998, p. A15(W).

"Fleet Street Sites," *Marketing Week*, April 12, 2001, p. 38.

"Government Bails Out UK Rail Operators," *BBC News*, posted March 7, 2002, http://news.bbc.co.uk.

Icon Group International Incorporated Staff, *National Express Group Plc: International Competitive Benchmarks and Financial Gap Analysis*, Icon Group International Incorporated, 2000.

——*National Express Group Plc: Labor Productivity Benchmarks and International Gap Analysis*, Icon Group International Incorporated, 2000.

Jones, Dominic, "Rock and Rail," *Project Finance*, January 2001, pp. 46–48.

"Manchester Buys East Midlands and Bournemouth Airports," *Business & Commercial Aviation*, April 2001, p. 32.

"National Express Buys US School Bus Firm," *European Report*, September 16, 1998.

National Express Group PLC and Central Trains Limited: A Report on the Merger SI Monopolies and Mergers Commission Report, London: Stationery Office Books, 1998.

"National Express Makes US Acquisition," *Corporate Money*, June 7, 2000, p. 5.

"Sema Group to Supply Ticketing System to National Express Group," *European Report*, March 28, 2001, p. 600.

"United Kingdom: Wave of Rail Privatisation Continues," *Transport Europe*, January 19, 1996.

—C. J. Gussoff

parmalat

Parmalat Finanziaria SpA

Via Oreste Grassi 26
Collecchio, Parma I-43044
Italy
Telephone: +39 (02) 806-8801
Fax: +39 (02) 869-3863
Web site: http://www.parmalat.net

Public Company
Incorporated: 1961
Employees: 38,303 (2000 est.)
Sales: US$6.92 billion (2000 est.)
Stock Exchanges: Italy
Ticker Symbol: PRF
NAIC: 311513 Cheese Manufacturing; 311514 Dry,
    Condensed, and Evaporated Dairy Product
    Manufacturing; 3115111 Fluid Milk Manufacturing;
    311421 Fruit and Vegetable Canning; 311941
    Mayonnaise, Dressing, and Other Prepared Sauce
    Manufacturing; 311812 Commercial Bakeries; 311821
    Cookie and Cracker Manufacturing; 311919 Other
    Snack Food Manufacturing; 311330 Confectionery
    Manufacturing From Purchased Chocolate; 311340
    Nonchocolate Confectionery Manufacturing; 312110
    Soft Drink Manufacturing; 312112 Bottled Water
    Manufacturing

Parma, Italy, is not only the home of fine Italian cheese and ham, but also Parmalat Finanziaria SpA, a diversified, international food company and one of the world's largest dairy processors. The company is best known for its revolutionary, ultra-high temperature (UHT) milk, which can sit unopened on an unrefrigerated shelf for six or more months without spoiling or souring. Parmalat also produces, distributes, and markets an ever-growing range of other food products, including dairy products, such as ice cream, yogurt, butter, and cheese; fruit and tomato juices; vegetable soups and tomato sauce; and bakery products like snacks, biscuits, pastry, pizza, and focaccia. Annual sales have exceeded US$6 billion, with roughly one-third made in each of

Europe, North and Central America, and South America, and with remaining sales made in Africa, Asia, and Australia. The founding Tanzi family remains an important part of the decades-old Parmalat, owning 51 percent of the company.

The 1960s: From Cold Cuts to Riches

In 1961, in a small town in Italy's Parma region, Calisto Tanzi founded Parmalat (meaning "milk from Parma"), expanding on the family tradition of operating a quality food business. Tanzi had just inherited his father's company, Tanzi Calisto e Figli: Salumi e Conserve (Tanzi Calisto & Sons: Cold Cuts and Preserves), which was established by his grandfather. But the 22-year-old entrepreneur wanted to produce a new range of distinctive foods. He decided to begin with dairy products and built a small pasteurizing plant in the town of Collecchio. The operation supplied fresh milk throughout Parma. By 1963, the Parmalat brand was born, establishing Tanzi's company as the first one in Italy to produce branded milk.

From the start, Tanzi's business pursued the creation of new milk products and innovative packaging. By 1966 those efforts resulted in what would become the company's signature product for decades to come: milk pasteurized at ultra-high temperatures (UHT milk). UHT milk was revolutionary because it maintained an unrefrigerated shelf life that exceeded six months before opening. One of the unique packages for this new milk product was equally novel, a tetrahedron-shaped paper package which soon became known as the Tetra Pak. Other appealing packages were introduced: the Zopak (1963) and the Pure Pak (1966), which featured Parmalat's new logo, later honored in New York's Museum of Modern Art. In 1969, Parmalat applied the UHT treatment to cream, creating a new product, Panna Chef.

Without question, the new UHT milk gave Parmalat an edge in the milk industry. Parmalat quickly became a successful business and was positioned to go well beyond its small region just as quickly. During its first decade of business, Parmalat recorded sales increases of 30 percent each year. A few years after that, the company business received a great opportunity to extend its distribution significantly and offer new products.

The 1970s and 1980s: Expanding in Italy and Abroad

The Italian milk industry saw changes in milk legislation throughout the early 1970s, which in effect, allowed Parmalat to sell its products beyond Parma, to other provinces throughout Italy and in grocery stores. Also, a major monopoly held by the Centrali del Latte (Municipal Milk distributing centers) was broken up in 1973, allowing Parmalat to go beyond producing part-skim milk and enter into the whole-milk market.

Parmalat expanded greatly throughout the 1970s. In 1971, Parmalat launched its yogurt operation, and in 1973, introduced Parmalat Vita7, a specialty milk enriched with seven vitamins. In 1974, Parmalat made its first international move, establishing a yogurt production facility in Itamonte, Brazil. The new venture went head-to-head with already established yogurt competitors Danone and Chambourcy, however. It was not long before Parmalat changed the Brazil facility's focus to UHT milk. The Brazil operation proved to be a good test of Parmalat's ability to maintain a successful business outside its home country.

On March 23, 1975, Parmalat became instantly famous throughout the world. It was the first company ever to sponsor a popular sports competition, the Ski World Cup in Val Gardena (the Italian Dolomites). The company paid roughly US$230,000 for the sponsorship. The Parmalat name and logo, posted all over the venue and worn by the athletes, was broadcasted for hours on prime-time television. Parmalat instantly became known as the "champion's milk." It was a branding tactic that the company repeated and other companies copied. Parmalat continued to sponsor other high-profile sports events, including the Formula One racing competition, and volleyball, baseball, and football events, among scores of others.

Parmalat continued to grow in more ways than one. It acquired companies in Italy and abroad: Bonlat SRL in Mantova, Dietelat SRL in Verona, and P. Paestum in Salerno; Molkerei Weissenhorn GmbH in Germany (1977); and Laiterie de Carpiquet S.A. in France (1979). The company's range of products expanded to include cheeses (1974), desserts (1976), butter (1978), and UHT béchamel sauce (1979). By the decade's end, Parmalat had already established the most efficient commercial network in Italy and was already established abroad. By this time, the company had 242 agents, 1,000 vehicles, 1,500 salespeople, and 150,000 points of sale. Sales during the 1970s increased yearly by 50 percent, turning Parmalat from an L6 billion company in 1970 to an L289 billion company by 1980.

The Parmalat brand debuted in the United States market in 1982 with its Pomi product brand of boxed tomatoes. One year later, the company established an operation in Spain. In 1987, Parmalat bought 25 percent of a little-known football team based in Parma, called the Parma AC. A few years later, after the death of the team's main shareholder, Parmalat took over altogether. The food company's investment helped turn the team into one of the best in Europe, and helped maintain Parmalat's strong product branding. In 1989, the holding company Finanziaria Centro Nord, which was controlled by the Tanzi family, acquired Parmalat, and in 1990, changed its name to Parmalat Finanziaria SpA in 1990.

The 1990s and Beyond: Capturing the American Market and Others

In terms of sales, new operations and businesses acquired, the 1990s marked a time for explosive growth for Parmalat. By 1990, Parmalat was already selling its products in more than 30 countries. Although that number did not grow much, the number of businesses within those countries producing, distributing, and marketing Parmalat products increased dramatically in the next ten years, as did revenues for those operations. Dairy sales in the United States, for example, ballooned from US$5 million in 1992 to US$650 million by 1999.

Parmalat was especially keen on developing its business in the United States. The milk industry in the country was regional, and in some instances ailing, since the collapse of Borden in the 1970s, which was the last company to produce, distribute, and market milk on a nationwide basis. Parmalat saw an opportunity to grow a national brand. Its strategy was to grow the national brand region by region.

According to Paul Betts of *the Financial Times*, "Parmalat's success has been its ability to exploit fragmented product markets formerly dominated by small and inefficient companies. It has acquired smaller companies, bringing the new subsidiaries' technology, production, and distribution know-how with a coherent marketing approach and brand." The company acquired an Atlanta dairy plant in 1991, from which a strong presence in the Southeast grew. The Atlanta facilities received a US$25 million face-lift, including a new 14,000-square-foot office building. And within the next year, the company acquired White Knight, West Dairies, and Farmland Dairies in the Northeast, as well as other large dairy processing plants. With Parmalat's new investment in White Knight, for example, the facility boosted its output from 160,000 to 500,000 cases of milk per month within less than a year. Parmalat U.S.A. was established in Wallington, New Jersey, part of a larger North American operation, which included Parmalat Canada and Parmalat Mexico.

In 1993, Parmalat introduced its UHT milk to the U.S. market, to lukewarm reviews, at best. Sales of the product that year reached a disappointing US$27 million. Analysts explained that the U.S. market was quite different from others: There was already a declining trend in drinking milk in general, with more and more teenagers opting for soft drinks; the con-

Key Dates:

1961: Parmalat is founded in Italy by Calisto Tanzi.

1966: Parmalat's revolutionary ultra-high temperature (UHT) milk is introduced, which is able to sit unopened and unrefrigerated for six months.

1969: Company applies the UHT treatment to cream creating a new product Panna Chef.

1974: First operation abroad is established in Brazil.

1975: Ski World Cup sponsorship makes Parmalat famous.

1977: Parmalat acquires three companies in Italy: Bonlat SRL (Mantova); Dietelat SRL (Verona); and P. Paestum (Salerno); and one company in Germany, Molkerei Weissenhorn GmbH.

1979: Parmalat acquires the French company Laiterie de Carpiquet.

1982: The company debuts in U.S. market with Pomi tomato product.

1990: The company name changes to Parmalat Finanziaria SpA.

1991: Parmalat acquires its first U.S. dairy plant in Atlanta, Georgia.

1992: The company acquires three more U.S. dairy processing plants: White Knight, West Dairies, and Farmland Dairies.

1993: The company introduces UHT milk to U.S. market.

1996: Parmalat launches its first ice-cream parlor in Brazil.

2001: Calisto Tanzi's son Stefano is named CEO and Parmalat restructures, combining its United States, Canada, and Mexico divisions into a single larger division called Parmalat of America based in Toronto, Canada.

cept and packaging were unfamiliar; and the price demanded a 10 percent to 15 percent premium. Also, another company, Dairymen, Inc., tried and failed to do the same thing in 1992. By 1994, Parmalat was organized into four main divisions: Liquid and Powdered Milk Products, which made up 60 percent of sales; Fresh Foods, which included yogurt, desserts, butter, and cheese (18 percent of sales); Vegetables (11 percent); and Baked Products (8 percent).

Still hopeful for success in capturing the U.S. market for UHT milk, Parmalat doubled its U.S. advertising budget to US$8 million in 1994. Thirty-second television commercials were developed to explain the convenience of UHT milk in a straightforward fashion. The UHT milk packaging was spiffed up to be more appealing and to make opening, pouring, and closing easier for the consumer. And the company launched a campaign to persuade stores to stock their products in the refrigerated section instead of next to the evaporated canned and dry milk shelves, or in the juice aisle. Parmalat insisted that its own permanent display unit designed for the refrigerated section could increase sales by as much as 10 times. By 1994, the company had a fleet of 125 additional route trucks to help distribute the products it expected to produce from the newly acquired facilities. Parmalat sales in the United States reached

US$128 million in 1995, about one half of 1 percent of the $22 billion U.S. milk market. Sales overall for the company grew 19 percent in the same year.

By 1997, Parmalat consisted of 62 companies, 84 plants, and 14,000 employees in 22 countries. Sales reached almost $5 billion that year. Sixty percent of its revenue came from North and South America, with U.S. sales reaching $400 million. All was not rosy, however. Parmalat was faced with some problems in Brazil and South Africa. For example, during 1997 the company entered the instant coffee market in Brazil, but ended that operation only a few years later in mid-2001 when its market share had fallen significantly. By that time, Parmalat's market share was a mere 2.1 percent, compared to Nestlé's huge 70 percent share. And in August 1999, a strike organized by 1,000 of Parmalat's 3,500 employees in South Africa led to a series of violent outbreaks including shootings, firebombs, hijackings, and death threats. According to *Africa News Service* on October 12, 1999, "the workers went on strike after failed negotiations concerning wage increases, an effort apparently prompted by the recently enacted labor laws."

Throughout the 1990s, Parmalat established many new operations, gaining a staggering reach into additional markets: Portugal (1990); Argentina, Uruguay, and the United States (1992); Russia and Hungary (1993); Ukraine, Venezuela, Chile, Paraguay, and Colombia (1994); Mexico, Ecuador, and China (1995); Rumania and Australia (1996); Canada, Mozambique, and Dominican Republic (1997); South Africa and Zambia (1998); and Nicaragua, Cuba, and Swaziland (1999). In 1996 the company also launched a new chain of ice-cream parlors, the first one in Brazil. Others were also opened elsewhere, including Spain and New York City. Parmalat also made more than 100 acquisitions during the same decade.

By the year 2000, Parmalat had spent $400 million to become the number 8 milk producer in the United States, although the brand is not well known outside the Northeast and Atlanta. Total U.S. sales reached $650 million. During 2000, Parmalat established new operations in the United Kingdom and Botswana. The company also made significant investments in e-commerce and e-marketing that same year, buying a 22 percent stake in NetGrocer.com and a $6 million stake in Transora.com. Parmalat also acquired two well-known U.S. cookie companies, Mother's Cake & Cookie Co. and Archway Cookies for $250 million. The company also introduced three new milks to the U.S. market: Milk-E, Lactose-Free Plus, and Skim Plus. In 2001, Parmalat also introduced its Omega3 milk, and in 2002, introduced an organic version of its signature shelf-stable whole milk. The new "functional" milks were promoted as healthful products.

In 2001, Calisto Tanzi's son, Stefano, was named CEO. In October of the same year, Parmalat acquired from Kraft Foods some of its dairy operations in Brazil, including the Gloria and Avare brands. The next month, Parmalat restructured, combining its U.S., Canada, and Mexico divisions into one larger one, called Parmalat of America, based in Toronto, Canada. By the end of 2001, Parmalat had sales offices in California, Florida, Georgia, Michigan, New Jersey, New York, and Texas. The retail distribution network had grown to include Georgia, eastern Alabama, South Carolina, and northern Florida in the Southeast; and New

York, Connecticut, New Jersey, Massachusetts, Rhode Island, Pennsylvania, Virginia, Maryland, Maine, Delaware, and New Hampshire in the Northeast. Other places in Parmalat's new U.S. distribution network included California, Illinois, Michigan, Ohio, Wisconsin, and Arizona. Barely into the new millennium, Parmalat was already a $6 billion company, with 162 plants and more than 40,000 employees in five continents.

Principal Divisions

Bakery; Fresh Foods; Milk; and Vegetables.

Principal Competitors

Cooperative Group; Dairy Crest; Dairy Farmers of America; Danone; Dean Foods; Express Dairies; George Weston; Kellogg; Kraft Foods North America; Lactalis; Leche Pascual; Nestlé; New Zealand Dairy Board; Saputo; Suiza Dairy Group.

Further Reading

Anderson, Virginia, "They've Got Milk! Dairy a Neighborhood Fixture," *The Atlanta Journal-Constitution*, May 25, 1998, p. E7.

"A Small Town's Big Cheeses," *The Economist*, May 31, 1997, p. 58.

Babej, Marc E., "How about a Nice Box of Warm Milk," *Forbes*, August 29, 1994, p. 86.

Betts, Paul, "Europe: Parmalat Adds to US Portfolio," *Financial Times*, September 13, 2000, p. 19.

——, "Europe: Parmalat Wins Bid for Ault: European News Digest," *Financial Times*, July 4, 1997, p. 32.

——, "Italy's Star Acquirers Aim to Defy a Trend: Paul Betts on Foreign Moves by Two Very Different Companies," *Financial Times*, October 22, 1997, p. 17.

Brandoo, Cristina, "The Right Stuff," *Food in Canada*, April 1998, p. 14.

Chandler, Susan, "Italian Dairy Giant Buys Two Baking Companies," *Knight-Ridder/Tribune Business News*, September 12, 2000.

"Clesa to Open Ice Cream Parlours," *Eurofood*, March 2, 2000, p. 14.

"Corporate Profiles: Parmalat Bakery Division," *Milling & Baking News*, October 1, 2000.

Crabb, Cheryl, "Can Parmalat Cream Its Rivals?," *Atlanta Business Chronicle*, January 24, 1997, p. A3.

"Daily Digest," *The Virginian Pilot*, September 10, 1996, p. D1.

Demarrais, Kevin G., "Parmalat Buying Farmland Dairies for $135M; Bergen Fixture Survived Long after Labor Battles," *The Record* (New Jersey), March 26, 1999, p. B1.

Doeff, Gail, "That's Italian! With Little Fanfare, Parmalat Takes Strong Position in US Dairy Market," *Dairy Foods*, February 1994, p. 24.

Dorrell, Kathryn, "Coming Home," *Food in Canada*, April 2000, p. 22.

Eggleston, Sheila, "Parmalat Takes Control of Dairytime," *Grocer*, November 11, 2000, p. 4.

Foster, Christine, "Going Bad," *Forbes*, October 21, 1996, p. 16.

Fusaro, Dave, "Parmalat USA Corp.," *Dairy Foods*, April 1997, p. 68.

Hill, Andrew, "Europe: Parmalat Boosts Turnover 19 Percent: News Digest," *Financial Times*, March 29, 1996, p. 28.

"Kraft Sells Brazilian Dairy," *Dairy Industries International*, November 2001, p. 7.

"Long-Life Milk in Recloseable Package," *Dairy Foods*, October 1994, p. 72.

Mans, Jack, "White Knight Plus Parmalat Equals Booming Growth," *Prepared Foods*, February 1994, p. 90.

"Moo," *Delaney Report*, April 5, 1999, p. 4.

Orr, Deborah, "Streetwalker," *Forbes.com*, October 2, 2000, http://www.forbes.com.

"Parmalat Ingredients," *Food Processing*, June 2001, p. 26.

"Parmalat Stops Instant Coffee in Brazil," *Eurofood*, August 2, 2001, p. 6.

"Parmalat USA," *Dairy Foods*, March 2002, p. 17.

"Parmalatte Coffee Cups," *Creative Review*, June 2000, p. 8.

Simon, Ellen, "Milk Money; Italian Milk Company Is Making Inroads in the U.S., Buying Dairies and Trying to Overcome Consumers' Perceptions about Its Boxed Beverage," *The Star-Ledger* (New Jersey), May 2, 2000, p. 2.

——, "Parmalat Using Online Partnership to Sell Milk," *The Star-Ledger* (New Jersey), August 4, 2000, p. 5.

"Tests Endorse Omega3 Health Claims," *Dairy Industries International*, January 2001, p. 11.

Theodore, Sarah, "An Eye on Quality," *Beverage Industry*, October 2001, p. 28.

——, "Functional Milk," *Beverage Industry*, July 2000, p. 16.

Wagner, Jim, "Moo-ving U.S. Consumers to Shelf-Stable Milk; Parmalat Reintroduces Long-Life Milk in Aseptic Cartons," *Food Processing*, August 1994, p. 61.

Waters, Oscar, "Glennon Co. Is Orchestrating Parmalat's Cookie Rollout," *St. Louis Post-Dispatch*, September 20, 1999, p. 16.

Wheatley, Jonathan, "Parmalat Enters Brazil Market," *Financial Times*, February 6, 1996, p. 24.

Williams, Murray, "Strike Havoc 'threat to SA,'" *Africa News Service*, October 13, 1999.

—Heidi Wrightsman

CONSTRUCTION LEADERS

PCL Construction Group Inc.

5410-99 St., Building #2
Edmonton, Alberta T6E 3P4
Canada
Telephone: (780) 435-9711
Fax: (780) 436-2247
Web site: http://www.pcl.ca

Private Company
Incorporated: 1913 as Poole Construction Company
   Limited
Employees: 5,500 (2002)
Operating Revenues: $3.23 billion (2002 est.)
NAIC: 233310 Manufacturing and Industrial Building
   Construction; 233320 Commercial and Institutional
   Building Construction

PCL Construction Group Inc. is the largest general contracting organization in Canada and extends its reach across the entire North American continent. PCL is active in commercial, industrial, institutional, residential, and agricultural-business sectors. PCL's contracts are directed out of district offices and major project offices located in over 20 cities across North America. Founded in 1906, historically the company has been primarily a builder of residential and commercial buildings. Over time the company has expanded its expertise to include the building of highways, bridges, and dams. The Poole family owns the company until ownership is shifted to its employees in 1977. In addition to being a respected contractor, the company has diversified its services to encompass the entire construction project life cycle from conception to design to actual construction.

Early 20th Century: Going West

PCL Construction was founded by partners James Martin and Ernest E. Poole in 1906. Martin and Poole both hailed from Prince Edward Island in Canada's Maritimes, but met in Saskatchewan. Poole first ventured to Canada's Western frontier in 1903. He and a group of friends traveled to the West on a Harvest Excursion, which is an organized expedition of men and women into the agricultural fields of the West to help

ensure a successful wheat harvest. In Melita, one of the first towns they stopped in, Poole was quickly recruited to work as a carpenter, even though he lacked formal carpentry skills or experience. After a successful season of carpentry work, Poole headed home to work at his father's saw, flour, and carding mills and to study at the Charlottetown Business College.

Over the next few years, Poole traveled back and forth between Prince Edward Island and the West and made friendships and business contacts while working a variety of jobs. In 1904 while working with a contractor named James Martin in Stoughton, Saskatchewan, Poole forged a friendship with Martin that resulted in a business partnership. Martin and Poole opened Martin and Poole Construction in 1906, and after one successful year of construction work, Martin retired. Poole, however, was far from retirement age and inclination, and when he returned to Saskatchewan from Prince Edward Island in the spring of 1907, he resumed operation of the business, changing the company's name to Poole Construction.

In turned out that Poole had started his construction business in the right place at the right time. Canada's West was growing rapidly with settlers pouring into the prairies and the Yukon gold rush in full swing. During this time, Poole Construction was building frontier towns, earning a reputation for turning out quality houses, barns, commercial banks, town halls, mercantile stores, and public schools. If the company ran out of work in one budding community, it moved its headquarters to another with more immediate construction needs. In this spirit, company headquarters moved from Stoughton to Rouleau to Moose Jaw and then to Regina by 1914. In 1913, Poole incorporated the company as Poole Construction Company Limited.

The War Years

When World War I broke out, construction work dried up, which made for hard years at the company. Many of the men who had worked for Poole enlisted. During these lean years, however, Poole was able to secure enough contracts to keep the business afloat. Poole recalled in an interview before his death in 1964, ''We secured a contract for the Saskatchewan Co-operative elevator office building in Regina, which was quite a large contract for us at that time, and because we did not have

Company Perspectives:

The right contractor offers experience, competitive pricing, financial strength, professionalism, integrity and a commitment to your project that is supported by quality and workplace safety initiatives. More importantly, the right contractor has a consistent track record of coming through for clients, no matter how big or small the project. PCL is that contractor.

much else to work on, we moved our residence to Regina.'' After this contract, PCL suffered a dry spell, during which they won no large contracts until 1918.

These difficult years ended in 1919 when the company won multiple large-scale contracts. That same year, the company built itself a brick office building that the company has been operating in ever since. In the years after the war, contracts continued to roll in, and the company flourished, growing to become one the most successful contractors in the area. Some of the contracts Poole Construction handled at this time included the Saskatchewan Cooperative Creameries, the Saskatchewan Provincial Police Department building, and the Weyburn Mental Hospital. Poole Construction was also one of the founding members of the Canadian Construction Association during this time. Until the Depression in 1929, the company remained busy and prosperous.

In the early 1930s, as with many businesses around the world, work at the Poole Construction Company came to a near standstill. The Poole family moved to Edmonton and kept the company afloat by diversifying into highway and irrigation work. In 1932, Poole moved his family and business to Edmonton, Alberta. The move proved to be successful when the company won a contract in 1935 to reconstruct the Calgary-Banff Highway from Cochrane to the Banff National Park Gate. This contract gave the struggling company the nudge it needed to recapture its former success. The company expanded rapidly as it geared up to meet Canada's once again growing construction needs. During this time, Poole's two sons, who had finished graduate school in civil engineering, took jobs with the company.

After the Wars: Expansion and Change

After the war, the company became the top builder of industrial power plants in Alberta, pioneered construction projects in the Yukon and Western Canadian Arctic, and expanded their highway work. The company also broadened its construction expertise to include dams, tunnels, and bridges. The Edmonton head office became the center for branches spread across Canada, including offices in Calgary, Regina, Toronto, Yellowknife, Lethbridge, and Winnipeg. Under Poole's stewardship, the company recruited and trained specialists in every area of the construction industry, and Poole remained active in the company's operation until his death in 1964.

After Ernie Poole's death, the company continued to be a part of the Poole family's legacy, with Ernie's sons John and George acting as co-chairmen of the board. However, in 1977, the Poole brothers agreed to sell their majority stake in Poole

Construction to the company's employees, and in 1979, the company's name was changed to PCL Construction Ltd.

Late 20th Century: Multiple Major Projects

Over the years, PCL has made a concerted effort to expand their business into the United States, and have achieved considerable success in the process. The company has district offices in Seattle, Minneapolis, Fort Lauderdale, Los Angeles, and in Canada in Calgary, Vancouver, Regina, Ottawa, and Winnipeg; operation offices in San Diego, Las Vegas, and in Canada in Saskatoon and Yellowknife; the corporate office is in Edmonton, Alberta; and the head office for U.S. Operations is in Denver, Colorado. In 1985, the Los Angeles district office was put to work on building the $650 million Citicorp Center as the contractor for the Center's 42-story tower located at Seventh and Figueroa, which represented the first phase of the planned complex.

In 1995, PCL won the contract to renovate the Seattle Coliseum. The project was notable because it went against the modern sports industry trend to build completely new arenas rather than renovate existing structures. John Donovan of PCL explained that what PCL did, however, went considerably beyond renovation, demolishing much of the original structure and sinking the event level 35 feet lower into the ground.

Also in 1995, PCL became involved in a legal dispute over the awarding of an airport construction contract. Historically, one of PCL's primary methods of securing contracts was through competitive bidding. Bidding is a complex practice that requires participating bidders to adhere to a rigid set of rules. To submit a bid that can be legally considered, a bidder must submit all stipulated forms and materials by an established deadline. It is not uncommon for a bidder to miss a deadline due to an incomplete submission. Generally, if a bidder misses a deadline—by omitting even a single form—their bid is discarded.

It was exactly this type of situation that caused PCL to seek legal resolution when the contract for the Ontario International Airport was awarded to TNT Grading Inc. of San Marcos, California. PCL maintained that TNT had submitted a flawed bid when the company neglected to include the necessary minority participation document by the required due date (TNT did submit the document at a later date). However, the airport commission decided that the requirement to submit the report on time was ''an informality, and the board [could] waive that informality and approve the bid.'' PCL felt that the airport commission had acted illegally, and Peter Jiacik, an administrative manager for PCL, noted that the commission's choice was ''a violation of the Subcontracting and Subletting Fair Practices Act.'' Despite PCL's objections, a month after the contract had been awarded to TNT, a judge upheld the bid award, allowing TNT to continue its work on the airport.

In 1997 when PCL was chosen to build a new Science Museum in St. Paul, Minnesota, the company could hardly have imagined their project would be impacted by a 19th-century bordello. Although the city had retained archaeologists to monitor building demolition, it was a surprise to everyone when, sifting through the site in search of artifacts, the scientists came across the limestone foundation of an historic bordello and saloon. The archaeologists' role was quickly expanded and PCL

Key Dates:

1906: Ernest E. Poole and James Martin start contracting in Stoughton, Saskatchewan, as Martin and Poole Construction Company.

1907: Martin retires to Prince Edward Island and Poole continues the contracting business under his own name, Poole Construction Company.

1910: The company headquarters are moved to Rouleau, Saskatchewan.

1913: The company incorporates as Poole Construction Company Limited.

1932: The company moves its headquarters to Edmonton, Alberta.

1964: Ernest Poole, the founder of the company, dies.

1977: Employees purchase majority ownership of the company from John and George Poole (sons of Ernest).

1979: The company changes its name to PCL Construction Ltd.

1985: The company becomes contractor for the $650 million Citicorp Center's 42-story tower in Los Angeles.

1995: The company wins the contract to renovate the Seattle Coliseum.

2001: The company is listed in the publication *Canada's Top 100 Employers* as one of the best companies to work for in Canada.

found itself eyeing a significantly elongated two-year construction schedule.

The New Millennium: Continuing to Invest in Employees

Amid its international success and significant growth and expansion, PCL has worked to retain the small-company atmosphere it has valued ever since Ernie Poole first founded the company in 1906. To that end, the company instituted a policy that every PCL employee must complete at least 35 hours a year of professional development training. Peter Greene, PCL's vice-president in charge of education programs, says the company has put such emphasis on continued education because "it shows that a company cares enough to help [its employees] develop the skills they'll need throughout their careers." PCL's education programs are developed internally and are taught through the PCL College of Construction. The college has a campus or a dedicated learning space in each of the company's operating centers and provides training and education through self-directed learning, instructor-led learning, and mentoring activities.

PCL's employee-oriented style has helped the company to be recognized two years in a row—2001 and 2002—as one of the best companies to work for in Canada, according to Richard Yerema's book *Canada's Top 100 Employers*. In addition, in the January 2002 issue of the *Globe and Mail*'s *Report on Business Magazine*, PCL ranked 37th among the *50 Best Companies to Work for in Canada*.

In addition to recognition as one of the best companies to work for in Canada, PCL has won award after award for busi-

ness and industry excellence. In 2001, the company was ranked Canada's No. 1 contractor by *Heavy Construction News*, a position PCL has held for 20 years. In 2002, for the seventh time, PCL was recognized as one of Canada's best-managed companies, an award sponsored by Andersen Consulting, Canadian Imperial Bank of Commerce, and Queen's School of Business and National Post.

Much of PCL's success has derived from the company's ability to recruit knowledgeable and skilled employees and to diversify their construction capabilities as market and business conditions indicated. The company has become as comfortable and capable at building residential high-rises as working on such high-technology projects as hydroelectric dams and steam facilities. The company has further diversified into pipe fabrication, module construction, mining operations, and construction design.

By moving into construction design, PCL has become capable of working on a project from inception to design and through construction. By assuming full-project ownership, PCL has been able to meet strict project design and construction requirements within stringent budget and schedule parameters—something that was often difficult to orchestrate when working solely as a construction management group.

Principal Subsidiaries

PCL Civil Constructors, Inc.; PCL Construction Management Inc.; PCL Construction Services, Inc.; PCL Constructors Canada Inc.; PCL Industrial Constructors, Inc.; Monad Contractors Ltd.

Principal Competitors

AMEC LC; Bovis Lend Lease; HOCHTIEF AG; Flour Corporation; Skanska AB.

Further Reading

"Airport Grading Project Overcomes Legal Challenge," *The Business Press*, October 16, 1995, p. 5.

Daniels, Stephen H., "Becoming More Rigid in Seattle," *ENR*, November 13, 1995, p. 49.

"History Lesson at New Museum Site," *ENR*, April 28, 1997, p. 12.

Hovde, Elizabeth, "Opinion: Union-Only Pacts Not in Interest of All," *Columbian*, October 25, 2001, p. C7.

"It Helps to Own a Piece," *Maclean's*, November 5, 2001, p. 53.

Korman, Richard, and David Kohn, "Design-Build? Ice Rink Runs Late," *ENR*, August 18, 1997, p. 9.

"Major Expansion Planned with New Terminal and Parking at Ottowa Airport," *Building*, November/December, 2000, p. 29.

McAfee, Paul, "Possible Lawsuit Puts Ontario Airport Bid in Turbulence," *The Business Press*, September 11, 1995, p. 1.

Mize, Jeffrey, "City, Events Center Contractor End Dispute," *Columbian*, December 1, 2001, p.C1.

——, "Events Center Builder Picked," *Columbian*, May 10, 2001, p. C1.

"Numbers 6, 5 Figure Largely in New Project," *Los Angeles Times*, September 22, 1985, p. 10.

Tulacz, Gary J., "PCL Construction Group Inc," *ENR*, October 13, 1997, p. 29.

Wright, Andrew, "Overhead Scheme Launches Bridge," *ENR*, July 27, 1992, p.4.

—Tammy Weisberger

Pennzoil-Quaker State Company

Pennzoil Place, 200 Milam
Houston, Texas 77002-2805
U.S.A.
Telephone: (713) 546-4000
Fax: (713) 546-8043
Web site: http://www.pennzoil-quakerstate.com

Public Company
Incorporated: 1998 (1968 as Pennzoil United, Inc.)
Employees: 7,467 (2001 est.)
Sales: $2,276 million (2001)
Stock Exchanges: New York
Ticker Symbol: PZL
NAIC: 324110 Petroleum Refineries; 3241910 Petroleum
   Lubricating Oil and Grease Manufacturing; 441310
   Automotive Parts and Accessories Stores; 421830
   Industrial Machinery and Equipment Wholesalers;
   421840 Industrial Supplies Wholesalers; 422720
   Petroleum and Petroleum Products Wholesalers
   (except Bulk Stations and Terminals); 811191
   Automotive Oil Change and Lubrication Shops;
   533110 Owners and Lessors of Other Non-Financial
   Assets; 551112 Offices of Other Holding Companies

The Pennzoil-Quaker State Company is a leading worldwide automotive consumer products company formed in 1998, through the spin-off of Pennzoil Company's marketing, manufacturing, and fast oil change businesses and the simultaneous acquisition of Quaker State Corporation. The company has leading brands in motor oils, appearance products, glass treatments, maintenance chemicals, engine treatments, tire and wheel cleaners, tire sealants, automotive organizers, air fresheners, and sunshades. It conducts business in the United States and 90 other countries through its five segments: lubricants, consumer products, international, Jiffy Lube, and supply chain investments. Its Pennzoil and Quaker State brand motor oils are the number one and two selling motor oils in the United States. The company also owns Jiffy Lube, the nation's leading fast oil change business.

Early History Was Centered in Pennsylvania

The companies that originally came together to form Pennzoil were all involved in the oil industry's early history in Pennsylvania and neighboring states. One of them, the South Penn Oil Company, was formed on May 27, 1889, by a unit of Standard Oil Company, John D. Rockefeller's enormous oil concern. Standard already controlled approximately 90 percent of the oil refining in the United States, but it had been slow to move into oil producing until the late 1880s, at which time it bought up a large number of ground leases in the Pennsylvania oil region and created South Penn to work them. Under first president Noah Clark, South Penn made rapid progress with its initial wells and was soon pushing across the border into the rich West Virginia fields. South Penn enjoyed all the benefits of membership in the Standard family of companies, including guaranteed sale of its crude to Standard distributors and refineries, ample provision of capital for expansion, and an absence of threatening competition. When Standard reorganized itself in 1892 into a closely interlocked trust of 20 operating companies, South Penn was capitalized at $2.5 million, a significant figure for the time, but among the smaller of Standard's holdings.

The reorganized South Penn received a new president as well. John D. Archbold had been a Pennsylvania oilman since the 1860s, and, after joining Standard, had rapidly risen to become one of the company's top five policy-makers and its director of all producing activity. As such, he became the president of South Penn upon its reorganization in 1892, when the Standard companies were responsible for over a quarter of all U.S. oil production. In the 1890s, South Penn increased tenfold its annual production of crude, and by 1898 it was the leader among the Standard interests with 7.6 million barrels per year, most of it pumped from its West Virginia fields. The year before, it had bought the drilling rights to some 20,000 acres of land in the Pennsylvania oil region, paying $1.4 million in what was described as the largest deal in the history of U.S. oil production.

In 1899, Standard Oil was again reshuffled, all of the affiliated companies becoming subsidiaries of the newly enlarged Standard Oil Company (New Jersey). John Archbold remained head of South Penn and was now effective head of New Jersey Standard as well, John D. Rockefeller having largely retired

from the scene. South Penn was thus well positioned to grow
into one of the giants of the U.S. petroleum business, with
unlimited financial backing, top management skills, and a
healthy share of the existing crude market. It soon became
apparent, however, that South Penn lacked the one indispensable
ingredient of the oil industry: oil. By 1900, the Appalachian
oil region had reached its all-time peak of production and
its many thousands of wells began to run dry. South Penn
production dropped by about 50 percent during the following
decade and would never again provide more than small amounts
of high-grade crude, in addition to useful quantities of the
recently harnessed natural gas.

In 1911, the Supreme Court ordered the dissolution of Standard
Oil Company (New Jersey). South Penn began life on its
own as one of the leading drillers of crude oil in a region that
was largely played out. About the time South Penn had been
formed, two independent refineries were built in nearby Rouseville,
Pennsylvania. The Pennsylvania Refining Company and
Nonpareil Refining Company were both founded in 1886 to
process the great stream of oil then produced by the region and
bound for the eastern seaboard. The founders of Pennsylvania
Refining (PRC), Henry Suhr, Samuel Justus, and Louis Walz,
invested $40,000 in their new company and commenced production
of kerosene, at that time the most valuable end product
of petroleum. Nonpareil Refining, on the other hand, designed
its facilities to make lubricating oil and enjoyed only mixed
success from the beginning.

The early oil industry was volatile, in more ways than one.
By 1893, Nonpareil had already changed hands once and was
then bought out by PRC for $50,000 at auction. Nonpareil's
name was changed to Germania Refining Company and its
offices consolidated with those of PRC. In the meantime, PRC
had suffered a catastrophic fire in 1892, which destroyed its
barrel factory and much of the adjoining refinery, killing 50
workers and causing an estimated $1 million in damage. Fires
were common in the early years of the petroleum industry, as
safety regulations were almost nonexistent and the product
naturally flammable. PRC rebuilt its facilities and within a few
months had restored production to full capacity.

Pennzoil Name First Used in the 1910s

The growing use of the automobile and other internal-combustion
engines gradually changed the relative value of oil's refined
products. Use of kerosene began a slow decline, its illumination
replaced by the cleaner and more-efficient electricity; while gasoline,
previously an unwanted oil byproduct, was increasingly required
by the new machines. Internal-combustion engines also

depended on efficient lubricants, which PRC recognized in 1904
when it expanded its lube facilities and five years later formed a
new company to market its lubricants, Oil City Oil and Grease
Company. Prevented by Pennsylvania's limited crude supplies
from becoming a major refiner of gasoline, PRC shifted more of its
production to lubricants and quickly developed a reputation for
manufacturing high quality products. PRC's president and part
owner was Charles Suhr, son of one of the company's founders,
and, in 1913, Suhr agreed to invest in a California company that
wished to distribute Germania lubricants on the West Coast. A few
years later, Suhr and his associates came up with the brand name
Pennzoil, which would henceforth become the company's trademark
and one of the country's more widely recognized logos. To
capitalize on Pennzoil's growing popularity, Suhr changed the
name of his two marketing companies in 1921 to the Pennzoil
Company (California) and the Pennzoil Company (Pennsylvania).

In the meantime, Suhr had merged his refining outfits in
1914 into a single company called Germania Refining Company,
soon changed for patriotic reasons to Penn-American
Refining Company. In 1924, Penn-American and its marketing
companies, now three in number with the addition a few years
before of Pennzoil Company (New York), were merged into an
umbrella corporation called Pennzoil Company. Pennzoil was
not only refining and marketing about 3,000 barrels per day of
crude oil; it also had bought gas stations in Detroit, Cleveland,
and Pittsburgh. Having organized the refining and marketing
aspects of the oil business, Pennzoil was still lacking crude-production
capacity, and in the mid-1920s it began talks with
South Penn Oil about a possible merger. South Penn, the former
Standard Oil producer, had limited refining and marketing
capacities, and in 1925 the two companies came together when
South Penn bought 51 percent of Pennzoil's stock. Though not a
merger, South Penn's purchase effectively united the two medium-sized
Pennsylvania oil concerns. South Penn completed
its purchase of Pennzoil in 1955.

While Pennzoil motor oils were racking up an impressive
series of Indianapolis 500 automobile racing and transcontinental
flight records, South Penn continued consolidating its holdings
in the Appalachian oil and gas region, which though
limited in scope remained a source of high-grade petroleum.
The focus of U.S. oil production had shifted to the South,
however, where the vast east Texas fields had begun pumping in
the early 1930s, and initial efforts were underway to tap the
offshore riches of the Gulf of Mexico. The immediate effect of
this surge in production was to depress the price of Pennsylvania
crude to an all-time low in 1933, but its long-term effect on
Pennzoil's future history was to be much more profound.

Zapata Petroleum Founded in 1953

After World War II, as the U.S. developed its love of the
automobile, investors continued to pour into the Texas oil
regions in search of more spectacular finds. One such wildcatting
firm, Zapata Petroleum Corporation, was founded in
1953 by two brothers, J. Hugh and William Liedtke, John
Overbey, and a young man named George Bush, later to abandon
oil for the richer field of politics. The Liedtkes had already
formed a useful friendship with another future U.S. president,
Lyndon Baines Johnson, at whose Austin, Texas, home they
rented rooms while attending law school at the University of

Key Dates:

1886: The Pennsylvania Refining Company (PRC) is founded.
1889: South Penn Oil Company is formed by a unit of Standard Oil Company.
1892: John D. Archbold becomes president of South Penn upon its reorganization.
1899: South Penn becomes a subsidiary of the newly enlarged and reorganized Standard Oil Company (New Jersey); John Archbold becomes effective head of New Jersey Standard as well as South Penn.
1909: PRC forms a new company to market its lubricants, Oil City Oil and Grease Company.
1911: The Supreme Court orders the dissolution of Standard Oil Company (New Jersey).
1924: Pennzoil Company is formed.
1925: South Penn, the former Standard Oil producer, buys 51 percent of Pennzoil's stock.
1953: Zapata Petroleum Corporation is founded.
1955: South Penn completes its purchase of Pennzoil and renames it South Penn Oil Company.
1962: J. Hugh Liedtke becomes president of South Penn.
1963: The Pennzoil Company is formed of the merger of South Penn with the Zapata companies.

1965: Pennzoil buys 42 percent of United Gas Corporation's stock.
1974: Liedtke spins off his United Gas Pipe Line Company, a subsidiary of United Gas.
1987: Texaco pays Pennzoil $3 billion in settlement of a suit.
1994: Liedtke retires as chairman.
1990: James L. Pate becomes president and chief executive officer of Pennzoil, with Liedtke remaining chairman.
1991: Jiffy Lube becomes a wholly owned subsidiary of Pennzoil.
1998: Pennzoil spins off the Pennzoil Products group, which joins with Quaker State Corporation in a merger acquisition; James L. Postl become president of Pennzoil-Quaker State.
1999: Devon Energy buys PennzEnergy.
2000: James L. Postl becomes president and chief executive officer; the company acquires assets of Auto Fashions, Sagaz Industries, Airfresh UK Limited and Bluecol Brands Limited; the company sells its Viscosity Oil Division.
2002: The company agrees to a takeover by Royal Dutch/Shell.

Texas. The four men all had some experience in oil, and in raising the $1 million to form Zapata planned to have a go at big-time oil gambling themselves. As it turned out, they were both lucky and talented: Zapata leased several thousand acres in Texas's West Jameson field and proceeded to drill 127 wells without once coming up dry.

Zapata soon moved offshore, creating Zapata Offshore Company and Zapata Drilling Company to pursue the oil fields then being uncovered in the gulf. In 1959, these two companies were spun off as independent concerns, with Bush remaining as Zapata offshore's head until his election to the House of Representatives in 1966. The so-called spinoff would become a favorite tactic of the resourceful Liedtke brothers, who were able time and again to realize substantial gains by relying on the willingness of shareholders to pay more for equity in a smaller, easily comprehended asset than they would for the same asset hidden in a large corporation. The Zapata partners were already wealthy men by the late 1950s, but the Liedtke brothers were eager to expand, and became interested in the fortunes of Pennzoil, whose corporate name had become South Penn Oil Company after the final merger of its partner companies in 1955. South Penn was well known as a producer of premium motor oil but its profits had never reached their potential. The company's largest shareholder was J. Paul Getty's Tidewater Oil, and the Liedtkes, who knew Getty through previous dealings, began buying large amounts of South Penn stock with Getty's approval. Convinced that South Penn's assets were not being fully exploited, the Liedtkes soon bought out Getty's position and, in effect, gained control of South Penn in the early 1960s. J. Hugh Liedtke became president of South Penn in 1962, and in the following year South Penn was merged with

the Zapata companies in a new entity called Pennzoil Company. Pennzoil was still a relatively small player among the oil giants, with sales in 1963 of only $77 million and a net profit of about $7 million. The corporation was headquartered in Houston, with regional offices in Los Angeles and Oil City, Pennsylvania.

Acquired United Gas Corporation in 1965

The Liedtkes next set their sights on a much richer prize, United Gas Corporation. United was formed in 1930 as a holding company for some 40 gas and oil concerns in the Gulf of Mexico region and, by the mid-1960s, had become one of the largest distributors of natural gas in the country, its United Gas Pipe Line Company carrying approximately 8 percent of the nation's supply. United also produced and processed natural gas and owned an important mining company, Duval Corporation. As with his friendly takeover of South Penn, Hugh Liedtke saw in United a company unable to exploit its large resources and hence undervalued in the market. He offered to buy one million shares of United at $41 per share; five million shares were promptly tendered, and Pennzoil bought all of them in 1965 for a total purchase of 42 percent of United's stock, borrowing $215 million of the $225 million required. The move was an early example of corporate raiding, in which a much smaller company—in this case, one-eighth the size of its target— gained control of a vast but underperforming competitor. As he did with Zapata, Liedtke proceeded to sell off much of United's assets, first spinning off its retail business and then, in 1974, the huge United Gas Pipe Line Company. According to Pennzoil, the latter divestment was made necessary by government regulations which inhibited Pennzoil's operation of both producing and distributing concerns, but the Liedtkes's handling of the affair resulted in a barrage of lawsuits and an investigation by the Federal Power Commission. In addition, the brothers agreed to pay $100,000 to former Pennzoil stockholders in settlement of insider trading charges brought at the time of the spinoff.

In any event, the absorption of the United companies turned Pennzoil into a large and diversified natural-resources company. Its 1970 sales hit $700 million, up tenfold from 1963, and its Duval Corporation mining subsidiary went on to make a series of quick strikes in sulfur, potash, copper, gold, and silver. To keep its natural gas production up, Pennzoil created two new companies in the early 1970s, Pennzoil Offshore Gas Operators (POGO) and Pennzoil Louisiana and Texas Off-shore, Inc. (PLATO), selling shares to the public in order to raise capital needed for further offshore drilling while also enjoying a sizable appreciation in the value of the stock it retained. By 1980, Pennzoil sales had passed $2 billion, the bulk of it generated by the company's traditional strength in the refining and sale of motor oil. Pennzoil had become the second-leading seller of motor oil, bolstered by its reputation for quality and by an increasing use of mass marketers instead of gas stations for its retail trade. Its assorted mining ventures brought in about 20 percent of corporate sales, while sulfur added another 10 percent. It was not surprising that Hugh Liedtke began pushing hard for more oil and gas production—though representing but one-fourth of sales, production accounted for fully 50 percent of net income, crude oil and gas always commanding a higher margin than refined products.

Legal Struggle with Texaco Over Getty Oil Dominated 1980s

With that in mind, in the early 1980s, Liedtke became interested in the squabbling heirs of J. Paul Getty. Liedtke calculated that Getty Oil Company stock was severely undervalued and began buying it up, and, in January 1984, he reached an agreement with Gordon Getty to buy three-sevenths of the company's shares at $112.50 per share, well over their current trading price. The $3.9 billion purchase would vastly increase Pennzoil's reserves of oil and gas, and probably precipitate the dissolution of Getty Oil at prices even higher than Liedtke had paid. The agreement was duly approved by Getty's board of directors and announced at a press conference, but Getty's investment bankers and lawyers continued to solicit higher offers for Getty stock. They got one from Texaco, which several days later announced that it had agreed to buy all of Getty's stock at $128 per share, or about $10 billion. At that point, Hugh Liedtke sued Texaco for tortuous interference with Pennzoil's prior contract with Getty, and shortly afterward a Texas jury agreed with him, deciding that Texaco owed Pennzoil about $10.5 billion in real and punitive damages—the highest such award to date.

With the exception of Hugh Liedtke, the award seemed to stun everyone. Texaco had not taken the suit seriously, assuming that at worst it would be forced to pay off Pennzoil with a nominal settlement fee. Not only did the Texas jury express the general public's growing dislike for big-money takeovers; its verdict was upheld upon appeal though the award was lowered to $8.5 billion. Texaco threatened to declare bankruptcy if Liedtke did not accept a "reasonable" settlement, but the Pennzoil chairman refused. In April 1987, Liedtke turned down an offer of $2 billion cash from Texaco, which promptly followed

through on its promise and filed under Chapter 11 of the bankruptcy code. Upon that news the stock value of Pennzoil dropped $631 million overnight. Liedtke was aware, however, that Texaco was a wealthy company even for the oil business, able to sustain a huge cash loss, and, by the end of 1987, Texaco agreed to pay Pennzoil $3 billion to have done with the case.

While this legal struggle was being waged, Pennzoil had decided to sell its various mining interests, with the exception of sulfur. Liedtke spun off the gold-mining subsidiary into an independent company, Battle Mountain Gold Company, whose stock tripled in a short time. The mining disposal left Pennzoil with a mix of motor oil refining and marketing, oil and gas production, and sulfur production, the last two far more profitable than the former; and about $3 billion in cash.

Based on a court ruling, Pennzoil management was led to believe that it could avoid paying taxes on the Texaco settlement if it invested the money in an asset similar to that of Getty. Liedtke, therefore, in 1989 spent the bulk of the money, $2.1 billion, for a big chunk of a larger oil concern, in this case 8.8 percent of Chevron. Anticipating the worst, Chevron immediately filed suit to prevent the purchase and readied itself for a hostile takeover bid. Nevertheless, Pennzoil, which was essentially making a tax-sheltered investment, did not follow through with a takeover bid. Meantime, money from the Texaco settlement also went into Pennzoil's purchase of Purolator, a maker of oil filters.

Restructurings and a Focus on Consumer Products in the 1990s

Unfortunately, over the next several years, company management had to pay considerable attention to the Chevron investment and to haggling with the Internal Revenue Service over whether it owed taxes on the Texaco settlement, all of which led management to be somewhat neglectful of its core operations. A subsequently weakened Pennzoil was forced to restructure its operations throughout the 1990s and operated with the threat of a hostile takeover hanging over it.

Nevertheless, Pennzoil began the decade with a promising acquisition. In January 1990, Pennzoil bought more than 80 percent of Jiffy Lube International, Inc., a franchiser, owner, and operator of automotive lubrication and fluid-maintenance centers. Jiffy Lube had successfully found a niche as a speedy-service center, but was deeply in debt. Pennzoil's $43.5 million purchase price bought a company with assets of $237.3 million and liabilities of $239.5 million. Two months later, James L. Pate, who had been company treasurer, was named president and chief executive officer, with Liedtke remaining chairman. In September 1991, Pennzoil paid $9.3 million for the remainder of Jiffy Lube, which then became a wholly owned subsidiary of Pennzoil.

Pennzoil began to reduce its Chevron holding in October 1992, when it exchanged 48 percent of its shares (worth about $1.2 billion) for Chevron PBC, which owned 240 million barrels of oil and gas reserves in and around the Gulf of Mexico. As part of the agreement, Pennzoil and Chevron also said they would not buy each other's stock for the next five years. In November 1993, Pennzoil sold 8.2 million shares of its remaining stake at $89 per share, gaining $171 million over what it paid for the stock. These deals left Pennzoil with just over 9 million shares of Chevron.

Continuing its 1980s sales of noncore assets, Pennzoil spun off Purolator in December 1992 in a public offering that generated $206 million. The following month, the company sold its Mt. Muro gold mine located near Kalimantan, Indonesia. In October 1994, after Pate had in May of that year succeeded the retiring Liedtke as chairman, Pennzoil sold the remaining U.S. assets of its sulphur division to Freeport-McMoRan Resource Partners LP.

Wanting to concentrate on rebuilding the company's long-neglected exploration operations, Pate moved quickly to close the chapter on the Texaco settlement by reaching an agreement with the IRS whereby, in October 1994, Pennzoil made a $556 million payment in cash for back taxes, including $294.3 million in interest charges. That same month, the company incurred a $500 million charge for the back taxes, a loss on its sale of its sulphur division, and bad real estate investments. Pennzoil was sufficiently weakened by this point that Pate feared the company was in danger of a hostile takeover. The company board therefore in early November adopted a "poison pill" defense to guard against any unwanted suitors.

For the year, Pennzoil posted a $288.7 million loss in 1994, which was followed by a 1995 loss of $305.1 million. The company was particularly hurt by a decline in the price of natural gas, which accounted for about two-thirds of the company's production, and continuing high debt. Pate subsequently restructured Pennzoil's operations, achieving savings in operating costs of more than $75 million a year, and reduced the company dividend in 1995 and 1996 to save cash. He was also able in 1996 to cut company debt by $300 million. With natural gas prices on the rise, 1996 showed a huge improvement with a net income of $133.9 million.

By mid-1997, Pennzoil had improved its financial picture and was enjoying long-awaited payoffs on its exploration investments in Azerbaijan and the Gulf of Mexico. The company had revenues of approximately $2 billion. In June 1997, Union Pacific Resources Group Inc.—an energy exploration and production company based in Fort Worth, Texas—launched a $4 billion hostile takeover bid of Pennzoil that the company board opposed, intent on its desire to let Pate's restructuring play itself out.

Under Pate's leadership, in 1998 Pennzoil spun off its motor oil, refined products, and franchise operations—Pennzoil Products Group—into a newly traded company that merged with all of Quaker State, which it purchased for $1 billion. The new company, called Pennzoil-Quaker State Company, became the world's largest automotive consumer products company with annual revenues of $3.2 billion and control of more than a third of the domestic lubricants market. Pate became chairman and chief executive officer of the new company, which began immediate trading on the New York Stock Exchange. Pennzoil Exploration and Production Company, one of the largest U.S.-based independent exploration and production companies, was renamed PennzEnergy Co. and also began separate trading on the New York Stock Exchange. Devon Energy Corp. of Oklahoma bought PennzEnergy in August 1999.

According to Pate, in a June 1999 article in *Management Review*, the new business's "blueprint included several avenues for growth": investing to build Pennzoil-Quaker State's name brands, developing new products, acquisitions, expanding Jiffy Lube operations (which now also included converted Q-Lubes), and expanding internationally. The company would attempt to leverage its most profitable products, its automotive accessories—glass treatments, maintenance chemicals for fuel systems, and wheel and tire care items. It would also invest in its fast-growing Jiffy Lube operations.

James Postl joined Pennzoil as president in late 1998, and the company continued in its efforts to become a world-class consumer products company. Postl, who had held key posts at National Biscuit Co., PepsiCo, and Proctor & Gamble, hired a new management team—many of whom came with a consumer products background and all of whom reported directly to him—including a head of research and development and a head of international sales. The company developed a five-year plan that focused on a major change in the way it did business: securing success for its operations independent of the ups and downs of oil and gas prices.

Divestment, Modest Growth, and Takeover in the 2000s

The late 1990s and early 2000s posed huge challenges for Pennzoil-Quaker State's growth. The company's ailing oil refining business wiped out cash flow and earnings for the company, and the company began to look for a buyer whose main business was refining. In 1999, it shut down its crude oil processing refinery in Rouseville, Pennsylvania, and in 2000 sold close to ten of its refineries and manufacturing products businesses, including the company's gold mining and sulfur gas divisions. The company continued selling off ancillary assets and businesses throughout 2001: a packaging plant for lubricants and its Louisiana-based refinery in the first quarter of the year.

With only modest earnings growth in 2000, the result of an unprecedented rise in the cost of motor oil, and rising fuel costs that curtailed consumer driving, Pennzoil-Quaker State nonetheless embarked on a spate of acquisitions. With Postl now chief executive, the company purchased Sagaz Industries, a seat cover, cushion, and auto floor mat company; Airfresh, a maker of air fresheners and fragrance products for autos; and Bluecol, a manufacturer of antifreeze, glass cleaners rust treatments, and cooling system treatments. It entered into a co-branding arrangement with Pickups Plus, Inc., a national truck accessory retailer to locate oil change centers at Pickups Plus stores in Pennsylvania. Also in 2000, Pennzoil-Quaker State completed expansion projects in South Africa, Spain, and Puerto Rico.

In mid-2001, Postl announced in a written statement quoted in *Lubricants World*, that his company had been "fighting an uphill battle" in recent years. Referring to the weak demand for automotive consumer products, he insisted that he felt confident that the industry would recover as it had in the past, although "we have not yet seen evidence that the recovery has begun." In an attempt to increase revenues, the company cut its quarterly dividend and restructured its lubricants, consumer products, and international segments.

By August 2002, Pennzoil-Quaker State had agreed to a takeover by Shell Oil Company, a unit of Royal Dutch/Shell and was awaiting completion of the merger in the second half of the year. In buying Pennzoil-Quaker State, Shell became the largest domestic lubricants company. For its part, Pennzoil-Quaker State anticipated tremendous benefits to accrue from putting the nation's top two brands of motor oil, Quaker State and Pennzoil, into Shell's massive worldwide distribution system.

Principal Subsidiaries

American Lubricating Company; Blue Coral/Slick 50; Jiffy Lube International, Inc.; Magie Brothers Oil Company; Medo Industries Incorporated; Pennzoil Co. Inc.; Wolf's head Oil Company.

Principal Competitors

Ashland; BP; ChevronTexaco.

Further Reading

Baldo, Anthony, "The Pennzoil Pickle: How Hugh Liedtke's Windfall from Texaco Could Be Torpedoed by the IRS," *Financial World*, November 26, 1991, pp. 30–31.

Barrett, William P., "Another Rabbit, Please," *Forbes*, December 10, 1990, p. 92.

Burrows, Peter, "Pennzoil Switches on Its Searchlight," *Business Week*, February 13, 1995, pp. 74–75.

Byrne, Harlan S., "Revving Up," *Barron's*, November 11, 1996, p. 20.

Carnes, Kathryn, "Pennzoil-Quaker State Announces Restructuring," *Lubricants World*, July 2001, p. 5.

Chubb, Courtney, "Pennzoil Emerges Dry from Sea of Red Ink, Prepares for Growth," *Oil Daily*, May 15, 1997, p. 1.

Durgin, Hillary, "Pennzoil's President is Busy Oiling the Wheels of Culture Change," *Financial Times* (London), December 14, 1999, p. 17.

Emond, Mark, "Pennzoil, Quaker State Shock the U.S. Fast Lube Business," *National Petroleum News*, July 1998, p. 36.

"Game Plan for a New Company," *Management Review*, June 1999, p. 13.

Gentry, Mickey, and Kimberly Patrick, *Pennzoil Company: The First 100 Years*, Houston: Pennzoil Company, 1989.

Ivey Mark, "Pennzoil's Trip Down a Slippery Slope," *Business Week*, July 22, 1991, p. 53.

Ivey, Mark, and Maria Shao, "What Does Liedtke Want?," *Business Week*, December 25, 1989, p. 42.

Lipin, Steven, Allanna Sullivan, and Terzah Ewing, "In Fight for Pennzoil, Old Suitor Becomes the Pursued: Union Pacific Resources' $4 Billion Offer Faces an Arsenal of Defenses," *Wall Street Journal*, June 24, 1997, p. B4.

"Love Her and Leave Her," *Forbes*, September 15, 1974.

Nulty, Peter, "How a Foxy Deal Became a Dog," *Fortune*, November 2, 1992, pp. 82, 86.

Petzinger, Thomas, *Oil and Honor: The Texaco-Pennzoil Wars*, New York: Putnam, 1987.

Shannon, James, *Texaco and the $10 Billion Jury*, Englewood Cliffs, N.J.: Prentice Hall, 1988.

Sherman, Stratford P., "The Gambler Who Refused $2 Billion," *Fortune*, May 11, 1987, p. 50.

"Slick Plan?," *Barron's*, July 12, 1999, p. 20.

—Jonathan Martin
—updates: David E. Salamie; Carrie Rothburd

Portland Trail Blazers

One Center Court, Suite 200
Portland, Oregon 97227
U.S.A.
Telephone: (503) 234-9291
Fax: (503) 236-4906
Web site: http://www.nba.com/blazers

Private Company
Incorporated: 1970
Employees: 249
Sales: $101 million (2001 est.)
NAIC: 711211 Sports Teams and Clubs

It seemed fitting that the board of governors of the National Basketball Association (NBA) saw a future for their sport in Portland, where pioneers settled in 1845 at the convergence of the Columbia and Willamette Rivers. Years earlier, from 1804 to 1806, explorers Meriwether Lewis and William Clark had blazed the Oregon Trail, opening the Pacific Northwest to development. So when Portland was granted an NBA franchise in 1970, perhaps no better name for the team could have been selected from nearly 10,000 entries than the Portland Trail Blazers.

Portland Trail Blazers Are in Business

Pioneering the cause of basketball in Portland was Harry Glickman, local entrepreneur, and professional sports promoter, who on February 6, 1970, proudly witnessed the granting of an expansion franchise to the city by the NBA Board of Governors at a cost of $3.7 million. Portland was one of three teams (Cleveland and Buffalo were the others) to begin playing in the 1970–71 season. Glickman, who became the executive vice-president and general manager of the Trail Blazers, and owners Herman Sarkowsky, Robert Shmertz, and Lawrence Weinberg, hired Stu Inman as Portland's first scout and Rolland Todd from the University of Nevada in Las Vegas as the first head coach. Geoff Petrie, a six-foot, four-inch shooter from Princeton was the first college draft selection and LeRoy Ellis, a rebounder with the Baltimore Bullets, was the first Trail Blazer selected in the NBA expansion draft.

The Trail Blazers began playing in Portland's Memorial Coliseum in an inter-squad game on June 27, 1970. High scorers for the game were Geoff Petrie and Ron Knight. The first pre-season game was played in September against San Francisco at Mark Morris High School in Longview, Washington, with the Blazers losing 119–118. Their first win came two days later in another pre-season game against San Francisco. The regular season started for the Blazers on October 16 before 4,273 fans in Portland's Memorial Coliseum with a 115–112 win over Cleveland.

Although Portland finished their inaugural season better than the other two new NBA franchises, their 29-win and 52-loss record was disappointing. This record, however, was the second-best ever by a first-year franchise. Geoff Petrie shared NBA Rookie of the Year honors with Boston's Dave Cowens and became the seventh rookie in NBA history to top the 2000-point mark. He was a unanimous pick for the NBA All-Rookie team and the first Blazer to be selected for the NBA All-Star game.

Providing thrills to Portland fans along with sharpshooting guard Petrie, who scored more than 40 points in ten games during his six years as a Blazer, was "Mr. Everything" Sidney Wicks who joined the team for the 1971–72 season. Wicks came to Portland from the University of California at Los Angeles (UCLA), where he had led the Bruins to National Championships in 1969 and 1970. By the season's end, Wicks had racked up Rookie of the Year honors, and was selected for the All-Rookie team and the NBA All-Star game.

Although the season ended with another disappointing record—18 wins and 64 losses—it was not without its highpoints. One came on November 19 when team captain Rick Adelman produced 17 assists against Cleveland, a team record that would last almost ten years. On March 18, Portland beat the NBA Finals-bound New York Knicks by 47 points (133–86). Coach Rolland Todd was dismissed on February 3, 1972, and was replaced as interim coach by former scout and Director of Player Personnel Stu Inman. LeRoy Ellis was traded to the Los Angeles Lakers for a future draft pick.

The 1972–73 season saw a steady improvement for the team under the coaching leadership of Jack McCloskey of Wake

<table>
<tr><td colspan="2"><h2 align="center">Key Dates:</h2></td></tr>
</table>

Key Dates:

1970: Portland is granted an NBA franchise; Roland Todd is named as the first head coach; and the first game is played at Portland's Memorial Coliseum.

1971: Geoff Petrie is named first Trail Blazer to play in the NBA All-Star game; and Rick Adelman is the first official captain of the Blazers.

1974: Bill Walton is chosen in the NBA draft; and Lenny Wilkins becomes head coach of the Blazers.

1976: Coach Wilkins is replaced by Jack Ramsay from Buffalo.

1977: Portland ends the season with 49 wins, 33 losses; and Blazermania is born when Portland wins the NBA Championships.

1978: Portland finishes the season with a 58–24 record, the best in the NBA.

1983: Portland sets an all-time club record with 156 points scored in a victory over Denver.

1986: Portland sells out its 400th consecutive game, the longest string of any organization in sports; and Mike Schuler is named head coach of the Blazers.

1987: Harry Glickman, founder of the club, is named president of the Trail Blazers; and Schuler wins NBA Coach of the Year honors.

1988: Seattle computer magnate and Microsoft cofounder, Paul Allen, buys the Trail Blazers.

1989: Rick Adelman is named interim head coach following the firing of Mike Schuler; and Bill Walton's No. 32 jersey is retired.

1990: Clyde Drexler scores his 10,000-career point to become the all-time leading scorer in the Trail Blazers' history.

1992: Portland becomes the first city outside New York to host the NBA draft.

1995: Portland moves to a new 20,000-capacity arena, the Rose Garden.

1996: Portland sets an all-time home attendance record with 21,567.

1997: Mike Dunleavy replaces P.J. Carlesimo as the head coach of the Blazers.

1999: Mike Dunleavy earns NBA Coach of the Year.

2001: The Blazers cinch a playoff spot for the 19th consecutive year, the longest streak in the NBA; and Maurice Cheeks becomes the tenth head coach of the Blazers.

Forest. The team ended with three more wins than the previous season, 21–61. Petrie and Wicks continued their high scoring and both finished among the league's top ten scorers. Petrie scored a team record of 51 points in two games against the Houston Rockets. The 1973–74 season ended only slightly better (27–55), but not enough for team management. McCloskey was let go at the end of the season.

Bill Walton Joins the Team

The 1974–75 witnessed two major personnel changes that breathed life into the Blazers. Lenny Wilkins was brought on as new head coach, and player Bill Walton, three-time College Player of the Year from UCLA, was taken as Portland's No. 1 choice in the 1974 NBA draft. Although injuries benched Walton in all but 35 games his rookie season, he averaged 12.8 points per game (ppg) and 12.6 rebounds per game (rpg). Sidney Wicks led the team with 21.7 ppg and 10.7 rpg in 82 games, and was selected to play in the NBA All-Star game. On February 26 in an overtime win over the Lakers, Wicks pulled down a club-record 27 rebounds. On October 18, Portland defeated Cleveland in a first-ever four-overtime win, 131–129.

Wilkins, who would go on to become one of the winningest coaches in NBA history and be inducted into the NBA Hall of Fame, could only lead the Blazers to a 38–44 record for the 1974–75 season. The following season saw the Blazers win one less game, ending with 37 wins and 45 losses. Although plagued again with injuries for most of the season, Walton exhibited signs of greatness during a winning 12–2 stretch mid-season, when he averaged 21.1 points and 17.8 rebounds, including a 36-point, 22-rebound game in a victory over Atlanta, and a 27-point, 22-rebound game in a win over the Lakers. He ended the season with an 18.1 point-per-game average, slightly below team leaders Wicks (19.1 ppg) and Geoff Petrie (18.9 ppg).

Coach Wilkins, unable to transform the Blazers into winners, was replaced by Jack Ramsay in June 1976. Ramsay, having come to Portland after leading the Buffalo Braves to the NBA Finals three straight years, was one of several factors that transformed a new era for the Trail Blazers.

Blazermania Is Born

Ramsay, known for his colorful wardrobe and disciplined-coaching style, was described by Blazer Executive Vice-President Harry Glickman as possessing "one of the best minds in the game.a brilliant teacher and motivator." Star players Wicks and Petrie had been replaced by forwards Maurice Lucas and Bobby Gross, and guards Dave Twardzik and Lionel Hollins. But a healthy Bill Walton proved to be the type of player Coach Ramsay could build a winning team around.

Blazermania was born on April 8, 1977, when a capacity crowd packed Memorial Coliseum to witness the Blazers take on the Phoenix Suns in a 122–111 win. That win began an 814-game sellout string, the longest-known sellout string in the history of professional sports.

The season ended with a 49–33 record, a tie for fourth in the league, third in the conference and second in the division. But more importantly, they were off to the Finals for the first time in franchise history. And what a finish! After getting past Chicago and Denver, the Blazers swept the Lakers, the team with the regular season's best record, and faced the Philadelphia 76ers in the Finals. The 76ers, lead by "Dr. J" Julius Erving, won the first two games. Portland took the next four, becoming only the second team in NBA history to win a title after losing the first two games in the series, and the second team ever to go all the way in their first post-season appearance. The following day 50,000 fans lined the streets of Portland for a victory parade. In true form, Bill Walton was named NBA Finals Most Valuable Player (MVP) with 20 points, 23 rebounds and a Finals-record eight blocked shots. Walton, an All-NBA Second team and All-Defensive team selection, led the league in rebounding (14.4 rpg) and blocked shots (3.25bpg).

Labeled the "team of destiny," Portland began the 1977–78 season looking like true NBA champions. Through their first 60 games, they racked up 50 wins, including a club-record 26 wins in a row and outscored their opponents by 9.9 points per game. Then disaster struck when Walton and several other players went out with injuries the second half of the season. Despite winning only eight of their final 22 games, Portland managed to finish the season with the league's best record, 58–24, and limped into the Finals. The Blazers were ousted in the Western Conference Semifinals by their neighbors, the Seattle Super-Sonics. Bill Walton, who had led the team in scoring (18.9 ppg), rebounding (13.2 rpg) and blocked shots (2.52 bpg), was selected as the NBA's MVP.

For the 1978–79 season, Walton and Lloyd Neal were sidelined with injuries and two rookies, Mychal Thompson and Ron Brewer, led the Blazers to the post-season again, after a 45–37 season. Phoenix knocked out Portland in the first round. Both Thompson and Brewer were selected to the NBA All-Rookie team. Neal, who had retired at the end of the season, became the first Trail Blazer to have his number retired (No. 36).

Walton Leaves Portland

Bill Walton, to the disappointment of Blazer fans, asked to be traded prior to the 1979–80 season, going to San Diego for Kermit Washington and Kevin Kunnert. Also joining the team were Calvin Natt, Jim Paxson, and Billy Ray Bates. Despite a strong start, the Blazers finished the season 38–44 and were below the .500 mark for the first time since the 1975–76 season. Calvin Natt was named to the NBA All-Star Rookie team.

Leading the Trail Blazers to a 45–37 season in 1981 were Kermit Washington, Mychal Thompson, and rookie Kelvin Ransey. For the fourth straight year since winning the NBA Finals, Portland exited the playoffs after the first round, losing to Kansas City. Kelvin Ransey was named to the NBA All-Rookie team and Kermit Washington was selected to the NBA's All-Defense Second team. But, once again, injuries to key players plagued the Blazers, including an ankle injury suffered by Kermit Washington prior to the season opener. Portland did not reach the Finals following the 1981–82 season, in spite of a 42–40 season record.

With a healthier squad the following season, Portland finished with a 46–36 record, and made it past the first round of the playoffs. After beating Seattle, the Blazers lost to the Lakers in the Western Conference Semifinals. Jim Paxson represented Portland in the NBA All-Star game.

With two more victories than the previous year, the Blazers posted the second-best record in the Western Conference in the 1983–84 season, but were bumped in the first round of the

playoffs by Phoenix. In a March 16 game against the Chicago Bulls, the teams went four overtimes before the Bulls pulled out a 156–155 win. The game, which lasted a club-record three hours and 24 minutes, was the highest-scoring game in Portland's franchise history. Jim Paxson, once again an All-Star selection, scored a career-high 41 points in the game. On March 23, Jack Ramsay became the second winningest coach in NBA history (703 career victories and second to Boston's Red Auerbach) when the Blazers defeated Phoenix 124–98.

Clyde Drexler Drafted from Houston

Clyde Drexler was selected from the University of Houston in the first round of the 1983 NBA draft. Joining him in Blazers' jerseys were Granville Waiters and Tom Piotrowski. In the second season with the Blazers, Drexler began to shine, along with Kiki Vandeweghe, the NBA's No. 3 scorer, who the Blazers acquired from Denver for Calvin Natt, Lafayette Lever, and Wayne Cooper. A key college draft pick was Sam Bowie, from Kentucky. At the end of the 1984–85 season, seven Blazers ended with double-digit scoring averages, including Vandeweghe (22.4 ppg), Thompson (18.4 ppg), Paxson (17.9 ppg), and Drexler (17.2 ppg). Bowie became the eighth Blazer in franchise history to be named to the NBA All-Rookie team.

The 1985–86 season was another disappointing season for the Blazers, finishing at 40–42, and losing in the first round of the playoffs. The second-half-of-the-season loss of Sam Bowie because of leg surgery had a major impact on the team. Clyde Drexler was selected to play in his first All-Star game.

Jack Ramsay, who had guided the Blazers to a 453–367 record, nine playoff appearances, and an NBA title, was replaced as head coach on May 28, 1986, by Mike Schuler. Schuler guided the Blazers to a 49–33 record, and was named NBA Coach of the Year. Another rising star in the Blazers' organization was Terry Porter, a rookie in 1985, who in a January 23 game against the Sacramento Kings, set a team record of 18 assists. Averaging 117.9 points per game, the Blazers advanced to the NBA Playoffs again but were upset by Houston in a first-round series.

Behind emerging stars Drexler and Porter, Portland ended their 1987–88 season with a 52–29 record. In a February 21 game against the Spurs, Jim Paxson became the first Trail Blazer to top 10,000 points. Other records set that season included Porter's 19 assists on April 14 against the Utah Jazz and Drexler's 2,185 points for the season, a club record. Once again, the Blazers failed to make it past the first round of the playoffs, this time falling to Utah.

Microsoft Cofounder Paul Allen Buys the Team

In May 1988, Blazers owner Larry Weinberg announced the sale of the organization to Microsoft cofounder and Seattle Seahawks owner Paul Allen. Coach Schuler left the Blazer organization in the middle of the 1988–89 season amid another losing season, 39–43. Rick Adelman, former Blazer player, took over as interim coach. High points of the season were Drexler's 50-point game on January 6 against Sacramento, and a club-record scoring average of 27.2 points per game. Kevin

Duckworth, acquired in the 1986–87 season, joined Drexler in representing Portland in the All-Star game.

Portland capped a winning season under Adelman in 1989–90, with a 59–23 record, second best in the league and earned the nickname, "Rip City." They won the Western Conference Semifinals against Phoenix and took on the defending champion Detroit Pistons in the Finals, who won in five games. Drexler led the team in scoring and represented the team for the fourth time in five years at the NBA All-Star game.

A franchise best-ever record was achieved in 1990–91, with 63 wins and 19 losses. Adding power to the lineup was Danny Ainge, acquired from Sacramento, who with Porter, ranked among the league's top 10 three-point shooters. Drexler, Porter, and Duckworth were selected to the All-Star game. Coach Adelman appeared set to take the Blazers back to the NBA Championships. After beating Seattle in the opening round, they beat Utah in five games to advance to the Western Conference title round for the second year in a row. Magic Johnson and the Los Angeles Lakers put a stop to their dreams by ousting them in six games. Despite the disappointment, Rick Adelman was named NBA Coach of the Month for the months of November and April, head coach of the West in the All-Star game, and runner-up for Coach of the Year. Three Blazers returned to the All-Star game: Drexler, Duckworth, and Porter.

The 1991–92 season was another stellar season for the Blazers. They ended the season with a 57–25 record and were once again off to the Playoffs, beating the Lakers, Suns, and Jazz. Drexler set a club playoff-high record of 42 points against the Lakers on April 29; the team racked up a team playoff-record 153 points against Phoenix on May 11. In the Finals, Portland met Michael Jordan and the Chicago Bulls, who beat the Blazers in six games.

For the fourth straight season, Portland won over 50 games, and ended with a 51–31 season. The season, however, was once again plagued by injury-stricken players, namely Drexler and Jerome Kersey. Adelman, who suffered through personal tragedies and player misconduct allegations, nonetheless achieved his 200-career win on November 22 against Detroit. Portland reached its 15th playoff berth in 16 seasons, but was stopped in the first round by the San Antonio Spurs.

In 1993–94, Portland continued their slow decline and ended the season with a 47–35 record. Rod Strickland replaced Terry Porter as point guard, and Harvey Grant was acquired from the Washington Bullets for Kevin Duckworth. Clifford Robinson replaced Drexler as the team's scoring leader and accompanied Drexler to his first NBA All-Star game. In the playoffs, Portland was ousted by the Houston Rockets, who went on to win the NBA title. Rick Adelman was fired after the playoff loss and replaced by P.J. Carlesimo, coach at Seton Hall University.

In July 1994, Blazers owner Paul Allen hired Bob Whitsitt as president and general manager of the Portland Trail Blazers and the Oregon Arena Corporation. A 1977 graduate in communications from Wisconsin-Stevens Point with a post-graduate degree in sports administration from The Ohio State University, Whitsitt came to Portland following an eight-year stint as president and general manager of the Seattle SuperSonics. While in Seattle, Whitsitt was named the 1994 NBA Executive of the Year.

A Transition of Eras: Clyde Drexler and the Rose Garden

On February 14, Clyde Drexler was traded to the Houston Rockets for Otis Thorpe. Drexler, a four-time NBA All-Star, was Portland's all-time scoring and rebounding leader. This was the last season for the Blazers in the familiar environs of Portland's Memorial Coliseum, their home for 25 years. The team was scheduled to move to their new Rose Garden arena the following season. The season ended at 44–38 and Portland was swept by the Phoenix Suns in the first round of the playoffs. Coach Carlesimo became the first coach in 25 years to move from the college ranks to the NBA and post a winning record in his first season.

The Oregon Arena Corporation was created in 1991 to develop a new arena for Portland. The result was the Rose Quarter, a 32-acre campus that encompasses the Blazer's Rose Garden arena, the Memorial Coliseum, the Rose Quarter Commons, and the One Center Court office complex which houses the Blazers' organization corporate offices.

The Blazers began their 1995–56 season in the 20,000-seat, $262 million Rose Garden against the Vancouver Grizzlies on November 3, 1995. After losing the game 80–92, Portland went on to finish the season with a 44–38 record. Lithuanian Arvydas Sabonis proved to be a key to the Blazer's successful season. The seven-foot, two-inch Sabonis was originally drafted by the Blazers in 1986, but spent six years in the Spanish league before joining the Blazers in 1995. Sabonis averaged 14.5 points per game and 8.1 rebounds, was named to the NBA All-Rookie First team, and was runner-up for the NBA Rookie of the Year Award and the Sixth Man Award. Chris Dudley won the J. Walter Kennedy Citizenship Award for exemplary service to the community. Portland lost to the Jazz in the first round of the playoffs. In game five, Portland lost by a score of 102–64, snapping the previous year's playoff record-low 68 points, set by the Knicks against the Pacers.

The changes in the team roster prior to the 1996–97 season resulted in a 49–33 finish. The team nucleus benefited from player acquisitions in July that saw Harvey Grant and Rod Strickland go to Washington for power forward Rasheed Wallace, shooting guard Isaiah Rider come from Minnesota, and Kenny Anderson sign to a free-agent contract. Together with Clifford Robinson, Arvydas Sabonis, and Gary Trent, the team embarked on an 11-game winning streak in late February that equaled the second longest in team history. For the fifth straight year, however, Portland exited the Finals in the first round, this time losing to the Lakers, and Coach Carlesimo exited after three seasons at the helm.

Headlining the 1997–98 season was the hiring of Mike Dunleavy as head coach and the trade of 1996 Rookie of the Year and Portland native Damon Stoudamire, and Walt Williams and Carlos Rogers from Toronto for Kenny Anderson, Gary Trent, and Alvin Williams. Dunleavy guided Portland to a 46–36 record and its 16th consecutive trip to the playoffs, the longest current streak in the NBA. Once again, the Blazers were sent packing by the Lakers in the first round.

Mike Dunleavy earned Coach of the Year honors in 1998–99 after the Blazers raced to a 35–15 record in a lockout-shortened season. In the post-season, Portland swept past Phoenix and Utah, before losing to the Spurs in the Western Finals.

The 1999–2000 season saw an outstanding season of 59 victories, the second-best season in franchise history, marred by losses on and off the court. On May 5, popular Assistant Coach Bill Musselman lost a six-month battle with a rare disease, primary systemic amyloidosis. Two weeks earlier, the Blazers lost their regular season finale to Denver, failing to post the franchise's second 60-win season. In June, Portland's loss to Denver quelled their hopes for another NBA Finals matchup. New to the lineup were Bonzi Wells from Detroit, and Scottie Pippin traded from Houston. Mike Dunleavy was named NBA Coach of the Month in November. Rasheed Wallace was fifth in the league in field goal percentage and played in his first NBA All-Star game.

New Season Brings Another New Coach

Fifteen-year NBA veteran player and Chicago native, Maurice Cheeks, was named Portland's head coach on June 27, 2001, the tenth coach in franchise history. Cheeks, a former assistant coach with the Philadelphia 76ers, played with the 76ers for 11 years and is credited with the development of All-Star guard Allen Iverson's career and helping coach the 76ers to the NBA Finals. Prior to the season opening, Brian Grant was traded to Miami and Gary Grant to Cleveland in a three-team, five-player trade that brought Shawn Kemp from Cleveland and sent Chris Gatling and Clarence Witherspoon from Miami to Cleveland. Joe Kleine and Jermaine O'Neal were traded to Indiana for Dale Davis. On January, Scottie Pippin suited up for this 1,000th NBA game and his 133rd as a Blazer; on April 26, he played in his 200th playoff game. The Blazers ended their season with a 50–32 record and lost in three games to the Lakers in the first round of the playoffs.

After three decades the Portland Trail Blazers have grown into one of the league's most successful franchise operations, on and off the court. Their story has included an NBA Championship, repeated visits to the Finals, and the opening of one of the nation's most impressive sporting arenas. The Blazers' organization has contributed not only entertainment, but service to the Portland community through involvement in youth development and educational programs, the Children's Hospital, Salvation Army, and Police Activities League. The team established the Hometown Hero of the Month Award, which honors players for outstanding community service; the NBA and WNBA Sportsmanship Awards; and has contributed to Prevent Child Abuse America, the Martin Luther King Holiday, Black History Month, Gallaudet University, and the Thurgood Marshall Scholarship Fund. On the court, the Blazers have rekindled memories of the exciting Portland teams of old, and will, hopefully bring back to the Rose Garden something else—another NBA championship trophy.

Principal Competitors

Los Angeles Lakers; Utah Jazz; Seattle SuperSonics; Sacramento Kings; San Antonio Spurs.

Further Reading

Carpenter, Sue, *2001–2002 Blazers Media Guide*, Portland, Ore.: Portland Trail Blazers Inc., 2001, p. 352.

"New Head Coach," *Jet*, July 16, 2001, p. 50.

Rambeck, Richard, *Portland Trail Blazers*, Mankato, Minn.: Creative Education, Inc., 1998, p. 32.

Taylor, Phil, "Six Portland Trail Blazers," *Sports Illustrated*, October 29, 2001, p. 166.

Wertheim, Jon, "Losing Their Grip," *Sports Illustrated*, December 24, 2001, p. 40.

—Carol D. Beavers

Powergen PLC

Westwood Way
Westwood Business Park
Coventry CV4 8LG
United Kingdom
Telephone: +44 (0) 24 7642 4000
Fax: +44 (0) 24 7642 5432
Web site: http://www.pgen.com

Wholly Owned Subsidiary of E.On AG
Incorporated: 1989 as The Power Generation Company
  PLC
Employees: 10,253
Sales: £5.65 billion (2001)
Stock Exchanges: Frankfurt New York
Ticker Symbol: EOA, EON
NAIC: 221112 Fossil Fuel Electric Power Generation;
  221121 Electric Bulk Power Transmission and
  Control; 221122 Electric Power Distribution; 221210
  Natural Gas Distribution

Powergen PLC is a leading integrated gas and electric company created from the breakup of the nationalized electricity industry in England and Wales. While privatization looms, Powergen is carved out as a separate division of the Central Electricity Generating Board in 1989 and is incorporated as a public limited company with the majority of its shares sold to the public two years later. Powergen and its larger rival at the time, National Power, constitute a virtual duopoly of electricity generation in England and Wales, though that scenario is expected to change as more and more competition enter the industry. Perhaps in response to this inevitable shift in the status quo, the company increasingly becomes involved in allied ventures including forays into international power markets, the provision of combined heat and power, and, most significantly, investment in natural gas.

Commercial Electricity, National Policy, and the Creation of Powergen

Electricity was first harnessed for practical use in the United Kingdom in the late 19th century with the introduction of street lighting in 1881. By 1921, over 480 authorized but independent electricity suppliers had sprung up throughout England and Wales, creating a rather haphazard system operating at different voltages and frequencies. In recognition of the need for a more coherent, interlocking system, the Electricity (Supply) Act of 1926 created a central authority to encourage and facilitate a national transmission system. This objective of a national grid was achieved by the mid-1930s.

The state consolidated its control of the utility with the Electricity Act of 1947, which collapsed the distribution and supply activities of 505 separate bodies into 12 regional Area boards, at the same time assigning generating assets and liabilities to one government-controlled authority. A further Electricity Act in 1957, created a statutory body, the Central Electricity Generating Board (CEGB), which dominated the whole electricity system in England and Wales. Generator of virtually all the electricity in the two countries, the CEGB, as owner and operator of the transmission grid, supplied electricity to the Area boards, which they in turn distributed and sold within their regions.

This situation continued for 30 years, until the government mooted the idea of privatizing the electricity industry in 1987. The proposal was enshrined in the Electricity Act of 1989, and a new organizational scheme was unveiled. The CEGB was splintered into four divisions, destined to become successor companies: Powergen, National Power, Nuclear Electric, and the National Grid Company (NGC). Powergen and National Power were to share between them England and Wales's fossil-fueled power stations; Nuclear Electric was to take over nuclear power stations; and the NGC was to be awarded control of the national electricity distribution system. The 12 Area boards were converted, virtually unchanged, into 12 Regional Electricity Companies (RECs), and these were given joint ownership of the NGC. The RECs' shares were the first to be sold to the public, at the end of 1990. Powergen and National Power's shares were offered for sale the following year.

Powergen before and after Industry Privatization

In order to understand Powergen's role within the electricity industry it is helpful to understand how the system operated until the extensive changes brought on by the Utilities Act of

Company Perspectives:

Powergen's vision is to create one of the world's leading independent electricity and gas businesses. It aims to grow by generating, distributing and supplying power both in the U.K. and other countries in which it operates. As a low-cost, innovative and environmentally responsible operator, it delivers value and quality to its customers, shareholders, employees, partners and communities.

2000. The provision of electricity consisted of four components: generation, transmission, distribution, and supply. In England and Wales, generation was the province of Powergen, National Power, and Nuclear Electric. Transmission is the transfer of electricity via the national grid, through overhead lines, underground cables, and NGC substations. Distribution was the delivery of electricity from the national grid to local distribution systems operated by the Regional Electricity Companies. Supply, a term distinct from distribution in the electricity industry, refers to the transaction whereby electricity is purchased from the generators and transmitted to customers. Under the terms of its license, Powergen had the right to supply electricity directly to consumers, but in the company's earlier years that right was little exercised. Powergen's usual customers were the RECs, which in turn sold the electricity to the end users.

A new trading market was devised with the privatization scheme for bulk sales of electricity from generators to distributors—the pool. A rather complicated pricing procedure existed in the pool, according to which each generating station offered a quote for each half-hour of the day, based on an elaborate set of criteria including the operating costs of that particular plant, the time of day, the expected demand for electricity, and the available capacity of the station. The NGC arranged these quotes in a merit order and made the decisions regarding when to call each plant into operation. The pool system was not relied upon exclusively, however, the generators frequently made contractual arrangements with distributors for a specified period of time as a means of mutual protection against fluctuations in the pool price.

At the end of 1990, National Power—divided into International Power and Innogy Holdings in 2000—Powergen's bigger rival at the time, boasted an aggregate Declared Net Capacity or Capability (DNC) of 29,486 megawatts (MW), where a megawatt was defined as the generating capacity of a power station in any given half-hour. Powergen, in second place, had 18,764MW DNC. Nuclear Electric's figure was 8,357MW, the National Grid Company controlled 2,088MW, and British Nuclear Fuels PLC, the United Kingdom Atomic Energy Authority, and small independent generators together accounted for about 2,900MW. Another, though limited, source was provided by linkages with the Scottish and French electricity systems, with which import or export deals were sometimes made. Powergen and National Power between them thus controlled some 78 percent of the electricity market in England and Wales, of which about 30 percent was held by Powergen.

Privatization of the utility was designed to promote a beneficial result through the free play of market forces. The introduction of competition in power generation, it was argued, would lead both to greater efficiency within the industry and to lower prices for the consumer. Within a few short years, however, concerns had already arisen, as critics of the scheme had predicted from the start. A duopoly, which at the time of its creation held such a significant majority of the electricity generating market, was never likely to embody the purest form of free market operations.

Government Regulation and the "Dash for Gas"

In 1994 the industry watchdog, the Office of Electricity Regulation (Offer), expressed concern about Powergen and National Power's continuing dominance of the market—and the fact that from June 1990 to January 1994 the wholesale price of electricity had risen by 50 percent. The market share of the big two had in fact declined since privatization, with National Power enjoying some 33 percent and Powergen controlling less than 25 percent, but nonetheless rumors were rife that Offer would refer the duopoly to the Monopolies and Mergers Commission. Offer eventually stopped short of that proceeding, but the regulator did lay strictures on the two generating companies, requiring that they should sell a specified amount of generating plant capacity—in the case of Powergen 2,000MW—and submit to price-capping for a period of two years.

The demand to sell plant capacity was expected to cause little hardship to Powergen; which plant to sell and when to sell was left to the company's discretion, provided it complied with Offer's deadline of December 31, 1995. Much of the plant capacity disposed of was expected to be less-attractive coal-fired plants, some of which Powergen would have closed anyway as the plants were unnecessary to its needs. In preference to an outright sale, it seemed possible that Powergen might be able to arrange an asset exchange with a foreign power company.

The required price caps, ironically, appeared likely to prove a less onerous burden to Powergen and National Power than to the state-owned Nuclear Electric and to small independents, both existing and potential. Nor would the new pricing rules result in lower electricity bills for the average household consumer—only for large corporate customers.

The government, apart from its concerns about fair competition and price, was particularly interested in resolving any controversy or questions regarding Powergen and National Power, as it intended to sell its remaining 40 percent share (which it had retained at privatization) in each of the two companies. The sell-off to the public, scheduled to take place in February 1995, was expected to raise a welcome £4 billion for the government; £1.5 billion of which would be attributable to Powergen.

Powergen followed the usual route of privatized companies in the United Kingdom by undertaking a rigorous program of cost-cutting, achieved primarily through improved efficiency, staff reductions, and plant closures. Employee redundancies had been dramatic: Powergen's staff as of 1994 was less than half its 1990 level. Several power stations were closed outright, while others were put into indefinite reserve. The strategy proved a successful one, with the company's profits healthy despite a reduction in sales.

In preparation for privatization, plans were laid to reorganize and modernize power generation, and during the 1990s the face of the industry accordingly changed. From a heavy reliance on coal-fired plants, Powergen, like its rival National Power, began moving to a more diversified base. As of 1994 coal was still the dominant source—figures for 1993 to 1994 proved that Powergen still relied very heavily on the resource, with coal accounting for a hefty 80.6 percent of total fuel used. Increasingly, coal was imported from abroad, as the foreign variety had a lower sulphur content than its British counterpart, obviating the need to fit special emission-reducing equipment to comply with environmental standards.

An emerging trend was toward combined cycle gas turbine (CCGT) plants—the so-called ''dash for gas.'' Excess generating capacity in the 1980s made some coal-fired capability redundant, and more was jettisoned in favor of natural gas, the use of which had both economic and environmental advantages. The use of gas, while relatively small at 10.6 percent, should be compared to 1992 to 1993 figures, when gas accounted for only 3.6 percent. And clearly, Powergen believed the future was in natural gas. Since privatization the company invested in some 3,000MW of new CCGT plant capacity, generated by three power stations: Killingholme, in South Humberside (completing its first full year of operations in 1993 to 1994); Rye House, Hertfordshire (finished in 1993); and Connah's Quay, in North Wales, which was expected to provide over half the electricity needs of Wales.

Thus a part of Powergen's long-term plan was to broaden its interests in natural gas. As early as 1989, with privatization on the horizon but not yet effected, Powergen, in a joint venture with Conoco UK Ltd., set up a gas trading company, Kinetica, to market gas downstream and construct gas transport pipelines. The venture became a clear success for Powergen, and the

company was confident that there would be ample scope for further development. The subsidiary Powergen (North Sea) Ltd. constituted an investment for the company's future business. In 1993, Powergen acquired from Monument Oil and Gas PLC a 3.9 percent stake in the Liverpool Bay development. This would supply gas to Powergen's own Connah's Quay power station. Further widening its scope, Powergen purchased in 1994 from a subsidiary of Lasmo an additional 5 percent of Liverpool Bay and a 12 percent interest in the Ravenspurn North field as well as a 3.75 percent stake in Johnston field, both located in the Southern Gas Basin of the North Sea.

Opportunities Abroad and Vertical Alignment

After becoming a PLC, Powergen increasingly looked abroad for opportunities and advancement. In 1993 to 1994 the company undertook, as a member of a consortium with two U.S. companies—NRG Energy, Inc. and Morrison Knudson Co., Inc.—to operate lignite mining and power generation in the Leipzig region of Germany. As a future investment in the area, and again in cooperation with NRG Energy, the company bought a 400MW share in the 900MW Schkopau power station. At Tapada do Outeiro in Portugal, Powergen became a member of a consortium charged to build and operate a 900MW CCGT power station.

Powergen began moving into the field of combined heat and power generation through its subsidiary Powergen CHP. Its first project in this area, initiated in 1993 to 1994, was a 14MW co-generation plant commissioned by SmithKline Beecham. The subsidiary has also undertaken to provide energy for three paper mills in Kent.

Powergen's sorties into ventures, related to but independent of its primary function as a U.K. power generator, were necessary for the company to grow. Its share of the home electricity market was undeniably dwindling, from a post-privatization inheritance of 30 percent to some 24.5 percent in 1994; and Nuclear Electric had edged out Powergen as the second largest power generator. Powergen's market share was expected to sink yet further as the government's plan to increase competition in power generation came to fruition. Nonetheless, it seemed likely that Powergen would continue to control a significant proportion of the industry.

The government sold its remaining 40 percent stock in Powergen in February 1995. The following year, the government rejected Powergen's bid to acquire Midlands Electricity PLC (MEB), which would have marked the first merger between a U.K. power generator and distributor. The government believed the merger would cause reduced competition and higher prices, ultimately operating against public interest.

Rebounding from the disappointment, Powergen entered into a new joint venture with Siemens in 1997, the development of the Cottam Development Centre, which went on to win a 1997 Strategic Partnership Industry All-Star Award. This collaboration wasn't the first between the two companies; they had worked together on other large-scale projects, including construction of the Killingholme station on South Humberside in 1993. The Cottam project would become a showcase for the latest design of high-efficient, environmentally mindful gas turbines, providing a solid platform for large-scale development ventures well into the future.

In July 1998, Powergen purchased East Midlands Electricity for £1.9 billion. This marked the company's entrance into the residential and smaller business electricity markets and allowed the distribution of electricity over a region of 16,000 square miles and 67,000 kilometers of overhead lines and underground cables. The following year, Powergen became the first U.K. company to sell electricity and gas to domestic customers via the Internet.

The New Millennium Brings Industry Changes

The year 2000 marked the beginning of a period of dramatic change for both the U.K. electricity industry and for Powergen as the company moved to reposition itself for the lucrative U.S. energy market. The company moved to acquired LG&E, a Kentucky energy service provider, for US$3.2 billion. But in order to make this happen, Powergen sold its Australian, Indian and other Asian assets, as well as three plants, including Cottam, which went as part of a £1.5 billion auction sponsored by Goldman Sachs.

In July 2000, the ACT Legislative Assembly created the Utilities Act, which was to commence on January 1, 2001. The Act instituted a new regulatory structure for electricity, gas, water and sewage utilities in the United Kingdom. A single energy regulator, the Gas and Electric Markets Authority, was established in November, and the offices for gas and electricity regulation were merged to form the Office of Gas and Electricity Markets (OFGEM). The biggest change brought on by the Act was the separation of distribution and supply, but another important component was the implementation of the New Electricity Trading Arrangements (NETA). Powergen took a positive tack, announcing that, "with our flexible generation, growing customer base and integrated trading strategy, NETA represents a business opportunity rather than a threat." The company went on to seal the LG&E deal in December, just four months before German company E.ON announced a preconditional offer to purchase Powergen.

The German utility giant's offer valued Powergen's share capital at roughly £5.1 billion. The acquisition was completed in July 2002, when Powergen became part of the world's largest investor-owned electricity and gas utility. It also found itself better positioned to achieve long-held ambitions in the United States and the United Kingdom. The Powergen board unanimously recommended the sale.

Principal Subsidiaries

Corby Power Limited (50%); East Midlands Electricity; LG&E Energy Corp. (US).

Principal Competitors

Centrica; Scottish Power; TXU Europe.

Further Reading

Beckett, Paul, "British Utilities Agree to Merge, But Concern Grows," *Wall Street Journal*, September 19, 1995, p. A18.

Benady, David, "Power Struggle," *Marketing Week*, October 14, 1998, pp. 27–28.

"Britain's Electricity Shocker," *Economist*, April 13, 1996, p. 14.

Butler, Daniel, "Power at Play," *Management Today*, November 1990, pp. 54–59.

"Customers Set to Benefit by up to £500m," *Financial Times*, February 12, 1994.

"Electricity Generator May Swap Assets," *Financial Times*, June 10, 1994.

"Electricity Generators to Escape Monopolies Reference," *Financial Times*, February 11, 1994.

Fuhrmans, Vanessa, "Germany's E.ON to Buy Powergen for $7.4 Billion," *Wall Street Journal*, April 10, 2001, p. A16.

"The Generation Game," *Economist*, September 1, 1990, p. 29.

"Generators in Deal to Sell Plant and Reduce Prices," *Financial Times*, February 12, 1994.

"Generators Stake to Be Sold for £4bn," *The Times* (London), March 5, 1994.

Gibson, Gina, "Powergen TV Ad First," *Marketing*, January 29, 1998, p. 5.

"Government Announces Last of Powergen Sell-off," *Birmingham Post*, March 5, 1994.

Kapner, Suzanne, "Germany's Top Utility Is Seeking a Global Presence," *New York Times*, January 18, 2001, p. W1.

Leslie, Keith, "Power Master-Stroke By Powergen," *Corporate Finance*, January 1998, p. 20.

"The Lex Column: Cash Power," *Financial Times*, June 10, 1994.

Maling, Nick, "Power Play," *Marketing Week*, March 25, 1999, pp. 26–29.

"Offer Proves a Party-Pooper for High-Flying Generators," *Independent*, January 5, 1994.

"Power Generators Meet Offer to Head Off MMC Enquiry," *The Times* (London), January 24, 1994.

"Power Sell-off in February," *The Times* (London), September 30, 1994, p. 21.

"Power to Generate Cash," *Management Accounting*, September 1995, p. 14.

"Powergen," *The Times* (London), November 16, 1994, p. 28.

"Powergen Hunts Top Marketer in Strategy Review," *Marketing*, November 1, 2001, p. 1.

"Powergen Looks for Role in Offshore Gas," *Lloyds List*, December 29, 1993.

"Powergen PLC to Purchase the LG&E Energy Corporation for 1.19 Times Revenue," *Weekly Corporate Growth Report*, March 6, 2000, p. 10.

"Powergen Sees Live Chances on Overseas Circuit," *Evening Standard*, January 21, 1994.

"Powergen Strengthens Gas Interests," *Birmingham Post*, December 12, 1993.

Rhoads, Christopher, "Germany's E.ON in Talks with Powergen of the U.K.," *Wall Street Journal*, January 18, 2001, p. A23.

Smith, Geoffrey T., "What Happened? Lessons from across the Seas," *Wall Street Journal*, September 17, 2001, p. R9.

"Special Report on Competitive Power," *Daily Telegraph*, March 11, 1994.

Tieman, Ross, "Powerful 27 Percent Payout from Powergen," *The Times* (London), November 16, 1994, p. 26.

"Uncertain Times," *Energy Economist*, July 1998, p. 1.

—Robin DuBlanc
—update: Stacee Sledge

Puget Sound Energy Inc.

Puget Power Building
Bellevue, Washington 98009
U.S.A.
Telephone: (425) 454-6363
Toll Free: (888) 225-5773
Web site: http://www.pse.com

Wholly Owned Subsidiary of Puget Energy Inc.
Incorporated: 1912
Employees: 2,852
Sales: $98.4 million (2001)
Stock Exchanges: Amsterdam London New York
Ticker Symbol: PSD
NAIC: 221111 Hydroelectric Power Generation; 221122
    Electric Power Distribution

Puget Sound Energy Inc. is the largest investor-owned utility in the state of Washington. The company serves more than 1.7 million people in a 6,000-square-mile service area that includes eight counties bordering Puget Sound in western Washington and part of Kittitas County in central Washington.

Over a Century of Power Begins

Puget Sound Energy's history began in 1885 when Sydney Z. Mitchell and F.H. Sparling opened an office in Seattle as northwest regional agents for the Edison Electric Light Company. In the early 1880s, Mitchell, at the age of 23, had been appointed exclusive agent for Edison Electric Light Company, covering the state of Oregon and the territories of Washington, Montana, and Alaska. Mitchell convinced Sparling, his best friend, to come west to Seattle with him. From their small office, the two launched a promotional campaign that would later become a model for developing electric services throughout the territory.

The first step was to convince the city of Seattle of the advantages the new incandescent electric light bulb offered. By the end of October 1885, Mitchell and Sparling had organized the Seattle Electric Light Company. The following month, the

Seattle City Council granted the company a 25-year franchise. On March 22, 1886, Mitchell and Sparling gave a successful demonstration of electricity to Seattle citizens, and soon after Seattle Electric's initial system had grown to 250 lamps, the first central station system for incandescent electric lighting west of the Rocky Mountains. Mitchell and Sparling quickly expanded their operation and over the next 15 years built steam-powered central station systems in Tacoma, Spokane, Portland, Bellingham, and many smaller towns in Washington, as well as Oregon, Idaho, and even British Columbia, Canada.

Meanwhile, other ambitious entrepreneurs founded other electric companies that would eventually become part of Puget Power. In the 1890s, civil engineer Charles H. Baker saw Snoqualmie Falls, located about 25 miles east of Seattle, and drew plans to harness the power of the Snoqualmie River. Remarkably, construction on the Snoqualmie Falls Plant, the first completely underground electric generating facility in the world, was begun and completed in 1898. The plant's power-house contained four great water wheels and generators capable of delivering a total of 6,000 kilowatts. In 1905 and 1910, two other generating units were added. In 1992, 93 years after their initial start-up, the original generators were still producing their rated output of 6,000 kilowatts.

Surviving New Competition

Meanwhile, Dr. E.C. Kilbourne, a Seattle dentist, founded the Pacific Electric Light Company in 1890 when he saw the advantages of serving lighting and streetcar power loads on combined systems. Many individual companies and systems, providing combinations of power, lighting, and streetcar loads, sprang up, including 12 in Seattle alone. Nearly all of them were wiped out in the financial panic of 1893. To revive the fledgling utilities industry in the Pacific Northwest, Mitchell called upon Charles Augustus Stone and Edwin Sidney Webster, partners in a Boston-based operation that advised or operated troubled electric utilities and also financed, refinanced, or even acquired them.

Stone and Webster realized that the utilities industry not only needed reorganization but strong local leadership. They approached Jacob Furth, a prominent Seattle banker, and con-

---

---

vinced him to become president in 1900 of the newly formed Seattle Electric Company. The new enterprise not only consolidated all the surviving lighting, traction, and related subsidiary businesses in Seattle, but began to expand its interests throughout the Puget Sound region. In 1912, Seattle Electric incorporated as the Puget Sound Traction, Light & Power Company. Later the word "traction" was dropped from the name.

Between 1912 and 1920, eight more utility companies in the Puget Sound region were bought and integrated within the company. From 1920 to 1940, the utility pursued an aggressive policy of acquiring utility companies in central and estern Washington, and ten more were added. During the first 50 years, the succession of mergers and consolidations involved more than 150 companies.

Innovation, Industry Leadership, and the Depression

During this formative period, Puget Power became a leader in the utilities industry. In 1913 near Lynden, for example, the company constructed what is believed to be the first power line in the United States built specifically to serve farm customers. In 1925 at Puyallup, it established the Farm Power Laboratory, a unique research center where laborsaving uses of electricity on the farm could be demonstrated and promoted. Another first for Puget Power came in 1926 when it installed a cross-Sound submarine cable from Richmond Beach, north of Seattle, to President's Point, south of Kingston on the Kitsap Peninsula.

In 1928, Puget Power began construction of the Rock Island Dam on the Columbia River, one of the most ambitious projects in its history. The first four units were brought online in 1933 with a capacity of 80,000 kilowatts. Unfortunately, construction on the dam was started one year before the stock market crash and the onset of the Depression, distressing events that brought a downturn to the company's fortunes.

Beginning in the 1930s, Puget Power began to face a series of problems that challenged the very existence of the utility. Company morale was low, due in part to salary cuts and layoffs. In 1930 state voters passed the District Power Bill, which allowed the formation of county Public Utility Districts (PUDs) to enter the electricity distribution business. Puget Power had fought hard against the bill, fearing that its passage would inhibit the company's financing of new construction projects. Other problems included the city of Seattle's default on payments of the streetcar revenue bonds it had issued to Puget Power to purchase the system and the Bremerton City Council's declaration of its intention to take over Puget Power's distribution system at the expiration of the current franchise in 1931.

The Growing Public Power Movement

Puget Power's greatest challenge was disarming the growing public power movement, which sought to disenfranchise the utility. The rallying cry of Puget Power's opponents was "this God-given water power resource belongs to the people—not the utility barons." The utility countered in a public campaign that tried to show what it considered to be the unfairness of tax-subsidized government competition. Initially, the company had some success. Bremerton decided against a takeover of the Puget Power operation in its city and renewed the Puget Power franchise in 1931. PUD elections in Skagit, Whatcom, Snohomish, and Island Counties were defeated in 1932. Despite these victories, by 1936 13 counties had voted to form PUDs. With the company's service area and revenue base threatened, the utility found that financing new construction projects was extremely difficult.

The struggle between public-owned and investor-owned utilities was temporarily suspended during World War II because the federal government mandated power pooling to serve the huge war industry, but it quickly resumed as the war drew to a close. In November 1943 the Seattle City Council adopted a resolution to expand its power-generating capacity with the intention of taking over service to Puget Power's customers at the expiration of the company's 50-year franchise in 1952. In 1950, Seattle made a formal offer to purchase Puget Power. The company's board of directors accepted the proposal, which became Proposition C on the November 7, 1950, ballot.

The proposition was hotly debated. Puget Power President Frank McLaughlin supported it as the best alternative for the company, and he urged employees to join him in support. In the late 1940s, the utility had been forced to sell off perimeter territories and non-electric subsidiary operations. In 1948 perimeter electric utility properties (excluding power plants), constituting about 10 percent of the company's customer and revenue base, were sold to eight county PUDs, reducing the company to 40 percent of its previous holdings.

The vote was extremely close: 65,616 for yes; 64,892 for no. On March 5, 1952, McLaughlin signed the papers completing the sale at a purchase price of $26,834,232. Following the vote, six country PUDs offered to pay $89.5 million for all the company's remaining properties except for those in Whatcom County. Puget Power accepted a purchase agreement calling for final closing on February 27, 1953. The utility's future, however, became complicated when another utility, Washington Water Power, proposed a merger with Puget Power.

By now, a controversy had been ignited, as many Puget Power customers opposed any sale of Puget Power. On November 12, 1953, the utility's board of directors voted not to accept either proposal. When McLaughlin emerged from the meeting, he told the press, "Puget will remain in business!"

Need for More Power Supply Sources

During the political turmoil, a new challenge for the utility had emerged: because demand for electricity had continued to grow, the utility needed to catch up in power supply sources. Puget Power began to purchase distribution system areas in an effort to regain the 60 percent of its business it lost in the late 1940s. At the same time, the utility began to reverse its reputation of instability, acquired through its difficulties in the previous decade, which had become a key roadblock to major financing. In 1956, McLaughlin presented his board with a

Key Dates:

construction budget of about $20 million—double the previous year's and the biggest in 25 years. Work began in that year on the $27 million Upper Baker River development, which was expected to provide 110,000 kilowatts, and the expansion of the Lower Baker River dam by 70,000 kilowatts for an additional $8 million.

In 1960, the Washington Utilities and Transportation Commission granted Puget Power a 10 percent rate increase, the first increase in the company's history. Financially more stable, Puget Power experienced an impressive period of growth in the 1960s. The number of customers and per capita use of electricity increased significantly. During this period, the utility sought to develop innovations that would improve the quality of electric services and the value of the homes served. In addition to developing new field installation techniques, including underground system installation, Puget Power worked with the Federal Housing Administration (FHA) for recognition of appropriate increases in the value of houses incorporating these advances. In 1964 the utility helped the U.S. government enact a treaty with Canada that substantially increased the energy production capacities of Columbia River hydropower dams.

In the late 1960s, Puget Power began planning for a new age when it joined with other private utilities to construct several coal and nuclear plants. It joined two nuclear power projects in the early 1970s—the Skagit Nuclear Power Plant and the WPPSS Nuclear Project No. 3—as well as a joint venture with the Montana Power Company, to build two units of a coal-fired thermal power-generating station at Colstrip in southeastern Montana.

Oil Embargo during the 1970s

In 1973, Puget Power, like other utilities across the country, faced an unexpected crisis when the Organization of Petroleum Exporting Countries (OPEC) instituted an oil embargo. Fuel costs skyrocketed and the utility was forced to implement emergency customer rate increases. Over the next decade Puget's costs increased dramatically, plant completion schedules lengthened, and concern over nuclear power increased.

After an accident at the Three Mile Island Nuclear Power Plant in Pennsylvania in 1979, the planned construction of Puget Power's Pebble Springs and Skagit Nuclear Power Projects were canceled. Fortunately for the utility, a ruling by the Washington Supreme Court in December 1985 allowed the utility to recover most of its investment in the two canceled projects.

During the 1980s and into the 1990s, Puget Power was faced with two major national trends: the growth of the environmental movement and the rise of public participation in the development of utilities. The company implemented a series of conservation measures, including the ''Power Conservation'' program, which provided incentives for large industrial customers and schools to interrupt their loads when requested at daily high-load periods during the high-demand months during the winter.

Panel Gains National Attention

In 1980 the utility instituted what was then the largest customer involvement program in the country, forming a series of 13 customer advisory panels throughout its service territory to review company policies. The program has been nationally recognized, and many other utilities have adopted similar programs.

Successful Despite Recession

Despite the recession of the early 1990s, Puget Power maintained a sound financial footing: from 1987 to 1991, the company experienced a rate of customer growth twice that of the national average for all other utilities in the nation, and net income was up from $120 million in 1987 to $133 million in 1991. The economy of its service area, while not immune to national problems, remained vigorous, and it was expected that the growth in both customers and usage that the company had experienced in the past would continue.

Puget Sound Energy struggled with mergers, drought, high-energy costs and shifting economies, yet maintained its position as the largest utilities provider in Washington. In a costly 1997 merger, Puget Sound Energy (PSE), was created by uniting Puget Sound Power & Light Co. with Washington Energy Co. After paying over $36 million in after-tax charges the company's net income dropped approximately 60 percent.

Technology Advancement

In 1999, PSE made wide strides in technology by installing meters that communicate with each other over a wireless network system. This proves to be cost efficient to consumers who can now access timely information regarding their energy use and prices. Another savvy move PSE made that year was to buy the PURPA Plant, which is a natural gas-fired co-generation plant that reduced their annual power cost by 17 percent.

In December 1999, PSE completed the year by being ranked one of the ten most efficiently run utility companies in the nation. *Electric Light & Power* magazine awarded this accolade based on quality customer relations and consistently low energy bills.

PSE lost one of it's biggest industrial clients, The Boeing Co., in the summer of 2001. Boeing wouldn't agree to pay daily market prices for power and PSE argued that if they gave Boeing a fixed-rate plan instead, they'd have to raise rates for residential customers. After a legal battle with PSE, Boeing discontinued their contract after 88 years.

The resilient energy company resumed its leader status with the inception of their Time-of-Day Rate Plan, in 2001. This innovative plan allows the consumer, either over the Internet or by calling the customer call center, to access pricing information daily which encourages energy use during cost-efficient times of day. The technological advancement and high efficiency of the program, which is included in the national energy policy, garnered PSE the "2001 Utility of the Year" from *Electric Light & Power* magazine.

Corporate Responsibility

Although their net income dropped from the previous year's $184.8 million to $98.4 million for 2001, and its credit rating was reduced to junk bond status by Wall Street in 2002, PSE stayed optimistic that their new CEO, Steve Reynolds, would turn things around. Reynolds expressed a commitment to make the company profitable and change the public's lackluster perception of PSE as well.

Aspects of the energy business that are consistent are the fluctuating weather, stock market, net income, and public opinion. Aware of changing conditions, over the years Puget Sound Energy has moved toward corporate responsibility and goodwill with programs such as their creation of "fish taxis" which enabled the almost extinct sockeye salmon to maneuver safely around hydroelectric projects.

PSE employees established TreeWatch, a program that removes trees that have the potential to fall during rainstorms. The removal of specific trees causes less danger and fewer power outages. Although PSE had laid off 500 employees, the company expected the remainder of 2002 to be profitable due to the hydroelectric system returning to a normal water level, unlike the previous year's drought. Reynolds stated that PSE is in good shape until 2004 for electricity generation and has expressed plans to "improve relations with the community, employees, customers, and investors. We need to be more collaborative."

Principal Competitors

PacifiCorp; Avista; Portland General Electric.

Further Reading

"Puget Sound Energy Leads the Pack in Demand Side Management," *Electric Light & Power*, December 2001.

"Puget Sound Energy Scores High in Service Quality While Positioning for Solid Growth," *Electric Light & Power*, September 2000.

"Tacoma, Wash., Area May Buy Water from Lake Owned by Puget Sound Energy," *News Tribune*, January 14, 2002.

"Washington State Allows Electric Utility to Extend Time-of-Day Rate Plan," *Seattle Times*, September 27, 2001.

Wing, Robert C., et al., *A Century of Service: The Puget Power Story*, Puget Sound Power and Light Company, 1987.

—Ron Chepesiuk
—update: Laura Rodriguez-Lowery

RAILTRACK

Railtrack Group PLC

Railtrack House, Euston Square
London NW1 2EE
United Kingdom
Phone: +44 (20) 7557-8000
Fax: +44 (20) 7557-9000
Website: http://www.railtrack-group.co.uk

Public Company
Established: 1996 as a privatized company
Employees: 11,776 (2001)
Sales: £1.797 billion (2002)
Stock Exchanges: London
Ticker Symbol: RTK
NAIC: 482111 Line-Haul Railroads; 488210 Support
   Activities for Rail Transportation; 485112 Commuter
   Rail Systems

Railtrack Group PLC (Railtrack) has become synonymous with the troubles that the United Kingdom has faced with the privatization of its rail network. When Railtrack was privatized in 1996 by the British government, the weight of controlling the country's rails rested entirely on its shoulders. While the company has had its ups and downs, in October 2001, against the protestations and counterproposals of Railtrack and its board of directors, the transport secretary of the United Kingdom placed Railtrack PLC, the main subsidiary of Railtrack Group, into railway administration, allegedly due to the company's inability to pay its accrued debt. By this action, the government removed control of Railtrack PLC from Railtrack Group. In its 2002 annual report, Railtrack Group classified Railtrack PLC as a discontinued operation.

A Private Company Is Born

After years of debating how, why, and when they would privatize British Rail, the U.K. Government decided, in 1994, to go ahead with a plan for privatizing the company. The government reorganized and fragmented out different areas of British Rail's responsibilities, creating four main component parts: track, rolling stock, maintenance, and train operators. The old railway companies Regional Railways, Network SouthEast, and InterCity were abolished and replaced with 25 train-operating units. The railway infrastructure (the track) was placed under the control of the newly formed, government-owned Railtrack. During 1995 and 1996 the government fell behind on their privatization schedule, and the U.K. Transport Secretary Sir George Young was concerned that the planned sell-off of Railtrack would be undermined by the slipping timetable. Sir George Young was further concerned when financial advisors stated that the success of the planned privatization rested largely on the success of Railtrack's successful privatization. Although the original plan had been for the government to sell Railtrack after all of the other rail franchises were sold and the operating companies had proven themselves, the government pushed Railtrack's sell date up to 1996. The estimated time schedule for selling Railtrack had originally been set at 2000.

In January 1996 the U.K. government confirmed the privatization of Railtrack. In October of the same year, Railtrack announced a plan to invest £1.5 billion in upgrading the West Coast Mainline railway. During its first year as a private company, Railtrack experienced its first of many deadly train crashes when in August 1996 a commuter train collided with an empty train, killing one person and injuring 66.

The Golden Years

Throughout 1997 and 1998, Railtrack entered into agreements with other rail companies, announced large-scale projects aimed at improving the rail network, and won important contracts. Some of these projects and contracts included: in January 1997, the company outlined a £560 million project called the Thameslink 2000; the following month, Railtrack unveiled a £15 billion plan to create the world's most efficient rail network; the company came to an agreement with Virgin Rail (Virgin) to an upgrade package that enabled Virgin to operate high-speed trains on certain intercity routes, and later, joined a partnership with Virgin wherein they promised to invest £600 million in the West Coast Mainline.

The company's expansion streak continued when, in 1988, Railtrack along with the U.K. government and London and Continental Railways (LCR), agreed to a public private partner-

---

Company Perspectives:

Our vision is the delivery of a safe, reliable, efficient, modern railway for our customers and the nation, using our railway skills to grow the company to reward our stakeholders and employees. We are making constant progress in improving operating performance, in delivering investment and in accommodating growth.

---

ship (PPP) deal to save the proposed Channel Tunnel project. The PPP involved the management of Eurostar (an LCR service that was intended to supply income while the railroad link was being constructed), based on the restructuring of LCR. This deal led to Railtrack's 1999 participation in the design, construction, finance, and operation of The Channel Tunnel Rail Link (CTRL). The CTRL was designed to carry high-speed services between London and the Channel Tunnel. The details of the CTRL deal enabled Railtrack to manage the construction of the CTRL, as well as assume responsibility for the operational management of the first phase of the project's infrastructure. As a result of their participation, Railtrack was granted the opportunity to purchase the entire new link upon completion of the project, although part of the plan was that the ownership of the link would eventually (in 2086) revert to the U.K. government.

Along with the partnerships and deals that Railtrack entered into during this period, they also experienced disaster in the form of one major train crash in 1997. Seven people were killed when an express passenger train crashed into a good train in a London suburb.

Government Dissatisfaction with Railtrack

Only two years after Railtrack's privatization, the company began to receive chastisement from the government for its failure to suitably upkeep the country's rail network. In December 1998, Rail Regulator Chris Bolt outlined a proposal that would cut future Railtrack profits and demand increased investment in the rail network; this proposal was scheduled to come into effect in 2001. The following year, an official report criticized Railtrack heavily for its failure to remedy train delays, run-down stations and out-of-date signaling. Soon after this report was released, the new Rail Regulator Tom Winsor informed Railtrack that if it did not improve passenger train performance by 12.7 percent by March 2000, the company would be fined from its profits. In November 1999, Tom Winsor began enforcement action against Railtrack for its failure to upgrade the West Coast Mainline as it had previously agreed to.

The chastisement did not have a noticeable effect on Railtrack. Indeed, not one month after the rail regulator started the process of enforcement, Railtrack announced that the cost of upgrading the West Coast Mainline would be almost three times the original estimate. This same year, a syndicate of 19 banks provided Railtrack with a £1 billion syndicated loan to rescue them from their monetary woes. Train crashes continued to occur, despite the government's attempt to goad Railtrack into improving rail safety, and in 1999 two trains collided outside London killing 31 people and injuring 400.

New Contracts

In February 2000, Railtrack signed a £98 billion public private partnership (PPP) with Tyne and Wear Passenger Transport Executive (Nexus) to develop the Sunderland Metro system. Railtrack undertook the design, construction, testing, and commissioning of the Northeast England network, including the parts of the network that connected to the Metro. Railtrack also agreed to build additional stations along the lines' extensions. Railtrack invested £40 million, Nexus provided £8 million, the European Regional Development Fund provided £12 million, and the central government invested £35 million.

In light of the number of accidents and difficult incidents that many of Railtrack's employees came into contact with, in March 2000 the company decided to consolidate the many different employee assistance providers and offer all of their employees assistance from one provider: Care First. Peter Turner, head of Railtrack's Compensation and Benefits department, said, "We were primarily concerned about the mental health of staff. Some staff come into contact with difficult incidents [and] some will never feel able to open up to people they are working with."

The Train Wreck That Changed the Company

On October 17, 2000, a broken rail caused a passenger train to derail near Hatfield; four people were killed and 34 were injured. The emergency recovery program that followed the crash cost Railtrack £644 million. Soon after the train wreck, in February 2001, Railtrack's Chief Executive Steve Marshall warned that Railtrack could have a net debt of approximately £8 billion come 2003. Marshall, in an article in the *Parliamentary House Magazine*, spoke of the "huge engineering consequences" of the Hatfield crash and the need for Railtrack to "rebuild and refocus our engineering function." Marshall also said that, "In the future the company will be seeking out partnerships which offer mutual benefits. My message to the industry is that they are very welcome to come to the party, but I want to be sure that they will bring a bottle. In the bottle should certainly be some money, some new ideas and some relevant skills would be even more welcome." He then added, "We are very clear that we have to put our house in order. We are up for partnership, but it has to be safe, it has to be operationally practical and it hinges on people's ability to share in the risks as well as the rewards."

The Downward Spiral Begins

On April 2, 2001, the government announced that it would give Railtrack an advance subsidy of £1.5 billion for sustaining the rail network. Along with this good news, the government announced some bad news; Railtrack would not get the originally agreed-upon option to build and then purchase a particularly "socially desirable" section of the CTRL line because of the company's past failings. Instead the government handed the project over to the Bechtel Group, a U.S. construction and project management company that had played a large role in rescuing the Channel Tunnel project. This announcement changed Railtrack's position in the U.K. Rail Network scheme; the company was no longer the only provider of rail infrastructure, and had lost out on the chance to earn unregulated profits on certain new ventures.

Key Dates:

1996: Railtrack, the government-owned operator of the British rail track network, is privatized.

1997: Railtrack unveils a £15 billion plan to create the world's most efficient rail network; and Virgin Rail group invests £600 million in Railtrack's West Coast Mainline.

1998: Railtrack wins the contract to manage construction of the Channel Tunnel Rail Link (CTRL).

1999: The rail regulator begins penalizing Railtrack for its failure to upgrade the West Coast Mainline.

2000: A passenger train derails (due to a broken rail) near Hatfield, killing four and injuring 34 people.

2001: The U.K. transport secretary petitions the High Court to place Railtrack PLC in railway administration; Railtrack Group requests the immediate suspension of trading in Railtrack Group shares.

2002: Railtrack Group receives offers from Network Rail and London and Continental Railways Ltd. (LCR) to acquire Railtrack PLC, Railtrack's interest in Section 1 link between the Channel Tunnel and London, the rights to operate the completed link, and the concession to manage St. Pancras Station in North-Central London.

At about this time, Railtrack announced that post-Hatfield repairs would cost well over the original estimate of £500 million; the actual post-Hatfield repairs would reach approximately £3 billion. Due in part to the Hatfield crash, on May 24, 2001, Railtrack posted a wider-than-expected full-year loss, £559 million (US$791 million) pre-tax in the year to March. The loss was attributed to penalty charges for late-running trains, and the cost of track repairs.

The Begg Paper

In light of the country's dissatisfaction with the state of the rail network, David Begg, chairman of the commission for Integrated Transport, and Jon Shaw, a transport economist, wrote a paper that recommended fundamental restructuring of the railways and network. They recommended that five regional train-operating companies be responsible for both train and track operations, and called for a review of the way the industry was regulated. David Begg also argued that the incentive structure that had been originally instituted with the privatization of the railways was flawed in that it gave Railtrack little incentive to invest in efficiency or growth. The paper came at a time when the government was forced to make a decision—many of the biggest train-operating companies franchises were due to be renewed in the coming months, and the franchises (as well as the country and the government) needed to know what was going to happen to the industry.

Railtrack Enters Administration

One year after the fatal Hatfield crash, Secretary of State for Transportation Stephen Byer, taking into consideration Railtrack's lack of success and fueled by the findings in the Begg paper, requested that Railtrack be placed into administration (the equivalent of receivership in the United States). Management of Railtrack PLC was removed from the Railtrack PLC board after the government refused to provide the requested £2 billion for emergency funding. The accountancy firm Ernst & Young LLP was chosen to be the administrator and reports said that a government-owned, nonprofit organization could eventually take over Railtrack's assets. This twist of events sent Railtrack shareholders into a tailspin; their shares had declined in value previously, but this unexpected turn of events had made their worth disappear altogether. Byer said that, ''Any shareholder payback will be a decision for the administrators. There will be no government money to bail out shareholders.'' The government would, however, guarantee the company's existing debts.

The day after the administration was announced, Railtrack CEO Steve Marshall resigned stating that the government had broken its commitments in a ''shoddy and unacceptable'' manner. The rating agencies, Moody's Investor Service and Standard & Poor's both responded to the administration announcement by downgrading Railtrack's credit rating. On this same day, a spokesperson for Railtrack announced that the company was considering legal action to force the administrators to hand over the £350 million that was frozen upon administration. The company argued that the money withheld belonged not to Railtrack PLC, but to its parent company Railtrack Group PLC. The government quickly agreed to return the money requested. The government also agreed to allow Railtrack the opportunity to borrow against that money. Railtrack at this point also put up a fight to regain rights to build the extension to the CTRL.

On October 11, 2001, the government announced that, although it had said it would not bail out Railtrack shareholders, it would enable the investors to get back 25 percent of their investments in the company. Railtrack employees, who were also shareholders, felt the acute pain of administration and issued this statement: ''Our staff feel as though they were mugged. Lots of people have used the share plan to provide for their future, whether it be for their retirement, paying off mortgages or their sons' and daughters' weddings. They feel that their good honest toil has been stolen.'' The company itself feared that the staff's discontent over their loss of investment would cause some of its 12,000 staff members to leave the company. The government during this time, stood firm, stating, ''The Government feels responsible to the traveling public. It respects, admires and appreciates the great work that many of the staff in the railways do, but when it comes to compensation, the Government has made its position clear.'' That position was that they were not willing to pay taxpayers' money into the bank accounts of shareholders in what was a private company. It turned out that Railtrack's concern about fleeing staff was well founded as the staff exited the company in droves.

After the company was placed into administration, contrary to government's expectations that the railways would continue to run normally, the state of the rail network deteriorated rapidly—there was a 46 percent increase in delays in the first two months since Railtrack went bust. Railtrack shareholders sued the government with the claim that the company was forced into administration not because of its failures, but for political reasons.

Railtrack Group PLC Moves On

With Railtrack PLC in administration, Railtrack Group PLC went about doing their best to conduct business-as-usual with its remaining contracts and responsibilities. The company's media agents, Maiden Outdoor invited publishing organizations to pitch for the exclusive London newspaper contract that was in the hands of Metro until the spring of 2002. The group published a paper that was distributed across Railtrack's network of stations in the United Kingdom, which, according to Maiden, delivered to an audience of around 8 million a week. Also in 2001, Railtrack signed a partnering agreement with United Switch & Signal Inc. to build and install a Network Mangement Centre System for Railtrack's West Coast Route Modernization Program; AEC-ACO won a $16 million order to supply 490 new Railtrack maintenance cars with it's advanced Axle Motion III suspension system; and optic-cable manufacturer Brand-Rex was approved to be Railtrack's sole supplier of thermoplastic signaling cable. To follow through on their commitment to upkeep the West Coast Main Line, Railtrack contracted GT Railway Maintenance to maintain the 418-mile southern section of the Line's infrastructure.

Railtrack in 2002

After much investigation it was revealed that Secretary of State for Transportation Stephen Byers' decision to place Railtrack into administration was indeed questionable. Byer rescinded his statement that, "There will be no taxpayers' money made available to support shareholders." Under the new plan, taxpayers ended up paying shareholders £300 million, and were liable for a further £200 million through a government-supported loan that was used to pay shareholders. The four banks that were chosen to refinance the Railtrack £4.4 billion debt were Barclays, Dresdner Kleinwort Wasserstein, Merrill Lynch, and Royal Bank of Scotland.

In March 2002, Railtrack received several bids on their troubled assets. The first bid came from Network Rail, a nonprofit company set up by the government in the wake of Railtrack's placement in administration, who offered £500 million for the assets of Railtrack PLC, plus the assumption of its liabilities. Several days later, a consortium called London and Continental Railways Ltd (LCR) offered £295 million for Railtrack Group's interest in the Section 1 link between the Channel Tunnel and London and another offer from Network

Rail of £80 million to operate the Channel Tunnel rail link and manage the St. Pancras Station in North-Central London. At the time of this writing, these offers were under review by the Railtrack Group board.

Principal Subsidiaries

Railtrack PLC; Railtrack UK.

Principal Competitors

Bechtel Group Inc.

Further Reading

Ascarelli, Silvia, "U.K. Government Throws a 25 Percent Bone to Railtrack Investors. Shareholders Hire Counsel, but Don't Comment on Offer," *Wall Street Journal* (Europe), October 11, 2001, p.13.

Board, Laura, "Two Bids Arrive for Railtrack Assets," *The Deal.com*, April 2, 2002, http://www.thedeal.com.

"End of the Line? Railtrack; Railtrack's Troubles," *The Economist*, April 7, 2001, p. 6.

"A Great Train Crash: Britain Railways Are Still Worth Privatizing," *The Economist*, January 21, 1995, p. 20.

"Mess on the Rails, Continued; Railtrack; More Trouble for Railtrack," *The Economist*, June 9, 2001, p.5.

Moreira, Peter, "Railtrack Bondholders May Suffer," *The Deal.com*, October 9, 2001, http://www.thedeal.com.

——, "Railtrack Gains Access to Some Funds," *The Deal.com*, October 10, 2001, http://www.thedeal.com.

——, "Railtrack's Future Remains Unclear," *The Deal.com*, October 8, 2001, http://www.thedeal.com.

——, "U.K.'s Railtrack Enters Receivership," *The Deal.com*, October 7, 2001, http://www.thedeal.com.

"Railtrack Appoints Single EAP Provider," *Employee Benefits*, March 2000, p. 8.

"Railtrack Could Have 8 bln stlg Net Debt by 2003, CEO Says," *Futures World News*, February 22, 2001.

"Railtrack Signs £98m Sunderland Metro Project," *Project Finance*, February 2000, p. 7.

Sames, Claire, "15 to 20 Publishers Pitch for Maiden Contract," *Media Business*, December 17, 2001, p.2.

"U.K. Private Sale: CTRL," *Privatisation International*, February 1999.

Willmott, Ben, "Staff Anger over Share Hijack," *Personnel Today*, November 13, 2001, p.1.

—Tammy Weisberger

Real Turismo, S.A. de C.V.

Dante 14
Mexico City, D.F. 11590
Mexico
Telephone: (525) 203-3113
Fax: (525) 250-4669
Toll Free: (800) 7-CAMINO or (888) 882-7325
Web site: http://www.caminoreal.com

Wholly Owned Subsidiary of Grupo Empresarial Angeles
Incorporated: 1980 as Casamar, Bienes Raices y
   Turismo, S.A. de C.V.
Sales: 958.86 million pesos (US$96.62 million) (1999)
NAIC: 721110 Hotels & Motels

Real Turismo, S.A. de C.V. is the operator of the Camino Real chain of Mexican luxury-class hotels. Camino Real is the third-largest Mexican-owned hotel chain and the longest in continuous operation. Real Turismo is a subsidiary of Grupo Empresarial Angeles, a privately owned conglomerate.

Growing Hotel Chain: 1959–1987

The first Camino Real hotel made its debut in Guadalajara in 1959. The owners were Jose Brockmann (or Brockman) Obregon and a group of local investors. The following year, Brockman formed a partnership with the U.S. company Western Hotels Inc., which soon changed its name to Western International Hotels Inc. (WIH) and then later to Westin Hotel Co. Western invested in the building and acquisition of other Camino Real hotels, taking a stake as high as 44 percent in what was named Western Hotels of Mexico (and, in 1963, Western International Hotels of Mexico). With Brockman at the helm, WIH built a Camino Real in Tampico in 1963, in Ciudad Juarez and Saltillo in 1965, and in Tapachula in 1967.

The enterprise's flagship was the 709-room Camino Real in Mexico City, constructed in 1968 to serve as the host hotel during the Summer Olympic Games held in the capital that year. It was built on 7.5 acres near Chapultepec Park at a cost of US$14 million and included duplex suites, each overlooking a private garden, a 570-car garage, a ballroom big enough to hold 1,500 people, four restaurants, seven bars, and two clubs. Also in 1968, WIH acquired a Guatemala City hotel that was converted into a Camino Real. Other Camino Real hotels were erected in Puerto Vallarta in 1969, Chapala in 1970, Mazatlan in 1971, San Salvador, El Salvador, in 1972, and Cancun in 1975. A hotel was acquired in Cabo San Lucas in 1970 and turned into another Camino Real. The company also assumed management of Acapulco's swank Las Brisas in 1976. Some of these ventures did not survive long in the chain: the Ciudad Juarez and Tapachula units were terminated in 1974 and the Cabo San Lucas and Chapala ones in 1975. Another beach-resort Camino Real was completed, in Ixtapa in 1981, and the Camino Real chain also constructed and opened the Galeria Plaza in Mexico City.

Banco Nacional de Mexico (Banamex), Mexico's largest bank, was providing much of the capital and held majority control of the chain by 1982, when the collapse of the national currency—the peso—resulted in the nationalization of Mexican banks. At this time, there were 12 hotels in the Camino Real roster, some of which were 100 percent owned by Banamex, others in which it held a minority of shares, and still others in which it had no stake at all.

During the following years, the holders of shares in Banamex received compensation from the government and used some of these credits to maintain a stake in the enterprise, which had been incorporated as Casamar in 1980. The Legorreta group, which had included major shareholders in Banamex, was especially prominent in this regard. In 1987, the enterprise was reorganized under a new holding company called Grupo Camino Real. At the end of that year, this group sold about 10 percent of its common stock on the Bolsa de Valores Mexicanos, Mexico City's stock exchange, collecting about US$20.55 million. The group had a five-year plan that called for an investment of US$300 million to add 5,000 rooms to the chain, building a new 500-room hotel in Cancun and others in the beach resorts of Cozumel, Huatulco, Los Cabos, and Puerto Vallarta. Starting more modestly, however, the chain began a program of adding 86 rooms to its existing Cancun hotel and constructing 76 more at its existing hotel in Puerto Vallerta. The company also was maintaining its affiliation with Western In-

Key Dates:

1959: The first Camino Real hotel opens in Guadalajara.
1960: Western International Hotels invests in the creation of other Camino Real hotels.
1968: Opening of the Mexico City Camino Real, the chain's flagship.
1982: The Camino Real chain opens its twelfth hotel.
1987: The enterprise goes public as Grupo Camino Real.
1989: The chain is controlled by a private holding company, Real Turismo.
1998: Following a banking scandal, a government agency obtains title to the chain.
2000: Grupo Empresarial Angeles purchases the hotels at auction.

ternational (now Westin Hotels & Resorts) under a 10-year contract signed in 1983. Also in 1983, Camino Real had acquired ownership of a hotel in Villahermosa that had formerly been a Holiday Inn.

Changing Hands Several Times: 1987–2000

Grupo Camino Real, still Mexico's largest luxury-class chain, recorded revenues of 211.88 billion pesos (about US$92.5 million) and earnings of 75.97 billion pesos (about US$33.2 million) during fiscal 1988 (the year ended August 31, 1988). Some of this money came not from owned hotels but from operating the Las Hadas resort hotel in Manzanillo (which the group purchased about this time), operating the Ambassador Hotel in Monterrey and Camino Real hotels the group no longer owned in Mazatlan and Saltillo, and from technical-assistance contracts with the hotels operating under the Camino Real name in El Salvador and Guatemala. By 1989, Grupo Camino Real had come under the control of two pairs of brothers—Israel and Pablo Brener and Moises and Anselmo (or Antonio) Cosio—and had been placed in a holding company named Real Turismo, S.A. de C. V., which also had other interests in the tourist sector.

The relationship quickly soured, and in early 1990, after months of bitter struggle, the Breners and Cosios split their holdings. The Breners retained the Real Turismo name, 10 Camino Real hotels—8 of them affiliated with Westin—and Las Hadas. The Cosios received the Camino Real in Ixtapa, Mexico City's Galeria Plaza, and management of Las Brisas. Real Turismo was operating nine Camino Real hotels in 1992, when it purchased the landmark 375-room Paso del Norte Hotel in El Paso, Texas, just a few blocks north of the Mexican border, and renamed it the Camino Real El Paso.

Expansion of the Camino Real chain continued in the 1990s, with hotels added in Acapulco (1993), Cuernavaca (1993, a former estate of Woolworth heiress Barbara Hutton), Tuxtla Gutierrez (1994), Chihuahua (1996), and Tijuana (1996). The company also purchased a Stouffer Presidente hotel in what had once been Oaxaca's Convento de Santa Catalina, converting it into a Camino Real in 1994, and Puebla's Convento de la Concepcion into another one in 1996. In 1996, the chain consisted of

14 hotels with 3,324 rooms, 2,351 employees, and revenues that year of 569.19 million pesos (US$73.41 million). However, the company had gone through numerous and wrenching changes. When Zonura Compania Hotelera, headed by Alvaro Lopez Castro, bought it around 1993, only the hotels in Mexico City and Guadalajara were profitable. Eighty-five percent of the purchase price came in the form of short-term credits from a consortium of seven Mexican banks, and the chain was spending another $30 million to remodel the four oldest properties in the system. The units in Cancun and Puerto Vallarta lowered their rates up to 20 percent in an attempt to capture a larger market share. Camino Real's affiliation with Westin was dissolved.

New Ownership: 2000–2002

The currency crisis and peso devaluation of December 1994 resulted in the failure of many Mexican enterprises and the banks that had been financing them. Banco Union, which held the Camino Real assets, went bankrupt after a banker allegedly embezzled as much as US$700 million before fleeing Mexico. The hotel chain fell into the hands of a government agency that did not succeed in divesting it until 2000, when most of the hotels were sold at auction to a private conglomerate called Grupo Empresarial Angeles for US$255 million. For this price, the buyers received many of the 16 Camino Real hotels, including a 22 percent stake in the Saltillo unit, and the assumption of the contracts to operate the hotels in Cuernavaca, Huatulco, and Oaxaca. It chose not to include the Camino Real in Mazatlan or the Las Hadas unit in Manzanillo. The operating unit for the chain was renamed Real Turismo.

These hotels were nominally five-star luxury lodgings, but under government administration they did not receive adequate funding and deteriorated in quality. As a result, the chain had to lower its rates for its most expensive rooms from about 1,800 pesos (about US$190) to an average of 1,100 pesos (about US$115). In 1999, the chain had an average occupancy rate of 62 percent and recorded an operating profit of US$24 million. Grupo Empresarial Angeles, which was already in the lodging business by virtue of its hospitals, was hoping to create synergies of operation by such means as contracting for the hotel chain's furniture and electrical apparatus through the furniture stores that were also owned by the group and by centralizing purchasing, inventories, and accounts receivable.

A US$48 million remodeling program was undertaken with, in the initial stages, the rooms, restaurants, bars, public areas, and recreational areas of the Cancun, Guadalajara, Mexico City, and Puerto Vallarta properties. Ricardo Legorreta, the architect of the Cancun and Mexico City hotels, was charged with the task of refitting the units within a unified architectural and decorative concept. Some US$19 million of that sum was earmarked for the Mexico City and Guadalajara hotels. The bulk of the US$14 million spent on the Mexico City Camino Real went for rooms upgraded with Internet hookups, work desks with ergonomic chairs and task lighting, and dual-line telephones. The hotel also opened two new restaurants, one featuring Spanish cuisine and the other a steakhouse. The Guadalajara makeover included replacement of the hotel's facade and a new business center and health club. The Puerto Vallarta unit received two restaurants and the Cancun one new meeting rooms and a new swimming pool for the exclusive use of guests staying in the more expensive Camino Real Club rooms.

The Camino Real hotels closed the year 2000 with an impressive list of honors from the travel industry. *Conde Nast Traveler* named the Cancun and Puerto Vallarta units to its Gold List of the best places in the world to stay. *Travel & Leisure* named the Puerto Vallarta unit among the top 25 destinations in the Americas other than the United States and Canada. Each Camino Real property scored ''excellent'' on more than 90 percent of the surveys filled out by vacationers for Apple Vacations. In 2001, Hilton Hotels Corp. signed an agreement with Hoteles Camino Real to affiliate 14 Camino Real hotels and resorts with the Hilton family of brands. The Camino Real hotels became active participants in the Hilton Honors guest-reward program, receiving sales and reservations support from Hilton Sales Worldwide and Hilton Reservations Worldwide offices around the globe.

The Camino Real hotels consisted at the time of the following: Acapulco, 157 rooms; Cancun, 391 rooms; Cuernavaca, 163 rooms; El Paso, 359 rooms; Guadalajara, 205 rooms; Huatulco, 120 rooms; Mexico City, 709 rooms; Oaxaca, 91 rooms; Puebla, 83 rooms; Puerto Vallarta, 83 rooms; Saltillo, 140 rooms; Tijuana, 250 rooms; Tuxtla Gutierrez, 210 rooms; and Villahermosa, 197 rooms. By the spring of 2002 another Camino Real resort hotel had been added, at Loreto, in Baja California Sur.

Hoteles Camino Real announced plans in 2001 to introduce a chain of limited-services hotels in secondary cities throughout Mexico. These hotels would target business travelers, with all rooms featuring dual-line phones, voice mail, fax machines, data ports, and work desks. The first of these Camino Real Ejecutivo hotels, a 137-room unit in or just north of Mexico City, was scheduled to open in December 2002. Four more were planned, including hotels in Guadalajara, Saltillo, and Torreon. It was believed that as many as 10 of these hotels could be in operation within three years.

Real Turismo's revenues fell from 994.92 million pesos (US$103.34 million) in 1998 to 958.86 million pesos (US$99.62 million) in 1999. Net profit fell from 108.19 million pesos (US$11.24 million) to 32.82 million pesos (US$3.41 million). Of the 1999 revenue, rooms accounted for 51 per cent; food and drink, 35 percent; other departments of operation, 7 percent; and operations for third parties and other revenues, 7 percent.

Principal Subsidiaries

Camino Real Guadalajara, S.A. de C. V.; Camino Real Mexico, S.A. de C.V. (96 percent); Camino Real Puerto Vallarta, S.A. de C.V. (98%); Caribe Resorts, S.A. de C. V.; Casanueva Inmobiliaria, S.A. de C. V.; Controladora Hotelera Acapulco, S.A. de C. V.; Controladora Hotelera Ixtapa, S.A. de C. V.; Desarrollos Turisticos del Pacifico, S.A. de C. V.; Hotel Camino Real Cancun, S.A. de C.V. (79%); Hotel Paso del Norte, Inc. (United States); Hoteles Camino Real, S.A. de C. V.; Inmobiliaria y Promotora Cancun, S.A. de C.V. (59%); Promociones C R, S.A. de C.V.

Principal Competitors

Grupo Posadas, S.A. de C. V.; Hoteles Presidente.

Further Reading

Alisau, Patricia, ''Hotel Giant Divides and Restructures,'' *Business Mexico,* December 1990, pp. 55–57.
Austin, Amanda A., ''Camino Real Seeks Stability After Rocky Year,'' *Hotel & Motel Management,* March 21, 1994, pp. 4, 32.
Bernstein, Lynne, ''Like a Prayer,'' *Travel Agent,* July 10, 1995, p. 66.
Budd, Jim, ''Mexicana, Real Turismo Set Major Expansion Plans, *Travel Weekly,* June 18, 1990, pp. 38, 43.
——, ''Real Turismo Eyes Role as Major Force in Mexico Travel Industry,'' *Travel Weekly,* May 1, 1989, p. 28.
''Camino Real Hotels Will Join the Hilton Family of Brands as Hilton Hotels Corporation Signs Affiliate Agreement With Hoteles Camino Real,'' *PR Newswire,* January 17, 2001 (on ProQuest database).
Copeland, Sid. *The Story of Western International Hotels.* Seattle: Western International Hotels, 1976.
Darling, Juanita, ''Mexican Company Is Buying Hotel in El Paso,'' *Los Angeles Times,* October 19, 1992, p. D2.
''El deslizamiento no facilita las cosas,'' *Expansion,* June 6, 1984, pp. 39, 41.
Flores Vega, Ernesto, ''Camino Real en el sendero bursatil,'' *Expansion,* October 12, 1988, pp. 87, 90, 92–93.
——, ''Los caminos de Real Turismo,'' *Expansion,* March 15, 1989, pp. 41–45.
King, Ralph, Jr., ''Mexican Contrarian,'' *Forbes,* September 4, 1989, pp. 288, 296.
''New Digs for Travelers,'' *Travel Weekly,* July 8, 2002, p. 18.
Reyes, Jorge Luis, ''Los Camino Real en terepia intensiva,'' *Expansion,* August 30, 2000, pp. 74–75, 77–79.
Rozenberg, Dino, ''Camino Real: Un largo camino,'' *Expansion,* July 6, 1994, pp. 80, 82.
Sidron, Jorge, ''Camino Real Plans New Brand,'' *Travel Weekly,* February 22, 2001, p. 4.
——, ''New Owner Refreshes a 'Stale' Camino Real,'' *Travel Weekly,* October 30, 2000, p. 54.
Zevallos, Victor R., ''Camino Real,'' *Architectural Forum,* November 1968, pp. 87, 89–90.

—Robert Halasz

The Reynolds and Reynolds Company

115 South Ludlow Street
Dayton, Ohio 45402
U.S.A.
Telephone: (937) 485-2000
Toll Free: (888) 473-9739
Fax: (937) 449-4213
Web site: http://www.reyrey.com

Public Company
Incorporated: 1889
Employees: 4,763 (2001 est.)
Sales: $1.004 billion (2001)
Stock Exchanges: New York
Ticker Symbol: REY
NAIC: 541512 Computer Systems Design Services

The Reynolds and Reynolds Company is one of the world's leading information management companies. Reynolds and Reynolds primarily serves the automotive industry, supplying them with software and services to manage a variety of operations, including parts procurement, retail and management enterprise systems, customer loyalty programs, document management, sales force education, accounting, leasing services, and the installation and maintenance of computer hardware and software. Reynolds and Reynolds also sells printed business forms, provides information technology consulting and training services, and offers integrated document solutions that combine paper and electronic capabilities. Reynolds and Reynolds also supplies document management services to companies outside of the automotive industry. Reynolds and Reynolds' success is due largely to their ability to expand with technology, offering their customers cutting-edge resources and ensuring that the tools they introduce are integrated seamlessly into their customers' business practices.

The Formative Years: 1866–1960

In 1866, Lucius D. Reynolds, a former Bellefontaine, Ohio, newspaper publisher, and his brother-in-law, James R. Gardner founded Gardner and Reynolds. The company made ledgers with removable carbon to allow originals and copies to be made simultaneously. Only one year later, Gardner sold his portion of the company to Lucius' father, Ira Reynolds, changing the firm's name to Reynolds and Reynolds. In 1869, Ira patented a system for duplicating sales books that utilized an inserted carbon leaf, and a removable and reusable hardcover.

The company's big break came when they won a contract in 1927 to produce business forms and paper-based accounting systems for Chevrolet's nationwide dealerships. The organization of data that Reynolds and Reynolds achieved while working this contract helped Chevrolet to overtake Ford in the marketplace. This success led Reynolds to establish an automotive division and set the wheels in motion for their becoming the major supplier of business forms to the entire automobile dealer market. The next ten years were spent expanding Reynolds and Reynolds' reach; they were busy opening sales offices across the United States. In 1939, when the Richard Hallam Grant family bought controlling interest in Reynolds and Reynolds, the company's ties to the automobile industry were strengthened; R.H. Grant, Sr., had played a leading role in General Motors' rise in the automobile market. At this point, 19 Reynolds and Reynolds sales offices were spread across the country. The opening of an office in Detroit to act as liaison between Reynolds and Reynolds and the automobile manufacturers' business management offices tied the knot, sealing the company's dedication to the automobile industry.

Expansion During the 1960s

The 1960s were an extremely eventful time period for Reynolds and Reynolds. With the purchase in 1960 of Controlomat, a Boston company that had computerized accounting for area auto dealers since 1956, Reynolds and Reynolds expanded their paper-only business approach to include electronic data processing. After two years of creating and testing a computerized accounting system specially designed for auto dealers, they released a product called Electronic Accounting.

In 1961 the company went public, and in 1963 the firm expanded internationally, forming Reynolds and Reynolds (Canada) Ltd. with the purchase of the automotive division of Windsor Office Supply at Windsor, Ontario, Canada. The purchase of the auto dealer forms business of Alger Press Ltd. based in Oshawa, Ontario, made Reynolds and Reynolds (Canada) Ltd. the predominant supplier of standard forms and systems to Canadian auto dealers.

Electronic Accounting took off immediately and the company opened more and more data processing centers across the United States. In 1963 the first centers were opened in Celina, Ohio, and Glendale, California. The year 1965 brought with it the opening of Electronic Accounting data processing centers in Burlingame (near San Francisco) and Chicago.

In 1966, Reynolds and Reynolds announced a new data processing service for auto dealers called EPIC (Electronic Parts Inventory Control). The service was offered to a limited number of firms until it was released for sale to all of the company's electronic data processing customers in 1967, when it emerged renamed RAPIC. Two other data processing tools were released in conjunction with RAPIC, a management report and account system for automobile lessors called LEASe and an accounts receivable system. With an eye to the future, the company installed their first third-generation computer in the Celina, Ohio, data processing center in 1968. They intended to install the same computers at all of their data processing centers spread across the United States. Soon the company entered the data transmission field, offering data transmission (as an alternate input method) to their Electronic Accounting customers.

A Technological Decade: The 1970s

In 1970 the company completed installation of third-generation computers at all seven of their data processing centers. The company's expansion reached a critical mass, and Reynolds and Reynolds broke ground on a $1.75 million expansion that would add 49,000 square feet of space to the Electronic Data Processing building. Another major milestone was reached in 1971 when the company launched their first electronic accounting service, called Vital Information Property (VIP), with online capability. VIP was soon renamed Vital Information for Management (VIM), and Reynolds and Reynolds added to the value of this product with the purchase and assimilation of two firms' business and customer base—Dealer-Management Analysis Corp. (D-MAC) and Computer Systems Corp. D-MAC provided computerized analyses of financial statements for auto dealers and Computer Systems Corp. carried an annual volume of about $120,000 in electronic data processing services to auto

dealers in the Denver area. The purchase of these two companies was just the beginning of an acquisitions spree for Reynolds and Reynolds. The company quickly followed the purchase of these two organizations with the 1973 purchase of World Wide Time Sharing, Inc. and Diversified Online Computing, Inc. (DOC). These two companies helped Reynolds and Reynolds expand their market into Chicago and Tucson and to expand their offerings by integrating World Wide Time Sharing, Inc.'s knowledge of online order-writing-invoicing and inventory control and DOC's minicomputer accounting and parts inventory technology. Minicomputer technology formed the basis of Reynolds and Reynolds' VIM II service.

The company followed the successful release of the VIM II service with the announcement in 1975 that they planned to offer a VIM III system that would provide services similar to the VIM II but would afford the customer a choice to either lease or purchase the software and hardware. A Dayton-based Chevrolet dealership was the first company to install the VIM III system. In order to market their VIM II service farther afield, Reynolds and Reynolds agreed in principle to a deal with an English company called Kalamazoo Limited of England to market VIM II in the United Kingdom.

By 1977 computer-related sales at Reynolds had risen to 45.5 percent of total sales, and to 50.6 percent in 1978. A reorganization of the company's sales and marketing operation resulted in dealer computer services and business forms becoming the two main groups. The end of the decade was marked with the company's first manufactured computer by ReyZon Computers, a joint-venture formed with Zonic Technical Laboratories, Inc. ReyZon was soon (in 1980) purchased outright by Reynolds and Reynolds, forming Reynolds and Reynolds' Computer Manufacturing Operation (CMO). Soon the computer ReyZon had designed, TC 1000, was upgraded to include two new systems for the dealer market. The updated computer system was called TC 1000 Dealer Management Systems and offered remote intelligent processing, low-cost accounting and parts inventory control applications. Computer manufacturing was not to be a long-lived aspect of the company's business plan. CMO was eventually phased out and the company returned its full attention to the more lucrative practice of purchasing the hardware their customers would need to run Reynolds and Reynolds software from others.

Growth Continues Throughout the 1980s

Reynolds and Reynolds continued their practice of constant growth throughout the 1980s. During this time, they acquired multiple companies that allowed them to continue adding value to the services they offered the automobile market. They formed a financial subsidiary, called Reyna Financial Corporation to assist customers in purchasing computers, hardware and software; they offered a new group of computer systems to auto dealers called VIM/NET that provided expandability, an array of systems for all sizes of dealers, and networking capabilities. The VIM/NET systems grew and expanded constantly, with the company frequently offering updated versions and expanding the VIM/NET reach into both France and Australia in 1983. The company also expanded in other areas including: marketing more of their products to auto dealers in Canada, Australia, France, New Zealand, and the United Kingdom; and purchasing

Key Dates:

1866: Lucius D. Reynolds and James R. Gardner found ''Gardner and Reynolds.''

1867: Gardner sells his share of the business to Lucius Reynolds' father Ira Reynolds. The firm becomes Reynolds and Reynolds.

1889: The firm is incorporated as The Reynolds and Reynolds Company.

1927: The company begins producing standard business forms and accounting systems for Chevrolet dealers.

1947: The company opens an office in Detroit to establish closer contact with the entire business offices of the automobile manufacturers.

1960: Reynolds and Reynolds becomes the first company to offer computer services to automobile dealers.

1961: The company sells its stock to the public.

1963: The company begins to expand in Canada, and in Ohio, California and Chicago.

1971: The company purchases Dealer-Management Analysis Corp. (D-MAC) and Computer Systems Corp.

1973: The company acquires World Wile Time Sharing, Inc. and Diversified Online Computing, Inc. (DOC).

1977: Annual sales hit $100 million.

1982: Reynolds and Reynolds announces a family of computer systems for auto dealers that includes networking—a feature new to the auto dealer market.

1994: The company purchases PD Medical Systems as part of its strategy to begin its expansion into the medical systems business.

1995: Reynolds and Reynolds is named one of *InfoWorld* magazine's ''Top 100 in Business Technology Innovations.''

2000: The company sells its Information Solutions Group to The Carlyle Group for $360 million cash.

2001: Reynolds and Reynolds is named in the top 25 percent of *eWeek*'s list of ''2001 FastTrack 500 eBusiness Innovators.''

the printing plant of the business forms division of Burroughs Ltd. at Sydney, Australia. The plant, under the management of Reynolds and Reynolds (Australia) Ltd., produced forms for Australian auto dealers.

In 1984, Reynolds and Reynolds brought David R. Holmes on board to head and revive their computer operation. The company's software was out-of-date; it did not allow for multiple users to access information. Holmes oversaw the development of a computer system called ERA (introduced in 1987) that allowed car dealerships to communicate with suppliers, databases, and to generate reports drawing from information found on 1,000 workstations. This new product addressed the needs of many different departments of a car dealership, giving salespeople a tool to access prices of vehicles and service department employees a tool to search for used-car parts. The same year the ERA system hit the market, Reynolds and Reynolds introduced an electronic parts catalog system, which used a combination of computer and CD-ROM technology to electronically deliver parts information and graphics to dealerships.

In 1988 when Holmes was named president and CEO, he addressed Reynolds and Reynolds' financial and organizational problems. For the first time in its 123-year history, the company went through a large-scale layoff. The downsizing of the company did not affect the string of successes and contracts that Reynolds and Reynolds signed in the last years of the 1980s. Reynolds broke into the *Fortune* 500; became the exclusive supplier of dealer communications systems for American Isuzu Motors Inc. (AIMI) and Saab-Scania of America, Inc.; signed agreements to market electronic parts catalog systems for Jeep/Eagle, Mercedes-Benz, Nissan, Honda Cars of North America, General Motors and Chrysler; and won a contract with Chrysler Motors to provide interactive video technology for Chrysler's Sales Effectiveness Training (SET). Reynolds also began expanding beyond the exclusivity of the automobile market with a contract to supply business forms and forms and management services to Insurance Services Office, General Dynamics, and General Electric.

Some of Reynolds' success may have been due to an innovative management move by new CEO Holmes. He observed that one of the byproducts of the acquisition of so many different companies in the past decade was that Reynolds and Reynolds was awash in many different management styles and personalities. Holmes and his corporate Vice-President of Human Resources Tom Momchilov devised a plan to create a formal education and training program that would give the company's executives a chance to come together to help create the vision and strategies that would focus the entire company in the years ahead. The education program was a success. Holmes noted ''The process defined, focused, and shaped our core values. In addition, it made management perceptibly more accountable for company performance.''

Additional Information Management Opportunities Arise During the 1990s

Throughout the 1990s, Reynolds and Reynolds continued its process of acquiring companies that possessed desired technology or market share, and integrating those companies' technology and reach into their offerings. The company continued to expand upon the ERA system's features. In 1994, Reynolds embarked upon a strategy to grow its medical system's business by purchasing PD Medical Systems and merging it with NMC Services, their wholly owned subsidiary, to form Reynolds and Reynolds Healthcare Systems. That same year, the company sold its subsidiary located in France and exited the French automobile market.

Among the slew of products that Reynolds and Reynolds offered to their customers in the 1990s, including the Vehicle Locator and Marketing Network (which allowed dealers to tap into an online database, locate, acquire, and resell used vehicles) was a product called SalesVision. SalesVision was a prospect—and management application that was designed to be a useful sales tool for dealerships of all sizes. It provided salespeople with all of the tools they might need to be successful, including a built-in prospective customer database, a daily list of contacts for calls and follow-ups, the ability to create personalized letters to clients, and even multimedia sales training that the salesperson could watch while not actively selling.

With the portion of Reynolds and Reynolds' business that focused on automobile dealerships doing well, Holmes focused some of his attention on expanding the company's burgeoning non-automotive integrated information management business. In 1997 alone, Reynolds Healthcare Systems acquired Crane-Drummond, a leading Canadian provider of business and document management services, and Fiscal Information, a company that primarily focused its business of providing management systems for radiologists in Florida and Colorado. In 1999 the company expanded its customer base with contracts to provide document management and other services to John Deere & Co. and TransAmerica Life, the insurance arm of Transamerica Corporation. *InfoWorld* magazine took note of Reynolds and Reynolds' practice of consistently offering innovative technologies by recognizing them as one of the "Top 100 in Business Technology Innovations." The company also won the largest contract in their history, a document-outsourcing contract with Novation a Texas-based supply firm.

The man chosen to replace Holmes upon his retirement was Lloyd "Buzz" Waterhouse. Waterhouse joined the company after working 26 years for IBM, where he had recently served as general manager of e-business services and was an early participant in the formation of the Internet. Waterhouse wasted no time in the formation of an eBusiness Group, a team tasked with making use of Internet technology to the benefit of Reynolds' automotive and document services markets. In February 2000, the company announced their intention to form a joint venture with Automatic Data Processing, Inc. and CCC Information Services, Inc. to build a Web-based dealer-to-dealer auto parts exchange. The company also quickly released the Internet-enabled version of their successful ERA system (ERA2). The purchase of HAC Group LLC, the world's leading provider of learning, customer relationship management, and Web services to automotive retailers and manufacturers, prompted the creation of Reynolds Transformation Services. They also changed the name of their National Customer Support service to the Technical Assistance Center (TAC). TACs across the country were repeatedly given awards like the STAR (Software Technical Assistance Recognition) Award from groups like The Help Desk Institute for high-quality technical assistance.

Also in 2000, the company sold its Information Solutions Group (ISG), the company's document-outsourcing and customer relationship management business, to Washington, D.C.-based global, private equity firm The Carlyle Group for $360 million cash. Carlyle, a firm that organizes, structures, and acts as lead equity investor in management-led buyouts, private placements, and venture capital transactions, renamed the business The Relizon Company. At the time of the sale, ISG's 12-month revenue run rate was about $800 million. Reynolds' intentions were to use the proceeds from the sale to fund its growth initiatives and share repurchase programs, as well as for general corporate purposes.

David R. Holmes, Reynolds chairman and CEO, said, "We're very proud of the ISG team. They've created a business with solid revenue growth and profitability, and the industry's highest customer satisfaction level and return on net assets. Now, with a clear focus on value-added document management and marketing solutions, we believe the future looks even brighter for ISG. . . . This is a great day for our ISG associates, the community and the 'new Reynolds,' which is now focused exclusively on leading the transformation of automotive retailing." In 2001, Reynolds and Reynolds formally entered the online automobile retail market when they launched CarsDirect Connect with CarsDirect.com, a buying process that offered consumers choices in the way they shop for and purchase vehicles.

The announcement in 2002 that Reynolds and Reynolds would phase out its Unix-based dealer system and replace it with a Microsoft system that utilizes .NET technology caused a flurry of discussion in the automobile dealership market. Some dealers were happy to hear of the change, noting that many of the released operating programs that their dealerships used were based on Microsoft Windows and that the switch would make future data transfer simpler. Other dealers were unhappy with the prospect of purchasing an entirely new system of hardware to support Reynolds' switch, particularly with the .NET platform being relatively new and untested compared with the familiar Unix-based system. The company announced that the transition to the .NET platform would be complete by 2012.

Principal Subsidiaries

Choiceparts LLC (founded jointly with Automatic Data Processing, Inc. and CCC Information Services); DealerKid; HAC Group LLC; Networkcar Inc.; Reyna Capital Corp.

Principal Competitors

Accenture Ltd.; Automatic Data Processing, Inc.; Avery Dennison Corporation; The Cobalt Group; Compaq Computer Corporation; Electronic Data Systems Corporation; Computer Sciences Corporation; Deluxe Corporation; The Standard Register Company.

Further Reading

Bowen, William J., "Once Company's Notes on Learning," *The Journal of Business Strategy*, May-June 1994, p. 58.
Gold, Jacqueline S., "All Ahead Full," *Financial World*, April 27, 1993, p. 64.
Grace, Tim, "SalesVision Makes Debut," *Manhasset*, February 5, 1996, p. 113.
Harris, Donna, "Dealer Systems Change Fires Up Competition," *Automotive News*, January 21, 2002, p. 60.
Icon Group International, Inc. Staff, *Reynolds and Reynolds Company (The): Labor Productivity Benchmarks and International Gap Analysis*, San Diego: Icon Group International, Incorporated, 2000, p. 20.
La Franco, Robert, "The Laziness Cure," *Forbes*, May 20, 1996, p. 84.
"Major Contracts Signed for Document Service," *Graphic Arts Monthly*, June 1999, p. 30.
"The Paper Chase," *Chain Store Age*, August 1997, p. B20.
Reynolds and Reynolds Co., "Reynolds and Reynolds Timeline," accessed March 11, 2002, http://www.reyrey.com.
"Reynolds' Push Beyond Car Dealers," *Business Week*, August 10, 1987, p. H66.
Wilson, Tim, "E-Biz Booms in These Parts," *InternetWeek*, February 14, 2000, p. 14.

—Tammy Weisberger

RIO TINTO

Rio Tinto PLC

6 St. James's Square
London SW1Y 4LD
United Kingdom
Telephone: +44 (20) 7930-2399
Fax: +44 (20) 7930-3249
Web site: http://www.riotinto.com

Public Company
Incorporated: 1962
Employees: 34,399 (2000)
Sales: US$10.4 billion (2001)
Stock Exchanges: Amsterdam Australia Brussels
    Frankfurt London New York Paris Zürich
Ticker Symbol: RTP (New York), RIO (London)
NAIC: 212234 Copper Ore and Nickel Ore Mining;
    212393 Other Chemical and Fertilizer Mineral
    Mining; 212221 Gold Ore Mining; 212222 Silver Ore
    Mining; 213113 Support Activities for Coal Mining

An estimated 79 percent of Rio Tinto PLC's assets are in Australia, New Zealand, and North America, with the rest divided among Africa, Asia, and Europe. The company owns mines worldwide, for coal and such metals as copper and gold, and the industrial minerals borax, silica and talc. In addition to being one of the largest producers of copper and coal in the United States, the company's boron mine in the Mojave Desert produces 50 percent of the world's borax. Among Rio Tinto's international mine holdings are Kennecott in Utah, which mines copper, coal, and gold; U.S. Borax, which mines borates and silica; and Palabora in South Africa, which mines copper.

The Origins of Rio Tinto Predecessors RTC and CZ

It had been the policy of the previously named RTZ Corporation PLC, since its formation in 1962 through the merger of the Rio Tinto Company (RTC) and the Consolidated Zinc Corporation (CZ), to invest only in first-class mining properties with large reserves and low-production costs. Both the RTC and CZ were formed during the years between 1870 and 1914, when London

rose to prominence as the hub of international mining and metallurgical activities. The number of overseas metal mining and processing companies listed on the London Stock Exchange climbed from 39 in 1875 to 913 in 1913, with the long-term capital employed in the industry rising at an average annual rate of more than 8 percent over the same period. In the city of London, for every prospective mine or group of mines, a new operating company would be created. A syndicate composed of city interests—specialist company promoters, bankers, stockbrokers, merchants, mining engineers, and others—would purchase a concession from a foreign vendor or exploration company, and a mining company would be formed to purchase the concession from the syndicate. Syndicates usually profited from the sale of the concession, and from securing contracts for financial or other services.

When launched in 1873, the RTC was by far the biggest international mining venture ever brought to market, and it remained the flagship of the British-owned sector of the international industry until well into the 20th century. The Rio Tinto mines, in the province of Huelva in southern Spain, had produced large quantities of copper, on and off, since before Roman times, most recently under the ownership of the government of Spain. In 1872, following a series of financial losses, the mines were offered for sale at a price equivalent to several million pounds sterling. The Spanish government was in a financial crisis and did not have the cash or the expertise needed to exploit the large reserves of cuprous pyrites known to exist at RTC. Substantial investments were needed to introduce opencast mining, and to build workshops, tramways, crushing and metallurgical plants, a railway from the mines to the seaport of Huelva, a shipping pier, and the many other works necessary to operate on a large scale.

The availability of the mines was brought to the attention of Matheson & Company, the London-based agent for the Far Eastern merchants Jardine Matheson, by Heinrich Doetsch of Sundheim & Doetsch, a general merchant of Huelva. Doetsch had the foresight to see that if the Rio Tinto mines were developed to their full potential, his business eventually stood to gain from a large increase in trade. A syndicate to purchase the Rio Tinto concession was organized by Hugh Matheson, senior partner in Matheson & Company, in London. The mines were

Company Perspectives:

Rio Tinto takes a long term and responsible approach to exploring for first class ore bodies and developing large, efficient operations capable of sustaining competitive advantage. In this way, Rio Tinto helps to meet the global need for minerals and metals which contribute to essential improvements in living standards as well as making a direct contribution to economic development and employment in those countries in which it invests.

purchased by the syndicate for £3.7 million, over a period of nine years, and immediately sold to the RTC. The new company was floated on the London Stock Exchange with an issued share capital of £2 million and debentures valued at £600,000. Hugh Matheson was appointed as first chairman of the RTC with Heinrich Doetsch as his deputy.

Matheson remained chairman of the RTC for a quarter of a century until his death in 1898. Matheson was a shrewd dealer in commodities, an outstanding entrepreneur with an ability to think on a scale that few could match, and a natural leader who could win the support needed to build very large enterprises in distant lands. The formation, survival, and ultimate prosperity of the RTC was the crowning achievement of his life. Matheson held together the original German and British banking, trading, and engineering consortium formed to launch the RTC in the crisis that followed the issue of its prospectus. The claims made in this document, especially the report of the mining engineer David Forbes, were vigorously denounced by the Tharsis Company, a Scottish-based firm set up in 1866 to work a group of mines not far distant from those at Rio Tinto. It was alleged that Matheson and his associates had falsely inflated potential revenues and grossly underestimated development and operating costs. The new company, it was said, could never earn a positive rate of return on the huge capital it was seeking to raise from investors. Matheson launched a massive press campaign, an early example of skillful public relations, and he won the day.

The Tharsis assault, however, did some damage, and this was further compounded by a three-year price war between the two companies. The pyrites mined in southern Spain and in Portugal were first burned to drive off the sulfur content. The sulfurous gases were used to make sulfuric acid, one of the fundamental products of the chemicals industry. The burnt ore from the chemical works was then treated to remove the copper and other valuable metals it contained. The iron cinders that remained were sent to ironworks for smelting. During these difficult years, revenues were low and development costs were running at more than £100,000 per month. The purchase agreement with the Spanish government was renegotiated on more favorable terms; the company was financially restructured, and additional funds were raised through the issue of mortgage bonds. Eventually, in 1876, a favorable price-fixing and market-sharing agreement was made with Tharsis, and the prospects for both companies began to improve.

The RTC was the major beneficiary of the 1876 agreement. Under this, the company gained control of the lucrative and

rapidly expanding German market for pyrites, and within a matter of years it had become the dominant firm—with a 50 percent market share—in an oligopolistic world industry, with some degree of control over prices. At the same time, more of the product of the mines was treated locally to recover the copper contained therein. By the end of the 1880s, RTC was the leading producer of copper in the world. The company had smelters in Spain and a smelter and refinery in south Wales. In 1887, when the French entrepreneur Hyacinthe Secrétan attempted to corner the world copper market to raise prices, RTC at first reaped the benefits of its participation in the scheme, whereby Secrétan undertook to buy all its copper at fixed prices, and was not severely affected when Secrétan's scheme backfired in 1889, resulting in a spectacular collapse in the copper market. The strong market position of the company—by 1887 it was responsible for 8 percent of the total world copper supply—was reflected from the 1880s onward in high profits. The larger part was returned to shareholders as dividends.

New Technology at the Dawn of the Century

Hugh Matheson laid the foundations for the subsequent prosperity of the RTC, which rose to a high level under the leadership of Sir Charles Fielding. In his first ten years as chairman, 1898 to 1908, the company paid an average annual dividend of 41 percent on a share capital of £3.5 million. Fielding built solidly on the achievements of the Matheson era, assuming personal responsibility for the introduction of a range of new technologies such as pyritic smelting. He also streamlined management, accounting, and decision-making practices, and, at a time of strong market growth, these innovations helped elevate the company to a higher level of profitability. The Spanish government, under pressure from nationalists of all descriptions, tried to lay claim to a larger share of company revenues, but these efforts were generally thwarted; nor did the laborers of the mining district have much success in raising the level of wages paid by RTC. The company showed scant regard for the argument that it could afford to pay much more than it did, pointing out that it already paid more in cash and kind than most other large employers in Spain. The real wages per head of the 15,000 workers employed by the RTC in Spain in 1913 were actually less than those paid to 10,000 workers employed 20 years earlier. Low-cost housing; discretionary pensions; and company stores, schools, taverns, and other recreational facilities as substitutes for higher wages began to cause resentment among the workers and their families.

Strikes of varying lengths and bitterness became commonplace at RTC following the outbreak of World War I, exacerbated by ever-rising prices and declining real wages. A violent and acrimonious nine-month strike in 1920 ended with the exhausted unions and resentment toward the company in many sections of Spanish society, across the political spectrum. From this time onward, the fate of the RTC in Spain was bound up with the turbulent course of national politics. There was a period of relative stability between 1923 and 1929 under the dictatorship of Miguel Primo de Rivera, and the company was fortunate to escape lightly when it was discovered to have been evading export taxes through under-recording of the copper content of minerals shipped from Huelva. After Primo de Rivera left office, however, there followed a long period of

Key Dates:

1873: The Rio Tinto Company (RTC) is launched.

1898: Hugh Matheson, the first chairman of the RTC dies, after serving 25 years, and laying the foundation for future prosperity.

1925: Sir Auckland Geddes serves as chairman of RTC until 1947.

1930: RTC, a major economic force in Northern Rhodesia, forms the Rhokana Corporation with Sir Ernest Oppenheimer of the Anglo American Corporation.

1951: Val Duncan is named managing director of RTC.

1954: After the Spanish Civil War and World War II, RTC sells its Spanish operation and mines.

1955: The company purchases a majority interest in the Algom group of uranium mines in the Elliot Lake district of Canada; and a controlling interest in the Mary Kathleen mine in Australia.

1962: RTZ Corporation PLC is incorporated through the merger of the Rio Tinto Company (RTC) and the London-based Consolidated Zinc Corporation (CZ)

1975: Through careful acquisitions worldwide— Bougainville Copper, Lornex Copper, Rössing Uranium, Atlas Steels, Borax Holdings, Capper Pass, and Pillar Holdings—RTZ achieves the geographically and geologically diverse pattern of operations long pursued by early Managing Director and eventual Chairman and Chief Executive Val Duncan.

1989: The company acquires BP Minerals, including Kennecott Corporation, making it one of the world's largest producers of gold outside South Africa.

1995: Kennecott's parent RTZ, merges with Australia's CRA Limited, creating the dual-listed RTZ-CRA Group, the largest mining company in the world.

1997: RTZ-CRA Group changes its name to Rio Tinto PLC and headquarters are established in London; and Sir Robert Wilson is appointed as chairman.

2002: Rio Tinto launches a EUR 750 million 5-year-bond issue in the Euro market, marking its first transaction in euros; the company stops its incursions into aboriginal land in Queensland, Australia.

disruption and uncertainty that lasted until the mines were sold to Spanish interests in 1954. As left- and right-wing political factions vied for power between 1929 and 1936, the RTC came to be seen as an economic Rock of Gibraltar that must concede more in the interests of Spain. Damaging labor laws and taxation policies were introduced at the very time when the company was suffering from depressed trading conditions around the world, and when the copper content of the ores mined at Rio Tinto was plummeting. The decision was made by the third chairman of the company, Sir Auckland Geddes, who served from 1925 to 1947, to invest only as much money in Spain as was needed to sustain the operation.

The 1936–1939 Spanish Civil War brought further problems. From an early date, the Rio Tinto mines were occupied by the Insurgent forces led by General Francisco Franco. The mineral wealth of the district was seen by Franco as a means of procuring arms from the Axis powers, and within months the RTC found itself caught up in a complex web of diplomatic intrigue involving London, Berlin, Rome, and the Franco regime. Control over the company's Spanish assets had been lost, and was never effectively regained. During World War II and the period of reconstruction that followed, the RTC had little control over production, prices, or the numbers of workers employed in Spain. The company was held in check by restrictive laws and regulations, causing the real value of its assets to fall with the passage of each frustrating year. It was with great relief that the RTC managed to sell its Spanish operations in 1954. After many years of negotiations, involving Franco himself, the business was sold to a newly formed Spanish company in exchange for a one-third interest in the enterprise plus £7.7 million in seven annual installments.

Global Expansion

Auckland Geddes involved the company in ventures in other parts of the world and brought to the RTC a new style of business leadership. Unlike previous chairpeople, he eschewed close involvement in day-to-day administrative matters in favor of major questions of policy and organization. He delegated responsibilities to full-time directors recruited from outside the business, and he initiated a search for major new investment opportunities in mining and related fields. Exploration subsidiaries were formed and research stations opened. A large minority shareholding in the Davison Chemical Corporation, a leading United States artificial-fertilizer manufacturer, was purchased. Together with Davison, the RTC set up a series of subsidiaries throughout Europe to manufacture and market the versatile chemical absorbent, silica gel. Substantial minority shareholdings were also acquired in several other companies devoted to exploration and the development of new products.

By far the most significant of the new departures inspired by Geddes was the involvement of the RTC in the development of the Northern Rhodesian (now Zambian) copperbelt. The opportunity to secure a stake in the field came early in 1929 when U.S. interests attempted to take over the promising N'Changa deposits. Along with Sir Ernest Oppenheimer and other members of the British-cum-South African business community, Geddes judged this move to be detrimental to British business interests, and led the resistance to it. By the time the struggle was over, the RTC had acquired sizable copperbelt holdings and valuable information which suggested that the deposits were amongst the richest and most extensive ever discovered. Further shares were purchased in major copperbelt development companies in the months following the N'Changa struggle, and by 1930 the RTC had become a major economic force in Northern Rhodesia. In that year Geddes and Sir Ernest Oppenheimer, whose Anglo American Corporation was the leading company in copperbelt finance, forced through the merger of three of the biggest development companies to form the Rhokana Corporation. Geddes was appointed chairman of the new company. Under his leadership Rhokana emerged during the next 17 years as one of the largest and lowest-cost copper companies in the world.

Not all of Geddes' business initiatives were so successful. The RTC's venture into chemicals proved in the end to be a financial disaster, and the firm's exploration activities never yielded anything of worth. Failure in these fields was largely a consequence of the world economic depression but in part such losses were due to ill-informed and hasty judgments on the part of the RTC board. The returns on the Northern Rhodesian investments, however, more than compensated for these setbacks, enabling the firm to survive the protracted decline of its Spanish business and laying the foundations for its emergence as a modern multinational enterprise.

The Postwar Period

The regeneration of the RTC after World War II was, to a great extent, the work of two men, Mark Turner and Val Duncan, who formed one of the most creative business partnerships of modern times. Turner, the elder of the two and an investment banker by training, was appointed acting managing director of the company in 1948 on a part-time basis. He was charged with finding a full-time replacement, and for the position he groomed Duncan, a younger lawyer he had met during the war. Duncan was appointed managing director of the RTC in January 1951, allowing Turner, who remained a leading member of the RTC board and Duncan's closest colleague, to devote more of his time to the banking business of Robert Benson, Lonsdale—later Kleinwort Benson. Together, Duncan and Turner persuaded their colleagues and leading shareholders that RTC should aim to become a growth-oriented, broadly based natural resource company with operations concentrated in politically stable parts of the world, especially the Commonwealth countries. In the late 1940s and early 1950s, interests in a range of potential mines were secured, from tin and wolfram in Portugal to diamonds in South Africa and copper in Uganda. Between 1952 and 1954, a network of amply funded exploration subsidiaries was established to search for mineral deposits that might be exploited on a large scale in Canada, Africa, and Australia.

The sale of the Spanish mines in 1954 released further human and financial resources for the task of rebuilding and reorienting the RTC. An intense period of exploration followed, which sent Duncan and other executives to all parts of the world to supervise exploration agreements and consider the mine-development deals put to the company from time to time. The first tangible result of this activity came in 1955 with the purchase of a majority interest in the Algom group of uranium mines in the Elliot Lake district of Canada. The authorized capital of the RTC was raised from £8 million to £12 million to accommodate the purchase, and a loan of US$200 million was raised against various supply contracts to fund the development of seven major mines. The company's position in the uranium industry was consolidated by the simultaneous acquisition of a controlling interest in the Mary Kathleen mine in Australia. By the end of the 1950s, RTC was responsible for the production of 15 percent of the world's uranium oxide, and along the way the company had gained control over two highly promising mineral prospects: the vast Hammersley iron ore deposits in Western Australia and the Palabora copper deposit in South Africa.

Merging RTC and Consolidated Zinc

By the early 1960s, Duncan was confident enough to take the decisive step toward realizing his vision of the RTC as a first-rank multinational enterprise. Merging was the obvious means of speeding the process of building up the organization, and he found an ideal prospective partner in the London-based Consolidated Zinc Corporation. This company had steadily expanded its activities since 1905 when it was launched to recover the large quantities of zinc remaining in the tailings dumps of the legendary silver-lead mines at Broken Hill in New South Wales, Australia. CZ's operations were still concentrated in Australia, but had been progressively extended to include a wide range of mining and metallurgical activities. The compatibility of CZ and the RTC was both strategic and structural. Strategically, the leading directors of CZ wished to attain major-company status through geographic diversification and the development of important new prospects, particularly the vast Weipa bauxite deposits of northern Queensland. Structurally, the company was about the same size as the RTC with net profits running at a little over £1 million per annum, and its major interests were in complementary rather then competing areas. The merger would, at a stroke, produce a large and broadly based organization with financial and technological resources to undertake a range of promising new ventures. In July 1962 the two companies came together to form RTZ. Duncan was appointed managing director of the new concern, and in 1963, on the retirement of A.M. Baer, he became chairman and chief executive of RTZ—positions which he retained until his death in December 1975.

Under Duncan's leadership, RTZ rapidly rose to prominence in the natural resources industries of the world. In partnership with Kaiser Aluminum, the firm established an integrated aluminum business in Australia, Comalco Limited. The Hammersley iron and Palabora copper projects were brought to fruition. Extensive exploration was continued, eventually yielding large-scale mines in Papua New Guinea (Bougainville Copper), Canada (Lornex Copper), and Namibia (Rössing Uranium). Meanwhile, the scale and the scope of the business was further expanded through the purchase of going concerns: Atlas Steels (high-grade specialty steels) in Canada; Borax Holdings (industrial raw materials) in the United States; and Capper Pass (tin refiners) and Pillar Holdings (aluminum fabricators) in the United Kingdom. By the early 1970s, RTZ had achieved the geographically and geologically diverse pattern of operations long pursued by Val Duncan.

Duncan made an important contribution to advancing the fortunes of the enterprise. He was the principal architect of the strategy of promoting growth through involvement in a stream of large-scale, capital-intensive natural resources projects. Potential financial limits to growth were overcome through the funding of massive projects with a high ratio of loan capital to equity. Multimillion-dollar loans were raised by Duncan and his team throughout the by offering long-term supply contracts as collateral. Potential organizational and managerial limits to growth were overcome by the progressive devolution of responsibilities to a series of nationally based companies, each charged with the goal of involving RTZ in substantial new projects. By the early 1970s, RTZ had emerged as a loosely knit family of companies with the activities of the parent concern limited to the provision of group services, the controlling of major strategic and financial decisions, and the appointment of top personnel.

RTZ Becomes One of the Largest Producers of Gold

The strategy, organization, and policies devised by Val Duncan remained in place in the 1980s. Duncan was succeeded as chief executive by Mark Turner. He continued in office until his death in December 1980. Turner saw no need to change course, nor did Anthony Tuke who replaced him, nor has Alistair Frame or Derek Birkin, the latest in the long line of distinguished chairpersons that began with Hugh Matheson. The essential integrity of RTZ was maintained while growth continued. New mines and smelters were brought on stream and new processing facilities developed. Some businesses were bought; others sold. The biggest boost to the enterprise came in 1989 with the acquisition of BP Minerals for £2.6 billion. This deal brought to RTZ one of the greatest names in world mining, the Kennecott Corporation, and a portfolio of assets in 15 countries, including the world's largest opencast copper mine and the world's largest producer of titanium dioxide feedstock. RTZ immediately became one of the world's largest producers of gold outside South Africa. The shares of world output accounted for by the much-enlarged company in 1989 were 55 percent of borates, 30 percent of titanium dioxide feedstock, 13 percent of zircon, 15 percent of industrial diamonds, 14 percent of vermiculite, 8 percent of talc, and 5 percent or more of uranium, copper, and molybdenum. RTZ also ranked amongst the world's largest producers of tin, bauxite, silver, iron ore, gold, lead, and zinc.

Sir Robert Wilson played a vital role in closing the BP Minerals deal. He joined the company in 1970, becoming managing director of its European zinc and lead smelting subsidiary in 1979. He moved to the head office in 1982 and was appointed to the main board in 1987 as executive director responsible for planning and development. It was in this capacity that he led the significant purchase that brought with it Kennecott Corporation. Wilson would go on to be named chief executive of Rio Tinto in 1991 and be appointed chairman in 1997.

When the London-based RTZ Corporation PLC and its Australian subsidiary CRA Limited completed a dual-listed companies merger in December 1995, the largest mining company in the world was created, RTZ-CRA Group. Combined revenues for the next year were US$8.4 billion, double the US$4.22 billion in sales reported by RTZ alone for 1995. As a result of the unique merger, both companies maintained separate identities and stock market listings.

The 1995 RTZ-CRA merger pulled in all of Kennecott's holdings, making the company an international giant in the mining and minerals industry. Kennecott had become a subsidiary of BP Minerals in 1987, when BP purchased an outstanding minority interest in Standard Oil in June 1989. BP Minerals was then acquired by RTZ Corporation PLC, Britain's largest mining company. The merger, while creating a multinational mining giant, also created the need for a management restructuring, which ultimately shook up the Kennecott operations.

In March 1997, RTZ-CRA announced a management restructuring into six new global product businesses, with three to be based in London and three in Australia. As a result, operations for copper, gold and other minerals, as well as operations for industrial minerals, were now based in London. In Australia, aluminum operations were headquartered in Brisbane, energy in Melbourne, and iron ore in Perth. These businesses were supported by the worldwide technology and exploration groups that remain headquartered in London. In June 1997, the company changed its name to Rio Tinto PLC.

Kennecott Corporation, the world's leader in copper output throughout most of the 20th century, by 1997 ceased to exist as a separate entity. That year it was divided into a group of wholly owned subsidiaries of Rio Tinto, who continued to operate Kennecott's chief U.S. businesses: Kennecott Utah Copper, Kennecott Minerals, and Kennecott Energy. However, these operations were absorbed into Rio Tinto's copper and energy units.

In the mid-1990s, Rio Tinto's exploration of mines around the world continued, with projects for gold in Papua New Guinea, prospecting in northern Norway's Finnmark region, and expanded coal-mining by buying U.S. operators Nerco and Cordero Mining. In 1997, copper and gold exploration looked promising at Famatina in northwestern Argentina.

As the 1990s drew to a close, Rio Tinto was looking at a strong world economy that would demand primary raw materials, such as copper, gold, and coal. Prices were holding, as well, but competition was a possible concern from emerging markets such as Russia and China.

Rio Tinto Hangs Tough in Difficult Market

But this stability would not hold. In January 1999, Rio Tinto deferred construction on its Hail Creek Coal Project, in Queensland Basin in reaction to an economic recession in Asia. (Development would resume in June 2001.) In April the company moved to shuffle chief executives in its copper, gold, and technology groups in an attempt to exchange best practices between the business groups. This came just two months after Rio Tinto declared a 10 percent drop in earnings to US$1.1 billion and a 2 percent decline in sales to US$9.2 billion. In September, Rio Tinto sold its Las Cruces copper deposit in Andalucia, southern Spain to MK Gold Company for US$42 million cash.

In February 2000, Rio put up a for-sale notice on its 40 percent stake in the rich Nevada gold mine, the Cortez Pipeline. Three years previously, Rio had considered spinning off its gold mines, but since a sizable proportion of production is a byproduct of copper companies, the idea was shelved. The sale never went through, but this period continued as an era of a fragile global economy.

Despite a tumultuous couple of years, a growth in demand would lead Rio Tinto to declare first-half net earnings in 2000 at US$677 million, a 33 percent increase over the previous year. Copper prices were averaging 23 percent above the low levels of first-half 1999 and aluminum prices were up 25 percent. Rio Tinto would go on to achieve a record level of earnings, helped by the full ownership of Comalco Limited and the acquisition of North Limited. Unfavorable economic conditions abounded in the United States, the European Union, and Japan, weakening demand and price for many Rio Tinto products. And yet, protected by the quality of the company's asset base, strength of its margins, and strong economic growth in China, Rio Tinto's adjusted earnings in 2001 would reach US$1.62 billion, up from US$1.51 billion in 2000.

By November 2001, Kennecott Utah Copper was taking steps to cut costs and improve productivity to secure its future. Record-low copper prices led to the permanent closing of its

North Concentrator. In February 2001, Rio Tinto posted a 23 percent drop in pre-tax earnings to US$1.93 billion in 2001 after taking an exceptional charge of US$583 million primarily due to the reduction in value of Kennecott Utah Copper.

In keeping with its reputation for high environmental and community standards, Rio Tinto stopped its incursions into aboriginal land in Queensland, Australia in early 2002, after increased pressure from the public and the NGO. The company also abruptly ended a decade-long battle against unions over individual workplace contracts, instead offering collective agreements in line with federal law to 4,000 workers at four mines in Western Australia. With its long view in production and project development, many new projects, open management style, and responsiveness to opportunity, Rio Tinto is expected to remain the world's top global mining company.

Principal Subsidiaries

Angelesey Aluminium Ltd. (UK; 51%); Bougainville Copper Ltd. (Papua New Guinea; 53.58%); Coal & Allied Industries (Australia; 71.46%); Comalco Ltd. (Australia; 50%); Cordero Mining Co. (U.S.); Dampier Salt Ltd. (Australia; 67.4%); Hammersley Iron Pty. Ltd. (Australia; 64.94%); Kennecott Corp. (U.S.); Nerco, Inc. (U.S.); New Zealand Aluminium Smelters Ltd. (79.36%); Novacoal Australia Pty. Ltd.; Palabora Mining Co. Ltd. (South Africa; 64.9%); P.T. Kelian Equatorial Mining (Indonesia; 90%); QIT-Fer et Titane Inc. (Canada); Queensland Coal Pty. Ltd. (Australia); Rio Paracatu Mineracao SA (Brazil; 51%); Rio Tinto Zimbabwe Ltd. (Zimbabwe; 56.04%); Rössing Uranium Ltd. (Namibia; 68.58%); Talc de Luzenac SA (France; 99.75%); U.S. Borax Inc. (U.S.).

Principal Operating Units

Minera Escondida (Chile); Argyle Diamonds (Australia); Talc de Luzenac (France).

Principal Competitors

Anglo American; BHP Billiton Ltd; WMC Limited.

Further Reading

Avery, David, *Not on Queen Victoria's Birthday: The Story of The Rio Tinto Mines*, London: Collins, 1974.

Burgert, Philip, "Rio Tinto Reports 10% Drop in Net Earnings," *American Metal Market*, February 26, 1999, p. 2.

——, "Rio Tinto Set to Shuffle Three Group Executives," *American Metal Market*, April 14, 1999, p. 2.

Eldridge, David, "Kennecott Copper Writedown Anticipated," *American Metal Market*, January 29, 2002, p. 5.

Green, William, "Lords of Dispassion," *Forbes*, January 12, 1998, p. 45.

Harvey, Charles E., *The Rio Tinto Company: An Economic History of a Leading International Mining Concern 1873–1954*, St. Ives: Alison Hodge (Publishers), 1981.

Lucas, Alastair, "How CRA and RTZ Went Dutch," *Corporate Finance*, December 1996, pp. 18–20.

"Northern Gems," *Maclean's*, March 4, 1996, pp. 54–55.

"Rio Tinto Plans $500M Issue as Agency Eyes Debt Levels," *Euroweek*, June 22, 2001, p. 4.

"Rio Tinto Pretax Earnings off 23%," *American Metal Market*, February 1, 2002, p. 5.

Webb, Toby, "Interview with Sir Robert Wilson, Chairman, Rio Tinto," *Ethical Corporation Magazine*, December 2001.

"When Will the Rio Carnival End," *Economist*, July 29, 1995, pp. 46–47.

—Charles Edward Harvey
—updates: Dorothy Kroll, Stacee Sledge

Robert Mondavi Corporation

P.O. Box 106
7801 St. Helena Highway
Oakville, California 94562
U.S.A.
Telephone: (707) 226-1395
Fax: (707) 251-4386
Web site: http://robertmondaviwinery.com

Public Company
Incorporated: 1966
Employees: 1000+ (seasonal) (2001 est.)
Sales: $481 million (2001)
Stock Exchanges: NASDAQ
Ticker Symbol: MOND
NAIC: 111332 Grape Vineyards; 312130 Wineries;
    551112 Offices of Other Holding Companies

Robert Mondavi Corporation, with its family of Robert Mondavi wineries, is one of the United States' premier winemakers and has done much to bring the Napa Valley region to the forefront of international winemaking. Dedicated to producing premium wines, the Mondavi wine family includes the brands Robert Mondavi, Woodbridge by Robert Mondavi, Vichon, Byron, Robert Mondavi Coastal, La Famiglia di Robert Mondavi, and a joint venture with Australian winery Rosemount Estates. Since 1979, Mondavi has also produced, in joint partnership with the Baron Phillippe de Rothschild wine family, the ultrapremium Opus One label. The company sells about 10 million cases of wine per year, with Woodbridge as its top-selling label. In 2001, the company earned $481 million in revenues and distributed wine in more than 80 countries. Founded by Robert Mondavi in 1966, the Robert Mondavi Corporation went public in 1993, although the Mondavi family controls 92 percent of voting stock. Robert Mondavi's oldest son, Michael, is president and CEO, and his youngest son, Tim, is managing director and winemaker.

Mondavi Family Beginnings

The Mondavi family's involvement in winemaking began in the early 1920s. Cesare Mondavi emigrated to the United States from Marches, Italy, in 1906, finding work in the iron mines of Minnesota. Two years later, he returned to Italy to marry. Returning to Minnesota with his bride, he opened a saloon and boarding house. Robert Mondavi was born in 1913 in the town of Virginia, Minnesota.

Prohibition brought the Mondavi family to California. A provision of the Prohibition laws allowed families to make up to 200 gallons of fruit juice per year. A member of the local Italian Club, Cesare Mondavi was sent to California to buy grapes, which could be processed into wine. Soon after, Mondavi settled in Lodi, California, with his family and set up a business shipping grapes from the Napa Valley and Central Valley regions. At age 13, Robert Mondavi began working for his father, including acting as the family's chauffeur, while attending high school. After high school, Robert Mondavi went on to study at Stanford University.

When the Prohibition laws were repealed, Cesare Mondavi moved from shipping grapes to pressing wine. In 1936, he bought a small winery in Napa Valley, the Sunny St. Helena, which produced bulk wines. Robert Mondavi, then in his last year of college, began taking chemistry courses in order to prepare to join his father's new business. After graduating, Robert Mondavi moved to St. Helena, and began learning to make bulk wines. His younger brother, Peter, then a student at the University of California at Berkeley, also turned his studies toward the making of wines, including cold fermentation techniques. The Mondavis incorporated cold fermentation into the making of their wine, producing a lighter, fruitier taste than the predominately sweet California wines available at the time. Before long, St. Helena's production reached more than a million gallons per year.

Mondavi Winery Gets Its Start

At the time, the bulk-wine market was dominated by a few large wineries, such as the Gallo Brothers, and bulk-wine making was made still less lucrative by a government imposed price-freeze that held the price of bulk wine at 27 cents per gallon. Robert Mondavi's interest began to lean toward producing the more sophisticated dry wines. In 1943, Robert learned that the Charles Krug Winery, one of the region's oldest, was up for sale. Robert planned to produce higher quality dry wines under the Krug label, while financing the purchase with the continued sale of St. Helena bulk wine. After Cesare Mondavi's initial reluctance, the family bought the Krug winery and its 160 acres of vines for $87,000. Robert and Peter Mondavi were each given 12 percent of the new business. Peter, then still in the Army, would join the business as its winemaker. Robert Mondavi became general manager, handling the development and marketing of their wines. The new company was called C. Mondavi & Sons.

The old Krug vines were torn out and replaced by Cabernet Sauvignon, Sauvignon Blanc, Riesling, and Chardonnay vines. The winery itself—which, in its later years, had served as a bulk wine factory—needed extensive renovations. Sales of the Mondavi's bulk wine, selling in half-gallon and gallon jugs, financed the new Krug operation. The bulk wine was renamed CK Mondavi, marking the first appearance of the Mondavi name on a label. The premium wine to be produced would be sold under the Krug label.

By then, Robert Mondavi had spent many years consulting wine-growing experts and experimenting with wine production techniques. In an effort to improve the quality of the Krug wines, he bought a number of used brandy barrels. By aging the wine in smaller barrels, in contrast to the giant aging vats common in the American wine industry at the time, Mondavi hoped to produce a finer wine. It was not long before the Krug wines began to win its first prizes at state fair competitions. Still more important to Krug's growth were Robert Mondavi's tireless promotional efforts. Mondavi was convinced that the Napa Valley region could produce a grape—and wines—equal to those of the renowned French and Italian wine-growing regions. He also insisted on blind tastings, which allowed his wines to stand on their own merits, uncompromised by the stigma still attached to Californian wine. Soon, the Napa Valley name— and Krug's—appeared on more and more wine lists and store shelves across the country.

Tensions Split the Family: Robert Mondavi Begins His Own Business

Unfortunately, tensions arose between Robert and Peter Mondavi. Peter Mondavi resented Robert's interference in the wine-making, and Robert's salesmanship also placed continuous pressure on the winery's production capacity. By 1946, the brothers faced a crisis: Robert had placed large orders for grapes from the local growers, but a bumper crop that year cut the price of grapes in half and the Mondavis faced a loss of nearly half a million dollars. Nevertheless, the family made good on its contracts with the growers, and the Krug winery went into debt. Robert Mondavi continued to promote the Krug wines, and continued to push his brother to expand the winery's production.

In order to meet the demand that Robert was creating, however, Peter was forced to release their wines before they were properly aged. Quality declined, followed shortly thereafter by sales. Robert appealed to Cesare Mondavi, who still controlled the majority of the company, and was placed in full control of the winery's production. When Cesare Mondavi died, however, Rosa Mondavi, inheriting the majority of the company, made herself president, and Rosa favored Peter's vision of running the Mondavi wineries. Meanwhile, both Peter and Robert were trying to establish their sons in the family business. Nonetheless, largely due to Robert Mondavi's abilities as a salesman, the Mondavis were showing pretax profits of $200,000 by 1965.

The tensions between Peter and Robert reached a head in that year and ended in a fistfight. Robert was dismissed as general manager and given a six-month leave from the company. At the same time, Robert's eldest son, Michael, then 23, who had grown up at the Krug winery and recently graduated from the University of Santa Clara, was barred from working at the company for ten years. It was then that Robert Mondavi decided to open his own winery.

Together with two partners, Mondavi raised $200,000 and purchased property in Oakville, California. Financing for construction was arranged through an insurance firm, while a glass company funded a bottling line. In September 1966, the Robert Mondavi Winery was ready for its first crush. It was the first new winery to appear in Napa Valley since Prohibition. From the outset, the Mondavi Winery was dedicated to producing premium wines. It was Robert Mondavi's ambition to produce wines that could compete with Europe's best.

The Krug side of the Mondavi family responded to the new winery by dismissing Robert Mondavi from the company altogether. This set the stage for a legal battle that would not be resolved until 1979. Robert Mondavi still controlled 24 percent of C. Mondavi & Sons, and remained on its board until 1973. The feud between the brothers extended to include the pronunciation of the family name. Peter called himself ''mon-day-vi,'' the Americanized pronunciation first adopted by Cesare Mondavi. Robert Mondavi began calling himself ''mon-dah-vi,'' the traditional Italian pronunciation.

Robert Mondavi Winery Begins

The new winery featured many of the innovations Robert Mondavi had introduced to California winemaking, including cold fermentation. On a trip through Europe in 1962, visiting the great chateaux and tasting their wines, Mondavi discovered what he considered a key element to the quality of French wines: they were aged in small barrels. Over the next several years, Mondavi experimented with a variety of wood types and barrel sizes, finally choosing small French oak barrels for his wines. At the new Mondavi winery, all wines were to be aged in French oak barrels.

Joined by Michael Mondavi and, later, by Tim Mondavi, the Robert Mondavi Winery produced its first wine for sale—a $3 Chenin Blanc—in 1967. By the following year, sales of this wine, previously known as White Pinot, increased fivefold. In that year, Mondavi also introduced a new wine, Fumé Blanc. This wine was, in fact, a Sauvignon Blanc, not a highly regarded wine variety. Mondavi changed the fermentation, blended the wine with Semillion, and aged it in French oak barrels, producing a drier wine. In order to distinguish his new wine, Mondavi coined the new name. The Americanized structure of the name—with the adjective first—connected it to California, while achieving a link to the renown of the French Blanc Fumé wines. Fumé Blanc was an immediate success, and did much to put Mondavi on the winemaking map.

The success of Robert Mondavi's wines was not enough, however. By 1969, Mondavi had run out of capital he would need to increase production beyond 25,000 cases per year, and he was forced to look for a fresh source of financial backing. Mondavi advertised for investors in the Wall Street Journal and received more than 250 responses. Both Suntory of Japan and Nestlé approached Mondavi with partnership offers, but Mondavi turned them down. Then Mondavi's two partners sold their share of the winery and vineyards to the Rainier Companies, a Seattle-based brewer, 48 percent of which was owned by the Molson Companies of Canada. The Mondavi Winery now had the capital to expand: over the next decade, Rainier poured more than $6 million into expanding the winery. At the same

time, Rainier had also gained 100 percent of the vineyards and 75 percent of the winery, with Robert Mondavi retaining only 25 percent of the winery. Importantly, however, he remained its president, still in control of its winemaking operations.

The feud over the C. Mondavi & Sons winery—which enjoyed considerable success through the 1960s and 1970s—gave way to a series of lawsuits and trials in the mid-1970s. Robert Mondavi emerged victorious in 1976, and by the following year, the courts ordered C. Mondavi & Sons to be sold in order to pay Robert Mondavi fair market value for his 24 percent interest. Eventually, the brothers reached an out-of-court settlement. Robert Mondavi received more the $5 million, which included five million gallons of wine and 430 acres of vineyards. The settlement enabled Mondavi to take back financial control of his winery. After Rainier sold its brewing operations to G. Heileman Brewing Co. in 1977, Molson agreed to sell its interest in Rainier to Robert Mondavi, at $9.40 for each of its one million shares. At the same time, Rainier, now little more than a holding company for the winery, began liquidation procedures, including buying back its stock from its shareholders. In the end, Robert Mondavi and his family regained full control of the Robert Mondavi Winery.

Mondavi Wines Gain Notoriety

Despite several years of losses and nearly $10 million in debt by 1978, Mondavi's wine enjoyed considerable success during the 1970s. In 1972 the Los Angeles Times named the Mondavis' 1969 Cabernet Sauvignon as its top wine. Production expanded to include red, rosé, and white wines by 1974, and by 1975, Mondavi wines were distributed nationwide. Two years later, Mondavi began exporting. In 1976, Napa Valley wines gained international renown when a 1973 Cabernet Sauvignon from the Stag's Leap winery won in a blind tasting of Californian and French wines that became known as the Paris Tasting.

Napa Valley's reputation was further enhanced when Baron Phillippe de Rothschild, of the famed Chateau Mouton Rothschild, announced plans to collaborate with Robert Mondavi on a new ultrapremium wine, to be called Opus One and to be produced in the United States. Importantly, the U.S. market for premium wines was beginning an explosion: by the end of the 1970s, U.S. wine consumption had grown to more than 450 million gallons per year. Robert Mondavi, with its commitment to quality, became one of the most powerful brand names in the U.S. wine industry. This, despite the fact that the company spent almost no money on advertising, relying instead on the salesmanship—and showmanship—of Robert Mondavi himself.

Through the 1980s, Mondavi continued to expand its product line. Its purchase of the Woodbridge Winery in 1979 allowed it to expand into California varietal wines, selling premium wines in the important $3–$7 per bottle market. In 1980, the first Mondavi vintage-dated wines were introduced, selling in the super premium, $14-per-bottle-and-over category. Mondavi purchased the Vichon Winery, in Napa Valley, in 1985, giving it greater vineyards and research capacity. Five years later, the company bought the Byron Vineyard & Winery in Santa Maria Valley in Santa Barbara County. Exports continued to grow, from 1 percent of the company's sales in 1980 to 6 percent in the 1990s, reaching more than 75 countries. By 1988, its revenues had reached $95 million, with earnings of $7.2 million.

New Generation of Mondavis Take Over

In 1990, at age 76, Robert Mondavi turned over active management of the company to sons Michael and Tim. Michael was named managing director and chief executive officer; Tim became managing director, and continued his role as head wine-maker. Robert Mondavi remained chairman of the company, and continued his role as promoter of California wines. By the following year, production had reached 500,000 cases per year. However, despite growing revenues—reaching $145 million in 1992—income had dropped, struggling to reach $7.1 million that year. By then, the company was carrying more than $126 million in debt.

A greater problem threatened the Mondavis, and the whole of Napa Valley, in the late 1980s and early 1990s. Grape phylloxera, a species of lice that attacks the roots and leaves of grape vines, had attacked much of the Napa and Sonoma valleys. With no cure for the disease, growers were forced to tear out their old vines and replace them with phylloxera-resistant varieties. Grape production throughout the Napa and Sonoma valleys, which accounted for some 80 percent of grapes used in the making of premium wines, was expected to drop by more than a third over the coming years. The majority of the Mondavis' grapes came from outside growers, however, so they were largely shielded from rising grape prices because most of their grape purchases were done through long-term contracts. Nevertheless, some 15 percent of their grapes were grown in their own vineyards, and the Mondavis were faced with spending $20 million or more to replace their damaged vines with new stock, which would take five years or more before they were ready to produce commercial quantities of grapes—which would require still more years of aging before they could be released as Mondavi wine. Meanwhile, growing competition from such countries as Chile and Australia, as well as increasing exports from Europe, forced U.S. wineries to keep their prices low despite rising grape costs. More and more wineries were being bought by large, cash-rich corporations.

Intent on maintaining control of their company, the Mondavis went public to raise funds. Despite misgivings from some industry analysts, the initial public offering of Mondavi stock, made in 1993, raised $32.3 million. A secondary offering two years later raised an additional $35.5 million. Yet the Mondavis still retained control of 92 percent of the voting stock. Production rose to 3.9 million cases in 1993 to 4.5 million in 1995. Revenues had grown to nearly $200 million in 1995, while net income more than doubled from $8.6 million in 1993 to $17.8 million in 1995. The company also discovered a hidden benefit of the phylloxera plague: the new disease-resistant vines could be planted closer together, allowing up to four times more vines per acre. In keeping with the Mondavi tradition, the company intended to grow fewer grapes per vine, producing a more intense flavor; nonetheless, it expected a 50–70 percent increase in yields.

Winery Expands With New Endeavors

In 1995 the company planned to spend $2.5 million on its first print advertising campaign, while Robert Mondavi contin-

ued to be the company's chief spokesman, salesman, and ambassador. By 1999, the advertising had expanded to radio and television, with a focus on the Woodbridge line in an attempt to increase everyday wine consumption in the United States "We want them to think of wine as a wonderful, social, everyday beverage to enjoy," said Michael Mondavi.

Big additions came to the winery during the last half of the 1990s, not only in terms of wine, but also in architecture, visitor experiences, and a return to age-old winemaking techniques. In 1998, the company embarked on a new kind of endeavor when it partnered with the Walt Disney Company to create a $10 million wine-country attraction at Disney's new California Adventure theme park. The experience offered a demonstration vineyard, tasting areas, and a film on wine.

In 2001, the interest in architecture expanded to yet another creation: Copia, the American Center for Food, Wine & the Arts, a museum dedicated to the culture of food and wine. Thirteen years in the making, it cost $55 million and covered 80,000 square feet. Robert Mondavi conceived it as a way to raise awareness of his region's wine profiles. The center boasted a cooking school, museum, restaurants, movies, concerts and picnics, a rare cookbook collection, wine tastings, kitchen showrooms and other attractions. Partners included UC-Davis, Cornell University, *Wine Spectator* magazine, and the area's large wineries. Julia Child and Martha Stewart have honorary board seats. Food masters hailed it as finally celebrating food and wine as a "serious subject." The Center anticipated 300,000 guests a year.

New changes to the winery itself were in order as well. By 2001, the winery was receiving 350,000 visitors a year; with a newly renovated visitor center the winery could now comfortably handle them all. The project cost $28 million and took two years to complete. It included a new red-wine fermentation cellar housing 56 French oak tanks, a departure from the stainless steel casks that caused a stir in the industry 40 years earlier. Two new public tasting rooms offered visitors a choice of eight different tours and samplings, and a reservations system ensured the experience ran smoothly.

On the wine front, global expansion and new offerings continued. In January 2001, the company introduced a new Chilean wine called Arboleda. Later that year, a new partnership with Southcorp's Rosemount Estates marked the company's foray into Australian wine. The family-owned winery, based in the Hunter Valley region of Australia, combined forces with Mondavi to create two new wine lines, one from California, one from Australia. Mondavi agreed to sell the Australian wines worldwide while Rosemount sold the Mondavi brands in Australia. CEO Michael Mondavi said: "This allows us to add a world-class Shiraz to our luxury wine portfolio while participating in the growth of the Australian super premium wine segment."

A Return to Old Traditions for the Mondavis

The new French oak tanks signified a return to old-fashioned, wood-barrel wine-making, coined the "To Kalon" project. The family concluded the best way to make wine was with as little technology as possible. Pumps were replaced by traditional gravity systems, grapes were grown too close for tractors to harvest (requiring human pickers), and bladder presses were replaced with basket presses. The temperature-controlled, steel fermenting tanks were reserved for the white wines. The new techniques also meant visitors could have more access to the winemaking process, with tours leading them through the oak-barrel-full cellars. The company also continued to experiment with grape-growing techniques, keeping true to its natural-farming practices.

However, not every endeavor was successful those years. The company canceled an $8 million project to create a winery in France, the first foreign-owned vin de terroir (a special designation for French wine), when the local French protested the move, fearing the loss of their forest and the creation of an industrial-sized winery. Some Napa Valley residents displayed much criticism for Copia, citing lost taxes and a decline in city resources. In 2001, the corporation cut its involvement in the Disney adventure, turning over day-to-day operations to them. The theme park failed to meet predicted attendance records, and Mondavi ended its 10-year agreement, taking a $12–$13 million loss.

Still the company continued to grow and give back to the community Robert Mondavi grew up in. The winery gave a $35 million gift to UC-Davis in September 2001, earmarked for creation of the Robert Mondavi Institute for Wine and Food Sciences. Although Robert Mondavi released control of the company to sons Michael and Tim—and new CEO Gregory Evans—in May 2001, he continued to serve as "ambassador-at-large." The senior Mondavi's autobiography, *Harvests of Joy*, was published in 1998, and in late 2001, *Forbes Magazine* named the Robert Mondavi company one of the "200 Best Small Companies in America." With the new Copia center, the advertising campaign, the return to traditional techniques, and a renovated visitor center, the winery looked forward to continuing its efforts in public education and appreciation of wine.

Principal Subsidiaries

Robert Mondavi Winery; Robert Mondavi Coastal; Seña; Caliterra; Woodbridge by Robert Mondavi; Vichon Winery; Bryon Vineyard & Winery; Opus One Winery (50%); Luce.

Principal Competitors

Allied Domecq; Bacardi USA; Beringer Blass; Brown-Forman; Cervecerias Unidas; Chalone Wine; Constellation Brands; Diageo; Zignago; Kendall-Jackson; Pernod Ricard; Ravens-wood Winery; Sebastiani Vineyards; Terlato Wine; Trinchero Family Estates; Stimson Lane Vinyards and Estates.

Further Reading

Abrams, Mara, "Improving with Age: Mondavi Gift Revamps UC-Davis Wine Program," *University Wire*, January 14, 2002.

Echikson, William, "How Mondavi's French Venture Went Sour," *Business Week*, September 3, 2001, p.60.

Erdman, Andrew, "Robert Mondavi," *Fortune*, March 11, 1991, p. 99.

Ferguson, Tim W., "Mondavi Bucks the Tide," *Forbes*, October 23, 1995, p. 203.

Grumbel, Andrew, "Hi-Tech Winery Dumps," *American Times*, January 8, 2002, p. 10.

Hall, Christopher, "Mondavi Expands Winery and Tours," *The New York Times*, April 15, 2001, p. 3.

Hubler, Shawn, and Fulmer, Melinda, "A Monument to the Good Life in Napa Culture," *Los Angeles Times*, November 17, 2001, p. A-1.

——, "Center Irritates Some," *The Seattle Times*, November 18, 2001, p. A13.

Johnson, Scott, "Mondavi in Languedoc," *Newsweek International*, September 24, 2000, p. 27.

Le Quesne, Nicholas, "A Case of Sour Grapes," *Time International*, June 18, 2001, p. 51.

Koselka, Rita, "A Pox on the Stox," *Forbes*, June 7, 1993, p. 46.

Mondavi, Robert, *Harvests of Joy: My Passion for Excellence*, Harcourt Brace & Co., 1998.

Morita, Jennifer K., "The Robert Mondavi Corp. Aims to Expand Wine's Everyday Appeal," *The Record*, November 7, 1999.

Nigro, Dana, "Mondavi Wins OK for Groundbreaking French Estate," *The Wine Spectator*, September 30, 2000, p. 14.

Prial, Frank, "There's a Genie in the Cellar," *The New York Times*, May 30, 2001, p. F1.

Quinn, Andrew, "California Wine Giant Robert Mondavi Steps Down," *Reuters Business Report*, May 1, 2001.

"Rosemount and Mondavi Form Alliance," *Grocer*, October 21, 2000, p. 55.

Shriver, Jerry, "Michael Mondavi California Winemaker," *USA Today*, December 29, 2000, p. D2.

——, "Napa Pours on the Hospitality; California Wineries Are Adding Luxury, and a Price Tag, to the Tasting Experience," *USA Today*, October 26, 2001, p. D9.

——, "Vintage Mondavi Winemaker at 85: They've All Been Very Good Years," *USA Today*, June 17, 1998, p. 1D.

Simeone, Lisa, "Profile: California Wine Grower Robert Mondavi's Attempt to Open a Winery in the South of France," *Weekend Edition* (NPR), March 17, 2001.

Tagliabue, John, "Robert Mondavi Abandons Plan to Make Wines in France," *The New York Times*, May 16, 2001, p. C4.

—M. L. Cohen
—update: Kerri DeVault

Roper Industries, Inc.

160 Ben Burton Road
Bogart, Georgia 30622
U.S.A.
Telephone: (706) 369-7170
Fax: (706) 353-6496
Web site: http://www.roperind.com

Public Company
Incorporated: 1981
Employees: 2,950 (2001)
Sales: $587 million (2001)
Stock Exchanges: NASDAQ
Ticker Symbol: ROP
NAIC: 333911 Pump and Pumping Equipment Manufacturing; 334514 Totalizing Fluid Meter and Counting Device Manufacturing; 421810 Construction and Mining (except Oil Well) Machinery and Equipment Wholesalers; 334516 Analytical Laboratory Instrument Manufacturing

A leader in the fluid handling, industrial controls, and analytical instrumentation industries, Roper Industries, Inc. manufactures and distributes highly engineered, application-specific products for a broad range of industries, including the oil and gas, chemical and petrochemical processing, research, medical, semiconductor, and power generation industries. In the early 2000s, Roper Industries operated in three business segments: industrial controls, which manufactured microprocessor-based turbomachinery control systems, pressure sensors, and thermostatic valves; fluid handling, which manufactured rotary gear pumps, air-operated diaphragm pumps, and centrifugal pumps; and analytical instrumentation which manufactured digital imaging, fluid properties test, industrial leak test, materials analysis, microscopy preparation and handling, and spectroscopy products. With slightly more than half of its sales derived from overseas, the company recorded resolute growth during the early 2000s by expanding internationally through several key acquisitions.

Stoves and Pumps: Early History

Roper Industries' historical roots reach back to its founder, George D. Roper, and the company he started in 1919, the Geo. D. Roper Corporation. Founded in Rockford, Illinois, as a manufacturer of gas stoves and gear pumps, Geo. D. Roper Corp. became best known for its production stoves, developing into a flourishing concern that eventually manufactured electric and gas kitchen ranges, power gardening tools, and a host of other home-related goods. The company's smaller business segment, the manufacture of pumps, which constituted the origins of Roper Industries, remained overshadowed by the association of the Roper name with kitchen appliances, existing for decades as a barely known enterprise, while the appliance segment garnered the bulk of Geo. D. Roper Corp.'s total sales and, consequently, nearly all of its publicity.

For much of the first half of the 20th century, the two businesses—gear pumps and kitchen stoves—operated together within the same corporate structure, but in the late 1950s the two segments were split into two different companies that 30 years later existed as Roper Corporation a large kitchen appliance manufacturer with more than $700 million in annual sales; and Roper Industries, a manufacturer of an assortment of pumps and controls with an annual sales volume roughly 25 times smaller than Roper Corporation.

The Postwar Years: Two Distinct Companies Emerge

The two distinct business segments embarked on their separate paths of development when the Florence Stove Company, founded in the early 1870s as a maker of wood-burning stoves, set its acquisitive sights on the Geo. D. Roper Corp. In 1957, Florence Stove sold its manufacturing facility in Florence, Massachusetts, and transferred production to Illinois, then purchased the inventories of finished products, receivables, and all capital stock of Geo. D. Roper Corp. The entire new operation took the name Geo. D. Roper Corp. in 1958. Meanwhile, Geo. D. Roper Corp.'s pump manufacturing operations were moved to Georgia, as the newly assembled corporation flourished under the beneficent corporate umbrella of retailing giant Sears, Roebuck & Co.

Sears not only was Geo. D. Roper Corp.'s largest customer but also owned nearly half of the Illinois-based appliance manufacturer. This relationship between Sears and Geo D. Roper Corp. was strengthened when Geo D. Roper Corp. merged with a wholly owned Sears subsidiary, Newark Ohio Co., in 1964. Newark Ohio, which manufactured electric ranges, lawn mowers, and other products for Sears, sold nearly all of its products to its parent company prior to the merger, while Geo D. Roper Corp. derived 55 percent of its annual revenue from sales to Sears before the merger. Once combined, the merged entity relied on its relationship with Sears to generate more than three-quarters of total sales, ranking as Sears' largest supplier of gas and electric ranges, rotary mowers, and a major supplier of drapery hardware.

When Geo. D. Roper and Newark Ohio merged, the Geo. D. Roper Corporation corporate title was retained for several years until Roper Corporation was adopted as the company's new name in April 1968, by which time the gas stove manufacturing business originally founded by George Roper was rapidly approaching the $200-million-a-year sales mark. Over the ensuing two decades, Roper Corporation broadened its product line and grew as Sears grew, developing into a more than $500 million company by the mid-1980s, when Roper Corp. implemented a major restructuring program. Nonessential businesses, such as the company's involvement in luggage and window blind production, were spun off; manufacturing facilities were relocated from the Midwest to Georgia and South Carolina; and 60 percent of its shares were bought back from Sears, making Roper Corporation a more cost-efficient maker of electric kitchen ranges than other major producers. The changes effected during the mid-1980s also made Roper Corporation a much more attractive acquisition target, and in 1988 a bidding war between Whirlpool Corporation and the General Electric Company was touched off, as the two giant appliance makers battled for the rights to acquire one of the few U.S. electric appliance manufacturers still in existence. In the end, General Electric emerged the victor, and acquired Roper Corporation's manufacturing capacity for stoves and lawn equipment, the core of its more than $700 million business at the time.

1980s and Beyond: New Leadership and Expansion at Roper Industries

As Roper Corporation slowly disappeared from the business press spotlight, existing in relative anonymity deep within the sundry organizational layers comprising behemoth General Electric, the other half of the former Geo. D. Roper Corporation—the pump manufacturing facilities that were relocated to Georgia in the late 1950s—was beginning to etch a new identity for the Roper name as Roper Industries Inc. During Roper Corporation's rise as a major supplier to Sears, the Georgia-based pump works—Roper Pump Company—operated as a public company until 1981, when a leveraged buyout transferred ownership of the company to private hands. The following year, the person chiefly responsible for Roper Industries' growing stature during the 1980s and 1990s arrived, marking the beginning of a new era in the company's history that would punctuate its decades of quiet existence with resolute, international growth.

This pivotal figure in the company's ascension was British-born Derrick N. Key, who was named vice president of Roper Industries in June 1982. A former consultant for Johnson & Johnson, Key put his experience in marketing consumer products to work at Roper Industries, and introduced a management system that had achieved considerable success at numerous consumer products companies, but rarely had been used at manufacturing companies like Roper Industries. Key's importation of the product manager system, which was adopted by Roper Industries following Key's arrival, pushed the decision-making process down the company's management ladder, ceding substantial control to company managers. Within Roper Industries, each major product was assigned its own manager, who was then put in charge of overseeing the full development of the product, wielding control over production, sales, and advertising.

As the success engendered by the implementation of the product manager system grew, Key moved up Roper Industries' corporate ladder, becoming president of Roper Industries' primary revenue-generating engine, Roper Pump Company, in November 1985. Less than four years later, in February 1989, Key was named president of Roper Industries, assuming the company's presidential post at a time when annual sales hovered around $35 million and earnings stood at $2 million. Under Key's direction, these modest financial totals would rise strongly, propelled by an aggressive acquisition and expansion program orchestrated by Key that would position Roper Industries as a considerably larger international competitor in the specialty controls industry. In the first five years of Key's leadership, annual sales more than quadrupled, while earnings recorded a more prodigious gain, increasing tenfold, as Roper Industries began to attract the attention long-accorded to Roper Corporation's appliance business.

The first pivotal move in Roper Industries bid to become a larger, more globally oriented competitor was executed a year after Key's promotion to president, when the company acquired Amot Controls Corporation and its U.K. and Switzerland subsidiaries in July 1990 for approximately $28 million. Amot Controls, which manufactured valves, switches, and sensors for the oil and gas, power generation, and transportation industries, represented an important addition to Roper Industries, giving the company one of the primary pillars supporting its existence during the 1990s. After its first full year as a Roper Industries' company, Amot Controls helped push companywide annual sales to $75 million, or more than twice as much as Roper Industries generated two years earlier, setting the tone for the rapid growth to follow during the early 1990s.

Another important acquisition, one that would play a leading role in Roper Industries' most publicized event in its history,

Key Dates:

1919: Geo. D. Roper Corporation is founded.
1957: The company is acquired by Florence Stove Company, and the combined new operation is renamed Geo. D. Roper Corporation.
1958: Geo. D. Roper Corporation's pump manufacturing is moved to Georgia, and is renamed Roper Pump Company.
1964: The company merges with New Ohio Co., a Sears subsidiary.
1968: Geo. D. Roper Corporation is renamed Roper Corporation.
1981: Roper Pump Company reorganizes as Roper Industries.
1989: Derrick Key becomes president of Roper Industries.
1990: The company acquires Amot Controls Corporation, a manufacturer of valves, switches, and sensors.
1992: Roper Industries becomes a public company.
1993: The company strikes a control systems deal with Russian natural gas conglomerate Gazprom.
1993: The company acquires Integrated Designs Inc. (IDI), a semiconductor manufacturer.
1994: Derrick Key is named chairman of Roper Industries.
1995: The company acquires Metrix Instrument Company, a manufacturer of equipment for the rotating machine industry.
1996: The company acquires Gatan International, a manufacturer of electron microscopy control systems.
1997: The company acquires Petrotech, a turnkey control systems company.
1998: The company acquires Acton Research, a maker of spectrographic systems and specialty optics, and Abel Pump, a manufacturer of water, industrial, marine, and mining pumps.
2000: The company acquires Hansen Technologies, a manufacturer of valves and controls for refrigeration systems.
2001: The company acquires Struers Holdings A/S, a producer of materialographic sample preparation equipment.

was completed two years after the purchase of Amot Controls. In September 1992, Roper Industries acquired Compressor Controls Corporation, the world's leading turbocompressor control manufacturer, for an estimated $35 million. Together, Amot Controls and Compressor Controls composed Roper Industries' industrial controls business segment, the smaller of the company's two business segments in 1992, but the segment that would provide the bulk of the company's growth between 1992 and the mid-1990s.

After an 11-year hiatus, Roper Industries once again became a publicly owned company in 1992, giving it the necessary capital to continue its acquisition and expansion campaign, which became increasingly international in focus following the purchase of Compressor Controls. Relying on the global connections it had realized through its two international acquisitions, Roper Industries made the headlines in the business press the year after its

public offering by striking a deal with the massive Russian natural gas conglomerate, Gazprom, to supply computerized control systems for Russia's enormous pipeline system. The agreement between Compressor Controls and Gazprom led to a seven-year contract worth $350 million, the announcement of which drew enough praise from certain sectors of the financial community to push Roper Industries' stock from a low of $5.75 a share to $78 a share before splitting two-for-one.

Although Roper Industries' Russian deal represented a potential boon to the company's business, it also represented a possible tinderbox, given the economic and political instability pervading Russia during the early and mid-1990s and the confounding vagaries of Russian bureaucracy. When shipments to Gazprom began in April 1993, however, expectations were high and largely substantiated by the year's end. By the end of 1993, in an abbreviated year as far as the company's contract with Gazprom was concerned, Roper Industries shipped $42 million worth of high-technology, high-speed controls to Gazprom, but in 1994, the difficulties inherent in doing business in Russia led to lackluster financial results. Installation delays and problems with financing in Russia hindered Roper Industries' Gazprom-related activities during the year, reducing the amount of the company's shipments to $35 million for the year.

The Gazprom deal continued to cause the company problems into the late 1990s. Starting in 1993, Roper worked with the U.S. Export-Import Bank (Ex-Im) to secure financing for shipments to Gazprom. In 1996, however, the company was forced to stop shipments because of congressional threats to block the financing. Senator Alfonse D'Amato of New York led the fight to suspend Ex-Im's dealings with Gazprom, citing Gazprom's dealings with Iran and the United States' increased sanctions on that country. As a result, Roper canceled a $12 million shipment to Gazprom in October 1997. That year, difficulties with the Russian gas conglomerate caused Roper's stock to fall by 24 percent. By December 1997, president Derrick Key announced that Gazprom would need to secure substantial funds by the middle of 1998, otherwise Roper would reduce its business or abandon the deal altogether. Gazprom then began efforts to arrange European bank financing to support the balance of its deal with Roper.

In January 1998, Roper announced a $12.3 million shipment to Gazprom (financed by Gazprom's general credit facilities). In May 1998, Gazprom had secured financing through a wholly owned European bank for its future business. This financing arrangement was expected to be available over the next five years for $128 million of additional turbomachinery controls purchases. By the time the company's 1998 annual report was released, Derrick Key was confident enough to pronounce that Roper had "finally achieve[d] the consistency of the Gazprom business that we have long striven for." In 2000, Gazprom extended its deal with Roper, committing to an additional $150 million of purchases over and above the original agreement and extended the term through the end of 2007.

Into a New Century: Growth in the 1990s and Beyond

Elsewhere in the family of Roper Industries companies, more consistently positive results were being achieved during the

1990s. In September 1993, Roper Industries acquired Integrated Designs Inc. (IDI) for $12 million, adding IDI's semiconductor-manufacturing equipment capabilities and its high profitability to the company's fluid handling business segment. The following year, as the company contended with the difficulties associated with Gazprom, it continued to focus on building other facets of its business by looking for industrial equipment companies to acquire, seeking to strengthen its involvement in the production of highly engineered, high-margin products. Roper Industries found such a company in August 1994 when it acquired Instrumentation Scientifique de Laboratoire, S.A. (ISL) for approximately $10.5 million. Headquartered in Verson, France with sales and service offices in the United States, the United Kingdom, Brazil, and Russia, ISL was one of the leading competitors in the world for oil refinery laboratory testing equipment. This acquisition bolstered Roper Industries' position in an industry—oil and refined petroleum products—it already served and it increased the company's international presence.

By the end of 1994, Roper Industries was deriving more than half its annual sales from outside the United States, largely through the foreign business developed by Key, who had been named chief executive officer in 1991, then finally chairman of Roper Industries in December 1994. Annual sales, which had reached $75 million in 1991, had climbed to $147 million by the end of 1994, thanks primarily to the development of the company's industrial controls segment, made up entirely of companies acquired since 1990. ISL, Compressor Controls Corporation, and Amot Controls Corporation composed Roper Industries' industrial controls segment, with Richmond, California-based Amot U.S. and Bury St. Edmunds, England-based Amot U.K. functioning as the two operating companies of Amot Controls Corporation. Combined, these companies generated $91 million of Roper Industries' 1994 total sales, with the company's fluid handling business segment, comprising Roger Pump Company, Cornell Pump Company and IDI, accounting for the balance.

As Roper Industries entered the mid-1990s, the company began mapping plans for the future, which included the strengthening of its U.S. businesses to offset any further problems with its contract to supply compressor controls to Russia. Toward this objective, the company announced the completion of its acquisition of Houston, Texas-based Metrix Instrument Company in October 1995. A manufacturer of vibration detection and analysis equipment for the rotating machinery industry, Metrix Instrument was incorporated into Roper Industries' burgeoning industrial controls segment. Roper continued to grow the segment through the 1990s with such acquisitions in 1997 as Petrotech, a turnkey control systems company, and in 2000 Hansen Technologies, a manufacturer of valves and controls for refrigeration systems. In 2001, Roper's industrial controls segment netted sales of $197 million.

In 1997 the company began expanding into the area of analytical instrumentation by making a series of acquisitions through the late 1990s and into the early 21th century. These acquisitions included Gatan International (a manufacturer of electron microscopy control systems) in 1996, Acton Research (a maker of high-end spectrographic systems and specialty optics) in 1998, and Struers Holdings A/S (a producer of materialographic sample preparation equipment) in 2001. In the first

quarter of 2002, Roper's analytical instrumentation segment had grown to net sales of $82 million.

The company carried over its strategy of acquiring small companies into its fluid handling segment, adding such companies as Abel Pump (a manufacturer of water, industrial, marine, and mining pumps) in 1998. In 2001, sales in the fluid handling segment netted the company $125 million.

The company was not immune from the economic downturn of the early 2000s, but Roper entered the early years of the 21th century optimistically and reported a strong start to the year 2002. The first quarter of that year saw a 9 percent increase in sales and a 240 basis point improvement in gross margins, and Roper remained confident in its ability to continue growing. "Roper is making good progress on the objectives we outlined for 2002," said president and CEO Brian Jellison in the company's first quarter report. "Despite the challenging first quarter economic environment, we are confident that our disciplined financial and operational processes will assure another record year for Roper Industries in 2002."

Principal Subsidiaries

ABEL Pump; Acton Research; Amot Controls Corp.; Antek Instruments; Compressor Controls Corp.; Cornell Pump Co.; Dynamco; Flow Technology; Fluid Metering, Inc.; Gatan; Hansen Technologies; Integrated Designs Inc.; Media Cybernetics; Metrix Instrument Co.; Petroleum Analyzer Company; Petrotech; Redlake/MASD; Roper Pump Co.; Roper Scientific.

Principal Operating Units

Analytical Instrumentation; Fluid Handling; Industrial Controls.

Principal Competitors

Agilent Technologies; Halliburton; SPX.

Further Reading

"Bottom-Fishing for Stocks during Volatile Markets," *On Wall Street*, June 1,1997, http://www.elibrary.com.

Byrne, Harlan S., "Russian Roulette," *Barron's*, July 31, 1995, p. 21.

Christy, John H., "Cheap and Unsexy," *Forbes*, March 24, 1997, p. 188.

Coleman, Zach, "Iran Sanctions Jeopardizing GA. Manufacturer, Roper Industries Fears Loss of Big Russian Customer," *Atlanta Business Chronicle*, November 14, 1997, p. A8.

Du Bois, Peter C., "Made-to-Order Profits: Companies Which Supply Sears Are Sharing in the Giant Retailer's Prosperity," *Barron's*, July 22, 1963, p. 3.

——, "On the Front Burner," *Barron's*, August 14, 1961, p. 11.

Eichenwald, Kurt, "G.E. in Deal to Acquire Roper," *New York Times*, April 1, 1988, p. D1.

"EQT Sells Struers," *European Venture Capital Journal*, October 2001, p. 16.

"George D. Roper—Special Situation," June 5, 1963, p. 9.

Glassman, James K., "No Excuse for Not Retiring Rich," *Washington Post*, May 16, 1999, p. H1.

Gordon, Mitchell, "Roper Recovery," *Barron's*, October 20, 1986, p. 60.

Gottschalk, Arthur, "Russian Deal 'Blessing and Curse' for Roper," *Journal of Commerce*, June 21, 1994, p. B5.

"How Georgia Stocks Fared: Roper Industries Downgraded after Russian Deal Stalls," *The Atlanta Constitution*, October 31, 1997, p. G4.

Husted, Bill, "With Georgia's Roper Industries, Only Thing Flashy Is Profit Line," *Knight-Ridder/Tribune Business News*, June 19, 1994, p. 6.

"In Brief," *Washington Post*, July 4, 2001, p. E5.

Joyner, Tammy, "Business Press: The Best Little Businesses in Georgia," *The Atlanta Journal and Constitution*, October 30, 1997, p. E9.

Karp, Richard, "The Home-Run Hitters," *Institutional Investor*, March 1989, p. 73.

Kempner, Matt, "Roper Acquisition Canceled, Earnings Outlook Reduced," *The Atlanta Journal and Constitution*, August 19, 1998, p. D12.

Lacroix, Edmond H., "Roper Corp.," *Wall Street Transcript*, November 4, 1968, pp. 14, 800.

"Leach Cancels Deal with Roper," *The Oil Daily*, August 20, 1998, http://www.elibrary.com.

Machan, Dyan, "Alchemist," *Forbes*, November 4, 1996, p. 182.

Matta, Mathew L., "NationsBanks Ropes in Roper Industries," *Bank Loan Report*, June 9, 1997, p. 13.

Music, Kimberley, "U.S. Equipment Firm Pulls Plug on Gazprom Deal," *The Oil Daily*, November 3, 1997, pp. 1–2.

"Net at Geo. D. Roper Cooking on All Burners," *Barron's*, March 21, 1968, p. 23.

O'Hanlon, John, "Derrick N. Key Chairman, President and Chief Executive Officer Roper Industries, Inc. Interview," *Wall Street Corporate Reporter*, March 29, 2001, http://www.elibrary.com.

Phadungchai, Naruth, "Roper Industries Borrows $300M," *Bank Loan Report*, March 27, 2000, http://www.elibrary.com.

Poole, Shelia, "Roper Earnings up 16 Percent, Gazprom Business in Doubt," *The Atlanta Journal and Constitution*, December 13, 1997, p. D1.

Quinn, Matthew C., "Roper Urges Russian Company to Find New Financing for Deal," *The Atlanta Journal and Constitution*, December 18, 1997, p. F5.

Rattle, Barbara, "Salt Lake Leak, Testing Company Sold to Georgia Firm for $4.8 Million," *The Enterprise*, December 1, 1997, p. 3.

"Roper Acquisition Brings Access to Aerospace Industry," *The Atlanta Constitution*, July 29, 1998, p. D12.

"Roper Completes Varlen Deal," *The Oil Daily*, June 23, 1999, http://www.elibrary.com.

"Roper Corp. Discloses It Is Talking Merger with Unit of Sears," *Wall Street Journal*, April 13, 1964, p. 20.

"Roper Corp. to Make Gas Ranges for Whirlpool," *Wall Street Journal*, March 14, 1962, p. 31.

"Roper Declines up to 23% after Warning Earnings Down," *The Atlanta Journal and Constitution*, July 1, 2000, p. F6.

"Roper Industries, Inc. Announces Acquisition of Metrix Instrument Company and a Fifty Percent Increase in Dividend Rates," *PR Newswire*, October 2, 1995, p.10.

"Roper Industries, Inc. Announces Record First Quarter Financial Results," *PR Newswire*, February 18, 1998, http://www.elibrary.com.

"Roper Industries, Inc. Announces Record Sales and Earnings for The Fiscal Year Ended October 31, 1998," *PR Newswire*, December 7,1998, http://www.elibrary.com.

"Roper Industries, Inc. Announces the Signing of a Definitive Purchase Agreement for the Acquisition of Photometrics, Ltd.," *PR Newswire*, March 30, 1998, http://www.elibrary.com.

"Roper Industries, Inc. Announces the Signing of a Letter of Intent for Its Largest Acquisition to Date," *PR Newswire*, July 28, 1998, http://www.elibrary.com.

"Roper Industries, Inc. Announces Third Quarter Financial Results," *PR Newswire*, August 17, 1998, http://www.elibrary.com.

"Roper Shares Decline as Company Tells of Acquisition, Warns of Profit Shortfall," *The Atlanta Constitution*, July 31, 2001, p. D5.

"Roper: Turncoat in a Takeover War," *Business Week*, April 11, 1988, p. 68.

"Sears' Unit and Roper Agree on Merger Plan," *Wall Street Journal*, April 20, 1994, p. 32.

Solomon, Goody L., "Nation of Magic Chefs?," *Barron's*, March 8, 1965, p. 11.

Stephens, Flo P., "Varlen Instruments, Inc.," *Hydrocarbon Processing*, November 1999, p. F116.

Walker, Tom, "How Georgia Stocks Fared: Roper's Prediction for Earnings Boosts Stock: Equipment Maker Expects to Beat Analysts' Estimates," *The Atlanta Journal and Constitution*, January 31, 1998, p. E04.

"Whirlpool Moves into the Kitchen," *Business Week*, March 14, 1988, p. 44.

—Jeffrey L. Covell
—update: Lisa Whipple

RWE AG

Opernplatz 1
45128 Essen
Germany
Phone: +49 (0) 201-12-00
Fax: +49 (0) 201-12-15199
Web site: http://www.rwe.com

Public Company
Founded: 1898 as Rheinisch-Westfälisches
Elektrizitätswerk Aktiengesellschaft
Employees: 155,634 (2001)
Sales: $29,498 million (2001)
Stock Exchanges: Frankfurt Düsseldorf XETRA Zürich
Ticker Symbol: 703712
NAIC: 221112 Fossil Fuel Electric Power Generation;
221113 Nuclear Electric Power Generation; 221121
Electric Bulk Power Transmission and Control;
221122 Electric Power Distribution; 221210 Natural
Gas Distribution; 211111 Crude Petroleum and
Natural Gas Extraction; 562111 Solid Waste
Collection; 562213 Solid Waste Combustors and
Incinerators

RWE AG is the holding company for the dominant electricity producer in Germany: RWE Group. That subsidiary supplies much of the country's electricity via a distribution and transmission network that extends over 139,000 kilometers—that is, a distance more than three times around the world. Founded at the end of the 19th century to supply electricity to the city of Essen, the subsidiary RWE Group now comprises six independently operating divisions. Electricity production remains the core business of RWE AG, but there has been some diversification in recent years into other energy sectors, namely oil, natural gas, water, and petrochemicals.

Turn of the Century Beginnings

The timing of RWE's foundation was fortuitous. At the end of the 19th century, Germany underwent the most rapid indus-trialization to date. In the decades before World War I, Germany moved into second place behind the United States among the world's industrial nations. Between 1880 and 1913, German coal output increased fourfold and production of steel tenfold. Chemicals manufacturing and heavy engineering were other strengths. Given its location at the heart of Germany's coal and steel industry and the presence of factories owned by Krupp, Thyssen, Siemens, and other German industrial giants, Essen was an appropriate base for the company that would come to dominate Germany's electricity supply. Even today, following the relative decline of heavy industry, Essen's state of North Rhine Westphalia still produces over one-quarter of German gross domestic product. Essen itself remains the energy center of Germany, playing host also to Ruhrgas and Ruhrkohle.

Such a dynamic economy, with its predominance of energy-intensive industries, needed power. Towards the end of the 19th century, only Friedrich Krupp AG generated electricity in Essen; this power was consumed primarily by Krupp plants. However, the municipal authorities were debating the desirability of establishing electricity supplies for electric trams and street lighting; small-scale electric street lighting was introduced in 1888 and the debate about power for trams was well under way in 1890.

In 1896, Elektrizitäts-Actien-Gesellschaft vorm W. Lahmeyer & Company (EAG) applied to the authorities of Essen for approval to build and manage a small power station. Despite heavy competition from Allgemeine Elektrizitäts-Gesellschaft (AEG) and Siemens & Halske, in 1898 Lahmeyer signed a 40-year contract to supply Essen with electricity. On April 25, 1898, Lahmeyer, together with banks from Frankfurt, founded the Rheinisch-Westfälisches Elektrizitätswerk Aktiengesellschaft (RWE). The company began operating with a steam generator to supply a few thousand consumers in the immediate environs of Essen. The first RWE-generated electricity was supplied on April 1, 1900.

The Market for Energy Broadens

From the beginning, RWE's leaders were conscious of the key role electricity would play in the industrial economy. Hugo Stinnes, a leading industrialist in the region, became chairman of the board. He was convinced the electricity industry would grow into an industrial giant and that an integrated supply industry able to take advantage of economies of scale was the best way forward. Throughout its history RWE has been heavily involved in the development of larger-scale generating units and high voltage transmission and distribution networks.

Stinnes also believed the task of developing this new industry was too important to be left solely to private enterprise. He concluded that the way forward lay in the coming together of private business and public authorities in a synthesis of the principles of private enterprise and public service. The city fathers of Essen, Mülheim an der Ruhr, and Gelsenkirchen, persuaded by Stinnes of the advantages of this approach, bought shares in RWE. By the beginning of World War I, a majority of the seats on the RWE board—17 out of 29—were occupied by public representatives. The mixed economy of RWE was established from an early stage. Private entrepreneurs managed the daily affairs of the company but the public authorities retained an influence on all fundamental policy questions.

It was in the first decade of the 20th century that the basic structure of Germany's industry took shape. In 1908, RWE and Vereinigte Elektrizitätswerke Westfalen AG (VEW) signed the first demarcation contract—a contract which remains in force to this day. Demarcation contracts mark out the supply areas of a utility and enable the larger companies to carve up the country by agreeing to keep out of each other's territory. Demarcation contracts are bolstered by concession contracts that grant utilities exclusive rights to public land for cables in return for concession payments to public authorities. In view of its growing contracts with a number of municipal authorities, RWE was rapidly able to build up its business and extend its supply area.

The system of concession contracts has persisted. However, attempts are being made to open up electricity supply to competition again. In 1980 a 20-year limit was placed on the duration of a concession contract, and, by the end of 1994, local authorities were free to chose alternative electricity suppliers. Large amounts of money are at stake; Essen, for example, receives 20 percent of RWE's nonindustrial tariff income, an arrangement the city may wish to leave intact. However, other utilities are known to wish to expand their activities into RWE's area and competition could become more intensive as the 1990s unfold.

The Importance of Coal

In 1899 Stinnes took on the young engineer Bernhard Goldenberg as technical adviser. By 1902 Goldenberg had become chairman of the technical board and was deciding company policy. Goldenberg shared Stinnes's belief that it was

necessary to take advantage of scale economies if electricity supply was to be cost effective. This strategy of maximizing sales needed a secure and plentiful supply of cheap fuel and technological advances in generation and distribution.

From the beginning, coal had been central to the growth of the German industrial economy and to the development of RWE in particular. In 1990 and 1991, brown coal and hard coal accounted for 48.1 percent and 23 percent, respectively, of electricity generated by RWE. Nuclear power was responsible for a further 21 percent, with water accounting for almost 4 percent. Gas and oil accounted for RWE's remaining primary energy consumption.

Hugo Stinnes, the driving force behind the creation of RWE, was originally a coal merchant and was most conscious of the direct connection between coal and electricity. In the early days of RWE, brown coal was not at first considered for use in electricity generation. The Reisholz power station built by Goldenberg to the south of Düsseldorf in 1908 and 1909, for example, was designed for hard coal. Goldenberg was, however, aware of the potential of brown coal, which is mined from open-cast mines and hence is much easier and cheaper to mine than hard coal, which is mined from deep pits. Goldenberg knew that Europe's largest reserve of brown coal was to be found west of the Rhine between Cologne and Aachen.

The end of World War I brought serious coal shortages as two million tons of hard coal had to be exported monthly as part of Germany's war reparations. This situation precipitated the use of brown coal in Germany and RWE set about securing its brown coal supplies. In 1920, a "common interest" contract involving an exchange of shares was signed between RWE and Roddergrube AG according to which Roddergrube, the first company to exploit brown coal commercially back in the 1870s, undertook to supply brown coal to RWE. Shortly afterwards, RWE acquired a majority holding in Roddergrube. Similar "common interest" contracts were signed with other coal producers in 1921.

In 1932 RWE developed its relationships with coal producers a stage further and acquired a majority shareholding in Rheinische Aktiengesellschaft für Braunkohlenbergbau (Rheinbraun). RWE's participation helped Rheinbraun, which owned the Fortuna power station—one of the largest power stations at that time and the subject of expansion plans—to extend its contract to supply electricity to the city of Cologne. Over the years, the Rheinbraun family of companies has been fully integrated into the RWE group. RWE's relationship with Rheinbraun is typical of the complex cooperation and ownership network that RWE gradually developed with coal producers and other electricity suppliers.

The Effects of World War II

German military requirements of the late 1930s and World War II made big demands on German heavy industry, including electricity. The end of the war brought with it the need for massive reconstruction, not only for the German economy but also for RWE. The Goldenberg works were destroyed, other plants were severely damaged, and coal mines, pipelines, and distribution networks were devastated. Massive external financial

Key Dates:

1896: The city of Essen signs a contract with utility company Elektrizitäts-Actien-Gesellschaft vorm. W. Lahmeyer & Company (EAG) to build a power plant.

1898: EAG and friends form the company Rheinisch-Westfälisches Elektrizitätswerk Aktiengesellschaft (RWE).

1900: The first RWE-generated electricity is supplied on April 1.

1906: With the acquisition of the utilities Elektrizitätswerk Berggeist AG, Brühl, and Bergische Elektrizitätswerke GmbH, Solingen, RWE extends its market beyond Essen and into the Kölner Bucht and Bergisches Land regions.

1933: National Socialists seize the seats on RWE's supervisory board held by the regional administrative bodies.

1948: At the initiative of RWE chairman, seven large electrical utilities join forces to form the interconnected power syndicate Deutsche Verbundgesellschaft (DVG).

1952: RWE is released from Allied Control.

1962: RWE and Bayernwerk decide to build Germany's first commercial nuclear reactor, Gundremmingen A.

1988: RWE further diversifies its Group with the acquisition of Deutsche Texaco AG, Hamburg; the chemicals and petroleum group is renamed RWE-DEA AG für Mineralöl und Chemie.

1990: Rheinisch-Westfälisches Elektrizitätswerk AG is renamed RWE Aktiengesellschaft.

1999: The company introduces a new vision of focusing their activities and resources, moving away from their past trend of diversification.

2000: RWE merges Lahmeyer AG into RWE AG.

2002: RWE agrees to buy U.K. power group Innogy Holdings.

assistance was required, as well as technical rebuilding. Reconstruction, however, brought technical opportunities. The plant was not merely rebuilt or repaired as obsolete equipment was replaced by the most modern, high pressure boilers and turbines.

The RWE leadership was more convinced than ever that the future of the electricity industry lay in the development of a fully integrated network of electricity producers, and was instrumental in the 1948 formation of the Deutsche Verbundgesellschaft (DVG). A forum for national electricity cooperation, DVG was composed of Germany's largest electricity utilities.

In 1952 RWE and its subsidiaries were finally released from the postwar control of the Allies. At this time Franz Hellberg, an internationally recognized expert on brown coal, joined the RWE board. He was charged with the task of building up the production of electricity from brown coal, a comparatively cheap source of fuel.

In the postwar years, brown coal was increasingly mined from new deep-lying open-cast mines. These mines, which could reach a depth of 300 meters, were part of a transition to bigger management units and required new mining technology. Excavators and diggers were developed which could move 100,000 cubic meters of coal a day.

By 1957, 45 percent of RWE's brown coal supply originated from the new open-cast mines. This transition made big investment demands. An extraordinary general meeting in October 1959 increased authorized capital by DM 147 million to DM 575 million. These funds were used to acquire 85 percent of the brown coal company Neurath AG.

The Demand for Electricity Feeds RWE Group's Growth

Increasing electricity demand necessitated productivity increases. RWE chose to bring these about through a major rationalization of Rhine brown coal. In December 1959 it transferred its shareholding in Neurath AG to Rheinbraun. In the same month, several other brown coal subsidiaries of RWE were brought under the umbrella of Rheinbraun. The assets so transferred included those of the Braunkohlen-und Brikettwerke Roddergrube AG, the Rheinische AG für Braunkohlenbergbau und Brikettfabrikation, and the Braunkohlen-Industrie AG (Biag).

As the German economic miracle got into its stride in the early 1960s, electricity demand surged ahead and a new phase of power station construction orders began. Brown coal provided the basis for this expansion, but it was also in the early 1960s that RWE became involved in the development of nuclear power. By 1990 nuclear power was responsible for over 20 percent of RWE-generated electricity. However, questions have been raised in Germany about the safety of nuclear power, which will limit the contribution of this source of electricity in the foreseeable future.

The development of secure and cheap fuel supplies was only one factor in RWE's growth. Bernhard Goldenberg initiated the policy of the development of coal and the technology of larger generating units, but Arthur Koepchen, Goldenberg's successor in 1917 as chairman of the technical board, was responsible for implementing the distribution of electricity over much longer distances than had hitherto been possible.

A Vision of Integration

Koepchen was firmly anchored in the RWE tradition of optimizing economies of scale. He believed electricity production was justified on economic grounds only through the generation of electricity in favorable locations and through the supply of large districts, and envisaged increasing cooperation between neighboring utility companies. In short, he had a vision of a fully integrated national electricity supply industry with cooperation between power stations regardless of fuel basis.

In order to achieve this, Koepchen had to connect RWE with the South where, since World War I, utilities in Prussia, Bavaria, and Baden had developed rapidly, with a particular reliance on hydroelectric power. Koepchen's goal was to connect the Alpine hydroelectric plants with the stations on the Rhine and the Ruhr. This brought legal, technical, and economic challenges.

Koepchen drew on the experience of the South Californian Edison Company which, since 1921, had demonstrated the possibility of transmitting electricity over high tension cables of 220 kilovolts, rather than the previous technical limit of 110 kilovolts. This breakthrough made possible a more extensive distribution network, and, in 1924, RWE began the construction of a north-south network with the assistance of Germany's biggest electrical engineering companies, Siemens and AEG.

By April 1930, Germany's first "electric highway" was completed, linking the densely populated areas of the Rhineland and Westphalia with the South. It was only within such a union that the development of the water power of Bavaria made economic sense, as Bavaria was sparsely populated in comparison to RWE's main supply area and by itself could not justify the construction of large production units. With work on the distribution network under way, RWE became involved in the construction of power stations in the southern part of the country. For example, in 1924 RWE participated, along with Grosskraftwerk Würtemberg, in the founding of the Voralpberge Illwerke, and, in 1928, work on the massive Schluchseewerk in the southern Black Forest began.

Moves Toward Diversification

Electricity production had always been one of the main sectors of RWE's activities. In 1988 RWE took a major step towards diversification with the acquisition of Deutsche Texaco. This deal prompted a reorganization of RWE's activities into the following divisions: energy, mining and raw materials; petroleum and chemicals; waste management; mechanical and plant engineering; and construction. All divisions operate independently. RWE AG fulfills the role of a holding company and serves to steer and coordinate Group interests in all strategically important matters.

The two main revenue-generating divisions were energy, organized under RWE Energie AG, and petroleum and petrochemicals, organized under RWE-DEA AG für Mineralöl und Chemie (RWE-DEA). In the fiscal year 1991, RWE Energie contributed 37 percent of the total earnings of the RWE group and RWE-DEA 41 percent (including petroleum tax).

The formation of RWE-DEA signaled the fact that, although electricity remained the core business of the RWE Group, diversification within the energy field was an important theme of the future. RWE-DEA had its roots in the 19th century. It was established in 1899 as the Deutsche Tiefbohr AG. In 1911 its name was changed to Deutsche Erdöl AG. In 1966 the Texaco Group acquired over 97 percent of the capital and altered the name to Deutsche Texaco in 1970. On June 29, 1988, Texaco sold its share in the company to RWE, giving rise to the reorganization is RWE and the creation of RWE-DEA. This new division of RWE was responsible for sales of DM 20.2 billion during fiscal year 1991. RWE-DEA was involved in exploration for and processing and marketing of crude oil and natural gas, and the production of petrochemicals.

The petroleum business was RWE-DEA's dominant source of income, but the company also engaged in some expansion in

eastern Germany and examined the possibility of involvement in other European countries. Interest in the former East Germany was not confined to petroleum products. In June 1991 an international consortium led by RWE and VEBA, with shares of 37.5 percent each, was reportedly poised to take over East Germany's largest oil refinery, Schwedt, which had an annual capacity of 11 million tons and a pipeline link to the former Soviet Union. RWE-DEA also intended to build up its chemical business, and, with a view to this, made a bid for Vista Chemicals of the United States in December 1990. The bid was ultimately successful. RWE-DEA finalized the acquisition in June 1991.

By taking over RWE's core business of electricity production, RWE Energie represented the greatest continuity with the past. The 1990s held out exciting possibilities for this division as a result of the unification of Germany in 1990. The East German electricity supply industry was unmodernized, inefficient, and polluting. The joint venture Vereinigte Energiewerke AG (VEAG) was formed in 1991 to rectify the situation. In return for investment in the supply of electricity to eastern Germany of DM 30 to DM 40 billion, VEAG was accorded a major slice of the market. The main participants in the venture were RWE Energie and PreussenElektra, with 35 percent each, and Bayernwerk, with 30 percent. However, the demands of European integration and continuing environmental vigilance provided major challenges in the 1990s.

Throughout the 1990s, RWE rode a telecommunication roller coaster. The company repeatedly sought out opportunities to merge with telecommunication companies and build their network up strong. In 1998, when the German telecommunication market opened up, competition became fierce for RWE's telecommunication subsidiaries. RWE disposed of some of their major telecommunication holdings by the end of 1998.

Moving into the Millenium with A New Group Vision

RWE introduced a new vision for the company in 1999. Rather than continuing to spread their interests thinly across a wide range of fields, RWE decided to focus their activities and resources on their core divisions: water, gas, electricity, and waste management. The new vision included the "multi-utility/multi-energy concept" which aimed at positioning RWE as Europe's leading international partner in the European energy and utility market. The company announced that they intended to sell the remaining non-core businesses by the end of 2003 (this included the unloading of their telecommunications interests that began in 1998). Conversely, RWE has focused attention on its core activities through strategic and global acquisitions. The company has acquired the United Kingdom's Thames Water and Innogy (electricity and gas), the United States' American Water Works, Slovakia's Nafta (gas storage), Itay's Elletra (electricity), the Netherlands' SSM Coal, and the Czech Republic's Transgas (gas). The 2001 purchase of Thames Water made RWE the third largest water supplier in the world. The purchase of Innogy made RWE Europe's second biggest electricity supplier behind Electricite de France and ahead of Italy's Enel. And the purchase of the Dutch coal trading company SSM Coal made RWE Europe's largest coal trading company. As RWE purchased up energy companies, concern grew over the decline in the number of choices available to customers. Concern about the privatization of utilities was also raised with the RWE's rash of utility purchases.

The high prices that RWE shelled out to acquire Innogy ($7.8 billion), American Water ($4.6 billion), and Thames Water ($6.29 billion) caused many spectators to question whether RWE would be able to continue without divesting interest in at least one of its divisions. Although the company focused its energy into the four core divisions, with the intent to transform itself into a one-stop-shop to cut costs on customer services, billing, and payment collection, the reality remained that RWE did not offer multiple utilities in each country where they operated. In 2002 RWE announced that the company intended to slow the rush of big money purchases. Dr. Richard Klein, head of corporate development and mergers and acquisitions at RWE, told *Utility Europe* in May 2002, "Our top priority is to integrate all our new businesses, as we did successfully with Thames Water." He continued, "However, our [acquisition] strategy is not necessarily on hold. We are still looking closely at new chances and observing markets for opportunities in Europe and the United States. However, their dimensions will be far smaller, more towards rounding off our current strong positions." Klein refused to discuss whether this statement could mean RWE was planning to bid for Vivendi Environment, an environment services company that RWE was interested in purchasing since their offer of EUR 30 billion was turned down in 2000.

Principal Subsidiaries

RWE Energie Aktiengesellschaft; Kernkraftwerke Gundremmingen Betriebsgesellschaft mbH (75%); Koblenzer Elektrizitätswerk und Verkehrs-AG (57%); Kraftwerk Aftwürttemberg AG (92%); Lech-Elektrizitätswerke AG (75%); Main-Kraftwerke AG (70%); Moselkraftwerke GmbH; Rhenag Rheinische Energie AG (54%); Rheinbraun Aktiengesellschaft; Maria Theresia Bergbaugesellschaft mbH; Reederei und Spedition "Braunkohle" GmbH; Rheinbraun Australia Pty Ltd; Rheinbraun U.S. Corporation; Rheinbraun Verkaufsgesellschaft mbH; RWE-DEA Aktiengesellschaft für Mineraloel und Chemie (99%); Condea Chemia GmbH; DEA Mineraloel Aktiengesellschaft; Vista Chemical Company (USA); RWE Entsorgung Aktiengesellschaft; American NuKEM Corp; R + T Entsorgung GmbH (51%); Lahmeyer Aktiengesellschaft für Energie-wirtschaft (64%); Rheinelektra AG (62%); Heidelberger Druckmaschinen AG (57%); Heidelberg Harris GmbH; Lahmeyer International GmbH (55%); NU.K.EM GmbH; Starkstrom-Anlagen-Gesellschaft mbH; Starkstrom-Gerätebau GmbH; Stierlen-Maquet AG; Hochtief Aktiengesellschaft vorm. Gebr. Helfmann (56%); D & M Partner, Inc (USA); MIT Gesellschaft für Management-Beratung, Informationssysteme und Technologie mbH (MIT-Beratung).

Principal Competitors

E.On AG; Royal Dutch/Shell Group of Companies; Vattenfall AB.

Further Reading

Bedell, Denise, "Powering Ahead of the Pack," *Corporate Finance,* November 2001, pp. 14–16.

Berghahn, V.R., *Modern Germany: Society, Economy and Politics in the Twentieth Century*, Cambridge: Cambridge University Press, 1987.

Fisher, Wolfram, "Germany in the World Economy During the Nineteenth Century," German Historical Institute, Annual Lecture, 1983.

"Germany Industry: REW Moves into U.K. Energy," *Country News Wire,* April 18, 2002.

Hardach, Kevin, *The Political Economy of Germany in the Twentieth Century*, Berkeley, Calif.: University of California Press.

Kitchen, Martin, *The Political Economy of Germany 1815–1914,* London: Croom Helm, 1978.

"Linklaters Seals $7.4 billion U.K. Energy Deal," *International Financial Law Review,* April 2002, p. 9.

Ockenden, Karma, "Hunger Turns to Thirst," *Utility Europe,* May 1, 2002, p. 18.

"RWE to Divest Condea Unit," *Chemical Market Reporter,* February 29, 2000, p. 1.

"RWE Launches New Gas Brand," *Gas Connections,* September 20, 2001, p. 8.

Spaccarotella, Nadia, and Kate Stanbury, "RWE," *Utility Europe,* January 1, 2002, p. 26.

—Debra Johnson
—update: Tammy Weisberger

Safeway PLC

6 Millington Road
Hayes
Middlesex UB3 4AY
United Kingdom
Telephone: 44 20 8848 8744
Fax: 44 20 8573 1865
Web site: http://www.safeway.co.uk

Public Company
Incorporated: 1977 (as James Gulliver Associates)
Employees: 92,000 (2001 est.)
Sales: £9.4 billion (US$14.4 billion) (2001)
Stock Exchanges: London
Ticker Symbol: SFW
NAIC: 445110 Supermarkets and Other Grocery (except
   Convenience) Stores

Considering its current annual sales of £9.4 billion, Safeway PLC has a remarkably short history. In 1987, just short of celebrating its tenth birthday, Argyll became the fourth-largest grocer in Britain, when it purchased the 133 U.K. Safeway stores from their U.S. parent, Safeway Stores, Inc. The Safeway purchase gave Argyll a place in the upper echelon of British retailing and encouraged the company to begin the conversion of its largest Presto stores to the widely recognized and well-respected Safeway name.

Gulliver Starts Small

James Gulliver is the person most responsible for Argyll's rapid rise. Gulliver was born in Cambeltown, Argyllshire (hence the Group's name), in 1930, and graduated from Glasgow University with a degree in engineering. He spent several years with the management consulting firm of Urwick Orr. In the mid-1960s, he joined the supermarket chain Fine Fare, then a division of Associated British Foods. He quickly became chief executive, and in a matter of seven years had more than tripled sales from £60 million to £200 million. One newspaper honored Gulliver as its ''Young Businessman of the Year'' for 1972, but

he resigned shortly thereafter, along with Alistair Grant, then managing director at Fine Fare.

Gulliver promptly bought a significant minority share Oriel Foods, a wholesaling firm doing about £10 million annually. Together with Grant and David Webster, an investment banker, Gulliver acquired management control of Oriel. Within a year, Oriel was bought out by RCA Inc., which was then trying to build a European food division. The three men stayed on, multiplying Oriel sales ten-fold by 1977. That year, Gulliver, Grant, and Webster left Oriel and formed James Gulliver Associates. After a first investment in a home improvements company, they began building their own grocery conglomerate, starting with the purchase of two food companies, Morgan Edwards and Louis C. Edwards, a Manchester meat business.

By 1980, the new organization had adopted the name Argyll Foods and made significant inroads into the U.K. grocery trade. Over the next few years, Argyll made several major acquisitions. Chief among these purchases were the 1981 acquisition of Oriel Foods for £19 million from RCA, which had apparently tired of the grocery business; and the June 1982 purchase of Allied Suppliers from James Goldsmith, for £101 million. Between them, these acquisitions gave Argyll a nationwide range of operations, but one concentrated in northern England and Scotland. Presto, the most important of the new holdings, was a chain of 136 large grocery stores. Argyll also now owned Templeton, a line of 84 medium-sized supermarkets in Scotland; Liptons, with some 500 supermarkets in England and Wales; Lo-Cost, which, as its name suggests, occupied the lower end of the price spectrum; and Cordon Bleu, a 125-unit chain selling frozen foods. Along with some limited food wholesaling activity, Argyll also owned a biscuit, tea, and coffee manufacturer and an oil refining business; both had been divested by 1987.

In 1983, Argyll Foods was merged with Amalgamated Distilled Products (ADP), a liquor company Gulliver and his associates had controlled since 1979. ADP produced Scotch whisky and dark rum, and ran a 300-unit discount liquor chain called Liquor-Save. It also owned Barton Brands, a U.S. liquor producer and distributor, which it had acquired in 1982.

Company Perspectives:

We believe that building sustainable advantage over our competitors can only be done through Safeway people. We are creating a business culture in which our people are passionate about our products, our stores and everything we do; have an unbreakable will to compete, and; have the skills, knowledge and resources to do their best, every day.

Argyll's Failed Bid for Distillers Company

In 1985, Argyll began a major reorganization of its food division, realizing that if it was to become a major force in British groceries, it would have to simplify and streamline its collected holdings, many of which were old, small, and out of touch with recent trends in marketing. The company therefore began converting all of its stores to either Presto or Lo-Cost, according to the demographics of each store. At the same time, the directors put a great deal of energy into lowering costs by taking advantage of the Group's greatly enhanced purchasing power and improving its distribution network. This reorganization, which was completed in 1986, put Argyll in a strong position to integrate its 1987 Safeway acquisition smoothly and efficiently.

One reason for Argyll's interest in Safeway was the debacle of its 1986 bid for the Distillers Company, Britain's largest producer and distributor of Scotch and other liquor products. Gulliver hoped to use Argyll's relatively minor liquor business as a springboard from which to enter the liquor market in a much more dramatic fashion.

In a carefully planned attack, Argyll made its bid for what Gulliver described as a once-great Scottish concern lately become moribund, offering to its shareholders a higher-than-market price for their stock and the prospect of fresh managerial expertise. Financial analysts heavily favored the proposed merger, which Gulliver and Alistair Grant hoped to consummate for reasons of Scots pride as well as profitability, but Distillers eventually rejected Argyll and accepted a possibly illegal bid from Guinness, the well-known British brewing conglomerate. The complex legal issues involved have not been fully sorted out, but it was clear that the failure of Gulliver's year-long struggle was a great disappointment to him. Although he remained at Argyll long enough to consummate the Safeway deal, he stepped down as chairman in September 1988.

Post-Gulliver: Argyll Becomes Safeway

Gulliver's successor, and the chief architect of the Safeway deal, was Alistair Grant. For many years Gulliver's closest adviser, Grant was an experienced food retailer who commanded great respect in London financial circles, as evidenced by the case with which he placed the £621 million worth of new stock needed to pay for the Safeway stores. (The total price of £681 million was made up with a £60 million interest-free loan from seller to buyer.)

It has been Grant's job to oversee the integration of Safeway and Argyll. The two companies were well matched; while Argyll's strength lay in the north, Safeway was predominantly a southern chain, though it had a significant business in Scotland.

In addition, Safeway, despite its size and high per-unit profits, was widely believed to have a weak purchasing policy, an aspect of the business that Argyll had honed to a fine art. In general, the merger brought together the old and the new: Argyll's older and smaller stores, closer to the English tradition of the independent shopkeeper, with Safeway's more efficient and more fashionable stores. Argyll essentially has set out to capitalize on Safeway's appeal by adopting not only its name but its merchandising concepts as well.

To that end, Argyll converted some 57 of its Presto stores to the Safeway logo in fiscal 1988 (and seven the year before), in addition to opening 19 entirely new Safeways. To supply its vast network of outlets in an efficient manner, Argyll continued to upgrade and consolidate its warehouse distribution centers, most recently adding a 510,000-square-foot facility in Bellshill, Scotland. In accordance with Argyll's policy of operating only in those markets in which it can be a major player, the Group sold off all of its liquor holdings, except its retail operation, Liquor-Save, after failing to capture Distillers. Argyll then became the third-largest grocer in the United Kingdom. The market analysts who once were suspicious of Argyll's unlimited ambition are now the company's most enthusiastic backers, predicting continued success under the Safeway logo and the likelihood of further acquisitions in the coming decade.

Safeway's Expansion Program

In 1991, Argyll accelerated its Safeway superstore opening program, opening 18 new stores, with a total of 503,00 square feet of sales area. The completion of nine Presto conversions to Safeways in 1990 added an additional 158,000 square feet. The company's intent was to open 20 to 25 stores a year, each with an averages sales area of 28,000 square feet that could include a cafeteria, a dry cleaner, and a gas station. Safeway's expansions over four years came to an investment of £568 million for store development, with an operating profit growth of £225.5 million, an increase of 40 percent.

In 1992, the Argyll group surprised everyone, especially Sainsbury's, who was down to the wire on signing for a 13-acre site in Glasgow, when the property was "swiped from under its nose," as was reported in *Super Marketing*, for a rumored £22 million. Safeway was criticized for its "outrageously aggressive manner" by Sainsbury's in being kept out of Scotland. In the meantime, Asda, a Scottish Co-op, remained Scotland's number two food retailer, while Tesco was not seen a major threat because of its concentration of stores in the south of England.

In the same article, Safeway's Gordon Witherspoon was quoted as saying, "The number of times we've been in direct competition with Sainsbury's for sites in Scotland are very few and far between. We saw an opportunity in Anniesland. I have to admit that if Sainsbury's was not around, then I doubt we would have paid the same price." Witherspoon stated that he had identified 38 potential development opportunities for Safeway in Scotland.

The year 1992 also saw the celebration of Safeway's 30 years in Britain, after coming to the United Kingdom from the United States in 1962, realizing that there was a need for higher quality food on a consistent basis and friendlier service. The Argyll Group purchased the Safeway chain in the United King-

Key Dates:

1977: Argyll Group PLC established.
1987: Purchased 133 U.K. Safeway stores from Safeway Stores, Inc. in the UnitedStates.
1988: Safeway launches aggressive growth program, converting Presto stores to Safeways.
1992: Safeway celebrates 30 years in the United Kingdom.
1993: Company split into Safeway, and Lo-Cost and Presto divisions.
1996: Symbol Personal Shopping System with hand-held scanners appears in superstores.
1997: Near merger with Asda.
1999: Carlos Criado-Perez comes to Safeway from Wal-Mart.
2000: Safeway web site launched.
2001: Online shopping Internet ventures ended.

dom in 1987; other stores owned by the group were Presto and Lo-Cost. In 1991, Argyll had record profits that were up 25 percent from the previous year. Given these profits, Argyll chairman and chief executive Sir Alistair Grant planned to open another 25 new Safeway stores in 1992, adding 650,000 square feet of sales area. The timing was right. Since Argyll had taken over Safeway, only two new Lo-Cost stores had been built, but there were plans to open five Presto stores, primarily in mid-sized Scottish towns, with the Lo-Cost stores to be placed in the Midlands, the south, and southwest England. As of 1992, the company had 212 Presto stores and 285 Lo-Cost stores.

In March 1993, Argyll split its retail operations into two divisions, Safeway Stores, and Presto and Lo-Cost Stores, with Argyll board director Charles Lawrie made managing director of Presto and Lo-Cost. Pat Kieran was made the new managing director of Safeway Stores. *Super Marketing* reported that Sir Alistair Grant stated in a memo, "The creation of Presto and Lo-Cost divisions is an important move which signifies our commitment to these important businesses and our wish that their direction and management should be given a strong specific focus." When Argyll had acquired Safeway, it had planned to phase out Presto, but these stores were expanded because of strong customer loyalty in the north.

The year 1993 also saw Safeway move into automated sales-based ordering (SBO) for its dry grocery lines that not only reordered products to replace those sold but provided feedback from the stores to create sales forecasts. With 345 stores and 12,000 to 16,000 lines of products per store, the system ensured that the right products were delivered to meet anticipated consumer demand. The SBO system was centralized in Safeway's main office. Individual store managers could not amend orders but could request a new order if he knew that local impacts would alter the volume of sales of a specific product.

Safeway vs. Costco

In late 1993, Safeway was criticized by consumers for its soaring profits, and found it difficult to please both shareholders and consumers. Profits had increased from 4 percent to 8.1 percent in ten years through own-label development and enor-

mous investment in infrastructure. However, in the wake of Safeway's rapid expansion to super stores, its returns were down 2 percent, Sainsbury's were down 3 percent, and Asda's were down 37 percent over a ten year period. David Webster, deputy chairman of Argyll, stated that this was due to increased price competition, which could increase still more if club warehouses came to the United Kingdom.

Indeed, in November 1993, Costco won a court battle against J. Sainsbury's PLC, Tesco PLC, and Safeway, who had taken Costco to the British High Court in their attempt to stifle the opening of the first European club in Thurrock, England. The court's ruling removed a major barrier to expansion of U.S.-style warehouse clubs in the United Kingdom. The food retailers wanted the Costco building site to be classified as retail, which would lead to more costly development and slim profit margins, perhaps discouraging other clubs from opening. Alas, Costco was granted wholesale status, even though 80 to 90 percent of the company's sales would be to individuals.

The logic of the Judge Schiemann's ruling was that Costco would be a wholesale operation focused on local businesses. As explained in *HFD, The Weekly Home Furnishings Newspaper*, the judge barred the three food retailers from the appeals process and required that they pay Costco's court costs. The ruling opposed a recommendation from the British Department of Environmental that local councils treat warehouse clubs as retail sites for planning purposes.

Creating Efficiency and Customer Service

In January 1994, Safeway launched pilots of secret electronic card trials, following pilot launches by Sainsbury's and Tesco in December. However, Safeway had already had air miles for its customers for more than a year on a trial basis. The card allowed customers to save more when using it. Throughout the United Kingdom, supermarket chains were technologically more advanced than those in the United States, with sales-based ordering very rare in the latter. Safeway introduced a customer-operated price scanning system in 1995, hoping to reduce checkout lines, a process that was already in use in the Netherlands. Customers could scan barcodes and obtain a printed receipt from the scanner.

The company also began to redesign its store layouts for ease of use by mothers with children, incorporating play areas and wider aisles. However, Safeway's sweeping changes resulted in the closure and sale of some Presto, Lo-Cost, and Safeway stores and the elimination of 1,800 jobs, with a further cut of 3,000 anticipated. Argyll chairman Sir Alistair Grant was quoted in *Super Marketing* as saying, "Changing the way Safeway is organized and managed is vital to our aim of ensuring that the business becomes more effective and efficient in responding to the needs of our customers. The significant savings we are making are coming not from simple cost-cutting, but from completely rethinking the way we work. Our head office functions, our store and field management structure, and our logistics network and supply chain are being completely redesigned. Some the of the benefit from our efficiency improvements will be reinvested in marketing and in improving our service to customers." The sale of ten stores to Iceland [food stores], seven in Scotland, and one in London was also announced.

Toward the end of 1995, shares of the top four companies in the highly competitive food retail market in Scotland were Sainsbury, 4.2 percent; Tesco, 16.5 percent; Asda, 15.7 percent; Safeway, 16.8 percent. Colin Massey, Scottish retail director for Safeway stated in *The Grocer*, "At the end of the day, food shopping is still about convenience, and retailing should be about convenience. The attraction to shoppers is what's convenient to them, whether it's a large superstore or an independent."

By mid-1996, the Symbol Personal Shopping System, developed by Symbol Technologies, Inc., was rolled out in the Safeway superstores throughout the United Kingdom. The system that allowed customers to scan bar-coded products in the aisle as they shop had been very successful when tested in trials in 24 Safeway stores beforehand. The customer could pick up a Scan & Go card to remove a Portable Personal Shopper device, about the size of a telephone handset, from a dispenser rack, and scan each product's bar code as items are placed in the cart. The "plus" key would be pressed as each item was scanned and added to the cart. If the shopper decided against a product already selected, pressing the "minus" key and scanning would remove the item from the total. A subtotal could be had at any time by pressing the "equals" key.

Facing Up

What led to this flurry of development, expansion, and customer service? As the competition between Tesco and Safeway increased in the early 1990s, it was not surprising that Safeway lost sight of some key points. While Tesco was focused on customer service and keeping prices down, Safeway leaned more toward customer service, and was shocked to discover in 1993 that its core customers, the "early nesters" were not able to afford its prices. Safeway was losing its over-thirty customers. As was pointed out in *Management Today*, it seemed that senior managers spent the majority of their time poring over the company's accounts instead of trying to learn what customers actually wanted from the grocery store.

These unpleasant truths became evident in the midst of the company's rush to develop superstores, and led Safeway to bring in McKinsey, a management consultant. McKinsey created Safeway 2000, a program designed to propel the retailer over the immediate hurdle and to keep it profitable in the long run. The first move was to learn which customers would be key to the company's success, pinpointing products and services that these people would need throughout their life cycles. The ranges of products were also modified to direct them more specifically to families, shifting the focus of products from premium products to more economical, standard items. One example of this strategy was the development of well-received Safeway sub-brands—not to be confused with own-label brands—which could be sold at lower rates while giving the stores better profit margins.

The Safeway 2000 program also re-evaluated the presentation of superstores that were being developed across England, Wales, and Scotland by Safeway. One innovation at a Safeway superstore in Camden, north London reflected the re-evaluation in that it had 30 parent and child parking spaces near the store entrance so parents would not have to struggle to get a parking space, then grapple with moving children and carts across expanses of tarmac. All of the combined changes helped Safeway attract back many customers, but it was uncertain whether the company would remain strong in the future.

A Proposed Merger And Other Innovations

In 1997, Safeway PLC, the newly renamed Argyll Group (1996), and Asda came close to merging, which would have pushed Tesco and Sainsbury's into second and third places in market share. Alas, the aborted merger was viewed as a public admission that Safeway needed outside help if it wanted to keep pace with the rest of the industry. There was also speculation about whether a merger would have worked because the two stores had very different customer bases and store portfolios. Apparently, the government took a hard line on takeovers and mergers, which led one analyst to suggest in *Marketing* that "after the initial price flurry, things would have settled down to a cozy three-way cartel."

Still on the lookout for new concepts, Safeway decided to replace 2,000 PCs with network computers (NCs). Safeway had found traditional client/server systems to be unreliable, costly, and hard to manage, and hoped that using centralized data management with mainframes, NCs, and Java would be a viable solution.

Unwilling to pass up any opportunity to please its customers, Safeway became the distributor for Teletubbies in December 1997 when thousands of these toys went into three stores: Brent Cross, London; Leicester; and Anniesland, Glasgow. Customers began to line up outside the Glasgow store at 3 a.m. When the store opened at 8 a.m., the Teletubbies sold out in three hours.

In 1998, Safeway announced that it would begin to supply stores in Scotland by rail in an effort to reduce costs and increase environmental awareness. This change would eliminate 3,000 truck deliveries per year between Glasgow and Inverness, although goods would still have to be transported by road from Inverness to stores at Nairn, Elgin, and Buckle in the outlying areas. The shift to rail shipping began early the following year.

In May 1999, Safeway installed a Hectronic Autofuel System for fleet of ten Compressed Natural Gas (GNG) vehicles. The controlled filling station was installed by Mobil and could complete the refueling process in six minutes while providing fuel that was cleaner than conventional diesel. Using this system reduced noise pollution, which allowed Safeway operate over a wider time scale. Because the site was less congested, exhaust emissions were also cut.

By December of 1999, competition among the giant food retailers was fierce for the sale of pre-paid mobile phones, with Tesco selling One2One mobile phones for £30 to £50, while Asda followed suit with Vodafone mobile phones that sold for as much as £50. Safeway then upped the ante by offering pre-paid mobile phone units from four companies: Vodafone, One2One, BT Cellnet, and Orange, noting that they expected the cell phones to be "incredibly popular." At about this time, Marks & Spencer also began to sell the Orange Just Talk package, later expanding to two types of phones. Research by Orange had shown that shoppers particularly liked the pre-paid phone packages as gifts, which made up about 80 percent of the mobile phone sales in December.

Wal-Mart Leader Comes to Safeway

Following a 20 percent loss in Safeway's pretax profits for the 28 weeks prior to 16 October 1999, Carlos Criado-Perez, the former chief operating officer of Wal-Mart, was named as the new Safeway chief operating officer. He leapt into operations with the promise to give managers the authority to drive sales and the ability to earn profit-sharing cash rewards. In addition, a new bonus plan allowed 2,000 managers an extra 20 percent of their salary if they met or exceeded sales targets, plus a further 30 percent for hitting separate profit goals.

Criado-Perez stated his philosophy for developing a family environment Safeway stores in *Super Marketing:* "We want to bring out the merchant in everyone and help them realize their will to win in each local market." He added that he wanted Safeway to be not the biggest but the best retailer by competitively taking market share from the other big grocery retailers, which would be achieved by making stores warmer and more interactive. Criado-Perez also shifted focus from national marketing campaigns to local markets.

Part of the struggle to keep profits up was the staggering cost of capital investments involved in grocery retail. As reported in *Super Marketing*, food retailers in the United Kingdom led the way in capital investment, not only in the United Kingdom, but internationally, seconded only by the oil and gas industry. One of the culprits was the high cost of property and land. In a report from the Department of Trade and Industry Innovations Unit, it was stated that Tesco, Sainsbury, and Safeway were among the top ten food retailers in investing worldwide, with the top spender the French Carrefour. Wal-Mart was considered to be in a different category.

The report also noted that the total capital investment per employee by British supermarkets came to about £47,000, which was 20 percent higher than the international average of £40,000. This extra expenditure was deemed intelligent by Norman Price, one of the authors of the report. "These figures show that the retail sector is making the necessary capital investment to achieve innovation and competitiveness." The biggest spender was Tesco, with an increased capital investment of 27 percent in 1998–1999, while Sainsbury's capital investment increased by 6 percent. Safeway had capital investment increase by 15 percent, while Asda was reduced by 4 percent.

In January 2000, Safeway launched its Web site, providing a recipe finder tool, games for children, a fact sheet on appropriate foods for allergies and pregnancy, and a catalog of the store's current promotions. Unfortunately, no online shopping appeared, nor did links to relevant related sites. *Management Today* expressed disappointment in the technology poor site, especially since Safeway stores provided cutting-edge technology with hand-held scanners and digital shopping lists. The article bemoaned the numerous unnecessary screens before "getting to the good stuff" and the "decorative graphics of winsome tots, which slow the download of the most extraneous pages."

Other more successful innovations for customers included an affiliation with the Automobile Association (AA) to offer discounted car breakdown services to customers holding loyalty cards. Customers could get a £20 discount off annual AA membership for 200 points, making the cost of AA's Option 200 service £58. Safeway also offered a £15 shopping voucher for customers who change to Powergen for gas or electricity supplies, and offered 20 percent discounts at Best Western hotels through its affiliation with the chain. Safeway cardholders used their points for holiday purchases in December, for such items as 60,000 tins of Mars Celebrations and 6,000 bottles of Glenfiddich malt whisky. PlayStation games also began to appear for sale in stores in February 2000, following a deal with Cork International.

Online Shopping

By mid-2001, Tesco was spending $22 million for a 35 percent stake in Safeway's online GroceryWorks.com in North America, which later relaunched under the Safeway brand name. The "store-picking" fulfillment model—which refers to employees rolling carts through the store to collect ordered groceries—was later expanded to 1,747 stores in the United States and western Canada. The alternative would have been a warehouse model with staff processing orders from a centralized location. The American Safeway stores, based in Pleasanton, California wanted to learn how Tesco created a successful commercial online shopping system in the United Kingdom. Tesco provided GroceryWorks with help in all aspects of the business, including web site development and the shopping service in individual stores.

In the meantime, Safeway in the United Kingdom was forced to terminate its only online home-delivery shopping service. The company's online partner, Madaboutwine, was purchased by the Australian drinks company Foster's, and caused the closure of the service, deemed a major setback for Safeway by *New Media Age*. Tesco was launching its own wine warehouse operation in September 2001 in 20 stores that allowed customers to order wines by the case, a very popular online service. Safeway's ending partnership with Madaboutwine came less than six months after the online shopping service was launched in April 2001, forcing the store to drop a planned major in-store promotion. Safeway Collect, the online service for ordering and collecting groceries was unaffected.

By November 2001, Safeway PLC was forced to end its two Internet ventures, returning its focus to tradition supermarket business. After running trials of Safeway Collect in eight stores, a service that allowed customers to buy groceries online, later collecting them at the store, Safeway decided that the service was too costly to continue. The company acknowledged that the venture was too ambitious. Other smaller rivals, Somerfield and Budgens, also had to abandon online operations. Tesco was clearly the leader in online sales, with sales of £1.46 million, a 77 percent increase over the same period in 2000.

Frenetic In-Store Promotions

Out of consideration for the country's farmers following the foot-and-mouth disease, both Safeway and Sainsbury's began offering tradition British meat dishes, such as shepherd's pie, beef casserole, and cottage pie. In October of 2001, Safeway also began selling Nordstrom gift cards, which were on sale in

1,500 stores. The Seattle-based Nordstrom decided on the strategy to boost its lagging sales.

As part of its nationwide store upgrade, Safeway prepared to open 40 Mediterranean style "Café Fresco" restaurants in the following two years, and installed CD listening posts, DVD preview screens, and provided wine experts in its stores. In addition to these changes in the stores, Safeway hired Newton 21 public relations firm in a departure from its previous reliance on in-store promotions.

The *Safeway* magazine, which had been around for five years and was initially developed to support the loyalty card, was editorially enhanced by emphasis on the everyday needs of shoppers and the use of more tips and advice. The improved caliber of the photography and design emphasized Safeway's "Best at fresh" philosophy, expressed in 84 instead of the previous 100 pages.

In 2002, Safeway launched a chain of a series of sandwich outlets that marketed its own label Eat Street to compete with fast food restaurants, such as Pret A Manger. The range of items to be sold included wraps, juices, sushi, sandwiches, salads, and cakes that would be kept in heated cabinets. Eat Street followed Eat Smart, the company's own-label low calorie brand of 150 products, none of which contained more than 3 percent fat.

One slightly different promotion was Safeway's demonstration of its interest in home entertainment, emphasized by its support of the second music benefit for the Prince's Trust charity. Working with Capital Gold, the Capital's Party in the Park format featured a Safeway Picnic 2002 in Hyde Park on June 29, 2002. Featured entertainers included Shirley Bassey, Gabrielle, Ronan Keating, Diana Ross, and Rod Stewart. The 2001 concert that had featured Pavarotti earned £500,000 for the Prince's Trust. Safeway sold tickets in its stores and on its web site for £20. Capital Gold featured ticket give-aways and special artist days, and broadcasted from the event.

In Spite of Promotions, Receipts Fall

By May 2002, Safeway was looking for a company to provide TV advertisement, a strategy it had abandoned years before as too costly and ineffective. However, receipts that had increased following the arrival of Criado-Perez began to wane, falling to 10.7 percent over the year. Asda's improved performance since its purchase by Wal-Mart in 1999 contributed to the loss, plus the tendency of Safeway customers to selectively zero in on the special offers only. Safeway evaluated its promotional and press ads, debating whether to return to television ads—which had ceased in 1999 when Safeway was criticized for using talking toddlers in its television ads.

What Lies Ahead

As of mid-2002, Safeway was still the United Kingdom's fourth largest grocery retailer, with the market as intense as ever. Safeway had four core styles in its stores: convenience, supermarket, superstore, and mega-store, all carrying the Safeway name. The Presto and Lo-Cost names no longer existed.

The five mega-stores sold much more than food, including health and beauty, electrical, home wares, and pharmacy goods, as well as cameras, TV sets, VCRs, DVD players, DVDs, videos, books, and CDs. Customers could also fill their gas tanks with diesel fuel. As ever, Safeway was attempting to draw customers away from other chains, but had not lost sight of the importance of its food products. The company stated that it is "Best at fresh" and has a Fresh to Go initiative, which let customers have their food cooked for them in the store.

The own-label brands, such as Eat Smart, indicated Safeway's future direction. Judith Batchelar, who was recruited from Marks & Spencer in 2001, worked with a team of 40 for new product development. She noted in *Marketing* that new vegetarian and snacking products would be available in 2002. Safeway also appointed Roger Hart, an ex-Seagram and Mars marketer, as its own-label brand manager. The company continued to be committed to its locally driven marketing strategy and wanted to be the best grocery retailer in the 484 areas where it had a presence. Safeway was beefing up its marketing capabilities; marketing chief Karen Bray drafted Comet marketer Martin Pugh to oversee the day-to-day running of the department as director of marketing, and operations chief Jack Sinclair became the group director for trading and marketing.

The market shares for grocery retailers in the United Kingdom as reported in *Marketing* in May 2002 by Taylor Nelson Sofres were: Tesco, 25.3 percent; Sainsbury's, 17.5 percent; Asda, 15.3 percent; Safeway, 10.5 percent; Morrisons, 5.7 percent; Waitrose, 3.1 percent; Iceland, 2.6 percent, and Kwik Save, 2.4 percent.

Principal Competitors

Tesco PLC; J. Sainsbury PLC; Asda Group PLC.

Further Reading

"1999 and All That," *Super Marketing*, December 17, 1999, p. 15.

Andrew, Don, "Jousting for The Crown," *Super Marketing*, September 25, 1992.

"Argyll Expands on Record Profits," *Super Marketing*, May 29, 1992, p. 8.

"Argyll Splits Retail Operations," *Super Marketing*, March 12, 1993, p. 12.

"Is Safeway Falling Too Far Behind?," *Marketing*, May 23, 2002, p. 17.

Lewis, Fiona, "Safeway Follows the Leader," *Management Today*, March 1997, p. 38.

"Safeway Speeds Up Expansion," *Super Marketing*, May 24, 1991, p. 10.

"Streamlined Safeway," *Super Marketing*, May 26, 1995, p. 5.

"Surfing USA; Tesco and Safeway Online: Tesco and Safeway Team Up Online," *The Economist*, June 30, 2001, p. 5.

"Tesco Won't Top Us, Insists Safeway," *The Grocer*, September 2, 1995, p. 69.

Wedbale, Jonathan, "Safeway's Online Plans Falter as Poster's Buys Wine Partner," *New Media Age*, August 23, 2001, p. 2.

Weiss, Todd R., "Safeway Turns to British Counterpart for Online Help," *Computerworld*, July 16, 2001, p. 39.

—update: Annette Dennis McCully

Sanpaolo IMI S.p.A.

Piazza San Carlo 156
10121 Turin (Torino)
Italy
Telephone: (39) 011 555-2289
Fax: (39) 011 555-2989
Web site: http://www.sanpaoloimi.com

Public Company
Incorporated: 1998
Employees: 35,729 (2000)
Total Assets: EUR 171.0 billion (2000)
Stock Exchanges: Borsa Italiana (BI) New York
Ticker Symbol: SPI (BI); IMI (New York)
NAIC: 522110 Commercial Banking

Building on a more than 400-year-old history of being managed by charitable foundations, the Sanpaolo IMI S.p.A. enters the 21st century as one of the largest banks in the world. In addition, the bank is still committed to helping the less fortunate throughout the northern Italian economic center where it began and beyond. Whether that will be true in years to come remains to be seen: modern analysts believe that continuing part ownership by charitable foundations will render the bank less able to compete in an increasingly global world market.

Due to a number of mergers that occurred mostly in the later part of the 21st century, the Sanpaolo IMI S.p.A. worldwide banking conglomerate of 2002 comprised three companies: the Instituto Bancario San Paolo di Torino, the Istituto Mobiliare Italiano (IMI), and the Banco di Napoli. Both Sanpaolo and Banco di Napoli have origins dating to the 16th century, but IMI is a relatively new institution, having been founded in 1931 (as a result of Italy's industrialization) as a medium- and long-term lending support institution.

Historic Origins

Sanpaolo IMI began in this northern Italian town in 1563, near the end of the Italian Renaissance. It was established as a charitable foundation, with both giving and banking activities,

under the name of Campagnia della Fede Cattolica sotto l'Invocazione di San Paolo.

Sanpaolo was centered in the city of Turin (i.e., Torino), part of the northern region of Italy long known for its commercial prosperity, starting in the 11th century. The Renaissance, during the 14th and 15th centuries, was a period of great artistic and musical achievements that has had lasting affects in Western culture today. Among them, the period strengthened the idea of a single nationality and the nationalist movement that occurred in Italy in the early 19th century.

Banco di Napoli originated with the foundation of the Sacro Monte di Pieta in 1539. Several regional credit institutions merged in 1809 to become the Banco delle due Sicilie, which was later renamed the Banco di Napoli when the reunification was complete and Kingdom of Italy proclaimed in 1860.

The Twentieth Century

The Italian-Turkish War in 1911 had a substantial effect on Italian economy. In particular, government expenditures financed by a large issue of five-year treasury bonds led to higher rates of inflation, a problem that persisted even into the next century. During WWI, Italy renounced an alliance with Germany, siding with the Allies. And, in 1922, Benito Mussolini took over and installed a fascist dictatorship known as the Corporate State.

Italian banks survived this period by facilitating material imports. Many were pushed to participate in wartime and other industries. Before the war, Italy's major banks were largely competitive. During the war, however, businesses and the government increased pressure for credit, which decreased the competition among banks. Then, in 1918, the larger banks formed a cartel to coordinate the rationing of credit and establish common policies.

The rampant and ill-planned growth of the early 20th century did not continue after the war, and the decreased activity in turn led to a depression in Italy. By 1921, businesses started to fail, slowing the growth of banks. By the 1930s, businesses were going bankrupt and the banks were severely affected. In

Company Perspectives:

Sanpaolo IMI's market position is based on its leadership in the retail savings market where it offers everything from current account and deposit facilities to sophisticated asset management products and in the business sector with leadership in corporate and investment banking. With the addition of Banco di Napoli, it extends its strengths from its traditional heartland in the north of Italy through to the south.

1933, the government stepped in to save the failing industry, creating the IRI, a government holding company that was intended to be a temporary organization.

The 1930s brought a period of regulation and reorganization among Italian banks. In 1931, IMI was established as a public law entity. The following year, Sanpaolo became a public law credit institution.

In 1936, Italy passed the Banking Law, which remained the main legislation governing Italian banks into the early 1990s. Under this reformed banking regulation, IMI focused on medium- and long-term lending, including lending for public works projects. Sanpaolo, meanwhile, remained centered in northwestern Italy and focused on short-term commercial banking, with divisions for mortgage activities and industrial lending. Banco di Napoli, one of the largest banks in the nation at the time, played a pivotal economic role in the financial development of Italy's southern region.

World War II and Beyond

In 1940 at the onset of World War II, Italy joined Germany in declaring war on France and the United Kingdom. The following year, it joined Germany and Japan to declare war on the United States. An anti-fascist movement, however, harassed German forces and eventually drove them out of Italy, before the monarchy ended in 1946. Mussolini's inability to dictate an effective economic strategy severely affected the nation's economy, and it was not until the 1950s and 1960s that the growth of exports led to sustained, long-term growth for the first time in a long time.

In 1969, the U.S. Federal Reserve Board began a policy of monetary restraint. Funds began flowing in the United States, and the Italian economy, forced to adjust to high U.S interest rates, was among those to suffer as a result. As domestic growth slowed, Italy reinvested itself overseas—as well as it could, with the nation's banking activities largely regulated by Italy's central bank, the Bank of Italy.

In the 1970s, many domestic clients began to demand increased services abroad, and banks accommodated them by expanding and opening branches in other countries. The oil crisis, which started in 1973, had a severe affect on Italy's economy, giving rise to high inflation and a growing public deficit. In 1976, the lira plummeted against the U.S. dollar. Adding to that instability, Italians feared that the growing Communist party might win election that year over the nation's longstanding party, the Christian Democrats.

In the later part of the decade, Italian banks were called upon to rescue some of the country's failing industrial groups, including some under state control. Bankers responded with concerns that banks would be forced to absorb the failing companies' losses.

In the next decade, losses from state-owned companies continued to increase, and by 1982, the IRI decided to raise money by issuing bonds and improving its relationship with the private sector. The economy was stronger by this time, however, and the Bank of Italy was able to relax some of its constraints on the banking industry. This allowed for more domestic competition and lower exchange controls. Eventually, the Bank of Italy, Italy's central bank and a public law institution since 1936, removed lending ceilings and began supporting previously denied requests for opening branches. The move helped institutions such as Sanpaolo expand beyond the regions in which they had operated for hundreds of years.

In the mid-1980s, decline of the U.S. dollar and the collapse of oil prices further boosted the Italian economy. While the economy surged, the money supply quickly increased. In 1987, the Bank of Italy responded by attempting to re-impose credit ceilings, and the approval of bank expansions led to heated discussions about reforming the stock exchange and the role of banks in the market in light of the coming single European monetary market.

In the late 1980s, there was a trend by Italian banks to join with insurers in an effort to broaden the range of services available. Nevertheless, the October 1987 stock market crash led to profit drops at Italian banks that year.

By the end of the decade and into the early 1990s, the Italian banking industry was once again the subject of reformation. Throughout the decade, alliances and joint ventures became increasingly commonplace. National banks in Italy, faced with the challenges of an increasingly global economy, acquired local commercial banks and the result was a significant increase in powerful and massive cross-functional banking groups.

Under a 1990 law, Italian banks (including savings banks and various credit institutions) were required to spin off banking activities into joint-stock corporations. Ownership shares of these corporations went into newly established charitable foundations. But, over the next decade, only nine foundations withdrew from spun-off banks. (Among them was the Fondazione Cassa di Risparmio di Venezia, which sold an 11 percent stake in Banca Cardine to Sanpaolo IMI at the beginning of 2001.)

The 1990 anti-trust law gave the government the right to review acquisitions where the merged entity would have combined sales of over 500 billion lire (adjusted over time for inflation). And, it gave the government the authority to block mergers under certain conditions, allowing certain industries to be more closely regulated or allowing the government to prohibit outright the involvement of foreign investors.

As part of that reformation in the early 1990s, the Bank of Italy again relaxed its rules on opening new branches in Italy. This gave Sanpaolo the encouragement it needed to expand beyond its traditional home base in Turin. The government also began encouraging banks to get more involved with private-sector activi-

Key Dates:

1539: The Sacro Monte di Pieta is founded.

1563: San Paolo di Torino is founded as a charitable foundation.

1809: Several regional credit institutions merge to become the Banco delle due Sicilie.

1860: The Banco delle due Sicilie is renamed the Banco di Napoli during the reunification of Italy.

1931: Istituto Mobiliare Italiano (IMI) is established to provide medium- and long-term lending in support of Italy's industrialization.

1957: Italy joins the agreement (known as the Treaty of Rome) to establish the European Economic Community, which later becomes the European Union (EU).

1983: Instituto Bancario San Paolo di Torino becomes the first bank to offer corporate home banking services in Italy.

1991: A restructuring project planned by the Instituto Bancario San Paolo di Torino leads to the creation of the Instituto Bancario San Paolo di Torino S.p.A.

1998: Italy's Istituto Bancario San Paolo di Torino and Istituto Mobiliare Italiano (IMI) merge to become Sanpaolo IMI, Italy's largest bank with assets in excess of $200 billion.

1999: Sanpaolo is the first Italian bank to receive approval for a Section 20 license from the U.S. Federal Reserve Bank.

2000: Sanpaolo acquires Banco di Napoli, a regional bank in Italy.

2001: The company acquires a 10.9 percent interest in the Bank of Cardine, the Turin-based regional 800-branch bank, for around 1 trillion lire ($464 million).

2002: Sanpaolo IMI announces plans for a merger with the Bank of Cardine and acquires a majority stake in Slovenia's fourth-largest bank, Banca Koper.

ties, supporting a series of legal measures (such as tax incentives) that aimed to strengthen the financial structure of Italy's banking system. The first of these was called the Amato Law and these reforms led charitable foundations with banking activities, such as Sanpaolo, to separate into businesses and charities through the sale of stakes in state-controlled banks, such as IMI.

Pursuant to the new law, Sanpaolo was established in early 1992 as San Paolo di Torino Società per Azioni with 21 percent of its capital floated in Italy and shares traded publicly. IMI also became a "Società per Azione" in 1991. In 1994, through the government's continuing privatization campaign, IMI took part in a global offering with more than a third of its shares listed on various stock exchanges; sales to institutional investors continued through 1996.

Sanpaolo bank's charitable foundation counterpart, the Compagnia di San Paolo, remained a majority stakeholder until 1997 when nearly a quarter (22 percent) of Sanpaolo's share capital was sold to 10 medium- and long-term shareholders. With the Bank of Italy's approval, another third (31 percent) was sold in public and global offerings.

This was a major directional change for the bank. When owned by a charitable foundation, Sanpaolo's board members in the past had ranged from city hall appointees to renowned authors, and they were often selected more for their cultural ingenuity than banking acumen. Some industry specialists at that time felt that bank foundation members tended to be more concerned with politics and personal power than turning a profit (sitting on the bank board was known for resulting in prestigious or lucrative appointments and other types of personal gain).

In 1997, Chairman Gianni Zandano said he wanted to change that system, in effect ending some 434 years of local control, by fully privatizing the company. Zandano decided the bank should focus less on philanthropy and more on profitability, an idea that was revolutionary for the Italian banking industry. For hundreds of years, the bank had been owned by charitable organizations and focused on spending money, rather than making it.

"The real problem of Italian banks is there's never been a shareholder holding a whip," Zandano told Wall Street Journal reporter Maureen Kline. He saw privatization as an opportunity for the bank to find local partners and reinforce its image as the bank from Italy's financial heartland. It was not only the institution of Sanpaolo that saw the need to adapt. In the last half of the decade, the banking sector worldwide went through a phase of rationalization and consolidation, influenced in part, and especially in Italy, by the advent of the European economic and monetary union.

With the European Union (EU), many Italian bankers and industry advisors saw the need for Italian banks to replace their medieval structures with more profit-driven, growth-oriented models. Italian banks were among the least profitable and most fragmented in Europe. According to the Italian Banking Association, the average equity return for Italian banks was only 2 percent, compared with 8 to 18 percent for those in Germany and the United Kingdom. Sanpaolo was the largest of Italy's 1,000 banks, yet it did not even rank among the top 20 in Europe.

Throughout Italy, bankers expressed concern that, at their current size, Italian banks would be "eaten alive" when they joined the EU. To encourage change, the Italian government drafted a bill giving incentives to banks that merged and privatized, with added incentives for making those changes quickly. Managers of both Sanpaolo and IMI determined that, in order to compete effectively in the changing banking environment, they needed to merge with an effective partner and create a bigger organization; they saw this as both a strategic move and one that would provide a basis for future consolidation and aggregation.

So, in November 1998, despite longstanding resistance to change and an industry tradition of patronage, the Instituto Bancario San Paolo di Torino S.p.A., Italy's largest retail bank, merged with the investment bank and mutual fund manager, Istituto Mobiliare Italiano S.p.A. This led to the creation of Sanpaolo IMI S.p.A., which continued into the next century under the leadership of former IMI General Manager Rainer Stefano Masero. The following year, the Euro officially appeared in the Italian market (replacing the Italian lira altogether by 2002), and Italy joined the Euro Monetary Area, which allowed for a fixed exchange rate across all member European countries.

The Twenty-First Century

Sanpaolo IMI was to grow again—geographically, as well as financially—in 2000 when it bought the Banco di Napoli; the acquisition included both the former Gruppo Banco di Napoli and its parent organization. (Previous to this, Sanpaolo lost its ranking as Italy's largest bank when Banco di Napoli, recapitalized and stripped of its bad loans, was sold and merged with Banca Nazionale del Lavoro S.p.A. Despite its near collapse and recovery, the bank remained inefficient prior to its sale to Sanpaolo.) Banco di Napoli brought to the group another 731 branches, mostly in southern Italy, a move that significantly complemented Sanpaolo's existing (mostly northern Italian) network.

Analysts said officials at both banks felt they needed to grow to avoid being taken over by foreign banks. The result of this latest consolidation was the Sanpaolo IMI Banking Group, which reported by year's end assets in excess of Euro 172 billion and total customer assets of Euro 304 billion. The group's return on equity that year was a notable 18.1 percent (just under Euro 1.3 billion); by midway through the next year, that amount had increased to 19 percent. According to the *Economist*, Italian banks previously were rated as tiny by world standards; now, thanks to new mergers in Italy, including Sanpaolo and the UniCredito Italiano bid for Banca Commerciale Italiana, Italian banks placed in the top 10. By the turn of the century, Sanpaolo and UniCredito had combined assets in excess of L1.1 billion.

Still early in the development of the EU, Italy's outlook for economic recovery looked positive, though it continued to lag behind its European counterparts and remained plagued by slow economic growth. The national debt had fallen, though it remained above the EU guidelines. Inflation remained high, increased by rising oil prices and government cutbacks. Unemployment hovered at a significant 10.5 percent in 2001 (though down from the previous year). And in March 2001, Fiat announced a joint venture with General Motors, claiming it could no longer compete in the global market.

The period of reformation and revitalization among banks continued. In 2000, Sanpaolo again strengthened its domestic ties, formalizing an agreement with the Cassa di Risparmio di Firenze that called for expanding operations in central Italy, where the Tuscan bank had a network of more than 400 branches.

In early 2002, Sanpaolo IMI was busy working out the details of another prospective merger, this time with the 800-branch Bank of Cardine. (Sanpaolo IMI already owned one-tenth stake in Cardine from the previous year.) Organizational and profit objectives were still to be worked out. Early details of the merger included a plan to retain Cardine's strong corporate identity, while helping Sanpaolo IMI expand into markets in Central and Eastern Europe. Measuring resources by capital, the move was expected to bump Sanpaolo IMI from third to second place among the Italy's largest banks.

Also, allowing for additional Eastern European expansion and still pending in early 2002, was Sanpaolo IMI's intention to purchase a majority stake in Banca Koper, Slovenia's fourth-largest bank. Announced in late 2001, that deal would provide Sanpaolo with another 37 branches and 7 percent of the Slovenian market. Sanpaolo planned to purchase a 52 percent stake and make a public offer for another 18 percent on the Ljubljana Stock Exchange. Both Italian and Slovenian authorities were expected to approve the deal in 2002.

With all this activity and in spite of the decade-old law that sought to discourage an involvement in banking, large regional nonprofit foundations in Italy continued to participate on a grand scale. Mergers across the industry at the end of the 20th century brought numerous large banks within their purview, and the trend seemed to be continuing into the next decade. Although the minister responsible for the 1990 law had since called his creation a monster, the measure didn't have completely negative outcomes. The law has required the foundations to spend their income on education, culture, health care, conservation and other endeavors for the deprived. Endowments over the past decade helped the elderly, funded museum restoration projects, and even provided aid to Italian-Americans affected by the U.S. terrorist attacks on September 11, 2001.

Whether the law was indeed a monster was still under debate, but certainly the foundations showed an undiminished appetite. In turn, this continuing control led many industry analysts to express concern that large banks in Italy were still in need of reform. The centuries-old foundations retained serious financial clout and, according to some, that was creating a barrier to faster consolidation among Italy's financial institutions.

In December 2001, Italy's Economic Minister Giulio Tremonti announced a new measure in the national budget, which would require the country's former banking foundations to identify nonprofit entities for channeling a significant part of their profits. The amendment simultaneously sought to prevent individuals from holding key posts on the boards of the foundations, along with positions in banks; it was a move that analysts felt would discourage those foundations from continuing to invest in the Italian banking sector.

With much to be determined in 2002, Sanpaolo's outlook as a world-class bank remained in many respects positive. Still among the nation's largest banks, the company boasted a full range of banking and financial services to corporate clients in Italy and around the world (including offices in Europe, Asia, and the Americas). The bank had a network of 1,300 branches throughout the country, but particularly in the financial centers of Turin, Milan, and Genoa, employing some 35,000 people in 2,170 offices worldwide.

Retail banking operations included the Sanpaolo network and the Banco di Napoli, as well as Banque Sanpaolo of France, the Inter-Europa Bank in Hungary, and the Cassa Risparmio Firenze. They also included fund manager Banca Fideuram, San Paolo IMI Asset Management, and the online brokerage company IMIWeb Bank. While continuing to provide basic banking services and loans to small- and medium-sized companies, the bank focused its services in four main areas: retail banking, wealth management, personal financial services, and wholesale banking. Those services included not only remote banking facilities, but a full range of retail payment services, with 1,800 automated teller machines (ATMs) and more than 2 million debit and credit cards.

Principal Competitors

IntesaBCI; UniCredito Italiano; Banca di Roma; Mediobanca.

Further Reading

Ball, Deborah, "Pair of Italian Banks Tantalize the Matchmakers," *Wall Street Journal*, June 16, 2000, p. A12.

Booth, Michael, "Online Retailers Getting Free Ride," *Denver Post*, March 23, 2000, p. B2.

Mandaro, Laura, "With Merger Finalized, SP-IMI Plans Section 20," *International Banker*, December, 14, 1998, p. 1.

"Finance and Economics: Odd Sort of Ownership; Italy's Charitable Foundations," *The Economist Newspaper,* October 27, 2001, p. 70.

"Italian Investors Buck Tradition and Back Funds," *Funds International*, July 1, 1998.

"Italy's Banks, Mired in Middle Ages, Face Revolution: Profits Before Charity," *Wall Street Journal*, March 24, 1997, p. A14.

"Italy's Largest Bank Is First to Get Sec. 20, *International Banker*, February 8, 1999, p. 1.

"Spaghetti Junction," *The Economist Newspaper*, March 27, 1999, p. 72.

Mondellini, Luciano, "Afternoon Mega-merger," *Euromoney*, April 1999, pp. 10–12.

O'Brian, Heather, "Italy Seeks to Curb Control of Banks," *The Daily Deal*, December 4, 2001, http://thedeal.com.

——, "Sanpaolo Buys Majority of Slovenian Bank," *The Daily Deal*, October 30, 2001, http://thedeal.com.

——, "Sanpaolo IMI and Cardine Outline Merger Plan," *The Daily Deal*, October 19, 2001, http://thedeal.com.

—Melissa London

Saudi Arabian Oil Company

Post Office Box 5000
Dhahran 31311
Saudi Arabia
Telephone: (966) 3-72-0115
Fax: (966) 3-873-8190
Web site: http://www.saudiaramco.com

State-Owned Company
Established: 1988
Employees: 56,500 (2001 est.)
Sales: $58.2 billion (2001 est.)*
NAIC: 324110 Petroleum Refineries; 213112 Support
    Activities for Oil and Gas Operations; 541360
    Geophysical Surveying and Mapping Services;
    213111 Drilling Oil and Gas Wells
*This number represents Saudi Aramco's revenues from crude
  oil exports only. It does not take into account Saudi
  Aramco's revenues from other product lines, nor its
  domestic revenues.

With production capacity of about ten million barrels of crude oil per day, the state-owned Saudi Arabian Oil Company (also known as Saudi Aramco) is without question the world's largest producer of crude oil. In the years immediately preceding and following the Persian Gulf crisis, the company worked to broaden its operations from the wellhead to include refining, marketing, distribution, and even retailing. By the mid-1990s, Saudi Aramco considered itself "a fully integrated global oil enterprise." In addition to its largely domestic quest for vertical integration, the oil company pursued joint ventures to extend its geographic reach into North America, Asia, and Europe.

Saudi Aramco is responsible for exploration, development, and production in a tract of land, which covers some 16 percent of the 2.2 million square kilometers that constitute the Saudi Arabian peninsula. The company's 260 billion barrels (bbl) of recoverable crude oil reserves constituted 26 percent of the world's total reserves in the early 1990s. Clearly, Aramco's crude oil operations, which account for 95 percent of total production, are vital not only to the Saudi Arabian economy but also global energy needs. The state-owned business also had natural gas reserves of 180 trillion cubic feet (tcf). Its assets include the world's largest onshore and offshore oilfields. Revenues generated through the export of Aramco crude oil production constitute over half of total Saudi government revenues, and have helped transform the country from, as one observer has noted, "a third world country in an inhospitable desert region, to one that is on the threshold of joining the ranks of developed nations."

Early-20th-Century Origins

The incorporation of Saudi Aramco on November 13, 1988, was largely a cosmetic operation, performed in order to remove the final legal attachments of the Arabian American Oil Company (Aramco) to the original U.S. company, registered in Delaware on January 31, 1944. However, the history of the Aramco concession, upon which the company's fortune has been forged, dates back to the early 1930s. In 1932 Standard Oil (California) (Socal), now known as Chevron, employed the energies of Harry St. John B. Philby, a close friend of Saudi King Ibn Saud, to obtain permission for Socal to conduct a geological survey in the eastern parts of the Saudi Peninsula. Although granting rights over Saudi Arabia's natural resources to a foreign company was against King Ibn Saud's better judgment, his need for money left him no alternative. King Ibn Saud insisted that no geological appraisal could take place until the full terms of a concession had been agreed. The king's fear was that Socal would discover that Saudi Arabia was barren before it had committed any capital. On May 29, 1933, the concession agreement was signed by the king's minister for finance, Abd Allah al Sulaiman, and the Socal representative, Lloyd N. Hamilton, at the royal palace in Jiddah.

In November 1933, the California Arabian Standard Oil Company (Casoc) was formed to manage operations within the concession on behalf of Socal. The original concession stretched from the Persian Gulf up to, and including, the western province of Dahna. In 1939, the concession was further enlarged to around 440,000 square miles to include Saudi Arabia's share of the neutral zone.

However, before any crude oil was discovered in its new Saudi concession, Socal was already experiencing problems in marketing its growing Bahraini oil production. Socal opted for

Company Perspectives:

These ten Corporate values have been the guiding principles by which Saudi Aramco has achieved extraordinary success: Excellence: We pursue excellence in everything we do. Human Resources: We encourage continuous learning and strive to develop our people to their highest potential. Fairness and Integrity: We strive for fairness and adhere to the highest ethical standards. Teamwork: We support each other and work together to achieve our business objectives successfully. Safety: We strive to maintain the highest levels of safety, security, health, and environmental standards. Responsiveness: We are responsive to the expectations of the government and our customers. Stewardship: We are proud of our company and are committed to preserving its assets and resources. Trust: We place authority where responsibility lies. Accountability: We are accountable for our actions. Citizenship: We support our communities and serve as a role model for others.

the quickest solution to this problem, which was to merge operations with a company that owned marketing facilities near the source of production, but that was short of crude. In 1936 Socal struck a deal with the Texas Company, now known as Texaco. The new joint venture was named Caltex and was charged with managing all of Texaco's marketing assets from the Middle East to the Pacific. As a part of the deal, Texaco was given half ownership of Casoc.

It took three years before the exploratory drilling of the Dammam Dome, a group of prominent limestone hills near what is presently called Dhahran, was rewarded. In March 1938, the seventh exploration well drilled on the Dammam Dome identified the Arab Zone, as the explorers named it. Crude oil exports started in the same year. The oil was piped from the well to the makeshift port of al-Khobar and from there was transported by sea to the Bahrain refinery. In the following year the now prolific Ras Tanura export terminal was used for the first time by Socal's tanker, the *D.G. Schofield*.

World War II

The advent of World War II impeded Casoc's operations. Production at the newly constructed Ras Tanura refinery lasted only six months before it was closed in June 1941 and all dependents of U.S. employees were sent home for the duration of the war.

The war years from 1940 to 1944 were significant, however, for the progressive rationalization of Casoc's management structure under the guidance of its new president, F.A. Davies. Davies had visited Saudi Arabia as a Socal representative in 1930 and had been closely involved in operations ever since. His election, together with that of a new board of directors in August 1940, marked the company's first step toward independence from Socal. Casoc set up its headquarters in San Francisco at 200 Bush Street. Symbolically, the final confirmation of the company's new identity came on January 31, 1944, when Casoc was renamed the Arabian American Oil Company.

The postwar years of the late 1940s witnessed the scramble to expand production from the Aramco concession and to establish a market for it. Between 1944 and 1949, Aramco expanded capacity in all spheres of operation, in no small way aided by the military cooperation in allocating materials and even providing transport. The strategic importance of oil had been proven in the defeat of Adolf Hitler, and the U.S. government had even set aside funds for possible direct investment in the Middle East to secure supplies. Aramco shunned the offer of direct government involvement but with its aid achieved a 25-fold increase in crude oil supply from 20 thousand barrels per day in 1944 to 500 thousand barrels per day in 1949. The Ras Tanura refinery's distillation capacity was expanded from 50 thousand barrels per day to 127 thousand barrels per day between 1945 and 1949, in part to supply the increasing requirements of the U.S. Navy.

Secure access to world markets was fostered in two ways. First, with regard to the European market, Aramco attempted to improve the competitiveness of its crude oil vis-a-vis Soviet and U.S. exports by cutting down on the time and, ultimately, costs of transporting crude from the Persian Gulf. In 1946 Aramco began to build, through its affiliate, the Trans-Arabian Pipe Line Company (Tapline), a 1,068-mile-long pipeline connecting the Abqaiq oilfield to the Mediterranean port of Sidon, Lebanon.

Second, Aramco tried to merge operations with the Standard Oil Company of New Jersey, later Exxon, and the Socony-Vacuum Oil Company, now known as Mobil. Harry Collier, the chairman of Socal at that time, supported the choice of these two companies not only because of their unrivaled marketing assets in the Far East, but also because the choice satisfied King Ibn Saud's explicitly stated wish that Aramco should remain American to avoid an extension of British influence in the region. Between 1946 and 1948, the two companies wrestled with the legal obstacle posed to the merger by the Red Line Agreement. This obstacle was overcome in December 1948. The companies' shares in Aramco and Tapline were divided as follows: Socal, Texaco, and Standard Oil of New Jersey each owned 30 percent and the Socony-Vacuum Company owned the remaining 10 percent.

Also in 1948, Aramco gave up its concessionary rights over the Saudi Arabian part of the neutral zone. This move was made in response to the severe terms accepted by the American Independent Oil Company (Aminoil) in the auction for the concession rights over the Kuwaiti half of the neutral zone. Unwilling to match Aminoil's offer, Aramco decide to preempt similar demands by the Saudi king by giving up the land. In return for this unilateral gesture, Aramco received a reaffirmation of its offshore concession rights in the Persian Gulf. In the auction that resulted from Aramco's cessation, the Pacific Western Oil Company agreed to terms even more onerous than those applied to Aminoil.

However, Aramco did not completely avoid compensating the government for the dramatic increase in the value of its concession. During the late 1940s and the first half of the 1950s, Aramco was progressively forced to relinquish small parts of its concession. Also, on December 30, 1950, following the example of Venezuela in 1948, the Saudi government authorized an increase in the government's share to 50 percent of Aramco's profits net of exploration, development, and production costs.

Key Dates:

1933: Standard Oil of California (Socal, later Chevron) is granted an oil concession to prospect Saudi Arabia's eastern parts. Socal forms The California Arabian Standard Oil Company (Casoc).

1936: The Texas Company (later Texaco) obtains 50 percent ownership in Casoc.

1938: Oil is discovered on Dammam Dome, near today's Dhahran.

1944: Casoc's name changes to Arabian American Oil Company (Aramco).

1945: The Ras-Tamura refinery begins continuous operations.

1948: Standard Oil Company of New Jersey (later Exxon) and Socony-Vacuum (later Mobil) obtain partial ownership in Aramco.

1973: The Saudi Arabian government acquires 25 percent of Aramco.

1974: The Saudi Arabian government increases its share in Aramco to 60 percent.

1980: The Saudi Arabian government obtains 100 percent ownership of Aramco.

1988: Aramco becomes a state-owned company, and renamed Saudi Arabian Oil Company (Saudi Aramco).

1993: Saudi Aramco takes over the Saudi Arabian Marketing and Refining Company (Samarec).

1995: Saudi Aramco's President and CEO, Ali al-Naimi, is named Saudi Arabia's minister of Petroleum and Mineral Resources.

1998: Saudi Aramco joins Shell and Texaco in creating Motiva Enterprises LLC, a refining and marketing operation in Eastern and Southern United States.

2002: Saudi Aramco and Shell complete a buyout of Texaco's shares in Motiva, assuming a 50–50 ownership of this joint venture.

Growth Slows in 1950s

The expansion of Aramco's operations continued through the 1950s, albeit at a slower pace. Crude oil production only increased from 761 thousand barrels per day in 1960 to 1.2 million barrels per day in 1959, despite an increase of 38 billion barrels to a total of 50 billion barrels in the Saudi Arabian proven recoverable reserves during the same period. This expansion of oil reserves was primarily attributable to two discoveries made by Aramco, the onshore Ghawar and the offshore Safaniya oil fields, in 1951. The onshore and offshore discoveries were the largest on record at the time and have remained unequaled to this day. 1951 marked Tapline's first full year in operation. By 1965, Tapline enabled Aramco to market some 44 percent of its total crude oil exports to Europe, a greater share than that of nearer markets in Asia.

Aramco's activities during the 1950s were distinguished from those of the postwar years by the mature approach that underlay them. Aramco did not ignore the U.S. lesson of the waste caused by over-rapid exploitation of oil reservoirs. In the early 1950s, Aramco began to implement oilfield pressure maintenance programs. At the Abqaiq oilfield, gas reinjection facilities started operation in March 1954, and, in February 1956, a similar water program was started. An added advantage with the gas program was that not only was Aramco able to utilize associated gas but that also the associated gas could be stored instead of burned off at the source.

Corporate Control at Issue in 1960s

Both Aramco's and Saudi Arabia's revenues increased dramatically during this period as a result of the expansion of crude oil exports and of rising posted prices. Like Aramco, Saudi Arabia ploughed these revenues into the development of infrastructure. As Saudi Arabia was overwhelmingly dependent on oil for revenues, it was vitally important that revenue stability was achieved to foster long-term development plans. Unlike the Aramco partners, however, the Saudi government had no influence on the two factors, production and price, that determined their revenues. The struggle for control, or the "participation" issue, emerged strongly in the 1960s.

Even though the general office had been moved to Dhahran and two representatives from the Saudi government were included on the board of directors, control of Aramco still rested firmly with the four partners. On August 9, 1960, the chairman of Standard Oil of New Jersey, Munroe Rathbone, decided unilaterally to shave 14 percent off the posted price, a cut of some 7 percent, in order to increase its competitiveness in Europe vis-à-vis Soviet crude exports. Not only did the chairman refuse to consult the Aramco board, but he also rejected the advice given him from, among others, the New Jersey company's representative on the Aramco board, Howard Page. Other companies followed suit with the price cut and fueled the outrage of the oil-exporting countries. One dissenting voice that rose above the rest was that of Sayyid Abdullah H. Tariki, the Saudi director general of petroleum and mineral affairs and member of the Aramco board. Tariki immediately set about arranging secret negotiations with other producer countries. The preparatory negotiations proved instrumental in the formation of OPEC in 1960. As it turned out, the formation of OPEC was to be decisive in the battle for control of Aramco.

On November 30, 1962, the General Petroleum and Mineral Organization of Saudi Arabia (Petromin) was founded. Its aim was to foster Saudi participation in all areas of the oil industry, including operations in the Aramco concession. Although Petromin was not producing any crude oil, by 1970 it had joint interests in many concessions and operated a refinery at Jiddah and a fertilizer plant in Dammam. The evolution of Petromin over the 1960s was central to the government's attempts to wrest control from the Aramco partners.

The weakness of the crude oil market continued through the 1960s, due to the emergence of Iran as the second major producer in the region. The freezing of posted prices over the 1960s meant that an oil exporter's only means to protect its revenues from being eroded by inflation was to increase production. The companies operating in the Gulf, including the Aramco partners, were each put under a great deal of pressure by concessionaire governments to increase production and maintain prices. These incompatible aims could only be satisfied if incremental world demand could be equitably divided between the producers. Howard Page was so concerned to appear to be representing the Saudi case for an increase in its market share that he refused the opportunity to involve Standard Oil of New Jersey in the very profitable exploration strategy being conducted in Oman, fearing that the company might be identified as aiding a direct competitor to enter the market. Between 1960 and 1970, Iran's production increased by 258 percent or 2.8 million barrels per day compared to the Saudi increase of 189 percent or 2.5 million barrels per day. However, by 1970, both Saudi and Iranian oil production had reached around 3.8 million barrels per day.

Aramco's fortunes were, and always have been, inextricably bound with those of the Saudi government. One way for both to overcome the constraint on revenue expansion imposed by the glutted crude oil market of the 1960s was to diversify into other markets. Expansion and progressive modernization of the Ras Tanura refinery increased crude oil throughput to 380,000 barrels per day in 1970, improved the quality of products, and enabled the blending of new products such as aviation gasoline. Aramco also began to establish the infrastructure necessary for the sale of liquid natural gas (LNG). Between 1962 and 1970, production of LNG increased 18-fold from 2,900 barrels per day to 52,100 barrels per day.

Tightening Markets Presage Gradual Government Takeover

The supply conditions in the crude oil market became markedly tighter in the early 1970s. In 1972, Aramco managed not only to increase production by an unprecedented 1.2 million barrels per day to six million barrels per day but also succeeded in increasing the posted price. The market conditions placed the government in a much stronger position from which to negotiate with the Aramco partners over Saudi participation.

In March 1972, after employing every delaying tactic possible, Aramco accepted the principle of 20 percent state participation in order to preempt unilateral action. The principle was worked out in detail in October 1972, when it was agreed that Saudi participation should be phased in from 25 percent on January 1, 1973, to 51 percent on January 1, 1982, and that compensation should be made for the updated book value of Aramco's assets.

By 1973, however, other oil-exporting countries had obtained or imposed terms far in excess of the Saudi government's demands. Negotiations restarted and continued through to 1980. In 1974, the Saudi interest in Aramco was increased to 60 percent. Between 1976 and 1980, the 100 percent Saudi takeover of Aramco was agreed upon and the financial provisions were made retroactive to January 1, 1976. By the terms of the agreement, the Aramco partners received a service fee of 18 to 19 cents per barrel and were obliged to market the crude that Petromin could not sell through its own channels.

The oil price rises of 1973–1974 had a dramatic effect on revenues. The effect on government revenues of increases in the oil price, taxation, and production—from 3.8 million barrels per day in 1970 to an all-time high of 9.9 million barrels per day in 1980—was such that the economy could no longer absorb the funds available to it and was, therefore, generating a surplus.

With their newly acquired interest, the Saudi government began to involve Aramco in the reinvestment of that surplus. In 1975, Aramco was given the task of constructing and operating a gas system that could fuel Saudi Arabia's drive towards industrialization. The master gas system (MGS), as it came to be known, started operation in 1980. In January 1977, Aramco formed a subsidiary, the Saudi Consolidated Electric Company (SCECO), to construct and operate an electric grid system for the Eastern Province. As a result of the agreement between the government and Aramco, SCECO became an independently managed company on January 1, 1983.

Although Aramco had become state-owned, the close ties between the original Aramco partners and the government were not lost. Their relationship was fostered through joint ventures outside Aramco's scope of operations. Mobil continued to hold a 29 percent interest in Petrolube and a 30 percent stake in Luberef. Both the Saudi-American joint ventures were formed to build lubricating oil refineries in Jiddah in the 1970s, and are still responsible for their operation. The other three of the original Aramco partners, Exxon, Texaco, and Gulf, are involved in industrial projects with the Saudi Arabian Basic Industries Corporation (SABIC) in Jubail.

Revenues, Profits and Production Fall in 1980s

However, Aramco's boom years of the 1970s and early 1980s did not last. The oil price rises of 1973 and 1979–1980 led to inter-fuel substitution, such as the substitution of oil for gas, and conservation measures being implemented by the Organization for Economic Cooperation and Development (OECD) countries that brought about a collapse in world oil demand. Coupled with the sharp increase in oil supplies from non-OPEC regions, such as the North Sea, from 32.9 million barrels per day in 1980 to 37.8 million barrels per day in 1985, Saudi Arabia was faced with the no-win choice of either cutting production to maintain the official selling price or cutting prices and flooding the market. Between 1980 and 1985, Saudi Arabia cut production from 9.9 million barrels per day to four million barrels per day.

By 1985, Saudi Arabia was tired of shouldering the full burden of price defense and looking on as its revenues declined. In September 1985, Sheikh Yamani, in conjunction with the Aramco partners, instituted a dramatic change of policy to regain Saudi Arabia's share of the crude oil market. Between August 1985 and August 1986, Saudi Arabian production increased from 2.2 million to 6.2 million barrels per day, and the spot price of many world crudes fell to less than $10 from their previous 1985 levels of around $26 to $29 per barrel. The real price of oil had returned to levels not seen since before the oil price shocks of 1973–1974.

Aramco did not emerge unscathed from the drastic fall in oil revenues. Between 1982 and 1989, Aramco's personnel fell from 57,000 to 43,000. Following the meeting of the Aramco board of directors in San Francisco on April 8 and 9, 1987, the decision was taken to cut its own membership from 20 to 13. Three Americans and four Saudis, among them the ex-oil minister Sheikh Yamani, were removed, leaving two representatives from each of the four original Aramco partners and five Saudi officials.

The trauma of the 1986 oil price crash led to a change in management, Hisham Nazer replacing Sheikh Yamani, and a change in oil policy. The primary aim of Saudi policy after the unbridled competition of 1986 was to secure market share just as it had been in the oil market glut of the 1960s. To secure long-term supply contracts, Hisham Nazer depended heavily on the close relationship between Aramco and the original shareholders. In his first attempt Nazer signed a 1.25 million barrels per day long-term supply arrangement with the four majors involved in the formation of Aramco, Chevron, Texaco, Mobil, and Exxon, on February 3, 1987. This agreement soon broke down, however, in the face of further price competition, and Nazer turned his attention to the possibility of securing market share through downstream integration—ownership of all phases of the industry from the wellhead to the service station.

In 1988, the first overseas downstream joint venture was concluded by the newly incorporated Saudi Aramco. On November 10, 1988, Saudi Aramco and Texaco signed an agreement committing themselves to the conditions of the joint venture named Star Enterprise. Aramco's share of the joint venture was to be managed by its subsidiary Saudi Refining Incorporated. From January 1, 1989, U.S.-based Star Enterprise was given the responsibility of operating Texaco's refining, distribution, and marketing assets in the east and gulf coasts. Texaco's assets were substantial in these areas and included three refineries—Delaware City, Convent, and Port Arthur—with combined distillation capacity of 625,000 barrels per day and, most importantly, 11,400 service stations. In return Saudi Aramco paid $1.5 billion and committed itself to supplying up to 600,000 barrels per day and to supplying a 30 million barrel inventory. By the mid-1990s, Star Enterprise ranked as the U.S.'s sixth-largest gasoline marketer. Aramco made subsequent acquisitions of 35 percent of South Korea's Ssangyong Oil and a 40 percent stake in Petron, the Philippines' leading refiner and marketer.

King Fahd Ibn Abdulaziz Al-Saud formally incorporated Saudi Arabian Oil Company by Royal Decree in 1988. The decree established a monarch-chaired Supreme Council and a board of directors led by the country's minister of petroleum and mineral resources. In addition to domestic government officials and top Aramco managers, the board included Exxon and Chevron chairmen into the early 1990s.

Persian Gulf Crisis, Management Shift Highlight Early 1990s

As a result of the 1990 Persian Gulf crisis, Saudi Aramco emerged as one of the most influential participants in the global oil industry. Within just a few weeks of Iraq's invasion of Kuwait, Saudi Aramco increased its daily production by over 2.5 million barrels per day. The conflict devastated Kuwait's oil-producing infrastructure and international sanctions prevented Iraq from trading oil, thereby eliminating over 4.5 million barrels of oil production per day and triggering what *Oil and Gas Journal* called "one of the most severe crises in the world's oil supplies since World War II." In fact, Petroleum Economist magazine asserted that Saudi Aramco "rescued the world from an oil supply crisis" by accelerating its plan to increase crude oil production capacity to ten million barrels per day from a target date of 1995 to 1992.

The company resumed its quest for vertical integration in the aftermath of the war, merging another state-owned firm, Saudi Arabian Marketing & Refining Co. (Samarec) in June 1993. *Oil and Gas Journal*'s L.R. Aalund noted that Samarec has "passed an acid test during the Gulf War when they supplied all allied air, land, and sea forces with their total fuel needs." The merger moved Saudi Aramco into the ranks of the world's ten largest refiners, and put the company in complete control of Saudi Arabia's crude oil, from refining to marketing and distribution. Less than one month later, the company added state-owned Petromin to its roster, thereby merging majority interests in Petromin Lubricating Oil Refining Co. (a.k.a. Luberef) and Petromin Lubricating Oil Co. (a.k.a. Petrolube), both joint ventures with Mobil Oil Corp.

After nine years as Saudi Arabia's minister of Petroleum and Mineral Resources, Hisham Nazer was succeeded by Saudi Aramco President and CEO Ali al-Naimi in 1995. The appointment by King Fahd was interpreted as an acknowledgement of the company's growing clout, and as a sign of a new emphasis on the domestic petroleum industry. Aramco Vice-President for International Operations Abdullah Jum'ah advanced to acting president and CEO of Aramco upon al-Naimi's promotion.

Moving into a New Millennium

The year 1998 was turbulent for oil-producing countries, and Saudi Arabia was no exception. The Asian financial crisis, combined with a warm winter, drastically reduced the demand for oil worldwide. The Saudi economy, so completely dependent on oil exports, was badly shaken as a result. At that time, Crown Prince Abdullah began talks that would eventually lead to the reopening of the country's oil and gas industry to foreign companies (the industry was closed to foreign competitors since 1975, when the oil and gas fields were nationalized). Also in 1998, the company joined forces with Texaco and Shell to form Motiva Enterprises LLC. The new joint-venture consolidated the refining and marketing efforts of the three companies in the southern and eastern United States. Three years later, as part of the Texaco-Chevron merger talks, Saudi Aramco and Shell bought Texaco's share in Motiva, and the company became a 50–50 joint venture.

Oil prices rebounded in 1999, but following the terrorist attacks on the United States on September 11, 2001 oil prices dipped sharply again. The economic roller coaster in Saudi Arabia underlined the country's need for economic diversification. In addition, Saudi demand for natural gas was increasing as the kingdom's industrial base grew. In May 2001, Saudi Arabia announced three major natural gas projects, totaling $25 billion, in which Saudi Aramco is an equity holder (Saudi Arabia holds approximately 4 percent of the world's gas reserves). Eight foreign companies were selected to participate in these projects. Saudi Aramco has been developing the kingdom's gas industry since the 1970s, but with no foreign investment.

Early in 2001, *Petroleum Intelligence Weekly* (*PIW*) named Saudi Aramco the top oil company in the world for the thirteenth consecutive year. *PIW*'s report also pointed out that the petroleum industry and Saudi Aramco's competition are both changing. Responded Abdullah Jum'ah, Saudi Aramco's President and CEO: "Increasing competition will encourage us to remain at our best in all respects and to maintain a high level of cooperation with key players in the petroleum industry.'' True to this sentiment, the company keeps pushing ahead with new and ambitious projects that will take several years to complete.

In 2000, Saudi Arabia established the Supreme Petroleum Council (SPC), which took over some responsibilities from Saudi Aramco. Although there are talks of increasing privatization in the Saudi oil sector, and despite recent decades' wholesale changes in the ownership, management, and function of Aramco, its place in Saudi Arabia and the world seems secure for the foreseeable future.

Principal Subsidiaries

Aramco Services Company (U.S.A.); Saudi Refining Inc. (U.S.A); Aramco Overseas Companies B.V. (various); Vela International Marine Limited (100%); Petromin Lubricating Oil Refining Co. (70%); Saudi Arabian Lubricating Oil Company (Petrolube) (71%).

Principal Competitors

Petroleos de Venezuela; ExxonMobil.

Further Reading

Aalund, L.R., ''Saudi Arabia,'' *The Oil and Gas Journal*, August 16, 1993, pp. 38–44.

''Energy: $3.8 billion Sale Clears Way for Chevron-Texaco Merger.'' *Chicago Tribune*, October 10, 2001, p. B2.

George, Dev, ''Safaniya, POEC, and the Saudi Power Play,'' *Offshore (incorporating The Oilman)*, November 1991, p. 11.

Gutkin, S., ''Belt Tightening in Oil Nations,'' Associated Press, March 23, 1998.

''King Of Oil Surges Ahead,'' *Petroleum Economist*, December 1991, pp. 6–9.

Longrigg, S.H., *Oil in the Middle East*, Oxford, England: Oxford University Press, 1969.

Mangan, David, Jr., and Marshall Thomas, ''Saudi Aramco Report Stresses Join Ventures,'' *The Oil Daily*, June 21, 1991, pp. 1–2.

Mollet, Paul, ''Aramco Man Gets the Top Job,'' *Petroleum Economist*, September 1995, p. 36.

Naimi, A.I., ''Saudi Aramco Staying On Course with Strategy for the '90s,'' *The Oil Daily*, November 21, 1991, p. 5.

O'Sullivan, E, ''Saudi Aramco Flexes its Muscles,'' *Middle East Economic Digest*, July 22, 1994, 38:29, pp. 8–9.

''Saudi Aramco Describes Crisis Oil Flow Hike,'' *The Oil and Gas Journal*, December 2, 1991, pp. 49–51.

Saudi Aramco tops Industry in PIW List, Dhahran: Saudi Aramco, 2002.

''Saudi Arabia in Pacts with Nine Global Oil Firms,'' *Los Angeles Times*, June 4, 2001, p. B2.

''Saudi Arabia Market Overview,'' Energy Information Administration, http://www.eia.doe.gov, accessed March 15, 2002.

Seymour, I., *OPEC: Instrument of Change*, London: Macmillan Press Ltd., 1980.

Yergin, D., *The Prize: The Epic Quest for Oil, Money and Power*, New York: Simon & Schuster, 1990.

—Adam Seymour
—updates: April Dougal Gasbarre; Adi Ferrara

Schering AG

13342 Berlin
Germany
Telephone: +49 (30) 468-1111
Fax: +49 (30) 468-15305
Web site: http://www.schering.de/eng/

Public Company
Incorporated: 1871
Employees: 25,556 (2001)
Sales: EUR 4.84 billion (US$4.31 billion) (2001)
Stock Exchanges: Basel Berlin Bremen Düsseldorf
Frankfurt Geneva Hamburg Hanover London
Munich New York Stuttgart Zurich
Ticker Symbol: SCH (Germany), SHR (New York)
NAIC: 325412 Pharmaceutical Preparation Manufacturing

Schering AG, the German pharmaceutical company, operates worldwide production facilities for fertility control and hormone therapy, diagnostics and radiopharmaceuticals, dermatology, and specialized therapeutics.

Although the company presently maintains a formidable presence in the United States, this has not always been the case. Schering's initial U.S. operations fell victim to the turmoil wrought by two world wars. The company's first U.S. subsidiary was dissolved during World War I. After being reestablished in 1929, it was then seized by the U.S. Alien Property Custodian during World War II. To Schering's chagrin, the subsidiary was eventually sold to private investors and was severed completely from its parent company. Having no other recourse, the firm occupied itself with rebuilding its virtually decimated facilities at home in Germany. In the years that followed, however, Schering regained its lost markets and expanded to become an impressive competitor around the world in its pharmaceutical specialties.

Schering's Origins and Early Successes

In 1851, at Berlin's Chausseestrasse 17, Ernst Schering opened a pharmacy he named Gruene Apotheke. Twenty years later, the founder incorporated the business as a stock company named Chemische Fabrik auf Actien. In December 1889, Schering died at the age of 65, one year before his company began marketing its first specialty product—a medication for gout. In 1901, the company's operations expanded into the area of electroplating. To facilitate the process of plating decorative metal, Chemische Fabrik manufactured baths and electrolytes. Later, these operations would expand to include the production of complete electroplating equipment as well as chemical compounds and machinery for printed-circuit manufacture.

At the dawn of the twentieth century, the German company also expanded into such diverse areas as industrial and laboratory chemicals. In the 1920s, agrochemicals were added to Chemische Fabrik's product line, and by the end of the decade the company made its first foray into an area that would become increasingly important in the future—female hormones. In 1937, the company merged with Oberkoks, a mining and chemical company, which resulted in the adoption of the current name, Schering AG.

As Germany entered World War II, Schering was widely recognized as a world leader in innovative chemical production and the scope of its operations. Exploratory work on sulfonamides, X-ray contrast media, and steroid hormones positioned the company on the cutting-edge of new technologies. Schering's successful innovations matched their expanding operations, with some 30 foreign subsidiaries worldwide.

Challenges of the World Wars

This expansion, however impressive, was not without setbacks. One of Schering's oldest subsidiaries, Schering & Glatz, was established in the United States in 1876 to distribute Schering products such as diphtheria medication. Yet during World War I, because it was affiliated with Germany, the operation was dissolved. In 1929 the company reestablished its presence in the United States by creating the Schering Corporation in New York City. This subsidiary specialized in hormone research developments, as company scientists became experts in synthesizing steroid drugs. These products accounted for 75 percent of total sales for the U.S. subsidiary.

While Schering's expertise would in time lead to the development of birth control products in the 1960s, its coveted knowledge became the target of espionage reports during World War II. Believing Schering research excelled in the area of corticosteriods, or hormones extracted from the renal cortex, the United States conducted a secret investigation resulting in an accusation that the company used its knowledge to develop highly sophisticated drugs to further the Nazi cause. The United States alleged that pilots under the influence of corticosteriods could perhaps withstand extremely high altitudes enabling them to fly well above antiaircraft flak. As it happened, Schering's corticosteroid research was not highly developed, and only after the espionage reports did Schering begin intense experimentation in this area.

Charges of military collusion with the Nazi regime aside, nothing could have prepared the company for its losses suffered after World War II. All of the company's foreign holdings disappeared. In 1942, Leo Crowley, acting as the U.S. Alien Property Custodian, seized assets to all German properties within America's borders—including Schering. Ten years later, the U.S. Attorney General announced that the company's U.S. subsidiary was for sale and a group of private investors headed by Merrill Lynch made the purchase to establish Schering Corporation independently from its German parent. The former subsidiary went on to post impressive financial gains with the discovery of two new corticosteriods that became the envy of the drug industry.

Post-World War II Recovery and a Return to the U.S. Market

Following the end of World War II in 1945, Schering AG's German factories were all but destroyed, and the company had lost valuable patents as well as the rights to its name in all 30 of its subsidiaries. The remaining employees searched the rubble for machine parts and usable wreckage. After a few years of scavenging, the company miraculously released a finished product, yet soon afterward its property was seized in East Germany by the new Communist regime. Nevertheless, in several years Schering succeeded in rebuilding its operations.

Manufacturing such products as lice powder and penicillin, the company soon exhibited signs of revitalization. Interestingly enough, by retaining headquarters in the city of its origin, Schering was the only company with a multinational orientation to remain in Berlin after World War II. In fact, its main headquarters was three blocks from where the Berlin Wall would be erected in 1961 separating East from West Berlin. For security reasons, Schering maintained a second corporate office along with all its business records in Bergkamen—200 miles west of the East German border. Board members who were committed to staying in their home city influenced the company's decision not to move.

A major step in Schering's postwar expansion involved pioneering work in the area of birth control. Using their expertise in steroid research, the company introduced the first birth control pill in the European market in 1961. By 1972 the company was responsible for supplying over 50 percent of the world market, excluding the United States, with hormonal contraceptives. Rather than relying on the success of ''the Pill,'' Schering made a concerted effort to diversify its product line. Out of $383 million in total sales, 65 percent came from a broad spectrum of pharmaceuticals, including 30 percent from X-ray contrast media and psycho-pharmaceuticals, 12 percent from phyto-pharmaceuticals, 18 percent from specialty industrial chemicals, and 5 percent from electroplating. While the Berlin facilities remained the center of all research, administrative, and some packaging operations, 50 subsidiaries operating throughout Europe, Asia, and Latin America finished and distributed Schering products worldwide.

With a strong financial position and an ambitious vision for research and development, the West German company prepared to make yet another entrance into the coveted U.S. market. Its purchase of a 50 percent interest in New Jersey's Knoll Pharmaceutical in 1972 was only the beginning for Schering. Between the years 1976 and 1980, five U.S. subsidiaries joined Schering's holdings—Nepera Chemical, Sherex Chemical, Berlex Laboratories (renamed from Cooper Laboratories), Chemcut, and Nor-Am Agricultural Products. The acquisitions directly corresponded to Schering's five divisions at the time: Drugs, Industrial Chemicals, Fine Chemicals, Agrochemicals, and Electroplating.

Horst Kramp, an executive board member of the six-man Vorstand at the time, directed Schering's U.S. operations. The unusual management structure, which did not allow a position for president, placed Kramp on equal footing with his five colleagues. While each Vorstand member held a distinct function, all policies were decided by consensus. Kramp, whose administrative specialties were marketing and sales, joined Schering in 1964 as a domestic sales manager. In the 1960s, he traveled to the United States to work at Nor-Am only later to return to Germany to become the only nonchemist on the Vorstand.

Schering Trademark Suit and Slow U.S. Growth in the 1980's

Although Schering AG eventually bought back many of its former subsidiaries after World War II, one former holding that was never repurchased was Schering Corporation in the United States. As industry observers watched the company's increasing financial success, the management at Schering AG realized, not without remorse, that its former subsidiary had grown too large to purchase back. Access to the use of the shared trademark in the United States had been an issue of contention between the two Scherings since their separation, and in 1983 their grievances led them to engage in a protracted legal battle. Schering-Plough (formed from the merger between Schering Corporation and a manufacturer of proprietary drugs) contended that Berlex,

Key Dates:

1851: Ernst Schering opens his pharmacy, Gruene Apotheke, in Berlin.

1871: Ernst Schering's operations are incorporated as Chemische Fabrik auf Actien.

1889: Ernest Schering dies.

1901: The company's operations expand into the area of electroplating.

1918: Schering's U.S. subsidiaries dissolve due to trading with the Enemy Act.

1929: The company returns to the United States by founding Schering Corporation in New York.

1932: The company merges with Oberkoks, a mining and chemical company, and adopts Schering AG as its name.

1942: The U.S. government takes control of all German properties in the United States, including Schering Corporation.

1945: Schering begins to rebuild destroyed factories and recover from the loss of patents and naming rights.

1952: Schering's U.S. subsidiary is sold to private investors, permanently separating the business from its German parent.

1961: The first birth control pill is introduced by Schering in the European market.

19702: The company gradually reenters the U.S. market through targeted acquisitions, such as Knoll Pharmaceutical.

1983: Legal conflict begins between Schering-Plough and Schering AG over the use of the Schering name in the United States.

1986: The company appoints Horst Witzel as its first chairman of the board since World War II.

1988: Schering-Plough is awarded exclusive rights to the Schering name in the United States, with certain exceptions; and Dr. Giuseppe Vita is named the new board chairman.

1993: The company releases Betaseron in the United States (known as Betaferon), the world's first drug to treat relapsing-remitting multiple sclerosis.

1999: The company broadens its pharmaceutical operations to include radiopharmaceuticals by purchasing Diatide Inc., a nuclear medicine specialist firm.

2000: The New York Stock Exchange lists the company for the first time and five-year sales and net income increase 90 percent and 165 percent, respectively.

2001: Dr. Vita retires and the board appoints Dr. Hubertus Erlen; and the company launches a new birth control pill, Yasim, in the United States.

Schering AG's pharmaceutical subsidiary in the United States, was infringing on its trademark. The German company asserted, however, that the company namesake stemming from founder Ernst Schering was widely recognized in Europe. To bar its use in the United States, Schering AG argued, would subject the company to unfair competition. The two companies reached an agreement in 1988 whereby Schering AG agreed to operate under the name Berlex in the United States and Canada, giving exclusive rights to the Schering name in the United States, with certain exceptions, to Schering-Plough.

By 1982, while Schering sales grew by 4 percent, the U.S. subsidiaries registered negligible earnings figures. The Vorstand members remained unconcerned, however, citing the time necessary before the companies could turn a profit. The next step was to remove unprofitable operations. Facilities manufacturing such products as adhesive chemicals or sulfuric chemicals were sold. In the meantime, $22.5 million was appropriated for the expansion of U.S. subsidiaries, including the building of new headquarters and research facilities. Similarly, management at Schering was conscientious in the provision and support of research expenditures for the U.S. holdings, investing as much as 14 percent of the company's gross income.

Sales for Schering's U.S. subsidiaries exceeded DM 1 billion for the first time in 1984. Worldwide sales first surpassed DM 5 million in the following year, with 82 percent derived from foreign operations. And in 1986, Schering appointed Horst Witzel as its first chairman of the board since the end of World War II. Shortly thereafter the firm sold Nepera, its weak fine chemicals U.S. subsidiary.

Focusing on Core Competencies in the 1990's

A year after the resolution of the legal battle between the German and U.S. Scherings in 1988, Dr. Giuseppe Vita was named Schering AG's new board chairman, with Klaus Pohle as his deputy. Schering created four strategic business units for the pharmaceutical division to enhance its commitment to this area—including Diagnostics, Fertility Control, Oncology and Dermatology, and Cardiovascular and Central Nervous System. By 1991, Schering's annual sales and profit levels reached new heights at DM 6.36 billion and DM 274 million, respectively.

In an effort to succeed as a niche player focusing on specialized areas within the pharmaceuticals industry, Schering sold its industrial chemicals and natural substances divisions to New York's Witco Corporation in 1992, and its electroplating division in 1993. These divested operations would have required tremendous levels of investment in order to be competitive globally, and Dr. Vita was confident in his focus on pharmaceuticals, which made up 95 percent of Schering's profits at the time. As evidence of this renewed pharmaceutical commitment, 1993 also marked the U.S. release of Betaseron (known as Betaferon elsewhere), the world's first drug to help treat relapsing-remitting multiple sclerosis. Betaseron would eventually yield more than 10 percent of Schering's annual sales. Schering's share price hit a new high of DM 1.160, although sales and profits experienced their second straight decline.

Shareholders agreed in 1994 to merge its Agrochemicals division into a new joint venture with Hoechst AG called AgrEvo, of which Schering would hold a 40 percent interest (five years later Hoechst merged the agrochemicals operations with Rhone-Poulenc to form Aventis Crop Science, with Schering controlling 24 percent of the venture). Despite decreases in sales and profitability, Schering was still ranked among the top 20 pharmaceutical companies worldwide in 1994 and was a world leader in agrochemicals.

After a turbulent year in 1995 with a 13 percent earnings drop, in large part due to an X-ray contrast medium recall, Schering soon rebounded and posted one of its most profitable years in 1997 with income of DM 446 million (against DM 6.2 billion in sales). The company achieved this success in part due to currency rates at the time combined with cost reduction in its acquisitions and strong sales of female health products. And amid rumors of a possible takeover by Roche Holdings AG, Schering's share price increased more than 3 percent.

Strategic Acquisitions Fuel Profitability in the New Century

In 1999, Schering decided to broaden its pharmaceutical operations to include radiopharmaceuticals in an effort to boost sales, so the company purchased Diatide Inc., a New Hampshire nuclear medicine specialist. Schering acquired 60 percent of Oris/Cis Bio in the following year to augment its diagnostics/radiopharmaceutical position even further, and two years later Schering exercised an option to purchase the remaining 40 percent of the firm.

To build up its Japanese presence, Schering purchased therapeutics specialist Mitsui Pharmaceuticals in 2000. But perhaps the firm's most public achievement of that year was that the New York Stock Exchange listed Schering AG for the first time. The new listing on the NYSE improved Schering's ability to attract top professionals to its U.S. subsidiaries through stock options, and provided Schering with added flexibility through the ability to utilize stock when making acquisitions.

Heading into the 21st century, Schering enjoyed strong sales and profit levels, which increased more than 20 percent in 2000 to EUR 4.49 billion and EUR 336 million, respectively. In fact, between 1995 and 2000, Schering's sales climbed 90 percent, and net income increased by an impressive 165 percent. Having exceeded the performance goals of Schering's five-year plan a year ahead of schedule, Dr. Vita set his sights on boosting sales to EUR 5.5 billion by 2006, with significant expansion in Japan and especially in the United States, where he aimed to increase sales from 21 percent of Schering's sales in 1999 to 30 percent by 2006.

Six new products were launched by Schering in the U.S. in 2001 through Berlex Laboratories, whose sales force was expanded as part of Schering's comprehensive marketing and public relations push that also included becoming a corporate sponsor for WNYC-FM, New York City's National Public Radio station. The newly released products in the United States included the new birth control pill Yasmin, introduced in Germany during the previous year. Yasmin helps reduce water retention, weight gain, and skin problems that have affected users of the traditional pill.

Dr. Vita retired as Schering's chairman in 2001, and the board appointed Dr. Hubertus Erlen, formerly head of manufac-

turing, as its new chairman. Schering and Aventis agreed to sell Aventis Crop Science to Bayer AG, marking Schering's return to its origin as a pharmaceuticals company exclusively. Despite the difficult economic climate of 2001, Schering reached record levels for the sixth consecutive year with net income up 24 percent to EUR 418 million (US $372 million) and sales 10 percent higher to EUR 4.8 billion (US $4.3 billion).

The Fertility Control and Hormone Therapy division experienced the most growth, with the introduction of Yasmin in more European countries as well as in the United States. In the specialized therapeutics area, sales of multiple sclerosis drug Betaferon increased 15 percent, making it Schering's top-selling product. With help from U.S. growth, in the company's Diagnostics and Radiopharmaceuticals division, Schering continued to be the worldwide market leader in contrast media for magnetic resonance imaging (MRI). Dermatology remained Schering's smallest area, and the company admitted to a poor launch of Levulan in the U.S. in 2001, while highlighting the successful U.S. introduction and significant potential of Finevin.

In 2002, Schering decided to pursue additional investment in external opportunities to further enhance core pharmaceutical specialties. In January, Schering reached a deal to obtain a 10 percent interest in MorphoSys to jointly develop diagnostic tests and antibody drugs. And to support Schering's interest in developing products to fight cardiovascular disease, in March the company announced plans to purchase the remaining 88 percent interest in Collateral, a California firm developing pharmaceuticals to fight heart disease through gene therapy. Further expanding U.S. biotechnology operations, in May, Schering purchased Leukine, a cancer drug by Immunex. At Schering's 2002 annual press conference, Dr. Erlen explained that future acquisitions were unlikely in the female healthcare and diagnostics fields due to Schering's global position and products, but purchases were more probable in the areas of specialized therapeutics and dermatology. And according to a March report by Goldman Sachs, large pharmaceutical companies were expected to continue the strategy of acquiring biotech companies in order to gain the rights to innovative new products—enhancing their product lines dramatically while earning a higher return than if they invested from the start.

Despite this trend, Schering retained its impressive commitment to innovation and research, with nearly 20 percent of sales invested in research and development in 2001. Important research areas highlighted by Dr. Erlen in 2002 included male hormones (to combat testosterone deficiency) and oncology, in addition to new products utilizing drospierenone, the principal ingredient behind the hormonal contraceptive Yasmin.

Schering AG's meticulous, well-planned reappearance and expansion in the United States and its focus on global market leadership in pharmaceutical niches, reflect a detailed program of long-term planning that has left executives optimistic about the company's growth potential.

Principal Subsidiaries

Asche AG, Germany; Berlex Canada; Berlex USA; CIS bio international, France; EnTec, Germany; Jenapharm, Germany; Leiras, Finland; Medrad, USA; Nihon Schering, Japan; Schering

Argentina; Schering, Austria; Schering Brazil; Schering Colombia; Schering Czech Republic; Schering Finland; Schering GmbH und Co. Produktions KG, Germany; Schering Health Care, UK; Schering Hungary; Schering Italy; Schering Mexicana; Schering Netherlands; Schering Poland; Schering Portugal; Schering Russia; Schering Scandinavia, Sweden; Schering Spain; Schering Switzerland; Schering Turkey; Schering Venezuela.

Principal Competitors

Amersham; Biogen; Johnson & Johnson.

Further Reading

Crabtree, Penni, ''Schering AG to Acquire its San Diego Gene-Therapy Partner,'' *San Diego Union-Tribune*, March 21, 2002, http://www.signonsandiego.com.

Herper, Matthew, ''Schering AG Makes Biotech Strides,'' *Forbes.com*, May 3, 2002, http://www.forbes.com.

Hill, George, ''Schering AG,'' *PharmaBusiness*, November 1998, http://www.pharmabusiness.com.

Hume, Claudia, ''Germany Invades Wall Street,'' *Chemical Week*, May 19, 1999, p. 45.

Mullin, Rick, ''More Biotech Deal-Making Ahead?,'' *Chemical Week*, April 3, 2002, p. 26.

Quinn, William T., ''Big Hopes for a Small Pill,'' *Business News New Jersey*, November 27, 2001, p. 10.

''Schering: Back to Its Roots,'' *Chemical Business Newsbase*, November 27, 2001, http://www.chemvillage.org.

''Schering Shows Healthy Figures,'' *Life Science Today*, April 2001, p. 6.

Scussa, Frank, ''Taking On the World,'' *PharmaBusiness*, November 2000, http://www.pharmabusiness.com.

Williams, Dede, ''Admiring Its New Image (Schering AG),'' *Chemistry and Industry*, January 2, 1995, p. 8.

Young, Ian, and Lyn Tattum, ''Companies Open Up to Outside Investors,'' *Chemical Week*, May 29, 1996, p. 36.

—update: Christopher W. Frerichs

Seattle City Light

700 5th Avenue, Suite 3300
Seattle, Washington 98104-5031
U.S.A.
Telephone: (206) 684-3000
Toll Free: (800) 862-1181
Fax: (206) 625-3709
Web site: http://www.ci.seattle.wa.us/light

Municipally Owned Company
Established: 1910
Employees: 1,700 (2002)
Sales: $396.1 million (2000)
NAIC: 221111 Hydroelectric Power Generation; 234920 Power and Communication Transmission Line Construction; 221119 Other Electric Power Generation

Seattle City Light has been providing Seattle with electricity since 1910. One of the largest municipally owned power companies, Seattle City Light serves more than 345,000 customers in their 131.3-square-mile service area. Seattle City Light owns or contracts the majority of its generating needs. The remainder of its energy is obtained from Bonneville Power Administration. The company is dedicated to producing environmentally responsible electricity.

Early 1900's: Seattle Supplies its Own Electricity

Before 1910, when Seattle City Light was founded, the City of Seattle's electricity came from a variety of neighborhood electric companies. The electricity was supplied by a hydroelectric facility that the residents of Seattle voted to finance in 1902. The hydroelectric facility was developed on the Cedar River, and it generated so much electricity that once it began generating power in 1905 the Seattle City Council decided to create a separate lighting department. on April 1, 1910, the separate lighting department was officially created and it was called Seattle City Light.

The large amount of electricity that the Cedar River facility produced gave rise to an increasing demand for power. Seattle City Light's second superintendent, J.D. Ross, hired into the position in 1911, approached his work with a clear goal in mind. Mr. Ross believed that the Skagit River was the river with the most potential for supplying Seattle City Light with hydroelectricity. He worked tirelessly toward the realization of his goal to dam the Skagit. In 1918, after a prior claim to develop the Skagit River expired, Mr. Ross received the federal government's go ahead to begin dam construction on the river. In 1924, Seattle City Light dedicated its first dam (the Gorge Dam) and it quickly began to supply Seattle with electricity. It took 30 more years, due partially to the interference of the Great Depression, for Ross's vision of two additional dams to be completed. The second dam, the Diablo Dam had been completed in 1930, but was waylaid by the Depression until 1936. The third dam, the Ross Dam, was finally completed and on line in 1951.

Mid-1900's: A Unified Power System Is Born

With their three dams in place, Seattle City Light in the mid-1900s was shaped by modernization and expansion. Seattle City Light focused on generating more electricity at existing facilities, building new substations, and an improved power distribution system. Another dam, the Boundary Dam located in Northeastern Washington, began generating electricity in 1967. Seattle City Light was extremely productive and successful during this time. Trouble was on the horizon, however. Just as in 1905, when increased availability of electricity spurred increased demand, Seattle City Light fell victim to unprecedented demand in the mid-1900s. High demand for electricity, combined with the regional draught of 1977 caused Seattle City Light to think increasingly more about conservation policy.

The company developed programs that educated and "incentivized" consumers to conserve energy. Seattle City Light also began to explore alternative energy resources. Streetlights were turned out in the interest of conservation, and a large thermometer was placed on one of Seattle City Light's buildings to motivate and track customers' conservation levels.

In order to comfortably supply the demanded electricity, and to keep electricity rates down to the low rate that Seattle customers were accustomed to, Seattle City Light contracted power from external sources like Canada, the Columbia Basin Irrigation Districts, Idaho's Lucky Peak hydro project, and the

Olympic Peninsula. Scarcity of water continued; the years between 1987 and 1989 were particularly bad, as were the years between 1992 and 1995. Throughout this period, it was common for Seattle City Light to raise electricity rates and surcharges and then reduce them as rainfall levels returned to normal. With the increased pressure of drought, Seattle City Light's dedication to conservation continued to grow.

1990s: Joining the Electronic Age

In the late 1980s and early 1990s, Seattle City Light in conjunction with five other major utilities, finalized a plan to automate the base map date for its 131-square-mile service area. The maps depicted the distribution system that served all of the company's customers. This system provided Seattle City Light with the ability to align their information with information supplied by other city departments, to improve management of the company's facilities, and to make production of detailed modeling applications and maps a much simpler prospect. The production of these models, and the capability to map the flow of electricity through the proposed distribution routes, allowed Seattle City Light to save money and make more informed decisions.

When Seattle City Light and Seattle Public Utilities agreed to consolidate services in July 1998, the utilities did so with an eye toward creating a technology-based future together. Their consolidation of services streamlined many of their customer-service based practices (they combined their databases, call centers, billings systems, and outreach efforts). The two companies also agreed to work together to add value to their customer offerings. John Gregg, the vice president of marketing for SCT Systems, the company that supplied Seattle City Light and Seattle Public Utilities with customer management, customer information software, and direct marketing programs, said, "Utilities are shifting away from being asset-based—that is, investing in transmission lines and power plants. The utility of the future may provide energy and gas, but if it has a good reputation and offers good value, it may provide cable TV service, or Web access, or home security."

Continuing with their trend toward investing in and exploring new technologies, in 1999, Seattle City Light partnered with Public Utility District (PUD) to develop a fiber optics communication system in Pend Oreille, Washington, in order to allow for improved communications between Pend Oreille and Spokane, Washington.

2000: Energy Crisis Calls for Conservation

Faced with the reality of a seemingly constant energy crisis, Seattle City Light tirelessly urged customers to conserve. The utility company also sought out new ideas for generating renew-

able-energy. In September 2000, in response to the utility company's call for propositions, the company received 62 offers from 30 different companies that proposed generating power from renewable sources like wind, sun, and the burning of landfill gases. Seattle City Light's goal was that, by 2010, their company's power portfolio would include approximately 5 percent non-hydro, renewable sources. As reported in the *Puget Sounds Business Journal*, "The utility received 23 proposals for wind projects, among them three from existing wind farms in Wyoming and California." The utility expected that the majority of its non-hydroelectric energy sources would be wind-generated.

The demand for energy was quickly exceeding Seattle City Light's capabilities to supply at the low rates that their customers were accustomed to. Not only was electricity production down due to poor weather but demand continued to rise. Partially because of the Northwest's legendary low electricity rates, data centers had begun to be moved into Seattle City Light's service area. Data centers were server farms, offices (or warehouses) that house the servers, routers, and switches that keep the Internet aloft. Data centers demand an extraordinary amount of energy for operation, and with the threat of more data centers moving to the Seattle-area, Seattle City Light feared that their infrastructure couldn't keep up with rising demand. In October 2000, the City of Seattle came to Seattle City Light's rescue and passed an ordinance that insisted that "large-load" customers (customers who demanded a certain amount of electricity) would have to pay for the cost upgrading the electrical infrastructure. The large-load customers were given the choice between a variety of pay-plans, but the underlying ordinance insisted that these customers would have to pay to upgrade Seattle's electrical infrastructure in order to operate within it. Heidi Wills, a Seattle City Council member told the *Puget Sound Business Journal*, "We left the language of the ordinance as flexible as possible to help in the contract negotiations. . . . It will depend on the customer if they want to pay more for the infrastructure costs upfront or pay more over time."

2001: The Energy Crisis

With the cost of electricity spiking on the wholesale market, Seattle City Light was forced to look for ways to raise their rates and continue to actively campaign and urge customers to conserve. In April 2001, Seattle City Light refinanced more than $100 million of its bonded debt in order to save several million dollars. Seattle City light spent $256 million buying outside power in the first three months of 2001, which is remarkable when compared with the fact that the utility spend $90 million for outside electricity for all of 1999. During 2001, Seattle City Light increased rates three times.

One of the major contributors to the Northwest's lack of energy was the California energy crisis. The Northwest had been involved in a share/trade plan with California which allowed for California to supply energy to Washington during the winter when Washington demanded large amounts of electricity to stay warm and Washington would supply energy to California during the summer when that state required additional energy to keep cool. Seattle City Light found themselves getting the short end of the stick at the end of 2000 and into 2001 when, as Tony Kilduff, a strategic advisor for Seattle City Light, told Janet Wood (writing for *International Water Power & Dam*

Key Dates:

1910: City of Seattle establishes Seattle City Light.
1924: Seattle City Light's first dam begins electricity generation.
1951: Seattle residents vote to buy-out privately owned Seattle City Light competitors, creating a unified power system.
1977: A drought hits Washington State and drastically effects electricity production.
2000: Seattle City Light announces a goal to have non-hydroelectric, renewable resources contribute approximately five percent of the company's power portfolio within ten years.
2001: Seattle City Light receives permission from the Seattle City Council to raise electricity rates by ten percent.
2002: Seattle City Light faces a $160 million budget deficit.

Construction) that, "Problems began in May 2000 when major generators in California figure out the possibilities. Supply contracted as they headed into the cooling season [that is, the summer season with increased use of air conditioning]. People can't adjust demand that quickly, and their utilities have an obligation to serve them. Generators, on the other hand, could choose to operate or not based on price and profit." Seattle City Light strained to locate enough energy to fulfill their customer's needs, but "By September we could see that these wildly high prices were not coming back down. We knew then we wouldn't meet our financial targets for the year and went to our City Council. We told them we had a US$60M hole—about 15% of our operating costs—and they agreed to a 10% rate adjustment." The situation worsened as the year progressed, and "We issued about US$700 million in debt. . . . Then everything changed on 19 June. That was when FERC finally decided to act. It imposed a west-wide price cap and issued a 'must offer' order for generators if they can generate. The bottom fell out of the market and our surplus is no longer the savior we thought it would be. We got hammered when prices shot up, and now we're being hammered as they go back to normal. . . . There are no fancy fixes for this. In the end the ratepayer will carry the cost." Seattle City Light was pushed almost to bankruptcy as a result of this energy crisis.

Seattle City Light attempted to fight some of the energy deficiency on the conservation front. Although Seattle City Light, by 2001, had already succeeded in imposing the toughest energy-efficiency standards in Washington State, the utility proposed even stricter standard for new buildings. Some of the standards included: more energy-efficient lighting in offices, medical centers, and schools; continuous sensors that adjust or turn off lights according to the amount of daylight in the room; a penalty for using electric heat; and energy-efficient windows.

When the electricity crises had begun to ease in August 2001, Ed Mosey, a spokesman for the Bonneville Power Administration, said that he believed that the lower rates reflected lower demand due to conservation measures, cooler-than-

expected weather, and the temporary closure of the state's aluminum smelters (as reported in the *Puget Sound Business Journal*). However, many big electricity users were cautioned against expecting lower rates, in fact, Seattle City Light still found it necessary to raise rates, although not as high as they had expected.

2001: Fighting Global Warming

Seattle City Light's dedication to conservation received national attention when they announced, in light of President George Bush's decision to not support the Kyoto Protocol, that they promised to reach zero net greenhouse gas (GHG) emissions, to achieve the equivalent of adding an average of 100 megawatts of capacity through conservation efforts, and 100 megawatts of non-hydro renewable energy within 10 years. Doug Howell, strategic advisor for Seattle City Light, told *Business and the Environment*, "The first part of the message is that while it is called global climate change, we very much understand the impacts here locally. We were a local cause of the problem [of GHG emissions]. We have very clear local effects. And we are going to be part of the solution." In July 2001, the city council announced its support for the Kyoto Protocol, and announced that they wanted to see a proposal on how Seattle could best achieve GHG reduction on par with the Kyoto Protocol's goal. Following this announcement, in November 2001, the city council unanimously approved a proposal to empower Seattle City Light to begin purchasing power from the State Line Wind Generating Plant in Walla Walla County. This movement by the city council made Seattle City Light the largest public power purchaser of wind power in the United States.

2002: More Trouble Ahead?

Despite all of Seattle City Light's conservation practices, the utility remains saddled with a projected $160 million budget deficit from the past years' energy crisis. In 2002, the average homeowner's electricity bill was $324 more per year than it was in 1999. Although electricity prices on the wholesale market dropped in late 2001, Seattle City Light was stuck with their own bills to pay. The utility company was forced to look toward the Seattle city council for help once more, and to continue charging high rates until the city would come to their rescue once again.

Principal Competitors

Avista Corporation; PacifiCorp; Puget Energy, Inc.

Further Reading

"City's Response to Climate Change Rebuffs U.S. President Bush," *Business and the Environment*, September 2001, p. 5.

Erb, George, "Tightening Energy Rules," *Puget Sound Business Journal*, June 8, 2001, p. 1.

Ernst, Steve, "Renewable-Energy Offers Pour in to Seattle Utility," *Puget Sound Business Journal*, September 22, 2000, p. 12.

——, "City Tried to Recover Cost of Power-hungry Data Centers," *Puget Sound Business Journal*, October 20, 2000, p. 5.

——, "Utilities Refinance Debt to Offset Part of Their Rising Costs," *Puget Sound Business Journal*, May 25, 2001.

Hecht, Linda, "Making Citywide Connections with GIS," *Electric Light & Power*, April 1997, p. 23.

Levey, Richard H., "Two Seattle Utilities Get Bright Idea: The Utility of the Future May Provide Cable TV Service, or Web Access, or Home Security," *Nation's Cities Weekly*, September 21, 1998, p. 4.

"Low Electricity Prices Could Mean Higher Rates for Seattle," June 2002, p. 4.

"Pend Oreille, Seattle Reach Agreement," *Northwest Public Power Association Bulletin*, June 1999, p. 16.

"Seattle Wants Wind Power for Five Percent of its Power," *Power Engineering*, November 2001, p. 40.

Willhelm, Steve, "Falling Electricity Prices Won't Help Many Firms," *Puget Sound Business Journal*, August 17, 2001, p. 5.

Wood, Janet, "Pushed . . . to the Limit: A Power Crisis in California . . ." *International Water Power & Dam Construction*, December 2001, p. 12.

—Tammy Weisberger

The Shaw Group, Inc.

4171 Essen Lane
Baton Rouge, Louisiana 70809
U.S.A.
Telephone: (225) 932-2500
Toll Free: (800) 747-3322
Fax: (225) 932.2661
Web site: http://www.shawgrp.com

Public Company
Incorporated: 1987
Employees: 20,000 (2002)
Sales: $1.5 billion (2001)
Stock Exchanges: NYSE
Ticker Symbol: SGR
NAIC: 332996 Fabricated Pipe and Pipe Fitting Manufacturing; 486990 All Other Pipeline Transportation

The Shaw Group, Inc. is the world's only vertically integrated provider of complete industrial piping systems and of comprehensive engineering, procurement, construction, and maintenance services to the power generation industry. It is the largest supplier of fabricated industrial piping systems in the United States and one of the leading suppliers worldwide. The company also performs work for the process industries, including petrochemical and chemical processing and petroleum refining, and for the environmental and public infrastructure sectors. A *Fortune* 1000 company, Shaw currently has offices and operations in North and South America, Europe, the Middle East, and Asia-Pacific.

Building a Pipe Fabrication Company: 1987–1994

James M. Bernhard, Jr., founded the Shaw Group in 1987. After graduating from college in the early 1970s, he worked his way through the ranks of various Baton Rouge pipe fabrication and contracting companies. This experience gave him an expert's education in the operations of the pipe fabrication industry.

The fabrication of complex piping systems for power generation facilities and process facilities, including petrochemical and chemical processing and petroleum refining, is complex and

demanding. Materials such as steel, titanium and aluminum are the raw materials of fabrication. These materials are formed into pipes with diameters as large 72 inches and walls as thick as seven inches. Some of these pipes become parts of "critical piping systems" used in high-pressure, high-temperature or corrosive applications. Such systems must withstand pressures up to 2,700 pounds per square inch and temperatures up to 1,020 degrees Fahrenheit. These critical systems are used in power generation.

By the mid-1980s, the U.S. pipe fabrication industry was experiencing significant difficulties. Power plant construction was at a low ebb domestically, as was refinery construction due to a decline in oil and gas exploration. At the same time, pipe fabrication was a craft performed by skilled welders brought to construction sites for that sole purpose. This handicraft approach kept piping prices high, and contributed to a large-scale exodus from the industry.

Bernhard believed that the industry could again become successful in the United States. He wanted to transform pipe fabrication from a craft industry to an industry that produced its product in factories using machinery to the extent possible. Such a change in fabrication practices, he believed, would reduce piping costs and allow the domestic pipe fabrication businesses to become profitable again.

To implement his ideas, Bernhard founded The Shaw Group in 1987 and purchased the Benjamin F. Shaw Company, a century-old pipe fabricator. In 1998, its first full year of operation, Shaw reported revenue of $29.3 million. By 1993 when the company went public, its revenue had increased to $120.7 million.

Becoming a Total Piping Resource: 1994–1997

The company began an aggressive but focused acquisition strategy with the proceeds of its initial public offering (IPO). In 1994, Shaw adopted the goal of becoming a "total piping resource." In pursuit of this end, it began a major expansion of its technical capabilities. It purchased Fronek Company to give it the nucleus of engineering and design capabilities in April. During the same month, it purchased a company that fabricated pipe supports. The company also began to purchase huge pipe-bending machines from the Danish company Cojafex.

Part of Bernhard's strategy was to substitute machinery for skilled humans. The Cojafex machine was an integral part of that strategy. Even when much of a custom-piping system was produced in a factory, the pipes themselves had to be shaped by expert pipe cutters and welders. The machine eliminated this human labor. This state-of-the-art piece of equipment could bend a pipe as much as 16 inches in diameter with walls as thick as 2.5 inches to the specifications of the customer. Although the Cojafex bending technology was not the sole similar machine on the market, it was the most advanced. The deployment of this machine gave Shaw a competitive advantage over other pipe fabricators.

Until 1994, Shaw supplied international customers by fabricating piping systems in its U.S. facilities and shipping them to the foreign site. U.S. fabricators could compete with foreign ones because labor costs were lower in the United States than in Germany and Japan, the home nations of some of their major competitors. U.S. manufacturers benefited from the greater availability of raw materials to them. The exchange rate of the dollar also contributed to the lower cost of U.S. produced systems.

International demand for pipe products, especially for use in the construction of power plants, continued to outstrip domestic demand in the early 1990s. Shaw, therefore, expanded internationally. Late in 1993, the company entered into a joint venture agreement to build and operate a pipe fabrication facility in Bahrain. From there, it could supply all Arab states of the Gulf Cooperation Council without paying tariffs. A year later, it purchased the 50 percent of a Venezuelan subsidiary it did not already own. This facility allowed Shaw to benefit from lower labor costs in competition for international projects.

Shaw continued its strategy of expanding its capabilities through focused acquisitions in 1996. In January, it acquired a fabrication facility and other assets in Oklahoma. The company followed this in March with the purchase of Alloy Piping Products (APP) located in Shreveport, Louisiana, a leading manufacturer of specialty pipe fittings—products such as elbows and caps that connect pipes or in some way modify them so they can be integrated into a system. It also added pipe insulation manufacturing to its capabilities by purchasing Pipe Shields, Inc. of California.

In 1997 and 1998, Shaw made two acquisitions that significantly increased the company's pipe-bending resources. First, it acquired NAPTech, Inc. of Utah, a piping systems and module designer and fabricator. NAPTech had experienced financial difficulties, including increasing net losses and liquidity problems. Nevertheless, it possessed three Cojafex bending machines, one capable of bending pipes with a diameter of up to 66 inches and a wall thickness of up to five inches. Shaw purchased Cojafex as a whole in 1998, thus taking control of the development and sales of a crucial pipe fabrication technology. Shaw considered these machines crucial enough to the pipe fabrication process that it stopped selling them to some competitors.

The company continued its international expansion. In October 1997, it bought a U.K. pipe fabrication company. The next month, it purchased Prospect Industries PLC also located in the United Kingdom. Prospect was deeply in debt, so purchase negotiations were not difficult. With this purchase, came piping systems fabrication subsidiaries in Virginia and the United Kingdom. It also established a base in the Asia-Pacific region with Prospect's subsidiary, Aiton Australia Pty. Ltd., a piping system, boiler refurbishment and project management enterprise. Shaw expanded its Venezuelan operations early in 1998 by purchasing a construction company. These acquisitions gave the company a total of four pipe fabrication facilities in regions outside the United States—a significant competitive advantage.

Becoming a Power Plant Builder: 1997–2000

The purchase in 1997 of two industrial construction and maintenance companies signaled the expansion of Shaw's business strategy to planning and constructing entire power and process plants. In pursuit of this expanded strategy, it acquired a construction and maintenance company specializing in offshore facilities in 1998.

This string of acquisitions greatly increased Shaw's financial resources and returns. Its current assets increased from $80.6 million in 1995 to $251 million in 1998. Sales increased from $113.2 million in 1994 to $506.1 million in 1998, while net income increased from $3.4 million to $19.2 million during the same period. In recognition of this growth, Shaw moved from the NASDAQ to the NYSE in 1996.

By the end of its 1999 fiscal year, Shaw had become a major supplier of pipe systems both domestically and internationally. It had provided services to some of the world's foremost multinational conglomerates, including AlliedSignal, Chevron, Mitsubishi, Monsanto, Raytheon, Hitachi, and Toshiba. It had formed strategic alliances with ABB, Air Products and Chemicals, Alstrom, BASF, Bechtel, Dow, General Electric, Orion Refining Company, Parsons Corporation, and Praxair, Inc.

Moreover, the demand for power plants, always strong internationally, had increased in the United States. The decommissioning of some nuclear plants had decreased domestic electrical supply; demand for electricity was increasing, and wholesale power markets had been deregulated. These events generated a surge in the construction of domestic power plants. Shaw benefited from this trend. Power generation projects amounted to only 30 percent of the company's backlog in 1997 and 1998. Such projects, some of them foreign, accounted for 64 percent of an $818.3 million backlog at the end of its 1999 fiscal year.

Despite its success in pipe design, engineering, fabrication and installation, Shaw had difficulties making the transition to

Key dates:

1987: The Shaw Group is incorporated.
1993: The company lists on the NASDAQ.
1994: Shaw acquires Fronek Company.
1994: Shaw enters into a joint venture in Bahrain to fabricate pipe.
1995: The company buys full ownership of a Venezuelan fabrication facility.
1996: Shaw buys Allied Piping Products (APP) in Louisiana and Pipe Shields, Inc. of California; moves from the NASDAQ to the NYSE.
1997: Shaw acquires NAPTech, Inc. of Utah, a piping systems and module designer and fabricator.
1997: Shaw buys Prospect Industries PLC of the United Kingdom.
1998: The company purchases Cojafex, BV of Holland, a leading company of pipe fabrication technologies.
2000: Shaw buys Stone & Webster (S&W), a provider of engineering, procurement, and construction services to the power plant industry.
2000: Shaw enters into an Entergy-Shaw joint venture.
2001: Shaw contracts with BASF to engineer and manage the construction of an ethylene plant in China; Shaw announces an agreement with PG&E's National Energy Group for the construction of four gas-fired power plants.
2002: Shaw purchases The IT Group, a leading environmental remediation firm.

providing engineering, procurement and construction (EPC) services for entire power plants. In part, these difficulties resulted from Shaw's inexperience in power plant construction, especially when it competed with large, established EPC contractors. Chairman Bernhard told *ENR* in 2002 that there was an additional problem: power plant engineers were reluctant to subcontract with Shaw to do engineering work on projects for which Shaw was the prime contractor, and Shaw lacked appropriate engineering capabilities of its own.

Shaw resolved this problem in 2000 by acquiring Stone & Webster (S&W), a century-old provider of EPC services to the power plant industry. S&W had experienced financial difficulties for much of the previous decade. In the mid-1990s, it completed a major downsizing resulting from a dependence on the nuclear power industry after construction of nuclear plants had virtually stopped and from losses generated by non-core assets, such as real estate.

By 1998, the company again experienced financial difficulties resulting in part from losses of Asian construction contracts when that region experienced a severe financial crisis. The company was experiencing such severe liquidity problems that it agreed in May 2000 to sell most of its assets to Jacobs Engineering Group. The agreement with Jacobs called for Jacobs to provide S&W with an immediate $50 million credit line to allow S&W to resolve its immediate liquidity problems. It also called for S&W to enter into Chapter 11 bankruptcy proceedings—a move that would protect S&W from potential lawsuits or adverse actions by its creditors.

The bankruptcy process, however, required that S&W's assets be disposed of by means of an auction administered by the bankruptcy court. This opened the way for Shaw to attempt to win S&W's assets. In July, Shaw won these assets after 20 rounds of bids lasting 18 hours. Shaw's final cash and stock bid was equal to about $163 million.

Not only did S&W bring EPC capabilities to Shaw, but the acquisition placed Shaw among the foremost companies with experience in the decommissioning and decontamination (D&D) of nuclear plants. S&W had built 17 of the reactors constructed in the United States in the 1970s and 1980s. It had done various kinds of work on 99 of the 104 nuclear facilities in the nation. Immediately before its bankruptcy, it was doing D&D work. This particular project was terminated because of the company's financial difficulties, but this was another new area opened to Shaw.

Shaw also took over a number of public infrastructure and environmental remediation projects started by S&W. In the environmental area, projects included remediation for former nuclear weapons production facilities and work on various Super Fund sites. In the infrastructure area, Shaw took over projects such as the construction and management of a water supply tunnel and the engineering and construction of a water treatment plant.

Financially, too, the S&W acquisition had a major effect on Shaw. Its current assets increased from $252.1 million in 1999 to $1.1 billion in 2001, the first full year it owned S&W. During the same period, its sales increased from $494 million to $1.5 billion, and its net income increased from $18.1 million to $61 million. Its total backlog increased from $818.3 million to $4.5 billion. Shaw debuted as number 835 on the *Fortune* 1000 in 2002.

Shaw quickly put its new capabilities and financial strength to work. In September 2000, after three years of discussions, Shaw formed a 50–50 joint venture, EntergyShaw, with the electric utility Entergy, to design and construct standardized power plants that could meet Entergy's increasing power needs. The partners also hoped the projected 10 to 15 percent cost savings of the plants would make them attractive to other North American and European customers.

In February 2001, the company contracted with BASF to engineer and manage the construction of an ethylene plant in China. Shaw agreed, in turn, to contract the construction of the plant to an independent Chinese company. This project allowed Shaw to profitably use some process industry equipment left with S&W when a contract was canceled.

The next month, Shaw announced an agreement with PG&E's National Energy Group for the construction of four separately sited gas-fired power plants, capable of producing a total of 4,400 megawatts of electricity on completion. Work on two of them started in 2001. Shaw initiated or extended similar agreements with other power generators, including NRG Energy and FPL Energy.

Into the 21st Century: Diversification

The continuation of the boom in power plant construction that had fueled much of Shaw's growth during the late 1990s began to show signs of weakening by 2002. The California energy crisis and consequent bankruptcy of two of the largest utilities in the nation, threats of volatile power prices and even blackouts in other states, and the collapse of the energy trading industry all raised questions about the longevity of the energy deregulation trend. This policy had stimulated the construction boom domestically.

Internationally, too, power plant construction had declined. The Asian financial crisis of the late 1990s had terminated many projects, and construction in that area had not yet recovered. The generalized economic uncertainty of the early 21st century contributed to construction declines in other regions as well.

Shaw had enough backlog at the beginning of 2002 to keep it busy for about 18 months, but it faced the twin dangers that some of the projects it had on its books would be canceled and that future projects would be harder to find. This prospect came as no surprise to the company. After all, Shaw came into being in the mid-1980s, at a time when construction of domestic power plants was not robust. In fact, such construction had always been notoriously cyclical.

In an effort to diversify Shaw's business focus beyond the power plant sector and to provide it with a diversified mix of income opportunities, the company agreed in January 2002 to bring The IT Group out of bankruptcy. The IT Group was a leading domestic and international firm specializing in environmental remediation, serving the government, commercial engineering and construction, solid waste, real estate restoration, and consulting sectors. The IT Group was especially strong in the government market.

When combined with the environmental business Shaw had acquired with its previous year's purchase of S&W, this new acquisition, approved by the Bankruptcy Court in April, gave Shaw a strong position in the environmental remediation industry. Shaw gained two major advantages from this. First, the business cycles of the environmental industry did not correlate with the cycles of the power production industry, thus Shaw's revenue stream became somewhat protected from the cyclical nature of that industry. Second, many of the contracts that came with The IT Group purchase were governmental. Usually contracted on a cost-plus-fixed-fee basis, an arrangement that was not as profitable to the contractor as were other alternatives, these government contracts, nevertheless, provided the contractor with a steady, reliable source of income.

As it entered the new century, The Shaw Group could look back with satisfaction at the massive growth it had achieved in its brief existence. Its most important challenge was to diversify its revenue sources from the very cyclical business of building or supplying components for power generation facilities. The company had begun to do just that.

Principal Subsidiaries

Cojafex BV (100%); EntergyShaw, LLC (50%); Manufacturas Shaw South America CA (100%); Power Technologies, Inc.

(100%); Shaw Alloy Piping Products, Inc. (100%); Shaw Aiton Australia Pty. Ltd. (100%); Shaw Environmental & Infrastructure, Inc. (100%); Shaw Group U.K. Ltd. (100%); Shaw Pipe Shields, Inc. (100%); Stone & Webster Consultants, Inc. (100%); Stone & Webster, Inc. (100%).

Principal Competitors

Bechtel Group Inc.; Fluor Corporation; Jacobs Engineering Group Inc.; Foster Wheeler Ltd.; ABB Ltd.

Further Reading

Angelo, William J., "Stone & Webster Is Short on Cash," *ENR*, November 8, 1999, p. 13.
——, "Stone & Webster Lures New Retirees in Cost-Cut Measure to Stem Red Ink," *ENR*, November 23, 1998, p. 19.
Angelo, William J., and Debra K. Rubin, "Jacobs Engineering Sees Value in Rescuing Stone & Webster," *ENR*, May 15, 2000, p. 13.
Basta, Nicholas, "Engineering and Construction Market Begins to Thaw," *Chemical Week*, April 24, 2002, pp. S3–S6.
"Business Brief—Shaw Group, Inc.," *Wall Street Journal*, November 10, 1997.
"EntergyShaw EPC," *Modern Power Systems*, October 2000, p. 11.
Guarisco, Tom, "New Digs for Shaw," *Greater Baton Rouge Business Report*, January 15, 2002, pp. 31–32.
"How Shaw Group Cuts the Risk on Turnkey Powerplant Work." *ENR*, April 2, 2001, p. 15.
Korman, Richard, "Beyond the Hype, Close Attention to Basics," *ENR*, April 1, 2002, p. 37.
——, "Shaw Wins Stone & Webster Assets," *ENR*, July 17, 2000, p. 12.
Korman, Richard, and Tony Illia, "The Shaw Group Branches Out," *ENR*, April 1, 2002, p. 34.
Korman, Richard, and Debra K. Rubin, "II Group Seeks Bankruptcy Move," *ENR*, January 28, 2002, p. 11.
McPadden, Mike, "BASF Moves Forward with Investment in Asia-Pacific," *Chemical Market Reporter*, February 12, 2001, p. 26.
Powers, Mary Buckner, "Stone & Webster Ex-Chief Speaks Out on Lawsuits," *ENR*, January 29, 2001, p. 12.
Schimmoller, Brian K., "Contracts and Construction," *Power Engineering*, February 2001, p. 23.
Shaw Group, *Form 10-K*, filed with the United States Securities and Exchange Commission, 1996–2001, accessed June 30, 2002, http://www.shawgrp.com.
"Shaw Group Inc: IT Group Inc," *Market News Publishing*, April 24, 2002.
"Shaw Group Inc. Signs Agreement," *Market News Publishing*, July 10, 2001.
"Shaw Just Keeps on Building," *Greater Baton Rouge Business Report*, October 9, 2001, p. 10.
Sissell, Kara, "IT Group Files Chapter 11," *Chemical Week*, January 23, 2002, p. 17.
Smith, Rebecca, "Entergy Forms Venture with Shaw for New Plants," *Wall Street Journal*, June 2, 2000, p. A4.
Swanekamp, Rob, and Robert J. Sansone, "Re-Regulation: Marching Forward, While Minding the Past," *Power*, January/February 2002, pp. 4–5.

—Anne L. Potter

Skandia Insurance Company, Ltd.

Sveavägen 44
S-103 50 Stockholm
Sweden
Telephone: +46 (08) 788-1000
Fax: +46 (08) 788-3080
Web site: http://www.skandia.com

Public Company
Incorporated: 1855
Employees: 7,200 (2001 est.)
Sales: SKr 198 billion (US$18.6 billion) (2000 est.)
Stock Exchanges: Copenhagen Frankfurt London Stockholm
Ticker Symbol: SDIA
NAIC: 524113 Direct Life Insurance Carriers; 525120 Health and Welfare Funds; 524114 Direct Health and Medical Insurance Carriers; 524126 Direct Property and Casualty Insurance Carriers; 523930 Investment Advice

Since its founding in 1855, Sweden's Skandia Insurance Company, Ltd. (*Försäkringsaktiebolaget Skandia* in Swedish) has grown from a small fire and life insurance company to that nation's top insurer and financial services group, operating in more than 20 countries worldwide. Skandia is headquartered in Sweden, but as of 2002, most of its business is conducted internationally. The company was among the seven firms listed on the Stockholm Stock Exchange when it opened in 1863, and in 2002 it is the only one of those original companies still listed there. While Skandia is still involved in the insurance business—selling and handling life, non-life, and pension insurances primarily—the company has shifted its main focus to financial services, offering loans, long-term personal savings products, mortgage loans, savings products for banking cardholders, financial and risk analyses, and new company development. As of 2000, Skandia leads the world in sales of unit-linked assurances, and the company achieves sales of SKr 198 billion (US$18.6 billion), a company record. These traditional measures of success are not the only by which Skandia measures itself: since 1994 the company has supplemented its annual reports with accountings of its "intellectual capital"—employee knowledge and expertise and other intangible assets—and is considered a pioneer in the movement to quantify such assets.

Early Days: 1850s–1890s

Skandia was established in 1855 as a mixed insurance company called Skandia Group Insurance Co. Ltd. by Carl Gustav von Koch when he acquired a series of small insurance companies throughout Sweden. In January 1855, Sweden's King Oscar I granted Skandia a concession to become the country's first life assurance company and nationwide fire insurance company. Its first offices were in a three-room apartment at Mynttorget 1 in Stockholm's Old Town, adjacent to the Royal Castle. Early company documents describe its business as "life assurance and fire insurance related therewith."

As European society became increasingly industrial, larger numbers of people became aware of a need for financial security for themselves and their families, sparking a wide interest in life insurance. Skandia benefited greatly from these new developments and the company expanded rapidly during those early years. Skandia was soon operating internationally with offices in Christiana (now known as Oslo), Copenhagen, Hamburg, and Rotterdam, and had significant operations in St. Petersburg, Russia. Skandia's stock shares began trading publicly for the first time on February 4, 1863, with the opening of the Stockholm Stock Exchange. By 1889 the company's life assurance business included 7,000 policyholders. Most of these policyholders were middle-class men; however, working-class people and women were showing a growing interest as well. The company introduced accident and disability insurance in 1890, and had expanded to 50 employees.

A New 20th Century

Skandia's robust expansion continued into the 20th century. In 1900 the company established operations in the United States and became the first non-British foreign insurance company to set up business there. At the dawn of the century, the company recognized that it could reduce the major risks involved with such disasters as the 19th century's great city fires by reinsuring fire premiums. As a result, most of the company's premium income

Company Perspectives:

Our vision at Skandia is a declaration of our interest in helping people achieve their goals for quality of life. Our products and services enable people to invest and build up the financial resources they need to make their dreams come true.

was soon resulting from sales of fire insurance. Ironically, it was the U.S. expansion and the increased focus on fire insurance that caused the company to suffer one of the greatest losses in its history with the 1906 San Francisco earthquake and fires, which resulted in the loss of 3,000 lives and over 28,000 buildings.

The losses caused by the earthquake were offset by the benefits the company enjoyed as a result of the advances made in Sweden's social legislation at the hands of the monarchs Oscar II and Gustav V. Besides progressive laws concerning factory conditions, voting rights, and working hours for women and children, Sweden adopted a statutory social insurance scheme during this time. Occupational accident insurance and pension insurance became obligatory in the first decades of the 20th century. Skandia became a pioneer in motor insurance, writing its first policy in 1920, almost a full decade before third-party motor liability insurance and vehicle damage insurance were mandated by law. In 1938 the company introduced home insurance—an innovation which enabled policyholders to hold a single policy that covered fire, burglary, flooding and liability insurance, with one premium and one due date.

Modern Skandia: 1950s through 1980s

Sweden's neutrality during the two world wars buffered the company from some of the damages suffered by other European companies, particularly during World War II, and the company began the second half of the 20th century in much the same way it had spent the first half—with rapid expansion and growth. In 1953 it entered the South American market with a venture in Colombia, and in 1955 made its first foray in Asia with an operation in India. The 1950s also marked a technological advance for Skandia—in 1957 it used a computer for the first time—the IBM650 Magnetic Drum Calculator, which is now on display at Stockholm's Museum of Science and Technology.

Skandia experienced a "rebirth" in the 1960s. At the beginning of the decade, the company purchased life insurer Thule (which had been established by the grandfather of Olof Palme, Sweden's late prime minister). Skandia followed that purchase with the merger of five companies—which originally consisted of 53 small Swedish insurance companies—and the new Skandia group was introduced in 1964. The company simultaneously unveiled its umbrella logo, which remained the company symbol in 2002.

Skandia began the 1970s with more expansion, opening an office for international reinsurance in Australia. In 1971 the company renamed its subsidiary Thule Skandia Liv, creating a separate, but wholly owned mutual insurance company. Also in 1971, the company shut down its India operations when that country nationalized its insurance industry. Skandia introduced child insurance in 1974. This insurance provided compensation for disability or handicaps—regardless of cause—for children up to age

20. In 1979 the company established Skandia Life UK in London. This company was one of the first to sell unit-linked pension insurance (also known as variable annuity)—a form of insurance that lets the policyholder invest a portion of the premium in a variety of investment alternatives—in the United Kingdom.

Skandia's growth continued unabated during the 1980s. In 1986 the company acquired the share capital of Almendahl Investment Co. and Internationell Assurans AB. It also began a series of real estate acquisitions with 20 percent of the shares in Fastighetsbolagets Hufvudstaden and the majority of the shares in Fastighets AB Stockholm Badhus. In 1987, Skandia opened a member financial services company, American Skandia Life Assurance, in Shelton Connecticut. The new company implemented innovations that would be later adopted throughout the financial services field: it worked with external money managers to help it remain unbiased, and it sold its products wholesale to brokers rather than to a network of distributors. American Skandia's business flourished, and by the year 2000 had more than US$36 billion in client assets. Skandia acquired Skandia International and Vesta-gruppen A/S, Norway in 1988; and in 1989 it acquired National Insurance & Guarantee Corp., Spain's Skandia Comp de Adm Immobilaria, the Netherlands' Argo Properties, and Reinhold International Properties in London, the United Kingdom, in Madrid, Spain, and in Lisbon, Portugal. Also in 1989, the company's shares were listed on the Oslo Stock Exchange (Skandia would be delisted from that exchange in 1995). In 1990 the company once again benefited from governmental changes when Sweden adapted its insurance industry legislation, allowing Skandia to introduce unit-linked assurance in its home country. That year, the company's shares were listed on the London Stock Exchange.

Development of the Intellectual Capital Concept

By the early 1990s, Skandia was heavily invested in real estate, beginning with its acquisitions in the mid-1980s, and during that time the Swedish real estate market suffered a collapse. Between the liabilities of its insurance contracts and the devaluation of its land assets, on paper, Skandia appeared to many analysts to be in serious trouble. To the company, however, the future looked good: it still had tremendous assets in its people, its customers, and its products. "Within Skandia, processes that create value for customers, shareholders, and the staff are carried out on a daily basis. Many of these are.invisible," wrote CEO Bjorn Wolrath, "Nevertheless, they are innovative, and they create value." Skandia felt that the traditional ways of financial reporting did not allow the company to tell its full story. "We needed a way to explain that we had a lot more value than just real estate," remembered Scott Hawkins of American Skandia.

In the fall of 1991, Skandia hired Leif Edvinsson, who had an M.B.A. from the University of California at Berkeley and a background in banking, as its first—and, indeed, the corporate world's first—director of intellectual capital. Edvinsson and others at Skandia developed a means by which to measure a company's intangible value, or its Intellectual Capital (IC). Skandia defined IC as the sum of "human capital" such as employee competence, expertise, and knowledge, and "structural capital" (software, customer lists, trademarks, and so on). Edvinsson felt that the value of a company's intellectual assets far exceeded the value of tangible assets that normally appear

Key Dates:

1855: The company is founded in Stockholm, Sweden, as Skandia Group Insurance Co. Ltd.

1863: Skandia's stock is listed on the Stockholm Stock Exchange.

1890: The company introduces accident and disability insurance.

1900: Operations in the United States are established.

1920: The company introduces motor insurance.

1938: Home insurance, a single policy covering fire, burglary, flooding, and liability is introduced.

1953: Operations in Colombia, South America are established.

1955: The company establishes operations in India.

1957: The company begins to computerize its operations.

1964: The company acquires Thule, merges five other companies, reorganizes, and unveils its umbrella logo.

1974: Child insurance is introduced.

1987: American Skandia Life Assurance opens in Shelton, Connecticut.

1990: Skandia is listed on the London Stock Exchange.

1993: Skandia supplements its annual report with its first Intellectual Capital (IC) report, which quantifies the value of the company's human capital.

2000: Skandia CEO Lars-Eric Petersson declares that the restructuring of Skandia into a savings and assets management company is complete.

on a balance sheet. By developing sophisticated tools to measure IC—such as its Dolphin Navigator and Skandia Intellectual Capital Index—Skandia was able to demonstrate how the company's knowledge could be converted into value.

In 1993, Skandia took the theory one step further and began supplementing its annual report—which reports on the company's traditional assets—with an IC report. This report quantified Skandia's IC, and made forecasts on how likely the company was to meet its strategic goals based on those quantifications. The theory proved highly successful: between 1993 and 1999, Skandia's share price quadrupled. Skandia was the first company to report on its IC in this manner, though many companies soon began emulating the approach. Edvinsson left the company in 1999, but Intellectual Capital remained a cornerstone of Skandia's corporate philosophy into the early years of the 21st century.

A New Focus for a New Millennium

Over the course of the 1990s, Skandia continued its tradition of expansion, and by the end of the decade had operations in more than 20 countries around the world, including Chile, the United Arab Emirates, China, and Poland. That decade also saw a major shift in the direction of the company. For 135 years, Skandia had focused on the insurance business; in the early 1990s, the company saw greater potential in the financial services industry and began to shift its core business in that direction. "The realization at the company was that growth comes from vigorously seeking out new market opportunities rather than calculating the market share of markets you're already in.

So we transformed Skandia from an old insurance company into an innovative financial services organization," said Leif Edvinsson in 2000.

Skandia made this transformation through a series of sales and acquisitions over the course of the decade, and by growing its financial services business unit (Skandia AFS). Skandia AFS adopted a new business model, setting itself up as a wholesaler of financial services with a wide range of products based on external funds management. These products were then sold by a sales force of carefully selected and trained independent financial advisors.

The new model proved highly successful: in 1990, Skandia AFS accounted for only 12 percent of the company's total income. In 1996 it represented nearly 50 percent; a year later, that total was 70 percent, and Skandia was garnering praise in Europe and the United States for the strength of its products. The company became a global *Fortune* 500 company in 1997. Also in 1997, Lars-Eric Petersson took over the role of CEO from Bjorn Wolrath, and continued steering the company in the financial services direction. When the company's core profits doubled in the first quarter of 2000, he declared, "the restructuring of the Skandia group into a pure-play savings and assets management company is.complete." In 2001, Skandia sold SINSER Holding A.B. to Aon Corporation, shedding the last of its risk management consulting services and property/casualty insurance operations.

Despite its successes, Skandia was not immune from the economic troubles of the early 21st century. After a peak in the first half of 2000, the world's stock markets experienced sharply falling prices—and the United States (where Skandia had significant interests) was particularly hit hard. Skandia's sales in Sweden dropped 10 percent, its growth in new markets slowed, and its sales fell by 37 percent. CEO Petersson, while regarding the downturn as an economic "blip," rather than a reflection of company weakness, nevertheless responded with a series of cost-cutting measures that included a 13 percent reduction in its U.S. workforce and an aggressive reduction in operating expenses. The company also sold its asset management operations to Den Norske Bank in 2002. "The prolonged duration and severity of the market pullback, along with the difficulty in predicting the timing of its culmination have led us to these hard decisions," Wade Dokken, CEO of America Skandia said in 2001.

Even with these economic difficulties, Skandia had reason to be optimistic for its prospects in the new millennium. In the company's 2000 annual report and its third-quarter 2001 interim report, CEO Lars-Eric Petersson pointed to several factors that indicated a healthy future for the company: the overhaul of social security systems in many countries and changes in the labor market were resulting in the need for more individual savings. Additionally, Skandia had no liability claims resulting from the events of September 11, 2001—such claims had a significant impact on the insurance industry—and the company's global focus insulated it from the worst effects of the decline in the U.S. market. The company also quickly launched a number of new products in response to the new economic climate. "Our rapid-response business model is our strength in turbulent times," wrote Petersson in the company's September 2001 interim report. He continued, "The ongoing process of refining our business activities, product development, and distribution strength creates solid opportunities for the future.''

Principal Divisions

Americas; Europe; UK; Asia Pacific.

Principal Operating Units

Global Business Development; Global Funds; Offshore.

Principal Competitors

Allianz; AIG; Generali.

Further Reading

"About American Skandia," January 30, 2002, *http://www.newcentury newdeal.com.*

Bender, Yuri, "Skandia Goes Back to Basics," *The European*, May 9, 1996, p. 22.

Bolton, Norah, "Your Organization's Most Important Asset," *The Canadian Manager*, Winter 1996, pp. 25–26.

Bradford, Michael, "Deal Makes Aon Top Captive Manager," *Business Insurance*, August 13, 2001, pp. 1, 27.

Bukowitz, Wendi R., and Gordon P. Petrash, "Visualizing, Measuring and Managing Knowledge," *Research Technology Management*, July/August 1997, pp. 24–31.

Cariner, Stuart, "1 + 1 = 11," *Across the Board*, November/December 2000, pp. 29–34.

——, "The Swedes Are Coming," *Across the Board*, June 1999, pp. 31–35.

"Commission Clears Sampo/Varma-Sampo/Skandia/Storebrand Venture," *European Report*, December 22, 2001, p. 362.

Deering, Ann, "The Insurance Professional in a Virtual World," *Risk Management*, November 1995, p. 37.

Duffy, Daintry, "Keeping Score," *Performance Management and Positive Reinforcement*, January 31, 2002, http://www.p-management.com/articles/2016.htm.

Edvinsson, Leif, and Michael S. Malone, *Intellectual Capital: Realizing Your Company's True Value by Finding Its Hidden Brainpower*, New York: HarperBusiness, 1997, p. 240.

"European Report: Commission Clears Diligentia/ Skandia Life Insurance," *European Report*, May 17, 2000, p. 1.

"FS Skandia, Storebrand ASA AND Pohjola-Yhtyma Notify New Life Insurance Company," *European Report*, July 17, 1999, p. 1.

Galagan, Patricia A., "Strategic Planning Is Back," *Training & Development*, April 1, 1997, pp. 32–36.

Garrity, Mike, "Skandia Adopting Novel Distribution Plan," *Mutual Fund Market News*, May 10, 1999, p. 1.

Gerwig, Kate, "Bandwidth: Skandia Seeks Network Insurance," *InternetWeek*, January 19, 1998, p. 33.

"Great Minds Write Alike," *Fast Company*, April 1, 1997, p. 44.

Haapaniemi, Peter, "Intellectual Capital," *Chief Executive*, January/February 1997, p. 59.

"Hafnia Humbled," *The Economist*, April 18, 1992, p. 78.

Hibbard, Justin, "Cover Story: Intellectual Capital," *InformationWeek*, February 22, 1999, p. 50.

Hobday, Nicola, "Den Norske Bank Buys Skandia Asset Management," *The Daily Deal*, January 8, 2002, http://www.TheDeal.com.

Icon Group International, Inc. Staff, *Forsakrings Ab Skandia: International Competitive Benchmarks and Financial Gap Analysis*, San Diego: Icon Group International, Incorporated, 2000, p. 24.

Icon Group International, Inc. Staff, *Forsakrings Ab Skandia: Labor Productivity Benchmarks and International Gap Analysis*, San Diego: Icon Group International, Incorporated, 2000, p. 20.

Kielmas, Maria, "Skandia Rumors Grow," *Business Insurance*, September 1, 1997, pp. 69–70.

"The Knowledge Gurus," *New Statesman*, September 27, 1999, p. 21.

LaBarre, Polly, "How Skandia Generates Its Future Faster," *Fast Company*, December 1, 1996, p. 58.

——, "The Rush on Knowledge," *Industry Week*, February 19, 1996, pp. 53–55.

Leavitt, Wendy, "Technology & Profit: Crunching More than the Numbers," *Fleet Owner*, October 1, 1998, pp. 51–55.

Maglitta, Joseph, "Smarten Up!," *Computerworld*, June 5, 1995, p. 84.

Melymuka, Kathleen, "Showing the Value," *Computerworld*, March 27, 2000, p. 58.

Merline, Kimberly, " 'Leading Lights' Interview with Leif Edvinsson," *Community Intelligence Labs*, November 1997, http://www.co-i-l.com.

Moberg, Gunnar, "How Skandia AFS Defines and Grows Its Customer Base," *Managing Service Quality*, 1996, p. 24.

Moore, Michael, "Insurance: Two Claimants for No. 1 in Variable Annuities," *American Banker*, September 14, 1999, p. 10.

Naiman, Linda, "Vision Quest: Transforming the Way We Live and Work," *Creativity at Work*, (Health Work and Wellness Conference proceedings), October 1, 1997, http://www.creativityatwork.com.

"Nordic Insurance: Scrapping over Skandia," *The Economist*, January 18, 1992, p. 82.

Racanelli, Vito J., "European Trader: Singing the Earnings Blues," *Barron's*, November 5, 2001, p. MW12.

Roos, Johan, Goran Roos, Nicola C. Dragonetti, and Leif Edvinsson, *Intellectual Capital: Navigating in the New Business Landscape*, New York: New York University Press, 1998, p. 208.

Simon, Emma, "Personal Equity Plans Guide: Charge of the Multi-Pep the Investment Industry Is Divided about the Rapid Growth of Umbrella Funds and the Price You Pay for Them," *The Sunday Telegraph*, February 28, 1999, p. 67.

"Skandia Adds Subordinated Feature to $800m Debt Shel," *Euroweek*, December 12, 1997, p. 8.

"Skandia Increases Pohjola Stake to 10.9%," *European Report*, January 5, 1996. p. 1.

"Skandia Sells Two Subsidiaries," *European Report*, September 16, 1998, p. 1.

Stewart, Thomas A., and Stephanie Losee, "Your Company's Most Valuable Asset: Intellectual Capital," *Fortune*, October 3, 1994, p. 68.

Strassman, Paul A., "Intelligence in Question," *Knowledge Management*, October 2000, http://www.destinationcrm.com/km.

——, "Behind the Hype," *Computerworld*, September 4, 2000, p. 4.

"Sweden," *Microsoft Encarta Encyclopedia*, Redmond, Washington: Microsoft Corporation, 1999.

"Sweden's Spat," *The Economist*, July 9, 1994, p. 78.

Syedain, Hashi, "A Helping Handicap," *Chief Executive*, May 2001, pp. 20–21.

Tapsell, Sherrill, "Making Money from Brainpower: The New Wealth of Nations," *New Zealand Management*, July 1998, pp. 36–43.

"Up the Fjord," *The Economist*, August 29, 1992, p. 70.

Weiss, Ruth Palombo, "Recipe for Innovation," *Training & Development*, June 2001, pp. 32–33.

Wormuth, Diana W., "Scandinavian Highlights: Insurers Open to Possibilities," *Best's Review*, October 1996, p. 22.

——, "Scandinavian Market Reflects Consolidation in Europe," *Best's Review*, February 1997, pp. 24–26.

Zimmerman, Eilene, "What Are Employees Worth?," *Workforce*, February 2001, p. 32.

—Lisa Whipple

Slough Estates PLC

234 Bath Road
Slough SL1 4EE
United Kingdom
Telephone: +44 (1753) 537 171
Fax: +44 (1753) 5 820 585
Web site: http://www.sloughestates.com

Public Company
Incorporated: 1920 as The Slough Trading Co. Ltd.
Employees: 549 (2001)
Sales: £135.1 million (US$197.2 million) (2001)
Stock Exchanges: London
Ticker Symbol: SLOU
NAIC: 233110 Land Subdivision and Land Development;
531190 Lessors of Other Real Estate Property;
221310 Water Supply and Irrigation Systems; 221122
Electric Power Generation, Transmission and
Distribution; 523999 Miscellaneous Financial
Investment Activities

Slough Estates PLC is Britain's largest industrial property investment company, with a property portfolio valued at about £3.8 billion. The development and management of industrial or trading estates, sites containing a number of units of industrial property occupied by several different companies, was pioneered by Slough in the 1920s and still forms the bulk of its business, both in the United Kingdom and overseas. In recent years the company has also diversified into other property and non-property activities.

Slough Estates' Extraordinary Beginnings

Slough Estates began life in 1920, when a syndicate of businessmen formed the Slough Trading Company to purchase a 600-acre site on Bath Road in Slough, England, which had been developed as a mechanical transport repair depot during World War I. The government's original intention was to repair and sell the assembled vehicles following the war, but lack of progress aroused public criticism and after publication of the report of a parliamentary joint select committee in July 1919, it was decided to sell the site to a private buyer. "The Dump," as the site was known, was sold for £7 million, and included thousands of used cars, trucks, and motorcycles left over after the war. Prominent among the syndicate of businessmen who bought the site were Sir (later Lord) Percival Perry, the managing director of the U.K. branch of the Ford Motor Company, and Noel Mobbs (later Sir), founder of the Slough Trading Company as well as chairman of the Pytchley Autocar Company Ltd., which he had founded in 1904.

Some 8,000 people, nearly half the population of Slough, were employed in repairing and selling the vehicles. About 15,000 derelict vehicles were cannibalized to produce 10,000 workable ones. Repaired vehicles were sold at auctions, and by the end of 1920 auction sales had already raised more than £5 million. To speed up the disposal of the vehicles, the company employed what was then an innovative labor management policy; the workforce was paid regular wages rather than piece rates and a 40-hour, five-day week was introduced, without any reduction in earnings despite the reduction of 10 percent to 20 percent in working hours. This policy proved successful, resulting in the productivity improvements that it was designed to achieve.

By 1925 the vehicle sales were completed and the company turned its attention to building fully serviced factories on the site. Machine shops, other plants, and offices had already been built by the company for vehicle repair operations, together with utilities, including a power station, gas-producing plant, water mains, roads, and railway tracks. The establishment of an integrated industrial estate of the type envisaged by the company's founder, Sir Noel Mobbs, involved further infrastructure provision. Utilities were extended and other services were organized; both Barclays Bank and the National Provincial Bank established themselves on the site to serve the new factories. Early tenants included Citroen Cars, Johnson & Johnson, Gillette, The Mentholatum Company, and the Hygienic Ice Company.

The site at Slough was ideal for such consumer-goods industries, with good road and rail links to London, which was only 20 miles away, and the Midlands. Slough's first chairman, Sir Percival Perry, was succeeded by Sir Noel Mobbs in 1922. Mobbs was to remain chairman at Slough for the next 35 years.

The passage of the Slough Trading Company Act 1925 permitted the company to build roads and lay water and steam mains, electricity cables, and drains. This facilitated large-scale industrial development on the site.

Within a few years the company had transformed itself from a motor-dealing firm to a property company, a transformation that was reflected in a change of name in 1926 to Slough Estates Ltd. A policy was developed in these early years regarding the management of the estate at Slough. Units were offered for rental rather than sale, thereby giving Slough Estates greater control over the estate and providing a continual source of revenue. Such a policy also proved popular with many small- and medium-sized tenants, who did not wish to tie up capital in the purchase of factory premises. Only light industry was to operate on the estate. Buildings were to be built in advance of requirements and were never custom built, although tenants' requirements were taken into account in their construction. The objective behind these policies was the provision of basic factories with a high degree of adaptability; units could be easily subdivided and could serve a wide variety of industrial needs. Adaptability was important since it meant that units could be easily re-leased, thereby overcoming a basic obstacle to successful long-term investment in industrial property.

The estate grew quickly and by 1930 had 100 tenants who employed 8,000 people on the site. As the businesses of some tenants grew, Slough was able to accommodate them in larger units on the estate, thereby enabling them to expand capacity easily without having to move to a new site or extend their premises. Sir Noel Mobbs envisaged the estate at Slough as an integrated industrial community. In addition to the provision of utilities and infrastructure on the site, he planned a variety of social and welfare services for the estate which would encourage a community atmosphere. His plans culminated in the establishment of the Slough Community Centre in 1937, and the Slough Industrial Health Service, launched in 1947 after delays caused by World War II.

The estate easily survived the 1930s, its variety of trades and concentration on the new light industries shielding it from the severe depression which hit Britain's older core industries. Slough claimed to have the lowest unemployment rate in the country, at 1 percent, and the estate was able to absorb unemployed workers from outside the area. This was encouraged by an extensive house-building program in Slough and the opening of a Ministry of Labour Training Centre for newcomers to the estate in 1929, which provided six-month courses in building, engineering, woodworking, and other skills required by the tenants. The growth of the town of Slough was closely linked with the fortunes of Slough Estates. When the company was established in 1920 the town had 16,000 inhabitants. By 1930 this figure had grown to 28,000 and by 1938 it had soared to 55,000.

In 1931 the company acquired a second industrial estate on a 55-acre site five miles south of Birmingham. Birmingham's diversified industrial structure made it an ideal location for the establishment of a trading estate to serve a variety of light industries. A year later, Slough Estates became the first company in England to provide metered steam for process and heating. This was particularly useful for industries such as food processing, where a high premium was placed on cleanliness, since it eliminated the coal dust resulting from an onsite boiler. The company's modern facilities and progressive outlook led a large number of foreign-based firms to establish themselves at Slough, something which Sir Noel Mobbs felt was impeded by the government's unsympathetic attitude to foreign companies. "The President of the Board of Trade," he complained, "can no more stop the tide of industry coming to sunlit open factories in pleasant surroundings than could Canute prevent the tide from advancing up the shores of Dover."

The estate at Slough escaped war damage during World War II. During the postwar reconstruction period, expansion was inhibited by shortages and government restrictions. Building materials were in extremely short supply due to wartime reductions in capacity. Government building licenses were difficult to obtain, due to local labor scarcity and a national economic policy that favored export-oriented industries at the expense of construction. Controls also extended to the provision of capital, and borrowing large sums for development required clearance from a government body known as the Capital Issues Committee. Despite a waiting list for new units, development at Slough in the early postwar years was restricted to expanding factory space for existing tenants.

In order to overcome these problems, Slough Estates sought further expansion outside Slough. During this time of tight government controls, undertaking government-sponsored projects provided one means of gaining the necessary official approval. Slough participated in such a scheme in 1945, developing an estate in Swansea at the request of the Board of Trade.

New Opportunities Following World War II

Just as Slough Estates' formation had resulted from government activity during World War I, demobilization following World War II brought new opportunities. In 1948 it obtained a 22-acre site at Greenford, Middlesex, which had been used as an ordnance depot, with 21 units leased to the War Department. As leases on these units were not due to expire until 1959, the investment offered little prospect of increasing returns in the short term, but the company's patience was rewarded by rising rental income after the leases terminated. Despite the shortages and government restrictions which inhibited expansion during these years, Slough Estates experienced rapid growth in asset values immediately after the war, reflected in an increase in the estimated value of its assets from £2.3 million to £3 million between 1945 and 1948. While postwar conditions had restricted the scope for expansion, they had increased the value of existing factories by allowing demand to outstrip supply.

Key Dates:

1920: Slough Trading Company is founded by Noel Mobbs (later Sir) to acquire a 600-acre site on Bath Road in Slough, England.

1925: The Slough Trading Company Act is passed.

1926: Slough Estates Ltd. is created.

1931: Slough Estates acquires a 55-acre site near Birmingham, England.

1937: The Slough Community Centre is founded.

1945: Slough develops an estate in Swansea at the request of the U.K. Board of Trade.

1947: Slough Industrial Health Service is founded.

1948: The company obtains a 22-acre site at Greenford, Middlesex.

1950: The company develops its first investment property in Ajax, Ontario Canada, near Toronto.

1957: Lieutenant Colonel W.H. Kingsmill succeeds Sir Noel Mobbs as chairman; and Gerald Mobbs, son of Sir Noel Mobbs, becomes managing director.

1961: Slough Estates Australia Pty. Ltd. is established after purchasing 1,500 acres at Altona, near Melbourne.

1967: The company purchases an industrial estate in Wakefield, to the north of England.

1969: Slough Estates acquires Hertford Industrial Estates and Yorkshire and Pacific Securities Ltd., a U.K.-based investment company.

1972: Gauntlet Developments is formed to develop offices in the United Kingdom and Europe.

1974: Slough Estates enters into a joint venture with Draper & Kramer of Chicago to form SDK Parks.

1976: Sir Nigel Mobbs, grandson of Slough founder Sir Noel Mobbs, becomes chairman and chief executive.

1984: Slough Estates merges with Allnatt London & Guildhall Properties.

1986: Slough Estates acquires equity interest in Tipperary Corporation of Denver, Colorado.

1998: The company begins development of Pegasus Business Park in Brussels, the site of a European center for the U.S. company Cisco Systems.

1999: Farnborough Business Park, the former Royal Aircraft Establishmen, is acquired.

2000: Cambridge Research Park development site is acquired; the city of South San Francisco grants Slough Estates consent to develop offices and R&D space at Oyster Point; and work commences on the Willingdon Park development outside Vancouver, B.C. Canada.

2001: Slough's Canada portfolio in Toronto is sold.

Slough Estates Holdings Extend to North America

Government restrictions and shortages continued to plague Slough Estates until 1954 when building license controls were lifted, although the Birmingham and Greenford estates had been virtually completed and let by this date. Other investments included the purchase of land in Canada and a large injection of capital to improve the power station at Slough. A large land bank was also acquired, which the company was able to put to good use in the less restricted environment of the 1950s and 1960s. Rents had risen only moderately in the years immediately following the war, since most property was still let on leases which had been negotiated in the interwar period. However, in 1951, when many leases came up for renewal, rental income jumped by 25 percent.

The property boom period, from the lifting of government restrictions on development in 1954, to the imposition of the government's so-called Brown Ban on office development in and around London in 1964, did not prove nearly so prosperous a time for industrial estate developers as it did for developers of offices or shopping malls. In addition, Industrial Development Certificate legislation held back development activity in this sector. Development funds were raised by a series of rights issues, while rising rents provided further capital for expansion. Sir Noel Mobbs retired as chairman in 1957, and was succeeded by Lieutenant Colonel W.H. Kingsmill, with Gerald Mobbs as managing director.

Restrictions in the domestic market prompted Slough's expansion overseas in the postwar period. From 1950 onward, parcels of land were accumulated gradually in the town of Ajax near Toronto, Ontario Canada. The choice of Ajax paralleled that of Slough, both being small towns close to large population centers with good transport facilities to major national and international markets. The establishment of the estate led to the formation of two new subsidiaries; Slough Estates (Canada) Ltd. and its construction subsidiary Slough Construction and Properties Ltd.

By the late 1950s, U.K. currency controls made it impossible to remit funds to Canada for the development of the Ajax estate investment. The company had sufficient security for local borrowing from the early 1960s, but funding continued to present problems until 1969 when Slough Estates acquired Yorkshire and Pacific Securities Ltd., a U.K.-based investment company whose assets were held by a Canadian subsidiary. A second Canadian estate was established in the mid-1960s, covering 109 acres in Malton, a mile from Toronto International Airport.

Slough Estates Enters Australian and European Markets

In 1949, Slough entered the Australian property market, a favorite area for U.K. developers wishing to expand overseas, with the purchase of 1,500 acres of land at Altona, near Melbourne. Unlike previous developments the land was not located in a town and it took over ten years to get the local authorities to extend utilities to the site. Eventually another industrial development was established nearby and the necessary services were extended. Slough Estates Australia Pty. Ltd., a wholly owned subsidiary, was established in 1961, but it was not until 1966 that a final agreement was reached with the Melbourne and Metropolitan Board of Works for the provision of amenities.

During the 1960s, influenced by the growing prosperity of the European Economic Community (EEC), Slough decided to expand into Europe. Britain's failure to gain entry to the EEC at that time led to Slough's decision to establish a factory in an EEC country. Belgium was chosen, since it had a highly developed industrial infrastructure, a rich domestic market, and close proximity to London. St. Nicholas, a textile town within easy reach of both Antwerp and Brussels, which wanted to diversity into other industries due to the depression in textiles, was chosen as a site. Designated by the government as an official development area, the site also offered financial concessions.

During the 1960s, Slough extended its operations to the north of England. In 1967 it purchased an industrial estate in Wakefield comprising 17 acres of land close to the M1 motorway. In an area of high unemployment, this development was not subject to Industrial Development Certificate legislation. The purchase of the site prior to the extension of the M1 was an example of Slough Estates' strategy of buying estates before the provision of infrastructure, which was also a factor behind the later acquisition of the estate at Yate. The Wakefield site also had features in common with the earlier estates in Slough and Birmingham, in that it was located in a major conurbation, with a skilled industrial workforce and a large local market for goods produced on the estate.

Slough Estates Acquires Hertford Industrial Estates

Growth was assisted by the takeover of another company specializing in industrial property, Hertford Industrial Estates, which was acquired in 1969 for £830,000. This company owned 24 acres of industrial buildings in Hertford, Bishop's Stortford, and Braintree. During the early 1970s the company expanded rapidly to take advantage of booming economic conditions. Sites were purchased in High Wycombe, Yate, near Bristol, and Aylesbury. New overseas operations included the purchase of a major site in Australia and the launching of a joint £9 million development program with Mackenzie Hill to develop sites in France and later in Germany.

The company was in a good position to take advantage of the rapid rise in industrial rents during the early 1970s. By 1970, 75 percent of the leases were tied to the wholesale price index and were adjusted annually. This system of leasing, which was unique to the company, led to rapid increases in rental income during the inflationary years of the 1970s. A further 10 percent of the properties were let on leases with seven-yearly rent reviews.

Diversification into the non-industrial commercial property market was also attempted, through a subsidiary, Gauntlet Developments, which was formed in 1972 to develop offices in the United Kingdom and Europe. This venture proved unsuccessful, leaving Slough Estates with offices in Brussels and Sheffield that remained vacant for several years. In 1974 the company turned its attention to the United States and entered into a joint venture with Chicago's Draper & Kramer to form SDK Parks, in which it took an 80 percent interest. Slough was the first British property company to tackle the industrial sector in the United States.

Following the property market crash in the same year and its aftermath, Slough was one of the few companies to achieve increases in profits. Industrial development did not suffer the same fate as the commercial market. Although the company had made minor excursions into commercial property, it emerged from the crisis largely unscathed. It was able to buy out the interest of Mackenzie Hill in their joint developments and successfully launched a £5.5 million convertible rights issue in 1975.

Improving property market conditions during the late 1970s allowed Slough Estates to enter a new phase of expansion, the most notable scheme being the Sutton Industrial Park at Reading, which was bought in 1976 and was intended to contain about 750,000 square feet of buildings. During 1976, Sir Nigel Mobbs, grandson of Sir Noel Mobbs, became chairman and chief executive succeeding his father Gerald Mobbs.

The early 1980s saw steady growth in Slough's profits, despite a depression in industrial property, as rent reviews led to increased rental income. Slough undertook a number of developments both at home and overseas. U.S. activities were expanded substantially with developments concentrated around the Chicago area.

Slough Estates Continues Expansion of Industrial Properties

In 1984, Slough merged with Allnatt London & Guildhall Properties, with assets valued at £159 million. Allnatt's properties were well suited to Slough's portfolio, since they were predominantly industrial.

In 1986, Slough Estates acquired an equity interest in Denver, Colorado-based Tipperary Corporation, an independent energy company, concentrating on the exploration and production of coal-bed methane, and owner of Tipperary Oil and Gas (Australia) Pty. Ltd. Slough planned to continue ownership in this company that holds a majority interest in the Cornet Ridge methane project in Southeast Queensland, with projected gas reserves valued at US$100 million.

During 1987 it was decided to broaden the company's asset base, with increased activity in the shop, office, and retail warehousing markets. Until 1987, only 8.5 percent of Slough Estates' U.K. portfolio was in nonindustrial property, though its commitment to other property areas increased sharply in 1986 with the purchase of a 52 percent stake in Bredero Properties, a development company that specialized in U.K. shopping malls.

Buoyant conditions in the industrial property market led to rising profits for Slough during the late 1980s. The company continued to expand its activities, launching a massive development program both at home and overseas, the eventual cost of which was estimated to be about £1 billion. Operations were extended into the French and German markets, while the company diversified into property and non-property activities unconnected with industrial estates in both U.K. and foreign markets. By 1990, investment in such activities amounted to £45 million.

In the late 1990s, Slough Estates eyed U.K. industrial specialist Bilton for possible takeover, culminating in a £276 million outlay in 1998 to acquire the company's £300 million portfolio of industrial estates in Southeast England. Later in the same year, Slough Estates announced plans to develop the Pegasus Business Park in Brussels, the site of a European technical assistance center for the U.S. Internet company Cisco Systems. Slough had also developed two additional business parks near Zaventem Airport, in Brussels.

Closer to home, Slough increased its presence in the U.K. with plans for the development in 1999 of a 180-acre commercial site near Farnborough Aerodrome, the former headquarters of Britains' Royal Air Force, and formerly the Royal Aircraft Establishment factory site in Hampshire. Its hometown of Slough also benefited from the company's development of a shopping mall complex, the Queensmere Shopping Centre. This location proved to be an extraordinary investment of the Slough Estates from its beginnings in 1920: a vibrant commercial center on the edge of London, close to M4, M40, and M25 motorways and Heathrow Airport. Slough commercial developments in the area attracted companies such as Leaseplan, Coca-Cola, and Unatrac. Slough upheld its reputation as the U.K.'s largest industrial property company with additional developments in Northampton and Southern Cross, near Southampton, in the Southeast corridor. Elsewhere in the United Kingdom, Slough's Buchanan Galleries, a shopping center complex in Glasgow, Scotland, set a U.K. opening-day record for first-day sales in April 1999.

Slough Estates Enters Hi-Tech Market Worldwide

In early, 2000 Slough Estates acquired Cambridge Research Park with plans to convert it into a hi-tech cluster, attracting tenants from the hi-tech, communications, and IT sectors. Motorola, once poised to open its European headquarters at Slough's Farnborough Aerodrome site, scaled back expansion plans in early 2001. At that time, only 20 percent of Slough's tenants were in the technology, media, and telecommunications sectors.

Through its U.K. and worldwide operations, Slough Estates continued to provide "Buildings for Better Business." In the South San Francisco, California, area, the Oyster Point Business Park and East Grand were acquired for the development of office and R&D facilities. San Diego provided the location for the company's largest ever pre-letting deal with Agouron, a research subsidiary of Pfizer. In Brussels, Belgium, Slough Estates acquired Pegasus Business Park near the airport for site expansion. Additional space acquired in the same area provided for the development of a hotel and buildings for tenants of Cisco Systems and Deloitte & Touche.

In Toronto, Ontario, Canada, industrial space was completed at Mississauga, Goreway, and Oakville. At Willingdon Park, Vancouver, construction began in early 2000 to meet the needs of high-tech industrial growth, including space committed to Nortel. Other worldwide developments included a 25-hectare site at Marly la Ville, north of the Charles DeGaulle Airport in France, and construction sites in Mönchengladbach, Ratingen, Glinde, and Kapellen, Germany.

The company's interests in the United Kingdom continued to be in the areas of business park and industrial space development, particularly in Southeast England and Thames Valley area. Additional buildings in the company's Bath Road location

were leased to health science occupiers. Industrial developments were being completed in Farnborough, Feltham, Acton, Uxbridge, Wokingham, Luton, High Wycombe, Southampton, Birmingham, Northampton, Elstree, and East Midlands Airport.

The Company's investment property portfolio for 2000 reflected worldwide interests in the United States (12 percent), Europe (6 percent), and Canada (5 percent). Types of businesses included office/business (18 percent), retail (14 percent), land (10 percent), and industrial (58%).

Slough Estates Continued Its Core Development in 2001

Slough Estates made notable progress with its major developments in the United Kingdom, Belgium, and the United States and grew its core investment property earnings by 13 percent in 2001. The Oyster Point, South San Francisco development began construction of four health science research businesses, with completion projected for 2005. The Group's San Diego Torrey Pines Science Center scheduled for completion in 2004, was developed for Pfizer, the world's largest pharmaceutical company. The Toronto, Ontario, Canada portfolio was sold at £2.5 million above book value. This property was Slough's first investment in Toronto in 1950. The Elk Grove, Illinois industrial property near Chicago was also sold as well as the Group's remaining Canadian assets in Vancouver.

The Brussels' Pegasus Park development continued its transformation with the completion of offices and hotel facilities in late 2001. Tenants at this location were Cisco Systems, DHL, and Deloitte & Touche. Other developments in the planning stages would be located in Antwerp and Düsseldorf.

The United Kingdom remained the largest piece of Slough's investment portfolio in 2001 at 78 percent. North American activity made up 16 percent, with 6 percent of activities concentrated in Europe. Approaching completion in early 2002 were the Farnborough Business Park and the Cambridge Research Park in the United Kingdom. Sales of buildings in London and Bournemouth raised £55 million.

The Group's strategy has continued through the years to follow the principles of owning and developing business parks, industrial and distribution estates, and retail centers in prime business locations, while creating flexible and economic accommodations. In the future, Slough Estates portfolios will be centered on prime business centers in the United Kingdom, Continental Europe, and the United States. Chairman Nigel Mobbs offers confidence in the Group's future earnings' growth potential from its existing portfolio and contributions from an extensive development program.

Principal Subsidiaries

Guildhall Properties Ltd.; Slough Commercial Properties GmbH (Germany); Slough Developments (France) SA; Slough Estates Australia Pty. Ltd.; Slough Estates Canada Ltd.; Slough Estates USA Inc. (USA); Slough Heat & Power Ltd. (England); Slough Properties NV (Belgium).

Principal Competitors

British Land Company; Brixton Land Securities; *io* Group; Mountcity Group.

Further Reading

Billingham, Erica, "Slough Touts Credentials as E-Commerce Landlord," *Estates Gazette*, March 25, 2000, http://www.egi.co.uk.

——, "Mobbs Eases Off the Accelerator at Slough," *Estates Gazette*, March 27, 1999.

"Buchanan Galleries Opens," *Estates Gazette*, April 3, 1999, http://www.egi.co.uk.

Cassell, Michael, *Long Lease!*, Tulsa, Okla.: PennWell Books, 1990, 200 p.

"Centres Take the State," *Estates Gazette*, November 6, 1999, http://www.egi.co.uk.

Cheesewright, Paul, "Slough Shares Fall as Its NAV Rises 35% and Its Profits 22%," *Financial Times*, March 30, 1989.

"Company File: Slough Estates," *Estates Gazette*, May 7, 1977, http://www.egi.co.uk.

Cooper, Mark, "Confident Slough Shrugs Off Economic Slowdown," *Estates Gazette*, March 24, 2001, http://www.egi.co.uk.

Erdman, Edward, *People and Property*, London: Batsford, 1982, 214 p.

Foster, Michael, "Company File: Slough Estates," *Estates Gazette*, May 7, 1983, http://www.egi.co.uk.

"New Front Opens in Bilton Battle," *Estates Gazette*, November 7, 1998, http://www.egi.co.uk.

"Slough Buys Aircraft Factory Site," *Estates Gazette*, April 17, 1999, http://www.egi.co.uk.

"Slough Estates Goes Commercial Again," *Investors Chronicle*, May 1, 1987.

"Slough Estates: Re-Rating Due?," *Investors Chronicle*, May 10, 1985.

"Slough Sells Canadian Estates," *Estates Gazette*, October 27, 2001, http://www.egi.co.uk.

Smyth, Hedley, "The Historical Growth of Property Companies and the Construction Industry in Great Britain between 1939 and 1979," Unpublished Ph.D. Thesis, Bristol: University of Bristol, 1982.

"U.S. Firms Make Cutbacks in U.K.," *Estates Gazette*, February 3, 2001, http://www.egi.co.uk.

—Peter Scott
—update: Carol D. Beavers

Sonera Corporation

Teollisuuskatu 15
Helsinki
Finland
Telephone: +358 (9) 20401
Fax: +358 (9) 2040 60025
Web site: http://www.sonera.com

Public Company
Incorporated: 1994 as Telecom Finland Ltd.
Employees: 10,000 (2001 est.)
Sales: EUR 2.187 billion (2001)
Stock Exchanges: NASDAQ Helsinki
Ticker Symbol: SNRA (NASDAQ); SRA1V (Helsinki)
NAIC: 513322 Cellular and Other Wireless Telecom-
    munications; 513310 Wired Telecommunications
    Carriers; 421690 Other Electronic Parts and
    Equipment Wholesalers; 514210 Data Processing
    Services

The largest provider of mobile and telecommunications services in its native Finland, the Sonera Corporation offers mobile communications, fixed network business, and the development of services and applications. With over 2.4 million mobile subscribers and a market share of 60 percent, Sonera remains, at heart, a mobile communications company, providing local, international, and long-distance voice services to its customer base. Sonera enjoyed a massive growth spurt in 1999 and 2000, taking advantage of the market's frenzy for new technologies that joined wireless and the Web, but the company's mounting debt and the downturn of the market forced Sonera to re-strategize. Sonera now concentrates on profitable business growth, improvement of customer focus, increasing cost-effectiveness, and capping their investments to ensure competitiveness in the long run. As its mission statement clearly indicates, Sonera ''intends to be ready, when the pace of development in the telecommunications market quickens again.''

Towards Deregulation in Finland: Sonera's Beginnings

The history of Sonera Corporation is closely tied to the early history of telecommunications in Finland. In 1855, when the first Finnish telegraph offices were opened, Finland was an autonomous Grand Duchy within the Russian Empire, and the telegraph offices were a state-controlled monopoly.

When Finland gained its independence in 1917, the Telegraph Office continued as a state controlled body. In 1927, the Telegraph Office merged with the Post Office. The Post and Telegraph Office had a dual role as regulator and operator of all forms of Finnish telecommunications. By 1935, the almost all Finnish long distance telephone traffic was transferred to the control of the Post and Telegraph Office.

This regulated telecommunications monopoly continued in Finland for over 50 years. By the mid-1980s, increasing internationalization and global competition made it evident that an industry-specific monopoly could economically cripple Finland. In 1981, the Post and Telegraph Office was renamed Posts and Telecommunications of Finland, and the Finnish state began to prepare for an eventual deregulation of the industry. Six years later, Finland passed the National Telecommunications Act of 1987, legislation geared towards quickly turning Posts and Telecommunications of Finland into a limited liability company. The first step was to transfer the regulatory functions of Posts and Telecommunications to another body, the Ministry of Transport and Communications, and to separate the operations of Posts and Telecommunications from the state budget. The second step was the actual formation of the state-owned limited liability company, now called Telecom Finland, which operated on more commercial terms than those of Posts and Telecommunications of Finland.

Telecom Finland was a very successful venture, connecting its 1.5 millionth mobile customer by 1997. One year later, the Finnish state released 18,850,000 shares of Telecom Finland. After this, the move toward the deregulation and privatization of the industry proceeded quickly. By the middle of the year, Telecom Finland's name was changed to Sonera, and the com-

441

Company Perspectives:

Sonera's goal is to grow as an operator and provider of transaction and content services in Finland and in selected international markets. In content production, we utilize our extensive network of partners. To achieve our goal, we combine its experience in mobile communications, the Internet, and customer-oriented services.

---

pany was listed on both the Helsinki Stock Exchange and on the NASDAQ. Sonera's IPO attracted strong retail and institutional demand, and on October 13, 1998, the public sale of Sonera shares commenced.

1999: Newly Privatized, Poised for Expansion

The newly privatized company hit the ground running, beginning the year by becoming a charter member of the Bluetooth cooperation, hoping to help construct a new wireless communications standard to connect various applications using radio technology instead of standard cable connections. It was this type of innovative drive that drew immediate positive attention to Sonera, who garnered various prestigious industry awards that year, including the World Billing Award for best customer care, the World Communications Award for Best Branding, Data Communications' Hot Product of the Year, and an award in Cannes for the most rapid GSM (global system for mobile communications) customer growth.

Sonera became the first operator in the world to launch commercial Wireless Application Protocol (WAP) services to mobile subscribers. WAP is an open, global specification that allows mobile users with wireless devices to access and interact with information. With Sonera's launch of Sonera Zed, a mobile portal, Zed users could access on-demand services such as news, games, dating, movie and restaurant guides, sports information, horoscopes, multi-language dictionaries, traffic reports, and directory information services. It also became a charter operator of CNN Mobile, the first mobile telephone news and information service to be available globally with pan-regional content, targeted at GSM mobile phone customers in Europe and Asia/Pacific.

Security issues have been long been considered to be one of the main obstacles to the successful deployment of wireless e-commerce services. Sonera made this a prime business focus, launching, along with Gemplus and EDS, a global initiative to define a standard security platform for mobile e-commerce. The initiative, called Radicchio, was created to promote the use of an environment based on a Public Key Infrastructure (PKI), and more specifically, Sonera's development of one such PKI-based framework, to provide security for financial transactions and information exchange over mobile networks. The Radicchio initiative was also formed to promote the use of this framework among certification authorities, mobile operators, systems integrators, device manufacturers, and financial institutions in order to create a standard security platform upon which all mobile commerce software, services, and devices can be based. Sonera teamed with Ericsson, the Swedish supplier of mobile systems, to

work on the first digital signature for secure wireless e-commerce using WAP phones. This digital signature allowed mobile operators and service providers to offer secure, transaction-based services in WAP environments, not unlike Sonera Zed. During this time, Sonera also became the first non-U.S. operator licensed to use 3DES encryption, which encrypts message data with three passes of the DES algorithm (symmetric key cryptography to safeguard remote network communications).

Sonera announced its intention to continue expanding its business outside Finnish borders with several global ventures. The most notable was Sonera's offering of QuickNet, its content-rich data-over-cable service, in the Netherlands.

Continued Growth in 2000

In 2000, Sonera was granted the opportunity to break entirely free of its past as a state controlled entity when the Finnish government authorized the reduction of the state's total holdings in Sonera to zero. This did not happen, however, and the Finnish government continued holding approximately 53 percent of Sonera's shares. During the year, the company continued to win accolades, awarded the Best Mobile Operator and Technology Foresight Award at 2000's World Communication Awards. Also in 2000, Sonera Plaza, the company's Internet transaction center and service provider, received over a million visitors per month.

The company made some organizational changes during this time. One such change was the transfer by Sonera's board of directors of the company's ASP (active server page) business to a new subsidiary called Sonera Juxto Ltd. Sonera Juxto was formed to offer solutions for wireless networks; services for external and internal communications; infrastructure management services covering workstations, mobile phones, and other wireless communications devices; LANs; remote networks; servers; and data processing platforms.

The year 2000 also found Sonera forming lucrative partnerships, one of which was with Equant, the Dutch data network operator, to offer GPRS (General Packet Radio Service) roaming solutions to mobile operators. Based on the concept of GPX (GPRS Roaming Exchange), a centralized IP routing network for interconnecting GPRS networks, the team's solution facilitated roaming between the networks of different GPRS operators. With this solution, subscribers could access data services such as e-mail, graphics, and video while outside their home network. With the importance of roaming services for mobile providers, particularly in the European market, offering this solution was a benchmark for Sonera.

In June, Sonera acquired iD2 Technologies and later, combined forces with Across Wireless to strengthen their existing SmartTrust venture and enrich their security offerings. SmartTrust offered wireless e-commerce enabling technologies, such as digital identification and digital signatures. The types of technologies developed by SmartTrust began to be used this year by institutions such as the Finnish Population Register Center (PRC) for electronic identification of a person into the wireless networks.

Sonera also spent time this year applying for digital TV licenses. Its cable television services had, by this time, over 50

Key Dates:

1994: The company is incorporated as Telecom Finland Ltd. in Finland.

1997: Connects 1.5 millionth mobile customer; Finnish Parliament approves partial privatization of Telecom Finland, who changes its name to Sonera.

1998: Changes name to Sonera Group Plc and is placed on the Helsinki Stock Exchange after Finnish government sells 22.2 percent of shares.

1999: Sonera wins the World Billing Award for best customer care; the company partners with CNN Interactive to form CNN Mobile, and its subscription base passes two million.

2000: Finnish Government reduces their holdings in Sonera to zero; Tedasys merges with Sonera, and the company sells its holding in VoiceStream.

2001: Mounting debt induces the company to sell their Deutsche Telekom AG (DT) shares; CEO Kaj-Erik Relander resigns, and Harri Koponen is appointed Sonera's new president and CEO; signs agreement with Nokia.

2002: The company opens a third-generation mobile communications UMTS network in Finland.

networks, but Sonera's interest was in developing a two-way, duplex network, or more specifically, interactive digital services accessed via a Web browser that plays on a television screen. This interest led to Sonera's decision to refuse a 34 percent purchase of media company Digita Oy because the Finnish Competition Council stipulated that neither Sonera nor a company under its authority would be allowed to apply for any digital television operating licenses if it owned Digita shares.

2001–2002: Bumps in the Road

The year 2001 brought challenges to the entire telecommunications industry and quickly altered the climate in which Sonera was operating. A downturn in market growth and increasing lags between mobile communications advances forced Sonera to concentrate their attentions on decreasing their debt and mapping strategies to increase company profitability. The company made several moves in this direction, scaling down their service businesses and capping future investments.

Sonera first showed signs of the strain with major leadership changes, some fraught with controversy. At the company's annual meeting in March 2001, six members of the Board of Directors were fired when the company's stock dropped 10 percent. In June, Executive Vice President Harri Hollmen announced his resignation, and a few days later, President and CEO Kaj-Erik Relander offered his resignation as well. Relander stepped down amid a cloud of criticism. During his brief six-month stint as CEO, he led Sonera in a decision to spend billions of dollars on third-generation (3G) mobile phone network licenses. These licenses were to allow the company to offer new Internet, e-mail, and video services to mobile phones—but at the time such services were years behind in development, costing the company huge amounts of revenue

with no guarantee of its eventual profitability. In October, Harri Koponen was appointed as Sonera's new president and CEO and was charged with reacting quickly to the investor unrest and changing market conditions.

Sonera immediately began selling its shares in other companies as a means to strengthen its financial position. The company sold approximately 19.7 million Deutsche Telekom (DT) shares, reducing Sonera's net debt to approximately EUR 2.8 billion. In May, Sonera sold 3.3 million VoiceStream shares for EUR 360 million and sold part of its fixed network business targeted at companies operating in Sweden to Song Networks (Tele 1 Europe).

Not all of Sonera's businesses suffered that year. Many continued to make advances and impressive agreements. SmartTrust partnered with Thomas Cook to offer the world's first secure mobile travel services using wireless devices. The Mobile FX Bureau service allowed customers to purchase, make conversion inquiries, arrange for remote collection of purchased currency, and access similar travel-related services. Sonera also introduced Sonera Shopper, a pilot program for mobile payment in the Helsinki, Finland, metropolitan area. Sonera Shopper turned a user's wireless device into a means of payment itself, much like a credit card. In the Helsinki metropolitan area, Tiimari, Pizza Hut, and Videofirma Makuuni all extended the use of Shopper for use throughout Finland. Sonera Zed formed an agreement with Telecom Italia, one of the largest mobile service operators in Europe, to distribute Zed services to Italian mobile phone customers. Sonera Carrier Networks Ltd participated in a project building a cable network connection for high-rate data transmission between Europe and the United States, part of Sonera's broadband connection that extends from Moscow to Western Europe and, with this project, into the United States.

Principal Divisions

Domestic Mobile Communications; International Mobile Communications; Media Communications and New Services; Sonera Telecom; Other Operations.

Principal Subsidiaries

Across Wireless AB; Across Wireless Ltd.; iD2 Holding AB; iD2 Technologies AB; Oy Infonet Finland Ltd. (90%); Primatel Ltd.; SmartTrust GmbH; SmartTrust Systems Oy; Sonera 3G Holding B.V.; Sonera Corporation U.S.; Sonera Entrum Ltd.; Sonera Gateway Ltd.; Sonera Info Communications Oy; Sonera Juxto Ltd.; Sonera Living Oy (51%); Sonera Plaza Ltd.; Sonera SmartTrust Holding B.V.; Sonera SmartTrust Ltd.; Sonera Solutions Ltd; Sonera Sverige AB; Sonera Systems Ltd.; Sonera Ventures Oy; Sonera Zed Ltd.; Spectrun Co Ltd (68%); Systems Consultant Partners Oy; Tedasys Inc.

Principal Competitors

Elisa Communications; TDC; Telia; Tele2 AB.

Further Reading

Brown-Humes, Christopher, "Sonera Talks to Several Groups: Finnish State Likely to Retain Holding in Telecoms Group as It Seeks an

International Partner,'' *The Financial Times*, August 29, 2000, p. 19.

Edmunds, Marlene, ''Finnish Digital Plans in Disarray,'' *Variety*, January 11, 1999, p. 65(1).

George, Nicholas, ''EUROPE: Sonera Warns on Earnings,'' *The Financial Times*, February 15, 2000, p. 32.

Kaihla, Paul, ''Will the Sun Rise Again for Sonera?,'' *Business 2.0*, posted April 19, 2001, http://www.business2.com.

''Killer Apps for a Wireless World,'' *Business Week*, September 18, 2000, p. 43.

Kuusela, Sami, ''Finland: POWER: Wireless Adoption,'' *Business 2.0*, January 2000, http://www.business2.com.

Lewis, Peter, ''Wireless Valhalla: Hints of the Cellular Future; What Do You Call a Scandinavian All-purpose Communication, Shopping and Entertainment Interface? A Phone,'' *The New York Times*, July 13, 2000, pp. D1(N), G1(L).

''On the Edge,'' *Communications International*, February 2002 p. 47.

Orman, Neil, ''Well-wired Finns Connect with Bay Area and Valley,'' *San Francisco Business Times*, March 30, 2001, p. 20.

Power, Carol, ''Finnish Bank Brings Digital Certificates to Mobile Phones,'' *American Banker*, January 18, 2000, p. 20.

Rubinsten, Roy, ''Sonera Launch First IP-based Network,'' *Company Business and Marketing*, October 23, 2000.

Shaw, William, ''In Helsinki Virtual Village,'' *Wired*, accessed March 19, 2002, http://www.wired.com.

''Sonera unveils shareholder rights issue,'' *The Wall Street Journal*, October 23, 2001, p. A18.

Spiegler, Marc, ''Behold the Power of the Videophone! A Finnish Company Offers Mobile Video-on-demand,'' *eCompany*, December 2000, http://www.business2.com.

''Wireless Web Portals Duke it Out,'' From the *McKinsey Quarterly*, Special to CNETNews.com, April 18, 2001, http://news.com.com.

—C. J. Gussoff

SPECIALIZED®

Specialized Bicycle Components Inc.

15130 Concord Circle
Morgan Hill, California 95037-5428
U.S.A.
Telephone: (408)-779-6229
Toll Free: (800)-245-3462
Fax: (408)-779-1631
Web site: http://www.specialized.com

Private Company
Incorporated: 1974
Employees: 300 (2002)
Sales: $200 million (est.) (2000)
NAIC: 336991 Motorcycle, Bicycle, and Parts
    Manufacturing

Specialized Bicycle Components Inc. is the United State's fourth-largest maker of high-end bicycles. Specialized is a leading innovator in the bicycle industry, consistently striving to create new and better bicycle technologies. In 1981, Specialized revolutionized the biking industry by introducing mountain bikes to the general public. The mountain bike Specialized sold in 1981, the StumpJumper, was such an important and groundbreaking product that an original model is on display in the Smithsonian Institute. Since 1981, Specialized has not backed off from its company motto, "Innovate or Die." The company, led by founder and CEO Mike Sinyard, has continued to create and introduce cutting-edge bicycle products such as lightweight helmets, physician-designed bicycle seats, a three-spoke wheel designed to cut bike racers' times, and bike frames made of high-tech materials. A minority share in the company was acquired by Merida, the Taiwan-based bicycle manufacturer in 2001.

Innovate or Die!

Specialized Bicycle Component's rags to riches story of Mike Sinyard's turning his passion for bicycling into a successful international business might sound like a cliché, but it is the honest-to-goodness story of Specialized's humble beginnings. After graduating from San Jose State University in 1974, 24-year-old Mike Sinyard sold his van for $1500 and flew off to Europe on a bicycling tour. While traveling, Sinyard met up with a woman at a youth hostel in Milan. The woman he met was acquainted with some of Italy's manufacturers of classic touring and racing bikes and their components. He went to meet the manufacturers and was surprised to find that they were willing to allow him to sell their bicycle components in the U.S. Sinyard knew that high-end bicycle parts were in short supply in the U.S. and that these products would be "as valuable as jewelry to people back home who were really into bikes." He used the remainder of his trip money to purchase bicycle components. When he returned home, he found that his intuition had been sound and that selling the components was a snap. He drew up a hand-written catalog listing his wares and sold the entire stock to local bike-shop owners.

After his first success—Sinyard had managed to turn his initial purchase of $1,100 worth of bike parts into $1,300—he found that the bike-shop owners were hungry for more. His lack of capital presented him with a problem, purchasing the parts up front was not an option with his current state of finance. Sinyard's answer to this conundrum was to persuade his bike shop customers to pay for their orders in advance. The shop owners agreed and Specialized was born. A few years of successful importing of bicycling parts gave Sinyard the taste for the bike business, and he decided that it was time for Specialized to manufacture its own products. In 1976, Specialized introduced its first home-grown bicycle component, a tire designed for the touring market. The years 1978 and 1979 were marked with Specialized's production of the first foldable clincher tire—the TURBO (with Kevlar bead) and the introduction of Specialized's first bicycles, the ALLEZ (road racing), and Sequoia (touring frames).

In 1981, Specialized changed the way that the world rode and thought about biking when they introduced mountain bikes to the general public. The bike Specialized sold was called the StumpJumper, and it revolutionized biking by moving the bicycle off of paved roads and into the great and uneven outdoors. The bike was a hybrid of durable bikes Sinyard rode in his childhood and the lightweight 10-speeds of his adolescence. The StumpJumper was advertised as the "bike for all reasons" and introduced the excitement and comfort of All-Terrain Bicycles

Company Perspectives:

At Specialized, building bikes isn't a job. It's a full-bore, hardcore religion. A religion that's helped us evolve as a company and as riders over the last 20 years. To some, our obsession may seem a little sick in the head. But then, those people probably don't ride. They don't understand that, to be the best at something, you need to be a fanatic. And believe us, there's plenty of those wandering around our hallways. People like our product designers, who pursue innovations like they were well-hidden single tracks. Or the masochistic group down in R&D, who probably have more scar tissue than the entire NHL combined. Even our founder, Mike Sinyard, has been known to cancel meetings just so he could spend more time on the trail. Weird? Not to us. We started Specialized for two major reasons: Number one: We love the sport. Number two: We want to build products that help people like you enjoy the sport as much as we do. Period.

(ATBs). The fat-tired and lightweight, 15-gear StumpJumper was so novel a product that the Smithsonian Institute had an original model placed in their museum. Specialized's 1981 production of 500 StumpJumper bicycles sold out quickly, and before long other high-volume bicycle manufacturers began to design and produce their own mountain bike models for the next model year.

Specialized's practice of selling their products exclusively in bike shops created a loyalty between the shops and Specialized. The shops knew and trusted Specialized's products and consistently recommended their products to customers. This close-knit relationship has served Specialized well. In the competitive bike market it is important that salespeople know and trust a company's product because when a customer enters a store they can easily be swayed from one product to another.

Moving on Up

Specialized grew quickly in the seven years after it was founded, and, in 1982, the company moved out of its warehouse in San Jose and into a much larger Morgan Hill space. The Morgan Hill site had 60,000 square feet and was surrounded by miles of trails perfect for Specialized's staff of biking enthusiasts. Specialized blazed new trails in 1983 with the creation of the world's first mountain bike racing team. Specialized's teams have been a great success, with team members and captains often winning competitions on Specialized products. Specialized's professional bikers test ride the company's equipment before it is released for sale to the public. The company's track record of releasing the professionally tested products within one year of testing works to their advantage as customers crave and appreciate the opportunity to ride the most technologically advanced products possible.

Specialized's founder and CEO Mike Sinyard's special contribution to the sport of mountain biking was honored in 1998 when he was inducted into the Mountain Bike Hall of Fame. During this year, Specialized released a few notable products—including the first affordable carbon fiber mountain bike, the

StumpJumper Epic and the Body Geometry bike seat. The Body Geometry bike seat was designed in response to growing concern that bicycling was linked to male impotence. The possibility of male impotence being liked to bicycling was not news to many long-distance cyclists, and Specialized was working on a solution when the scientific study, written by Dr. Irwin Goldstein asserting the impotence connection, was released. Specialized's Body Geometry seat was designed by a physician and intended to shift the bulk of the rider's weight from the perineal area to the seat. Cycling enthusiasts and recreational riders alike made the switch from the traditional seat to the new design.

In 1989, Specialized once again made tracks where other bike companies had not dared venture. In a deal with Duralcan Corp., a San Diego-based aluminum fabricator, Specialized ordered 5,000 metal-matrix composite bicycle rims. Sinyard noted that the new rims are a ''major break-through in the industry'' and other bicycle manufacturers agreed. Michael D. Milton of Huffy Corp.'s Bicycle division (a competitor of Specialized) noted that Huffy had experimented with the metal-matrix composites but faced problems and ended their research. The metal-matrix rims made their debut mounted on Specialized mountain bikes and were also sold in the aftermarket (in bike shops for individual purchase). The making of a metal-matrix rim was an international affair with companies in the United States, England, and France working on different aspects of its production. The first metal-matrix rim was introduced in 1990, and Specialized's global reach expanded when it opened Specialized Canada and Europe.

A New Kind of Advertising

An advertising campaign that Specialized launched in 1990, featuring Soviet leader Mikhail Gorbachev, attracted a significant amount of attention to the company and characterized their advertising methods to be almost as revolutionary as their bicycling technology. Specialized purchased a photo of Mr. Gorbachev and altered it so that Gorbachev was pictured on a bicycle wearing the bicycling uniform of the Soviet national team, his famous mole was altered to resemble the Specialized symbol, and he was holding a Specialized racing helmet. The caption of the photo read, ''Mr. Gorbachev is riding a Specialized 'Sirrus.''' The company chose to use Gorbachev's image for a multitude of reasons, including the fact that the Russian National Team was, at the time of the advertisement, wearing Specialized helmets when they raced. Some members of the advertising community felt that the ad was breaking the spirit of privacy laws and was a violation of advertising ethics. The company continued to use the advertisement as they had planned and characteristically spun the ad in a press release to be a declaration of Specialized ''setting the standard for ads in the 1990s and creating a new brand of advertising for the cycling industry: advertising with an attitude; advertising with an edge.''

Bumpy Road Ahead

The early 1990s were a hard time for the mountain biking industry. The popularity of the bikes attracted a lot of competition so that companies were flooding the market with mountain bikes while at the same time sales were flat or in decline. Specialized faced management and production problems and floundered in the now competitive market. The other bicycling

Key Dates:

1974: Specialized is founded by Mike Sinyard.
1976: Specializes produces and sells their first self-made product, a tire designed for the touring market.
1981: Specialized introduces the StumpJumper, the first mountain bike sold to the general public.
1982: Specialized moves from its small warehouse space in San Jose to a 60,000 square foot space in Morgan Hill.
1989: Specialized introduces the composite wheel, a joint venture with DuPont.
1990: Specialized introduces M2 metal-matrix composite technology into bicycles for the first time.
1995: Specialized announces plans to distribute bicycles and accessories to sporting goods dealers and discount retails under the Full Force brand.
1996: Specialized discontinues the Full Force brand.
2001: Merida, a Taiwan-based bicycle manufacturer, acquires a minority share of Specialized Bicycles.

companies (like Trek, Cannondale, and Schwinn-Scott) had begun innovating as quickly as Specialized had been, and Specialized was left in the dust of these more established companies. Specialized's special relationship with dealer-customers slipped when salespeople grew lax: some bike shops did not receive new bike models until a year after the models had been announced and introduced.

Many of Specialized's competitors had begun selling low-end mountain bikes in sporting goods chain stores. Specialized saw the potential to boost its sales, and in 1995 announced that they, too, would begin selling bikes to sporting goods stores and discount retailers, but that they would be selling bikes under the Full Force brand.

Specialized's decision to expand their retail channel beyond bike shops was met with skepticism from Specialized dealers. Many bike shop owners saw this move as a serious mistake. It was easy for Specialized's customer-dealers to see the move as a breach of their trust and loyalty—they had been loyally selling Specialized's products only to have their customers stolen from them by discount sports stores. Sinyard reasoned that the customers who purchased bikes at the discount stores were customers who would not have ventured into specialty bike shops, and he hoped to hook them on the purchase of the bike in the discount store, and then reel them into the specialty bike shops to purchase additional Specialized parts.

Some dealers were extremely angry at Specialized's move, but most dealers took the news in stride and waited to see what would happen. Two years after Specialized distributed their low-end Full Force line, they discontinued it. Sinyard, in what some people believed to be a mark of his graduation into a mature businessman, wrote a formal letter of apology to all Specialized dealers.

Specialized followed up their attempt to distribute low-end bikes by releasing a slew of top-of-the-line bike products, including 7-ounce to 9½-ounce helmets, concept bicycles, and

the Ultralight Composite Wheel designed and produced with Dupont. The Ultralight Composite Wheel had a 1 mph advantage over a conventional wire spoke wheel tested at 30 mph. Specialized was so sure of their new wheel's superiority, that they issued a $5,000 challenge to any manufacturer who could prove their wheel to be more aerodynamic.

Although competition was fierce and internal company organization faced problems, low U.S. bike sales also had a hand in Specialized's trouble in the early 1990's. Ironically, the downturn in bike sales might have been the fault of Specialized's earlier success; "As it turned out, mountain bikes were a catalyst for all kinds of outdoor activities," said Specialized's marketing director Chris Murphy. "Once people got outdoors, they discovered lots of new things they wanted to do."

Innovative Partnerships

Specialized's success moving into the late 1990s had something to do with the formation of innovative partnerships with popular brands. Mountain Dew and Specialized joined forces when Mountain Dew signed on to sponsor the Mountain Dew Specialized Team and to sponsor the Specialized BMX program. With the increased support and sponsorship of Mountain Dew, Specialized began a national BMX project in inner cities. Specialized renovated deteriorated parks and constructed permanent fixtures for kids to use for riding BMX, skateboarding, and inline skating in New York, Los Angeles, Chicago, and Miami. Specialized's partnership with Subaru was equally community-minded. Subaru helped to support some of Specialized's grass roots programs including Friends o' Trails, which teaches off-road biking. While many other bike and car companies joined forces and offered buy-a-car-get-a-bike deals, Specialized and Subaru's deal did not include a similar promotion.

In 1996, in a strange twist of fate, one of Specialized's bicycles made the leap from backcountry trails to museum galleries. A San Francisco gallery's exhibit, entitled "Wild Design: Design for the Wild," showcased the artful design of many modern sporting goods. A Specialized mountain bike, made from lightweight aluminum typically used in airplanes, caught the curator's eye and was included in the display shown in both San Francisco and Minneapolis, Minnesota.

World Ride Web

Building a highly functional and dynamic Web site was a top priority for Specialized. Because their products were sold primarily out of their catalog and through bike shops, the company saw the Web as a prime opportunity to build brand awareness and cultivate even deeper customer loyalty. When a customer sends e-mail to the site, they do not receive a blanket response, said global E-marketing manager Mike Regan, instead they get a response with the name of a Specialized employee attached so the "customer has a clear sense that they're dealing with an individual who cares about their needs."

Specialized Sells Minority Share

In June 2001, Merida—the second-largest bicycle manufacturer in the world—acquired a minority share of Specialized. It was not revealed exactly what percentage of the company had

448   **Specialized Bicycle Components Inc.**

been sold. Sinyard stated that Specialized needed the capital to meet the company's long-term goals to increase sales efforts, increase its service to specialty retailers, continue its dedicated attention to research and development, and to expand further into Europe. Specialized's relationship with Merida continued what was already a strong bond between the manufacturer and supplier. Although Sinyard claimed that Specialized would continue to use all of its suppliers, many people in the industry believed that suppliers external of Merida would be used only for products that Merida had no interest in producing.

Principal Subsidiaries

Specialized Central Europe, Inc.; Specialized Italy, Inc.; Specialized UK, Inc.; Specialized Canada, Inc.

Principal Competitors

Giant Manufacturing Co., Ltd; Trek Bicycle Corporation; Pacific Cycle, LLC.

Further Reading

Abbe, Mary, "Design is a Sporting Proposition: Exhibit Shows the Artful Ways that Sporting Goods are Taking," *Star Tribune*, September 14, 1996, p. 09E.

"Cycling and Impotence: New Seats are Among the Potential Solutions," *The Seattle Times*, September 13, 1998, p. L4.

Barrier, Michael, "Wheels of Change in Bicycle Retailing," *Nation's Business*, February 1996, p. 40.

Barry, David, "But Will Gorbachev Make Wheaties Box?," *The Business Journal*, February 19, 1990, v.7, p.1.

Gelsi, Steve, "Subaru Outback onto Slopes, Trails," *Brandweek*, October 7, 1996, p. 4.

Holzinger, Albert G., "A Cyclist Who is Riding High," *Nation's Business*, August 1992, p.16.

Irving, Robert R., "Metal-Matrix Composite Rims Ordered by Specialized Bicycle," *Metalworking News*, December 19, 1998, p.1.

Liebmann, Lenny, "E-Service at Hub on Online Push," *InformationWeek*, September 27, 1999, p. 373.

Mazzante, Lou, "Specialized, Merida Ink Major Deal," *Bicycle Retailer and Industry News*, July 1, 2001, p.1.

"Mountain-Bike Innovator Now Rolling with the Punches Specialized has Matured with Founder," *The Seattle Times*, December 26, 1996, p. D1.

"Reinventing the Wheel: Bicycle Makers," *The Economist* (US), August 1, 1992, p.61.

Sani, Mark, "Spinning Wheels," *Sporting Goods Business*, November 1995, p.38.

—Tammy Weisberger

The Stash Tea Company

7204 S.W. Durham Road Suite 200
Tigard, Oregon 97224
U.S.A.
Telephone: (503) 684-4482
Toll Free: (800) 547-1514
Fax: (503) 684-4424
Web site: http://www.stashtea.com

Wholly Owned Subsidiary of Yamamotoyama of America
Incorporated: 1972
Employees: 50 (2002 est.)
Sales: $11.8 million (2002 est.)
NAIC: 311920 Coffee and Tea Manufacturing; 312111
    Soft Drink Manufacturing

The Stash Tea Company (also know as the Universal Tea Co., Inc.) ranks among the top five specialty tea companies in the United States, offering a complete line of specialty teas: traditional black teas, flavored and spiced teas, herbal teas, green teas, organic teas, rare and exotic teas, and specialty iced teas. The company's specialty-tea mail-order business is the largest in the United States, based on an extensive mail order catalog that offers more than 200 blends of tea, tea accessories, tea gifts, and savory baked delicacies and sweets (gourmet cookies, scones, honeysticks, Stash bread mix, jam, and biscotti). Stash Tea products are also available worldwide, through foodservice, grocery stores, tea and coffee shops, club stores, mass merchandisers, natural foods stores, and the Internet. Headquartered in Tigard, Oregon, the company is privately owned by the U.S.-based subsidiary of Yamamotoyama Co., Ltd., a 300-year-old tea company based in Tokyo, Japan.

Early Years: 1970s to Mid-1980s

In 1972, Steve Lee, Dave Leger, and Steve Smith founded The Stash Tea Company in suburban Portland with $7,000 and a Victorian house basement full of herbs, spices, teas, and dreams. Named for the special reserve of precious teas that many sea captains kept for their personal use aboard ship, the fledgling company quickly became a viable purveyor of fine teas. With Lee's mail-order marketing background with Sears, Roebuck and Co., Leger's work with Frito-Lay, and Smith's management experience at nearby Sunshine Natural Foods, the business took off during its first year, making $50,000 selling bulk herbs and spices and loose teas to natural foods stores. The company even began to work directly with Oregon mint farmers to grow and cultivate Oregon peppermint, later recognized by the tea industry to be the world's best. By 1974, the company reaped $290,000 in revenue.

By 1975, the company began marketing tea bags and a complete line of traditional, specialty blend, and herbal teas to restaurants and through mail-order catalog. Then the company dropped the wholesale, bulk aspect of the business and concentrated almost exclusively on restaurants and other segments of the food service industry. To appeal to the college food service market, for example, the company devised a promotion, which offered a European vacation to the food service supervisor who sold the most Stash tea. Restaurants sales soon became the company's bread and butter, at one point accounting for 80 percent of total sales. Success in the restaurant business allowed Stash Tea to later break into other markets, including grocery stores and international sales.

In 1977, a worldwide coffee shortage made coffee less affordable, causing many consumers to switch to tea. However, when Stash Tea's Pennsylvania-based packager could not keep up with the new surge in tea demand, Stash began to look for a packager on the West Coast. They partnered with Yamamoto of America, based in Los Angeles, which was the United States' arm of Japan's Yamamotoyama Co., Ltd., one of the oldest tea companies in the world (established in 1690). Alongside the green teas, seaweed, and dried enoki mushrooms packaged under the Yamamotoyama brand, the Japanese company packaged tea leaves imported from Ceylon, China, Indonesia, Sri Lanka, and Kenya for Stash Tea.

The demand for tea was not completely dependent on the fluctuations of the world's coffee supply, however. Since the 1950s (for at least 35 years, according to the Tea Council of the U.S.A.), tea imports had been steadily increasing by about 4 percent each year. Stash was well positioned to ride the crest of that wave. The tea industry's growth and Stash Tea's increasing success turned out to be an irresistible investment opportunity for Yamamotoyama. In 1979, Yamamotoyama acquired 25 percent of Stash for only $112,000. Two years later, when another Stash shareholder wanted to sell out, Yamamotoyama bought an additional stake for $120,000, which brought the Japanese company's stake in Stash Tea to 48 percent. That left the company with only a handful of shareholders, including Yamamotoyama (48 percent), Lee (about 23 percent), Leger (about 23 percent), and Barbara Longaker, who was a sister of a friend of Lee's (about 6 percent).

Growing Pains: Mid-1980s to Early 1990s

In 1987, the U.S. tea market crossed the billion-dollar threshold for the first time, when per-capita brewing reached 1.54 pounds. Although iced tea accounted for 75 percent of total sales, herbal teas, at about 4 percent of the market share at the time, was the most rapidly growing segment of the industry. By this time, Stash Tea's employee count had grown to 26. Stash Tea's 1987 restaurant sales accounted for about 50 percent of total sales, with grocery stores and international sales becoming a larger part of the sales picture. Still, restaurant sales had increased dramatically, in large part due to an 18-month-old association with the makers of the Sweet 'N Low sugar substitute, Sugar Foods Corp. Sugar Foods sold and shipped Stash Tea to food service distributors throughout the United States, mainly on the East Coast. The relationship easily doubled the number of distributors carrying Stash Tea products. During this time, Stash Tea went well beyond its limited international sales presence in Canada by securing sales in Japan, New Zealand, Australia, and Norway.

To gain even more customers, and keeping marketing costs low, Stash Tea established a marketing strategy that became quite successful. Instead of sending mass mailings to an unsuspecting public, the company opted to simply print a simple invitation on each tea bag envelope: "Send for our Stash Tea catalog of premium teas, gifts and accessories. P.O. Box 610R Portland, OR 97207." According to Susan McIntyre, director of Stash's mail-order division, "The sad fact is that most names on any list wouldn't be interested in your product or won't be interested today. In package-based solicitation, your effort's placed directly in the hands of prospects who have selected themselves for interest in your product and have done so today. Also, the waste of scatter-shot solicitation is eliminated."

This low-cost advertising made it possible for the company to aggregate an extensive database of customer data, and a long mailing list that would become the envy of the industry. By 1987, for example, the company already had more than 100,000 customers on their mailing list, 20 percent of whom made an average $25 purchase. The mailing list had continued to grow at a healthy pace, with the company receiving about 2,000 catalog requests per month. Once someone bought a Stash Tea product, the company used gifts, discounts, and, eventually, free shipping to create a loyal customer. Although mail orders account for only 6 percent of Stash tea sales and contribute just 10 percent of total revenues, they represent 35 percent of the company's profits. Stash Tea's later marketing efforts were also successful and savvy, with a form of "added-value" advertising. The company adopted a foster child in India, named Kenda, and began featuring photos and letters from her in the mail order catalog.

The early 1990s were looking good for Stash Tea. The company was already considered the second largest purveyor of specialty teas in the United States, after Bigelow. By 1991, Stash Tea's offerings had grown to 30 different tea blends, including "Earl Grey," "Ruby Mist," "Orange Spice," "Friendship," "Lapsang-Souchong," and "Oolong." In 1992, industry-wide sales of herbal tea bags in supermarkets increased by 5 percent. However, the Stash Tea-Yamamotoyama relationship became more entwined when Stash began borrowing money from the larger, more successful Japanese company to help ease some growing pains. Even though Stash Tea had some difficulty making payments, Yamamotoyama restructured the debt several times, often loaning Stash Tea even more money during the process. From the mid-1980s, Stash was paying about $20,000 a month in principle and interest to Yamamotoyama. In 1991, after Stash Tea lost about $250,000 for its expansion efforts into the Eastern U.S., and once West One Bank of Oregon demanded repayment on a $500,000 line of credit, Yamamotoyama moved to acquire the remaining shares of Stash Tea, much to the dismay of Stash Tea's founders.

Lee and Leger were able to stave off the immediate acquisition by Yamamotoyama with a compromise: Stash Tea had 11 months to find another buyer who would agree to pay $1,800 per share, or a total of $3.6 million. They found two interested parties who would partner together in a bid against Yamamotoyama: Windsor, Connecticut-based Redco Foods, a company Stash Tea had had a more amicable relationship with in a previous joint venture, and Endeavor Capital, a Portland merchant banking firm. After some intense counter-bidding between Yamamotoyama and the newly formed Redco-Endeavor partnership, Yamamotoyama resorted to a secret meeting with Longaker, who finally agreed to sell her remaining shares. She had also convinced the Japanese company to buy the remaining minority shareholders' stock for $3,200 per share, or $6.4 million. The deal closed in the summer of 1993. By that time, the Tigard-based tea company was already a $10-million-a-year operation. Lee left the company a millionaire, and within the next year, without the restraint of a non-compete agreement, he partnered with two other entrepreneurs to found another tea company, Tazo Tea Company, which was later bought by Starbucks.

Post-Takeover Successes: Mid- to Late-1990s

Throughout the 1990s, sales in the specialty tea market had doubled, from about $1.8 billion in 1990 to $4.5 billion by the end of 1997. Specialty black and herbal teas accounted for about 25 percent of the tea market. According to Stash Tea spokesperson Catharine Trapasso, the company's sales had more than doubled during 1992 to 1997. By early 1997, the company's sales broke down into three main categories: mail order (24 percent), foodservice (14 to 15 percent), and the retail trade (60 to 61 percent).

In 1993, Stash Tea created a bed and breakfast promotion, which became a very popular aspect of its business. The company teamed up with more than 1,000 bed and breakfast inns throughout the United States to offer consumers a great deal: when they pay for one night at a participating inn, they could stay a second night for free. In exchange, participating inns received a sampler box of tea and could order refills at a discount. For consumers to receive a directory of participating inns and a certificate for one free night, they have to send in three Stash Tea UPC codes, a check for $2.95, and a completed offer form. By 1996, the company averaged 2,000 certificate requests per month via the catalog, retail, and new Web site.

In 1995, The Stash Tea Web site debuted on the Internet, and was quickly recognized as a valuable source of information about tea. Not only did the Web site function as another way to do business, but it also shared entertaining and education information about tea in general. The site offered a history of tea, descriptive Stash Tea product information, an online version of its popular print catalog, tea trivia and quotes, clips from its humorous radio campaign, and a directory of bed and breakfast inns for its "free night at a bed and breakfast inn" promotion. The Stash Tea Web site was also very accessible, as it was fully indexed and searchable, and the home page could be translated from English into 13 other languages. Since its debut, an average of 1,000 people have visited the site each month. The Stash Tea Web site was rated among the top 5 percent of all Web sites in a review conducted by Point Survey, a guide referred to as the Zagats guide to the World Wide Web. Also in 1995, the company's first radio commercial was chosen as the world's best radio commercial for 1995 in the Non-Alcoholic Beverages category at the London International Awards competition.

By 1996, Stash Tea sold about 80 different blends of tea. In response to consumers' quickly and ever-evolving palates, Stash Tea introduced several new lines of exotic and unusual teas in attractive, descriptive packaging, offering new teas available loose or in teabags. One example is the "Exotica"

line, which features nine exquisite teas including champagne "Oolong," pure golden-tipped "Darjeeling," "Silver Jasmine," rare "China White," "Ceylon Estate Earl Grey," "Dragonwell Green Tea," robust "Assam Breakfast," fragrant "Osmanthus," an "Exotic Reserve" blend, and a sampler collection. The tea company also began selling Yamamotoyama teas, introducing to Stash Tea customers a new world of Japanese and Chinese teas, such as "Genmai Tea," "Kukicha Tea," "Chrysanthemum Tea," and "Special Occasion Green Tea." Stash Tea also introduced a new line of medicinal teas, to appeal to consumers interested in the increasingly popular field of naturopathic medicine. With names like "Sharpness," "Sleep," "Well," and "Stress Relief Tea," these new teas featured ingredients such as ginseng and echinacea promising medicinal benefits. A premium organic line of teas was also introduced in the late 1990s.

2000 and Beyond

By the start of the new millennium, Stash Tea was one of the more successful tea companies in the industry, and certain trends seemed to indicate that the company could stay successful for some time to come. Consumer demand for tea continued to increase, while demand for coffee generally declined. From 1995 to 2000, the overall retail coffee category declined in sales from about $4 billion to $3.5 billion, while sales of tea bags and loose leaf teas grew from about $637 million to $751 million, according to an industry overview report published in the September 2000 issue of *Beverage Industry*. Although sales in black tea remained strong from 1995 to 2000, the true leaders in the tea industry segment were chai teas, herbal teas, and green teas—segments in which Stash Tea was already quite successful.

In response to rising consumer demand for loose teas, the company had begun offering loose versions of some of its popular teas in handy, resealable, nitrogen-flushed pouches. By 2000, Stash Tea's offerings had grown to more than 200 varieties and blends. During 2000 to 2002, the company introduced several more teas, including a "Teas of India" line, which won "Best of Show" in the Beverage Packaging Global Design Awards in 2000, and other teas, including "Ti Kuan Yin Deluxe Oolong," "Organic Pinhead Gunpowder," "Energy Tea with Mate and Guarana," "Wild Lychee White Tea," "Monkey King Jasmine," "Chocolate Peppermint," and "Triple Ginseng."

Principal Competitors

The Hain-Celestial Group, Inc.; Nestlé; R.C. Bigelow; R. Twining and Company, Ltd.; Reily Foods Company; Starbucks; Tazo Tea Company; Tetley GB Ltd.; Unilever.

Further Reading

Altman, Randy, "Defining Specialty Tea," *Tea & Coffee Trade Journal*, April 20, 2001, p. 125.

"Coffee and Tea Run Hot and Cold," *Beverage Industry*, September 2000, pp. NP24–NP25.

Drummer, Randyl, "Yamamotoyama of America Giant Tea Maker is Quietly Stashed Away in Pomona," *The Business Press*, May 18, 1998, p. 15.

Cirillo, Joan, "Chai Becomes More People's Cup of Tea," *The Baltimore Sun*, August 16, 1995, p. 1E.

——, "Using Tea Leaves to Flavor Foods Keeps Them Out of Hot Water," *The Baltimore Sun*, December 29, 1993, p. 8E.

Durbin, Barbara, "Stash's Specialty Tea Sales Heat Up in 5 Years," *The Portland Oregonian*, February 22, 2000, p. FD2.

Flaccus, Gillian, "Tea Company Finds Success with Starbucks," *Associated Press Newswires*, April 7, 2001, http://www.ap.org.

"A Fresh Cup," *Beverage Industry*, October 2001, pp. 14–15.

Friedman, Martin, "Tea Market Quietly Simmers," *AdWeek*, September 28, 1987.

Hogue, Kendra, "Teamakers Stash Away a Cupful of Revenue," *Business Journal-Portland*, May 18, 1987, p. 1.

Kiley, Kathleen, "B&B Promotion Stirs Up Stash," *Catalog Age*, May 1996, p. 7.

Levenson, Lisa, "Tea for the Masses," *The Portland Oregonian*, June 29, 1997, p. C1.

Levine, Michael, "A Stash of Tea to Please Your Palette," *Tea & Coffee Trade Journal*, March 1997, p. 54.

Manning, Jeff, "Takeover in a Teapot: The Zen Battle Over Stash Tea," *Business Journal-Portland*, May 13, 1994, p. 1.

McIntyre, Susan, "Added-Value Advertising for the '90s," *Direct Marketing*, December 1991, p. 20.

McMath, Robert, "Whether Regular or Herbal, It's Increasingly Time for Tea," *Brandweek*, May 31, 1993, p. 36.

Nicholas, Jonathan, "Tea for Two (or 200 million) from Tigard," *The Portland Oregonion*, February 26, 1990, p. 1.

Perry, Sara, "He's Got Tea tasting Down to a T," *The Portland Oregonian*, January 14, 1993, p. L14.

"Predictions from a Group of Industry Experts on Tea Industry Trends in 1997," *A World of Tea Web Site*, April 16, 1998, http://www.stashtea.com.

Savini, Gloria, "Something's Brewing in Oregon," *Direct Marketing*, January 1987, p. 84.

"Selling by Mail Suits This Company to a Tea," *Sales & Marketing Management*, January 1991, p. 21.

Sturdivant, Shea, "Tea Trends," *Tea & Coffee Trade Journal*, October 1997, p. 14

"Surfing for Tea," *Direct Marketing*, January 1996, p. 34.

"Tea Times: International Tea Yearbook 1994," *World Coffee & Tea*, March 1995.

"A World of Tea," *Link-Up*, July 2001, p. 30.

—Heidi Wrightsman

SUPERVALU

Supervalu Inc.

11840 Valley View Road
Eden Prairie, Minnesota 55344-3691
U.S.A.
Telephone: (952) 828-4000
Fax: (952) 828-8998
Web site: http://www.supervalu.com

Public Company
Incorporated: 1926 as Winston & Newell Company
Employees: 57,800 (2002)
Sales: $20.98 billion (2002)
Stock Exchanges: New York
Ticker Symbol: SVU
NAIC: 445110 Supermarkets and Other Grocery (except
   Convenience) Stores; 446110 Pharmacies and Drug
   Stores

Minnesota-based Supervalu Inc. is the leading grocery wholesaler in the United States, supplying products to more than 4,200 stores—regional and national chain supermarkets, corporate owned and licensed retail locations, mass merchandisers, and e-tailers—in 48 states and abroad. The company also offers retailers a variety of business support services, including consumer and market research; private labeling; personnel training; accounting; insurance brokerage and services; store site selection, construction and design; category management; and business planning. Major clients include Bruno's, Dahl's, Jewel, Kroger, and SuperTarget. Supervalu is also the 11th largest food retailer in the United States, running more than 1,000 retail stores across 36 states, including Save-A-Lot, bigg's, Cub Foods, Shop'n Save, Scott's, Shoppers Food Warehouse, Metro, Farm Fresh, and Hornbacker's. In addition, Supervalu has franchise and licensing agreements for stores operated by others companies, including 55 Cub Foods and 764 Save-A-Lot stores.

Late 1800s to Early 1900s:
Minneapolis Wholesaler Roots

Supervalu's origins lie in the 1871 merger of the Minneapolis wholesale grocery firms B.S. Bull and Company and Newell and Harrison Company. The new Newell and Harrison existed for only three years; in 1874 George R. Newell bought out his partners and renamed the company George R. Newell Company.

Meanwhile, one of Newell's former partners, Hugh G. Harrison, formed a wholesaling venture called H.G. Harrison Company in 1879. After a series of reorganizations (including Harrison's sale of his interest), this company became Winston, Harper, Fisher Company in 1903, headed by F.G. Winston, a Minneapolis railroad contractor; J.L. Harper, a merchandiser; and E.J. Fisher, a financier. In 1916, Harrison's grandson, Perry Harrison, joined Winston, Harper, Fisher as vice-president and co-owner.

In 1926, George R. Newell Company and Winston, Harper, Fisher Company merged to form Winston & Newell Company, with Perry Harrison and L.B. Newell, Winston's son-in-law, as principal shareholders. Winston & Newell was incorporated in 1926 in response to the threat that independent retailers faced from the emerging grocery store chains that began developing in the 1920s. Winston & Newell hoped to improve services to these independent retailers so they could withstand the competitive impact of the chain stores. At the time of its creation, Winston & Newell was serving some 5,000 small grocery stores and had sales of $6 million—making it the largest grocery wholesaler in the Midwest.

With Minnesotan Thomas G. Harrison at its helm, Winston & Newell became one of the first wholesale distributors in the nation to join the new Independent Grocers Alliance (IGA). Harrison, the son of Perry Harrison, had joined Winston, Harper, Fisher Company in 1919 as an assistant sales manager. He successively became assistant treasurer and executive vice-president, directing the operations of Winston & Newell and later Super Valu in a variety of executive positions from 1926 until his retirement as CEO in 1958.

Harrison, in guiding the company through the Great Depression, was primarily responsible for introducing many practices that changed the way in which grocery stores conducted business. Cash-and-carry and self-service shopping, almost unheard of at the time, were two of his innovations at Winston & Newell. He broke with tradition again when he stopped using a pricing structure with an arbitrary markup and began charging instead

Company Perspectives:

The philosophy of Supervalu companies will always be a "total commitment to serving customers more effectively than anyone else could serve them." We believe the pursuit of this meaningful goal is the continuing and overriding responsibility from which every corporate activity must evolve. We value today's success as merely the beginning of a constantly expanding level of achievement.

We believe that customers are most knowledgeable, skilled, and capable buyers who will always seek out and do business with that supplier which most effectively serves their wants and needs.

Therefore, by serving our customers more effectively than anyone else could serve them, and by efficiently managing our business with highly skilled and dedicated people, we are confident that we shall continue to increase Supervalu's sales and share of market. We believe that this philosophy and practice will result in continuing profitable growth for Supervalu and provide security and opportunity for our many thousands of loyal employees.

the manufacturer's price plus a percentage fee that declined with volume. This practice gave the company impressive cumulative profits. During the 20-year period from 1942 to 1962, *Fortune* reported that the company's sales volume increased from about $10 million to more than $300 million.

Early 1940s to 1960s: Formation of Voluntary Associations

It was during World War II that Winston & Newell began the march to becoming Supervalu and attaining its position as the world's largest food wholesaler and distributor. Although no acquisitions were made during the 1940s, in 1942 the company ended its affiliation with IGA and formed its own association, known in the industry as a "voluntary." Winston & Newell offered independent retailers services such as food processing and packaging, preparation of advertising for individual store use in local newspaper advertising, and store-planning assistance, in addition to supplying most of the merchandise sold. This voluntary association introduced the Super Valu name and operated independently from the wholesale business. Super Valu and another voluntary association called U-Save (which was also formed under the auspices of Winston & Newell) were familiar to grocers in Iowa, Minnesota, and North Dakota. By 1942 the company had wholesale sales of $10 million and some 400 stores belonged to its wholesale-retail team.

In 1954 Winston & Newell Company changed its name to Super Valu Stores Inc. in order to clarify the connection between itself and the voluntary association. During the 1950s Super Valu began to grow by acquiring other voluntary associations. In 1955 it purchased Joannes Brothers of Green Bay, Wisconsin, a firm that had begun serving stores in northern Michigan and northeastern Wisconsin in the 1870s. Joannes Brothers became Super Valu's Green Bay Division. In 1958 Russell W. Byerly became president of Super Valu. Byerly, a North Dakota native who joined Winston & Newell in 1932 as a

bookkeeper, served as president until 1964 and later was chairman of the board and chief executive officer.

Series of Acquisitions in the 1960s

Acquisition followed acquisition during the 1960s as Super Valu expanded throughout the Midwest. In 1961 Super Valu moved into the Ohio Valley with the purchase of the Eavey Company, one of the nation's oldest food wholesale distributors. In 1963 the company acquired the J.M. Jones Company of Champaign-Urbana, Illinois, and the Food Marketing Corporation of Fort Wayne, Indiana. Each of these companies could trace its beginnings to the early days of the grocery business. Jones began as a general store and developed into a large wholesale business; Food Marketing dated back to the early 1800s, as Bursley & Company and the Bluffton Grocery Company. The Food Marketing acquisition also brought Super Valu into the institutional market. After the acquisition, these two companies were operated as autonomous divisions in a company that historically gave its divisions and stores as much free rein as possible.

In 1964 Super Valu expanded its area of operation outside the Midwest by acquiring Chastain-Roberts Company, which had begun in 1933 as a wholesale flour and feed company, and the McDonald Glass Grocery Company, Inc. of Anniston, Alabama. These acquisitions formed the basis for Super Valu's Anniston Division.

In 1965 Super Valu acquired the Lewis Grocer Company of Indianola, Mississippi. The Lewis Grocer Company was founded by Morris Lewis, Sr., in 1895 and eventually became a multimillion-dollar wholesale grocer, branching out later into the retail grocery business.

The 1960s were a growth period for Super Valu in ways other than acquisition. The company expanded its retail support services to include accounting, efficiency studies, budget counseling, and store format and design advice. In 1962 Super Valu established Planmark, a department that offered engineering, architectural, and design services to independent retailers, subsidiaries, and corporate stores. Planmark became a division in 1975. With Studio 70, its commercial design arm, Planmark used computer-assisted design to analyze and develop plans for construction, expansion, or remodeling. This innovation, implemented in the recessionary years of the late 1970s, allowed Super Valu retailers to take a project from planning to opening faster than their competition. Super Valu also began providing financial assistance for retailers building new stores, bankrolling some 500 stores in a three-year period in the 1960s. Super Valu also signed leases on its retailers' behalf, allowing them to locate in prime space in shopping centers and other locations.

In 1968 Preferred Products, Inc. (PPI) was incorporated as a subsidiary of Super Valu to develop its private label program. A food packaging and processing division, it was started in the 1920s as a department of Winston & Newell.

Super Valu also formed an insurance agency—Risk Planners, Inc.—in 1969. This wholly owned subsidiary began by providing insurance on retail property for the company and its retail affiliates. Tailored specifically to the needs of retailers, its products have expanded to include all types of insurance for

Key Dates:

1871: Minneapolis wholesale grocery firms—B.S. Bull and Company, and Newell and Harrison Company—merge to form the early forerunner to Supervalu.

1926: Earnings reach $6 million. The company incorporates as Winston & Newell Company.

1954: The company changes its name to Super Valu Stores, Inc.

1955–88: The company acquires 12 regional food wholesalers, primarily in the Midwest, Southeast, and Northwest.

1962: Sales surpass $300 million.

1971: With the acquisition of Shopko, the company begins major investments in the nonfood, general merchandise business.

1989: Supervalu opens its first hypermarket (a Cub Foods-ShopKo combination) in Cleveland, Ohio, and company sales reached $1.28 billion.

1992: The company changes its name to Supervalu Inc.

1999: Supervalu acquires Richfood Holdings, Inc., a leading Mid-Atlantic food distributor and retailer.

2000: Sales surpass $20 billion.

2002: Supervalu opens its 1,000th Save-A-Lot store, and is faced with an accounting scandal centering on its pharmaceutical business.

Super Valu and its stores and franchisees, as well as independent retailers' employees and families.

Diversified Operations in the 1970s

Diversification was the moving force at Super Valu in the 1970s, in part because the U.S. government in the late 1960s made it clear that it was not going to allow further consolidation of the food industry. Beginning with the 1971 acquisition of ShopKo, a general merchandise discount chain, Super Valu began what proved to be a highly profitable program of nonfood marketing operations. ShopKo, founded by James Ruben in Chicago in 1961, opened its first store in Green Bay, Wisconsin, in 1962. In 1971 Super Valu acquired Daytex, Inc., a textile goods company, but the venture proved unsuccessful and its assets were liquidated in 1976. Meanwhile, Super Valu sales surpassed $1 billion for the first time in 1972.

When Jack J. Crocker became chairman and CEO of Super Valu in 1973, he initiated another diversification venture, County Seat. A success story in its own right, County Seat opened its first store in 1973 selling casual apparel, including the complete Levi's jeans line. By 1977 there were 183 County Seat stores, and the chain's earnings were $8 million in that fiscal year. When it was sold for $71 million to Carson Pirie Scott and Company of Chicago in 1983, there were 269 stores in 33 states.

Crocker, a CPA who came to Super Valu from the presidency of the Oregon-based grocery and pharmacy chain Fred Meyer, Inc., also directed the company's continuing acquisition and expansion program. Very much a part of the trend toward consolidation in the food wholesale industry, Super Valu continued to purchase smaller food wholesalers, acquiring Pennsylvania-based Charley Brothers Company in 1977. Charley Brothers, which began as a retail grocery store in 1902 and moved into wholesaling in 1918, served Shop 'n Save stores and other independent retailers in Pennsylvania.

The advent of universal price codes and scanning equipment in the grocery business led to the introduction, in the mid-1970s, of Testmark, an independent research center providing store measurement data. This data had been available from Super Valu stores since 1965 and, during the period before Testmark was established, had been handled by Super Valu merchandising research, an internal department for clients who preferred not to use commercial research companies. In direct competition with these commercial research companies, Testmark, with Super Valu's backing, offered its customers the advantage of cooperation within the Super Valu network and with major chains and independents nationwide. Testmark's autonomy was enhanced by its Hopkins, Minnesota, location, separate from Super Valu's corporate headquarters.

Crocker's tenure at Super Valu was characterized by his success in running what was one of the better-capitalized and stronger wholesalers in the country and by the casual no-frills operation he ran. Company headquarters were in a warehouse, not a plush office. Crocker personally founded a professional soccer team, the Minnesota Kicks, in 1976. They, too, were a Crocker success story, becoming popular in their home territory.

Crocker's successes were apparent on the bottom line, as well. By fiscal 1978 earnings per share had increased approximately 50 percent since Crocker's first year with Super Valu, but, Crocker explained to *Financial World* in 1977, ''I don't think about profits very much. If you're doing things right, profits always follow.'' By the end of the 1970s Super Valu's sales were $2.9 billion.

Move into Retail Grocering with Acquisition of Cub Foods in 1980

Super Valu ushered in the 1980s with the acquisition of Cub Foods, a discount grocery store operation. Warehouse stores, with bare bones facilities and prices, were a phenomenon of the 1970s. Cub Foods was founded by the Hooley family, grocers since 1876 in Stillwater, Minnesota. The Hooleys opened their first warehouse store with the Cub name in a Minneapolis suburb in 1968. When Super Valu purchased the chain in 1980, there were five Cub stores and a Hooley supermarket in Stillwater. Culver M. Davis was appointed president and chief executive officer of Cub Foods in 1985. Davis had joined the Hooley organization in 1960 and was a founder, with the Hooley family, of the discount stores.

Super Valu originally acquired the Cub chain to boost its wholesale sales, but, *Business Week* reported in 1984, the company soon realized it had a ''tiger by the tail,'' and that Cub had ''taken on a (retailing) life of its own.'' Super Valu improved the atmosphere of Cub Foods stores by using attractive decor, keeping the stores clean, and increasing product offerings, including perishables, which the early warehouse stores did not offer. As a result, Cub Foods evolved into a combination of the conventional grocery store and the warehouse store, known in the industry by the late 1980s as a "super warehouse."

Although Cub Foods competed directly with a number of Super Valu's customers' stores and its own corporate stores, the company saw a benefit in the opportunity Cub offered its retailers to learn about warehouse-store operations from the inside. Several of its retailers did not totally agree, citing a 10 to 15 percent reduction in business when a Cub Foods store opened in their market area. To address this complaint, Super Valu started franchising its Cub stores and also developed County Market, a downsized version of Cub with the same low prices, but aimed at smaller communities and at independent retailers who could not meet the financial commitment that buying a Cub franchise required. By 1989, 74 Cub Foods stores (of which Super Valu owned 34) were in nine states and had sales of approximately $3 billion.

By 1986 Super Valu had introduced another variation on the Cub theme. Developed for retailers who needed to improve their stores' look and style to meet competition, the Newmarket format combined warehouse pricing with an upscale product line and services such as video rental, check cashing counters, and baggers. The first Newmarket store opened in the St. Paul-Minneapolis area, and was so successful that the company opened more stores in other locations.

In June 1981 Jack Crocker, at age 57, stepped down from his position as CEO. Crocker, who headed Super Valu for nine years, brought the company to just over $4 billion in sales. He is reported to have handpicked Michael W. Wright, who had joined Super Valu as an executive vice-president in 1977 and become president in 1978, to be the next CEO. Wright had first come to Crocker's attention when he handled some legal matters for the company in Minneapolis. Wright, a former captain of the University of Minnesota football team, had put himself through law school by playing professional football with the Canadian Football League.

The 1980s: Expansions in the West and the South

Super Valu took its expansion west in 1982 when it acquired Western Grocers, Inc. Western had distribution centers in Denver, Colorado, and Albuquerque, New Mexico; in 1984 these two centers became separate divisions. Super Valu also moved into Nebraska in 1982 by acquiring the Hinky Dinky distribution center near Omaha from American Community Grocers, a subsidiary of Texas-based Cullum Companies. In 1984 Super Valu sold the center back to Cullum.

With intentions of gaining a strong market presence in Florida, in 1983 and 1984, respectively, Super Valu purchased Pantry Pride's Miami and Jacksonville distribution centers. In what Super Valu considered a breach of their agreement, Pantry Pride began selling off its stores. With this and the fact that the Florida market had historically been dominated by the chains, Super Valu, claiming that the Florida market would take a large amount of capital to develop, sold the Miami center to Malone & Hyde in 1985, and the Jacksonville center to Winn-Dixie in 1986.

In 1985, Super Valu created its Atlanta Division when it acquired the warehouse and distribution facilities of Food

Giant. Through this division the company supplied Food Giant, Big Apple, Cub Foods, and independent stores. Food Giant, according to a 1988 *Financial World* report, "refused to implement Super Valu's turnaround plan for store upgrading," and the retail stores that Super Valu owned through the original transaction and a later acquisition of stock lost money for the company. By 1988 the company had divested itself of these stores, but operated or franchised seven Cub stores in the Atlanta area.

Also in 1985, Super Valu acquired West Coast Grocery Company (Wesco) of Tacoma, Washington. Wesco, founded by the Charles H. Hyde family in 1891, was Super Valu's largest acquisition to that time. Wesco had distribution centers in two Washington cities and Salem, Oregon, and a freezer facility in another Washington city. Super Valu's West Coast operations were hurt when the Albertson's chain opened a distribution center to supply its own stores in Washington.

In 1986 and 1987 Super Valu acquired two more distribution centers in Albuquerque and Denver, respectively. These centers were owned by Associated Grocers of Colorado, which, at the time of the Denver purchase, was in Chapter 11 bankruptcy proceedings. In December 1988, Super Valu acquired the Minneapolis; Fargo, North Dakota; and Green Bay, Wisconsin, distribution centers of Red Owl Stores, Inc.. The former Denver and Albuquerque divisions of Western Grocers were moved into these new facilities.

By the mid-1980s Super Valu had developed a substantial presence in the military commissary marketplace. The company had been supplying both product and retail support to military commissaries in the United States and abroad and, in 1986, demonstrated its commitment to international operations by appointing a military and export product director. Super Valu International had its beginnings with the Caribbean and Far East markets and eventually supplied fresh goods and private label canned goods, general merchandise, and health and beauty aids to most countries of the world.

During the 1980s ShopKo continued to expand and to turn in substantial profits for the company. At the end of fiscal 1989 ShopKo operated 87 stores in 11 states from the Midwest to the Pacific Northwest and had sales of $1.28 billion. Super Valu's only nonfood retail operation at the time, ShopKo had its headquarters and distribution center in Green Bay, Wisconsin, and distribution centers in Omaha, Nebraska, and Boise, Idaho.

It was perhaps the successes of ShopKo and of Cub Foods that led Super Valu to its biggest venture in retailing in the 1980s—the "hypermarket," a retailing concept that originated in Europe after World War II. The first hypermarkets introduced in the U.S. in the early 1970s were not successful, but in the mid-1980s Hyper Shoppes, Inc., a predominantly French consortium, reintroduced the hypermarket in the United States. Super Valu was a 10 percent investor in the venture, which opened bigg's, a 200,000-square-foot food and general merchandise store in the Cincinnati, Ohio area.

With the experience of this venture under its belt, Super Valu created its own version of the hypermarket, Twin Valu. A combination of a Cub Foods and a ShopKo, this 180,000-square-foot store opened in early 1989 in Cleveland. A second

Twin Valu opened in Cleveland in 1990. The hypermarket concept as executed by Super Valu emphasized low prices, good selection, and brand name merchandise.

In 1988 Super Valu lost its position as the world's largest wholesaler when Oklahoma City-based Fleming Companies bought Malone & Hyde, a purchase Super Valu declined to make. At the end of the 1980s, Super Valu served some 3,000 independent retailers in 33 states. The company still owned and operated 70 conventional grocery stores and some Cub Foods stores and served its corporate stores and customers from 18 retail support and distribution centers.

Acquisition of Wetterau Inc. and Other Purchases Highlight Early 1990s

Super Valu entered the 1990s having to contend with the loss of $220 million in business from the sale or closing of three major customers in 1989: Red Owl stores in Minneapolis, Skaggs Alpha Beta stores in Albuquerque, and two Cub Foods stores in Nashville. The loss of business through acquisition of its independent retail customers by major chains—nearly all of whom were self-distributing—would continue to pose a threat to Super Valu and other wholesalers throughout the 1990s. Part of Super Valu's response to this threat was to further bolster its own retail operations.

Meanwhile, Super Valu's ShopKo subsidiary had grown so rapidly it was beginning to be too large for Super Valu to manage. The company decided to divest itself of part of ShopKo through an initial public offering (IPO). In October 1991 the IPO resulted in the sale of 54 percent of ShopKo to the public, netting Super Valu $420 million. Wright told *Grocery Marketing* that if Super Valu had not taken this step, "it was a case where we would have ended up with the tail wagging the dog."

The very next month Wright began to reinvest the cash, and to boost the company's retail sector through the purchase of Scott's Food Stores, a 13-store chain based in Fort Wayne, Indiana. With the addition of Scott's, Super Valu became the 25th largest retailer in the United States.

In early 1992, Super Valu Stores Inc. changed its name to Supervalu Inc. Later that year, the company made its largest acquisition to date when it acquired Wetterau Inc., the fourth largest wholesaler in the country, in a $1.1-billion deal. The addition of Wetterau's $5.7 billion in sales volume to Supervalu's $10.6 billion leapfrogged Supervalu over rival Fleming and back into the top spot in U.S. grocery wholesaling. Wetterau, founded in 1869 and based in Hazelwood, Missouri, was led at the time of the merger by Ted C. Wetterau, a member of the fourth generation of Wetteraus to run the company. With Wright, Wetterau became vice-chairman of Supervalu and a company director. Wetterau retired late in 1993, leaving Wright in sole control of Supervalu once again.

In addition to bolstering Supervalu's wholesaling operation, Wetterau brought Supervalu a significant retail operation—180 stores in 12 states (added to Supervalu's stable of 105 stores in 11 states). Most significantly, Wetterau's stores included the Save-A-Lot chain of limited-assortment stores, a format new to the Supervalu fold and one that would expand under Supervalu's supervision. The newly combined retail operations

moved Supervalu into 14th place among U.S. food retailers. The company set a long-term goal of being one of the top ten retailers by the end of the 1990s.

The Wetterau acquisition was soon followed by additional acquisitions, several in retail. Late in 1993 Supervalu acquired Sweet Life Foods Inc., a wholesaler based in Suffield, Connecticut, with $650 million in revenues and a few retail operations in New England, one of Supervalu's weaker regions. In March 1994, the 30-store Texas T Discount Grocery Stores chain was acquired. Then in July, Supervalu bought Cincinnati-based Hyper Shoppes, Inc., which ran seven bigg's stores in Cincinnati, Denver, and Louisville, Kentucky, and had more than $500 million in annual revenues. Meanwhile, in June 1994, Fleming leapfrogged back over Supervalu into the number one wholesaling position when it acquired Scrivner Inc., then number three. At that time, Fleming claimed $19 billion in revenue to Supervalu's $16 billion.

Mid-1990s to 2002: Supervalu Restructures While Still Growing

Supervalu announced in late 1994 that it would begin to implement a restructuring program called Advantage in early 1995. Over a two-year period, the company eliminated about 4,300 jobs (10 percent of the total workforce) and divested itself of about 30 underperforming retail stores. The Advantage program also centered around three chief aims: revamping the distribution system into a two-tiered system in order to lower the costs to retailers; creating a new approach to pricing called Activity Based Sell; and developing "market-driving capabilities" that would increase sales for Supervalu's retail customers, chiefly through category management. The last of these goals also involved the realignment of the company's wholesale food divisions into seven marketing regions: Central Region, based in Xenia, Ohio; Midwest Region, Pleasant Prairie, Wisconsin; New England Region, Andover, Massachusetts; Northeast Region, Belle Vernon, Pennsylvania; Northern Region, Hopkins, Minnesota; Northwest Region, Tacoma, Washington; and Southeast Region, Atlanta, Georgia. Supervalu took a $244 million charge in 1995 to implement the Advantage program, which was the company's response to increasing market pressures—low inflation, industry consolidation, a slowdown in growth, and changes in the promotional practices of manufacturers—which had yet to hurt the company's earnings but were certain to begin to do so if the company took no action.

In late 1996 Supervalu bought the 21-store Sav-U Foods chain of limited assortment stores from its rival, Fleming Companies. The purchase provided Supervalu its first southern California retail presence. The stores were to be converted to Save-A-Lot stores, and the company made plans to eventually open 200 to 300 Save-A-Lot stores in the area.

Also in late 1996, ShopKo and Phar-Mor Inc., a chain of more than 100 deep-discount drug stores, merged under the umbrella of a new holding company called Cabot Noble Inc.. Although initially Supervalu was to have no stake in the new company, the final agreement gave Supervalu 6 percent of Cabot Noble in order to reduce the amount of financing needed for the merger. Supervalu also gained about $200 million as a result of the purchase of most of its shares in ShopKo. In 1997, the company exited its 46 percent investment in ShopKo, making about $305 million in the net proceeds. Supervalu had also started to take some tentative steps toward expanding its presence overseas, through a 20 percent stake it held in an Australian wholesaler and its agreement to supply products to a new supermarket in Moscow.

By mid-1998, the company had a strong first quarter to boast about, a two-for-one stock split, and opened or completed acquisitions of 73 stores. The company focused its expansion efforts that year to growing the Save-A-Lot unit. That same year, Supervalu began its investment in the pharmacy business: Scott's Foods stores acquired Keltsch Pharmacy of Northeast Indiana, which included 11 freestanding pharmacies and three in-store ones. Supervalu also lost one of its bigger customers, Bellevue, Washington-based QFC, which was acquired by Portland's Fred Meyer.

In 1999, Supervalu reported record sales of $17.4 billion for 1998, and shortly thereafter, still riding the crest of the previous year's revenue wave, acquired Richfood Holdings, Inc., the leading Mid-Atlantic food distributor and retailer. As a result, Supervalu took over the Shoppers Food Warehouse, Metro, and Farm Fresh retail food chains and gained about 800 new customers. Supervalu then divested of Hazelwood Farms Bakeries to focus its investments on core food distribution and retail businesses, but maintained its link with the bakeries (and new owner Pillsbury Bakeries & Foodservice) as a supplier.

Along with various cost-reduction initiatives, Supervalu's continued focus on core businesses and the boost from the Richfood acquisition helped Supervalu see yet another record year for sales: By mid-2000, Supervalu's sales surpassed the $20-billion mark. An ever-growing, increasingly more efficient company, Supervalu was operating more than 194 price superstores (including Cub Foods, Shop'n Save, Shoppers Food Warehouse, Metro, and bigg's), 839 limited assortment stores (including 662 licensed locations under the Save-A-Lot banner), and 85 other supermarkets. It was also the primary supplier to about 3,500 supermarkets and franchises of its own retail chains, and a secondary supplier to approximately 2,600 stores, including 1,350 Kmart stores. The company also joined the Worldwide Retail Exchange, a premier retail-focused, business-to-business exchange, and signed a multiyear national supply agreement with Webvan Group, Inc. of Foster City in California.

As was the trend among wholesalers at this time, Supervalu planned to continue its expansion of retail stores in order to gain more control of its core businesses. By 2001, Supervalu's retail food business represented about 60 percent of total company operating earnings, and was growing even more. One of the company's goals was to increase retail square footage by about five percent for the 2001 fiscal year. The pharmacy side of Supervalu's retail business, however, was apparently not considered a core one, as the company closed 30 stores in three states, 18 of which contained pharmacies.

The distribution side of Supervalu's business took a blow when Kmart ended its contract with the company, resulting in $2.3 billion in reduced revenue for the year. Supervalu also lost a $400 million annual supply contract with the Genuardi's chain, once the East Coast chain was bought by Safeway in mid-

2001. Supervalu continued to consolidate its distribution centers and announced that it would cut 4,500 jobs, or 7.3 percent of its workforce.

During fiscal year 2002, Supervalu opened 115 new stores, including 103 Save-A-Lot stores, 11 price superstores, and one conventional supermarket, and closed 49 stores. In mid-2002, the company announced its aggressive plans for 2003: It would open 10 to 15 superstores and at least 150 extreme value food stores. And in yet another move to gain control over its core business, Supervalu announced that it would purchase St. Louis-based Deal$-Nothing Over a Dollar LLC, adding 53 stores to its general merchandise business. Supervalu's Save-A-Lot chain also opened its 1,000th store in 2002.

In June 2002, Supervalu faced an embarrassing major setback, however. The company's shares dropped 22 percent in value after the company announced that profits for its pharmacy business were deliberately inaccurate for three years. While preparing for a scheduled, internal audit, the company discovered that a former Supervalu comptroller deliberately misstated earnings for the company's pharmaceutical stores, artificially inflating profits. Although Supervalu entered into the new millennium with great momentum for expanding its retail business and consolidating its distribution business, any possible long-term effects from the accounting scandal remained to be seen.

Principal Competitors

Ahold USA; Albertson's; Alex Lee; Allou; AWG; Associated Wholesalers; Bozzuto's; C&S Wholesale; D&W Food Centers; Delhaize America; Di Giorgio; Dierbergs Markets; Fleming Companies; Fresh Brands; Giant Eagle; A&P; Jetro Cash & Carry; Krasdale Foods; The Kroger Co.; Marsh Supermarkets; McLane; Meijer; Nash Finch; Roundy's; Safeway; Schnuck Markets; Sherwood Food; Shurfine International; Spartan Stores; Topco Associates; Wakefern Food; Wal-Mart; Winn-Dixie.

Further Reading

Barth, Brad, "IT Drives Supervalu's Turnaround; Setbacks in Its Wholesale and Retail Operations Lead the Food Wholesaling Giant to Roll Out a Wide-Ranging Technology Program," *Supermarket News,* May 6, 2001, p. 71.
Byrne, Harlan S., "Super Valu Stores: Food Wholesaler Gives Thanks for Its Retail Operations," *Barron's,* November 19, 1990, p. 51.
——, "Super Valu Stores Inc.: It Looks to the Unconventional for Growth in Retailing," *Barron's,* April 24, 1989, p. 49.
Hamstra, Mark, "Wall Street Pounds Supervalu Stock after Disclosure," *Supermarket News,* July 1, 2002, p. 1.
Levy, Melissa, "Supervalu's Third-Quarter Earnings Slip 19 Percent," *Star Tribune* (Minneapolis), December 19, 2000, p. 2D.
Lewis, Len, "Plan-A-Lot: Supervalu's Noddle Charts a Course That Combines Aggressive Expansion with Fiscal Prudence," *Progressive Grocer,* November-December 2001, p. 71.
Merrefield, David, "The New Super Valu," *Supermarket News,* June 22, 1992, p. 1.
Merrill, Ann, "Dented But Undaunted; A New Supervalu Executive Team Aims to Freshen Earnings, in Part by Rejuvenating Some Cub Foods Stores," *Star Tribune* (Minneapolis), December 11, 2000, p. 1D.
——, "Supervalu Bags $305 million from ShopKo Deal," *Star Tribune* (Minneapolis), July 3, 1997, p. 3D.

——, "Supervalu Loses $400 Million Deal, Affirms Earnings," *Star Tribune* (Minneapolis), August 8, 2001, p. 3D.

——, "Supervalu Reports Strong First Quarter, Stock Split; 40 New Stores are Planned," *Star Tribune* (Minneapolis), July 2, 1998, p. 4D.

——, "Supervalu Sales Pass $20 Billion Threshold," *Star Tribune* (Minneapolis), March 31, 2000, p. 2D.

——, "Supervalu Seeks the Advantage; Goal Is to Streamline Food Delivery System," *Star Tribune* (Minneapolis), October 6, 1997, p. 1D.

Morris, Kathleen, "Beyond Jurassic Park: Meet the First Big Company Likely to Make It Out of 'Dinosaur-Hood,' " *Financial World,* June 22, 1993, p. 28.

"No National Link for Kmart," *Food Logistics,* September 15, 1999, p. 13.

Parr, Jan, "Leader of the Pack," *Forbes,* February 8, 1988, p. 35.

"Retailer Roundup," *The Food Institute Report,* February 26, 2001, p. 5.

Schifrin, Matthew, "Middleman's Dilemma," *Forbes,* May 23, 1994, p. 67.

Sciacca, Patrick, "Supervalu Helps Launch Retailers into Cyberspace," *Supermarket News,* January 4, 1999, p. 17.

Smith, Rod, "Supervalu to Create Extreme-Value Centers," *Feedstuffs,* June 3, 2002, p. 9.

"Supervalu: 50 Years on the Road to Excellence," special section of *Grocery Marketing,* 1992.

"Supervalu Announces Major Restructuring," *The Food Institute Report,* April 9, 2001, p. 1.

"Supervalu Announces Store Closings, Restructures," *MMR,* June 25, 2001, p. 138.

"Supervalu Boosts Spending, Plans Expansion, Acquires Discount Retailer," *The Food Institute Report,* April 8, 2002, p. 1.

"Supervalu Closes Stores," *Drug Store News,* July 23, 2001, p. 4.

"Supervalu Falls 22% after Revealing False Accounting," *The New York Times,* June 27, 2002, p. C10.

"Supervalu Inc. (The Bottom Line)," *Business Record* (Des Moines), February 4, 2002, p. 24.

"Supervalu Inks Richfood Deal," *Food Logistics,* July-August 1999, p. 12.

"Supervalu Is Stung by Accounting Fraud," *Drug Store News,* July 22, 2002, p. 6.

"Supervalu Posts Record Results," *The Food Institute Report,* April 3, 2000.

"Supervalu Posts Record Sales, Earnings," *Supermarket News,* December 20, 1999, p. 8.

"Supervalu Takes $17.6 Million Charge in Earnings Restatement," *Supermarket News,* July 8, 2002, p. 4.

"Supervalu to Buy 29-Unit Retailer," *Supermarket News,* October 26, 1998, p. 4.

Tosh, Mark, "Wholesale Changes," *Progressive Grocer,* January 1999, p. 29.

Weinstein, Steve, "The Reinvention of Supervalu," *Progressive Grocer,* January 1996, p. 26.

——, "Tomorrow the World," *Progressive Grocer,* October 1992, p. 58.

Zwiebach, Elliot, "SuperValu Set to Reposition Six Chains as One Operation," *Supermarket News,* June 7, 1999, p. 1.

——, "Supervalu's Strength; Though Acquisitions and Consolidation, the Super Distributor Continues to Strengthen Its Position as a Leader in the Nation's Food Industry," *Supermarket News,* September 27, 1999, p. 1.

——, "SuperValu to Buy Fleming California Chain," *Supermarket News,* September 30, 1996, p. 1.

——, "SuperValu to Buy Wetterau," *Supermarket News,* June 15, 1992, p. 1.

—Nina Wendt
—updates: David E. Salamie, Heidi Wrightsman

Svenska Handelsbanken AB

Kungstragardsgatan 2
S-10670 Stockholm
Sweden
Telephone: +46 (8) 701-1000
Web site: http://www.handelsbanken.se

Public Company
Incorporated: 1987
Employees: 9,800 (2002)
Total Assets: SKr 1.2 billion (US$123 million) (2002)
Stock Exchanges: Stockholm
Ticker Symbol: SHB
NAIC: 522110 Commercial Banking; 524113 Life
    Insurance Carriers, Direct

In its infancy, Svenska Handelsbanken AB was a small bank, with operations confined to the city of Stockholm. In the first half of the 20th century, it was the foremost financier of Swedish heavy industry. And in the latter half of this century, it has led Scandinavian banks into the brave new world of international finance. The bank has 540 branches in the Nordic counties and seven subsidiaries including finance, mortgage, mutual funds, life insurance companies, and a telephone and Internet bank.

A Bank Is Formed

Svenska Handelsbanken began its life in 1871 under the name Stockholms Handelsbank. Its founders were former directors of Stockholms Enskilda Bank who left that bank after losing an internal power struggle. Their new bank, Stockholms Handelsbank, was one of the nation's first joint-stock banks (along with Skandinaviska Bank) and engaged primarily in small-scale commercial lending.

The bank remained small throughout most of the remainder of the century. Sweden was a poor, mostly agrarian nation with little heavy industry, and the authorities that oversaw the banking system kept it regional in nature, believing that a bank should be able to carve out its own geographical domain. All of this began to change, however, in the 1890s, as Sweden indus-

trialized. Under managing director Louis Fraenckel, who led the bank from 1893 to his death in 1911, Stockholms Handelsbank pursued an aggressive lending policy to take advantage of this development; between 1893 and 1913, its loan volume increased nearly sevenfold, from SKr 17 million to SKr 114 million. Fraenckel also used his extensive connections with the nation's industrialists to secure underwriting and investment banking business. Of Sweden's ten largest industrial concerns in 1912, eight of them had done business with Stockholms Handelsbank at some point.

Corresponding changes were taking place in the banking industry as well. Larger industrial undertakings required larger financing packages, which in turn required larger banks to extend the credit. Swedish banks began to amalgamate and the old regional fiefdoms dissolved. Stockholms Handelsbank embarked on a series of mergers in 1914, when it acquired a bank in northern Sweden and along with it, ties to the lumber and paper industry. In 1917 it acquired another northern bank. In 1919 it purchased a bank in the South that was involved in agriculture and the textile industry. The bank exploded in size through these mergers; its branch network expanded from seven offices in 1914, all of them in Stockholm, to more than 250 nationwide. Its assets totaled SKr 1.6 billion in 1919, making it the largest bank in the nation. To reflect this, the bank changed its name to its present form, Svenska Handelsbanken, in 1919.

World War I and Ivar Kreuger's Effect on Handelsbanken

Sweden remained neutral during World War I, so while the hostilities produced much anxiety about the nation's economy, they did little damage to it. Industry continued to prosper and banking power continued to concentrate. By 1924, four institutions, including Svenska Handelsbanken, were accounting for 56 percent of Sweden's banking activity. The early 1920s, however, were marked by a severe Depression. In 1922 the bank decided to write off more than SKr 100 million in bad loans and additions to its reserves.

The economy began to recover in 1923, and so did Swedish banks. But renewed prosperity also brought with it a dizzying

Company Perspectives:

Handelsbanken's overall objective is to have higher profitability than a weighted average of the other listed Nordic banks. The quality of the Group's services should meet the expectations of demanding customers. Handelsbanken should charge a fair price for its services. The cost level should be lower than at other banks. Profitability must always be given higher priority than volumes. When granting credits, this means that the quality of the credits must never be neglected in favor of a large lending volume. Higher profitability should benefit the shareholders via greater growth in dividends than the average for other Swedish banks. Handelsbanken aims to have more satisfied customers than other banks. The bank seeks to employ young, well-educated staff and train them within the Group. As far as possible, managers should be recruited internally. The bank's activities should benefit its customers, the bank itself and society as a whole.

wave of speculation. Before the decade was out, an ambitious Swede named Ivar Kreuger pulled Svenska Handelsbanken into what has been called the largest financial fraud in history. An engineer by training, Kreuger made a small fortune in the construction business in the early 1910s, and he used that stake to start building his own financial empire. His main goal was to turn his family's match business into a worldwide monopoly, but he also involved himself in other ventures, including a corporate-raider-style takeover of telecommunications giant L.M. Ericsson in 1925. Kreuger obtained most of his financing from U.S. sources, but he also borrowed heavily from Swedish banks, including Svenska Handelsbanken. The problem was that he lied extensively and convincingly about his net worth and offered assets that did not exist as security. His practice of hiring accountants based either on their lack of accounting skill or their vulnerability to blackmail helped him in this regard.

Kreuger killed himself in 1932 when the Great Depression threatened to unravel his pyramid-financing game. An audit undertaken after his death revealed the extent of the fraud he had perpetrated, and Svenska Handelsbanken could not help but be involved in the bankruptcies and restructurings that followed. Not only had Kreuger embezzled $5 million from L.M. Ericsson, but he had endangered its independence by borrowing against his controlling interest in the company. Svenska Handelsbanken, along with rival Stockholms Enskilda Bank, was closely involved in Ericsson's reconstruction. The bank also took control of what remained of Svenska Cellulosa Aktiebolaget (SCA), a Kreuger venture for which it was the major creditor. It formally bought out SCA in 1934 for SKr 3 million, and considered itself fortunate when it resold an 83 percent stake in the company to industrialist Axel Wenner-Gren later that year for SKr 10 million.

Sweden's economy fared better than the rest of the world's in the 1930s. Whereas the overvalued kronor in the 1920s encouraged capital flight and banks struggled to keep their deposits, in the 1930s the opposite happened. Undervalued currency kept money at home and banks had to fight to maintain a profitable loan volume. During this time, Svenska Handelsbanken benefited from its geographical diversity; deposit surpluses in areas where economic activity was especially slow could be sloughed off on areas where lending was brisker. The bank also continued its close involvement with heavy industry, despite that sector's growing independence from the big banks in general. In 1935 more than one-third of all money loaned to large Swedish industrial concerns came from Svenska Handelsbanken.

World War II

During World War II, Sweden once again remained neutral, but its aloofness failed to keep Swedish banks entirely insulated from the shock of war. Political uncertainty kept deposits high and it became even more difficult to maintain profitable loan volumes than it had been in the 1930s. The government helped alleviate the banks' difficulties by selling them large quantities of securities; Sweden found a large military buildup necessary to protect its neutrality and financed it through war bonds.

For Svenska Handelsbanken in particular, the 1940s were marked by divestiture of its industrial holdings. Banking laws enacted in reaction to the Kreuger crash and the Depression restricted, among other things, the amount of stock that banks could own in other companies. In 1943 the bank organized Industrivärden, a holding company devoted to managing its portfolio. Between 1943 and 1946, it sold Svenska Handelsbanken's entire interest in the steelmaker Fagersta for more than SKr 37 million. After years of struggle, SCA gained solid financial footing during World War II and the bank bought out Axel Wenner-Gren in 1947 for nearly SKr 18 million, then resold the company in 1950. Also in 1950, the bank sold the agricultural machinery firm Bolinder Munktell to Volvo.

Svenska Handelsbanken then began to reorient itself toward small- and medium-scale lending. In 1955 it acquired Stockholms Intecknings Garanti, a real estate lender. It also began to expand its branch network after a 1954 study commissioned by the bank found that convenience was of paramount importance to retail customers. By 1968, it had 500 branch offices throughout the nation. It also sold its controlling interest in Reymersholm, a chemical and mining company, to Boliden Mining in 1963.

Foreign Expansion

By the mid-1960s, Svenska Handelsbanken had not only become the largest bank in all of Scandinavia, but it was also a leader among Swedish banks in recognizing the increasing importance of international markets. Major Swedish companies had always conducted much of their business abroad, but the lack of a Swedish banking presence in those countries meant that foreign banks wound up supplying their credit needs. In 1964, Svenska Handelsbanken joined with three other Scandinavian banks—Kjobenhavns Bandelsbank of Denmark, Den norske Creditbank of Norway, and Kansallis-Osake-Pankki of Finland—to establish Nordfinanzbank in Zürich and Banque Nordique du Commerce in Paris. Over the next several years, it also acquired stakes in banks in Greece and Spain to help Swedish companies capitalize on foreign markets.

Key Dates:

1871: The former directors of Stockholms Enskilda Bank found Stockholms Handelsbank.

1919: Stockholms Handelsbank changes its name to Svenska Handelsbanken.

1943: The bank organizes Industrivärden, a holding company to manage its portfolio.

1964: The company joins three other Scandinavian banks—Kjobenhavns Bandelsbank of Denmark, Den norske Creditbank of Norway, and Kansallis-Osake-Pankki of Finland—to establish Nordfinanzbank in Zürich and Banque Nordique du Commerce in Paris.

1968: The company has 500 branch offices throughout Sweden.

1971: Jan Wallander becomes CEO and introduces a new organization and policy.

1974: The company opens a representative office in Moscow.

1978: The company sets up a subsidiary bank, Svenska Handelsbanken SA in Luxembourg.

1982: Handelsbanken establishes its own merchant-banking subsidiary in London, Svenska International.

1984: The company forms a subsidiary in Singapore, Svenska Handelsbanken Asia Limited.

1990: The bank acquires the Swedish Skanska Banken and Norway's Oslo Handelsbank.

1991: The bank acquires Norway's Stavanger Bank.

1992: The bank acquires RKA, the life insurance company, and changes its name to Handelsbanken Liv.

1997: The company joins ten European banks in forming a nonexclusive association they call the Trans-European Banking Services.

1999: The bank offers Internet banking and wireless banking services.

2001: *Privata Affärer*, a periodical for private finances, names Svenska Handelsbanken Bank of the Year.

Svenska Handelsbanken continued to prosper and expand its foreign operations in the 1970s. It took a merger between Stockholms Enskilda Bank and Skandinaviska Bank in 1972 to overtake it as Scandinavia's largest bank. In 1970, Svenska Handelsbanken participated in the formation of Nordic Bank Limited in London, along with Den norske Creditbank and Kansallis-Osake-Pankki. In 1974 it opened a representative office in Moscow, responding to increased trade between Sweden and the Soviet Union. The next year, it established a subsidiary in New York, Nordic American Banking Corporation, devoted largely to import and export financing for North and South American clients doing business with Nordic countries. And in 1978, it set up a subsidiary bank in Luxembourg, Svenska Handelsbanken SA, Luxembourg.

Shorter-Term Forecasting Pays Off

Svenska Handelsbanken raised a few eyebrows in 1971 when, under the guidance of Chairman Jan Wallander, it abandoned most forms of long-range economic forecasting and

planning, deciding to rely instead on shorter-term forecasting and greater flexibility of action. Writing in *Euromoney* ten years later, President Jan Ekman announced that the policy had produced results above the industry average. "Forecasting is an exercise in meaningless impossibilities," he declared, deriding the large margins of error that characterized long-range prognostication.

By the early 1980s, Svenska Handelsbanken had grown to the point where it no longer needed consortium partners to carry out its international business. In 1982 it established its own merchant-banking subsidiary in London, Svenska International. The next year, it sold its interest in Nordic Bank Limited to Den norske Creditbank. In 1984 it formed a subsidiary in Singapore, Svenska Handelsbanken Asia Limited, and sold much of its stake in Nordfinanzbank to Kansallis-Osake-Pankki, giving its Finnish partner a controlling interest. In 1985 it sold its 25 percent share of Nordic American Banking Corporation to Den norske Creditbank. And in 1988 it established a subsidiary bank in Norway.

The 1980s have also been marked by a decline in the influence of banks over other segments of the Swedish business community as major corporations set up their own in-house financing units. Svenska Handelsbanken was no longer the kingmaker of industry that it once was. But Svenska Handelsbanken had made up for the end of this role by playing its newer one to the hilt. While profiting from the smaller end of the domestic market, it had also led Scandinavian banks into the modern financial world of international, integrated markets.

Continued Expansion

Svenska Handelsbanken was the only Swedish bank to survive the country's banking crisis in the early 1990s without having to be bailed out by the government. The bank's success rested largely on decentralization, cost-cutting, and increased earnings. One successful aspect of the bank's decentralization lay in the day-to-day operations of the bank's many branches. The branches of Handelsbanken were organized to be separate businesses, with the responsibility for earning profits and controlling costs resting entirely on the shoulders of each branch manager. The branch managers were given the freedom to decide which products to emphasize in their own market and were held accountable for keeping the cost ratio in line—this organization succeeded in motivating branch managers to cut costs. Another aspect of the bank's success resided in their determination to cut out unnecessary layers of bureaucracy. The branch managers, in addition to having a large amount of control and responsibility of the individual branches, also had an almost direct route to the bank's chief executive. The only level between the branch managers and the bank's chief executive was a group of eight regional mangers.

The economic crisis of the early 1990s did nothing to hamper Handelsbanken's drive to expand. In 1990, the bank kicked off its expansion marathon with the acquisition of the Swedish Skanska Banken and Norway's Oslo Handelsbank. Stavanger Bank, another Norwegian commodity was purchased in 1991. In 1992, Handelsbanken expanded its life insurance holdings when it acquired the life insurance company RKA (its name was quickly changed to Handelsbanken Liv). The flurry of Nordic acquisitions continued throughout the decade.

In 1997, Svenska Handelsbanken joined forces with ten European banks to form a nonexclusive association called the Trans-European Banking Services Group. The Group was founded to provide transnational banking services to business-people. The bank hoped to make accessing money easier for traveling businesspeople. The bank expanded their service base by taking their business to the Internet in 1997. In 2000, Handelsbanken had 200,000 registered Internet customers, about 20 percent of its customer base. The bank also offered Internet customers the opportunity to pay their bills electronically. Handelsbanken follwed their successful Internet banking service with the launch in 1999 of wireless banking services. The launch was a shoe-in for success, considering that 60% of the people in Handelsbanken's Nordic region carried mobile phones. The bank planned to offer more Internet and wireless banking options, from access to stock market information to bill payments in the coming years.

Bank of the Year

Privata Affärer, a periodical for private finances, named Svenska Handelsbanken Bank of the Year in 2001. In a 2001 press release issued by Svenska Handelsbanken, they stated that *Privata Affärer* explained the award in this way: "At a time when many banks are closing branches, Handelsbanken stands out as a bank which offers good personal service at branch offices and combines an extensive branch network with free banking services over the Internet. Loyal customers have every opportunity of negotiating better conditions for themselves. This year, Handelsbanken has also opened up for increased competition by removing mutual fund charges and allowing customers to move their pension savings." The bank is poised to meet their customers needs for many years to come.

Principal Subsidiaries

Handelsbanken Finance; Handelsbanken Fonder; Handelsbanken Hypotek; Handelsbanken Liv; SPP; Stadshypotek; Stadshypotek Bank.

Principal Competitors

Danske Bank Aktieselskab; Nordea AB; Skandinaviska Enskilda Banken AB.

Further Reading

"Culture of Thrift: Bank Management," *The Economist* (US), July 12, 1997, p. 67.
"Eleven European Banks Set Up Cross-Border Group," *American Banker,* October 23, 1997, p. 12.
"For Scandinavian Banks, Web Is Business as Usual," *American Banker,* January 19, 2000, p. 14.
Hildebrand, Karl-Gustaf, " *Banking in a Growing Economy: Svenska Handelsbanken Since 1871*," Svenska Handelsbanken, Stockholm, 1971.
Shaplen, Robert, "Kreuger, Genius and Swindler," New York: Garland Publishing, 1986.
"Sitting Pretty," *Euromoney,* October 1993, p. 70.
"Two Approaches to Expansion," *Euromoney,* October 1998, p. 92.
Uimonen, Terho, "Swedish Bank in Big Wireless App Test," *Computerworld*, October 11, 1999, p. 25.

—update: Tammy Weisberger

Telekomunikacja Polska SA

3 Swietokrzyska
00945 Warsaw
Poland
Telephone: +48 (22) 657-1111
Fax: +48 (22) 826-5653
Web site: http://www.tpsa-ir.pl

Public Company
Incorporated: 1991
Employees: 68,437 (2001)
Sales: EUR 4.7 billion (2001)
Stock Exchanges: London Warsaw
Ticker Symbols: TPSD (London), TPSA (Warsaw)
NAIC: 513310 Wired Telecommunications Carriers;
513320 Cellular and Other Wireless
Telecommunications; 541618 Other Management
Consulting Services

Telekomunikacja Polska SA (TPSA) is Poland's leading telecommunications company. It is also Eastern Europe's largest. The company provides fixed-line and cellular telephone services, Internet and other data transmission services, and radio and television transmission services throughout Poland. TPSA is the successor of the Communist-era state-run telephone company. The state still has a 23 percent interest in the company.

Telecommunications in Immediate Post-Communist Poland: 1989

When Poland's first post-Communist government took office in 1989, the nation's telephone system was one of the least adequate in Eastern Europe. A report by the Polish Electrical Engineers Association labeled telephone availability "catastrophic." Estimates put the number of telephone lines per 100 people at seven, compared with 43 in Western Europe and 23 in East Germany. Only Bulgaria and Albania showed lesser rates of penetration.

This average, however, did not illustrate the full extent of the system's inadequacy. Almost 10,000 villages had no telephones at all; many others had only one telephone, usually in the mayor's home; about one of four homes in urban areas had phones, but only about one in 30 had phones in rural areas. About 2 million businesses and households were on waiting lists for phones, some for many years. Even the possession of a phone was no guarantee that its possessor could use it. The network was antiquated and poorly maintained. Consequently, it was difficult or impossible to complete calls.

A lack of money, the assignment of a low priority to the provision of communications services and an embargo by Western governments on the export of advanced technologies to the Communist bloc all contributed to the poor system the new Polish government inherited. At the beginning of the 1990s, the means to improve the telephone system appeared obvious: privatize it and encourage Western telecommunications companies to invest in it. To comply with this prescription was not, however, as easy as it might seem.

For most of the preceding 42 years, the government had owned, controlled, and administered almost every industry and business in Poland. Only a few small businesses had any experience with private ownership. Virtually nobody had relations of any kind with Western businesses. Moreover, the state enterprises, inefficient though they might be, provided employment for much of the population, and the Post, Telegraph and Telephone Ministry (PTT) was a major employer. Its privatization, therefore, raised both political and social questions.

Even more important, Poland had no system of laws and regulations establishing fair processes for the sale of state enterprises. It had no laws to govern the operations of businesses once they were in private hands. Its guarantees surrounding private ownership of property and assets were vague. It also lacked any of the economic infrastructure that modern capitalist enterprises depended on for their very existences. For example, Poland had no stock exchange; it had no accounting standards and nobody to apply them. The new government had to create all of this while simultaneously opening the nearly 7,000 state enterprises to private ownership.

Company Perspectives:

Telekomunikacja Polska Capital Group is no longer satisfied with its role of the market leader in Poland. Aiming much higher, we are interested in being ranked at least sixth in terms of Europe. What this means in practice is that we need to be comparable with other European telecoms in all aspects of our activity, particularly effectiveness, productivity and labour intensity.

Privatization: The First Steps during 1990–1995

It is no surprise, then, that the privatization of the telecommunications system was a lengthy process. In January 1990, the PTT called for proposals to operate two analog cellular phone systems in Poland. One license would allow its holder to construct and operate a wholly private system. The other would allow its holder to build a system in alliance with the PTT. By April, the PTT announced that more than 20 consortia, including many of the largest European and U.S. companies, had submitted bids.

In March, the government submitted a telecommunications reform law to Parliament. Reports stated that the Polish government was planning a sweeping de-monopolization and privatization of the system. Some believed that the PTT would be broken into a postal company, a long-distance telecommunications provider, and several regional providers. The reports also suggested that private and foreign companies would be allowed to compete with the state companies in each of these areas.

A hint that the award of the cellular licenses might not go as easily as many Western bidders had expected came in July when the PTT announced that it was postponing the selection of the winning consortia until September and requested extensive new information from the nine finalists.

In January 1991 the entire process began to unravel. The Polish Parliament, after a year's delay, passed the Telecommunications Law. The law as enacted differed from the one introduced by the government. Competition would be allowed only for local networks; the PTT would retain its monopoly over the more-profitable long-distance and international connections. This provision originated from a fear that if allowed to compete in those areas, private and especially foreign companies would neglect the local networks and focus their efforts only on the most remunerative portions of the system.

This law also created Telekomunikacja Polska when it split the PTT into TPSA to handle telecommunications and Poczta Polska to provide postal services. The company incorporated in 1991. Through the Ministry of Communications, the government maintained ownership of 100 percent of the new company's shares—a provision to which Western businesspeople objected. The Ministry was also charged with interpreting the law and with licensing private competitors. The potential for conflicts of interest were evident, and there were calls for a separate and independent regulator.

The new law required that all foreign investment in the system be through joint ventures with majority ownership by Polish partners. This restriction had been absent from the government's initial request for the cellular tenders. At first, the government announced that new conditions for the bids would be issued and that a final decision would be issued at the end of April. By the end of January, however, intensive lobbying by Ameritech, which did not participate in the first competition, and by the U.S. government on its behalf, persuaded the government to invalidate the first competition and open a new one. Many of the original competitors failed to submit new bids, and in June 1991 Ameritech and France Telecom each received 24.5 percent of the venture. This gave them a combined 49 percent of the venture, named "Polska Telefonia Komorkowa" (PTK). TPSA, which officially took responsibility for the system in December, would control 51 percent.

In a transaction that would create problems for PTK in later years, Ameritech and France Telecom made a "donation" to Poland's telecommunications system of $75 million above the license fee. In exchange, they received a letter of intent signed by the Communications Minister guaranteeing them the opportunity to build and operate a system based on the next generation of cellular technology when it became available in Poland. The technology was unavailable in 1991 because Western prohibitions on the import of advanced technology into Poland were still in force.

PTK launched Centertel, the brand assigned to the cellular system, in Warsaw in June 1992. It planned to extend the service to seven additional cities by the end of the year and to enroll 6,500 subscribers by the end of 1993. The consortium surpassed this goal, reaching 10,000 subscribers by October 1993.

The creation of Centertel was, however, a relatively minor event in the overall effort to improve Poland's telecommunications system. The cellular system had a maximum capacity of 125,000 subscribers, and cellular service was far too expensive for most Poles. The massive expansion Poland needed would require the installation of modern fiber-optic landlines. TPSA focused on this task.

Confronting both a lack of money and a dearth of contemporary technology, the government and TPSA reached out to foreign companies again, not to plan and operate the telecommunications system, but to supply and help finance it. As part of its broader privatization program, the government identified the dominant state manufacturers of switching and transmission equipment. It combined these into three enterprises and encouraged foreign telecom companies to submit competitive bids for them. Since these enterprises were not directly part of Poland's telecommunications system, their ownership was not subject to the requirement that they be 51 percent Polish-owned. They were subjected to a requirement that 50 percent of the content of their products be of Polish origin.

By 1993, three foreign companies had purchased the manufacturers. AT&T, with a commitment to spend $86 million modernizing the product line, took ownership of one enterprise. Alcatel of France paid $46 million and made a commitment to increase its investment for another. Siemens of Germany bought the largest of the three for $57 million.

Key Dates:

1991: Telekomunikacja Polska (TPSA) incorporates and takes over the operation of the Polish telephone system; Polska Telefonia Komorkowa (PTK) is formed as a TPSA subsidiary to build and operate a cellular phone system; the subsidiary is a partnership among TPSA, Ameritech, and France Telecom.

1992: Centertel, PTK's cellular brand, begins operations in Warsaw.

1993: First contracts for upgrade of Polish telephone systems are awarded to foreign companies.

1996: Digital cellular licenses are issued to Polska Telefonia Cyfrowa (PTC) and Polkomtel, and TPSA does not participate in the bidding process.

1998: First 15 percent of TPSA is sold to individual investors.

1999: Another 15 percent of TPSA is given to a TPSA employee stock ownership plan.

2000: TPSA loses its monopoly of Poland's long-distance services; and France Telecom and Kulczyk Holding purchase 35 percent of TPSA.

2001: France Telecom and Kulczyk Holding purchase an additional 12.5 percent of TPSA and an option to bring their ownership to a majority of shares; and TPSA announces restructuring, beginning with a 20 percent reduction of its workforce.

2002: TPSA is scheduled to lose its monopoly on international services in December.

The government guaranteed that these three entities would face no other competition to serve Poland's telecom needs, but it required that they compete among themselves for business. By late 1993, under contracts with TPSA, AT&T was installing networks in five cities and laying 1,500 kilometers of fiber-optic line worth $30 million; Alcatel was installing systems in two cities, and Siemens was installing DM 72 million worth of local and international switches in the region of Silesia.

The highly profitable TPSA provided about one-third of the financing. The rest of the money came from a combination of credits arranged by the three suppliers, the World Bank, the European Investment Bank, and the European Bank for Reconstruction and Development.

While TPSA moved forward with its construction plans, the Ministry of Communications issued about 50 licenses to private companies allowing them to compete in local markets. Most of these ventures floundered from lack of financing and obstructions from TPSA in such matters as arranging for connections to the national network. One effort did see some success. RP Telekom, a newly formed Polish company, joined US Sprint promising to invest up to $2 billion in the modernization of fiber-optic networks in eight cities. They began with a $120 million investment to build 120,000 lines in Pila and Katowice.

The export restrictions applying to advanced technology imposed on Eastern Europe during the Cold War were progressively weakened after 1991 and were eliminated in 1994. In 1995, the Polish Parliament authorized the issuance of two licenses to construct GSM digital cellular networks in the country. Ameritech and France Telecom, part owners with TPSA of Centertel, believed that the letter of intent issued to them in 1991 guaranteed Centertel one of the licenses. But the law authorizing the licenses immediately called that belief into question. The Parliament specified that there would be a public bid process for both licenses, and a government spokesperson stated that Centertel would not be given favored treatment. This seeming change in purpose resulted from four factors. Poland had begun to nurture ambitions to join the European Union and wanted to apply EU standards of transparency and competition to the award process. There had been intense lobbying in opposition to Centertel by the Polish business community, which objected to the high prices and low quality of its services. Reports in Polish newspapers that the U.S. ambassador had intervened to press Ameritech's right to receive a license without competing for it further raised the political temperature. TPSA also expressed its displeasure with what it saw as a lack of influence in the operations of Centertel.

TPSA resolved this question by announcing that Centertel would not bid for the new licenses. Since France Telecom and Ameritech were contractually obligated to undertake any development of a digital system only in cooperation with TPSA, this decision effectively eliminated both companies from the competition.

By the January 3, 1996 deadline, three consortia, all of which met the requirement for more than 50 percent Polish participation, had submitted bids. Polska Telefonia Cyfrowa (PTC) included U.S. West and DeTeMobil, the cellular subsidiary of Germany's Deutsche Telekom which each held a 22.5 percent share; and on the Polish side were Elektrim with a 32.5 percent ownership stake; and a variety of groups, including entrepreneur Jan Kulczyk, with 5 percent or smaller stakes. Polkomtel was formed by AirTouch Communications and Tele Denmark, each with a 19.25 percent ownership; by a Polish oil refinery and a Polish copper-mining company, each of which held 19.25 percent of the consortium as well; and by a group of Polish partners who held the remaining 23 percent. C-Line was formed by STET of Italy and Ciech SA of Poland. In February 1996, PTC and Polkomtel won the licenses, agreeing to pay EUR 520 million over five years. By October, PTC had initiated service in five cities, while Polkomtel had begun service in Warsaw.

Both Ameritech and France Telecom initiated legal proceedings, in Poland and later in international fora, to try to enforce what they believed was a contract guaranteeing them a GSM license. When these initiatives failed, Ameritech withdrew from PTK/Centertel, selling its interest to TPSA and France Telecom. Both minority partners dropped their legal challenges.

Privatization and the Initiation of Competition: 1995–2002

Despite many expectations that TPSA itself, rather than only PTK/Centertel, would undergo significant privatization in the early 1990s, the company remained 100 percent in state hands in 1995, and there had been little movement toward privatization and de-monopolization until then. By 1995, however, discussion of some kind of sale of shares began. Two options for such a sale surfaced. Some argued that a substantial share of the company ought to be sold to a foreign "strategic investor," which could provide the company with increased technical expertise and easier access to capital. Others, including TPSA's managers who did not wish to lose control of the enterprise, advocated a sale of stock through the Warsaw and foreign exchanges, to individual investors.

The government announced a commitment to both approaches early in 1996. It would first sell a portion, perhaps 15 percent, to individual investors to test both the government and individual investors and to help establish free market share prices. Several months later, it would sell a larger share, but not one that would exceed 50 percent, to a strategic investor or to institutions generally. It would, however, maintain TPSA's monopoly on international connections until 2001.

After lengthy discussion and some delay, TPSA sold 15 percent of its shares to Polish and international investors in November of 1998. The government received about US$1 billion in exchange. In 1999, TPSA gave another 15 percent of the company to an employee stock ownership plan. It also announced that it would sell shares to a strategic partner in two stages: 25 to 35 percent would be sold almost immediately; later another portion would be sold, perhaps bringing private ownership above 50 percent. In April 1999, Parliament amended the Telecommunications Act to allow the government to reduce its interest in TPSA below 51 percent.

More difficult was the sale of a 25 to 35 percent interest to a strategic partner. The government expected to receive bids from a number of international telecommunications companies. At the August 30, 1999 deadline, though, only France Telecom and SBC Communications had tendered bids. Reports stated that SBC had bid only about US$1.8 billion while France Telecom bid about US$3 billion. In November, amid reports that it had made only a token effort, SBC withdrew from the competition. As the sole bidder, France Telecom was unwilling to meet the government's price expectations. The government therefore canceled the tender at the end of the year.

The government initiated a new competition in January 2000. By that time an international telecom rally raised TPSA's stock price and generated more interest in the company. The government stated that it received four bids and identified the makers of three of them: France Telecom; Telecom Italia, and Spain's Telefonica. France Telecom and Telecom Italia were short-listed. France Telecom, in partnership with Kulczyk Holding SA, won the competition, paying US$4.33 billion for 35 percent of TPSA.

The final phase came in September 2001, when the France Telecom/Kulczyk Holding partnership bought another 12.5 percent of TPSA for EUR 988.4 million. With this purchase, the partnership also received an option to purchase an additional 2.5 percent plus one share before the end of 2002. If this offer is exercised, France Telecom and Kulczyk Holding will control 50 percent plus one share of the company. The state would then maintain about a 20 percent share of TPSA.

With TPSA's privatization behind it, the company lost little time in initiating a major restructuring to increase its efficiency.

In December 2001, the company took a first step announcing a 20 percent reduction of its workforce.

By the end of 2001, TPSA had made major strides in improving Poland's telecommunications infrastructure. There had been about 3 million telephone lines in the nation, or about seven per 100 persons in 1989. In 2001, there were about 10.5 million fixed-lines, or 30 per 100 persons. TPSA, with about 30 percent of the market, also served about 3.2 million cellular customers.

The future was not without challenges, however. In 2000, TPSA lost its monopoly on long-distance services, and at the end of 2002, it would lose its monopoly on international connections. Moreover, the revised Telecommunications Act that took effect on January 1, 2001, established legal barriers to the entrance of new competitors to the market and for the expansion of existing ones. Even though Centertel had purchased a digital concession in 1998, both PTC and Polkomtel still had more customers and were aggressively targeting Centertel's profitable business customers. There were even indications that the Ministry of Communications was encouraging TPSA's stronger competitors to combine in order effectively compete with it for the long-distance market.

The international financial environment was harsh for telecommunications companies that had accumulated massive debts at the dawn of the 21st century. Although TPSA denied that it had such problems in 2002, this environment could only add to the above challenges.

Principal Subsidiaries

Incenti SA (51%); OTO Lublin Sp zoo (100%); Otwarty Rynek Elektroniczny SA (100%); Pracownicze Towarzystwo Emeytaine Telekomunikacji Polsidej SA (100%); PTK Centertel Sp zoo (66%); TP Ditel SA (100%); TP Emitel Sp zoo (100%); TP Internet Sp zoo (100%); TP Invest Sp zoo (99.99%); TP MED Sp zoo (100%); TPSA Finance BV (100%); TP SIRCOM Szkolenia i Rekreacja Sp zoo (100%); TP Teltech Sp zoo (100%); TP Wypoezynek Poludnie Sp zoo (100%); TPSA Finance BV (100%).

Principal Competitors

Polska Telefonia Cyfrowa; Polkomtel; Netia; Telefonia Lokaina; NOM.

Further Reading

Adonis, Andrew, et al., "The West Rings the Changes in Eastern Europe," *Financial Times* (London), October 1, 1993, p. 21.

"Ameritech Reportedly Has Sold Polish Cellular Interest," *Washington Telecom Newswire*, December 18, 1996.

Barnes, Hilary and Reuters, "France Telecom Sues Poland for $500m," *Financial Times* (London), January 4, 1996, p. 18.

Bashford, Ray, "Survey of Poland," *Financial Times* (London), June 17, 1993, p. IX.

Bobinski, Christopher, "Poland Poised to Re-open Tenders for Telecom Deals," *Financial Times* (London), September 28, 1993, International Company News, p. 20.

——, "Poland Postpones Decision on $150m Telecom Contract," *Financial Times* (London), January 23, 1991, p. I6.

——, "State Operator Mobilises for Phones Battle," *Financial Times* (London), October 30, 1996, p. 4.

——, "Survey of Poland," *Financial Times* (London), March 18, 1994, p. IV.

——, "Western Partners Stranded by Polish Mobile Phone Move," *Financial Times* (London), October 2,1995, p. 26.

——, "World Telecommunications 29; So Much Ground to Make Up-Poland," *Financial Times* (London), October 1, 1993, p. XXIX.

Bobinski, Christopher, and Anthony Robinson, "Poland Awards GSM Mobile Phone Licences," *Financial Times* (London), February 2, 1996, p. 21.

Dixon, Hugo, "International Telecommunications 5; Liberal Market in the Offing," *Financial Times* (London), April 19, 1990, p. V.

——, "Poland to End Telecom Monopoly," *Financial Times* (London), April 6, 1990, p. I3.

"France Telecom, Ameritech Proceeds with Arbitration in Poland," *Mobile Phone News*, January 8, 1996.

"France Telecom to Raise Stake in Polish Operator TPSA," *Tech Europe*, February 2, 2001, p. 303.

"France Telecom Unit TPSA Plans to Cut 12,500 Jobs in 2002," *Tech Europe*, December 13, 2001, p. 307.

"GSM Row: Ameritech Goes to Arbitration," *Finance East Europe*, October 20, 1995.

Jeffrey, Peter, "World Watch," *Wall Street Journal*, November 1, 1999, p. A41.

"Legal Action Launched," *Communications Daily*, August 26, 1996, p. 4.

Leighton, Oonagh, and Guy Norton, "At TPSA's Beck and Call," *Central European*, September, 1999, pp. 34–36.

"News: France Telecom/Ameritech Wins in Poland," *Mobile Communications*, June 20, 1991.

Pate, Kelly, "Ameritech Fights for Right to New Polish GSM Cellular Network," *RCR Radio Communications Report*, January 1, 1996, p. 16.

——, "Polkomtel Begins Polish GSM Service on Its Competitor's Heels," *RCR Radio Communications Report*, October 7, 1996, p. 40.

——, "Three Groups Compete to Operate Poland's GSM Digital System," *RCR Radio Communications Report,* January 8, 1996, p. 18.

Pawlicki, Machiej, "Polish Telephone Industry Opened for Foreigners," January 28, 1991, p. 3.

"Poland's Ambitious 2000 Programme," *Privatisation International*, October, 1999.

"Poland Could Launch More Telecom Sales," *Tech Europe*, November 18, 1999.

"Poland Defers Cellular Decision," *Mobile Communications*, August 2, 1990.

"Poland Launches Controversial Contest for Two GSM Licences," *Mobil Communications*, June 15, 1995.

"Poland Looks Abroad to Remedy Its 'Catastrophic' Telecoms," *Telecom Markets*, December 14, 1989.

"Poland Poised to Award Cellular Telephone Licences," *Mobile Communications*, April 26, 1990.

"Poland's Cellular Winners to Be Announced," *East European Markets*, May 31, 1991.

"Polish Cellular Licence Contest Could Be Re-opened," *Mobile Communications*, January 31, 1991.

"Polish Cellular Telephone Network Launches in Warsaw," *Mobile Communications*, June 18, 1992.

"Polish Government Prepares for Sale of Polish Telecom," *Newsbytes*, January 8, 1996.

"PTT to Be Split," *Finance East Europe*, December 18, 1991.

Reed, John, "Companies and Finance Europe: TPSA Prepares for Competition," *Financial Times* (London), May 14, 2002.

Robinson, Anthony, "New Company Breaks into Polish Telecoms," *Financial Times* (London), September 1, 1993, p. 6.

Schares, Gail E., et al., "The East Bloc's $100 Billion Phone Bill," *Business Week*, November 20, 1989, p. 139.

Smosarski, Grog, "Poland Seeks Finance for Ambitious Expansion of Telecommunications," *Central European*, June 1994, pp. 33 + .

"Sorry, Reformer, the Line is Dead," *The Economist* (US), July 21, 1990, p. 52.

"Sprint and RP Telekom to Build and Operate Local Telecommunication Network in Poland," *PR Newswire*, January 18, 1994.

"Telekomunikacja Polska Announces That the Polish Parliament Has Adopted Two New Amendments," *PR Newswire*, April 26, 1999, p. 3,071.

"TPSA Doesn't Want Strategic Investor," *Finance East Europe*, November 8, 1996.

"US Telecoms Company in JV," *Finance East Europe*, January 21, 1994.

Williamson, Elizabeth, "French Buy into Polish State Firm," *Wall Street Journal*, July 25, 2000, p. A14.

——, "Poland to Name Bidder for Stake in Telecom Firm," *Wall Street Journal*, May 22, 2000, p. C11E.

—Anne L. Potter

Telstra Corporation Limited

242 Exhibition Street, Level 41
Melbourne, Victoria 3000
Australia
Telephone: +61 (3) 9634-6400
Fax: +61 (3) 9632-3215
Web site: http://www.telstra.com

Public Company
Incorporated: 1992 as Overseas Telecommunications
    Corporation Limited
Employees: 50,761
Sales: A$19,840 million (2000)
Stock Exchanges: New York Australia New Zealand
Ticker Symbol: TLS
NAIC: 513310 Wired Telecommunications Carriers;
    513320 Wireless Telecommunications Carriers
    (Except Satellite); 513322 Cellular and Other Wireless
    Telecommunications; 514191 Online Information
    Services; 514210 Data Processing Services;

Telstra Corporation Limited is a full-service telecommunications, information services, and network platform company that competes in all telecommunications markets throughout Australia. The former state-owned monopoly provides traditional telephone service to residences and businesses, local and long distance service, mobile telecommunications, and a comprehensive array of data services, including Internet and online services. Telstra is Australia's leading Internet service provider. The company also provides wholesale services to other carriers and service providers, creates and maintains telephone directories, and offers pay-television services through its Foxtel subsidiary.

In addition, Telstra has literally wired Australia from coast to coast. Its fixed telephone network extends from major cities to the rural outback. Telstra also has developed a variety of delivery platforms over which services are provided, including transaction and digital data networks, a hybrid fiber coaxial cable broadband network, Internet protocol networks, and access to international satellite infrastructure.

Telstra's Roots

In 1901 the Australian Postmaster-General's Department was established to manage all domestic telephone, telegraph, and postal services. In 1946 the Overseas Telecommunications Commission was established to manage Australia's international telecommunications. The Australian Telecommunications Commission, trading as Telecom Australia, was created as a separate entity in July 1975 following the breakup of the Postmaster-General's Department. In 1980 a group called Business Telecommunications Services began lobbying for deregulation. A 1982 task force was recruited in response to requests for a public inquiry into telecommunications. The task force issued the Davidson Report, which recommended that Telecom be divided into two organizations. One of these organizations would be allowed to compete with privately owned carriers. The ruling Liberal-National coalition government accepted the report but did not implement the findings.

Meanwhile, Telecom unions protested against deregulation, which would lead to higher telephone bills, decrease the number of jobs, and lessen service quality. When the Australian Labor Party was elected to power in 1983, it affirmed its commitment to an ongoing telecommunications monopoly with state-run Telecom. But demands persisted from the private sector to privatize Telecom. While continuing to trade as Telecom Australia, the Commission became the Australian Telecommunications Corporation beginning January 1989.

The Early 1990s

The Australian telecommunications market was first liberalized in 1991 when new entrant Optus was allowed to build and own fixed and mobile networks. The Overseas Telecommunications Commission and Telecom Australia became the Australian and Overseas Telecommunications Corporation Limited (AOTC) following a February 1992 merger. The new company had posted annual revenues of around US$7 billion, assets of US$17 billion, and profits of US$1.5 billion. AOTC was the sixth-largest user of the Intelsat communications system and the third-largest owner of submarine communications cables. At this time its global network connected 218 destinations in 185 countries. Former AT&T executive Frank Blount was the surprise choice as chief executive for AOTC, and he planned to pursue global expansion for the company.

Telstra Corporation Limited became the legal corporate name of the merged entity in 1993. The domestic trading name, Telecom Australia, was changed to Telstra on July 1, 1995 to distinguish Telstra from other telecommunications companies in increasingly competitive and deregulated markets. The company had been trading as Telstra internationally since 1993.

In the early 1990s the competitive landscape began to change for Telstra and the Australian telecommunications market in general. In 1991 Telstra became subject to competition in the national long distance and international telephone service markets for the first time.

In 1992 Telstra faced increased competition for mobile phone service from Optus Communications, the consortium made up of Bell South, Cable and Wireless, Mayne Nickless, and institutional investors. In order to offset the potential loss of market share within Australia to new rivals, Blount embraced a service expansion plan to mainland Asia. The company already had strong footing in the Asian markets of Indochina, Hong Kong, Thailand, the Philippines, and Kazakhstan, but Blount looked to expand the company's reach even further into Indonesia, China, Taiwan, South Korea, Malaysia, and Japan. AOTC's strong domestic base in Australia would prove its biggest asset in this effort.

Optus Communications also became a competitor to Telstra in cable television in 1994, when Optus TV built its own cable network. This prompted Telstra to accelerate the building of its own high-bandwidth network and form a joint venture with Rupert Murdoch's News Corporation. Dubbed Foxtel, the joint venture delivered pay-television services along with regular cable television. Service overlaps with Optus proved costly for Telstra, which later scaled back its cable television services.

The telecommunications landscape changed once again for Telstra in July 1995, when the company's local telephone network was opened to provide access to other service providers. The move was forced by the Australian Competition and Consumer Commission, which ruled that other telecommunications providers should be allowed to provide services directly to homes and workplaces via the copper local loop owned by Telstra. The move greatly benefited two Telstra rivals, Cable & Wireless Optus and AAPT Limited. Competitors were also allowed to provide high-speed Internet access, data and pay-television services to add further competition for Telstra.

Telstra's Road to Privatization

In the meantime, Telstra was generating respectable profits. The company reported record earnings of US$2.3 billion for the year ending June 30, 1996, despite the fact that Telstra had been investing heavily in infrastructure during this time. It also planned to double its projected spending to US$20 billion for the next five years for goods and services. Outsourcing was also on the horizon, which meant that a significant number of staff would be eliminated over the next few years. Telstra had already sold off its technology division to IBM, which cost 1,200 employees their jobs. Another 2,000 staff were released in late 1996 when Telstra sold its cable-laying operation to Leighton Holdings. Another sale, this time its conformance testing division, to Comtest Laboratories was also pending. In September 1996, Telstra management released an employee reduction plan to reduce staff levels by 23,000 to nearly 51,000 over the next three years. The board of directors framed the layoffs in the context of a leaner, newly deregulated telecom marketplace. However, critics felt the reduction represented an overreaction to weak competitors.

Although public opinion polls told Australia's politicians that the majority of citizens were against the privatization of Telstra, the issue came to the forefront of the Coalition government. The nation was under mounting financial pressure due to the growing economic crisis in the Asia-Pacific region, and the Coalition government hoped that the A$8 billion gained from the sell-off its shares in Telstra would ease its fiscal burden. In a controversial move, the Coalition linked an A$1 billion environmental policy to the partial privatization of Telstra. In doing so, it hoped to gain the support of the minority parties in the Senate which were more concerned about the environment than with the privatization of Telstra.

The fate of the government's bill to privatize one-third of its stake in Telstra was in the hands of two independent members of the Australian Senate. Brian Harradine and Mal Colson previously wanted Telstra to remain a public entity, but at the last minute the two had a change of heart. With the support of Harradine and Colson, Telstra offered the Liberal-National coalition the crowning achievement of its first term. The two Senate members placed personal conditions on the Telstra sell-off: at least A$100 million had to be earmarked for ecological advances in Tasmania, home of Harradine; and Telstra was required to create jobs in both Tasmania and Queensland, Colson's home. The most far-reaching concession was demanded of Telstra by the parliament, which retained the right to direct the company in the best interests of the nation.

Australians eventually began to look forward to a new, open telecommunications market. Local investors were expected to show heavy support for the Telstra share sale, just as they had for the recent privatization of the Australian airline company Qantas and the Commonwealth Bank. Foreign investment was to be capped at 35 percent of the privatized portion of the company.

Australia's telecommunications markets had opened to full competition on July 1, 1997. This meant that there was no limit on the number of carriers that own transmission infrastructure able to enter the Australian market. On November 17, 1997, the Commonwealth of Australia successfully floated one-third of Telstra on the Australian, New York, and New Zealand stock exchanges. Brokers were inundated with applications for shares of the telecom giant. The flotation made Telstra the biggest

Key Dates:

1901: Postmaster-General's Department is established to manage domestic telephone, telegraph, and postal services.

1975: Australian Telecommunications Commission is created as a separate entity.

1989: Australian Telecommunications Corporation Act establishes Austel.

1990: Approved merger of Telecom and Overseas Telecommunications Commission (OTC).

1992: OTC and Austel become Australian and Overseas Telecommunications Corporation Limited (AOTC).

1993: Telstra Corporation Limited becomes legal corporate name of merged entity.

1997: Australia's telecommunications markets opened to full competition.

1997: Commonwealth of Australia successfully offers one-third of Telstra on the Australian, New York, and New Zealand stock exchanges.

2000: Telstra builds a communications network to bring the Syndey 2000 Olympic Games to more than 400 billion worldwide viewers.

company by market capitalization in Australia, with a value of A$43 billion and more than 1.8 million shareholders. At the time, Telstra represented the sixth-largest telecommunications listing in the previous two months worldwide.

In March 1998 just months after the wildly successful initial public offering, the Australian government announced plans to sell its remaining two-thirds stake in Telstra after the next election, or by March 1999. The sale was valued at US$30 billion based on the Telstra share price at the time. But in July 1998 the Telstra privatization bill was defeated in the Senate. Lawmakers cited concerns that service in rural areas would suffer if Telstra were given completely to the private sector. A week later, the Cabinet approved a plan to privatize another 16 percent of the company, which would still leave 51 percent in state hands. The plan would include service guarantees to rural customers, but leave the government with less money to pay down debt.

Telstra launched a new range of wholesale high-speed voice and data services in August 1998. The products were aimed at Internet service providers and other carriers needing high-bandwidth paths between major cities in Australia. Although deregulation had chipped away at the former telecom monopoly's market share, Telstra was able to counter the effect with productivity gains. During the previous six months, Telstra doubled earnings to A$1.1 billion.

In 1999 Telstra reported Australia's largest-ever profit when it announced US$2.2 million in earnings for the fiscal year ending June 30. CEO Ziggy Switkowski boasted that the company was succeeding in the face of intense competition in a changing industry. Telstra's priorities were to improve the quality of service and reduce faults on its Customer Assess Network, and provide further investment in the new digital Code Division Multiple Access (CDMA) network. The company said CDMA would bring a new era in Australian mobile communications, particularly for those living in rural and remote parts of the country.

Ready to Compete

Telstra continued to devote significant resources to upgrade and modernize its networks and systems. The evolution of the marketplace demanded that Telstra change its corporate culture to be more commercially oriented and customer-focused. It also continued to form strategic alliances in order to expand its range of products and services.

Telstra announced in December 1999 that it would partner with Phone.com Inc. to offer wireless Internet access to its customers. The next month, Telstra planned to buy Internet service provider Ozmail for A$197 million. In August 2000, Telstra substantially increased the capacity of its Internet Protocol network in the United States due to an agreement with Cisco Systems.

At this time, Telstra planned to double its existing Internet capacity between Australia and the U.S. before the Sydney 2000 Olympic Games. Telstra built a A$400 million communications network to bring the Olympic Games to more than four billion worldwide viewers. The Telstra Millennium Network was nine years in the making. It consisted of 1.5 million kilometers of fiber-optic cable feeding Telstra's growing national network, but it was also used to provide voice, video, and data transmissions during the Olympics. The project included 30,000 new telephone lines, the ability to handle 300,000 mobile phones, and 280 video links. Telstra had the sole responsibility of supplying all telecommunications for the 2000 Games. The network was continually used in Australia after the Games finished.

In October 2000 Telstra and Hong Kong-based Pacific Century CyberWorks (PCCW) announced plans for a new Pan-Asian telecommunications alliance. After lengthy negotiations, the two companies agreed to develop a global IP backbone, provide bulk carrier services for Internet-based information, and a Pan-Asian mobile phone firm. The deal significantly boosted Telstra's regional reach. The deal, after some revisions, gave Telstra more control over PCCW's mobile telephone assets and reduced its cash commitment by US$532 million. Telstra also said it would buy 60 percent of PCCW's mobile telephone unit HKT Mobile for US$1.68 billion.

Telstra completed an alliance it sought for more than a year with Centura Software Corporation in April 2001. Telstra and Centura Software planned to aggressively mobilize securely transmitted data from anywhere in the world. The two along with Powerlan announced joint efforts to form the Enterprise Mobility Alliance.

The next month, Telstra said it expected less favorable industry conditions to affect the second half of the fiscal year. Also in May 2001, the Australian government said it would delay any further privatization of Telstra until the fiscal year ending June 30, 2004.

Principal Competitors

Cable & Wireless Optus; One.Tel; Telecom Corporation of New Zealand.

Further Reading

"All Australian Telstra," *Economist*, July 19, 1997, p. 57.
"Australia Sweetens Telstra Sale for Rural Areas," *Financial Times*, July 10, 1998.
"Deregulation in Australia, by Design or Default," *Telecommunications Policy*, December 1984.
"Long-Distance Vision," *Far Eastern Economic Review*, June 4, 1998.
"Not Exactly One Nation," *Economist*, July 18, 1998, p. 38.

Pease, Robert, "Telstra Readies Fiber Network for 2000 Olympics," *Lightwave*, February 1999, p. 29.
"Telstra Brokers Were Swamped," *Financial Times*, November 19, 1997.
"Telstra Privatisation," *Asian Business Review*, April 1996, p. 33.
"Telstra Shapes up for Competition," *Communications International*, June 1997.

—Rebecca Rayko Cason

Tennessee Valley Authority

400 West Summit Hill Drive
Knoxville, Tennessee 37902-1499
U.S.A.
Telephone: (865) 632-2101
Web site: http://www.tva.gov

Self-Financed Government Agency
Established: 1933
Employees: 13,000 (2002 est.)
Sales: $6.99 billion (2001)
Stock Exchanges: New York
Ticker Symbol: TVC
NAIC: 221111 Hydroelectric Power Generation; 221112
Fossil Fuel Electric Power Generation; 221113
Nuclear Electric Power Generation; 221119 Other
Electric Power Generation; 221121 Electric Bulk
Power Transmission and Control; 221122 Electric
Power Distribution

Established by the U.S. Congress in 1933 as a critical component of President Franklin Roosevelt's Depression-era "New Deal," the Tennessee Valley Authority (TVA) was initially created primarily to manage the Tennessee River's navigation and flood control problems, to encourage reforestation and proper land use, and to foster agricultural and industrial development. In time, the TVA grew to become the nation's largest public power provider serving more than 8 million customers over an 80,000-square mile region covering the Tennessee Valley. This area includes most of Tennessee and portions of Mississippi, Kentucky, Alabama, Georgia, North Carolina, and Virginia. Following decades of operations as a massive bureaucracy, the TVA has dramatically streamlined itself in recent years in order to boost its competitiveness in preparation for the anticipated onset of deregulation.

The Genesis of the TVA in the Early Twentieth Century

The federal government purchased a site in 1916 on the Tennessee River in Muscle Shoals, Alabama, where a sudden drop in river depth resulted in strong rapids that inhibited ships from progressing further upstream. Dam construction began in this location to produce power for the manufacturing of explosives needed during World War I, but the war had concluded before this new project was operational. During the 1920s, Congress considered whether the property should remain a public site or be sold to the private sector.

Nebraska Senator George W. Norris fought for the property to remain under public control. He had little support from his Congressional colleagues, until the advent of the Depression, when government economic assistance became more widely accepted. President Franklin Roosevelt supported Senator Norris' plan, and envisioned it as one way to help achieve the success of his "New Deal," which aimed to save the U.S. economy from the Depression. With a lack of national investment in the Tennessee Valley region, President Roosevelt requested that Congress create "a corporation clothed with the power of government but possessed of the flexibility and initiative of a private enterprise." In agreement with the President's goal, Congress passed the Tennessee Valley Authority Act on May 18, 1933. Through this legislation, which far exceeded Norris' initial plan, TVA was established as a federal agency charged with improving the navigation and flood control of the Tennessee River, encouraging reforestation and proper land use in the area, leading regional agricultural and industrial development, and operating national defense-related properties in Muscle Shoals, Alabama.

By June 1934, 9,173 people were already employed by the TVA, and 16 dams were built by the agency between 1933 and 1944. Before the TVA, dams were engineered exclusively for either electricity generation or flood control. The agency was able to address both needs within a single dam, which soon became the global standard.

At the time, the Tennessee Valley included some of the most under-served areas of the South. While 90 percent of Americans in urban areas had electricity by the 1930's, merely 10 percent of rural Americans enjoyed the same benefit. Most utility companies avoided powering rural areas due to the significant expense of setting up electric lines over such expansive areas, and because of a concern that rural Americans would not be able to afford electricity. This inequity between urban and rural communities in the United States led to President Roosevelt's resolve that the government must become involved.

Company Perspectives:

In keeping with its mission of generating prosperity in the Tennessee Valley, TVA's leadership standard is to deliver excellence in business performance and public service by supplying low-cost reliable power, supporting a thriving river system, and stimulating economic growth across a seven-state region of the southeastern United States.

Private power companies took issue with the cheaper energy the federally-subsidized TVA provided. President Roosevelt saw the TVA as a benchmark by which the rates of private utility companies could be evaluated. Seen as a threat to the private sector, the TVA was sued by many power companies during the 1930s. One such suit claimed that the government had overstepped its Constitutional powers by creating an electric utility corporation. Testifying before Congress regarding the TVA in 1935, John D. Battle, Executive Secretary of the National Coal Association, stated that, "we are willing to be put out of business if it can be done in a plain straightforward business-like manner, but we do object to our government putting us out of business." The TVA was victorious in a case ruled on by the Supreme Court in February 1936, and in 1939, the TVA Act was upheld by the Supreme Court as constitutional.

Beyond the electricity generated by newly built dams, the founding of the TVA soon resulted in a variety of other important benefits to the Tennessee Valley. The agency provided farmers with advice to boost crop yields, aided in reforestation and forest fire control, and developed fertilizers. Rather than carrying out a predetermined federal master plan, the TVA aimed to develop the region by working with community members and their state and local agencies.

From its inception until 1938, the three members of the TVA's board jockeyed for control of the overall vision for the Authority. President Roosevelt removed Arthur E. Morgan as the TVA's chairman in March 1938 due to internal organizational conflicts, obstruction of the work of the agency, and unsubstantiated allegations Chairman Morgan made against fellow directors.

TVA in the 1940s and 1950s: Becoming the Top United States Electric Utility

In the 1940s during World War II, the TVA conducted a remarkable hydropower construction program, one of the largest ever in the United States, to provide electricity for aluminum plants that supplied the much-needed metal to manufacturers of bombs and planes. The TVA had finished a 650-mile navigation channel as long as the Tennessee River by the conclusion of World War II. It had also become the largest supplier of electricity in the country, although demand still exceeded the capacity of its hydroelectric dams.

During the 1950s, unable to secure federal funding of coal-fired plant construction, the TVA lobbied Congress for the ability to issue bonds. President Dwight Eisenhower was not enamored of the TVA, however, citing the agency in 1953 as an example of "creeping socialism." Nonetheless, in 1959, Congress passed legislation which made the TVA a self-financing

operation, provided that the TVA would restrict its operations to the existing Tennessee Valley region. More than a dozen public operations similar to the TVA had been created around the world since its creation, with thousands of international visitors having visited the Tennessee Valley to learn about the agency's integrated regional development.

Strip mining and coal burning increased significantly in the 1950s as the TVA worked to meet energy demand—actions that a later chairman of the TVA, S. David Freeman (1978–1981), cited in *Environment* in April 1985 as causing "environmental problems that spoiled land, degraded waters, and polluted air." Chairman Freeman added that although the TVA's dams protected against flooding, they also created lakes that in turn flooded farmland.

The Advent of the TVA's Nuclear Power Program in the 1960s

In the early 1960's, the TVA developed "Land Between the Lakes," a 170,000-acre national park on a 40-mile strip of wooded land located between two reservoirs in western Kentucky and Tennessee. This outdoor education and recreation area attracts 2 million visitors annually.

The Tennessee Valley experienced strong economic growth throughout the 1960s, as farms and forests were in top condition and residents enjoyed some of the lowest electric rates in the nation. To address the continued growth in demand for economical power, the TVA designed a colossal plan in 1966 calling for the eventual construction of 17 nuclear power plants throughout the region.

Energy Crisis and Environmental Cleanup in the 1970s

The international oil embargo in 1973 dramatically altered the Tennessee Valley's economy, along with that of the rest of the country. Fuel costs continued to rise for the remainder of the decade. In some regions of the Tennessee Valley, alternative energy sources were virtually eliminated over the years, and this became clear with the spiraling energy costs of the 1970s. Many environmentalists opposed the TVA's coal and nuclear power programs, and environmental organizations initiated lawsuits against the TVA with a variety of allegations—including violations of the National Environmental Protection Act of 1969 and the Endangered Species Act of 1973. A serious fire at the Browns Ferry, Alabama nuclear plant in 1975 could have resulted in a catastrophe, but the situation was controlled before reaching that level. The TVA had become the worst United States sulfur dioxide polluter by 1977 (2 million tons emitted annually and one-tenth of U.S. emissions), putting it in violation of the Clean Air Act. In 1978, the TVA began a billion-dollar cleanup initiative to reduce sulfur dioxide emissions from its 12 coal-fired plants. Six years later, sulfur dioxide emissions were cut in half and all plants had become compliant with the Clean Air Act.

A Move Toward Conservation in the Late 1970s and Early 1980s

By the end of the 1970s, the TVA's new leadership headed by Chairman S. David Freeman began to steer the agency in a

Key Dates:

1916: The United States federal government purchases a Tennessee River site in Muscle Shoals, Alabama, for damn construction—to become part of the Tennessee Valley Authority (TVA).

1933: The Tennessee Valley Authority Act passed by the U.S. Congress.

1939: The TVA Act upheld by the U.S. Supreme Court as constitutional.

1959: The U.S. Congress passes legislation making the TVA a self-financing agency.

1966: The TVA develops a plan to create a system of nuclear power plants.

1975: Fire at the TVA's Browns Ferry, Alabama, nuclear power plant.

1978: Billion-dollar cleanup effort by the TVA to reduce sulfur dioxide emissions from coal-fired plants.

1983: The TVA board halts new construction of dams or structures along the Tennessee River.

1985: Five functioning TVA nuclear reactors shut down due to regulatory concerns.

1995: Termination of three remaining TVA nuclear reactor construction projects.

1999: The U.S. Department of Energy announces plan to produce radioactive tritium gas at a TVA nuclear reactor for use in nuclear weapons. Congressional appropriations to the TVA's non-power programs are eliminated.

2002: The TVA board approves restarting Browns Ferry nuclear reactor.

new direction with conservation programs, experiments in alternative energy sources like solar power, and strengthened relationships with the international community. The TVA started to focus on conservation rather than power-plant construction as a top priority for its customers—offering free audits and low-interest financing in order to foster the winterization of buildings to save energy. The agency's investment in nuclear power was also reduced significantly. Soil erosion due to inferior farming techniques, a problem in the early years of the TVA, returned as a concern in the 1970s and 1980s, which led the TVA to offer technical advise on the problem once more. This work resulted in 1.2 million tons of topsoil saved each year. With the TVA's tree planting projects, the valley reached a forestation level of 60 percent. The TVA's renewed commitment to conservation was also exemplified in a 1983 board policy that halted construction of additional dams or structures along the Tennessee River, and ended the channeling of more streams in the Tennessee Valley.

Hard Times for the TVA's Nuclear Program in the mid-1980s

By the early 1980s, Tennessee Valley electric rates were five times higher than a decade earlier. As was the case with other U.S. utilities, several nuclear plant construction projects were terminated due to lower energy demand and higher construction costs, with billions already spent on these sites. The TVA's management of its nuclear power program came under serious attack in the mid-1980s. The agency had received 12 Nuclear Regulatory Commission fines since 1980, and was under Congressional investigation for alleged mismanagement and cover-ups. The TVA had to shut down its five functioning reactors in 1985, due to tough new federal nuclear regulations. The TVA's plans to recover from these closings were in disarray, and responsibility for the nuclear power program had been shared across multiple divisions, making it difficult to proceed with an integrated plan. Eventually, the TVA obtained new consultants and staff with expertise in nuclear power. During 1988, almost one-third of the TVA's 33,000 employee workforce was laid off and management salaries were frozen. By 1989, two nuclear reactors were operational. The massive borrowing practices of the TVA, keeping the agency on the verge of bankruptcy, led to $20 billion of nuclear debt. Congress placed a debt ceiling of $30 billion on the TVA.

1990s: The TVA's Return to Nuclear Power

In an effort to return to a stronger position in the industry, the TVA's Chairman Marvin Runyon focused the agency on cutting costs and boosting efficiency and productivity. Electric rates stabilized in the late 1980s, and this stability continued well into the 1990s. Much of the TVA's lauded 1985 energy conservation program was scrapped, in favor of a renewed interest in nuclear power to meet anticipated growth in energy demand, much to former Chairman S. David Freeman's dismay. By 1991, three inactive nuclear reactors went back on-line after years of inactivity.

In May 1992, the TVA purchased emissions allowances from Wisconsin Power and Light, considered one of the cleanest operations in the United States This type of transaction, enabling the TVA to emit 10,000 tons of sulfur dioxide, became permissible under the 1990 Clean Air Act and was cheaper than using alternative fuels. The TVA's 1992 net income of $120 million had fallen significantly from the previous year's total of $286 million. By 1993, having exceeded requirements of the Clean Air Act, the TVA earned its own emissions allowances for its use and sale.

The TVA continued to pursue adding additional nuclear power capacity in 1994, with three reactors operational at the time. Two reactors in Watts Bar, Tennessee remained under construction, originally budgeted at $625 million 22 years previously, with $7.7 billion spent as of 1994. In February 1995, the TVA announced plans to terminate its three remaining nuclear reactor construction projects, which would have required at least another $8.8 billion to complete, if not more. This decision brought an end to a 28-consecutive-year program of nuclear reactor construction. The TVA sought partners to help convert one of those sites into a gas-firing plant. One reactor at Watts Bar was still able to begin operations later that year, with commercial power generation starting the following year.

The U.S. General Accounting Office questioned the TVA's long-term sustainability in 1995, but with its recent change in direction, the TVA was optimistic about its prospects for achieving a more competitive position. As the $208 billion electric power industry moved towards deregulation as an inevitability, the TVA formed a Public Power Alliance with Municipal Electric Authority of Georgia, Old Dominion Electric Cooperative of Virginia, and the Municipal Energy Agency of Mississippi in order to serve as an effective lobbying entity and to share strategies and innovations with each other. A deregulated industry would create a free market environment where customers and distributors could openly select utilities regardless of their location in the country.

Regaining Competitive Position in the Late-1990s

During the 1990's, the TVA significantly reduced its operating costs, cut its workforce by more than 50 percent, and boosted plant capacity, earning the company a third place ranking for lowest production costs by a major electric utility in 1997. Early that year, the TVA Chairman Craven Crowell offered, but soon retracted, a suggestion that Congress spin off the TVA's non-power-related operations to other public agencies and eliminate the federal funding it received for those programs—enabling it to focus on the electric utility industry. The TVA had been receiving just over $100 million from Congress each year, which was less than 2 percent of the agency's $5.7 billion budget. The TVA's private utility competitors argued that the public agency's indirect subsidies, mostly tax exemptions, totaled $1.2 billion annually—making it difficult for private utilities to compete. Southern lawmakers were shocked that such a proposal could be suggested by someone within the TVA, rather than by the agency's opponents, as was usually the case. They worried that this situation would lead Congress to eventually sell off the TVA as a private utility, which might bankrupt the organization due to the agency's $27 billion of debt.

In July 1997, the TVA settled a lawsuit with several private utilities that accused the TVA of selling electricity beyond its limited region mandated by Congress. As part of the settlement, the TVA promised to cooperate in future deregulation efforts by the electric industry. With especially high energy demands during the summer of 1997, the TVA found that purchased power was not as reliable as it needed. This led the TVA to plan on establishing firm contracts with others for power and exploring the possibility of purchasing other utility operations entirely to guarantee reliability.

The U.S. Department of Energy decided in 1999 it would eventually produce radioactive tritium gas at one of the TVA's nuclear reactors for use in nuclear weapons—anticipated to begin during 2003. This would mark the first time a commercial U.S. nuclear reactor would be used for military purposes—a prospect that led critics of the decision to express grave concern about the blurring of the separation between civilian and military operations. The TVA switched to cleaner coal for its plants in June 1999, helping the agency adhere to environmental regulations. In September, the TVA announced it would not raise rates for the following year, and planned to keep rates stable for the following decade through increased productivity and controlled operating costs.

The Environmental Protection Agency (EPA) charged the TVA in November with violating pollution regulations of the Clean Air Act in seven coal-fired plants, with a cleanup that would cost upwards of $1 billion. The TVA challenged the EPA's interpretation of the Clean Air Act, and a U.S. Court of Appeals ordered in 2002 that the two parties use a mediator to

resolve the issue, though this approach failed which put the case back to the court. The TVA's Congressional appropriations were terminated for fiscal year 1999, though the TVA was permitted to refinance some of its high interest debt, which will result in significant savings in the future. Despite the loss of Congressional appropriations, the TVA posted net income of $119.3 million in 1999.

In 2000, a new Public Power Institute was formed by the TVA, marking a return to its past conservation and energy development initiatives. The TVA began to explore means to produce electricity drawn from the sun, wind, and landfill gas sources, while charging customers a premium price for "green power." A $3.4 million wind-powered generator construction project was announced in September 2000 for Knoxville, Tennessee, and demand for cleaner energy continued to grow. Five nuclear reactors were operational in 2000, although $10 billion of investment from terminated reactors had not yet been written off. Debt reduction was not progressing as rapidly as planned, but $1.7 billion had been cut since 1996's debt cap of $27 billion.

Heading Towards Deregulation in the Twenty-First Century

The TVA's board voted in May 2001 to invest in the upgrading of two nuclear power plants in order to meet growing demand for electricity and avoid relying on outside providers. Having been among the nation's worst nuclear programs in the 1980's, the TVA had made significant progress in the 1990s and, by 2001, was ranked in the top quartile in the United States Partnering with the British corporation Innogy PLC, the TVA also announced plans to construct a $25 million energy storage plant—the first of its kind in the United States—using regenerative fuel cell technology to store energy in bulk. In July 2001, President George W. Bush named TVA board member Glenn McCullough to replace outgoing Chairman Craven Crowell. Later in the year, Chairman McCullough voiced his support for an electric utility deregulation bill that would provide competition and choice throughout the TVA's current region, and this bill was under consideration by Congress in 2002.

The TVA wrote off $3.4 billion in assets from unfinished nuclear reactors, resulting in a $3.3 billion deficit for fiscal year 2001. With a $7.1 billion budget adopted for fiscal year 2002, the TVA launched a $2.5 billion capital spending plan—its largest since the mid-1990s—focused on new transmission lines, pollution reduction from coal-fired plants, and increased productivity from current and future plants. At this point, residential customers' rates had only been raised once since 1987. Chairman McCullough pledged to improve industrial rates, which had been kept at an average level over the years.

In April 2002, the TVA partnered with Southern Co. of Atlanta, Entergy of New Orleans, and Midwest Independent Transmission System Operator of Carmel, Indiana in an agreement to provide "seamless wholesale power trading" in the Southeast and Midwest, providing uniform access and more effective transmission of electricity. In May, the TVA's board approved restarting the Browns Ferry nuclear reactor, the agency's oldest, which was shut down in 1985 due to safety concerns and would cost an estimated $1.8 billion to restart. Repairs were slated to begin in 2003, with the reactor expected to restart in 2007. A 2002 U.S. General Accounting Office study of the TVA found that its customers rates were between 14 and 22 percent less than competitors, and that the agency functions with a smaller staff than other electric utilities.

The Tennessee Valley Authority has faced a variety of significant challenges and controversies over the course of its lengthy history. Although the TVA began as a dynamic new model for regional integrated resource development and ballooned into an immense bureaucratic agency with billions in debt that remain today, it has transformed itself in recent years into a much leaner operation that appears to be committed to debt reduction and is preparing for the arrival of deregulation.

Further Reading

Dumaine, Brian, ''Nuclear Scandal Shakes the TVA,'' *Fortune*, October 27, 1986, p. 40.

Freeman, S. David, ''The Nine Lives of TVA,'' *Environment*, April 1985, pp. 6–11.

Higgins, Benjamin, ''The American Frontier and the TVA,'' *Society*, March/April 1995, p. 34.

Hodge, Clarence Lewis, *The Tennessee Valley Authority: A National Experiment in Regionalism*, New York: Russell & Russell, 1968.

Martin, Roscoe C., *TVA: The First Twenty Years*, Knoxville: University of Alabama Press and University of Tennessee Press, 1956.

Moore, J. R., *The Economic Impact of TVA*, Knoxville: University of Tennessee Press, 1967.

Neuse, Steven M., ''TVA at Age Fifty: Reflections and Retrospect,'' *Public Administration Review*, November/December 1983, pp. 491–499.

Sheffield, Christopher, ''TVA Looks to New Alliances, Both Foreign and Domestic,'' *Mississippi Business Journal*, November 25, 1996, p. 18.

Upbin, Bruce, ''The Tennessee Valley Anachronism,'' *Forbes*, May 19, 1997, p. 52.

—Christopher W. Frerichs

TOTAL FINA ELF

Total Fina Elf S.A.

2, Place de la Coupole
La Défense 6
92078 Paris La Défense Cedex
France
Telephone: +33 (1) 47 44 45 46
Web site: http://www.totalfinaelf.com

Public Company
Incorporated: 1924 as Compagnie Française des Pétroles
Employees: 122,025 (2001)
Sales: EUR105.3 billion (US$105.76 billion) (2001)
Stock Exchanges: Euronext London New York
Ticker Symbols: FR0000120271 (Euronext), TOF (London), TOT (New York)
NAIC: 212111 Bituminous Coal and Lignite Surface Mining; 211112 Natural Gas Liquid Extraction; 211111 Crude Petroleum and Natural Gas Extraction; 213111 Drilling Oil and Gas Wells; 541360 Geophysical Surveying and Mapping Services; 213112 Support Activities for Oil and Gas Operations; 324110 Petroleum Refineries; 212113 Anthracite Mining; 447110 Gasoline Stations with convenience Store; 447190 Other Gasoline Stations; 324210 Asphalt Paving Mixture and Block Manufacturing; 324191 Petroleum Lubricating Oil and Grease Manufacturing; 324199 All Other Petroleum and Coal Products Manufacturing; 326220 Rubber and Plastics Hoses and Belting Manufacturing; 339991 Gasket, Packing and Sealing Device Manufacturing; 326192 All Other Rubber Product Manufacturing; 325510 Paint and Coating Manufacturing; 325520 Adhesive Manufacturing; 325199 All Other Basic Organic Chemical Manufacturing; 325998 All Other Miscellaneous Chemical Products and Preparation Manufacturing; 325910 Printing Ink Manufacturing; 325411 Medicinal and Botanical Manufacturing; 325412 Pharmaceutical Preparation Manufacturing.

Total Fina Elf S.A. is one of the four largest oil, natural gas, and specialty chemicals companies in the world, along with BP Amoco PLC, Exxon-Mobil Corporation, Royal Dutch/Shell Group PLC, and Chevron Texaco Corporation. Its activities are organized into three main areas: upstream, downstream, and chemicals. The company's upstream sector consists of the exploration for and production of crude oil and natural gas, along with development activities in gas and electricity and operations in coal mining. Its downstream unit focuses on refining, marketing, and trading of petroleum products; while the chemicals sector includes rubber products made by its Hutchinson subsidiary (the bulk of which are products for the automotive industry), resins, paints, inks, and adhesives. The French state held a more than one-third stake in Total for much of the company's history, but by 1996 France owned less than 1 percent.

The expanded Total Fina Elf has a refining capacity of 2.4 million barrels per day equivalent (boe/d), and has more than 22,000 service stations and 29 refineries in 100 countries. The company's activities in the energy business run from oil and gas exploration and production to refining and marketing of refined products, as well as international trading in both crude and refined products. Total Fina Elf has also been heavily involved in the chemical market through its branch Atofina. By 2002, the company focused on heating fuels, liquefied petroleum gas, solvents, waxes, bitumens, lubricants, and aviations fuel. The company is also reaching out to potential high-growth areas, such as Southeast Asia, Africa, and the Mediterranean Basin.

Roots in World War I French Oil Crisis

The foundation of Total Fina Elf's initial company, Compagnie Française des Pétroles, France's oldest and, for most of its life, largest oil company, in 1924 came on the heels of France's realization that it needed secure energy supplies. In late 1917, France had come within three months of running out of fuel and seeing its World War I effort grind to a halt.

At the turn of the century the United States and the Russians, with their huge domestic resources, had supplied 90 percent of the world's oil needs. Since then, the British had developed a powerful presence through the activities of the Anglo-Persian

Company Perspectives:

As a global energy group of European origin, our ambition is to meet society's energy needs by offering an ever broader range of products and services. We carry out that mission with commitment, professionalism, service and loyalty—all values to which we are deeply attached. Finding, manufacturing and distributing reliable quality products is the goal we seek to achieve, drawing on innovation and state-of-the-art technologies to do so. We conduct our oil and gas and chemicals activities in an ongoing spirit of transparency, outreach, partnership and solidarity, in order to meet society's expectations and rise to the crucial challenges of ensuring the safety of people and property, preserving natural resources and protecting the environment.

Oil Company—today's British Petroleum—and Royal Dutch Shell. The French found that the key to acquiring oil was the 25 percent stake in the fledgling Turkish Petroleum Company (TPC) held by Germany's Deutsche Bank.

The TPC had been founded in 1911 to exploit the oil fields of Mesopotamia on either side of the German-built railway to Baghdad. The British-owned National Bank of Turkey had originally been TPC's major shareholder with 50 percent, but in 1914 the British government persuaded the bank to sell out to Anglo-Persian. An additional 25 percent was held by Royal Dutch Shell. In 1915, the 25 percent stake in TPC still held by Deutsche Bank was sequestered by the British.

CFP Founded in 1924

Four years later, a new French government concluded that it was unacceptable that a foreign company should control the exploitation of France's oil rights in Mesopotamia, and the Compagnie Française des Pétroles (CFP) was established.

CFP's function was not limited to Mesopotamia. In the interests of developing an oil producing capacity "under French control," Chairman Ernest Mercier was charged with acquiring stakes in "any enterprise active in whatsoever oil producing region" of the world. CFP was to co-operate, with the support of the government, in "exploiting such oil wealth as may be discovered in France, her colonies, and her protectorates." The Compagnie Française des Pétroles was set up as a private, not a state-owned, firm.

On October 15, 1927, the Turkish Petroleum Company struck oil—a large find—at Baba Gurghur in Iraq. The discovery ended a debate among the TPC shareholders, some of whom wanted to receive dividends on their investments, others of whom wanted to be remunerated in crude oil. The French had favored crude, having no oil fields of their own; after Baba Gurghur they received it.

The TCP was restructured in 1928, with Anglo-Persian ceding half its stake to a consortium of five U.S. oil companies. The shareholders in the TPC signed a non-aggression pact known as the Red Line Agreement in circling a large area of the map of the Near and Middle East with red crayon. The area within the red line corresponded to the old Ottoman Empire at the end of World War I, encompassing Turkey, Syria, Saudi Arabia, Lebanon, Iraq, and Palestine. Within that region, the TPC shareholders, now including the U.S. giants Standard Oil of New York and Standard Oil of New Jersey, undertook not to compete with one another.

Entered Refining in 1929

Mercier came up against opposition from some of the company's shareholders to his cherished plans to delve into refining, but some of the oil distributors who backed CFP objected, not wanting to disrupt close ties with foreign refiners. A plan was developed for the French state to acquire a 25 percent stake in CFP and a 10 percent stake in a new refining subsidiary to be created by CFP, the Compagnie Française de Raffinage.

The Compagnie Française de Raffinage (CFR) was founded in April 1929; its first refinery was opened at Normandy in 1933. The first shipment of CFP's own oil came from Iraq the following year when the pipeline from the wells to the Lebanese port of Tripoli went into operation. In the years up to World War II, CFR's refining capacity grew steadily, outstripping CFP's ability to supply it with crude. Further crude shipments came from Venezuela and the United States.

By 1929, all the Turkish Petroleum Company's oil came from Iraq under a concession awarded by the Iraqi monarch, King Feisal, installed by the British in 1921. TPC changed its name to the Iraq Petroleum Company in June 1929. By 1936, CFR was supplying nearly 20 percent of French demand for refined oil from two plants located at either end of the country, one in Normandy and the other in Provence.

Elf Aquitaine's Beginnings

Elf Aquitaine, which became the substantial Elf portion of the Total Fina Elf name decades later, got its start before World War II as three small companies: RAP, SNPA, and BRP. The group was founded by the French government in 1939 as Régie Autonome des Pétroles (RAP) to exploit modest gas reserves discovered at Saint-Marcet in southwest France. But, the group's origins could be said to go back much further than that—to 1498 when Jacob Wimpfeling, a theologian from Alsace, was surprised to note mineral oil welling out of the ground at a place called Pechelbronn (fountain of pitch).

Almost 500 years later, in 1970, the Antar group, which then owned Pechelbronn, was taken over by Elf. A close historical connection might be perceived between the history of Elf and the history of France's energy policy as practiced by successive governments since World War II.

The discovery of gas at Saint-Marcet in the summer of 1939 was made by a small exploration syndicate set up with public funding earlier in the decade to prospect for oil and gas in the region. The Compagnie Française des Pétroles, Royal Dutch Shell, and Standard Oil of New Jersey could not be expected to plow much money into looking for oil or gas in France. The oil giants were wrong, but it was not until after the war that they were to discover it. The find at Saint-Marcet was modest, although it continued to produce gas until 1988. The Régie

Key Dates:

1920: Petrofina (Compagnie Financiére Belge des Pétroles) is founded by investors from Antwerp.

1924: Total is founded as Compagnie Française des Pétroles (CFP).

1929: New refining subsidiary, Française de Raffinage, is established jointly with French state.

1939: Gas field discovery in France leads to founding of Régie Autonome de Pétroles (RAP).

1941: Société Nationale des Pétroles d'Aquitaine (SNPA) is established.

1945: Bureau de Recherches de Pétrole (BRP) is established.

1954/55: Trademark "Total" is created and registered.

1965: TOGB, with Petrofina, constructs and operates a new refinery near Killingholme.

1967: Elf logo and name chosen as the brand name for ERAP and Société Nationale des Pétroles d'Aquitaine (SNPA).

1980: Acquires Vickers Petroleum.

1985: CFP becomes Total-Compagnie Française des Pétroles (Total-CFP).

1991: Company's name becomes Total.

1995: Thierry Desmarest is made CEO of Total. Total is the first foreign oil company to produce in Iran since 1979.

1999: Total acquires Belgium's Petrofina for $12 billion and becomes Total Fina.

2000: Total Fina merges with Elf Aquitaine and becomes Total Fina Elf.

2001: Total Fina Elf merges with Spain's Cepsa to expand Spanish market. The company partners with Kazakhstan's state Kazakoil for exploration in the Caspian Sea.

2002: Total Fina Elf invests in Russina Vankorskoye project in East Siberia with Anglo Siberian Oil Company. Deepwater oil find in the Campos Basin off the shore of Brazil.

Autonome des Pétroles (RAP) was immediately formed to exploit the new resource by extracting the gas and building a plant for its treatment near Boussens.

In 1941, CFP set up a new company, the second of Elf's forerunners, Société Nationale des Pétroles d'Aquitaine (SNPA), to look for oil and gas in the Aquitaine region, with the state owning 24 percent. CFP wound up owning 14 percent, along with the National Nitrogen Board (ONLA), Saint Gobain, Pechiney, and Rhône-Poulenc. It was obvious that this project would include petrochemicals. Through the efforts of SNPA, Aquitaine was to become the oil and gas province of France. During the German occupation, the management of SNPA slacked off in its efforts to find oil. SNPA's reluctance to help in the German war effort resulted in the deportation of the company's first chairman, Pierre Angot.

At the end of the war, President Charles de Gaulle was eager for the government to play an active role in restoring the country's control over its energy supplies. In 1945, he created the third of Elf's forerunners, the Bureau de Recherches de Pétrole (BRP), to help the process along. The role of this publicly funded venture was—according to its founding charter—to encourage oil and gas exploration in France, its colonies, and protectorates "in the exclusive interest of the nation." BRP was to identify and invest in exploration projects. It owned both the RAP and the government's share of SNPA.

African Exploration Begins After World War II

De Gaulle chose Pierre Guillaumat as the first chairman of BRP. Then 36 years old, Guillaumat was to prove the single most influential figure in the history of Elf Aquitaine, later retiring as chairman of Elf in 1977.

In the first years of its life, the most important investments made by BRP were in the French colony of Algeria and in equatorial Africa. Exploration operations in the Congo and Gabon were largely carried out through Société des Pétroles d'Afrique Equatoriale (SPAFE), a joint venture with various French banks. Consortia were formed between SPAFE, Mobil, and Shell. In Algeria, the beneficiary of BRP's funding was SN Repal, a joint venture with colonial government and the Compagnie Française des Pétroles. Also established was Compagnie de Recherché et d'Exploitation du Pétrole du Sahara (CREPS), a further oil exploration joint venture in Algeria—this time between RAP with 65 percent and Royal Dutch/Shell with 35 percent.

BRP's failure to discover oil in the 1940s appeared to confirm the skepticism of those who doubted that oil would ever be discovered in the Algerian Sahara. Paradoxically, it was precisely this skepticism that had encouraged the French government to set up BRP in the first place—the privately owned oil companies, with shareholders' dividends to pay out, were not about to see large investments swallowed up by the sands of north Africa. In 1950, Guillaumat left BRP to become head of France's new Atomic Energy Commission.

Total Vertically Integrated Oil Company by World War II

Following Ernest Mercier's resignation in 1940, the new chairman Jules Mény entrusted the French interests in IPC to Harold Sheets, the chairman of Standard Oil of New York. The rapid succession of chairmen at CFP during the war reflected the instability of those times. Mercier departed peacefully, but Jules Mény was taken hostage by the Nazis in 1943 and deported to Dachau. Mény's successor, Marcel Champin, died in 1945, leaving the task of determining CFP's postwar strategy to his deputy, Victor de Metz, who was to serve as chairman for 25 years.

Rapid Postwar Expansion at Home and Abroad

The nationalization drive that affected so many French companies after the war did not engulf CFP; its private shareholders were powerful and not worth alienating. More threatening for CFP in the long run was President Charles de Gaulle's creation in 1945 of the Bureau de Recherches de Pétrole (BRP), which was much later to form one of the constituent parts of Elf Aquitaine.

At its creation, however, BRP was charged exclusively with searching for oil in France, its colonies, and protectorates.

In the late 1940s and early 1950s, CFP expanded rapidly both at home and abroad. The company's annual supply of oil from the Middle East increased from 806,000 tons in 1945, to 1.61 million tons in 1950, to 8.824 million tons in 1953. The security of these supplies depended on the continuing stability of the region and its rulers' continuing respect for the oil companies' prewar concessions. Victor de Metz recognized that CFP needed to diversify its sources of supply.

After a fruitless venture in Venezuela from 1948 to 1951, CFP began exploration in Canada, then in French Equatorial Africa and Algeria. CFP's venture to develop the oil wealth of Algeria fared well. In 1946, the state-owned Bureau de Recherches des Pétroles had established, jointly with the French colonial government in Algeria, an oil exploration company, the Société Nationale de Recherché de Pétrole en Algérie (SN Repal). In 1947, CNP sent a geologist to Algeria to evaluate the region's prospects, teaming up in the 1950s with CFP to explore a huge promising region.

In 1956, a huge oil field was discovered and an equally impressive gas field. CFP and Repal were able to organize a vast industrial complex that provided French engineers with the opportunity to gain priceless technological knowledge in all aspects of oil and gas exploration, production, transport, gas treatment, and maritime shipping.

Major Discoveries in the 1950s

The Lacq gas field, discovered by SNPA in southwest France in December 1951, was huge by French standards and impressive enough by any standards with reserves estimated at 250 billion cubic meters. Extracting the gas was to prove technically awkward on account of its highly toxic and corrosive impurities, notably hydrogen sulfate. However, in the longer term, SNPA was to turn these initial difficulties to its advantage. France became a net exporter of sulfates, and the expertise SNPA acquired in treating highly sulfurous natural gas also proved eminently exportable.

The other forerunners of Elf Aquitaine, RAP and SNPA, also struck oil in the Algerian desert at about the same time. In 1956, CREPS, the RAP and Shell joint venture, brought the Sahara's first marketable oil to the surface at Edjeleh. The following year, SNPA discovered oil at El Gassi. In 1956 and 1957, there were the first discoveries of oil in equatorial Africa, in Gabon, and in the Congo, and in the early 1960s, a very big discovery was made in the Gulf of Guinea.

However, the Compagnie Française des Pétroles was far from being a household name in France. CFP petrol stations did not cover the land, even though a large proportion of the fuel that the independent distributors sold had been refined at the plants of a CFP subsidiary. Distribution was not a particularly profitable activity, but a major oil producer without distribution facilities of its own risked being held for ransom by its distributors with the threat of losing their business. From 1946, Victor de Metz worked to remove this risk by creating the Compagnie Française de Distribution en Afrique to sell CFP's refined oil products in francophone Africa.

Total Brand Debuted in 1954

CFP pursued the professionalization of petroleum marketing operations and the concentration of retail networks. The unveiling of the Total brand name in 1954. The distributors of oil refined by CFR were now entitled to deck out their service stations in the Total colors and logo, giving them a stronger market identity. First tested in Africa and then brought to France in 1957, the plan was a success. In 1961, refineries belonging to CFP or working on its behalf treated 12 million tons of oil, seven million tons of which went on to be distributed under the Total brand name.

However, France's independent fuel distributors still were experiencing hard times, losing ground when competing with the big foreign oil companies. One by one they sold out— usually to CFP, as CFP expanded its market to Europe and Africa where it had begun marketing in 1968.

Because French authorities had urged CFP to gain a stake in the Sahara oil fields in the 1950s, and CFP refused, the French government withheld its approval when CFP considered taking over its partner's retail network. Instead, the government consolidated the foundations for the future Elf Group by establishing the Union Générale des Pétroles (UGP), that united RAP, Repal, SPAEF, and SNPA, all groups of which BRP was a driving force.

UGP thus gained the SNPA network in southwestern France, including French downstream assets owned by Caltex. These assets encompassed a refinery near Bordeaux, four oil tankers, and 1,400 service stations. In taking this step, the French government had set up a significant French company with assets in upstream, transport, downstream, and gas. The stage was set for vertical integration of the company.

While CFP was making strides in refining and selling its oil, the process of extracting it was becoming increasingly difficult. The model for a new relationship with the Middle Eastern governments was the 50–50 profit-sharing agreement signed by the Saudi government and the U.S. oil producers' consortium Aramco in 1950. In the same year, IPC struck a similar profit-sharing deal with the Iraqi government. The risks posed by nascent nationalism in the Middle East were made clear in 1951, when Muhammad Mussadegh came to power in Iran. He nationalized the assets of the Anglo-Iranian Oil Company— formerly the Anglo-Persian Oil Company and forerunner of British Petroleum—and an international embargo of Iranian crude failed to change his attitude.

More effective than either of these actions was a revolt linked to the British and U.S. intelligence services, which led to the restoration of the shah and Mussadegh's imprisonment in 1953. A year later, the oil companies and the Iranian government created an international consortium of oil companies led by Anglo-Iranian with a 40 percent share. CFP took a modest 6 percent stake in the venture.

Increased Reliance on Algerian Oil in the 1960s

Upheavals such as the one in Iran spurred the French effort to develop oil production in its Algerian colony. However, both CFP and BRP knew that that any oil or gas discovered in

Algeria would lie within the franc zone. The IPC installations in Iraq did not fall into this category and CFP had to fund its share of investment in the Iraq Petroleum Company in pounds sterling. In the late 1940s and early 1950s, when the franc was fast losing its purchasing power, this arrangement was not very satisfactory.

By 1962, the future Total and Elf groups realized that they needed to find resources other than those in Algeria, and to examine the political risks associated with their reserves. The French government revised its oil policy, making it vital that French oil companies be able to explore for oil beyond the borders of France and its former colonies.

Consolidation and Formation of Elf in the Late 1960s

Large-scale nationalization took place in 1966, presided over by Pierre Guillaumat. BRP and RAP were transformed into ERAP. The majority stake in Société Nationale des Pétroles d'Aquitaine (SNPA) held by BRP thus passed to ERAP. Guillaumat became chairman both of the ERAP holding company and of its most dynamic subsidiary SNPA. The group was still receiving funds from the sales tax on petroleum products; these funds, known as support grants, increased as the government encouraged the group to diversify its oil supplies.

Government involvement in the oil industry was hardly unique in Continental Europe at the time. The Italians had created Ente Nazionale Idrocarburi (ENI) in 1953, and in 1965, the Spanish had restructured their oil industry, leading to the creation of Hispanoil.

Guillaumat and ERAP were more original in the deals they struck with oil-producing nations. ERAP's pioneering contrats d'entreprise were signed first with Iran in 1966 and two years later with Iraq. These were service contracts under which ERAP agreed to provide exploration and production skills in return for long-term crude supplies at preferential rates. The success of this arrangement in Iraq provided a framework for the amicable resolution of Franco-Iraqi differences when the Iraqi government nationalized the assets of the Compagnie Française des Pétroles, among others, in 1972. ERAP was also able to set up new operations in Nigeria (1962), Indonesia (1963), and Canada (1964), later launching a venture in Mexico.

ERAP and SNPA still lacked a recognizable brand name in France. This was remedied in 1967, when the Elf name and logo were unveiled at thousands of service stations around the country. The name "Elf" was chosen—by a computer, according to corporate folklore—for its attractive connotations of nimbleness and sprightliness, and was not an acronym. Also significant was the partnership of BRP and RAP before the merger in an effort to expand oil and gas exploration and production in the British, Norwegian, and Dutch offshore zones in the North Sea.

Despite the Iraqi nationalization of the assets of the Iraq Petroleum Company in 1971, CFP announced in its annual report that it would be maintained as before. On de Metz's retirement in 1971, the Compagnie Française des Pétroles was one of the largest oil companies in the world; the company's oil production had risen at a rate 30 percent faster than global oil production in the 1960s.

Elf's Diversification in the Difficult 1970s

The oil and gas reserves of the future Total Group increased by 3.5 times between 1960 and 1971, to a total of 68 million metric tons. At the same time, those of the future Elf Group tripled to nearly 33 million metric tons. Both groups began searching for sites for new refineries. Total ultimately built at Dunkirk in Northern France and at Vlissingen in the Netherlands. Elf took over the Antar Group, doubling its downstream sector, and inherited a stake in refineries in Alsace-Lorraine. During this time, SNPA kept its close ties with the major French chemical firms. However, none of the Elf component companies could envision the fast growing demand for chemicals in France and Europe, not even CFP, which had diversified into chemicals in the late 1950s.

To make a greater commitment to chemicals, Total brought together as Total Chimie all the chemicals businesses run by CFP and CFR in 1968, also diversifying into polyethylene in partnership with German firms. The Group joined SNPA in founding the Compagnie de Pétrochimie the following year. In 1971, the future Elf and Total formed Ato Chimie, which grouped all their chemical activities under one roof.

Following the oil crisis in 1973, Elf and Total cooperated in chemicals and upstream operations in the North Sea. Both companies had to learn to better handle risk, as oil prices were very unstable. The challenge for Elf at this time was to increase the proportion of oil in its resources and to expand its production base, which was primarily in the North Sea and West Africa. CFP, however, had a wide spread of production, with operations in Algeria, the Middle East, Indonesia, and the North Sea, as well as new operations in Yemen. It had also begun to explore in Argentina and Columbia.

The year 1975 found joint operations with ATO Chimie becoming increasingly difficult. Even so, the government encouraged the formation of Chloé Chimie in 1979, a second joint venture specializing in chlorochemicals, with the assets coming from Rhône-Poulenc, with Elf and Total holding 80.5 percent of the newly established company's equity.

Because Total had been absorbed in consolidating its refining and marketing operations, its profitability in chemicals plunged. Total sold its stakes in Ato Chimie and Chloé Chimie in 1983, eliminating its chemical assets by 1985. Elf was in better shape financially and wanted to build up a refining and marketing operation as well in the 1970s, and expanded its chemical operations, building a vast chemicals complex of base chemicals, specialty chemicals, and a hygiene-pharmaceuticals division.

In 1977, the year after the final merger between ERAP and SNPA to form the new Société Nationale Elf Aquitaine, Pierre Guillaumat retired. Albin Chalandon, who became chairman, raised Elf Aquitaine's profile in the United States through the acquisition in 1981 of Texas Gulf. The combination of Texas Gulf's strength as a producer of mined sulfur and Elf's existing production at Lacq made the group the world's largest producer of sulfur. Texas Gulf also had huge phosphate reserves and was one of the largest U.S. potassium-based fertilizer producers. The purchase tripled Elf's overall U.S. business at a stroke, and included interests in mining and oil exploration.

Elf and Total in the 1980s

The oil crisis that extended into the 1980s forced both Total and Elf to reduce their refining capacities, sell off most of their tankers, and boost the productivity of their retail networks. The number of service stations owned by both was halved as supermarkets were gaining a foothold in the motor fuel market. Both groups began trading in both crude and refined products, launching aggressive market expansion programs aimed at Latin America, Southeast Asia, and Central Europe.

In 1985, the name by which CFP had come to be known universally was incorporated in its official title: CFP became Total CFP. At the same time the Compagnie Française de Raffinage and its distribution subsidiary, Total CFD, merged to become CRD Total France. By the end of the 1980s, CFP had an output of 520,000 barrels of oil equivalent per day (boe/d) over five zones. Now that it was known as Total, the company had also diversified into coal, nuclear power, and renewable energy sources. Total enlarged its portfolio rapidly in the early 1980s, doubling its overall chemicals turnover during the decade, even before gaining Petrofina assets.

In the meantime, the Elf Group carved out a position for itself in the U.S. market, taking over a division of American Can, Metal, and Thurmit Chemicals. In 1989, Atochem expanded into performance chemicals. In 1990, Elf swapped with Total, taking over the base chemicals division of Orkem in exchange for the paints company La Seigneurie. By this time, chemicals had become a major component of the Elf Group, as the company had the strongest commitment to chemicals of all the major oil companies.

Elf gained a vital foothold in Spain and eastern Germany, and was engaged in a modernization program while trying to reduce production costs, strengthening its brand image. By the end of the 1980s, Elf had made several major deep offshore discoveries in Africa and the Gulf of Mexico, and moved back into Iran where Total was already well established. The Elf Group had major assets and had gained considerable knowledge in medium and deep offshore operations.

Total had reduced excess refining capacity but continued to enter into new markets, divesting assets in the United States to make investments in China. The company also made its refining operations more efficient and tightened environmental standards. Total beefed up its presence in Africa and around the Mediterranean Basin, while planning growth in Southeast Asia. Total's merger with Petrofina strengthened the company's position as it added competitive refining operations and boosted market share in some European markets where Total lacked the critical mass for long-term profit.

In 1994, the French government sold all but 13 percent of its controlling interest in Elf, generating nearly $6 billion in the process. Ironically, the company suffered its first-ever net loss—a $1 billion shortfall—that same year.

Serge Tchuruk an Aggressive Leader for Total in the Early 1990s

Serge Tchuruk, Total's CEO, moved quickly to transform Total—which had, by the early 1990s, ceded its position as France's largest oil company to Elf Aquitaine—from a bureaucratic, complex, sleepy firm into a sleeker, more modern, and more aggressive company. Two hundred subsidiaries were abolished and were replaced by a mere six profit centers; one-seventh of Total's service stations network was closed in 1991; and about 6,500 jobs were eliminated. The company's marketing operations reached into new potentially more lucrative markets, as Total purchased interests in service station chains in Spain, Portugal, Czechoslovakia, Hungary, and Turkey.

On the production side, Tchuruk aimed to increase oil and gas production outside the Middle East by 50 percent by 1995. In 1991, a joint venture—40 percent owned by Total—with British Petroleum and Triton Energy discovered an oil field at Cusiana in Colombia, while Total on its own discovered a significant gas field in Indonesia. In 1993, production began at a gas field in Thailand. By 1995, Tchuruk's emphasis on beefing up the company's gas business had made Total the world's third largest gas producer, trailing only Royal Dutch/Shell (Royal Dutch Petroleum Company) and Mobil Corporation.

In June 1991, the company changed its name to Total SA, and soon began trading on the New York Stock Exchange for the first time. The French government reduced its direct share holding in the company to 5.4 percent, increasing Total's independence and ability to act quickly and aggressively.

Thierry Desmarest Comes to Total in the Late 1990s

In 1995, Tchuruk was replaced by 15-year company veteran Thierry Desmarest, who almost immediately closed a $610 million deal to develop two offshore oil fields in Iran. Total thus became the first foreign oil company allowed back in Iran since the overthrow of the shah in 1979.

Because of Total's willingness to operate in controversial countries, it had fewer competitors for its projects and was able to make better deals, leading to exploration and development costs among the lowest in the industry. These lower costs contributed to steadily increasing profits, with net income rising from FFr2.85 billion (US$600 million) in 1992 to FFr7.61 billion (US$1.26 billion) in 1997.

In 1997, the company announced that it would invest US$2 billion to develop an Iranian gas field. Prior to signing the deal, however, Desmarest got advance backing from the French government and the European Union (EU), lessening the possibility that U. S.-sponsored sanctions would threaten it. Total had just days before signing this Iranian deal to complete its sale of Total Petroleum (North America) Ltd.—its North American refining and marketing arm—to Ultramar Diamond Shamrock Corporation for an approximate eight percent stake in Ultramar, and Ultramar assumed about $435 million in Total Petroleum debt.

Despite quite a large exposure to the Asian financial crisis that arose in 1997, Total's results for that year were extremely healthy: a 7.9 percent increase in sales to FFr191.09 billion (US$31.75 billion) and a 35 percent increase in profits to FFr7.61 billion (US$1.26 billion). Total's aggressive approach in the 1990s had turned the company into one of the most profitable in the industry as well as one of the most fearless in terms of controversial deal making.

Total Fina Becomes Third Largest Oil Company in Europe

Total S.A. moved from being the second largest oil company in France to the third largest in Europe through its acquisition of Petrofina S. A., the Belgian oil and petrochemicals company. In a FFr74 billion (US$13 billion) deal, essentially a share swap, Total agreed with a group of shareholders to acquire a 41 percent stake in the company, beating out rivals Elf Aquitaine and ENI. Fina also had 2,500 service stations in the United States, most of which were in Texas, Arizona, and New Mexico.

A Brief Overview of Petrofina

Petrofina was a Belgium-based integrated oil company that had interests in oil and gas production, refining and marketing, and chemicals, principally in the United States and Europe. When it was established in 1920 as Compagnie Financiére Belge des Pétroles (Belgian Petroleum Finance Company) by a group of Belgian financiers in Antwerp, the company's main strengths were refining and marketing, but chemicals became an important part of the company's business through production of polypropylene, polyethylene, and polystyrene. The company's upstream assets were in the United States, the United Kingdom, and Norway, and its refining assets were in the United States, Belgium, Italy, the Untied Kingdom, and Angola.

Starting out to extract and refine petroleum products, Petrofina had found oil in Romania through the Concordia Company. In the 1920s, with Pure Oil of Delaware, Petrofina founded Purfina, a distribution company in Belgium and Holland that became a wholly own subsidiary of Petrofina in 1923. Purfina paraffin was produced at a warehouse in Antwerp and sold in bottles in grocery stores. The later purchase of the factory and a small refinery opened the way for car lubricants, medicinal oils, and products used in the preparation of foods. The Société Industrielle Belge des Pétroses SIBP (Belgian Industrial Petroleum Company) was founded in Antwerp in 1949, beginning production in 1951. By the 1950s, the Congo, Angola, French Equatorial Africa, and Tunisia formed the African core of the group, with exploration, production, and distribution being developed in these areas. Major discoveries in Mexico, Canada, Angola, and Egypt followed.

Petrofina expanded throughout Europe, North America, and Africa, preparing for a boom in the car market. The company delved into chemistry in 1954, the beginning of the plastics age. At this time, Laurent Wolters of Petrofina achieved his vision of ''going to America'' through the acquisition of Cosden Chemicals, marking Petrofina's entry into petrochemicals in America. The company also had crude oil and finished products cross the world in ships, and entered into the aircraft fuels market in 1960, establishing Belgo Chim at Geluy, Belgium's center region. Petrofina began a large-scale exploration of the North Sea, finding gas in 1966 in the British Sector.

In 1972, Petrofina diversified into paints. The group expanded under the leadership of Adolphe Demeure de Lespaul, with the profitable sale of the Canadian Petrofina, which helped Petrofina strengthen its assets in the United States in the midst of the 1970s oil crisis. Petrofina later bought back its shares in Société Industrielle Belge de Pétroses to focus on refining

activities. In 1988, Fina Italia successfully launched exploration and production in Italy, and Fina Europe built a new high tech factory for lubricants in 1991 at Ertvelde. In 1995, the refinery at Antwerp was equipped for deep conversion, which meant it could stay ahead of market developments and accomplish high levels of efficiency.

Wood Mackenzie Consultants Ltd. of Edinburgh stated in the *Oil and Gas Journal* that the merged Total Fina would have an estimated overall product market share of about 8 percent, which placed it fourth behind Shell (12.5 percent), BP-Mobil (11 percent), and Exxon (10 percent). The new company's market share of 25 percent in France and Belgium made it a market leader and put it ahead of rival Elf. The combined workforce of the two companies was about 69,100. The two companies combined then had a processing capacity that exceeded crude production by more than 500,000 barrels per day (boe/d).

Total Fina's upstream division was based in Paris, with its refining, marketing, and petrochemicals division in Brussels. Total Chairman Thierry Desmarest was made Chairman of Total Fina, while Petrofina CEO Francois Cornelis became vice-chairman of Total Fina's executive committee, over which Desmarest presided.

In February 1999, Elf Aquitaine and Eni of Italy signed a 10-year, US$998 million contract to redevelop an Iranian oil field. The two European oil companies and Tehran were to refurbish the Doroud offshore field near Kharg Island in the Gulf. This kind of foreign investment in Iran had been in opposition to U.S. policy to restrict far-reaching investment in Iran's strategic oil industry, although Clinton had waived these sanctions when Total also defied policy and with a $2 billion gas exploration contract in Iran in 1997. The United States had threatened sanctions against any country that invested more than $20 million in Iran or Libya. Clinton waived these potential sanctions if the European Union (EU) would press Iran to stop encouraging international terrorism and developing nuclear weapons.

Another Stunning Acquisition

In July 1999, the newly named Total Fina launched a hostile bid for oil group Elf Aquitaine for US$44 billion. Elf Aquitaine fought back, offering its own US$53 billion cash and stock counterbid to acquire Total Fina. Ultimately, Total Fina acquired Elf Aquitaine for US$54 billion, making the new Total Fina Elf the fourth largest oil company in the world. Thierry Desmarest was to continue as chairman, while Elf chairman Philippe Jaffre, who instigated the counteroffer in July resigned.

Elf Aquitaine S. A., known simply as Elf, was one of France's largest oil companies and one of the world's top ten petrochemical companies when it was acquired by Total Fina. Its more than 800 subsidiaries included hydrocarbon, chemical, and health care interests. At its core, Elf was a fully integrated oil and gas company, combining upstream production capacity from fields in more than a dozen countries worldwide with downstream operations encompassing five refineries and over 6,500 gas stations throughout Europe and West Africa, and churned out the equivalent of over one million barrels of oil a day (75 percent oil and 25 percent natural gas). Through its Elf Atochem subsidiary, the conglomerate also ranked among the world's top chemical companies, manufacturing both basic and specialty chemicals.

Total Fina and Elf have complementary strategies and would be able to strengthen their geographic presence in Africa and the Middle East. Total Fina had operations east of the Suez Canal Southeast Asia, and Latin America, while Elf was a major presence in West Africa and the North Sea. This configuration apparently worked well, as Total Fina Elf's net income was up by 24 percent at the end of the first quarter of 2000.

What Lies Ahead

Demarest stated that Total Fina Elf's plans were to expand its exposure in the Gulf of Mexico, and that lack of involvement in the United States was based on the lack of attractiveness of projects, not an aversion to the United States because of George Bush's "axis of evil" speech about Iran and Iraq where Total had extensive operations. Total's upstream strategy focuses on four major projects, each of which provided more than 200,000 barrels of oil per day equivalent. The first was the US$2.5 billion Elgin-Franklin development in the U.K. North Sea; the second was the $4.3 billion Sincor heavy oil project in Venezuela; the third was the US$2.6 billion Girassol field in Angola; and the last was the $2 billion South Pars gas development in Iran.

Since Total's merger with its rival Elf Aquitaine in 2000 and the purchase of Belgium's PetroFina in 1999, Desmarest has met the goals he set at the start of the merger, and continued to expand to new goals. In May 2002, Total bought into the Russian Vankorskoye project in East Siberia through an agreement with the U. K.-registered Anglo Siberian Oil Company, making Total the operator and 52 percent owner of the 900 million bbl/d field through the deal with Anglo Siberian, which held a 59 percent interest. The company has continued its strategic successes, with a deepwater oil find in the waters of the Campos Basin off the shore of Brazil in June 2002. Brazilian state oil company Petrobras held a 35 percent interest in the well with Royal Dutch/Shell and Enterprise Oil each owning 15 percent. Also in June 2002, Atofina, the chemicals branch of Total Fina Elf, launched two major projects: the installation of an ethane cracker in Ras Laffan and a polyethylene (LLDPE) plant in Mesaieed, both in Qatar.

However, Total's profits fell 36 percent in the first quarter of 2002 because of lower commodity prices and a plunge in European refining margins. Fortunately, this decline was less severe than that of its rivals. The top six U. S.-based oil companies had first quarter earning of about 65 percent less than 2001. Rivals in Europe—BP, Royal Dutch/Shell, and Eni—had first quarter losses of 57 percent, 48 percent, and 27 percent respectively.

Principal Subsidiaries

Chemicals: Atofina Chemicals, Inc.; Atofina Petrochemicals, Inc.; Atofina UK Ltd; Australia Atofina Pty Ltd; Belgium Atofina Bruxelles; Brazil Atofina Do Brasil; Canada Atofina Canada Inc.; China Atofina Investment Co., Ltd; Colombia Atofina Colombia S.A.; Egypt Atofina Middle East-Branch Office; France Atofina; Germany Atofina Deutschland BmgH; Great Britain Atofina UK Ltd; Italy Atofina Italia S.r.l.; Japan Atofina Japan K.K.; Korea Atofina Korea Ltd; Portugal Atofina

Portugal Produtos Quimicos e Industriais, Lda; Spain Atofina Espana; The Netherlands Atofina Nederland BV; The Netherlands Atofina Rotterdam B.V.; The Netherlands Atofina Vlissingen B.V.; United States Atofina Chemicals Inc.; United States Atofina Chemicals Inc. Atoglas Division; United States Atofina Petrochemicals Inc.; Vietnam Atofina Vietnam Ltd; Australia Atotech Australia Pty Ltd; Belgium Bostik Findley Belux SA-NV; China Atotech Asia Pacific Ltd; France Alphacan; France Altumax Europe; France Atoglas Europe; France Atotech France; France Bostik Findley S.A.; France Ceca; France Cerexagri; France Cray Valley; France Dorlyl; France Eco-Per; France Gaxaro; France Grande Paroisse; France Hutchinson; France MLPC International; France Naphtachimie; France Oxochimie; France Oxysynthése; France Résinoplast; France Société Béarnaise du Synthéses; Germany Atotech Deutschland GmbH; Great Britain Altumaz UK Ltd; Great Britain Atotech UK Ltd; India Max Atotech Ltd; Ireland Evode Industries Ltd; Israel Safepack Products Ltd; Italy Atotech Italia S.r.l.; Italy Cerexagro S.r.l.; Italy Mydrin Findley S.r.l.; Korea Cray Valley Kirea; Korea Sigma Coating Korea Ltd; Spain Alphacan España SA; Spain Cerexagri Iberica; Spain Dequisa; Spain Plasgom S.A.; The Netherlands Atotech Nederland B.V.; The Netherlands Bostik Findley Nederland B.V.; The Netherlands Cerexagri B.V.; The Netherlands Signakalon Group B.V.; United States Atotech USA Inc.; United States Bostik Findley Inc.; United States Bostik Inc.; United States Cerexagri Inc.; Venezuela Produven C.A.

Principal Subsidiaries

UPSTREAM—Exploration and Production: Africa: Algeria; Angola; Cameroon; Congo; Equatorial Guinea; Gabon; Libya; Nigeria. *Australia, Asia, Russia, and Southeast Asia:* Indonesia; Kazakhstan; Myanmar (Burma); Russia; Thailand. *Europe:* France; Italy; Norway; the United Kingdom. *North, Central and South America:* Argentina; Bolivia; Brazil; Honduras; Mexico; Salvador; Venezuela; the United States. *DOWNSTREAM—Refineries and Marketing: Africa:* Algeria; Angola; Benin; Botswana; Burindi; Cameroon; Central Africa; Congo; Equitorial Guinea; Eritrea; Ethiopia; Gabon; Ghana; Guinea; Guinea-Bissau; Ivory Coast; Kenya; Liberia; Madagascar; Mali; Mauritania; Morocco; Mozambia; Namibia: Niger; Nigeria; Rwanda; Senegal; Sierra Leone; Somalia; South Africa; Sudan; Tanzania; Togo; Uganda; Zaire; Zimbabwe. *Australia, Asia, Russia, and Southeast Asia:* Australia; Bangladesh; Belarus; Cambodia; China; French Polynesia; Hong Kong; India; Indonesia; Japan; Kazakhstan; Malaysia; Myanmar (Burma); Nepal; New Caledonia; North Korea; Pakistan; Philippines; Russia; South Korea; Turkmenistan; Ukraine; Viet Nam. *Europe:* Austria; Bulgaria; Croatia; Czech Republic; Estonia; Finland: Germany; Greece; Hungary; Iceland; Ireland; Latvia; Lithuania; Macedonia; Norway: Poland; Portugal; Romania; Slovak Republic; Slovenia; Spain; Sweden; Switzerland; the United Kingdom. *North, Central and South America:* Argentina; Bolivia, Brazil; Canada; Chile; Colombia; Costa Rica; Cuba; Dominican Republic; Equador; French Guyana; Guadeloup; Guatemala; Haiti; Lesser Antilles; Mexico; Panama; Paraguay; Peru; the United States; Uruguay; Venezuela.

Principal Competitors

BP Amoco PLC; Exxon-Mobil Corporation; Royal Dutch/Shell Group PLC; Chevron Texaco Corporation.

Further Reading

Avati, Helen, "Total Wants to Be the Best of the Rest," *Petroleum Economist*, January 1993, pp. 4+.

Bahree, Bhushan, and Thomas Kamm, "Total Seeks More Pacts with Iran, Despite U.S.," *Wall Street Journal*, March 17, 1998, p. A13.

Beckman, Jeremy, "Total Beginning Program of Global Expansion," *Offshore*, August 1993, pp. 126+.

Catta, Emmanuel, *Victor de Metz: de la CFP au Groupe Total*, Paris: Total Edition Presse, 1990.

Corzine, Robert, "Maverick Total Stays Relaxed Under Fire," *Financial Times*, February 12, 1997, p. 32.

Dawkins, William, "Shaping Up for Competition," *Financial Times*, November 12, 1990.

Fleming, Charles, and Bhushan Bahree, "France's Total Dismisses U.S.-Sanctions Threat," *Wall Street Journal*, September 30, 1997, pp. A18, A19.

"French, Italian Investment in Iran Oil," United Press International, March 2, 1999.

George, Dev, "Total Focuses on Offshore and Gas," *Offshore*, August 1994, pp. 80+.

Giraud, André, and Xavier Boy de la Tour, *Géopolitique du Pétrole et du Gaz*, Paris: Editions Technip, 1987, 418 p.

Grayson, Leslie E., *National Oil Companies*, New York: John Wiley, 1981.

Guillon, Eric, and Gérard Pruneau, *Total Vôtre Groupe*, Paris: Total CFP, 1988.

"Merger à la Française," *The Economist*, September 18, 1999, p. 73.

Michelson, Marcel, "Total, Petrofina an Another Mega Merger," *Indian Express*, December 2, 1998.

Milmo, Sean, "Total Buys Petrofina in $13 Billion Deal," *Chemical Market Reporter*, December 7, 1998, p. 7

Reed, Stanley, and Stan Crock, "Total Loves to Go Where Others Fear to Tread," *Business Week*, October 13, 1997, p. 52.

Reier, Sharon, "State of Grace," *Financial World*, October 13, 1992, pp. 34–37.

Rondot, Jean, *La Compagnie Française des Pétroles—du Franc-Or au Petrole-Franc*, Paris: Librairie Plon, 1962; reprinted, New York: Arno Press, 1977.

"Sprint Start: France's Total," *Economist*, August 8, 1992, pp. 60–61.

"Total Hits Oil Offhsore Brazil," *The Oil Daily*, June 18, 2002.

"Total Profits Fall 36% in Q1, Helped by Lack of US Exposure," *The Oil Daily*, May 23, 2002.

"Total Reports Weaker Results, Plays Down US Acquisition Talk," *The Oil Daily*, January 31, 2002.

"Total Sees Profits Double," *The Oil Daily*, November 27, 2000.

Toy, Stewart, "Total May Pull Off a Total Turnaround," *Business Week*, September 25, 1995, pp. 114F, 114H.

"Trouble in the Pipeline," *Economist*, January 18, 1997, p. 39.

Vielvoye, Roger, "Modern Management Style Brings New Look to Total," *Oil and Gas Journal*, February 25, 1991, pp. 15+.

—William Pitt
—updates: David E. Salamie, Annette D. McCully

Trader Joe's Company

800 South Shamrock Avenue
Monrovia, California 91016
U.S.A.
Telephone: (626) 599-3700
Toll Free: (800) 746-7857
Fax: (626) 301-4431
Web site: http://www.traderjoes.com

Private Company
Incorporated: 1967
Employees: 7,488 (2001)
Sales: $1.67 billion (2001)
NAIC: 445110 Supermarkets and Other Grocery (Except
    Convenience) Stores; 445310 Beer, Wine, and Liquor
    Stores

Trader Joe's Company operates a chain of unique grocery stores that have been described as equal parts discount warehouse club, natural foods store, specialty grocer, and neighborhood store. A credit to the company's resourceful buying practices, the Trader Joe's stores offer an ever-changing inventory of about 2,000 unusual and appealing food items, wine, and other products. About 98 percent of the product assortment is food, much of it natural, cruelty-free, and made without artificial ingredients: pastas, seafood and meatless foods, baked items, frozen meals, chips and other snacks, coffee and tea, nuts, cheeses, vitamins, candies, pet food, wine and beer, and fresh produce. Business has grown steadily since its inception, through innovation and sharp management techniques. The company was purchased in 1979 by the Albrechts, a wealthy German family who also owns the ALDI discount food stores. In 2002, there were at least 160 Trader Joe's stores operating in 15 states.

Transforming a Little-Known Grocery Chain into Trader Joe's: 1950s–1960s

Although Trader Joe's was not officially founded until 1967, its origins can be traced back to the Pronto Markets chain of food stores that were started in the late 1950s. Pronto Markets was initiated by the Rexall Drug Co. in 1958. The venture reflected the intent of Rexall, an operator of a chain of drugstores, to get in on the burgeoning convenience and corner food-stand market. Rexall appointed Joe Coulombe to head up the new division. Coulombe was only 26 years old at the time and had been with Rexall for only three years. Nevertheless, his managers were impressed with his performance and believed that he could handle the job. During the late 1950s and early 1960s, Coulombe managed to build Pronto into a chain with a considerable presence in Orange County, California.

Despite its expansion, Pronto was experiencing growing profit pressures by the mid-1960s as a result of increased competition. Southland Corp.'s successful 7-Eleven chain, in particular, was bearing down on smaller competitors like Pronto and was even planning an aggressive expansion in Pronto's region. Rexall elected in 1966 to jettison its Pronto Markets division and escape the convenience store industry. Coulombe, still at the helm, was faced with a choice—attempt a buyout of the chain that he had built and remain as chief executive, or bail out and look for a new niche in the retail industry. Coulombe took an extended Caribbean vacation before deciding to stick with Pronto. With the financial backing of Bank of America, he purchased Pronto from Rexall and went to work.

Coulombe knew when he bought Pronto that the strategy he had used to grow the business in the past would be ineffective in the face of growing competition. 7-Eleven was targeting his customers, and his organization lacked the resources to compete with the national chain. The ever-innovative Coulombe considered two prevalent social trends as he devised a new marketing scheme. First of all, consumers were becoming increasingly educated and sophisticated, and were expecting more from their shopping experiences. Secondly, the surge in global travel, made possible by plummeting jumbo-jet airfares, was exposing Americans to new foods. Coulombe decided to develop a food store at which well-educated, well-traveled, but not necessarily wealthy, people could buy foods that would impress themselves and their friends. "I wanted to appeal to the well-educated and people who were traveling more," he explained in the October 2, 1989 issue of *Forbes*, "like teachers, engineers and public administrators. Nobody was taking care of them." Coulombe opened the first Trader Joe's outlet in South Pasadena in 1967—the rest of the Pronto chain would soon become transformed into other Trader Joe's outlets.

Defining the Trader Joe's Store: 1970s

Coulombe's initial concept was to reposition Pronto as an upscale food market/convenience store located near educational centers. That decision was influenced by the health of the liquor business at the time, which, for Pronto, was still very profitable. That scheme was scrapped in 1971, however, when the aerospace industry collapsed and the local Orange County economy plunged. The recession squarely hit Coulombe's targeted customers, who were no longer throwing many parties. To overcome the slowdown, Coulombe drew on his own travel experiences and fashioned a sort of combination health-food shop and liquor store during the early 1970s. He ordered unique food items from different parts of the world to attract customers, and he labeled the foods with sprightly, entertaining labels like "Kiwi from Paradise Juice," and "Look Ma! No Refined Sugar!" Coulombe's new Trader Joe's stores experimented with all types of health foods and beverages, and generally avoided marketing mammoths like Coca-Cola and Budweiser.

Among Coulombe's most successful tactics in the early 1970s was his biting journal *Fearless Flyer* (originally called *Trader Joe's Insider Report*), which aroused environmental awareness through stinging commentary on conservation issues. Distributed to the general public, the *Fearless Flyer* brought hordes of environmentally conscious customers into Trader Joe's, which began stocking increasing amounts of vitamins, biodegradable products, and health foods. Focused on that key market, Trader Joe's boosted sales and profits steadily until 1976. In that year, California legislators deregulated the supermarket industry. The change boded poorly for Trader Joe's liquor segment. Indeed, since the Depression the state had effectively subsidized the sale of milk and liquor by markets. Many smaller convenience stores, in fact, had come to rely on milk and liquor sales, even to the point of advertising other items below cost just to get customers in their shops. Deregulation quashed that practice, and many mom-and-pop stores failed.

As the giant supermarkets flexed their muscles in the newly deregulated grocery industry, Trader Joe's quickly adapted to

the new environment. Coulombe rejected traditional convenience store inventory and began to market Trader Joe's as an upscale, but value-oriented, seller of trendy, hard-to-find beers and wines. The strategy was a success and Trader Joe's maintained its profitability. Trader Joe's continued to sell its inexpensive, unique wines and imported cheeses and coffees as it had since the early 1970s. But Coulombe gradually began expanding the chain's inventory to include a wide array of singular nuts, pastas, fish, vegetables, and prepared snacks and meals. In 1979, Trader Joe's was purchased by German billionaires Karl and Theo Albrecht, who also owned the immensely successful ALDI discount stores in Europe. The company retained Coulombe as CEO.

Perfecting the Trader Joe's Strategy: 1980s

During the early and mid-1980s Coulombe continued to perfect Trader Joe's inventory and market position and to slowly grow the California chain. He gradually moved away from the intense environmental rhetoric in the *Fearless Flyer*, for example, and evolved with his core market. That meant positioning the Trader Joe's stores to appeal to the emerging upwardly mobile, or "Yuppie" crowd, which was exhibiting increasingly sophisticated shopping patterns. Unique beers and wines remained a major attraction, but Coulombe also began bringing in more perishables and unique dry food items. The *Fearless Flyer* continued to be a primary marketing tool, but it was toned down and used to provide entertaining and useful information such as health tips and new store items. In the June 5, 1995, *Business Week* article, Coulombe said, "I wanted it to be a marriage of *Consumer Reports* and *Mad Magazine*."

Importantly, Coulombe bolstered the attraction of his inventory by keeping a sharp focus on value and targeting the well educated, but less-than-affluent consumer. Wines and other alcoholic beverages were often displayed in cases and most stores had only a few rows of shelving. And while the average store size increased during the 1970s and 1980s, the average Trader Joe's store was still only about 6,000 square feet by the late 1980s—about half the size of the typical Los Angeles supermarket. Although his strategy of maintaining a continually changing inventory may have seemed like an expensive and daunting proposition to larger markets and superstores, Coulombe managed to keep prices low. Trader Joe's efficiency was partly the result of its cash policy; the company paid cash for all purchases and funded growth internally as well as through the deep-pocketed Albrecht family. Innovative, low-cost advertising was a major money saver as well. Trader Joe's cost-saving private label comprised about 80 percent of the company's product offering.

Also minimizing expenses was the company's unusual purchasing program. The store's own branded items—fresh salsa and unique pastas, for example—were supplied by a constantly changing set of small, independent contractors. The foods they supplied were often discontinued items that Trader Joe's bought at a discount. Those contractors and other suppliers were found by Trader Joe's own buying team, which traveled throughout America and Europe in search of interesting items and bargains. The result of Coulombe's innovative inventory and pricing strategy was huge profit margins. In 1989, Trader Joe's chalked up an estimated $150 million in sales. That figure reflected

Key Dates:

1958: Joe Coulombe manages the new Pronto Markets chain in California, which later becomes Trader Joe's.

1967: The first Trader Joe's store debuts in South Pasadena, California.

1979: The Albrecht family buys the Trader Joe's chain.

1988: Coulombe retires and is succeeded by longtime friend and colleague John V. Shields.

1989: The company reaches about $150 million in sales.

1993: The company expands outside California and opens stores in Phoenix, growing the Trader Joe's chain to 59 stores.

1994: The company reaches about $600 million in sales; and opens stores in Seattle and Oregon.

1996: The Trader Joe's Web site debuts online; and the company expands stores on the East Coast in Boston, Washington, D.C., and New York.

1998: Trader Joe's expands its nonfood specialty business.

2000: Trader Joe's headquarters moves to Monrovia, California.

2001: The company begins to eliminate genetically modified ingredients from its private-label products.

2002: More than 160 stores in 15 states make up the Trader Joe's chain.

gross sales of more than $800 per square foot—extremely high compared to grocery industry norms. Furthermore, because its stores were usually located on non-prime real estate, the company's fixed overhead was relatively low.

By the late 1980s the nearly 60-year-old Coulombe had built Trader Joe's into a chain of 30 outlets, most of which were in the Los Angeles and San Diego regions. Besides his efforts at Trader Joe's, moreover, Coulombe became involved with Denny's Restaurants Inc. as a board member in the early 1980s and had been instrumental in taking the company private in a $700 million buyout. "I was approaching coronary age and I wanted to retire," Coulombe recalled in the February 26, 1990, *Los Angeles Business Journal.* "But I wanted to leave the company in good hands," he added. In 1988, Coulombe selected 55-year-old John V. Shields to succeed him at the helm. Following a short transition period, Coulombe stepped aside and the Albrecht family welcomed Shields as the new chief.

Shields had known Coulombe for about 40 years when he joined Trader Joe's. The two had met in 1950 as fraternity brothers at Stanford University and had kept in touch over the years; Coulombe had always been impressed by Shields' retail sense. Shields' first exposure to retailing occurred at Stanford, where he worked as a salesperson at a men's clothing store. After college he accepted a job with R.H. Macy in New York and set a goal of becoming senior vice-president by the age of 40. He began by turning around the women's department, converting it from a money loser into one of the store's most profitable departments. Following similar feats, he was promoted to senior vice-president before he was 40. In 1978 he took a job at Mervyn's and helped that retail chain grow from 38 stores to 180 within nine years. His next move was to Trader Joe's.

Growing the Trader Joe's Business: 1990s and Beyond

Shields maintained much of Trader Joe's unique product mix and marketing strategy, as evidenced by a transaction conducted shortly after he took control of the chain. In a rapid-fire deal, Trader Joe's wrote a check for $1 million worth of wine from the Napa Valley Mihaly winery. The winery had just been purchased by a group of Japanese investors who planned to make sake, or rice wine, at the winery. They did not need the inventory of wines that were popular in the United States, so Trader Joe's moved quickly in a deal that brought it 240,000 bottles of wine at a bargain price. "We never buy anything unless we've tasted it, and we turn down more than 90 percent of the wine that is offered to us," Shields said a the *Los Angeles Business Journal* article, "but we knew we wanted the Mihaly inventory . . . [and] if we didn't move fast, someone else might have." A similar deal about the same time brought 3,000 cases of a mid-level chardonnay to Trader Joe's; Trader Joe's was selling the bottles for $2.99 while nearby liquor stores were charging $8.50.

Deals like these kept Trader Joe's cash registers ringing into the early 1990s. Indeed, despite an economic downturn and another depression in the California defense industry, the Trader Joe's stores continued to perform. Inventory was broadened to include a variety of wines, nuts, cheeses, dairy products, frozen foods, candies, bakery items, juices, and even dog food. Moreover, Trader Joe's became the largest retailer of pistachio nuts, whole bean coffee, and brie in California, and was among the largest retailers of maple syrup and wild rice, among other distinctions. Meanwhile, Shields was working to expand the enterprise. By late 1991 there were 43 Trader Joe's operating in California, including several new stores in the San Francisco Bay area. Total sales for the company were topping $250 million annually, and the average size of the outlets had grown to about 7,500 square feet.

Shields stepped up Trader Joe's expansion activity in 1992 and 1993, moving outside of California into Phoenix and growing the chain to 59 stores by late 1993. By that time, the chain was generating revenues of about $500 million annually (about 40 percent of which came from imported goods) and was eyeing expansion possibilities in Seattle and Portland. Trader Joe's inventory had swelled to include about 1,500 items in each store, including many goods from former Soviet-bloc countries like Hungary and the Czech Republic. The company was also boosting purchases from Caribbean nations as a result of new trade agreements signed by the United States in that region. Its major advertising tool continued to be its *Fearless Flyer* and word of mouth, but it was also promoting through radio spots and ads in local media by the mid-1990s.

Trader Joe's expansion efforts would not end there, however; the mid- to late 1990s saw the company's most aggressive expansion campaign yet. Trader Joe's grew to about 65 outlets in 1994 and grossed about $600 million, representing average annual per-store sales growth of about 10 percent over the past five years. The company established stores in Seattle late in 1994 and opened several more outlets throughout Oregon and Washington within a few years. By mid-1995, Trader Joe's was operating 72 outlets and was generating an estimated $1,000 per square foot. In 1996, Trader Joe's began its aggressive East

Coast expansion. Twenty-one stores were quickly established in Boston, Washington, D.C., and New York within three years.

Evidencing the rising popularity of Trader Joe's was the circulation of the *Fearless Flyer*, which had grown to 800,000 before rising delivery costs forced the company to begin distributing it in the stores rather than through the mail. Trader Joe's quickly moved to leap over the *Fearless Flyer* postage barrier, however. In 1996, the company went online, offering customers state-specific *Fearless Flyers* and other useful information via the World Wide Web, including detailed product listings, special announcements, recipes, contact information, and directional maps to stores.

Trader Joe's made another savvy technology investment, this time in 1997, which enabled it to quickly cut costs and position itself for improved communications and data sharing. The company invested in a satellite network which enabled the company to get a volume discount on credit transaction costs for all of its stores on the network, a huge savings overall. By centralizing all the credit card data from various stores, the company was able to deliver the transactions to the bank in a way that the bank prefers. The network was also capable of carrying other kinds of data for the company, including sales data, product availability and spoilage information, delivery schedules, personnel and payroll data, and e-mail messages.

In 1998, Trader Joe's moved to expand its specialty food business and began going upscale by regularly stocking imported items at higher price points. New imported items include ceramicware and crystalware from Italy and Germany. Previously, the company had offered such items on a limited basis, as two-week specials. The specials proved to be so popular with customers (many of whom kept asking store employees about the next special) that it made sense to feature them as regular items. Overall, imported selections in the nonfood, general merchandise category at Trader Joe's doubled from the previous year.

Trader Joe's continued to grow into the new millennium. In 2000, the company moved its headquarters to a much larger site in Monrovia, California. Plans were made to expand into the Midwest beyond Chicago, into Cleveland and Detroit. In 2001, Trader Joe's outlets were averaging 8,000 to 12,000 square feet, which was about more than double the size of some of the original Trader Joe's stores. Despite the still relatively small size of its stores, Trader Joe's president, Doug Rauch, boasted that the company had "the highest sales per square foot of any grocery chain in America." At the end of that same year, the company announced that it would eliminate genetically modified ingredients from its private-label products within one year—a major undertaking, considering that the company's private-label products made up about 85 percent of the stores' inventory. According to Trader Joe's Web site, "Our goal for existing private-label products is to have all such products reformulated, if necessary, and certified within one year." But perhaps such a bold move is not so daunting to such a successful company. By 2002, more than 160 stores in 15 states made up the Trader Joe's chain, with sales reaching $1.67 billion.

Principal Competitors

Albertson's; Arden Group; Cost Plus; GNC; A&P; Haggen; Hannaford Bros.; Hickory Farms; The Kroger Co.; NBTY; Raley's; Royal Ahold; Safeway; Stater Bros.; Stop & Shop; Whole Foods Market; Wild Oats Markets.

Further Reading

Aoki, Naomi, "Trader Joe's Agrees to Eliminate Genetically Altered Ingredients," *Boston Globe*, November 12, 2001, p. E4.

Armstrong, Larry, "Trader Joe's Atlantic Overtures," *Business Week*, June 5, 1995, pp. 86–87.

Blair, Adam, "Trader Joe's Satellite Network Cuts Credit Transaction Costs," *Supermarket News*, September 8, 1997, p. 31.

Elson, Joel, "Trader Joe Adds Imports to General Merchandise," *Supermarket News*, May 4, 1998, p. 167.

Frook, John Evan, "A Well-Developed Sense of Retailing Trade Winds," *Los Angeles Business Journal*, February 26, 1990, p. 22.

Goldfield, Robert, "Trader Joe's Is Trading Up; The Off-Beat Retailer Adopts New Merchandising Tactics," *Business Journal-Portland*, April 16, 1999, p. 13.

Goodman, Stephanie, "Trader Joe's Thrives on Inconsistency," *Adweek's Marketing Week*, April 24, 1989, p. 32.

Hannon, Kerry, "Let Them Eat Ahi Jerky," *U.S. News & World Report*, July 7, 1997, pp. 61–62.

Hicks, Larry, "Yuppie Foods at Bargain Prices," *Sacramento Bee*, November 20, 1991, p. D1.

Hill, Jim, "Trader Joe's On Way to Portland Area," *Oregonian*, January 25, 1995, p. B16.

Hutton, Erika, "Not Your Average Joe," *Shopping Center World*, December 2000, p. 20.

Julian, Sheryl, "West Coast Retailer Trader Joe's Drops Anchor in Boston," *Boston Globe*, June 12, 1996, p. 77.

Kim, Nancy, "Trader Joe's in 3 New Sites," *Puget Sound Business Journal*, October 3, 1997, p. 1.

Law, Steve, "Trader Joe's Sprouts in Portland; California Grocer Takes Aim at Nature's Niche," *Business Journal-Portland*, July 26, 1993, p. 1.

Lazzareschi, Carla, "BeGATTing an End to Food Fight Era," *Los Angeles Times*, December 10, 1993, p. D1.

Lewis, Len, "Feeding Frenzy," *Progressive Grocer*, May 1997, pp. 72–80.

Mozingo, Joe, "A Buffet for the Mind; Trader Joe's Founder Peppers Library Lecture with an Array of Observations," *Los Angeles Times*, March 15, 1998, p. B3.

Mulligan, Thomas S., "Easter Trader Route; Joe's Heads to Other Coast with Its Natural Recipe for Success," *Los Angeles Times*, February 8, 1997, p. 1.

"New Angles from Trader Joe's," *Mass Market Retailing*, November 1, 2001, p. 21.

Paris, Ellen, "Brie, but Not Budweiser," *Forbes*, October 2, 1989, p. 235.

"Presence Information Design Helps Trader Joe's Take Its Expansion to the World Wide Web," *Business Wire*, October 29, 1996.

Prishva, Natasha, "L.A.'s Fastest Growing Companies," *Los Angeles Business Journal*, November 12, 2001.

Retchin, Mark, "Back at the Helm," *Orange County Business Journal*, August 6, 1990, p. 9.

Sanchez, Jesus, "Trader Joe's Looks East: 68-Store Grocery Firm Plans to Conquer New Markets," *Los Angeles Times*, February 27, 1995, p. D1.

Sather, Jean, "Trader Joe's Will Open String of Gourmet-Food Emporiums," *Puget Sound Business Journal*, March 10, 1995, p. 1.

Shiver, Jr., Jube,, "Pacific Enterprises Appoints Trader Joe's Founder to Oversee Its Ailing Retail Chains," *Los Angeles Times*, March 12, 1992, p. D1.

Sur, Indraneel, "Trader Joe's Planning to Move to Monrovia," *Los Angeles Times*, May 31, 2000, p. C2.

—Dave Mote
—update: Heidi Wrightsman

Tyson Foods, Inc.

Tyson Foods, Inc.

2210 West Oaklawn Drive
Springdale, Arkansas 72762-6999
U.S.A.
Telephone: (479) 290-4000
Toll Free: 1-800-4-CHICKEN (1-800-424-4253)
Fax: (479) 290-4061
Web site: http://www.tysonfoodsinc.com

Public Company
Incorporated: 1947 as Tyson Feed & Hatchery,
    Incorporated
Employees: 120,000 (2002 est.)
Sales: $10.751 billion (2001)
Stock Exchanges: New York
Ticker Symbol: TSN
NAIC: 311615 Poultry Processing; 311999 All Other
    Miscellaneous Food Manufacturing; 311412 Frozen
    Specialty Food Manufacturing; 311611 Animal
    (except Poultry) Slaughtering; 311612 Meat Processed
    from Carcasses

Founded in 1935, Arkansas-based Tyson Foods, Inc. is the world's largest processor and marketer of chicken, beef, and pork. The company produces a wide variety of brand name, processed food products—including fresh meats, processed and precooked meats, refrigerated and frozen prepared foods, and animal feeds—and is the recognized market leader in almost every retail and foodservice market it serves. A $24-billion operation, Tyson supplies about 25 billion pounds of chicken, beef, and pork per year to McDonald's, Wal-Mart, and most major supermarket and restaurant chains in the United States. The company employs about 120,000 people and operates in 32 states and 22 countries. The Tyson family controls 80 percent of the company's voting power.

1935 to Early 1960s: The Early Years

During the Depression, John Tyson moved to Springdale, Arkansas, with his wife and one-year-old son Don. In 1935, he bought 50 "springer" chickens and hauled them to Chicago to sell at a profit. Two years later, he named his business Tyson Feed & Hatchery. Over the next 13 years the company prospered by buying and selling chickens, aided by the postwar boom, which brought improved kitchen appliances and the first supermarkets. Gradually, however, Tyson became involved in raising chickens, which allowed him better control over the quality of what he sold. In 1947, the company was incorporated.

Five years later, Don Tyson graduated from college and joined the company as head of operations. Father and son were said to have made a dynamic team, the older Tyson more cautious and the younger one pushing forward. For example, Don convinced his father to raise rock cornish game hens, a market that Tyson would one day dominate.

For the next six years, Tyson focused on expanding production facilities, and, in 1957, the company opened a processing plant in Springdale, Arkansas, the site of the company headquarters. Tyson also introduced its first ice-pack processing line, which brought the company into a more competitive industry bracket. By achieving more complete vertical integration, its dependence on other suppliers lessened.

During the early 1960s, many amateur chicken producers were lured into the market by the drop in feed-grain prices and the easy availability of credit. As a result, broiler production rose about 13 percent between 1965 and 1967. The glut that followed caused big price cuts and accounted for about $50 million in losses in the industry. Several small companies were forced out of business, but the demand for low-priced chicken soared. People were eating four times as much chicken as they did in 1950.

Mid-1960s through 1970s: A Growing Company in a New Industry

In 1963, Tyson went public and changed its name to Tyson's Foods, Incorporated. It also made its first acquisition, the Garrett Poultry Company, based in Rogers, Arkansas. In 1966, John Tyson and his wife died in an automobile accident, and Don Tyson took over the business as president.

Technological improvements in the 1960s fundamentally changed the poultry industry. Broiler production had become one of the most industrialized, automated parts of U.S. agriculture. Through the development of better feeds and better disease control methods, chickens were maturing more quickly. These improvements, combined with increased competition, meant lower prices for consumers, but, for processors, it meant lower earnings. In 1967, despite a 37 percent gain in sales, Tyson lost more than a dollar per share in earnings. Nonetheless, the company took advantage of a situation in which several smaller companies were floundering, and, with its acquisition of Franz Foods, Inc., continued its pattern of buying out smaller poultry concerns. It also began to give its corporate name more visibility, printing ''Tyson Country Fresh Chicken'' on its wrappers instead of the name of the supermarket to which the chickens were sold.

In 1968, Tyson went to court with two other processors when an Agriculture Department officer alleged that the processors had discriminated against Arkansas chicken farmers who were members of an association of poultry farmers. At that time, processors customarily hired farmers to raise their chickens; Tyson and the others had been accused of ''boycotting and blacklisting'' association members in 1962. In 1969, a federal appeals court ruled that the Agriculture Department had ''erred'' in treating the chicken processors like meatpackers and, therefore, did not have the authority under existing laws to take any action against them.

Also in 1969, Tyson acquired Prospect Farms, Inc., the company that became its precooked chicken division. That year Tyson produced more than 2 percent of the nation's chickens, 70 percent for retail sale and 30 percent for institutions. The company had grown from 15 to 3,000 employees and operated five chicken-processing plants and four protein-processing plants in northwest Arkansas and southwest Missouri.

During the 1970s, Tyson continued to grow and diversify. In 1970, a new egg facility was built, and, in 1971, a computerized feed mill and a plant in Nashville, Arkansas, were completed. Also in 1971 the company's name was changed from Tyson's Foods to Tyson Foods. In 1972, Tyson acquired the Ocoma Foods Division of Consolidated Foods Corporation, including three new plants, as well as Krispy Kitchens, Inc., and the poultry division of Wilson Foods. That year Tyson began selling the Ozark Fry, the first breaded chicken breast patty, and also bought a hog operation in Creswell, North Carolina, from First Colony Farms.

1972 was a shakeout year in the poultry business, and several large processors sold out to those with better prospects of survival, easing competition. Because of the rising prices of beef and pork, chicken consumption was increasing at a rapid rate, and new products and technological developments seemed to promise improved profits for the industry. Tyson was already a leader in introducing new products like its chicken patty, chicken hotdog, and chicken bologna; by 1979, it had 24 specialty products. Tyson also operated three plants that used the new deep chill (rather than ice-pack) process, in which the moisture of the bird was frozen at 28 degrees—one degree warmer than the temperature at which chicken meat freezes, leaving the meat still tender and doubling shelf life to about 25 days.

In the early 1970s Tyson closed its unprofitable plant in Shelbyville, Tennessee, but reopened it in 1974 to produce more popular processed and precooked chicken products. In 1973, Tyson bought Cassady Broiler Company, another small poultry concern, and in the next year acquired Vantress Pedigree, Inc. A civil antitrust lawsuit brought against Tyson and other broiler processors in 1974 for conspiring to fix, maintain, and stabilize broiler prices was settled in 1977. Tyson agreed to pay a $975,663 fine to about 30 chicken purchasers. In 1978, Tyson acquired the rest of Wilson Foods Corporation. A year later the company sold its two North Carolina chicken processing plants.

1980s to Early 1990s: Bigger Gains and Growing Pains

By the early 1980s, consumers' nutritional concerns and the continuously high prices of beef and pork had caused the nation's poultry consumption to increase 30 percent since 1970. This increase was also partly due to innovative, easy-to-prepare products from companies like Tyson and the industry's ability to improve breeding and feed techniques. Some of Tyson's experiments had produced six-pound chickens in just six weeks.

In 1980, Tyson introduced its Chick 'n Quick line of products, which included a variety of chicken portions that were easy to prepare. By then Tyson was the largest grower of Rock Cornish game hens and one of the nation's largest hog producers. As it perfected its precooked chicken patty for restaurants, its institutional sales grew. In 1983, Tyson implemented its new advertising slogan, ''Doing our best . . . just for you'' with television commercials on all three major networks in the United States. The company also acquired Mexican Original Products, Inc., a manufacturer of tortillas, taco shells, tostados, and tortilla chips.

In 1984, Cobb, Inc., and Tyson began a joint venture called Arkansas Breeders to breed and develop the Cobb 500, a female with fast growth, low fat, and high meat content. Later that same year, Tyson acquired 90 percent of another poultry firm, Valmac Industries. By then, Tyson had expanded its operations into six states—Georgia, North Carolina, Missouri, Tennessee, Louisiana, and Arkansas—and many of its products were being distributed internationally. In 1986, *The Wall Street Transcript* named Don Tyson the gold award winner in the meat and poultry industry. The company acquired Lane Processing Inc., a closely held poultry-processing firm that had been bankrupt since 1984.

In October 1988, Tyson made a takeover bid for Memphis-based Holly Farms Corporation, the national leader in brand

Key Dates:

1935: Company founder, John Tyson, begins selling chickens in Springdale, Arkansas.
1947: Tyson Feed & Hatchery is incorporated.
1957: The company's first processing plant opens on the north side of Springdale.
1963: The company goes public and changes its name to Tyson's Foods, Incorporated.
1966: The founder's son, Don, becomes president of the company.
1970: Tyson's debuts on the Fortune 1000.
1971: The company name changes to Tyson Foods.
1977: Tyson becomes the nation's largest hog producer.
1982: Tyson debuts on the Fortune 500.
1986: Tyson becomes number one in poultry processing.
1989: Tyson acquires Holly Farms and nearly doubles its national market share.
1992: Tyson goes into the seafood business with the purchase of Arctic Alaska Fisheries, Inc., and Louis Kemp Seafood.
1998: Tyson merges with longtime competitor Hudson Foods. The founder's grandson, John Tyson, becomes chairman of the board.
2000: Tyson celebrates its 65th anniversary. John Tyson becomes CEO.
2001: Tyson acquires IBP and becomes the world's largest processor and marketer of chicken, beef, and pork.

name chicken sales. Holly Farms had begun more than a century before as a cotton compressor. Over the years it had evolved into a chicken and foodservice firm with vast holdings and a 19 percent share of the brand name chicken market. It had been the first processor to use its own name rather than the retail seller's on its packaging, which gave the company a longstanding credibility with consumers and made it a very attractive purchase. Holly Farms rejected the bid, nodding to Tennessee takeover laws, and agreed to merge with ConAgra, Inc., one of the nation's largest food companies and a leading poultry producer based in Omaha, Nebraska. Holly Farms also agreed to sell its poultry assets to ConAgra should the merger not come to fruition. In mid-November, Tyson sued Holly Farms and ConAgra to stop the merger. A few days later, a federal judge ruled that Tennessee's anti-takeover laws were unconstitutional and could not be used to halt Tyson's bid, opening an eight-month fight between Tyson and ConAgra for control of Holly Farms.

Tyson's rapid growth in the fast-food chicken business had put a strain on its production facilities, and Tyson needed Holly Farms's chicken supply. More than half of Tyson's business now was with institutions and restaurants, and Tyson's name was not as popular as Holly Farms's in grocery stores. Finally in June 1989, Don Tyson agreed to pay $1.29 billion for Holly Farms, and the company was fully merged into Tyson later that year. In 1990, its first full year with Holly Farms under its wing, Tyson's sales increased 50.7 percent. The purchase of Holly Farms made Tyson the undisputed king of the chicken industry. It also gained a stronger position in beef and pork through Holly Farms's further-processing operations. Tyson's Beef and Pork

Division grew substantially over the next several years and claimed 11 percent of the company's revenue by 1995.

In 1991, Leland E. Tollett, a college classmate of Don Tyson whom Tyson had brought into the firm in the late 1950s, was named president and chief executive officer; Tyson remained chairman of the board, but was slowly reducing his responsibilities.

Tyson next turned its attention to seafood in an effort to further diversify its operations. In 1992 Tyson acquired Arctic Alaska Fisheries Corporation, a vertically integrated seafood products company, and Louis Kemp Seafood Company, which was purchased from Oscar Mayer Foods Corporation. Tyson's resulting Seafood Division experienced some rocky initial years, and the firm was forced to take a write-down of $205 million on its seafood assets in 1994, the first major write-down in Tyson's history. The Seafood Division was subsequently revamped and then bolstered by the 1995 acquisition of the seafood division of International Multifoods Corp., which had $65 million in sales in 1994 and produced simulated crabmeat, lobster, shrimp, and scallops.

Arkansas Governor Bill Clinton's presidential election campaign and his subsequent term in office brought unwanted attention to the condition of Tyson's chicken processing plants and eventually embroiled the company in controversies. As governor of Arkansas, Clinton had strongly supported the chicken industry, and Don Tyson was a major contributor to Clinton's presidential bid. During the campaign several journalistic investigations of the chicken industry in Arkansas, such as one published in *Time*, revealed that many of the plants were unsanitary and dangerous and staffed by low-paid workers often subject to such difficult conditions as line speed-ups. Environmentalists had also charged that Clinton, while he was governor, had allowed the Arkansas poultry industry to dump tons of chicken waste in Arkansas streams.

After Clinton took office, the close ties between Tyson and the president aroused controversy first when reports stated that James Blair, Tyson's general counsel and a close friend of Bill Clinton and Hillary Rodham Clinton, had helped Hillary Rodham Clinton make a killing in the commodity markets. Then came reports in 1994 that Mike Espy, agriculture secretary under Clinton, had accepted a trip on a Tyson jet and football tickets from Tyson in exchange for favorable treatment from poultry inspectors. Espy subsequently resigned over this matter. Tyson denied any wrongdoing.

Tyson had traditionally expanded its chicken processing capacity through the purchase of existing facilities, but when it decided it needed to expand in 1994, no suitable plants could be found that were for sale. The company then decided to build— at a cost of about $400 million—four new poultry plants over a four-year period, each of which would be able to process 1.3 million chickens a week. That year Tyson also bought a controlling interest in Trasgo, S.A. de C.V., a Mexican joint venture started in 1988. Trasgo held the number three position in the growing chicken market in Mexico.

Also in 1994, Tyson acquired Culinary Foods, Inc., a maker of specialty frozen foods mostly for the foodservice market, and Gorges Foodservice, Inc., a further processor of beef for the foodservice market. Tyson failed, however, to acquire a much larger prize, WLR Foods Inc., a $700 million Virginia-based producer of high-quality turkey and chicken products sold primarily under the Wampler-Longacre brand. Similar to Tyson's experience with Holly Farms, WLR management fought Tyson's $330 million attempt to take over the company in early 1994, an attempt that then turned hostile. WLR instituted a takeover defense, which Tyson fought in federal district court as unconstitutional. This time, unlike the Holly Farms case, the judge ruled against Tyson in a decision that summer. Early in 1995, Tyson announced it would appeal the decision to the U.S. Circuit Court of Appeals.

The Seafood Division write-down had soured Tyson's 1994 results and it posted a $2 million loss, its first in years. Not to be deterred, the company continued its aggressive expansion in 1995 with the purchase of the chicken plants of Cargill, which had decided it could no longer compete with Tyson's chicken empire. This purchase added more than 2.5 million chickens per week to Tyson's processing capacity. Another 2.4 million chickens per week were added later in the year with the acquisition of McCarty Farms Inc., a Mississippi-based closely held firm.

An important era for Tyson ended in April 1995 when Don Tyson retired as chairman, denying that the firm's recent controversies had prompted the move. Tyson remained involved in the firm as senior chairman, but day-to-day operations were handed over to Tollett, who became chairman in addition to his previous position as CEO, and Donald ''Buddy'' Wray, who became president in addition to his previous position as chief operating officer. Like Tollett, Wray was another college classmate of Tyson's and had joined the firm in 1961. John Tyson, Don's then-41-year-old son, was reportedly being groomed to eventually run the company and held the position of president of the Beef and Pork Division.

Mid-1990s and Beyond: Tyson's Plate Gets Crowded

By 1995, Tyson Foods enjoyed a strong position as the leading chicken firm in the United States and looked forward to continuing tremendous growth. Sales had more than doubled from the pre-Holly Farms level of $2.54 billion in 1989 to $5.11 billion in 1994. Tyson was diversifying its operations to become more than just a poultry company, aiming to be a leader in all ''center-of-the-plate'' proteins. In 1994, poultry accounted for only 75 percent of Tyson's revenues. From this strong position, Tyson appeared ready to more aggressively pursue overseas opportunities, evidenced by the formation of a joint venture in the People's Republic of China in 1994, the opening of an office in Moscow in 1995, and the formation in 1995 of a subsidiary, World Resource, Inc., designed to help Tyson's customers throughout the world source products. About 10 percent of the firm's revenues (about $500 million) derived from international sales.

Tyson's past investment in seafood continued to be problematic. In February 1996, the company agreed to pay Alaska up to $5.85 million over ten years to settle allegations of illegal fishing off the Alaska Peninsula in the early 1990s, a legal problem Tyson assumed when it purchased Arctic Alaska Fisheries Corp. in 1992. Later in 1996, the Securities and Exchange Commission accused Donald Tyson of tipping off a friend who then made a quick profit in the stock of Arctic Alaska Fisheries while the sale of the seafood company to Tyson was pending. Tyson quickly agreed to pay a civil penalty of $46,125.

In the fall of 1997, Tyson announced that it planned to acquire the fourth-largest U.S. poultry processor, Hudson Foods Inc., for $642.4 million. The move meant that Tyson would gain control of 30 percent of the U.S. poultry market. However impressive the move, the year ended on an embarrassing note for Tyson, with the company pleading guilty to giving former agriculture secretary Mike Espy $12,000 in illegal gratuities. According to Susan Schmidt writing for *The Washington Post*, ''Tyson Foods admitted to lavishing gifts on Espy—including football tickets, airline trips, meals and scholarship money for his girlfriend—at a time when his department was considering action on several matters affecting the company's business, including safe handling instructions on poultry packaging.'' Tyson consented to pay $6 million in fines and costs.

As the poultry industry was faced with an oversupply and low prices, Tyson took a number of measures designed to reduce production, improve its product mix, and focus on higher added-value products. Consequently, 1998 and 1999 for Tyson were years marked by restructuring and streamlining, including some divesting of nonchicken businesses. In 1998, Tyson closed a laying-hen-processing plant in Bloomer, Arkansas, and sold off a turkey processing plant in Minnesota. That same year, the company created a new division, the Tyson Prepared Foods Group, under which many of Tyson's businesses realigned. In 1999, Tyson sold its seafood and pork groups.

After about twenty years of double-digit profit growth, Tyson shares peaked in late 1998, and then dropped sharply over the next two years. Despite its efforts to address a chicken oversupply and low prices, Tyson saw a dramatic 45 percent drop in its second quarter profits for 2000. Still, Tyson had its 65th anniversary to celebrate. As part of the celebration, the company launched a major campaign to fight hunger. Partnering with Share Our Strength (SOS), Tyson committed to providing $10 million in product and support to local communities over three years. The company also announced that it would donate 650,000 pounds of chicken to local hunger organizations. Total sales for 2000 fell just short of the previous year's, at $7.158 billion, compared to 1999's $7.363 billion. Year 2000 net income fell to $151 million, from the previous year's $230 million. In 2001, Tyson began test marketing an organically grown chicken product, Nature's Farm Organic Chicken, in an effort to find a way to compete in the growing organic and natural foods markets.

Even though Tyson's past was checkered with failed attempts to diversify into beef, pork and seafood, the company still sought a way to go beyond chicken. In mid-2001, Tyson made its boldest move to diversify, and this time, the company seemed to get it right. Tyson acquired IBP, the world's largest beef processor, for $4.4 billion, transforming the company from a giant chicken-only operation into the largest diversified meat company in the world. The acquisition made Tyson a $23-billion enterprise, responsible for processing nearly one-quarter of all meat sold in the United States, and earned the company a third-place U.S. ranking as a packaged food company, behind

Philip Morris's Kraft Foods division and ConAgra. Profits and sales surged after the acquisition: profits tripled in the most recent quarter after the sale; chicken prices rose during the summer as glut-busting production cuts took effect and demand for wings and legs improved; and pork sales grew by more than tenfold to $508.7 million.

The year for Tyson ended on a negative note, however, as the company faced serious allegations of illegal hiring practices, brought on by a two-and-a-half-year investigation by the Department of Justice. Tyson and several employees were indicted for conspiring to smuggle illegal immigrants across the United States-Mexico border and put them to work with false documentation. Tyson was investigated for financial gains derived from the alleged offense, which was estimated to be in excess of $100 million.

IBP's businesses continued to benefit Tyson's bottom line into 2002. Tyson's mid-year profits jumped to a sixfold increase, raising net income to $107 million, compared to 2001. Also, in that same time frame, revenue tripled to $5.9 billion from $1.92 billion. International sales, however, were less successful. Russia, the world's leading poultry importer, halted purchases from the United States, citing concerns over sanitation and handling practices. China also imposed import restrictions, further hurting Tyson's foreign sales.

Principal Operating Units

Foodservice and International Unit; Retail and Consumer Products Unit; Fresh Meats.

Principal Competitors

Cagle's; Cargill; ConAgra; ContiGroup; Farmland Industries; Foster Farms; Gold Kist; Hormel; Keystone Foods; Perdue; Pilgrim's Pride; Sanderson Farms; Sara Lee Foods; Smithfield Foods.

Further Reading

"After Acquiring Beef Producer, Tyson Foods Says Profit Is Up," *The New York Times*, November 13, 2001, p. C4.

Barboza, David, "Why Is He on Top? He's a Tyson, for One," *The New York Times*, March 4, 2001, p. 1.

Behar, Richard, "Arkansas Pecking Order," *Time*, October 26, 1992, pp. 52–54.

Bloomberg News, "Profit Increases Sixfold at Tyson Foods," *The New York Times*, July 30, 2002, p. C8.

Buckler, Arthur, "Tyson Foods Isn't Chicken-Hearted about Expansion," *Wall Street Journal*, January 18, 1994, p. B4.

Edmundson, Sheila, "Real Home of the McNugget Is Tyson," *Memphis Business Journal*, July 9, 1999, p. 21.

Hamon, John, "Tyson Foods Plans to Close Bloomer Plant," *Arkansas Business*, May 18, 1998, p. 11.

Heath, Thomas, "A Booming Business Runs Afowl of Politics: Tyson Foods' Troubles Escalated Following Clinton's Election," *Washington Post*, July 23, 1995, p. H1.

Manning, Earl, "Don Tyson: The Chicken King Spreads His Wings," *Progressive Farmer*, March 1994, pp. 24–25.

McGraw, Dan, "The Birdman of Arkansas," *U.S. News & World Report*, July 18, 1994, pp. 42–46.

Miller, Bill, "Tyson Foods Executive Sentenced in Espy Case," *The Washington Post*, September 26, 2000, p. A6.

Ruggless, Ron, "Don Tyson: Chairman, Tyson Foods Inc., Springdale, Arkansas," *Nation's Restaurant News*, January 1995, pp. 213–14.

Schmidt, Susan, "Tyson Foods Admits Illegal Gifts to Espy; Firm to Pay U.S. $6 Million; Executives to Testify at Trial of Former Cabinet Member," *The Washington Post*, December 30, 1997, p. A1.

Schwartz, Marvin, *Tyson: From Farm to Market*, Fayetteville, Ark.: University of Arkansas Press, 1991, 158 p.

Smith, David, "Tyson Foods Country's Largest Poultry Exporter," *Arkansas Business*, September 11, 1995, p. 26.

Stein, Nicholas, "Son of a Chicken Man," *Fortune*, May 13, 2002, pp. 136–46.

Stewart, D. R., "Tyson Forecasts Its Future in Faster Foods," *Arkansas Democrat-Gazette*, January 14, 1995, pp. D1–D2.

Taylor, John, "Tyson, Kroger, ConAgra Test Health Market: Food Giants Discover Money in Organic Products, Labels Natural vs. Organic," *Omaha World-Herald*, July 6, 2002, p. 1d.

Tyson Corporate Fact Book, Springdale, Ark.: Tyson Foods, Inc., 1994, 40 p.

Tyson Corporate Fact Book, Springdale, Ark.: Tyson Foods, Inc., 2002, 40 p.

"Tyson Foods Ex-Chairman to Pay Fine," *The Seattle Times*, September 24, 1996, p. D4.

"Tyson Foods Expands International Interests," *Nation's Restaurant News*, June 25, 2001, p. 154.

"Tyson Launches Major Campaign to Fight Hunger," *Food Management*, July 2000, p. 24.

"Tyson Seafood Agrees to Pay Alaska Up to $5.85 Million," *The Seattle Times*, February 6, 1996, p. E3.

"Tyson Struggles as Low Prices Take Their Toll," *Eurofood*, May 11, 2000.

"Tyson to Sell Pork Group," *ID: The Voice of Foodservice Distribution*, December 1999, p. 20.

"Tyson Will Realign Several Food Businesses," *The News & Record* (Piedmont Triad, N.C.), September 11, 1998, p. B6.

Walsh, Sharon, "Tyson Foods to Buy Competitor Hudson; Rival Had Been Hit by Massive Beef Recall," *The Washington Post*, September 5, 1997, p. G1.

Young, Barbara, "Tyson Foods' Karma," *National Provisioner*, June 2002, p. 10.

—updates: David E. Salamie, Heidi Wrightsman

UnionBanCal Corporation

400 California Street
San Francisco, California 94104
U.S.A.
Telephone: (415) 765-2969
Fax: (415) 765-2950
Web site: http://www.uboc.com

Public Company
Incorporated: 1952
Employees: 9,100 (2001 est.)
Total Assets: $35.2 billion (2001)
Stock Exchanges: New York
Ticker Symbol: UB
NAIC: 522110 Commercial Banking

San Francisco-based UnionBanCal Corporation is a commercial bank holding company that was incorporated in California in 1952. UnionBanCal's primary subsidiary is the Union Bank of California, which was formed April 1, 1996, when the Union Bank of San Francisco merged with the Bank of California. This merger formed one of the 35 largest banks in the United States. The consolidation of these two banks was brought about by the merger of the Bank of Tokyo Ltd., which owns Union Bank, and Mitsubishi Bank Ltd., which owns the Bank of California.

In the years since the merger, the Union Bank of California has grown to become the third largest commercial bank in the state of California. The Bank of Tokyo-Mitsubishi, Ltd. owns 67 percent of UnionBanCal Corporation. Union Bank of California offers numerous customer services, including ATM/Debit Cards, home mortgages, supermarket branches, real estate financing, asset-based finance and leasing, import/export financing, electronic letters of credit, trust and money management, Internet banking, and other state-of-the-art financial services.

Early History of Union Bank of San Francisco

The founder of Union Bank, Kaspare Cohn, was a highly successful businessman in the wool-growing industry in the state of California. During the late 19th century and early years of the 20th century, California was still a pastoral state with huge tracts of land upon which cattle and sheep used to graze. During one period of the state's history, over seven million sheep roamed the California landscape. In his capacity as a wool merchant, Kaspare Cohn worked with Basque shepherds who supplied him with the wool for his business. Since these shepherds tended their sheep far from the city of Los Angeles, they were naturally inclined to ask Cohn, with whom they had developed a close working relationship, to safeguard the proceeds of their wool sales until there came a time when the money was needed. Occasionally, when one shepherd needed an advance to help him during a financially difficult time, or another needed credit to improve or add to his flock of sheep, Cohn would provide the necessary funds.

When the California Banking Department became aware that Cohn was functioning like his own bank, namely, accepting deposits from customers and arranging loans, the state authorities gave him the choice of either formalizing his activities by creating a bank or desisting from any further financial transactions. Cohn, already a wealthy man from his various investments in land and vineyards, decided that he had all the contacts necessary to establish and organize a bank. In 1914, he founded the Kaspare Cohn Commercial & Savings Bank. Some of the more important decisions Cohn made while serving as president of the bank included the financing of the San Gabriel Light & Power Company, and another small natural gas company that ultimately became part of Pacific Lighting Corporation.

Kaspare Cohn died in 1916 and was followed by Ben Meyer as president of the bank. Just before the U.S. entry into World War I, the city of Los Angeles and the state of California were starting their long period of growth and development. Businesses, restaurants, and civic organizations were being created all over the state, and many of these enterprises were being founded by new residents. The search for capital was at an all-time high, yet risks were understandably great, and the banking community was conservative in its loan policies. A new bank like Kaspare Cohn Commercial & Savings Bank saw an opportunity to manage customer deposits by providing exceptional service. In addition, under the direction of Meyer, the bank began to garner a reputation as an astute lender. Meyer had an uncanny ability to provide loans to those entrepreneurs who not only were successful in their business endeavors but who were also able to promote the development of the city of Los Angeles.

In 1918 the name of the bank was changed to Union Bank & Trust Company. In 1922 the bank was growing at such a fast rate that it opened a new headquarters on Eighth and Hill Streets and, just five years later, the bank's continued growth required an enlargement and significant improvement of these facilities. Much of the bank's business during this time was based on the civic leadership and personal qualities of Ben Meyer. As president of Cedar Hospital, Meyer visited the hospital every morning, greeting both staff and patients. While attending a ballet one evening at the Hollywood Bowl, Meyer discovered that the performance was in danger of being canceled since the stagehands had not been paid their wages. Meyer went backstage, presented the stagehands with a personal check for what they were owed, and the show was performed.

During the entire decade of the 1920s, Meyer presided over Union Bank's period of uninhibited growth. Deposits were increasing, the loan department was successful in its choice of entrepreneurs, and assets continued to rise at an astounding rate. Like every bank across the nation, however, Union Bank was affected by the stock market crash of 1929. Yet the bank survived the crash and the worst of the Depression. After Franklin Delano Roosevelt's Bank Holiday Proclamation in 1933, Union Bank was one of the banks allowed to reopen for business. The deft management of the bank's assets and business activities during this time was largely due to the talent of Ben Meyer.

Expanded Services in the 1940s, 1950s, and 1960s

The early 1940s were disruptive for the entire United States since men of all ages were involved in the military conflicts of World War II. Yet even below normal staff levels, Union Bank continued to expand its services and extend its asset base. The bank was the first bank throughout the entire western part of United States to implement a program known as "bank-by-mail service." This program involved free postage both ways for customers doing banking business. Since the bank had a policy of not opening branch offices, the nearby mailbox was a highly successful substitute. Union Bank was also one of the first banks throughout the western United States to provide its customers with "lock-box banking," a new development for collecting payments. During the latter part of the decade, Union Bank's slogan became, "The Bank of Personal Service."

Ben Meyer retired in 1950, and Herman Hahn, an executive with 20 years service in Union Bank, became president. Hahn was an energetic leader and active in many civic groups in the

Los Angeles area. Within the bank, he had built a reputation for his ability to structure complex loans and had thereby brought a good deal of visibility to the loan department. Unfortunately, Hahn unexpectedly died in 1954, and the bank was forced to look for a successor. Meyer came out of retirement to temporarily assume the responsibilities of president, as the bank's board of directors searched for a new candidate. In 1957 the bank appointed Harry J. Volk to serve as president. Volk brought with him extensive experience from the insurance industry, having left a job at The Prudential Insurance Company to accept the presidency at Union Bank. Two months following Volk's appointment, Ben Meyer died.

Soon after Volk became president, he assembled his staff and members of the bank's board of directors to discuss the changes in the banking industry and how Union Bank should respond to the challenges ahead. The overwhelming response was that the bank had to take advantage of as many growth opportunities as possible. As a result, management decided to expand its presence throughout the state of California, but rather than imitate the branch banking system of most retail banks, Union Bank decided to organize semiautonomous offices staffed with senior bank officers that would provide all the services normally available at the bank's headquarters on Eighth and Hill Streets in San Francisco. The bank adopted the phrase, "Regional Banking," in order to describe this comprehensive, yet highly innovative, banking system.

Over the next decade, Union Bank opened 16 regional head offices, including facilities in major areas such as Beverly Hills, Sacramento, and San Diego. Along with its development of regional offices, Union Bank acquired Occidental Bank, located in the heart of the San Fernando Valley. This was Union Bank's first acquisition. While concentrating on expanding geographically, the bank also initiated new and highly creative customer service practices. The bank was the first financial institution to calculate a daily compounded interest rate on individual savings accounts, the first to introduce savings statements for customers that were computer generated, and the first to introduce original techniques for interim construction financing.

A New Concept in Banking

The year 1967 was one of the most important years in the history of Union Bank. The bank was the first major bank in the United States to form and establish a one-bank holding company. This new concept in banking completely transformed the banking industry. The holding company, Union Bancorp (subsequently changed to Unionamerica, Inc. in 1969) was formed to assume the ownership of Union Bank and to create new opportunities for expanding into diversified areas of financial services. The day after the formation of the bank holding company, Union Bank acquired one of the largest mortgage firms in the United States, Western Mortgage Corporation.

When the Bank Holding Company Act was passed in 1970, describing strict limitations on the activities of bank holding companies and requiring that some of these activities be divested, Unionamerica changed its name back to Union Bancorp and reorganized its operations, including the operations of all its subsidiaries. The company's new headquarters on Bunker Hill were occupied by this time, and new acquisitions of banks were

Key Dates:

1914: Kaspare Cohn founds the Kaspare Cohn Commercial & Savings Bank.

1918: The bank's name is changed to Union Bank & Trust Company of Los Angeles.

1922: The bank opens a new headquarters in San Francisco.

1958: The bank's name is shortened to Union Bank.

1967: The bank establishes Union Bancorp, a one-bank holding company.

1972: The bank enters international banking and opens offices in Rio de Janeiro, Tokyo, and London.

1979: Union Bancorp is acquired by Standard Chartered PLC of London.

1988: Union Bancorp is acquired by California First Bank (which is owned by The Bank of Tokyo California) and retains the Union Bank name.

1996: The Mitsubishi Corporation of Japan and The Bank of Tokyo, Ltd. merge, resulting in the consolidation of The Bank of California and Union Bank into UnionBanCal Corporation and its primary subsidiary Union Bank of California, N.A.

1998: The bank redesigns its product line and enhances its technological capabilities for customers.

2001: Due to a rash of bad loans, the bank announces its intent to shift its emphasis from lending to a fee-oriented business and to expand business nationwide.

made in Oakland, San Francisco, Palo Alto, and Long Beach. By 1972 the bank's deposits in its Northern California regional office were greater than those of the entire bank. It was during this period that the bank entered the field of international banking and opened offices in Rio de Janeiro, Tokyo, and London.

Ownership by the Bank of Tokyo

The late 1970s and the entire decade of the 1980s were highly profitable years for the bank. Under astute management, the bank continued to improve upon its already-attractive customer services. Most important, however, the bank continued to expand throughout California. Not content with regional offices anymore, management decided to go into branch banking. By the mid-1980s, Union Bank had an extensive network of branch locations up and down the coast of California. One of the surprises within the state banking industry occurred when the Bank of Tokyo, Ltd., a Japanese-based bank holding company, purchased Union Bank in October of 1988. Although Union Bank was performing admirably, the acquisition by the Bank of Tokyo signaled that the bank's board of directors was willing to use the resources of its Japanese parent to grow even larger. Under the direction of the Bank of Tokyo, Union Bank continued its expansion program, and the result was an impressive increase in the assets of the bank. By the mid-1990s, assets had grown to approximately $18 billion. In addition to its ever-increasing asset base, however, the bank built its branch network to include a total of over 200 offices in the state. Union Bank was widely regarded as one of the financial institutions with the best customer services on the West Coast.

Merger with the Bank of California in 1996

In 1995, the Bank of Tokyo and Mitsubishi Bank, Ltd., also a Japanese-based bank holding company, agreed to merge in order to create the world's largest bank. The two financial titans established a private bank whose assets totaled approximately $820 billion. At the same time, the Bank of Tokyo and Mitsubishi Bank, Ltd., agreed to merge their two most prominent subsidiaries, Union Bank and the Bank of California, and created UnionBanCal Corporation, a holding company, and its primary subsidiary Union Bank of California. The Bank of California was less than half the size of Union Bank, with only $7 million in assets and 46 branch offices in Washington, Oregon, and California. Effective April 1, 1996, the merger between the two subsidiaries formed the fourth largest bank in the state of California, with over $25 billion in assets. The combined resources of Union Bank and the Bank of California meant improved services in such areas as commercial markets, specialized lending, trust services, private banking, treasury services, retail markets, and international banking.

Union Bank of California continued a number of the more important strategies that management at Union Bank was working on at the time of the merger. Union Bank had a long-established policy of providing support services to individual entrepreneurs and businesses from Asia and the Pacific Rim that wanted to establish themselves in the United States. At the time of the merger, Union Bank was helping over 1,200 Japanese corporations with their operations in California. Union Bank of California planned to continue assisting these business pioneers by offering such services as cash management, pension plans, investment products, wire transfers, expedited loan approvals, and general financial advice. Another policy continued at Union Bank of California was the bank's commitment to community involvement. In the past, Union Bank had sponsored 5k runs for charity, funded the construction of low-income family dwellings in Los Angeles, and contributed $150,000 to the brand-new San Francisco Main Library.

The merger between Union Bank and the Bank of California has provided a wider range of financial services, including trust and investment services, retail banking, private banking, business banking, and international banking.

Changes after the Merger

In 1997, Union Bank of California was the first licensee of software called Mobile Solutions for Banking. The software, jointly developed by American National Bank & Trust Co. and KPMG Peat Marwick LLP, allowed sales staff working outside of the office access to information about all of the bank's customers and prospective customers, as well as up-to-date listings of exactly which products and services the bank offered in the region they were working. Union Bank of California was not the only institution to find this new system groundbreaking, The Smithsonian Institute felt it was distinguished enough to include in the permanent collection of exponents of technological innovation, at the National Museum of American History. Other technological resources that the bank added to their offerings in the late 1990s included: CLEAR/IMAGE International Positive Pay service, a tool that gave businesses the ability to view suspicious checks online to detect fraudulent activity before a decision to pay or not pay the check was made; ImageMark proof-of-deposit (POD), which allowed the bank to deliver image statements via the Internet and perform other useful functions; and the development of an online service that permitted customers to set up and manage 401(k) plans from any device connected to the Internet. The online 401(k) service joined the many resources that the Union Bank of California had available for its customers, including the ability for bank customers to call up their accounts, check balances, and gain access to information from online financial sources.

Due to a spattering of bad loans in 2000, Union Bank of California shifted its emphasis from lending to a fee-oriented business. Two of the bad loans were to Pacific Gas and Electric Corporation and Southern California Edison Company; both of these companies' finances were affected by the 2001 California energy crisis. Norimichi Kanari, appointed to president and CEO of the bank in 2001, announced plans to adhere to the strategy adopted in late 2000 by then president and CEO Takahiro Moriguchi to lessen the bank's dependency on lending. Additionally, Kanari set the bank on a path toward expanding the Union Bank of California's private banking business in the West and expanding its institutional trust and custodial business nationwide. The stock market responded positively to Kanari's shift in strategy, raising the bank's stock price 112 percent between September 2000 and July 2001. This remarkable spike in stock price caused some analysts to speculate that a takeover may be in Union Bank of California's future. Regardless of speculation, the company continues to maintain a strong position in the Californian banking industry.

Principal Subsidiaries

Armstrong/Robitaille; Union Bank of California.

Principal Competitors

AmSouth Bancorporation; BB&T Corporation; Comerica Incorporated; Compass Bancshares, Inc.; Fifth Third Bancorp; Huntington Bancshares Incorporated; National Commerce Financial Corporation; Regions Financial Corporation; SouthTrust Corporation; Zions Bancorporation.

Further Reading

"Another Redo," *American Banker*, February 2001, p. 16.

Baljko, Jennifer L., "Union Bank of California Adds Fraud Safeguard," *Bank Systems & Technology*, February 1998, p. 39.

"Bank Offers Wireless 401(k) Management," *Nokomis*, July 2001, p. 56.

Clark, Don, "Union Bank to Buy Bank of California as Parents Merge," *Wall Street Journal*, September 29, 1995, p. A7(E).

Crockett, Barton, "Bank of California, Union Bank Put Merger Savings at $90 Million," *American Banker*, September 29, 1995, p. 4.

——, "Japanese Giants' California Jewels Are Seen as Takeover Target," *American Banker*, August 28, 1995, p. 4.

Icon Group International, Inc. Staff, *UnionBanCal Corp.: Labor Productivity Benchmarks and International Gap Analysis*, San Diego: Icon Group International, Incorporated, 2000, http://www.icongrouponline.com.

"Japanese Megamerger to Create California Giant," *American Banker*, May 30, 1995, p. 26.

"Kanari: Cleaning Up the Mess," *American Banker*, August 2001, p. 20.

Kraus, James, R., "Japan Likely to Create the Biggest Foreign-Owned Bank in the U.S.," *American Banker*, March 30, 1995, p. 1.

Marlin, Steven, "Union Bank of California to Deploy POD System," *Bank Systems & Technology*, June 1998, p. 26.

Monahan, Julie, "Union Bank of California Plans to Speed New Accounts Using the Local Area Net," *American Banker*, March 22, 1995, pp. A10–11.

O'Sullivan, Orla, "Bringing Your Commerical Customers into Focus," *ABA Banking Journal*, December 1997, p. 52.

Pesek, Jr., William, "Union Bank Rings Up Retail Profits with Phone-Based System," *American Banker*, May 24, 1993, p. A8.

"Union Bank of California," *Manhasset*, September 24, 2001, p. 41.

"Union Bank Purchase of Branches Approved," *American Banker*, May 29, 1992, p. 8.

Volk, Harry J., *Union Bank*, New York: Newcomen Society, 1974.

—Thomas Derdak
—update: Tammy Weisberger

United States Steel Corporation

600 Grant Street
Pittsburgh, Pennsylvania 15219
U.S.A.
Telephone: (412) 433-1121
Toll Free: (866) 433-4801
Fax: (412) 433-5733
Web site: http://www.ussteel.com

Public Company
Incorporated: 1901 as United States Steel Corporation
Employees: 37,161 (2001)
Sales: $6.4 billion (2001)
Stock Exchanges: New York
Ticker Symbol: X
NAIC: 331513 Steel Foundries (except Investment);
421520 Coal and Other Mineral and Ore Wholesalers;
212112 Bituminous Coal Underground Mining;
331210 Iron and Steel Pipe and Tube Manufacturing
from Purchased Steel; 213114 Support Activities for
Metal Mining; 324199 All Other Petroleum and Coal
Products

The United States Steel Corporation is the largest integrated steel company in the United States and the 11th largest in the world. It produces and sells a wide range of semi-finished and finished steel products, coke, and taconite pellets. It operates smaller businesses in real estate, engineering, mining, and financial services. The company owns and operates a steel production facility in the Slovak Republic that supplies the Eastern European market. It also engages in joint ventures with Japanese and Korean steelmakers.

Origins: 1873–1915

The origin of United States Steel Corporation (U.S. Steel) is virtually an early history of the steel industry in the United States, which in turn is closely linked to the name of Andrew Carnegie. The quintessential 19th-century self-made man, Carnegie began as a bobbin boy in a cotton mill, made a stake in the railroad business, and, in 1864, started to invest in the iron industry. In 1873 he began to establish steel plants using the Bessemer steelmaking process. A ruthless competitor, he led his Carnegie Steel Company to be the largest domestic steelmaker by the end of the century. In 1897 Carnegie appointed Charles M. Schwab, a brilliant, diplomatic veteran of the steel industry who had worked his way up through the Carnegie organization, as president of Carnegie Steel.

At about the same time, prominent financier John Pierpont Morgan became a major participant in the steel industry as a result of his organization of the Federal Steel Company in 1898. Morgan's personal representative in the steel business was Elbert Henry Gary, a lawyer, former judge, and director of Illinois Steel Company, one of the several steel companies co-opted into Federal Steel, of which Gary was made president. Carnegie, Schwab, Morgan, and Gary were the key participants in the organization of U.S. Steel.

By 1900 the demand for steel was at peak levels, and Morgan's ambition was to dominate this market by creating a centralized combine, or trust. He was encouraged in this by rumors of Carnegie's intention to retire from business. U.S. President William McKinley was known to approve of business consolidations, and his support limited the risk of government antitrust claims in the face of a steel industry combination. In December 1900 Morgan attended a now-legendary dinner at New York's University Club. During the course of the evening Schwab gave a speech that set forth the outlines of a steel trust, the nucleus of which would be the Carnegie and Morgan steel enterprises, together with a number of other smaller steel, mining, and shipping concerns. With Schwab and Gary as intermediaries between Carnegie and Morgan, negotiations were concluded by early February 1901 for Carnegie to sell his steel interests for about $492 million in bonds and stock of the new company. The organization plan was largely executed by Gary, with Morgan arranging the financing. On February 25, 1901, United States Steel Corporation was incorporated with an authorized capitalization of $1.4 billion, the first billion-dollar corporation in history. The ten companies that were merged to form U.S. Steel were American Bridge Company, American Sheet Steel Company, American Steel Hoop Company, American Steel & Wire Company, American Tin Plate Company, Carnegie Steel Company, Federal Steel Company, Lake Superior Consolidated Iron Mines, National Steel Company, and National Tube Company.

At Morgan's urging Schwab became president of U.S. Steel, with Gary as chairman of the board of directors and of the executive committee. Two such strong personalities, however, could not easily share power. In 1903 Schwab resigned and soon took control of Bethlehem Steel Corporation, which he eventually built into the second-largest steel producer in the country. Gary stayed on as, in effect, chief executive officer to lead U.S. Steel and to dominate its policies until his death in August of 1927. His stated goal for U.S. Steel was not to create a monopoly but to sustain trade and foster competition by competing on a basis of efficiency and price. Steel prices did drop significantly in the years after the company began, and, because of competition, U.S. Steel's market share of U.S. steel production dropped steadily over the years from about 66 percent in 1901 to about 33 percent from the 1930s to the 1950s. U.S. Steel's sales increased from $423 million in 1902 to $1 billion during the 1920s, dropped to a low of $288 million in 1933, reached $1 billion in 1940, and climbed to about $3 billion in 1950. Except for a few deficit years, U.S. Steel's operations have been generally profitable, though earnings have been cyclical.

U.S. Steel's history is notable for continual acquisitions, divestitures, consolidations, reorganizations, and labor disputes. In 1901 U.S. Steel acquired the Bessemer Steamship company, a shipping concern engaged in iron-ore traffic on the Great Lakes. Shelby Steel Tube Company was purchased in 1901, Union Steel Company in 1903, and Clairton Steel Company in 1904; a number of other, smaller acquisitions were made in those early years. In 1906 U.S. Steel began construction on a large, new steel plant on Lake Michigan together with a model city designed primarily for its employees. The new town was named Gary, Indiana, and was substantially completed by 1911. A major acquisition in 1907 was that of Tennessee Coal, Iron and Railroad Company, the largest steel producer in the South. A presence in the West was established with the purchase of Columbia Steel Company in 1910. In addition to steel manufacture, U.S. Steel also maintained large coal-mining operations in western Pennsylvania. These operations were based on former properties of H.C. Frick Coke Company, which included some of Carnegie's coal properties and which became a part of U.S. Steel when it was formed in 1901. The coal produced by these mines was used to fuel U.S. Steel's operations.

The 12-hour workday, standard in industry during U.S. Steel's early years, was a major labor issue. U.S. Steel's workers originally were unorganized, and Gary was a staunch enemy of unionization, the closed shop, and collective bargaining. He took a leading role among businessmen, however, by calling in 1911 for the abolition of the 12-hour workday. Little was actually done, however, and a general strike was called against the steel industry in 1919. The strike failed and was abandoned in 1920. The 12-hour workday eventually was abolished, and in 1937 U.S. Steel signed a contract with the Steel Workers Organizing Committee, which in 1942 became the United Steelworkers of America. U.S. Steel's labor relations have historically been adversarial, characterized by divisive negotiations, often bitter strikes, and settlements that were sometimes economically disastrous for the company and, in the long run, for its employees.

The U.S. government's tolerant view of big corporations ended with the administration of President Theodore Roosevelt. On Roosevelt's instructions, an antitrust investigation of U.S. Steel was begun in 1905. Gary cooperated with the investigation, but the final report to President William Howard Taft in 1911 led to a monopoly charge against U.S. Steel in the U.S. Circuit Court of Appeals. This court's 1915 decision unanimously absolved U.S. Steel from the monopoly charge and largely vindicated Gary's claim that U.S. Steel was designed to be competitive rather than a monopolistic trust.

Growth: 1915–1963

U.S. Steel's business boomed during World War I with sales more than doubling between 1915 and 1918 and remaining strong at about $2 billion annually through the 1920s. Gary's personal domination of U.S. Steel ended with his death in 1927. J.P. Morgan, Jr., became chairman of the board of directors from 1927 to 1932, but during this period U.S. Steel essentially was under the leadership of Myron C. Taylor, chairman of the finance committee from 1927 to 1934 and chairman of the board from 1932 until his resignation in 1938. Taylor brought about extensive changes in U.S. Steel's makeup. Numerous obsolete plants were closed, others were modernized, and a new plant was added with total capital expenditures of more than $500 million. By the end of Taylor's tenure, about three-quarters of U.S. Steel's products were different or were made differently and more efficiently than they had been in 1927, with the principal realignment being the change from heavy steel for capital goods to lighter steel for consumer goods.

After Taylor's resignation in 1938, Edward R. Stettinius, Jr., served as chairman of the board until he left in 1940 to undertake government service and eventually to become secretary of state. Benjamin F. Fairless, an important figure in U.S. Steel history, became president in 1938, and Irving S. Olds succeeded Stettinius as chairman of the board in 1940. Olds served as chairman until 1952, when he was succeeded in that office by Fairless.

During this period U.S. Steel's business recovered from its Depression slump, buoyed by the enormous demand for steel products generated by World War II and the postwar economic boom. Revenues more than quintupled from $611 million in 1938 to more than $3.5 billion in 1951. U.S. Steel was present in every geographical market in the United States except the East, so in 1949 it announced plans to build a large integrated steel plant in Pennsylvania on the Delaware River to be known as the

Key Dates:

1873: Andrew Carnegie founds Carnegie Steel Co.
1898: J.P. Morgan founds Federal Steel Co.
1901: Ten steel companies, including Carnegie and Federal, merge to form the United States Steel Corporation.
1911: Antitrust charges are brought against U.S. Steel.
1915: U.S. Steel is cleared of antitrust charges.
1937: U.S. Steel signs a contract with the Steel Workers' Organizing Committee, the predecessor of the United Steel Workers of America.
1952: President Truman seizes U.S. Steel properties to assure the supply of steel for the Korean War; Supreme Court rules the seizure is unconstitutional.
1962: President Kennedy protests a steel price increase and causes its reversal.
1979: U.S. Steel closes 13 facilities.
1982: U.S. Steel acquires Marathon Oil Company.
1991: A restructuring renames U.S. Steel USX and creates two tracking stocks: USX-U.S. Steel Group and USX-Marathon Group.
1992: USX-Dehli Group is created as a third tracking stock.
2000: USX acquires a steel producer in the Slovak Republic.
2002: USX is broken into independent companies: United States Steel Corporation and Marathon Oil.

Fairless Works. This plant, operational in 1952, was intended to compete with Bethlehem Steel for the eastern market and to take advantage of ocean shipment of iron ore from U.S. Steel's large ore reserves in Venezuela.

In 1951 a change intended to simplify the structure of United States Steel Corporation took place when a single company was formed from its four major operational subsidiaries. This reorganization, completed in 1953, created a tightly knit, more efficient organizational structure in place of the former aggregate of semi-independent units. In 1953 Clifford F. Hood was appointed president and chief operating officer, sharing overall responsibility for the company with board chairman Fairless and Enders W. Voorhees, who continued as chairman of the finance committee.

Fairless's tenure as chairman of the board included one of the longest strikes in U.S. Steel's history, resulting from the company's refusal to allow substantial wage increases and tighter closed-shop rules. Just before the strike was to begin in April 1952, President Harry S. Truman seized the company's properties in order to ensure steel production for the Korean War. This unusual action was declared unconstitutional by the U.S. Supreme Court in June 1952. An industry-wide strike ensued that was settled in August, ending a unique episode in U.S. Steel's labor history. A more productive occurrence was the ground breaking in 1953 for the building of a new research center near Pittsburgh. Fairless retired in May 1955 and was succeeded by Roger M. Blough as chairman of the board and chief executive officer.

Due to improved administrative, operating, and plant efficiencies, U.S. Steel set a postwar record for profitability in 1955, although market share continued to decline to around 30 percent. In 1958 a further corporate simplification took place when wholly owned subsidiary Universal Atlas Cement Company was merged into U.S. Steel as an operating division, as were the Union Supply Company and Homewood Stores Company subsidiaries. Profits were being squeezed between rising operating costs and relatively stable prices, and in April 1962 U.S. Steel unexpectedly announced an across-the-board price increase that triggered a storm of criticism, including an angry protest to Blough from U.S. President John F. Kennedy. Within a week U.S. Steel was forced to rescind the price increase, using the face-saving excuse that other steel companies had not agreed to support the new price level. This situation resulted from U.S. Steel's continued decline in market share to about 25 percent in 1961, together with deteriorating profitability, in part caused by excessive capital spending in relation to market volume.

Decline and Consolidation: 1963–2002

In response to its difficulties, U.S. Steel announced in 1963 a further reorganization and centralization of its steel divisions and sales operations in order to concentrate management resources to a greater extent on sales and consumer services. In 1964 U.S. Steel created a new chemicals division called Pittsburgh Chemical Company. Effective in 1966 United States Steel Corporation was reincorporated in Delaware to take advantage of that state's more flexible corporation laws. In 1967 Edwin H. Gott became president and chief operating officer, and in 1969 he succeeded Blough as chairman of the board and CEO. Edgar B. Speer, a veteran steel man, moved up to the presidency. In 1973 Gott retired and Speer assumed his duties as chairman and CEO. Significantly, Speer immediately announced plans to expand U.S. Steel's diversification into nonsteel businesses. Prospects for long-term growth in steel were fading rapidly because of rising costs, competitive pricing, and foreign competition.

During Speer's tenure, U.S. Steel closed or sold a variety of facilities and businesses in steel, cement, fabricating, home building, plastics, and mining. Capital expenditure, much of it for environmental purposes, remained high. There was little significant diversification, however. In 1979 U.S. Steel lost $293 million. Also that year, former president David M. Roderick became chairman and CEO. He announced a major liquidation of unprofitable steel operations and increased efforts to diversify. In 1979, 13 steel facilities were closed with an $809 million write-off. Universal Atlas Cement—once the United State's largest cement company—was sold, and various real estate, timber, and mineral properties were leased or sold. The long-promised diversification move came in 1982 with United States Steel Corporation's $6.2 billion acquisition of Marathon Oil Company, a major integrated energy company with vast reserves of oil and gas. Marathon's revenues were about the same as those of U.S. Steel; thus, the company's size was doubled, with steel's contribution to sales dropping to about 40 percent.

Marathon had been incorporated on August 1, 1887, as Ohio Oil Company by Ohio oil driller Henry Ernst and four of his fellow oil men, primarily in order to compete with Standard Oil Company. Ohio Oil quickly became the largest producer of crude oil in Ohio and was bought out by Standard Oil in 1889. When Standard was broken up on antitrust grounds by the U.S. government in 1911, Ohio Oil again became an independent company with veteran oilman James Donnell as president. Under Donnell and his successors, Ohio Oil grew into an international integrated oil and gas company with large energy resources and extensive exploratory and retail sales operations. Its name was changed to Marathon Oil Company in 1962.

U.S. Steel continued to improve the efficiency and profitability of its steel operations with the 1983 closing of part or all of 20 obsolete plants. By 1985 Roderick had shut down more than 150 facilities and reduced steelmaking capacity by more than 30 percent. He cut 54 percent of white-collar jobs, laid off about 100,000 production workers, and sold $3 billion in assets. U.S. Steel continued its diversification program in February 1986 with the $3.6 billion acquisition of Texas Oil & Gas Corporation. Founded in 1955 as Tex-Star Oil & Gas Corporation, the company is engaged primarily in the domestic production, gathering, and transportation of natural gas. In July 1986 United States Steel Corporation changed its name to USX Corporation to reflect the company's diversification.

In October 1986 corporate raider Carl Icahn threatened to make a $7.1 billion offer for USX after purchasing about 29 million USX shares. Roderick fought off the takeover attempt by borrowing $3.4 billion to pay off company debts with the provision that the loan would be called in the event of a takeover. Icahn gave up his attempt in January 1987 but kept his USX shares and began a long program of urging USX management to spin off or sell its under-performing steel business. In 1987 Roderick shut down about one-quarter of USX's raw steelmaking capacity, but by 1988 U.S. Steel, the steel division of USX, had become the most efficient producer of steel in the world.

In May 1989 Roderick retired and was succeeded as chairman and CEO by Charles A. Corry, a veteran of the USX restructuring. In October 1989 Corry announced a plan to sell some of Texas Oil & Gas's energy reserves in order to pay off debt and implement a large stock buyback. In June 1990 the company stated that it would consolidate Texas Oil's operations with Marathon Oil in order to cut costs. On January 31, 1991, Icahn won his long battle to have USX restructured when the company announced that it would recapitalize by issuing a separate class of stock for its U.S. Steel subsidiary although both businesses, energy and steel, would remain part of USX. In May 1991 USX shareholders approved the plan. Common shares of USX Corporation began trading as USX-Marathon Group, and new common shares of USX-U.S. Steel Group were issued. In May 1992 USX shareholders approved the creation of a third common share, USX-Delhi Group, which reflects the performance of the Delhi Gas Pipeline Corporation and related companies engaged in the gathering, processing, and transporting of natural gas.

In 1991 the two stocks rose 28 percent and the steel shares actually outperformed the oil. Several factors influenced the positive performance of the company and its stock. Marathon, unlike many of its competitors, had prepared for growth in the 1990s. The 1991 discovery of what may be a large oil field in Tunisia and two new Gulf of Mexico strikes had the early 1990s looking promising for USX-Marathon. The addition of its East Brae field in the North Sea in 1995 could also boost crude output by 25,000 barrels per day from about 200,000 barrels per day. In addition, while other oil companies reduced their exploration budgets, USX-Marathon increased its capital and exploration budget by almost one-third.

In the early 1990s, USX-U.S. Steel reduced its fixed costs and boosted productivity by cutting its raw steel capacity in half, closing four of its seven plants and reducing its total number of employees by 56 percent between 1983 and 1990. From 1991 to 1992 alone U.S. Steel reduced its operating capability by 3 million tons to 13.5 tons. The drastic cuts paid off for U.S. Steel; by 1993 the company was the lowest-cost fully integrated steel producer in the United States.

U.S. Steel has also worked to bring its quality up to par with foreign competitors, especially the Japanese, by forging joint ventures with such companies as Japan's Kobe Steel and Korea's Pohang Iron and Steel Co. The company also spent $1.5 billion in the early 1990s to upgrade its facilities to industry benchmark standards.

As the decade proceeded, however, these measures proved insufficient to remedy USX's many problems. Internationally, the industry suffered from production that exceeded demand. Domestically, the traditional integrated steel companies, including USX, bore the crushing burden of "legacy costs," the pension and health benefits that union contracts obligated them to pay to the thousands of retired and laid-off employees that had resulted from the restructurings of the previous decades.

Facing this difficult environment, USX cooperated with the rest of the industry in bringing "antidumping" trade suits against foreign producers. In 1992 and 1998, the industry accused foreign companies of selling steel in the United States at prices below those they sold it for at home. If successful, these actions would cause the U.S. government to impose prohibitive tariffs on foreign steel, thus eliminating foreign competition. These efforts were not, however, initially successful. Only in 2001 did the industry succeed in invoking such antidumping penalties.

Internally, the company continued to suffer the extreme cyclicality of the industry, moving into and out of profitability during the decade. By 1998, USX cut production at its Fairless Works and planned to spend $10 million to encourage 540 management and salaried employees to retire early.

In 1997 USX, the largest U.S. steel producer but only the 11th largest globally, began a search for a company or companies that would allow it to become a strong international competitor. The search extended over several continents and three years. In October 2000, USX announced the acquisition of a nearly bankrupt former communist steel maker in the Slovak Republic. U.S. Steel-Kosice, as the unit was renamed, was expected to sell steel to automobile makers in much of Eastern Europe.

The tracking stock structure, in which USX-Marathon and USX-U.S. Steel Group remained units of a single parent but traded separately on the stock exchange, came under criticism in 1999. The oil industry had been suffering a down cycle, and several large companies had merged. The tracking stock arrangement made Marathon an unattractive acquisition target because payment for its acquisition would be taxable to USX unless a purchaser bought the entire company—an unlikely happening. The existence of the Marathon unit also made it more difficult for the U.S. Steel unit to seek acquisitions or acquirers. Marathon Oil and the United States Steel Corporation became independent companies on January 1, 2002.

As it entered the new century, United States Steel reclaimed its original name and identity as an integrated steel manufacturer. The environment in which it operated, however, was still an exceedingly difficult one. At the end of 2001 it took a $35–$45 million charge to close most operations at its Fairless Works.

By the beginning of 2002, U.S. Steel proposed a major reorganization of the entire U.S. integrated industry. It began discussing a merger with bankrupt Bethlehem Steel. The company quickly followed this move with a more comprehensive proposal that all integrated companies consolidate in order to improve their efficiency and compete better with foreign producers and the domestic minimills that made steel by less costly methods.

The prospects for such a consolidation were not good. As prerequisites, the industry, represented by U.S. Steel, demanded that the government establish very high barriers to protect it from foreign competition. They also asked that the government take over responsibility for paying the industry's legacy costs. Even if these conditions were met, the consolidation would undoubtedly meet strong protests by foreign governments for violations of international trade agreements, including World Trade Organization rules. At the beginning of the 21st century, the future of U.S. Steel and of the rest of the U.S. integrated steel industry appeared cloudy.

Principal Subsidiaries

Acero Prime, S.R.L. de CV (44%); Chrome Deposit Corporation (50%); Clairton 1314B Partnership, L.P. (10%); Delta Tubular Processing (50%); Double Eagle Steel Coating Company (50%); Feralloy Processing Company (49%); Olympic Laser Processing (50%); PRO-TEC Coating Company (50%); Republic Technologies International, LLC (16%); Straightline Source, Inc. (100%); Transtar, Inc (100%); UEC Technologies, LLC (100%); U.S. Steel-Kosice, s.r.o. (100%); USS-POSCO Industries (50%); Worthington Specialty Processing (50%).

Principal Competitors

AK Steel Holding Corporation; Arcelor; Bethlehem Steel; Commercial Metals Company; Corus Group; Kawasaki Steel; Kobe Steel; Nippon Steel; NKK Corporation; Nucor; POSCO; ThyssenKrupp.

Further Reading

Adams, Chris, "Ailing Steel Industry Launches a Battle Against Imports," *The Wall Street Journal,* October 1, 1998, p. B4.

——, "USX's U.S. Steel Goes Scouting for Deals," *The Wall Street Journal,* April 4, 1997, p. A3.

Ansberry, Clare, and Dana Millbank, "Small-Midsize Steelmakers Are Ripe for a Shakeout," *The Wall Street Journal,* March 4, 1992, p. B4.

Bahree, Bhushan, et. al., "European Deal to Forge No. 1 Steel Firm," *The Wall Street Journal,* February 20, 2001, p. A3.

Beck, Robert J., "Industry to Trim Spending in U.S. During 1992," *Oil & Gas Journal,* February 24, 1992.

"Business Brief: USX Corp.," *The Wall Street Journal,* November 5, 1998, p. A4.

Cooper, Helene, "Move to Impose Steel Duties May Fail," *The Wall Street Journal,* February 16, 1999, p. A24.

Cotter, Arundel, *The Authentic History of the United States Steel Corporation,* New York: Moody Magazine and Book Co., 1916.

Crandall, Robert W., "Whistling Past Big Steel's Graveyard," *The Wall Street Journal,* March 19, 1999, p. A18.

"Feds Are Asked to Support a Big Steel Combination," *Mergers and Acquisitions,* January 2002, pp. 14–15.

Fisher, Douglas A., *Steel Serves the Nation, 1901–1951,* Pittsburgh: United States Steel Corporation, 1951.

Hoffman, Thomas, "USX Diversifies into Information Services Arena," *Computerworld,* August 31, 1992.

Jackson, Stanley, *J. P. Morgan,* New York: Stein and Day, 1983.

Matthews, Robert Guy, "A Big Stick: The U.S. Won't Take 'No' for an Answer At Paris Steel Summit," *The Wall Street Journal,* December 14, 2001, p. A1.

——, "Smelting Point: U.S. Steel's Plunge Into Slovakia Reflects Urgent Need to Grow," *The Wall Street Journal,* October 12, 2000, p. A1.

——, "Trade Panel Rules for U.S. Steelmakers," *The Wall Street Journal,* October 23, 2001, p. A2.

——, "USX Rethinks 2 Tracking Stocks," *The Wall Street Journal,* December 1, 2000, p. B7.

——, "USX to Split U.S. Steel and Marathon Oil," *The Wall Street Journal,* April 25, 2001, p. A2.

——, "USX-U.S. Steel, Bethlehem May Merge," *The Wall Street Journal,* December 5, 2001, p. A3.

——, "USX-U.S. Steel Plans to Cut 600 Jobs, Close Mills," *The Wall Street Journal,* August 15, 2001, p. A2.

Milbank, Dana, "Changing Industry: Big Steel Is Threatened by Low-Cost Rivals," *The Wall Street Journal,* February 2, 1993, p. A1.

——, "Technology: Minimill Inroads in Sheet Market Rouse Big Steel," *The Wall Street Journal,* March 9, 1992, p. B1.

Norman, James R., "U.S. Oil (& Steel)," *Forbes,* September 19, 1991.

Normani, Asra Q., and Dana Milbank, "Trade Panel Backs Foreign Steel Concerns," *The Wall Street Journal,* July 28, 1993, p. A3.

Norton, Erle, "Metal Fatigue," *The Wall Street Journal,* July 18, 1996, p. A1.

Sheridan, John H., "Steel-makers Face Growing Pressures," *Industry Week,* February 2, 1998, pp. 73–75.

"U.S. Steel Sees Charge Due to Buyout Program," *The Wall Street Journal,* November 9, 1998, p. B6.

—Bernard A. Block
—update: Anne L. Potter

UPM

UPM-Kymmene Corporation

Eteläesplanadi 2
P.O. Box 380
FIN-00101 Helsinki
Finland
Telephone: +358 (9) 204 15 111
Fax: +358 (9) 204 15 110
Web site: http://www.upm-kymmene.com

Public Company
Incorporated: 1872 as Kymmene Aktiebolag
Employees: 36,298
Sales: EUR 9.92 million (2001)
Stock Exchanges: Helsinki New York
Ticker Symbol: UPMIV (Helsinki), UPM (New York)
NAIC: 113310 Logging; 321113 Sawmills; 321211
Hardwood, Veneer, and Plywood Manufacturing;
322110 Pulp Mills; 322121 Paper (Except Newsprint)
Mills; 322214 Fiber Can, Tube, Drum, and Similar
Projects Manufacturing; 322221 Coated and
Laminated Packaging Paper and Plastics Film
Manufacturing; 322222 Coated and Laminated Paper
Manufacturing; 322223 Plastics, Foil, and Coated
Paper Bag Manufacturing; 322224 Uncoated Paper
and Multiwall Bag Manufacturing; 322298 All Other
Converted Paper Product Manufacturing

UPM-Kymmene Corporation is Finland's leading forestry company and Europe's largest papermaking concern. The company consists of approximately 100 production facilities in 14 countries and more than 170 sales/distribution companies. It owns nearly one million hectares of forest in Finland, the United States, and Great Britain. UPM-Kymmene's operations consist of four main divisions: Paper division (includes Magazine, Newsprint, Fine and Specialty Paper subdivisions); Converting division; Wood Products division; and Other Operations division which includes Forest, Energy, and Real Estate departments. The Paper division is the largest and covers 67 percent of the company's turnover. UPM-Kymmene is the world's largest producer of magazine paper. The Converting division's products include labels, packing, and envelope materials; it covers 14 percent of the turnover. Wood Products manufactures sawed timber, plywood, planed timber, and derivatives such as parquet flooring; this division covers 14 percent of the turnover. UPM-Kymmene's quality products, dedication to growth, and environmental considerations have made it one of the strongest international companies in the world.

Kymmene Corporation: From 1873 to the 1980s

The inception of Kymmene Corporation almost 120 years ago reflects the early stages of Finland's paper industry as a whole. The art of making groundwood pulp was discovered in 1846. Axel Wilhelm Wahren, one of the great Finnish industrialists, recognized the potential afforded by hydroelectric power, vast forests, and the proximity of the Russian market and in 1870 leased a section of the largest rapids on the River Kymi flowing through southeast Finland at Kuusankoski. At around the same time Count Carl Robert Mannerheim, father of Finland's military leader and President C.G.E. Mannerheim, purchased an island in the same rapids and part of the riverbank. The founding meeting of Wahren's company, Kymmene Aktiebolag, was held on May 21, 1873. A company by the name of Kuusankoski Aktiebolag, established by Mannerheim, began operating in January 1872. In 1896 a third businessman, Rudolf Elving, purchased the Voikkaa Rapids farther upstream and over the next five years built four paper machines, a groundwood plant, and a sulfite pulp mill. The founding of three large mills in the same area within a short period of time raised the prices of the local forestlands and timber, while the resulting competition reduced the prices of the end products. The rival enterprises soon became aware of the advantages of joining forces and in 1904 signed an agreement whereby Kymmene bought both the Kuusankoski Company and the Voikkaa Mill in exchange for shares in the company. The resulting company, the predecessor of today's Kymmene Corporation, was the largest limited company in Finland and the largest papermaker in the Nordic countries.

By the time of the merger, the individual companies had acquired 76,000 hectares of forest, an area that grew as more mergers took place. The purchase of Strömsdal Board Mill—the supplier of groundwood (used in paper manufacturing) to the company's paper mills—in 1915 increased the forest area by 21,000 hectares, and it increased by a further 119,300 with the purchase of the Halla sawmill. Halla also had some inland sawmills, and Kymmene became a major exporter of sawed goods.

During Rudolf Elving's four years as managing director beginning in 1904, Kymmene installed more production machinery than any other firm in Finland to that date. But a disastrous fire at the Voikkaa Mill, in which three machines were destroyed, and a slump in prices on the paper market caused a setback from which the company recovered only under its next managing director, Gösta Serlachius.

The building of the railway from Helsinki to St. Petersburg in the early years opened up new prospects for Finnish groundwood, board, and paper on the Russian market. At the outset Kymmene sold goods on commission at certain points in Russia. The sales areas covered by the local agents were extended between 1910 and 1915, and 1916 saw the establishment in St. Petersburg of the Kauppaosakeyhtiö Kymmene Aktiebolag trading company, registered as a Russian limited company, with sales offices in Moscow, Nizni Novgorod, Rostov, Tiflis, Odessa, Baku, Samara, St. Petersburg, Krakow, and Kiev. Serlachius was followed by Gösta Björkenheim as the new managing director. By that time World War I had broken out—initially placing obstacles in the way of deliveries to Russia but later increasing the demand for paper—and Kymmene Corporation's leading position in the Russian paper market attracted international attention. In October 1916, the London *Times*, in an article headed ''A Russian Paper King,'' wrote: ''the joint stock company Kymmene is now regarded as the biggest enterprise of the paper industry, not only in Russia, but in all Europe.'' In 1917 paper exports to Russia were hindered by the revolution. Lenin's rise to power put an end to private trade.

In the early decades of the 20th century, Western Europe was not regarded as a major market. Paper exports to the United Kingdom had begun in the first decade, but the first major agreement, for 2,000 tons, was not signed until 1910.

Research into the potential of Western European markets began to advance around 1910. That year Rafael Jaatinen, a correspondence clerk in the company's sales office, traveled to England to study trading methods. In 1919 the Finnish government sent a trade delegation to Western Europe and North America. One of its members was Gösta Serlachius. In the autumn of 1921, Kymmene laid the foundations for its own export marketing organization. Its first new foreign agency agreement was made with H. Reeve Angel & Co. of England.

Kymmene was one of the first Finnish companies to make acquisitions abroad. Fearing that the United Kingdom would levy customs duties to protect its own paper industry, Kymmene acquired a majority stake in the Star Paper Mill Co. Ltd., which had a paper mill at Blackburn. The following year Star took over Yorkshire Paper Mills Ltd. at Barnsley.

Meanwhile, the company had increased its forest holdings in Finland. The need to guarantee its supply of timber led Kymmene to purchase Högforsin Tehdas Osakeyhtiö, one of the largest ironworks in Finland, in 1933. Kymmene Corporation thus branched out into a completely new field—engineering. By the end of 1935, Kymmene owned more land than at any other time until its later mergers with Kaukas and Schauman. In this year it bought Oy Läskelä Ab, which had 100,000 hectares of forest and two paper mills, as well as a sulfite pulp mill situated north of Lake Ladoga. Läskelä's mills and most of its forests were, however, lost to the Soviet Union during World War II.

During the war the production of sawed timber, pulp, and paper had to be curtailed to correspond to the reduction in demand and workforce. Some of the company's engineering capacity was put toward making munitions, and its Paper division made utility articles both for the Soviet front and for the areas behind it. One-third of the war reparations paid by Finland to the Soviet Union under the terms of the peace treaty ending World War II consisted of products of the wood-processing industry. Because of its size, Kymmene was the chief supplier.

The demand for forestry products remained brisk until the late 1940s, but price controls imposed by the Finnish government at home reduced profitability. The company was also forced to relinquish about 60,000 hectares, some of it land expropriated by the Finnish government, for the resettlement of evacuees from the parts of Karelia ceded to the Soviet Union. Not until the late 1950s and early 1960s was the company again in a position to extend its production, with a new newsprint machine at Voikkaa. A new sulfate pulp mill went on line at Kuusankoski in 1964.

By 1966 the company was ready to expand its operations abroad. This time it joined forces with Oy Kaukas Ab to found a German subsidiary, Nordland Papier. In the latter half of the 1960s, Kymmene was one of the partners in Finland's largest forest industry project to date, Eurocan Pulp & Paper Ltd., in British Columbia, Canada.

As one of the suppliers of chlorine for the petrochemical industry, Kymmene decided to expand its chemical interests in the late 1960s and early 1970s. The year 1970 also saw the establishment of Oy Finnish Peroxides Ab—in collaboration with the U.K. company Laporte Industries Ltd. and Solvay & Cie S.A. in Belgium—for the manufacture of peroxide.

The output of the paper industry increased together with expansion into other fields. A large machine making supercalendered paper grades went on stream at Voikkaa in 1968 and was followed two years later at Kuusankoski by what was at that time the largest fine-paper mill in Europe. Expansion was also visible in the restructuring of the organization. In 1969, on the appointment of Kurt Swanljung as managing director, the company's industrial operations were divided into seven fields

Key Dates:

1873: Kymmene Aktiebolag founded by Axel Wilhelm Wahren.

1904: Kymmene, Kuusankoski Aktiebolag, and Voikkaa Mill merge.

1917: Kymmene is the largest paper company in Europe when World War I begins.

1921: The company begins to export and forms an agreement with H. Reeve Angel & Co. of England.

1930: The company purchases a large share in Star Paper Mill Co. Ltd. in England.

1966: Oy Kaukas Ab and Kymmene start Nordland Papier in Dorpen, West Germany.

1969: Kymmene divides into paper, pulp, conversion, chemicals, metal, sawmill, and board production fields.

1977: U.S. company Leaf River Forest Products Inc. is started by Kymmene in Mississippi.

1982: Kymmene merges with Strömberg to become Kymmene-Strömberg Corporation.

1986: Kymmene-Strömberg and Oy Kaukas Ab merge and sell Strömberg to become Kymmene Corporation.

1988: Kymmene Corp. merges with Oy Wilh. Schauman Ab.

1996: Kymmene Corp. merges with Repola Ltd. and its subsidiary, United Paper Mills Ltd., to become UPM-Kymmene.

2000: UPM-Kymmene purchases the Changshu fine-paper mill in China and Repap in Canada.

2001: The company restructures to manage increasing growth, purchases majority of shares in ZAO Chudovo-RWS in Russia, and purchases G. Haindl'sche Papier Fabriken KgaA company in Germany.

of production: paper, pulp, conversion, chemicals, metal, sawmill, and board.

Kymmene purchased Soinlahti Sawmill and Brick Works in 1975, and with its subsidiary Star Paper Mill Co. Ltd. it acquired the majority holding in the French company Papeteries Boucher SA in 1977. The same year also saw the start-up of the U.S. company Leaf River Forest Products Inc. in Mississippi. There were also plans for building a pulp mill in Mississippi. In 1979 the company reorganized its foreign interests in the forestry industry by selling its 50 percent holding in Eurocan Pulp & Paper and buying all the shares in the Wolvercote Paper Mill at Oxford in England.

By the 1970s, Kymmene had steadily upgraded its range of paper products. In order to establish closer contacts with its customers and improve its marketing, it decided in 1975 to resign from the Finnish Paper Mills' Association (Finnpap), which it had rejoined in 1946 after having left it in 1920. The main products not covered by its own sales organization were the newsprint and magazine papers made by the Voikkaa Mill.

The company cut down its range of activities in 1981. It discontinued its petrochemical manufacturing because of struc-

tural reorganization in the industry, and it closed the Barnsley paper mill, which was unprofitable. An agreement was made with the Great Northern Nekoosa Corporation for the building of a pulp mill in Mississippi (in which Kymmene would have a minority holding). In order to even out fluctuations in the forestry and metal industries, Kymmene at the end of 1982 purchased the majority holding in Strömberg, a company producing electrical equipment. The parent company was renamed the Kymmene-Strömberg Corporation. In mid-1985, Kymmene-Strömberg sold a major part of its Engineering division, the Högforsin foundry, and closed the Boucher Mill in Calais, France.

The first in a chain of mergers resulting in the present Kymmene Corporation took place in 1985, when Kymmene procured 45 percent of the shares in Oy Kaukas Ab. Shareholders of the two companies approved the merger on January 7, 1986. The result was a highly integrated forestry concern. Casimir Ehrnrooth, chairman of the board of Kaukas, was appointed Kymmene-Strömberg's chairman of the board and CEO at the end of 1985, and Fredrik Castrén continued as managing director.

In 1986 the company decided to concentrate exclusively on the forest industry. On June 19 the board of Kymmene-Strömberg approved an agreement selling Strömberg's business operations to ASEA Ab. The company took the name Kymmene Corporation.

Cooperation with Oy Wilh. Schauman Ab became increasingly close in the course of 1986. A Schauman-Kymmene merger was approved in 1987 and came into force in 1988. The company decided to concentrate on two major fields of production, and consequently Kymmene's Juankoski board mill, the printing works in Kouvola, and the self-copying paper mill were sold. The emergence of Kymmene Corporation in the late 1980s as Finland's largest wood-processing enterprise marked the joining of three companies, each dating from the 19th century.

Gösta Björkenheim had been managing director of both Kaukas and Kymmene. He was the son of Robert Björkenheim, the founder, director, and owner of Kaukaan Tehdas Osakeyhtiö—the name under which the Kaukas Mill was originally established. Gösta Serlachius, nephew of Schauman's founder Wilhelm Schauman, had taken the helm of Kymmene Corporation at the beginning of this century.

Gösta Björkenheim was one of the first Finnish industrial leaders to recognize the vital need for employers to band together against growing unionism, and he invited the pulp and paper manufacturers to join him in founding an employers' association. Meanwhile, Gösta Serlachius was building up trade relations with the European and U.S. markets. At his suggestion the manufacturers set up three joint sales organizations: the Finnish Pulp Association (Finncell); the Finnish Paper Mills' Association (Finnpap); and the Finnish Paper Agency.

Oy Kaukas Ab: From 1873 to Its 1986 Merger with Kymmene

One of the pioneers in spotting the potential of birch wood was Robert Björkenheim, who had birch in his own forests in southern Finland. Being engaged in the sawmill industry, he saw machine bobbins being made in his father's homeland,

Sweden, and went on to Glasgow to pursue the idea further. On February 6, 1873, Björkenheim and three others signed an agreement for the establishment of a bobbin factory at Mäntsälä on the banks of the Kaukas Rapids.

The first bobbin deliveries went to Scotland, where the largest buyer was Clark & Co. The production figures rose, but little profit was made, and it was 1882 before a dividend could be issued. The dwindling birch resources in the timber supply area, combined with the favorable outlook for this industry, prompted the decision to found a new factory near Lappeenranta in 1890. For 20 years the Kaukas Mill struggled to produce bobbins before selling out to Hugo Standertskjöld in 1894. Gösta Björkenheim, who later took over the management of Kymmene, was chiefly instrumental in steering the company into clearer waters.

In 1903, Kaukas became a limited company. Gösta Björkenheim suggested that a pulp mill be built to use up the waste timber from the bobbin factory, and the mill began operating in March 1897. The customs duty levied on imported pulp was one reason for Kaukas's decision to build a new sulfite pulp mill in 1904. The first major extensions were carried out in 1912, after which Kaukas was for a time Finland's largest producer of sulfite pulp.

Initially more than half of the pulp was sold to Russia, while the rest went to the domestic market. On the completion of the second mill, it was necessary to look abroad for markets—first to Germany and later to the United States. The years 1895 to 1914 were a golden era for the bobbin factory. The number of customers rose to 100, but the bulk of production went to large, regular customers in Russia, Germany, Austria, France, England, and Belgium.

In 1916, Kaukas expanded further by buying up all the shares in the Kaltimon Puuhiomo groundwood plant, as well as a considerable area of good forest. Later in the year, Kaukas purchased Osakeyhtiö T. & J. Salvesen, thereby acquiring four sawmills and 69,500 hectares of well-stocked forest. The most significant investment in terms of enlarging the company's forest reserves was the purchase of all the shares in Osakeyhtiö Gustaf Cederberg & Co. in 1920, which brought with it 105,000 hectares of forest.

The voice of Jacob von Julin, managing director of Kaukas between the two world wars, was frequently heard on the committees set up on behalf of the industry as a whole to further matters of industrial and economic policy and to boost exports. He was also the chairman of the trade delegation sent by the Finnish government to Western countries in 1919. World War I brought a slump in the bobbin industry, and Kaukas had to look around for other ways of converting timber.

A plywood industry had begun in Finland in 1912, with the start-up of the Jyväskylä Mill belonging to Oy Wilh. Schauman Ab, which was later to merge with Kymmene Corporation. The decision to build a plywood mill at Kaukas was made in 1924, and it began production in 1926. The main product was plywood to produce chests for tea, meat, and tobacco transport. The output of sulfate pulp tripled and that of sulfite pulp quadrupled in the period between the wars. Between 1933 and 1935 the sulfite pulp mill underwent major expansion. As a result of World War I, Kaukas lost many of its forests and timber procurement areas. During this period Kaukas evacuated many of its most valuable machines. The Kaukas bobbin factory was modernized after the war, and the U.S. method was introduced. Production of bobbins came to an end in 1972.

Kaukas's plywood industry underwent modernization, including the addition of about 63,000 cubic meters of space, in the mid-1950s. New lathes and glue presses were installed in the early 1960s. These were followed in the 1970s by peeling and drying lines suitable for making spruce plywood. In the 1970s and 1980s the company placed emphasis on further processing of plywood.

The sawmills at Lappeenranta operated along traditional lines until the 1950s, when work began on a new mill, which would increase capacity to 330,000 cubic meters between 1967 and 1971. Later in 1977 a medium-sized sawmill was bought in the northern timber procurement area at Nurmes.

The pulp market was buoyant after World War II. Later the war in Korea sent raw materials prices skyrocketing. But this was followed by a cost crisis in the Finnish wood-processing industry, the result of fears of impending raw materials shortages and political conflict with the Soviet Union, a major buyer of dissolving pulp used for chemical conversion. The company debated whether to stop manufacturing dissolving pulp altogether, but capital investments brought about a rise in quality and demand.

In the early 1960s the company decided to build a new sulfate pulp mill, which went online in 1964. With a view to the further development of pulp production, Casimir Ehrnrooth, managing director from 1967, proposed that the sulfite pulp mill be closed down and a second line producing long-fibered pine pulp be built at the sulfate pulp mill. This construction was done in the 1970s, and the mill was extended in two stages in the 1980s.

In order to diversify production, a paper mill was established at Dörpen in the Federal Republic of Germany. On the withdrawal of the Canadian company from the joint venture, its place was taken by Kymmene Corporation. Nordland Papier's first paper machine started up in 1969.

While paper production was starting up in the Federal Republic of Germany, Kaukas began to seek a suitable paper grade to be manufactured from its own bleached sulfate pulp. One of the central figures in the investigations and later in the start-up of production was Harri Piehl, who eventually became CEO of Kymmene Corporation. The choice fell on lightweight coated (LWC) paper, a new type of magazine paper made from pulp, ground wood, and coating. The first production line at the mill started up in 1975 and the second in 1981. The choice of paper grade proved to be right because, with the steady increase in demand, a good price level could be maintained.

Oy Wilh. Schauman Ab: 1873 to the 1988 Kymmene Merger

Schauman, the company that merged with Kymmene in 1988, was likewise founded in the 19th century. Wilhelm Schauman, the founder of Oy Wilh. Schauman Ab, having left his job in a gun factory in St. Petersburg, settled in Pietarsaari and there began processing chicory in 1883.

In 1892, Schauman turned to timber, which soon overtook chicory in importance. In 1895, the year in which his sawmill started up, he started expanding in the Pietarsaari district. He ceased buying his timber ready-cut in favor of standing timber. His exports of roundwood timber brought in good profits.

The second sawmill bought by Schauman in 1900 operated for many years at a loss, but his Pietarsaari sugar mill proved to be a profitable investment. His involvement with sugar nevertheless came to an end in 1919 with the merging of Finland's sugar mills.

Having sold its sugar interests, the company concentrated on projects that led to the establishment of what is now a market leader in plywood products. He began with boxboard and later added plywood. The Jyväskylä plywood mill represented a completely new departure. During the early years of World War I, the mill flourished. Sales were good and profits large. Production in Savonlinna began in 1921, and in 1924 all the shares in a plywood mill at Joensuu were acquired.

Plywood was converted into chair bottoms, furniture, and board, and in 1931 a Building Joinery department was set up in Jyväskylä. Its main products were interior doors. Blockboard production began in Jyväskylä in 1933 and subsequently moved to Savonlinna. The mills at Jyväskylä, Savonlinna, and Joensuu merged in 1937 to form Oy Wilh. Schauman Ab.

During World War II the proportion of plywood products rose considerably. One of the most important products was a plywood tent for military use. In 1958 a chipboard mill was opened in Jyväskylä, in 1962 Schauman purchased a chipboard mill from Viiala Oy, and in 1969 a chipboard mill, built by Schauman, went into production at Joensuu.

By the early 1990s the company had chipboard mills in Joensuu, Ristiina (Pellos chipboard mill), and Kitee (Puhos chipboard mill). The chipboard mills in Jyväskylä and Viiala were no longer in operation, but Kymmene's subsidiary, Finnish Fiberboard Ltd., had a fiberboard mill in Heinola.

Schauman's second cornerstone was laid with the construction of a sulfite pulp mill in Pietarsaari begun in 1934 by a separate company, Ab Jakobstads Cellulosa-Pietarsaaren Selluloosa Oy. Pulp production doubled in the 1950s. The addition of a sulfate pulp mill, a paper mill, and a paper sack plant in the early 1960s meant a great increase in value-added products.

The next major investment in pulp manufacturing came in the first half of the 1970s, making Schauman the largest producer of market pulp in Finland. The Wisapak paper sack plant soon became the largest of its kind in Finland, and in 1969 Schauman purchased the Craf'Sac plant in Rouen, France. The establishment of an industrial wrappings unit raised the output considerably. All the former Schauman industrial divisions in Pietarsaari—Sawn Timber, Pulp, Paper, and Packaging Materials—were grouped together to form the Kymmene subsidiary, Wisaforest Oy Ab. The divisions were known as Wisatimber, Wisapulp, Wisapaper, and Wisapak.

Product development and the increase in plywood production continued at a brisk pace beginning in the 1960s. The most important technical innovations were in the field of plywood gluing and the development of a wide range of coated and processed plywood products, as well as the use of spruce as a raw material. Schauman became a world leader in plywood product development and the leading European plywood manufacturer.

Schauman at various points in its history also made furniture, along with more conventional converted panel products. Half a century of joinery production came to an end in 1969. In 1971, Schauman became a producer of large sailing yachts after buying Nautor, a boatyard near the Pietarsaari mills.

Among the advantages of the Kymmene-Kaukas-Schauman merger were greater financing potential and more effective operation and marketing. In order to exploit the advantages of a small company, Kymmene split up its five industrial divisions in Finland in 1990. The registered companies—Kaukas Oy, Kymi Paper Mills Ltd., Wisaforest Oy Ab, and Schauman Wood Oy—became fully owned subsidiaries of Kymmene Corporation. Similar status had already been granted to the subsidiaries abroad: Nordland Papier GmbH, Kymmene France SA, Kymmene U.K. PLC, and Caledonian Paper PLC. This last mill project became the first and only one of its kind in the United Kingdom when it began LWC paper production in the spring of 1989. Kymmene U.K. PLC's mills at Blackburn and Oxford were sold in the spring of 1990. Expansion through acquisition continued in 1990, when Kymmene bought the large French LWC and newsprint manufacturer Chapelle Darblay SA.

The 1990s: The Establishment of UPM-Kymmene Corporation

In the early 1990s plans were made to merge Kymmene Corporation and Repola Ltd. The merger was approved by both companies' shareholders and the EU (European Union) Commission, and the two companies operated as a single unit beginning in November 1995. The merger officially took effect in April 1996.

As a result of its merger with Repola Ltd. and its United Paper Mills (UPM) subsidiary, Kymmene changed its name to UPM-Kymmene Corporation. On May 2, 1996, it began trading shares on the Helsinki Stock Exchange, but the company decided not to apply for a listing on the London Stock Exchange, opting instead to have its shares listed on the Stock Exchange Automated Quotations International System in London. The companies hoped eventually to save up to Fmk 2 billion in transportation, logistics, timber procurement, and sales as a result of the merger. Combined products of the merged companies made it the largest paper producer in Europe, with a capacity of over 7 million metric tons per year, and the second-largest worldwide producer, behind the International Paper Co. in the United States.

Shareholders chose Juha Niemala as UPM-Kymmene's president and CEO once the merger was completed. Formerly he had been executive vice-president of UPM. His broad marketing background gave him the advantage over candidates with more substantial experience in the forestry industry. A strategic committee of three forest-industry veterans—Tauno Matomaki, Yrjo Niskanen, and Casimir Ehnrooth—was formed to act as a spending watchdog for the new president, but shareholders took much of its power away at their annual meeting in April 1997. Niemala did not take the shareholders' decision to mean he could go on a spending binge. Instead, he put several large investments on hold, although he continued with plant upgrading where necessary.

In May 1996 the UPM-Kymmene Kaipola plant began upgrading its paper machine number 6 (PM 6), which produced lightweight coated printing paper. Already the fastest and mostefficient machine of its kind, PM 6 produced in 1995 approximately 240,000 metric tons of paper, which amounted to 1,518 meters of paper per second. In July 1996 the company started up paper machine number 8 (PM 8), which produced release paper (used in the production of self-adhesive labels), at its Tervasaari Mill in Valkeakoski, in the process increasing the production of release paper to 100,000 metric tons per year. Previously Tervasaari's capacity for release paper was only 55,000 metric tons per year.

In December 1996, UPM-Kymmene and Nokio Corporation each agreed to sell their 50 percent share of the joint venture Finnish Chemicals to Erikem Oy. Finnish Chemicals provided bleaching chemicals to the wood-processing industry. Including this transaction, UPM-Kymmene sold assets totaling Fmk 3.8 billion in 1996.

Growing into the 21st Century

In August 2000, UPM-Kymmene acquired the Changshu fine-paper mill in China, thereby establishing a key stronghold in the East Asian market. This same year, the company also purchased Repap in Canada, increasing production in North America by 20 percent and complementing the company's existing Blandin Paper Mill in Minnesota.

In 2001, subsidiary Shauman Wood purchased the majority of shares in ZAO Chudovo-RWS, a birch plywood mill in the Novgorod area, strengthening the company's position in Russia. UPM-Kymmene purchased all the shares of G. Haindl'sche Papier Fabriken KgaA in Germany. The merger was finalized in November 2001 after scrutiny by the EU regulatory council that was concerned it could create a monopoly. UPM-Kymmene agreed to sell two of the six Haindl mills to its competitor Norske Skog to prevent this. It retained four: Augsburg, Shongau, and Schwett in Germany, and Steyrermuhl in Austria. The addition of these Haindl facilities allowed for a production increase of 11.8 million ton of paper.

A New Structure in 2001

In January 2001, UPM-Kymmene implemented a new structure that organized the company into four main divisions: Paper (that included Magazine, Newsprint, Fine, and Specialty Paper subdivisions); Converting; Wood Products; and Other Operations. The Other Operations division included a Forest Department, Real Estate Unit, and Energy Department. The Paper division comprised the largest division in the company, and the magazine paper subdivision comprised the company's largest, operating 25 paper machines in seven countries with a turnover

in 2001 of EUR 3.5 million. It is also constituted the largest magazine paper producer in the world. The Newsprint division was the largest producer in Europe at the time and included 14 machines in five countries. Likewise, the Fine and Specialty Papers division represented the largest in Europe, operating 17 paper machines in four countries.

Working with the Environment for the Future

UPM-Kymmene is not only the largest private forest owner in Finland, but also one of the largest consumers of natural wood resources. In 1999 they consumed nearly 23 million cubic meters of wood supplied mainly by its private forests in Finland, the United States, and Great Britain. In 2002 the company planned to donate 560 hectares of their forestland to Finland for the development of Repovesi National Park.

UPM-Kymmene generates its own power to run its Finnish mills, utilizing a method that the company states does not generate carbon dioxide emissions or require use of other biofuels. UPM-Kymmene has announced plans to invest EUR 127 million in a recycling facility to begin operation in 2004. The Recycling Fibre Pulp facility, to be located at the Shotton Paper Mill in North Wales, is slated to produce 100 percent recycled paper. In addition, the 2001 merger with Haindl helped raise UPM-Kymmene's environmental standards because Haindl uses 60 percent recycled paper in their papermaking process.

Also in 2001 the company joined forces with competitor Stora Enso and the Tapere University of Technology to research the development of biodegradable barrier-coated and laminated paper/board products and investigate strategies for promoting and expanding recycling efforts. In their efforts to mitigate their enormous consumption of natural resources, UPM-Kymmene has spent EUR 40 million on environmental protection initiatives.

Principal Divisions

UPM-Kymmene Fine Papers; UPM-Kymmene Converting (Raflatac, Loparex, Walki Wisa, Walki Films, Rosenlew, and Walki Can); UPM-Kymmene Forest (Rauma Corporation); UPM-Kymmene Magazine; UPM-Kymmene Newsprint; UPM-Kymmene Other Operations (Timber, Schauman Wood Oy, UPM Stationery, Walkisoft, Oy Nautor Ab); UPM-Kymmene Wood Products (Schauman Wood).

Principal Competitors

Stora Enso; Abiti-Consolidated; International Paper Co.; Norske Skog; Asia Pulp & Paper.

Further Reading

"Europe: UPM Buys Repap to Fuel US Expansion—Forestry Products Finnish Group Becomes World's Largest Producer of Magazine Paper," *Financial Times*, August 30, 2000, p. 24.

"Finnish Marketing Organizations Dissolve," *Pulp & Paper*, May 1996, p. 21.

"Forest Industry Giants Align on R&D Cooperation," *Paperboard Packaging*, May 2001, p. 18.

"Haindl Renames," *Printing World*, March 4, 2002, p. 32.

"Haindl Split Up Between UPM-Kymmene and Norske Skog," *PIMA'S.Papermaker*, July 2001, p. 16.

Hong, Victorya, ''Paper Merger to Get EU Clearance,'' *The Daily Deal*, November 8, 2001, http://www.TheDeal.com.

''Kymmene, Repola Agree to Merger,'' *Pulp & Paper*, November 1995, p. 17.

''Papermakers Bring Out the Best in Dealmakers,'' *Corporate Finance*, December 2001, p. 32.

Tiller, Alan, ''Early Riser Reaches Top of the Tree,'' *The European*, April 17, 1997, p. 32.

''UPM-Kymmene Starts Up World's Largest Release Paper Machine,'' *Pulp & Paper*, September 1996, p. 29.

''UPM-Kymmene Strengthens Its Foothold in China,'' *Pulp & Paper International*, February 2001, pp. 34–36.

—Reijo Virta
—updates: Terry Bain, Peggi Swan Skjelset

UST Inc.

100 West Putnam Avenue
Greenwich, Connecticut 06830
U.S.A.
Telephone: (203) 661-1100
Fax: (203) 622-3493
Web site: http://www.ustinc.com

Public Company
Incorporated: 1911 as Weyman-Bruton Co.
Employees: 4,691 (2001)
Sales: $1.67 billion (2001)
Stock Exchanges: New York
Ticker Symbol: UST
NAIC: 312229 Other Tobacco Product Manufacturing;
422940 Tobacco and Tobacco Product Wholesalers;
312130 Wineries

UST Inc., the top dog in the only part of the U.S. tobacco market experiencing growth, is a holding company for four subsidiaries: United States Smokeless Tobacco Company, International Wine & Spirits Ltd., United States Tobacco Manufacturing Ltd., and United States Smokeless Tobacco Brands. United States Smokeless Tobacco Company is the country's leading producer of moist smokeless tobacco products and is the central business of UST.

Although health concerns cut down on growth in the rest of the tobacco industry, snuff sales were on the increase during the first part of the 1990s, a trend that continued into the new millennium. Snuff is pulverized tobacco that is placed between the cheek and gums. Snuff, practically a UST monopoly, was the fastest growing segment of the U.S. tobacco industry, increasing at 3 to 5 percent a year. UST controls between one-third and one-half of the oral tobacco market, which includes chewing tobacco, dry tobacco, moist snuff, and several other products.

Company History—Beginnings

The formation of the United States Tobacco Company dates back to 1911, when the U.S. government dissolved the tobacco monopoly of James Buchanon Duke. From that dissolution,

several cigarette companies, including R.J. Reynolds, Liggett & Myers, and Lorillard, as well as several smaller tobacco concerns, including Weyman-Bruton Co., were formed. Weyman-Burton Co., a snuff manufacturer in 1911, eventually became United States Tobacco Company and came to control about 85 percent of the U.S. snuff market.

Although oral tobacco products have been UST's mainstay, it has been in and out of many businesses. In 1958 it acquired Circus Foods, a candy bar and nut products manufacturer. However, the market was already dominated by Planters, according to Louis Bantle, UST's chief executive officer from 1972 to 1992. Shortly after that, UST purchased pet food company B.A. Bernard and marketed Cadillac dog food. According to Bantle, UST was a few years too late with that venture as well, since Alpo already had established itself as the top-premium dog food company.

W.H. Snyder & Sons, a Pennsylvania cigar company, became a subsidiary of UST in 1965. It was later merged into Wolf Brothers Cigar Co., and the name was changed to House of Windsor, Inc. In 1981, UST acquired the assets of Havano Cigar Corp. of Tampa, Florida, and transferred its operations to House of Windsor. House of Windsor, however, was sold to its employees in 1987. UST continued to produce and market Don Tomas premium cigars, handmade in Honduras, in the early 1990s.

In 1969, United States Tobacco acquired Henry, Leonard & Thomas Inc., which manufactured Dr. Grabow Pre-Smoked pipes. UST added to its pipe business in 1974 by acquiring Mastercraft Pipes, Marxman Imports, Inc., and Manhattan Briar Pipes, Ltd. UST continues to market Borkum Riff, the best-selling brand of imported tobacco in the United States, as well as Dill pipe cleaners.

While UST had been testing the waters in outside industries for decades, the 1980s saw both further diversification and the divestiture of incompatible businesses. In 1980, UST acquired WPBN-TV and WTOM-TV but five years later sold these broadcast holdings. A year later, UST bought Heritage Health, which operated 14 drug- and alcohol-abuse clinics in hospitals. A few years later, however, UST sold it because it was not consistent with the company's core business. It also sold its interests in its pen and pencil company and its cigar company. UST considered its diversification into the premium-wine business a good com-

Key Dates:

1822: George Weyman, inventor of Copenhagen snuff, opens his tobacco shop in Pittsburgh, Pennsylvania.
1870: Following their father's death, William and Benjamin Weyman officially adopt the name Weyman & Bro.
1905: Weyman & Bro. is acquired by the American Tobacco Company.
1911: Following the breakup of American Tobacco in 1907, Weyman-Bruton Company incorporates.
1921: Weyman-Bruton acquires the United States Tobacco Company.
1922: Weyman-Bruton becomes the United States Tobacco Company.
1934: U.S. Tobacco Company introduces Skoal, a wintergreen-flavored smokeless tobacco.
1965: W.H. Snyder & Sons, a Pennsylvania cigar company, becomes a subsidiary of UST.
1969: The company acquires Henry, Leonard & Thomas, Inc., manufacturer of Dr. Grabow Pre-Smoked pipes.
1970: U.S. Tobacco Company headquarters relocates from New York City to Greenwich, Connecticut.
1973: The company's sales top $100 million for the first time.
1974: The company enters the wine business by acquiring Chateau Ste. Michelle, Washington state's largest winery.
1983: Columbia Crest winery is opened.
1987: UST Inc. is established as a holding company with its primary subsidiaries being U.S. Tobacco Compa-

ny and International Wine & Spirits Ltd; its cigar-making subsidiary, House of Windsor, is sold; and UST is sued by Betty Ann Marsee for $147 million over the death of her 19-year-old son, which she attributes to his use of UST products.
1988: U.S. Tobacco Company begins its association with NASCAR by sponsoring the Skoal Bandit Grand National Race Car.
1992: UST sales surpass $1 billion.
1995: UST begins to print warning labels and "Not for sale to minors" on its product packaging.
1996: UST and Philip Morris announce a plan to limit advertising of tobacco products; and a class-action suit is filed in Texas against several tobacco companies, including UST.
1998: U.S. Tobacco Company signs a master settlement agreement with 45 state attorneys general, and the company agrees to a set of marketing restrictions.
1997: UST launches the value-priced Red Seal brand.
1998: UST launches the premium Rooster brand.
2000: A federal judge requires UST to pay $1.05 billion in damages to its rival Conwood in an antitrust case.
2001: U.S. Tobacco Company changes its name to U.S. Smokeless Tobacco Company; and UST launches Revel, which is packaged in a cigarette-pack-shaped container.

plement to its core tobacco business, and kept its ownership of Washington-State wineries Chateau Ste. Michelle and Columbia Crest and California's Conn Creek and Villa Mt. Eden.

Old Products and New

UST's top brand, Copenhagen, the world's best-selling brand of moist smokeless tobacco, is one of the oldest-packaged consumer brands in the United States, according to the company. Skoal, a wintergreen-flavored moist smokeless tobacco and UST's other flagship brand, was launched in 1934. While United States Tobacco Company had been making inroads into new regional markets, it was not until the last half of the 1970s that moist smokeless tobacco use and UST sales soared. Between 1974 and 1979, sales had increased by more than 10 percent annually, bringing 1979 United States Tobacco sales to more than $233 million, with 60 percent of that total coming from sales of moist smokeless tobacco products Happy Days, Skoal, and Copenhagen. Its earnings were $32 million, up 15 percent from the year 1978. Most of the company's growth was from sales to young men between the ages of 18 and 35. According to a University of Nebraska study, snuff use increased 30 percent between 1988 and 1992 and one in five male high-school seniors used the smokeless tobacco product. Adolescent tobacco use remained relatively stable throughout the 1990s, and as recently as 1999, smokeless tobacco experienced renewed popularity among teenagers.

According to CEO Louis F. Bantle, the company's primary markets had been "Chicago through North and South Dakota,

Minnesota, Montana out to Washington State." UST had not even introduced its products to the Southwest until 1950 or to the Southeast until the mid-1960s. Between 1974 and 1979, sales in the Southeast and Southwest leaped 145 percent and 108 percent respectively. Bantle told *Forbes*, "If you go to high school in Texas and you don't have a can of snuff in your pocket, you're out." The company growth strategy included ads featuring sports and rodeo stars attesting to the sense of "individuality" expressed by snuff users. Since then, the tobacco industry agreed to stop using athletes in advertising and smokeless tobacco has been banned at some levels of pro baseball and in some college conferences. Some Major League teams banned distribution of free samples in their clubhouses.

Research showed that in the 1970s the moist tobacco market was comprised mostly of men whose work or activities made cigarette smoking inconvenient or even hazardous. Users were miners, lumberjacks, and petroleum workers—men who had to keep their hands free for their work or for whom a burning cigarette could cause fire or explosion. This was a small market compared to the cigarette industry's market, but UST practically had a monopoly on this smokeless market. Bantle predicted that the snuff market would increase to 100 million pounds by the dawn of the century and that most of the users would be people who had quit smoking but could not give up tobacco use. By 1992, males in the southeast, mountain/plain, and southwestern regions had per capita use of more than ten cans of smokeless tobacco annually. The Northeast region had a per capita use of only two cans. UST had an 85 percent share of the moist smokeless tobacco market, the largest segment of the smokeless tobacco market.

In 1983, UST introduced Skoal Bandits, small, ''tea-bag'' pouches of wintergreen-flavored tobacco designed for novice snuff users. Its four-week $2 million ad campaign for New York City touted the Bandits as an alternative to smoking and invited potential users to ''take a pouch instead of a puff.'' By 1990, Bandits comprised 5 percent of UST's business.

A Health Hazard?

According to *FDA Consumer*, moist smokeless tobacco use caught on among teens because of UST's aggressive ad campaigns, which specifically targeted them. The campaigns featured popular sports heroes, including the Yankees' pitcher Catfish Hunter, Houston Oilers' running back Earl Campbell, and Dallas Cowboys' running back Walt Garrison. *FDA Consumer* claimed that with this campaign, ''smokeless tobacco became a socially acceptable symbol of virility, machismo and coolness.'' The article added that UST attracted teens with free samples of low-nicotine and fruit-flavored tobaccos. Although UST had been accused of promoting Skoal and Copenhagen among minors, UST denied the allegation. Walt Garrison also denied the charge. In addition, UST donated money to addiction treatment centers in Maryland and Connecticut.

Although smokeless tobacco had been touted as a non-hazardous alternative to smoking, results of a study published in the *Journal of the American Medical Association* in June 1999 suggested that smokeless tobacco could be dangerous to consumers' health. University of Miami researchers concluded that smokeless tobacco users were at risk for oral cancer and other diseases, as well as nicotine addiction. ''These findings,'' the article stated, ''underscore the need for intensive efforts to prevent children and adolescents from using any tobacco product, including smokeless tobacco.'' And although a few months later, cigarette manufacturers were admitting that their products were potentially addictive, UST and other smokeless tobacco companies were not. On October 20, 1999, *US Newswire* reported that Joe Garagiola, national chairman of the National Spit Tobacco Education Program, called specifically for UST to admit the addiction potential of their products: ''All the facts are in. Spit tobacco is addictive and its use can lead to very serious health conditions and even death.''

By 2002, UST was insisting that it specifically avoided targeting minors with its products and advertising. In a letter to *Sports Illustrated* in March of that year, President Murray Kessler wrote, ''We are the only smokeless tobacco company to sign an agreement to work with various state attorneys general to significantly reduce youth access to tobacco products and have voluntarily adopted an array of advertising and promotional restrictions.'' Although the health risks of smokeless tobacco, as compared to smoking, have not been studied as extensively, a March 2001 article in the *Journal of School Health* considered both types of tobacco use when studying the prevalence of use among high-school students. And in 2002, UST asked the Federal Trade Commission to allow it to advertise its products as less hazardous than cigarettes. Matthew Myers, president of Campaign for Tobacco-Free Kids, objected, saying on February 6, 2002 in *US Newswire*, ''A tobacco company that continues to deny the harm caused by its products should not be allowed to make health claims about them.''

Tobacco's Day in Court

Like other tobacco products, snuff and chewing tobacco have been criticized as menaces to health. In 1986, Betty Ann Marsee brought a $147 million lawsuit against UST. Marsee claimed her son's death at age 19 from mouth cancer was the direct result of his use of UST's smokeless tobacco. The trial was closely covered by the national news media, bringing the issue of the safety of smokeless tobacco to the public's attention even though Marsee's lawyers were unable to prove that UST was liable for her son's health problems.

Snuff had been touted by UST as a safe alternative to cigarettes, capitalizing on the growing evidence that smoking was responsible for many life-threatening conditions. The 1986 Smokeless Tobacco Act, passed during the same spring the Marsee trial occurred, ended snuff's exemption from the restrictions placed on cigarettes in the 1960s and 1970s. The 1986 law called for three rotating labels warning that the products could cause mouth cancer; that they could cause gum disease and/or tooth loss; and that smokeless tobacco is not a safe alternative to cigarette smoking.

The 1986 legislation enacted an excise tax on smokeless tobacco of about two cents a can, although a nine-cent tax had been proposed by some legislators and anti-tobacco lobbyists. Senate Majority Leader Robert Dole of Kansas promised a hike would be considered if a forthcoming Surgeon General's report on smokeless tobacco was unfavorable. Despite a Surgeon General's report which concluded that ''smokeless tobacco can cause cancer and a number of noncancerous oral conditions and can lead to nicotine addiction,'' the tax remained at two cents until several years later, when it was raised about one cent per can. State excise taxes varied widely, from 65 percent of wholesale price per can in Washington to no tax in a majority of states. Meanwhile, health officials called for an excise tax comparable to that on cigarettes as well as an extra $1.00 or $2.00 per can to discourage teen use of the products.

The 1986 law also imposed a ban on broadcast ads for smokeless products, a tactic popular since the 1950s. However, the act did not allocate sufficient funds to finance the anti-smokeless tobacco campaign that the act legislated. In 1993, Congress did allocate slightly more than $10 million for public education about snuff and other smokeless products. In 1991 alone, however, UST had spent $14 million just to distribute free samples of its products. According to company officials, the individual approach is important because novices need a personal introduction to the use of snuff. In addition, UST spent millions of dollars annually on political contributions and lobbying in Washington to block anti-snuff legislation; the company was one of the largest donors to George W. Bush's campaign for the U.S. presidency. Bantle called legislation and taxes the greatest threats to his company and the industry.

Since the Marsee case, the threat of litigation against UST diminished. A ruling by the National Academy of Sciences concluded that there was no epidemiological or clinical data that proved that moist smokeless tobacco caused cancer. While this ruling was reassuring to investors, it also was likely to deter users or their families from filing suit against the company. A recent Supreme Court ruling that said cigarette companies could not be sued for failure to warn was also likely to be a deterrent to litigation against UST, which now included warnings on its products and began labeling packages "Not for sale to minors" in 1995.

In the mid-1990s, however, litigation against UST was renewed. In 1994, the state of West Virginia filed suit against several tobacco and tobacco-related companies, including UST. In 1995, a federal judge in Oklahoma ruled that tobacco companies could be sued for concealing the addiction potential of their products, clearing the way for a nationwide class-action lawsuit against several companies, UST included. The same year, a suit was filed specifically against smokeless tobacco companies, again including UST, claiming while the companies' products were smokeless, they were still addictive. The financial world reacted immediately, and UST lost share value, sales, and market share that year.

A separate agreement was signed with UST at about the same time. As the majority stakeholder in the smokeless tobacco market, UST was viewed as posing a similar health risk to consumers as companies which manufactured cigarettes. The company agreed to pay $100 million over ten years to the American Legacy Foundation, for the purposes of research into tobacco and addiction prevention. Also in 1998, the city of San Francisco and the Environmental Law Foundation sued UST, as well as five other smokeless tobacco companies and several retailers, for targeting youths in their advertising and sales. And in 2000, UST was required by a federal judge to pay $1.05 billion in damages to its rival Conwood, the outcome of an antitrust case. The company received $1 billion in credit from Goldman, Sachs and the Bank of Nova Scotia, most of which would be used to finance the payment.

A Smokeless Future

Despite health concerns and the threat of litigation, UST expected to benefit from the growing trend toward banning smoking in public places and office buildings. Of the oral tobacco market, which included chewing tobacco, dry tobacco, and moist snuff, moist snuff was the only product showing sales increases. UST controlled half of the oral tobacco market through its 85 percent share of the moist snuff market. UST marketed ten products in its Skoal line, but Copenhagen was responsible for 50 percent of sales. In 2001, the company launched Revel, a snuff packaged in a cigarette-pack-shaped container. The plastic container, and an advertising campaign with the tagline "Anytime. Anywhere," were expressly designed to appeal to cigarette smokers who might find themselves in situations where they were unable to smoke.

The company continued to rely on its core business for its success, with relatively modest contributions from its wine subsidiary and its other smaller concerns, including Dr. Grabow Pre-Smoked pipes, Dill's pipe cleaners, and Cabin Fever Enterprises, which developed, produced, and marketed video programming with a U.S. theme.

In the early 1990s, exports to countries other than Canada accounted for about 1 percent of sales. Moist smokeless tobacco products were little known outside of the United States and Sweden, where they originated. Several nations had imposed stiff

restrictions on snuff, including Australia, Hong Kong, Ireland, Israel, New Zealand, Saudi Arabia, Singapore, Tasmania, Thailand, the United Kingdom, and other European nations. However, Bantle considered the international market, especially the countries of Eastern Europe, UST's greatest opportunity for growth. That emphasis continued into the new millennium; as Edward J. Deak, an economist at Fairfield University, told the *Connecticut Post* in March 2002, "Most of the expansion for tobacco products is going to be outside the United States."

In 1993, Bantle and Ralph L. Rossi, president, chairman, and CEO of U.S. Tobacco's parent company, both retired, making way for Joseph R. Taddeo and Vincent A. Gierer, Jr., to take their respective places. This marked the first significant executive changes at UST in 20 years, but both new executives emphasized that there would be no dramatic changes in how the company was run. Taddeo stated that the company would continue to improve and expand its moist tobacco products, while Gierer noted that changes in the social acceptability of cigarette smoking indicated a particular opportunity for smokeless tobacco. "Some smokers are becoming our customers," he noted in a May 1994 interview with *U.S. Distribution Journal*. "People like to enjoy the pleasure of tobacco but just can't light up, so they smoke sometimes and they enjoy snuff at other times."

Throughout the 1990s, UST worked to expand its presence and visibility in the smokeless tobacco market. A brighter, more appealing can design for its Skoal brand in 1998, a promotional partnership between Skoal and NASCAR that same year, the launch of the discount Red Seal line in 1997, and a merchandise promotion in 1997 where consumers traded tobacco can lids for Skoal-branded products. Also in 1997, UST introduced its Copenhagen Long Cut brand, as an alternative to the regular fine cut. The recent tobacco-related litigation had inspired a few advertising changes as well; ads for the Skoal Fine Cut Straight brand, introduced in 1996, included labeling warning of the risk of mouth cancer, and prohibiting sale of the product to minors. Other new flavors and products, as well as commercial tie-ins such as concert and sports promotions, attempted to maintain and increase UST's visibility and market share.

In the third quarter of the year 2000, however, UST experienced a drop in tobacco sales. Murray Kessler, just recently appointed president of the company's principal subsidiary, responded with an announced intention of raising corporate earnings 10 percent annually over the following five years. New products, brands, and packaging were reported to be in the works, all with the intention of increasing snuff's social acceptability. Among other innovations, Kessler wished to introduce a non-spit tobacco, as well as new flavors. One of the new flavors, launched in 2001 under the Copenhagen brand, was the Black Bourbon Flavor Smokeless Tobacco. UST also did not neglect its bargain brands, launching a Fine Cut Wintergreen flavor in its value-priced Red Seal line in April 2000. Although in 1999, UST had a 78 percent share of the moist snuff market, and a 38.8 percent share of the smokeless tobacco market overall, a single-digit growth rate and a shrinking price cap spelled trouble for the industry as a whole. Therefore, UST's new marketing and pricing would involve emphasis on value and discount brands. The company also increased the size of its cans of Skoal tobacco, selling the new 1.2-ounce cans at the same price as the older 1-ounce cans. The advertising cam-

paign accompanying the change included the tagline "Skoal
. . . Always There in a Pinch."

In 2001, the company raised its wholesale prices between 10
to 15 cents a can. It also consolidated its advertising at the
Warwick Baker O'Neill agency, which had handled UST's Copenhagen brand for 82 years. Under the new agreement, the
agency would also handle advertising for the Skoal and Rooster
brands, plus the company's principal subsidiary's name change
from United States Tobacco Company to United States Smokeless Tobacco Company. The stated purpose of this name change,
which took effect in early 2001, was to more accurately reflect the
company's business; according to a February 2001 article in
Convenience Store News, "Most consumers believed the subsidiary manufactured cigarettes." President Kessler was quoted in
the January 2001 issue of *World Tobacco* as saying that the new
name was "a more accurate reflection of who we are—the
world's largest manufacturer and marketer of moist smokeless
tobacco products." UST also increased its advertising spending,
nearly doubling it from $8 million a year to $14 million a year, in
an effort to offset a drop in market share due to competition from
other brands. If 1 percent of U.S. cigarette smokers switched to
snuff, the company claimed, UST would own 10 percent of the
tobacco market overall. In the same *World Tobacco* article,
Kessler stated the company's long-term goal: "Our vision is to
have our smoke-free products recognized by adults as the preferred way to experience tobacco satisfaction."

By early 2002, the company was predicting 10 percent
earnings growth over the following three years, although it
declined to make any concrete statements concerning the potential health risks of smokeless tobacco, as opposed to cigarette
smoking. In 2001, the company reported a net income of $491.6
million. A general rise in value for tobacco stocks in 2001 also
boded well for UST.

Principal Subsidiaries

International Wine & Spirits Ltd.; Stimson Lane Ltd.; United
States Smokeless Tobacco Brands Inc.; United States Smoke-
less Tobacco Company; United States Tobacco Manufacturing
Limited Partnership.

Principal Competitors

Conwood; Swedish Match; Swisher International.

Further Reading

Abramson, Jill, and Barry Meier, "Tobacco Braced for Costly Fight,"
New York Times, December 15, 1997.
Beirne, Mike, "Skoal Bulks Up, Seeks Fishing Fans," *Brandweek*,
February 7, 2000, p. 6.
Broder, John M., and Barry Meier, "Tobacco Accord, Once Ap-
plauded, Is All But Buried," *New York Times*, September 14, 1997.
"Chewing Tobacco Firms Are Targeted by Lawsuit," *Wall Street
Journal*, April 1, 1998, p. A8.
"Copenhagen Black Smokeless Tobacco—Bourbon Flavor," *Product
Alert*, September 11, 2000.
"Copenhagen Smokeless Tobacco—Long Cut," *Product Alert*, Janu-
ary 27, 1997.

Dawkins, Pam, "Greenwich, Conn.-Based Tobacco, Wine Firms' Par-
ent Honors 90 Years of Trading," *Connecticut Post*, March 29,
2002.
"Democracy 21: President Bush's Fortune Seeking 100 Investors in
White House Portfolio," *US Newswire*, March 11, 2001.
Denny, Jeffrey, "The King of Snuff," *Common Cause Magazine*,
Summer 1993, p. 20.
"Determination of Nicotine, pH, and Moisture Content of Six US
Commercial Moist Snuff Products," *Journal of the American Medi-
cal Association*, June 23, 1999, p. 2,279.
Deveny, Kathleen, "With Help of Teens, Snuff Sales Revive," *Wall
Street Journal*, May 3, 1990, p. B1.
"Dipping into New Product Pipeline, Ailing UST Turns to Flavored
Snuff," *Brandweek*, November 20, 2000, p. 5.
Elvin, John, "Ups and Downs of Drug Use," *Insight on the News*,
January 29, 2001, p. 34.
Everett, Sherry A., Corinne G. Husten, Charles W. Warren, Linda
Crossett, and Donald Sharp, "Trends in Tobacco Use Among High
School Students in the United States, 1991–1995," *Journal of
School Health*, April 1998, p. 137.
"Executive Business Briefing," *United Press International*, May 14,
2001.
Fairclough, Gordon, "UST Is Hoping Smokers Switch to Snuff
Packets," *Wall Street Journal*, January 22, 2001, p. B1.
——, "UST Pursues No-Spit Image for Its Snuff," *Wall Street Jour-
nal*, August 1, 2001, p. B2.
Geer, John F., "Smoke Signals," *Financial World*, August 29, 1995,
p. 39.
"Global Investing: Tobacco Companies Find a Little Respect," *Finan-
cial Times*, May 23, 2001, p. 32.
Goldstein, Josh, "Campaign Contributions to Both Parties Give To-
bacco Industry a Loud Voice in Public Affairs," *Knight-Ridder/
Tribune News Service*, August 23, 1996.
"If You Can't Smoke in the Office, Snuff Can Be a Secret Vice," *Wall
Street Journal*, February 11, 2000, p. A1.
"It's Smokeless but Addictive, Suit Charges," *New York Times*, July
22, 1995, p. 19.
"Judge Allows Big Suit against Tobacco Industry," *New York Times*,
February 18, 1995, p. 27.
Kemper, Vicki, "The Inhalers," *Common Cause Magazine*, Spring
1995, p. 18.
Lappen, Alyssa A., "Just a Pinch," *Forbes*, September 9, 1985, p. 134.
"Letters," *Sports Illustrated*, March 25, 2002, p. 12.
Lewis, Paul C., Joanne S. Harrell, Shibing Deng, and Chyrise Bradley,
"Smokeless Tobacco Use in Adolescents: The Cardiovascular
Health in Children Study," *Journal of School Health*, October
1999, p. 320.
Loeffelholz, Suzanne, "Raider Bait," *Financial World*, September 20,
1988, pp. 24–25.
Meier, Barry, "Big Tobacco on the Line in Congress," *New York
Times*, January 5, 1998.
——, "Cigarette Makers and States Draft a $206 Billion Deal," *New
York Times*, November 14, 1998.
——, "Companies Refocus Efforts as the Litigation Cloud Lifts," *New
York Times*, January 4, 1999.
——, "Trimmed Tobacco Plan Takes Center Stage," *New York Times*,
October 6, 1998.
Mintz, Morton, "The Artful Dodgers," *Washington Monthly*, October
1986, pp. 9–16.
"New York," *AdWeek East*, February 26, 2001.
Pope, Charles, "Tobacco Officials Admit Nicotine Is Addictive, Ask
for Congress to Pass Settlement," *Knight-Ridder/Tribune News
Service*, January 29, 1998.
Prezioso, Jeanine, "UST Predicts 10 Percent Earnings," *Fairfield
County Business Journal*, January 7, 2002, p. 2.
"Red Seal Chewing Tobacco—Fine Cut Wintergreen," *Product Alert*,
April 24, 2000.

"Red Seal Smokeless Tobacco," *Product Alert*, August 11, 1997.

Rosenbaum, David E., "Tobacco Leaders Refuse to Budge on Pact," *New York Times*, February 25, 1998.

Shaw, Joy C., "U.S. Tobacco Raises Litigation Funds," *Bank Loan Report*, October 9, 2000.

"Should Programs Take Tobacco Money? Just Say 'I Don't Know'," *The Addiction Letter*, July 1993, p. 5.

"Skoal Smokeless Tobacco—Original Fine Cut Straight," *Product Alert*, December 9, 1996.

"Skoal Straight Smokeless Tobacco," *Lookout-Nonfoods*, February 11, 1997.

"Skoal Undergoes Packaging Redesign," *Tobacco Retailer*, December 1998, p. 42.

"Smokeless Tobacco: No Minors Allowed," *USA Today*, April 4, 1995, p. B1.

"Snuff Maker UST Is Hit by $1.05 Billion Verdict," *Wall Street Journal*, March 30, 2000, p. A3.

"State Files Tobacco Suit," *Wall Street Journal*, September 21, 1994, p. B11.

Stevens, Kathleen R., A. Marie Barron, Carol A. Ledbetter, Katie M. Foarde, and Shirley W. Menard, "Legislation, Policy, and Tobacco Use Among Youth: Implications for Health Care Providers," *Journal of School Health*, March 2001, p. 89.

"TFK: Proliferation of Nicotine Lollipops Underscores Need for FDA Regulation of All Nicotine Products," *US Newswire*, April 3, 2002.

"TFK: UST Puts Profits Ahead of Public Health in Seeking to Claim that Smokeless Tobacco Products Are Safer than Cigarettes," *US Newswire*, February 6, 2002.

"Time for U.S. Tobacco to Step Up to the Plate, Says Joe Garagiola," *US Newswire*, October 20, 1999.

"Tobacco Firms Try to Sow Seeds of Self-Regulation," *USA Today*, May 16, 1996, p. B1.

Traczek, Chris, "What Price Glory?," *Tobacco Retailer*, April 2000, p. 16.

"UST Changes Name," *Convenience Store News*, February 12, 2001, p. 10.

UST Company Web Site, accessed May 6, 2002, http://www.ustinc .com.

"U.S. Tobacco Co.," *Advertising Age*, January 26, 1998, p. 34.

"U.S. Tobacco Repositions Skoal," *Tobacco Retailer*, December 1998, p. 8.

"UST's 'New' Generation," *U.S. Distribution Journal*, May 15, 1994, p. 31.

"UST's New Name," *World Tobacco*, January 2001, p. 4.

"UST Unveils Strategic Initiatives," *U.S. Distribution Journal*, September-October 1997, p. 58.

"When Diversification Doesn't Pay," *Institutional Investor*, August 1990, pp. 39–40.

White, Larry C., "Tobacco on Trial," *Merchants of Death*, New York: William Morrow, 1988, pp. 88–115.

Wyatt, John, "Tobacco's Future: Up in Smoke?," *Fortune*, April 29, 1996, p. 195.

—Wendy J. Stein
—update: Genevieve Williams

Vincor International Inc.

441 Courtneypark Drive East
Mississauga, Ontario L5T 2V3
Canada
Telephone: (905) 564-6181
Toll Free: (800) 265-9463
Fax: (905) 564-6909
Web site: http://www.vincorinternational.com

Public Company
Incorporated: 1993
Employees: 1,372 (1999 est.)
Sales: $187.0 million (2001)
Stock Exchanges: Toronto
Ticker Symbol: VN
NAIC: 312130 Wineries

Vincor International Inc. is the largest producer and marketer of wine in Canada, the fourth largest in North America, and ranks among the 15th largest in the world. While the company's primary focus is the sale of premium wines (which account for about half of its sales), it also produces and markets wine coolers, hard lemonade and cider, and winemaking kits. Vincor's wine brands include such well-known Canadian and U.S. producers as Inniskillin, Jackson-Triggs, Jordan, Okanagan Vineyards, and Hogue Cellars; its other brands include Canada Cooler, Vibe and Grower's Cider, Vex hard lemonade, and R.J. Spagnol's wine kits. Additionally, the company also owns Wine Rack, an independent wine retailer in Ontario that operates more than 250 stores. Besides earning Vincor financial success (sales reached a record C$111.3 million for the quarter ending December 31, 2001), the company's products also garner critical acclaim: at the 2001 Canadian Wine Awards, Vincor wines earned Best White Wine of the Year, Best Cabernet Franc, and Best Cabernet/Merlot Meritage, and the company's Inniskillin winery was named Best Canadian Winery at the London International Wine and Spirits Competition for the third year in a row.

Historical Roots: T.G. Bright & Co.

Vincor International is the result of the consolidation of several Canadian wineries and wine companies with historical roots dating back to the nineteenth century. The oldest of these companies was founded in 1874 in Toronto as the Niagra Falls Wine Company by Thomas G. Bright and Francis A. Sherrif. In 1911, Bright bought out Sherrif's interests in the winery and renamed it T.G. Bright & Co., and over the next 80 years the company grew to be the largest winemaking company in Canada, acquiring such wine interests as Jordan and Ste-Michelle Cellars. In 1992, T.G. Bright & Co. was acquired by Wine Acquisitions International. The new company assumed the name T.G. Bright & Co. and would later participate in the merger that created Vincor International.

Birth of a Company

In 1989, Donald Triggs and Alan Jackson purchased Ridout Wines (where Triggs had been president until 1982), the wine division of venerable Canadian brewing company John Labatt, Inc., which was getting out of the wine business due to the advent of new free trade laws that promised to make it difficult for Canadian wine producers to prosper. The trade laws would result in the importation of high-quality foreign wines at a relatively low price—and in the wake of the new laws, Canadian wineries lost 24 percent of their market share in just five years. "You had two choices as a Canadian wine producer," Triggs recalled in 2001, "Go to higher price points if you wanted to stay small. Or get bigger fast if you were in the popular-priced segments." Triggs and Jackson chose to pursue both segments of the market with their new company, Cartier Wines. First they attacked the higher-end market when they acquired the prestigious Inniskillin Wines.

Inniskillin was founded in 1975 by Donald J.P. Ziraldo and Karl J. Kaiser in Niagara-on-the-Lake, Ontario. The winery received the first winery license given in Ontario since 1929 and pioneered the estate winery movement in Canada. Inniskillin became particularly well know for its ice wine (derived from the German *eiswine*), a highly concentrated dessert wine made from grapes that are naturally frozen on the vine, and thus can only be produced in cooler climates such as Ontario. Inniskillin produced its first icewine in 1984, and its 1989 vintage won the Citadelle d'Or Award (Grand Prix d'Honneur) at Vinexpo in Bordeaux, France. Inniskillin was also instrumental in forming the Vintners Quality Alliance (VQA), Canada's organization for quality assurance in winemaking. After the acquisition, Inskillin continued to operate as an autonomous company under Ziraldo's direction.

After acquiring Inniskillin, Triggs and Jackson's once again renamed the company—Cartier Inniskillin Vintners, Inc.—and set about tackling the lower end of the market. They merged Cartier Inniskillin with the more popular-price-oriented T.G. Bright & Co. in November of 1993, forming Vincor International, Inc. The merger instantly created the largest wine merchant in Canada, and doubled the company's annual sales to C$125 million.

A New Company

Vincor soon set about winning back market share from imported wines. Despite the dim view most investors took of the future of premium (wines that retail for over US$10 a bottle) Canadian wines, Vincor CEO Donald Triggs saw a brighter future. A C$100 million government program in Ontario was encouraging grape farmers to replace the traditional labrusca grapes with the higher-quality vinifera grapes. Vinifera grapes produce premium wine varietals such as Cabernet Sauvignon, Chardonnay, and Pinot Noir, and Triggs believed that a new abundance of these grapes would greatly raise the quality of domestic brands. He also predicted that the aging baby-boom generation would soon drive up the demand for quality wine—industry studies indicated that while beer consumption peaks at age 35, wine consumption does not peak until age 50. "We saw a growing market for premium wine, which was starting to show dramatic growth," Triggs recalled in 1997.

In 1993, Vincor established Jackson-Triggs winery in Niagara-on-the-Lake, Ontario. The winery initially produced only two wines, a Chardonnay and a Cabernet Sauvignon. The wines were made partly with Ontario grapes, supplemented by grapes from Chile and California. The wines were an immediate hit, and over the next five years the brand became one of the top 10 best-selling in Canada. The company also began growing through a series of acquisitions that would continue through the decade. In 1996, Vincor acquired Dumont Vins et Spiritueux, Okanagan Vineyards, and London Winery. Also that year,

Vincor's shares were publicly traded for the first time. The shares opened at C$8, and by the autumn of 1997, they had climbed steadily to C$13. Besides its excellent products and prudent acquisitions, Vincor owed much of its success to its chain of Ontario retail stores called Wine Rack. The chain sold only wines from Ontario produced by Vincor wineries. The stores allowed the company to aggressively market its premium wines. "[The Wine Rack stores] are a very important tool in what I call the 'missionary work' of developing an awareness of Ontario wines," said Trigg in 1997. The stores also gave Vincor substantial advantage over international wineries, which were not permitted to open stores in Canada.

Continued Growth

As the 1990s progressed, Vincor continued to grow through acquiring wineries and wine companies. In 1997, the company entered the home winemaking market with its purchase of R.J. Grape Company, a producer of wine kits. High tax jurisdictions in Canada resulted in a greater interest in home winemaking among Canadian consumers than those in other countries. By March of 2001, Vincor's wine-kit sales were the equivalent of three million cases of wine a year. Vincor further grew in the winemaking market with its purchase of Spagnol's Wine and Beer Making Supplies Ltd. in 1998. That year, Vincor also acquired Montreal wine distribution company Groupe Paul Masson. By 1999, just three years after going public, Vincor's net sales had grown to C$253.2 million and the company's sales represented 25 percent of Canada's wine, wine kit, cooler, and cider sales. The company had wineries in British Columbia, Ontario, Quebec, and New Brunswick and was producing a variety of wines, from its premium brands such as Inniskillin and Jackson-Trigg to lower-priced wines such as L'Ambiance and Notre Vin Maison.

International Expansion

Vincor began the 21st century with its first international venture. The company signed a joint venture with Boisset, France's largest Burgundy producer, to purchase a 77-acre tract of land on the Niagara Peninsula, where they would produce a high-end Pinot Noir. The new winery was called Le Clos Jordan. "We could have invested anywhere," said Boisset vice-president Jean-Charles Boisset, "We searched the globe from Argentina to New Zealand and ultimately decided that this was the most perfect piece of land for soil analysis, exposure, and climactic similarity to Burgundy." Le Clos Jordan was staffed with winemakers and viticulturists from France and Canada and planted with eight clones of French Pinot grapes in the traditional Burgundian manner, using techniques such as high vine density, close canopy management, and green harvesting to reduce yield. The new winery's first bottling—slated for sale in Canada and the United States—was expected in 2005.

Vincor followed the venture with Boisset with a second French alliance, this time with Groupe Taillan, France's largest producer of Appelation Controleé wines. The two wine giants created Osoyoos Larose in British Columbia's Okanagan Valley. The vineyard's 50 acres were planted with classic Bordeaux varietals, and its first bottling—Merlot, Cabernet Sauvignon, Cabernet Franc, and Malbec, produced by renowned French winemaker Michel Rolland—was expected in 2005. "Osoyoos

Larose is a formidable demonstration of our absolute belief in the world class quality and future of Okanagan wine, coupled with our respect for the wines of Bordeaux," said Donald Triggs at the time of the venture.

The year 2000 saw more growth for Vincor. In May of that year, the company acquired Sumac Estate Winery, one of British Columbia's first wineries, for approximately C$7 million. In June, Vincor bought Hawthorne Mountain Vineyards, and in August, the company acquired Canuck Brewing, Ltd. In October, Vincor made its first U.S. venture with its purchase of premium winery R.H. Phillips, located in the Dunnigan Hills region northeast of California's Napa Valley. The acquisition gave the company a network of 90 distributors and 30 salespeople to market Vincor products in the United States, made the company the fourth largest wine producer in North America, and added three labels—R.H. Phillips, Toasted Head, and EXP—to Vincor's growing portfolio of premium brands. "With this closing, Vincor International has become truly international," said Donald Triggs, "We look forward to demonstrating the tremendous benefits to our company of this acquisition over the months and years to come." Those benefits were quick in coming: by May 2001, premium wines represented 59 percent of the company's sales, compared with 17 percent only five years before.

In August 2001, Vincor continued its U.S. growth with the purchase of Hogue Cellars winery in Prosser, Washington, for US$36.4 million. Hogue, which produced 400,000 cases a year, brought the company's yearly U.S. production to one million cases and its yearly U.S. revenues up to US$60 million. The acquisition also doubled Vincor's dedicated sales force in the United States to 50. At the time of the acquisition, Vincor planned to integrate Hogue with R.H. Phillips to create a single company. Industry experts praised Vincor's move into the U.S. markets. "Phillips in particular was a very smart move," said Toronto wine writer Tony Aspler, "By undertaking the expansion in production, Vincor won't be able to sell it all in Canada.

They'll need another market." Aslper anticipated that the company would develop a niche market for its ice wine, which retailed in Canada for between C$35 and C$85 for a half bottle.

Vincor's near uninterrupted success since its 1992 founding gave the company cause for optimism for the early years of the 21st century. In September 2001, CEO Donald Triggs hoped to increase the company's production of higher-priced wines from 50 percent to 60 percent and increase annual Canadian sales to C$400 million by the year 2006. He also anticipated U.S. sales to rise to US$300 million by that year—through an expanded profile for ice and table wines and through boosting the output of R.H. Phillips and Houge. R.H. Phillips alone had the capacity to produce 750 million cases a year. And, Triggs had his eye on further international expansion for Vincor. "Basically, what we are doing is charting a course to develop an international portfolio of products," he said in 2001, "Our long-term goal is to vertically integrate into vineyards of California, Canada, Australia, and perhaps Chile and Argentina and to market those wines to consumers around the world in Canada, the United States, Europe, and Asia."

Principal Subsidiaries

Vincor (Quebec) Inc.; Inniskillin Okanagan Vineyards Inc; Inniskillin Wines Inc; Sumac Ridge Estate Winery (2000) Ltd.; Hawthorne Mountain Vineyards (2000) Ltd.; Spagnol's Wine & Beer Making Supplies Ltd.; R.H. Phillips, Inc.; The Hogue Cellars, Ltd.

Principal Competitors

Constellation Brands; Gallo; Robert Mondavi.

Further Reading

Ashton, Linda, "Washington Winemakers Toast Cooperation and Competition," *Columbian*, October 2, 2001, p. E1.

"Background Information: Le Clos Jordan," *Wineward.com*, accessed March 19, 2002, http://www.wineward.com.

Bateman, Anne, and Samir Zabaneh, "A Toast to Inniskillin . . . ," *Food in Canada*, September 1, 1995, pp. 35–37.

Bertin, Oliver, "Red Wine Lovers Chug Their Choice into No. 1 Spot," *The Globe and Mail*, July 2, 2001, p. B3.

"Brights Wines," *Canada's Digital Collections*, accessed March 19, 2002, http://collections.ic.gc.ca.

"Continued Growth in Sales and Net Income Highlight Strong Third Quarter Results For Vincor," *Market News Publishing*, May 17, 2001, http://www.elibrary.com.

de Villiers, Marq, "The Big Turnaround at Brights Wines," *Canadian Business*, February, 1980, p. 56.

Dunphy, Stephen H., "State Winery Gets Canadian Owner Hogue Cellars Has Been Sold for $36.4 Million," *Seattle Times*, August 17, 2001, p. E2.

Ejbich, Konrad, "Burgundy Giant Plans Joint-Venture Pinot Noir from Canada," *Wine Spectator Online*, posted February 26, 2000, http://www.winespectator.com.

——, "Merger Madness Strikes," *The Eye*, posted March 2, 2000, http://www.eye.net.

Fisher, Lawrence M., "Foster Deal to Buy Beringer Puts Other Wineries in Play," *New York Times*, August 30, 2000, p. C2.

"Focus Ontario—Jackson-Triggs," *Vintages*, posted April 7, 2001, http://www.vintages.com.

"French Winemaker to Set up Pelham Vineyard, Boutique," *Welland Tribune*, December 5, 2001, p. A7.

Jenish, D'Arcy, "Cool Wines, Hot Market: Canada's Two Biggest Wine, Makers Are on an Expansion Binge, But Their Strategies Are Very Different: One Is Going Global While the Other Targets Canadians," *Maclean's*, August 27, 2001, p. 38.

Kim, Sheila, "Clearly Canadian: A KPMB-Designed Winery Takes Its Cues from the Earth," *Interior Design*, January, 2002, pp. 214–16.

Lane, Judith, "The Birth of a Winery: Osoyoos Larose," *Alberta.com,* accessed March 19, 2002, http://www2.alberta.com.

Lubliner, Murray, "Build It, They Will Come," *Beverage World*, November 15, 2000, pp. 84, 91.

"Master Architect, Frank Gehry, Designing Estate Winery for Le Clos Jordan in Niagara Peninsula, Canada," *PR Newswire*, June 8, 2000, http://www.infotrac.gale.com.

McFarland, Janet, "Bidding Group Extends Bright Deadline," *The Financial Post*, March 27, 1993, p. 29.

Menzies, David, "Sour Grapes," *Canadian Business*, February 26, 1999, p. 28.

O'Hanlon, John, "Donald L. Triggs President and Chief Executive Officer Vincor International, Inc—Interview," *Wall Street Corporate Reporter*, March 19, 2001, http://www.elibrary.com.

"Proprietors of Several of the World's Most Prestigious 'Grand Cru Classe' Chateaux in Bordeaux Bring Their Legendary Talents and Expertise to Canada's Okanagan Valley," *PR Newswire*, August 22, 2000, http://www.infotrac.gale.com.

Ryval, Michael, "Glass Half Full: Trumping All the Politics of Free Trade, Donald Triggs of Vincor International Has Purchased Winer-ies in the U.S. He's Also Selling Wines to the French," *The Globe and Mail Online*, posted September 28, 2001, http://www.theglobe andmail.com.

"Success on the Vine," *WorldLink*, posted January/February 1998, http://backissues.worldlink.co.uk.

Verburg, Peter, "Bring a Corkscrew," *Canadian Business*, October 8, 1999, pp. 54, 58.

"Vincor and Andres Toast Profits," *Welland Tribune*, February 8, 2002, pp, A7.

"Vincor—New Building with a Familiar Look," *Business News Niagra Falls,* posted January 1999, http://www.city.niagarafalls .on.ca.

"Vincor International Inc.," *Canadian Shareowner*, July/August 1998, pp. 23, 27.

"Vincor International Inc. Completes Tender Offer for R.H. Phillips, Inc. Vincor Becomes Fourth Largest North American Winery," *Canadian Corporate News*, October 5, 2000, http://www.infotrac .gale.com.

"Vincor International, Inc.," *Food & Drink Weekly*, May 8, 2000, p. 5.

"Vincor International, Inc. Declares Quarterly Dividend," *Business Wire*, February 27, 1995, http://www.infotrac.gale.com.

Waal, Peter, "What's Red and White and Drunk All Over?," *Canadian Business*, September 26, 1997, pp. 110–13.

Ziraido, Donald J.P., "History of Inniskillin," *Winerack.com,* accessed March 19, 2002, http://www.winerack.com.

—Lisa Whipple

W.R. Grace & Company

7500 Grace Drive
Columbia, Maryland 21044
U.S.A.
Telephone: (410) 531-4000
Fax: (410) 531-4367
Web site: http://www.grace.com

Public Company
Incorporated: June 20, 1899
Employees: 6100 (2001)
Sales: $1,597.4 million (2000)
Stock Exchanges: New York
Ticker Symbol: GRA
NAIC: 325110 Petrochemical Manufacturing; 325188 All
   Other Inorganic Chemical Manufacturing; 325220
   Adhesive Manufacturing; 325998 All Other
   Miscellaneous Chemical Product and Preparation
   Manufacturing; 551112 Offices of Other Holding
   Companies

W.R. Grace & Compainy is one of the oldest and most adaptable U.S. corporations. Over the course of its 150-year existence, it has been involved in areas of business ranging from fertilizer to shipping to consumer goods to specialty chemicals. At one time or another, the company, in addition to its current role as one of the most comprehensive, specialty chemical and packing companies in the world, has been the world's largest distributor of spaghetti, a cowboy apparel retailer, and owner of an airline. Despite a tumultuous history—most recently involving extensive asbestos litigation and a resulting Chapter 11 filing—W.R. Grace has survived, with an adaptability and flexibility unusual in large companies. It may be hard to believe that W.R. Grace & Company started out shipping guano, or bird droppings, from South America.

In the Beginning

In 1854, William Russell Grace and his father, James Grace, traveled to Callao, Peru. James, a prosperous Irish landowner, wanted to establish an Irish agricultural community. He hoped to rebuild the family fortune which had been depleted during the Irish famine of 1847–48 when he provided employment to a large number of people from the countryside around his estate. Not finding the prospects he had hoped for in Peru, James soon returned to Ireland.

William, however, remained in Peru and became a clerk in the trading firm of Bryce & Company. His value to the company was recognized after a few years when he was made a partner in the firm, which was then renamed Bryce, Grace & Company. Under William's direction, the commercial house soon became the largest in the country.

Poor health forced William to retire from the Peruvian business in 1865. He returned to New York City where he had spent a year during his youth. His brother, Michael P. Grace, who had joined him earlier in South America, remained behind to manage the growing family business in Peru which was soon named Grace Brothers & Company.

With his health fully recovered, William established W.R. Grace & Company in New York. William had long been a confidant of the Peruvian president, and through this connection the company became the Peruvian government's agent for the sale of nitrate of soda.

The Chile-Peruvian war of 1887–81 severely weakened Peru's economy, and the government had difficulty repaying its foreign debt. In 1887, a group of foreign bondholders in the Peruvian government, mostly British, called on Grace Brothers & Co. to attempt a settlement of the debt. Michael accepted the offer and in the settlement he negotiated, known as the Grace-Donoughmore Contract, two Peruvian bond issues amounting to $250 million were cancelled in exchange for equally valuable concessions to the bondholders. Bondholders received shares in a newly-established company, The Peruvian Corporation, which received the rights to two state-owned railroads for 66 years, all Peruvian guano output up to 3 million tons (except for that on Chincha Island), a government promise to pay shareholders 80,000 pounds sterling annually for 30 years, and ownership of the lucrative Cerro de Pasco silver mines. In return, the shareholders agreed to finish uncompleted railroads and repair existing

Company Perspectives:

Grace is a leader in catalysts and silica products, construction products and container products. Our products enhance the performance of your petroleum products, ensure the integrity of some of the world's major buildings and bridges, increase the quality of images on ink jet paper, improve the appearance of your fine wood furniture and preserve the safety of your foods.

ones within certain time limits. (Most of the contracts for supplying the railroad building program went to the Grace company.)

At the time of the company's incorporation in Connecticut in 1899, Grace listed capital of $6 million. The amount, however, undervalued the company's worth. since it did not include Grace Brothers & Co. Limited in London and its branches in San Francisco, Lima, and Callo, Peru as well as Valparaiso, Santiago, and Concepcion Chile.

The Next Generation

When William Grace died in 1904, control of the company passed to his brother Michael, who became chairman. In 1907, he negotiated a new agreement with the Peruvian government annulling the terms of the previous agreements and extending the Peruvian corporation's lease for 17 years. The government agreed to continue paying £80,000 annually to shareholders for 30 years, but made claims to one half of the company's net proceeds.

William's son, Joseph, who started working for the company's corporate offices in New York in 1894 when he graduated from Columbia University, became President in 1909. The company underwent a period of rapid growth during Joseph's presidency, and, in the process, greatly expanded South American production and trade.

In 1929, the year Joseph became chairman of the board, W.R. Grace and Pan American Airways together established the first international air service down the west coast of South America, Pan American Grace Airways otherwise known as Panagra.

After suffering from a stroke in 1946, Joseph retired. A feud subsequently broke out among family members over who should run the company. Eventually, Joseph prevailed, and his son, J. Peter, after some misgivings of his own, became president.

Expansion and Diversification

At the age of 32, Peter inherited a company with $93 million in assets and whose primary interests were in Grace Steamship Lines, Grace National Bank, Panagra, sugar plantations and cotton mills in Peru and Chile. The company also produced paper and biscuits, mined tin, and grew coffee.

From the very beginning, Peter was concerned about the political and economic instability of South American nations that he believed threatened Grace's operations. In particular, many companies had shown resistance to U.S. domination of their

economies. With what proved to be remarkable foresight, Peter embarked on a plan of diversifying into U.S. and European investments, seeking to reduce South American investments from 100 percent to 5 percent. To raise the capital necessary for his expansion the company went public in 1953. The board of directors resisted his plan of broadening investment and, though the Grace family owned more than one-half of the company's stock, he nearly lost his position as chief executive officer.

Attracted by profits achieved by Dupont, Peter began searching for investments in the chemical industry. He purchased two major chemical companies which made Grace the nation's fifth largest chemical producer. In 1954 Grace completed a merger with Davison Chemical Corporation, a manufacturer of agricultural and industrial chemicals. Later that year, Grace purchased Dewey & Almy Chemical Company, an investment one industry analyst later called "among the greatest acquisitions of all time." A producer of sealing compounds and batteries, Dewey and Almy grew rapidly and earnings quickly surpassed the $35 million purchase price. This became the foundation for one of the world's largest specialty chemical operations. Over the next 11 years, Grace acquired 23 more chemical companies for four million shares of stock.

Seeking to enter markets that could compensate for the cyclic nature of the fertilizer industry, Grace set out to build the "General Foods of Europe." Over the decade, Peter Grace purchased a chocolate producer in the Netherlands, a Danish ice cream maker, and an Italian pasta company. Critics charge that he was searching for companies he could shape and manage himself, attempting to prove he was his ancestors' equal as an entrepreneur.

Peter continued selling the company's old businesses and using the money to acquire new ones. In August 1965, he sold Grace National Bank to what is now Marine Midland Bank. The next year, he acquired a 53 percent interest in Miller Brewing Company. And in 1967 Peter sold the company's 50 percent interest in Pan American Grace Airways to Braniff Airways for $15 million.

The late 1960s proved a difficult time for Grace. The fertilizer market became severely depressed, where it had once been a source of substantial profit. Facing falling profits, Grace attempted to boost efficiency by closing marginal plants, but in the process the company incurred huge losses.

In the meantime, relations between Grace and Miller Brewery's minority stockholder, an heir to the company's founder, had turned for the worse. Peter realized he would never be able to buy the rest of the company. Thus, in 1969, Grace sold its holdings in Miller for $130 million, resulting in a net profit of $53.9 million.

In the early 1960s, the company management had reversed its previous policy in regard to South American investment and began pouring funds into paper, food and chemical companies. Later that year, however, Grace's fears about these investments came true when the Peruvian government seized the company's sugar mills and a 25,000 acre sugar plantation. Earnings on South American operations tumbled from $12 million the previous year to zero on sales of $256 million. Peter, not discounting the possibility of pulling completely out of the region, said that

Key Dates:

1854: William Russell Grace becomes a partner in Bryce, Grace & Co., in Peru.

1865: The company, now called W.R. Grace & Co., moves to New York.

1899: W.R. Grace & Co. incorporates.

1904: Death of William Grace. His brother, Michael, succeeds as chairman.

1914: Grace National Bank established. Grace sends first commercial ship through Panama Canal.

1945: J. Peter Grace, grandson of William, becomes president of W.R. Grace & Co.

1953: W.R. Grace & Co. lists on New York Stock Exchange.

1954: Grace acquires Davison Chemical Company and Dewey & Almy Chemical Company. Cryovac spins off from Dewey & Almy as a separate subsidiary.

1958: Grace constructs Washington Research Center, a chemicals research facility in Maryland.

1960: Grace introduces Cryovac Type L shrinkwrap for meat and poultry.

1963: Grace introduces pellet silica gel for use as a packaging desicant.

1964: Grace Davison introduces XZ-15, a catalyst that increases gasoline efficiency.

1965: Grace introduces Bituthene waterproofing membrane, replacing paint-on waterproofing.

1968: Grace introduces Cryovac Market-Ready packaging for beef and Monokote spray-on fireproofing.

1972: Grace Davison introduces CO Combustion Promoter Additive.

1978: Grace introduces Ice & Water Shield for roofing.

1979: Grace introduces Darex Corrosion Inhibitor for concrete.

1984: Grace introduces Cryovac cook-in bags for institutional cooking.

1985: Grace acquires Chomerics, Inc., a packaging and coating manufacturer.

1986: Grace settles with eight Woburn, Massachusetts families in a water pollution case.

1987: Grace becomes first wholly foreign-owned company to do business in the People's Republic of China.

1991: Grace announces major restructuring plan, to culminate in a company with two lines of business, instead of dozens.

1992: First asbestos-related lawsuit is filed against W.R. Grace.

1993: J. Peter Grace retires as CEO of W.R. Grace & Co. and is succeeded by J.P. Bolduc. Grace introduces beer bottle seals that help retain freshness without preservatives.

1994: Grace settles out of court regarding the violation of Clean Air Act asbestos standards near Libby, Montana.

1995: J. Peter Grace dies at age 82; Balduc resigns. Albert J. Costello is named president, chairman, and CEO. Grace is challenged on its patent of its extraction of natural pesticide from Indian neem trees.

1996: Grace divests extensively, streamlining the company to six core businesses. *Merchant Adventurer*, a long-suppressed biography of William Grace, is published by S.R.

1998: Cryovac merges with Sealed Air Corporation. Grace further streamlines to two essential businesses: specialty chemicals and container products.

1999: Paul Norris becomes chairman. Grace relocates headquarters from Boca Raton, Florida, to Columbia, Maryland.

2000: Grace makes acquisitions in keeping with its new focus, including Crosfield Groups, International Protective Coatings, Hampshire Polymers, and more.

2001: Grace files for Chapter 11 on April 2. The company acquires $250 million in financing to continue day-to-day operations, and names senior executive David Siegel to the newly-created position of chief restructuring officer.

---

company investments in future would be made on the attitude of each individual country.

In the early 1970s, W.R. Grace made a move into consumer goods. In 1970, the company purchased Baker & Taylor, a supplier of books to libraries, as well as FAO Schwarz, the New York toy store. Hoping to cash in on the U.S.'s love affair with leisure-time activities, the company acquired Herman's World of Sporting, a landmark in New York's financial district.

Grace saw a chance for substantial returns in the sporting goods business. Involvement in the market was especially attractive since there were no national sporting goods chain stores. Department stores, preferring the profits and turnover of apparel and other "soft" product lines, had shunned sporting goods. The company sought to expand Herman's from three stores with $10 million in sales into the first national chain. As part of the plan, Grace bought Mooney's of Boston, Atlas of

Washington, and Klein's of Chicago and converted them to Herman's sporting goods stores.

In 1971, the year that Peter became chairman, the company's profit was at its lowest point in years, after hitting a high of $82 million in 1966, and its return on equity was well below that of other conglomerates. Extraordinary (or, one time only) write-offs, became such a regular part of the company's financial statements (just that year the company wrote off $7.8 million from closing fertilizer plants) that some security analysts had come to consider them a regular part of Grace's operations. Consequently it was not surprising that in 1972, company executives produced a 700-page memo, establishing 20 criteria for acquiring a new business. Most importantly, these executives decided that in order to be purchased a company must have $20 million in sales and $1 million in profits.

In 1974, Peter began to reduce the company's holdings by selling a grocery products venture, and began to concentrate company investments in three areas: consumer goods, chemicals, and natural resources. Fertilizer profits had rebounded because of low supply and high worldwide demand, but the consumer groups showed lackluster profits even with large sales in sporting goods. In addition, Grace's final investment in Peru was severed later in the year. The Peruvian government nationalized its paper and chemical operations, leading to a loss of $11.5 million for the company, despite $23.6 million in compensation from the government.

By 1976, the company was ready to continue its move into consumer goods and services. Later in the year, when the company was about to make a public stock offering to raise capital for further expansion, it received an offer from Peter's old friend Friedrich Karl Flick, who during the 1950's had worked for Grace National Bank for three years. Flick, head of Friedrich Flick Industrial Corporation, Germany's largest family-owned company, was looking for somewhere to invest the $900 million it had recently made from the sale of its 29 percent interest in Daimler-Benz to Deutsche Bank. Wanting to take advantage of German laws that granted tax free capital gains and dividends earned on investments of more than 25 percent ownership in foreign companies, Flick eventually bought a 30 percent stake in Grace.

Although Grace family interest in the company had dwindled to 3 percent, Peter made it clear that Flick would not run the company. Receiving seats for only three of the company's 35 directors, Flick nonetheless obliged, since he was concerned with his own business ventures in Europe.

The consumer divisions' growth accompanied increasing internal strife at the company. In 1979, after years of watching the company's stock trading at low earnings multiples, management proposed splitting up the company into seven or eight separate companies which would command higher stock prices. Worried about the company's increasing reliance on consumer products, they also suggested selling the energy division whose market value could have been as much as $1 billion over book value. Peter, unwilling to give up his control of the company which might also have resulted from these proposals, rejected both ideas.

1980s: The Beginning of Specialization

At the beginning of the 1980s, Grace's move into natural resources appeared as if it was going to be as profitable as its venture into chemicals. The company's energy reserves had grown to 73 million barrels of oil, 300 billion cubic feet of natural gas, and 239 million tons of coal. Specialty chemicals sales and earnings, meanwhile, rose an average of 15 percent annually over the last decade. The company had 85 product lines, ranging from plastic packaging materials to petroleum cracking catalysts, many of which were market leaders.

However, the company suffered with falling energy prices in 1981. Moreover, in 1982, the combination of a poor natural resources profit and a further decline in the fertilizer business led to a 50 percent decrease in the company's profitability. As a result, Grace petroleum was put up for sale in 1984. The retail and consumer goods divisions, which were returning just 14 percent of profits on 36 percent of sales, looked like they might be next.

At the same time, however, Grace began to pursue business interests that would eventually become the main focus of the company: specialty chemicals and materials. Particularly significant was the 1985 acquisition of Chomerics, Inc., a packaging and coating manufacturer. The company, which had been losing money, was acquired through a $99 million stock swap.

The company's problems were compounded in 1984, when Flick became the target of a government bribery scandal and was forced to confront a $260 million dollar tax bill. Rumors abounded in West Germany that Flick was looking for someone to buy the family business, putting Grace at risk of a hostile takeover.

The rumors about Flick proved true, when Deutsche Bank acquired the company and put its holdings in Grace on the market. The company immediately seized the attention of takeover specialists, since Grace's assets could be sold at a profit of $20 to $25 more than the market price. GAF Corporation Chairman J. Heyman approached Grace about a friendly takeover, causing Grace's stock to rise 30 percent.

Although already strapped for cash, Peter, fearing a takeover, was forced to buy Flick's holdings for $598 million. The acquisition put Grace's debt at $2.6 billion and caused a downgrade of Grace's credit rating.

Critics, both inside and outside the company, regarded this as an unthinking decision. Complaints about Peter's domination of the company and an incoherent business strategy put mounting pressure on him to sell the consumer division. Since Grace was desperate for cash, this forced Peter to comply. Energy and fertilizer investments were reduced. Herman's was sold to Dee Corporation for $227 million, realizing a profit of $144 million. The remaining consumer goods businesses were sold for $500 million, but because of high expansion costs at the 317-store home center operations, Grace barely broke even on the sale. In addition, in 1986, Peter agreed to selling 51 percent of the restaurant division to its management in a leveraged buyout, although Grace did not bail out of the newly created Restaurant Enterprises Group until 1993. In 1986, William Baldwin wrote in *Forbes* that a $1 investment in W.R. Grace in 1945 would be worth $23 23 years later; but, the same investment in the S&P 500 would be worth a corresponding $77. Some speculated that Peter wished to live up to his grandfather's entrepreneurial spirit by remaking the company his own way, and Peter himself said that ''My grandfather didn't found any of the things we have now. He didn't found this company. I did.'' While Peter Grace was definitely onto something, *Forbes*' Thomas Jaffe considered the company severely undervalued in 1989. Speculation arose that Peter might resign.

The 1990s: A Leaner, Meaner Company

In January 1993, J. Peter Grace did stepped down as CEO, ending the longest term of any CEO in history. His successor, J.P. Balduc, had been groomed for the position since joining Grace in 1983, eventually becoming COO and president in 1990. In contrast to Peter Grace, of whom Smith Barney analyst James Wilbur said, ''You never knew what business he'd be in next,'' Balduc took the reins of an ambitious restructuring plan, stating, ''There is no backing up. The days of Grace buying companies that are not strategic are gone." First announced in 1991, this plan was to cut back Grace's operations to two lines of business, specialty chemicals and health care, and called for a divestment of 25 percent of the company's assets. Although Peter Grace retained his position as chairman, it was clear that Balduc was in charge as the company began to lose all resemblance to a family-run operation, becoming more like a standard corporation.

This transformation, it seemed, was long overdue. Although Grace topped $6 billion a year in sales in 1993, its profit on those sales was only $26 million, and the sprawling company was so heavily diversified that it owned over 100 subsidiaries. When Balduc trimmed it to six core businesses, the sold-off assets, which included divisions ranging from organic chemicals to restaurants to book distribution, were worth nearly $1.5 billion. Some argued, reflecting the emphasis on specialization in business that had become a 1990s trend, that even six was too much, particularly when the six ranged from specialty chemicals to health care to food packaging. Under Balduc's leadership, health care emerged as the most prominent part of Grace's business, in the form of the National Medical Care division, and the company's goal of $10 billion by 2000 seemed possible.

However, Balduc's term had barely begun when the company—and, Balduc himself—was once again embroiled in controversy. On March 2, 1995, Balduc abruptly resigned from Grace, citing philosophical differences with the board of directors. Inevitably, further—and, less abstract—details surfaced, among them allegations that Balduc had threatened to disclose details of previously unreported financial compensations to J. Peter Grace and to his son, J. Peter Grace III. Additional allegations of sexual harassment on Balduc's part toward five female Grace employees surfaced as well, although the harassment allegations came not via Grace's official procedure on sexual harassment, but via the company's board of directors, with no formal complaint being filed. This gave rise to suspicions that the company wished to avoid placing Balduc in the chairman's seat. The chairman's seat had recently been vacated by Peter Grace due to pressure from major shareholders, who also influenced the company's decision to reduce its board of directors from 22 members to 12. Whatever the truth may have been, both Balduc and Peter Grace departed; the latter, already ill from lung cancer, died a few weeks later, and Albert J. Costello was named CEO.

If anything, Costello was more aggressive about streamlining the company than his predecessor. This included spinning off Grace's medical care division, National Medical Care, in a sale to German-based medical company Fresenius AG, despite a federal investigation into the division's handling of Medicare charges and an FDA citation regarding importation of dialysis equipment from its Dublin plant. In addition, Grace sold its Dearborn water treatment business—then the third largest in the United States—to Betz Laboratories; its transgenic plant business to Monsanto; its TEC systems division to Sequa Corporation; its specialty polymers business to National Starch and Chemical Co.; its cocoa business to Archer Daniels Midland; and more. Other actions included a buyback of 10 million shares of common stock, amounting to approximately 10 percent of the total, as well as a new two-year corporate reorganization, inaugurated late in 1995. This move, designed to cut costs

by $100 million, reduced the company's staff by 800. Over 50 percent of the cost reduction was due to decreased staff as Grace sought to reduce its number of core businesses from six to three. Those businesses were streamlined also; for instance, in June 1997, Grace set out to restructure its packaging business on a global basis, saving an estimated $25 million a year.

Costello was not only focused on selling, however. At the annual shareholders' meeting in 1996, he said, "We are a much more focused and financially disciplined company, targeting performance levels that will put us in the top quartile of our peer companies." While Grace's divestments had increased its value and decreased its liability, its CEO sought acquisitions and joint ventures in keeping with the company's newer, narrower focus. In April 1998, Grace's remaining divisions essentially split: the specialty chemicals divisions, consisting of Grace Davison, Grace Construction Products, and Darex Container Products, kept the W.R. Grace name, while the Cryovac packaging business merged with Sealed Air Corporation. Now in essence a chemicals company, W.R. Grace & Co. bore no remaining resemblance to its namesake's initial venture.

On November 2, 1998, the top chair at the new Grace changed hands again. This time the new name was former Allied-Signal executive Paul Norris, who was named president and CEO, and was slated to take the chairman position as well. Norris immediately announced a plan of divestiture, streamlining, and job cutting, and was quoted in trade publication *Chemical Week* that "We can't just offer products to our customers anymore. We have to control our costs as well as help control our customers' costs by providing services to them." The following year, Grace moved its corporate headquarters from Boca Raton, Florida, where it had been quartered since 1991, to Columbia, Maryland, the location of its specialty chemicals division. The move cut costs both by reducing staff and by moving the headquarters closer to its business divisions. Also in 1999, Grace cut 370 jobs, or approximately 8 percent of its workforce, as part of a restructuring designed to streamline the company still further. Grace was not alone; in 1999, the trade publication *Chemical Week* noted an industry-wide trend toward reducing spending, as a slowing economy cut into profits. *Chemical Week* noted that Grace's capital spending in 1998 was $95 million, as opposed to $137 million in 1997, a 30 percent reduction. In addition, *Chemical Week* reported that in 1999, of the 40 top publicly traded chemical companies, 11 had new CEOs.

By 2000, it appeared that Norris had succeeded in his aim. W.R. Grace had slimmed down from a $5.7 billion conglomerate to a $1.5 billion company specializing in chemicals. Instead of 30 business divisions, it had only two: Grace Davison, and its performance chemicals division. In 1999, the company had $1.47 billion in sales, with a goal of 15 percent earnings growth for 2000. By 2001, Norris intended to reach the $2 billion sales mark, partly through acquisitions, partly through the introduction of new products, and to boost the company's sagging stock price. This reflected the two-fold strategy he described to *Chemical Specialties* in July 2000: "We have a number of initiatives. The majority involve bringing new products to existing markets. But in some cases we want to enter new markets with new applications for existing products." He added that "Growth is the most difficult of all strategic agenda items, but I think it's the most important." Although Grace continued to acquire new companies, the deals involved were relatively small, and in keeping with the company's new goals: purchases of coating and sealant manufacturer Bayem SA in 1996, food packaging manufacturer Schurpack in 1997, the construction chemicals division of Sociedad Petreos in 2000 (incidentally, returning Grace to its original region of business in South America), Crosfield Group's hydroprocessing catalyst business in 2000, International Protective Coatings Corporation in 2000, and similar acquisitions were examples of the company's more focused acquisitions approach. Acquisitions continued into 2001, even as Grace faced redoubled legal problems.

With the new millennium, Grace faced a new obstacle: asbestos litigation. And, while Norris claimed that publicity from the asbestos suits against the company—numbering in the hundreds of thousands by 2001—had little to do with the stock price, it is a fair bet that Grace's bankruptcy filing did.

The 1990s also saw the long-overdue publication of William Russell Grace's biography, *Merchant Adventurer*, by the Pulitzer Prize-winning author Marquis James. The book, commissioned by William Grace's son Joseph, and originally scheduled for publication by Viking Press in 1948, was suppressed by the Grace company, for reasons that remain unclear. Discovered in a disused storage room in 1978 by historian Lawrence Clayton, himself the author of *Grace: W.R. Grace & Co., the Formative Years, 1850–1930*, the book was finally published by Scholastic Resources in 1993.

2001: The Final Chapter?

Legal action, of course, is a way of corporate life, and a company the size and breadth of W.R. Grace was certainly no exception. A high-profile pollution case in 1986 pitted Grace against eight families in Woburn, Massachusetts over the question of drinking-water contamination; Grace settled for a reported $8 million, and the case was a subject of the book and film "A Civil Action." In 1995, Grace's patent on the extraction of the natural pesticide, azadirachtin, from Indian neem trees was challenged, as the substance had been used for that purpose in India for hundreds of years. In 1998, the company agreed in a settlement to pay $32 million for remediation of a radioactive waste site, and the SEC sued Grace that same year over reserves pertaining to former subsidiary National Medical Care (the suit was settled out of court). 1999 brought an emergency order from the Environmental Protection Agency to clean up ammonia near Lansing, Michigan, which threatened the local water supply. The ammonia was a byproduct of Grace fertilizer production from the 1960s. In 2000, Grace agreed to pay the major portion of a $15.5 million settlement against book distributor and former subsidiary Baker & Taylor.

The asbestos suits, however, were a different kind of legal action. For one thing, there were more of them; for another, they dealt not only with damage done, but with potential injury as well. The trouble had been brewing for a while. As far back as 1985, Matthew Schifrin reported in *Forbes* that gypsum suppliers, including W.R. Grace as well juggernaut USG, could expect a flood of litigation in the wake of a high-profile personal injury suit related to asbestos, and in fact the first asbestos-related suit had been filed against Grace in 1982. In 1994, Grace settled charges of violating asbestos standards at its Libby,

Montana tremolite mine, for over half a million dollars; in 2000, the EPA ordered Grace to spend an additional $5 million to clean up the site. Then, in 1999, Grace was party to a $200 million settlement to residents of Cook County, Illinois, who were exposed to asbestos in the 1960s and 1970s.

On October 5, 2000, Owens Corning, the United States' largest building materials manufacturer, filed for bankruptcy. While this did not affect Grace's fortunes directly, it did cause a general fall in stock prices among companies with asbestos liability—including Grace. More serious, however, was how removal of players from the field affected those remaining; as Merrill Lynch analyst Karen Gilsenan put it in *Chemical Market Reporter*, "Grace and the other remaining players could face increased liability . . . co-defendants in many of these cases could end up shouldering a larger part of the financial burden." As of June 30 that year, Grace was named in over 53,000 asbestos lawsuits and had paid out a total of $1.15 billion in judgments and settlements. By April of the following year, that amount had risen to $1.9 billion, and the number of personal injury claims against the company topped 325,000.

By early 2001, Grace's stock price had fallen to under $2 a share, and President and CEO Norris admitted in the company's fourth-quarter conference call that Grace was reviewing the choice of actions available, and that "these include . . . resolving our asbestos liability through a reorganization under Chapter 11." The decision was not long in coming; Grace filed for Chapter 11 on April 2, 2001. The filing included 61 of Graces 70 domestic subsidiaries, but none of its foreign subsidiaries.

Grace's troubles did not end there. An investigation related to the filing looked into whether Grace's massive divestitures in the 1990s, particularly National Medical Care and Cryovac, were meant to shield the assets tied up in these companies from asbestos liabilities. Atlanta attorney Sally Weaver noted in an affidavit related to the Libby case, "the asbestos liability faced by W.R. Grace & Co. was sufficiently large to constitute a strong inducement to insulate the company's assets."

Grace acted immediately to keep the company afloat, acquiring $250 million in financing to maintain day-to-day operations. The company also created the position of chief restructuring officer, naming Senior Vice-President and General Counsel David Siegel to the post. In fact, the outlook for Grace was generally considered good; Norris was quoted in *Chemical Week* as saying that "We are confident that once we can finally resolve this difficult issue, the company can emerge from reorganization as a strong, financially sound enterprise." And analyst Fred Siemer told *Adhesives Age* that "Grace is a really strong company . . . the lawsuits simply got out of hand. The courts will set up a payment schedule, and Grace will meet it." Some saw the situation as illustrative of a fundamental imbalance between business and law; consultant Stephen Einhorn told the same publication that "W.R. Grace is another example of how the legal profession is in a battle with the business world for survival." Lehman Brothers analyst Timothy Gerdeman agreed, saying that "Grace is an excellent company, possessing an attractive portfolio, solid management, and solid cash flow, but it is a victim of the U.S. legal system." There seemed little doubt, despite the overwhelming volume of lawsuits and the bankruptcy filing, that the company that had persisted for 150 years would continue, and perhaps even thrive.

Principal Subsidiaries

Grace Performance Chemicals; Grace Davison Chemicals; Gloucester New Communities; Grace Logistics Services.

Principal Competitors

BASF AG; DuPont; Engelhard; Cytec Industries; GenTek Incorporated; Great Lakes Chemical Corporation.

Further Reading

"Ammonia Cleanup Ordered," *Water World*, April 1999.

"Asbestos Firms to Pay $200 Million," *Chicago Tribune*, February 9, 1999, p. 1.

"B&T Settles Lawsuit; Libraries Get Money," *Library Journal*, September 1, 2000, p. 129.

Baldwin, William, "The Greener Pastures Syndrome," *Forbes*, May 5, 1986, Vol. 137, p. 91.

"Betz Signs to Purchase Grace's Dearborn Business," *Chemical Market Reporter*, March 18, 1996, p. 3.

Boraks, David, "In Brief: Grace's Chapter 11 Filing Names Big Banks," *American Banker*, April 3, 2001, p. 19.

Brennan, Terry, "W.R. Grace Probe Gets Messy," *The Daily Deal*, July 19, 2001.

Burns, John, "W.R. Grace Division Under FDA Fire—Again," *Modern Healthcare*, April 17, 1995, p. 9.

Cecil, Mark, "USG Filing Chapter 11: Will It or Won't It, Sources Wonder," *Mergers & Acquisitions Report*, June 18, 2001.

Chang, Joseph, "Chemical Industry Ramps Up Stock Buybacks as Prices Fall," *Chemical Market Reporter*, August 14, 2000, p. 1.

——"Grace's New $1.5 Billion Incarnation is Off to a Flying Start in M&As," *Chemical Market Reporter*, April 6, 1998, p. 1.

——"W.R. Grace's Stock Implodes on Asbestos Liability Concerns," *Chemical Market Reporter*, October 16, 2000, p. 1.

"Chemical Industry Trims Down in '99," *Chemical Week*, March 3, 1999.

Clayton, Lawrence, *Grace: W.R. Grace & Co., the Formative Years, 1850–1930*, New York: Jamison Books, 1985.

Colodny, Mark M., "Apparently Grace Has An Heir," *Fortune*, September 24, 1990, Vol. 122 No. 7, p. 211.

"Conglomerate W.R. Grace to Vacate Florida for Columbia, MD," *Florida Sun-Sentinel*, January 28, 1999.

"Dark Days for Toxic Polluters," *U.S. News & World Report*, August 11, 1986, p. 8.

De Sacada, C., and G. Alexander, "Arms, Guano, and Shipping: The W.R. Grace Interests in Peru, 1865–1885," *Business History Review*, 1985, p. 59.

"Died, J. Peter Grace," *Time*, May 1, 1995, Vol. 145, No. 18, p. 33.

Dorman, Dan, "A Whistle-Blower's Lawsuit Triggers a Justice Probe that May Derail W.R. Grace," *Money*, August 1995, Vol. 24, No. 8, p. 15.

Farnham, Alan, "Don't Miss This Annual Meeting!," *Fortune*, April 3, 1995, Vol. 131, No. 6, p. 17.

——"Straight Talk from a New Boss," *Fortune*, April 19, 1993, Vol. 127, No. 8, p. 85.

Feil, Stuart, "Dynamit Buys Grace Stake in Joint Venture," *Electronic News*, March 17, 1986, Vol. 32, No. 1593, p. 47.

"Final Payments," *Time*, October 6, 1986, Vol. 128, p. 35.

"For the Record: W.R. Grace to Settle SEC Charges," *Business Insurance*, July 12, 1999, p. 17.

Ford, Tom, "Grace Adds Coextrusion Plant," *Plastics News*, November 6, 1995, p. 3.

Gain, Bruce, "Grace Restructuring Will Save Money," *Chemical Week*, June 11, 1997, p. 16.

Giltenan, Edward, "Amazing Grace, Finally?," *Forbes*, November 11, 1991, Vol. 148, No. 11, p. 10.

"Grace Acquires Pieri SA, Construction Chemicals Business," *PR Newswire*, July 31, 2001, p. 306.

"Grace Acquires Schurpack, Maker of Food Packaging," *Supermarket News*, April 21, 1997, p. 60.

"Grace Acquires Silicas Business," *American Ink Maker*, January 2001, p. 10.

"Grace and Chevron in Catalysts," *Chemical Market Reporter*, October 16, 2000, p. 3.

"Grace Approves Stock Buyback," *Chemical Market Reporter*, October 9, 1995.

"Grace Buys Container Firm, Merges Unit with Packaging," *Chemical Market Reporter*, August 19, 1996, p. 3.

"Grace Buys Hampshire Polymers," *Chemical Market Reporter*, July 24, 2000, p. 3.

"Grace Buys Separations Group," *Chemical Market Reporter*, March 19, 2001, p. 6.

"Grace Buys Silicas," *Chemical Market Reporter*, April 2, 2001, p. 3.

"Grace Controversy Takes Shine Off Earnings Gains," *Chemical Market Reporter*, March 13, 1995.

"Grace Davison Launches Syloid W 300 for Waterborne Systems," *Chemical Market Reporter*, November 6, 1995, p. 28.

"Grace Debuts Asbestos-Eating Product," *Chemical Week*, December 17, 1997, p. 5.

"Grace Enters New Markets Via Hampshire," *Adhesives Age*, August 2000, p. 10.

"Grace Guilty of Tainting Woburn Water," *Science News*, August 16, 1986, Vol. 130, p. 105.

Grace, J. Peter, "Burning Money: The Waste of Your Tax Dollars" (transcript), *Vital Speeches*, July 1, 1993, Vol. 59, No. 18, p. 566.

"Grace Names Restructuring Chief," *Chemical Week*, April 19, 2001, Vol. 163, No. 16, p. 9.

"Grace Sells Health Care Services Unit," *Chemical Week*, June 30, 1999, p. 30.

"Grace Settles," *Chemical Week*, May 13, 1998.

"Grace Reports Second Quarter Operating Earnings," *PR Newswire*, July 25, 2001.

"Grace Starts Cost Cutting," *Chemical Market Reporter*, November 6, 1995.

"Grace to Buy Chomerics in $99M Stock Swap," *Electronic News*, March 11, 1985, Vol. 31, No. 1540, p. 44.

"Grace to Focus on Specialties and Packaging," *Chemical Market Reporter*, May 20, 1996, p. 12.

"Grace's Cryovac Under the Gun, Fresenius Pact Okayed," *Chemical Market Reporter*, August 12, 1996, p. 18.

"Grace's DARAMEND Bioremediation Technology Selected for Soil Treatment at Major Department of Defense Installations," *PR Newswire*, July 30, 2001.

"Grace's Neem Patent is Challenged," *Chemical Market Reporter*, September 18, 1995, p. 7.

Green, Meg, "Calpers Wins: $3.7 Million Will Be Returned to W.R. Grace & Co.," *Bestwire*, October 15, 1999.

Greenwald, John, "Sex, Lies and W.R. Grace," *Time*, April 10, 1995, Vol. 145, No. 15, p. 58.

Henry, Brian, "Getting Down to Basics," *Chemical Market Reporter*, January 13, 1997.

Homer, Eric, "144A Market Ripe with Issues," *Private Placement Letter*, June 25, 2001, p. 4.

"Hydroprocessing Catalyst Business Acquired by W.R. Grace," *Adhesives Age*, February 2000, p. 20.

"Inside Track: A Legal System Insulated from Logic: A New Surge of Asbestos Lawsuits is Bankrupting U.S. Businesses and Exposing the Failings of the Law," *Financial Times, Ltd.*, June 7, 2001, p. 12.

Jaffe, Thomas, "Grace's Graceful Exit?," *Forbes*, July 2, 1984, Vol. 134, p. 50.

——"Grace Note," *Forbes*, February 20, 1989, Vol. 143, No. 4, p. 152.

James, Marquis, *Merchant Adventurer: The Story of W.R. Grace*, Wilmington, DE: Scholarly Resources, Inc., 1993.

"Justice Department Throws the Book at Grace," *Chemical Week*, August 9, 2000, p. 5.

King, Roger, "Grace Enters China Venture," *Plastics News*, November 13, 1995, p. 4.

Lacayo, Richard, "Tales from the Elevator," *Time*, April 17, 1995, Vol. 145, No. 16, p. 51.

Lemonick, Michael D., "Seeds of Conflict," *Time*, September 25, 1995, Vol. 146, No. 13, p. 50.

Lerner, Ivan, "Grace Silicas Acquisition is Indicative of Growing Market," *Chemical Market Reporter*, July 24, 2000, p. 19.

"Libby Cleanup Ordered," *Chemical Week*, June 7, 2000, p. 48.

Lovel, Jim, "Fayetteville, Arkansas-Based Firm Sells Staffing Division," *Arkansas Democrat-Gazette*, March 20, 2001.

Lunan, Charles, "New President of Grace Packaging Has Some Novel Ideas," *Florida Sun-Sentinel*, October 11, 1995.

"Manufacturing's Might: Part 13," *Industry Week*, June 11, 2000, p. 36.

McCabe, Robert, "W.R. Grace Executive Accused of Sexual Harassment," *Florida Sun-Sentinel*, April 4, 1995.

"Merchant Adventurer: The Story of W.R. Grace" (review), *Publishers Weekly*, July 19, 1993 Vol. 240, No. 29, p. 243.

Moore, Samuel K., "Catalysts," *Chemical Week*, March 15, 2000, p. 41.

Mullin, Rick, "CS Interview: Finishing the Job at W.R. Grace," *Chemical Specialties*, July 2000, p. 36.

"News Briefs: W.R. Grace & Co.," *Food & Drug Packaging*, September 1997, p. 10.

"News Capsule: Grace Inks Sale to Monsanto," *Chemical Market Reporter*, May 27, 1996, p. 7.

O'Brien, Maureen, "B&T Sale Finalized; Reorganized as Solo Corporation," *Publishers Weekly*, March 30, 1992, Vol. 239, No. 16, p. 8.

Pedersen, Martin, "SR Books Sponsors Suppressed Biography," *Publishers Weekly*, June 14, 1993, Vol. 240, No. 24, p. 30.

Plishner, Emily S., "Grace: Parting is Sweet," *Financial World*, July 18, 1995, Vol. 164, No. 16, p. 18.

"Regulatory Briefs: W.R. Grace & Co.," *Chemical Market Reporter*, September 26, 1994, p. 31.

Reingold, Jennifer, "Leon Black's Debt to Society: Bond Investors May Find the W.R. Grace Restaurant Bailout Hard to Stomach," *Financial World*, December 13, 1993, Vol. 162, No. 24, p. 32.

Ruquet, Mark E., "Expect Asbestos Claims to Rise: Tillinghast Study," *National Underwriter Property & Casualty*, June 4, 2001, p. 2.

Schifrin, Matthew, "Selling Gypsum Short," *Forbes*, June 3, 1985, Vol. 135, p. 258.

Schmitt, Bill and Kerri Walsh, "Tough Market Still Hard to Crack," *Chemical Week*, May 9, 2001, p. 35.

Schwartz, Jody, "Saving Grace," *Adhesives Age*, May 2001, p. 47.

"Sealed Air," *Food & Beverage Marketing*, June 1998, p. 42.

"SEC Sues Grace," *Chemical Market Reporter*, December 28, 1998.

"Sequa Completes TEC Acquisition," *Package Printing & Converting*, December 12, 1997, p. 12.

Seewald, Nancy, "Demand is Brewing for the PET Beer Bottle Market," *Chemical Week*, July 18, 2001, p. 27.

Shriver, Kelly, "One Probe Down, Two to Go for Grace Unit," *Modern Healthcare*, June 24, 1996, p. 28.

"Specialties Briefs: W.R. Grace & Co.," *Chemical Market Reporter*, April 3, 2000, p. 24.

Steele, Karen Dorn, "W.R. Grace Accused of Shifting Assets to Avoid Asbestos Liability," *Spokesman-Review*, January 28, 2001.

"Strategies: Grace Reorganization Picking Up Speed with Business Sales," *Chemical Market Reporter*, March 3, 1997, p. 3.

"To be or not to be: W.R. Grace," *The Economist*, April 2, 1994, Vol. 331, No. 7857, p. 65.

"Tyumen Oil Makes Alliance, Acquires Ukraine Refinery," *Oil & Gas Journal*, September 4, 2000, p. 61.

Walsh, Kerri, "An Altered State for Grace," *Chemical Week*, January 26, 2000, p. 53.

——"Grace Considers Bankruptcy Protection," *Chemical Week*, February 7, 2001, p. 8.

——"Grace Enters Precipitated Silicas with Acquisition of Akzo-PQ," *Chemical Week*, April 4, 2001, p. 19.

——"Grace Files Chapter 11," *Chemical Specialties*, March 2001, p. 8.

——"Grace Files for Chapter 11," *Chemical Week*, April 11, 2001, p. 7.

Walsh, Kerri, Samuel K. Moore, Claudia Hume, and Bill Schmitt, "Specialty Chemicals: The New CEOs Ride into Town," *Chemical Week*, April 28, 1999.

"Whistleblower Targets Florida W.R. Grace Unit," *Modern Healthcare*, September 9, 1996.

Wipperfurth, Heike, "Problem Loans Dog N.Y. Banks," *Crain's New York Business*, February 12, 2001, p. 3.

Wolfgang, Lori, "Patents on Native Technology Challenged," *Science*, September 15, 1995, Vol. 269, No. 5230, p. 1506.

Wood, Andrew and Alex Scott, "Combinatorial Chemistry," *Chemical Week*, July 18, 2001, p. 18.

"W.R. Grace," *Food & Drug Packaging*, August 1996, p. 9.

"W.R. Grace & Co.: Restructuring, Large Investment on Three Core Businesses, Targeting Asia," *Japan Chemical Week*, December 12, 1996.

"W.R. Grace Buyback Is Planned to Follow Spinoff of Subsidiary," *Wall Street Journal*, September 24, 1996, p. A14.

"W.R. Grace Cashes in Its Restaurants," *Fortune*, June 9, 1986, Vol. 113, p. 9.

"W.R. Grace Develops Asbestos Treatment," *New York Times*, December 11, 1997, p. C16.

"W.R. Grace Expands in South America," *Chemical & Engineering News*, January 10, 2000, p. 18.

"W.R. Grace Has New Business, But Needs a New Image," *Wall Street Journal*, March 16, 2000, p. B4.

"W.R. Grace Ponders Bankruptcy with Mounting Asbestos Claims," *Chemical Market Reporter*, February 5, 2001, p. 4.

"W.R. Grace Seeks Bankruptcy Protection in the Face of Asbestos-Related Litigation," *Wall Street Journal*, April 3, 2001, p. B8.

"W.R. Grace Switches to Expansionary Policy," *Japan Chemical Week*, November 12, 1994.

"W.R. Grace to Cut 370 Jobs, Earnings Up," *Chemical Week*, February 17, 1999.

"W.R. Grace to Cut Sealed Air Corporation Work Force by 5 Percent," *The Record*, July 28, 1998.

"W.R. Grace Under Pressure to Break Up Following the Ouster of the Chairman," *Wall Street Journal*, March 20, 1995, p. A2.

—Genevieve Williams

Whole Foods Market, Inc.

601 North Lamar Boulevard, Suite 300
Austin, Texas 78703
U.S.A.
Telephone: (512) 477-4455
Fax: (512) 477-1301
Web site: http://www.wholefoods.com

Public Company
Incorporated: 1980
Employees: 20,800
Sales: $2.3 billion (2001)
Stock Exchanges: NASDAQ
Ticker Symbol: WFMI
NAIC: 445110 Supermarkets and Other Grocery (except
    Convenience) Stores

Whole Foods Market, Inc. is the leading chain of natural food supermarkets in the United States. The company's stores average 28,500 square feet in size and feature foods that are free from artificial preservatives, colors, flavors, and sweeteners. They also offer many organically grown products. Many locations include in-store cafes and juice bars. Whole Foods has also developed a growing line of private label products such as organic pasta, freshly roasted nut butters, oak-aged wine vinegars, and aromatic teas. After the company was founded in 1980 with a single store, it grew dramatically into a chain of more than 130 stores in 25 states, the District of Columbia, and Canada. It is a *Fortune* 1000 company, ranked as the 41st largest U.S. supermarket and the 730th largest U.S. company overall.

1980–1988: Foundation and Expansion in Texas

The company was founded in Austin, Texas, in 1980 when the first Whole Foods Market opened on September 20. The company's founders were Craig Weller and Mark Skiles, owners of the Clarksville Natural Grocery, and John Mackey, owner of Safer Way Natural Foods. Mackey, a self-described hippie who had dropped out of the University of Texas a few credits shy of gaining a philosophy degree, had cajoled $45,000 out of

family and friends to open Safer Way, a small health food store, in Austin in 1978. Age 25 at the time, Mackey had, as he described it, "had the natural foods conversion," and wanted to convert others.

Natural food stores first began to appear in the United States in the late 1960s as an outgrowth of the 1960s counterculture. Well into the 1970s, these stores were typically small, rather dingy and unattractive, and often poorly managed. The Whole Foods Market that Mackey, Weller, and Skiles opened in 1980 after they decided to merge their businesses was huge—12,500 square feet—by comparison; it was, in fact, a supermarket. This was not the first natural food supermarket but there were less than half a dozen others at the time, and the immediate success of Whole Foods Market showed that the founders had gotten the formula right.

That first store included but went well beyond the typical fare of natural food stores—organic fruits and vegetables, dried beans, and whole grains. Also available were fresh fish, all-natural beef, locally baked bread, and selections of cheese, beer, wine, and coffee that far exceeded that offered by conventional supermarkets. The store's selection, neat and clean appearance, and helpful staff of 19 attracted not only those already "converted" to natural foods, but also people who had never stepped into one of the smaller health food stores. Mackey and his partners also found out early on that many people were willing to pay a premium price for food products considered more healthful, more nutritious, or simply devoid of artificial ingredients.

Unfortunately, on Memorial Day in 1981, Austin suffered from its worst flood in 70 years. The Whole Foods Market was caught in the flood's path, with $400,000 in resulting uninsured losses; the entire store inventory was wiped out and much of the equipment was damaged. Nevertheless, the store was reopened only 28 days later thanks to the cooperation of creditors, investors, customers, and staff alike.

By 1985, two more Whole Foods Markets had opened in Austin and another in Houston. The company suffered a setback, however, when it ventured beyond retailing by opening a restaurant in 1985 that subsequently failed, costing Whole Foods $880,000 in the process. In these early years, Mackey

clearly emerged as the company leader; Skiles left the company
in 1986, while Weller headed up Texas Health Distributors, the
wholesale division of the company founded in 1980, which
served both the company's stores and other natural food stores
and restaurants.

In October 1986 Whole Foods made its first purchase of an
existing store, when it bought the Bluebonnet Natural Foods
Grocery in Dallas and converted it into a Whole Foods Market.
From this point forward, the company expanded both by purchasing existing natural food stores or chains and by opening
new stores. The expansion program was a gradual one, ensuring
that Whole Foods did not grow too quickly. Typically, each
year saw the addition of one new store in each existing region as
well as the addition of a new region.

1988–1991: Company Expands Beyond Texas

In May 1988 Whole Foods ventured outside Texas for the
first time when it acquired the Whole Food Company, which
operated a large natural food supermarket in New Orleans. This
store had opened in 1981, having replaced the Whole Food
Company's first store that had debuted in October 1974. Later
in 1988, the seventh Whole Foods Market was opened in Richardson, Texas.

The president of the Whole Food Company, Peter Roy,
stayed with Whole Foods following the purchase and in July
1988 moved to California to help launch a new region. In
January of the following year, the first California store opened
in Palo Alto.

Whole Foods next launched a private label called Whole
Foods in January 1990. For the majority of the products in this
line, the company sought out smaller manufacturers located in
the ''right'' region—a salsa maker in Texas, a producer of pasta
in Marche, Italy—who were committed to producing quality
organic products. The private label proved quite successful,
generating healthy margins and brand loyalty that helped to
encourage customers to return to Whole Foods Market despite
an increasingly competitive market. In just a few years, the
Whole Foods label included more than 500 stock-keeping units
(SKUs) within 22 categories.

From the beginning Mackey espoused a team-oriented atmosphere at Whole Foods, believing that management and staff
should work together to attain the company's goals. In such an
environment he believed that workers did not need unions, that
they were ''beyond unions.'' Nonetheless, he and his company
were at various times accused of being anti-union, a charge that

first surfaced in 1990 when the company opened its second California store in Berkeley at the location of a Berkeley Co-Op that
had closed. Starting on the day of the grand opening, the United
Food and Commercial Workers local set up a picket line to protest
that the store paid its workers from $1 to $5 less per hour than
other supermarkets paid comparable employees and that Whole
Foods had practiced discriminatory hiring in terms of age and
race, the store having failed to hire a single person who had
worked at the Co-Op. Picketing continued for the next 18 months
to no avail. In the years that followed, similar union protests
occurred at newly opened Whole Foods Markets in such union
strongholds as Los Gatos, St. Paul, and Madison, Wisconsin.

During 1991 Texas Health Distributors (THD) moved into a
new, 85,000-square-foot facility. As Whole Foods expanded,
however, the company decided that it needed a warehouse and
distribution center in each of its regions to better serve its
increasingly far-flung stores. THD was eventually transformed
into the central distribution center for the Southwest Region,
serving stores in Texas and Louisiana.

In November 1991 the company acquired Wellspring
Grocery, Inc. and its two natural food supermarkets in Durham
and Chapel Hill, North Carolina. Wellspring had been founded
in March 1981 by Lex and Anne Alexander. This buyout
marked the beginning of Whole Foods' Southeast region. Unlike in previous purchases, this time Whole Foods decided to
retain the Wellspring Grocery name, in order not to alienate
existing customers. In October 1992, a third Wellspring opened
its doors in Raleigh, along with Wellspring Distributors, which
was launched to serve as the region's central distribution center.
Lex Alexander stayed with Whole Foods, becoming director of
private label products.

1991–1997: Challenges of a National Operation

By the end of 1991 Whole Foods had 10 stores, more than
1,100 employees, sales of $92.5 million, and net profits of $1.6
million. It had quickly become the largest chain of natural food
stores in the country. The company went public in January 1992
through an initial public offering, raising $23.4 million in the
process. A secondary offering in 1993 raised an additional
$35.4 million. Backed by this war chest, Whole Foods subse-
quently grew rapidly, moving in concert with a rapidly expanding industry. From 1990 to 1996, sales of natural products in the
United States more than doubled, increasing from $4.22 billion
to $9.14 billion, while organic sales grew from $1.0 billion to
$2.8 billion during this same period.

Whole Foods' $26.2 million acquisition of Bread & Circus in
October 1992 brought with it six stores in Massachusetts and
Rhode Island and a central distribution center in Boston which
served Whole Foods' new Northeast region. Bread & Circus was
founded by two students of macrobiotics, Anthony and Susan
Harnett, when they purchased a store in Brookline, Massachusetts,
in 1975. The name derived from the first store's unusual product
line: natural foods and wooden toys. The Harnetts subsequently
opened stores in Cambridge, Wellesley, Hadley, and Newton, all
in Massachusetts; and in Providence, Rhode Island. In 1991 they
relocated the Brookline store to Brighton, Massachusetts. When
acquired by Whole Foods, Bread & Circus was the Northeast's
largest retailer of natural foods and enjoyed an outstanding reputa-

Key Dates:

1980: Whole Foods Market incorporates; opens first store in Austin, Texas.

1985: The company owns three stores in Austin and one in Houston.

1986: The company buys Bluebonnet Natural Foods Grocery in Dallas, converts it to a Whole Foods Market.

1988: The company buys Whole Food Company of New Orleans, its first venture outside Texas.

1989: The company opens store in Palo Alto, California.

1990: The company launches a private label, Whole Foods.

1991: The company acquires Wellspring Grocery of North Carolina.

1992: The company buys Bread and Circus of Massachusetts and Rhode Island.

1993: The company launches a Midwest Region with the opening of a store in Chicago.

1995: The company buys Bread of Life in San Francisco area, the Unicorn Village Marketplace in North Miami Beach, and Oak Street Market in Evanston, Illinois.

1996: The company acquires the 22-store Fresh Fields chain.

1997: The company buys Amiron, a manufacturer and distributor of natural supplements, and acquires Merchant of Vino of Detroit and the Allegro Coffee company.

1999: The company buys Nature's Heartland of Boston and acquires a 16% interest in the Real Goods Trading Corporation; also launches Wholefoods.com, which is soon transformed into Wholepeople.com.

2000: The company purchases Natural Abilities of Sonoma County, California, and Harry's Farmers Markets of Atlanta; sells Wholepeople.com.

2001: The company sells Amiron.

2002: The company opens a store in Toronto, Ontario, Canada.

tion for its produce, meat, and seafood departments. As with Wellspring Grocery, Whole Foods decided to keep the Bread & Circus name. Following the acquisition, two additional Bread & Circus stores opened in the Boston area. One other consequence of the buyout was that Mackey was accused of union busting, since the stores' employees had been unionized but voted against union representation following the takeover.

In February 1993 Whole Foods acquired a majority interest in The Sourdough: A European Bakery, which had been providing breads to the stores in Texas and Louisiana for a number of years. The move enabled the company to leverage the expertise of master bakers through an apprenticeship program. Whole Foods also went on to open bake houses in all of its operating regions.

Whole Foods launched a Midwest region in March 1993 with the debut of a Lincoln Park store in Chicago. Over the next few years, additional stores were opened in the Chicago area, as well as in Ann Arbor, Michigan; St. Paul, Minnesota; and Madison, Wisconsin. Also in 1993, Peter Roy, who had been serving as president of the company's northern California region, was appointed president and chief operating officer in August. Mackey remained chairman and chief executive officer (he had also been president; the COO position was new). With the appointment, Whole Foods' regional presidents now reported directly to Roy, who was also charged with coordinating national purchasing, distribution, and vendor programs.

In September 1993 Whole Foods made an even larger acquisition than Bread & Circus when it paid $56 million for Mrs. Gooch's Natural Food Markets, a chain of seven stores in the Los Angeles area with 1992 sales of approximately $85 million. Mrs. Gooch's, which was the nation's number two retailer of natural foods at the time of the buyout, had been founded in 1977 by Sandy Gooch, a homemaker and former grade school teacher, and Dan Volland, who ran three health food stores in southern California. The two opened the first Mrs. Gooch's in west Los Angeles in January 1977, then added six more over the next decade. In 1987 the chain opened a distribution center, which, following the takeover, became Whole Foods' central distribution center for its new southern California region.

Mrs. Gooch's stores, which operated under the name Mrs. Gooch's Whole Foods following the acquisition, traditionally had a slightly different product mix than Whole Foods Markets. Sandy Gooch did not sell any product that contained white flour or sugar and did not offer beer or wine, either. Whole Foods subsequently added these products to the stores, as well as its Whole Foods private label items, although it did keep some Mrs. Gooch's brand products.

During fiscal year 1995, Whole Foods made several small acquisitions. In February the company acquired Bread of Life and its two stores in the San Francisco Bay area, as well as the Unicorn Village Marketplace in North Miami Beach, Whole Foods' first location in Florida. In December, the Oak Street Market in Evanston, Illinois, was added to the company fold. All four of these stores subsequently operated under the Whole Foods Market name.

In July 1996, as part of a restructuring of the southern California operations, the company began to transform the Mrs. Gooch's stores so that they would completely resemble other Whole Foods stores, including having them adopt the Whole Foods Market name. The change in name apparently resulted in a 5 to 10 percent sales drop—in a testament to customer loyalty—but company officials were confident that this was a temporary phenomenon. Nevertheless, in the future Whole Foods was more cautious about changing the names of acquired stores.

By January 1996 the company had 43 stores in ten states, with plans for about a dozen more to be opened in 1996 and 1997. Many of the newer stores were much larger than the 22,000-square-foot company average. With 30,000 to 40,000 square feet, Whole Foods was finding that it could generate sales of $15 million a year from a single store. Company management, meanwhile, was setting aggressive expansion targets: 100 stores and $1.5 billion in sales by 2000 (fiscal 1995 sales were $496.4 million).

Whole Foods took a giant step toward achieving these goals in September 1996 when it acquired the 22-store Fresh Fields chain, its closest rival, for $135 million in stock. Fresh Fields had been founded only in May 1991 but had grown more rapidly than any other natural food chain. It had stores in four different market areas: Washington and Baltimore; Philadelphia; New York, New Jersey, and Connecticut; and Chicago. One of Fresh Fields' founders was Leo Kahn, who had previously found retailing success by building the Purity Supreme and the Staples office supplies superstore chains.

Following the acquisition, Fresh Fields stores in Chicago and Washington, D.C., were closed, while three other Chicago stores became part of Whole Foods' Midwest region. Four stores in the greater New York City area were folded into the Northeast region, a store in Charlottesville was added to the Southeast region, and the remaining 12 Philadelphia and Baltimore area stores were combined with four Bread & Circus stores to create a new Mid-Atlantic region. The Chicago stores were converted to the Whole Foods Market name because the company was already established there, but name changes at other Fresh Fields stores were placed on the back burner.

In March 1997 Whole Foods bolstered its operations in Florida with the purchase of a two-store Bread of Life chain. Bread of Life had been founded in 1990 by James Oppenheimer and Richard Gerber with the opening of a 7,000-square-foot location in Fort Lauderdale. The cofounders then opened a 30,000-square-foot store in Plantation in 1995 and had in development a 33,000-square-foot store in Coral Springs scheduled for opening in fiscal 1998. At least initially these stores would retain the Bread of Life name, and, along with the Whole Foods Market in North Miami Beach, formed a newly created Florida region, headed up by Oppenheimer as regional president and Gerber as regional vice-president.

1997–2002: Centralization, Abortive Moves Beyond Grocery Business and Retrenchment

In the spring of 1997, in a move designed to contain costs and improve productivity, Whole Foods began to roll out a centralized purchasing system. Installed systemwide by the end of 1997, the system enabled the company to track product movement and prices. Also that spring, Whole Foods launched a low-priced private label called 365, which was meant to denote value every day of the year. The 365 line differed from the Whole Foods line in that 365 did not feature organic products and the 365 products were priced about 20 percent cheaper. The new label was meant to attract more value-conscious customers, people who typically shopped at conventional supermarkets.

In June 1997 Whole Foods acquired Amiron Inc.—a manufacturer and marketer of nutritional supplements and natural medicinals based in Boulder, Colorado—in a stock swap that translated into about a $138 million purchase price. Amiron was formed in 1987 by Mark Crossen and his father, Henry Morgan Crossen. The father had read about a compound that was supposed to strengthen the heart muscle; the Crossens then ordered some and found that it relieved their genetically caused irregular heartbeats. Amiron was founded to market this compound to others and the company expanded into other nutritional supplements, eventually producing more than 200 such products. The Crossens took the company public in 1988 and by 1996 posted net income of $4.5 million on sales of $54 million, 85 percent of which was generated through direct mail and catalog orders.

In 1996 the Crossens decided that it was time to sell Amrion or merge it with another firm, since they wanted to reach a broader market and knew that they had to step up their retail presence to do so. By joining forces with Whole Foods, Amrion would gain dozens of outlets at which its products could be sold. Amrion would take over the manufacture of the Whole Foods brand of nutritional supplements and further expand this line. Whole Foods would also gain Amrion's expertise in selling these items through catalogs and the World Wide Web. Following the acquisition, Amiron became an "autonomous subsidiary" of Whole Foods and Mark Crossen remained Amrion's CEO and also joined Whole Foods' board of directors.

Whole Foods ended 1997 with two additional acquisitions, both in December. It entered the Detroit area with the purchase of Merchant of Vino for $41.2 million in stock. This company owned four natural foods supermarkets and two wine and gourmet stores with 10-month sales of $42 million. It also acquired its longtime supplier, Allegro Coffee Company, for about $7.5 million in stock.

By 1998, Whole Foods and its sole major competitor, Wild Oats Markets, Inc., had purchased most natural foods businesses that had a significant number of stores. The company therefore slowed its pace of acquisition. It further expanded its Boston-area holdings in 1999 with the purchase for $24.5 million in cash of Nature's Heartland, the owner of four natural foods supermarkets. Later that year, Whole Foods spent about $3.6 million to buy 16 percent of Real Goods Trading Corporation, a retailer of environmental and renewable energy products by means of retail stores, catalogs, and the Internet.

In 2000, Whole Foods purchased Natural Abilities, the operator of three stores in Sonoma County, California, for $25 million. This transaction brought the company's Northern California presence to 12 stores. The 2001 acquisition of Harry's Farmer's Markets for about $35 million brought Whole Foods to Atlanta. This purchase also contributed to what Chairman Mackey called the company's "intellectual capital." The three stores were much larger even than Whole Foods', averaging over 70,000 retailing square feet. More important was the business' focus on perishables, with about 75 percent of its sales fitting that category. Mackey expected to "leverage" Harry's large store and perishables experience "across the Company."

Not only did Whole Foods expand geographically, it also tried to add the Internet to its methods of distribution. In March 1999, it launched Wholefoods.com, with the stated intention "of being the number one retailer of natural products online." By September further plans were announced to merge Amirn, the company's natural supplement subsidiary, with Wholefoods.com to create Wholepeople.com. This venue would combine Whole Foods offerings with those of Amiron, Real Goods Trading Corporation and other businesses focused on "the natural lifestyle." The company hoped to create a site that would "become the homepage for a community of people who share common values about healthy lifestyles and supporting the environment and who are looking for a wide range of high-quality products at competitive prices that are consistent with those values and interests." Whole

Foods hoped to be able to spin Wholepeople.com off as a separate public company within a year.

Before Wholepeople.com could be launched, however, the bottom fell out of Internet stocks. Moreover, Amiron itself was suffering from a downturn in the natural supplement market. Whole Foods quickly exited both businesses, selling Whole people.com to the successful Internet company Gaiam.com in exchange for Gaiam stock in 2000, and selling Amiron (then named NatureSmart) to NTBY for about $28 million cash in 2001.

As Whole Foods entered the 21st century, it was by far the dominant natural foods supermarket in the United States. With the opening of a store in Toronto, Ontario, Canada, in May 2001 and plans to open one in Vancouver, it became an international company. It was also making plans to compete more directly with traditional supermarkets.

Principal Subsidiaries

Whole Foods Market Services (100%); WFM Beverage Corp. (100%); Whole Foods Market Southwest I, Inc. (100%); Whole Foods Market Southwest Investments, Inc. (100%); Whole Foods Market California, Inc. (100%); Mrs. Gooch's Natural Foods Markets, Inc. (100%); Whole Foods Market Group, Inc. (100%); Allegro Coffee Company (100%); Whole Foods Market Distribution, Inc. (100%); Whole Foods Market IP, Inc. (100%); Whole Foods Market Finance, Inc. (100%); Whole Foods Market Purchasing, Inc. (100%); Fresh Fields Markets Canada, Inc. (100%).

Principal Competitors

Wild Oats Markets; Trader Joe's Co.

Further Reading

Algeo, David, "Whole Foods Buying Colo. Vitamin Maker," *Denver Post,* June 11, 1997, pp. 1C, 8C.

Appin, Rick, "Natural Food Has Healthy M&A Levels," *Merger and Acquisitions Report,* August 16, 1999.

Breyer, R. Michelle, "Whole Foods Spells Out Recipe for Growth," *Supermarket News,* March 31, 1997, pp. 1, 7.

Brooks, Nancy Rivera, "From Gooch to High Gloss," *Los Angeles Times,* July 24, 1996, pp. D1, D7.

Del Franco, Mark, and Moira Cotlier, "Mergers and Acquisitions," *Catalogue Age,* September, 2000, Financial Update.

Gattuso, Greg, "Nature Trails: The Two Main Natural-Food Players Chart a Course for Rapid Growth," *Supermarket News,* March 24, 1997, pp. 1, 11, 14, 61.

George, Lianne, "Green Grocer," *Report on Business Magazine,* April 26, 2002, http://www.robmagazine.com.

Hammel, Frank, "Green Goes Gourmet," *Supermarket Business,* April 1996, pp. 103–7.

Ismail, Adam H., "Feeling Just Fine," *The Daily Deal,* May 21, 2001, Industry Insight.

Lee, Louise, "Whole Foods Swallows up Nearest Rival," *Wall Street Journal,* June 19, 1996, pp. B1, B6.

Locke, Tom, "Colorado Pharmaceutical Amrion Inc. at a Crossroads," *Daily Camera* (Boulder, Colo.), November 19, 1996.

Loro, Laura, "Doing What Comes Naturally: Whole Foods and Fresh Fields Grow Their Own Strategies," *Advertising Age,* August 6, 1994, p. 22.

Mack, Toni, "Good Food, Great Margins," *Forbes,* October 17, 1998, pp. 112–13, 115.

Mackey, John, "Beyond Unions: The CEO of Whole Foods Market Explains Why Workers Don't Need Unions," *Utne Reader,* March/April 1992, pp. 75–77.

Murphy, Kate, "Organic Food Makers Reap Green Yields of Revenue," *New York Times,* October 26, 1996, pp. 37, 39.

Patoski, Joe Nick, "John Mackey: Winning the Food Fight," *Texas Monthly,* September 1996, pp. 119, 148.

"Real Goods Sells 16% of Company to Whole Foods Market," *PR Newswire,* September 23, 1999, http://www.prnewswire.com.

Riedman, Patricia, "Whole Foods Enters Tough Online Grocery Sales Arena," *Advertising Age,* March 22, 1999, p. 40.

Saxton, Lisa, "Leo Kahn's Fresh Start," *Supermarket News,* August 17, 1992, pp. 1, 40–41, 46–47.

Tosh, Mark, "Whole Foods' Natural Progression," *Supermarket News,* December 20, 1993, pp. 1, 44–45.

"Whole Foods Buys Natural Abilities," *DSN Supercenter & Club Business,* January 24, 2000, p. 3.

"Whole Foods Market," *Chain Store Age Executive,* April 2002, p. 20.

"Whole Foods Market to Launch E-commerce Subsidiary," *PR Newswire,* February 22, 1999, http://www.prnewswire.com.

"Whole Foods Market to Sell NatureSmart," *Neutraceuticals World,* June 2001, p. 107.

"Whole Foods Merger," *MMR,* July 24, 2000, p. 12.

"Whole Foods to Buy Merchant of Vino," *The New York Times,* November 6, 1997, p. D4.

"A 'Whole' Lot of Living Going On," *Internet Retailer,* May 2000, p. 12.

—David E. Salamie
—update: Anne L. Potter

Wyeth

Wyeth

Five Giralda Farms
Madison, New Jersey 07940
U.S.A.
Telephone: (973) 660-5000
Fax: (973) 660-7026
Web site: http://www.wyeth.com

Public Company
Incorporated: 1926 as American Home Products
Employees: 52,289 (2001)
Sales: $14.1 billion (2001)
Stock Exchanges: New York
Ticker Symbol: WYE
NAIC: 325412 Pharmaceutical Preparation
    Manufacturing; 325414 Biological Product (except
    Diagnostic) Manufacturing

Wyeth is a global pharmaceutical research and manufacturing company. It develops and markets traditional pharmaceuticals, vaccines, and biotechnology products that serve both human and animal health care. It has strong product lines in both prescription medications and in consumer health products, including over-the-counter (OTC) medications and nutritional supplements. Wyeth markets its products in more than 140 countries, and has manufacturing facilities on five continents. During the 1990s, Wyeth—which at the time was called American Home Products (AHP)—began selling off the wide-ranging businesses it had acquired over the years, retaining a focus on medicine and pharmaceuticals. In 2002, the company changed its name from American Home Products to Wyeth.

1926–1965: Birth and Development of a Conglomerate

Incorporated in 1926 as American Home Products (AHP), the company came to be known as "Anonymous Home Products" or the "withdrawn corporate giant." Though the company marketed such popular products as Black Flag insecticides, Easy-Off oven cleaner, Woolite, and Chef Boyardee, as well as the familiar pharmaceuticals Anacin, Advil, Dristan, Robitussin, and Dimetapp, the corporate name has never appeared on its products' labels. Public relations was considered such a low priority that switchboard operators answered the phone with the company phone number instead of the company name. And although executives at AHP had made few efforts to influence Wall Street analysts, the company's many consecutive years of increased sales and earnings made AHP shares a very popular investment.

AHP's unusual combination of anonymity and financial success stems from its history of competent management, product diversification through acquisition, and closefisted expenditures on virtually everything except advertising. AHP has been able to strike a balance between the aggressive advertising of its consumer package goods and maintaining a reputable name within the medical community.

AHP's strict management policy allowed for a minimal margin of error. If a product did not show promise before money was spent on promotion, it was dropped. If a division did not increase sales and earnings by 10 percent annually, a division president could be out of a job. Until the 1990s, AHP found little reason to invest in research, preferring to wait for competitors to release innovative products, and then launch its own improved line. Or it would simply buy the competitor.

Expenditures are so closely monitored at AHP that, in 1983, employees at the Whitehall division paid $20 each to attend their own Christmas party. A journalist from *Business Week*, researching a rumor in 1970 that then-AHP Chairman and President William F. LaPorte had reduced the size of the toilet paper in the executive washrooms to save money, discovered that, in fact, the paper was $\frac{9}{16}$-inch narrower than typical size. As late as 1980, LaPorte was personally approving any expenditures more than $500, including anything from the purchase of a typewriter to a secretarial pay raise.

AHP's knack for acquiring little-known products and companies at a reduced price and turning them into money-makers dates back to AHP's earliest years. In 1926, a group of executives associated with Sterling Products Inc. and Household Products Inc. consolidated several independent nostrum makers into a holding company. Its subsidiaries sold such medicinal products as Hill's Cascara Quinine, St. Jacob's Oil, Wyeth's Sage and Sulphur, Kolynos dental cream, and Old English No Rubbing Floor Polish.

W.H. Kirn was named chairman of the new company in 1930 and served until 1935, when Alvin G. Brush, a salesman of Dr. Lyon's toothpaste, took over as president and chief executive officer, a position he held for the next 30 years. Brush's penchant for expansion through acquisition, while maintaining a sizable amount of cash in reserve, set the pattern for AHP's operating style. In his first eight years as president, Brush acquired 34 food and drug companies for a total of $25.6 million in cash and stock. One of AHP's earliest prizes was the acquisition of a sunburn oil in 1935 that the company transformed into Preparation H, which became one of the world's best-selling hemorrhoid treatments.

Other purchases included the 3-in-One Oil Company and Affiliated Products Inc., which made cosmetics and toiletries under such names as Outdoor Girl, Kissproof, and Neet. In 1938, AHP acquired Eff Laboratories, a manufacturer of commercial vitamin products, and S.M.A. Corporation, a producer of infant foods and vitamins. In 1939, the Black Flag Company came under the AHP umbrella, followed in 1943 by the G. Washington Coffee Refining Company, a manufacturer of grocery specialties. In 1946, another grocery specialties firm, Chef-Boy-Ar-Dee Quality Foods Inc., came aboard.

1965–1983: Expansion Through Advertising

AHP's marketing genius transformed its newly acquired products into household names. Preparation H is a good example. By 1981, Preparation H had captured 64 percent of the hemorrhoid treatment market, and its success was attributable exclusively to the company's aggressive advertising. In 1968, AHP spent more than $2 million on radio spots and $6 million on television advertising for Preparation H. These amounts may seem exorbitant for a single product; the figures become even more impressive when one realizes that the radio code standards only readmitted the controversial advertisements for hemorrhoid medications in 1965 and that the National Association of Broadcasters continued to debate approval for television. AHP advocated a broadened scope of code approval even as it appropriated more funds for advertising on noncode television stations.

The struggle for an expanded consumer audience was fought not only over advertising codes for personal products; AHP's aggressive marketing style also brought investigations of the company's advertising copy. In 1967, the Federal Trade Commission (FTC) ordered AHP and three other companies to refrain from making false claims with regard to the therapeutic value of their hemorrhoid treatments. Citing the advertisements' unsubstantiated claims, the FTC prohibited any future misrepresentation.

Company executives were not intimidated by the FTC ruling. AHP, deeming the commission's findings "capricious" and "arbitrary," asked for a review before a federal appeals court. The company continued to run advertisements in more than 1,100 newspapers, 700 radio stations, and 100 television stations. In response, the FTC temporarily enjoined AHP from continuing to run the advertisements. The court finally upheld most of the commission's findings, and the advertising copy for Preparation H had to be permanently modified.

Throughout this controversy AHP executives remained characteristically unavailable for comment. This combination of persistent product promotion (at the risk of damaging company reputation) and a united but anonymous executive front came to the fore in the promotion of another AHP product. In 1930, the company had purchased the rights to manufacture a little-known painkiller called Anacin, previously promoted through samples to dentists. AHP's Anacin grew in popularity and became the nation's leading over-the-counter analgesic. As with Preparation H, it took aggressive marketing to propel Anacin into this position.

By 1971, AHP had spent more money on the promotion of Anacin than had any other analgesic manufacturer on a comparable product. Total costs for radio advertising reached $1.5 million, and costs for television advertising surpassed $25 million. In 1972, the FTC charged that AHP and two other analgesic manufacturers were promoting their products through misleading and unsubstantiated claims. Because no reliable scientific evidence existed as to the superiority of one brand over another, or the ability of analgesics to relieve nervous tension, the FTC disputed therapeutic claims and advertisements that did not identify generic ingredients such as aspirin and caffeine.

AHP and the other manufacturers refused to negotiate consent agreements, and so the FTC issued formal complaints and ordered hearings before an FTC administrative judge. The case was finally settled in 1981 and permanent limits were placed on misleading claims in Anacin advertisements. In 1982, a federal appeals court upheld the FTC ruling after AHP attempted to have it overturned.

During the hearings on aspirin advertisements, Johnson & Johnson's Tylenol made its market appearance. To maintain their market share, AHP and other aspirin manufacturers launched a campaign to promote aspirin's anti-inflammatory action. After several suits and countersuits between AHP and Johnson & Johnson, a federal court judge in 1978 ordered the discontinuance of the advertising of Anacin's anti-inflammatory property as a claim of superiority over Tylenol.

Competition in the pain-reliever market was intensified by the introduction of ibuprofen. The drug is a non-steroidal anti-inflammatory agent that is as effective as aspirin and aspirin substitutes, but without the side effect of digestive tract irrita-

Key Dates:

1926: Company incorporates as American Home Products (AHP).

1930: AHP purchases the rights to manufacture the painkiller Anacin.

1932: AHP acquires pharmaceutical manufacturer Wyeth Chemical Company.

1935: AHP acquires the maker of a sunburn oil that is made into Preparation H.

1938: AHP acquires vitamin manufacturer Eff Laboratories and vitamin and infant food manufacturer S.M.A. Corporation.

1939: AHP acquires the Black Flag Company, an insecticide manufacturer.

1943: AHP acquires grocery specialties manufacturer G. Washington Coffee Company.

1946: AHP acquires Chef-Boy-Ar-Dee Quality Foods Inc., a grocery specialty firm.

1967: Federal Trade Commission orders AHP to stop making false advertising claims.

1978: Federal judge orders company to terminate false advertising.

1981: Federal Trade Commission again orders company to cease making misleading advertising claims.

1983: AHP acquires medical-device maker Sherwood Medical Group.

1989: The company acquires over-the-counter drug manufacturer A.H. Robins Co.

1992: AHP buys a majority interest in biotechnology company Genetics Institute.

1993: AHP acquires jam maker M. Polaner.

1994: AHP acquires pharmaceutical and agricultural chemicals firm American Cyanamid, which includes a majority interest in the biotechnology firm Immunex.

1995: AHP sells its oral-care product line.

1996: AHP purchases full ownership of Genetics Institute.

1996–98: AHP disposes of its food businesses.

1997: AHP is forced to withdraw diet drugs Pondimin and Redux and faces a wave of lawsuits that eventually costs AHP more than $16 billion; AHP sells its ophthalmic business.

1998: AHP sells its medical-device business.

2000: AHP sells its agricultural chemicals business.

2001: AHP sells Immunex interest in exchange for an interest in biotechnology firm Amgen.

2002: AHP sells its generic, injectable product line and changes its name to Wyeth.

---

tion. AHP marketed its ibuprofen under the name Advil. Industry analysts suggested that ibuprofen could capture as much as 30 percent of the pain-reliever market.

The pattern of controversy and investigation established in the marketing for Preparation H and Anacin continued with several other AHP products. Easy-Off oven cleaner, Black Flag insecticide, Easy-On starch, and Aero Wax were all involved in an FTC investigation into deceptive advertising. Yet, for all of the controversy, no one can dispute AHP's success in capturing markets and acquiring products that have become household staples.

AHP's advertising budget for 1985 was estimated at more than $412 million. Despite or perhaps because of this great expenditure, AHP gained a notorious reputation among advertising agencies as a demanding and uncompromising client. Paying the lowest possible commission rates, the company will, nonetheless, demand the best price for prime-time spots on television and expect promotion to be effective on strict budgets. In 1967, Ted Bates & Company, the fifth largest advertising agency in the world at that time, resigned AHP's $20-million account because of "differences in business policy." This was not the first time an AHP account had been abandoned by an agency. Grey Advertising Inc. and J. Walter Thompson similarly dropped the demanding company's account. The Bates agency was replaced with an in-house agency called the John F. Murray Company. At the time of the replacement, industry-owned agencies were rare.

By 1983, AHP grudgingly began to change its attitude toward promotion. The company hired world-renowned photographer Richard Avedon and actress Catherine Deneuve to promote its line of Youth Garde cosmetics. But despite this willingness to "upscale" its advertising, AHP was voted as one of the ten worst clients of 1983 by *Adweek*.

1932–1994: Development of a Pharmaceutical Business

The success of AHP's proprietary goods has overshadowed the company's position as a leading manufacturer of ethical drugs. In 1932, AHP acquired Wyeth Chemical Company (now Wyeth Laboratories), a pharmaceutical manufacturer with a long history, under unusual circumstances. Wyeth was run by family descendants until the death of Stuart Wyeth, a bachelor. He bequeathed the laboratory to Harvard, his alma mater, and the university in turn sold the company to AHP at a generous price. In the early 1940s, AHP also acquired two other pharmaceutical laboratories, Ives and Ayerst.

AHP's prescription drugs and medical supplies accounted for 47 percent of sales and 62 percent of profits in 1983. Among the ethical drugs AHP produces are Ovral, a low-dosage oral contraceptive, and Inderal, a drug that reduces blood pressure and slows the heartbeat. Inderal was introduced in 1968, and by 1983 supplied more than half of the U.S. market for beta-blocker drugs. The company was also busy developing new pharmaceuticals: AHP filed 21 new drug applications with the Food and Drug Administration (FDA) in 1985 alone.

In 1981, company President John W. Culligan was promoted to chairman and chief executive officer. LaPorte, who had been chairman since 1965, continued as chairman of the executive committee. Culligan, 64 years old at the time of the promotion, had been with the company since 1937. John R. Stafford, a lawyer recruited from Hoffmann-LaRoche in 1970 as general counsel, was named company president on December 1, 1986. Some observers predicted that AHP's management changes would herald a modernization of LaPorte's highly centralized style of management and financial control, which contradicted contemporary theories of corporate management.

Nevertheless, this anachronistic approach guaranteed shareholders a handsome return on investment. In 1982, *Fortune* magazine's directory of the 500 largest U.S. industrial corporations ranked AHP 76th in sales and 24th in profits. The company had no long-term debt, and it paid out 60 percent of earnings in dividends. Despite a chronically low stock price in the late 1980s and early 1990s, AHP saw higher earnings and increased dividends every year from 1951 to 1993.

In 1983, AHP spent $425 million to buy the Sherwood Medical Group. A manufacturer of medical supplies, Sherwood placed AHP in a competitive position to capture the lion's share of the growing medical-device market. That subsidiary was supplemented with the 1992 acquisition of Symbiosis Corp., a developer and manufacturer of disposable instruments for minimally invasive laparoscopic and endoscopic surgery.

Under Stafford's guidance in the late 1980s and early 1990s, AHP worked to transform itself into a health care company through acquisitions and divestments. In 1989, the firm divested its Boyle-Midway division and purchased A.H. Robins Co., an over-the-counter drug manufacturer that complimented the Whitehall laboratories subsidiary. In response to criticism of its low research and development expenditures, AHP spent a record 11 percent of sales on R&D in 1990. The firm invested in Genetics Institute, Inc., a biotechnology firm specializing in blood cell regulation, bone repair, and immune system modulation, in 1992.

AHP's marketing of infant formula came under intense scrutiny and criticism in the late 1980s and early 1990s. Prior to 1988, infant formula was marketed strictly as a pharmaceutical product. Given historical product loyalty, formula makers offered their products free to pediatricians and hospitals in the hopes that the first formula a mother used would be the one she continued to purchase. According to a 1990 *Business Week* article, many doctors began to allege that hospitals promoted infant formula over breast-feeding—despite the inherent advantages of breast-feeding—because of the money and services received from manufacturers. And when the federal government directed the states to purchase all their formula from one manufacturer to garner lower prices, formula manufacturers were forced to compete directly for Women, Infants and Children (WIC) contracts, which constituted about 35 percent of state formula purchases. In June of 1993, *Advertising Age* reported that the FTC had charged the top three formula marketers—divisions of Abbott Laboratories, Bristol-Myers Squibb Co., and AHP Corp.—with price-fixing in government nutrition programs.

Although food products received less attention in the 1990s, AHP did augment its Chef-Boy-ar-dee line with the 1992 purchase of Ro*Tel, the leading brand of canned tomatoes and green chilies in the Mexican food category. In 1993, the company added M. Polaner Inc., a jam maker, to the food products segment.

Into the 21st Century: Becoming a Leading Pharmaceutical and Biotechnology Firm

By 1993, over 60 percent of AHP's global revenues came from pharmaceuticals. The company was not yet a strong pharmaceutical manufacturer, though. In 1994, it reported only four products with patents extending beyond 1997; its two lengthiest patents lasted until 2007. In an industry such as the brand name pharmaceutical industry, which depended on the profits derived from monopolies conferred by patent protections, AHP was not in a good competitive position.

The company initiated a series of acquisitions and divestitures aimed at transforming itself into a major pharmaceutical company in 1994. In that year, AHP spent about $9.7 billion to acquire American Cyanamid. This purchase expanded its product line to vaccines, cancer agents, and antibiotics. AHP also got a majority interest in Immunex Corp., a biotechnology firm. A major agricultural chemical business also came with the acquisition. Immunex rejected its 1995 attempt to purchase the remainder of the company. In 1996, AHP bought the remainder of Genetics Institute. In 1997, it purchased an animal health products company, and in 1998, a vitamin and nutritional supplement manufacturer.

To help pay for these purchases and to narrow its focus to human and animal pharmaceuticals, AHP sold many of its traditional product lines during these same years. It disposed of its oral-care products in 1995, of its ophthalmic business in 1997, of its medical-device business in 1998, of its agricultural chemicals business in 2000, and of its branded generic injectable products in 2002. Between 1996 and 1998, AHP also sold all of its food product business. In 2001, AHP sold its interest in Immunex to Amgen and acquired a ten percent interest in that biotechnology company.

AHP's restructuring efforts encountered several challenges. During the 1990s, the pharmaceutical industry was undergoing a major consolidation through mergers and acquisitions. AHP tried unsuccessfully to join the trend. In 1998, AHP initiated separate merger negotiations with SmithKline Beecham and with Monsanto. Both of these proposed mergers failed. AHP followed this with an attempt to merge with Warner-Lambert in 1999. Although Pfizer eventually won Warner, AHP collected a $1.8-billion breakup fee in the transaction. Despite continued rumors that AHP was a suitor or target of takeover attempts, management denied such ambitions.

The company also confronted major legal problems. In 1996, studies implicated two of the company's weight-loss drugs, Redux and fenfluramine (Pondimin), in damage to users' heart valves, damage that might be fatal and sometimes required surgical replacement of the valve. At the FDA's request, AHP withdrew the drugs in 1997. Since 1992, millions of overweight Americans had used Pondimin in combination with phentermine, a combination known as fen/phen, to help them lose weight. Later, AHP introduced Redux for the same purpose.

The 1996 findings unleashed a wave of product liability lawsuits. Eventually AHP spent over $13 billion defending itself and paid as much as $3.75 billion in settlements. As late as 2002, the company was not entirely sure of its total eventual liabilities. This uncertainty about its liability costs contributed greatly to AHP's inability to reach merger agreements during the 1990s.

Despite these problems, AHP, which changed its name to Wyeth in 2002, entered the 21st century with a strong pharmaceutical franchise. With strengths in vaccines, biotechnology, and traditional pharmaceuticals, Wyeth's products spanned a wide range of treatment areas, and, on average, its pharmaceuticals had one of the longest remaining patent lives in the industry. It had about 60 potential products in its research pipeline. It had a powerful presence in the consumer health market. Through its Fort Dodge division, Wyeth also maintained a significant presence in the animal health market.

Principal Subsidiaries

Ayerst-Wyeth Pharmaceuticals Incorporated (100%); Cyanamid International Corporation Limited (100%); MDP Holdings, Inc. (100%); Route 24 Holdings, Inc. (100%); American Cyanamid Company (100%); Wyeth-Ayerst International Inc. (100%); Wyeth-Ayerst Pharmaceuticals, Inc. (100%); Wyeth-Ayerst Lederle, Inc. (100%); Wyeth-Whitehall Pharmaceuticals, Inc. (100%); Berdan Insurance Company (100%); Laboratorios Wyeth-Whitehall Ltda. (100%); Wyeth-Ayerst Canada Inc. (100%); John Wyeth & Brother Limited (100%); Wyeth-Lederle (100%); Wyeth-Pharma GmbH (100%); AHP Finance Ireland Limited (100%); Wyeth Lederle S.p.A. (100%); Wyeth Lederle Japan, Ltd. (100%); Wyeth S.A. de C.V. (100%); AHP Manufacturing B.V. (100%); Wyeth Philippines, Inc. (100%); Wyeth Nutritionals (Singapore) Pte. Ltd. (100%); Wyeth Pharmaceuticals (Singapore) Pte. Ltd. (100%); Wyeth Farma S.A. (100%); Wyeth Lederle Nordiska A.B. (100%); Dimminaco AG (100%); Cyanamid Taiwan Corporation (100%).

Principal Competitors

Aventis; Merck; Novartis; Pfizer; Bristol-Meyers Squibb; Johnson & Johnson; GlaxoSmithKline; Abbott Laboratories; Eli Lilly; AstraZeneca; Hoffmann-La Roche; Schering-Plough.

Further Reading

Barrett, Amy, "AHP-Warner: No Panacea, But," *Business Week,* November 15, 1999, p. 44.

Burton, Thomas M., and Scott Kilman, "Monsanto's Cost-Cutting Steps," *The Wall Street Journal,* November 12, 1988, p. A4.

Golden, Frederic, "Who's to Blame for Redux and Fenfluramine?," *Time,* September 29, 1997, pp. 78–79.

Gopal, Kevin, "Life Science Living," *Pharmaceutical Executive,* July 1998, pp. 28–30.

Harris, Gardiner, "American Home, Warner-Lambert Post Earnings," *The Wall Street Journal,* April 20, 2000, p. 15.

Hensley, Scott, "American Home Plans to Reduce Stake in Immunex," *The Wall Street Journal,* August 10, 2000, p. A12.

"Immunex Corp.," *The Wall Street Journal,* November 9, 1995, p. B6.

Koberstein, Wayne, "Executive Profile: Team AHP—Parting the Clouds," *Pharmaceutical Executive,* June 2000, pp. 46–62.

Levin, Gary, "Time for Bottle: Infant Formula Ads May Spurt," *Advertising Age,* June 7, 1993, pp. 3, 42.

Moore, Samuel K., "AHP Seeks a New Pharmaceutical March," *Chemical Week,* January 26, 2000, p. 16.

"More Megadeals Loom in the Drug Industry," *Mergers and Acquisitions,* April 2000, pp. 10–11.

Ono, Yumiko, "Colgate to Buy Oral Care Line in Latin America," *The Wall Street Journal,* January 10, 1995, p. A3.

Papanikolaw, Jim, "BASF to buy AHP-Cyanamid," *Chemical Market Reporter,* March 27, 2000, p. 1.

Siler, Julia Flynn, "The Furor over Formula Is Coming to a Boil," *Business Week,* April 9, 1990, pp. 52–53.

Steinmetz, Greg, and Elyse Tanouye, "American Cyanamid Agrees to Takeover by American Home," *The Wall Street Journal,* August 18, 1994, p. A3.

Wood, Andrew, "Smithkline, AHP Plan Merger," *Chemical Week,* January 28, 1998, p. 9.

—updates: April Dougal Gasbarre, Anne L. Potter

The York Group, Inc.

8554 Katy Freeway, Suite 200
Houston, TX 77024
U.S.A.
Telephone: (713) 984-5559
Toll Free: (800) 223-4964
Fax: (713) 935-7636
Web site: http://yorkgrp.com

Public Company
Incorporated: 1996
Employees: 1,667 (2000)
Sales: $150.7 million (2001)
Stock Exchanges: NASDAQ
Ticker Symbol: YRKG
NAIC: 339995 Burial Caskets and Manufacturing

The York Group, Inc. is the second largest casket and funerary product manufacturer in the United States. (Hillenbrand's Batesville Casket is the largest.) Based in Houston, Texas, the company also produces cremation containers, memorial plaques, and other bronze memorial products. York's services include financial planning and insurance for funerals, as well as such nonfunerary services as architectural and interior design. The company also runs The York Children's Foundation, a nonprofit division that donates portions of casket sales to charitable children's organizations nationwide. In May of 2001, York is purchased by Matthews International Inc., the largest maker of cremation urns and bronze memorials in the United States.

Company Beginnings

The York name can be traced back to 1892 when the company was a wooden horse-drawn carriage manufacturer in York, Pennsylvania. At the dawn of the century, York Wagon Gear Company literally changed gears when it switched from manufacturing wagon bodies to hardwood caskets. For the next 60 years the company (now called York Hoover due to an earlier acquisition) continued to make hardwood caskets, when it was bought by the Simmons Mattress Co., who also owned Elgin Metal Caskets.

Ten years later, Simmons was acquired by Gulf + Western, who in turn bought several other casket companies. Gulf then sold these to Amedco, a manufacturing company, in 1982, and in 1986 Amedco was acquired by Service Corporation International (SCI), the nation's largest funerary services company.

In 1990, SCI decided to return to its core business of funeral services and cemeteries. They sold two of its casket divisions: the Distribution division, which became Houston Casket Co., and the Supply division, which was sold to a group of independent investors who incorporated as York. The group paid $55 million for a new start of selling caskets in Houston.

Rapid Acquisitions Focus of First Years

During its first few years, York operated as a supplier of wood and metal caskets through about 60 domestic distributors, who in turn sold the caskets to funeral directors. The funeral industry was booming by 1996 with death-care stocks in general showing attractive gains. The death rate in the U.S. was rising by 0.8 percent a year and was forecasted to rise by 1.4 percent after 2040. However, because caskets were sold mainly by local funeral directors, competition was soft. Often funeral homes clustered around other funerary services such as embalmers or cemeteries, which cut down on costs, but which also limited their proximity to customers. With a $6 to $8 billion industry at hand, York saw a significant opportunity and quickly got started with a rapid growth plan.

In 1996 the company completed its initial public offering (IPO) of stock at $13 a share, raising $29.9 million. With this capital the company began to expand through acquisitions, starting with acquiring their own distributors. This opened the door for expanding their product base as well. While it broadened the company, one analyst deemed their moves as "low-risk acquisitions that don't give you a lot of bang for your buck." However, York was expanding according to plan.

The next year was pivotal for York as the business grew. They created a former-SCI reunion when they acquired the Houston Casket Company. Soon after, they bought West Point Casket Co., a metal- and cloth-covered casket manufacturer, adding one more type of casket to their product line. West Point distributed both their own caskets and York's in seven Southern states. Venturing into California for its potential sales—due to its higher death rate than most of the nation—York then bought the Sacramento Casket Co. Branching out into the growing cremation industry, they purchased Elder Davis, Inc., also a cloth-covered casket and cremation container manufacturer. These purchases allowed York to reach a whole new customer need and to extend their product offering, a move that "... expands the full complement of products and programs we offer, serving both funeral and cremation customers," said President and CEO Bill W. Wilcock in a press release. By 1997 the company was producing 300,000 caskets and 200,000 casket components each year, and with all their acquisitions they had operations in ten states: Missouri, Georgia, Alabama, Kentucky, North Carolina, Florida, New Mexico, Texas, California, and Louisiana.

The later 1990s continued to see rapid growth for the company. In March 1998 they acquired Colonial Guild, Ltd., a company that specialized in bronze memorials and commemorative products. This marked York's foray into products other than caskets. That year, they also acquired Cercueil Lauzier, Inc., establishing the company's first foothold in Canada. Cercueil Lauzier manufactured wood caskets. In 1999, York added another metal casket business to their family when they bought Star Manufacturing Corporation of Indiana. York moved the product manufacturing to their other production facilities but kept the distribution intact.

New Burial Options Threaten Traditional Casket Sales

The middle of the 1990s brought new challenges to the funeral industry. The Internet provided an opportunity for discounters to sell lower-priced caskets, undercutting funeral directors' prices. No expensive showrooms meant lower overhead. Large discount stores, including some found in shopping malls, also entered the marketplace. While a traditional funeral-home funeral cost an average of about $5,000, discounters and Internet sellers were offering simpler funerals and caskets for as little as half that amount. One Internet seller, Casket Royale, even called itself the "Wal-Mart of the funeral industry." Other business threats included growing interests by consumers in biodegradable caskets, custom-decorated caskets, and cremation.

By 1999, one in four burials involved cremation. The number of cremations had been rising one percentage point a year and was forecasted to continue increasing. Cemeteries also started encroaching on funeral directors' traditional markets by offering flowers and burial ceremonies. Customers were becoming more

interested in simpler, non-traditional ceremonies, or sometimes no ceremony at all. Cemeteries were willing to offer different options. Even though by 1999, discount casket sales totaled less than $35,000 a year in a $10 billion industry, the threat was enough to cause funeral directors to demand some regulations from the Federal Trade Commission (FTC). They wanted the same strict regulations on sales, manufacturing, and quality that were imposed on the traditional funeral industry.

York had to face these new challenges in the marketplace at the same time they had to deal with challenges within their own company as it struggled with the very expansion it had spawned. At the end of 1999, the company carried $80 million in debt, partly due to massive loans and rapid growth. As a result, York closed the Star Manufacturing plant in Indiana that it had acquired a year earlier, paying $4.5 million in severance expenses, and absorbing the product production into their other manufacturing plants.

In February 1998, York suffered another blow when they lost their contract with Service Corporation International. SCI was Houston's largest funeral home and cemetery company, and its purchases accounted for about 24 percent of York's revenues. In a major setback for York, SCI had decided to buy all its caskets from Hillenbrand, York's biggest competitor. Consequently, York's stock plunged 32 percent. To accommodate the lost revenue, York planned to concentrate on its remaining business with independent funeral homes. Reflecting on these times (before he was at the helm), CEO Tom Crawford attributed the troubles to "[the company growing] too far, too fast in [its] desire to become a larger organization and overran the capabilities of the management and information systems."

During the 1990s, the funeral industry had been evolving toward a higher awareness of customer service and satisfaction. York adapted to these changes by tapping into consumers' desires for a more personal touch in their casket buys. One example was York's introduction of caskets that buyers could personalize with handwritten messages. (Examples of other popular casket offerings of the time included custom-designed vinyl casket art, novelty caskets, and themed-caskets.) New product lines were emerging at trade shows annually, even though historically casket models lasted 10 to 15 years on the market. With York's new write-on casket and the earlier purchase of cremation container manufacturer Elder Davis, the company started to gain a foothold in the growing custom casket and cremation markets. However, the real boon for York came in 1997 with a concept that overhauled the funeral business itself.

Revamping the Casket Business: The York Merchandising System

As the choices in the death-care industry became more abundant and traditional practices were threatened by consumers' changing attitudes, it became apparent a change was needed in the funerary sales business. Since York was barely keeping its second-place position to Batesville, they decided to bring in extra help.

The York Merchandising Systems (YMS) was the brainchild of Alton F. Doody, who based the practice on systems he'd seen in Europe. Up to this point, traditional funeral homes and casket

Key Dates:

1990: York Group is formed by a group of private investors after the sell-off of casket businesses by Service Corporation International (SCI).

1996: York Group goes public; later acquires The Doody Group, Inc.

1997: The company acquires Sacramento Casket Co. and Houston Casket Co.

1997: York Group introduces The York Merchandising Systems (YMS), which displays caskets in a non-traditional way.

1998: The company acquires Colonial Guild, Ltd. and Cercueil Lauzier, Inc.

2000: Wilbert Inc. tries to take over company and Tom Crawford is the appointed CEO.

2001: Matthews International Corporation purchases The York Group.

makers had displayed full coffins in stark rooms; the first move Doody made was to create a showcase system that featured partial caskets, drawers of lining material, and displays of hardware. By using this system casket sellers could remove the harsh reality of a full coffin from the buyer, while maximizing their space for more options. The prevailing theory behind it was that consumers, when given a wide range of choices, would gravitate toward the higher-priced goods.

After unsuccessfully pitching the idea to Batesville, Doody turned to York, who bought Doody's consulting company. They gave the concept a name and pitched it to morticians. It was a hard sell at first. Morticians were used to full caskets and traditional setups. The costs in overhauling a funeral home were substantial. And morticians did not like that they could not sell other casket brands. The concept had a slow start.

But once funeral directors took a chance on the system, favorable results were apparent. Those who employed the systems lauded them. Large inventories of full caskets were gone. Personalization was easier, since caskets were made to order. One funeral director called it the "first new innovation in caskets in 75 years," in a *Wall Street Journal* article. York's first 50 displays showed an average gain of $438 per sale under the new system, with the next batch following suit. Some funeral directors also found they could create a more-friendly atmosphere with additions such as coffee bars, bookstores, greeting cards, and memorial items. By 2000 more than 500 funeral homes were using the York system.

Wilbert Inc. Tries to Take Over

New CEO Tom Crawford had a lot to manage when he took charge of York in March 2000. That month, Wilbert Inc. proposed to buy York by investing $6.50 per share, 40.5 percent above the market price. Based in Illinois, Wilbert was the world's largest burial vault company. They were already the largest shareholders of York stock with 14.1 percent. Wilbert also wished to replace the entire board of York with six of its own members.

York mulled over the offer for several months, even bringing in a financial advisor to assess their situation. Industry analysts noted the absence of a shareholder meeting date and proxy filing early on, causing speculation that York was considering the Wilbert offer. But in May, the company sold its metal vault business to Doric Products, Inc., reducing York's debt to $30 million from $40 million. Wilbert Inc. increased their offering price to $7.75 per share. York indicated that they were exploring several options, including merging with another firm, staying independent, or not taking any action. In September, York rejected Wilbert's offer. York CEO Crawford said the deal was "inadequate and substantially undervalues" the York company.

When the talks fell through, Wilbert bought an additional 11 percent of York in a continued attempt to gain control of the business. They then offered individual shareholders the opportunity to sell their shares to Wilbert for 39 percent higher than York's closing price of $4.69 on March 16, 2001, a year after Wilbert's first acquisitions attempt. They also offered to swap York shares for Wilbert shares. While the York stock jumped, the company still spurned Wilbert thanks in part to a shareholder rights plan, called a "poison pill," that was designed to fend off hostile takeover attempts. Exercisable only in the event that a group or company acquired more than 15 percent of York stock, the plan entitled York shareholders to purchase York stock in bulk and also acquire stock in the acquiring company at 50 percent of its market price. In Security Exchange Commission (SEC) documents filed by York in December 2001, explaining its rejection of Wilbert's offer, the company stated, "We believe continuing to pursue discussions with Wilbert is not in the best interest of York's shareholders."

The Future of York and Matthews International

The Wilbert ordeal had taken its toll. York's stock dropped 29 percent in 2000. CEO Crawford was at the helm of a company that needed refinancing strategies and some new plans. He started by taking a $10 million write-off for the fourth quarter of 2001 and sold 32 of York's distribution centers. (Three-quarters of the company's caskets were sold through independent distributors anyway.). "We primarily are manufacturers," said CFO Dan Malone.

York had another plan fermenting when in early 2001 the company announced that Matthews International Corporation had bought York for $10 a share, marking Matthews International's foray into the casket business. Matthews also bought the commemorative products division of York for $45 million. Fresh on the heels of the unsuccessful Wilbert takeover bid, it was a move that surprised the industry, though Crawford indicated in *Today in Deathcare* that they had established a relationship with Matthews as early as 1996. Matthews, based in Pittsburgh, Pennsylvania, was a leading designer of custom identification products and made 60 percent of the industry's bronze grave markers and cremation urns, including Hall of Fame plaques and Elvis Presley's grave marker at Graceland. They also produced printing plates, pre-press services, imaging systems, mausoleums, cremators, and other memorialization products. In 2000 they made *Forbes* magazine's "Eleven to Watch" list as one of the country's most promising companies.

The company had set a goal to reduce net debt to $30 million by the end of May 2001, and when Matthews bought the company a few weeks later the debt was reduced to zero. Now York could focus on building their casket business while battling new challenges in an evolving industry. "Our priorities continue to be executing our strategic plan, organizing the company's assets in the most efficient way possible, improving our cash flow, strengthening our organization and refinancing [debt]," said Crawford in a *Houston Business Journal* article in late 2000.

With refocused attention, the York Merchandising System was expanded, and plans to offer more features to the Funeral Resource Center concept were made. The company started to think about a new direction in the death-care industry, called "pre-need." This new direction involved advance sales of caskets and specific burial insurance, as well as other prepayment practices and funding plans.

The next few years looked to be lucrative for the death-care industry as the nation's 78 million Baby Boomers aged. The National Funeral Directors Association estimated that annual deaths would increase 50 percent by 2020, to three million a year. Given those statistics, and given new challenges in the sales market, and a new parent company, York plans to expect many new challenges in the years to come.

Principal Divisions

The Doody Group, Inc.; Elder Davis; York Agency, Inc.; The York Children's Foundations.

Principal Competitors

Hillenbrand Industries; Rock of Ages; DirectCasket.com.

Further Reading

Ahles, Andrea, "Making Its Mark: Casket Maker Builds on Tradition," *Houston Chronicle*, August 16, 1997, p. B1.

Anton, Nelson, "Bye-Bye SCI/Funeral Giant Drops York Group," *Houston Chronicle*, February 7, 1998, p. B1.

Beachy, Debra, "Hillenbrand to Buy SCI Unit," *Houston Chronicle*, November 21, 1989, p. 1.

Cecil, Mark, "York Employs Hostile Takeover Defenses," *Mergers & Acquisitions Journal*, May 1, 2001, http://web.lexis-nexis.com.

Charleton, Linda, "FTC Asks Rules to Curb Funeral Home Practices," *The New York Times*, August 29, 1975, p.1.

Davies, Dick, "Helping People Pay 'Tribute,' " *The Muskegon Chronicle*, March 22, 2000, p. D1.

"Deal for Coffin Maker," *The New York Times*, May 25, 2001, p. C6.

Elder, Laura Elizabeth, "York Group Acquiring Casket Distributors," *Houston Business Journal*, March 28, 1997, http://houston.bcentral.com.

Fixmer, Rob, "Discounted Urns and No Overhead," *The New York Times*, December 28, 1998, p. C3.

"FTC Crackdown Is Urged on the Funeral Industry," *The New York Times*, August 17, 1977, p. 86.

Glanton, Eileen, "Eleven to Watch," *Forbes*, October 30, 2000, pp. 194–218.

Greer, Jim, "Casketmaker Buries Deal for Sell-Off," *Houston Business Journal*, May 14, 2001, http://houston.bizjournals.com.

——, "Funeral Firm Buys York Stock after Casket Maker Buries Merger," *Houston Business Chronicle*, September 29, 2000, p. 16.

Hopkins, Jim, "Technology Changes Casket Makers' Work," Tech Report, *USA Today*, November 12, 2000, http://www.usatoday.com.

"Houston Casket Maker Being Sold," *Houston Chronicle*, May 24, 2001, p. C2.

Johnson, Kelly, "Local Casket Firm Sells Up," *Sacramento Business Journal*, November 14, 1997, http://sacramento.bcentral.com.

Kirkpatrick, Keith, "No Funeral Needed for Casket Maker," *Going Public, the IPO Reporter*, April 8, 1996, p. 6.

Lewine, Edward, "Thinking Ahead," *The New York Times*, October 13, 1996, p. 13-A.

Morse, Dan, "Cold Comfort," *The Wall Street Journal*, January 7, 2000, p. A1.

Parker, Suzi, "Get Your Laws off My Coffin!," *Salon.com*, January 12, 2001, http://www.salon.com.

Patterson, Demetrius, "Funeral Industry Sees Boom," *Seattle Times*, February 6, 1994, p. A6.

"Plant Closes," *Houston Business Journal*, July 28, 2000, p. A34.

Siwolop, Sana, "Mortality Wears a Profitable, Noncyclical Edge," *The New York Times*, March 30, 1997, pp. 3–4.

Tahmincioglu, Eve, "Funeral Homes Branch Out to Catch No-Frills Wave," *The New York Times*, April 30, 2000, p. 3.16.

"Will York Bury the Hatchet with Wilbert?" *Mergers & Acquisitions Report*, May 21, 2001, http://www.mareport.com.

Willing, Richard, "Net Poses Challenge for Funeral Industry," Tech Report, *USA Today*, October 8, 1999, http://www.usatoday.com.

Wyman, Thomas P., "Death a Way of Life in Small, Southeastern Indiana Town," *Seattle Times*, September 6, 1998, p. A13.

Yardley, Jim, "Savings Are Large, but Some Find the Setup Unnerving," *The New York Times*, May 29, 1998, p. B1.

Yip, Pamela, "SCI Finds a Buyer for Casket Division," *Houston Chronicle*, February 23, 1990, p. 1.

"York Group Buys Colonial Guild," *The Wall Street Journal*, March 18, 1998, p. B7D.

"York Group Inc. Stock Plunges 32% on Loss of Service Corp.," *The Wall Street Journal*, February 9, 1998, p. B4.

"York Group to Close Indiana Casket Plant," *Houston Chronicle*, July 22, 2000, p. C2.

"York Holders Wooed after Company Rebuffs Merger," *The New York Times*, March 20, 2001, p. C4.

"York Is Determined Not to Go Gently into Wilbert's Grasp," *Mergers & Acquisitions Report*, April 2, 2001, http://www.mareport.com.

—Kerri DeVault

Zumtobel AG

Höchster 8
A-6850 Dornbirn
Austria
Telephone: +43 (5572) 390-575
Fax: +43 (5572) 390-602
Web site: http://www.zumtobel.com

Private Company
Incorporated: 1976
Employees: 9,515 (2001 est.)
Sales: EUR 1.3 billion (2001 est.)
NAIC: 335122 Commercial, Industrial, and Institutional
Electric Lighting Fixture Manufacturing

Zumtobel AG has emerged as Europe's leading supplier of commercial, industrial and public sector lighting fixtures and components. Starting as a post-World War II manufacturer of fluorescent light ballasts, the Austrian holding company now oversees five autonomous operating units: Thorn, Zumtobel Staff, Tridonic Atco, Luxmate Controls and Reiss International. Together these companies manufacture and market lighting systems for hospitals, stadiums, tunnels, airports, office buildings, factories, museums, and similar facilities. The zealous pursuit of export markets and product innovation—plus acquisitions and mergers—has enabled family-owned Zumtobel to climb to the top. The usually quiet company made its biggest splash in 2000 when it acquired UK-based conglomerate Wassall and its important subsidiary Thorn Lighting Group. Industry analysts believe the nearly $1 billion deal made Zumtobel the largest lighting company in Europe, surpassing Dutch lighting giant Philips.

1950: Walter Zumtobel Saw Fluorescent Future

Austrian-born Walter Zumtobel (1907–1990) provided the technical aptitude, determination and charisma that launched Zumtobel. Enrolling at Munich Technical University in 1924, Zumtobel earned a doctorate in engineering there eight years later. During his studies, he met Gertrude Kappler, his future wife. In 1934, Zumtobel became plant manager of a German-owned company in Vienna that manufactured gas masks and gas filters. When Germany, under Adolph Hitler, annexed Austria in 1938, Zumtobel's work shifted to designing a high-altitude breathing system for German fighter pilots. In 1943, with the war in Europe well underway, he became general operations manager for another German company in Vienna that produced electrical components for the military.

After Germany surrendered to the Allies in 1945, Zumtobel—never a member of Germany's National Socialist party—was appointed by French occupation forces as administrator for three local German-owned manufacturing companies in Austria. One was the electric component company Michel-Werke, located in Hard. Zumtobel saw limited prospects for these company's products. But the energetic engineer did detect a budding opportunity in fluorescent lighting. Using one-fifth the energy of incandescent lights, fluorescent lamps had been developed prior to World War II, and were just making their marketplace debut in the late 1940s. In 1950, in his hometown in Dornbirn, he founded Elektrogeräte und Kunstharzpreßwerk W. Zumtobel KG/, a partnership with his wife. Housing the business in two rented rooms, Zumtobel planned to produce starters and ballasts, key fluorescent light components.

In the early days of fluorescent lights, the starter functioned as a switch to deliver electricity to electrodes at each end of the tube-shaped lamp. The ballast served as a transformer, providing an initial electric arc that started a current flowing through ionized gases contained in a lamp. Critical to Zumtobel's business plan was his license to manufacture an improved starter developed by the Swiss lighting company Knobel AG. Whereas conventional starters often required flipping a switch two or three times to light the lamp, the Knobel starter consistently triggered the lamp the first time. Zumtobel's interest in the more reliable starter illustrated his enthusiasm for innovation and gaining a technology edge on his competition. A year later, he had already improved on the idea by developing ballast that incorporated the starter.

At the end of his first year in business, Zumtobel had 31 employees, an Austrian sales network, and sales totaling 1.32 million Austrian schillings (ATS). In spring 1951, the company opened its first production plant in Dornbirn. Michel-Werke, which Zumtobel began leasing in 1950, also relocated into the

Company Perspectives:

Using light to create worlds of experience—this is the corporate mission of the Zumtobel group. Our products and services are designed to make an innovative contribution to raising the quality of the spaces we live in, while conserving the resources of our natural environment through reduced usage of materials, intelligent control technology, user-friendliness and timeless design. Together with its various partners, the Zumtobel group is targeting global leadership. The key to our success lies in consistent attention to customer requirements, proactive cooperation with our partners in a spirit of mutual trust, and confidence in the commitment and competence of our employees. Our top-priority values are: technology leadership, an unshakeable faith in creativity and innovation, and growing the value of the Zumtobel group in the medium- to long-term. Our objective of becoming global market leader as an innovative supplier of quality lighting components, lighting solutions and lighting management systems, means that each division of Zumtobel AG faces its own demanding strategic objectives.

new building. At the start of 1953, Zumtobel's two companies merged and began operating under a shorter name: W. Zumtobel KG.

1952: Debut of First Light Fixture

Zumtobel soon decided to build complete fluorescent light fixtures—also called "batten luminaries"—in addition to ballasts. His inspiration came from two sources. One was the costly cancellation of a large ballast order for a Vienna railway station lighting project, exposing the young company's single product vulnerability. The other was the suggestion from his corporate ballast customers—Siemens and AEG—that he build light fixtures they could sell through their catalogs. At the risk of competing with these powerful German patrons, the company developed its first complete Zumtobel light fixture in 1952. Sold under the brand name Profilux, the fixtures carried the first company patents and were marketed as "the slimmest batten luminaries in the world." The Profilux line proved a market success. Zumtobel developed a moisture-proof version the following year. Then versions that included louvers, lenses, and a one-man installation rail that made it easy to attach to the ceiling.

Zumtobel ballast design kept moving ahead as well. Using a random wiring and transverse interleaving, Zumtobel engineer Ernst Wiesner in 1957 developed the new LXG ballast that required less copper and silenced the humming often associated with fluorescent lighting. Most leading lighting component manufacturers soon adopted the breakthrough. The late 1950s also saw light experiments begin in the company's first light laboratory located inside a Dornbirn barn with painted black walls.

By the mid-1950s, neighboring Germany and Switzerland had already become export markets for the company, partly due to Walter Zumtobel's regular and engaging appearances at trade fairs. But Zumtobel especially concentrated on Germany, the largest national market in Europe. He exhibited company products for first time at the 1958 Hanover Fair, the country's annual high-profile industrial design showcase. He also established a sales company in Munich that same year, then another in Lindau in 1959.

At the end of its first decade, and by offering the lighting products Europe needed for the rebuilding process, Zumtobel looked like it had survived the business startup frenzy that followed the war. Zumtobel ended the 1959/1960 fiscal year with an average of 323 employees on the payroll, and sales of ATS 47.6 million.

1960s: Product Line Expands

Company growth continued in all directions in early 1960s. New production facilities were added at the main Dornbirn plant, and the growing employee population led to company-sponsored sports clubs and even a volunteer fire brigade. New sales offices with showrooms opened in Austria. The company began producing its first recessed ceiling lights and track lighting. To define lighting effects and more precisely plan lighting solutions, color charts came into use to test the reflecting properties of walls and surfaces.

Second-generation Zumtobel family members also began to join the company. Jürg Zumtobel (1936–), Walter Zumtobel's oldest son, took over production planning in 1961. Younger son Fritz Zumtobel (1939–) joined the company in 1966. Walter Zumtobel not only added family, but he also added specialized companies during this period. To offset the lack of suppliers in post-war Austria, he bought nearby toolmaking and machine shops. In 1964, he co-founded Electro-Terminal to produce junction and power supply boxes, terminal blocks and strips, and other "connection technology."

Development of fiberglass-reinforced polyester fixtures—which resisted impacts, corrosion, water and fire—helped make Zumtobel a supplier for tunnel lighting projects, starting with the Karaj Tunnel near Teheran, Iran, in 1962. Product evolvement also moved ahead in 1967 with the successor to the Profilux fluorescent fixtures. Designed for industrial settings, the "Z System" included a variety of reflectors, optics, and grilles. In 1969, Zumtobel introduced the first European "air-handling" lights that removed lighting heat along with warm air from the room. The cooled lamps also yielded better light.

The increasing production of light fixtures—many of them earning industrial design awards—prompted an organizational change at Zumtobel. The company created separate lighting and ballast development departments in 1968. At the same time, the company simplified its name, dropping the "W" and settling on Zumtobel KG. At the end of the 1969/1970 fiscal year, sales for the company year had reached ATS 277.3 million and the average employee count totaled 820.

1970s: Beyond Bavaria

Zumtobel celebrated its 20th anniversary in 1970. The anniversary event coincided with the opening of yet another new production plant in Dornbirn. Ballast evolution moved ahead in the early 1970s with introduction of the LXYG, a compact unit with fewer parts and built on a highly automated production line. Improvements also were made to tunnel light fixtures, metal vapor HID lamps, and flat recessed lights used with false ceilings. Zumtobel also worked with office furniture makers—without marketable results—on developing small flat illuminators that fit into chairs and desks.

Zumtobel extended its market even further beyond Bavarian country borders during this period. In 1970, the company acquired a small stake in a Spanish light manufacturer and, in 1976, purchased a 24 percent stake in British lighting company Tridonic. In 1973 it established an Italian sales company in Bolzano. That same year it crossed into the southern hemisphere, acquiring a 20 percent stake in an Australian ballast producer Soltra, with an agreement to manufacture Zumtobel lighting components at a new plant in Sydney. The production work at Soltra was later moved to a new Australian venture, Atco Controls. In 1976, Zumtobel slipped into the South African market creating a subsidiary lighting company in Johannesburg.

Zumtobel ventured into other new territory, too. It opened its first computer center in 1973 to handle bookkeeping. In 1978, it began using desktop computers to handle complex lighting calculations. The company also adopted an electronics focus. In 1979,

it established an Electronic Components Department and, in conjunction with Vienna Technical University, started development work on electronic ballasts. And, the company pondered its first sizeable merger. Serious merger talks began with German light fixture company Staff, a strong industry player that developed the Variolux electronic phase dimmer and innovative track lighting and spotlight systems. Walter Zumtobel eventually balked at the cost of acquiring Staff, however.

The oil crisis and global recession in 1973 caused Zumtobel management to reassess the company and consider a new diversification strategy. Management consultants presented the idea of creating four autonomous company divisions and allowing executives outside the family manage them. The company took a first step in that direction in 1974 by creating the Luminaires, Electrical Components, Toolmaking, and Investment divisions. It took another step in December 1976, when it incorporated as Zumtobel AG. The restructuring paved the way for professional outside management to help run the company. Walter Zumtobel was elected chairman of the new management board. Zumtobel executives Jürg Zumtobel, Fritz Zumtobel, Walter Dünser, and Helmut Hutter were appointed board members. At the end of the 1969/70 fiscal year, Zumtobel had sales of ATS 824.2 million and employment averaged 1,189.

1980s: Design Focus Elevated

At a development meeting in 1979, Walter Zumtobel suggested elevating design elements in Zumtobel light fixtures. Company management agreed, and product development gained a strong aesthetic orientation in the 1980s. The company sought out notable industrial designers to fashion its fixtures and began to sponsor symposiums and exhibitions related to lighting design issues. In the mid-1980s, the company began working closely with German lighting designer Hans T. von Malotki and Ettore Sottsass' Italian design studio. The design emphasis was later extended to corporate communications, with top graphic artists contracted to prepare Zumtobel annual reports.

During the decade, the company also pushed forward in research, production automation, and cutting-edge products. Zumtobel debuted its EC magnetic ballast in 1980. Over the next two decades, more than 403 million units were built at plants in Austria, South Africa, and Australia. Contracts for electronic ballasts were also being signed, with lighting projects at Innsbruck railway station (1983) and Frankfurt/Main airport (1984) among the first to use them. Other high-profile projects included lighting systems for a new BMW plant at Steyr, Austria, and the control center of the nuclear power plant in Leibstadt, Switzerland. Zumtobel light fixtures, and their designers, garnered a raft of awards over the period.

Corporate changes during this time carried less impact than the previous decade's. Retiring as chairman of the company's management board, and from day-to-day involvement in the company, Walter Zumtobel became chairman of the supervisory board of Zumtobel AG in 1981. Jürg Zumtobel took over as chairman of the management board. The company adopted its first mission statement in 1989, and it continued to invest in computer technology. Computer-aided design (CAD) workstations came to Zumtobel in 1984 following the company's development of the lightning design software package Cophos. Over time, Cophos became a standard tool in the lighting industry. Zumtobel also worked with the regional government to create a CAD training center at the company in 1987. Company employees were among the instructors.

Zumtobel established new sales companies in Great Britain in 1983 and Spain in 1989. In 1984, the company also arrived in the U.S., opening a sales office in Garfield, New Jersey. Five years later it would build a light fixture production facility there. Political uncertainty prompted Zumtobel to decrease its presence elsewhere. It combined its South African operations with other companies to minimize risks and sold its interest in an Iranian lighting company. At the end of the 1989/1990 fiscal year, Zumtobel revenues totaled ATS 3,123.4 and employment had averaged 2,654. The company also said goodbye to founder Walter Zumtobel, who died in 1990.

1990s: Transition to Holding Company

At the turn of the decade, Zumtobel management and its consultants concluded that European lighting industry was heading toward the same kind of consolidation seen in the U.S., where five lighting suppliers had cornered 65 percent of market. They decided changes were required if Zumtobel wanted to become a dominant supplier in Europe. "The decisive step came in 1989 when a strategic analysis conducted in conjunction with external consultants revealed that we were too big to retreat into the role of a niche provider, but still far too small to hold our own in the face of the foreseeable market trends," explained board chairman Jürg Zumtobel in an interview in *Light Years*, Zumtobel's corporate history. "Our only option was to adopt a proactive expansion strategy."

Management's "expansion strategy" mirrored the restructuring that occurred in the mid-1970s but took it to another level. The plan called for repositioning Zumtobel as a holding company and transforming the Luminaires and Electrical Components divisions into independent operating companies. The changeover occurred in 1991, with the Luminaire Division becoming Zumtobel Licht and the components divisions taking the name of subsidiary Tridonic. Jürg Zumtobel became chairman of the holding company, which retained the Zumtobel AG name. Other members of the executive board were Fritz Zumtobel and Walter Dünser. Fritz Zumtobel assumed the chairman title in 1996.

A mergers and acquisition binge followed the reorganization. In 1993, Zumtobel Licht succeeded in bringing long-coveted German light manufacturer Staff into the fold by acquiring a majority stake. Staff transferred the remaining shares to Zumtobel in 1994, and two years later Zumtobel Licht was renamed Zumtobel Staff. The merger brought a critical product sector—display lighting—to Zumtobel.

In 1996, Tridonic took over the Swiss lighting component manufacturer Knobel AG, which had licensed its starter technology to Walter Zumtobel in 1950. In 1998 the Australian company Atco Controls came under the wing of Tridonic, which changed its name to Tridonic Atco. The Luxmate electronic lighting management system, jointly developed by Tridonic and Zumtobel Licht, had made its debut in 1992. By 1998, Luxmate Controls had become a separate operating company of the Zumtobel group, focusing on lighting management services that improve energy efficiency and automatically adjust lighting levels. Finally, the group acquired the German lighting manufacturer Reiss International as a subsidiary in 1999.

The company meanwhile continued to pursue new markets. Sales offices were opened in Sweden in 1990 and, following the reunification of Germany, the East German city of Jena in 1991. Zumtobel Staff added the first Asian sales offices in Hong Kong and Kuala Lumpur in 1997 and in Norway in 1999. New products included the Orea waveguide luminaire, which helped drive the trend for glare-free workplace lighting. Awards and honors rolled in again during the 1990s for Zumtobel products and their designers.

2000: Zumtobel Doubles in Size

Zumtobel entered the new millennium proposing the largest merger in the European lighting industry, and one that would make it among the largest lighting companies in the world. On February 11, 2000, Zumtobel and international financial investment group Kholberg, Kravis Roberts (KKR) announced it had made an offer for the British mini-conglomerate Wassal. Wassal subsidiary Thorn Lighting Group—Europe's second largest light fixture maker—was Zumtobel's target. The corporate strategy was to bring Thorn's outdoor and airfield lighting segments into the group to round out its product and service portfolio and gain access to the company's core markets in the U.K., France, Scandinavia, and the Far East. A Zumtobel corporate fact sheet stated that with the addition of Thorn the company had attained "the global critical mass required for future market success."

The European Commission sanctioned the merger and Zumtobel acquired Wassal two months later. Zumtobel immediately integrated Thorn as an autonomous operating company. The transaction gave KKR a 34 percent holding, leaving the Zumtobel family with a 66 percent majority holding. Thorn's lighting component manufacturer, Atlas, was folded into Tridonic Atco. Overnight, Zumtobel almost doubled its volume of business. Sales for the group rose almost 94 percent to ATS 18.4 billion (EUR 1.33 billion). The employee count rose to an annual average of 9,515.

Looking Ahead

Strategic product innovation, market development, and corporate restructuring propelled Zumtobel into the new century as a powerful international player in the lighting industry. Looking forward, the company had begun to anticipate new industry movements. Management recognized the impact of new lamp technology such as T5 fluorescents, LEDs (light-emitting diodes), and ceramic metal halides, and the trend toward using indirect general office lighting. And, while the company had yet to establish itself in the huge North American market, it was casting an optimistic eye toward South America.

Principal Operating Units

Thorn; Zumtobel Staff; Tridonic Atco; Luxmate Controls; Reiss International.

Principal Competitors

Siemens AG (OSRAM SYLVANIA); Koninklijke Philips Electronics N.V. (Philips Lighting); General Electric Company (GE Lighting); SLI, Inc.

Further Reading

Dawley, Heidi, ''Storming Fortress Europe,'' *Business Week Online*, October 16, 2000, http://www.businessweek.com.

Dorman, Paul, ''Austrian Link-up Ahead as Wassall Backs KKR Offer,'' *The Times (London)*, February 12, 2000, *Lexis-Nexis Academic Universe*, accessed March 26, 2002, http://www.lexis-nexis.com/universe.

Harris, Tom ''How Fluorescent Lamps Work,'' *How Stuff Works*, accessed March 15, 2002, http://www.howstuffworks.com/fluorescent-lamp.htm.

''Kohlberg Kravis Buys Britain's Wassall PLC in $998.7 Million Deal,'' *Wall Street Journal*, February 14, 2000. p. B16.

''Light Management,'' *Der Standard*, May 15, 1999, p.6.

Riewoldt, Otto, ed. *Light Years: Zumtobel, 2000–1950*, Basel, Switzerland: Birkhäuser, 2000.

Yee, Roger, ''Light the Way,'' *Architecture*, December 2001, p. 28.

Zumtobel, Jürg, ''Of Courage and Change,'' *Zumtobel AG Editorial*, accessed March 15, 2002, *http://www.zumtobel.com.*

''Zumtobel AG Invests Sch760m,'' *Wirtschaftsblatt*, November 3, 1999, p. 2.

''Zumtobel Announces Opening of U.S. Manufacturing Plant,'' *Business Wire*, June 9, 1989, *Lexis-Nexis Academic Universe*, accessed March 26, 2002, http://www.lexis-nexis.com/universe.

''Zumtobel Turns On the Light in the U.S.,'' *Wirtschaftsblatt,* August 29, 1998, p. 8.

—Doug Cooley

INDEX TO COMPANIES

Index to Companies

Listings in this index are arranged in alphabetical order under the company name. Company names beginning with a letter or proper name such as Eli Lilly & Co. will be found under the first letter of the company name. Definite articles (The, Le, La) are ignored for alphabetical purposes as are forms of incorporation that precede the company name (AB, NV). Company names printed in bold type have full, historical essays on the page numbers appearing in bold. Updates to entries that appeared in earlier volumes are signified by the notation **(upd.)**. Company names in light type are references within an essay to that company, not full historical essays. This index is cumulative with volume numbers printed in bold type.

Bozell, Jacobs, Kenyon, and Eckhardt Inc. *See* True North Communications Inc.
Bozell Worldwide Inc., 25 89–91
Bozkurt, **27** 188
Bozzuto's, Inc., 13 111–12
BP. *See* British Petroleum Company PLC.
BP Amoco plc, **31** 31, 34; **40** 358
BP Canada. *See* Talisman Energy Inc.
BP p.l.c., 45 46–56 (upd.), 409, 412
BPB, **III** 736
BPD, **13** 356
BPI Communications, Inc., **7** 15; **19** 285; **27** 500
BR. *See* British Rail.
Braas, **III** 734, 736
Braathens ASA, 47 60–62
Brabant, **III** 199, 201
Brabazon, **III** 555
Brach and Brock Confections, Inc., 15 63–65; 29 47
Brad Foote Gear Works, **18** 453
Bradbury Agnew and Co., **IV** 686
Braden Manufacturing, **23** 299–301
Bradford District Bank, **II** 333
Bradford Exchange Ltd. Inc., **21** 269
Bradford Insulation Group, **III** 687
Bradford Pennine, **III** 373
Bradlees Discount Department Store Company, II 666–67; **12 48–50; 24** 461
Bradley Lumber Company, **8** 430
Bradley Producing Corp., **IV** 459
Bradstreet Co., **IV** 604–05; **19** 133
Braegen Corp., **13** 127
Bragussa, **IV** 71
BRAINS. *See* Belgian Rapid Access to Information Network Services.
Brake Bros plc, 45 57–59
Bramalea Ltd., 9 83–85; 10 530–31
Brambles Industries Limited, III 494–95; **24** 400; **42 47–50**
Bramco, **III** 600
Bramwell Gates, **II** 586
Bran & Lübbe, **III** 420
Brand Companies, Inc., **9** 110; **11** 436
Branded Restaurant Group, Inc., **12** 372
Brandeis & Sons, **19** 511
Brandenburgische Motorenwerke, **I** 138
Brandt Zwieback-Biskuits GmbH, **44** 40
Brandywine Asset Management, Inc., **33** 261
Brandywine Holdings Ltd., **45** 109
Brandywine Insurance Agency, Inc., **25** 540
Brandywine Iron Works and Nail Factory, **14** 323
Brandywine Valley Railroad Co., **14** 324
Braniff Airlines, **I** 97, 489, 548; **II** 445; **6** 50, 119–20; **16** 274; **17** 504; **21** 142; **22** 406; **36** 231; **50** 523
Branigar Organization, Inc., **IV** 345
Brannock Device Company, 48 68–70
Brascade Resources, **IV** 308
Brascan Ltd., **II** 456; **IV** 165, 330; **25** 281
Braspetro, **IV** 454, 501–02
Brass Craft Manufacturing Co., **III** 570; **20** 361
Brass Eagle Inc., 34 70–72
Brasseries Kronenbourg, **II** 474–75
Braswell Motor Freight, **14** 567
Braud & Faucheux. *See* Manitou BF S.A.
Brauerei Beck & Co., 9 86–87; 33 73–76 (upd.)
Braun, **III** 29; **17** 214–15; **26** 335

Braunkohlenwerk Golpa-Jessnitz AG, **IV** 230
Brauns Fashions Corporation. *See* Christopher & Banks Corporation.
Brazilian Central Bank, **IV** 56
Brazos Gas Compressing, **7** 345
Brazos Sportswear, Inc., 23 65–67
Breakstone Bros., Inc., **II** 533
Breakthrough Software, **10** 507
Breckenridge-Remy, **18** 216
Breco Holding Company, **17** 558, 561
Bredel Exploitatie B.V., **8** 546
Bredell Paint Co., **III** 745
Bredero's Bouwbedrijf of Utrecht, **IV** 707–08, 724
BREED Technologies, Inc., **22** 31
Breedband NV, **IV** 133
Brega Petroleum Marketing Co., **IV** 453, 455
Breguet Aviation, **I** 44; **24** 86
Breitenburger Cementfabrik, **III** 701
Bremer Financial Corp., 45 60–63
Bremner Biscuit Co., **II** 562; **13** 426
Brenco Inc., **16** 514
Brenda Mines Ltd., **7** 399
Brennan College Services, **12** 173
Brenntag AG, 8 68–69, 496; **23 68–70 (upd.)**, **23** 453–54
Brent Walker Ltd., **49** 450–51
Brentwood Associates Buyout Fund II LP, **44** 54
Bresler's Industries, Inc., **35** 121
Breslube Enterprises, **8** 464
Bresser Optik, **41** 264
Brewster Lines, **6** 410
Breyers Ice Cream Co. *See* Good Humor-Breyers.
BRI Bar Review Institute, Inc., **IV** 623; **12** 224
BRI International, **21** 425
Brian Mills, **V** 118
Briarpatch, Inc., **12** 109
Brickwood Breweries, **I** 294
Bricorama, **23** 231
Bricotruc, **37** 259
Bridas S.A., **24** 522
Bridel, **19** 49–50; **25** 85
Bridge Communications Inc., **34** 442–43
Bridge Oil Ltd., **I** 438; **50** 200
Bridge Technology, Inc., **10** 395
Bridgeman Creameries, **II** 536
Bridgeport Brass, **I** 377
Bridgeport Machines, Inc., 17 52–54
Bridgestone Corporation, V 234–35; 15 355; **20** 262; **21 72–75 (upd.)**
Bridgestone Liquefied Gas, **IV** 364
Bridgestone/Firestone, **19** 454, 456
Bridgeway Plan for Health, **6** 186
Bridgford Company, **13** 382
Bridgford Foods Corporation, 27 71–73
Brier Hill, **IV** 114
Brierly Investment Limited, **19** 156; **24** 399
Briggs & Stratton Corporation, III 597; **8 70–73; 27 74–78 (upd.)**
Briggs and Lundy Lumber Cos., **14** 18
Brigham's Inc., **15** 71
Bright Horizons Family Solutions, Inc., 31 71–73
Bright of America Inc., **12** 426
Bright Star Technologies, **13** 92; **15** 455; **41** 362
Brighter Vision Learning Adventures, **29** 470, 472

Brighton & Hove Bus and Coach Company, **28** 155–56
Brighton Federal Savings and Loan Assoc., **II** 420
Brightpoint, Inc., 18 74–77
Brightwork Development Inc., **25** 348
Briker, **23** 231
Brillion Iron Works Inc., **23** 306
Brimsdown Lead Co., **III** 680
Brin's Oxygen Company Limited. *See* BOC Group plc.
Brinco Ltd., **II** 211
Brink's, Inc., **IV** 180–82; **19** 319
Brinker International, Inc., 10 176–78; 18 438; **38 100–03 (upd.)**
Brinson Partners Inc., **41** 198
BRIntec, **III** 434
Brinton Carpets, **III** 423
BRIO AB, 24 81–83
Brio Technology, **25** 97
Briones Alonso y Martin, **42** 19
Brisbane Gas Co., **III** 673
Brisco Engineering, **41** 412
Bristol Aeroplane, **I** 50, 197; **10** 261; **24** 85
Bristol-BTR, **I** 429
Bristol-Erickson, **13** 297
Bristol Gaming Corporation, **21** 298
Bristol Hotel Company, 23 71–73; 38 77
Bristol-Myers Squibb Company, I 26, 30, 37, 301, 696, 700, 703; **III 17–19**, 36, 67; **IV** 272; **6** 27; **7** 255; **8** 210, 282–83; **9 88–91 (upd.)**; **10** 70; **11** 289; **12** 126–27; **16** 438; **21** 546; **25** 91, 253, 365; **32** 213; **34** 280, 282, 284; **37 41–45 (upd.); 50** 538
Bristol PLC, **IV** 83
Bristol-Siddeley, Ltd., **I** 50; **24** 85
Britannia Airways, **8** 525–26
Britannia Security Group PLC, **12** 10
Britannia Soft Drinks Limited, **38** 77
Britannica Software, **7** 168
Britannica.com, **39** 140, 144
Britches of Georgetowne, **10** 215–16
BRITE. *See* Granada Group PLC.
Brite Voice Systems, Inc., 20 75–78
BriteSmile, Inc., **35** 325
British & Commonwealth Shipping Company, **10** 277
British Aerospace plc, **48** 81, 274
British Aerospace plc, I 42, 46, **50–53**, 55, 74, 83, 132, 532; **III** 458, 507; **V** 339; **7** 9, 11, 458–59; **8** 315; **9** 499; **11** 413; **12** 191; **14** 36; **18** 125; **21** 8, 443; **24 84–90 (upd.); 27** 474
British Airways plc, I 34, 83, **92–95**, 109; **IV** 658; **6** 60, 78–79, 118, 132; **14 70–74 (upd.); 18** 80; **22** 52; **24** 86, 311, 396, 399–400; **26** 115; **27** 20–21, 466; **28** 25, 508; **31** 103; **33** 270; **34** 398; **37** 232; **38 104–05; 39** 137–38; **43 83–88 (upd.)**
British Aluminium, Ltd., **II** 422; **IV** 15
British American Cosmetics, **I** 427
British American Financial Services, **42** 450
British American Insurance Co., **III** 350
British American Nickel, **IV** 110
British-American Tobacco Co., Ltd.,
British American Tobacco PLC, V 396, 401–02, 417; **9** 312; **29** 194–95; **34** 39; **49** 367, 369; **50 116–19 (upd.)**
British and Foreign Marine, **III** 350

Tuboscope, **42** 420

Tucker, Lynch & Coldwell. *See* CB Commercial Real Estate Services Group, Inc.

TUCO, Inc., **8** 78

Tucson Electric Power Company, **V** 713; **6 588–91**; **42** 388

Tucson Gas & Electric, **19** 411–12

Tuesday Morning Corporation, **18 529–31**

Tuff Stuff Publications, **23** 101

TUI. *See* Touristik Union International GmbH. and Company K.G.

TUI Group GmbH, **42** 283; **44 432–35**

Tuileries et Briqueteries d'Hennuyeres et de Wanlin, **14** 249

TUJA, **27** 21

Tultex Corporation, **13 531–33**

Tumbleweed, Inc., **33 412–14**

Tunhems Industri A.B., **I** 387

Tunisair. *See* Société Tunisienne de l'Air-Tunisair.

Tupolev Aviation and Scientific Technical Complex, **24 58–60**

Tupperware Corporation, **I** 29; **II** 534; **III** 610–12;, **15** 475, 477; **17** 186; **18** 67; **28 478–81**

Turbinbolaget, **III** 419

Turbine Engine Asset Management LLC, **28** 5

TurboLinux Inc., **45** 363

Turcot Paperboard Mills Ltd., **17** 281

Turkish Engineering, Consultancy and Contracting Corp., **IV** 563

Turkish Petroleum Co. *See* Türkiye Petrolleri Anonim Ortakliği.

Türkiye Garanti Bankasi, **I** 479

Türkiye Petrolleri Anonim Ortakliği, **IV** 464, 557–58, **562–64**; **7** 352

Turnbull, **III** 468

Turner Broadcasting System, Inc., **II** 134, 149, 161 **166–68**; **IV** 676; **6 171–73 (upd.)**; **7** 64, 99, 306, 529; **23** 33, 257; **25** 313, 329, 498; **28** 71; **30** 100; **47** 272

The Turner Corporation, **8 538–40**; **23 485–88 (upd.)**; **25** 402; **33** 197

Turner Entertainment Co., **18** 459

Turner Glass Company, **13** 40

Turner Network Television, **21** 24

Turner's Turkeys, **II** 587

Turnstone Systems, **44** 426

TURPAS, **IV** 563

Turtle Wax, Inc., **15 506–09**; **16** 43; **26** 349

Tuscarora Inc., **17** 155; **29 483–85**

Tussauds Group Ltd., **IV** 659

Tutt Bryant Industries PLY Ltd., **26** 231

Tuttle, Oglebay and Company. *See* Oglebay Norton Company.

TV & Stereo Town, **10** 468

TV Asahi, **7** 249

TV Azteca, S.A. de C.V., **39** 194–95, **398–401**

TV Food Network, **22** 522

TV Guide, Inc., **43 431–34 (upd.)**

TVA. *See* Tennessee Valley Authority.

TVE. *See* Television Española, S.A.

TVE Holdings, **22** 307

TVH Acquisition Corp., **III** 262, 264

TVI, Inc., **15 510–12**

TVN Entertainment Corporation, **32** 239

TVS Entertainment PLC, **13** 281

TVW Enterprises, **7** 78

TVX, **II** 449; **13** 449

TW Kutter, **III** 420

TW Services, Inc., **II 679–80**; **10** 301–03

TWA. *See* Trans World Airlines *and* Transcontinental & Western Airways.

Tweco Co., **19** 441

Tweeds, **12** 280

Tweeter Home Entertainment Group, Inc., **30 464–66**; **41** 379, 381

Twen-Tours International, **II** 164

Twentieth Century Fox Film Corporation, **II** 133, 135, 146, 155–56, **169–71**, 175; **IV** 652; **7** 391–92; **12** 73, 322, 359; **15** 23, 25, 234; **25** 327, **490–94 (upd.)**; **43** 173; **46** 311

Twentsche Bank, **II** 183

"21" International Holdings, **17** 182

21 Invest International Holdings Ltd., **14** 322

21st Century Food Products. *See* Hain Food Group, Inc.

21st Century Mortgage, **18** 28

Twenty-Second National Bank, **II** 291

Twenty-third Publications, **49** 48

24/7 Real Media, Inc., **49 421–24**

TWI. *See* Trans World International.

Twin City Wholesale Drug Company, **14** 147

Twin Disc, Inc., **21 502–04**

Twin Hill Acquisition Company, Inc., **48** 286

Twining Crosfield Group, **II** 465; **13** 52

Twinings' Foods International, **II** 465–66; **III** 696

Twinings Tea, **41** 31

Twinlab Corporation, **34 458–61**

Twinpak, **IV** 250

Two Guys, **12** 49

2-in-1 Shinola Bixby Corp., **II** 497

21st Century Mortgage, **41** 18, 20

TWW Plc, **26** 62

TXEN, Inc., **18** 370

TXL Oil Corp., **IV** 552

TXP Operation Co., **IV** 367

Ty-D-Bol, **III** 55

Ty Inc., **33 415–17**

Tyco International Ltd., **21** 462; **28 482–87 (upd.)**; **30** 157; **44** 6; **50** 135

Tyco Laboratories, Inc., **III 643–46**; **13** 245–47

Tyco Submarine Systems Ltd., **32** 217

Tyco Toys, Inc., **12 494–97**; **13** 312, 319; **18** 520–21; **25** 314

Tyler Corporation, **23 489–91**

Tymnet, **18** 542

Tyndall Fund-Unit Assurance Co., **III** 273

Typhoo Tea, **II** 477

Typpi Oy, **IV** 469

Tyrolean Airways, **9** 233; **33** 50

Tyrväan Oy, **IV** 348

Tyskie Brewery, **24** 450

Tyson Foods, Inc., **II 584–85**; **7** 422–23, 432; **14 514–16 (upd.)**; **21** 535; **23** 376, 384; **26** 168; **39** 229; **50 491–95 (upd.)**

U.C.L.A.F. *See* Roussel-Uclaf.

U-Haul International Inc. *See* Amerco.

U.K. Corrugated, **IV** 296; **19** 226

U.S. Aggregates, Inc., **42 390–92**

U.S. Appliances, **26** 336

U.S. Bancorp, **12** 165; **14 527–29**; **36 489–95 (upd.)**

U.S. Bank of Washington, **14** 527

U.S. Banknote Company, **30** 43

U.S. Bearings Company. *See* Federal-Mogul Corporation.

U.S. Billing, Inc. *See* Billing Concepts Corp.

U.S. Biomedicals Corporation, **27** 69

U.S. Bioscience, Inc., **35** 286, 288

U.S. Borax, Inc., **42 393–96**

U.S. Brass., **24** 151

U.S. Can Corporation, **30 474–76**

U.S. Cellular Corporation, **31 449–452 (upd.)**

U.S. Computer of North America Inc., **43** 368

U.S. Delivery Systems, Inc., **22** 153, **531–33**; **47** 90. *See also* Velocity Express Corporation.

U.S. Electrical Motors, **II** 19

U.S. Elevator Corporation, **19** 109–11

U.S. Envelope, **19** 498

U.S. Food Products Co., **I** 376

U.S. Foodservice, **26 503–06**; **37** 374, 376

U.S.G. Co., **III** 762

U.S. Generating Company, **26** 373

U.S. Geological Survey, **9** 367

U.S. Graphite. *See* Wickes Inc.

U.S. Guarantee Co., **III** 220; **14** 108

U.S. Healthcare, Inc., **6 194–96**; **21** 16

U.S. Home Corporation, **8 541–43**

U.S. Industries, Inc., **7** 208; **18** 467; **23** 296; **24** 150; **27** 288

U.S. Intec, **22** 229

U.S. International Reinsurance, **III** 264

U.S. Investigations Services Inc., **35** 44

U.S. Land Co., **IV** 255

U.S. Lawns, **31** 182, 184

U.S. Life Insurance, **III** 194

U.S. Lines, **I** 476; **III** 459; **11** 194

U.S. Lock Corporation, **9** 543; **28** 50–52

U.S. Long Distance Corp. *See* Billing Concepts Corp.

U.S. Marine Corp., **III** 444

U.S. News and World Report Inc., **30 477–80**

U.S. Office Products Company, **25 500–02**; **41** 69, 247; **47** 91

U.S. Overall Company, **14** 549

U.S. Plywood Corp. *See* United States Plywood Corp.

U.S. Realty and Improvement Co., **III** 98

U.S. RingBinder Corp., **10** 313–14

U.S. Robotics Inc., **9 514–15**; **20** 8, 69; **22** 17; **24** 212; **34** 444; **36** 122, 357; **48** 369; **49** 184

U.S. Rubber Company, **I** 478; **10** 388

U.S. Satellite Broadcasting Company, Inc., **20 505–07**

U.S. Satellite Systems, **III** 169; **6** 285

U.S. Shoe Corporation, **43** 98; **44** 365

U.S. Smelting Refining and Mining, **7** 360

U.S. Software Inc., **29** 479

U.S. Steel Corp. *See* United States Steel Corp.

U.S. Telephone Communications, **9** 478

U.S. Tile Co., **III** 674

U.S. Timberlands Company, L.P., **42 397–400**

U.S. Time Corporation, **13** 120

U.S. Trust Co. of New York, **II** 274

U.S. Trust Corp., **17 496–98**

U.S. Vanadium Co., **9** 517

U.S. Venture Partners, **15** 204–05

U.S. Vitamin & Pharmaceutical Corp., **III** 55

INDEX TO INDUSTRIES

Index to Industries

SkyWest, Inc., 25
Société Tunisienne de l'Air-Tunisair, 49
Southwest Airlines Co., 6; 24 (upd.)
Spirit Airlines, Inc., 31
Sun Country Airlines, 30
Swiss Air Transport Company, Ltd., I
Swiss International Air Lines Ltd., 48
TAP—Air Portugal Transportes Aéreos
  Portugueses S.A., 46
Texas Air Corporation, I
Thai Airways International Public
  Company Limited, 6; 27 (upd.)
Tower Air, Inc., 28
Trans World Airlines, Inc., I; 12 (upd.); 35
  (upd.)
TransBrasil S/A Linhas Aéreas, 31
Transportes Aereos Portugueses, S.A., 6
TV Guide, Inc., 43 (upd.)
UAL Corporation, 34 (upd.)
United Airlines, I; 6 (upd.)
US Airways Group, Inc., 28 (upd.)
USAir Group, Inc., I; 6 (upd.)
VARIG S.A. (Viação Aérea Rio-
  Grandense), 6; 29 (upd.)
WestJet Airlines Ltd., 38

AUTOMOTIVE

AB Volvo, I; 7 (upd.); 26 (upd.)
Adam Opel AG, 7; 21 (upd.)
Aisin Seiki Co., Ltd., 48 (upd.)
Alfa Romeo, 13; 36 (upd.)
Alvis Plc, 47
American Motors Corporation, I
Applied Power Inc., 32 (upd.)
Arvin Industries, Inc., 8
Automobiles Citroen, 7
Automobili Lamborghini Holding S.p.A.,
  13; 34 (upd.)
AutoNation, Inc., 50
Bajaj Auto Limited, 39
Bayerische Motoren Werke AG, I; 11
  (upd.); 38 (upd.)
Bendix Corporation, I
Blue Bird Corporation, 35
Bombardier Inc., 42 (upd.)
Borg-Warner Automotive, Inc., 14; 32
  (upd.)
The Budd Company, 8
CARQUEST Corporation, 29
Chrysler Corporation, I; 11 (upd.)
CNH Global N.V., 38 (upd.)
Consorcio G Grupo Dina, S.A. de C.V., 36
CSK Auto Corporation, 38
Cummins Engine Company, Inc., I; 12
  (upd.); 40 (upd.)
Custom Chrome, Inc., 16
Daihatsu Motor Company, Ltd., 7; 21
  (upd.)
Daimler-Benz A.G., I; 15 (upd.)
DaimlerChrysler AG, 34 (upd.)
Dana Corporation, I; 10 (upd.)
Deere & Company, 42 (upd.)
Delphi Automotive Systems Corporation,
  45
Don Massey Cadillac, Inc., 37
Donaldson Company, Inc., 49 (upd.)
Douglas & Lomason Company, 16
Ducati Motor Holding S.p.A., 30
Eaton Corporation, I; 10 (upd.)
Echlin Inc., I; 11 (upd.)
Edelbrock Corporation, 37
Federal-Mogul Corporation, I; 10 (upd.);
  26 (upd.)
Ferrari S.p.A., 13; 36 (upd.)
Fiat SpA, I; 11 (upd.); 50 (upd.)
FinishMaster, Inc., 24

Ford Motor Company, I; 11 (upd.); 36
  (upd.)
Ford Motor Company, S.A. de C.V., 20
Fruehauf Corporation, I
General Motors Corporation, I; 10 (upd.);
  36 (upd.)
Gentex Corporation, 26
Genuine Parts Company, 9; 45 (upd.)
GKN plc, 38 (upd.)
Harley-Davidson Inc., 7; 25 (upd.)
Hayes Lemmerz International, Inc., 27
The Hertz Corporation, 33 (upd.)
Hino Motors, Ltd., 7; 21 (upd.)
Hometown Auto Retailers, Inc., 44
Honda Motor Company Limited (Honda
  Giken Kogyo Kabushiki Kaisha), I; 10
  (upd.); 29 (upd.)
Insurance Auto Auctions, Inc., 23
Isuzu Motors, Ltd., 9; 23 (upd.)
Kelsey-Hayes Group of Companies, 7; 27
  (upd.)
Kia Motors Corporation, 12; 29 (upd.)
Lear Seating Corporation, 16
Les Schwab Tire Centers, 50
Lithia Motors, Inc., 41
Lotus Cars Ltd., 14
Lund International Holdings, Inc., 40
Mack Trucks, Inc., I; 22 (upd.)
The Major Automotive Companies, Inc., 45
Masland Corporation, 17
Mazda Motor Corporation, 9; 23 (upd.)
Mel Farr Automotive Group, 20
Metso Corporation, 30 (upd.)
Midas International Corporation, 10
Mitsubishi Motors Corporation, 9; 23
  (upd.)
Monaco Coach Corporation, 31
Monro Muffler Brake, Inc., 24
National R.V. Holdings, Inc., 32
Navistar International Corporation, I; 10
  (upd.)
Nissan Motor Co., Ltd., I; 11 (upd.); 34
  (upd.)
O'Reilly Automotive, Inc., 26
Officine Alfieri Maserati S.p.A., 13
Oshkosh Truck Corporation, 7
Paccar Inc., I
PACCAR Inc., 26 (upd.)
Pennzoil Company, 20 (upd.)
Pennzoil-Quaker State Company, 50 (upd.)
Penske Corporation, 19 (upd.)
The Pep Boys—Manny, Moe & Jack, 11;
  36 (upd.)
Peugeot S.A., I
Piaggio & C. S.p.A., 20
Porsche AG, 13; 31 (upd.)
PSA Peugeot Citroen S.A., 28 (upd.)
Regie Nationale des Usines Renault, I
Renault S.A., 26 (upd.)
Republic Industries, Inc., 26
The Reynolds and Reynolds Company, 50
Robert Bosch GmbH., I; 16 (upd.); 43
  (upd.)
RockShox, Inc., 26
Rockwell Automation, 43 (upd.)
Rolls-Royce plc, I; 21 (upd.)
Rover Group Ltd., 7; 21 (upd.)
Saab Automobile AB, 32 (upd.)
Saab-Scania A.B., I; 11 (upd.)
Safelite Glass Corp., 19
Saturn Corporation, 7; 21 (upd.)
Sealed Power Corporation, I
Sheller-Globe Corporation, I
Sixt AG, 39
Skoda Auto a.s., 39
Spartan Motors Inc., 14
SpeeDee Oil Change and Tune-Up, 25
SPX Corporation, 10; 47 (upd.)

Standard Motor Products, Inc., 40
Superior Industries International, Inc., 8
Suzuki Motor Corporation, 9; 23 (upd.)
Sytner Group plc, 45
Tower Automotive, Inc., 24
Toyota Motor Corporation, I; 11 (upd.); 38
  (upd.)
TRW Inc., 14 (upd.)
Ugly Duckling Corporation, 22
United Auto Group, Inc., 26
United Technologies Automotive Inc., 15
Valeo, 23
Volkswagen Aktiengesellschaft, I; 11
  (upd.); 32 (upd.)
Walker Manufacturing Company, 19
Winnebago Industries Inc., 7; 27 (upd.)
Woodward Governor Company, 49 (upd.)
ZF Friedrichshafen AG, 48
Ziebart International Corporation, 30

BEVERAGES

A & W Brands, Inc., 25
Adolph Coors Company, I; 13 (upd.); 36
  (upd.)
Allied Domecq PLC, 29
Allied-Lyons PLC, I
Anchor Brewing Company, 47
Anheuser-Busch Companies, Inc., I; 10
  (upd.); 34 (upd.)
Asahi Breweries, Ltd., I; 20 (upd.)
Bacardi Limited, 18
Banfi Products Corp., 36
Baron Philippe de Rothschild S.A., 39
Bass PLC, I; 15 (upd.); 38 (upd.)
BBAG Osterreichische Brau-Beteiligungs-
  AG, 38
Beringer Wine Estates Holdings, Inc., 22
The Boston Beer Company, Inc., 18; 50
  (upd.)
Brauerei Beck & Co., 9; 33 (upd.)
Brown-Forman Corporation, I; 10 (upd.);
  38 (upd.)
Cadbury Schweppes PLC, 49 (upd.)
Canandaigua Brands, Inc., 34 (upd.)
Canandaigua Wine Company, Inc., 13
Carlsberg A/S, 9; 29 (upd.)
Carlton and United Breweries Ltd., I
Casa Cuervo, S.A. de C.V., 31
Cerveceria Polar, I
The Chalone Wine Group, Ltd., 36
Clearly Canadian Beverage Corporation, 48
Coca Cola Bottling Co. Consolidated, 10
The Coca-Cola Company, I; 10 (upd.); 32
  (upd.)
Corby Distilleries Limited, 14
D.G. Yuengling & Son, Inc., 38
Dean Foods Company, 21 (upd.)
Delicato Vineyards, Inc., 50
Distillers Company PLC, I
Dr Pepper/Seven Up, Inc., 9; 32 (upd.)
E. & J. Gallo Winery, I; 7 (upd.); 28 (upd.)
Ferolito, Vultaggio & Sons, 27
Florida's Natural Growers, 45
Foster's Brewing Group Ltd., 7; 21 (upd.)
Foster's Group Limited, 50 (upd.)
Fuller Smith & Turner P.L.C., 38
G. Heileman Brewing Company Inc., I
The Gambrinus Company, 40
Geerlings & Wade, Inc., 45
General Cinema Corporation, I
Golden State Vintners, Inc., 33
Grand Metropolitan PLC, I
Green Mountain Coffee, Inc., 31
The Greenalls Group PLC, 21
Greene King plc, 31
Grupo Modelo, S.A. de C.V., 29
Guinness/UDV, I; 43 (upd.)

Praxair, Inc., 11
Quantum Chemical Corporation, 8
Reichhold Chemicals, Inc., 10
Rhodia SA, 38
Rhône-Poulenc S.A., I; 10 (upd.)
Robertet SA, 39
Rohm and Haas Company, I; 26 (upd.)
Roussel Uclaf, I; 8 (upd.)
RPM, Inc., 36 (upd.)
RWE AG, 50 (upd.)
The Scotts Company, 22
SCP Pool Corporation, 39
Sequa Corp., 13
Shanghai Petrochemical Co., Ltd., 18
Sigma-Aldrich Corporation, 36 (upd.)
Solvay & Cie S.A., I; 21 (upd.)
Stepan Company, 30
Sterling Chemicals, Inc., 16
Sumitomo Chemical Company Ltd., I
Takeda Chemical Industries, Ltd., 46 (upd.)
Terra Industries, Inc., 13
Teva Pharmaceutical Industries Ltd., 22
Total Fina Elf S.A., 50 (upd.)
TOTAL S.A., 24 (upd.)
Ube Industries, Ltd., 38 (upd.)
Union Carbide Corporation, I; 9 (upd.)
Univar Corporation, 9
The Valspar Corporation, 32 (upd.)
Vista Chemical Company, I
Witco Corporation, I; 16 (upd.)
Zeneca Group PLC, 21

CONGLOMERATES

Accor SA, 10; 27 (upd.)
AEG A.G., I
Alcatel Alsthom Compagnie Générale d'Electricité, 9
Alco Standard Corporation, I
Alexander & Baldwin, Inc., 40 (upd.)
Alfa, S.A. de C.V., 19
Allied Domecq PLC, 29
Allied-Signal Inc., I
AMFAC Inc., I
The Anschutz Corporation, 36 (upd.)
Aramark Corporation, 13
ARAMARK Corporation, 41
Archer-Daniels-Midland Company, I; 11 (upd.)
Arkansas Best Corporation, 16
Associated British Ports Holdings Plc, 45
BAA plc, 33 (upd.)
Barlow Rand Ltd., I
Bat Industries PLC, I
Berkshire Hathaway Inc., 42 (upd.)
Bond Corporation Holdings Limited, 10
BTR PLC, I
Bunzl plc, 31 (upd.)
Burlington Northern Santa Fe Corporation, 27 (upd.)
Business Post Group plc, 46
C. Itoh & Company Ltd., I
Cargill, Incorporated, 13 (upd.); 40 (upd.)
CBI Industries, Inc., 7
Chemed Corporation, 13
Chesebrough-Pond's USA, Inc., 8
CITIC Pacific Ltd., 18
Colt Industries Inc., I
Compagnie Financiere Richemont AG, 50
The Connell Company, 29
CSR Limited, 28 (upd.)
Daewoo Group, 18 (upd.)
De Dietrich & Cie, 31
Deere & Company, 21 (upd.)
Delaware North Companies Incorporated, 7
Desc, S.A. de C.V., 23
The Dial Corp., 8
EBSCO Industries, Inc., 40 (upd.)

El Corte Inglés Group, 26 (upd.)
Elders IXL Ltd., I
Engelhard Corporation, 21 (upd.)
Farley Northwest Industries, Inc., I
Fimalac S.A., 37
First Pacific Company Limited, 18
Fisher Companies, Inc., 15
Fletcher Challenge Ltd., 19 (upd.)
FMC Corporation, I; 11 (upd.)
Fortune Brands, Inc., 29 (upd.)
Fuqua Industries, Inc., I
General Electric Company, 34 (upd.)
GIB Group, 26 (upd.)
Gillett Holdings, Inc., 7
Grand Metropolitan PLC, 14 (upd.)
Great American Management and Investment, Inc., 8
Greyhound Corporation, I
Grupo Carso, S.A. de C.V., 21
Grupo Industrial Bimbo, 19
Gulf & Western Inc., I
Hagemeyer N.V., 39
Hankyu Corporation, 23 (upd.)
Hanson PLC, III; 7 (upd.)
Hitachi, Ltd., I; 12 (upd.); 40 (upd.)
Hutchison Whampoa Limited, 18; 49 (upd.)
IC Industries, Inc., I
Ilitch Holdings Inc., 37
Inchcape PLC, 16 (upd.); 50 (upd.)
Ingram Industries, Inc., 11; 49 (upd.)
Instituto Nacional de Industria, I
International Controls Corporation, 10
International Telephone & Telegraph Corporation, I; 11 (upd.)
Istituto per la Ricostruzione Industriale, I
ITOCHU Corporation, 32 (upd.)
Jardine Matheson Holdings Limited, I; 20 (upd.)
Jason Incorporated, 23
Jefferson Smurfit Group plc, 19 (upd.)
The Jim Pattison Group, 37
Jordan Industries, Inc., 36
Justin Industries, Inc., 19
Kanematsu Corporation, 24 (upd.)
Kao Corporation, 20 (upd.)
Katy Industries, Inc., I
Kesko Ltd. (Kesko Oy), 8; 27 (upd.)
Kidde plc, 44 (upd.)
Kidde, Inc., I
KOC Holding A.S., I
Koninklijke Nedlloyd N.V., 26 (upd.)
Koor Industries Ltd., 25 (upd.)
K2 Inc., 16
The L.L. Knickerbocker Co., Inc., 25
Lancaster Colony Corporation, 8
Larry H. Miller Group, 29
Lear Siegler, Inc., I
Lefrak Organization Inc., 26
Leucadia National Corporation, 11
Litton Industries, Inc., I; 11 (upd.)
Loews Corporation, I; 12 (upd.); 36 (upd.)
Loral Corporation, 8
LTV Corporation, I
LVMH Moët Hennessy Louis Vuitton SA, 33 (upd.)
Marubeni Corporation, 24 (upd.)
Marubeni K.K., I
MAXXAM Inc., 8
McKesson Corporation, I
Menasha Corporation, 8
Metallgesellschaft AG, 16 (upd.)
Metromedia Co., 7
Minnesota Mining & Manufacturing Company (3M), I; 8 (upd.); 26 (upd.)
Mitsubishi Corporation, I; 12 (upd.)
Mitsubishi Heavy Industries, Ltd., 40 (upd.)

Mitsui & Co., Ltd., 28 (upd.)
Mitsui Bussan K.K., I
The Molson Companies Limited, I; 26 (upd.)
Montedison S.p.A., 24 (upd.)
NACCO Industries, Inc., 7
National Service Industries, Inc., 11
New World Development Company Limited, 38 (upd.)
Nichimen Corporation, 24 (upd.)
Nissho Iwai K.K., I
Norsk Hydro A.S., 10
Novar plc, 49 (upd.)
Ogden Corporation, I
Onex Corporation, 16
Orkla A/S, 18
Park-Ohio Industries Inc., 17
Pentair, Inc., 7
Philip Morris Companies Inc., 44 (upd.)
Poliet S.A., 33
Powell Duffryn plc, 31
Power Corporation of Canada, 36 (upd.)
Preussag AG, 17
Pubco Corporation, 17
Pulsar Internacional S.A., 21
R.B. Pamplin Corp., 45
The Rank Organisation Plc, 14 (upd.)
Red Apple Group, 23
Roll International Corporation, 37
Rubbermaid Incorporated, 20 (upd.)
Samsung Group, I
San Miguel Corporation, 15
Sara Lee Corporation, 15 (upd.)
Schindler Holding AG, 29
Sea Containers Ltd., 29
Seaboard Corporation, 36
ServiceMaster Inc., 23 (upd.)
Sime Darby Berhad, 14; 36 (upd.)
Société du Louvre, 27
Standex International Corporation, 17; 44 (upd.)
Stinnes AG, 23 (upd.)
Sudbury Inc., 16
Sumitomo Corporation, I; 11 (upd.)
Swire Pacific Ltd., I; 16 (upd.)
Talley Industries, Inc., 16
Tandycrafts, Inc., 31
TaurusHolding GmbH & Co. KG, 46
Teledyne, Inc., I; 10 (upd.)
Tenneco Inc., I; 10 (upd.)
Textron Inc., I; 34 (upd.)
Thomas H. Lee Co., 24
Thorn Emi PLC, I
Thorn plc, 24
TI Group plc, 17
Time Warner Inc., IV; 7 (upd.)
Tokyu Corporation, 47 (upd.)
Tomen Corporation, 24 (upd.)
Tomkins plc, 11; 44 (upd.)
Toshiba Corporation, I; 12 (upd.); 40 (upd.)
Tractebel S.A., 20
Transamerica–An AEGON Company, I; 13 (upd.); 41 (upd.)
The Tranzonic Cos., 15
Triarc Companies, Inc., 8
Triple Five Group Ltd., 49
TRW Inc., I; 11 (upd.)
Unilever, II; 7 (upd.); 32 (upd.)
United Technologies Corporation, 34 (upd.)
Universal Studios, Inc., 33
Valhi, Inc., 19
Valores Industriales S.A., 19
Veba A.G., I; 15 (upd.)
Vendôme Luxury Group plc, 27
Viacom Inc., 23 (upd.)
Virgin Group, 12; 32 (upd.)
W.R. Grace & Company, I; 50

ELECTRICAL & ELECTRONICS

ENGINEERING & MANAGEMENT SERVICES

ENTERTAINMENT & LEISURE

National Presto Industries, Inc., 43 (upd.)
National Sea Products Ltd., 14
Nestlé S.A., II; 7 (upd.); 28 (upd.)
New England Confectionery Co., 15
Newhall Land and Farming Company, 14
Newman's Own, Inc., 37
Nippon Meat Packers, Inc., II
Nippon Suisan Kaisha, Limited, II
Nisshin Flour Milling Company, Ltd., II
Northern Foods PLC, 10
Northland Cranberries, Inc., 38
Nutraceutical International Corporation, 37
NutraSweet Company, 8
Ocean Spray Cranberries, Inc., 7; 25 (upd.)
OJSC Wimm-Bill-Dann Foods, 48
Ore-Ida Foods Incorporated, 13
Oscar Mayer Foods Corp., 12
Otis Spunkmeyer, Inc., 28
Papetti's Hygrade Egg Products, Inc., 39
Parmalat Finanziaria SpA, 50
PepsiCo, Inc., 38 (upd.)
Perdue Farms Inc., 7; 23 (upd.)
Pet Incorporated, 7
Pez Candy, Inc., 38
Philip Morris Companies Inc., 18 (upd.)
PIC International Group PLC, 24 (upd.)
Pilgrim's Pride Corporation, 7; 23 (upd.)
Pillsbury Company, II; 13 (upd.)
Pioneer Hi-Bred International, Inc., 9
Pizza Inn, Inc., 46
Poore Brothers, Inc., 44
PowerBar Inc., 44
Prairie Farms Dairy, Inc., 47
Premium Standard Farms, Inc., 30
The Procter & Gamble Company, III; 8 (upd.); 26 (upd.)
Purina Mills, Inc., 32
Quaker Oats Company, II; 12 (upd.); 34 (upd.)
Quality Chekd Dairies, Inc., 48
Ralston Purina Company, II; 13 (upd.)
Ranks Hovis McDougall Limited, II; 28 (upd.)
Reckitt & Colman PLC, II
Reckitt Benckiser plc, 42 (upd.)
Rica Foods, Inc., 41
Rich Products Corporation, 7; 38 (upd.)
Riviana Foods Inc., 27
Roland Murten A.G., 7
Rowntree Mackintosh, II
Royal Numico N.V., 37
Russell Stover Candies Inc., 12
Sanderson Farms, Inc., 15
Sara Lee Corporation, II; 15 (upd.)
Savannah Foods & Industries, Inc., 7
Schlotzsky's, Inc., 36
Schwan's Sales Enterprises, Inc., 7
See's Candies, Inc., 30
Seminis, Inc., 29
Smithfield Foods, Inc., 7; 43 (upd.)
Snow Brand Milk Products Company, Ltd., II; 48 (upd.)
Sodiaal S.A., 36 (upd.)
SODIMA, II
Sorrento, Inc., 24
Spangler Candy Company, 44
Stock Yards Packing Co., Inc., 37
Stolt-Nielsen S.A., 42
Stouffer Corp., 8
Südzucker AG, 27
Suiza Foods Corporation, 26
Sun-Diamond Growers of California, 7
Sunkist Growers, Inc., 26
Supervalu Inc., 18 (upd.); 50 (upd.)
Suprema Specialties, Inc., 27
Sylvan, Inc., 22
Taiyo Fishery Company, Limited, II
Tasty Baking Company, 14; 35 (upd.)

Tate & Lyle PLC, II; 42 (upd.)
TCBY Enterprises Inc., 17
TDL Group Ltd., 46
Thomas J. Lipton Company, 14
Thorn Apple Valley, Inc., 7; 22 (upd.)
Thorntons plc, 46
TLC Beatrice International Holdings, Inc., 22
Tombstone Pizza Corporation, 13
Tone Brothers, Inc., 21
Tootsie Roll Industries Inc., 12
Tri Valley Growers, 32
Tropicana Products, Inc., 28
Tyson Foods, Inc., II; 14 (upd.); 50 (upd.)
U.S. Foodservice, 26
Uncle Ben's Inc., 22
Unigate PLC, II; 28 (upd.)
United Biscuits (Holdings) plc, II; 42 (upd.)
United Brands Company, II
United Foods, Inc., 21
Universal Foods Corporation, 7
Van Camp Seafood Company, Inc., 7
Vienna Sausage Manufacturing Co., 14
Vlasic Foods International Inc., 25
Wattie's Ltd., 7
Wells' Dairy, Inc., 36
White Wave, 43
OJSC Wimm-Bill-Dann Foods, 48
Wisconsin Dairies, 7
WLR Foods, Inc., 21
Wm. Wrigley Jr. Company, 7
World's Finest Chocolate Inc., 39
Worthington Foods, Inc., 14
YOCREAM International, Inc., 47

FOOD SERVICES & RETAILERS

Advantica Restaurant Group, Inc., 27 (upd.)
AFC Enterprises, Inc., 32 (upd.)
Albertson's, Inc., II; 7 (upd.); 30 (upd.)
Aldi Group, 13
Alex Lee Inc., 18; 44 (upd.)
America's Favorite Chicken Company, Inc., 7
American Stores Company, II
Applebee's International, Inc., 14; 35 (upd.)
ARA Services, II
Arby's Inc., 14
Arden Group, Inc., 29
Argyll Group PLC, II
Ark Restaurants Corp., 20
Asahi Breweries, Ltd., 20 (upd.)
Asda Group PLC, II
ASDA Group plc, 28 (upd.)
Associated Grocers, Incorporated, 9; 31 (upd.)
Association des Centres Distributeurs E. Leclerc, 37
Au Bon Pain Co., Inc., 18
Auchan, 37
Auntie Anne's, Inc., 35
Autogrill SpA, 49
Avado Brands, Inc., 31
Back Bay Restaurant Group, Inc., 20
Back Yard Burgers, Inc., 45
Bashas' Inc., 33
Bear Creek Corporation, 38
Benihana, Inc., 18
Big Bear Stores Co., 13
Big V Supermarkets, Inc., 25
Blimpie International, Inc., 15; 49 (upd.)
Bob Evans Farms, Inc., 9
Bon Appetit Holding AG, 48
Boston Chicken, Inc., 12
Boston Market Corporation, 48 (upd.)

Brinker International, Inc., 10; 38 (upd.)
Brookshire Grocery Company, 16
Bruno's, Inc., 7; 26 (upd.)
Buca, Inc., 38
Buffets, Inc., 10; 32 (upd.)
Burger King Corporation, II
C.H. Robinson, Inc., 11
California Pizza Kitchen Inc., 15
Cargill, Inc., II
Caribou Coffee Company, Inc., 28
Carlson Companies, Inc., 22 (upd.)
Carr-Gottstein Foods Co., 17
Casey's General Stores, Inc., 19
CBRL Group, Inc., 35 (upd.)
CEC Entertainment, Inc., 31 (upd.)
Chart House Enterprises, Inc., 17
Checkers Drive-Up Restaurants Inc., 16
The Cheesecake Factory Inc., 17
Chi-Chi's Inc., 13
Chicago Pizza & Brewery, Inc., 44
Chick-fil-A Inc., 23
Cinnabon Inc., 23
The Circle K Corporation, II
CKE Restaurants, Inc., 19; 46 (upd.)
Coborn's, Inc., 30
Compass Group PLC, 34
Comptoirs Modernes S.A., 19
Consolidated Products Inc., 14
Controladora Comercial Mexicana, S.A. de C.V., 36
The Cooker Restaurant Corporation, 20
The Copps Corporation, 32
Cracker Barrel Old Country Store, Inc., 10
D'Agostino Supermarkets Inc., 19
Dairy Mart Convenience Stores, Inc., 7; 25 (upd.)
Darden Restaurants, Inc., 16; 44 (upd.)
Dean & DeLuca, Inc., 36
Delhaize "Le Lion" S.A., 44
DeMoulas / Market Basket Inc., 23
DenAmerica Corporation, 29
Diedrich Coffee, Inc., 40
Domino's Pizza, Inc., 7; 21 (upd.)
Eateries, Inc., 33
Edeka Zentrale A.G., II; 47 (upd.)
Einstein/Noah Bagel Corporation, 29
El Chico Restaurants, Inc., 19
Elior SA, 49
Elmer's Restaurants, Inc., 42
Embers America Restaurants, 30
Etablissements Economiques du Casino Guichard, Perrachon et Cie, S.C.A., 12
Famous Dave's of America, Inc., 40
Fazoli's Systems, Inc., 27
Flagstar Companies, Inc., 10
Fleming Companies, Inc., II
Food Lion, Inc., II; 15 (upd.)
Foodarama Supermarkets, Inc., 28
Foodmaker, Inc., 14
The Fred W. Albrecht Grocery Co., 13
Fresh Choice, Inc., 20
Fresh Foods, Inc., 29
Friendly Ice Cream Corp., 30
Frisch's Restaurants, Inc., 35
Fuller Smith & Turner P.L.C., 38
Furr's Supermarkets, Inc., 28
Garden Fresh Restaurant Corporation, 31
The Gateway Corporation Ltd., II
Genuardi's Family Markets, Inc., 35
George Weston Limited, II; 36 (upd.)
Ghirardelli Chocolate Company, 30
Giant Food Inc., II; 22 (upd.)
Godfather's Pizza Incorporated, 25
Golden Corral Corporation, 10
Golden State Foods Corporation, 32
The Golub Corporation, 26
Gordon Food Service Inc., 8; 39 (upd.)
The Grand Union Company, 7; 28 (upd.)

HEALTH & PERSONAL CARE PRODUCTS

INFORMATION TECHNOLOGY

INSURANCE

MATERIALS

Daishowa Paper Manufacturing Co., Ltd., IV
Deltic Timber Corporation, 46
Dillard Paper Company, 11
Domtar Inc., IV
Enso-Gutzeit Oy, IV
Esselte Pendaflex Corporation, 11
Federal Paper Board Company, Inc., 8
FiberMark, Inc., 37
Fletcher Challenge Ltd., IV
Fort Howard Corporation, 8
Fort James Corporation, 22 (upd.)
Georgia-Pacific Corporation, IV; 9 (upd.); 47 (upd.)
Groupe Rougier SA, 21
Guilbert S.A., 42
Honshu Paper Co., Ltd., IV
International Paper Company, IV; 15 (upd.); 47 (upd.)
James River Corporation of Virginia, IV
Japan Pulp and Paper Company Limited, IV
Jefferson Smurfit Group plc, IV; 49 (upd.)
Jujo Paper Co., Ltd., IV
Kimberly-Clark Corporation, 16 (upd.); 43 (upd.)
Kruger Inc., 17
Kymmene Corporation, IV
Longview Fibre Company, 8; 37 (upd.)
Louisiana-Pacific Corporation, IV; 31 (upd.)
MacMillan Bloedel Limited, IV
The Mead Corporation, IV; 19 (upd.)
Metsa-Serla Oy, IV
Mo och Domsjö AB, IV
Monadnock Paper Mills, Inc., 21
Mosinee Paper Corporation, 15
Nashua Corporation, 8
National Envelope Corporation, 32
NCH Corporation, 8
Oji Paper Co., Ltd., IV
P.H. Glatfelter Company, 8; 30 (upd.)
Packaging Corporation of America, 12
Papeteries de Lancey, 23
Plum Creek Timber Company, Inc., 43
Pope and Talbot, Inc., 12
Potlatch Corporation, 8; 34 (upd.)
PWA Group, IV
Rayonier Inc., 24
Rengo Co., Ltd., IV
Reno de Medici S.p.A., 41
Rexam PLC, 32 (upd.)
Riverwood International Corporation, 11; 48 (upd.)
Rock-Tenn Company, 13
St. Joe Paper Company, 8
Sanyo-Kokusaku Pulp Co., Ltd., IV
Sappi Limited, 49
Scott Paper Company, IV; 31 (upd.)
Sealed Air Corporation, 14
Sierra Pacific Industries, 22
Simpson Investment Company, 17
Specialty Coatings Inc., 8
Stone Container Corporation, IV
Stora Enso Oyj, 36 (upd.)
Stora Kopparbergs Bergslags AB, IV
Svenska Cellulosa Aktiebolaget SCA, IV; 28 (upd.)
Temple-Inland Inc., IV; 31 (upd.)
TJ International, Inc., 19
U.S. Timberlands Company, L.P., 42
Union Camp Corporation, IV
United Paper Mills Ltd. (Yhtyneet Paperitehtaat Oy), IV
Universal Forest Products Inc., 10
UPM-Kymmene Corporation, 19; 50 (upd.)
West Fraser Timber Co. Ltd., 17
Westvaco Corporation, IV; 19 (upd.)
Weyerhaeuser Company, IV; 9 (upd.); 28 (upd.)
Wickes Inc., 25 (upd.)
Willamette Industries, Inc., IV; 31 (upd.)
WTD Industries, Inc., 20

PERSONAL SERVICES

AARP, 27
ADT Security Services, Inc., 12; 44 (upd.)
American Retirement Corporation, 42
Arthur Murray International, Inc., 32
Berlitz International, Inc., 39 (upd.)
Carriage Services, Inc., 37
Childtime Learning Centers, Inc., 34
Chubb, PLC, 50
Corinthian Colleges, Inc., 39
Correctional Services Corporation, 30
CUC International Inc., 16
Davis Service Group PLC, 45
DeVry Incorporated, 29
Educational Testing Service, 12
The Ford Foundation, 34
Franklin Quest Co., 11
Goodwill Industries International, Inc., 16
Jazzercise, Inc., 45
The John D. and Catherine T. MacArthur Foundation, 34
Kaplan, Inc., 42
KinderCare Learning Centers, Inc., 13
The Loewen Group Inc., 16; 40 (upd.)
Management and Training Corporation, 28
Manpower, Inc., 9
Michael Page International plc, 45
Regis Corporation, 18
The Rockefeller Foundation, 34
Rollins, Inc., 11
Rosenbluth International Inc., 14
Rotary International, 31
The Salvation Army USA, 32
Service Corporation International, 6
SOS Staffing Services, 25
Stewart Enterprises, Inc., 20
Supercuts Inc., 26
Weight Watchers International Inc., 12; 33 (upd.)
The York Group, Inc., 50
Youth Services International, Inc., 21
YWCA of the U.S.A., 45

PETROLEUM

Abu Dhabi National Oil Company, IV; 45 (upd.)
Agway, Inc., 21 (upd.)
Alberta Energy Company Ltd., 16; 43 (upd.)
Amerada Hess Corporation, IV; 21 (upd.)
Amoco Corporation, IV; 14 (upd.)
Anadarko Petroleum Corporation, 10
ANR Pipeline Co., 17
Anschutz Corp., 12
Apache Corporation, 10; 32 (upd.)
Arctic Slope Regional Corporation, 38
Ashland Inc., 19; 50 (upd.)
Ashland Oil, Inc., IV
Atlantic Richfield Company, IV; 31 (upd.)
Baker Hughes Incorporated, 22 (upd.)
Belco Oil & Gas Corp., 40
Benton Oil and Gas Company, 47
Berry Petroleum Company, 47
BJ Services Company, 25
BP p.l.c., 45 (upd.)
The British Petroleum Company plc, IV; 7 (upd.); 21 (upd.)
British-Borneo Oil & Gas PLC, 34
Broken Hill Proprietary Company Ltd., 22 (upd.)
Burlington Resources Inc., 10
Burmah Castrol PLC, IV; 30 (upd.)
Callon Petroleum Company, 47
Caltex Petroleum Corporation, 19
Chevron Corporation, IV; 19 (upd.)
ChevronTexaco Corporation, 47 (upd.)
Chiles Offshore Corporation, 9
China National Petroleum Corporation, 46
Chinese Petroleum Corporation, IV; 31 (upd.)
CITGO Petroleum Corporation, IV; 31 (upd.)
The Coastal Corporation, IV; 31 (upd.)
Compañia Española de Petróleos S.A., IV
Comstock Resources, Inc., 47
Conoco Inc., IV; 16 (upd.)
Cooper Cameron Corporation, 20 (upd.)
Cosmo Oil Co., Ltd., IV
Crown Central Petroleum Corporation, 7
DeepTech International Inc., 21
Den Norse Stats Oljeselskap AS, IV
Deutsche BP Aktiengesellschaft, 7
Diamond Shamrock, Inc., IV
Dynegy Inc., 49 (upd.)
E.On AG, 50 (upd.)
Egyptian General Petroluem Corporation, IV
Elf Aquitaine SA, 21 (upd.)
Empresa Colombiana de Petróleos, IV
Enbridge Inc., 43
Energen Corporation, 21
Enron Corporation, 19
Ente Nazionale Idrocarburi, IV
Enterprise Oil PLC, 11; 50 (upd.)
Entreprise Nationale Sonatrach, IV
Exxon Corporation, IV; 7 (upd.); 32 (upd.)
Ferrellgas Partners, L.P., 35
FINA, Inc., 7
Flying J Inc., 19
Forest Oil Corporation, 19
OAO Gazprom, 42
General Sekiyu K.K., IV
Giant Industries, Inc., 19
Global Industries, Ltd., 37
Global Marine Inc., 9
GlobalSantaFe Corporation, 48 (upd.)
Grey Wolf, Inc., 43
Halliburton Company, 25 (upd.)
Helmerich & Payne, Inc., 18
Holly Corporation, 12
Hunt Consolidated, Inc., 27 (upd.)
Hunt Oil Company, 7
Husky Energy Inc., 47
Idemitsu Kosan Co., Ltd., 49 (upd.)
Idemitsu Kosan K.K., IV
Imperial Oil Limited, IV; 25 (upd.)
Indian Oil Corporation Ltd., IV; 48 (upd.)
Kanematsu Corporation, IV
Kerr-McGee Corporation, IV; 22 (upd.)
Kinder Morgan, Inc., 45
King Ranch, Inc., 14
Koch Industries, Inc., IV; 20 (upd.)
Koppers Industries, Inc., 26 (upd.)
Kuwait Petroleum Corporation, IV
Libyan National Oil Corporation, IV
The Louisiana Land and Exploration Company, 7
OAO LUKOIL, 40
Lyondell Petrochemical Company, IV
MAPCO Inc., IV
Maxus Energy Corporation, 7
McDermott International, Inc., 37 (upd.)
Meteor Industries Inc., 33
Mitchell Energy and Development Corporation, 7
Mitsubishi Oil Co., Ltd., IV
Mobil Corporation, IV; 7 (upd.); 21 (upd.)
Murphy Oil Corporation, 7; 32 (upd.)
Nabors Industries, Inc., 9

PUBLISHING & PRINTING

WASTE SERVICES

GEOGRAPHIC INDEX

Geographic Index

Società Finanziaria Telefonica per Azioni,
V
Società Sportiva Lazio SpA, 44
Telecom Italia S.p.A., 43
Tiscali SpA, 48

Japan

Aisin Seiki Co., Ltd., III; 48 (upd.)
Aiwa Co., Ltd., 30
Ajinomoto Co., Inc., II; 28 (upd.)
All Nippon Airways Co., Ltd., 6; 38 (upd.)
Alpine Electronics, Inc., 13
Alps Electric Co., Ltd., II; 44 (upd.)
Asahi Breweries, Ltd., I; 20 (upd.)
Asahi Glass Company, Ltd., III; 48 (upd.)
Asahi National Broadcasting Company,
Ltd., 9
Bank of Tokyo-Mitsubishi Ltd., II; 15
(upd.)
Bridgestone Corporation, V; 21 (upd.)
Brother Industries, Ltd., 14
C. Itoh & Company Ltd., I
Canon Inc., III; 18 (upd.)
CASIO Computer Co., Ltd., III; 16 (upd.);
40 (upd.)
Central Japan Railway Company, 43
Chubu Electric Power Company, Inc., V;
46 (upd.)
Chugai Pharmaceutical Co., Ltd., 50
Chugoku Electric Power Company Inc., V
Citizen Watch Co., Ltd., III; 21 (upd.)
Cosmo Oil Co., Ltd., IV
Dai Nippon Printing Co., Ltd., IV
Dai-Ichi Kangyo Bank Ltd., The, II
Daido Steel Co., Ltd., IV
Daiei, Inc., The, V; 17 (upd.); 41 (upd.)
Daihatsu Motor Company, Ltd., 7; 21
(upd.)
Daikin Industries, Ltd., III
Daimaru, Inc., The, V; 42 (upd.)
Daio Paper Corporation, IV
Daishowa Paper Manufacturing Co., Ltd.,
IV
Daiwa Bank, Ltd., The, II; 39 (upd.)
Daiwa Securities Company, Limited, II
DDI Corporation, 7
DENSO Corporation, 46 (upd.)
Dentsu Inc., I; 16 (upd.); 40 (upd.)
East Japan Railway Company, V
Fanuc Ltd., III; 17 (upd.)
Fuji Bank, Ltd., The, II
Fuji Electric Co., Ltd., II; 48 (upd.)
Fuji Photo Film Co., Ltd., III; 18 (upd.)
Fujisawa Pharmaceutical Company Ltd., I
Fujitsu Limited, III; 16 (upd.); 42 (upd.)
Furukawa Electric Co., Ltd., The, III
General Sekiyu K.K., IV
Hakuhodo, Inc., 6; 42 (upd.)
Hankyu Corporation, V; 23 (upd.)
Hino Motors, Ltd., 7; 21 (upd.)
Hitachi Ltd., I; 12 (upd.)
Hitachi Metals, Ltd., IV
Hitachi Zosen Corporation, III
Hitachi, Ltd., 40 (upd.)
Hokkaido Electric Power Company Inc., V
Hokuriku Electric Power Company, V
Honda Motor Company Limited, I; 10
(upd.); 29 (upd.)
Honshu Paper Co., Ltd., IV
Idemitsu Kosan Co., Ltd., 49 (upd.)
Idemitsu Kosan K.K., IV
Industrial Bank of Japan, Ltd., The, II
Isetan Company Limited, V; 36 (upd.)
Ishikawajima-Harima Heavy Industries Co.,
Ltd., III
Isuzu Motors, Ltd., 9; 23 (upd.)
Ito-Yokado Co., Ltd., V; 42 (upd.)

ITOCHU Corporation, 32 (upd.)
Itoham Foods Inc., II
Japan Airlines Company, Ltd., I; 32 (upd.)
Japan Broadcasting Corporation, 7
Japan Leasing Corporation, 8
Japan Pulp and Paper Company Limited,
IV
Japan Tobacco Inc., V; 46 (upd.)
Jujo Paper Co., Ltd., IV
JUSCO Co., Ltd., V
Kajima Corporation, I
Kanematsu Corporation, IV; 24 (upd.)
Kansai Electric Power Co., Inc., The, V
Kao Corporation, III; 20 (upd.)
Kawasaki Heavy Industries, Ltd., III
Kawasaki Kisen Kaisha, Ltd., V
Kawasaki Steel Corporation, IV
Keio Teito Electric Railway Company, V
Kenwood Corporation, 31
Kikkoman Corporation, 14; 47 (upd.)
Kinki Nippon Railway Company Ltd., V
Kirin Brewery Company, Limited, I; 21
(upd.)
Kobe Steel, Ltd., IV; 19 (upd.)
Kodansha Ltd., IV; 38 (upd.)
Komatsu Ltd., III; 16 (upd.)
Konica Corporation, III; 30 (upd.)
Kotobukiya Co., Ltd., V
Kubota Corporation, III; 26 (upd.)
Kumagai Gumi Company, Ltd., I
Kyocera Corporation, II; 21 (upd.)
Kyowa Hakko Kogyo Co., Ltd., III; 48
(upd.)
Kyushu Electric Power Company Inc., V
Lion Corporation, III
Long-Term Credit Bank of Japan, Ltd., II
Makita Corporation, 22
Marubeni Corporation, I; 24 (upd.)
Marui Co., Ltd., V
Maruzen Co., Limited, 18
Matsushita Electric Industrial Co., Ltd., II
Matsushita Electric Works, Ltd., III; 7
(upd.)
Matsuzakaya Company Limited, V
Mazda Motor Corporation, 9; 23 (upd.)
Meiji Milk Products Company, Limited, II
Meiji Mutual Life Insurance Company,
The, III
Meiji Seika Kaisha, Ltd., II
Minolta Co., Ltd., III; 18 (upd.); 43 (upd.)
Mitsubishi Bank, Ltd., The, II
Mitsubishi Chemical Industries, Ltd., I
Mitsubishi Corporation, I; 12 (upd.)
Mitsubishi Electric Corporation, II; 44
(upd.)
Mitsubishi Estate Company, Limited, IV
Mitsubishi Heavy Industries, Ltd., III; 7
(upd.); 40 (upd.)
Mitsubishi Materials Corporation, III
Mitsubishi Motors Corporation, 9; 23
(upd.)
Mitsubishi Oil Co., Ltd., IV
Mitsubishi Rayon Co., Ltd., V
Mitsubishi Trust & Banking Corporation,
The, II
Mitsui & Co., Ltd., 28 (upd.)
Mitsui Bank, Ltd., The, II
Mitsui Bussan K.K., I
Mitsui Marine and Fire Insurance
Company, Limited, II
Mitsui Mining & Smelting Co., Ltd., IV
Mitsui Mining Company, Limited, IV
Mitsui Mutual Life Insurance Company,
III; 39 (upd.)
Mitsui O.S.K. Lines, Ltd., V
Mitsui Petrochemical Industries, Ltd., 9
Mitsui Real Estate Development Co., Ltd.,
IV

Mitsui Trust & Banking Company, Ltd.,
The, II
Mitsukoshi Ltd., V
Mizuno Corporation, 25
Nagasakiya Co., Ltd., V
Nagase & Company, Ltd., 8
NEC Corporation, II; 21 (upd.)
NHK Spring Co., Ltd., III
Nichii Co., Ltd., V
Nichimen Corporation, IV; 24 (upd.)
Nihon Keizai Shimbun, Inc., IV
Nikko Securities Company Limited, The,
II; 9 (upd.)
Nikon Corporation, III; 48 (upd.)
Nintendo Co., Ltd., III; 7 (upd.); 28 (upd.)
Nippon Credit Bank, II
Nippon Express Co., Ltd., V
Nippon Life Insurance Company, III
Nippon Light Metal Company, Ltd., IV
Nippon Meat Packers, Inc., II
Nippon Oil Company, Limited, IV
Nippon Seiko K.K., III
Nippon Sheet Glass Company, Limited, III
Nippon Shinpan Company, Ltd., II
Nippon Steel Corporation, IV; 17 (upd.)
Nippon Suisan Kaisha, Limited, II
Nippon Telegraph and Telephone
Corporation, V
Nippon Yusen Kabushiki Kaisha, V
Nippondenso Co., Ltd., III
Nissan Motor Company Ltd., I; 11 (upd.);
34 (upd.)
Nisshin Flour Milling Company, Ltd., II
Nisshin Steel Co., Ltd., IV
Nissho Iwai K.K., I
NKK Corporation, IV; 28 (upd.)
Nomura Securities Company, Limited, II; 9
(upd.)
Norinchukin Bank, II
NTN Corporation, III; 47 (upd.)
Odakyu Electric Railway Company
Limited, V
Ohbayashi Corporation, I
Oji Paper Co., Ltd., IV
Oki Electric Industry Company, Limited, II
Okura & Co., Ltd., IV
Omron Corporation, II; 28 (upd.)
Onoda Cement Co., Ltd., III
Orix Corporation, II
ORIX Corporation, 44 (upd.)
Osaka Gas Co., Ltd., V
Pioneer Electronic Corporation, III; 28
(upd.)
Rengo Co., Ltd., IV
Ricoh Company, Ltd., III; 36 (upd.)
Roland Corporation, 38
Sankyo Company, Ltd., I
Sanrio Company, Ltd., 38
Sanwa Bank, Ltd., The, II; 15 (upd.)
SANYO Electric Company, Ltd., II; 36
(upd.)
Sanyo-Kokusaku Pulp Co., Ltd., IV
Sapporo Breweries, Ltd., I; 13 (upd.); 36
(upd.)
Seibu Department Stores, Ltd., V; 42
(upd.)
Seibu Railway Co. Ltd., V
Seiko Corporation, III; 17 (upd.)
Seino Transportation Company, Ltd., 6
Seiyu, Ltd., The, V; 36 (upd.)
Sekisui Chemical Co., Ltd., III
Sharp Corporation, II; 12 (upd.); 40 (upd.)
Shikoku Electric Power Company, Inc., V
Shionogi & Co., Ltd., III; 17 (upd.)
Shiseido Company, Limited, III; 22 (upd.)
Showa Shell Sekiyu K.K., IV
Snow Brand Milk Products Company, Ltd.,
II; 48 (upd.)

United States

NOTES ON CONTRIBUTORS

Notes on Contributors

BEAVERS, Carol. Washington-based freelance writer, editor, and documentation specialist.

CASON, Rebecca Rayko. Business editor of the *Northwest Florida Daily News* and contributor to *Flight International*; former editor of AeroWorldNet.com and U.S. editor of *Commercial Aviation Report*.

COOLEY, Doug. Seattle-based business writer and editor at State Street Writing Works (statestreetwriting.com).

DeVAULT, Kerri. Seattle-based freelance writer, editor, and Web designer.

DOGIL, Arianna. Writer and editor.

FEDER, Michelle. Freelance writer in Seattle, Washington.

FERRARA, Adi. Freelance writer and editor based in Brooklyn, New York.

FRERICHS, Christopher W. Freelance writer, editor, and non-profit development consultant based in New York, NY.

GUSSOFF, Caren. Writer and editor.

GWILYM, Linda M. Seattle-based writer, editor, and movie reviewer.

HALASZ, Robert. Former editor in chief of *World Progress* and *Funk & Wagnall's New Encyclopedia Yearbook*; author, *The U.S. Marines* (Millbrook Press, 1993).

LONDON, Melissa. Freelance writer who has published articles in newspapers and magazines throughout the United States on subjects ranging from business to education; she also works as a technical editor and information technology instructor and currently lives in North Bend, Washington (www.melissalondon.com).

LOWERY, Laura. Writer and editor.

McCULLY, Annette Dennis. Freelance writer based in the Seattle area who has written about science and business for *International Environmental Systems Update (IESU)*, *globeNet, Quality Digest,* and the American Management Association.

POTTER, Anne L. Policy analyst and writer living in Portland, Oregon.

ROTHBURD, Carrie. Creative and technical writer and editor based in Portland, Oregon; also a consultant and grant writer for nonprofit organizations.

SLEDGE, Stacee. Freelance writer living in Bellingham, Washington, and restaurant critic for the *Bellingham Herald*; her work has appeared in several publications, including *Better Homes & Gardens*, *Northwest Life & Times*, and *USA Today*.

SWAN SKJELSET, Peggi. Writer and editor.

WEISBERGER, Tammy. Seattle-based writer and editor.

WHIPPLE, Lisa. Freelance writer living in Seattle, Washington; writings include reviews, technical documentation, and poetry for such companies as Amazon.com, Microsoft, AOL Time Warner, and Hasbro; her articles have appeared in several publications, including *McSweeney's* and *Arcade*.

WILLIAMS, Genevieve. Seattle-based freelance writer and fact-finder; former content editor at Amazon.com.

WRIGHTSMAN, Heidi. Seattle-based writer, editor, and researcher.